THE LAW OF ANTITRUST: AN INTEGRATED HANDBOOK

Second Edition

By

Lawrence A. Sullivan

*Professor of Law, Emeritus Southwestern
Law School and
Emeritus Professor of Law
University of California School of Law, Berkely*

and

Warren S. Grimes

*Professor of Law,
Southwestern Law School*

HORNBOOK SERIES®

THOMSON
WEST

Mat #40155321

© West, a Thomson business, 2000
© 2006 Thomson/West
     610 Opperman Drive
     P.O. Box 64526
     St. Paul, MN 55164–0526
     1–800–328–9352
Printed in the United States of America

ISBN–13: 978–0–314–14706–6
ISBN–10: 0–314–14706–3

 TEXT IS PRINTED ON 10% POST CONSUMER RECYCLED PAPER

*To: Joan Sullivan
and
Amity Hume Grimes*

*

Foreword to First Edition

The Hornbook on the Law of Antitrust by one of the authors was published by West in 1977 to meet the needs of students and practitioners for adequate treatment of major antitrust areas. Although the purposes of this volume are essentially the same and its title similar, this is not a revision of that work but a new book that is responsive to changes in the economy (e.g., increasing dynamism and globalization), in economic theory (e.g., analysis of network efficiencies), in prevailing attitudes about how theory should be applied (e.g., post-Chicago analysis), in related policy areas (e.g., deregulation) and, reflexively, in antitrust itself. The book addresses new areas, treats a number of areas more fully, and thoroughly reassesses core concepts like monopolization and horizontal and vertical restraints.

We think of antitrust as law, not free form policy. Antitrust, at any stage, is shaped by the interplay of the legal rules previously laid down (however broad or general these may be) with current political, economic and theoretical forces. Our effort has been to describe this process and to distill from it what we view as antitrust law today. Because antitrust law is constantly evolving, we have sought to describe the law's central principles in their developmental contexts. While we have often disclosed our own (usually consistent) views on significant policy issues, we have tried fairly to summarize alternative positions and contentions. Because we are convinced that each of antitrust's developmental stages is related to an existing or emerging consensus about the needs and opportunities of the economy, we view current policy debates less as efforts to stake out solid, normative base lines than as parts of the ongoing developmental process.

Our debts are many. Few can be specifically recognized, none adequately. We are especially grateful to Southwestern University School of Law for encouragement and support in the form of released time, summer stipends and funding for research assistants. We must also stress out gratitude to Ms. Antoinette Shilkevich, librarian of the law firm of Blecher and Collins in Los Angeles, who took time from busy professional involvements to proof read and correct the book.

Los Angeles, California
February 1, 2000.

*

Foreword to Second Edition

In the 6 years since publication of this Hornbook, there have been a number of significant antitrust developments in the marketplace, in the case law, and in the theoretical literature. This revision addresses a number of these important developments.

These developments include: (1) the challenges raised by the increasingly global reach of competition and antitrust enforcement; (2) potential competitive abuses of intellectual property holders that have sought to enhance or extend the rewards of government-granted exclusivity; (3) awareness of the buying power of large chain retailers and the "gatekeeper" nature of their power, and (4) new and reinforced learning concerning distribution restraints, including insights into the anticompetitive potential of deferred-purchase requirements ties.

The competitive effects of distribution restraints require more than a single stage analysis that focuses on the producer. Instead, a proper approach requires, at a minimum, a dual-level analysis. Distribution restraints are best understood and legitimately classified based on whether the source of power is upstream or downstream. This revision of the Hornbook follows that learning, treating downstream power restraints such as vertical minimum price fixing and exclusive territories in one chapter while upstream power restraints such as tying, exclusive dealing and vertical maximum price fixing are addressed in a subsequent chapter.

Developments in the literature and in the case law do not necessarily go hand in hand. The Supreme Court has signaled the need for increased freedom of action for a monopolist at the same time that some theorists have offered new insights into the substantial anticompetitive risks of exclusionary conduct.

I am responsible for the choice and treatment of new developments in this revision. Prof. Sullivan provided valuable counsel and editorial suggestions.

WARREN S. GRIMES
LOS ANGELES, CALIFORNIA

February 1, 2006

*

WESTLAW® Overview

The Law of Antitrust: An Integrated Handbook offers a detailed and comprehensive treatment of the basic rules, principles, and issues relating to antitrust law. To supplement the information contained in this book, you can access Westlaw, West's computer-assisted legal research service. Westlaw contains a broad array of legal resources, including case law, statutes, expert commentary, current developments, and various other types of information.

Learning how to use these materials effectively will enhance your legal research abilities. To help you coordinate the information in the book with your Westlaw research, this volume contains an appendix listing Westlaw databases, search techniques, and sample problems.

The instructions and features described in this Westlaw overview are based on accessing Westlaw via westlaw.com® at **www.westlaw.com**.

THE PUBLISHER

*

Summary of Contents

*

Table of Contents

Chapter VII. Distribution Restraints Based on Downstream Power: Vertical Minimum Price and Other Distribution Restraints **370**

THE LAW OF ANTITRUST:
AN INTEGRATED HANDBOOK
Second Edition

*

Chapter I

ANTITRUST AND THE MARKET MECHANISM

Table of Sections

---

§ 1.1 Introduction

This book is about the antitrust law of the United States, a system of law to maintain and, where necessary, restore competition. Outside of the United States, a comparable set of legal rules would generally be known as competition law. By whatever label it is known, antitrust law is subject to development and change. The economy is dynamic; relevant economic theory grows and accumulates; social, political and philosophical thought about the economy also shift. All such changes can influence antitrust over time. Because the United States and increasingly the world economy is market oriented, the market mechanism is at the core of antitrust. Of the more than 90 nations that have now adopted competition laws,[1] each has to a considerable extent embraced the

§ 1.1

1. William J. Kolasky, Deputy Assistant Attorney General, Antitrust Division, US Department of Justice, *International Con-* *vergence Efforts: A U.S. Perspective,* Speech of March 22, 2002, available at http://www.usdoj.gov/atr/public/speeches/10885.htm

1

market as the optimal allocator of productive resources and distributor of the goods and services these resources produce. Although competition laws differ widely in coverage, methods of enforcement, and effectiveness of enforcement, these laws have one clear element in common. Each responds to oppressive use of economic power. Markets do not always function optimally. When market actors accumulate power, that power can distort allocation and be exercised in a manner society deems oppressive. As medicine is to good health, antitrust is to well-functioning markets. By occasionally performing surgery on a market and, more frequently, treating behavioral symptoms of abuse, antitrust seeks to maintain and restore optimally functioning markets.

After first exploring the universal basis for competition law, this chapter turns to the circumstances that underlay adoption of the Sherman Antitrust Act in 1890[2] as the basic U.S. antitrust law. The United States has one of the oldest competition laws and is the first nation to establish credible enforcement institutions that built a substantial body of precedent. Here, as elsewhere, antitrust law and policy have adapted to unique national experiences. Chapter 1 then shifts forward to examine the goals of U.S. antitrust law at the onset of the twenty-first century. The chapter concludes with a description of the role of economics in contemporary antitrust analysis.

§ 1.2 Antitrust as a Response to the Oppressive Use of Economic Power

The rapid growth of competition laws throughout the world has multiple causes, among them the trend away from centrally planned economies in favor of more decentralized, market oriented systems. Antitrust has no place in an economy in which resource allocation and pricing decisions are made by government officials.

For many of the nations that have chosen to embrace market competition, enacting a new competition law is relatively easy. Implementing it in an effective manner may prove a formidable task. Enforcing a competition law means challenging the very firms that possess economic power (and inevitably political power as well). To take on a powerful firm requires independence and professionalism in the enforcement agency as well as in the courts that may review any enforcement initiative. For government institutions to achieve this expertise and political insulation may require long-term education of citizens and officials accompanied by basic political reform.

For those nations that succeed in implementing an effective competition law, the benefits may be substantial. In a world in which the most competitively fit enterprise survives and thrives, a nation with vigorous-

---

2. As amended, the Sherman Act is set forth in 15 U.S.C.A. §§ 1–7.

ly enforced competition laws may have a comparative advantage over other nations. That nation's enterprises, honed by competition in the home market, may be better equipped to compete in global markets. Conversely, nations lacking vigorous competition law enforcement may be more likely to tolerate firms unsuited for worldwide competition.[1]

Switzerland, a nation that adopted its first comprehensive competition law in 1995, provides an interesting test for the comparative advantage thesis. Well before 1995, many large Swiss firms in areas such as pharmaceuticals were highly competitive on international markets despite the lack of a Swiss competition policy. But the lack of competition in domestic markets led to higher costs in Switzerland that forced large Swiss companies to move production facilities outside Switzerland. That cost disadvantage along with the heightened competition from foreign firms that were disciplined by competition ultimately led Switzerland to adopt its own comprehensive competition law.[2]

Although recent growth in competition law may reflect an awareness that competition at home makes firms more fit for the international marketplace, the roots of antitrust law are much older. Antitrust is a response to the universal pursuit of economic power. Those with power may seek to gather and retain wealth at the expense of the less powerful. Although societies tolerate or even encourage some exercises of economic power, they have developed a variety of responses to uses of power deemed oppressive. A few examples from different eras and civilizations illustrate the point.

Over two thousand years ago, the City of Athens in Greece was engaged in a war with Sparta to the south. The Athenians had strict regulations governing the sale of grain, a commodity in short supply because of the sparseness of the soil in their home province of Attica. One goal of the regulations was to prevent importers from limiting output.[3] In the Winter of 388–387 B.C., when the grain trade was disturbed by Spartan military conquest, grain dealers took advantage of the crisis and combined to limit sales and charge prices said to be six times the legal profit. The case was vigorously (and apparently successfully) prosecuted by Athenian authorities.

The Roman Emperor Diocletian (284–305 A.D.) responded quite differently to popular disaffection over high prices—inflation in the Roman Empire is said to have been as high as 800 percent during the last half of the third century. The Emperor decreed maximum prices on goods and services ranging from meat and beer to haircuts and school

---

§ 1.2

1. M. PORTER, THE COMPETITIVE ADVANTAGE OF NATIONS 662 (1990) ("Few roles of government are more important to the upgrading of an economy than ensuring vigorous domestic rivalry").

2. See Zäch, *Competition Law as Comparative Advantage*, in TOWARDS WTO COM-
PETITION RULES 395, 402–03 (R. Zäch, ed. 1999).

3. The regulation of grain trade in ancient Athens and the prosecution of cartelizing dealers described here are related in Kotsiris, *An Antitrust Case in Ancient Greek Law*, 22 INT'L LAW. 451 (1988).

tuition charges. The edict threatened the death penalty to violators.[4] These efforts at direct state control over the market mechanism apparently did not survive the Emperor's reign.

In England in 1602, an importer of playing cards brought suit to enforce the monopoly on the distribution of playing cards that the Queen of England had granted him.[5] The Court of the King's Bench refused to enforce the monopoly, both perhaps as a general response to the Queen's widespread grants of monopoly without the concurrence of the Parliament and to the particular economic oppression inherent in this monopoly. The recorded views of the English judges are impressive for their recognition of the benefits (lower prices, higher quality, and the freedom to enter and maintain a trade) that competition brings.

Another response to economic oppression grew out of the Tenpo famine in Osaka, Japan in 1837. Oshio Heihachiro, a reformer, visionary and Confucian scholar, petitioned the local magistrate (machi bugyo) to release the city's rice reserve. Oshio Heihachiro criticized local officials for corruption and extravagance for shipping rice from Osaka to Edo (Tokyo) during times of scarcity, and for failing to punish merchants guilty of exploitative accumulation of wealth and land. When the local government refused to respond, he led a local revolt that set fire to a quarter of the city. The revolt failed to generate wide support from the people of Osaka, but apparently served as an inspiration for later reform efforts.[6]

There were no sophisticated antitrust laws in the pre-twentieth century societies described here, but each had a response to economic repression. In Ancient Greece and in Renaissance England, the response came through application of the law in a manner that, by attempting to restore competition, replicates twentieth-century competition law. In Ancient Rome, the Emperor attempted a more intrusive form of state control of the price mechanism. In premodern Japan, the response was a revolt that contributed to subsequent reforms of government. Although the responses differed, the apparent universality of the challenge suggests that societies of diverse traditions, facing varying economic conditions, share a common hostility toward the oppressive use of economic power. That same human response underlies the adoption of competition laws in more than ninety countries throughout the world.

§ 1.3 The Evolution of United States Antitrust Laws

Although arising from a basic aversion to abuse of power, the form and intensity of antitrust laws are shaped by each nation's experience. As Congress debated the Sherman Act in 1890, most Americans lived in rural and small town settings. The majority were farmers and many

4. R. Zimmermann, The Law of Obligation, Roman Foundations of the Civilian Tradition 260–61 & nn.162–65 (1990).

5. Case of Monopolies, 1602, 11 Coke 84, 77 Eng. Rep. 1260.

6. These events are described in C. Totman, Early Modern Japan 514–18 (1993).

more were tradesmen or small businessmen. In the nineteenth century, the dominance of an agrarian economy was common throughout the world. But it is instructive to compare the dominant nineteenth-century agrarian patterns outside the United States. The agrarian culture in Japan, for example, was strikingly different. In Japan, land suitable for farming was in short supply. Japanese farmers learned to produce exceptional yields, in many areas two crops per year, with the help of irrigation systems constructed and maintained through the cooperative efforts of all living in the farming village. Cooperation and consensus were critical to the success of this type of farming.[1]

The nineteenth-century United States was still a place where almost anyone who wanted to farm could find arable land. Farmers lived and worked independently. An American farmer did not live in a village, but rather in a separate home built on the farmer's land, perhaps out of sight of any neighbor's house. Although American farmers were quick to aid one another during harvesting or other times of need, cooperation and consensus were not primary virtues for the American farmer. Each was, to an extent perhaps unfathomable in more densely populated countries, free to farm as he wished. Farmers tended to be fiercely independent, nurtured in the freedom to look elsewhere if the land did not provide a bountiful existence. Throughout most of the nineteenth century, if land was in short supply in one region, a family could move west to areas where land was still available.

America has long embraced the notion of equality enshrined in Thomas Jefferson's words in the Declaration of Independence in 1776 ("all men are created equal"). Although the United States has never quite succeeded in making this aspiration a reality, the independence and freedom of the nineteenth-century American farmer fit nicely with the notions of equality it embodies. The rapid industrialization of the second half of the nineteenth century brought unwelcome change that threatened this ideology. Farmers and small tradesmen resented the economic power of railroads and other large firms. Farmers quickly became dependent on these firms to supply transportation and machinery needed for farming. The resentment was fueled by a sense that they were targets of discriminatory treatment, as in the case of railroad rates that favored large businesses and disfavored the small tradesman and farmer.[2]

Mistrust of large corporate entities left Americans with something of a dilemma. Large firms could be countered by government, which might assume ownership or control of these firms or their assets. But Americans were no more trusting of government than of large private firms. Power concentrated in a few hands, whether those hands were private or governmental, was offensive. The Jeffersonian ideal was diffused power left in the hands of citizen farmers and small businessmen. Thus, late-

§ 1.3

1. See generally E. REISCHAUER, JAPAN: THE STORY OF A NATION (1990).

2. Letwin, *Congress and the Sherman Antitrust Law: 1887–1890,* 23 U. CHI. L. REV. 221 (1956).

nineteenth-century reformers tended to favor breaking up monopolies, not a government takeover of these firms.

Antitrust laws place primary reliance on market forces to discipline economic behavior. If a monopoly or a cartel is created, the antitrust laws may be invoked to restore a situation of diffused power, but once that competitive balance is restored, there should be no need for continuing government oversight. The "invisible hand" of the market provides the discipline,[3] so no regulators or bureaucrats are required once the proper competitive balance is restored. For Americans who mistrusted both big government and big corporations, the antitrust laws seemed well-suited as a remedy for the abuses of large corporations.

The name "antitrust" was derived from combinations of large firms that, in that time, were first organized in the form of, and thus became known as, trusts. For most Americans, the Sherman Act probably was understood, if at all, as a weapon to be used against such combinations— favorite targets, in addition to the railroads, were the oil, sugar, and whiskey trusts. But from the recorded proceedings of that Congress, we can identify other more narrowly tailored goals.[4] Chief among them were preventing the high prices associated with monopoly or cartel activity (transfers of wealth from consumers to monopolists), a basic pocketbook issue that every voter could grasp. Another goal was protecting the right of every person to practice a trade of choice. Both of these goals were seen as consistent with suppressing or restraining the growth of big business.

The revisionist efforts of some later commentators notwithstanding,[5] the goal of economic efficiency tended to be ignored by the public and largely by the legislature. Seen as a central goal in modern antitrust analysis, the efficient operation of the economy was not central to the debates in Congress. Another widely accepted goal of antitrust today—to foster research, development and innovation—was also at best dimly reflected in the legislative debates in 1890.

The Sherman Antitrust Act contains two core provisions. Section 1 of the Sherman Act condemns contracts, combinations, or conspiracies in restraint of trade. Because even a simple contract between a buyer and seller can be viewed as a restraint of trade, a major challenge for the courts has been in determining which restraints are forbidden. Although classic cartel behavior involving the limiting of output or fixing of prices has been condemned with regularity throughout the last century,[6] the courts have shown greater inconsistency in decisions on other forms of

---

3. The term "invisible hand" was first used by Scottish economist A. SMITH, AN INQUIRY INTO THE NATURE AND CAUSES OF THE WEALTH OF NATIONS 423 (N.Y. Mod. Lib. ed. 1937).

4. For a discussion of the goals reflected in congressional debate, see H. THORELLI, THE FEDERAL ANTITRUST POLICY: ORIGINATION OF AN AMERICAN TRADITION 226–29 (1955).

5. R. BORK, THE ANTITRUST PARADOX: A POLICY AT WAR WITH ITSELF 10–11, 66 (1978) ("The Sherman Act was clearly presented and debated as a consumer welfare prescription.").

6. There have been exceptions, e.g., Appalachian Coals, Inc. v. United States, 288 U.S. 344, 53 S.Ct. 471, 77 L.Ed. 825 (1933).

restraints, such as cooperation among rivals that limits competition while offering efficiencies, or restraints in the distribution system (vertical restraints) that may foster a producer's distribution network.

Section 2 prohibits monopolization or attempts to monopolize. The words suggest not a condemnation of the mere existence of monopoly, but of the *active behavior* associated with monopolization or attempts to monopolize. As commonly construed today, a monopolist violates Section 2 only if it engages in abusive or anticompetitive behavior. Still, there remain conceptual problems in applying Section 2, including the extent of its application to single brand monopolies, as may occur, for example, in aftermarkets for parts or service for a manufacturer's products or in markets associated with the products of a franchisor.

Both core provisions of the Sherman Act were written in broad language leaving the courts a great deal of interpretive freedom. Over the past century, court decisions have gradually filled in the body of what we know today as antitrust law. The process is one of evolution, but not always in a constant direction. U.S. antitrust policy has adjusted to changes in interrelated social and economic conditions such as the increasing urbanization of the population, rapid technological progress, the growth in mass markets of branded goods, severe swings in the cycle of economic growth and recession, and the increasing internationalization of markets. Changes in antitrust policy have also been influenced by political currents, changes in economic theory, and even changes in the membership of the judiciary.

Some of the major shifts in U.S. antitrust policy can be briefly described. During the Presidency of William Howard Taft (1909–1913), antitrust enforcement was vigorous. For a fifteen-year period extending from 1920 through 1935, antitrust enforcement was tepid, perhaps reaching a low point during the first years of the Great Depression. During the first term of President Franklin Roosevelt, the Government experimented with government-sanctioned cartels as a means of dealing with depressed industries. But in Franklin Roosevelt's second term, antitrust gained new vitality after the appointment of a forceful new head of the Justice Department's Antitrust Division, Thurman Arnold. By the late 1930s, cartel conduct had become widely associated with totalitarian governments, increasing the political support for a strong antitrust policy.[7] This period of active antitrust enforcement probably reached its peak in the 1960s. By the mid–1970s, a sense that some court decisions had suppressed conduct that was efficient and the contemporaneous growth in influence of the Chicago School of Economics began tempering enforcement policy. The shift to a less active enforcement accelerated during the Presidency of Ronald Reagan (1980–1988). Under the first President Bush enforcement became somewhat more active, a trend that continued during the Clinton years. Under President George

7. Temporary National Economic Commission, S. Doc. No. 35, 77th Congress, 1st Sess. (1941).

W. Bush, enforcement remains active albeit at levels below those of the 1990s. With the past three Presidents, shifts in antitrust enforcement have been largely at the margins, leaving the core of antitrust largely unaltered.

§ 1.4 Who Makes Antitrust Policy?

One significant change during the past century has been in who establishes antitrust goals and priorities. In 1890, there seemed little doubt that Congress could specify antitrust policy, but Congress accepted that responsibility only in part. In the legislative debates of 1890, it was suggested on more than one occasion that the Sherman Act was merely an effort to codify the English common law governing restraints of trade and monopolies, as that law had been applied in the United States.[1] The courts have, in any event, become important in determining antitrust policy. The broadly worded provisions of the Sherman and Clayton Acts have invited—indeed required—judicial construction. The Supreme Court has described the Sherman Act as a "charter of freedom," asserting for itself broad interpretative discretion more often associated with provisions of the Constitution.[2] Indeed, the Sherman Act might have had little relevance to much of the economy were it not for constitutional change worked by the Supreme Court. Early case law interpreting the Sherman Act limited its application by construing the interstate commerce requirement strictly. The Sherman Act did not apply to most local business operations or even a merger of manufacturers or producers (because the act of production was not seen as interstate in character).[3] However, by the mid–1930s, the Supreme Court had greatly expanded its interpretation of what constituted interstate commerce, with the result that the federal antitrust laws could assume a central role in maintaining competition at all levels of the economy.

The federal antitrust agencies (the Antitrust Division of the Department of Justice and the Federal Trade Commission) have also assumed a preeminent role in framing antitrust goals and policies. By choosing enforcement targets and shaping theories of prosecution, federal enforcers have always had a significant role in antitrust policy. But that role has expanded substantially. One reason is the use of antitrust guidelines issued by the federal agencies. Beginning with merger guidelines in the

---

§ 1.4

1. H. Thorelli, The Federal Antitrust Policy: Origination of an American Tradition 228 (1955) ("There is ample evidence that not only the bills reported by Sherman in the 51st Congress but also the bill finally passed were intended by their sponsors primarily to be federal codifications of the common law of England and the several states.").

2. Appalachian Coals, Inc. v. United States, 288 U.S. 344, 359–60, 53 S.Ct. 471, 77 L.Ed. 825 (1933).

3. United States v. E. C. Knight Co., 156 U.S. 1, 15 S.Ct. 249, 39 L.Ed. 325 (1895) (a monopoly of manufacturing only "incidentally and indirectly" affected interstate commerce and was beyond the reach of the Federal Constitution and the Sherman Act). See Grimes, *The Seven Myths of Vertical Price Fixing: The Politics and Economics of a Century-Long Debate,* 21 Sw. U. L. Rev. 1285, 1287–88 & nn.7–8 (1992) (citing early-twentieth-century court decisions that declined to apply the Sherman Act to vertical restraints on the ground that no interstate commerce was involved).

1960s, the agencies now issue guidelines and policy statements in a number of areas including intellectual property, international operations, health care and joint ventures. Although these guidelines purport to describe only the agency's approach to determining which cases to bring, their influence on courts and members of the private bar extends beyond cases investigated by a federal agency. Another development that has greatly enhanced the influence of the federal enforcers is the 1976 legislation creating the premerger reporting program.[4] Because almost all acquisitions that are challenged under the antitrust laws are reported to the federal agencies before the acquisition occurs, the agencies have substantial bargaining leverage that allows them to negotiate agreements with the merging parties. The courts have little or no input into these agreements, so that the locus of power in mergers has shifted to a considerable extent to the federal agencies.

Members of the private antitrust bar also influence antitrust policy and goals. Private suits outnumber public enforcement initiatives at roughly a 10 to 1 ratio. Almost all of the Supreme Court's important decisions of the last three decades have come in privately initiated antitrust suits.[5] Additionally, through advice to in-house or outside clients, private antitrust attorneys are instrumental in assuring antitrust compliance by countless firms.

Finally, academic commentators or theorists, often with economics backgrounds, have an indirect influence on the shaping of antitrust policy. These theorists sometimes propose new economic models or frameworks for antitrust analysis; at other times, their role is more in restating and criticizing the interpretive law announced by the courts or the administrative decisions of the agencies. There have been and continue to be significant differences of opinion among such commentators. Much of the current debate has been among three groups: free market theorists (the "Chicago School"), traditionalists, and post-Chicago theorists. Chicago School commentators rely heavily on deductive analysis from standard economic assumptions and generally favor a smaller role for antitrust. Traditionalists recognize a range of goals for antitrust and are more likely to envision a more vigorous role for antitrust that may include some expansion. Post–Chicago thinkers focus on two goals—maximizing efficiency and assuring that wealth is not shifted from consumers to firms with power; they, like Chicagoans, rely on microeconomic analysis but try to work inductively on the basis of

---

4. Hart–Scott–Rodino Antitrust Improvements Act of 1976, Pub. L. No. 94–435, 90 Stat. 1383 (codified in scattered sections of 15 U.S.C.A.).

5. E.g., State Oil Co. v. Khan, 522 U.S. 3, 118 S.Ct. 275, 139 L.Ed.2d 199 (1997); Brooke Group Ltd. v. Brown & Williamson Tobacco Corp., 509 U.S. 209, 113 S.Ct. 2578, 125 L.Ed.2d 168 (1993); Eastman Kodak Co. v. Image Technical Servs., Inc., 504 U.S. 451, 112 S.Ct. 2072, 119 L.Ed.2d 265 (1992); Business Elecs. Corp. v. Sharp Elecs. Corp., 485 U.S. 717, 108 S.Ct. 1515, 99 L.Ed.2d 808 (1988); Matsushita Elec. Indus. Co. v. Zenith Radio Corp., 475 U.S. 574, 106 S.Ct. 1348, 89 L.Ed.2d 538 (1986); Aspen Skiing Co. v. Aspen Highlands Skiing Corp., 472 U.S. 585, 105 S.Ct. 2847, 86 L.Ed.2d 467 (1985); Broadcast Music, Inc. v. CBS, Inc., 441 U.S. 1, 99 S.Ct. 1551, 60 L.Ed.2d 1 (1979); Continental TV v. GTE Sylvania, 433 U.S. 36, 97 S.Ct. 2549, 53 L.Ed.2d 568 (1977).

rigorous inquiry into particular market facts. Although the future flow of the ongoing theoretical debate cannot be charted, with the possible exception of treatment of parallel behavior by oligopolists, there is general agreement on the main points of horizontal restraints policy. More uncertainty remains over antitrust's proper response to strategic conduct, often involving the vertical exercise of power over upstream suppliers or downstream customers.

§ 1.5   The Goals of United States Antitrust Policy Today

From all of the sources described in § 1.4, the contemporary goals of U.S. antitrust policy can be traced. Antitrust's overriding goal is to maintain public confidence in the market mechanism by deterring and punishing instances of economic oppression. Antitrust preserves and protects markets as an alternative to more intrusive government regulation or control of the economy. To fulfill this role without overstepping, theorists have offered more specific economic and social goals that serve to delimit antitrust.

1.5a.   Antitrust as a Protector of the Market Mechanism

Properly implemented, antitrust policy would prevent economic oppression by maintaining competition. Market forces, not regulation or government control, would allocate resources among market players and consumers. Herein lies the critical distinction between the antitrust ideal and other methods of preventing economic oppression, such as government ownership or regulatory control.

The United States has never foresworn all government ownership. The federal government has owned and operated its military and its post office system. Public utilities that provide gas and electricity are often owned by local governments. When not government-owned, such utilities are frequently subject to government rate regulation. Other forms of government regulation, such as regulation of health, safety, working conditions and the environment, are pervasive. The body of government regulation of businesses began expanding rapidly roughly at the same time the Sherman Act was passed, growing even more rapidly in the 1930s after the onset of the Great Depression. Occasional government ownership and substantial government regulation are a part of the overall economic scheme in the United States. Still, a commitment to private enterprise and the discipline of the market remain central tenants of U.S. economic policy. Recent deregulatory initiatives have sought to bring market discipline to industries such as telecommunications and electric power. Some selective reregulation may be integral to the process, but the underlying commitment to market discipline remains.

The United States has no agency comparable to Japan's Ministry of International Trade and Industry (MITI). The U.S. Department of Commerce is charged with promoting and aiding American businesses at home and abroad, but it simply does not have the same influence or responsibility for economic planning that MITI has in Japan. Although there are large exceptions (such as in the defense industry) and small ones (such as policies to subsidize loans for homes, education or other socially encouraged activities), the United States does not plan or coordinate industrial policy for American businesses. To be sure, the United States has not always been firm in its resolve to oppose industrial planning. During its first term, the administration of President Franklin Roosevelt experimented with, but subsequently abandoned, various forms of closer cooperation between government and depressed industries. More recently, there was a period during the 1980s when many began to question whether the United States needed a MITI to better coordinate the activities of U.S. businesses, particularly in high technology industries. As the American economy rebounded and the Japanese economy lost ground in the 1990s, these calls have abated.

Using the market to discipline business behavior has undeniable advantages over a more centralized coordination of business. One of these advantages is that decentralized decision-making allows players to experiment with differing strategies. Many firms will make wrong decisions and fail miserably. There is substantial social cost to these failures. But the positive side is that every entrepreneur must constantly adjust to changing market conditions to stay competitive, which reinforces reliance on the market, where competition ensures that conditions are set by forward-looking, progressive firms. In such an environment, an entrepreneur who does not adjust risks failure. Moreover, because market decisions are decentralized, markets reduce the risk of a costly error, a risk that is high in industrial planning. As recent Japanese economic history testifies, centralized resource allocation decisions can lead to costly missteps not just for one firm but for an industry or the entire economy. Finally, a market-driven economy may reduce the risk of corruption and wasteful expenditures designed to win government influence or approval. Thus, outright bribes and buying of governmental influence are reduced in a system that relies primarily on the market. For example, the heaviest contributors to election campaigns are not necessarily the largest firms, but usually those that are heavily regulated or dependent upon the government for subsidies.[1]

The experience of the European Union (EU) highlights another advantage of relying on market forces instead of a centrally planned industrial policy. Within the EU, the various members frequently feud over the amount of government benefits that should flow to each country. These disagreements are a major source of friction within the Community. But the EU's competition policy has been a major positive force for strengthening the union. Competition policy helps to break down trade barriers between member states, assisting greatly in the task of creating a single market. Moreover, reliance on market forces rather

§ 1.5

1. Vartabedian, *Corporate Traffic Heavy on U.S. Political Money Trail*, LOS ANGELES TIMES, Sept. 21, 1997, at A1 (reporting the heaviest campaign contributions typically come from the "financial, defense, tobacco, oil and telecommunications sectors").

than the decision of some EU industrial policy body tends to reduce friction among member states. When allocation decisions are made by the market, it is more difficult to blame an EU official or body for the results. Dispassionate and relatively invisible market discipline decides which firms will succeed and which will not. To be sure, the enforcement of the EU's competition laws has obvious national political ramifications. But such enforcement is one step removed from actual allocation decisions and, thus, more insulated from the inter-member feuds that promote disunity.

1.5b. Consumer Welfare Goals of Antitrust Policy

In addition to maintaining public confidence in the market system, reasonably precise goals delimit contemporary American antitrust policy. These goals generally fall into four categories: (1) consumer welfare goals, including the efficient allocation of existing resources, avoiding wealth transfers to participants with market power, and preserving consumer choice; (2) fostering innovation and technological progress; (3) protecting individual firms through fairness and equity goals; and (4) maintaining decentralized economic power. This section describes the consumer welfare goals.

1.5b1. *Maintaining Allocative Efficiency*

If there is universal agreement on one antitrust goal, it is that antitrust should strive for the *efficient allocation of society's available goods and services*. One of the costs of monopoly is the loss to consumers that would have purchased the monopolized product or service at a competitive price, but forego the purchase because of the monopoly surcharge. When compared to competition, the monopolist's output is reduced and fewer desired goods or services are distributed (economists call this a deadweight loss). When a dominant buyer exercises monopsony power, output is again suppressed when the buyer forces sellers to accept a lower price for their goods. The deadweight loss to society is reflected in the buyer's reduced purchase of input and the commensurate reduction in outflow from the monopsonist.

1.5b2. *Preventing Wealth Transfer*

What makes monopoly pricing lucrative for the monopolist are those consumers who continue to buy at the monopoly price. These consumers suffer loss in the form of a wealth transfer to the monopolist. This wealth transfer loss can be, and probably is, more substantial than any deadweight loss. Thus, a second widely recognized and important goal of antitrust policy is to ensure that sellers (or buyers that are monopsonists) do not use market power to capture wealth from consumers or sellers.

Some theorists claim, however, that antitrust should be concerned only with resource allocation. The argument is that any wealth transfer produced by market power is a matter of wealth distribution within the society. Under this view, wealth distribution should be addressed, if at all, by other legal rules, perhaps tax law or welfare policies. The antitrust laws and the courts that must resolve litigated cases should not be influenced by judgments about who should receive what allocation of society's wealth.[2] If accepted, this narrower view of antitrust goals would have ramifications in the calculation of damages in private suits as well as in the substantive outcome of cases in which the goals of efficient allocation and wealth transfer avoidance are in conflict.

Accepting efficient allocation as the exclusive consumer welfare goal of antitrust runs counter to statutory intent. The Congress that enacted the Sherman Act and subsequent Congresses that have amended it from time to time intended to stop powerful firms from shifting wealth from consumers to themselves.[3] But even on its own terms, the position of theorists who accept this view is deficient. For example, Bork asserts that the antitrust laws are meant to establish and protect competitive markets. He recognizes competition as normative, monopoly markets as aberrational. That being so, his own conception marks the distributional characteristics associated with competition—that is, the existence of the full consumer surplus—as normative, and marks the transfer of that surplus to firms with power—the major consequence of monopoly and the incentive that drives firms to seek monopoly—as aberrational.

In most antitrust enforcement initiatives, the wealth transfer injury is more prominent than any deadweight loss that may occur. Even during President Reagan's Administration when the leadership of the Antitrust Division embraced allocative efficiency as the exclusive goal of antitrust,[4] the Division aggressively prosecuted road and airport construction cartels that allowed conspirators to capture consumer surplus without any evident suppression in output. In most (perhaps all) of those cases, the Division brought a criminal action after the government agency had already agreed to pay the cartel price, so any suppression in output would be speculative and based on availability of funds for the next government's future road or airport construction contracts.

Avoiding undue transfers of wealth does not stand alone as an antitrust goal, but protecting consumer pocket books from market power overcharges is probably at the core of political support for the antitrust laws.[5] Sound economic policy also requires that antitrust address the wealth transfer issue. In most cases, market power will bring both a misallocation of resources and a wealth transfer injury. But these harms

---

2. R. BORK, ANTITRUST PARADOX: A POLICY AT WAR WITH ITSELF 427 (1993); Rule, *Merger Enforcement Policy: Protecting the Consumer,* 56 ANTITRUST L.J. 739, 740 (1987). See also the views expressed in Baxter, *Separation of Powers, Prosecutorial Discretion, and the 'Common Law' Nature of Antitrust Law,* 60 TEX. L. REV. 661, 693–94 (1982).

3. This is a key point in Lande, *Wealth Transfers as the Original and Primary Concern of Antitrust: The Efficiency Interpretation Challenged,* 34 HASTINGS L.J. 67 (1982).

4. See the positions expressed by Assistant Attorneys General Baxter and Rule, *supra* note 2.

5. The political strength of the wealth transfer concern is reflected in the large number of commentators who now embrace this goal. Lande, *The Rise and (Coming) Fall of Efficiency as the Ruler of Antitrust,* 33 Antitrust Bull. 429, 455–63 (1988).

are not always complementary. Suppose that a merger results in substantial efficiencies. If the postmerger market remains competitive, the efficiencies will be passed on to consumers in the form of price reductions. But suppose the merger produces not only efficiencies but also market power. After the merger, there will be various possible outcomes. For one, the merged entity may be able to continue charging the same price, capturing the full efficiency gain as a gain in its revenue. Under these circumstances, society could not achieve the efficiency gain without tolerating an increase in market power. Allowing the merger to go forward would achieve the efficiency gain. There is no net allocative loss due to the merger (because the merged entity does not increase price above the premerger level). But there is a wealth transfer (the extent of the merged entity's revenue gain) directly tied to the increase in market power. Alternatively, in the postmerger market the new entity may face some competition to which it responds by reducing the price below premerger levels, thus sharing the efficiency gain with consumers, although exercising enough power to keep part of that gain in supracompetitive profits—a producer surplus.

Wealth transfer and efficient allocation goals could also conflict in certain cases of price discrimination. Suppose that a powerful seller of a machine requires that buyers purchase spare parts or service only from an approved source. The seller might impose supra-competitive prices on the aftermarket sales, effectively charging intensive users a high price and less intensive users a lower price for the bundled products and services. At least in theory, this price discrimination scheme might result in a more efficient allocation of the seller's machines because low intensive users would be able to procure a machine that they would not buy at a higher packaged price. Whatever allocative gain might be reflected in this arrangement would have to be weighed against the wealth transfer losses to more intensive users who were forced to pay a higher price for the bundled products and services.[6]

Those who claim that a wealth transfer should be of no concern to antitrust often assume that any revenue gains from the exercise of market power will be passed on to stockholders, either in the form of dividends or increased value of the firm stock.[7] But this assumption, too, is on shaky ground. Over time, a firm enjoying market power is likely to incur additional costs of two types: *x-inefficiencies* and *rent-seeking*, costs that will prevent much (or all) of the revenue gain from benefitting stockholders.

An x-inefficiency is the increase in cost linked to relaxed or self-indulgent behavior by a firm possessing market power. A firm in a secure position, for example, might pay less attention to efficient production and marketing, buy labor peace at excessive cost or fail to shop or bargain aggressively for other inputs. There is some evidence that the

6. For a more detailed description of the potential allocative and wealth transfer effects of this bundled sale, see §§ 8.3b2, 8.3c1, 8.3c3.

7. Rule, *Merger Enforcement Policy*, supra note 2, at 740–42.

salaries and amenities of top management and the wages of rank and file employees tend to be higher in industries in which concentration is high.[8] Regulated public utilities, for example, may tolerate high costs that are passed on to the ratepayer. In a more competitive environment, no rival can afford to ignore such a cost. Although measurement of x-inefficiencies is difficult, Scherer and Ross find it plausible that the loss from these inefficiencies is "at least as large as the welfare losses from resource misallocation."[9]

Rent-seeking behavior of a firm possessing market power occurs when the firm incurs expenditures to extend or entrench its position of power. Once having enjoyed the fruits of market power, most sellers will resist its erosion. For example, a monopolist may spend substantial funds, probably up to the point of its monopoly gain (and, for short periods, perhaps even more than that gain) in order to maintain market position. Money might be spent to lobby legislators or regulators to forestall an undermining of the seller's market power. Litigation might be used to thwart competitors. A powerful firm might also advertise more heavily in order to thwart a potential entrant. Or a seller might spend extra money redesigning a product in a manner that does not improve performance but does make it more difficult for competitors to sell aftermarket parts in competition with the seller. There may be numerous strategies open to a firm with power that will be profit-maximizing for it only because the strategy protects or enhances power.

1.5b3. Preserving Consumer Choice

All else being equal, consumers would prefer having a choice of suppliers or brands available to purchase. Even if differing brands are deemed equal in some overall price-quality assessment, individual buyers may prefer one brand's features over another. Large buyers often prefer to divide their purchases among available suppliers for reasons that may have nothing to do with quality or price differences. Over-reliance on a single supplier is perceived to raise business risks to the buyer. If a single source supplier has labor difficulties, imposes an abrupt price increase, has a fall-off in quality, or the begins defaulting on critically timed deliveries, the buyer may face losses that could have been avoided had other suppliers been available and familiar with the buyer's needs. Based on these and other concerns, consumer choice has been identified as a goal of antitrust policy.[10] Indeed, it has been suggested that consumer choice may be a comprehensive analytical model for all antitrust policy, one that avoids an undue emphasis on price at the expense of non-price competition.[11] Preserving consumer choice is also important

---

8. F. Scherer & D. Ross, Industrial Market Structure And Economic Performance 681–82 (3d ed. 1990).

9. Id. at 672.

10. FTC v. Indiana Fed'n of Dentists, 476 U.S. 447, 459, 106 S.Ct. 2009, 90 L.Ed.2d 445 (1986)(horizontal agreement that limits "consumer choice by impeding the 'ordinary give and take of the market

place,' cannot be sustained under the Rule of Reason.")(quoting National Soc'y of Prof. Engineers v. United States, 435 U.S. 679, 692, 98 S.Ct. 1355, 55 L.Ed.2d 637 (1978)).

11. Lande, Consumer Choice as the Ultimate Goal of Antitrust, 62 U.Pitt. L.Rev. 503 (2001).

because it ensures a market structure conducive to innovation and technological improvement, addressed separately below.

If a dominant firm exercises monopsony power, it is the sellers who may suffer from reduced choice. Aside from deadweight loss or wealth transfer injuries, sellers confronting powerful buyers may also incur greater business risks based on reduced choice in sellers who would purchase their product.

1.5c. Promoting Innovation and Technological Progress

Another widely accepted goal of antitrust policy is to promote innovation, or what the economists refer to as the *dynamic efficiency* of the economy. Allocative efficiency means producing and distributing more efficiently through the use of existing technology. Dynamic efficiency refers to improvements in the technology: improving the product, producing it more efficiently, or perhaps replacing it with an entirely different product that outperforms the old one. Dynamism in the economy can also generate new and more efficient methods in distribution. Economists believe that society benefits far more (real income rates grow faster) from dynamic efficiency than from allocative efficiency.[12] But the role of competition in promoting dynamic efficiency is less understood, creating a challenge for fixing the most desirable antitrust policy toward research and development.

There is agreement that the market fosters innovation by rewarding those who bring new and better products into the market. A diverse market with multiple players competing to be the first to introduce meaningful innovation should increase the pace and variety of innovation—both the development of new processes or products and their use and commercialization. A monopolist has a reduced incentive to innovate; if it does innovate, it may be motivated to suppress or delay commercialization. Indeed, to protect its monopoly, a firm may even attempt to suppress or discourage others from marketing available innovation. Based upon the foregoing, one might safely conclude that antitrust policy is consistent with fostering innovation and its subsequent commercialization. But an inventor's reward is bolstered by the patent system, which provides a legal monopoly for a term of years as additional compensation to the inventor. Such a monopoly may but need not be at odds with the market principles underlying antitrust. The patent system, like antitrust, is aimed at improving efficiency, but each system responds to a different market deficiency. While antitrust seeks to limit or redress allocative and wealth transfer problems resulting from market power, the patent system seeks to encourage adequate allocation of investment in research and development by overcoming a "free rider" problem. Consistency between the two systems is achieved when the protection granted by the patent system is sufficient to encourage needed research and development investment, but does not unnecessari-

12. F. SCHERER & D. ROSS, INDUSTRIAL   ANCE 31 (3d ed. 1990).
MARKET STRUCTURE AND ECONOMIC PERFORM-

ly stifle competition. Excessive patent protection, like excessive market power, may be hurtful to efficiency goals, not helpful. If powerful firms obtain large numbers of overlapping patents, they may be asserted to hinder or prevent rivals from innovating. Lengthy patent protection may also over-reward a firm for its innovation while preventing competition that would bring down consumer prices. There may also be situations other than those covered by patent and other intellectual property law in which antitrust principles should defer to the greater social interest in innovation. In particular, when massive resources are required to innovate and develop, as may be the case in industries such as computers and aerospace, a single firm acting alone may be incapable of pursuing the innovation. Joint activity that might confer market power (and might be condemned under Section 1 of the Sherman Act) may be necessary to foster that innovation. The United States Congress has made concessions to these interests by providing limited antitrust exemptions for certain joint research and development activity.[13]

1.5d. Protecting Individual Firms: Fairness and Equity Interests

Another goal of the framers of the Sherman Act was to protect the right of any person to enter and pursue a line of work or business. Today, that goal has been rejected by some theorists and courts, and given low priority by others. Competition is a dispassionate mechanism that will cause many business failures. The Supreme Court has said that "[i]t is competition, not competitors, which the Act protects."[14] The Court has given weight to this principle by requiring that a private plaintiff prove "antitrust injury" as a precondition for pursuing an antitrust claim,[15] a concept apparently limited to allocative and wealth transfer injuries. The antitrust laws should avoid constructions that allow an inefficient or incompetent business to survive at the expense of higher prices or lower quality for consumers. But protecting an individual firm's interests is often consistent with these antitrust goals. For example, many antitrust violations raise rivals' costs or discriminate against targeted rivals. A tie-in that exploits the buyer's sunk costs (a lock-in) will make it difficult for the buyer to compete against rival buyers who are not so exploited. Predatory pricing by a powerful firm can drive rivals from the market, or discipline them to accept subservient status. Under such circumstances, the defendant's conduct can be harmful to consumer welfare goals as well as to individual firms. In addition, it has been argued that noneconomic factors, such as injury to competitors, may validly tip the scales when, in a particular case, the evidence of competitive injury and competitive benefits is evenly bal-

---

13. The National Cooperative Research Act of 1984, Pub. L. No. 98–462, 98 Stat. 1815 (codified in 15 U.S.C.A. §§ 4301–4306). See §§ 5.3l and 13.2a1v.

14. Brown Shoe Co. v. United States, 370 U.S. 294, 344, 82 S.Ct. 1502, 8 L.Ed.2d 510 (1962).

15. Brunswick Corp. v. Pueblo Bowl–O–Mat, Inc., 429 U.S. 477, 97 S.Ct. 690, 50 L.Ed.2d 701 (1977). See § 17.2b.

anced.[16] The Supreme Court has also given weight to the injury to competitors in cases such as Aspen Skiing Co. v. Aspen Highlands Skiing Corp.[17] and Klor's, Inc. v. Broadway–Hale Stores, Inc.[18] Because many antitrust cases are tried before a jury, any conduct by a defendant that is perceived as unfair may influence outcomes.[19] By the end of the twentieth century, there was no longer (if there ever was) a right of a displaced competitor to claim that the displacement in and of itself was grounds for antitrust relief. But given allocative or wealth transfer effects, evidence of such injury (and perhaps the unfairness associated with it) may weigh in favor of finding an antitrust violation.

1.5e.   Decentralized Economic Power: Populist Values

The populist goal of preventing the growth of big business motivated many supporters of the Sherman Act and still had some force during the activist period of antitrust enforcement that lasted into the 1960s. In *United States v. Aluminum Co. of America*, Judge Learned Hand wrote: "It is possible, because of its indirect social or moral effect, to prefer a system of small producers, each dependent for his success upon his own skill and character, to one in which the great mass of those engaged must accept the direction of a few."[20] Picking up on this theme, Chief Justice Warren wrote in 1962:

> [W]e cannot fail to recognize Congress' desire to promote competition through the protection of viable, small, locally owned businesses. Congress appreciated that occasional higher costs and prices might result from the maintenance of fragmented industries and markets. It resolved these competing considerations in favor of decentralization. We must give effect to that decision.[21]

As allocative efficiency became a more dominant goal of antitrust, the goal of maintaining a decentralized economy lost force. The internationalization of markets has reenforced this change. When major U.S. industries lost ground in competition with foreign rivals, it became clear that the efficiency of American firms should be a priority in crafting antitrust policy. A second consideration was the difficulty in formulating a workable test for pursuit of a decentralization goal: unless all moves toward concentration were to be condemned, courts were faced with an impossibly subjective balancing of how much lost efficiency should be tolerated in order to maintain dispersed economic power.

Nonetheless, the inherent power of the Jeffersonian ideal of dispersed economic power has not disappeared entirely from antitrust. For

---

16. Pitofsky, *The Political Content of Antitrust,* 127 U. Pa. L. Rev. 1051, 1074–75 (1979).

17. 472 U.S. 585, 105 S.Ct. 2847, 86 L.Ed.2d 467 (1985).

18. 359 U.S. 207, 79 S.Ct. 705, 3 L.Ed.2d 741 (1959).

19. An example of a case in which conduct toward rivals appeared blatantly un-

fair and may have influenced the outcome is Conwood Co., L.P. v. United States Tobacco Co., 290 F.3d 768 (6th Cir. 2002).

20. 148 F.2d 416, 427 (2d Cir.1945).

21. Brown Shoe Co. v. United States, 370 U.S. 294, 344, 82 S.Ct. 1502, 8 L.Ed.2d 510 (1962).

example, merger enforcement policy still is based on an incipiency standard: Section 7 of the Clayton Act forbids increases in concentration that "may" substantially reduce competition.[22] Although recent iterations of federal merger guidelines have shifted to allow greater levels of concentration, a premise of these guidelines remains that trends toward concentration are to be halted in their incipiency–well before levels of monopoly power are reached. In the merger guidelines the federal enforcement agencies have found objective bases for determining how great a risk of reduction is sufficient by considering concentration ratios and entry barriers, and focusing on whether the risk of price fixing is noticeably increased by the structural change caused by the merger. The incipiency standard serves the goal of maintaining dispersed economic power and is also consistent with the consumer welfare goals of avoiding deadweight and wealth transfer injuries. The goal of maintaining dispersed economic power may still serve as a tiebreaker in much the same way as the goal of protecting an individual firm's right to compete.

§ 1.6   The Role of Economics in Antitrust

The law and economics movement has affected most branches of law in the United States. But antitrust differs from other legal topics because the subjects with which antitrust deals have always been central to the social science of microeconomics. Economics is dedicated to explaining the production, distribution and consumption of wealth. Microeconomic theory focuses on the workings or dysfunctions of the market system, precisely the system antitrust is intended to preserve and protect. Competition and the kinds of industrial structures that stimulate competition are also the explicit subjects of a related branch of economics, that of industrial organization. Today, one interested in antitrust must do some economic thinking. Effective antitrust lawyers must understand not only the strengths, diversity and breadth of economics, but also some of its limitations, and both are matters addressed in this section.

During the century plus period since antitrust became national policy, change has marked economics as it has the law. Early on, economists tended to be indifferent or even hostile to antitrust. Most of them saw tariffs as the predominant cause of monopoly and regarded the issues addressed by the Sherman Act as something less than momentous. The courts in the early cases did their own analyzing of competition without much scholarly help. Concepts that industrial organization theorists addressed in the mid-twentieth century were dealt with much earlier by courts attempting to piece together an understanding of competition. In time, all this changed. By the 1930s, economists were addressing competition theoretically, and by mid-century sustained theoretical and empirical studies were becoming available. This allowed courts to turn more and more toward theoretical economics for insight

22. 15 U.S.C.A. § 18.

and aid in the development of antitrust doctrine. Chapter 2, addressing market power, introduces a number of basic economic terms and concepts that have come to be touchstones for antitrust analysis.

Although the specific limitations of various economic approaches are best left until the substantive topics are addressed, there are four noteworthy limits on the use of economics in antitrust analysis: (1) economic learning is an evolving and incomplete source, in part because the target of this study—the economy—is itself an everchanging phenomenon; (2) many conclusions even by leading economists are not a matter of consensus and some are highly controverted; (3) two of the most basic models of neo-classical economic analysis–the model of monopoly and the model of perfect competition–are based upon assumptions that are never fully met in real life markets; and (4) the assumptions that underlie economic analysis are often difficult or impossible to prove in an agency investigation or litigated case.

Economists have examined competition issues at least since Adam Smith, but practices that become the focus of antitrust enforcement have not always been studied thoroughly. In a rapidly changing economy, economic theory is often a step or two behind the wave. For example, as the information-based economy advances, many markets are becoming clusters of interconnected units. The power of computer chips doubles every eighteen months, the value of networks increases exponentially with increases in the number of users, and the need for compatibility of communication devices and input and output devices evokes a need for industrywide standards. If standards are proprietary, they can yield power that can be leveraged, perhaps throughout large segments of interrelated markets. Economists are only beginning to fully understand the resulting "network externalities," and both the antitrust and intellectual property laws have yet to fully integrate either the new market realities or the emerging economic insights. Also, while economists have for decades been explaining the size and vertical links of firms in terms of maximizing scale economies and minimizing transaction costs, they have scarcely begun to think about whether, in an economy in which all players at every vertical level can be in instant communication, cost minimization can be achieved by further horizontal and vertical disaggregation, rather than through horizontal and vertical mergers.[1] As another instance, the explosion in franchising has led to considerable economic analysis, but this material is still evolving and disagreements are substantial. Even in areas long subject to antitrust enforcement, such as vertical restraints, disagreements and debates among economists are continuing and vigorous.

In many cases, economic debate leading to refinements in analysis will occur only after courts have addressed an alleged anticompetitive practice. But the problem goes beyond debate about critical issues. Economic orthodoxy changes over time and can be expected to continue

§ 1.6

1. See generally, L. Downes & C. Mui, Unleashing the Killer App: Digital Strategies for Market Dominance (1998).

to do so. This is a forceful reason for not prematurely integrating economic assumptions into legal doctrine. It is better to keep the legal norms goal-oriented and general, allowing the theoretical and empirical debate to inform the fact finder. Otherwise, the risk of premature closure on inadequate or even erroneous theoretical propositions is significant. As noted above, a typical turn of the century economist would have supposed that monopoly was no threat, except as sustained by government through tariffs or other interventions. Later, during the mid-twentieth century, economists turned to structural analysis as a means of understanding market power. Meanwhile, some contemporary economists seem to stand where their forefathers stood at the turn of the century—they feel that monopoly can only be sustained by direct governmental intervention. Others, by contrast, focus on firm strategies that raise the costs of rivals. In addition to changes in orthodoxy, the very methods used by economists vary widely and are subject to change. Microeconomic theorists traditionally have reasoned deductively from simplified economic models subject to rigorous mathematical proof. More recently, game theorists have expanded the ability of economists to use deductive logic to analyze oligopolistic behavior not subject to a simplified model. Industrial organization economists make use of empirical data in their efforts to draw conclusions about structure, conduct and performance. The strength of such empirical research obviously is increased as new and more statistically valid data sources become available to economists, and as the methodologies for statistical analysis are developed and improved.

The models of monopoly and perfect competition, discussed in Chapter 2, are the careful and largely unchallenged product of deductive logic. But the assumptions upon which they are based (e.g., one seller or many sellers) are a far cry from the markets typically encountered—markets with from two or three to several sellers, not just one, nor yet a crowd. Game theory expands an economist's ability to study oligopoly, a condition much more descriptive of real markets than the monopoly or competition models. But while allowing an analysis of differing variables that affect outcome, a game theorist's conclusions are also valid only to the extent the underlying premises conform with market realities. Finally, the economist's theoretical positions, once accepted, are often difficult or impossible to apply to actual markets—or can be applied to them only with considerable risk of error—because factual indeterminacies cannot be resolved, or can be resolved only at excessive cost. To the law, it avails nothing to conclude that a particular legal intervention will yield greater allocative efficiency in a market characterized as a tight oligopoly, especially when barriers to entry are substantial, if there is no satisfactory technique for determining whether a particular set of firms do constitute a "tight oligopoly" or whether entry barriers exceed the threshold that the theoretical position deems crucial.

§ 1.7 Antitrust Challenges

Antitrust faces a number of critical unresolved issues, some old, some new. Three of these challenges are highlighted here.

1.7a.   The Oligopoly/Oligopsony Problem

Oligopolists can, through tacit parallel conduct, achieve output reductions and inflated prices comparable to those engendered by a cartel or monopolist. Because tacit parallel conduct by either powerful sellers or powerful buyers may be insufficient to constitute a conspiracy, it may, unlike cartel conduct, be beyond the reach of Sherman Section 1. This result would leave a broad category of anticompetitive conduct outside the coverage of federal antitrust law.[1]

Society's concern with oligopoly and oligopsony may be reduced because of emergence of countervailing power. Countervailing power is widely present in the economy and allows powerful buyers to obtain lower prices even from oligopolistic sellers. There are, however, many classes of small buyers (or small sellers confronting oligopsonistic buyers) for whom the exercise of countering power is not a realistic option.[2] For these small players, the unresolved oligopoly problem presents an acute issue because of discriminatory terms that raise their costs and threaten their survival even if they are innovative and efficient players.

1.7b.   Unresolved Vertical Restraints Issues

Another unresolved issue is developing a proper platform for analyzing the competitive effects of vertical restraints–those restraints imposed by a power player in a customer-supplier relationship. This analysis has been largely frozen by the Supreme Court's 1977 decision in Continental TV v. GTE Sylvania, which has dictated the parameters of lower court and subsequent Supreme Court decisions addressing vertical restraints. This paradigm fails to recognize the competition that occurs between vertical players and the opportunity for abuse that arises when an upstream or downstream players wields power. These abuses can undermine intrabrand competition, often at the retail level, and harm interbrand competition at all levels.[3] Intrabrand competition can never be a fully adequate substitute for interbrand competition, yet where interbrand rivalry is undermined by brand selling or the presence of patents or copyrights, intrabrand competition may be all that stands between the consumer and the abusive behavior of power players at various levels of the distribution system. These issues are addressed in Chapters VI and VII.

1.7c.   Can Competition Policy Work in High Tech Markets?

High tech industries involve fast-moving developments in highly complex factual settings. Many of these industries involve networking

---

§ 1.7

1.   See the discussion in § 5.2a.

2.   See Grimes, *The Sherman Act's Unintended Bias Against Lilliputians:*

Small Players' Collective Action as a Counter to Relational Market Power, 69 ANTITRUST L. J. 195 (2001).

3.   Chapters 6 and 7.

efficiencies: the larger the network of users, the more useful and cost-efficient the product becomes. Can antitrust react with sufficient speed and expertise to play a constructive role in these industries? How, if at all, should the standards of antitrust be adjusted to account for networking efficiencies? Or for the infeasibility of marginal cost pricing in some of these industries? These and other related issues are addressed at various points throughout this book.[4]

High tech industries also make extensive use of, and arguably depend upon, intellectual property rights. Firms that possess intellectual property are constantly pushing to extend the exclusive rights accorded to them. For example, filings with the Patent Office are said to have achieved record levels and have raised concerns that firms are using ill-founded patents tactically to prevent legitimate competition and not as a reward for a legitimate and valuable research break-through.[5] The FTC has held extensive hearings that address these and other related issues. The underlying policy concerns color many of the interpretive questions involving the interaction of antitrust and intellectual property law addressed in Chapter XV.

§ 1.8 Conclusion

It is sometimes said that every business favors antitrust, except for enforcement against its own activities. After more than a century, antitrust policy is well established, yet constantly subject to attack and to developmental vacillations fueled by changing political and economic currents, and special interest politics. The resiliency of antitrust is reinforced by tradition and the momentum provided by well-established enforcement agencies, a large private bar, and emphasis on consumer welfare goals that the general public can understand and support. Yet, these forces alone will probably not ensure antitrust's survival. It will survive and thrive only if antitrust decision-makers can adopt antitrust policy to rapidly changing industrial and commercial conditions, and can show the relevancy of enforcement activities in light of consumer welfare and resistance to economic oppression. If antitrust cannot effectively deter abuse, those exercising market power, however oppressively, will have free sway, and calls for regulation or other more intrusive steps by government will follow.

As a protector of the market mechanism, antitrust's primary goal is in maintaining a system of economic allocation that decentralizes power while leaving decisions, as much as possible, in the hands of individual firms. A decentralized market system promotes progress and efficiency, reduces risks of mistakes, minimizes opportunities and reduces incentives for corruption of government officials, and generally increases public confidence in the fairness and equity of the allocation of available resources.

---

4. For an overview of these issues, see L. Sullivan, *Is Competition Policy Possible in High Tech Markets?: An Inquiry Into Antitrust, Intellectual Property, and Broadband Regulation As Applied to "The New Economy"*, 52 CASE W. RES. L. REV. 41 (2001).

5. Id. at 62–75.

Chapter II

MARKET POWER AS A BASIS FOR ANTITRUST ENFORCEMENT: EFFECTS AND MEASUREMENT

Table of Sections

§ 2.1 Introduction

Antitrust is concerned with the power of market participants to distort the competitive process. This distortion can misallocate resources, transfer wealth from consumers and other protected groups to market participants with power, or stifle new entry or innovation and commercialization. Without power, a market participant can do none of these things but is, instead, itself subject to the discipline of competition. In many cases, an exercise of power that distorts competition will also implicate fairness values. Market participants may be treated in a discriminatory fashion because they lack the power or knowledge of larger or better informed participants. But the root of antitrust harm is power.

The power relevant for antitrust is called *market power*. It is power that is exercised by commercial means and should be distinguished from other forms of power such as military power or political power. A large market player may exercise political as well as market power, and a state enterprise may have the direct backing of military power. But these other forms of power need not be present in order for market power to be exercised.

For some antitrust offenses market power may be inferred from the violative conduct. For example, conspiracies among competitors to affect price or output are generally treated as *per se* unlawful. The plaintiff who establishes such behavior by the defendants need not make a separate showing that the defendants possess market power.[1] Still, whether market power is so inferred or must be separately established, its presence is a prerequisite for finding an antitrust violation. Some such power is, moreover, too light or transitory to warrant antitrust intervention. The threshold may vary depending upon the type of antitrust violation and the remedy that is sought.

This chapter begins by explaining that market power is, at its core, linked to elasticity of supply or demand. For sellers, market power may be defined as the ability to raise the price without losing sales sufficient to offset increased revenues from the higher price. The Chapter then describes various contexts in which market power may occur, including power associated with a single dominant seller (monopoly), with a market of few sellers (oligopoly), with agreement among competitors about price (cartelization) and with various types of single-brand sellers. It addresses the question of how market power may be measured and proven in antitrust cases. Finally, it addresses the special set of issues related to the existence and exercise of power on the buyer's side.

§ 2.1

1. See generally § 5.4.

§ 2.2 Market Power Defined

Although market power can be exercised by a participant either as a seller or as a buyer, it is most typically defined from the point of view of the seller: market power is the seller's ability to raise and sustain a price increase without losing so many sales that it must rescind the increase.[1] Some economists refer to this power as "monopoly power."[2]

Market power is directly correlated with the steepness of the demand curve. Demand curves are representations of buyer responses to changes in prices. In the theoretical model of perfect competition, the individual seller confronts a horizontal or flat demand curve. There is no market power because the seller has no ability to raise its price above the market level, even by a small amount, without losing all of its business. See Figure 2.2A below. In such a market each seller will set its output at the level at which the market price will just cover its costs (including a return on its capital adequate to attract and sustain its investment).[3] A competitive market price is thus a price directly related to cost.

Most sellers of branded products confront a downward sloping demand curve. Consumer demand for the seller's product will decrease with increased price, but will not disappear. If the seller can earn a higher return by raising its prices above its costs (including a reasonable return on capital)—that is, if the revenue gained from the increased price exceeds the revenue lost from fewer sales, the seller has market power.

Elasticity of demand is a concept used to signify for a particular demand curve the relationship between changes in price and responsive changes in demand. If consumer demand drops one unit for each one unit of increase in price, the demand curve will drop at a 45° angle from the horizontal axis. If demand drops less rapidly, creating a slope only slightly downward sloping, demand is said to be *elastic*. Even relatively small increases in price will cause large numbers of consumers to stop buying the seller's product, a condition consistent with limited market power. See figure 2.2A below. If the demand curve drops more sharply than a 45° angle, creating a more nearly vertical slope, demand is said to be *inelastic*. Even relatively large price increases may cause few customers to stop buying the seller's product, a condition consistent with substantial market power.

§ 2.2

1. Landes & Posner, *Market Power in Antitrust Cases,* 94 HARV. L. REV. 937, 939 (1981). See also a similar definition offered in D. CARLTON & J. PERLOFF, MODERN INDUSTRIAL ORGANIZATION 8, 281 (2d ed. 1994).

2. F. M. SCHERER & D. ROSS, INDUSTRIAL MARKET STRUCTURE AND ECONOMIC PERFORMANCE 17 (3d ed. 1990).

3. See generally M. SEIDENFELD, MICRO ECONOMIC PREDICATES TO LAW AND ECONOMICS, Chap. 3 (1996).

Figure 2.2A
Market Power Illustrated Through Demand Curves

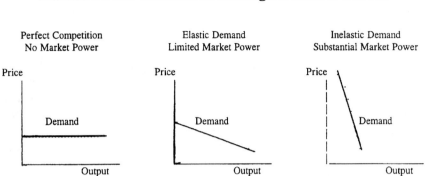

The demand curves presented here are simplified models with straight lines to represent demand response. In real markets, the demand curves may have varying slopes, with some portions falling away from the horizontal only slightly (elastic) while other portions slope downwards sharply (inelastic). A seller may enjoy substantial pricing discretion for those outputs associated with an inelastic slope, but little pricing discretion for the elastic portions of the slope. See figure 2.2B below. The larger the price range over which the demand curve remains inelastic, the greater the seller's potential market power. A hypothetical monopolist could be expected to continue to push price upward to the point where greater elasticity of demand causes a large enough drop in sales to make further price increases unprofitable. Thus, although the monopolist may peg its price at a point on the curve at which demand has become elastic, it is the existence of a relatively inelastic segment of the curve that defines the monopolist's market power.

Figure 2.2B
Market Power in a Hypothetical Real Market

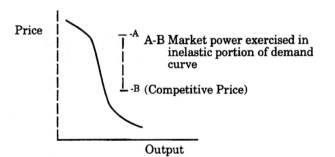

Some writers draw a distinction between the term "market power" as used in economic literature and the use of that term in antitrust. In economics, any downward sloping demand curve may describe a measure of market power. In antitrust, the focus is on substantial and nontransitory market power that suggests injury to competition. Inelasticity of demand that is transitory or, although nontransitory, is sustained over a very narrow range of prices, would not be considered the type of market power that warrants antitrust intervention. Each of these points may be illustrated. If a firm markets an improved product that performs better than competing offerings, it may increase its price, lowering its output below the level that perfect competition would produce. Or, if a retailer's newly adopted warehouse mode of operations allows it to sell more efficiently, it may sell at a price that passes only part of that gain on to consumers, preserving the remainder as a higher return. Each firm faces a downward sloping demand curve consistent with market power for each has the ability to raise or maintain price above the competitive level without losing substantial sales. In each of these cases, the higher profitability, although it may be substantial, may prove transitory. High profits will encourage rivals to emulate the improved product or innovative retailing method. The high profits serve as an incentive for rivals to mimic a new competitive initiative.

Other forms of power over price, although nontransitory, may prove too insignificant to be the basis of antitrust intervention. Some market power may, for example, be based on the seller's location. Suppose that there are four grocery stores in a small community, each located in a different geographic quadrant of that community. Consumers who are close to one store may prefer to shop there, even if prices are slightly higher (perhaps 1 percent higher) than the rival stores. Indeed, each of the four stores may similarly exploit its geographic advantage, each charging prices that are slightly higher than would be possible if all four stores were located in the same shopping center. The willingness of local consumers to tolerate slightly higher prices in order not to travel longer distances creates a downward sloping demand curve, an indication of some power over price. If such a location advantage were to allow great pricing discretion—say, in the first supermarket located near a new housing development—high profits should attract new entrants to that location. On the other hand, a small but enduring amount of power over price associated with location advantage should generally not be a concern of antitrust.

For antitrust purposes, then, market power must involve inelasticity of demand that is both nontransitory and covers more than a narrow range of prices. Such power might be exercised, for example, by a monopolist; by an oligopolist engaging in strategic behavior; by a cartel; by a patent holder or branded product seller that has differentiated its product in a way other sellers cannot easily replicate; by a seller controlling its aftermarket; by a seller that exploits buyer information voids to extract a higher return; or by a seller or buyer in a vertical relationship with a smaller and dependent firm (as in franchising). These exercises of power are possible targets of antitrust, but are not uniformly vulnerable. Certain exercises of market power may be tolerated to attain other social goals. A patent monopoly is tolerated (indeed fostered) to encourage innovation. Some manifestations of franchisor power over franchises may be tolerated as enhancing the efficiencies of franchising.

Other monopolies thought to be efficient (such as utilities providing gas, electricity, or water) may be permitted subject to public regulation of rates.

2.2a. Varying Market Power Thresholds in the Courts

The courts have offered a variety of market power definitions over the years but have consistently recognized the importance of a seller's power over price. Not surprisingly, Judge Posner has expressly endorsed a classic economic definition of market power that he and Landes articulated in a leading article.[4] The Supreme Court has defined market power in a variety of ways that either expressly or, by implication, look to the seller's power over price, as indicated by elasticity of demand. For example, in merger cases such as *Brown Shoe*, the Supreme Court has focused on the "cross-elasticity of demand" among products as the key to determining the confines of a market.[5] In monopolization cases, the Court has said that the existence of market power can be determined by examining elasticities ("the responsiveness of the sales of one product to price changes of the other").[6] In the predatory pricing context, the Supreme Court has described market power as the ability of a seller "to set higher than competitive prices."[7] And in the tying context, the Supreme Court has said that market power is the power " 'to force a purchaser to do something that he would not do in a competitive market.' "[8] Such definitions do not all unambiguously adopt the power-over-price definition of market power, but most imply that definition and all are consistent with it.

This brief survey suggests that the Court's efforts to define market power is still a work in progress. Although elasticity of demand remains the common core in the Supreme Court's treatment of market power, it

---

4. Landes & Posner, supra note 1. Judge Posner has restated this definition in various opinions. In re Brand Name Prescription Drugs Antitrust Litigation, 123 F.3d 599, 603 (7th Cir.1997) (market power or monopoly power is "the power to raise price above cost without losing so many sales as to make the price rise unsustainable"), cert. denied, 522 U.S. 1153, 118 S.Ct. 1178, 140 L.Ed.2d 186 (1998); Olympia Equip. Leasing Co. v. Western Union Tel. Co., 797 F.2d 370, 373 (7th Cir.1986) (market power is "the power to raise prices without losing so much business that the price increase is unprofitable"), cert. denied, 480 U.S. 934, 107 S.Ct. 1574, 94 L.Ed.2d 765 (1987); Valley Liquors, Inc. v. Renfield Importers, Ltd., 678 F.2d 742, 745 (7th Cir.1982) (market power is the "power to raise prices significantly above the competitive level without losing all of one's business").

5. Brown Shoe Co. v. United States, 370 U.S. 294, 325, 82 S.Ct. 1502, 8 L.Ed.2d 510 (1962) (boundaries of a product market de-

termined by "interchangeability of use or the cross-elasticity of demand between the product itself and substitutes for it").

6. United States v. E. I. du Pont de Nemours & Co., 351 U.S. 377, 400, 76 S.Ct. 994, 100 L.Ed. 1264 (1956). The Court also said that the relevant market is defined by whether there is "cross-elasticity of demand" between cellophane and other wrappings. Id. at 393–404.

7. Matsushita Elec. Indus. Co. v. Zenith Radio Corp., 475 U.S. 574, 590, 106 S.Ct. 1348, 89 L.Ed.2d 538 (1986).

8. Eastman Kodak Co. v. Image Technical Servs., Inc., 504 U.S. 451, 464, 112 S.Ct. 2072, 119 L.Ed.2d 265 (1992) (quoting Jefferson Parish Hosp. Dist. No. 2 v. Hyde, 466 U.S. 2, 14, 104 S.Ct. 1551, 80 L.Ed.2d 2 (1984)). The Kodak Court, 504 U.S. at 464, also cited with approval the market power definition in Fortner Enters., Inc. v. United States Steel Corp., 394 U.S. 495, 503, 89 S.Ct. 1252, 22 L.Ed.2d 495 (1969) (market power is "the ability of a single seller to raise price and restrict output").

is unlikely that the Court can specify precise tolerance levels for the amount or durability of market power.

The case survey also suggests tolerance for different levels of market power depending on the nature of the violation. For example, there tends to be higher tolerance of market power in monopolization cases, less tolerance in horizontal restraint cases. Even within a narrower category, such as intrabrand distribution restraints, market power may be more readily tolerated in some manifestations (vertical nonprice restraints) than in others (vertical price restraints).[9] Variation in tolerance levels for market power may be reflected in differing descriptions of market power, or in differing threshold showings of that power. Under Section 2 of the Sherman Act, the degree of power required for monopolization is greater than for attempted monopolization, where the plaintiff need only show a dangerous probability of success in achieving a monopoly.[10]

Another factor that may influence varying market power thresholds is the feasibility of remedial action. For example, a tie-in may be addressed through relatively straight-forward behavioral sanctions, whereas a claim of monopolization under Section 2 of the Sherman Act may require a far more difficult and expensive structural remedy such as divestiture of parts of the monopolist's business. The substantive requirements for these violations may be influenced by the perceived feasibility of relief. In individual cases, although remedial issues should not control the market power inquiry, there may be a tendency to demand a greater showing of market power when the requested relief is seen as intrusive or more difficult to impose.

The willingness to tolerate market power will also vary with the importance of an industry to consumers. A prosecutorial judgment might accept a given level of market power in an industry that affects only a small number of buyers, but be quick to challenge that degree of power in the oil industry that sells large amounts of its products to millions of consumers. A 1 percent overcharge by the oil industry might deprive consumers of hundreds of millions of dollars each year, whereas a 10 percent overcharge in an obscure industry may have a relatively trivial overall impact on consumers.

An awareness that antitrust has different thresholds of market power should not undermine the core definition of market power, which is as firmly rooted in principle as the politically driven vicissitudes of antitrust allow. Inelastic demand—the ability to raise or maintain price above the competitive level—is the starting point for antitrust analysis of market power.

2.2b. Criticisms of a Market Power Definition Keyed to Inelastic Demand

A market power definition keyed to inelastic demand has won near universal acceptance among economists, whose discipline leads them to

---

9. See the discussion in Chapter VI.

10. The power element in monopolization and attempted monopolization cases is addressed in § 3.3 and § 3.6.

describe and predict economic phenomena regardless of whether they implicate antitrust. Basic industrial organization texts use variations on this definition of market power.[11] The influential Landes and Posner article developed this definition and explained its relevance for antitrust.[12] The article generated a great deal of comment—much of it critical of the manner in which Landes and Posner proposed to measure market power in antitrust cases, but largely accepting of the definition itself.[13]

Despite wide acceptance among economists that market power equates with the power to raise or maintain prices above the competitive level, and numerous antitrust decisions consistent with this conception, a number of theorists reject this definition as a basis for antitrust intervention.[14] Sparked by the *Kodak* decision and its language confirming that market power may exist in a single brand, these theorists are less concerned with economic fundamentals and more with the perceived antitrust consequences of acceptance of the definition.[15] Critics argue that: (1) the definition is based upon a model of perfect competition that does not comport with market realities; (2) adoption of the definition will promote an activist antitrust agenda that could suppress a variety of procompetitive behavior; and (3) the definition is inconsistent with antitrust jurisprudence.

Much of this criticism is apparently driven by concern that a power over price definition could lead to expansion of antitrust intervention in single brand markets and is addressed in that context in § 2.4e1. Whatever antitrust's role in addressing single brand market power has been or will become, there is no principled basis for excluding a fundamentally sound economic definition from the world of antitrust.

In the view of some critics, a broad definition of market power represents overly rigorous adherence to the economic model of perfect

---

11. Carlton & Perloff, supra note 1, at 8, 281 (market power is the ability "to price profitably above the competitive level" or "above marginal cost"); Scherer & Ross, supra note 2, at 17 (market power or monopoly power is "some degree of power over price" or the ability to use changes in output to influence price); see also H. Hovenkamp, Federal Antitrust Policy: The Law of Competition and Its Practice § 3.1, at 79 (1994) ("Market power is the ability of a firm to increase its profits by reducing output and charging more than a competitive price for its product."); Hay, *Market Power in Antitrust*, 60 Antitrust L.J. 807, 813 (1992) (market power definitions "are satisfied by any firm facing a downward sloping demand curve" (emphasis omitted)).

12. Landes & Posner, supra note 1.

13. See the comments on Landes & Posner by Schmalensee, Kaplow, Brennan, and Ordover, Sykes, and Willig, in 95 Harv. L. Rev. 1787 (1982).

14. Klein, *Market Power in Aftermarkets*, 17 Managerial & Decision Econ. 143 (1996); Arthur, *The Costly Quest for Perfect Competition: Kodak and Nonstructural Market Power*, 69 N.Y.U. L. Rev. 1 (1994). For a more recent statement of Klein's position, see Klein & Wiley, *Competitive Price Discrimination as an Antitrust Justification for Intellectual Property Refusals to Deal*, 70 Antitrust L. J. 599, 621–633 (2003). A different view is offered by Baker, *Competitive Price Discrimination: The Exercise of Market Power Without Anticompetitive Effects (Comment on Klein & Wiley)*, 70 Antitrust L. J. 643 (2003).

15. Thus, Klein accepts inelastic demand as a definition of "economic power", but seeks to distinguish the type of power required for antitrust intervention. Klein, supra note 14, at 155–157.

competition. As Klein points out, many sellers of goods or services face a declining demand curve, i.e, one that allows them to raise prices without losing sufficient business to offset the revenue gain.[16] Any seller who offers a superior product or service, for example, probably has the ability to raise its prices above levels demanded by less proficient rivals. Such an exercise of power often leads to procompetitive results by attracting the capital and skill of new entrants that wish to take advantage of the high margin of profit. These observations are accurate. But the definition of market power (as described in § 2.2 above) requires, in addition to inelastic demand, a demonstration that the inelasticity is more than transitory and that it involves a significant range of pricing discretion. No court has held, nor has any theorist suggested, that the market power associated with competitive proficiency is, by itself, a basis for an antitrust relief.

Even a showing of market power (nontransitory, inelastic demand over a significant price range) does not establish an antitrust violation. To the contrary, antitrust tradition and precedent suggest that a competitor's "superior skill, foresight and industry"[17] are exculpatory. The courts regard the presence of some market power, either expressly shown (as in most monopolization or attempted monopolization and some horizontal restraint cases) or implied (as in many horizontal restraints cases) as necessary but not sufficient to establish an antitrust violation. In a monopolization case, the mere existence of power, even that associated with a 100 percent market share, does not establish a violation; the market power must be associated with some form of abusive conduct.[18] Many horizontal restraints are unlawful only upon a showing of power acquired or used in ways threatening to competition. Even some horizontal restraints subject to a *per se* rule are, since Broadcast Music, Inc. v. CBS, Inc.,[19] analyzed under a rule of reason analysis if they involve cooperative endeavors that, whether or not associated with an exercise of market power, offer substantial procompetitive gain.

As this suggests, power over price by itself should not be a basis for antitrust intervention. But that well-established principle is not under-

---

16. Id. at 157.

17. United States v. Aluminum Co. of America, 148 F.2d 416, 430 (2d Cir.1945). These words of Judge Learned Hand echo a sentiment expressed by Senator Hoar, the Chairman of the Senate Judiciary Committee, during the Senate debate on passage of the Sherman Act:

I suppose * * * that a man who merely by superior skill and intelligence, a breeder of horses or raiser of cattle, or manufacturer or artisan of any kind, got the whole business because nobody could do it as well as he could was not a monopolist, but that it involved something like the use of means which made it impossi-

ble for other persons to engage in fair competition, like the engrossing, the buying up of all other persons engaged in the same business.

21 Cong. Rec. 3,152 (1890).

18. See United States v. Grinnell Corp., 384 U.S. 563, 570–71, 86 S.Ct. 1698, 16 L.Ed.2d 778 (1966). See § 3.4 for a discussion of the conduct requirement.

19. 441 U.S. 1, 99 S.Ct. 1551, 60 L.Ed.2d 1 (1979) (applying the rule of reason to a cooperative arrangement that fixed the rates for certain copyright licenses). The increasing integration of rule of reason and *per se* analysis is addressed in § 5.3f.

cut by defining market power in a comprehensive manner consistent with economic learning. A definition keyed to elasticity of demand is more accurate and comprehensive than any alternative. Because direct measurement of elasticity will often not be possible, surrogates are used and are important. Analysts should be mindful, however, that they are only surrogates and that their function is to warrant inferences about elasticity. The most widely used surrogate measure of market power is to define the relevant market and to examine market shares, entry barriers and potential competition.[20] But adjustments may be made, given the purpose of the exercise. Indeed, even in the merger area, where the surrogate relevant market approach is strongly entrenched, the Justice Department/FTC 1992 Horizontal Merger Guidelines call for an adjustment in product market definitions based upon the degree to which products are differentiated or there exists a closeness of products as substitutes in a differentiated market.[21] Often referred to as the unilateral effects doctrine, this process is a refinement of the market definition approach designed to respond to differences in demand elasticities. See discussion in § 11.2e2.

§ 2.3   The Effects of Market Power

Market power can cause injury to the three key goals of antitrust policy: the efficient allocation of resources used to produce goods and services; avoiding undue wealth transfers from consumers to powerful sellers; and preserving and promoting the dynamic element of competition that ensures that innovative products and services are developed and efficiently allocated in the future. Market power can also be exercised to injure efficient market players by raising their costs, depriving them of business opportunities, or driving them out of business. Before examining these potential injuries and the economic policy debate that has swirled around them, we first examine the economic models for perfect competition and monopoly.

2.3a.   Monopoly and Perfect Competition

The term "monopoly" has a precise meaning in neo-classical economic analysis. It identifies an analytically useful theoretical construct, not a real market or market actor. A monopolist is a seller that has no rivals. The pure monopolist is the exclusive seller of a product or service for which there is no close substitute. There are few, if any, such pure monopolists. Some public utilities may come close. A company that provides electricity, water or natural gas to local residents may have no rivals either because it has an exclusive franchise or because it is a natural monopolist; the consumer must buy from the monopolist, or do without. Of course, even for such exclusive services, however necessary, consumers may have alternatives. If a resident is not hooked up to the natural gas service provided by the local monopolist, the resident may

20. The market definition approach is discussed in § 2.6b.

21. Department of Justice/FTC Horizontal Merger Guidelines §§ 2.21, 2.211 (1992).

still purchase bottled gas or obtain energy from other sources (electricity, fuel oil or coal). Electricity might be generated by purchasing a home generator, or the resident may find other ways of performing the tasks that electricity does so well—for example, by using candles or gas lamps for lighting. Bottled water may be purchased in the supermarket. So even basic utilities may fall short of the analytical model for pure monopoly.

Another condition for the theoretical model of monopoly is that the seller must set a single price for all sales of its product; price discrimination must not be possible. All buyers, of course, do not have the same *reservation* price (the highest price each is willing to pay). If the seller must sell at a single price, that price will be set at the level of the lowest reservation price of a buyer whose purchase is required to achieve a given level of output. If consumer demand falls off rapidly as the price is increased, the nondiscriminating monopolist will have to set a lower price in order to achieve a given level of output. The theoretical basis for the no discrimination assumption is arbitrage: that if the monopolist tried to discriminate, low price buyers would resell to high price buyers at an intermediate price until the monopolist's prices were forced to a single level. But powerful sellers in real markets may well have success in discriminating. See § 2.5. Such discrimination distinguishes their conduct from that of the pure monopolist in a manner that may reduce the adverse allocative effects but increase the income transfer effects of exercising the power. See § 2.3b.

Economists compare the power that can be exercised by a pure monopolist with that which would occur under perfect competition. Conditions of perfect competition, like those of pure monopoly, are unlikely in real markets. Perfect competition requires a large number of producers, none with a substantial market share, and each producing a fungible or undifferentiated product. Thus, product differences based on physical characteristics, transportation or brand image are inconsistent with this model. Industries lacking the minimum number of participants, say thirty or more, or in which one or more of the rivals has more than five percent of the market, are also unlikely to fit the model. The closest we can come to perfect competition in real markets may be undifferentiated agricultural products, such as corn or wheat, that are produced by a large number of farmers.[1]

Despite the inconsistency between real markets and the models of monopoly and perfect competition, economists use the models because they allow for rigorous mathematical proofs that help explain the workings of competitive or noncompetitive markets. The models also help in understanding the injury that can arise from market power.

A pure monopolist has substantial ability to raise price by limiting output. The model assumes that a monopolist sets the price at a level

§ 2.3

1. Even these markets will fall short of the perfect competition model, for example, to the extent that they are subject to government subsidies or regulation.

that brings maximum profits. If the price is set too high, buyers will shun the product altogether. To sell more, the monopolist can lower its price, but that will decrease the per item revenue (marginal revenue) the seller earns. The monopoly model illustrated in Figure 2.3A predicts that the monopolist will set its price (PM) and output (OM) at the point where the monopolist's marginal cost (the cost of producing one more unit) equals its marginal revenue (the revenue received from sale of one more unit). In other words, the monopolist will keep producing and keep reducing its price to sell the output until the point at which an additional sale no longer brings enough revenue to meet the cost of that additional item. It can be inferred that real firms that approach the model for pure monopoly will have significant, though widely varying, ability to control price. Each such firm will have unique constraints, based in part on the closeness of substitute goods and on the ease with which other firms can enter its business. But within these constraints, it, like the pure monopolist in the model, may vary output so as to price at the profit-maximizing point at which marginal cost and marginal revenue are equal.

Figure 2.3A: Price and Output Under Pure Monopoly

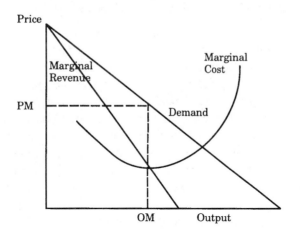

Under the model of perfect competition, a large number of sellers offer a fungible product to consumers who will buy only the lowest priced item offered. To survive, a producer must sell at this price. In addition, because the market consists of numerous sellers, no one seller, by increasing or decreasing its output, can affect the market clearing price. As a result, each seller perceives its own demand curve as flat and will increase output (OC) until the cost of producing one additional item no longer brings in enough revenue to cover that cost. In other words, the price (PC) will be set at the point at which a firm's marginal cost intersects the consumer demand curve. This is illustrated in Figure 2.3B.

Figure 2.3B: Price and Output Under Perfect Competition

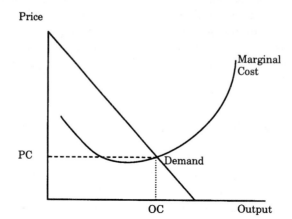

Again, few real markets will meet all the conditions of this model. But some markets may come close, and producers in such markets may act in ways like the price-takers in the model of perfect competition.

2.3b. Allocative, Wealth Transfer and Other Injuries from Monopoly

When the monopoly model is compared to that of perfect competition, significant differences are evident. If all other aspects of the two markets are the same, the price at which the monopolist sells will be higher than the price under perfect competition. In addition, because price and output are inversely linked and the monopolist is incapable of discriminating, the output of the pure monopolist is necessarily less than the aggregate output of producers in a perfectly competitive market. Economists describe this injury from monopoly in terms of this lost output. Some buyers that would have purchased the product at a competitive price will no longer do so at the higher monopoly price. Society's resources are allocated differently, to the detriment of consumers who would have purchased this product at a competitive price—that is, who would have paid for it at its social cost. As Adam Smith put it, monopoly frustrates an allocation of resources "as nearly as possible in the proportion which is most agreeable to the interests of the whole society."[2] The injury from reduced output is shown in Figure 2.3C as the difference between OC (output under competition) and OM (output under monopoly).

2. A. Smith, An Inquiry into the Nature and Causes of the Wealth of Nations, 594–95 (Mod. Lib. ed., 1937).

Figure 2.3C: Injury From Monopolization

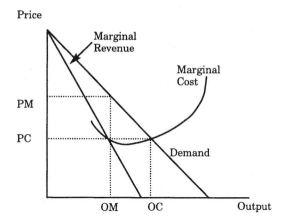

When demand falls off rapidly as price is increased a seller may be able to lessen the revenue loss by discriminating in price. See § 2.5. Contrary to the theoretical assumption about the pure monopolist, to the extent that a seller with power is able to discriminate in price, the allocative injury from that seller's market power may be reduced; the discrimination may facilitate higher output (sales), with the result that distribution may more closely approximates the optimum allocation that would result from competition. For instance, if a firm with monopoly power could "perfectly discriminate"—that is, charge each buyer the maximum amount that buyer would pay for the product (thus "pricing down" the demand curve)—that firm would produce and sell the same amount of the product, and would draw the same resources into its production as would result from perfect competition. The only difference from a perfectly competitive market would be the prices paid.

Of course, perfect discrimination is never possible; any significant amount of price discrimination by a monopolist may be difficult or impossible because of arbitrage—the practice of buyers that receive lower prices reselling to buyers that the monopolist intended to charge higher prices. Hence, a significant injury to resource allocation is likely from a substantial amount of market power even if the theoretical assumption that the monopolist cannot discriminate at all is abandoned. Moreover, because price discrimination often targets smaller and less-informed buyers, its use in many instances may be based on exploitation of information asymmetries, further distorting allocation from the competitive ideal.

In addition to doing allocative injury, monopoly transfers wealth from consumers to the monopolist, and this harm persists whether or not discrimination is possible. When competitive prices prevail, all consumers that would have been willing to pay more than its cost to obtain the product—that is, every consumer represented on that part of the industry demand curve above the point where that curve intersects with marginal cost—are benefitted by being able to obtain the product for less than their respective reservation prices for it. The aggregate of these benefits is the consumer surplus yielded by competition. But monopoly, because it enables the monopolist to charge more for the product, shifts part of this surplus from consumers to the monopolist. This harm to consumers occurs whether or not the monopolist is able to price discriminate. Indeed, to the extent that the monopolist successfully discriminates this wealth transfer injury increases. If perfect discrimination were achieved, the entire consumer surplus would be shifted to the monopolist. Take this example: A salt monopolist raises its price to increase return. Because of the inelastic nature of demand for the monopolist's product, a large percentage of buyers continue to purchase at the monopolist's increased price. For them, the injury is the additional wealth transferred to the seller in order to purchase at the monopoly price. If the salt monopolist could price discriminate, the amount of that transfer would increase. The prevention of this wealth transfer injury is widely acknowledged as a major, some say the primary, purpose of antitrust.[3] See the discussion in § 1.5b1.

Market power may also undermine dynamic efficiency. Some firms lacking power may be too small or too constrained by the narrow spread between income and production costs to engage in some types of research and development. One would not expect a sole entrepreneur to have the resources, time and expertise to experiment with the nuances of complex modern technology. However, notwithstanding adequate technological and financial resources, firms with substantial market power may lack incentives to research actively or aggressively. Or, what is perhaps worse, they may seek to dampen the flow of technological change discovered by others. As a telephone monopolist, AT & T was well known for its research successes (for example the discovery of the transistor), but was often the last to introduce change into its telephone systems. For example, many independent telephone companies introduced automatic switching machines well before the Bell System did.[4] In *Berkey Photo, Inc. v. Eastman Kodak Co.*, the court found that Kodak, alleged to have monopoly power in the instant camera market, had conspired with developers of camera flash devices (Sylvania and General Electric) to keep innovative devices out of the hands of competing camera producers.[5] Technological progress in some industries may require a minimum level of size and concentration, but substantial market power can dis-

---

3. Lande, *Wealth Transfers as the Original and Primary Concern of Antitrust: The Efficiency Interpretation Challenged*, 34 Hastings L. J. 67 (1982) (which explores the legislative history). See also Lande, *The Rise and (Coming) Fall of Efficiency as the Ruler of Antitrust*, 33 Antitrust Bull. 429, 455–63 (1988)(listing antitrust theorists who agree that wealth transfer is a key concern of antitrust).

4. Telecommunications Act of 1980, Report of the House Comm. On the Judiciary, H.R. Rep. No. 96–1252 Pt. 2, 96th Cong., 2d Sess. 4–5 (1980).

5. 603 F.2d 263, 299–302 (2d Cir.1979), cert. denied, 444 U.S. 1093, 100 S.Ct. 1061, 62 L.Ed.2d 783 (1980). This portion of the *Berkey* decision rested on a conspiracy found to violate Section 1 of the Sherman Act. Nonetheless, the real source of power in this case was probably Kodak's dominance of the instant camera market—power that allowed the delay in the introduction of new flash technology and made General Electric and Sylvania willing to agree not to make that technology available to Kodak's camera competitors.

courage new research and ideas. Research and development serves dynamic change. Change, never wholly predictable in effect, can threaten the dominant firm. Its incentive to invest in innovation may be much weaker than would be the aggregate incentives of several smaller but still substantial competitive firms.[6]

Finally, there are social concerns about market power. Large firms with concentrated power may stifle or prevent the growth of small, independent businesses. Some theorists stress the importance for a democratic system of an economy open for entry by small firms and for significant citizen involvement in economic activity, including decision-making, that can increase overall owner/worker satisfaction. Large firms with concentrated power, in contrast, are said to increase worker feelings of alienation. As Judge Hand said in *Alcoa*, it is possible, "because of its indirect social or moral effect, to prefer a system of small producers, each dependent for his success upon his own skill and character, to one in which the great mass of those engaged must accept the direction of a few."[7]

§ 2.4   Forms of Market Power

2.4a.   Monopoly Power

Both in economics and in antitrust, the term "monopoly power" often has a broader definition than the textbook definition of the pure monopolist. Because few, if any, monopolists possess a pure monopoly— an exclusive, nondiscriminating seller of a product for which no substitutes exist—monopoly power is often used to describe a seller or group of sellers that possess something that approaches the power of a pure monopolist. In this sense, the term monopoly power may be used to describe the power of a dominant (but not exclusive) seller of a product, a cartel which involves all or most of the competitors selling a product, or oligopolists that, with the benefit of strategic pricing, can price at levels that approach those a pure monopolist would charge.

Such monopoly power is often readily visible. Perhaps this visibility made it a natural target for supporters of the Sherman Antitrust Act. Whether attacking a monopolist (Standard Oil Co. v. United States)[1] or a cartel (United States v. Addyston Pipe & Steel Co.),[2] the most frequent focus of early antitrust enforcement was on the market power that was held by participants with a large percentage of the market. Of course, as the discussion below indicates, market participants with a high market

---

6. F.M. Scherer & D. Ross, Industrial Market Structure and Economic Performance 654–60 (3d ed. 1990)(summarizing the theory and evidence concerning innovation and concluding that, although minimal size and scale efficiencies contribute to research and development, high concentration and entry barriers probably undermine innovation and its marketing).

7. United States v. Aluminum Co. of America, 148 F.2d 416, 427 (2d Cir.1945).

§ 2.4

1. 221 U.S. 1, 31 S.Ct. 502, 55 L.Ed. 619 (1911).

2. 85 Fed. 271 (6th Cir.1898), modified and aff'd, 175 U.S. 211, 20 S.Ct. 96, 44 L.Ed. 136 (1899).

share may exercise little or no market power. But a high market share enhances not only the visibility of that power, but also the psychological effect of strategic behavior that may result in control of price and output.

Finally, it should be noted that the term "monopoly power" may or may not denote a greater concentration of power than that associated with brand differentiation. As discussed in § 2.4e below, some firms may enjoy substantial and enduring market power as the result of consumer loyalty to their differentiated brands. A seller with a small market share in an industry of differentiated products could possess more market power than does a high market share participant in an industry of relatively undifferentiated products. Whether this market power has been exercised abusively is a separate issue addressed in subsequent chapters.

2.4b. Oligopoly

Most sellers that possess a degree of market power are not monopolists in the sense of being the exclusive seller of a product or service. More often, they are oligopolists—one of a few sellers active in a particular market. Although it is widely accepted that an oligopolist possesses a degree of market power, defining the extent of this power has been a challenge for theoretical economists. There is no single model for an oligopolistic industry that describes the extent of an oligopolist's power.

One reason for the difficulty in describing and delimiting oligopoly power is the large number of variables that confront any theorist building an oligopoly model. Pure monopoly is akin to a single player game such as solitaire; the oligopoly model may be more like a multi-handed poker game. In a solitaire game, the single player knows the choices based on the cards that are displayed. A theoretician can assess what choices the rational solitaire player (monopolist) would make given those options. Multi-handed poker, in contrast, involves not only a number of players but a different set of incomplete information for each player—each player has a different set of cards and no direct knowledge of what cards the opponent holds. Players also vary widely in their propensity to bluff or take risks.

Unlike poker, where for any hand one player will win all of the money bet, the players in an oligopolistic market can actually increase the returns that all of them receive through disciplined pricing. To achieve this discipline, the oligopolists must recognize their interdependence and act accordingly. This is distinguished from the independent behavior assumed for the theoretical models of perfect competition or pure monopoly. But in most real markets, each market participant recognizes that its output and pricing decisions will have an impact on and will draw a response from competitors. For such players, output and pricing decisions are taken with an eye to what the competitive response will be.

The difficulties in predicting how oligopolists will behave have not deterred economists from attempting descriptive models. Under the 1838 model of the economist Cournot, the seller's monopolistic return decreases as the number of sellers participating in the oligopoly increases, ultimately approaching marginal cost, the price that would be set in a perfectly competitive market. Although the Cournot model has been partially discredited because of questionable assumptions, the correlation between the number of participants in an oligopolistic market and the price that they charge is consistent with common observation and may be correct.[3]

More recent theoretical literature has relied upon game theory to explore oligopolistic behavior. In game theory, two or more competitors are assumed to have the same objective: to maximize payoff. The choices of one player are analyzed against a range of choices made by other players. Most oligopolists are likely to realize that each may receive a higher payoff through interdependent behavior. For example, if each of three oligopolists pursued profit without sensitivity for the response of the other two firms, a price war might ensue, resulting in reduced profits for all three participants. Firms are likely to recognize that by foregoing aggressive price cutting and limiting production, each can earn a higher return.

When oligopolists recognize their interdependence and restrain their price competition, the results can approach those of a monopolist seeking to maximize its return. Injuries to allocation and the transfer of wealth to sellers may occur as in the case of monopoly. Whether players actively collude to limit output and fix prices (an antitrust violation) or simply engage in parallel pricing without direct communication, there could also be an increase in cost among the seller participants in the form of x-inefficiencies or rent-seeking. If a cartel is formed, cartel administration costs, not a factor in the case of monopoly, always will raise costs to some degree. Collusive behavior may deter innovation by limiting the number of participants in an industry, and may deter entry.

Although the benefits of coordinated pricing may be clear to all participants in an oligopolistic industry, the difficulty in achieving successful supracompetitive pricing may still be substantial. Each competitor will likely have its own idea about what its fair share of the market should be. Doubts and uncertainties about other players may foster mistrust. These differences can preclude coordination either through agreement or without it and can cause a breakdown of pricing discipline, if once achieved, thus reducing profits for each firm. Even if pricing discipline is established and preserved for a time, discipline may break down when market conditions change. For example, a decline in demand can be expected to result in price reductions. But when an oligopolist experiences weaker demand for its own product and downward pressure

3. F.M. SCHERER & D. ROSS, INDUSTRIAL MARKET STRUCTURE AND ECONOMIC PERFORM- ANCE 200–06 (3d ed. 1990).

on its price, it may not be sure whether a marketwide reduction in demand is occurring, or whether a rival has been "cheating"—that is, attracting some customers away from other sellers by selective reductions below the previously maintained supracompetitive price. A likely reaction to such uncertainty is a price war, which will continue until pricing discipline is restored, either by agreement or by tacit, interdependent conduct.[4]

2.4c. Cartels and Collusion

The difficulties in coordinating prices are likely to increase as the number of players increases. Similarly, more complex and differentiated products probably reduce the gain from coordination and make it more difficult to implement. One way of achieving cooperation and avoiding breakdown is by negotiating an agreement among competitors—that is, forming a cartel. Cartels, which are prohibited under long-established interpretations of Section 1 of the Sherman Act, have a purpose, and usually also an effect—of attaining a supracompetitive price.

A tightly organized cartel can, in theory, achieve the same price as a pure monopolist. But even when cartels are legal, they are unstable and tend to self-destruct over the long term. Successful cartels, particularly if they involve a large number of members, may need the benefit of government authorization or support, as in the case of some domestic agricultural cooperatives, international ocean carrier cartels and OPEC. Absent such government support, cartels may take other steps to make it easier to achieve pricing discipline. One possible step is to simplify the way in which products are offered or sold. For example, to eliminate transportation as a factor in bids to sell cement, the cement industry agreed to a base point pricing system, calculating all transportation costs from a single base point regardless of the actual point of origin of the cement.[5] Product standardization programs can also be used as cartel-facilitating devices, although these programs can bring benefits to sellers and consumers that may offset competitive risks.

Another mechanism for coordinating pricing is for the cartel to appoint a single agent for making its sales. This mechanism was, for example, chosen by the defendants in *Appalachian Coals, Inc. v. United States*.[6] To the extent that the cartel is able to limit its members' output, there may be no need for the cartel to control prices directly. In American Column & Lumber Co. v. United States,[7] lumber producers were alleged to have used their association to disseminate information about prices, but also to urge and cajole members to limit production at times of slack demand. The Standard Oil Company, later found to have monopolized petroleum refining, has also been viewed as the agent

4. See generally Parter, *On the Incidence and Duration of Price Wars*, 33 J. INDUS. ECON. 415 (1985). As noted in § 2.4d, price wars, perhaps orchestrated by a price leader, may be a strategic weapon for maintaining oligopolistic price discipline.

5. FTC v. Cement Institute, 333 U.S. 683, 68 S.Ct. 793, 92 L.Ed. 1010 (1948).

6. 288 U.S. 344, 53 S.Ct. 471, 77 L.Ed. 825 (1933).

7. 257 U.S. 377, 42 S.Ct. 114, 66 L.Ed. 284 (1921).

through which late-nineteenth-century American railroads cartelized rail rates.[8]

Even if oligopolists are able to reach a disciplined pricing strategy that pushes price toward monopoly level, there is the problem of cheating. Any member of the industry can increase its sales and profits by selling slightly below the oligopoly price level. Some of the pressure to cheat can come from large buyers that promise a large volume of business in return for a discount. The response of the remaining members of the industry may be to abandon coordinated pricing, with a loss of the gains of oligopolistic pricing for all. To prevent cheating, a tightly organized cartel may agree to constrict output. Achieving these goals may be easier if participation in an industry requires a patent license. Assuming antitrust laws permit such activity, the license can be used to restrict entry, assign exclusive territories, or impose other restrictions to prevent price competition. Another response to the threat of cheating is the use of most-favored-nation (MFN) clauses. An MFN clause is inserted into a contract for the sale of goods, committing the seller to meet the lowest price offered to any buyer at the time of sale. If all sellers in an industry use MFN clauses, each has an added incentive not to discount its price lest other purchasers be entitled to the same discount. MFN clauses are likely more effective if these contract provisions are known to rival buyers and sellers.

An even stronger enforcement mechanism was used in the electric turbogenerator market. The only two major U.S. producers (General Electric and Westinghouse) followed a parallel practice of promising purchasers a retroactive rebate if subsequent purchasers were given a lower price. This public mechanism created a strong disincentive for any firm to discount and assured the purchaser that such price discounting would not occur.[9]

2.4d.　Strategic Parallel Behavior

Short of forming a cartel, and if centripetal forces outweigh centrifugal ones in their industry, oligopolists may find other ways to cooperate on prices. Given the severe antitrust penalties for collusion, other mechanisms for maintaining parallel pricing are probably more common in many industries.

For example, the largest firm may play the role of price leader. During the first half of this century, U.S. Steel, the largest domestic steel producer, played a price leadership role for the industry. Changes in prices by U.S. Steel were usually followed by all other major domestic competitors. During the early years, the mechanism for this price leadership role was apparently lubricated by meetings (the Gary Dinners) among top executives of the firms involved, increasing the incentive to

8. Granitz & Klein, *Monopolization By "Raising Rivals' Costs": The Standard Oil Case*, 39 J. L. & Econ. 1 (1996).

9. United States v. General Electric Co., 1977–2 Trade Cas. (CCH) ¶ 61,659 (E.D.Pa. 1977).

cooperate rather than obstruct the pricing arrangements.[10] A more recent case in which price leadership was alleged involved the market for antiknock gasoline additives.[11] Although claims of conscious parallel pricing have not always fared well in the courts, there may be no difference in economic effect between an overt cartel arrangement and a lockstep pricing pattern based upon price leadership. Price leadership may be more likely to occur in industries with a smaller number of firms and in which one (usually the largest firm) can naturally assume the leadership mantel. In the automobile industry, General Motors was the price leader until the time that its dominance fell into question because of Japanese imports.[12]

Price leadership may work more effectively if it is backed up with occasional "punishment" of other industry players that do not follow the pricing pattern. An industry that experiences longer periods of supra-competitive pricing punctuated by occasional price wars demonstrates this punitive mechanism. When an industry player fails to follow the pricing pattern, the other participants may initiate a price war. Although all industry participants may suffer reduced profits or even loss as the result of the price war, it may demonstrate to maverick members the advantage of interdependent behavior and maintaining the system of price leadership.[13]

2.4e. Single Brand Market Power

When market power is properly defined as power over price,[14] it is clear that sellers of branded products often exercise market power. Just as a pure monopolist, the seller of a branded good may face an inelastic demand curve, allowing it to raise price without losing offsetting sales revenues. The origins of single brand market power are varied, but are often linked to the flow of information available to buyers. A seller with a powerful brand, for example, may have brand-loyal consumers who will absorb price increases rather than switch to a different brand. The basis for this brand loyalty may be accurate information about the characteristics of the favored brand and all rival offerings. But brand loyalty may also be based on inaccurate, out-of-date or incomplete information. Brand loyalty will be reinforced by "satisficing" conduct—where market actors are not constantly reevaluating their alternatives and patterns tend to stabilize and be repeated until something disorienting occurs. Single brand market power may also be generated by the sales methods used by the seller. Intrabrand (vertical) distribution restraints[15] may

---

10. United States v. United States Steel Corp., 251 U.S. 417, 440, 40 S.Ct. 293, 64 L.Ed. 343 (1920).

11. E.I. du Pont de Nemours & Co. v. FTC, 729 F.2d 128 (2d Cir.1984).

12. Scherer & Ross, supra note 3, at 254–55.

13. Baker & Bresnahan, *Empirical Methods of Identifying and Measuring Mar-*

ket Power, 61 Antitrust L.J. 3, 13–15 (1992) (explaining how the punishment method may work and how the underlying market power may be measured by econometric methods).

14. See § 2.2.

15. Addressed in Chapter VI.

generate brand loyalty. Or interbrand restraints[16] such as tie-ins may create market power in aftermarkets because of incomplete information in the hands of the buyer. Yet another source of single brand market power is relational, arising out of long-term business relationships such as those between a franchisor and franchisee. Finally, a seller may also enjoy market power if the buyer can pass on the costs of a purchase to a third party that does not exercise cost discipline over the buyer's purchase decision. Such buyer pass-on may sometimes occur in health care, where many patients pay little or nothing to receive health care services that are covered by government or private health insurance.

In its 1992 *Kodak* decision, the Supreme Court stressed that a single brand could occasionally be a separate market. In dealing with tie-in and attempted monopolization claims, the Supreme Court confronted the question of whether market power could be found in a single brand market: the aftermarket for parts of Kodak-brand micrographic equipment. The Court described the market power issue in this way: "The extent to which one market prevents exploitation of another market depends on the extent to which consumers will change their consumption of one product in response to a price change in another, i.e., the 'cross-elasticity of demand.' "[17] The Court went on to explain why the plaintiff's theory of market power in a single brand's aftermarket for parts could not be rejected at the summary judgment stage.[18] Later, and more explicitly, in dealing with the attempted monopolization claim, the Court said:

> Kodak also contends that, as a matter of law, a single brand of a product or service can never be a relevant market under the Sherman Act. We disagree. * * * This Court's prior cases support the proposition that in some instances one brand of a product can constitute a separate market. The proper market definition in this case can be determined only after a factual inquiry into the 'commercial realities' faced by consumers.[19]

There can be no single brand market power without brand differentiation. A market in which every product is sold subject to brand differentiation may give each producer considerable, perhaps even substantial latitude to limit output and raise prices. Firms in such a market engage in what economists call "monopolistic competition."[20] A seller's

---

16. Addressed in Chapter VII.

17. 504 U.S. at 469.

18. The plaintiff alleged that Kodak used its power over aftermarket parts to charge high prices in the service market. In discussing this theory, the Court stated that, "What constrains the defendant's ability to raise prices in the service market is the elasticity of demand faced by the defendant—the degree to which its sales fall * * * as its price rises." Id. at 469 n.15 (quoting P. AREEDA & L. KAPLOW, ANTITRUST ANALYSIS ¶ 342(c), 576 (4th ed. 1988)).

19. 504 U.S. at 481–82 (citations omitted)(footnote omitted).

20. SCHERER & ROSS, supra note 3, at 17. The term "monopolistic competition" was initially used in the 1930s to describe what theorists suggested was the state of competition in most markets. See J. KEPLER, MONOPOLISTIC COMPETITION THEORY: ORIGINS, RESULTS, AND IMPLICATIONS 78–89 (1994) (describing the work of Edward Chamberlin and other economists who first developed monopolistic competition theory). The theory was later dismissed or ignored be-

market power in these circumstances may be based on performance differences, transportation costs, variation in style or appearance, or on perceived differences fostered by advertising or promotion. As noted below, the brand loyalty that produces this power is by no means a wholly negative development; it contributes to scale efficiencies and incentives for quality control and innovation. Still, the producer's ability to play on brand loyalty to reduce output and raise price can distort allocation and transfer wealth—the same injuries that other forms of market power cause.

As with other forms, market power based on brand differentiation should not by itself be the basis for condemning a firm's behavior. Only when exploitatively used should such power be vulnerable under the antitrust laws. A major motive for brand merchandising is that the seller's differentiated brand may be sold for a higher price than its rival's goods. Such merchandising can be used to sell goods superior in quality and features. The producer of branded goods has an incentive to maintain quality and performance to maintain consumer loyalty to its brand. Also brand advertising may allow for a broader market, increasing the seller's production or distribution efficiencies.[21] Differentiated brands and brand merchandising can also benefit consumers. The range of product alternatives is widened and, once a consumer chooses among them, the consumer can shop in a more focused manner and be reasonably confident that the product purchased will meet expectations. If consumers obtain full and accurate information about branded goods, they will make wise purchasing decisions that result in a better allocation of resources.

Exercises of market power associated with brand differentiation may create less injury to society than those of a pure monopolist because the seller's latitude to raise prices above a competitive level may be smaller and because rival firms may more easily break down the brand loyalty. But this injury may be substantial. Large firms with substantial sales volume may exercise brand differentiated market power. Even if the firm initially exercising brand power has a small share, emulation of that firm's behavior may become widespread, so that the collective societal injury may be equivalent to that of a cartel. This risk is particularly evident with respect to certain intrabrand and interbrand distribution restraints discussed in Chapters VI– VIII.

Should the power exercised by a seller of a powerful brand be considered, as some would claim, beyond the reach of antitrust? How fundamental is the distinction between the power exercised by a brand

cause it was associated with unwelcome government intervention in nations subject to fascist or communist governments and because, unlike the theory of perfect competition, it was unable to describe a model that could be rigorously tested. Id. at 191– 96. But monopolistic competition theory has enjoyed a resurgence through more recent economic endeavors such as game theory, which assume the strategic power of market players to control price and output. Id. at 176–77 ("By its very nature the theory of games is linked to the idea of monopolistic competition, since under perfect competition no strategic interdependence exists.").

21. These and other benefits of brand merchandising are discussed in § 6.2a.

seller and that exercised by an interbrand monopolist? In some cases, brand differentiation may be based entirely on consumer perception and not on any objective differences in the product the seller markets. But the distinction between these two types of power is slippery. Even a seller whose product is differentiated only in the consumer's mind may enjoy substantial ability to raise its price through limited output. Indeed, the monopolist may face relatively close substitutes for its product, so that its market power may be less than that possessed by a firm that has effectively differentiated its brand through advertising and other promotion methods. One might also attempt to distinguish various forms of market power based on durability.[22] Market power based on brand differentiation may seem inherently ephemeral, particularly if rival brands display no meaningful differences in physical characteristics. Any rival producer, it would appear, could embark on a promotion campaign that would bring its product into close competition with the relevant brand. But the marketplace suggests that brand-differentiated power can be enduring, difficult to challenge and an effective means of thwarting competition. Strong brands such as Coca Cola, Mercedes Benz, Sony and Chanel have hard won reputations that endure over decades. A rival wishing to challenge the strength of such brands would have to spend substantial funds over a long period with uncertain prospects of success. Moreover, the creation of a second or third strong brand may or may not pressure the owner of the original strong brand to lower its price. Instead, owners of the brands with newly won consumer loyalty may simply join a higher price segment of the market that maintains margins through strategic, parallel behavior. The owner of a strong brand is not by virtue of that fact an antitrust violator. But neither should that owner be able shield itself from antitrust claims of abusive conduct made possible by the brand's market power.

2.4e1. Criticisms of the Concept of Single Brand Market Power

Perhaps the primary motivating concern of critics of a comprehensive market power definition is that it will promote an activist antitrust agenda, particularly with respect to questions of single brand market power. As one critic put it:

> A major problem in using the economic definition of market power * * * as the standard by which to measure antitrust market power is that it leads economists to label every real world deviation from the perfectly competitive model that results in a less than perfectly elastic demand, such as the conditions that produce discriminatory marketing arrangements, as 'market imperfections'. The implication that then appears to follow is that these 'imperfections' require fixing.[23]

---

22. Schmalensee discusses the difficulty of basing market power analysis on durability. For example, in the popular song market, each song may enjoy only short term popularity. But industrywide marketing practices for all popular songs may still cause substantial wealth transfer and allocation injuries. Schmalensee, *Another Look at Market Power*, 95 HARV. L. REV. 1789, 1795–96 (1982).

23. Klein, *Market Power in Aftermarkets,* 17 MANAGERIAL & DECISION ECON. 143,

A variation on this concern was offered in the *Kodak* dissent, where Justice Scalia complained that recognition of single brand market power in the aftermarket context invites "a torrent of litigation" and creates an "all-purpose remedy against run-of-the-mill business torts."[24]

These concerns are overstated. Antitrust case law, although based upon statute, displays many of the features of a common law jurisprudence. The general language of key provisions of the Sherman and Clayton Acts leaves the courts a large measure of control over interpretation. The resulting jurisprudence is one of incremental evolution, not revolution. Stare decisis and judicial deference to the constitutional prerogatives of the legislature limit change. Furthermore, even when incremental change occurs, it is not necessarily in an activist direction, as the line of cases beginning in 1977 with *Sylvania* convincingly show.[25] No doubt it is possible—conceivably even likely—that the inelastic demand definition will provide a platform for those who would extend antitrust law into new areas. But demand elasticity is not a platform from which ambitious extensions could be launched. Its use imposes the rigorous discipline of microeconomics, the very discipline that has narrowed the range of antitrust in recent years. This constraint together with stare decisis imposes an appropriate barrier to any extreme agenda to expand or contract antitrust. The likely and desirable consequence of embracing inelasticity as a market power definition is that it will assist in rationalizing and explaining existing case law, perhaps refining precedents at the margins, but doing so in an evolutionary rather than revolutionary manner.

Another criticism asserts that recognition of single brand market power could lead to overly broad remedies that compel inefficient or second best strategies for achieving legitimate commercial goals. It has

---

157 (1996). Similar arguments are advanced in Arthur, *The Costly Quest for Perfect Competition:* Kodak *and Nonstructural Market Power,* 69 N.Y.U.L. REV. 1, 60–71 (1994). Arthur urges a distinction be made between "structural" and "nonstructural" market power. Id. at 32–38. Arthur apparently would include only high market share manifestations of market power in the structural category, grouping market power based on information asymmetries or product differentiation in the nonstructural category. Although sympathetic to Arthur's policy position, Klein suggests that Arthur's distinction between structural and nonstructural market power is not workable because "it fundamentally begs the question of the relevant product market." Klein, supra, at 153 n. 31. A different view is offered in Grimes, *Antitrust Tie-in Analysis After Kodak, A Reply to Larson's Comment,* 63 ANTITRUST L.J. 267, 268–69 (1994).

24. Eastman Kodak Co. v. Image Technical Servs. Inc., 504 U.S. 451, 489, 503,

112 S.Ct. 2072, 119 L.Ed.2d 265 (1992)(Scalia J., dissenting). For a more comprehensive attack on the use of micro economic models of perfect competition as justification for regulatory intervention, see Johnson, *Hayek and Markets,* 23 SW. U. L. REV. 547, 555–58 (1994). Although Justice Scalia and critics of *Kodak* have sought to highlight the risks of an expansive market power definition, the majority in *Kodak* doubtless saw its holding as, at most, evolutionary, and, more likely, as a reaffirmation of precedent. Although *Kodak* invokes economic theory pertaining to information and lock-in, the result the Court reaches might have been the same even in the absence of that learning. As the discussion of the case law later in this section suggests, the Supreme Court has long recognized antitrust claims involving a variety of single brand market power.

25. Continental T. V., Inc. v. GTE Sylvania, Inc., 433 U.S. 36, 97 S.Ct. 2549, 53 L.Ed.2d 568 (1977).

been asserted, for example, that an antitrust intervention to stop price discrimination against a small group of customers might lead to a remedy costly to "the entire market."[26] This might occur if the remedy were divestiture or compulsory licensing in circumstances that deprived the defendant of minimum efficient scale or other efficiencies. But here again, the concern hardly comports either with the allocative efficiency value (which use of the inelasticity definition serves) or with the bench's well-known reluctance to impose such far-reaching remedies, particularly when a more narrowly drawn behavioral sanction can address the injury.[27] Especially when market power is limited to a single brand, one would expect that judicial relief would be limited to behavioral sanctions, such as prohibiting tying or unlawful vertical restraints. An example of single brand market power might be that of a German automobile manufacturer, with limited North American market presence, that advertises extensively to promote brand image, and sets export prices at levels substantially above those charged for comparable models in the German market. Such a manufacturer may engage in substantial rent-seeking activity, such as lobbying for legislation blocking parallel or gray market imports of its cars into the North American market. Measured by its power over price, such a manufacturer may clearly possesses significant, sustained market power in the North American market. That market power alone is not an antitrust violation. But assume further that this manufacturer requires its North American dealers to buy only aftermarket parts manufactured by the German company. If such conduct were successfully challenged as an unlawful tie,[28] it is not credible to suggest that a court would order divestiture or compulsory licensing for this single brand market power abuse.[29]

26. Arthur, supra note 20, at 29.

27. Thus, even during a more activist era of antitrust, the courts evidenced reluctance to impose a divestiture sanction. As Judge Wyzanski wrote (when denying the government's request for divestiture against United Shoe Machinery Corporation found guilty of monopolization):

> Judges in prescribing remedies have known their own limitations. * * * Judicial decrees must be fitted into the framework of what a busy, and none too expert, court can supervise. Above all, no matter with what authority he is invested, with what facts and opinion he is supplied, a trial judge is only one man, and should move with caution and humility.

United States v. United Shoe Mach. Corp., 110 F.Supp. 295, 347–48 (D.Mass.1953), aff'd per curiam, 347 U.S. 521, 74 S.Ct. 699, 98 L.Ed. 910 (1954). The court used similar words of caution in rejecting the government's request for divestiture relief in United States v. General Elec. Co., 115 F.Supp. 835, 864–71 (D.N.J.1953) and in restricting divestiture relief in United States v. Alumi-

num Co. of Am., 91 F.Supp. 333, 346–47 (S.D.N.Y.1950).

28. Metrix Warehouse, Inc. v. Daimler–Benz Aktiengesellschaft, 828 F.2d 1033 (4th Cir.1987), cert. denied, 486 U.S. 1017, 108 S.Ct. 1753, 100 L.Ed.2d 215 (1988); see also United States v. Mercedes–Benz of North America, Inc., 517 F.Supp. 1369 (N.D.Cal. 1981), where the Government first successfully pursued (to the point of partial summary judgment), then (after President Reagan assumed office) abandoned, a spare parts tie-in case against an automobile importer.

29. The Supreme Court has also indicated that establishing a violation of Section 2 of the Sherman Act requires more market power than would be needed to show an unlawful tie-in. *Kodak,* 504 U.S. at 481. Among Section 2 offenses, there may be additional variation in market-power thresholds. The threshold for attempted monopolization, for example, is likely to be lower than for monopolization cases. See United States v. E.I. du Pont de Nemours & Co., 351 U.S. 377, 396 n. 23, 76 S.Ct. 994,

It has also been argued that a market power definition based upon demand inelasticity is inconsistent with antitrust jurisprudence because "very few cases adopt the technical economic (own elasticity) definition of market power."[30] In dicta from *du Pont,* the Court stated that the power that "automobile or soft-drink manufacturers have over their trademarked products is not the power that makes an illegal monopoly."[31] But the Supreme Court in *Kodak* expressly refused to read this language as precluding recognition of single-brand market power.[32] When one looks at a broader collection of judicial definitions of market power (see § 2.2a), almost all of them utilize, allude to, or are wholly consistent with a "power-over-price" definition, and many are inconsistent with any more restrictive definition.[33]

For almost a century, the Court has found certain vertical restraints and tying arrangements involving the sale of a single brand or line of goods to be a violation of antitrust law. In 1911, the Supreme Court first held resale price maintenance to violate the Sherman Act, and did so without any analysis going beyond the manufacture and distribution of a single brand of patent medicine.[34] Although the *per se* rule against vertical price fixing that evolved from that line of cases, long under attack, has been narrowed in recent Court holdings,[35] the Court has not overturned the *per se* rule, nor has it suggested that nonprice vertical

---

100 L.Ed. 1264 (1956) (distinguishing prior holdings because they involved attempted monopolization, not monopolization claims).

30. Klein, supra note 20, at 157. Arthur claims that before the 1992 decision in *Kodak*, "nonstructural" market power was not addressed by antitrust (except in a few scattered lower court decisions). Arthur, supra note 23, at 40–42.

31. United States v. E.I. du Pont de Nemours & Co., 351 U.S. 377, 392–93, 76 S.Ct. 994, 100 L.Ed. 1264 (1956).

32. *Kodak*, 504 U.S. at 482 n.30. The meaning of the *du Pont* language is ambiguous, because the Court goes on to state that "illegal power must be appraised in terms of the competitive market for the product", a statement that is consistent with measuring market power by demand elasticity. *du Pont,* 351 U.S. at 392, 393.

33. Although Klein's 1996 article clearly rejects a power-over-price definition of market power for antitrust purposes, what he proposes to replace it is unclear. At one point, Klein suggests that antitrust market power requires inelastic demand *and* a "large market share." Klein, supra note 23, at 155. Later he describes offending market power as a firm's ability to "influence market outcomes." Id. at 157. This latter statement is ambiguous, and could be read as adopting a definition alluding to demand inelasticity. Courts usually define a relevant market by looking at cross-elasticity of de-

mand, a method that could still produce a single brand market when buyer demand for that brand is inelastic. In a 1993 article, Klein suggested that a market be defined by looking not only at elasticity of demand, but also by viewing a firm's ability to control output in a broader market of homogeneous products. Klein, *Market Power in Antitrust: Economic Analysis After Kodak,* 3 S. Ct. Econ. Rev. 43, 78 (1993) Such an approach leaves open the question of what constitutes this broader "homogeneous market" and fails to explain the market power in single brands implicitly found in venerable Supreme Court precedents involving monopolization, vertical restraints and tie-ins. See the discussion in the text following this note.

34. Dr. Miles Medical Co. v. John D. Park & Sons Co., 220 U.S. 373, 31 S.Ct. 376, 55 L.Ed. 502 (1911).

35. The plaintiffs successfully invoked the *per se* rule against vertical price fixing in Monsanto Co. v. Spray–Rite Serv. Corp., 465 U.S. 752, 104 S.Ct. 1464, 79 L.Ed.2d 775 (1984); California Retail Liquor Dealers Ass'n v. Midcal Aluminum, Inc., 445 U.S. 97, 100 S.Ct. 937, 63 L.Ed.2d 233 (1980). In the Court's most recent decision involving vertical minimum price fixing, the Court read the *per se* rule narrowly, but did not overturn it. Business Elecs. Corp. v. Sharp Elecs. Corp., 485 U.S. 717, 108 S.Ct. 1515, 99 L.Ed.2d 808 (1988).

restraints measured under the rule of reason are out of bounds simply because the restraint involves a single brand. Similarly, the Court's jurisprudence involving tie-ins has often focused on their use by a single seller purveying a single brand or line of goods. Although the Court's opinion in *Jefferson Parish* may be read as requiring that the *per se* rule against tying applies only if the tying defendant has market power in an interbrand setting,[36] the same opinion offers a more traditional definition of market power in the tying context: whether the defendant could "force" the buyer to purchase the tied product.[37] In cases such as Northern Pacific Ry. Co. v. United States,[38] United States v. Loew's, Inc.,[39] and Fortner Enterprises, Inc. v. United States Steel Corp.[40], the Court relied on the uniqueness of the tying product and the defendant's concomitant ability to force a buyer to purchase the tied product, rather than the defendant's interbrand market share, to establish the defendant's ability to force an unlawful tied purchase.[41] Also before *Kodak,* there were numerous lower court precedents to support antitrust claims of single brand market power exercised through tie-ins.[42]

36. In *Jefferson Parish Hosp. Dist. No. 2 v. Hyde,* Justice Stevens wrote that the defendant hospital's 30 percent share of local hospital patients failed to establish "the kind of dominant market position that obviates the need for further inquiry into actual competitive conditions." 466 U.S. 2, 26–27, 104 S.Ct. 1551, 80 L.Ed.2d 2 (1984). But this discussion was in the context of determining whether the Court should apply the *per se* rule against tie-ins. Justice Stevens went on to analyze whether the plaintiff could prevail under the rule of reason, an indication that the Court did not feel the interbrand market share was a *sine qua non* for showing an antitrust violation. Id. at 29–31.

37. Id. at 13–14.

38. 356 U.S. 1, 5–7, 78 S.Ct. 514, 2 L.Ed.2d 545 (1958). For a discussion of the Supreme Court's tie-in jurisprudence, see Grimes, *Antitrust Tie-in Analysis After Kodak: Understanding the Role of Market Imperfections,* 62 ANTITRUST L.J. 263, 299–307 (1994).

39. 371 U.S. 38, 45–47, 83 S.Ct. 97, 9 L.Ed.2d 11 (1962).

40. 394 U.S. 495, 498–500, 89 S.Ct. 1252, 22 L.Ed.2d 495 (1969).

41. Using variations on the "forcing" definition, the Court has proscribed tie-ins involving a single firm's card-sorting machines, IBM Corp. v. United States, 298 U.S. 131, 56 S.Ct. 701, 80 L.Ed. 1085 (1936), and a single company's salt injection machines, International Salt Co. v. United States, 332 U.S. 392, 68 S.Ct. 12, 92 L.Ed. 20 (1947). In both the *IBM* and *International Salt* cases, there was evidence that competitors of the defendants used similar tie-in practices. There was no indication that the Court deemed this parallel behavior of rivals to be pivotal in determining the outcome. See the discussion of these cases in Grimes, supra note 38, at 299–300.

42. Parts & Elec. Motors, Inc. v. Sterling Elec., Inc., 866 F.2d 228, 232–33 (7th Cir.1988) (upholding a jury verdict of an unlawful tie of spare parts and electric motors), cert. denied, 493 U.S. 847, 110 S.Ct. 141, 107 L.Ed.2d 100 (1989); Metrix Warehouse, Inc. v. Daimler–Benz Aktiengesellschaft, 828 F.2d 1033 (4th Cir.1987) (upholding a jury verdict of an unlawful tie of dealership franchise and aftermarket parts), cert. denied, 486 U.S. 1017, 108 S.Ct. 1753, 100 L.Ed.2d 215 (1988); Digidyne Corp. v. Data General Corp., 734 F.2d 1336 (9th Cir.1984)(upholding a jury verdict finding an unlawful tie of computer software to computer hardware), cert. denied, 473 U.S. 908, 105 S.Ct. 3534, 87 L.Ed.2d 657 (1985). Three other cases that followed the language of *Jefferson Parish* in finding that the seller of a tying product may have market power because of the "uniqueness" of the tying product are: Thompson v. Metropolitan Multi–List, Inc., 934 F.2d 1566, 1576–77 (11th Cir.1991), cert. denied, 506 U.S. 903, 113 S.Ct. 295, 121 L.Ed.2d 219 (1992); Monument Builders of Greater Kansas City, Inc. v. American Cemetery Ass'n, 891 F.2d 1473, 1482 (10th Cir.1989), cert. denied, 495 U.S. 930, 110 S.Ct. 2168, 109 L.Ed.2d 498 (1990); Tic–X–Press, Inc. v. Omni Promotions Co., 815 F.2d 1407, 1420 (11th Cir.1987).

In horizontal cases, the Court has routinely assumed that single brand restraints were subject to the same *per se* rules as multibrand horizontal restraints.[43] In monopolization litigation, the Supreme Court has accepted a jury finding of market power in a single seller's operation of three local ski resorts, notwithstanding competition in a broader market of destination ski resorts.[44] And in an attempted monopolization case, the Court found that a publisher of a local newspaper violated Section 2 of the Sherman Act based upon " 'bold, relentless, and predatory commercial behavior' " without any analysis of the existence of market power.[45] Although critics may disapprove of some or all of these cases, *Kodak's* implicit affirmation of such holdings hardly portends open-ended activism. What *Kodak* invites is a fact-focused analysis to determine whether a defendant possesses and has abused sustained, nontrivial power based on sustained inelastic demand.

Market power—defined as power-over-price that is more than transitory and involves a significant price range—is a necessary but not a sufficient basis for antitrust intervention. This fundamental precept of antitrust is not revolutionary—but offers hope of greater clarity and transparency in antitrust analysis.

2.4e2.   *Types of Single Brand Market Power*

2.4e2i.   *Single Brand Market Power and Intrabrand Distribution Restraints*

A seller that imposes a restraint on the distribution of its product generally does so in order to shift its demand curve in a way that will increase sales and profits. But such distribution restraints, often called vertical restraints, can raise competitive concerns, as discussed in Chapters VI–VIII. The impact of such vertical restraints in reducing the elasticity of demand may be similar to the impact of brand loyalty that a seller wins by convincing consumers—through means other than vertical restraints—of the quality and features of the seller's brand. But exploitation can occur, as when the buyer misperceives the quality or features of the brand being purchased, or fails to pay attention to these factors. The exploitation of such information gaps may involve price discrimination directed at less knowledgeable buyers.[46]

---

43. E.g., United States v. General Motors Corp., 384 U.S. 127, 86 S.Ct. 1321, 16 L.Ed.2d 415 (1966); cf. Palmer v. BRG of Georgia, Inc., 498 U.S. 46, 111 S.Ct. 401, 112 L.Ed.2d 349 (1990)(per curiam). See also United States v. Sealy, Inc., 388 U.S. 350, 87 S.Ct. 1847, 18 L.Ed.2d 1238 (1967); United States v. Topco Assocs., Inc., 405 U.S. 596, 92 S.Ct. 1126, 31 L.Ed.2d 515 (1972).

44. Aspen Skiing Co. v. Aspen Highlands Skiing Corp., 472 U.S. 585, 596 n. 20, 105 S.Ct. 2847, 86 L.Ed.2d 467 (1985). In two cases involving Sherman Act claims against sponsors of sporting events, the Court has adopted narrow market definitions that encompass only college football, National Collegiate Athletic Ass'n v. Board of Regents of Univ. of Okla., 468 U.S. at 101–102, 111–112 (1984), and professional boxing, International Boxing Club of New York, Inc. v. United States, 358 U.S. 242, 249–52, 79 S.Ct. 245, 3 L.Ed.2d 270 (1959).

45. Lorain Journal Co. v. United States, 342 U.S. 143, 149, 72 S.Ct. 181, 96 L.Ed. 162 (1951).

46. See § 2.5.

A unique feature of such restraints is that they can both create and exploit market power in a single transaction. Thus, market power may not have existed prior to use of a distribution restraint, but may be created by the very transaction that also constitutes an abuse. For example, in the case of a restraint such as vertical minimum price fixing, the dealer is assured a high margin that encourages it to promote the producer's brand. That promotion may be based on accurate and complete information, inaccurate or incomplete information, or hard sell tactics that have no information content. Many intrabrand distribution restraints may be benign or procompetitive, but when they are used in connection with multibrand retailing and other risk factors, the anticompetitive potential is substantial. The dealer may push the customer to purchase the favored brand, a sort of on-site brand conversion that precludes the beneficial effects of intrabrand competition. The consumer, even if converted for valid reasons to the brand pushed by the dealer, may have no opportunity to shop for a lower price on that brand because the purchase is made simultaneously with the on-site brand conversion.

Because the exploitation of buyer informational deficiencies creates the same sort of allocative injuries as other forms of market power, no competitive analysis of distribution restraints is complete without assessing the risk of that exploitation.[47] As discussed in § 6.3, the instant market power that can be created by such distribution restraints is not, by itself, the basis for condemning a vertical restraint, but is integral to understanding its anticompetitive potential.

2.4e2ii. Single Brand Market Power and Interbrand Distribution Restraints

Interbrand distribution restraints such as tie-ins can also create and exploit market power where none pre-existed. Interbrand restraints are harmful if the seller has the ability to coerce the buyer. But if this power to coerce could be lawfully exercised without the use of the interbrand restraint, the restraint may create additional harm as, for example, when a tie-in exploits buyer information deficiencies. Restraints such as tie-ins, unlike many intrabrand restraints, do not work through on-site conversion. Instead, these restraints can complicate the buyer's transaction, exploiting the information gaps that prevent a consumer from predicting future needs or market conditions associated with the purchase of the tied product. Although the bundled sale of goods can

---

47. At the very least, this risk tends to undercut an argument of theorists who suggest that the greater output engendered by a distribution restraint necessarily implies a better allocation of goods and services. R. BORK, THE ANTITRUST PARADOX: A POLICY AT WAR WITH ITSELF 437–38 (1993); Posner, *The Rule of Reason and the Economic Approach: Reflections on the Sylvania Decision*, 45 U. CHI. L. REV. 1, 18–19 (1977); Easterbrook, *Vertical Arrangements and the Rule of Reason*, 53 ANTITRUST L.J. 135, 155–56 (1984).

Intrabrand distribution restraints are traditional focuses of antitrust enforcement as the result of statutory directives—Section 1 of the Clayton Act and Section 5 of the FTC Act. Any ambiguity with respect to the statute's applicability to vertical restraints has been narrowed through almost a century of judicial decisions applying Section 1 to intrabrand and foreclosure restraints such as vertical price fixing and tie-ins.

simplify a buyer's decision, a tie-in that compels a buyer to commit to the subsequent purchase of a tied product is more likely to be troublesome. Even if the buyer tries to learn about the tied product, information about the competitive terms on which this product might be available in the future is likely to be difficult or impossible to obtain. The market power associated with a tie-in might also arise because of a buyer pass-on, as when the cost of the tied product is paid by a third party such as an insurance company. These and other factors contributing to a high risk of exploitation in tie-ins are discussed in § 8.3c3.

When interbrand restraints exploit information deficiencies, the allocative and wealth transfer injuries that can result are no different than those from other market power abuses. As with a pure monopolist, allocation is distorted and wealth is transferred in a manner that would not occur under competitive conditions. In his dissent in *Kodak*, Justice Scalia acknowledged that this form of market power may exist, but questioned whether misallocations prompted by exploitation of buyer information deficiencies belong in antitrust analysis.[48] Market distortions are, as Justice Scalia recognized, ubiquitous and an inevitable part of commerce. But distortions fostered by harmful distribution restraints such as the tie-in alleged in *Kodak* can be identified and deterred. Such distortions are not adventitious, but the result of a conscious decision by the seller imposing the exploitive vertical restraint. The injury is not the result of a seller's passive reliance on informational asymmetries such as may commonly occur in many sales.

2.4e2iii.　*Power in Aftermarkets*

An aftermarket is the market for replacement and supplementary parts and/or repair services for a product that the buyer has previously acquired, or for products consumed through use of the original product. Market power in an aftermarket is premised on brand differentiation. Unless products are differentiated in physical characteristics, or at least in the buyer's mind, interbrand competition will occur in the aftermarket. If, on the other hand, the consumer believes that only aftermarket products designed for its original product are suitable, the seller of aftermarket products may exercise market power. This power in the aftermarket could be the basis of a claim for an unlawful tie-in (as discussed in the previous section) or a claim for attempted monopolization or monopolization under Section 2 of the Sherman Act.

Restraints involving aftermarket products and services have frequently produced litigation, albeit with mixed signals about the lawfulness of any market power that may be exercised. Every producer of a product that may require replacement parts, additional complementary parts, or supplementary items consumed through use of the product or

---

48. Eastman Kodak Co. v. Image Technical Servs., Inc., 504 U.S. 451, 493–97, 112 S.Ct. 2072, 119 L.Ed.2d 265 (1992) (Scalia, J., dissenting). Some commentators have argued that such power is capable of being constrained contractually, and therefore ought not to give rise to antitrust concerns. See the discussion of aftermarket power in § 2.4e2iii.

service may be the beneficiary of some aftermarket power. That power tends to increase with the complexity and originality of the product subject to the original sale. For example, a producer of a novel copy machine, even assuming no patent protection, would probably have a lock on the aftermarket for replacement parts and service for a period after the product is first introduced. During that period, the seller might lawfully extract a higher price in the aftermarket.

A market can be defined to include only aftermarket goods or services. The Supreme Court agreed in *Kodak* that a single brand market was possible and declined to allow summary judgment against the plaintiff whose monopolization and tie-in claims were based upon a single brand market theory.[49] Under a single brand approach, many producers with little or no market power in the original equipment market might still be considered monopolists in aftermarkets. But, as in other claims of violations of Section 2 of the Sherman Act, the mere existence of market power does not, by itself, constitute a violation. The plaintiff's evidence must also meet the high Section 2 requirements for abusive conduct.

Market power in aftermarkets, as with all forms of market power, is limited by the possibility of new entry. In the case of an aftermarket product or service, such entry may be relatively easy if it is not constricted artificially through tie-ins, other foreclosure restraints, or the redesigning of a product to make it more difficult for competing suppliers to copy. If the aftermarket is large (based on the sales of the original product), other firms have a substantial incentive to enter the market and can provide competitive discipline.

Two additional constraints on aftermarket power may limit the potential for abuse. The first is the seller's concern with reputation. If the seller charges too much for aftermarket parts, repeat buyers or even first time buyers may shun the seller's original equipment. The second constraint is the ability of sophisticated buyers to seek contractual adjustments that mitigate anticompetitive effects. Those constraints may limit—but not eliminate—the injury from an exercise of aftermarket power.[50]

The seller's concern with reputation is not a complete substitute for competition in the aftermarket. A seller is constrained by concern with reputation only to the extent of information flow to future buyers. One would expect that large and repeat buyers would become sensitive to the price and quality of aftermarket supplies and, in response, adjust future purchases of original equipment. But some such buyers may be locked-in to a line of original equipment because of a large investment in training,

---

49. *Eastman Kodak*, 504 U.S. at 481–82.

50. Borenstein et al., *Antitrust Policy in Aftermarkets*, 63 ANTITRUST L.J. 455 (1995) (explaining the economic theory behind antitrust injury from some exercises of aftermarket power). For a contrasting view, see Shapiro, *Aftermarkets and Consumer Welfare: Making Sense of Kodak*, 63 ANTITRUST L.J. 483 (1995) (arguing that the damage from exercise of aftermarket power will be limited, difficult to remedy, and an inappropriate target for antitrust law).

equipment, and parts. In addition, many first time buyers may not receive the information available to experienced buyers and would be unaware of life cycle pricing considerations for the product. If a seller can discriminate in price between knowledgeable and less knowledgeable buyers, the seller may more easily exploit aftermarket power.

A seller may be less constrained by reputation concerns if the seller confronts stagnating sales of the original product.[51] Particularly if the product is to be discontinued, the seller may be disposed to charge high prices in the aftermarket to maximize short term revenues. Regardless of the future of the product, if the seller is insecure about its own financial prospects, it may seek high short term returns with less concern for its reputation. But even if the seller continues to enjoy modest and stable sales growth, the incentive to charge supracompetitive prices for aftermarket products may control if the seller has a large base of previous customers, each of whom must pay the higher price for all sales of aftermarket products. The higher returns for aftermarket sales are immediate, and are less likely to be offset by the discounted value of lost future sales of original equipment. Moreover, the seller can compensate future or repeat buyers of original equipment for higher aftermarket prices by offering discounts on the original equipment.

Who is harmed if, when measured against competitive prices, original equipment prices are lower and aftermarket prices are higher? Previous customers are harmed because they do not benefit from the discount on original equipment. In addition, the higher aftermarket prices may cause allocative distortions: users may reduce their rate of use of aftermarket products, while buying more original equipment. These harms may be transitory if rival firms enter the aftermarket to bring aftermarket prices closer to marginal cost. But sellers may engage in behavior to forestall or obstruct such entry through practices such as tie-ins or strategic design changes. These practices, rather than the isolated act of charging high prices for aftermarket products or services, are likely to warrant antitrust intervention.

Some economists argue that the injurious effects of aftermarket power can be offset through contract.[52] A sophisticated and powerful buyer can contract for more favorable treatment from the seller, in effect obtaining reduced prices on the aftermarket products and services. This result is likely if there is viable competition in the original equipment market, but is less likely if oligopolistic behavior constrains such competition. Even if there is some competition in the sale of original equipment, all buyers may not be protected. Antitrust cases involving tie-ins often are linked to discrimination in favor of the powerful and against the less powerful, less sophisticated buyer. The resulting competitive injury (misallocations and wealth transfer losses) may be more limited

---

51. The analysis presented in this paragraph and the following paragraphs follows Borenstein et al., supra note 50.

52. Klein, *Market Power in Antitrust*, supra note 33, at 43; Shapiro, supra note 50 at 488, 489, 496.

than in the case of power in a more broadly defined market, but no different in kind and no less real.

The sophisticated buyer's ability to contract for more favorable aftermarket prices and terms is also limited because neither buyer nor seller can predict future developments in a dynamic market. New providers of aftermarket products and services may inject new competitive elements. For example, new entrants in the service aftermarket may offer more service, varying levels of service, or more competitively priced service. Neither the buyer nor the seller of service can predict these developments in advance. A most-favored-nation contract clause may provide the buyer some protection, but these clauses may in themselves facilitate other anticompetitive injury. Such clauses (addressed in § 7.5) probably deter entry into aftermarkets and facilitate cartel-like behavior at the seller level or among participants in certain buyer industries.

Even if antitrust injury is present, Shapiro argues that no readily manageable antitrust remedy is available to the courts. The high prices charged for aftermarket products and services cannot reasonably be regulated through judicial decree.[53] The point is well taken, and demonstrates the folly of an antitrust policy that is directed at market power detached from additional abusive or exploitative conduct. But antitrust has addressed, and should continue to address, the abusive conduct itself by prohibiting a harmful intrabrand distribution restraint (such as an anticompetitive tie-in).

2.4e2iv. *Relational Market Power*

Enduring vertical relationships can give rise to supplier market power over a dealer for reasons closely related to the lock-in that can occur in aftermarkets. This lock-in may occur, for example, in franchise relationships. There are three evident sources of lock-in power that a supplier may exercise over a dealer: (1) the dealer's sunk costs reasonably incurred in connection with carrying the supplier's line; (2) the supplier's ability to impose additional costs on a disfavored dealer; and (3) the supplier's ability to deprive a disfavored dealer of favorable business opportunities available to other dealers. Each of these sources of supplier market power are considered below.

Sunk Costs- Sunk costs are fixed costs that cannot be recovered if a business is sold or abandoned. If a dealer invests substantial amounts in carrying the supplier's line, some of this investment may be sunk. For example, dealer personnel may undergo training at the dealer's expense, the dealer may make changes to his premises required by the supplier (including signs or non-functional design changes) and may purchase equipment unique to the supplier's line that cannot be resold except at a substantial loss. For some franchisees, these sunk costs may include a non-refundable franchise fee that must be paid before the franchisee can begin operations.

---

53. Shapiro, supra note 50, at 502.

To some extent, a dealer's incurred sunk costs are like poker chips already committed in a poker hand. Just as a rational poker player would not consider chips already wagered in determining whether to stay in the hand, a dealer that has incurred sunk costs (such as a franchise fee or training costs) should not allow them to dictate future investments that the dealer, based on business experience, considers ill-advised. But unlike the poker player's chips already on the table that will be won or lost in toto, the dealer's investment is paid-for assets that will have a wide range of values depending on the relative success of the business. Consider the situation confronted by a fast food franchisee who has invested $500,000 to get a franchise outlet underway. If the fast food franchise is abandoned after one year of unprofitable operation, the franchisee may recover only $300,000 through the sale of the assets (leaving $200,000 in unrecoverable or sunk costs). But if the franchisee stays the course, there is a chance to turn the business around, building the good will of the business through profitable operation. If the business makes a healthy profit, it might be sold at this point for $1 million, more than offsetting the sunk costs. Perhaps more realistically, the franchisee might achieve a small, below market rate of return on its investment that would still allow it to sell the business for $400,000, partially mitigating the loss it would have suffered if the business had been sold at the end of the first year. Thus, although a franchisee considering whether to sell or abandon its business should disregard already incurred sunk costs in determining the future profit flow, the franchisee must recognize that the assets purchased in part through the sunk investment will have a variable resale value based on the degree of success of the business. It's as if the poker player was given an opportunity to achieve partial success or mitigate loss by staying in the game. Under these modified rules, if the player drops out of the bidding, all of the invested chips are lost. But if the player continues, there is a chance to win it all, and perhaps a statistically more significant chance to reduce the amount that would be lost if the player folded (abandoned the hand).

The franchisee's ability to mitigate or wholly offset the loss from sunk costs will tend to make the franchisee more reluctant to abandon the franchise and more willing to accept franchisor conduct that results in higher franchisee costs or a "squeezed" resale margin. It is not only the financial aspects of a sunk investment, but also the dealer's personal commitment to the supplier and the supplier's line, the dealer's credibility to customers, and the difficulty of acknowledging that an investment decision and much hard work may have been erroneous. The dealer's reluctance to walk away from a combined financial and personal commitment can give the supplier power over price, the power to raise the price charged the dealer or to squeeze the dealer's margin through a supplier-imposed maximum resale price. In some supplier-dealer relationships, this power is amplified by the supplier's ability to impose additional costs on the dealer or to withhold financial benefits from the dealer.

A supplier's ability to impose additional costs on a dealer- A supplier may have the ability to impose additional costs on a dealer. Consider a dealer that is subject to supplier monitoring and inspection. At the supplier's discretion, inspections can be made more frequent or more rigorous; minor departures from the norm that would be overlooked for other dealers can be pursued vigorously if a dealer is disfavored.[54] Or a supplier that is displeased with some aspect of a dealer's performance might demand that the dealer purchase unwanted inventory that cannot be sold profitably. Some franchisors may be able to impose additional costs on a franchisee that decides to sell or abandon its business. The franchise contract may forbid the franchisee from using the premises for a competing business should the franchise be terminated. Equipment useful only in the franchise system may have no resale market, or may be repurchased by the franchisor at a substantial loss to the franchisee. Some franchisors may retain the power to dictate the terms and the identity of the buyer for the sale of the franchise, forcing down the resale price below a level that the market would have sustained. Facing these potential additional costs, the dealer may go to great lengths to avoid offending the supplier. This supplier will have power over price in its dealings with the dealer.

A supplier's ability to deny business opportunities to the dealer- Suppliers in continuing relationships with their dealers may have numerous opportunities to reward favored dealers. The supplier may offer to the dealer training or services, advertising and promotion benefits, or a favorable allotment of new or scarce products. In franchising, all of this and more may occur. The franchisor may provide waivers to favored franchisees, allowing them to experiment with new products or services not a part of the franchisor's line while denying these waivers to other franchisees. The franchisor can also offer favorable new locations to favored franchisees. As in the case of costs that the supplier might impose, the supplier's ability to confer business benefits on favored dealers will enhance the supplier's power over price in its dealings with a dealer.

A supplier's market power arising from its continuing relationship with a dealer is a variant of the "lock-in" that the Court addressed in Eastman Kodak Co. v. Image Technical Services, Inc.[55] But the potentially coercive nature of some supplier relationships over dealers was recognized in earlier Supreme Court decisions involving franchise relationships. For example, in *FTC v. Texaco, Inc.,* the Court upheld the Commission's challenge to "inherently coercive" arrangements by which Texaco, in return for a 10 percent commission from Goodrich, required independent Texaco dealers to purchase tires, batteries and accessories from Goodrich.[56]

---

54. Franchisors apparently used discriminatory enforcement to wield power over disfavored franchisees in Blanton v. Mobil Oil Corp., 721 F.2d 1207 (9th Cir. 1983) and in Milsen Co. v. Southland Corp., 454 F.2d 363 (7th Cir.1971).

55. 504 U.S. 451, 112 S.Ct. 2072, 119 L.Ed.2d 265 (1992).

56. 393 U.S. 223, 89 S.Ct. 429, 21 L.Ed.2d 394 (1968)(upholding the Commission's conclusion that Texaco had coerced dealers to purchase tires, batteries and accessories in violation of Section 5 of the

The issue of whether a market can be limited to a franchisor's line of goods has generated a debate in many respects parallel to the debate over aftermarket power.[57] Those who argue that a franchisor has no significant market power over a franchisee may concede a franchisor's ability to impose costs or confer benefits on franchisees, but argue that a franchisor will not exploit its market power in order to preserve its reputation enabling it to sell additional franchise outlets.[58] But under widely occurring circumstances, the discipline afforded by a need to maintain its reputation will not prevent a franchisor from abusing a franchisee. For example, a franchisor facing a fall-off in demand or threatened financially may discount concern with reputation in favor of short-term gain or even survival. Franchisors may also be able to target exploitative behavior on less informed franchisees in a manner that does relatively little harm to the franchisor's reputation. The circumstances in which reputational discipline may be inadequate to limit the franchisor's abusive conduct are further developed in § 6.4c3ii.

§ 2.5   Market Power and Price Discrimination

The theoretical models for perfect competition and monopoly assume that a seller sets a single price for its entire output. Monopolists are likely to strive in various ways to discriminate in price for the obvious reason that they can sell more and make more money if discrimination is possible. A seller whose brand lacks market power cannot discriminate in price—a buyer is unwilling to pay more to receive this brand and will instead readily substitute other brands. Of course, if rivals engage in the same discriminatory practice, as is the case with the multitiered but relatively standardized fares for domestic airlines, discrimination will be possible.

When a firm has market power, price discrimination can be constrained or precluded by arbitrage: buyers that pay a relatively low price may resell a product to other buyers. Arbitrage will make it difficult for the monopolist to set discriminatory prices—if a seller demands a higher price from a particular buyer, that buyer will likely seek to purchase the product from another buyer that was charged a lower price. But when sellers are able to discourage arbitrage, as, for example, appears to be the case with airline tickets and many service industries, the seller may be able to discriminate in price in a manner that increases its overall revenue. Sellers may use devices such as tie-ins to make it easier to implement discriminatory prices. See § 8.3b2.

FTC Act). See Atlantic Refining Co. v. FTC, 381 U.S. 357, 85 S.Ct. 1498, 14 L.Ed.2d 443 (1965)(upholding the FTC order against a similar tie-in imposed by Atlantic Refining). In Perma Life Mufflers, Inc. v. International Parts Corp., 392 U.S. 134, 88 S.Ct. 1981, 20 L.Ed.2d 982 (1968), the Court, without addressing the nature of the franchisor's market power, held that the franchisees' acquiescence to various clauses that re- stricted their procurement options did not bar their recovery under the Sherman Act.

57. See the discussion in § 2.4e2iii.

58. Klein & Saft, *The Law and Economics of Franchise Tying Contracts*, 28 J.L. & Econ. 345, 356 (1985); Rubin, *The Theory of the Firm and the Structure of the Franchise Contract*, 21 J.L. & Econ. 223, 231–32 (1978).

Many manifestations of price discrimination cause no meaningful competitive injury and a few (some would say more than a few) price discrimination schemes can be procompetitive. Examples of widely practiced and probably harmless or beneficial price discrimination include restaurants that grant a discount to early diners or movie theaters that sell lower-priced tickets for children or seniors. College tuition, selectively reduced by a school's financial aid, is probably another good example. It has been argued that high fixed (and low marginal) cost industries (such as airlines) may be forced to use price discrimination to survive in a competitive market.[59] Although it would be a mistake for antitrust to challenge many common manifestations of price discrimination, it should be recognized that some forms of discrimination, such as those implemented through a tie-in, can exploit a consumer's information gaps. Moreover, any price discrimination, even if it enhances the efficient allocation of a seller's product, will raise wealth transfer issues.

The antitrust goal of protecting consumer surplus, addressed in § 1.5b1, has special significance when addressing price discrimination. For many monopolization and cartel abuses, the view one takes of consumer surplus does not alter the outcome of a competitive analysis. A monopolization abuse that captures consumer surplus is also likely to skew allocative efficiency, so antitrust theorists of all stripes are likely to condemn it. But some forms of price discrimination appear designed to absorb consumer surplus while enhancing allocative efficiency. A perfect form of price discrimination would measure the demand level of each purchaser, extracting the highest price each buyer is willing to pay (the buyer's reservation price). If this scheme could be perfectly implemented, it would absorb all consumer surplus without reducing allocative efficiency. Indeed, allocative efficiency might be enhanced because a new buyer with a low reservation price might be reached: this buyer might decline to purchase under a uniform price that exceeded the buyer's reservation price. Although perfect price discrimination cannot be achieved, some price discrimination schemes probably do enhance sales while absorbing buyers' consumer surplus. This might be true, for example, of an airline pricing scheme that extracts higher fares from business travelers who book seats with little or no advance notice but offers substantial discounts to travelers who plan a trip long in advance. The net effect may be that the airline will allow more people to travel, a benefit both to them and to the airline.

Political support for antitrust may rest in large part on its ability to protect consumer surplus. That protection should not be to the exclusion of other antitrust goals and concerns. It is likely that many forms of price discrimination will diminish consumer surplus. This fact alone should not be a basis for condemning a broad category of variegated pricing schemes. But neither should it be ignored. For most consumer goods or services, we are accustomed to buying at a fixed, pre-announced

---

59. Baumol & Swanson, *The Economy and Ubiquitous Competitive Price Discrimination: Identifying Defensible Criteria of* *Market Power*, 70 ANTITRUST L. J. 661 (2003).

price. A consumer takes comfort in knowing that she is paying no more than the next person. Fixed prices also reduce search costs: customers know that, at least at this store, no one can get a lower price. Indeed, many customers probably make the assumption, perhaps based on the store's reputation, that the price they are paying is as low as, or almost as low as, the price that the same item would be sold for at other nearby stores.

Another pragmatic concern with price discrimination is that in many of its forms, it is unlikely to increase allocative efficiency. In theory, perfect price discrimination increases output by providing a product or service to low-reservation price buyers who would not have purchased at a higher, uniform price. In service industries such as airlines, restaurants, hotels, movie theaters, and university education, a system of price discrimination that provides a low end price for targeted groups may succeed in increasing output. This conclusion, however, assumes that a uniform price would have been set at a level higher than the low end discriminatory price. A seller facing a downward sloping demand curve and high marginal costs may choose not to lower its low end discriminatory price, but simply to raise prices charged to targeted groups with higher reservation prices. In addition, an efficient price discrimination may not be possible because of the exigencies of the market place. Products that are purchased can be resold, so that any seller that attempts to extract a higher price from those with higher reservation prices may find its pricing scheme undercut by arbitragers.[60] Moreover, if the seller can obfuscate or muddy the buyer's cost calculations, the price discrimination may be a way to raise prices for all customers. This might occur, for example, in aftermarket tying in cases in which the need for and competitive availability of the aftermarket tied product cannot be known with precision at the time the buyer purchases the tying product. This form of tying is addressed in § 8.3c3. Particularly when contrasted with strategically implemented price discrimination that would exploit information asymmetries, uniform pricing protects less powerful or less knowledgeable buyers. In a world in which power buyers constantly pressure vendors to discriminate in their favor, uniform pricing assures that rivals of the power buyers can compete on equal terms. This recognition should play a role in formulating antitrust policy toward price discrimination.

§ 2.6   Measuring Market Power

2.6a.   A Universal Measure of Market Power

If sustained and significant power over price constitutes market power, one way of measuring it is to examine the difference between a seller's price and its marginal cost. A high markup over marginal cost sustained for a length of time shows that competition is not effective—

---

60. It is no accident that most examples of widely used price discrimination involve servicing where arbitraging is more difficult.

perfect competition would require sale at marginal cost.[1] Theoretically, this measure, known as the *Lerner Index*, may be the best way of measuring market power, for it would measure all types of market power, regardless of whether the power is based upon industrywide structural factors or upon brand differentiation. Successful use of this method would eliminate the need for defining the market. Market share would become irrelevant if it could be established that a market participant was charging a price that could only be consistent with market power. Put another way, if a firm can sustain prices significantly in excess of marginal cost, the market would have to be defined in a way that confirms the existence of this power. Still, this performance index, however valid in theory, has limited practical value. It is not widely used in litigated cases, probably because of the difficulty in establishing marginal cost.[2]

Determining true marginal cost is difficult because the many conventions of generally accepted accounting principles often have little to do with economic costs. Calculating true marginal cost would require second-guessing cost accounting decisions about how costs are allocated among product lines. Even the costs appearing in the accounting data may be inflated because of x-inefficiency or rent-seeking behavior. Furthermore, even if one could establish a single firm's marginal cost, the competitive analysis would not be complete without determining marginal cost for the entire industry. A firm with the lowest costs in the industry, for example, would not necessarily have substantial market power simply because its markup above cost was higher than its competitors.

Given these rather substantial difficulties with the Lerner Index, economists rely widely on alternate methods of estimating market power based upon structure and conduct. The most widely used of these measures—and virtually always the beginning of the analysis—is through assigning shares in a market deemed relevant for purposes of the market power inquiry.

2.6b. Measuring Market Power Through Market Share

A second-best but often more usable approach for determining whether market power exists is to define the market, determine market share and evaluate other structural data. A firm's market share is generally correlated with market power, but market share often does not indicate a firm's actual market power. A firm with a high percentage of

§ 2.6

1. F. M. SCHERER & D. ROSS, INDUSTRIAL MARKET STRUCTURE AND ECONOMIC PERFORMANCE 70–72 (3d ed. 1990). Although originally proposed in 1934, A.P. Lerner, *The Concept of Monopoly and the Measurement of Monopoly Power*, 1 REV. OF ECON. STUDIES 157 (1934), the concept was explained to a broader antitrust audience in Landes & Posner, *Market Power in Antitrust Cases*, 94 HARV. L. REV. 937, 939–943 (1981). The authors rejected use of the Lerner index not because it was incorrect, but because it was difficult to use in antitrust counseling and litigation.

2. The Government sought unsuccessfully to employ a Lerner Index analysis in United States v. Eastman Kodak, 63 F.3d 95 (2d Cir.1995).

the market is more likely to have market power than one with a low percentage of the market. However the contrary may also hold. Some firms with high market shares may have relatively little market power; others with low market shares may possess substantial market power. For example, a firm with 90 percent of the sales of a product may possess relatively little market power if entry barriers are low and the product being sold is often interchanged with a product from another market. Similarly, a pattern of strategic pricing or high brand differentiation in an oligopolistic market may confer substantial market power, even on a seller with a relatively low percentage of the market. The utility of a traditional interbrand market share analysis diminishes as differentiated brands become dominant. By itself, the method tells us nothing about the market power associated with a particular brand.

Although market definitions are contested in a great many proceedings, although the cost of resolving these contested markets is high for both litigants and the tribunals, and although market definitions, once resolved, often are blindly applied as a surrogate for more sensitive market analysis, lawyers and courts continue to rely on market definitions as the key to disposing of market power issues. Judge Posner has suggested that "[i]t is only because we lack confidence in our ability to measure elasticities, or perhaps because we do not think of adopting so explicitly economic an approach that we have to define markets instead."[3] But the momentum against change may also lie in the common law principle of stare decisis and in lawyers' familiarity with the deficient but familiar market definition approach. In addition, whatever its shortcomings, the use of market definitions remains a constructive approach in merger and monopolization litigation if it is accompanied by an analysis of a consumer's willingness to substitute products, the height of barriers to entry, and other factors that may determine whether a particular market share confers market power on the seller. This is essentially the approach of the merger guidelines discussed in Chapter XI.

The first step in determining market shares is defining the market. A market definition has two components: identifying the relevant product or service market and then identifying the relevant geographic area. These questions often consume a great deal of a lawyer's time and resources in merger and monopolization counseling and litigation. In many cases, there may be no single correct market definition, but a series of reasonable definitions, each with its own strengths and weaknesses. Although the market definition adopted by the court may often determine the outcome of the case, that suggests undue reliance on definitions that might be better seen as a first step to understanding the likelihood of market power being exercised.

2.6b1. *Defining the Product or Service Market*

The difficulty in defining the product market stems from the interchangeability of many products. Some products, (salt is sometimes cited

---

3. R. POSNER, ANTITRUST LAW: AN ECONOMic Perspective 125 (1976).

as an example) may have few satisfactory substitutes, but many do. Consider the example of a producer of copper cookware. Should the market be confined to cookware made from copper, or should it include cast iron, steel, aluminum and other cookware? What if a particular manufacturer specializes in Teflon-coated pots and pans? Does that suggest a separate market? If so, should only cookware coated with Teflon be considered, or should porcelain-coated cookware, also having nonstick characteristics, be included? In theory, the answer to such questions should turn on the cross-elasticity of consumer demand: if consumers would not readily shift between coated and noncoated cookware, there is a coated cookware market. If consumers would readily shift from Teflon-coated to porcelain-coated cookware, then both of the products are in the same market. But cross-elasticity questions cannot be answered with a yes or no. There are countless variations of cross-elasticity along a continuum, making predictable and consistent results to a cross-elasticity inquiry an elusive goal.

In many consumer goods markets, products are highly differentiated, making the choice of product definition particularly difficult. Assume that there are seven widget producers in a tentatively defined market. The brand of widget that each produces is differentiated by quality reputation, features, style, packaging and image. Each is priced differently. Two brands are grouped in a low price range, three more are in a mid-price range, and the final two are in the highest price range. Within any one of these three groups, cross-elasticity may be high. Between any two neighboring groups (say the low-and mid-priced widgets), there is some cross-elasticity. But cross-elasticity is very low (or nonexistent) between the high-and low-priced groups. If the high-and low-priced widgets are grouped along with the medium-priced in a single, inclusive widget market, a single firm's market share may significantly understate its power. But considering any one of the three groups as itself a relevant market will result in shares that tend to overestimation of power. The lack of any clear gaps on the pricing continuum for the seven widget brands makes it extremely difficult to carve out functionally effective market definitions.[4] These difficulties again counsel against blind reliance on any product market definition.

In the Merger Guidelines, cross-elasticity is measured by taking the narrowest descriptive product definition, and asking whether a nontransitory price increase of 5 percent for that product would cause consumers to shift to the second product.[5] In practice, this measure of cross-elasticity can be difficult because there may be little or no accurate empirical data indicating buyer responses to price movements. Moreover, the Merger Guidelines approach must account for the possibility that prices for a product are already set at levels reflecting market power. A profit-maximizing firm possessing market power would be expected to

---

4. This difficulty in finding gaps in which to draw the lines for product market definitions for differentiated products is explored in Schmalensee, *Another Look at* *Market Power*, 95 HARV. L. REV. 1789, 1799–1800 (1982).

5. DOJ/FTC Horizontal Merger Guidelines § 1.11.

raise its price up to but not beyond a point where further increases might cause large numbers of consumers to switch to a less desirable product. Hence, in estimating market power, the crucial question concerns cross-elasticity at prices closely related to cost—cross-elasticity at competitive prices—not cross-elasticity at the price a firm is now charging. If a firm has already raised its price to a level substantially above cost, the willingness of consumers to switch in response to further small increase would not reflect such "true" cross-elasticity of demand but rather consumers' decisions to walk away from a desired product at some level of supracompetitive pricing. These decisions both reflect and identify the deadweight loss from market power. Another indication of cross-elasticity of demand, and one perhaps less susceptible to the above concern about premeasurement monopoly pricing, is whether producers of the closest substitute product (outside the tentative definition) tend to follow price changes made by producers of the first product. If there is little or no sensitivity to price changes for the other product, cross-elasticity is not established.

Although a market is usually defined initially based upon consumer demand, it may be appropriate to also examine the supply side of the market. For example, if three producers currently produce cast-iron cookware, but a fourth producer, not currently producing such cookware, produces related cast-iron products using similar machinery and production techniques, the presence of this fourth firm can limit the market power of the cookware producers. If profits were high among these producers, the fourth firm might decide to shift some of its machinery and resources to production of competing cookware.

However, using supply side considerations to define the product market can be problematic. In the cast-iron cookware example, assuming that the fourth firm, engaged in production of noncookware products, could switch to cookware, how much of its production capacity should be included in the market? This firm will not likely wish to abandon an existing market where it has substantial investments, dealers, and goodwill over a customer base. Thus, its ability or willingness to shift its capacity to cookware is limited. It would be misleading to count its entire production as part of the cast-iron cookware market. One response to such supply side flexibility is not to alter the market definition to include the fourth firm, but to consider apparent flexibility of potential entrants as a factor limiting market power after the market has been defined.

Another problem that arises in connection with the product market definition is the status of any captive production of a vertically integrated firm. In United States v. Aluminum Co. of America,[6] Alcoa produced a large amount of virgin aluminum for its own internal use in fabricating other aluminum products. Because this aluminum ingot was not sold to outsiders, it arguably was not part of the market. Judge Hand, however, decided that such captive production was part of the ingot market

6. 148 F.2d 416 (2d Cir.1945).

apparently because Alcoa's captive production, which could be quickly switched to other uses, represented part of the downstream demand.[7]

Aggregation of several products into a single product market can also raise issues. Some retailing examples are obvious, of course, such as drugs and notions for a drugstore market. But others may be debatable. The Supreme Court has held banking services to be a product cluster, though depositors and borrowers might be quite different groups with different demand functions.[8] In determining whether a cluster of products or services should be considered a single market, the Court has been influenced by supply side efficiencies. But the basic test should remain consumer demand. Do consumers choose the supplier based upon the cluster of services available? If the answer is yes for a substantial number of buyers, then the cluster of services should be considered a single market. The "all parts" market in the remand decision in Image Technical Services, Inc. v. Eastman Kodak Co. is an example.[9]

2.6b2. Defining the Geographic Market

The geographic component of market definition is the second phase in evaluating market concentration. Markets can be local, regional, national or even international in scope. Once again, consumer demand is the primary measure of a market's geographic scope. Where do consumers look when considering the purchase of a product or service? For some products, groceries for example, the market may be local, perhaps as small as a neighborhood in a New York City borough where most residents can shop without cars. Even in suburban areas, many shoppers may prefer to shop within five minutes drive of their home. On the other hand, if a consumer is considering a major and less frequent purchase, such as an automobile or television set, a broader geographic range of sellers may be appropriate. And when the buyer is a large firm with substantial long-term needs, the firm may shop worldwide, particularly if transportation costs are an insignificant part of the product's costs. This may be true, for example, with computer chips that are relatively expensive to manufacture, but relatively inexpensive to transport. On the other hand, cement is heavy and relatively inexpensive to produce, making transportation a major factor in setting price. For cement, the importance of transportation costs may rule out a market that is national in scope.

When a market is defined with a national scope (and, on some occasions, even when it has a regional scope), there is a question of how to treat imports. For example, if the market for aluminum ingot is defined as national in scope, and 10 percent of current aluminum ingot sales to U.S. buyers is produced abroad, should this 10 percent be

---

7. Id. at 424.

8. United States v. Philadelphia Nat'l Bank, 374 U.S. 321, 356–57, 83 S.Ct. 1715, 10 L.Ed.2d 915 (1963); see also, United States v. Grinnell Corp., 384 U.S. 563, 86 S.Ct. 1698, 16 L.Ed.2d 778 (1966) (central station protective services of various kinds aggregated into a single market).

9. 125 F.3d 1195 (9th Cir.1997), cert. denied, 523 U.S. 1094, 118 S.Ct. 1560, 140 L.Ed.2d 792 (1998).

included in the market? In *United States v. Aluminum Co. of America*, Judge Hand said yes, but did not include any additional production capacity of foreign producers as part of the market.[10] The crucial question here is whether all or part of the additional foreign capacity will influence the U.S. market because it could easily be diverted to the U.S. if prices increased further. The better answer is probably a presumption that no additional foreign capacity should be included in the market. Foreign producers are unlikely to abandon existing customer relationships to move a large percentage of their production to U.S. customers. Indeed, were they to attempt such a move, they might well be confronted with challenges by U.S. producers under trade legislation restricting imports. This presumption, however, should be open to rebuttal. Do foreign suppliers have substantial unused capacity that could be quickly brought on line? Is current trade policy committed by relevant and enforceable treaty to open markets? Is there available transport capacity? Are the trade relationships needed for distribution accessible or in place? The proponent of a wider market may be able to produce evidence on such issues. If so, the trier of fact should hear and evaluate that evidence and any rebuttal.

Once the product or service and geographic component of a market are identified, the market is defined, and market shares can be determined. It bears repeating, however, that this definition is a guide and should never be regarded as determinative of whether market power exists. Many market definitions are rather fragile constructs, based on a number of disputed or even subjective determinations. No market definition is a substitute for careful market analysis. After the market has been defined, there are, for example, important questions involving barriers to entry still to be resolved.

2.6b3. Barriers to Entry

If firms outside the market could easily enter the market, a high market share may not reflect a great deal of market power. Entry barriers include all factors that allow incumbents to maintain a price significantly in excess of marginal cost without stimulating entry by new firms.[11] Examples include economies of scale (because a new entrant would have to enter on a large scale and win substantial patronage in order to survive); product differentiation (because a new entrant would have to convince consumers to turn away from brands to which they are loyal); or government laws and regulation that require licensing or impose regulatory hurdles on new entrants. Although entry barriers of various kinds are widespread, their existence is critical in determining the extent of market power. If entry barriers are insubstantial, even a monopolist may have no significant ability, based upon industry structure, to misallocate resources through control of price or output.[12]

---

10. 148 F.2d 416, 426 (2d Cir.1945).

11. J. BAIN, BARRIERS TO NEW COMPETITION: THEIR CHARACTER AND CONSEQUENCES IN MANUFACTURING INDUSTRIES (1956).

12. Such a firm might be able to exercise single brand market power, based, for example, on brand advertising and distribution restraints.

In the economic literature, there is controversy about the proper definition of entry barriers. Though the Bainian approach, which treats as a barrier any factor that as a realistic matter discouraged entry, has generally been accepted by courts[13] and adhered to by leading economists,[14] Stigler has proposed a narrow definition that appeals to some commentators. Stigler treats as a barrier only costs that a new entrant must incur that were not incurred by incumbents when they entered.[15] Under this definition, economies of scale would not be considered a barrier. Although incumbents enjoying economies of scale might have some market power allowing them to charge higher prices without inviting entry, this may be a necessary result of minimum efficient scale (MES) for the industry. For example, an industry with three firms, each barely meeting the MES requirement, cannot accommodate a fourth firm without a threatened loss of efficiency. Even if these three firms enjoy some leverage that allows them to price above competitive levels, that price increase may be more than offset by efficiencies of production, so that the consumer does not pay any more (and may pay less) than would occur if the market was made up of a larger number of firms. Product differentiation also might not qualify as an entry barrier under the Stigler definition because each firm entering would presumably incur the costs of establishing consumer brand loyalty. On the other hand, incumbents that entered the market early may have substantially lower costs in establishing brand loyalty than later entrants.[16]

Even if a new entrant faces no entry costs beyond those paid by existing firms, the new entrant may face a higher risk of losing the sunk costs associated with entry. The sunk costs may make the entrant more vulnerable to strategic behavior, such as targeted price cuts, by existing firms. Faced with large sunk costs and the risk of a strategic response, there is a substantial deterrent to entry for this firm regardless of whether its entry costs are higher than those for existing firms.[17]

The Stigler definition of entry barriers is also inconsistent with the definition of market power, used here and elsewhere (the ability to misallocate resources by limiting output to raise prices above costs, causing allocation and other antitrust injuries). An industry made up of three MES firms may perform more efficiently than would the same industry made up of ten firms, none large enough to meet MES. But it is not unlikely that the three MES firms possess market power as mea-

13. The courts have paid little attention to the academic debate about the definition of barriers to entry, focusing instead on an analysis of entry barrier arguments put forward by the parties in light of the conditions extant in the particular industry and the past record for entry in that industry. FTC v. Staples, 970 F.Supp. 1066, 1086–88 (D.D.C.1997). This fact-intensive analysis is consistent with the approach to entry analysis outlined in agency enforcement guidelines. E.g., DOJ/FTC Horizontal Merger Guidelines § 3.0.

14. SCHERER & ROSS, supra note 1, at 56. D. CARLTON & J. PERLOFF, MODERN INDUSTRIAL ORGANIZATION 110–14 (2d ed. 1994)(arguing that all barriers that increase the entrant's long term costs are significant).

15. G. J. STIGLER, THE ORGANIZATION OF INDUSTRY 67 (1968).

16. SCHERER & ROSS, supra note 1, at 407.

17. CARLTON & PERLOFF, supra note 14, at 113.

sured by control over price. There is no assurance that the greater efficiency of the three-firm industry will be passed on to consumers. Much or all of that gain may be lost in the higher firm costs often associated with market power: x-inefficiency or rent-seeking. The higher costs imposed on potential new entrants can also have unpredicted effects on the dynamic element of competition: new firms that might bring innovative and more efficiently produced products may never have the opportunity to do so. A distinction like that which Stigler builds into his definition of barrier—a concept intended to evaluate power–is simply not relevant to the power analysis, however relevant such distinctions might be at a later analytical stage where the legality of conduct is considered or, if a violation is found, possible remedies evaluated.

Smaller countries may more frequently confront the problem of MES. Because of a small population base, some countries may be able to accommodate only a single firm in the domestic industry that is sufficiently large to achieve scale economies. In the United States, there is empirical evidence that most industries can accommodate a significant number of firms that have MES.[18] The concerns that led Stigler to adopt a narrower definition of entry barriers may, in any event, be weighed in applying particular antitrust laws. The presence of market power is not, in and of itself, an occasion for invoking antitrust remedies. If a proposed merger would allow two firms to achieve market power, but they establish that the merger is required in order to achieve MES, decision-makers have discretion to decide whether or not this merger should be permitted. See the discussion in Chapter XI.

Entry barriers can be naturally occurring, as in the case of economies of scale, or they may be artificial, in the sense that they are created by the conduct of a competitor. For example, a firm wishing to deter entry may redesign its product to make it more difficult for competing parts suppliers to enter. Or, a firm seeking to ward off entry might intensify an advertising campaign, or seek to lock up large customers through long-term contracts. Although all types of entry barriers would be relevant in evaluating market power, antitrust is more often concerned with strategically instituted barriers within the control of a firm. The creation of such entry barriers may, for example, raise conduct issues under Section 2 of the Sherman Act. See § 3.4.

2.6b4. *Measures of Industry Concentration*

Particularly in oligopolistic industries, a firm's individual market share does not tell the whole story in terms of its market power. The likelihood of interdependent behavior will likely vary not only with a single firm's market share, but with the shares of its competitors as well. Recognizing that a firm's market share is better understood in the context of concentration in the entire market, two measures of overall market concentration have been widely used. The first, the four figure concentration share, is simply the sum of the market shares of the four

18. Id. at 114–18.

largest firms in the industry. In an industry with the four largest firms each holding 20 percent of the market, four figure concentration is 80 percent. A variation on four figure concentration is eight figure concentration, or the sum of the market shares of the largest eight firms in an industry.

A second widely used measure of market power is the Herfindahl–Hirschman Index (HHI).[19] The index is the sum of the square of the market share for each firm in the industry. Thus, if the four largest firms each have 20 percent of the market, and the remaining twenty firms have 1 percent each, the Index would be 1620 $(20^2 + 20^2 + 20^2 + 20^2 + 20(1^2) = 1620)$. The HHI has the advantage of reflecting higher degrees of concentration with greater refinement. For example, the following two markets would have identical four figure concentration measures but markedly different HHIs (assuming that firms ranked number five and below have insignificant market shares):

Market No. 1: Firm No. 1 (60 percent)
    Firm No. 2 (10 percent)
    Firm No. 3 (10 percent)
    Firm No. 4 (10 percent).

 Four figure concentration = 90 percent
 HHI = 3900

Market No. 2: Firm No. 1 (22.5 percent)
    Firm No. 2 (22.5 percent)
    Firm No. 3 (22.5 percent)
    Firm No. 4 (22.5 percent)

 Four figure concentration = 90 percent
 HHI = 2025

Market No. 1 presents greater risks of parallel, oligopolistic behavior because the largest firm far outdistances its competitors and may possess leverage to affect price and output acting alone, or may have enhanced abilities to exercise price leadership with respect to the remaining competitors. Although the 1968 Department of Justice Merger Guidelines used the four figure concentration measure, more recent versions of those guidelines (beginning with the 1982 version) use the HHI to measure concentration.

2.6c. Alternative Measures of Market Power

Although assigning market shares is the most widely used method of estimating market power in monopolization and merger litigation, it is expensive and uncertain in application. Many antitrust cases involve protracted disputes about market definition and courts sometimes place undue reliance on such a definition instead of using it as a starting point

---

19. The history of the HHI is explained in Hirschman, *The Paternity of an Index*, 54 Amer. Econ. Rev. 761 (1964).

for analysis. More fundamentally, market shares are useless as a measure of market power when that power is based on brand differentiation.[20] Thus, when measuring the legality of a distribution restraint, the use of a market share test as the exclusive measure of market power is difficult to justify. Although the Lerner Index would work well to measure market power in this context, it is not used because of the difficulties in determining a firm's marginal costs. There are, however, a number of alternative approaches for determining the existence of market power, as checks on the use of a market share approach, when the market share approach is not relevant, or when that approach will not work.

Other methods of determining market power that have been suggested include profitability and past market behavior.[21] These measures, too, are imperfect. Low profitability may be consistent with market power if rents are consumed in an effort to obtain or keep market power (rent-seeking behavior) or by inefficient management not sufficiently disciplined by competition (x-inefficiency). High profitability may be a short-term phenomenon, necessary to entice rivals to shift resources into new competitive areas, and not reflective of long-term market power. Substantial accounting problems also confront the use of profitability evidence.[22] Still, when persistent high profitability can be demonstrated, it is a useful indicator of market power.[23]

Behavioral indicators can also be useful. Baker and Bresnahan describe three possible econometric methods for measuring market power.[24] Econometrics processes data through statistical methods to determine the magnitude of a concept (such as market power) developed by economic theory. For example, data might be gathered and analyzed to support or refute the existence of market power by: (1) determining whether the target firm can sustain an increase in price against rivals that do not likewise raise their prices (if the target firm can sustain the price increase, market power is present); (2) determining whether the target firm can sustain price increases when producers of a related product, interchangeable for some uses, do not raise their prices (if the narrower market for the target firm's product is competitive, the target firm could not sustain a price increase); and (3) determining whether an industry engages in a pattern of long periods of high prices interspersed with short price wars (a condition that economic theorists find consistent with strategic and interdependent pricing that demonstrates market

20. Schmalensee, supra note 4, at 1800 ("If substantial differentiation can be demonstrated, market share computation is unlikely to yield reliable information" concerning market power).

21. Id. at 1804–07.

22. Baker & Bresnahan, *Empirical Methods of Identifying and Measuring Market Power*, 61 ANTITRUST L.J. 3, 5 (1992) (summarizing the difficulties in use of evidence of profitability).

23. The dissent cited du Pont's high profits for cellophane as evidence of the appropriateness of its market definition (confined to cellophane) in United States v. E.I. du Pont de Nemours & Co., 351 U.S. 377, 422–23, 76 S.Ct. 994, 100 L.Ed. 1264 (1956).

24. Baker & Bresnahan, supra note 22.

power). Because each of these three econometric examples requires the gathering of substantial data, they have been employed primarily in connection with branded consumer products, where point-of-sale scanner data is available.[25]

In the distribution restraints context, evidence of persistent price discrimination in the sale of the same brand, or in the sale of two brands that are identical except for brand image, may signal the presence of the requisite market power.[26] Although it is true that such price discrimination may not be a precise indicator of the degree of market power, it may be used in vertical restraints litigation to show a minimum threshold has been met. For distribution restraints, another behavior indication of market power may be the use of the restraint in a manner likely to exploit consumer information gaps. As described in § 2.4e2, the use of such restraints may create "on-site" market power as a result of a dealer's promotion of the relevant brand, or because a buyer is uninterested or unable to assess the competitive virtues of a deferred purchase of a tied product. In the context of cases involving these restraints, it is not difficult to isolate conditions that are conducive to the creation and exploitation of this form of market power.[27] For example, market power based on the exploitation of informational or motivational market imperfections is more likely in consumer goods markets involving complex products. It is less likely when sales are to large, business buyers. If the transaction targets buyers that lack cost sensitivity because costs are passed on to a third party, there is also a high risk the seller may be exercising some sort of market power. Some tie-ins, for example, are selectively applied to smaller or less sophisticated buyers. Tie-ins in health care may involve buyer pass-on. See § 8.3c4ii. Market power based on brand differentiation may be associated with large advertising expenses. Or, its presence may be detected by a large price differential between a particular brand and competing goods. Independent pricing patterns of a seller whose brand seems relatively insulated from pricing changes of competitors may also establish market power.

Market power in aftermarkets may lend itself to some structural measurements. For example, the existence of competing suppliers of aftermarket parts tends to show reduced market power in the same manner as in the original equipment market. In many cases, however, a seller of original equipment may be the sole supplier of aftermarket parts and still be subject to some market discipline because of the threat of entry and because of the seller's desire to protect its reputation for the original product. The case for adequate competitive discipline is strengthened if there are relatively few informational problems associated with the sale of aftermarket parts. If, on the other hand, the seller takes additional steps to thwart entry in the aftermarket (through the use of tie-ins, exclusive dealing or redesigned products), this action

25. Id. at 15.

26. See the discussion in § 2.5.

27. See Chapters VI and VII.

suggests rent-seeking behavior consistent with inadequately disciplined market power.

In determining the existence of relational market power (such as a franchisor often has in dealings with its franchisees), the key question may be the existence of high franchisee sunk costs or the ability of the franchisor to impose additional costs on franchisees or deny them services or business opportunities available to other franchisees. The vulnerability of a franchisee will vary with its size and the number of outlets that it owns. A corporate franchisee that owns a large number of outlets from a single franchisor will likely possess considerable counter-leverage to offset the leverage that a franchisor possesses as the result of the franchisee's sunk costs. On the other hand, a small franchisee that owns a single outlet may have no other means of countering the franchisor's relational market power.

2.6d. A Showing of Anticompetitive Effect May Obviate the Need for Market Definition

Antitrust focuses on abusive exercise of market power. The exercise of defining the market is merely a tool for determining if that has occurred; it should not be an end in itself. In *Eastman Kodak Co. v. Image Technical Services, Inc.*, the Supreme Court stressed that "legal presumptions that rest on formalistic distinctions rather than actual market realities are generally disfavored in antitrust law."[28] Confronted with Kodak's arguments that aftermarkets were not appropriate for measuring market power, the Court wrote: "It is clearly reasonable to infer that Kodak has market power to raise prices and drive out competition in aftermarkets, since respondents offer direct evidence that Kodak did so."[29]

Disputes about market definition, then, are of little consequence in the face of actual evidence of anticompetitive effects. The Seventh Circuit recognized this in a case in which Toys "R" Us (TRU) was found to have violated the Sherman Act and the FTC Act through its efforts to limit toy manufacturers' sales to warehouse clubs.[30] The court rejected arguments that the FTC had failed to allege and prove market power in a properly defined market:

> TRU seems to think that anticompetitive effects in a market cannot be shown unless the plaintiff ... first proves that it has a large market share. This, however, has things backwards. As we have explained elsewhere, the share a firm has in a properly defined relevant market is only a way of estimating market power, which is the ultimate consideration. *Ball Memorial Hospital, Inc. v. Mutual Hospital Insurance*, 784 F.2d 1325, 1336 (7th Cir. 1986). The Supreme Court has made clear that there are two ways of proving market power. One is through direct evidence of anticompetitive

28. 504 U.S. 451, 466–67, 112 S.Ct. 2072, 119 L.Ed.2d 265 (1992).

29. Id. at 477.

30. Toys "R" Us v. FTC, 221 F.3d 928 (7th Cir. 2000).

effects. See *FTC v. Indiana Federation of Dentists*, 476 U.S. 447, 460–61, 106 S.Ct. 2009, 90 L.Ed.2d 445 (1986).[31]

§ 2.7 Market Power on the Buyer's Side: Monopsony, Oligopsony and Gatekeeper Power

Writers who address the subject of monopsony often describe it as the flip side of monopoly. Competition can be distorted, and efficient allocation undermined, by either a power-wielding seller or a power-wielding buyer. Yet the case law and literature addressing buyer power is much thinner than that addressing seller power. It is worth reflecting on why this has been the case and why, in recent years, more attention has been focused on buyer power issues.

The most obvious reason for antitrust's relative inattention to buying power is that harm to consumers was a prime focus when the Sherman Act was enacted and for the century that followed. Every individual consumes. Unless we are self-sufficient farmers or hunter gathers, we must buy (or have someone else buy for us) what we consume. A consumer is the classic atomistic buyer. Although consumers have been known to form buyers' cooperatives or occasionally boycott certain sellers, most make buying decisions as individuals or as a part of a family unit. Such buyers lack power to influence a seller's price except through the invisible hand of the market place: i.e., through competition. Sellers, on the other hand, even relatively small sellers, may exercise market power in a local geographic market or in a broader geographic market for a unique product or service. This sort of power was widely recognized in 1890. Farmers of that time were relatively unconcerned about buying power in the then relatively unconcentrated slaughter-house market but very concerned about the discriminatory high railroad rates they had to pay to ship livestock to markets. Still, buying power existed in 1890 (see the example of the Standard Oil trust below) and was a major concern of those who urged enactment of the Sherman Act.

Emphasis on seller power abuse pushed the vocabulary and analysis of power abuses in 1890 and in the years that followed. Although atomistic sellers existed in 1890 (family bread winners who sold their products and services to make a living), there are fewer individual sellers than there are consumer-buyers, and the circumstances under which individuals sell their services vary substantially. Many are employees, a few function primarily as capitalists, and many are independent contractors or professionals. Among employees, antitrust has to a considerable extent ceded its function to labor law that governs collective bargaining.

With the emergence of the Chicago School after the 1960s, the term "consumer welfare" gave perhaps unintended but added weight to antitrust's focus on seller power. If consumer welfare is the equivalent of

---

31. *Id.* at 937. Accord, Law v. NCAA, 134 F.3d 1010, 1020–21 (10th Cir. 1998)(price fixing violation involving a limited class of assistant basketball coaches for Division I universities sustained based on showing of "actual anticompetitive effects").

efficient allocation, a buyer power abuse is just as much an abuse of that efficiency as a seller power abuse. On the other hand, if one focuses just on low prices for consumers (as followers of the Chicago concept of consumer welfare tend to do), it can be argued that buyer power is less threatening to consumers and, in some cases, will benefit them. Because a monopsonist is able to buy for less, the monopsonist may also sell its output product for less, resulting in a lower price for consumers. This conclusion, it turns out, is often misleading. It is possible that a power buyer will exercise power only in a regional market served by its suppliers and sell its output product in a highly competitive national market. Under these circumstances, the power buyer will price its output good competitively, perhaps benefitting consumers through lower prices. Still, although a monopsonist is able to buy for lower prices, it does so by restricting input purchases, which can also result in a decline in output and higher prices for the output good. As the economist Warren–Boulton has put it:

> When firms with monopsony power drive down supplier prices, they do so by restricting their purchases of these inputs. Less inputs means less output. Less output means higher prices to consumers. The gross margin of the monopsonist increases both because the price he charges for his output goes up and the prices he pays for his inputs go down.[1]

Warren–Boulton concludes that both "monopsony and monopoly transfer wealth (usually from lower to higher-income individuals) and ... both ... result in lower output/production, less inputs purchased, higher prices to consumers, and lower prices to suppliers."[2]

It does not follow, however, that all monopsony abuses produce higher consumer prices, nor does it follow that, in the absence of such higher prices, there is no harm to competition. If monopsony abuses are truly the mirror image of monopoly abuses, the focus for monopsony ought not to be on consumers as atomistic buyers, but on the atomistic or small sellers in the market who are harmed by monopsony abuse. Thus, the relevant market in a monopsony case is not based on alternative sellers of products or services available to consumers, but on alternative buyers available to the small or atomistic seller. This important distinction was recognized by the Second Circuit in *Todd v. Exxon*.[3]

Another reason that less attention has been paid to monopsony is because a monopsonist buyer is often (although by no means always) a monopolist in its downstream sales. Any antitrust challenge to the monopsonist's conduct may be framed as a challenge to monopoly power.

§ 2.7

1. F.R. Warren–Boulton, The Case Against an "Agrarian Antitrust Policy", Agricultural Outlook Forum 2000, available at <http://www.usda.gov/oce/waob/oc2000/speeches/warren-boulton.txt>

2. Id.

3. 275 F.3d 191, 202 (2d Cir. 2001). This analysis would suggest that proving harm to consumers is irrelevant in a monopsony case. David Balto, *Punishing Monopsony Without Proving Consumer Harm?* (unpublished paper presented at the Sedona Conference, Nov. 20–21, 2003).

If a large firm has market power in both purchasing and selling, the easier path for an antitrust challenge may be to focus on the selling conduct. An antitrust challenge to this firm's conduct would tend to focus on its higher priced output, not on its suppressed price paid for input. An example is the conduct of Standard Oil that led to the landmark 1911 Supreme Court case. The Government brought this case under Sections 1 and 2 of the Sherman Act, claiming in part that the Standard Oil trust was a monopoly. Yet, to build his trust, Rockefeller relied on his firm's buying power as a purchaser of railroad services.[4]

None of these considerations suggest that antitrust should have no role in addressing abuses of buyer power. Indeed, antitrust already has a substantial track record in addressing competitive abuses by powerful buyers, even if the theoretical literature has been slow to recognize this. The need for this role grows as power buyers become an increasingly common feature of the marketplace. Mergers and acquisitions that may present relatively few competitive issues on the selling side may, because of the vulnerability of the small or atomistic seller, present significant problems on the buying side.

2.7a. Buying Power Abuses Involving Atomistic Sellers

There are a substantial number of buying power cases involving small and vulnerable sellers, including farmers, ranchers, fishermen, independent contractors (such as truck drivers or taxi cab drivers) not covered by the labor laws, or professional service providers (such as doctors, lawyers, or pharmacists). In cases involving agricultural produce, animal stock, or seafood, the small sellers are particularly susceptible to abuse because of the rapid spoilage of their products: the seller must move the product quickly or risk a total loss when the product spoils. Abusive conduct has included individual buyers who have exercised monopsony power or buyers who act collectively to limit output and fix the prices of their purchases.[5]

The classic case of an atomistic seller may be a skilled or unskilled laborer selling her services. These employees receive a degree of protection from federal labor law. Agricultural producers have attempted to counter buyer power by creating agricultural cooperatives when federal and state law allow this.[6] Doctors and nurses have sought the protection of an antitrust exemption so that they too might bargain collectively.

2.7b. Buying Power and Sunk Costs: Athletes, Professionals and Skilled Employees

Professional athletes and coaches of sports teams invest a great deal of time in obtaining the skill set to perform at a high level in their

---

4. See the discussion in § 3.8.

5. See, e.g., United States v. Griffith, 334 U.S. 100, 68 S.Ct. 941, 92 L.Ed. 1236 (1948) (theater chain's monopsony abuse); Mandeville Island Farms v. American Crystal Sugar Co., 334 U.S. 219, 68 S.Ct. 996, 92 L.Ed. 1328 (1948)(sugar refiners unlawful conspiracy to suppress price of California sugar beets).

6. See Parker v. Brown, 317 U.S. 341, 63 S.Ct. 307, 87 L.Ed. 315 (1943).

profession. These investments in a particular sport are often difficult for an individual to translate into work outside of the chosen sport. The training is therefore a sunk investment, making the player or coach vulnerable to the leverage possessed by the sports leagues that may be the only outlet, or one of very few outlets, for the player or coach. Preeminent athletes or coaches are handsomely compensated (some would say over-compensated), but journeyman athletes and coaches may fare poorly. Antitrust claims against leagues or college athletic associations are not unusual.[7]

The sunk investment that athletes and coaches have made is of course not unique to sports occupations. Professionals, such as doctors and nurses, also have made a substantial investment in their training. Although medical professionals generally have a range of employment options, those options may become increasingly limited as buyers of health care services consolidate.

2.7c. Buyer Power in Retailing

For a number of reasons, buying power among retailers creates a unique set of analytical issues. There are substantial scale economies attached to retailing. If there were not, all producers would presumably choose to sell directly to consumers, bypassing the retailing stage.[8] One example of these scale efficiencies involves transportation costs. Consider a lawn mower manufacturer's transportation costs in selling directly to the public. The expense of shipping individual lawn mowers to a particular customer would add substantially to the manufacturer's cost, perhaps in the amount of $40 for each mower sold. But if a truckload of mowers can be transported directly to a retail distribution center, the cost of this transportation may go down to $5.00 per unit. To reduce these costs, each lawn mower producer could operate its own retail stores, but this too has risks and costs; a retail store dedicated only to a single brand may have less variety and draw fewer customers, reducing retail scale efficiencies.

A producer's dependency on multi-brand retailers can give large retailers substantial power in the vertical relationship. Walmart is said to sell 22% of all toys sold in the United States,[9] giving it very substantial leverage over any toy manufacturer that wishes to sell in this country. But a retailer's leverage may begin at much lower levels. The UK Competition Commission has concluded that retail buyer power can distort competition with as little as 8 percent of the total market.[10]

---

7. See, e.g., NCAA v. University of Oklahoma, 468 U.S. 85, 104 S.Ct. 2948, 82 L.Ed.2d 70 (1984); Brown v. Pro Football, Inc., 518 U.S. 231 (1996); Clarett v. NFL, 369 F.3d 124 (2d Cir. 2004).

8. The scale economies associated with retailing are addressed in Lynch, *Why Economists are Wrong to Neglect Retailing and How Steiner's Theory Provides an Explanation of Important Irregularities*, paper presented at American Antitrust Institute Conference, June 21, 2004 (forthcoming in Antitrust Law Bulletin).

9. Michael Barbaro, Washington Post, May 31, 2004 Page E01.

10. These and other insights on retail buying power with particular reference to grocery retailing in the UK are presented in P. Dobson, Exploiting Buyer Power: Les-

Although sellers with strong brands have some leverage to offset this buying power, even a powerful brand may not be sufficient to remove a supplier's dependency on a retail chain with as little as 10 percent of the market. Consider the producer of a preeminent brand of laundry detergent with 25% of the national market, selling its detergent to a retail grocery chain which sells 10% of all detergent sold in the national market. If the chain decides to drop this preeminent brand, it may lose some sales to customers who will go elsewhere to buy the preeminent brand. But the chain can replace the preeminent brand with other brands (and its own private label), perhaps earning a higher margin on slightly reduced sales of laundry detergent. Overall, the chain's profit lost on laundry detergent sales may be 1 or 2 percent, whereas the producer, having lost access to a chain that sold 10% of its detergent, may lose significantly more. The producer may find it impossible to reach the consumers who are loyal customers of the chain and could lose most of the sales that had been made through the chain, perhaps 8 or 9 percent of its profits. This *relative economic dependency* of the producer on the retail chain translates to buying power in this vertical relationship.[11]

Power retail buyers often exercise power over suppliers because they are also competitors of these suppliers (through the retailer's private label sales) and suppliers in their own right (selling shelf space and advertising to the producers). This has led at least one observer of the retail scene to conclude that retail power can trump even the power of a supplier of a major brand.[12]

For most sellers, creation of their own distribution system is not a satisfactory option. Most sellers will end up relying in whole or in part on the retailers who sell the bulk of consumer goods in a multibrand setting. These retailers perform a gatekeeper function: unless a retailer carries the sellers' brand, the brand will be relatively inaccessible to customers who shop at that retailer's outlets. The power that a gatekeeper retailer exercises may be local,[13] national or international in its reach.[14] The power retailer may wield its power strategically, making it more difficult for rivals to compete with it.[15]

2.7d. Determining the Likelihood and Extent of Buying Power

A leading treatise on monopsony proposes a buying power index (BPI) as a measure of the degree of market power possessed by a buyer (or group of buyers). According to the authors, there are three components that influence the BPI: (1) market share of the buyer; (2) the

sons from the British Grocery Trade 72 ANTITRUST L.J. 529 (2005).

11. Id. at 532–36 & n.21.

12. Id.

13. See Business Electronics Corp. v. Sharp Electronics Corp., 485 U.S. 717, 108 S.Ct. 1515, 99 L.Ed.2d 808 (1988); Klor's,

Inc. v. Broadway–Hale Stores, Inc., 359 U.S. 207, 79 S.Ct. 705, 3 L.Ed.2d 741 (1959).

14. Toys "R" Us v. FTC, 221 F.3d 928 (7th Cir. 2000).

15. See Toys "R" Us v. FTC, 221 F.3d 928 (7th Cir. 2000).

elasticity of supply; and (3) the elasticity of fringe demand.[16] This approach is sufficiently flexible to address most of the buying power abuses that are likely to occur. For example, in their treatment of the elasticity of supply, the authors seem willing to embrace a range of factors that could influence that elasticity, including information issues, sunk costs, and the perishability of supply.[17] As in any antitrust matter, the details of the industry setting are critical to the analysis. There must also be sensitivity to the role of multibrand retailers who, with relatively low market shares, can wield substantial power over even large producers.

2.7e. Monopsony and Countervailing Power

Buying power is often seen as a potentially beneficial means of countering concentration in the seller's market. Countervailing power on the buyer's side could pressure oligopolistic or monopolistic sellers to reduce the price charged to the power buyers.

On the subject of countervailing power, Scherer & Ross conclude that while a bilateral monopoly (monopsonist buyer dealing with monopolist seller) may produce results better than either of these power firms dealing with competitive markets, the conditions required for this to occur are unlikely in real markets. A bilateral oligopoly, however, probably occurs quite often. Here the results are more difficult to predict, but the authors offer the following tentative conclusion:

> By bringing their bargaining power to bear, strong buyers are in at least some cases able to restrain the price-raising proclivities of oligopolistic sellers. If the buyers in turn face significant competition as resellers, consumers benefit.[18]

Whether this produces a net competitive benefit is a more complex question because the power buyers will obtain a discriminatory lower price that less powerful buyers will not receive. Price discrimination that harms the remaining less powerful buyers will make it more difficult for them to compete and survive in the market. The trend toward concentration in the buyer industry will be accelerated. This can produce indeterminate effects on innovation, perhaps harming society through lost dynamic efficiency far more than it benefits society through increased allocative efficiency. Thus, for example, a concentrated buyer industry that settles into passive oligopolistic pricing behavior may lose the competitive edge needed to produce and market technological breakthroughs.

---

16. R. BLAIR & J. HARRISON, MONOPSONY, ANTITRUST LAW AND ECONOMICS, 52–53 (1993).

17. Id. at 71–72 (discussing buying power exercised by a cartel of macaroni producers that purchased durum wheat or by sports leagues that purchase the services of professional athletes).

18. Scherer & Ross, at 536.

Chapter III

MONOPOLY, MONOPSONY AND ATTEMPTS OR CONSPIRACIES TO MONOPOLIZE

Table of Sections

§ 3.1 Introduction

A true monopoly possesses classic market power that vitiates the discipline of competition, providing a model against which other forms of market power can be measured. The Greek roots of the word "monopoly" provide a straightforward definition: a sole seller. A buyer that wants the monopolist's offering has no alternate source. The monopolist, in consequence, may demand a very high price. Not surprisingly, monopoly has been the target of public ire and was the occasional subject of legal action well before passage of the Sherman Act. Since 1890, Section 2 of the Sherman Act has been the primary antitrust tool for challenging monopolization.

The courts have construed Section 2 to cover both abuses of buyer and seller power. The word "monopsony," or a sole buyer, was not used until the 1930s, but is commonly used today to describe a powerful buyer.[1]

3.1a. Summary of the Law

Section 2 of the Sherman Act makes it a criminal offense: (1) to monopolize; (2) to attempt to monopolize; or (3) to combine or conspire to monopolize. Each of these offenses may also be attacked under Section 5 of the Federal Trade Commission Act or, if the conspiracy requirement is met, under Section 1 of the Sherman Act. The broad wording of Section 5 may also reach monopolization-related conduct that is beyond the reach of either section of the Sherman Act. Section 2 does not make it unlawful to be a monopolist. The statutory term, "to monopolize," proscribes the *conduct,* the acts of monopolization, of attempting to monopolize, and of conspiring to monopolize. To address monopolization first, the Supreme Court has ruled that a firm has unlawfully monopolized if it has deliberately followed a course of market conduct through which it has obtained or maintained power to control price or exclude competition.[2] The offense has two elements. The first is a matter of capacity—the possession of power to control prices or exclude competition. But even when a defendant possesses this power, there must be an additional showing of conduct or intent. Although it is well settled that both of these elements must be present, the case law offers varying

§ 3.1

1. See § 3.8.

2. Standard Oil Co. v. United States, 221 U.S. 1, 31 S.Ct. 502, 55 L.Ed. 619 (1911); United States v. E. I. du Pont de Nemours & Co., 351 U.S. 377, 76 S.Ct. 994, 100 L.Ed. 1264 (1956); United States v. Grinnell Corp., 384 U.S. 563, 86 S.Ct. 1698, 16 L.Ed.2d 778 (1966).

interpretations both about how much power is needed and how it can be shown, and about the types of conduct or intent that must be shown.

An attempt to monopolize is an offense separate and distinct from monopolization or conspiracy to monopolize. There are three elements that must be proven: a specific intent to monopolize, predatory or anticompetitive conduct, and a dangerous probability of success.[3] Conspiracy to monopolize is also a distinct Section 2 offense. It requires proof of concerted action, deliberately entered into with the specific intent to accomplish monopoly and the commission of at least one overt act in furtherance of the conspiracy. Both attempt to monopolize and conspiracy to monopolize are frequently alleged along with a monopolization claim under Section 2 and a restraint of trade claim under Section 1, a circumstance that may have clouded the clarity of judicial rules governing some of these offenses.

Although the attempt or conspiracy to monopolize offenses may be assuming a more significant role, the core of Section 2 remains the monopolization offense. Much of the law governing attempt to monopolize, for example, is derived directly or indirectly from the interpretations that the courts have given to the monopolization offense. The FTC's monopolization enforcement under Section 5 of the FTC Act also remains heavily influenced by Section 2 interpretations.

3.1b. Critical Policy Issues in Monopolization Litigation

3.1b1. *Limiting Power Without Stifling Competition*

The tension between tolerating or even facilitating the development of market power, on the one hand, and constraining its creation or condemning its exercise, on the other hand, is reflected in the shifting enforcement policy toward Section 2. In the 1960s, a high point in antitrust activism, Congress considered legislation to move more aggressively to break up monopoly power. Today, the pendulum has swung markedly in the direction of tolerating a monopolist's conduct. Emblematic of this shift is the language of Justice Scalia, writing for the Court in Verizon Communications v. Trinko. The Court said that "the mere possession of monopoly power, and the concomitant charging of monopoly prices, is not only not unlawful; it is an important element of the free market system" because "the opportunity to charge monopoly prices—at least for a short period—is what attracts 'business acumen' " and is productive of "innovation and economic growth."[4]

The case for more relaxed treatment of a monopolist's conduct can be briefly summarized. The possibility of monopoly returns can be an incentive for innovation, a circumstance constitutionally recognized as a basis for intellectual property laws. Once the monopoly has been achieved, too much constraint on the monopolist's conduct can under-

---

3. Spectrum Sports, Inc. v. McQuillan, 506 U.S. 447, 456, 113 S.Ct. 884, 122 L.Ed.2d 247 (1993).

4. Verizon Communications Inc. v. Trinko, 540 U.S. 398, 407, 124 S.Ct. 872, 157 L.Ed.2d 823 (2004).

mine the monopolist's flexibility in responding to potential or residual competition, perhaps undermining consumer welfare. False positives, unwarranted proscriptions on a monopolist's conduct, can undermine both innovation and competition in the delivery of existing goods and services. Although fairness values are usually not openly invoked by proponents of these views, there may be a sense that it is unfair to saddle power-wielding players with conduct restraints that are not imposed on their smaller rivals.

In isolation, one can accept each of these points as valid concerns. The Court's language in *Trinko*, however, ignores the larger picture. The risk of false positives can indeed deter a monopolist from efficient behavior that could benefit society. But the tolerance of false negatives (anticompetitive conduct that is deemed beyond the reach of antitrust) can serve to embolden a monopolist to initiate abusive conduct that entrenches or extends monopoly.[5] As detailed in Chapter 2, society objects to monopoly power because, as explained in theory and in borne out in practice, monopoly injures consumer welfare in the form of higher prices, reduced quality, or more limited consumer choice. Monopolists can be efficient, but over time they tend to squander these gains in x-inefficiencies and rent-seeking behavior (non-productive outlays intended to shield their monopoly power from a rival's inroads). While superior skill and foresight should be rewarded and may produce a "deserved" monopoly power, once that power has been attained, the incentive and opportunity is there to engage in strategic behavior that stifles innovation by rivals. This was the basis of the Justice Department's 1998 case against Microsoft.

To the extent that *Trinko* suggested that monopoly power (apart from that conferred by the intellectual property laws) is necessary for economic growth, it is overreaching. The first mover advantage from marketing a new product or service may allow the charging of high prices, and this advantage does promote innovation. But this advantage should not be equated with monopoly power. Monopoly power is something less transitory and arguably less closely linked to innovation. Indeed, monopoly power can be and often is strategically employed to stifle the development or marketing of innovative products and services. As Trinko suggests, there is a risk that condemnation of a monopoly power achieved through skill and foresight could constrain the very competition that antitrust is designed to protect. This recognition, however, should not be the basis for overturning the collective wisdom of a century of Section 2 jurisprudence and economic learning.

The dichotomy between tolerating and constraining power gives rise to a uniquely American, market-affirming response to power: to end dominance when attained or maintained in unapproved ways, yet to give dominance wide latitude when it is inevitable or earned by merit. The

---

5. For criticism of *Trinko* and its rhetorical concern with false positives, see Gavil, *Dominant Firm Distribution: Striking A* *Better Balance,* 72 ANTITRUST L. J. 3, 30–51 (2004).

response assumes that strong incentives promote efficiency, and that power, unless bolstered either by abusive conduct or by government support, will erode under the pressure of market developments. Moreover, where supracompetitive pricing accompanies power, erosion of the power is thought to be more likely because high prices signal the need and promise a reward for entry.

Because the earliest successful monopolization cases involved industry-dominating trusts, put together by merger, that engaged in manifestly abusive conduct, the tension between the power and conduct strains of monopoly law was not immediately evident. But it became apparent quite early and has persisted. On the one hand, the law abhors the use of monopoly power to engage in exclusionary tactics, such as foreclosing the public from access to alternative goods or services, avoiding the rigor of competition by encumbering smaller, less powerful rivals, or engaging in inefficient activities that prolong or increase monopoly returns. Because such "exclusionary," "restrictive," or "exploitative" conduct elevates power over merit, the law condemns dominance so obtained, exploited or protected. On the other hand, a firm's ability to accrue power by innovation and development, to expand sufficiently to attain scale economies, and to operate a benignly acquired monopoly in an efficient, effective manner should be shielded from attack.

Balancing these interests requires a series of inevitable compromises. Courts, and sometimes juries, must distinguish a monopolist's fair exploitation of superior financial, productive or marketing capabilities from abusive tactics that inhibit or foreclose competition. The dilemmas can be formidable. Even those that seem not to confound judgment may defy articulation, at least with the precision in which a workable rule of law will ideally be clothed. The usual formulation, that "exclusionary" conduct by a monopolist is forbidden, is inevitably overbroad. Certainly some conduct that no rational rule would forbid may block opportunity for competitors. Of course, instructive precedents exist that can guide the inquiry and permit courts and juries to evaluate some situations with reasonable confidence. A judicially manageable situation might arise if, for example, a dominant firm deliberately engaged in one of the following: (1) acquiring blatantly excessive resources or technology to discourage entrants; (2) stifling development of a market for recycling the monopolized product to reduce price competition; or, (3) paying a critical supplier to cut off rivals. Such strategies could make economic sense for the dominant firm only because they are likely to discourage or burden rivals. Although such "monopoly rent-seeking" activities are legally vulnerable, lines are seldom crystal clear, and most litigated cases are fact intensive.[6]

One area of continuing controversy is evaluating whether conduct of a monopolist challenged as exclusionary is efficient. If so, it may be

---

6. 3 P. Areeda & H. Hovenkamp, Antitrust Law: An Analysis of Antitrust Principles And Their Application ¶¶ 605–658 (rev. ed. 1996). This source includes comprehensive analysis of the case law.

lawful for that reason. As an example, an upstream monopolist may restrict downstream sales by refusing to deal with or raising its price to downstream competitors in a manner that raises the costs of such rivals. Although eliminating competitors, such behavior may enhance efficiencies through vertical integration, removing, for example, the costs of bargaining with downstream players. Also, it is argued, there is little or no likelihood of extending the monopolist's return, but only of shifting that return back and forth among upstream and downstream products. But the model from which these conclusions are deduced is confined to rather sterile, textbook conditions.[7] A pure monopoly must exist at the upstream level, a perfectly competitive market at the downstream level, and buyers must have perfect information. Even if all these conditions are met, and assuming that the monopolist enhances its efficiency, there is no assurance that any of the social gain will be passed on to consumers and not retained by the monopolist. Moreover, in real market situations the three conditions are not likely to be fully met. For example, perfect information, or even a workable substitute for it, is often lacking when complex products are offered to consumers. Indeed, sellers often exercise their monopoly power to discriminate in prices, charging powerful, better informed buyers lower prices, but charging the smaller and less knowledgeable buyers higher ones. A more detailed discussion of the benefits and risks of vertical integration is offered in Chapter 12.

To lessen the risk of condemning efficiency enhancing conduct, a profit sacrifice test might be employed. Unless the plaintiff can demonstrate that the defendant's conduct resulted in foregoing profits that would have flowed in the absence of the conduct, the conduct would not violate Section 2. The Supreme Court has used language suggesting the significance of a profit sacrifice.[8]

3.1b2. The Definition of Monopoly Power

A central issue in interpreting Section 2 is whether the section should be applied to extensive market power of all types, or applied only to one form of such power: a single firm with (interbrand) marketwide dominance. Under one possible approach, the term "monopoly" would signify a strong form of market power, regardless of origin. For example, a "monopolist" might include not only a firm that had a dominant market share, but also each of the following: (1) a firm exercising oligopoly power in cooperation with other firms; (2) a firm facing rivals in a primary product market, but exercising power over price and output through its dominance of aftermarkets for parts, services or the like; or (3) a firm exercising dominance over price or output through a strong brand or through the exploitation of buyer information imperfections.

---

7. These arguments are set forth in detail and criticized in Sullivan, *Section 2 of the Sherman Act and Vertical Strategies by Dominant Firms*, 21 Sw. U. L. Rev. 1227, 1240–47 (1992).

8. Verizon Communications v. Trinko, 540 U.S. 398, 408–11, 124 S.Ct. 872, 157

L.Ed.2d 823 (2004)(citing and discussing Aspen Skiing Co. v. Aspen Highlands Skiing Corp., 472 U.S. 585, 593–94, 105 S.Ct. 2847, 86 L.Ed.2d 467 (1985)). For criticism of the profit sacrifice test, see § 3.5.

Each of these forms of power can be real and, at least theoretically, can be measured by the Lerner Index (the difference between price and marginal cost), so that a comparable quantitative standard for monopoly could be utilized regardless of the source of the power. Each form could cause the same types of allocative or wealth transfer injuries through higher prices and reduced output. An argument for an inclusive interpretation of Section 2 is that only such an interpretation comprehends all situations in which serious social harms resulting from monopoly power occur. It reaches allocative injury, regardless of the source of the power, but avoids problems of over-or under-inclusion. For example, a firm with some of the external trappings of a monopoly will not be included if its power is disciplined by likely entrants or by significant crossover demand for related products or services. On the other hand, oligopolists or sellers exercising some form of intrabrand market power will be included where they inflict the same economic injury as a market-dominating monopolist.

There may be some indirect support for a broad reading of the "power" requirement of Section 2 in early Supreme Court opinions.[9] There is also support in Eastman Kodak Co. v. Image Technical Services, Inc.[10] In its unsuccessful "shared monopoly" case brought against the cereal industry, the Federal Trade Commission used Section 5 of the FTC Act to attack interdependent, oligopolistic behavior among cereal producers.[11] Still, for the most part, the enforcement agencies and courts appear to have followed a more limited, "market dominance" concept of monopoly. Under this approach, a firm is characterized as a monopoly only when it dominates pricing and output decisions within a well-defined market or industry. Thus, Section 2 would not cover most manifestations of intrabrand market power (such as exploitation of brand differentiation power), nor would it cover such forms of market dominance as nonconspiratorial coordination among oligopolists. The leading case taking such a market dominance approach is United States v. Aluminum Co. of America,[12] in which Judge Learned Hand required a showing of both monopoly power (as measured by market share) and anticompetitive conduct designed to create, preserve or extend that power.

The design and wording of the Sherman Act provides support for this more limited reading of Section 2. The word "monopoly" had a common usage dating back at least as far as *The Schoolmasters' Case* decided by an English court in 1410.[13] Under that usage, a monopolist is a firm that holds an exclusive or at least dominant position in the market as measured by structural indicia. By addressing "restraint of trade" in Section 1 of the Sherman Act, Congress may have been

---

9. These early opinions paid relatively little attention to power, focusing on the conduct of alleged monopolists. See § 3.2.

10. 504 U.S. 451, 112 S.Ct. 2072, 119 L.Ed.2d 265 (1992) (leaving open the possibility that the exercise of a seller's power in an aftermarket could violate Section 2).

11. In re Kellogg Co., 99 F.T.C. 8 (1982).

12. 148 F.2d 416 (2d Cir.1945).

13. 11 Hen. IV. f. 47, pl. 21 (1410).

signaling that Section 2, dealing with monopolization, was targeted at a narrower category of market power abuses. If Section 2 is read broadly, it could envelop much conduct also addressed in Section 1 of the Sherman Act. On the other hand, a narrow reading can leave major areas of anticompetitive conduct untouched by the Sherman Act, particularly if the "conspiracy" requirement of Section 1 is also read strictly.[14] For example, the coordinated behavior of a tight oligopoly may create the same economic injury as a monopoly, yet be beyond the reach of either section of the Sherman Act. Although the FTC might attack such an oligopoly under the broader wording of Section 5 of its enabling act, that agency has so far failed to do so successfully in cases involving oligopolistic behavior.[15] The logic for a narrower reading of monopolization may also erode when addressing the attempt to monopolize or conspiracy to monopolize language of Section 2. The wording of these offenses suggests that at least some exercises of market power by those that have not yet achieved a dominant market share may be unlawful. See the discussion in § 3.4. Thus, questions about the breadth of application of Section 2 are by no means wholly settled.

3.1b3. *Monopolization Suits as a Tool for Restructuring Industry*

Beginning with a 1904 case brought during Theodore Roosevelt's Presidency,[16] major monopolization litigation seeking to restructure an industry has become a major political event. As one would expect of a court challenge that threatens the very existence of one of the nation's largest corporations, defendants have not confined themselves simply to defending the litigation. In an effort to thwart monopolization litigation, they have, for example, resorted to collateral litigation and to major lobbying and political initiatives directed to the Executive and Legislative branches. During the 1970s, four major monopolization cases were underway simultaneously: the Department of Justice's proceedings against AT & T[17] and IBM,[18] and the FTC's proceedings against the oil[19] and cereal industries.[20] Although the Justice Department's success in the AT & T litigation is historic, no relief was achieved in any of the other three cases.

---

14. The conspiracy requirement is addressed in § 5.2.

15. For example, the FTC staff was unsuccessful before the Commission in the shared monopoly case against the cereal industry, In re Kellogg Co., 99 F.T.C. 8 (1982), and the Commission was unsuccessful before the reviewing court on its complaint alleging oligopolistic pricing behavior against producers of antiknock gasoline additives, E.I. du Pont de Nemours & Co. v. FTC, 729 F.2d 128 (2d Cir.1984).

16. Northern Sec. Co. v. United States, 193 U.S. 197, 24 S.Ct. 436, 48 L.Ed. 679 (1904).

17. United States v. AT & T Co., 524 F.Supp. 1336 (D.D.C.1981).

18. U.S. Dept. of Justice, Antitrust Division, Memorandum for the Attorney General, Re United States v. IBM Corp., reprinted in E. Fox & L. Sullivan, Cases and Materials on Antitrust 237–41 (1989).

19. In re Ethyl Corp., 101 F.T.C. 425 (1983), vacated sub nom. E. I. du Pont De Nemours & Co. v. FTC, 729 F.2d 128 (2d Cir.1984).

20. In re Kellogg Co., 99 F.T.C. 8 (1982).

AT & T, like the defendants in the other cases, was active in nonjudicial forums. It instituted: (1) a major campaign to obtain legislation from Congress that would have largely mooted the case; and (2) an intra-Executive branch war that pitted the Departments of Defense and Commerce against the Department of Justice. At one point, this effort forced Antitrust Division head William Baxter to request (unsuccessfully) the court to stay the monopoly case while the Executive branch pursued a legislative solution. AT & T's efforts to thwart the litigation failed, in part because AT & T's competitors were also actively lobbying, because presiding Judge Harold Greene refused to agree to a stay in the litigation, and because the determined leadership of Assistant Attorney General Baxter ultimately carried the day within the Executive branch.[21]

The collateral warfare pursued in the other three monopolization cases contributed to delay and, in all probability, the ultimate success of the defendants. The IBM case was litigated for 13 years, lasting through significant changes in the industry, long enough to find an Administration (the fifth President to serve during the pendency of the litigation) that was less sympathetic to the case and willing to drop it in 1982. Both of the FTC's monopoly cases were also dropped or dismissed during the 1980s after spanning at least three Presidents. The length of these proceedings prevents a single Administration from evolving and executing a cohesive program for monopolization enforcement. The problems are compounded, moreover, when focus moves from relatively stable, "smokestack" industries to dynamic high tech industries. Conditions change so rapidly in some dynamic industries that relief attained after several years of litigation may be irrelevant. That obstacle, along with the very substantial costs and decidedly mixed results, calls into question the effectiveness of monopolization litigation as a tool for restructuring American industry.

The Government's most recent major Section 2 case was its 1998 complaint against Microsoft. The Justice Department achieved a substantial success on the merits but no meaningful structural relief.[22]

Despite these difficulties, monopolization litigation against major firms has played a significant restructuring role at critical developmental stages during the last century. Section 2 challenges led to the breakup of the oil and tobacco trusts in 1911,[23] to du Pont's divestiture of its substantial holdings of General Motors in 1957,[24] and to the major divestiture by AT & T in 1982.[25] Assuming such basic structural change

---

21. The comprehensive story of the AT & T litigation and the collateral wars that it sparked is told in P. TEMIN, THE FALL OF THE BELL SYSTEM: A STUDY IN PRICES AND POLITICS 160–276 (1987).

22. See the discussion of the Microsoft litigation in §§ 3.4b2, 3.4b5.

23. Standard Oil Co. v. United States, 221 U.S. 1, 31 S.Ct. 502, 55 L.Ed. 619 (1911); United States v. American Tobacco

Co., 221 U.S. 106, 31 S.Ct. 632, 55 L.Ed. 663 (1911).

24. This action was brought under Section 7 of the Clayton Act, but required du Pont to divest a 23 percent stock interest that it had held in General Motors since 1919. United States v. E. I. du Pont de Nemours & Co., 353 U.S. 586, 77 S.Ct. 872, 1 L.Ed.2d 1057 (1957).

25. United States v. AT & T Co., 552 F.Supp. 131 (D.D.C.1982), aff'd sub nom.

in an industry is occasionally necessary, there is no risk-free mechanism for accomplishing it. A political component is inevitable in any attempt to restructure elephantine business institutions. The lesson of the 1970s and 1980s may be *not* that monopolization litigation seeking structural relief should never be attempted, but rather that it should be used sparingly with carefully chosen targets. The economic, legal and factual underpinnings of the case should be strong: it should be based on consensus concepts likely to survive a change of administration; and there should be sufficient political will within the Administration to withstand inevitable aggressive lobbying. Even so, there will be a measured chance of success in major cases, given the defendant's opportunity to delay resolution and to seek extrajudicial relief in legislative or executive decisions. The all-important choice of the judge assigned to such a case may also remain a matter of chance. Yet, when measured against other avenues of obtaining such relief—for example, by legislation—the relative independence and professionalism of a federal enforcement agency and the federal judiciary may still render the monopolization case the preferred approach.

Not all monopolies are possessed by Fortune 500 corporations. Government or private suits against local or regional monopolies, or monopoly in small, national niches may meet with fewer political obstacles and more success when restructuring is sought. Assuming that major restructuring is not practical or desirable, monopolization cases may attain other meaningful relief. The agencies have imposed conduct remedies such as prohibiting acts that restrict entry or reduce buyer options (for example, restricting lease only policies or prohibiting the use of ties or other foreclosure restraints) or requires licensing of competing firms.[26] The problems in designing and the mixed results from using such remedies are discussed in the next section.

3.1b4. *Remedial Issues*

In addition to the controversy surrounding divestiture (§ 3.1b3), there is debate about the conduct sanctions that are used to limit the freedom of action of dominant firms. One view is that remedies in successful monopolization suits cause large, successful firms to pull their punches rather than to compete aggressively on the merits, with the result that inefficient rivals are protected.[27] Some behavioral sanctions may also require substantial and continuing judicial scrutiny and therefore be both difficult to enforce and disruptive of self-regulatory efficiencies associated with market incentives and interactions. On the other hand, the dynamic component of competition, including entry by effi-

---

Maryland v. United States, 460 U.S. 1001, 103 S.Ct. 1240, 75 L.Ed.2d 472 (1983).

26. E.g. United States v. United Shoe Mach. Corp., 110 F.Supp. 295 (D.Mass. 1953) (prohibiting certain leasing and tying practices), aff'd per curiam, 347 U.S. 521, 74 S.Ct. 699, 98 L.Ed. 910 (1954); In re Xerox Corp., 86 F.T.C. 364 (1975) (prohibit-

ing certain leasing practices and requiring licensing of technology).

27. Baxter, *How Government Cases Get Selected—Comments from Academe*, 46 ANTITRUST L.J. 586 (1977); *Report from Official Washington: Interview with William F. Baxter, Assistant Attorney General, Antitrust Division*, 52 ANTITRUST L.J. 23, 27 (1983).

cient and innovative firms, can be severely obstructed by a monopolist. There seems little doubt that monopolists can and do pursue strategies that make a rival's entry or market penetration difficult. The record in the *AT & T* litigation, for example, is replete with examples of efforts to prevent or discourage rivals of AT & T that sought to provide long-distance service or telephone equipment.[28] If divestiture is not feasible, constraint on predatory strategies is warranted even at the risk of some over-constraint.

In American law the tendency is to resolve these tensions by enjoining blatant predation but granting monopolists a wide discretion to push the edges where the line between exploitative and aggressive competition grows vague. The reluctance of courts to impose behavioral limits on dominant firms is evident in many such areas, including claims of predation in research and innovation strategies. For example, in Berkey Photo, Inc. v. Eastman Kodak Co.,[29] the court declined to require Kodak to predisclose new camera models and new film types to competing firms in the film manufacturing and processing businesses. On the other hand, the European Union has imposed mild predisclosure remedies in its antitrust proceeding against IBM.[30] Although *Berkey's* influence has been substantial, the Supreme Court has yet to rule definitively on the issue of predisclosure relief. Other sorts of behavioral limits are imposed, many of them not difficult to enforce. A court order to end tying practices or lease only practices, for example, may be relatively easy to enforce.[31]

Neither predisclosure nor any other conduct remedy ought to be rejected categorically. Inquiry into particulars is often warranted. On the negative side, predisclosure could lessen the monopolist's return for innovative products and services and thereby discourage innovation. It could also create enforcement problems. But enhancing the return to innovation at the expense of competitive values otherwise attainable once an innovation is on-line is always a complex and often a difficult tradeoff. In contexts in which Congress has not established categorical intellectual property rules, any unqualified answer to whether innovators can be compelled to disclose will risk giving too much weight to the social value of encouraging innovation and too little weight to the social value of making technological information accessible, or vice versa. Moreover, an information disclosure may be less intrusive and easier to enforce than other possible behavioral provisions (such as one that seeks to limit the monopoly profit on a product). Although a predisclosure requirement will decrease the monopolist's freedom of action, such a remedy is imposed, if at all, only after a showing of monopoly power and

---

28. United States v. AT&T Co., 524 F.Supp. 1336, 1349–50 (D.D.C.1981).

29. 603 F.2d 263 (2d Cir.1979), cert. denied, 444 U.S. 1093, 100 S.Ct. 1061, 62 L.Ed.2d 783 (1980).

30. IBM Corp. v. Commission of the European Communities, [1981] E.C.R. 2639,

[1979–1981 Transfer Binder] Common Mkt. Rep. (CCH) ¶ 8708 (1981).

31. See, e.g., United States v. United Shoe Mach. Corp., 110 F.Supp. 295 (D.Mass.1953).

an evaluation of the social costs and benefits of the monopolist's effort to expand its power through secrecy.

3.1b5. *International Reach of Monopolization Enforcement*

A firm that possesses monopoly power in the United States may possess it in other nations as well. The international reach of many forms of commerce increases the likelihood of this circumstance. An example of this reality is the enforcement initiatives brought against the Microsoft Corporation. Its dominance in the operating software market has sparked competition law proceedings not only in the United States, but in other jurisdictions including the European Union, Japan, and Israel. Other jurisdictions may be unlikely to impose structural remedies on a U.S. based firm, but the European Union has imposed conduct remedies on U.S. firms in the IBM and, subject to review, in the Microsoft case.[32]

§ 3.2 Historical Overview of the Law Governing Monopolization

Monopolies were attacked under English common law well before enactment of the Sherman Act in 1890. *The Schoolmasters'* Case is an early example of the common law's antipathy to the power exercised by a monopolist, although at this point, in 1410, the court did not find the act of monopolization itself unlawful. A local grammar school that had long enjoyed monopoly status filed a writ of trespass against a new entrant that offered schooling to children for a smaller fee. The court, after noting that the public interest was served by the new entry, held that a monopolist could not use the writ to recover damages from a new entrant that deprived the monopolist of revenues.[1] A more proactive stance against a monopoly is reflected in the Case of Monopolies, a 1603 ruling that the Queen's grant of a monopoly on the manufacture and importation of playing cards was invalid. The court's reasoning, although colored by the rivalry between monarch and Parliament, reflected a grasp of the injury from monopoly not only to competing firms, but also to the public interest. The court suggested this public injury would occur because of "inseparable incidents to every monopoly against the commonwealth," namely that: (1) the price of the commodity would be raised by the monopolist; and (2) the quality of the product would decrease as the monopolist pursued only its own private benefit.[2] Both arguments anticipate modern economic theory, including the x-inefficiency linked to monopoly power (cost increases associated with a lack of competitive discipline).[3]

Despite early expressions of concern, monopolies were widely tolerated in England and the United States in 1890. A monopoly such as a

---

32. See the discussion of EU Article 82 enforcement in §§ 18.7a, 18.7e.

§ 3.2

1. 11 Hen. IV, f.47, pl. 21 (1410).

2. Case of Monopolies, 11 Coke 84, Eng. Rep. 1260 (K.B. 1603).

3. See § 2.3.

public utility may be embraced as the most efficient way to deliver products or services to the public. But in 1890 the Sherman Act responded to the darker side of monopolies. The rhetoric surrounding the enactment of the Sherman Act is full of references to monopolies as powerful, unscrupulous businesses that held the fate of consumers, small businesses and farmers in their hands.[4] Although the Act's supporters lacked sophisticated understanding of the economic theory of monopoly, they doubtlessly understood that monopoly represented the antithesis of competition, and that competition benefitted consumers and other protected groups. This sentiment led Congress to include Section 2 in the Act.

The Supreme Court's early cases showed understandable uncertainty about which monopolies were prohibited by Section 2. Northern Securities Co. v. United States[5] was prosecuted by Theodore Roosevelt's administration with the President's open support.[6] As with many monopoly cases then and now, the complaint alleged both a violation of Section 1 and Section 2 of the Sherman Act. The Court found that a holding company formed to control competing major railroads—and pilloried in the populist press because it consolidated interests of Morgan, Hill and Harriman, leading figures in a new capitalistic autocracy—violated the Sherman Act. Although the majority opinion offered no clearly stated rule for assessing the lawfulness of monopolies, it implied, at least, that all consolidations leading to substantial market power were unlawful. Thus, the opinion stated that "every combination or conspiracy which would extinguish competition between otherwise competing railroads," thereby restraining interstate trade, was rendered illegal.[7] Justice Holmes, in a famous dissent ("Great cases * * * make bad law."), took a diametrically different view—that consensual consolidation did not "suppress competition" even though it ended competition.[8]

Two more major monopoly cases were successfully prosecuted by the Taft Administration, which was uncompromisingly critical of all powerful trusts.[9] Standard Oil Co. v. United States[10] resulted in the breakup of the powerful Standard Oil trust formed by John D. Rockefeller. Rockefeller began his empire with a single oil refinery in Cleveland.[11] As the refinery grew in output, it was able to command a substantial secret rebate from the railroads that shipped the refined product to the East.

---

4. A sampling of this rhetoric can be found in a source such as 1 E. Kintner, The Legislative History of the Federal Antitrust Laws and Related Statutes (1978).

5. 193 U.S. 197, 24 S.Ct. 436, 48 L.Ed. 679 (1904).

6. In his campaign oratory, Roosevelt purported to distinguish between good and bad trusts. *Northern Securities* and other early cases are discussed in W. Letwin, Law and Economic Policy in America: The Evolution of the Sherman Antitrust Act (1965) (see especially Chapter 7). See also Fox & Sullivan, *The Good and Bad Trust Dichoto-*

my: A Short History of a Legal Idea, 35 Antitrust Bull. 57 (1990).

7. *Northern Securities,* 193 U.S. at 331 (emphasis omitted).

8. Id. at 400, 410–411.

9. Letwin, supra note 6.

10. 221 U.S. 1, 31 S.Ct. 502, 55 L.Ed. 619 (1911).

11. The story of Rockefeller's consolidation of power is told in M. Josephson, The Robber Barons 112–19, 161–63 (1962).

Ultimately, Rockefeller formed a pool in which favored members were given not only secret low rates from the railroads; they were also given a "drawback," a percentage of the higher rates paid by nonmember refiners. This enormous transportation advantage was a lever forcing noncooperating refiners to sell out at bargain prices.

Perhaps responding to the broad and controversial approach that the majority took in *Northern Securities,* Chief Justice White for the majority in *Standard Oil* announced a tempering rule of reason that emphasized the conduct of the defendants. Chief Justice White also wrote the opinion in United States v. American Tobacco Co.,[12] again focusing on conduct. The interest in conduct, and the relative inattention to power, is understandable. In both these cases, the Government presented overwhelming evidence of the economic domination of the defendants, and the defendants apparently made no substantial effort to argue that they lacked economic power.

These decisions do not suggest that market dominance is irrelevant to a finding of unlawful monopolization. Chief Justice White noted that Standard Oil had obtained "mastery over the oil industry" through which it was "able to fix the price of crude and refined petroleum."[13] The Court's concern with this structural power was addressed in a pragmatic manner, with few of the trappings of the more rigorous approach to structural analysis that was to develop later. It was enough for Chief Justice White to know that Standard Oil had control over 90 percent of the refining business. He inferred from this—and from the cost advantage over rivals obtained through railroad rate discounts and drawbacks—an absolute power to control the price of refined petroleum. On the basis of a very limited discussion and analysis he concluded that this mastery over refined petroleum gave a "substantial power over the crude product" which had to be sold to the refiners, despite the fact that the defendants had very little direct control over crude production.[14]

Neither of Chief Justice White's opinions tightly define or narrowly limit the values that underlie the law's concern with market power. In *Standard Oil,* he repeatedly referred to the interest of consumers ("the general public") whose pocketbooks were adversely affected by conduct violative of the act.[15] He noted that a monopolist can fix prices, limit production and allow quality to deteriorate. But there is also reference to the "right of individuals" to engage freely in trade,[16] and to the purpose of the act to restrict limitations imposed upon that right which arise out of combination or monopoly.[17] Indeed, he suggested that respect for an individual's right to contract is the reason Congress did not forbid "monopoly in the concrete."[18] In *American Tobacco*, a record of predatory and malicious behavior arrested the Court's attention. That opinion stresses the purpose of the act to protect against market conduct

---

12. 221 U.S. 106, 31 S.Ct. 632, 55 L.Ed. 663 (1911).

13. *Standard Oil*, 221 U.S. at 33.

14. Id. at 77.

15. Id. at 50, 58.

16. Id. at 58.

17. Id.

18. Id. at 55.

"designed to injure others" by "driving competitors out of business," and erecting "barriers to the entry."[19] Both opinions embrace consumer welfare as a goal, but insist, also, upon the interest of other traders that entry not be blockaded.

The failure in either *Standard Oil* or *American Tobacco* to articulate a clear rule with respect to market dominance and how it was to be evaluated may have contributed to the result in United States v. United States Steel Corp.,[20] decided a decade later. Once again the Court marked out conduct and purpose for particular attention. While it expressly held that power to control price, and either its use, or its continued existence, or both, is a prerequisite to the offense of monopolization, it declined to draw from the defendant's massive holding in basic steel the inference about market power that had been drawn from seemingly comparable evidence in *Standard Oil*. Apparently, the Court concluded that because the oil trust had coerced recalcitrants to join, whereas all steel trust participants willfully entered the consolidation, the two cases could be distinguished. Influenced by the seeming lack of "bad acts" other than deliberate consolidation, the Court affirmed the finding below that power over price was never obtained or, if it was obtained, was never exercised and soon dissipated as the strength of competitors grew. It is true that United States Steel's share of the market fell and the industry was transformed from what initially had the look of monopoly into an oligopoly.[21] The Court read this development well. Yet, it failed to perceive or react to indications of power in the original formation, or to be concerned about (or even to consider the relevance of) the oligopoly which had developed, or the relevance of the fact that even before the consolidation the defendants had attempted to cartelize.

Modern structural analysis of monopoly issues begins with the opinion in United States v. Aluminum Co. of America,[22] rich in concepts pertinent to the evaluation of single firm power. Although not a Supreme Court opinion, Judge Learned Hand's opinion has enjoyed a prominence which few Supreme Court opinions have enjoyed. The United States had appealed an initial judgment for the defendants to the Supreme Court.[23] Recusals prevented the Court from mustering a quorum, so the case was referred to the Second Circuit, which reversed the judgment of the district court. The two step process which Judge Hand used to determine market power, first defining the market and then measuring power, has been followed at least in form in most subsequent cases. Later cases have added refinements, both in determining whether monopoly power was present and in evaluating conduct.

19. United States v. American Tobacco Co., 221 U.S. 106, 181–83, 31 S.Ct. 632, 55 L.Ed. 663 (1911).

20. 251 U.S. 417, 40 S.Ct. 293, 64 L.Ed. 343 (1920).

21. Id. at 437–39 & n.1.

22. 148 F.2d 416 (2d Cir.1945).

23. Under the Expediting Act, then in effect, appeals in Sherman Act cases brought by the United States in the district courts went directly to the Supreme Court. Ch. 544, 32 Stat. 823 (1903) (codified as amended at 15 U.S.C.A. §§ 28, 29).

The two strands of monopoly law require an examination of power and conduct in every monopolization case. Evaluation of power included delimiting the market in geographic as well as product terms.[24] It also required giving consideration to entry barriers and seeking to evaluate with greater refinement the degree of concentration attained in order to make a judgment about power. And it necessitated developing norms or guides that would assist fact finders in specifying the bounds of the product or geographic market.[25]

In articulating a conduct test there was less effort at refinement. During the Sherman Act's formative era, from about 1900 to 1930, and during the long political consensus period favoring tough enforcement, from about 1940 to 1975, the Supreme Court consistently articulated the conduct test in very general terms. The leading decisions yielded a series of epithets against which courts and enforcement agencies would measure a monopolist's challenged conduct. In *Standard Oil*, the Court stressed that the defendant's growth was "not * * * a result of normal methods of industrial development."[26] In United States v. Griffith, the Court spoke of intent to use power to exclude competitors.[27] More than half a century after *Standard Oil,* in United States v. Grinnell Corp., the Court contrasted the "willful acquisition or maintenance of that power" with growth or development as a consequence of "superior product, business acumen, or historical accident."[28] These formulations suggest, as Judge Wyzanski recognized in *United Shoe Machinery,*[29] that the test confronts the decision-maker with a binary choice between sweeping characterizations: has defendant engaged in exclusionary conduct which impairs competitive opportunity, distorts competitive process and makes market outcomes turn on power, or has it, however aggressively, been pressing competition on the merits?[30]

Throughout the formative and consensus periods, courts used this norm regardless of whether the monopolist allegedly cut prices to drive out a competitor,[31] built excess capacity to discourage entry,[32] engaged in limit pricing,[33] merged with competitors,[34] stockpiled scarce technology, talent or resources,[35] or refused to deal with a downstream rival.[36]

---

24. § 3.3a.

25. § 3.3b.

26. 221 U.S. 1, 74–76, 31 S.Ct. 502, 55 L.Ed. 619 (1911).

27. 334 U.S. 100, 107, 68 S.Ct. 941, 92 L.Ed. 1236 (1948).

28. 384 U.S. 563, 570–71, 86 S.Ct. 1698, 16 L.Ed.2d 778 (1966).

29. United States v. United Shoe Mach. Corp., 110 F.Supp. 295 (D.Mass.1953), aff'd per curiam, 347 U.S. 521, 74 S.Ct. 699, 98 L.Ed. 910 (1954).

30. Id. at 341–43.

31. United States v. American Tobacco Co., 221 U.S. 106, 31 S.Ct. 632, 55 L.Ed. 663 (1911).

32. In re E.I. du Pont de Nemours & Co., 96 F.T.C. 653 (1980).

33. See Transamerica Computer Co. v. IBM Corp., 698 F.2d 1377 (9th Cir.), cert. denied, 464 U.S. 955, 104 S.Ct. 370, 78 L.Ed.2d 329 (1983).

34. Standard Oil Co. v. United States, 221 U.S. 1, 31 S.Ct. 502, 55 L.Ed. 619 (1911); United States v. United States Steel Corp., 251 U.S. 417, 40 S.Ct. 293, 64 L.Ed. 343 (1920).

35. United States v. Aluminum Co. of America, 148 F.2d 416 (2d Cir.1945).

36. Otter Tail Power Co. v. United States, 410 U.S. 366, 93 S.Ct. 1022, 35 L.Ed.2d 359 (1973).

Whatever the practice or strategy, courts and enforcement agencies asked the same general question: Did the monopolist deliberately engage in exclusionary tactics that distorted competition on the merits, or did it compete by exercising its own skill, foresight and industry? While not altering very much the way in which issues were phrased, beginning in the late 1970s, courts began to give greater weight to the monopolist's freedom to compete aggressively.[37]

Looking at the flow of Supreme Court opinions involving monopolization issues, a significant development is the near disappearance of cases brought by the Department of Justice and Federal Trade Commission.[38] Of course, the Department has been involved as a party in fewer Supreme Court cases in all areas, not just Section 2 litigation. But federal enforcers have reduced the flow of Section 2 cases substantially. During the 1980s, four major monopolization cases were resolved, only one resulting in relief.[39] No new monopolization litigation was initiated seeking structural relief.[40] Although the *AT & T* case brought the largest divestiture in the history of antitrust, the fact remains that no major restructuring cases have been filed since the 1970s. This trend began due to the ideological leadership of the Department during the 1980s, but has deeper, more persistent, causes that were explored in § 3.1b3. Of course, private Section 2 litigation has continued, including two cases which led to important Supreme Court opinions.[41]

The one hundred year history of the Sherman Act has demonstrated that enforcement ebbs and flows with changing political tides and economic thinking. There is little reason to expect that the pendulum has come to its final resting place for major monopolization cases. Monopolization cases were restored to the Department's agenda in the 1990s. A major Federal Trade Commission investigation of the Microsoft Corporation produced a deadlock among voting members and was passed on to the Department of Justice. The Department pursued the investigation and obtained a consent settlement against Microsoft in 1994, directed at certain predatory conduct of the firm.[42] The Department did not seek structural relief in this case. In a later complaint filed in 1997, the Department obtained a strong ruling and a structural remedy from the district court.[43] A strong court of appeals opinion affirmed critical

---

37. See the discussion in § 3.5.

38. Major Section 2 cases brought by the Department of Justice were the case against IBM (filed in 1969), voluntarily dismissed before trial, and the case against AT & T (filed in 1974) settled by consent decree.

39. See § 3.1b3.

40. The Department of Justice did initiate an attempted monopoly case against American Airlines during the 1980s, but sought no structural relief. United States v. American Airlines, Inc., 743 F.2d 1114 (5th Cir.1984), cert. dismissed, 474 U.S. 1001, 106 S.Ct. 420, 88 L.Ed.2d 370 (1985).

41. Aspen Skiing Co. v. Aspen Highlands Skiing Corp., 472 U.S. 585, 105 S.Ct. 2847, 86 L.Ed.2d 467 (1985); Eastman Kodak Co. v. Image Technical Servs., Inc., 504 U.S. 451, 112 S.Ct. 2072, 119 L.Ed.2d 265 (1992).

42. United States v. Microsoft Corp., Proposed Final Judgment and Competitive Impact Statement, 59 FED. REG. 42,845 (Aug. 19, 1994).

43. United States v. Microsoft Corp., 87 F. Supp. 2d 30 (Dist. D.C. 2000).

portions of the district court's monopoly maintenance holdings, but remanded the district court's decision to impose structural remedies.[44] In November 2001, the Department settled the case on terms that imposed relatively modest conduct restrictions on Microsoft.[45] Private litigation against Microsoft continues, as do proceedings brought against Microsoft outside the United States.

§ 3.3 Market Power in Monopolization

The ultimate question concerning power is whether the defendant possesses power over price and the power to exclude competition. A distinction is often drawn between market power—some degree of power to affect price by increasing or reducing output—and monopoly power— the power to set a price significantly above the competitive level and to sustain such a price for a substantial period of time. Any firm facing a downward sloping demand curve possesses some degree of market power, perhaps sustained through product differentiation and brand identity which depend upon advertising or other expenditures that increase costs and reduce supracompetitive returns. By contrast, monopoly power in the classic form is power possessed through market dominance, idealized in the pure monopolist that possesses 100 percent of the market, fears no competitive entry, and sells a product or service for which there is no substitute. Perhaps the local electric utility may approach this description, but few unregulated firms are likely to do so. As Judge Hand saw it in United States v. Aluminum Co. of America, the market should be defined analytically, not just taken to be the given industry, and the market dominance needed to trigger the statute need not reach 100 percent. In *Alcoa*, "over ninety per cent" of the aluminum ingot market was found to give the firm "complete control within certain limits,"[1] sufficient to find a Section 2 violation.

The ultimate power question concerns whether the defendant possesses power over price and the power to exclude competition. It might be phrased: does the defendant possess sufficient market power to set price substantially above cost and to sustain that price for a substantial period without losing so much trade that it will be obliged to reduce price to a level closely related to cost? The conventional way in which courts have addressed this question uses approaches that are drawn from industrial organization economics. First, courts define the relevant market. Then they evaluate power within that market on the basis of evidence of market share, the closeness of substitutes, whether there are constraints on entry, and other structural indicia. There is implicit contrast between the evidence and the extreme form of such power—a

---

44. United States v. Microsoft Corp., 253 F.3d 34 (D.C. Cir. 2001)(en banc).

45. The settlement was approved with minor modifications by the district court and has survived appellate review. Massa-

chusetts v. Microsoft Corp., 373 F.3d 1199 (D.C. Cir. 2004).

§ 3.3

1. United States v. Aluminum Co. of America, 148 F.2d 416, 425 (2d Cir.1945).

single firm with blatant market dominance—but to constitute monopoly the facts need not approach this extreme very closely.

As a practical matter, the question becomes, does the defendant possess enough power of that kind to be labeled a monopolist and so evoke the law's conduct constraint? There may be ways other than defining the market and evaluating structural features in which a judgment on this question could be made. If it were feasible to measure demand elasticity directly, that would be an ideal way. Extrapolating from this insight, it might be possible to do a performance evaluation by applying econometrics techniques to available price and related data that might signify power, or its lack, more directly than does market definition and share analysis. The Federal Trade Commission successfully challenged a merger between two office supply superstores using this approach.[2] Conventional power analysis would ask, should the market be defined as all sales of office supplies or as sales of office supplies by superstores? The FTC contended that an answer to the power question was available from data that indicated there were only three superstores nationally and, when all three were present in a local market, prices were substantially lower than when less than three of the firms was present. The FTC did not argue that this data directly established power (which it might rationally have done). Instead, it contended that the evidence showed that superstores constituted a relevant market. This shorthand surrogate for a measure of supply elasticity would be feasible in a monopolization case as well. The law values competitive structure and disapproves monopoly structure because the one generates competitive performance, the other monopoly performance. If performance can be reliably characterized directly, these structural characteristics can be inferred from the performance, instead of the reverse.

In the earliest monopolization cases, the Supreme Court was hardly methodical about analytical technique in evaluating whether a firm had power. It supposed that monopoly, if it occurred, involved dominance of an industry, and it assumed that what constituted an industry, whether oil, steel, tobacco or railroads, was a matter of common knowledge, not leaving much room for dispute. But since *Alcoa* courts have consistently used the two step process: define the market; then evaluate power within the market as defined. In § 3.3a we comment on market definition in monopolization cases. The evaluation of monopoly power is addressed in § 3.3b.

3.3a. Market Definition in Monopolization Litigation

The analytical process for defining the relevant product and geographic market is thoroughly discussed in § 2.6b. Essentially, the process is the same for monopolization cases as it is for merger. Neither the differing substantive law requirements for violation, nor the different thresholds at which power becomes problematical, alters the process of

---

2. FTC v. Staples, Inc., 970 F.Supp. 1066 (D.D.C.1997); cf. Woods Exploration & Producing Co. v. Aluminum Co. of America, 438 F.2d 1286 (5th Cir.1971), cert. denied, 404 U.S. 1047, 92 S.Ct. 701, 30 L.Ed.2d 736 (1972).

market definition. Our purpose here is to review examples of definitions accepted by courts in monopolization cases. Such a review highlights uncertainties and problems that are inevitable parts of the process. It also demonstrates not that courts or juries gerrymander definitions to reach predetermined outcomes, but that market definition is an aspect of a holistic process—that of deciding whether, after integrating information about demand, supply, buyer alternatives and producer conduct, judicial sanction is warranted.

In *Alcoa*,[3] which ushered in the now conventional analytical process, Judge Hand faced troubling questions about market definition. One arose out of Alcoa's vertical integration. The firm not only produced ingot, but also fabricated some of its production into sheet which it sold in competition with other fabricators that purchased ingot from Alcoa. Should this "captive" ingot production be excluded when computing Alcoa's share of ingot production? If so, Alcoa's market share would fall from approaching 90 percent to about 60 percent. Judge Hand recognized that Alcoa's integrated use of some of its production reduced the amount of ingot Alcoa brought to market, but also proportionately reduced demand for ingot: Alcoa's noncaptive production share of the smaller non-Alcoa market for ingot was only slightly smaller than its total production share of total ingot market (including Alcoa's internal use). Ingot Alcoa processed itself was, therefore, included. Another question was whether the market should include secondary ingot refabricated from junked aluminum products, which could be used for many, but not all, purposes for which virgin ingot was sought, and that sold at a modest differential in price from virgin. Though recognizing that secondary ingot constrained Alcoa's pricing discretion Judge Hand excluded it because the original ingot that was later reprocessed came from ingot that had been produced by Alcoa, putting Alcoa in a position to control the recycling flow by output decisions at the time of initial ingot production. A third issue was whether to included the total output of foreign ingot producers, thus reducing Alcoa's share significantly. The court included only that part of foreign production that overcame transportation cost, tariff and other barriers and actually entered the U.S. market. By the court's definition Alcoa had a share of 90 percent which the court found showed monopoly power.

The last two of the *Alcoa* conclusions about market definition (or, at any rate, the justification given for them) remain debatable. Would a firm like Alcoa, even if equipped with today's computerized technology and econometric sophistication, be able to integrate recycled product flow expectations back into its pricing and output decision for current ingot production? Was there any evidence that Alcoa or any firm similarly situated in fact attempted such a task? Another possible reason for excluding secondary ingot would be if such ingot was produced by a different technology under different cost constraints than virgin ingot. Secondary ingot might well have faced a very different price elasticity of

3. United States v. Aluminum Co. of
America, 148 F.2d 416 (2d Cir.1945).

supply than virgin. The responsiveness of secondary supply to an increase in the price of virgin should not be assumed without exploration of relevant information and experience. Limiting foreign output only to foreign product already in this country is also debatable. Foreign virgin ingot already reaching the United States presumably experiences aggregate costs for production, transportation and tariffs, etc., that make sale here at current prices profitable. If prices here were to go up, more foreign product could presumably be diverted here unless there were some new, additional, offsetting constraint. But whether additional constraints exist or may arise might be difficult or impossible to determine. Would tariffs increase here? Would export countries constrain further exports? Today, in the era of global markets and the World Trade Organization (WTO), negative answers to both of these questions might seem presumptively correct. But there are other complexities on which market expanding presumptions are probably not warranted. Are foreign supply sources inelastic or fully committed elsewhere? Is shipping capacity limited? Is demand highly price elastic?

These problems, and others as confounding, recur. Another, not mooted in *Alcoa*, although opaquely present there, is exemplified by United States v. E. I. du Pont de Nemours & Co.,[4] decided a decade later. Here the Supreme Court held that du Pont's cellophane production was part of a larger relevant market made up of numerous flexible packaging materials. Du Pont produced about 75 percent of all cellophane sold in the United States, but only 20 percent of all flexible wraps, not enough, the Court concluded, to warrant an inference of power. The Court articulated two approaches to choosing between the wider and the narrower of the markets suggested: (1) comparing similarities and differences in prices and in functional characteristics of cellophane and other wraps to determine whether they were "reasonably interchangeable"; and (2) evaluating cross-elasticity of demand between cellophane and other wraps. The first approach is still used today, at least as a metaphor. The answer in *du Pont* was (and often is) indeterminate, for both similarities and differences were (and usually are) evident. As to the second test, there was clearly some cross-elasticity of demand between cellophane and other flexible wraps, which led the Court to choose the wider market. But as the dissent stressed, the price for cellophane was substantially higher than for most materials included in the wider market, and the manufacturers of other wraps did not respond to cellophane price reductions. Du Pont may well have been pricing at supracompetitive levels before buyers began to switch in substantial numbers when they encountered even a higher cellophane price. Buyers of any monopolist's product begin to turn to less attractive alternatives or forego purchases entirely at some extremely high price. Such a falloff in volume does not result from competitive discipline. It occurs because the monopolist has exceeded the limit price of too many buyers of the

---

4. 351 U.S. 377, 76 S.Ct. 994, 100 L.Ed. 1264 (1956).

monopolized product; it has gone above the profit-maximizing monopoly price.[5]

Perhaps the majority thought that if du Pont were earning monopoly returns at current prices, the plaintiff had the burden of proving it. If so, its holding is in tension with *Alcoa*, which the Court had earlier gone out of its way to embrace. Judge Hand in that case had discussed the significance of profits in rejecting Alcoa's proposal that the market should be widened to include foreign capacity. He assumed with Alcoa that the threat of foreign competition may have placed a ceiling on Alcoa's prices that prevented exploitation. But he concluded that by proving Alcoa stood alone in the domestic ingot market, the Government had "gone far enough."[6] If foreign capacity not now being shipped to the U.S. precluded Alcoa from supracompetitive prices, it was Alcoa's burden to prove that fact. Nor did bookkeeping evidence of market profit alone establish such a constraint because bookkeeping and economic profits can vary and because a monopolist can dissipate profits, pursing the "quiet life" at the cost of x-inefficiencies.

Because product markets often entail a series of ever wider concentric restraints, it is well to emphasize that factual issues about market definition are within the province of the trial judge or jury. Consider prizefighting as an example. Is the "appropriate market" that for promoting professional sports events, prizefights, championship fights, or heavyweight championship contests? Both approaches used in *du Pont*—cross-elasticity and reasonable interchangeability in light of characteristics and prices—might be pressed into service to support any of the plausible alternatives. In International Boxing Club, Inc. v. United States,[7] the Supreme Court refused to make resolving the conundrum an appellate task. The trial court had defined the market as championship fights in light of evidence that they yielded larger revenues and attracted greater demand than did other professional fights, and that media professionals regarded them as attracting a "special demand." Refusing to view *du Pont* as warrant for making its own independent comparison of characteristics and its own determination of reasonable interchangeability, the Supreme Court affirmed.[8] This distinction between the trial court and appellate roles is a sound step. Any designation of "the" appropriate market should be a nuanced summation of impressions derived from alternative market data by academic experts and market professionals, all processed in a context requiring a holistic judgment about market power. Reading briefs and a truncated record may not provide an appellate court with guidance comparable to that available to

5. Many of these criticisms of the *du Pont* holding were offered in Turner, *Antitrust Policy and the Cellophane Case,* 70 HARV. L. REV. 281, 282–83 (1956).

6. *Alcoa,* 148 F.2d at 427.

7. 358 U.S. 242, 79 S.Ct. 245, 3 L.Ed.2d 270 (1959).

8. Id. at 249–51; see also Syufy Enters. v. American Multicinema, Inc., 793 F.2d

990, 994 (9th Cir.1986) (court found sufficient evidence for a rational jury to conclude that first run movies which the industry anticipated would be top grossing films constituted a separate market from other first run films), cert. denied, 479 U.S. 1031 & 1034, 107 S.Ct. 876, 93 L.Ed.2d 830 (1987).

trial judge or jury. They alone can build an integrated conception which places definitional evidence in a wider context, including information about entry constraints, competitive strategies and tactics all of which may contain interactive implications about power. Appellate courts have occasionally overturned lower courts' market definitions, and should continue to do so in appropriate cases, provided that the reviewing court gives proper weight to the nuances of the fact-intensive inquiry that underlies the trial court's determination.

The problem is not limited to proper division of tasks between fact finder and lawgiver. As eminent commentators remind us there is an essential second step when courts, as often as they do, face extremely close relevant market questions. The trial court must be mindful, and should remind the jury, that "market definition is no more than a tool for estimating market power, not a scientific test."[9] The grave risk is that a "market share figure" yielded by a costly, ultimately futile search for "some ideal of relevant market" will be given undue weight or even treated as dispositive.[10] Discipline by both the trial judge and the appellate court are needed. The telling question is not share, but power. For example, if in a close call a fact finder opts for the narrower of two plausible definitions, it can and should give appropriate weight to any evidence of potential competition from substitutes, or about the vulnerability of barriers. The last thing a court should think, or lead a jury to think, is that coming up with a share percentage ends the inquiry.

United States v. Grinnell Corp.[11] also continues to influence market definition outcomes. There, the Court made or accepted several instructive choices. For one, it clustered different alarm services, such as fire and police, into a single market. Although each may face a separate demand curve, scope and scale efficiencies resulted in consistent clustering by suppliers.[12] For another, it accepted a narrow market for "[underwriter] accredited central station service," thereby excluding not only integrated "in-house" protection systems,[13] watchman or guard services and nonautomatic alarm systems, but also noncertified automatic systems (even those limited to municipal agencies), stating that such substitutes appear to have "marked differences," reflected in insurance rates and municipal rules, and noting that "for many customers, only central station protection will do."[14] Also, pragmatically attenuating demand elements, the Court accepted a national geographic market

9. M. HANDLER ET AL., TRADE REGULATION, CASES AND MATERIALS 215 (4th ed. 1997).

10. Id.

11. 384 U.S. 563, 86 S.Ct. 1698, 16 L.Ed.2d 778 (1966).

12. The Court cited United States v. Philadelphia Nat'l Bank, 374 U.S. 321, 83 S.Ct. 1715, 10 L.Ed.2d 915 (1963), where, in a merger case, based upon similar supply side justification, the Court recognized "commercial banking" as a market, although demand for loans and demand for depository services are manifestly distinct.

For an important recent case affirming a cluster market, see Image Technical Servs., Inc. v. Eastman Kodak Co., 125 F.3d 1195 (9th Cir.1997) (affirming a monopolization verdict based on power in an "all [repair] parts" market), cert. denied, 523 U.S. 1094, 118 S.Ct. 1560, 140 L.Ed.2d 792 (1998).

13. Contrast the inclusion in the market in *Alcoa* of ingot made and processed by Alcoa (discussed earlier in this subsection).

14. *Grinnell,* 384 U.S. at 573–74.

notwithstanding that service was local and limited to about a twenty-five mile radius, because major suppliers operated nationally and at least one had a national price list and dealt with multistate businesses through national contracts, and insurance company accreditation was national.

The cases thus reinforce the conviction that the market definition process in Section 2 cases is essentially eclectic and guided both by the policy goal of deciding whether power is present and the pragmatic need to work with available data and confine the analysis to manageable limits. The position of any seller can be diagrammatically represented within a series of concentric circles, each representing groups of other sellers which affect the subject seller less and less directly. In Alcoa's case, other American virgin producers (if any) would be within the innermost circle; domestic secondary producers might be next, followed by Canadian virgin producers, other foreign virgin producers, and producers of copper, or other substitutes.[15]

The court, however, is compelled to simplify. It cannot explore the world economy in order to decide a single monopoly case. When the court draws a line round a relevant market it is making a critical judgment. In effect it is saying, "this data will be weighed and considered in deciding whether defendant is violating the law; that data will not." That judgment is always in part intuitive. Is there a systematic way to inform the intuition? Consider Judge Hand's intuition in *Alcoa*—to drop from consideration all data less proximate than domestic virgin production. Was this more or less valid than an alternative intuition—say, to press the inquiry far enough to include the circles that would comprehend domestic secondary and imported aluminum ingot, but not so far as to pick up other competitive or potentially competitive metals?

There is no Geiger counter that will identify the regions where data will be significant and the regions that may safely be ignored. Nonetheless, there is a methodology that will be an aid to judgment. The "significance" of data is neither a self-defining nor an irreducible concept. In deciding whether to draw a particular set of data into consideration, the court is mediating between two competing interests, the potential utility of the data to refine the court's ultimate substantive judgment about the extent of the firm's power, and the demands of administrative convenience.[16]

For example, before deciding whether to consider data as to recycled ingot production or data as to steel production the *Alcoa* court might survey in a preliminary way the kind and quality of data available and then inquire along two distinct lines. First, how complex and extensive are the problems of judicial administration which are likely to be encountered if an effort is made to absorb and analyze the data in question and to relate it to other data in the case? Secondly, what if anything is likely to be gained in terms of reducing the likelihood of substantive error in evaluating power if that effort is made? To deal with

---

15. United States v. Aluminum Co. of America, 148 F.2d 416 (2d Cir.1945).

16. Cf. FED. R. EVID. 403.

data about some entirely different industry, such as steel, might complicate the inquiry immensely. It might be necessary to absorb information
about a wholly different technology and industrial structure. Unless
there is a convincing, preliminary showing that the substantive advantages would be compellingly high, a balancing test indicates that this
complexity should be avoided. To deal with the market for foreign virgin
aluminum might also be complex. It would be necessary to determine,
not only the extent of historical movements, but the potential for
increases in foreign shipments that might be stimulated by Alcoa's price
increases. This would require information as to total foreign production,
the nature and elasticity of the foreign supply and of alternative demands now absorbing part of foreign production, and whether limits on
shipping facilities might inhibit increased movement. But in a WTO
world, efforts of this kind may become increasingly essential.

In *Alcoa*, however, the provisional showing of the importance of
some of the excluded data had perhaps been made; buyers did purchase
the foreign product on a parity with the domestic one. Thus, it might be
concluded that this data should have been taken into account. To deal
with the domestic secondary aluminum market would perhaps be easier;
a different technology is entailed, but the industry may not be exception-
ally complex. Furthermore, the close relationship between secondary
prices and those for virgin ingot suggests that a full inquiry into the
elasticity of secondary and its relationship to virgin would be fruitful. If
this approach is accepted, the ultimate determination—whether this firm
has monopoly power—will often not turn on the one dimensional measure of the firm's share of a single relevant market. Several submarkets
might be comprehended by the widest market deemed to be both
relevant and material and data as to these narrower markets would also
be relevant. Also, the significance of a particular percentage share of the
market will vary with whether the market definition is relatively broad
or narrow. From all of the relevant structural data (and from the process
of analysis through which the court decided which data were relevant
and material) the court or jury would then decide the ultimate issue:
Does the firm possess such a high degree of market power that it could,
if it wished, substantially foreclose competition by reducing price and
increasing production, thus driving others from the market? This task
need not be unduly complex or unmanageable. In a post-Chicago litigation context, the judge will be required to comprehend and constrain if
need be the data that experts for the contesting parties are assessing. If
any expert proposes to use data of remote relevance, the court must
decide whether allowing reliance on that data adds enough value to
warrant the increased complexity and the expansion of the proceeding
brought about by exploring a complex new area. Once these metes and
bounds of relevance are in place, the fact finder, whether court or jury,
will have to evaluate the conflicting expert opinions about whether all of
the relevant data warrants an inference of market power.

The approach here suggested refines, but is not inconsistent with,
the case law. In *Alcoa*, for example, Judge Hand obviously did do the

underlying analytical task as well as he could on the evidence presented; his ultimate simplification, that Alcoa had 90 percent of one discernible market, and therefore was a monopoly, can be seen as a symbolic statement of the ultimate analytical conclusion: Alcoa had enough power over price to foreclose effective competition.

There are more recent cases harkening back to earlier simplicities, perhaps to the notion suggested (though not adequately developed) in *Standard Oil*[17]: that monopoly power may be identified judicially much as it might be identified by informed participants in the marketplace, on the basis of a confluence of size, history and conduct.[18] For example, in *Eastman Kodak Co. v. Image Technical Servs., Inc.*, the Supreme Court upheld a refusal to grant summary judgment on the plaintiff's Section 1 and 2 claims involving abuse of markets for aftermarket parts and services.[19] The Court found "it reasonable to infer that Kodak has market power to raise prices and drive out competition in the aftermarkets, since respondents offer direct evidence that Kodak did so."[20] The Supreme Court was likewise focused on conduct and effects in its 1985 Section 2 holding in *Aspen Skiing Co. v. Aspen Highlands Skiing Corp.*[21] In appropriate cases, courts may move away from the deductive techniques of the micro economist to reassert the wisdom of empirical observation.[22]

3.3b. Evaluating Power in Monopolization Litigation

We have noted, above, the complexity of market definition and the danger that courts would overvalue the implications of the defendant's share of the market chosen as appropriate. Other structural elements should be considered.[23] Entry barriers and barriers to expansion are particularly important. If the industry is one in which existing firms

---

17. Standard Oil Co. v. United States, 221 U.S. 1, 31 S.Ct. 502, 55 L.Ed. 619 (1911).

18. In Woods Exploration & Producing Co. v. Aluminum Co. of America, 438 F.2d 1286, 1304–07 (5th Cir.1971), cert. denied, 404 U.S. 1047, 92 S.Ct. 701, 30 L.Ed.2d 736 (1972), the court held that if actual power to exclude competition was observable from its exercise, there was no need to analyze market shares. Other similar approaches are seen in Case–Swayne Co. v. Sunkist Growers, Inc., 369 F.2d 449, 454–55 (9th Cir.1966), rev'd on other grounds, 389 U.S. 384, 88 S.Ct. 528, 19 L.Ed.2d 621 (1967); Philadelphia World Hockey Club, Inc. v. Philadelphia Hockey Club, Inc., 351 F.Supp. 462 (E.D.Pa.1972); Twin City Sportservice, Inc. v. Charles O. Finley & Co., 365 F.Supp. 235 (N.D.Cal.1972), rev'd, 512 F.2d 1264 (9th Cir.1975), cert. denied, 459 U.S. 1009, 103 S.Ct. 364, 74 L.Ed.2d 400 (1982); United States v. IBM Corp., 60 F.R.D. 654, 658 (S.D.N.Y.1973).

19. 504 U.S. 451, 112 S.Ct. 2072, 119 L.Ed.2d 265 (1992).

20. Id. at 477.

21. 472 U.S. 585, 105 S.Ct. 2847, 86 L.Ed.2d 467 (1985).

22. See the discussion in Cooper, *Attempts and Monopolization: A Mildly Expansionary Answer to the Prophylactic Riddle of Section Two*, 72 MICH. L. REV. 373, 383–84 (1974). For more recent statements on the value of empiricism in antitrust analysis, see Salup, *The First Principles Approach to Antitrust*, Kodak *and Antitrust at the Millennium*, 68 ANTITRUST L. J. 187 (2000); Grimes, *Antitrust and the Systemic Bias Against Small Business:* Kodak, *Strategic Conduct, and Leverage Theory*, 52 CASE W. RES. L. REV. 231 (2001).

23. See pertinent language in United States v. Columbia Steel Co., 334 U.S. 495, 528, 68 S.Ct. 1107, 92 L.Ed. 1533 (1948); Ball Memorial Hospital, Inc. v. Mutual Hospital Insurance, Inc., 784 F.2d 1325, 1335 (7th Cir.1986).

could rapidly expand production and in which outsiders could rapidly enter if prices were pushed significantly above competitive levels, even a share as large as 90% of a plausibly defined market or submarket may not confer massive power. By contrast, even a firm with substantially less than 50 percent, because of a significant natural advantage (like prime ore sources) or a comparable patent advantage, might be operating at substantially lower costs than other firms and be the only firm capable of expanding output without significantly increasing its per unit cost. If other firms are already making no more than a competitive return, they would not be able to counter a price cut without significant loss. The firm below 50 percent would possess the power to drive all others out of the market at any time it elected to do so. Despite statements in some of the cases about 60 percent being borderline, such a firm, having massive market power—being able to control access to the market—ought to be called a monopolist. A firm does not cease to be a monopolist when it permits others to share its market by sufferance, particularly in instances in which that firm is charged with conduct that is the very antithesis of that sufferance.[24]

Conceding the importance of entry barriers, how does a court or a lawyer determine whether they are present? What is known about the nature of entry barriers?

Scale economies can be an important barrier. Suppose that there are three firms in an industry, the smallest with 20 percent of output, and that the most efficient scale for operation in the industry is so large, relative to total industry output, that no firm can operate at the lowest possible per unit cost without producing an amount equal to 20 percent or more of current total industry production. Entry will be greatly inhibited. Any firm considering entry would not expect the existing firms to suffer such a large diversion. Aggressive price cuts and other responses could be expected. Few would-be entrants would be eager to take on the battle of ousting others from such a large share of the market. Entry at a smaller scale might be possible, of course, but only by a firm ready to accept a cost disadvantage such that it would be able to sell profitably only if the existing firms priced high enough above their (lower) costs to allow the new firm to continue operating. There are industries where barriers of magnitudes comparable to these enhance significantly the power attributable to any given market share.[25] In such a market an

24. Broadway Delivery Corp. v. United Parcel Serv. of America, Inc., 651 F.2d 122 (2d Cir.1981), cert. denied, 454 U.S. 968, 102 S.Ct. 512, 70 L.Ed.2d 384 (1981).

25. Bain lists minimum plant scale for tractors as 10–15 percent of national capacity, that for typewriters as 10–30 percent, that for auto component production and car assembly as 5–10 percent. J. BAIN, BARRIERS TO NEW COMPETITION: THEIR CHARACTER AND CONSEQUENCES IN MANUFACTURING INDUSTRIES 72, 84 (1956). Another study shows minimum plant scale for household refrigerators

and freezers as 14.1 percent. F. SCHERER ET AL., THE ECONOMICS OF MULTI-PLANT OPERATION: AN INTERNATIONAL COMPARISONS STUDY chap. 3 (1975). Consideration of products having regional markets could be expected to increase the number of industries in which scale barriers are significant. For a detailed study illustrating many of the problems, see, e.g., McGee, *Economies of Size in Auto Body Manufacture*, 16 J.L. & ECON. 239 (1973). Today, scale economies in software development are a significant barrier to entry into some high tech fields such as the

entrant would be at best a fringe firm operating at the sufferance of the existing firm or firms. Entry barriers may also result from ownership of scarce resources, from vertical integration, from patent research and development policies, from the level and type of promotion expenditures,[26] and from various resource acquisition and product marketing policies.

United Shoe Machinery is instructive about the significance of entry barriers. The evidence showed a large market share but the court did not predicate a finding of power on this fact alone; it identified numerous barriers to entry, which, conjunctively, indicated that United Shoe's market share gave it massive power. These barriers included: an accumulation of patents which in their multiplicity and complexity would deter an entrant from seeking ways to breach United Shoe's defense against competitive technology;[27] a pricing policy which kept returns low on the simplest of the company's machines (those most likely to attract would-be competitors to enter) and high on more complex machines;[28] a static or declining aggregate industry demand that tended to make the industry unattractive to new investment;[29] and various marketing practices (such as a "lease only" policy which also encouraged a firm which leased one United Shoe machine to lease other machines from it).[30] The court concluded that these factors greatly reduced the opportunities for rivals to attract business from United Shoe.[31]

This was significant doctrinal movement. Judge Wyzanski drew upon Judge Hand's opinion in *Alcoa*,[32] but refined the analysis. There was frank recognition that defining the market is not an act of discovery, but an act of judgment. There was also recognition that no share of any market accords power (at least beyond the very short run) except to the extent that the market is insulated from rapid and easy entry by firms beyond its borders. The dynamics of market power were delineated.

In gauging power, the availability of substitutes from outside of the market as defined is always relevant. Products that might have been included in a wider definition retain relevance as a beyond-market constraint. Also, other structural features, in addition to concentration ratios and entry barriers, may be important in particular settings. One circumstance which may be relevant is the manner in which the shares of the nondominant firms are distributed. A firm having 60 percent of a market may have greater single firm power if the remaining 40 percent

---

manufacture of telephone switching equipment.

26. See generally F. M. SCHERER & D. ROSS, INDUSTRIAL MARKET STRUCTURE AND ECONOMIC PERFORMANCE 360–61 (3d ed. 1990).

27. United States v. United Shoe Mach. Corp., 110 F.Supp. 295, 332–33 (D.Mass. 1953), aff'd per curiam, 347 U.S. 521, 74 S.Ct. 699, 98 L.Ed. 910 (1954).

28. Id. at 325–29.

29. Id. at 301.

30. Id. at 314–25.

31. Id. at 338–46; see also Philadelphia World Hockey Club, Inc. v. Philadelphia Hockey Club, Inc., 351 F.Supp. 462 (E.D.Pa.1972) (holding that a reserve clause in league player contracts was exclusionary); cf. United States v. Standard Oil Co., 362 F.Supp. 1331 (N.D.Cal.1972), aff'd mem., 412 U.S. 924, 93 S.Ct. 2750, 37 L.Ed.2d 152 (1973).

32. United States v. Aluminum Co. of America, 148 F.2d 416 (2d Cir.1945).

is held by 20 firms, each with about five percent, than if it is held by four firms each with about 10 percent.[33] If one of the four firms had an ambition to grow and a taste for competition, it might discipline the dominant firm pricing significantly. Yet another relevant circumstance is whether the market displays network effects. Whenever the utility of a product to its user varies directly with the number of other users of the same brand, any significant lead in market share will yield significant power. Another factor which might have significance is the degree to which industry products are homogeneous.[34] For example, successful product differentiation might make a large firm's market share more significant than it would be if other firms were producing an identical product. If other firms tried to increase their shares by lowering price, their chances of success would be greater in a market for a homogeneous product where price would be of predominant importance and cross-elasticity between suppliers within the industry very high. Another factor is the long-run condition of the industry. If it is expanding, a given share will have less significance than if it is contracting. Justice Wyzanski took note of this in *United Shoe Machinery*.

In sum, the selection of the market and the calculation of the defendant's share poses the questions that must be addressed to determine whether power is exercised: are there few or many firms close to the market's fringe? What barriers exclude them? What are the characteristics of firms within the market: feisty? compliant? vulnerable? stable? well-or ill-managed? Is the defendant vertically integrated? Are customers and suppliers large or small, concentrated or not? Does the industry perform well or poorly over time? And what has been its structural history?

3.3c. Intrabrand Market Power in Monopolization

Not until recently did a leading case expressly recognize that intrabrand market power could be sufficient to meet the Section 2 power requirement. If the test for monopolization is the ability to control price and exclude competition, and markets are always defined in interbrand terms, then intrabrand market power may establish the former but not the latter, at least in cases in which the intrabrand power is exercised by a firm with a modest share of the interbrand market. Such a firm may be able to control price and output through brand differentiation, perhaps even within a significant range above cost, and for a prolonged period. But it will likely have difficulty in excluding competition in its market or in downstream markets defined in interbrand terms. However, even if analysis is limited to interbrand markets, as the market share of such a firm grows it may attain the power to exclude competition, especially in downstream markets, without attaining the market share threshold indicated in *Alcoa*. If rivals pursue parallel practices, the

---

33. On the other hand, the joint exercise of power through direct or indirect collusion might be easier in a market of fewer sellers. See § 2.4.

34. SCHERER & ROSS, supra note 26, at 600–610.

collective ability of these firms to exclude competition may approach that of a monopolist. Moreover, if an aftermarket for repairs, service or compatible ancillary products for a single brand is insulated from competition from firms offering like services or products in such aftermarkets for other brands, a firm may also be able to both raise price and exclude competition in that single brand aftermarket.

In *Eastman Kodak Co. v. Image Technical Services, Inc.*, the Supreme Court held that a market definition that included only aftermarket products or services—a form of intrabrand market power because it related to a single manufacturer's line of goods and services—was sufficient to survive a summary judgment motion.[35] On the trial of this case after remand Image Tech obtained a substantial treble damages verdict and an injunction against Kodak for monopolizing a market for servicing Kodak equipment by cutting off its competitors in that market from access to needed Kodak repair parts.[36] This judgment was affirmed in significant part, although the damages were reduced and the injunction narrowed, on review by the court of appeals.[37] Although earlier cases had occasionally drawn market definitions narrowly for the purpose of Section 2 analysis,[38] the Supreme Court had never expressly held that an aftermarket product or service could be a relevant market and lower courts, although split, were predominantly resistant to the idea that a market could be defined in terms of a nondominant manufacturer's brand.[39] Kodak apparently had only 30 percent of the original equipment market. Nonetheless, under the facts alleged (and which, given the procedural posture, the Supreme Court properly assumed to be true and

35. 504 U.S. 451, 112 S.Ct. 2072, 119 L.Ed.2d 265 (1992).

36. Image Technical Servs., Inc. v. Eastman Kodak Co., 1996–2 Trade Cas. (CCH) ¶ 71,624 (N.D. Cal. Feb. 28, 1996).

37. Image Technical Servs., Inc. v. Eastman Kodak Co., 125 F.3d 1195 (9th Cir. 1997), cert. denied, 523 U.S. 1094, 118 S.Ct. 1560, 140 L.Ed.2d 792 (1998).

38. International Boxing Club of New York, Inc. v. United States, 358 U.S. 242, 249–52, 79 S.Ct. 245, 3 L.Ed.2d 270 (1959) (professional boxing is a relevant market); Aspen Skiing Co. v. Aspen Highlands Skiing Corp., 472 U.S. 585, 105 S.Ct. 2847, 86 L.Ed.2d 467 (1985) (affirming a verdict based upon a market consisting of ski resorts in the Aspen, Colorado area).

The circuits had occasionally drawn market definitions to include only a particular brand of equipment. International Logistics Group, Ltd. v. Chrysler Corp., 884 F.2d 904, 905, 908 (6th Cir.1989) (parts for Chrysler cars), cert. denied, 494 U.S. 1066, 110 S.Ct. 1783, 108 L.Ed.2d 784 (1990); Dimidowich v. Bell & Howell, 803 F.2d 1473, 1480–81 & n. 3 (9th Cir.1986), modified, 810 F.2d 1517 (1987) (service for Bell & Howell equip-

ment); Heatransfer Corp. v. Volkswagenwerk, A.G., 553 F.2d 964 (5th Cir.1977) (air conditioners for Volkswagens), cert. denied, 434 U.S. 1087, 98 S.Ct. 1282, 55 L.Ed.2d 792 (1978). Another appellate decision accepting a narrow market in the context of an attempted monopoly claim is Photovest Corp. v. Fotomat Corp., 606 F.2d 704 (7th Cir.1979) (affirming a judgment in which the submarket was confined to the franchisor's drive-thru film development kiosks), cert. denied, 445 U.S. 917, 100 S.Ct. 1278, 63 L.Ed.2d 601 (1980). The FTC has also drawn market definitions limited to a single brand. In re General Motors Corp., 99 F.T.C. 464, 554, 584 (1982) (crash parts for General Motors cars).

39. Smalley & Co. v. Emerson & Cuming, Inc., 808 F.Supp. 1503, 1512–13 (D.Colo.1992), aff'd, 13 F.3d 366 (10th Cir. 1993); PSI Repair Servs., Inc. v. Honeywell, Inc., 104 F.3d 811, 815–21 (6th Cir.), cert. denied, 520 U.S. 1265, 117 S.Ct. 2434, 138 L.Ed.2d 195 (1997); Queen City Pizza, Inc. v. Domino's Pizza, Inc., 124 F.3d 430, 439–40 (3d Cir.), reh'g denied, 129 F.3d 724 (1997) (drawing an unusual written dissent from the denial of the petition for rehearing).

which, on remand, the jury found to be true), Kodak was in a position both to influence price and output and to exclude competition in aftermarkets for parts and servicing. Servicing competitors of Kodak could cite testimony that their service was both superior to and less expensive than that provided by Kodak, yet they were being driven out of the market by Kodak's policy.

The Court's holding, challenged in Justice Scalia's dissent,[40] has drawn scholarly criticism and support.[41] Many manufacturers of differentiated products that require aftermarket support will probably enjoy a degree of market power.[42] Each of these manufacturers could be subject to the scrutiny of Section 2 for behavior that, but for the aftermarket power, would not be scrutinized at all, or at least not with the same heightened prospect of antitrust liability. But this scrutiny is hard to fault as policy. The aftermarket power that such a manufacturer possesses can create the same allocative and wealth transfer injuries that arise from market dominance. Although intrabrand market power may be less threatening than is market dominance to the dynamic component of competition in the important interbrand upstream market, its threat both to allocation and to dynamic innovation in downstream aftermarkets can be substantial even if the manufacturer holds a modest share of the upstream market. Moreover, this threat will grow with the size of the defendant's share of the original equipment market, or if the defendant's rivals impose similar restraints on downstream competition. Furthermore, aftermarket power can also discourage innovation in the upstream product market. Especially in high tech industries aftermarket competitors often compete on quality as well as price. When they do, this encourages the upstream manufacturer to invest more in innovation and to commercialize more rapidly. If the upstream manufacturer can exclude such downstream intrabrand competition its incentives to innovate and commercialize may be significantly reduced.

Even if aftermarket power satisfies the power requirement for a Section 2 violation, a firm possessing that power is not guilty of any violation unless its conduct invokes willful acquisition or maintenance of that power. Thus, a manufacturer possessing aftermarket power is in no worse a position than any firm that, through superior skill and foresight, has gained a dominant market position. Nor does it follow that every producer of a uniquely designed product that requires aftermarket servicing meets the power requirement. The threat to the dynamic

---

40. *Kodak*, 504 U.S. at 486.

41. Critics of some aspects of *Kodak* include Carlton, *A General Analysis of Exclusionary Conduct and Refusal to Deal– Why* Aspen *and* Kodak *are Misguided*, 68 ANTITRUST L.J. 659 (2001), Arthur, *The Costly Quest for Perfect Competition:* Kodak *and Nonstructural Market Power*, 69 N.Y.U. L. REV. 1 (1994), and Hovenkamp, *Market Power in Aftermarkets: Antitrust Policy and the* Kodak *Case*, 40 UCLA L. REV. 1447, 1452–53 (1993). Among those supporting

the decision are Grimes, *Antitrust and the Systemic Bias Against Small Business: Kodak, Strategic Conduct, and Leverage Theory*, 52 CASE W. RES. L. REV. 231 (2001), Borenstein, *Antitrust Policy in Aftermarkets*, 63 ANTITRUST L.J. 455 (1995) and Lande, *Chicago Takes It on the Chin: Imperfect Information Could Play a Crucial Role in the Post-*Kodak *World*, 62 ANTITRUST L.J. 193 (1993).

42. See § 2.4e.

component of downstream aftermarket competition becomes substantial only if the defendant's share of the primary market is significant, as in the 30 percent share held by Kodak, or if the defendant's upstream competitors also use the same exclusionary practices downstream. A firm with a small market share—say less than 10 percent—whose competitors do not control their aftermarkets is unlikely to significantly affect aftermarket competition because competitive options at all levels are open to buyers at the time they make their initial choice of brand.

The court's recognition that aftermarket power can fulfill the power requirement of Section 2 places considerable importance on the Section 2 conduct requirement. This should be interpreted in a manner that allows a firm freedom of action to design new and improved products, including those with unique aftermarket requirements, without incurring the risk of Section 2 enforcement. When a manufacturer possesses aftermarket power no presumption is warranted about how that power was obtained. A producer of a new and innovative product, for which there is no competition, will have at least a short-term lock on the aftermarket and is, in this sense, innocent of any intentionally aggrandizing behavior. But most products are in competition with other existing lines, allowing the producer a choice in designing its product. If the product is designed in a manner that is compatible with competing products, then aftermarket power is less likely—the aftermarket will be served by more than one firm. If, on the other hand, a firm designs its product so that only uniquely designed parts will be compatible, unless that choice was dictated by technological needs, it has made a conscious choice to obtain and exercise power in the aftermarket. The conduct issues that may arise when a firm gains power by the later choice are discussed in § 3.4b9.

The *Kodak* decision leaves open the question of whether, in addition to aftermarket power, other forms of intrabrand market power, including substantial dealer sunk costs, brand differentiation and exploitation of information asymmetries would satisfy the power requirement of Section 2. The economic logic for extending *Kodak* in that direction is straightforward: these other forms of intrabrand market power, like aftermarket power, create the same types of allocative and wealth transfer injuries—the essence of antitrust injury—as does market dominance. Such power can also be exercised in a manner that tends to exclude procompetitive, downstream competition.[43] The unassailable economic logic of this position notwithstanding, placing the intrabrand power obtained through brand differentiation or information exploitation within reach of Section 2's monopolization is seen by critics as a major extension beyond the mainstream of Section 2 case law. If courts are to avoid converting antitrust law into an all-purpose consumer protection remedy, Section 2 should not be available for each and every victim of consumer fraud or asymmetric information. It is true that any consumer fraudulently induced to buy can claim a distortion of competi-

43. The example of a procompetitive buyer's cooperative injured through use of brand differentiation market power is discussed in § 7.5b.

tion that is common to traditional abuses of monopoly power. In effect, fraudulent statements can lead to heightened and inelastic demand for a product that gives the seller an ability to raise price, just as a traditional monopolist might do. What distinguishes market power in the antitrust context is its systemic or enduring nature and the inability to undermine that power by disseminating readily available and accurate information. The *Kodak* case provides an example: Kodak's market power in the aftermarket for parts might have been mitigated somewhat if consumers had received full information before buying Kodak's original equipment. But gathering and disseminating that information was impossible–the long life cycle of ownership would have required omniscient consumers with a grasp of unpredictable future market events.

§ 3.4   The Conduct Test for Monopolization

Being a monopolist does not alone violate Section 2. That result, if not evident after the early Section 2 cases ending with *United States Steel*,[1] was articulated clearly (if left ambiguous in application) by *Alcoa's* bifurcated test for monopolization. To establish unlawful monopolization, the defendant must be shown to have willfully acquired or maintained its monopoly position.[2] Although unquestioned in recent years, the wisdom of requiring a showing of harmful conduct to prove monopolization was questioned at earlier stages. Under a policy of no-fault monopolization, Section 2 could become a statutory platform for restructuring American industry to enhance competitive performance. One problem with construing Section 2 to reach power attained without bad conduct is that Section 2 provides for criminal as well as civil remedies for its violation. It would be anomalous, to say the least, to sanction with a felony conviction a defendant that had done nothing wrong. During the 1970s, advocates of no-fault monopolization proposed no-fault monopolization legislation that would have eliminated any criminal violation.[3] But a prohibition against no-fault monopolization was criticized because it might deter vigorous competition to gain market share. Proposals for no-fault monopolization never gained substantial support. The political consensus supporting antitrust has consistently presupposed a response to bad conduct, not an unprovoked response based on government planning to redesign important markets. Looking beyond the United States, most provisions of competition law that challenge power also include a conduct requirement. For example, Article 82 (formerly 86) of the European Economic Community's charter requires "an abuse * * * of a dominant position."[4]

The closest any court has come to embracing a no-fault monopoly rule was *Alcoa*, where Judge Hand found that the firm's expansion

---

§ 3.4

1. United States v. United States Steel Corp., 251 U.S. 417, 40 S.Ct. 293, 64 L.Ed. 343 (1920).

2. United States v. Aluminum Co. of America, 148 F.2d 416 (2d Cir.1945).

3. Monopolization Reform Act of 1976, S. 3429, 94th Cong., 2d Sess., 122 Cong. Rec. 13,872.

4. See the discussion in § 18.6b.

activity—building new plants in anticipation of increased demand—was conduct that showed an intent to maintain monopoly power in violation of Section 2.[5] If strictly followed, that holding could injure consumers by deterring large market participants from competing aggressively. The only monopoly safe from attack would be power attained through passive behavior or through government license, such as patent. But elsewhere in the opinion, Judge Hand made clear that a monopoly gained through superior skill or foresight was also lawful.[6] The apparently contradictory dicta in Judge Hand's opinion leaves us with a somewhat muddled rule of that case for determining what constitutes improper conduct.[7]

In a subsequent Section 2 action brought by the Department of Justice against United Shoe Machinery, Judge Wyzanski described three alternative rules for determining whether the conduct element of Section 2 was satisfied, each with some support in earlier case law: (1) the classic test—whether the defendant obtained a monopoly by means of conduct that independently violated Section 1's prohibition on restraints of trade; (2) the exclusionary test—whether the defendant obtained a monopoly by means of conduct that was predatory or exclusionary in purpose or effect; and (3) the prima facie approach—allowing a rebuttable prima facie showing of monopolization if the defendant took affirmative steps, however benign, to attain that power.[8]

The first test, reflecting early precedents such as *Standard Oil*, is clearly sufficient to show monopolization, but has too narrow a reach. Conduct that violates Section 1 will create competitive injury, but conduct that falls short of a Section 1 violation (perhaps because the conspiracy requirement is not met) may also injure competition. For example, *United Shoe Machinery* used a lease only policy that prevented development of a secondary market for shoe machines. While this was a part of an apparently successful scheme to obstruct competitors, it probably would not violate Section 1. Judge Wyzanski's exclusionary test could cover such practices if engaged in by a dominant firm and probably comes closer to describing current law. Conduct of a monopolist that makes it difficult for rival firms to compete, or has similar effects in downstream markets, could meet the exclusionary test regardless of whether it violates Section 1.

Under Judge Wyzanski's third test, the plaintiff makes a prima facie case of monopolization upon any showing of affirmative steps, however benign, taken by the monopolist to obtain power. A defendant could then counter this prima facie showing by establishing that the monopoly was attained through means such as through superior skill and foresight or the grant of a lawful patent. This third test is perhaps implicit in *Alcoa*

---

5.   148 F.2d at 430–32.

6.   Id. at 429–30.

7. Compare the language in United States v. Grinnell Corp., 384 U.S. 563, 570–71, 86 S.Ct. 1698, 16 L.Ed.2d 778 (1966), to the effect that Section 2 is violated when a firm willfully acquires or maintains monopoly, rather than gaining it from "superior

product, business acumen, or historical accident."

8. United States v. United Shoe Mach. Corp., 110 F.Supp. 295, 342–43 (D.Mass. 1953), aff'd per curiam, 347 U.S. 521, 74 S.Ct. 699, 98 L.Ed. 910 (1954).

(in that Judge Hand's opinion criticized Alcoa's expansion to meet projected increases in demand and stressed the similarities in effect between monopoly and concerted price fixing). To the extent this test makes the possession of monopoly power presumptively unlawful, it clearly extends beyond current law, which accords a monopolist substantial freedom of action.

There is at least one more test for evaluating the propriety of conduct by a monopolist: it focuses on the intent underlying the monopolist's conduct. Some of the language in *Alcoa* speaks in terms that support intent analysis. For example, Judge Hand suggests that a market participant that has a monopoly "thrust upon" it does not violate the Act.[9] An influential 1955 report indicated that monopoly power acquired through an "element of deliberateness" did violate the Act.[10] In *United States v. Griffith*, the Supreme Court wrote that the power to exclude competitors violates Section 2 if it is "coupled with the purpose or intent to exercise that power."[11] Of course, the fact finder often infers intent from overt conduct, so that the intent test, in many instances, will still focus on conduct. But direct evidence of intent, if probative, may clarify ambiguous conduct and aid in evaluating a Section 2 claim.[12]

Each of the conduct or intent tests described above captures elements of the earlier cases. The Court has most recently applied the *Griffith* test in *Verizon Communications Inc. v. Trinko*.[13] Other recent Section 2 case law looks for "predatory" or "exclusionary" behavior by a monopolist. The formulation in Otter Tail Power Co. v. United States[14] and Aspen Skiing Co. v. Aspen Highlands Skiing Corp.[15] requires the jury to determine whether the monopolist engaged in exclusionary or otherwise impermissible conduct by considering: (1) the defendant monopolist's intent; (2) the effect of the defendant's conduct on the plaintiff, on consumers, and on the defendant itself; and (3) whether the defendant had "efficiency based" business justifications for its course of conduct.[16] This phrasing, although general, invites discernment of antitrust policy and goals.

Sound application of the conduct norm for firms with power would forbid only conduct displaying each of these three elements: (1) competitive harm results (the conduct threatens to reduce competitive opportu-

9. United States v. Aluminum Co. of America, 148 F.2d 416, 429 (2d Cir.1945).

10. Report of the Attorney General's National Committee to Study the Antitrust Laws 43 (1955).

11. 334 U.S. 100, 107, 68 S.Ct. 941, 92 L.Ed. 1236 (1948).

12. Olympia Equip. Leasing Co. v. Western Union Tel. Co., 797 F.2d 370, 379–80 (7th Cir.1986) (Judge Posner discounted a statement of defendant's officer that Western Union wanted to "flush these turkeys"), cert. denied, 480 U.S. 934, 107 S.Ct. 1574, 94 L.Ed.2d 765 (1987). See also the discussion of intent in Sullivan, *Monopolization: Corporate Strategy, the IBM Cases, and the Transformation of the Law*, 60 Tex. L. Rev. 587, 632–37 (1982).

13. 540 U.S. 398, 124 S.Ct. 872, 157 L.Ed.2d 823 (2004).

14. 410 U.S. 366, 93 S.Ct. 1022, 35 L.Ed.2d 359 (1973).

15. 472 U.S. 585, 105 S.Ct. 2847, 86 L.Ed.2d 467 (1985).

16. Id. at 605–11; *Otter Tail*, 410 U.S. 366, 93 S.Ct. 1022, 35 L.Ed.2d 359.

nities of rivals significantly); (2) effective competition by the monopolist is not inhibited (forbidding the conduct will leave ample room for business skill, innovation and efficiency by the monopolist); (3) anticompetitive intent can be inferred (the conduct's likely adverse effects and the monopolist's capacity to compete effectively without resorting to it will be evident to the monopolist). If each of these elements is present, a procedural desideratum will be met: the case will be capable of discovery and proof by manageable judicial inquiry. These elements and this desideratum provide a basis for evaluating some of the judicial responses to conduct that has been challenged in Section 2 cases.

3.4a.   Direct Acquisition of Monopoly Power

One way to gain monopoly power is to combine with competitors by acquisition or joint action. In early monopolization cases such as *Standard Oil*, the record showed acquisitions of competitors, often under circumstances in which the competitor was economically coerced to sell out.[17] Horizontal acquisition that results in monopoly stifles competition, can be identified by structural inquiry, and can normally be forbidden without discouraging efficient competition. In policy terms such conduct is a paradigmatic violation of Section 2. Proof of it is sufficient to establish unlawful monopolization, regardless of whether there is coercion.[18] But suppose a case where an acquisition offers efficiency benefits but also threatens monopoly power.[19] In policy terms it is relevant that if significant scale economies are available the market will motivate some firm to invest in sufficient growth to attain them. Also, if a natural monopoly is involved it may be protected by state law, by the state action doctrine or by Congress itself. If there is no regulation or ineffective regulation, when monopoly is attained by combining existing competitors any efficiency benefits may be short-term because of the x-inefficiency and rent-seeking behavior associated with monopoly power. Also, with the loss of competitive discipline, the efficiency gains attained through unregulated monopoly will not benefit consumers; even if not dissipated by x-inefficiency or rent-seeking behavior, any efficiency gains will go to stockholders. Preventing such wealth transfer losses is widely if not universally accepted as a major goal of antitrust enforcement.[20]

While willful attainment of a monopoly is undesirable, attaining power by internal growth should be distinguished from doing so by acquisition. Internal growth is a gradual and indirect process. It is far easier to target, prevent, or even undo acquisitions that lead to immedi-

---

17. Standard Oil Co. v. United States, 221 U.S. 1, 31 S.Ct. 502, 55 L.Ed. 619 (1911); cf. Northern Sec. Co. v. United States, 193 U.S. 197, 24 S.Ct. 436, 48 L.Ed. 679 (1904) (apparently holding that combining two or more significant competitors violated Section 1 of the Act).

18. United States v. Grinnell Corp., 384 U.S. 563, 576–77, 86 S.Ct. 1698, 16 L.Ed.2d 778 (1966); United States v. Southern Pac. Co., 259 U.S. 214, 42 S.Ct. 496, 66 L.Ed.

907 (1922). Merging to monopoly is also a clear violation of Section 7 of the Clayton Act. See § 11.2e.

19. Section 7 of the Clayton Act is clearly relevant too. See §§ 11.2e, 11.2h2.

20. Lande, *Chicago's False Foundation: Wealth Transfers (Not Just Efficiency) Should Guide Antitrust*, 58 ANTITRUST L.J. 631 (1989). See the discussion in § 1.5b.

ate monopoly than to intervene in a growth process that may reach the same end. But the most forceful distinction is substantive: Internal growth often comes from efficient, effective, perhaps aggressive competition that benefits consumers. Its suppression would reduce incentives to innovate, improve product, or control costs and could encourage higher, oligopolistic pricing with concomitant x-inefficiency.

Concerted action by firms that results in their joint exercise of monopoly power violates Section 2 even if there is no acquisition.[21] For example, concerted pricing or division of markets can produce monopoly power. Of course, this type of behavior may also be an unlawful conspiracy to monopolize under Section 2 of the Sherman Act or a conspiracy in restraint of trade under Section 1.

3.4b. Exclusionary Strategies

Competition is the critical disciplining mechanism for unregulated firms. When abused by overly aggressive or predatory strategies, competition can also lead relentlessly and effectively to the creation and maintenance of market power. Harmful, exclusionary strategies sufficient to violate the conduct test must be distinguished from beneficial or benign competitive methods that will be tolerated even from a monopolist. It is a beginning to say that "competition on the merits" is protected. The phrase is descriptive, but too vague and susceptible to subjective interpretation to provide a clear rule for distinguishing conduct that should be proscribed under Section 2. A wide variety of marketplace conduct has been challenged under Section 2. Examples include: predatory (below cost) and discriminatory pricing; predatory or excessive advertising, brand introduction, or capacity increases; design manipulation; patent exploitation; foreclosing restraints of numerous kinds; and refusals to deal, price squeezes and leveraging power from one market to another. In evaluating any conduct challenged as unreasonably exclusionary context is crucial. The inquiry always involves the rule of reason. Possible harms and benefits must both be identified and gauged. The basic guides are purpose and effect. Given the structural setting and its performance implications, why did the defendant select this strategy or collection of strategies? What is the likely effect? Will the strategy improve the defendant's product or service, protect or enhance its goodwill, reduce or stabilize its costs? Will the strategy constrain competitors by differentially increasing their costs or foreclosing them from needed resources or outlets? Is adverse impact upon competitors the only or a major factor making the strategy a profit-maximizer for the defendant? If the strategy both harms competitors and gives the defendant additional benefits, could those benefits have been attained in a less restrictive way?

In subsections following, we discuss several theories often used to explain whether conduct violates Section 2. There is a substantial body

21. United States v. Paramount Pictures, Inc., 334 U.S. 131, 68 S.Ct. 915, 92 L.Ed. 1260 (1948); American Tobacco Co. v. United States, 328 U.S. 781, 66 S.Ct. 1125, 90 L.Ed. 1575 (1946).

of Section 2 law which holds that a monopolist may violate the law by leveraging power in the monopoly market to obtain unfair advantage in a related market that is not monopolized. Leverage theory, however, is out of fashion and some would say defunct. One sign of this is that in its 1998 complaint against Microsoft, the Government, despite inviting factual circumstances, did not rely on leverage theory. The Supreme Court, in its 2004 holding in Verizon Communications Inc. v. Trinko, disposed of leverage arguments in a single footnote, indicating that leverage theory is valid only if the plaintiff establishes a threat to monopolize the new market.[22] The *Trinko* language tends to equate a leveraging abuse with an independent claim of attempted monopolization of the new market, and undermines the utility of leverage theory as a means of attacking genuinely abusive conduct. These developments come against a backdrop of strong criticisms of traditional leverage theory by Chicago theorists who have argued that a monopolist's freedom to compete would be unduly constrained by leverage theory.[23]

Despite these developments, leverage theory deserves careful treatment here. It has resonated through Section 2 law for the better part of a century, has continued standing in the law of the European Union, and seems assured of survival under Sherman Act jurisprudence in some form. Chicago has made a convincing case that traditional leveraging theory sweeps too broadly and can threaten a monopolist's procompetitive or benign conduct. This critique is logical and forceful if its premises are accepted, but its limitations have been recognized. Even if a leveraging claim by that name can no longer be vindicated, alternative theories, including raising rivals' costs or maintaining or extending an existing monopoly, seem likely to offer plaintiffs many of the same opportunities for establishing a Section 2 violation that leverage theory has offered. No matter the label placed on the conduct, the critical issue for a court does not involve theoretical debate about the validity of leverage theory but whether the particular facts before it constitute an abuse of the monopoly power possessed by the defendant.

The remaining subsections discuss more specifically the types of conduct often used to establish a violation of Section 2. Omitted from this list are two types of conduct often associated with monopolization or attempted monopolization, price predation and intellectual property strategies, which are addressed in separate chapters.[24]

3.4b1. Leveraging Theory

"Leveraging" is a monopolist's use of power in one market to gain an advantage in a related market, or power held in one time period to gain advantage in a later period. Often, the leveraging occurs in a vertical context, as when an upstream producer with monopoly power

---

22. 540 U.S. 398, 415 n.4, 124 S.Ct. 872, 157 L.Ed.2d 823 (2004).

23. R. Bork, The Antitrust Paradox: A Policy at War with Itself 299–309 (1978).

24. Price predation is addressed in Chapter IV; intellectual property strategies are addressed in Chapter XV.

uses that power to gain advantage in a downstream market.[25] Leveraging may also occur in the aftermarket context—involving the sale of aftermarket products or services.[26] Or, leveraging can occur in a primary market, as when a producer uses monopoly power over one geographic segment of that market to gain an advantage in another segment.[27]

3.4b1i. Traditional Leveraging Theory

The essential elements of leveraging are monopoly power in one market; abuse or exploitation of that power; and resulting competitive harm in a different market.[28] It is settled that when, by such conduct, monopoly is obtained or threatened in the second market, and no offsetting efficiency justification can be shown, Section 2 is violated; no abusive conduct in the second market need be shown.[29] There had been debate, however, about whether leveraging without offsetting efficiencies violates Section 2 of the Sherman Act, when shifting power from a monopolized market does serious competitive harm in a second market but does not threaten monopoly there.[30] The *Berkey* opinion stressed that there "is no reason to allow the exercise of [monopoly] power to the detriment of competition, in either the controlled market or any other"[31] and the *Kerasotes* opinion asserts that inferior products in a market "should not be allowed to prosper * * * as a result of its producer's exploitation of its monopoly position [elsewhere]."[32] The *Alaska Airlines* opinion, by contrast, feared that leveraging by "efficient and natural

---

25. Otter Tail Power Co. v. United States, 410 U.S. 366, 93 S.Ct. 1022, 35 L.Ed.2d 359 (1973); Paschall v. Kansas City Star Co., 727 F.2d 692 (8th Cir.), cert. denied, 469 U.S. 872, 105 S.Ct. 222, 83 L.Ed.2d 152 (1984).

26. Eastman Kodak Co. v. Image Technical Servs., Inc., 504 U.S. 451, 479 n. 29, 112 S.Ct. 2072, 119 L.Ed.2d 265 (1992).

27. This is the basis of many predatory pricing cases, such as Utah Pie Co. v. Continental Baking Co., 386 U.S. 685, 87 S.Ct. 1326, 18 L.Ed.2d 406 (1967), and United States v. Griffith, 334 U.S. 100, 68 S.Ct. 941, 92 L.Ed. 1236 (1948).

28. Jones, *Leveraging: The Legality Of Monopolists' Efforts to Increase Sales in Related Markets*, ABA Section of Antitrust Law, Spring Meeting, April 9, 1997. A summary of leveraging elements and history appears in Grason Elec. Co. v. Sacramento Mun. Util. Dist., 571 F.Supp. 1504, 1512–19 (E.D.Cal.1983).

29. Sargent–Welch Scientific Co. v. Ventron Corp., 567 F.2d 701, 711–12 (7th Cir. 1977), cert. denied, 439 U.S. 822, 99 S.Ct. 87, 58 L.Ed.2d 113 (1979); Mid–Texas Communications Sys., Inc. v. AT & T Co., 615 F.2d 1372, 1385–86 (5th Cir.), cert. denied 449 U.S. 912, 101 S.Ct. 286, 66 L.Ed.2d 140 (1980); Greyhound Computer Corp. v. IBM

Corp., 559 F.2d 488, 503 (9th Cir.1977), cert. denied, 434 U.S. 1040, 98 S.Ct. 782, 54 L.Ed.2d 790 (1978).

30. Compare Berkey Photo, Inc. v. Eastman Kodak Co., 603 F.2d 263, 274–75 (2d Cir.1979), cert. denied, 444 U.S. 1093, 100 S.Ct. 1061, 62 L.Ed.2d 783 (1980), and Kerasotes Mich. Theatres, Inc. v. National Amusements, Inc., 854 F.2d 135, 136–37 (6th Cir.1988), cert. denied, 490 U.S. 1087, 109 S.Ct. 2461, 104 L.Ed.2d 982 (1989), with Alaska Airlines, Inc. v. United Airlines, Inc., 948 F.2d 536, 546–48 (9th Cir. 1991), cert. denied, 503 U.S. 977, 112 S.Ct. 1603, 118 L.Ed.2d 316 (1992), and Fineman v. Armstrong World Indus., Inc., 980 F.2d 171, 205–06 (3d Cir.1992), cert. denied, 507 U.S. 921, 113 S.Ct. 1285, 122 L.Ed.2d 677 (1993). See, e.g., Key Enters., Inc. v. Venice Hosp., 919 F.2d 1550, 1566–68 (11th Cir. 1990), vacated per curiam, 979 F.2d 806 (11th Cir.1992), cert. denied, 511 U.S. 1126, 114 S.Ct. 2132, 128 L.Ed.2d 863 (1994); Advanced Health–Care Servs., Inc. v. Radford Community Hosp., 910 F.2d 139, 149–50 (4th Cir.1990); Eastman Kodak Co. v. Image Technical Servs., Inc., 504 U.S. 451, 479 n. 29, 112 S.Ct. 2072, 119 L.Ed.2d 265 (1992).

31. *Berkey*, 603 F.2d at 275.

32. *Kerasotes*, 854 F.2d at 138.

monopolies" might be challenged if leveraging were unlawful without it threatening a second market monopoly,[33] and the Third Circuit read the language of Section 2 to require a second market monopoly.[34] The Supreme Court appears to have resolved this dispute in *Verizon Communications Inc. v. Trinko*, indicating in a footnote that leveraging requires " 'a dangerous probability of success' in monopolizing the second market."[35] Older Supreme Court language in leveraging cases that seemed to favor the *Berkey* view[36] went unmentioned, a circumstance that might leave the door open for more nuanced consideration of leveraging in a future case.

Another consideration might well be factored in: Is the conduct likely to yield efficiencies, as well as to move power to the second market? If it is tying, long-term exclusive or package dealing, or other aggressive conduct not used to gain efficiencies but only to target power on the second market, in all likelihood the conduct can be forbidden without inhibiting any efficiency gains in the first market and without dampening efficiencies in the second market. Such non-efficiency enhancing conduct will likely distort second market outcomes without regard to the competitive merits, and it also can be identified with reasonable clarity. It is therefore consistent with Section 2 policy to forbid such conduct, absent any convincing showing of offsetting efficiencies.

3.4b1ii.   *Chicago School Challenge to Leveraging Theory*

The theoretical challenge to leverage theory is that a monopolist seeking to sell products or services related to a monopoly product may be enhancing innovation or efficiency and will generally not be able to extend or increase its monopoly power in doing so.[37] According to this critique, the power a monopoly confers can be exploited only once. If the monopolist extracts a high price for a good or service in which it holds monopoly power, it cannot extract any second premium by selling another good or service for which it holds no monopoly. The buyer will pay no more than the sum of the monopoly price for the monopolized good and the competitive price for the second good. To be able to extract a higher than competitive price for the second good, the monopolist must

---

33. *Alaska Airlines*, 948 F.2d at 548.

34. *Fineman*, 980 F.2d at 203–06.

35. 540 U.S. 398, 415 n.4, 124 S.Ct. 872, 157 L.Ed.2d 823 (2004).

36. United States v. Griffith, 334 U.S. 100, 107, 68 S.Ct. 941, 92 L.Ed. 1236 (1948). In *Kodak*, 504 U.S. at 479 n. 29, the majority, while not directly addressing leverage theory, seemed to leave ample room for traditional leverage concepts in responding to Justice Scalia's dissent:

The dissent urges a radical departure in this Court's antitrust law. It argues that because Kodak has only an "inherent" monopoly in parts for its equipment, post, at 489–490, the antitrust laws do not apply to

its efforts to expand that power into other markets. The dissent's proposal to grant per se immunity to manufacturers competing in the service market would exempt a vast and growing sector of the economy from antitrust laws. Leaving aside the question whether the Court has the authority to make such a policy decision, there is no support for it in our jurisprudence or the evidence in this case.

37. BORK, supra note 23, at 299–309. For an economist's critique of leverage theory in the context of tying, see Bowman, *Tying Arrangements and the Leverage Problem*, 67 YALE L.J. 19 (1957).

make an offsetting reduction in the price for the monopoly good. In other words, when a monopolist experiments with different ways of exercising its power, it plays a zero sum game. A monopolist can switch the return from one product to another, but cannot extend or increase the return by such tactics. Moreover, if the conduct thought to be leveraging has efficiency benefits, a prohibition will undermine the performance of the firm and the monopoly incentive to innovate.

This critique is most telling when there are clear and substantial efficiency benefits associated with the leveraging conduct. The logic that leveraging cannot harm competition, however, is based upon assumptions that are unlikely in real markets. For example, the theory may not hold up if the monopolist cannot fully exploit its power over the monopoly product or if information problems complicate the buyer's purchase decision for the secondary product. Under such real market conditions, the monopolist may be able to increase its aggregate return through non-efficiency enhancing leveraging behavior.

Recent economic literature has emphasized the limiting assumptions that underlie the Chicago view of leveraging and has identified a number of specific conditions in which leveraging is a viable strategy for increasing monopoly returns. As one leading theorist has put it, while "there are some special cases in which leverage does not lead to higher profits, in the general case, a monopolist can earn higher profits by leveraging its power into a competitive market."[38]

3.4b1iii.   *Obscuring the Monopoly*

The Chicago critique of leveraging assumes that a firm that has achieved a perfect monopoly (based on the theoretical model) cannot improve on its pure monopoly power. But few power-wielding firms enjoy anything approaching perfect monopoly power. Through leveraging, the imperfect monopolist may play on buyer knowledge imperfections to obtain higher returns approaching those of a perfect monopolist. Indeed, leveraging may be a means of effecting price discrimination against less knowledgeable buyers, increasing returns beyond those available by the theoretical monopolist (who cannot discriminate in prices).

The monopolist may obscure transactions by spreading increased price into two or more markets. A monopoly return on a single product is obvious to most buyers and an attractive target for any new entrant to challenge. But when the monopoly return is spread among two or more products in separate markets, the picture seen by many buyers will be clouded. Some careful buyers may have experience in and information from both markets; they may see through the obfuscation. Still, the

38. Nalebuff, Bundling as a Way to Leverage Monopoly, Yale SOM Working Paper No. ES–36 (2004), available at <http://ssrn.com/abstract=586648>. See also Grimes, *Antitrust and the Systemic Bias Against Small Business: Kodak, Strategic Conduct, and Leverage Theory*, 52 Case W. Res. L.Rev. 231, 253–261 (2001); Sullivan & Jones, *Monopoly Conduct, Especially Leveraging Power from One Product or Market to Another, in* Antitrust, Innovation, and Competitiveness 171–75 (Jorde & Teece, eds., 1992).

prescience of some buyers may not preclude the seller from leveraging. Many leveraging schemes are designed to discriminate in price, charging higher prices to less powerful or less knowledgeable buyers. The risk that a leveraging scheme involves exploitation of information deficiencies increases with the complexity of the product and the inexperience of buyers. In *Kodak*, the plaintiffs alleged that the intrabrand market power possessed by Kodak was based in part on exploitation of market information deficiencies, exploited more efficiently because large buyers were given favored, discriminatory treatment.[39]

3.4b1iv. *Isolating Market Participants*

In United States v. Griffith,[40] a regional movie theater chain was alleged to have used its power in towns in which it had the sole theater (closed towns) to obtain favorable dates for desired films in towns in which it competed with other theater owners (open towns). The chain exhibitor's power stemming from control of closed towns might have limited effect if distributors as a class could maintain a solid front. But any one distributor, when confronting the exhibitor chain alone, might fear loss of trade to other distributors in the closed towns if the other distributors agreed to the theater chain's terms. In effect, although distributors acting collectively might call the bluff of the theater chain, a distributor when acting alone would not be willing to take the risk of losing to rival distributors its access to the closed towns. And once one movie distributor accommodates the theater chain, a bandwagon effect may occur, with the remaining distributors rushing to make similar accommodations.

Griffith illustrates use of a divide and conquer strategy by a monopsonist buyer. But the same strategy can work for a monopolist seller. In United States v. United Shoe Machinery Corp.,[41] the monopolist probably was successful in imposing its lease only, contract penalty provisions in part because it negotiated individually with shoe manufacturers, no one of which was willing to stand up to United Shoe at the risk of losing a critical supplier.[42]

3.4b1v. *Limit Pricing and Leveraging*

Many monopolists may engage in limit pricing, a practice designed to discourage new entry into the monopolist's market. By limiting the monopoly markup to a point below the maximum monopoly return, a monopolist earns a lower return but makes it less attractive for other firms to enter the market. Although limit pricing is intended to assure that power remains intact for a longer period, it yields an offsetting

39. Eastman Kodak Co. v. Image Technical Servs., Inc., 504 U.S. 451, 464–65, 477, 112 S.Ct. 2072, 119 L.Ed.2d 265 (1992). These information deficiencies are discussed in the context of foreclosure restraints in § 8.3c3.

40. 334 U.S. 100, 68 S.Ct. 941, 92 L.Ed. 1236 (1948).

41. 110 F.Supp. 295 (D.Mass.1953), aff'd per curiam, 347 U.S. 521, 74 S.Ct. 699, 98 L.Ed. 910 (1954).

42. See Kaplow, *Extension of Monopoly Power Through Leverage,* 85 Colum. L. Rev. 515 (1985). See also the discussion in § 3.4b5 and § 3.4b6.

allocative gain, to the extent it brings the monopolist's price closer to a competitive level. Thus, when limit pricing is pursued without any concomitant leveraging, it probably should remain beyond antitrust attack. But a monopolist may limit its price below the monopoly level and then capture that lost monopoly profit on a secondary product, perhaps by requiring the buyer to purchase the secondary product as a condition of purchasing the monopoly product. This behavior might be seen as "phony" limit pricing because the allocative gain from limiting the price on the monopoly product is lost when the monopolist captures it in the secondary sale.

This form of leveraging may allow the monopolist to have the best of both worlds. Because of the complicating and market obscuring features of the tie-in, the lower price on the monopoly product may have much the same impact as a true limit price: it may discourage entry and prolong the life of the monopoly. But the monopolist will also distort the market for the secondary product, perhaps raising costs of rivals in that market or foreclosing a substantial share of the secondary market.

3.4b1vi.   Remedial Aspects of Leverage Abuses

The conduct associated with leveraging generally presents manageable remedial problems for a court. Prohibiting the leveraging conduct requires no complex and politically difficult divestiture. For example, if the leveraging is accomplished through a tie-in, prohibiting the tie-in often can be straightforward and relatively unproblematic. Such a prohibition usually raises few risks that competitively beneficial competition on the merits will be obstructed. Although some theorists argue that distribution restraints invoked by a firm possessing market power will enhance efficiencies, there are almost always less anticompetitive avenues for obtaining any such efficiencies.[43]

3.4b2.   Exclusionary Conduct that Raises Rivals' Costs

The continuing effort to understand the economics of exclusionary strategies was advanced in the 1980s by a trio of law and economic scholars.[44] Conventional analysis suggests that firms with power raise prices by directly constraining output. It is not the only possibility. If a firm with power can take steps that confront rivals with increased costs, the rational response for rivals, in the face of unchanged demand, will be to reduce their output. Indeed, the theory suggests even strategies that increase the monopolist's own costs can raise entry barriers and increase supracompetitive returns if the costs imposed on rivals are relatively greater. Foreclosure strategies of various kinds, including denial of access to an essential facility, tying, predatory design changes, and

---

43. A tie-in can have efficiency benefits, notably in ensuring quality control and protecting the reputation of the seller of the primary product, but these benefits usually can be attained through means short of a tie-in. See the discussion in §§ 8.3b3, 8.3b4.

44. See Krattenmaker & Salop, *Anticompetitive Exclusion: Raising Rivals' Costs to Achieve Power over Price*, 96 YALE L.J. 209 (1986); Krattenmaker et al., *Monopoly Power and Market Power in Antitrust Law*, 76 GEO. L.J. 241 (1987).

enforcement of contract penalty clauses, can also be explained as strategies to increase rivals' costs.

To some extent, a claim of a monopolist's strategic behavior that raises a rival's costs may be seen as a narrower category of leveraging behavior. Often, the claim may be phrased in terms of monopoly maintenance, as it was in the Justice Department's 1998 suit against Microsoft.[45] In this suit, the Justice Department made no claim that Microsoft was leveraging its operating system monopoly into related markets such as the market for an Internet browser. Instead, it viewed Microsoft's strategy from the perspective of its existing monopoly, claiming that Microsoft sought to raise rivals' costs of competing in the Internet browser market in order to maintain its monopoly over the operating system market. The court of appeals upheld the district court's judgment that Microsoft had violated Section 2 through its strategic conduct directed at rival Internet browser providers, concluding that Microsoft had employed various tactics to make rivals' distribution of browser software more difficult. Microsoft had not barred rivals from all methods of distribution, but "did bar them from the cost efficient ones."[46]

3.4b3. Denying Access to an Essential Facility

Though limited in application, the notion that one in possession of a scarce resource should deal with all comers in a nondiscriminatory fashion was well established long before the Sherman Act. An innkeeper's common law duty to accommodate travelers is an example. Sherman Act cases have imposed this duty for some market participants possessing monopoly power.[47] In limited contexts, a firm possessing even a lawful monopoly may nonetheless be found to have monopolized in violation of Section 2 if it exploits its unique resource in ways that exclude or disadvantage customers arbitrarily or invidiously. The anticompetitive effects may be in the primary market in which the defendant operates[48] or in downstream markets in which the defendant also competes.[49]

The least problematical applications of this concept to antitrust occur where two or more firms in a venture have together developed a facility that cannot be duplicated, that conveys monopoly power giving the venturers a great advantage and that it would be feasible for them to share with other competitors.[50] In United States v. Terminal Railroad

---

45. 253 F.3d 34 (D.C. Cir. 2001)(en banc).

46. Id. at 63.

47. E.g., United States v. Terminal R.R. Ass'n, 224 U.S. 383, 32 S.Ct. 507, 56 L.Ed. 810 (1912); Associated Press v. United States, 326 U.S. 1, 65 S.Ct. 1416, 89 L.Ed. 2013 (1945); Otter Tail Power Co. v. United States, 410 U.S. 366, 93 S.Ct. 1022, 35 L.Ed.2d 359 (1973).

48. Terminal R.R., 224 U.S. 383, 32 S.Ct. 507, 56 L.Ed. 810.

49. Otter Tail, 410 U.S. 366, 93 S.Ct. 1022, 35 L.Ed.2d 359.

50. See Terminal R.R., 224 U.S. 383, 32 S.Ct. 507, 56 L.Ed. 810; Associated Press, 326 U.S. 1, 65 S.Ct. 1416, 89 L.Ed. 2013; Silver v. New York Stock Exchange, 373 U.S. 341, 83 S.Ct. 1246, 10 L.Ed.2d 389 (1963). But cf. Northwest Wholesale Stationers, Inc. v. Pacific Stationery & Printing Co., 472 U.S. 284, 105 S.Ct. 2613, 86 L.Ed.2d 202 (1985).

Ass'n,[51] several railroads owned rail facilities that provided the only access to the City of St. Louis and rail lines on either side of the Mississippi. The arrangement that the defendants enjoyed is sometimes referred to as an "essential facility" or a "bottleneck monopoly." The Court held that the company must provide access to nonparticipating railroads upon reasonable terms that did not discriminate between participants and nonparticipants. There are two features of the relief, both of which are common in public utility regulation: (1) that access to the product or service be available to all comers on a nondiscriminatory basis; and (2) that the rates not exceed reasonable levels. The second aspect, limiting rates, challenges a court to undertake a task whose solution has often defied even the most expert regulatory agency. Note, however, that without some control on rates, the relief accorded to nonmember railroads could be meaningless. The railroads owning the Terminal Railroad Association could set high, nondiscriminatory rates, knowing that they, as owners, would receive a substantial rebate in the form of the Association's high profits. In the case of *Terminal Railroad*, enforcement problems may have been manageable because the industry was independently subject to rate regulation and relatively few railroads were involved. The assumption is that where access for others is feasible, essential facility cases can often be managed by a decree simply directing the defendants to grant access on reasonable, nondiscriminatory terms. Such a decree establishes a context for bargaining in the shadow of the law. At least in instances where the bargainers are informed and sophisticated, as would be the railroads in this landmark case, accord is likely to be reached without more explicit court activity. While a price term is likely to be problematic, there are often alternative means by which access could be provided: access as a member of the venture, access to the venture's output on sale, rental or license terms appropriately related to cost, or others.

In joint facility cases there are other litigated issues in addition to power and the terms for access: whether the facility is essential or at least confers a great competitive advantage; whether it could be duplicated by the plaintiff alone or with other excluded competitors;[52] whether it is feasible for the defendants to accommodate additional participation; and whether there are reasonable justifications for excluding one or more particular applicants. In addition to *Terminal Railroad, Associated Press* and *Silver*,[53] a considerable amount of lower court case law has accumulated.[54]

51. 224 U.S. 383, 32 S.Ct. 507, 56 L.Ed. 810 (1912).

52. *Associated Press,* supra note 47, a leading case in this area, is addressed in § 5.7b.

53. These cases cited in note 50, supra.

54. E.g., United States v. Realty Multi–List, Inc., 629 F.2d 1351 (5th Cir.1980); Time Warner Entertainment Co. v. FCC, 93 F.3d 957 (D.C.Cir.1996) (per curiam); Mt. Mansfield Television, Inc. v. FCC, 442 F.2d 470 (2d Cir.1971); Phil Tolkan Datsun, Inc. v. Greater Milwaukee Datsun Dealers' Advertising Ass'n, Inc., 672 F.2d 1280 (7th Cir.1982).

Suppose, however, that the allegedly essential facility was developed by one firm which, because of it, becomes a monopolist. Compelling a monopolist to grant competitors access to a facility that the monopolist has alone developed is problematic. The very idea collides with three commonplace propositions: that not even monopolists need give positive assistance to competitors; that innovation should be encouraged and rewarded; and that the law should not turn against those that competition has encouraged merely because they have thoroughly prevailed. The leading case is Otter Tail Power Co. v. United States.[55] Otter Tail was a vertically integrated power company that produced electricity, transferred ("wheeled") it over its owned lines, and sold it at retail in Minnesota and the Dakotas. Municipalities that operated their own utilities could buy power from Otter Tail, but the company declined to wheel to them power that they purchased from other suppliers. The Court held that Otter Tail must wheel power from any source where to do so would not inhibit its ability to serve other customers. Thus, Otter Tail's duty to deal even extended to situations where it would be displacing its own business as a seller of electricity. The dissent was highly critical of this result, noting that Otter Tail had invested substantial sums in constructing the network of power lines that wheeled electricity throughout the region.[56] The decree, however, would allow Otter Tail to continue to exact reasonable charges for performing the wheeling function. Moreover, it facilitated competition at the producer level, bringing the potential of lower costs to local utilities and their customers.[57]

A retail electric utility's delivery lines might be a natural or legal monopoly no matter who controlled it, and no matter who supplied its power. In the context of *Otter Tail*, denying the defendant the right to control retail operations would not prevent someone else, also a monopolist, from extracting the same return from consumers of electricity. Reasoning from this, it could be argued that the relief in *Otter Tail* at best could shift profits among monopolists, but not benefit consumers.[58] But who owns the local electric utility can make a difference. In *Otter Tail*, two municipalities sought to operate their own utilities and obtain power from an apparently cheaper source, the Bureau of Reclamation. Even if such local utilities maximized their allowed profits, charging consumers the same rates that Otter Tail would have charged had it controlled the local utility, the municipally owned utility might benefit the local community through better or more comprehensive service, through higher employment in the community, or in other ways. Local

---

55. 410 U.S. 366, 93 S.Ct. 1022, 35 L.Ed.2d 359 (1973).

56. Id. at 382 (Stewart, J., dissenting).

57. For a critical view of *Otter Tail* and a pessimistic attitude about whether antitrust can deal with the accompanying regulatory problems, see Hale & Hale, *The Otter Tail Power Case: Regulation by Commission or Antitrust Laws*, 1973 S. Ct. Rev. 99;

see also 1A P. Areeda & H. Hovenkamp, Antitrust Law: An Analysis of Antitrust Principles and Their Application ¶ 240, at 9, ¶ 251, at 155 (1997); Lipsky & Sidak, *Essential Facilities*, 51 Stan. L. Rev. 1187 (1999).

58. Arguments that vertical integration is unlikely to harm consumers are examined in § 12.3.

officials running the municipal utility might be brought under greater political pressure to provide benefits, including lower rates, than would a privately owned company with its headquarters in a faraway city. The diversity of ownership furthered by the decree in *Otter Tail* may also provide more opportunities for independent, innovative behavior that has long-term benefits to the economy. And, there are potential social benefits to diversified ownership.[59]

Nevertheless, the conventional policy underpinnings of monopolization law will often argue against a single firm essential facility doctrine. Denying access may limit the opportunities of rivals and can be detected by conventional inquiry, but can it be forbidden and effectively remedied without discouraging innovative initiative? If it cannot, conventional antitrust analysis suggests that the innovator should have its reward.[60] These concerns were prominent in *Verizon Communications Inc. v. Trinko*, a case in which the Court declined to apply the essential facilities doctrine.[61] The plaintiff was a law firm that claimed that Verizon, the dominant local exchange carrier (LEC) had failed to provide prompt access to the local network for rival LECs that sought to offer local telephone service to the plaintiff and other class members. Although three dissenters would have disposed of this case on antitrust standing grounds, the Court, after addressing the merits, concluded that no valid claim had been stated under Section 2 of the Sherman Act. In response to claims that rival LECs required access to Verizon's local exchange network, the Court distinguished *Aspen Skiing* and *Otter Tail*. The Court then cautioned that despite lower court applications of an essential facilities doctrine, it had "no need either to recognize it or to repudiate it here."[62] The Court concluded that access to the network was governed by 1996 federal legislation that assigned regulatory supervision to the FCC, a circumstance that ruled out any application of the essential facilties doctrine. This conclusion was bolstered by the Court's concern that any "forced access" ordered by the courts might create intractable problems of court supervision and deter innovative or efficient conduct.[63]

Trinko may be confined to its facts, but undeniably stands as a warning flag to undisciplined application of the essential facilities doctrine. At the same time, despite intuitive or analytical resistance to compelling a firm to share its significant assets, there is some case law in addition to *Otter Tail* applying the essential facility doctrine to individual dominant firms. Hecht v. Pro–Football, Inc.,[64] applied it to a sports stadium; United States v. Standard Oil Co.,[65] to oil storage facilities;

---

59. See § 1.5e.

60. If that reward amounts to a natural monopoly, perhaps regulation is indicated, but neither rate of return nor price cap regulation is a task conventionally assigned to a court.

61. 540 U.S. 398, 124 S.Ct. 872, 157 L.Ed.2d 823 (2004).

62. Id. at 411.

63. Id.

64. 570 F.2d 982 (D.C.Cir.1977), cert. denied, 436 U.S. 956, 98 S.Ct. 3069, 57 L.Ed.2d 1121 (1978).

65. 362 F.Supp. 1331, 1341 (N.D.Cal. 1972), aff'd mem., 412 U.S. 924, 93 S.Ct. 2750, 37 L.Ed.2d 152 (1973).

Venture Technology, Inc. v. National Fuel Gas Co.,[66] to natural gas distribution; Byars v. Bluff City News Co., to a newspaper distribution system.[67] A case of great prominence was the government's suit against AT & T, which led to the consent decree that broke up AT & T's vertically integrated monopoly.[68]

Any given single firm essential facility may, of course, satisfy the rationale for antitrust intervention. It can be asked, did the defendant's innovation require unique or special initiative? Would application of the doctrine to this and similar fact situations discourage investment in efficient, socially valued innovations? Perhaps the doctrine should apply to single firm facilities only when the market power attained is attributable in significant part to sources other than the skill, initiative and innovation of the owner. In both *Otter Tail* and *AT & T*, for example, the defendants' facilities depended upon exclusive government grants. In some other instances, even if entry is not blocked by law, the defendant may be exploiting a natural monopoly, its own initiative being limited to having made the first entry. There may also be situations where the defendant, though entitled to appropriate reward for innovation, is seeking to enhance that return by leveraging its power into adjacent markets or inhibiting or delaying duplication by foreclosure devices. A rebuttable presumption against antitrust constraints on the use of a single firm facility may be warranted. But one cannot confidently generalize. Particular arrangements must be examined in their own structural setting and apparent dynamic interests given appropriate weight. Only then can a policy evaluation be fully and soundly made.

3.4b4. Duty to Deal or Continue to Deal on Nondiscriminatory Terms

A monopolist's duty to deal under Section 2 has been extended beyond situations comprehended by the essential facilities concept. A monopolist's duty to deal is likely to be found when such dealings enhance consumer welfare and when the refusal to deal raises rivals' costs and has no efficiency or welfare-enhancing justification. The Supreme Court has recognized that a news-gathering organization has a duty to deal with competitors to allow access to the news[69] and that a ski lift operator has a duty to continue cooperating with a competitor to issue efficient, consumer-desired joint-tickets for ski lifts in a resort area.[70] In addition, the duty to deal may under some circumstances extend to customers of rivals. The Court has found that a newspaper publisher had a duty to sell advertising space to customers of a radio station that competed for advertising revenue.[71]

---

66. 1980–81 Trade Cas. (CCH) ¶ 63,780 (W.D.N.Y.1981), rev'd on other grounds, 685 F.2d 41 (2d Cir.), cert. denied, 459 U.S. 1007, 103 S.Ct. 362, 74 L.Ed.2d 398 (1982).

67. 609 F.2d 843 (6th Cir.1979)

68. United States v. AT & T Co., 524 F.Supp. 1336 (D.D.C.1981).

69. Associated Press v. United States, 326 U.S. 1, 65 S.Ct. 1416, 89 L.Ed. 2013 (1945).

70. Aspen Skiing Co. v. Aspen Highlands Skiing Corp., 472 U.S. 585, 105 S.Ct. 2847, 86 L.Ed.2d 467 (1985).

71. Lorain Journal Co. v. United States, 342 U.S. 143, 72 S.Ct. 181, 96 L.Ed. 162 (1951).

Aspen Skiing raises the interesting question whether a duty to deal arises in some circumstances only because of a pattern of past cooperation with rivals, or whether that past cooperation is merely a tool for demonstrating the welfare-enhancing effect and feasibility of dealings with rivals.[72] Aspen drew skiing customers from its own catchment area and also substantial business from distant skiers who traveled to Aspen rather than to other competing "destination ski resorts." Aspen had four developed mountains operated for a time by three independent corporations. To enhance Aspen's appeal among destination resort shoppers, the three operators began offering multiday tickets that were usable in any of the four facilities, revenues being divided in a manner proportionally to the frequency of each mountain's use. Defendant, Ski Co., which owned two of the four facilities then acquired one of the two competing ones. Thereafter it sold three mountain tickets on its own. However, it also continued selling four mountain tickets, as did its remaining competitor, plaintiff Highlands. This practice continued for some years. Disappointed with its share of total revenues, Ski Co. ultimately ended this cooperation with Highlands. It offered to continue issuing a four mountain ticket only if Highlands would accept a fixed share of revenue substantially below its historic usage. When Highlands declined, four mountain ticket sales ended. Highlands tried to respond by offering a four ticket package including bank guaranteed vouchers for skiers to use to pay Ski Co. These would have yielded Ski Co. the price of its own daily lift tickets, but Ski Co. refused to honor the vouchers and later raised the price of its daily ski passes to make Highlands' package uneconomical. Highlands' monopolization suit against Ski Co. followed.

The trial court instructed the jury to discriminate between a monopolist's unlawful conduct—described as conduct primarily intended to exclude competition without benefitting consumers—and lawful conduct—described as conduct the monopolist selected for valid business reasons. At trial Ski Co. proposed as justification that it did not want to be associated with an inferior facility, and that maintaining records of usage was inaccurate and a cumbersome burden. A jury verdict for Highlands led to a judgment upheld by the court of appeals. In affirming, the Supreme Court stated that the instructions were accurate and that the jury was warranted on the evidence in finding that Ski Co. acted to stifle competition and that its justifications were pretextual. Signifying that a valid business justification should be limited to steps taken to lower cost, improve product or service and enhance consumer welfare, the Court said:

> The question whether Ski Co.'s conduct may properly be characterized as exclusionary cannot be answered by simply considering its effect on Highlands. In addition, it is relevant to consider its impact on consumers and whether it has impaired competition in an unnecessarily restrictive way. If a firm has been '*attempting to exclude*

72. 472 U.S. 585, 105 S.Ct. 2847, 86 L.Ed.2d 467.

rivals on some basis other than efficiency,' it is fair to characterize its behavior as predatory.[73]

The Court went on to summarize evidence warranting the conclusion that consumers would prefer a four mountain choice, that Ski Co. was interested in reducing competition in the Aspen market, a conclusion "strongly supported by Ski Co.'s failure to offer any efficiency justification whatever for its pattern of conduct."[74]

In sum, *Aspen Skiing* teaches that a monopolist may have to continue to deal with a competitor when doing so would enhance consumer welfare, when the monopolist is aware of this welfare benefit, and when the monopolist can show no offsetting benefit to consumers from an efficiency achieved by means of the monopolist's exclusionary conduct.[75] Ski Co. could not have prevailed by showing knowledge that, although aggregate Aspen business would fall slightly without a four mountain ticket, Ski Co., with its three mountain ticket, would increase its share of the smaller aggregate. Such a defense by Ski Co. would be an open admission that it was using a tactic which, far from yielding efficiencies accessible to consumers, manifestly reduced consumer welfare in order to increase its own revenues at the expense of competition.

It is often supposed that had the custom or tradition of joint tickets never been established, the result might have been otherwise. To place such weight on tradition creates a tension of its own: Conduct with equally anticompetitive results will be lawful or unlawful depending solely on whether there was an earlier custom of behaving in a less anticompetitive way. But viewed pragmatically a distinction based on whether or not the monopolist had ever cooperated can be understood. Highlands' experience and its reaction to that experience was the source of proof both that Ski Co.'s excuses were pretextual and that consumers preferred the four mountain option. The past cooperation was also a concrete demonstration that a decree ordering such behavior was workable and not simply a fabrication of lawyers or judges lacking business experience. In addition, the transaction costs involved in depriving a once participating lift operator from joint participation gave a concreteness to the dispute. Highlands' sunk investment was placed at risk by Ski Co.'s refusal to continue past, welfare-enhancing cooperation. When a current, concrete loss to competitors is linked to a concretely evident antitrust injury to society, there is reason for a court to offer strong relief.

The remand decision in Eastman Kodak Co. v. Image Technical Services, Inc.,[76] although not involving refusal-to-deal analysis, seems consistent. Kodak supplied parts to downstream independent service

---

73. Id. at 605 (emphasis added) (footnote omitted) (quoting Bork, supra note 21, at 138).

74. *Aspen Skiing*, 472 U.S. at 608.

75. See Data Gen. Corp. v. Grumman Sys. Support Corp., 36 F.3d 1147, 1183 (1st Cir.1994).

76. Image Technical Servs., Inc. v. Eastman Kodak Co., 125 F.3d 1195 (9th cir. 1997), cert. denied, 523 U.S. 1094, 118 S.Ct. 1560, 140 L.Ed.2d 792 (1998).

providers and, indeed, encouraged their entry when it thought alternative options for service would enhance its position in the upstream product and parts markets. Later, it decided that it would maximize its own returns, even though reducing slightly the aggregate sales of its own products and parts, if it leveraged its upstream power to cut off the downstream service competition it had earlier fostered. Absent any showing by Kodak of any business justification that resulted in offsetting efficiency, consumer welfare was clearly hurt by the reduction in price and quality competition in the market for services.[77]

The Court's most recent duty to deal holding came in *Verizon Communications Inc. v. Trinko*.[78] The Court declined to recognize a Sherman Act duty on Verizon to deal with its rival local telephone service providers, describing *Aspen* as a "limited exception" to the rule that a firm need not deal with rivals and further characterizing the decision as "at or near the outer boundary of § 2 liability."[79] The Court found *Aspen* distinguishable because of the past pattern of cooperative conduct among rivals that was not evidenced in the record before it. In strong language, the Court also cautioned of the risks that a judge-ordered duty to deal might entangle the court in difficult enforcement issues and deter procompetitive conduct by the monopolist.[80] It is uncertain whether the Court would have reached the same result had 1996 Federal legislation not already imposed an FCC regulated duty on Verizon to deal with its local rivals. Nonetheless, the tone of the Court's opinion suggests a strong inclination not to extend the law governing a monopolist's duty to deal.

3.4b5. *Tying and Loyalty Rebates That Violate Section 2*

Tying, exclusive dealing and other vertical arrangements that unreasonably foreclose access by competitors to suppliers or outlets can violate Sherman Section 1 and Clayton Section 3; illegality requires market power but does not require monopoly power by the perpetrator. See §§ 8.3c and 8.4c. Where the instigator of such a competitive strategy possesses monopoly power an arrangement that would violate either Sherman Section 1 or Clayton Section 3 also becomes vulnerable under Sherman Section 2. Eastman Kodak Co. v. Image Technical Services, Inc.[81] is a more recent example. United States v. Standard Oil Co.,[82] involving a long-term supply contract that dampened entry possibilities in an oligopolistic market, applied a comparable principle when those contracts were challenged under Sherman Section 2.

---

77. For a discussion of Kodak's attempt to justify by asserting intellectual property rights in some parts, which the court of appeals dismissed as pretextual, see § 15.8a.

78. 540 U.S. 398, 124 S.Ct. 872, 157 L.Ed.2d 823 (2004). The facts are described in § 3.4b3.

79. Id. at 409.

80. Id. at 414–15.

81. 504 U.S. 451, 112 S.Ct. 2072, 119 L.Ed.2d 265 (1992); Image Technical Servs., Inc. v. Eastman Kodak Co., 125 F.3d 1195 (9th Cir.1997) (after remand), cert. denied, 523 U.S. 1094, 118 S.Ct. 1560, 140 L.Ed.2d 792 (1998).

82. 362 F.Supp. 1331 (N.D.Cal.1972), aff'd mem., 412 U.S. 924, 93 S.Ct. 2750, 37 L.Ed.2d 152 (1973).

When a market is not already dominated or threatened with domination, competitive strategies with some possible foreclosure effects may provide attractive options to consumers and may threaten little harm from foreclosure. In most manifestations such competitive conduct is not likely to be at risk under Sherman Section 1 or Clayton Section 3. A lease only policy or package sales of a product and service are familiar examples. Yet, as *United Shoe Machinery*[83] demonstrates, when a firm already possesses power, if it markets in a way that forecloses competitors, it may be vulnerable under Sherman Section 2 for having deliberately used an "exclusionary" tactic.

Lower court cases have varied in their treatment of foreclosure effects. A leading case is the en banc court of appeals decision United States v. Microsoft Corp.[84] At the core of this case was the government's allegations that Microsoft had used various exclusionary and tying tactics to maintain its monopoly over personal computer operating system software. The decision shows that neither complexity nor the deliberateness of judicial procedure precludes effective Sherman Act enforcement in dynamic, high tech markets. Coming scarcely three years after the filing of the complaint, this thorough, convincing, full bench opinion upheld in their entirety the detailed trial court findings that were the basis for finding Section 1 and Section 2 liability. Not all of the court's holdings favored the government. The court reversed the trial court holdings on attempted monopolization and tying. Microsoft's monopoly maintenance tactics, however, were found to violate Section 2. Among these tactics were restrictive software licenses; exclusive contracts with internet access providers; a product design that locked Microsoft's browser (Explorer) into Windows by commingling software supporting each functionality without any add/remove capacity; and subverting Sun Microsystem's Java technologies to favor Microsoft's Java version so that compatible applications would not run on operating systems other than Windows. Although not directly attacking other operating systems, all these tactics helped to maintain the Windows monopoly by handicapping both Netscape's browser and Sun's Java, two "middleware" products with potential to ultimately erode that monopoly. After describing Microsoft's strategic conduct related to the sale of Internet browser programs, the court concluded that Microsoft had not denied all channels of distribution to rival producers Internet browsers, but had deprived rivals of the most cost efficient methods.[85]

The tendency of such tactics to bolster the Windows monopoly can be illustrated with Netscape's browser. Because Windows is the standard for PCs, most applications are written for it. Comparatively few are available for competing operating systems. This reinforces and protects the Windows monopoly by creating (an applications barrier) to its

---

83. United States v. United Shoe Mach. Corp., 110 F.Supp. 295 (D.Mass.1953), aff'd per curiam, 347 U.S. 521, 74 S.Ct. 699, 98 L.Ed. 910 (1954).

84. 253 F.3d 34 (D.C. Cir. 2001)(en banc). This case is also discussed in § 15.8c4.

85. United States v. Microsoft Corp., 253 F.3d 34, 64 (D.C. Cir. 2001)(en banc).

erosion. The most significant facet of this holding is what the court refused to do. Microsoft contended that courts should never second guess the purposes or effects of any software design decision—that any integration of any previously separate functionalities is per se lawful. The court first rejected this "Gates principle" when it ruled that integrating Explorer into Windows violated Section 2. It did so again when it remanded the Section 1 tying claim for fuller efficiency analysis.

Earlier lower court decisions involving high technology industries were mixed in their results. In *Telex Corp. v. IBM Corp.*,[86] IBM faced erosion of its market share in peripheral equipment sales. It responded by deep price cuts in return for long-term leases with heavy penalties for early termination and by integrating memory components, previously sold as peripherals, into its CPU. Relying largely on *Alcoa*, the trial court found "willful acquisition or maintenance" of monopoly power.[87] The court of appeals, however, rejected this view of the breadth of the monopolization offense. It excused the IBM tactics as ordinary business practices typical of those used in competitive markets, thus implying that the possession of monopoly power put a firm under no greater tactical restraint. Violation would result only when the monopolist's strategy depended on use by the monopolist of its power.

While *Telex* may or may not have reached the right result, it certainly misread Section 2 by overstating the scope of a monopolist's tactical discretion. If there are numerous equal sized firms in a market and one of them uses lease only, long-term requirements, or even tying contracts, competitors are not seriously foreclosed, competitive process is not seriously encumbered, and competitive structure is not seriously threatened. A foreclosure theory was successfully used in the Justice Department's 1994 case against Microsoft which led to a consent decree that prohibited certain strategic conduct apparently designed to foreclose or raise the costs of rival producers of operating system software.[88]

Another type of conduct closely related to tying is the loyalty or bundled rebate. A dominant firm may offer a rebate to customers who buy not only its monopoly product but related products as well. Or, in order to maintain its dominance, a firm may simply provide a progressively larger rebate as the customer buys increasing amounts of the product. These rebates can be a means of enforcing a tie-in or exclusive dealing arrangement and, as such, can be attacked under Section 1 of the Sherman Act or Section 3 of the Clayton Act.[89] In *Le Page's Inc. v. 3M (Minnesota Mining & Manufacturing) Co.*, the court of appeals addressed claims that the defendant was guilty of monopoly maintenance

86. 367 F.Supp. 258 (N.D.Okla.1973), rev'd per curiam, 510 F.2d 894 (10th Cir.), cert. dismissed, 423 U.S. 802, 96 S.Ct. 8, 46 L.Ed.2d 244 (1975).

87. Id. at 335, 341.

88. United States v. Microsoft Corp., 56 F.3d 1448 (D.C.Cir.1995) (per curiam). The Justice Department failed in its effort to use the consent decree for relief against Microsoft's integrated sale of operating software and its browser software. United States v. Microsoft Corp., 147 F.3d 935 (D.C.Cir.1998).

89. See the discussion of tying in § 8.3.

in violation of Section 2.[90] 3M offered bundled loyalty rebates on a product group that included its famous Scotch tape, which nearly all retailers needed, and including its cheap private label tape, which it introduced as a fighting brand "to kill" Le Page's offering. The buyers received no rebate unless they met their quota in purchasing each of six products in the rebate program. 3M had a 90% share of the transparent tape market but never priced below cost. A divided court of appeals upheld a jury verdict for Le Page's, concluding that there was "ample evidence that 3M used its market power over transparent tape, backed by its considerable catalog of products, to entrench its monopoly to the detriment of Le Page's, its only serious competitor."[91]

3.4b6. Aftermarket Abuses

Leveraging frequently occurs in an aftermarket context. Although a seller's concern with reputation may limit to some degree its exercise of aftermarket leverage, the discipline afforded by reputational concerns is, for reasons already discussed, unlikely to be a substitute for competition in the aftermarket.[92] The market power that a producer of original equipment naturally enjoys in the sale of aftermarket products and services can be extended or reinforced in various ways, including through (1) redesign of the original equipment in ways that make existing aftermarket supplies incompatible (discussed in § 3.4b9); and (2) the use of ties and other interbrand foreclosure devices (discussed in § 3.4b5).[93]

3.4b7. Contract Penalty Clauses

Another tactic by which a monopolist may leverage or extend its power is by contract penalty provisions which place heavy costs on buyers or lessees that default on (often long-term) commitments to use the monopolist's product or service.[94] Such provisions seem designed to increase the costs of future entrants. To win business from a buyer, a new entrant must offer a price sufficiently low to offset the buyer's penalty in failing to fulfill an existing contract with the monopolist. Such a barrier to new entry can undercut the critical dynamic component to competition.

The analysis that led Judge Wyzanski to conclude in 1953 that such provisions were harmful has received recent vindication in game theory economic literature.[95] The buyer or lessee who agrees to a contract containing a penalty provision may receive, in return, a lower rate from

90.   324 F.3d 141 (3d Cir. 2003).

91.   Id. at 169.

92.   See § 2.4e2ii.

93.   United States v. United Shoe Mach. Corp., 110 F.Supp. 295 (D.Mass.1953), aff'd per curiam, 347 U.S. 521, 74 S.Ct. 699, 98 L.Ed. 910 (1954); see Eastman Kodak Co. v. Image Technical Servs., Inc., 504 U.S. 451, 112 S.Ct. 2072, 119 L.Ed.2d 265 (1992).

94.   United States v. United Shoe Mach. Corp., 110 F.Supp. 295 (D.Mass.1953), aff'd per curiam, 347 U.S. 521, 74 S.Ct. 699, 98 L.Ed. 910 (1954).

95.   Brodley & Ma, *Contract Penalties, Monopolizing Strategies, and Antitrust Policy*, 45 STAN. L. REV. 1161 (1993) (applying the game theory analysis of Aghion & Bolton, *Contracts as a Barrier to Entry*, 77 AM. ECON. REV. 388 (1987)).

the monopolist. Viewed alone such a rate is a form of limit pricing that discourages entry, conduct that by itself may not be unlawful. But this is limit pricing with an added punch. At the point at which a competitor enters the market, the competitor must offer a price that is not only lower than that of the monopolist, but lower by a margin sufficient to offset the penalty that the contract-breaching buyer must pay. The injury to competition may be substantial.

Game theory analysis assumes that the monopolist offers a discount from the price that it would extract without a penalty clause. In effect, the monopolist-seller and the buyer are sharing the premium that a subsequent entrant must pay. But this relatively benign characterization of the effect on the buyer assumes that the buyer is well informed, a condition that may or may not prevail, and that the buyer will not be influenced by the cartel features of this arrangement. The monopolist-seller such as United Shoe may have offered its contract on a most-favored-nation basis—telling buyers in effect: "you will get the same terms as every other buyer in your industry." The seller is orchestrating cartel-like behavior at the buyer level that tends to dampen the buyer's incentive to bargain for a better deal.[96]

Despite possible cartel features to this conduct at the buyer level, the power remains with the monopolist-seller. Contract penalty clauses offer a further example of leveraging conduct that depends upon isolating the buyer. If the customers of the monopolist could act collectively, they might well decline to sign the monopolist's contract imposing heavy penalties. These customers would, after all, have an interest in leaving the door open for future suppliers who might offer a better or cheaper product. But when confronted in isolation with the monopolist's offer of a lower price in return for agreeing to the penalty clause, most buyers will not resist, fearing that they may otherwise lose ground against rivals who will accept the offer.

3.4b8.   *Control of a Secondary Market—Lease Only Provisions*

In United States v. United Shoe Machinery Corp.,[97] Judge Wyzanski found that the defendant's lease only policy on critical shoe manufacturing machines contributed to the anticompetitive effects of monopolization. One probable effect of lease only policies is to give the monopolist greater control over any secondary, arbitrage market that might exist for its machines. If ownership is retained by the lessor-monopolist, no machines need ever enter the market for resale unless the monopolist itself permits it. As in the case of a contract penalty provision, a customer might prefer to purchase the machine, but may acquiesce in a leasing arrangement because it is the only one offered, particularly if assured that its competitors will likewise not be allowed to purchase.

96. See the discussion of this phenomenon in Krattenmaker & Salop, supra note 44.

97. 110 F.Supp. 295 (D.Mass.1953), aff'd per curiam, 347 U.S. 521, 74 S.Ct. 699, 98 L.Ed. 910 (1954).

Although the anticompetitive effects of this arrangement may have been self-evident to Judge Wyzanski, this has not prevented theorists from advancing arguments that the lease only policy was efficiency-enhancing, allowing the monopolist to earn a higher return without cost to customers (shoe manufacturers) and the ultimate shoe consumer.[98] But the cost of administering the lease only policy almost certainly exceeds the cost of a simple sale, creating an offset to any efficiency gains the monopolist may receive.[99] Moreover, the model on which these arguments are based apparently assumes that customers of United Shoe were prescient and omniscient, knowing in advance whether terms to which they agreed were favorable in light of developments that had not yet occurred. Customers would not, for example, know the quality and price of any competitive offerings that might be made in the future. Indeed, a major purpose of the lease only policy may have been to enhance the effect of exclusive use provisions and contractual penalties. Collectively, these measures appear designed to forestall competitive offerings altogether. Thus, the lease only policy seems to undermine the vital dynamic component to competition. Even assuming that static efficiency gains outweigh anticompetitive losses for such lease only policies, it seems unlikely that any gain that the monopolist receives will be passed on to its customers. Thus, even a small loss to the dynamism of competition brings a loss to the consumer, who receives no wealth transfer gain from the monopolist's greater efficiency.

3.4b9. *Design Change or Product Integration Tying*

Design change or product integration tying, either alone or in combination with other tactics, has been aggressively used at times in the marketplace. A firm that has been selling a unique product that spawns sales for aftermarket products or services may redesign its product to make it more difficult for aftermarket rivals. Or a firm selling a monopoly product and a related non-monopoly product may redesign its offering as a single product. When used by a dominant firm, these tactics can sometimes generate a monopolization complaint. We have emphasized in several subsections that the Section 2 conduct inquiry involves the rule of reason. Under this measure, benefits that can lead to lower prices or improved products for consumers can offset possible harms.

Design changes may involve intellectual property rights, an intersection with antitrust law that is discussed in Chapter 15. Courts doubt the capacity of judicial process to gather enough information and evaluate it sufficiently to sensibly oversee such business judgments. Initial court decisions on design changes are suggestive. In the prior subsection we

---

98. Wiley, et al., *The Leasing Monopolist*, 37 UCLA L. Rev. 693 (1990).

99. Wiley, et al. argue that leasing can be efficient, saving transaction costs. Id. at 710. The authors cite the greater efficiency of renting a car for a short period of use as opposed to buying it and reselling it at the end of the period of use. But the long-term leases involved in *United Shoe Machinery* do not appear to offer these efficiencies because the customer is far less likely to be involved in short-term use of machinery.

discussed *Telex*, where the court rejected a competitor challenge to IBM's decision to "inboard" memory, making it part of the CPU which IBM supplied, rather than a freestanding peripheral which others might supply. California Computer Products, Inc. v. IBM Corp.[100] is similar although the plaintiff offered evidence of " 'technological manipulation' which did not improve performance" and inhibited competitors.[101] Nonetheless, the court concluded that because there was evidence that the design changes also offered consumer advantages, "[t]he reasonableness of IBM's conduct * * * did not present a jury issue."[102] Judge Schnacke's district court opinion in In re IBM Peripheral EDP Devices Antitrust Litigation[103] is the most hospitable to contentions about product change predation. He thought that "[a] more generalized standard, one applicable to all types of otherwise legal conduct by a monopolist" should apply. Thus, "[i]f the design choice is unreasonably restrictive of competition, the monopolist's conduct violates the Sherman Act."[104] While he found no such violation on the evidence before him, he gave this hypothetical example of a violation:

> [I]f a monopolist frequently changed the teleprocessing interface by which its computers communicate with remote terminals in such a way that its terminals would continue to function while others would fail, and, if the only purpose and effect * * * was to gain a competitive advantage * * * that use of monopoly power would be condemned.[105]

Even this formulation can give scant comfort to a competitor adversely affected by the dominant firm's product strategies. No real case will be as easy as the hypothetical. The crucial question is what would be enough to warrant the characterization, "unreasonably restrictive." In a dynamic technological market, one plausible goal of any product manipulation strategy is to increase the capital costs of existing competitors or entrants. In such markets there may be network externalities that magnify the significance both of interoperability and any initial-entry advantage obtained by the dominant firm in an adjacent market. Any tactic which can discourage possible sources of start-up capital and increase the cost of working capital by increasing risks and reducing returns may be devastating to competition. Perhaps a few well-timed changes in the dominant system will be enough to signify a credible threat. Surely, a dominant firm will find it easily possible, in order to gain strategic advantage, to make a design change that can be defended by pointing to some technological advantages for some users.

Design changes that integrate one product (say, a competitive one) into another product (a monopolized one) present a different and perhaps more manageable issue. When, on the basis of consumer demand

100. 613 F.2d 727 (9th Cir.1979).

101. Id. at 744.

102. Id.

103. 481 F.Supp. 965 (N.D.Cal.1979), aff'd sub nom. Transamerica Computer Co. v. IBM Corp., 698 F.2d 1377 (9th Cir.), cert. denied, 464 U.S. 955, 104 S.Ct. 370, 78 L.Ed.2d 329 (1983).

104. Id. at 1003.

105. Id.

and supply-side efficiencies, two distinct products can be identified, each with its own supply and demand curves, integrating those products together and offering them at a single price constitutes a tie. That practice may be perfectly legal. If a grocer offers to sell flour and sugar in a single bundled package, no antitrust violation is involved even though flour and sugar are separate products. Because there is ample competition both for flour and for sugar with or without their bundled sale, the bundling could not harm competition. But if a competitive product is integrated into a monopolized product there is nothing obscure about the effect—it constitutes exclusionary tying. Unless there are demonstrable offsetting efficiency effects not attainable by less restrictive means, significant competitive harm results.[106]

It has been argued that a more relaxed standard should be imposed for product integration bundling. The risk of anticompetitive harm is said to be lower because of the sunk costs and high risks facing a producer who errs in integrating two products that the public would prefer to buy separately.[107] Indeed, the stakes are likely to be higher when a seller makes a substantial investment in integrating two formerly separate products. Some of these costs may be sunk or non-recoverable if the strategy is unsuccessful. If there are networking efficiencies associated with the tied product, the stakes (potential benefits and potential losses) may be greater still. A tie-in implemented through product integration may also be more efficient to enforce. The customer has no choice but to purchase the tied product, so the seller need not worry about a buyer who "cheats" on the contractual tie.[108] But alone or collectively, these distinctions between contractual and product integration ties do not determine overall competitive effect. The distinctions simply show that both the costs and benefits of a product-integration bundling are likely to be higher.

Higher risks mean only that a seller will consider product integration if it is confident of a higher or more certain return on its investment. That return might arise from an efficiency gain but it might also arise from an anticompetitive market distortion. So higher stakes, by themselves, do not support a policy to impose a more relaxed standard on product integration ties. Indeed, if product integration is treated more leniently than contractual tying, a tying seller could be expected to choose product integration precisely when it has reason to expect an antitrust challenge to its conduct.[109]

---

106. But *cf.* United States v. Microsoft Corp., 147 F.3d 935, 946 (D.C.Cir.1998) (majority of the panel held that a consent decree that covered some but not "all 'tying' law under the [Sherman] Act" was not violated by integration of Windows 95 and Explorer).

107. Hylton & Salinger, *Tying Law and Policy: A Decision–Theoretic Approach,* 69 Antitrust L.J. 469, 516–17 (2001).

108. Because product integration ties involve the simultaneous sale of the tying and tied products, one substantial source of a tying seller's power over under-informed consumers is eliminated: there is no deferred purchase of the tied product. There is, however, another major source of exploitable information asymmetries that is often present in high tech industries: the complexity and sophistication of the tying and tied products.

109. This result was predicted by Lessig. See *Microsoft III,* 87 F.Supp.2d 30 (No.

In addition, the high sunk costs involved in product integration may make it less likely that a court will force a reversal of the integration strategy. Consider a judge who is confronted with two anticompetitive tie-ins. The first is effected by contract; the second by product integration. It is relatively simple for a judge to enjoin future use of the contractual tie-in. There is probably little sunk investment in such a tie and less concern about excessive interference with the defendant's operations. In contrast, the same judge may be reluctant to order a redesign of an integrated product. Thus, even if the legal standards for tying by contract or by product integration are identical, a tying seller may perceive tactical advantage in proceeding by product integration. Once the integration is accomplished, momentum favors the tying seller in any litigation that might ensue.

A judge's reluctance to interfere with product integration decisions is well founded. But the risk is that this reluctance will compromise the integrity of tying law and encourage sellers to prefer product integration tying over contractual tying, especially when they believe their conduct may have anticompetitive consequences. Some courts that have examined product integration tying, including the 1998 court of appeals opinion in United States v. Microsoft, have signaled more lenient treatment of product integration tying.[110] The same court addressing similar issues in its 2001 en banc decision, although imposing a rule of reason test for "platform software products," wisely drew no distinction in the legal standard between contractual and product integration tying. Nor did the court, in its analysis of Microsoft's bundling conduct under Section 2, suggest that different legal standards for contractual and product integration tying should apply in a monopolization claim.[111]

An overall assessment of the competitive effects of high tech, product-integration tying is not complete without a careful examination of the role of networking efficiencies. A dominant firm is likely in industries with strong networking efficiencies. As in any industry, superior skill and foresight can lead to a firm earning a substantial market share. But once a firm has become the largest in the industry, networking efficiencies may create a momentum that leads to dominance. This momentum is directly linked to efficiency—the more people in the network, the more useful the network. So how is antitrust law to deal with such industries? The *en banc* 2001 *Microsoft* court, citing dis-

---

98–1233), Brief of Professor Lawrence Lessig as *Amicus Curiae* (filed Feb. 1, 2000).

110. United States v. Microsoft Corp., 147 F.3d 935 (D.C.Cir.1998). In Caldera, Inc. v. Microsoft Corp., 72 F. Supp. 2d 1295, 1322–23 (D. Utah 1999), the court criticized the *Microsoft* court's suggestion that a product integration is lawful as long as the seller offers a "plausible claim that it brings some advantage." The Utah court said:

> Certainly a company should be allowed to build a better mousetrap, and the courts should not deprive a company of the op-

portunity to do so by hindering technological innovation. Yet, antitrust law has developed for good reason, and just as courts have the potential to stifle technological advancements by second guessing product design, so too can product innovation be stifled if companies are allowed to dampen competition by unlawfully tying products together and escape antitrust liability by simply claiming a "plausible" technological advancement.

111. United States v. Microsoft Corp., 253 F.3d 34 (D.C. Cir. 2001)(en banc).

agreements in the literature, drew no definitive conclusions. The court contrasted two views[112]—one that such industries deserved heightened antitrust scrutiny[113]—the other that antitrust should move cautiously because the drive to obtain incumbency in an industry with networking efficiencies can encourage innovation.[114]

Assume that Firm M desires to become the incumbent provider of operating software for personal computers. Networking efficiencies are a powerful incentive for firm M to create an appealing product that will become the industry standard. But once dominance has been achieved, while Firm M still has an incentive to innovate (in order not to lose its incumbent position to a rival offering), Firm M now has an obvious and effective avenue for anticompetitive conduct that will maintain its incumbent position. Consider, for example, how Firm M might integrate two formerly separate products (thereby raising the costs of rivals to offer a substitute product); exercise leverage over writers of applications[115] software not to write, or to write only on less favorable terms, software for rival operating systems; or exercise leverage over computer hardware manufacturers not to load rival operating systems into its machines. The list is not exhaustive, but illustrative of the type of anticompetitive conduct Firm M might be driven to employ in order to maintain its dominant position.

Before Firm M became the dominant firm in the industry, heightened antitrust scrutiny of its conduct would be inappropriate. The predominance firm has no heightened ability to engage in anticompetitive conduct and, at this stage, the potential benefits of innovative change in product offerings are substantial. However, once dominance has been achieved, Firm M will have heightened opportunity (and no reduced incentive) to engage in anticompetitive conduct because of the likely absence of significant competitive discipline. The most likely conditions that lead to reduced competitive discipline are: (1) market dominance (a likely result in networked industries) and (2) exploitable information asymmetries (possible, for example, when complex and sophisticated products are being bundled). The traditional analyses employed in tying cases, then, are very much relevant to the actions of Firm M. If it is demonstrated that the seller's conduct is taken when one or both of these underlying conditions are present, heightened antitrust scrutiny is warranted.[116]

112. *Microsoft III*, 253 F.3d at 49–50.

113. Steven C. Salop & R. Craig Romaine, *Preserving Monopoly: Economic Analysis, Legal Standards, and Microsoft*, 7 Geo. Mason L. Rev. 617, 654–55, 663–64 (1999)(heightened scrutiny of exclusionary conduct in high tech networked industries is necessary because such conduct may deter innovation).

114. Ronald A. Cass & Keith N. Hylton, *Preserving Competition: Economic Analysis, Legal Standards and Microsoft*, 8 Geo. Mason L. Rev. 1, 36–39 (1999)(antitrust implications of networking are unclear because efficiencies of networks may encourage innovation by providing a more durable monopoly to innovating winners).

115. 110 F.Supp. 295, 345 (D. Mass. 1953), citing *Alcoa*, 148 F.2d 416, 431 (2d Cir. 1945).

116. Based upon their premise that a great deal of tying conduct is benign or procompetitive, Hylton and Salinger would disagree with heightened antitrust scrutiny for tying conduct in the context of network

3.4b10.   Miscellaneous Predation: Predatory Overcapacity and Abusive Advertising

The most widely challenged form of predation, price predation, is addressed in Chapter 4. The range of nonprice strategies that firms with power might use to leverage power from one market to another, heighten entry barriers, or raise rivals' costs are as varied as are markets themselves. *Alcoa* and *United Shoe Machinery* used metaphors like "honestly industrial" to distinguish legitimate conduct from conduct exclusionary "in economic effect." Jury instructions often incorporate such phrases, and such an instruction was approved in *Aspen Skiing*, which also emphasized the need to evaluate effects on consumers, intent and the possibility of justification on the basis of efficiency increases. Generalizing, if a plaintiff proves conduct by a monopolist that burdens competitors is serious enough to threaten competitive structure or process, that conduct is unlawfully exclusionary unless the defendant can justify it as reasonably necessary to attain efficiencies yielding offsetting consumer benefits. Possibly valid business justifications are also as varied as markets. They include scale and scope economies, cost reductions in production, marketing and delivery processes, product or service improvements, and the like. A defendant can, of course, introduce evidence to counter the plaintiff's prima facie case—evidence showing that the defendant's conduct does not stifle the plaintiff's competitive efforts or threaten structure or process. If a defendant introduces evidence intending to show resulting efficiencies, the plaintiff would have an opportunity to refute this showing.[117] Each tactic in the caption is certainly capable of providing such benefits, just as are price cuts. Not one of them can be characterized as a threat to competition without being qualified by a negative adjective: excessive or misleading ads; exclusionary, inefficient design changes; predatory plant or equipment expansions leading to exclusionary overcapacity.

The foregoing suggests why there is little solid law dealing with such miscellaneous tactics. In areas such as these, courts are reluctant to intrude into conventional business decision-making. Courts fear stifling constructive and efficient development. There are, however, cases where egregious conduct not associated with any credible efficiency has been condemned under Section 2. A recent example is *Conwood Co., L.P. v. United States Tobacco Co.*, a case in which the defendant monopolist was found to have allowed its sales representatives to destroy or remove retail sales racks placed in stores by rival producers of moist snuff, a chopped smokeless tobacco.[118]

3.4b11.   Disclosure and Nondisclosure Tactics

Disclosure and nondisclosure of product changes are tactics related to product development and change. In the IBM litigation discussed in

---

efficiencies. But their premise, as previously pointed out, is vulnerable because the modified per se rule is likely to screen out almost all beneficial bundling arrangements.

117.   Cf. Data Gen. Corp. v. Grumman Sys. Support Corp., 36 F.3d 1147 (1st Cir. 1994).

118.   290 F.3d 768 (6th Cir. 2002).

§ 3.4b9, peripheral equipment manufacturers complained not just about IBM's interface changes but of its failure to give adequate advance notice of these and other changes so that rivals could respond in timely fashion.[119] Sophisticated firms competing with Microsoft in application fields also complained that where Microsoft plans changes in its operating system, it discloses in advance to important application system suppliers in fields where it has no application software of its own or has a weak market share, but withholds this information from firms competing in application fields where Microsoft itself has a significant position.[120] When used by a monopolist, should strategies of these kinds be unlawful?

A pointed authority is Berkey Photo, Inc. v. Eastman Kodak Co.[121] Kodak, a camera, film and film processing monopolist, had great success with a new, smaller instamatic camera and associated film, seriously reducing the market share of the plaintiff, a rival camera manufacturer. One of Berkey's claims was that Kodak's plans should have been predisclosed to competitors so that they could come to market with competing products before being overwhelmed. The trial court instructed that nondisclosure of new products is an ordinary and acceptable business practice, but that if

> Kodak had monopoly power * * * [that] was so great as to make it impossible for a competitor to compete * * * unless it could offer products similar to Kodak's, you may decide whether in the light of other conduct * * * Kodak's failure to predisclose was on balance * * * exclusionary * * *.'[122]

The Court of Appeals held this to be error. In rejecting predisclosure, the appellate court said:

> But it is difficult to comprehend how a major corporation * * * could possess the omniscience to anticipate all the instances in which a jury might one day in the future retrospectively conclude that predisclosure was warranted. And it is equally difficult to discern workable guidelines that a court might set forth to aid the firm's decision. For example, how detailed must the information conveyed be? And how far must research have progressed before it is "ripe" for disclosure? These inherent uncertainties would have an inevitable chilling effect on innovation. They go far, we believe, towards explaining why no court has never imposed the duty Berkey seeks to create here.[123]

Although the administrative difficulties associated with predisclosure relief may be considerable, the court overstated at least some of

119. IBM Corp. v. Commission of the European Communities, [1981] E.C.R. 2639, [1979–1981 Transfer Binder] Common Mkt. Rep. (CCH) ¶ 8708 (1981).

120. In its 1995 and 1998 proceedings against Microsoft, DOJ did not challenge this type of conduct under § 2 of the Sherman Act.

121. 603 F.2d 263 (2d Cir.1979), cert. denied, 444 U.S. 1093, 100 S.Ct. 1061, 62 L.Ed.2d 783 (1980). The nondisclosure aspects of Berkey are discussed in § 3.5.

122. Berkey, 603 F.2d at 281.

123. Id. at 282 (footnote omitted).

these concerns. For example, it seems clear that research in progress would not have to be disclosed; only concrete plans to introduce a new product that could adversely affect a rival's ability to compete. In some situations there may be a "benchmark" against which to evaluate predisclosure. Microsoft was criticized by some industry participants for nondisclosure allegedly in the following context: it predisclosed planned operating systems improvements to developers of highly successful application programs (even when it offered competing application software itself) because success of its new operating system would require that compatible versions of these operating programs be immediately available. However, in application areas where it thought it could gain significant ground by having its own program compatible with its new operating system ready substantially ahead of competitors, it selectively refused advance disclosure to such competitors. Were the allegations proven, the extent and nature of Microsoft's disclosure practices (where it deemed predisclosure advantageous) could have been used as a benchmark defining the scope of its obligation in those situations where it refused to predisclose. Perhaps because of the broad reach and intrinsic force of the *Berkey* language, perhaps because of doubt about the force of the factual case, perhaps because Microsoft was ready to consent to a decree on narrower grounds, or because of the cumulative force of all three, the Department of Justice did not press this predisclosure claim.[124]

It is also possible to require predisclosure only prospectively, as the EEC did when it required predisclosure of certain IBM products.[125] If this approach were taken by U.S. courts, a firm would be subject to damages only if it failed to carry out a decree that required predisclosure, eliminating concern that damages would be imposed retrospectively to remedy a past failure to disclose. Under this approach, a monopolist's failure to predisclose would not be a conduct abuse sufficient to invoke Section 2, but could be imposed as a remedy to counter other past conduct abuses.[126]

The *Berkey* court's concern that a disclosure duty could discourage innovation is substantial. But in particular cases—*Berkey* may well have been one—there is much to weigh against that concern. For this reason, *Berkey* raises again the issue about whether (or when) rules of reason are tolerable or fixed rules of conduct essential. This is an issue first debated by Justices Peckham and White at the turn of the century[127] and about which Supreme Court sentiment has shifted, first toward *per se* unreasonableness[128] then toward open analysis later in this century.[129]

124. United States v. Microsoft Corp., 56 F.3d 1448 (D.C.Cir.1995) (per curiam).

125. IBM Corp. v. Commission of the European Communities, supra note 94.

126. See § 3.1b4.

127. E.g., United States v. Joint–Traffic Ass'n, 171 U.S. 505, 19 S.Ct. 25, 43 L.Ed. 259 (1898).

128. E.g., United States v. Socony–Vacuum Oil Co., 310 U.S. 150, 60 S.Ct. 811, 84 L.Ed. 1129 (1940); United States v. Topco Assocs., Inc., 405 U.S. 596, 92 S.Ct. 1126, 31 L.Ed.2d 515 (1972).

129. E.g., Broadcast Music, Inc. v. CBS, Inc., 441 U.S. 1, 99 S.Ct. 1551, 60 L.Ed.2d 1 (1979); NCAA v. Board of Regents of Univ. of Okla., 468 U.S. 85, 104 S.Ct. 2948, 82 L.Ed.2d 70 (1984). But cf. Arizona v. Maricopa County Medical Soc'y, 457 U.S. 332, 102 S.Ct. 2466, 73 L.Ed.2d 48 (1982).

Especially when disclosure issues arise in potentially dynamic, high tech markets with strong network advantages for the standard setter, any severe risks that power will be extended through leveraging must be weighed against any danger of discouraging dominant firm innovation. In such markets, it may not be the dominant firm, but one of its competitors, that innovates in ways that redefine the industry. Also, there may be times where the social interest in post innovation competition outweighs the risk of leading firm deterrence. This is possible, for example, if the leading firm's innovation investment would have been made in any event and if early dispersion of any innovation it achieves would lead to improvements in the innovation. Nondisclosure may result in less efficient resource allocation and deadweight loss and to a significant shift from consumer surplus to producer surplus. The Microsoft strategies that Judge Sporkin criticized the Department of Justice for not challenging in the 1995 *Microsoft* suit may illustrate these risks.[130]

What differentiates the current *per se* rule of reason debate from the judicial debate in earlier years is that ideological sides have shifted. At that earlier stage it was those who trusted markets highly and championed allocative efficiency as an antitrust goal who urged judicial analysis and balancing under the rule of reason. They feared excessive *per se* illegality. Today, it tends to be those most cautious of market failures and who insist that antitrust should be concerned about wealth transfers as well as allocative efficiency who urge that courts can balance well enough. Their fear is excessive *per se* legality.

§ 3.5   Monopolization Cases in the Lower Federal Courts

The enduring tension between restraining a monopolist's anticompetitive behavior and protecting a monopolist's right to compete effectively has produced varying formulations of Section 2 enforcement standards. In recent years, a shift has occurred that favors the monopolist's freedom of action. Although this shift is reflected in the language of Supreme Court opinions such as Verizon Communications Inc. v. Trinko[1] and Spectrum Sports, Inc. v. McQuillan,[2] the Court's decision in Aspen Skiing Co. v. Aspen Highlands Skiing Corp.[3] reflects a more traditional concern: Any abuse of a dominant position undermines both fairness and consumer welfare. But with relatively few Supreme Court holdings, the lower courts have had room to establish new law. While their decisions place greater emphasis on the dominant firm's right to compete aggressively, most do so within the framework of traditional Section 2 analysis. However, a few have gone beyond that framework, to the point of

---

130. See the discussion in § 3.1b4.

§ 3.5

1. 540 U.S. 398, 124 S.Ct. 872, 157 L.Ed.2d 823 (2004).

2. 506 U.S. 447, 458, 113 S.Ct. 884, 122 L.Ed.2d 247 (1993) ("this Court and other

courts have been careful to avoid constructions of § 2 which might chill competition, rather than foster it").

3. 472 U.S. 585, 105 S.Ct. 2847, 86 L.Ed.2d 467 (1985).

undermining, if not flatly rejecting, traditional concepts of abusive conduct.

United States v. Dentsply International is a recent example of traditional application.[4] The Third Circuit applied Section 2 to the exclusionary conduct of a defendant enjoying a 75–80 percent market share, 15 times larger than its closest competitor. Dentsply International made prefabricated artificial teeth and sold them primarily through a dealership network. Its dealers resold to dental laboratories that made the dentures supplied to dentists. The Third Circuit reversed a lower court decision and held that Dentsply violated Section 2 when it required its dealers not to purchase artificial teeth from rival producers.

A few decades ago, this decision would have been tantamount to a painless extraction of a loose baby tooth. Against the backdrop of increasing tolerance of dominant firm behavior, the appellate court's vindication of traditional Section 2 case law was more difficult restorative dentistry. Dentsply convinced the district court that the ban on dealer purchases from Dentsply rivals did not contravene the Sherman Act, in part because rivals could bypass dealers and sell directly to dental laboratories. In reversing and imposing liability on Dentsply, the court of appeals reaffirmed Section 2 law and offered a number of noteworthy analytical points.

The court offered a detailed analysis of the gatekeeper power of the dealers and used this analysis to counter the district court's decision that direct sales to dental labs (bypassing the dealers) were a meaningful distribution alternative for Dentsply rivals. The dealers performed an important efficiency-enhancing role for dental labs. A lab could purchase all needed dental supplies, not only artificial teeth but other supplies as well, through one-stop shopping at the dealer. A Dentsply rival seeking to sell directly to a lab would confront the lab's preference for maintaining a single account with a dealer who may offer a volume discount.

The court paid homage to buyer choice as a legitimate goal of antitrust, reasoning that Dentsply's exclusive dealing denied dental labs the opportunity of efficiently choosing among rival producers' artificial teeth through one-stop dealer orders. The court found no credible procompetitive rationale for Dentsply's exclusionary conduct. This decision gives further momentum to the DC Circuit's *Microsoft* opinion and its vindication of a "monopoly maintenance" claim. *Dentsply* may also quiet the interest, sparked by the Supreme Court's decision in *Verizon*, in use of a "profit sacrifice" test that would be the exclusive measure to determine the legality of a dominant firm's exclusionary conduct. The Third Circuit did not employ this test. Indeed, it appears that Dentsply's requirement that dealers buy only *its* teeth, however anticompetitive, resulted in sustaining or increasing, not decreasing, Dentsply profits. *Dentsply* is a strong example of harmful exclusionary conduct that would escape liability if the profit sacrifice test were the sole basis for finding liability.

4.   399 F.3d 181 (3d Cir. 2005).

Dentsply reminds us that a dominant firm's conduct still remains subject to tighter restrictions than its smaller rival. More traditional Section 2 analysis is also reflected in cases such as LePage's Inc. v. 3M Co.[5] and Conwood Co. L.P. v. United States Tobacco Co.[6] In the health care industry, Section 2 has found application in three court of appeals decisions involving the durable medical equipment industry.[7] Durable medical equipment (DME) includes reusable products such as wheelchairs, crutches, walkers and oxygen equipment. Although hospitals provide these products for inpatients, discharged patients have to purchase or rent them for home use. Although the facts varied somewhat, each of the three cases was brought by a provider of DME that had lost business because of alleged predatory or exclusionary practices of a hospital that had acquired an interest in, or made a financial arrangement with, a rival DME provider. The hospital could then influence discharged patients to use only the favored DME provider, to the exclusion of all rivals. Monopoly power was arguably present in these cases because the hospital served a high percentage of hospital patients in the local market.[8] To sustain a monopolization claim, the plaintiff still had to show that this power was leveraged unfairly into the market for DME. The defendants used a number of techniques to influence patients to purchase DME from the favored provider, including denying competing DME suppliers access to hospital patients,[9] pressuring home health care nurses (who received referrals from the hospital) to recommend exclusively the favored DME supplier,[10] or simply ordering DME for outgoing patients from the favored supplier, without informing the patients of alternative sources.[11] The conduct was apparently effective in giving the favored supplier a substantial gain in market share.[12] The courts in each case vindicated leverage theory by reversing an adverse district court holding and reinstating a verdict for the plaintiff,[13] by reversing the lower court's order granting a motion to dismiss,[14] or by reversing summary judgment for the defendant.[15]

5. 324 F.3d 141 (3d Cir. 2003)(discussed in § 3.4b8).

6. 290 F.3d 768 (6th Cir. 2002)(discussed in § 3.4b11).

7. Key Enters., Inc. v. Venice Hosp., 919 F.2d 1550 (11th Cir.1990), vacated per curiam, 979 F.2d 806 (11th Cir.1992), cert. denied, 511 U.S. 1126, 114 S.Ct. 2132, 128 L.Ed.2d 863 (1994); Advanced Health–Care Servs., Inc. v. Radford Community Hosp., 910 F.2d 139 (4th Cir.1990); M & M Medical Supplies & Serv., Inc. v. Pleasant Valley Hosp., Inc., 981 F.2d 160 (4th Cir.1992) (en banc), cert. denied, 508 U.S. 972, 113 S.Ct. 2962, 125 L.Ed.2d 662 (1993). In these three cases, the plaintiffs brought various combinations of claims under Section 2 of the Sherman Act, including monopolization, attempt to monopolize, and conspiracy to monopolize.

8. For example, in the Venice, Florida area, the defendant hospital was found to serve around 80% of the hospital patients. *Key Enters.*, 919 F.2d at 1553.

9. *Advanced Health–Care*, 910 F.2d at 150.

10. *Key Enters.*, 919 F.2d at 1555.

11. *M & M Medical Supplies*, 981 F.2d at 166–68.

12. For example, in *Key Enterprises*, the favored supplier had only 9.2% of the DME market before it entered into a joint venture with the hospital. Afterwards, its market share rose to 61%. *Key Enters.*, 919 F.2d at 1555.

13. Id. at 1550, 1566–68.

14. *Advanced Health–Care*, 910 F.2d at 149–50.

15. *M & M Medical Supplies*, 981 F.2d at 166–68.

The Second Circuit's 1945 decision in *Alcoa*[16] may have been the high point of restricting competitive options for dominant firms. Some thirty years after *Alcoa*, the same court in Berkey Photo, Inc. v. Eastman Kodak Co., signaled a shift in the balance favorable to the dominant firm's freedom of action.[17] Kodak dominated the film, camera and processing markets and had recently developed a new pocket-sized camera requiring small format film. Kodak simultaneously tried to develop a new film that would produce high definition pictures in the small format. Despite problems with the film's quality, Kodak went ahead with joint promotion efforts for the new film used in the new camera.

Berkey, a camera competitor, alleged that Kodak's conduct violated Section 2 of the Sherman Act in three ways. In § 3.4b11 we mentioned Berkey's contention that because of Kodak's great power in the camera market, Kodak had a duty to predisclose specifications about its new camera before introduction. Berkey also argued that Kodak engaged in cross-leveraging between camera and film markets that enhanced its power in each by selling its new camera and film as an integrated system. Here, Berkey stressed that the conduct was improperly exclusionary because it was both deliberate and avoidable. Finally, Berkey argued that by producing its new film only in a size that fit the new camera, Kodak was leveraging its power in the film market into the camera market, giving Kodak an advantage in the camera market that had nothing to do with the relative merits of competing cameras. The jury agreed with Berkey's allegations and awarded damages, which after trebling and attorneys' fees amounted to $87 million.[18]

The Second Circuit reversed.[19] Rejecting Berkey's first theory, the court held that a requirement that a monopolist predisclose its innovations would discourage innovation by the monopolist.[20] The worry about dampening innovation incentives is legitimate, but the analysis is one-sided and incomplete.[21] Any fine tuning of the levels of protection available to innovators, whether by granting more protection or reducing the scope of protection, can only be adequately evaluated by considering both the effect of the change on the level of investment in innovation and the rate at which inventions, once achieved, are dispersed, commercialized and improved upon. This would obviously be true for any change in the law making patents easier or more difficult to obtain. But it is also manifestly true for refinements such as how innovation investments and their outputs are evaluated under the antitrust laws.

16. United States v. Aluminum Co. of America, 148 F.2d 416 (2d Cir.1945).

17. 603 F.2d 263 (2d Cir.1979), cert. denied, 444 U.S. 1093, 100 S.Ct. 1061, 62 L.Ed.2d 783 (1980).

18. Id. at 268.

19. Id.

20. See the discussion in § 3.1b4 about the possible relevance of this holding to the *Microsoft* litigation.

21. See the discussion in § 3.4b9. See also the theoretical discussion in Sullivan, *Section 2 of the Sherman Act and Vertical Strategies by Dominant Firms,* 21 Sw. U. L. REV. 1227, 1248–50 (1992).

Consider a possible change in the patent law in order to illustrate the analytical issues. Suppose that the standards that had to be met to obtain patent protection were greatly reduced. Such a policy change would surely encourage some additional investment in innovation. But is there any reason for predicting that it would serve the goal of more efficient resource allocation? More investment in innovation might come at an appalling cost, including: supracompetitive returns on all innovation resulting from reduced dispersion of and access to newly patentable inventions and suppression through noncommercialization of many newly patentable inventions that now reach the market. Monopolists are often slow to market innovative products, processes or capital equipment even when they own the rights to them. Older capital may not be fully amortized, or older products may offer a better cost-price ratio than those anticipated for the innovation. During the early part of this century, for example, the Bell System monopoly was slow to introduce automatic switching machines that eliminated manually operated local switchboards. Small independent companies were the first to bring this cost-saving and convenience-enhancing technology into local telephone exchanges.[22] Similar behavior is evident in the record in the *Berkey* case. In a portion of the opinion applying Section 1 of the Sherman Act, the court found that Kodak had unlawfully conspired to delay introduction of a new electronic flash device developed by General Electric, making it unavailable to consumers and competitors such as Berkey that could have incorporated it into their cameras.[23]

Although the issue of innovation is complex, there is neither conclusive empirical evidence nor a convincing theoretical case that protecting a monopolist from competitive discipline will produce more innovation or ensure its more rapid marketing.[24] After surveying both theory and available empirical evidence, Scherer and Ross conclude that while some degree of concentration may further innovation, very high concentration levels are more likely to retard progress by restricting the number of independent providers. They also conclude that barriers to entry must be kept low to allow for the benefits of "technically audacious newcomers."[25] The strongest impetus for innovation in many industries may be the need of any firm to stay current in technology so that consumers, in the exercise of a natural competitive function, will continue to value the firm's products. Moreover, the monopoly rewards that flow from allowing a monopolist to leverage its power into another market will create rewards for the monopolist that may have little bearing on the underlying value of the invention to society. A patent monopoly is likely to be profitable in direct proportion to the value that society places on the invention. But when a monopolist innovator withholds an invention from the market, or attempts to use it to leverage power into different

22. H.R. Rep. No. 96–1252 Pt.2, 96th Cong., 2d Sess. 5 (1980).

23. 603 F.2d at 301–03.

24. F. M. Scherer & D. Ross, Industrial Market Structure and Economic Performance 626–30, 644–60 (3d ed. 1990).

25. Id. at 653–54, 660.

markets, additional variables affect profitability that may have little or nothing to do with the underlying value of the invention.[26]

On the question of what market share is adequate to trigger a finding of monopoly power, a 1981 decision of the Second Circuit provides some useful language. In Broadway Delivery Corp. v. United Parcel Service of America, Inc.,[27] the plaintiff alleged a relevant market consisting of the pickup and delivery in the New York area of wholesale packages weighing less than 50 pounds. Based on a jury instruction that the defendants must be found to have at least 50 percent of the relevant market, the jury found for the defendants. Although the court found this jury instruction to be harmless error on the facts before it, the court's opinion provides useful guidance on market share requirements:

> The trend of guidance from the Supreme Court and the practice of most courts endeavoring to follow that guidance has been to give only weight and not conclusiveness to market share evidence * * *.

> * * *

> The extent to which market characteristics should be explained to the jury in a particular case will vary with the nature of the underlying facts and the expert testimony. Sometimes, but not inevitably, it will be useful to suggest that a market share below 50% is rarely evidence of monopoly power * * * and a share above 70% is usually strong evidence of monopoly power. But when the evidence presents a fair jury issue of monopoly power, the jury should not be told that it must find monopoly power lacking below a specified share or existing above a specified share.[28]

§ 3.6 Attempts to Monopolize

Plaintiffs bringing suit under Section 2 of the Sherman Act frequently combine a claim for monopolization with one for attempt to monopolize. If it cannot be shown that a defendant has achieved monopoly power, a lesser showing may still suffice for the attempt claim. A plaintiff makes a showing of attempt to monopolize by proving "(1) that the defendant has engaged in predatory or anticompetitive conduct with (2) a specific intent to monopolize and (3) a dangerous probability of achieving monopoly power."[1] A showing of dangerous probability of monopolization in turn requires the plaintiff to establish a relevant market in which to measure the defendant's power.[2]

26. This issue is analyzed in Grimes, *Antitrust Tie–In Analysis After* Kodak: *Understanding the Role of Market Imperfections,* 62 ANTITRUST L.J. 263, 290–91 (1994).

27. 651 F.2d 122 (2d Cir.1981), cert. denied, 454 U.S. 968, 102 S.Ct. 512, 70 L.Ed.2d 384 (1981).

28. Id. at 128–29.

§ 3.6

1. Spectrum Sports, Inc. v. McQuillan, 506 U.S. 447, 456, 113 S.Ct. 884, 122 L.Ed.2d 247 (1993).

2. Id.; Walker Process Equip., Inc. v. Food Mach. & Chem. Corp., 382 U.S. 172, 177, 86 S.Ct. 347, 15 L.Ed.2d 247 (1965).

3.6a. Policy Issues in Attempt to Monopolize Cases

3.6a1. Balancing Power and Conduct

Many attempt to monopolize cases might be characterized as embryonic monopolization cases. Even if lacking the requisite monopoly power to establish monopolization, the defendant may be well on its way to achieving that power. Although the Supreme Court's test for attempt to monopolize does not directly require a showing of monopoly or near monopoly power, the necessity to show significant power is inherent in demonstrating a dangerous probability of achieving a monopolization. Doing this "requires inquiry into the relevant product and geographic market and the defendant's economic power in that market."[3] Although at least one lower court has attempted to set a market share limit,[4] the Supreme Court has so far declined to do so. As a practical matter, a firm with a small market share is an unlikely target of an attempt to monopolize claim unless a single brand market is accepted as, for example, may occur in aftermarket sales. The Supreme Court's decision in Eastman Kodak Co. v. Image Technical Services, Inc.[5] leaves the door open for such a showing. Of course, the mere existence of an aftermarket does not by itself show sufficient power to undermine competition. Success in efforts to extend or maintain this power at the expense of competitive discipline is also required.[6]

Although significant power is requisite, near monopoly power ought not to be required if the defendant's conduct is unambiguously anticompetitive. In Lorain Journal Co. v. United States,[7] the defendant operated the only newspaper to serve Lorain and adjoining communities. The relevant market for purposes of the Court's analysis was the "mass dissemination of news and advertising, both of a local and national character."[8] When an independently owned radio station based in a nearby community began to serve Lorain, the defendant refused to accept newspaper advertisements from any firm that advertised on the radio station. The conduct had no apparent explanation other than an intent to drive the radio station from the market. Indeed, many purchasers evidently preferred the option of advertising on the radio as well as in the local newspaper, so consumer welfare would have been enhanced had the Journal accepted business from radio advertisers. Although an implicit finding of some market power is apparent (otherwise the defendant would not have constituted a threat to the radio station), the Court

---

3. *Spectrum Sports*, 506 U.S. at 459.

4. M & M Medical Supplies & Serv., Inc. v. Pleasant Valley Hosp., Inc., 981 F.2d 160, 168 (4th Cir.1992) (en banc) (indicating market shares above 50% will be sufficient, but allowing some room for a showing of a violation with shares between 30% and 50%), cert. denied, 508 U.S. 972, 113 S.Ct. 2962, 125 L.Ed.2d 662 (1993). See also Sixth Circuit case saying 50–55% insufficient in medical practice group case, cited 72 ATRR 1809, pg.432 (5/1/97).

5. 504 U.S. 451, 112 S.Ct. 2072, 119 L.Ed.2d 265 (1992).

6. See the discussion of aftermarket abuses in § 3.4b6.

7. 342 U.S. 143, 72 S.Ct. 181, 96 L.Ed. 162 (1951); see also United States v. American Airlines, Inc., 743 F.2d 1114 (5th Cir. 1984), cert. dismissed, 474 U.S. 1001, 106 S.Ct. 420, 88 L.Ed.2d 370 (1985).

8. *Lorain Journal*, 342 U.S. at 147.

made no finding that the defendant possessed monopoly or near monopoly power in the mass media market.

Lorain Journal suggests a sliding scale for determining an attempt to monopolize. As the severity of the anticompetitive conduct increases, a lesser showing of market power may suffice. On the other hand, if the defendant has achieved near monopoly measured in market share, a lesser showing of anticompetitive conduct may suffice to establish an attempt to monopolize. Such flexibility increases the utility of attempt claims in filling the loophole for single firm anticompetitive conduct that escapes prohibition under Section 1 while also falling short of full-fledged monopolization. When economic theory and supporting evidence show a genuine anticompetitive injury, the use of the attempt to monopolize claim to challenge the abusive conduct is consistent with the language of Section 2 and with the intent of the antitrust laws.

This broader use of the attempt claims has met with some success in the courts (see § 3.4b), but is countered by the need to avoid interpretations of Section 2 that " 'will dampen the competitive zeal of a single aggressive entrepreneur.' "[9] It is also clear that no matter how blatantly anticompetitive the conduct, there is no attempt offense if the defendant's position in a contestable market impeaches all possibility of monopolization.[10] But as *Lorain Journal* demonstrates, many actions of single firms that do not yet approach monopoly are unambiguously anticompetitive. At least at the margin where claims about risk of monopoly become credible, the interdiction of such conduct should be no more threatening to aggressive competition than other well-reasoned applications of the Sherman Act.

3.6a2. *The Role of Intent*

The genesis of the intent requirement for attempt to monopolize is Justice Holmes' opinion in Swift & Co. v. United States.[11] Justice Holmes kept Section 2 in line with other "attempt" offenses recognized by the law. If conduct in and of itself did not monopolize, "an intent to bring it to pass is necessary in order to produce a dangerous probability that it will happen."[12] Other language in the opinion was construed by one court of appeals as waiving the dangerous probability requirement when the requisite intent requirement was otherwise met.[13] That minority view was rejected by the Supreme Court in Spectrum Sports, Inc. v. McQuillan.[14] After *Spectrum,* it is clear that there must be a showing of a

9. Spectrum Sports, Inc. v. McQuillan, 506 U.S. 447, 456, 113 S.Ct. 884, 122 L.Ed.2d 247 (1993) (quoting dicta from Copperweld Corp. v. Independence Tube Corp., 467 U.S. 752, 768, 104 S.Ct. 2731, 81 L.Ed.2d 628 (1984)).

10. United States v. Empire Gas Corp., 537 F.2d 296 (8th Cir.1976), cert. denied, 429 U.S. 1122, 97 S.Ct. 1158, 51 L.Ed.2d 572 (1977).

11. 196 U.S. 375, 25 S.Ct. 276, 49 L.Ed. 518 (1905).

12. Id. at 396.

13. Lessig v. Tidewater Oil Co., 327 F.2d 459, 474 (9th Cir.), cert. denied, 377 U.S. 993, 84 S.Ct. 1920, 12 L.Ed.2d 1046 (1964).

14. 506 U.S. 447, 457–59, 113 S.Ct. 884, 122 L.Ed.2d 247 (1993).

dangerous probability of monopolization even if the intent requirement is met.

Other questions remain about the nature of the intent and how it must be demonstrated. The Supreme Court has indicated that the intent must be "more than an intent to compete vigorously."[15] But a showing of predatory or anticompetitive conduct "may be sufficient to prove the necessary intent to monopolize."[16] Thus, a strong showing of an unambiguously anticompetitive act may obviate the need for any further showing of intent. This result is sound. The conduct and its effects are at the core of antitrust and may be the surest indicator of probable intent. Other types of intent evidence, such as internal firm documents written by employees, may reflect the biased views of someone not privy to all of the facts or seeking to influence their interpretation. Still, such evidence can be relevant to establishing a violation. For one thing, internal documents are not always ambiguous, nor mere arguments presented in the course of policy formation. Sometimes they may be clear reflections of settled, consensus policy. In close cases in which the court has difficulty determining the competitive effect of conduct, internal documents may also be useful in showing how the firm views its own conduct. Despite some risks that such documents may be rhetorically biased, they may be valuable evidence of persons with expertise and first hand knowledge of the likely effect of commercial conduct.[17]

3.6b. Attempt to Monopolize Cases in the Courts

Because claims of attempt to monopolize are frequently married to monopolization claims, delimiting the unique case law that applies only to attempt cases is difficult. There are some areas, however, where claims of attempt have resulted in specialized rules of interpretation. One such area is predatory pricing. Plaintiffs who bring predatory pricing suits under Section 2 of the Sherman Act routinely include attempt to monopolize claims (see the discussion in chapter 4). Perhaps the largest group of attempt cases involves unilateral conduct by a firm that possesses a degree of market power insufficient to sustain a finding of monopoly power. The same tension exists in these cases that is found in monopolization cases. On the one hand, the courts have sought to strike down unilateral conduct that is unambiguously anticompetitive.[18] On the other hand, they have sought to avoid broad interpretations of the attempt offense that could stifle legitimate competitive initiatives.[19]

In *Spectrum Sports, Inc. v. McQuillan,* a terminated regional distributor of a shock-absorbing plastic product useful in medical, athletic and equestrian products sued the patent-holder and manufacturer for attempted monopolization. The distributor had used the patented plastic

15. Id. at 459.

16. Id.

17. See the discussion of the role of intent in establishing predatory pricing in § 4.3c.

18. Lorain Journal Co. v. United States, 342 U.S. 143, 72 S.Ct. 181, 96 L.Ed. 162 (1951).

19. Spectrum Sports, Inc. v. McQuillan, 506 U.S. 447, 113 S.Ct. 884, 122 L.Ed.2d 247 (1993).

to develop a horseshoe pad. Relying on language from a 1905 Supreme Court case involving attempted monopolization[20] and Ninth Circuit interpretation of that language,[21] the distributor argued that no showing of power in the relevant market was required and that a showing of the defendant's unfair or predatory conduct would satisfy both the specific intent and the dangerous probability elements of the offense. Verdict was entered for the distributor and the Ninth Circuit affirmed. The Supreme Court reversed and remanded. The Court held, in line with the larger number of circuits, that a showing of intent did not obviate the need to establish a dangerous probability of monopolization. In remanding the case to the circuit, the Court did not challenge the lower courts' conclusion that the defendant had engaged in predatory conduct.

The narrow issue resolved in *Spectrum Sports* is unlikely to return. Instead, *Spectrum* may be more frequently cited for its dictum that favors antitrust interpretations that allow competitor freedom to compete aggressively. Indeed, a bent favoring even a risky freedom of action has governed the result in a number of recent circuit holdings.[22] Thus, in United States v. Empire Gas Corp.,[23] the court was faced with a record of unambiguously anticompetitive conduct. Empire was a large wholesaler and retailer of liquefied petroleum, including propane and butane. Although it operated in 24 other states, Empire's conduct was specifically challenged only in local markets in Missouri. In these markets, Empire had apparently sought to coordinate oligopolistic price increases for liquefied petroleum products. There was evidence that if a local rival refused to cooperate, Empire drastically reduced its prices in the rival's territory; Empire's salesmen told customers that the rival was going out of business; and Empire occasionally acquired the supply source (after which it raised the wholesale price to the rival). Despite this record of conduct, the district court found for the defendant and the Eighth Circuit affirmed. The court of appeals found no dangerous probability of success. In two local markets in which Empire's market share was highest (around 50 percent), the court found no evidence that Empire's threats or actions had forced a rise in retail prices. In other areas where the conduct may have been more successful in damaging rivals, Empire's market share was significantly lower. Implicit in the court's holding is a rigidity of interpretation (requiring strict adherence to a 50 percent market share and predatory conduct in the same market) that seems at odds with the Court's decision in *Lorain Journal*,[24] where unambiguous-

---

20. Swift & Co. v. United States, 196 U.S. 375, 25 S.Ct. 276, 49 L.Ed. 518 (1905).

21. Lessig v. Tidewater Oil Co., 327 F.2d 459 (9th Cir.), cert. denied, 377 U.S. 993, 84 S.Ct. 1920, 12 L.Ed.2d 1046 (1964).

22. Alaska Airlines, Inc. v. United Airlines, Inc., 948 F.2d 536 (9th Cir.1991), cert. denied, 503 U.S. 977, 112 S.Ct. 1603, 118 L.Ed.2d 316 (1992).

23. 537 F.2d 296 (8th Cir.1976), cert. denied, 429 U.S. 1122, 97 S.Ct. 1158, 51 L.Ed.2d 572 (1977).

24. Lorain Journal Co. v. United States, 342 U.S. 143, 72 S.Ct. 181, 96 L.Ed. 162 (1951).

ly anticompetitive conduct led to liability without extensive analysis of market share.[25]

§ 3.7   Conspiracy to Monopolize

To establish a conspiracy to monopolize in violation of Section 2 of the Sherman Act, a plaintiff must show, in addition to the conspiracy itself, an intent and purpose to exercise monopoly power.[1] In line with common law conspiracy requirements, at least one overt act in furtherance of the conspiracy is required. The plaintiff need not show that the defendants possessed monopoly power, or even that there was a dangerous probability of monopolizing, but merely that they conspired to and made some effort to attain it. If all the cigarette manufacturers in the country met and signed an agreement to merge into a single firm, they would have conspired to monopolize even though they remain as yet vigorous competitors.

Despite the advantage of not having to demonstrate attained or threatened monopoly power, plaintiffs allege conspiracy to monopolize less often than monopolization or attempt. One reason is that the conspiracy element requires more than unilateral conduct. If a showing of conspiracy can be made, many plaintiffs prefer to proceed under Section 1 of the Sherman Act, perhaps because the plaintiffs hope to gain the benefits of a *per se* rule or other standard requiring a lesser showing on the merits. Indeed, the conspiracy showing itself is more difficult under Section 2 than Section 1. Showing conspiracy under Section 2 probably requires maneuvering around all of the pitfalls for establishing a conspiracy under Section 1,[2] and also requires a showing of intent to monopolize and at least one overt act in furtherance of the conspiracy. In addition, it must be shown that if the conspiracy is successful, monopoly will result.

Despite these difficulties, plaintiffs often advance a conspiracy to monopolize claim in conjunction with a monopolization claim under Section 2 and a conspiracy in restraint of trade claim under Section 1.[3] This gives the fact finder an additional opportunity to find for the plaintiff.[4] It is possible that a conspiracy claim will meet with success

---

25. Three decisions reflecting a more sympathetic response to attempted monopoly claims involve the durable medical equipment industry (reusable health aids such as crutches, wheel chairs, walkers, and oxygen equipment). See § 3.5 n.7. These cases sustained attempt to monopolize claims involving conduct that appeared unambiguously anticompetitive.

§ 3.7

1. American Tobacco Co. v. United States, 328 U.S. 781, 809, 66 S.Ct. 1125, 90 L.Ed. 1575 (1946).

2. For example, the plaintiff cannot show a conspiracy between two subsidiaries of the same firm. See the discussion in § 5.2c.

3. See, e.g., Key Enters., Inc. v. Venice Hosp., 919 F.2d 1550 (11th Cir.1990), vacated per curiam, 979 F.2d 806 (11th Cir. 1992), cert. denied, 511 U.S. 1126, 114 S.Ct. 2132, 128 L.Ed.2d 863 (1994); Advanced Health–Care Servs., Inc. v. Radford Community Hosp., 910 F.2d 139 (4th Cir.1990); Monument Builders of Greater Kansas City, Inc. v. American Cemetery Ass'n, 891 F.2d 1473 (10th Cir.1989), cert. denied, 495 U.S. 930, 110 S.Ct. 2168, 109 L.Ed.2d 498 (1990); Directory Sales Management Corp. v. Ohio Bell Tel. Co., 833 F.2d 606 (6th Cir.1987).

4. For example, the jury found a conspiracy to monopolize, a finding that was upheld on appeal, in *Key Enters.*, 919 F.2d at 1564–65.

when other Section 2 claims fail because of an inability to show that sufficient market power has been attained. Although a conspiracy to monopolize claim obviates the need to establish monopoly power or a dangerous probability of attaining it, questions of market structure cannot be eliminated. A plan to merge a candy manufacturer with a railroad, for example, could hardly be found a conspiracy to monopolize. To establish such a conspiracy, the defendants' plans must be aimed toward achieving market power in an identified relevant market.[5]

§ 3.8   Monopsony

Monopsony is often thought of as the flip side of monopoly. A monopolist is a seller with no rivals; a monopsonist is a buyer with no rivals. A monopolist has power over price exercised by limiting output. A monopsonist also has power over price, but this power is exercised by limiting aggregate purchases.[1] Monopsony injures efficient allocation by reducing the quantity of the input product or service below the efficient level.

Monopsony is thought to be more likely when there are buyers of specialized products or services or when the seller of the product or service has substantial sunk costs that make it more difficult for the seller to abandon its business. For example, a sports league may exercise monopsony (or oligopsony) power in purchasing the services of professional athletes, in part because of the sunk costs that an athlete has invested in developing a relevant set of skills. An owner of a chain of movie theaters, some of which are the sole theaters in small towns, may have monopsony power in the purchase or lease of movies. Cable TV franchises may exercise monopsony power in purchasing television channels that will be offered to their subscribers. Even when the products are not highly specialized, a buyer with a dominant market share may exercise monopsony power. Cattlemen have complained that beef slaughterhouses are now concentrated in the hands of a few, giving these firms oligopsony power in the purchase of cattle. Although not a monopsonist, a retailer with as little as 10 per cent of the market may have substantial gatekeeper power over suppliers who have a much larger market share. See the discussion in § 2.7. Because retailer buying power is exercisable at relatively low market share levels, it may be less suited to attack under Section 2. This power, however, is very much relevant to the competitive assessment of vertical restraints, addressed in Chapters VI and VII.

Antitrust law has been slow to develop a coherent set of principles for assessing monopsony power. One reason for this is that many firms

---

5. Two cases in which conspiracy to monopolize claims were upheld are *Key Enters.*, 919 F.2d 1550 (reversing district court and restoring a jury verdict for the plaintiff), and *Advanced Health–Care*, 910 F.2d 139 (reversing a district court order granting a motion to dismiss).

§ 3.8

1. For a discussion of the economic injury underlying monopsony power, see R. BLAIR & J. HARRISON, MONOPSONY: ANTITRUST LAW AND ECONOMICS (1993); D. CARLTON & J. PERLOFF, MODERN INDUSTRIAL ORGANIZATION 152–57 (2d ed. 1994).

possessing monopsony power in the purchase of goods or services also possess monopoly power when the goods or services are resold. For example, the monopsony power that a cable TV franchise possesses in purchasing television programming becomes monopoly power when that programming is distributed to the franchise's cable subscribers. When a monopsonist is also a monopolist, attacking the monopoly conduct may be the politically more viable enforcement option because the monopoly conduct has a direct impact on the price paid by consumers. But a monopsonist is not necessarily also a monopolist. In labor markets, a buyer of specialized workers (or the sole employer in a geographic region) may possess monopsony power, yet may compete with other firms in the sale of its finished product. Sports leagues often enjoy a degree of monopsony power in contracting with specialized athletes. Those same leagues may also be oligopolists in staging athletic contests for their particular sport. Yet, because spectators may have choices in deciding which sport or other leisure time entertainment to patronize, the league may be subject to a degree of competitive discipline at the output end that is not present when the league exercises its monopsony power to purchase the services of specialized athletes.[2]

Although there is no theoretical basis for assuming that monopsony power is less injurious to consumer welfare than monopoly power, the direct injury that monopsony occasions is to the seller of goods and services, not to the end consumer. To the extent antitrust chooses politically popular enforcement initiatives, it is understandable that it would focus on a monopoly that raises prices to consumers rather than a monopsony that depresses prices to sellers. But antitrust attacks on monopsony abuses do occur and enforcement efforts can lead to a potentially wider interest in market power abuses of powerful buyers. For example, in addressing vertical restraints, the theoretical literature has increasingly recognized that some restraints are a product of market power in the hands of downstream dealers that buy from their suppliers.[3] Increased public interest also followed the Federal Trade Commission's pursuit of a vertical restraints case against Toys "R" Us alleging that the powerful retail chain exercised monopsony power in preventing suppliers from selling on equal terms to other retailers.[4]

The Supreme Court has mentioned monopsony power only rarely.[5] Still, although the Court did not use the term "monopsony," it has not hesitated in a number of cases to apply Section 2 of the Sherman Act to monopsony power. An early example of this was the 1911 *Standard Oil* case, involving allegations that Standard Oil used its monopsony power

2. Ross, *The Misunderstood Alliance Between Sports Fans, Players, and the Antitrust Laws*, 1997 U. ILL. L. REV. 519.

3. See Klor's, Inc. v. Broadway–Hale Stores, Inc., 359 U.S. 207, 79 S.Ct. 705, 3 L.Ed.2d 741 (1959); Business Elecs. Corp. v. Sharp Elecs. Corp., 485 U.S. 717, 108 S.Ct. 1515, 99 L.Ed.2d 808 (1988); Grimes, *Brand Marketing, Intrabrand Competition,*

and the Multibrand Retailer: The Antitrust Law of Vertical Restraints, 64 ANTITRUST L.J. 83 (1995).

4. The *Toys "R" Us* case is discussed in § 7.6.

5. NCAA v. Board of Regents of Univ. of Okla., 468 U.S. 85, 93, 104 S.Ct. 2948, 82 L.Ed.2d 70 (1984).

over the railroads to dictate the terms by which the railroads would deal with rivals of Standard Oil. Standard Oil was by no means the sole purchaser of railroad transportation, but its substantial position in the oil industry and the relative importance of a railroad maintaining its petroleum business probably gave Standard Oil a substantial measure of monopsony power. The Justice Department directed another Section 2 attack on monopsony power at movie theater owners in United States v. Griffith.[6] In *Griffith,* the defendants owned movie theaters in towns in Oklahoma, Texas and New Mexico, some of them in competition with rival theaters in the same town, others operating as the sole theater in town. The Justice Department successfully invoked Section 2 in condemning the defendants use of their buying power to gain favorable terms from movie distributors. Each of these historic Section 2 cases is discussed in § 3.2.[7]

The unspoken premise of *Griffith* is that the Court will apply the same standards of proof to a monopsony claim under Section 2 that it would apply to a monopolization claim. Thus, a plaintiff would have to establish that the defendant possesses monopsony power in a relevant market and that the defendant is guilty of a conduct abuse. The lower courts appear to follow this supposition.[8]

6. 334 U.S. 100, 68 S.Ct. 941, 92 L.Ed. 1236 (1948).

7. The Supreme Court has also not hesitated to apply Section 1 of the Sherman Act against conspiracies among buyers to exercise monopsony power in the purchase of livestock or sugar or in the leasing of motion pictures. Swift & Co. v. United States, 196 U.S. 375, 25 S.Ct. 276, 49 L.Ed. 518 (1905) (conspiracy among buyers not to bid against one another at livestock auctions); Mandeville Island Farms, Inc. v. American Crystal Sugar Co., 334 U.S. 219, 68 S.Ct. 996, 92 L.Ed. 1328 (1948) (conspiracy among sugar refiners to keep down the price paid farmers for sugar beets); Interstate Circuit, Inc. v. United States, 306 U.S. 208, 59 S.Ct. 467, 83 L.Ed. 610 (1939) (conspiracy involving both exhibitors and distributors in which the exhibitors exercised monopsony power to dictate the terms of film leasing to rivals of the exhibitors).

8. Chicago Professional Sports Ltd. Partnership v. NBA, 95 F.3d 593 (7th Cir. 1996); Silverman v. Major League Baseball Player Relations Comm., Inc., 67 F.3d 1054 (2d Cir.1995); U.S. Healthcare, Inc. v. Healthsource, Inc., 986 F.2d 589 (1st Cir. 1993).

Chapter IV

PRICE PREDATION

Table of Sections

---

§ 4.1 Introduction

4.1a. Price Predation Defined

Price predation, like other antitrust violations, is a power offense. Although definitions of price predation vary, all encompass a market participant's use of low prices to injure competition. An encompassing definition that should include all instances of competitive injury—and one used throughout this chapter—is that price predation occurs when a market participant with market power uses low prices in a manner that creates allocation injuries or undermines the dynamic component of competition (by discouraging entry or innovation). A narrower definition employed in recent Supreme Court decisions would limit price predation to the use of low prices that are below some measure of the seller's cost and that may reasonably be recouped by the seller.[1]

---

§ 4.1

1. Brooke Group Ltd. v. Brown & Williamson Tobacco Corp., 509 U.S. 209, 222, 113 S.Ct. 2578, 125 L.Ed.2d 168 (1993); Matsushita Elec. Indus. Co. v. Zenith Radio Corp., 475 U.S. 574, 584 n. 8, 588–89, 106 S.Ct. 1348, 89 L.Ed.2d 538 (1986). Although the Supreme Court's definition is narrower in its coverage, it is at least theoretically broader in one respect because it is not

Price predation should be distinguished from competitive below cost pricing. In conditions of overcapacity, firms in industries with relatively high fixed costs and relatively low variable costs may, competing intensely, cut prices below full costs. Each firm is under pressure to make sales that will cover all of the associated variable costs and contribute something toward the implacable fixed costs. Section 1 case law has consistently rejected the contention that competition is bad in such situations and that competing firms should be permitted to agree that none will engage in below cost pricing.[2] So-called "predatory pricing" is price-cutting in a different context: One firm possesses or is ambitious to possess significant market power. It cuts its prices to some or all buyers hoping to drive competitors out of the market or to force them to give up some aggressive strategy that the predator wants to stifle. Competitors can be hurt by such tactics. Can consumers? Resource allocation? In the short run such pricing obviously helps consumers. If, however, the predatory strategy succeeds and targeted competitors are driven out or effectively disciplined, the predator may be able to raise prices and to sustain them at supracompetitive levels. Predatory pricing such as this may be vulnerable under Sherman Section 2 or, if it involves some form of price discrimination (for example, predatory prices in the target firm's geographic market, not elsewhere), it may violate the Robinson–Patman Act.[3]

Nonprice predatory practices by those possessing market power are addressed in § 3.4b9. Predatory pricing is here addressed separately because its legality is measured by unique standards arising out of Section 2 of the Sherman Act and Section 2a of the Robinson–Patman Act and because price predation implicates a bedrock principle of competition. Any act of price-cutting will have at least some short-term benefit to consumer welfare: Lower prices, assuming no falloff in quality, will increase output and benefit consumers. This benefit will occur whether the monopolist is adjusting a profit-maximizing to a limit price, reducing (but not eliminating) a limit price, moving from a supracompetitive price to a competitive price, or moving from a price above to a price below full or variable cost. A limit on a powerful firm's pricing practices may do more harm than good if it prevents legitimate discounting that passes production or distribution gains on to the consumer.

A key to analyzing the anticompetitive effects of possible price predation is determining what market power, if any, is exercised by the would be predator. Once that power is determined, much of the confusion surrounding price predation is cleared away. A market player lacking power cannot, without the help of misinformation or deception, injure competition. On the other hand, a firm possessing market power may find it quite possible to take predatory actions that eliminate

---

expressly limited to instances in which the price discrimination is imposed by a firm with market power. As a practical matter, a firm lacking market power will not be able to show an ability to recoup.

2. See the early development of Section 1 case law in § 5.3b.

3. Robinson–Patman Act, 15 U.S.C.A. §§ 13–13b, 21a.

competitors, deter future entrants, or enhance its ability to play a price leadership role in an oligopolistic pricing scheme.

4.1b. Summary of the Law

Assuming no conspiracy can be shown, price predation can be attacked under Section 2 of the Sherman Act and (provided the requisite price discrimination can be established) under Section 2(a) of the Robinson–Patman Act. To apply Section 2 of the Sherman Act, a plaintiff must establish each of the elements of monopolization (the defendant has monopoly power and has engaged in conduct designed to maintain or extend that power) or attempted monopolization (a specific intent to monopolize, predatory or exclusionary acts, and a dangerous probability of success). See the discussion of these elements in §§ 3.3–3.6. Perhaps because the plaintiff regards the evidentiary burden as favorable, most predatory pricing cases brought under Section 2 of the Sherman Act include an attempted monopolization claim.

Section 2(a) of the Robinson–Patman Act requires no showing of monopolization. This provision addresses a seller's price discrimination in the sale of commodities of like grade or quality. A plaintiff must show that the effect of the price discrimination "may be substantially to lessen competition or tend to create a monopoly in any line of commerce."[4] The overlap with Section 2 of the Sherman Act occurs primarily when Section 2(a) of the Robinson–Patman Act is applied to price discrimination that causes injury in the seller's own market (primary line). Although Section 2(a) applies to injury to downstream markets (secondary or tertiary lines), these cases are less likely to meet the requirements for a monopolization or attempted monopolization claim.

These general requirements for monopolization, attempted monopolization and primary line price discrimination have effectively been merged into a more or less uniform requirement in price predation cases. In Brooke Group Ltd. v. Brown & Williamson Tobacco Corp.,[5] the Supreme Court indicated that price predation claims under Section 2 of the Sherman Act and Section 2(a) of the Robinson–Patman Act are "of the same general character."[6] In language that is dicta insofar as it relates to Section 2 of the Sherman Act, the Court indicated that the same screening tests—a showing of pricing below some measure of cost and a reasonable likelihood of recouping losses (or a dangerous probability of recouping losses under Section 2 of the Sherman Act)—would apply in claims under either statute.[7] These same two tests would also appear to apply when the plaintiff invokes Section 1 of the Sherman Act to attack a conspiracy to engage in price predation.[8] This convergence of the law governing price predation may bring desirable simplification and lessen the likelihood of inconsistent results depending on which statute

---

4. 15 U.S.C.A. § 13(a).

5. 509 U.S. 209, 113 S.Ct. 2578, 125 L.Ed.2d 168 (1993).

6. Id. at 221.

7. Id. at 222–24.

8. Matsushita Elec. Indus. Co. v. Zenith Radio Corp., 475 U.S. 574, 584 n. 8, 589, 106 S.Ct. 1348, 89 L.Ed.2d 538 (1986).

is invoked. For reasons addressed in § 4.1c, however, the screening tests chosen by the Court may permit a great deal of predatory pricing that is harmful to allocative efficiencies and to the dynamic component of competition. These tests may also create legal loopholes for a powerful firm to engage in significantly harmful predatory conduct that would have been proscribed in earlier Supreme Court interpretations.

4.1c. The Narrow View of Price Predation

Predatory pricing has been deemed as rare as a white tiger or as fanciful as a unicorn.[9] This rhetoric is an outgrowth of the Chicago theory, under which price predation is viewed as irrational and unlikely behavior. A Chicago description of predatory pricing begins with the observation that true price predation requires the defendant to sacrifice revenues, incurring a loss on the sale of the items sold at predatory prices. The loss will be substantial, particularly if the predator has a large market share and must reduce price on all of the goods of the type subject to predation. Consequently, rational sellers would not risk these certain losses unless they believed that recoupment of the lost income was likely. But recoupment is said to be unlikely under any of a number of widely applicable circumstances. For example, recoupment is unlikely if rivals of the predator remain in the market and are not deterred by the predatory acts; if entry into the relevant market is easy so that new entrants will keep down monopoly profits; or if the product or service on which monopoly profits are sought becomes obsolete. When the accused predators are oligopolists, recoupment is said to be even less likely because monopoly profits can be maintained only if there is coordinated pricing among the oligopolists and because a single predator only reaps a percentage of monopoly profits (usually proportionate to its market share). Reliance on such future coordination is risky—coordination may be destroyed if even a single participant decides to discount its prices.

In support of this narrow view of predation, theorists also express concern that predatory pricing litigation will produce errors in measurement of costs, creating "false positives"—misapplications of the law that result in the suppression of legitimate price competition that benefits society. Measuring a seller's costs is difficult for many reasons, among them that allocations of costs are governed only loosely by accounting and legal standards, so that disagreements are likely as to how much cost should be allocated to the production and distribution of a given product.

In recent cases, the Supreme Court has embraced much of this narrow view of price predation. For example, the Court has said that "predatory pricing schemes are rarely tried, and even more rarely

---

9. Baker, *Predatory Pricing After Brooke Group: An Economic Perspective*, 62 Antitrust L.J. 585, 586 (1994) (citing remarks of two FTC Commissioners as to the most apt metaphor for describing predatory pricing). The ensuing discussion in the text borrows heavily from Baker's description of the positions of Chicago and post-Chicago theorists.

successful."[10] The Court has also stressed that "because 'cutting prices in order to increase business often is the very essence of competition * * * ; mistaken inferences * * * are especially costly, because they chill the very conduct the antitrust laws are designed to protect.' "[11] Despite the acceptance that these orthodox Chicago positions have found in the Supreme Court majority, they are not consensus views among theorists.[12]

4.1d. An Alternate View of Price Predation

The view that predatory pricing is rare or even fanciful is based on theoretical constructs that ignore the realities of markets in which oligopolistic structure, incomplete information and strategic behavior are commonplace. Initially, the premise that a powerful firm will undertake price predation only if it can reasonably expect recoupment of its losses may be incorrect. Most acts of price predation may be coldly rational, profit-maximizing decisions. But business players may act at odds with profit maximization in the face of information vacuums, particularly if anger or a desire for retribution enters the picture. And in publicly traded firms in which ownership and control are separated, management may occasionally pursue selfish interests that do not further the share-holders' interest in profit maximization. For example, a management insulated from stockholder pressure, absent conduct that seriously depresses stock prices, may pursue a higher market share at the expense of some profitability. The power that flows from a leading market position may be its own reward to individuals controlling such firms. A management team that achieves substantial gains in market share is likely to increase overall profit even if the percentage of profitability is somewhat reduced by the losses of predation. Unless predation losses are substantial, a short-term decrease in the rate of profitability may be little more than a blip on the screen for even the most attentive stockholders.

Still, Chicago theorists are surely correct that most firms will not engage in price predation if this conduct seems inconsistent with long term profit maximization. But this narrow view of price predation overlooks the ability of powerful firms to act strategically so that the costs of predation are limited and the gains potentially large. In a marketplace in which information is not shared equally by all players and bluffing is a standard tactic, a powerful firm may target its predato-

---

10. Matsushita Elec. Indus. Co. v. Zenith Radio Corp., 475 U.S. 574, 589, 106 S.Ct. 1348, 89 L.Ed.2d 538 (1986).

11. Cargill, Inc. v. Monfort of Colo., Inc., 479 U.S. 104, 122 n. 17, 107 S.Ct. 484, 93 L.Ed.2d 427 (1986) (quoting *Matsushita,* 475 U.S. at 594).

12. For a summary of conflicting views on price predation, see F. M. Scherer & D. Ross, Industrial Market Structure and Economic Performance 468–79 (3d ed. 1990). For a more recent critique of the Chicago School's view of predation, see Bolton et al., *Predatory Pricing: Strategic Theory and Le-* *gal Policy,* 88 Geo. L. J. 2239 (2000); Elzinga & Mills, *Predatory Pricing and Strategic Theory, Reply to Bolton et. al.,* 89 Geo. L.J. 2475 (2001); Bolton, et al., *Predatory Pricing: Response to Critique and Further Elaboration, Reply to Elzinga et al.,* 90 Geo. L. J. 2495 (2001); Baker, *supra* note 8, at 586–89. For a critique of the *Matsushita* holding and a discussion of price predation in the international context, see First, *An Antitrust Remedy for International Price Predation: Lessons from* Zenith v. Matsushita, 4 Pac. Rim L. & Pol'y J. 211 (1995).

ry prices at a smaller rival. This divide and conquer strategy may work to drive the rival from the market or chasten it to cease pricing that undercuts oligopoly levels. Thus, a powerful firm may limit its costs from predation by limiting the geographic reach or the duration of the predation, or by limiting the brands or models to which it applies. The goal of these limitations is price discrimination that targets a rival while maintaining the predator's higher prices in nontargeted sales. One effective way to achieve this goal is to design a new product or service that directly competes with the rival that is to be disciplined. Thus, an international ocean shipping cartel has used "fighting ships" to follow the same routes and schedules as rivals that were undercutting cartel rates.[13] The American Tobacco monopoly was accused of using "fighting brands" to target a rival's business.[14] In other cases, a predator may lower its prices on a geographic basis to challenge a rival that operates only in those markets.[15] In this manner, at relatively low cost, the powerful firm may win a reputation as a predator not to be challenged, either by existing rivals or future entrants. The benefits of the powerful firm's predator image may extend well beyond the geographic or product market in which the predation occurred.[16]

Perhaps the single most telling omission from the Chicago theory is the failure to recognize that many price predators are acting not in the hope of gaining new monopoly revenues in the future, but to maintain established oligopolistic price levels that may be threatened by an aggressive rival. In an oligopolistic industry in which supracompetitive pricing has been the rule, some occasional "disciplining" steps are taken to prevent new entrants or smaller rivals from breaking the pattern of high, oligopolistic prices. Targeted price predation may be the ideal tool for such a disciplining step. The losses incurred by the sponsors of "fighting ships" or "fighting brands" were doubtlessly seen as one of the costs of maintaining the cartel or tacit interaction of the oligopoly. Seen in this light, price predation in an oligopolistic industry is a form of rent-seeking behavior by a firm possessing market power.

Particularly when a predator is able to target its predatory low prices, the consumer benefit from short-term low prices is likely to be minimal and will be far outweighed by the longer term welfare injury of oligopolistic prices.[17] Thus, a rule that favors granting a powerful firm maximum pricing freedom, such as would be the probable result under the below cost and recoupment screening tests in *Brooke Group*,[18] may bring a few short-term welfare benefits that are more than offset by welfare losses from long-term, higher prices.[19]

13. § 14.7c1.

14. Scherer & Ross, *supra* note 12, at 451.

15. E.g., Utah Pie Co. v. Continental Baking Co., 386 U.S. 685, 87 S.Ct. 1326, 18 L.Ed.2d 406 (1967); Borden, Inc. (ReaLemon), 92 F.T.C. 669 (1978).

16. Baker, *supra* note 9, at 589–92.

17. Scherer & Ross, *supra* note 12, at 472–79.

18. Brooke Group Ltd. v. Brown & Williamson Tobacco Corp., 509 U.S. 209, 222–24, 113 S.Ct. 2578, 125 L.Ed.2d 168 (1993).

19. Scherer and Ross discuss the possibility that a price predator will be unsuccessful in deterring new entry. Under such

A large firm selling multiple brands or lines can use its predator image to discourage discounting across its full product line. An occasional and strategic price cut on one product may be sufficient to deter price cutting on any of its products. The multiple lines also give the predator a broader capability to cross-subsidize the predation. For example, a regulated utility may rely on its guaranteed rate base, allocating fixed costs of the firm's operation to the rate payers, then using its organization to compete against rivals in nonregulated areas. The utility may be in a position to use predatory pricing against rivals that are easily deterred by the utility's ability to subsidize predation by allocating costs to ratepayers.[20]

As a justification for stiff screening tests, Chicago theorists also point to cost measurement risks that may lead to false positives. But measurement risks may equally create false negatives. Moreover, even if they appear to be above some measurement of cost, prices still can be predatory in effect, dampening beneficial price competition or eliminating or deterring rivals.

Following Chicago orthodoxy, the Supreme Court has stressed that price competition is at the heart of a competitive system and substantial risks ought to be borne in order not to stifle this competition. But the costs of false negatives—the failure to interdict true instances of predation—may be even greater. The strategic use of predation may be a key method of coordinating oligopolistic pricing patterns, a widespread and largely untouched area of antitrust injury. Moreover, strategic price predation may be a barrier to the vital dynamic component of competition, including innovation and new entry into markets. Through strategically employed predation, a firm with market power may raise the costs of new entrants, perhaps precluding their successful entry even in instances in which they offer a more efficiently produced or superior product. There is evidence that over time, the dynamic component of competition enhances consumer welfare far more than static efficiency, so these concerns should not be lightly dismissed.[21]

A predator's costs of predation may also be easily overstated. A powerful firm with unsold inventory may view its losses from discount sales more in terms of opportunity cost, not by some absolute measure of cost.[22] For example, a firm may have a substantial unsold inventory of a particular model of television set. Regardless of the cost of producing the sets, the most relevant inquiry for the firm is: "What use can be made of

circumstances, a narrow rule such as the Supreme Court has adopted might result in broader welfare benefits because the new firm enters on a broader scale with more depressing effects on price. SCHERER & ROSS, *supra* note 12, at 472–78. The authors conclude that the circumstances governing these outcomes are sufficiently complex so that sound application of a simple below cost pricing screen is beyond the competence of an antitrust court. Id. at 478.

20. United States v. AT & T Co., 524 F.Supp. 1336, 1365 (D.D.C.1981).

21. The role of dynamic competition is discussed in § 1.5c.

22. First, supra note 12, at 231–32 (in the context of *Matsushita*, explaining why the lost opportunity cost from a below cost sale might be substantially less than the difference between the cost of production and the sale price).

this unsold inventory that will maximize revenues?" It may be impossible to sell the sets at any price that would meet their production costs. If the firm chooses to market them at a deeply discounted price in a manner that injures a rival, the lost opportunity cost would be limited to the difference between the discounted price and the best available price at which the sets could be sold.

§ 4.2 Historical Overview of Price Predation

Early price predation cases focused on the conduct of monopolists and cartel members. The Supreme Court found that price predation was a part of the unlawful conduct of monopolists in Standard Oil Co. v. United States[1] and in United States v. American Tobacco Co.[2] The low prices of Standard Oil have been defended as efficiency based,[3] but the swashbuckling behavior of American Tobacco may be more difficult to defend.

Another classic example of predatory pricing was the use of "fighting ships" by international ocean carrier cartels that served the United States. The cartels would assign a ship to follow the route and schedule of a rival's ship that was not adhering to the cartel's prices. The fighting ship would undercut the prices of the rival, attempting to drive it from the market or discipline it to adhere to the cartel's rates. The cost of maintaining the fighting ship was borne by the cartel, but that cost was limited because there was no general reduction of rates by cartel members—the rate war was conducted only by the specially designated ships. Use of such fighting ships was apparently never successfully attacked under the Sherman Act, but Congress stepped in to outlaw the use of fighting ships in the 1916 Shipping Act.[4]

The use of the Sherman Act to attack predation has continued, but enactment of the Robinson–Patman Act in 1936 gave plaintiffs a new vehicle for attacking price discrimination that was injurious to the seller's rivals. The Robinson–Patman Act's more relaxed treatment of the power requirement can be traced to the concerns that underlay its passage. Responding to protests from small retailers that felt that suppliers treated them less favorably than large retail chains, the sponsors of the Robinson–Patman Act focused on preserving equity among rivals and protection of the small firm's opportunity to compete. These values are not alien to the Sherman Act. But especially in more recent Sherman Act interpretations, courts tend to give greater emphasis to broader concerns with consumer benefits. Likewise, although the Su-

§ 4.2

1. 221 U.S. 1, 31 S.Ct. 502, 55 L.Ed. 619 (1911).

2. 221 U.S. 106, 31 S.Ct. 632, 55 L.Ed. 663 (1911).

3. McGee, *Predatory Price Cutting: The Standard Oil (N.J.) Case*, 1 J.L. & ECON.

137 (1958)(arguing that Standard Oil's low prices must have derived from its efficiencies).

4. The 1916 Shipping Act, a response to fighting ships and other abuses of ocean carrier cartels, is addressed in § 14.7c1.

preme Court has stressed that " 'the Robinson–Patman Act should be construed consistently with broader policies of the antitrust laws,' "[5] that statute's greater emphasis on equity and protection of small competitors remains indelibly imprinted in its wording, legislative history and court interpretations.[6]

The Robinson–Patman Act has drawn criticism—some of it justified—for enforcing competitors' rights to the point that consumer welfare may be sacrificed.[7] The concern is that ill-grounded price predation suits will dampen price competition. Any firm threatened with losses because of the aggressive price competition of a rival, and able to show some difference in the prices that the rival charges for a commodity of like grade or quality, could bring suit with some hope of a settlement, or at least of discouraging such price competition in the future. The dampening of price competition may undercut the preeminent antitrust interest in consumer welfare.

§ 4.3 Price Predation Screens

Theorists have advanced and the Supreme Court to a degree has embraced various screens to prevent unwarranted price predation claims. Each of these screens has a common policy objective: eliminating claims that might serve to inhibit effective price competition by a firm while still allowing meritorious cases (or the most weighty of them) to go forward.

Two of these screens are typically associated with Section 2 monopolization litigation: a showing of monopoly power and a showing of intent. Litigation involving Section 2(a) of the Robinson–Patman Act has generated a somewhat different list of screens: a showing of intent; a showing of pricing below some measure of cost; and a showing of likelihood of an ability to recoup losses incurred as a result of the predatory behavior. As the result of dicta in *Brooke Group*, it would now appear that a below cost pricing and a recoupment screen will be applied in price predation cases under either Section 2 of the Sherman Act or Section 2(a) of the Robinson–Patman Act.[1]

---

5. Brooke Group Ltd. v. Brown & Williamson Tobacco Corp., 509 U.S. 209, 220, 113 S.Ct. 2578, 125 L.Ed.2d 168 (1993) (quoting Great Atl. & Pac. Tea Co. v. FTC, 440 U.S. 69, 80 n. 13, 99 S.Ct. 925, 59 L.Ed.2d 153 (1979)).

6. See Hansen, *Robinson-Patman Law: A Review and Analysis*, 51 FORDHAM L. REV. 1113 (1983).

7. Bowman, *Restraint of Trade by the Supreme Court: The Utah Pie Case*, 77 YALE L.J. 70 (1967); Kintner & Bauer, *The Robinson–Patman Act: A Look Backwards, A View Forward*, 31 ANTITRUST BULL. 571 (1986).

§ 4.3

1. Brooke Group Ltd. v. Brown & Williamson Tobacco Corp., 509 U.S. 209, 222–24, 113 S.Ct. 2578, 125 L.Ed.2d 168 (1993). The Court's statement is dictum to the extent that it applied to Section 2 of the Sherman Act because there was no Sherman Act claim before it. The Court first discussed recoupment in Matsushita Electric Industrial Co. v. Zenith Radio Corp., 475 U.S. 574, 106 S.Ct. 1348, 89 L.Ed.2d 538 (1986).

4.3a. Below Cost Pricing

Courts began to impose below cost pricing screens after Areeda and Turner's 1975 law review article.[2] Their pricing benchmark—average variable cost—has been challenged by other theorists, who have pointed out that prices that will be found nonpredatory under this standard can still have welfare-reducing effects.[3] This undercoverage has prompted proposals for other cost-based standards, including one that is based in part on average total cost,[4] or another that would allow a finding of predation under some circumstances when pricing is above average total cost.[5] Williamson has proposed yet another standard, a "quantity rule" that would bar an incumbent monopolist from increasing output when confronted with a new entrant.[6]

Although Areeda and Turner chose the average variable cost measure in part because it was thought to be a judicially manageable measure of cost, determining average variable cost has proven difficult and costly. Variable costs are any costs that are not fixed. Typical examples of variable costs might include the cost of raw materials used to fabricate a manufactured product, energy costs associated with a production run, and the manufacturer's transportation costs incurred in the distribution of the product. Fixed costs, in contrast, might include the cost of plant and equipment, or any costs that will have to be borne regardless of the level of production. Disagreements about how to delimit variable costs are significant and can affect the outcome of cases. For example, assembly line labor costs are often regarded as variable because they vary with the level of production. The salaries of research and management employees may be regarded as fixed because they remain constant through business cycles of varying output. Yet these categorizations are hardly etched in stone. Some management and research employees may receive lower compensation or be terminated in times of severe recession, suggesting that some of these costs are variable in the

---

2. Areeda & Turner, *Predatory Pricing and Related Practices Under Section 2 of the Sherman Act*, 88 Harv. L. Rev. 697 (1975). This rule is refined and restated in 3 P. Areeda & H. Hovenkamp, Antitrust Law: An Analysis of Antitrust Principles and Their Application ¶¶ 722–749 (rev. ed. 1996). A number of courts have applied the average cost standard, or a comparable standard. *E.g.,* Clamp–All Corp. v. Cast Iron Soil Pipe Inst., 851 F.2d 478, 483 (1st Cir.1988), cert. denied, 488 U.S. 1007, 109 S.Ct. 789, 102 L.Ed.2d 780 (1989); Northwestern Tel. Co. v. AT & T Co., 651 F.2d 76, 88 (2d Cir.1981), cert. denied, 455 U.S. 943, 102 S.Ct. 1438, 71 L.Ed.2d 654 (1982).

Other courts have held that prices below average total cost *may* be unlawful. *E.g.,* McGahee v. Northern Propane Gas Co., 858 F.2d 1487, 1503 (11th Cir.1988), cert. denied, 490 U.S. 1084, 109 S.Ct. 2110, 104 L.Ed.2d 670 (1989); William Inglis & Sons Baking Co. v. ITT Continental Baking Co., 668 F.2d 1014, 1035–36 (9th Cir.1981), cert.

denied, 459 U.S. 825, 103 S.Ct. 58, 74 L.Ed.2d 61 (1982). In *Brooke Group,* the Supreme Court did not opt for a particular measure of cost but referred to "an appropriate" measure. *Id.* n.1.

3. Scherer, *Predatory Pricing and the Sherman Act: A Comment*, 89 Harv. L. Rev. 869, 883–89 (1976).

4. Joskow & Klevorick, *A Framework for Analyzing Predatory Pricing Policy*, 89 Yale L.J. 213 (1979).

5. Baumol, *Quasi-Permanence of Price Reductions: A Policy for Prevention of Predatory Pricing*, 89 Yale L.J. 1 (1979)(suggesting a standard that would prohibit some above cost pricing cuts but would allow such cuts if they were maintained more or less permanently, an indication that they are sustained by the dominant firm's cost advantages).

6. Williamson, *Predatory Pricing, A Strategic and Welfare Analysis*, 87 Yale L.J. 284 (1977).

long run. For Japanese firms, many of whom are committed to retain employees for their working careers, the wages of assembly line workers might properly be regarded as fixed, and the same might be said of some western firms that follow similar employment policies.[7]

Many of the problems incurred in measuring cost go beyond any distinction between fixed and variable costs. In firms producing a variety of products, difficult allocation questions will always plague cost determinations. For example, how are the costs of management, research and development, and image advertising allocated among the various product lines that a firm produces? The task will be aided through development of standardized rules. Still, at the margins, allocation disputes are inevitable. Any determination of cost is likely to be expensive, adding substantially to the resources required to litigate a price predation case.

Other cost measurements will encounter many of the same difficulties incurred in determining average variable cost, although an average total cost standard, adopted by some lower courts,[8] may be somewhat more manageable if only because it eliminates the need to separate fixed from variable costs. But the broader policy question is whether a below cost screening test is ever appropriate, regardless of the cost measure employed. One critic has described the Areeda–Turner standard, and related cost measurements, as "too complicated to be handled competently by the antitrust courts."[9] Even if the complexity of cost-based rules could be overcome, there is still the substantial issue of undercoverage—some competitively injurious conduct will escape enforcement under virtually any cost-based formula that is rigidly applied.

The dominant tenor of case law and commentary implies that while prices below average variable cost or some other surrogate are at least highly suspect, prices above full cost are lawful. Yet, under some circumstances even prices above full cost may intentionally discourage entry or aggressive price competition, or drive a rival from the market.[10] Indeed, a powerful firm is more likely to engage in aggressive temporary, disciplining price cuts when the cost it incurs is less substantial. Low prices, even when above any measure of cost, still represent an opportunity cost to both the predator and the target of the predation. Either could sell its product at a higher rate but for the predation. A price sufficiently low to deny an adequate return on investment may force a rival to abandon the market in favor of alternate uses of capital that promise a higher return. Or, perhaps more likely, predation above cost levels might chasten a target firm to stop discount pricing and follow a comfortable, coordinated oligopolistic pricing. Under this scenario, the predator firm is trying to establish or reestablish price leadership or coordination, forestalling future attacks on oligopoly price levels.

---

7. First, *An Antitrust Remedy for International Price Predation: Lessons from Zenith v. Matsushita,* 4 PAC. RIM L. & POL'Y J. 211, 240–41 (1995).

8. See the discussion of lower court decisions on the proper cost standard in note 2, supra.

9. F. M SCHERER & D. ROSS, INDUSTRIAL MARKET STRUCTURE AND ECONOMIC PERFORMANCE 478 (3d ed. 1990).

10. See Edlin, *Stopping Above–Cost Predatory Pricing,* 111 YALE L.J. 941 (2002).

The below cost pricing requirement may still be desirable if it prevents predatory pricing litigation lacking in merit. This it may do quite effectively, but crudely, forestalling meritorious and meritless cases alike. Undercoverage of true predation may be justified as a necessary cost of preventing a greater anticompetitive injury: the overdeterrence of aggressive price competition by powerful firms. But the harm from strategic predation may be even more substantial, linked as it is to widespread oligopolistic pricing patterns and the deterrence of entry or innovation. The measure of the harms and benefits on either side is difficult to draw. But this debate may be tangential and largely irrelevant if it can be demonstrated that, without blocking legitimate cases, other, more effective screens can be devised for preventing predatory pricing litigation lacking in merit. That question is addressed in § 4.4.

4.3b. Recoupment

Under the narrow model now accepted by the Supreme Court, a rational predator would not undertake predation unless it could reasonably anticipate recoupment through future supracompetitive profits. Moreover, recoupment is said to be unlikely because of unpredictable market developments following the predation, particularly if supracompetitive pricing is based upon oligopolistic pricing coordination. See § 4.1c. Recoupment is now a screen that will allow courts to dismiss a predatory pricing case on a summary judgment motion (or a motion for judgment as a matter of law) if the plaintiff fails to show a reasonable likelihood of recoupment (Section 2(a) of the Robinson–Patman Act) or a dangerous probability of recoupment (Section 2 of the Sherman Act).[11]

Rational market players will not engage in predation when to do so would court major losses and when the chances of recouping those losses are low. To do so would be to court financial disaster. When mechanically applied, however, the recoupment test will often lead to anomalous results, inconsistent with market realities. In particular, a predator (1) may be indifferent to some lost profitability (see the discussion in § 4.1d); (2) may be able to achieve its goals through above cost pricing, particularly if its behavior is a way of signaling displeasure with a rival's undercutting of oligopolistic pricing (see the discussion in § 4.3a); or (3) may be unconcerned with recoupment because the firm incurs little or no lost opportunity cost even when it is pricing below cost.

What is most relevant to a firm is not a loss measured against average variable cost or average total cost, but a loss measured against opportunity cost. Opportunity costs are a measure not of the actual cost of producing and distributing a product, but of the available alternative uses that the seller can make of an unsold product. Thus, if a manufacturer has an overcapacity problem, and needs to keep plant equipment running at or near maximum levels to pay off debt and other fixed costs, the seller may have to reduce its price in order to sell the excess

---

11. Recoupment screens have been used in Israel Travel Advisory Service, Inc. v. Israel Identity Tours, 61 F.3d 1250, 1256 (7th Cir.1995); Dial A Car, Inc. v. Transportation, Inc., 82 F.3d 484, 488 (D.C.Cir. 1996).

inventory. Faced with the prospect of making discounted sales, the seller can make targeted, strategic use of unsold inventory with little or no lost opportunity cost.[12] Discounted sales of the overstocked merchandise can be directed at a rival that the predator wishes to discipline. Such selective use of inventory can build the firm's predator image and ensure a pattern of oligopolistic price leadership at little or no opportunity cost.[13]

A part of the narrow model of predation is the notion that recoupment is unlikely, particularly if it depends upon coordinated pricing in an oligopolistic industry. Oligopolists may find it difficult to coordinate supracompetitive pricing. In addition, the oligopolist-predator reaps only a percentage of the gains from subsequent supracompetitive pricing—the remaining gains will benefit the other oligopolists. Endorsing this reasoning, the Supreme Court has described the recoupment challenge facing an oligopolist as foreboding, suggesting that an "anticompetitive minuet is most difficult to compose and to perform, even for a disciplined oligopoly."[14] But the argument is easily overstated. In many instances, what the predator is trying to do is not to build a structure and pattern of oligopolistic pricing where none existed, but to restore discipline to one that has functioned in the past. To paraphrase Justice Stevens in dissent, the defendant had been dancing the minuet with the same oligopolistic partners for some forty or fifty years and could predict the behavior of their favorite partners.[15] The existence of past oligopolistic pricing may also give the predator an advance cushion with which to pay the costs of the predation, and even a sense of righteous indignation against the rival that has disrupted a comfortable status quo of high profitability. Seen in this light, the predator's costs are not ill-considered attempts to *build* oligopolistic pricing, but rather selective rent-seeking behavior designed to *preserve* supracompetitive profits. The predator, by building or restoring its predator image, may be able to maintain oligopolistic prices for many years and in brands or lines that were not the direct subject of the predation. Thus, the recoupment may occur not simply in sales of the brand subject to predation, but in all brands that

---

12. A firm's targeted and strategic use of overcapacity may be relatively harmless if the firm has no significant market power. But the question takes on a different light when the firm has market power enabling it to raise a rival's costs or deter entry.

The problem of putting underused plant and equipment to use may explain the behavior of the Japanese cartel in *Matsushita*. See First, supra note 7, at 230–31. More generally, high fixed costs are likely to be a problem in some transportation industries, where a ship, plane or train traveling a scheduled route generates substantial costs regardless of whether it travels full or empty.

13. A manufacturer making use of overcapacity to engage in predation has at least two opportunities to escape liability under the current dual screening tests (below cost pricing and likely recoupment). If average variable cost is used as the cost test, the manufacturer's high fixed costs will not be included in the cost calculation, so the manufacturer may not be considered a predator. If, however, average total cost is used as a cost measure, the manufacturer is less likely to escape under the cost measure, but may well be able to show that recoupment of lost total costs is unlikely.

14. Brooke Group Ltd. v. Brown & Williamson Tobacco Corp., 509 U.S. 209, 227–28, 113 S.Ct. 2578, 125 L.Ed.2d 168 (1993).

15. Id. at 257 (Stevens, J., dissenting).

the defendant sells. To be sure, the defendant's targeted price-cutting behavior, unlike other rent-seeking behavior, brings short-term benefits to consumers through lower prices. But it is undertaken for the same purpose and effect as other forms of rent-seeking. If the predatory strategy is effective, it may injure consumers in the long term not only in sales of the brand in which the predation occurred, but in all brands that the defendant sells. These losses could easily far outweigh any short-term benefits for consumers. The more targeted the predation, the more limited are the short-term consumer gains (and the predator's costs) and the easier it will be to recoup those losses.

In Brooke Group v. Brown & Williamson, the Court described as "demanding" the chain of logic underlying its conclusion that no reasonable jury could find that the defendant could reasonably expect to recoup its losses.[16] The dissent was less restrained, calling it a "hodgepodge of legal, factual, and economic propositions."[17] One of the difficulties confronting the majority was the well-documented cigarette oligopoly dating from the early twentieth century.[18] Aside from the industry's long-standing oligopolistic structure, it had a record of high profitability. Even after the complaint was filed, the industry continued parallel pricing practices, as indicated by the lockstep, semi-annual price increases that all members of the industry implemented for their branded cigarettes.[19] These facts seem wholly consistent with a rent-seeking explanation for Brown & Williamson's predation—the company was engaged in behavior that was designed to forestall future price competition from the plaintiff (Liggett Group) and to restore and maintain oligopolistic, high industry profits.

The Court's silence on the issue of rent-seeking predation might be explained by the failure of the plaintiff to press this theory. The plaintiff apparently argued more narrowly that the defendant could reasonably expect recoupment solely from future sales of its generic and branded cigarettes.[20] Other Supreme Court cases involving oligopolistic industries, including *Matsushita*[21] and *Utah Pie*,[22] also were not presented on rent-seeking theories of predation. Although the Court may have limited itself by embracing Chicago rhetoric concerning the irrationality of predation, it cannot be faulted for not considering theories of predation that have yet to be forcefully presented to it.

The critiques of the recoupment test are compelling, at least when predation occurs within the context of an oligopolistic industry, unless some other justification exists for imposing a recoupment showing on a

---

16. Id. at 243.

17. Id. at 254 (Stevens, J., dissenting).

18. SCHERER & ROSS, *supra* note 9, at 340–41. Some of this background is detailed in American Tobacco Co. v. United States, 147 F.2d 93 (6th Cir. 1944).

19. Id. at 213, 217–18.

20. Baker, *Predatory Pricing After Brooke Group: An Economic Perspective,* 62 ANTITRUST L.J. 585, 597 (1994).

21. Matsushita Elec. Indus. Co. v. Zenith Radio Corp., 475 U.S. 574, 106 S.Ct. 1348, 89 L.Ed.2d 538 (1986).

22. Utah Pie Co. v. Continental Baking Co., 386 U.S. 685, 87 S.Ct. 1326, 18 L.Ed.2d 406 (1967).

plaintiff. That reason may lie in the belief of some theorists that a powerful firm's freedom of action to price without interference from the antitrust laws is procompetitive or serves some other overriding social value. The premise that false positives are more damaging to competition than false negatives is difficult to substantiate. Even if correct, that premise should not be the basis for tolerating a large risk of false negatives if more refined and workable screens for determining predation can be devised. See § 4.4.

4.3c. Intent

Courts have long used evidence of a defendant's intent in determining Section 2 claims of attempted monopolization. See § 3.6a2. Where price predation is concerned, the Supreme Court has also looked to intent in cases brought under Section 2(a) of the Robinson–Patman Act. In *Utah Pie Co. v. Continental Baking Co,*[23] the Supreme Court appeared to give substantial weight to intent evidence in restoring a jury verdict in favor of the plaintiff in a price predation case. The Court cited record evidence that a manager for one of the defendants had identified the plaintiff "as an 'unfavorable factor,' one which 'd[u]g holes in our operation' and posed a constant 'check'" on the defendant's performance in a local market.[24] In *Brooke Group*, another case involving application of Section 2(a) of the Robinson–Patman Act, the Court had before it even more detailed evidence of the defendant's alleged intent.[25] But the Supreme Court declined to give weight to this evidence, finding it implausible in light of its belief that predation is irrational, particularly in the context of an oligopolistic industry.[26] Perhaps the Court would have found the intent evidence more compelling had it been supported by post-Chicago economic theory. But *Brooke Group* appears to invite courts to disregard intent evidence, creating a tension with the Court's earlier holding in *Utah Pie*.

Intent evidence can play a constructive role in resolving price predation cases. Although evidence of intent alone should not be decisive, as Justice Brandeis stated in another context, "knowledge of intent may help the court to interpret facts and to predict consequences."[27] Economists, lawyers and judges may react to a given set of facts based on ideological bias or currently fashionable economic theories. Business participants may be less schooled in theoretical ruminations of antitrust theorists, and may be biased by participation in marketplace battles. But

---

23. 386 U.S. 685, 87 S.Ct. 1326, 18 L.Ed.2d 406 (1967).

24. Id. at 697.

25. Glazer, *Predatory Pricing and Beyond: Life After* Brooke Group, 62 Antitrust L.J. 605, 610–13, 625–29 (1994). Glazer suggests that evidence in *Brooke Group* went far beyond the conclusory statements of sales personnel that were on the record in *Utah Pie*.

26. Brooke Group Ltd. v. Brown & Williamson Tobacco Corp., 509 U.S. 209, 232,

113 S.Ct. 2578, 125 L.Ed.2d 168 (1993). Some theorists have joined in urging that intent evidence be given no weight in price predation cases. Scherer & Ross, supra note 9, at 478 (listing a number of theorists who have concluded that intent evidence should not be considered).

27. Board of Trade of Chicago v. United States, 246 U.S. 231, 238, 38 S.Ct. 242, 62 L.Ed. 683 (1918).

evidence of the intent of business players has offsetting strengths. Business players know the market in which they participate from firsthand experience. In arguing that courts should not condemn business practices that they do not understand, Judge Easterbrook noted: "Wisdom lags far behind the market. * * * [L]awyers know less about the business than the people they represent. * * * The judge knows even less about the business than the lawyers."[28]

Judge Easterbrook's observations, though offered in support of a noninterventionist agenda, suggest the merit of a careful use of intent evidence. Although statements from a single company's employee may or may not accurately capture the firm's motivation for an allegedly predatory act, exclusion of evidence from those closest to and most knowledgeable of the firm's action invites lawyers and judges, whose vicarious experience with marketplace realities is limited, to fill the vacuum with their own relatively uninformed views.

4.3d. Market Power

All price predation cases brought under Section 2 of the Sherman Act have a built-in market power screen (monopoly power for monopolization cases or a dangerous probability of achieving monopoly power for attempted monopoly cases). These screens are discussed in Chapter 3. Although Section 2(a) of the Robinson–Patman Act does not expressly employ a market power screen, it does so indirectly: a use of price discrimination is unlawful only if its effect may be to reduce competition substantially or tend to create a monopoly. A price discrimination is unlikely to reduce competition unless its use is connected with some form of market power. Such a market power screen, in addition to being derived from statute, has a sound foundation in economic theory. Because price predation is a power offense, it is unlikely to be successfully employed unless the predator has market power. As Joskow and Klevorick put it, absent such power, firms "can do anything they please with price."[29] Requiring a showing of the defendant's market power should eliminate many "false positive" risks from the universe of price predation claims.

The defendant's market power is likely to be based on either the monopolistic or oligopolistic structure of the industry. Other forms of market power, such as forms of single brand market power (see § 2.4e), are less likely to lead to competitively injurious predation. A firm that has achieved a high degree of brand differentiation, for example, is somewhat insulated from rivals' price competition and is, therefore, less likely to be motivated to engage in price predation.

The dicta in *Brooke Group* place no importance on the underlying market power of the predator. Indeed, without explanation, the Court

---

28. Easterbrook, *The Limits of Antitrust,* 63 Tex. L. Rev. 1, 5 (1984).

29. Joskow & Klevorick, *supra* note 4, at 245; see also Shepherd, *Assessing "Predatory" Actions by Market Shares and Selectivity,* 31 Antitrust Bull. 1 (1986)(stressing the relevance of market share in determining which price cutting actions are predatory).

appears to be erecting an even tougher hurdle in a Section 2 case where monopoly power or near monopoly power is a prerequisite. Thus, in a Section 2 Sherman Act case, the Court will require a "dangerous probability" of recoupment (instead of a reasonable likelihood of recoupment required under Section 2(a) of the Robinson–Patman Act). When the alleged predator is a monopolist, showing a likelihood of recoupment is easier in one sense: as long as entry barriers are high, the alleged predator would be insulated from competition or potential competition that would drive down the predator's monopoly price that leads to full recoupment. But an apparent anomaly of the recoupment test is that the higher the defendant's market share, the greater the amount of lost profits the predator might have to recoup, making it more difficult for the plaintiff to establish a likelihood of recoupment. In most real markets, a higher market share will increase the threat of injurious predation. One reason for this is that a firm with a high market share is more likely to be feared by smaller rivals, giving the large firm a stronger predator image to deter potential discounting activity by rivals. Another reason is that most predators with market power are able to pick targets of predation selectively so as to minimize lost profits. A predator with a high market share might target a small regional rival as the target of its predation, in this manner ensuring that the predation would not undercut its profits outside the geographic market of the rival.

§ 4.4 A Structured Rule of Reason for Price Predation

Whatever their expectations, the Areeda and Turner below-cost pricing screen has proven expensive and difficult to apply. The test creates a great deal of tangential litigation about a matter (whether the defendant's prices are below some measure of cost) that is not determinative of whether predation has occurred. If the test is applied mechanically, many competitively injurious price predations will be beyond the reach of the law. The recoupment standard may be subject to similar criticisms. Collectively, application of these two screens seems likely to exculpate a great deal of conduct that will be competitively harmful, particularly in oligopolistic industries in which price leadership or coordination are common.

A structured rule of reason analysis for price predation could avoid the inflexibility of the below cost pricing and recoupment screens while still providing the courts with concrete guidance in furthering their inquiry and eliminating meritless cases. Such an inquiry might focus on two pivotal questions: (1) whether the defendant possesses monopoly or oligopoly power; and (2) whether there is a credible theory of predation and facts to sustain it. On the latter point intent evidence might be relevant. The plaintiff would be required to make a showing as to each of these matters in order to survive summary judgment. As an additional practical rule that may focus the inquiry and advance the analysis, courts should examine whether the price reduction is strategically targeted in terms of product, region or duration such that it appears not to be a durable price reduction that will pass long-term benefits to the consumer.

4.4a. Monopoly or Oligopoly Power

A market power screening test is judicially manageable, and largely free of risk that it would create false negatives. Moreover, as explained in § 4.3d, it is already a requirement for any price predation case brought under Section 2 of the Sherman Act. To the extent that a monopolization or an attempted monopolization claim under Section 2 requires a high market share (e.g., 50 percent or higher), it may screen out some meritorious price predation claims involving oligopolists. But such cases should still be picked up in suits brought under Section 2(a) of the Robinson–Patman Act, which would appear to require a lesser showing of market power (a showing that effect of the defendant's action "may be substantially to lessen competition or tend to create a monopoly").[1] The application of this screen should ensure that the antitrust laws are not invoked to restrict the pricing freedom of firms that possess no significant power to use price predation to injure competition.

One area of difficulty will be delimiting those cases in which an oligopolist possesses sufficient power to make price predation a threat. The factual setting of the *Brooke Group* provides a case in point.[2] The Supreme Court found that the industry was oligopolistic, dominated by six firms. Brown & Williamson, the alleged predator, was the third largest firm, with around 12 percent of the total market, trailing well behind the first and second firms (with 40 percent and 28 percent, respectively). Liggett, the plaintiff, had around 5 percent of the market. Aside from industry structure, the Court also referred to the conduct (lockstep, semi-annual price increases for cigarettes, irrespective of changes in costs) and performance (one of the nation's most profitable industries with no significant price competition among rival firms) that tended to show oligopoly power. On the other hand, although the prices of branded and generic cigarettes were unquestionably on the rise, the majority could point to evidence that newly introduced "subgeneric" cigarettes had sparked another round of deep discounting.[3] The examination of structure, conduct and performance collectively would give the court a more complete picture of whether oligopoly power is feasible and is being exercised.

4.4b. A Credible Theory of Predation

The market power screen will not address the concern that price predation litigation may unduly restrain the pricing freedom of a market player possessing monopoly or oligopoly power. Although theorists who have stressed this concern often understate the competitive threat from

§ 4.4

1. 15 U.S.C.A. § 13(a).

2. Brooke Group Ltd. v. Brown & Williamson Tobacco Corp., 509 U.S. 209, 212–15, 113 S.Ct. 2578, 125 L.Ed.2d 168 (1993).

The industry statistics in this paragraph are taken from the referenced pages of the Court's opinion.

3. Id. at 236.

price predation, the concern that price predation law may deter legitimate procompetitive pricing initiatives is legitimate and ought to be addressed. A substantial answer to these concerns may lie in requiring a plaintiff, in addition to establishing market power, to offer a credible economic theory of predation and make a showing of facts to sustain its application. Such a test is consistent with the Court's summary judgment teachings in Eastman Kodak Co. v. Image Technical Services, Inc.[4] and more recently in Brooke Group Ltd. v. Brown & Williamson Tobacco Corp.[5] These decisions allow the courts to grant summary judgment (or judgment as a matter of law) when economic learning suggests no credible economic theory supports the plaintiff's claim, but also make clear that the plaintiff should survive summary judgment when it has advanced such a theory and made a preliminary showing of facts to support it.

To establish a credible theory for predation a plaintiff must show that the predation was likely to cause an anticompetitive injury, such as a raising of the targeted rival's costs or a disciplining of a rival to adhere to an oligopolistic pricing pattern. In a general sense, the theory must also show that the predation is a commercially reasonable response to a rival's competition. Usually, this will require a showing that the predation does not generate costs out of line with the anticompetitive benefit the predator hopes to attain. But the test should not be a tight mathematical calculation of short-term results because a predator might well accept some short-term losses for their longer term strategic value, or even because of a desire for retribution.

One of the strengths of the common law approach to interpretation of the Sherman Act has been the flexibility it has left the Supreme Court in adjusting to new economic learning. In an area of theoretical turmoil such as predatory pricing, some differences of view and occasional missteps are inevitable in determining whether a theory of price predation is a credible one. But the common law wisdom derived from past precedents as well as the considerable body of theoretical literature should guide a court in determining which theories are acceptable. *Brooke Group* may be criticized for its insensitivity to post-Chicago theories of predation, but some of that insensitivity may be traced to the absence of a forceful presentation of these theories to the Supreme Court.[6]

4.4c. Targeted Price Cuts—A Practical Guide

As an additional tool for focusing and advancing its inquiry, a court should examine whether the alleged predatory prices are targeted at a

4. 504 U.S. 451, 112 S.Ct. 2072, 119 L.Ed.2d 265 (1992).

5. 509 U.S. 209, 113 S.Ct. 2578, 125 L.Ed.2d 168 (1993). In *Brooke Group* the Court majority thought plaintiff's theory of predation was not credible. In evaluating it the majority gave little weight to the history of lock-step oligopolistic pricing and ignored the fact that defendants offered no alternative theory at all that could explain their unusual pricing responses.

6. Baker, *Predatory Pricing After Brooke Group: An Economic Perspective*, 62 ANTITRUST L.J. 585, 595–98 (1994).

particular product, geographic market or rival, and do not appear to be durable, broad-based price reductions that might pass efficiencies on to consumers. This rule is based on common law wisdom (and perhaps underlying the Robinson–Patman Act as well) that most predatory pricing is likely to be targeted rather than across-the-board. Price discrimination is often a part of such a scheme because its use enables the predator to lessen the cost of predation. The classic example of targeted predation is the fighting ship (designed to undercut the business of the ships of a discounting rival) or the fighting brand (designed to undercut the trade of a particular rival's brand of cigarette). When a court intervenes to stop targeted price-cutting, it is also lessening the risk of deterring beneficial competitive behavior. Although some selective price-cutting may be procompetitive (as discussed at the end of this section), such price cuts will bring fewer short-term benefits than an across-the-board price cut that benefits all purchasers of a product. If price predation is limited to a powerful firm's targeted and strategically employed price reduction, even a monopolist will be free to use broad-based and durable price reduction as a legitimate procompetitive tool that can pass efficiencies on to buyers, a result that finds support in the literature.[7]

Th concept of "targeted price reduction" is intended as a guide, not an inflexible mechanical test. The test runs the risk of being over-and under-inclusive in some respects, although those errors of coverage may be infrequent. Broad-based and durable price reductions would be exculpated under this approach. Such enduring price reductions may be a form of limit pricing which, though not as favorable to consumers as competitive pricing, is likely to be an improvement over the oligopolistic price level that would otherwise prevail. In addition, for all the reasons suggested by Chicago theorists, durable price reductions are likely to be very expensive to the predator and, as a consequence, predatory use of such reductions will probably be rare.

The targeted price reduction guide leaves the powerful firm vulnerable to antitrust attack for certain pricing initiatives that may be legitimate, including limited promotional discounts and efforts to match competitors' prices. To prevent such false positives, the defendant should be allowed to prove promotional intent and to use any exceptions to liability under the Robinson–Patman Act. Thus, for example, a defendant should be exculpated if it can show that its low prices were an effort to meet the competition (Section 2(b) of the Robinson–Patman Act)[8] or were a legitimate volume discount that reflects cost savings in the manufacture or distribution of a product (Section 2(a) of the Robinson–Patman Act).[9] These exceptions are not in the text of the Sherman Act, but should easily fit within an interpretive framework that provides

---

7. Baumol, *Quasi-Permanence of Price Reductions: A Policy for Prevention of Predatory Pricing*, 89 YALE L.J. 1, 26 & n.50 (1979); Joskow & Klevorick, *A Framework for Analyzing Predatory Pricing Policy*, 89 YALE L.J. 213, 224–25 (1979).

8. 15 U.S.C.A. § 13(b).

9. 15 U.S.C.A. § 13(a).

for the application of the Act only in instances when significant competitive injury is threatened.[10]

The law with respect to a promotional discount is less clear.[11] Such a discount will often be targeted in a manner similar to true predation. But the distinction may lie in the very limited duration of promotional discounts and in their failure to seek to discipline a rival or rivals. If such a discount operates for a short period, it is unlikely to have enduring anticompetitive effects on rivals. Promotional discounts may be offered in the hope that a customer may become familiar with a product, then continue to buy it after the promotion is discontinued. On the other hand, if the discount, based on timing and geographic reach, appears aimed at a particular rival's pricing, it is more likely to be predatory in effect.

§ 4.5 Price Predation Cases

The Supreme Court's major price predation decisions in the last three decades have involved private antitrust suits. Of those, the two most recent, *Brooke Group*[1] and *Matsushita*,[2] were clear victories for the defendants. The preponderance of private suits and the very high success rate for defendants are reflected in lower court decisions as well.

Brooke Group, already discussed throughout this chapter, deserves a last look. The Supreme Court embraced the below cost pricing and recoupment screening tests. But how would the case have fared under a more balanced test (as proposed in § 4.4) that isolates predatory acts harmful to wealth allocation or the dynamic component of competition? Looking only at the facts as presented by the Court, it is quite possible that the plaintiff could have made a winning case that harmful predation was involved. The Court found an oligopolistic industry with high profitability and a history of lockstep pricing. The Liggett Group's introduction of a black and white generic cigarette was a new competitive element that threatened price coordination in this industry. When Liggett's generic began winning sales from branded competitors, it made its heaviest inroads against a brand of defendant Brown & Williamson.[3] Thus, although Brown & Williamson was only the third largest member of this industry, it had perhaps the largest incentive to strike back against this break in oligopolistic pricing and could do it against a significantly smaller rival. It could also target the predation, introducing a black and white generic cigarette that was precisely patterned on

10. Flair Zipper Corp. v. Textron Inc., 1980–2 Trade Cas. (CCH) ¶ 63,555, at 76,-959 (S.D.N.Y.1980), aff'd mem., 659 F.2d 1059 (2d Cir.1981). See Denger & Herfort, *Predatory Pricing Claims After* Brooke Group, 62 ANTITRUST L.J. 541, 553 (1994)(discussing the applicability of the meeting competition defense to Sherman Act cases).

11. Denger & Herfort, supra note 10, at 552–53.

§ 4.5

1. Brooke Group Ltd. v. Brown & Williamson Tobacco Corp., 509 U.S. 209, 113 S.Ct. 2578, 125 L.Ed.2d 168 (1993).

2. Matsushita Elec. Indus. Co. v. Zenith Radio Corp., 475 U.S. 574, 106 S.Ct. 1348, 89 L.Ed.2d 538 (1986).

3. 509 U.S. at 214.

Liggett's black and white generic. Because most downstream sellers of cigarettes needed only to carry one of these two largely fungible lines, Brown & Williamson's lower prices would have a devastating affect on Liggett's ability to market its line.[4]

Under these facts, it would appear that Brown & Williamson had market power as a member of a long-standing oligopoly. A credible theory of predation could also be advanced. Brown & Williamson may have been engaged in rent-seeking behavior, designed to forestall the threat to oligopolistic pricing that Liggett's generic cigarette represented. The predation was targeted (copying Liggett's black and white format) to limit the costs of the predation and to enhance the impact on Liggett.

The evidence of whether Brown & Williamson's predation was successful was mixed. If Brown & Williamson's goal was merely to bring prices for Liggett's generic closer to prices for branded cigarettes, the predation may have succeeded. After the alleged predation, lockstep price increases on branded and generic cigarettes apparently substantially raised the prices of both types of cigarettes and narrowed the gap between them.[5] But rebates offered to wholesalers may have clouded this picture, and new competition shortly emerged from subgeneric cigarettes, also introduced by Liggett and subsequently by the other major industry participants.[6] Taken collectively, the introduction of first generic and later subgeneric cigarettes and the discounting of each suggests a breakdown in uniformity of marketing, a serious problem for an oligopoly hoping to coordinate its pricing. Industry overcapacity may have made such coordination highly unlikely in the near term. Still, when Liggett introduced its generic brand, it represented a major and procompetitive departure from oligopolistic marketing and pricing patterns that had prevailed in this industry. As the Supreme Court's decision stands, it appears to invite oligopolists to target and attack such procompetitive departures from oligopolistic pricing. The hindsight that gave the Court some comfort—that other procompetitive departures (such as the introduction of subgeneric cigarettes) were to follow—was known neither to Liggett nor to Brown & Williamson at the time the alleged acts of predation occurred. Thus, it is not unreasonable to assume that Brown & Williamson was confident that its predation would achieve its goal of restoring some competitive discipline to cigarette pricing.

Matsushita,[7] like *Brooke Group*, involved the alleged use of predatory pricing by an oligopoly. The major Japanese producers of consumer electronic products were alleged to have formed a cartel for the purposes

---

4. The Court notes that the first competitive response to Liggett's black and white generic came from one of the industries two largest firms, R.J. Reynolds. Reynolds reduced the price on its "Doral" brand to generic levels. 509 U.S. at 215. This response seemed less targeted than that of Brown & Williamson because Reynolds did not copy the marketing format that Liggett had used with the black and white (non-branded) cigarette.

5. 509 U.S. at 235.

6. Id. at 236.

7. Matsushita Elec. Indus. Co. v. Zenith Radio Corp., 475 U.S. 574, 106 S.Ct. 1348, 89 L.Ed.2d 538 (1986).

of gaining control of the U.S. market through acts of price predation. The plaintiffs (U.S. competitors of the Japanese firms) alleged that the conspiracy in violation of Section 1 of the Sherman Act was implemented in part through: (1) check price agreements (entered into with the participation of the Japanese Ministry of International Trade) that set minimum prices for sale of consumer electronic products on the U.S. market; and (2) a "five company rule" which limited each Japanese producer to five American distributors. After the court of appeals had reversed a trial court's order granting summary judgment for the defendants, the Supreme Court (in a 5–4 decision) reversed and remanded on the ground that the appellate court had improperly applied the standards governing predatory pricing and summary judgment.[8]

The Court applied the Chicago theory that suggests that price predation among oligopolists is difficult to achieve and highly unlikely. In particular, the Court concluded that it was unreasonable to assume that the Japanese producers' could expect to recoup their losses from the predation in the U.S. market. The Court also found that the check price agreements to maintain minimum prices in the United States favored the defendants because they showed a desire "to place a floor under prices rather than to lower them." Likewise, the five distributor rule was said to have a natural effect of raising rather than lowering U.S. prices.[9]

The Court's objections notwithstanding, the plaintiffs appear to have presented a credible theory of predation. That theory was that the Japanese producers had already cartelized the Japanese market, maintaining supracompetitive prices in that market (evidence of that cartelization introduced by the plaintiffs has since been supplemented by others).[10] Faced with higher fixed costs than their American rivals (because of the Japanese tradition of guaranteeing career employment to employees) and with substantial overcapacity, the Japanese producers needed a large market in which to sell overflow production. The United States was an obvious choice for the Japanese producers, but some means had to be devised for preventing a breakdown of oligopolistic coordination while developing the U.S. market. A breakdown in cooperation in the U.S. could undercut the coordinated high prices charged in the Japanese producers' domestic market. Both the check price agreements (maintaining minimum prices in the American market) and the five distributor rule seem well designed to this end. They would limit the costs of predation, allowing the predators to undercut U.S. rivals without causing losses that were too severe to the predators. With losses to the Japanese firms limited in this manner, it is quite possible that the firms had achieved an equilibrium (high profits in the Japanese market countered by minimal losses in the U.S. market) that could be sustained indefinitely, with no need to recoup losses. Indeed, there may have been no loss at all in the U.S. market if the Japanese firms' behavior is

8. Id. at 595, 598.

9. Id. at 596.

10. First, *An Antitrust Remedy for International Price Predation: Lessons from*

Zenith v. Matsushita, 4 Pac. Rim L. & Pol'y J. 211 (1995).

assessed in terms of opportunity cost. Had the Japanese firms been unable to sell in the U.S. market, they might have suffered even greater losses from high fixed costs that were not adequately offset. Any losses in the United States market constituted rent-seeking behavior needed to sustain the cartelized Japanese market.

Although the plaintiffs presented essentially this theory to the Court, it was found implausible by five of the nine sitting justices. The Court's position may have been bolstered by the Justice Department's amicus brief, also reflecting a Chicago orthodoxy. Since *Matsushita* was decided, additional literature critical of the Chicago view of price predation has emerged.[11] The Court has also signalled a greater sensitivity to post-Chicago theories in Eastman Kodak Co. v. Image Technical Services, Inc.,[12] only to retreat again to Chicago orthodoxy in *Brooke Group*. Whatever the Court's view on these subjects, it is difficult to erase the evidence, both within and outside the record in the case, that the Japanese defendants were engaged in cartel-like conduct with obvious anticompetitive potential both in the United States and in their home market. This is not to say that the plaintiffs should necessarily have prevailed in *Matsushita*. There were difficult issues of foreign relations involved because of the Japanese Government's involvement in establishing the Japanese firms' export policy, including their check prices rule. The Court did not reach these issues.[13]

Beginning in the 1980s, the enforcement agencies were for a long period inactive in bringing predatory pricing cases. However, in 1999, the Antitrust Division filed a significant predatory pricing case against American Airlines. The complaint alleged that American violated Section 2 of the Sherman Act by anticompetitive and predatory behavior directed at three low cost carriers that had begun offering service to American's Dallas hub.[14] The Government alleged that American was a monopolist in the relevant city-pair markets, that it increased the number of available flights and priced below some measure of cost as a targeted predatory strategy to drive the low cost carriers out of the Dallas market, and that it had been or would be able to recoup its losses after the low cost carriers no longer served Dallas. The district court granted summary judgment for American Airlines "because it at most matched the prices of its competitors, and because there is no dangerous probability (even assuming below-cost pricing) of recoupment of American's supposed profits by means of supra-competitive pricing."[15] On appeal, the Tenth Circuit affirmed, concluding that the Government had failed to show that American's pricing was below an "appropriate" level of

---

11. See the summary of some of this literature in Baker, *Predatory Pricing After Brooke Group: An Economic Perspective*, 62 ANTITRUST L.J. 585, 589–92 (1994).

12. 504 U.S. 451, 112 S.Ct. 2072, 119 L.Ed.2d 265 (1992).

13. For a view that the facts of *Matsushita* suggest a Sherman Act remedy for "dumping", see First, *supra* note 10, at 245–46.

14. United States v. AMR Corp., 140 F. Supp. 2d 1141 (D. Kan. 2001).

15. Id. at 1218.

cost.[16] Although the court declined to adopt a specific measure of cost, it used marginal cost, or average variable cost as a proxy for marginal cost, as a basis for rejecting the Government's expert testimony. The appeals court did not reach the recoupment issue.

The appropriate measure of cost remains an unresolved issue. The possibility that courts may move away from strict use of such measures is opened by the aggressive challenge to the cost screening test in the literature. The Tenth Circuit cited one such study in suggesting that the "incredulity that once prevailed" with respect to predatory pricing is no longer warranted.[17] The facts of AMR are a case in point. American Airlines did not price below the level of the new entrants in the Dallas city-pair markets. It did, however, expand capacity in these routes, adding new flights or larger planes. It also increased the number of seats sold at its lowest fare. After the new entrants left these city pair markets, American reduced capacity and raised its prices to pre-entry levels. There was also intent evidence from statements made by various American officials. The Government argued that American's aggressive response, with no demonstrated link to any efficiency, was intended to convey a "no-holds-barred" reputation that would discourage any would-be entrant from future challenges to American routes.[18] Both lower courts disregarded these factors in favor of the mechanical "below-cost" screening test.

Spirit Airlines, Inc. v. Northwest Airlines, Inc. is a second and even more recent case involving an airline's alleged price predation.[19] The case seems at odds with the Eighth Circuit's ruling in AMR in several respects. Spirit, a small independent carrier, operated flights out of Detroit. Spirit focused its marketing on local leisure or price-sensitive customers whose travel by air is discretionary. In 1995 and 1996, Spirit began head to head competition with Northwest, the dominant hub carrier operating out of Detroit Metropolitan Airport, by offering discount flights to Philadelphia and Boston. Prior to Spirit's entry, Northwest had a 72% market share for the Detroit-Philadelphia route and an 89% market share for the Detroit-Boston route. Northwest responded by decreasing the cost of its advance purchase fares to levels at or below those charged by Spirit and by increasing flights to Boston and Philadelphia. Within three months of Northwest's action, Spirit withdrew from the Boston and Philadelphia markets.

Spirit brought suit for predatory pricing and other predatory conduct under Section 2 of the Sherman Act (monopolization and attempted monopolization claims). The district court granted summary judgment to Northwest, dismissing Spirit's claims. On appeal, the Sixth Circuit reversed the grant of summary judgment and remanded the case for further proceedings. In reaching this decision, the appellate court found

---

16. United States v. AMR Corp., 335 F.3d 1109, 1121–22 (10th Cir. 2003).

17. Id. at 1114–15 (citing Bolton, et al.), *Predatory Pricing: Strategic Theory and Legal Policy*, 88 Geo. L.J. 2239, 2241 (2000).

18. Id. at 1114–15.

19. 429 F.3d 190 (6th Cir. 2005).

that Spirit's experts had made a credible claim that the market for determining price predation was not all air passenger travel to Boston or Philadelphia, but only the discretionary or leisure travel for which Spirit sought to compete. Using this market definition, the court proceeded to evaluate Spirit's evidence that Northwest was pricing below its average variable costs and that Northwest was able to recoup its losses within 4 months of Spirit's withdrawal from the market. The expert for Spirit had reached different conclusions on these issues than the expert for Northwest. On this record, the court held that the district court should not have granted summary judgment for Northwest.

The Spirit court also concluded that the predatory effects of Northwest's actions were linked to its decision to expand capacity at the same time it lowered its price. Thus, even if Northwest's prices exceeded average variable cost, the Section 2 claims were not at an end. Discounted prices, even if above average variable cost, might together with the substantial expansion of output, constitute a violation of Section 2.

Chapter V

HORIZONTAL RESTRAINTS

Table of Sections

---

§ 5.1   Introduction

This chapter deals with horizontal restraints—power jointly exercised by two or more rival firms. By cooperating or conspiring, such rivals can exercise market power in much the same way that a single firm can. Common forms of concerted conduct among rivals include price fixing, division of markets, and boycotting or joint refusals to deal. An arrangement among rivals to divide the market or set prices is often called a cartel—an organization with rules of operation and enforcement powers. Less organized concerted action—sometimes called interdependent conduct or coordinated interaction—may have the same effects as a cartel. Although these restraints may involve close knit cooperation, as in the case of a cartel, the firms remain under separate ownership and control. As rival firms meld their operations more closely, their cooperation may take on the form of a joint venture—addressed in Chapter 13— or a horizontal merger—addressed in Chapter 11.

Horizontal restraints are to be distinguished from vertical restraints—also involving two or more firms. Vertical restraints, which are addressed in Chapters 6–8, involve players on more than one level of the distribution chain—for example, a supplier and its customers. Because horizontal restraints involve combinations among rivals that can increase their market power—perhaps to near dominant or dominant levels—many horizontal restraint issues are corollaries of monopoly issues, addressed in Chapter 3.

5.1a. Summary of the Law

Horizontal restraints of trade are addressed under Section 1 of the Sherman Act and under Section 5 of the Federal Trade Commission Act. Section 2 of the Sherman Act may also come into play—especially Section 2 offenses that require less than monopoly power, such as attempt to monopolize or conspiracy to monopolize. But Section 1 has provided the touchstone for horizontal restraint enforcement since 1890. Section 1 forbids "[e]very contract, combination * * * or conspiracy, in restraint of trade." Chief Justice Hughes described the Sherman Act as a "charter of freedom" that possesses "generality and adaptability comparable to that found * * * in constitutional provisions."[1] These words have pointed application to Section 1 of the Act which is more spacious in sweep and more open to development and change than is Section 2. The phrase "restraint of trade" invites a variety of interpretations of business conduct. The words "contract, combination or conspiracy" also cover a broad range—potentially every business deal. Thus, from the outset, the Supreme Court has struggled to give these words content that is true to the goals of antitrust without overcoverage that could stifle legitimate and efficient business conduct.

Before 1978, there were two approaches to the application of Section 1. The first—the rule of reason—called for a broad inquiry into the nature, purpose and effect of any challenged arrangement before a decision is made about its legality. The second—the *per se* doctrine–made every practice to which it applied illegal, regardless of the reasons for or the effects of any particular use. Although the two approaches purported to seek the same statutory goals, they signified quite distinct attitudes toward the appropriate role of the courts in the regulation of economic conduct. Lawyers and judges tended to see the two approaches to Section 1 as distinct antitrust categories. They also assumed that the consequences of placing an alleged offense in one category or the other were profound; both the scope of litigation and the likely outcome were directly and substantially affected.

Beginning with United States v. Socony–Vacuum Oil Co.[2] shortly before World War II, the trend was toward increasing the reach of the *per se* doctrine. But this tendency was reversed beginning in the late 1970s, when Broadcast Music, Inc. v. CBS, Inc.,[3] suggested a return to wider application of the rule of reason. At about the same time, the Court suggested in National Society of Professional Engineers v. United States[4] that a rule of reason inquiry could be truncated, offering an

§ 5.1

1. Appalachian Coals, Inc. v. United States, 288 U.S. 344, 359–60, 53 S.Ct. 471, 77 L.Ed. 825 (1933).

2. 310 U.S. 150, 60 S.Ct. 811, 84 L.Ed. 1129 (1940).

3. 441 U.S. 1, 99 S.Ct. 1551, 60 L.Ed.2d 1 (1979).

4. 435 U.S. 679, 98 S.Ct. 1355, 55 L.Ed.2d 637 (1978).

intermediate position between the polar extremes of the traditional *per se* and rule of reason treatment. In sum, developments since 1978 have not obliterated the distinction between the two categories, but they have suggested increased reliance on a modified rule of reason in cases that cannot safely be assessed under the more or less mechanical formula of a *per se* rule. While naked price fixing and territorial allocations among rivals may still be *per se* illegal, some conduct tending toward similar effects may still be subject to the rule of reason—and be lawful if it is a part of a larger scheme with overriding competitive benefits.

5.1b. Horizontal Restraints and Market Power

Power and the potential for or actual abuse of that power is the common thread running through the fabric of antitrust. So it is with horizontal restraints, where the concerted conduct of rivals can create or extend power and use it to the detriment of key antitrust goals, in particular maintaining efficient allocation, ensuring against unfair transfer of wealth to those wielding power, and providing a competitive framework in which initiative and innovation can thrive. A cartel that limits output and fixes prices can undercut each of these goals, lowering production below the level of efficient allocation, transferring wealth from consumers to the cartel, dampening entry opportunities and discouraging innovation or its commercialization.

The text of Section 1 of the Sherman Act—forbidding combinations "in restraint of trade"—provides only the most amorphous reference to power. As one might expect, a showing of market power has not been a rigorous requirement in interpretations of Section 1. Yet, if the provision is to be applied in a manner that furthers the interests of competition without stifling legitimate and creative initiatives, some attention must be paid to power, a root of antitrust abuse. Even so, a *per se* rule that requires no proof of market power is still warranted when a quick look discloses an abuse routinely associated with an exercise of market power and devoid of efficiency potential.

5.1b1. Cartels

In a perfectly competitive market, each firm will assume that it must sell at the current market price and will set output at a level expected to maximize returns at that price. A monopolist, by contrast, since its output is the output of the industry, will recognize that the higher its output, the lower will be the price at which it will be able to market that output. It will therefore lower output so that supracompetitive prices can be charged and the overall return maximized. If an industry has a relatively small number of participants, they may be able to act concertedly in the manner of a single monopolist. Even if industry participants cannot perfectly duplicate a monopolist's control, they may be able to reduce output sufficiently to increase prices and thus share a higher overall industry return.

The likelihood of a cartel will vary with the gain from its formation and implementation and with the difficulties that hinder effectuating it.

Impediments to a cartel can be substantial.[5] Information must be gathered and dispersed. Mechanisms must be developed and utilized for the concerted making of complex business decisions and these decisions must be executed by all of the independent firms. The difficulty of achieving a successful cartel changes with a number of key variables discussed below.[6] But some of the conditions that make cartel coordination more difficult may also suggest increased gain from—and incentive for—such coordination.

The number of firms in the industry—As the number of firms in an industry increases, coordination is likely to become more difficult. This factor is a key to merger control policy, which bases enforcement decisions in large part on the number of firms that will remain in an industry after the merger. But a larger number of firms is not an absolute bar to successful horizontal restraints. Indeed, large numbers may increase the industry's political influence, enabling them to pressure the government to tolerate or actively assist an organization of competitors that affects the restraints. For example, professional associations—sometimes acting with tacit or express government approval—may facilitate cartel practices among a large number of market actors.

The number of potential entrants into the market—As the number of potential entrants into a market increases, the risk of injury from coordinated action decreases. Of course, potential entrants vary widely in terms of their ability and willingness to enter the market. But if entry constraints are low enough and the number of firms that could overcome them large, potential entry can be a significant restraint on anticompetitive cooperation.

The complexity, differentiation and stability of the product—Homogeneous products that do not change in characteristics over time are thought to be the most susceptible to cartel activity. This description might fit, for example, agricultural commodities such as fruits, grains or vegetables. The uniform characteristics of the product may make it easier for market participants to find common ground in establishing the terms of sale. But differentiation among products, although it may make formal cartel activity less likely, may facilitate tacit interaction, as discussed in § 5.1b2. If support or service is frequently needed with the product and usually supplied by the seller, significant differentiation may result from ancillary service activities even if the product itself is highly standardized.

The proportion of fixed (overhead) costs to total costs—As fixed costs (overhead) increase in proportion to overall costs, cartel practices become more difficult because a market participant with high fixed costs has a

---

5. F. M. SCHERER & D. ROSS, INDUSTRIAL MARKET STRUCTURE AND ECONOMIC PERFORMANCE 277–315 (3d ed. 1990); Hay & Kelley, *An Empirical Survey of Price Fixing Conspiracies*, 17 J.L. & ECON. 13 (1974); McGee, *Ocean Freight Rate Conferences and the American Merchant Marine*, 27 U. CHI. L. REV. 191, 197–204 (1960)(describing the conditions favoring cartelization and the organization and behavior of a cartel).

6. SCHERER & ROSS, supra note 5, at 315 (summarizing factors that make concerted conduct more difficult).

strong incentive to increase production to lessen the per item burden of these costs. Even if a cartel is organized, the incentive to cheat will be strong and may lead to under-the-table rebates or discounts as members fight *sub rosa* to increase their output. Many transportation industries have high fixed costs—a plane or train that travels with a 20 percent load may cost almost as much to operate as one that travels with a full load. But cartel activity is still possible under these conditions, especially if government entities tolerate or assist that activity. Indeed, the incentive for cartel activity is increased. An industry with high fixed costs will have more to gain by avoiding competition that might drive rates below the level needed to cover those costs. Although cheating may be more likely, the cartel's ability to tolerate some cheating—and still earn a higher return than would be earned in the absence of cartel organization—may be substantial.

Depressed business conditions—When a market is depressed, firms will be struggling with excess capacity, a condition that tends to raise a firm's proportion of fixed costs. Here, again, the incentive to cheat on the cartel is increased. But the incentive to engage in cartel activity is probably also increased. Political tolerance for cartels may also grow when an industry is depressed. During the early years of the Franklin Roosevelt Administration, the United States experimented with cartel activity in an effort to regulate excess capacity and prevent further precipitous declines in prices. Other nations have recognized an antitrust exemption for the operation of crisis cartels. See the discussion in § 5.3c.

The proportion of large sales to infrequent purchasers—The buying power of large, infrequent purchasers can undermine a cartel. As these large purchasers occupy an increasing percentage of the market, it becomes increasingly difficult for sellers to maintain output and plan ahead without winning a share of the long-term contracts. Competition for the large buyers' trade may thwart efforts to discipline cartel members. A government enforcement mechanism may still overcome this difficulty. Or cartel members might establish a cartel that includes a price discrimination scheme that favors large buyers.

Opportunities for secret discounting—As opportunities for secret discounting increase, the discipline of a cartel becomes more difficult. A transparent market—one in which all transactions are known to the members of the industry—may facilitate cartel discipline.

Distrust and animosity among industry executives—To successfully cartelize each participant must see its own self-interest in ways similar to those of the other participants. If all major competitors enter the industry at about the same time, use the same technology, and produce in plants of about the same age, their respective conceptions of the profit-maximizing price will tend to converge. As such factors differ, conceptions about realistic cartel goals will diverge. Variation in corporate culture can also make a difference. For example, if all participants operate only in a single industry, cartelization may be easier than if several participants are conglomerate, each having entered the subject market for different, perhaps inconsistent reasons. Indeed, as a number of unsuccessful merger attempts also suggest, differences in management style and temperament can be disruptive even if much else is conducive to cooperation. As distrust and animosity among industry executives increases, cartel discipline will be harder to maintain. Indeed, the presence in an industry of even a single maverick—say, a firm that entered late and aggressively and gained its place by hard competition—may be sufficient to thwart effective cartel practices.

Cumulative effects—Even when there are fewer than ten firms in an industry, cartelization can be difficult. For example, how does an industry of eight agree on a common price or the output assigned to each? Because of firm variances, the output required to attain maximum efficiency may be a different percentage of each firm's total capacity. Even if output is fixed so that each can operate at maximum efficiency, each is likely to have different costs, so that the profit-maximizing price will be different for each. Since each firm is anxious to maximize its own returns, each would desire to make and sell more at the cartel price than it would have elected to sell at a lower and truly competitive price. Even though each firm would like to increase its own output, a depressed industrywide output must be maintained to operate an effective cartel.

Of course, a successful cartel will still benefit all members as increased aggregate returns are shared. Obstacles can be overcome, even when there are a large number of participants. For example, although the large number creates substantial coordination difficulties, it may give the industry added political clout needed to achieve a regulatory program that facilitates cartelization. Consider agriculture; it looks like a paradigmatic competitive industry structurally, but cooperatives controlling output may be sanctioned under state or federal law. Sometimes, a cartel actually attains the assistance of a government mechanism to enforce cartel decisions. For example, for many years, the tariffs jointly negotiated and set by carriers participating in international ocean shipping cartels were routinely filed with and enforced by the Federal Maritime Commission. The international oil cartel (OPEC) is also illustrative. It is a cartel that has survived because of the support of the governments of oil exporting countries. As that experience demonstrates, government support may not completely insulate a cartel either from market forces or underlying difficulties of coordination.

Even when no government assistance is available, industry members may establish a workable cartel, perhaps even in quite unconcentrated markets. Firms may adopt a convention or formula that successfully divides markets or establishes a minimum price. Because overt cartels are almost sure to be prosecuted in the United States, firms seek to keep any concerted action a secret. That such arrangements are not only possible but likely is suggested by the vast array of successful price fixing cases brought by the government and by class action plaintiffs over the years. The record begins with such early cases as United States v.

Addyston Pipe & Steel Co.[7] and extends through the large number of bid-rigging cases that the Justice Department brought during the 1970s and 1980s against firms seeking road or airport construction contracts, to matters like the Department's international cartel case against ADM and its case against NASDAQ market makers for the concerted manipulation of the spread between buying and selling prices—a conspiracy first identified by scholars, then challenged in a class action,[8] later enjoined in a Government consent decree and finally sanctioned by the Securities and Exchange Commission. While covert cooperation among rivals may be widespread, it entails substantial risks. Detection puts participants at risk of criminal prosecution by the Justice Department and of treble damage litigation brought on behalf of injured buyers. Some of the sanctions can be economically and socially severe.

The other key variable affecting the likelihood of cartelization is incentive. The incentive for cartelization is probably stronger if products are fungible (because there are fewer opportunities for niche marketing), if the industry is depressed, or if the industry has high fixed costs or is confronted with long-term overcapacity. For example, the high fixed costs—and relatively low variable costs—associated with many transportation industries create a substantial incentive for individual firms to join in a cartel arrangement. A cartel can ensure industry participants a return that covers the high fixed costs. Those same high fixed costs create a substantial incentive to cheat on the cartel—eliminating idle capacity means that a greater percentage of a firm's high fixed costs are met. But this incentive to lower prices to attract business will be present regardless of whether the industry has cartelized. From each participating firm's point of view, even if some cheating occurs, it may be better off with than without the cartel.

5.1b2. *Interdependent Conduct*

There may be ways for firms to achieve the benefits of cartel-like conduct while staying within the confines of the law. The starting point is oligopoly, perhaps with five or fewer firms in the industry. If the product is relatively homogeneous and cost structures are similar, each firm will recognize that price competition in the industry is adverse to its interest. Each firm's profits, and those of its rivals, will be maximized if the price settles at a level that approximates the level each firm would charge if it were a monopolist. When firms are so few, and when the advantages of cooperation and the path to cooperation are both evident, each firm may well see as its own profit-maximizing price the noncompetitive price that maximizes returns for the industry. Thus, without any explicit accord on any course of conduct—an accord that would greatly increase the risk of antitrust liability—each firm may set and adhere to a supracompetitive price. One firm initiates a price at a level it thinks will maximize not only for itself but also for others, hopeful that they will

---

7.   85 Fed. 271 (6th Cir.1898), modified and aff'd, 175 U.S. 211, 20 S.Ct. 96, 44 L.Ed. 136 (1899).

8.   In re NASDAQ Market–Makers Antitrust Litig., 169 F.R.D. 493 (S.D.N.Y.1996).

perceive the advantage of following rather than cutting price. An effort to increase share through price cuts would be in vain because any reduction below the leader's price would be followed by the leader and others.

Of course, things do not always work smoothly. Just as cartels may be unstable, efforts at oligopolistic coordination may also be. But conventions may aid firms in determining price. For example, at the retail level, a convention for a particular percentage markup—say a 100 percent markup over wholesale price—may aid retailers in dampening price competition. Price leadership may be institutionalized in some fashion. If one industry member is significantly larger than other participants, others may routinely follow its price initiatives.[9] And strategic behavior by one or more members may discipline less cooperative members of the oligopoly to adhere to higher price levels. At its simplest, this strategic behavior may be nothing more than an occasional price war. If a firm deviates from a higher price level, it may be "punished" by other firms in the industry by means of a price war. True, all firms in the industry will suffer a decline in profitability as a result of this price war. But its effect may be to remind all participants, especially the firm that instituted the discounting, of the value of tacit interaction in maintaining the higher price level. An oligopolistic industry in which higher price levels are maintained most of the time, with short interruptions for price wars, is likely to be engaging in strategic behavior designed to maintain supracompetitive prices.[10]

Strategic behavior to enforce monopoly level prices will be most effective and most likely to occur if it can be targeted. For example, a market leader may respond to a smaller firm's discounting by cutting its prices only in the geographic region in which the smaller firm sells. In this way, the smaller firm can be "punished" at relatively low cost to the market leader, which can subsidize any losses from its strategic price cuts with higher profits earned elsewhere.

Although more rigorous cartel conduct is generally associated with homogeneous products, highly differentiated products may facilitate tacit coordination when there is market segmentation. For example, if most buyers of automobiles usually choose among offerings in a particular segment of the automobile market—luxury, mid-priced or economy— there may be relatively little competition across these segmental lines. For tacit interaction to operate successfully, it may have to account mainly for players in the same segment of the market, not the entire automobile industry. This makes tacit interaction easier and more likely.[11]

9. General Motors is said to have long held a price leadership role in the domestic automobile industry. SCHERER & ROSS, supra note 5, at 254–56.

10. Baker & Bresnahan, *Empirical Methods of Identifying and Measuring Mar-* *ket Power*, 61 ANTITRUST L.J. 3, 13–15 (1992).

11. See the discussion of tacit interaction in differentiated markets in § 11.2e1.

Firms may develop and use, sometimes individually, sometimes imitatively, sometimes by express or implicit agreement, practices that facilitate oligopolistic price coordination. To illustrate, the preannouncement of planned price changes or arrangements to exchange industry information will, by making pricing decisions by each participant more transparent, tend to facilitate coordinated, interdependent pricing. Strategies that firms can undertake to encourage interdependent conduct may at times cross the line of legality. But some forms of interdependent conduct can offer participants supracompetitive returns at low risk of antitrust liability. If such interdependent conduct works to limit output or raise prices in the same manner as a cartel, it will undermine efficient resource allocation and cause wealth transfer. These are precisely the adverse effects that the antitrust laws are intended to sanction. Section 1 of the Sherman Act has been used to try to attack interdependent conduct, so far with limited success.[12]

5.1b3. Cartel Variations

The prototypical cartel possesses market power that allows it to limit output and raise prices. But an organization of rivals may exercise market power in other ways that do not directly limit output, yet still lead to higher prices and to both resource allocation and wealth transfer injuries often associated with higher prices. Two theories have been offered to explain such behavior: (1) a conspiracy among rivals to raise the costs of nonparticipating rivals; and (2) a conspiracy among rivals to raise their own costs, or the costs of their customers in ways that, to their relative advantage, make the market less competitive.

Rival firms that possess market power may cooperate to increase the costs of nonparticipating firms.[13] To do so effectively, the firms must control a vital input that can be denied nonparticipating rivals, or made available to them only on discriminatory terms. Thus, nonparticipating manufacturers might be denied access to a needed raw material controlled by the conspirators. Or, nonparticipating doctors may be denied admitting privileges to a hospital, or realtors denied membership in a multiple listing service. The upstream input gives such conspiracies a vertical dimension. Despite the vertical element, plaintiffs often attack such arrangements as horizontal conspiracies, seeking more favorable legal standards. Theorists who see this conduct as distinct from traditional cartel behavior emphasize its failure to directly limit output or raise price.[14] But an effort to raise a rival's costs may also be an effort to enforce discipline in a cartel, whose major purpose is limiting output and raising price. Despite this competitive threat, when there is no evidence

---

12. The success or failure of such enforcement efforts under Section 1 may turn on the court's interpretation of the words "contract, combination or conspiracy," a matter addressed in § 5.2.

13. Krattenmaker & Salop, *Anticompetitive Exclusion: Raising Rivals' Costs to Achieve Power over Price*, 96 YALE L.J. 209

(1986); Salop & Scheffman, *Raising Rivals' Costs,* 73 AM. ECON. REV. 267 (1983).

14. Langenfeld & Silvia, *Federal Trade Commission Horizontal Restraint Cases: An Economic Perspective*, 61 ANTITRUST L.J. 653, 661–65 (1993).

of direct attempts to limit output or raise price, or when the conduct that leads to these results is tacit cooperation, the conduct may be beyond the reach of current antitrust law. But failure of a plaintiff to show that the cartel has directly limited output or raised prices should not bar successful prosecution if these injuries flow indirectly from cooperative conduct designed to raise rivals' costs. The Federal Trade Commission has instituted a number of cases based upon this theory and if the facts alleged are proved, relief should be available under Section 5.[15]

A second variation involves rivals in possession of market power that attempt to raise their own costs or those of their own customers, when by doing so they can injure rivals relatively more severely than any harm to themselves.[16] A professional association, for example, may ban advertising, a ban supported by firms already in the market and operating at efficient scale. The effect of this ban may be both to discourage entry to limit some market participants' ability to obtain scale economies that advertising could help them to achieve and to increase the search costs of consumers seeking alternatives to their present trading patterns (because the absence of advertising could make a consumer search more difficult and costly). Even if direct conduct to limit output or raise prices cannot be shown, such facilitating practices should be prohibited. The impact of the professional association's advertising ban, for example, will be to increase participants' profits, create allocation injuries, and transfer wealth from consumers to association members.[17] These are classic antitrust harms. Concerted conduct to achieve them should violate Section 1 of Sherman and Section 5 of the FTC Act.

5.1b4. Coercion With or Without Market Power

The exercise of power takes many forms. Market power as described in Chapter 2 is a market player's power over price. But some market participants may engage in coercive anticompetitive conduct even though they lack market power.[18] If a firm engages in coercive conduct of a kind associated with some form of injury to competition that has little or no potential for competitive benefits, almost always it can be rationally condemned without a power analysis. For example, a firm may attempt

15. An example of such a case is Detroit Auto Dealers Ass'n, 111 F.T.C. 417 (1989), aff'd in part and remanded, 955 F.2d 457 (6th Cir.), cert. denied, 506 U.S. 973 (1992)(challenging the association's limit on dealer hours of operation, conduct that did not directly decrease output or raise price, but denied consumers a convenience that they preferred and indirectly may have raised prices by limiting consumer shopping time). For a listing of other FTC cases involving non-traditional cartel theories, see Langenfeld & Silvia, supra note 14, Appendix B, at 690–93.

16. Langenfeld & Silvia, supra note 14, at 665–78.

17. The question of the whether the *per se* rule, quick look, or more expansive rule of reason should be the standard for illegality of advertising restrictions was addressed in California Dental Ass'n v. FTC, 526 U.S. 756, 119 S.Ct. 1604, 143 L.Ed.2d 935 (1999) and is discussed in § 5.3f.

18. Sullivan, *The Viability of the Current Law on Horizontal Restraints*, 75 Cal. L. Rev. 835, 849 (1987)(pointing out that some coercive conduct has no potential for improving competition and its use, therefore, might be rationally condemned without a showing of market power).

to drive a rival from the market by disparaging its product, by sabotaging its production, or by convincing a labor union to target the rival in a strike action. Most of these actions are likely to violate laws other than the antitrust laws, but they may also violate Section 1 of the Sherman Act. In many cases, the disparagement of a rival's product may be undertaken as part of a boycott, a practice condemned in traditional antitrust enforcement. Despite venerable roots in boycott law, coercion as a basis for antitrust intervention is not a well-defined concept. Its use as an independent basis for antitrust intervention could produce undisciplined interpretations.[19] But when coercion is linked to some form of market power, or when its use is condemned because it has no possible competitive benefits, as may be the case with some boycotts or vertical restraints, it is a proper determinant of antitrust intervention.

5.1b5. Buyer Cartels

Traditional cartel theory addresses conspiracies among sellers. Buyers too can and do form cartels. As a seller cartel is to monopoly, so is a buyer cartel to monopsony. Buyer cartel cases are not new, but early court holdings had little economic theory and failed to distinguish between buyer and seller cartels or between monopoly and monopsony power. An early Supreme Court Sherman Act case involved a conspiracy among buyers not to bid against one another at livestock auctions.[20] Over the years, there have been many other cases involving buyer conspiracies for fish, livestock, or agricultural commodities.[21] Sports law cases, involving league restrictions on the recruitment and hiring of players or coaches, have also been common.[22] Buyer cartels are by no means restricted to these areas, as is demonstrated by Todd v. Exxon Corp., a Second Circuit case involving an alleged cooperative arrangement among large oil companies to share salary data for managerial, professional, and technical employees in order to suppress the amount paid to these

19. Kauper, *The Sullivan Approach to Horizontal Restraints*, 75 CAL. L. REV. 893, 910–11 (1987)(suggesting that coercion as a basis of antitrust intervention introduces "considerable discretion into judicial analysis").

20. Swift & Co. v. United States, 196 U.S. 375, 25 S.Ct. 276, 49 L.Ed. 518 (1905).

21. E.g., American Tobacco Co. v. United States, 328 U.S. 781, 66 S.Ct. 1125, 90 L.Ed. 1575 (1946)(3 major cigarette producers conspire to rig terms of tobacco auctions); Swift & Co. v. United States, 196 U.S. 375, 25 S.Ct. 276, 49 L.Ed. 518 (1905)(conspiracy among buyers not to bid against one another at livestock auctions); Eagle v. Star–Kist Foods, 812 F.2d 538 (9th Cir. 1987)(tuna canneries alleged price fixing of tuna purchased); United States v. Portac, 869 F.2d 1288 (9th Cir. 1989)(buyers of timber rights); Betaseed Inc. v. U & I Inc., 681 F.2d 1203 (9th Cir. 1982)(processor of sugar beets exercises buying pow-

er through forced reciprocal dealing with sugar beet farmers); Live Poultry Dealers' Protective Assoc. v. United States, 4 F.2d 840 (2d Cir. 1924)(178 wholesale poultry buyers collude to set price); Reid Brothers Logging Co. v. Ketchikan Pulp Co., 699 F.2d 1292 (9th Cir.), cert. denied, 464 U.S. 916 (1983)(two logging companies refuse to bid against one another); U.S. v. Champion International Corp., 557 F.2d 1270 (9th Cir.), cert. denied, 434 U.S. 938 (1977)(logging case).

22. E.g., Maurice Clarett v. NFL, 369 F.3d 124 (2d Cir. 2004)(unsuccessful challenge to NFL's restrictions on recruitment of college-age athletes); Law v. NCAA, 134 F.3d 1010 (10th Cir. 1998)(NCAA members suppress salaries of a class of Division IA assistant basketball coaches); Smith v. Pro Football, Inc., 593 F.2d 1173 (D.C.Cir. 1978)(NFL football teams concertedly declined to deal with would-be players before the draft).

employees.[23] A buyers cartel, just as a sellers cartel, will suppress output, but the direct injury is to the seller (who receives a lesser payment than would occur under competitive conditions) rather than to a buyer who pays an inflated price. The market power that a buyers cartel exercises would be measured by examining the alternative buying sources to which the seller might turn.

Many buyer power cases involve atomistic sellers, comparable to the atomistic buyer (the consumer) victimized in seller cartel cases. Farmers, ranchers, fishermen, health care professionals, or individual journeyman athletes or coaches may lack meaningful countervailing leverage in dealings with the cartel. Moreover, many of these sellers have added vulnerability because of sunk costs or the perishable nature of the product or service that they are selling. For example, an athlete that has spent years developing a skill set that allows her to play a professional sport may be able to sell her services only to a professional league that is the only available buyer for that sport. If the athlete abandons sport for another profession, a major portion of her investment in the sport may be lost. A farmer or rancher often sells a commodity that is perishable, so that there is no opportunity to hold the product in inventory while awaiting more favorable terms. It has been said that any person seeking employment is dealing with a perishable resource because a day's lost employment can never be recouped.[24]

There is a need for the antitrust bar and for courts to more directly confront the unique issues involved in a buyer cartel. Although much of the law applicable to a seller cartel will continue to be directly transferrable to buyer cartels, there are important differences, in particular in the nature of the market analysis (focusing on options available to the seller, not to the buyer) and as to the nature and target of the injury (usually an atomistic seller). In particular cases, there may be difficult theoretical and empirical questions about the impact of a buyer cartel on consumers. Under limited conditions, it is possible, for example, that a buyer cartel that directly injures atomistic sellers may benefit consumers by passing along lower prices. See the discussion in § 2.7e2.

§ 5.2 Definition of a Conspiracy

Section 1 of the Sherman Act applies to "[e]very contract, combination * * * or conspiracy, in restraint of trade." The quoted words fuse into a single concept—concerted action. On its face this language requires two or more participants to accomplish the unlawful conduct. The language implies a judgment that conduct of a single firm is less threatening than that engaged in by a collective. Of course, if the single firm is dominant or near dominant in the industry, its conduct is within the reach of the monopolization proscriptions of Section 2. But once concerted action has been shown, the conduct of the collective is more tightly circumscribed by Section 1 (prohibiting a restraint of trade) than

23. Todd v. Exxon Corp., 275 F.3d 191 (2d Cir. 2001).

24. Id. at 211.

is the conduct of the dominant firm or would-be dominant firm by Section 2 (prohibiting monopolization or attempted monopolization). Although Section 1 makes no explicit reference either to competition or to power, perhaps the drafters had an intuitive sense that firms were unlikely to engage in concerted action to restrain trade except in an effort to create, extend or harvest the rewards of market power. In hindsight, we know any such generalization to be overbroad. Many combinations limiting the trade freedom of two or more firms may be efficiency enhancing while not presenting a significant threat to competition.

Whatever the Congressional intent behind the words, it is now well established that Section 1 reaches a variety of collective conduct, at least some of it in circumstances that, if engaged in unilaterally, would not violate Section 2. The definition of the words "contract, combination, or conspiracy" is crucial in many of these situations. Controversy has centered on three points: (1) how broadly or narrowly should the requirement for concerted action be construed—does it reach interdependent but noncollusive conduct; (2) what sort of evidentiary showing will be required to establish the existence of a conspiracy; and (3) when does joint ownership of part or all of two market participants or joint commitment by two or more separate owners to a unified enterprise preclude a showing of conspiracy between those participants.

5.2a. Interdependent But Noncollusive Conduct

The early Section 1 cases involved classic conspiracies; the evidence in each showed an express agreement among competitors to engage in a common course of conduct. United States v. Addyston Pipe & Steel Co.[1] and United States v. Trenton Potteries Co.[2] exemplify express agreement on the model of the classic cartel. American Column & Lumber Co. v. United States[3] involved an express agreement for common conduct in exchanging price and related data, conduct that was deemed likely to inhibit price competition and discourage production increases to keep market prices high. And United States v. Socony–Vacuum Oil Co.[4] involved an express agreement to enter the market and buy from identified "dancing partners," conduct aimed at bolstering market price.

The early cases did not address the circumstance of interdependent but noncollusive behavior by oligopolists. In the absence of any agreement, an industry of, say, three firms may price in supracompetitive fashion because each recognizes that its own interests are best served by pricing in parallel fashion. The economic impact of this conduct may be the same as if collusion were established. Posner has suggested that a showing of prolonged supracompetitive pricing along with conscious

§ 5.2

1. 85 Fed. 271 (6th Cir.1898), modified and aff'd, 175 U.S. 211, 20 S.Ct. 96, 44 L.Ed. 136 (1899).

2. 273 U.S. 392, 47 S.Ct. 377, 71 L.Ed. 700 (1927).

3. 257 U.S. 377, 42 S.Ct. 114, 66 L.Ed. 284 (1921).

4. 310 U.S. 150, 60 S.Ct. 811, 84 L.Ed. 1129 (1940).

parallelism should be sufficient to warrant or even require the inference of an agreement, thus establishing concerted action.[5] But if, in fact, all that was involved was successful interdependent pricing, such an approach could subject defendants to criminal prosecution for not competing aggressively, a result that may be politically unacceptable. Even if criminal prosecution were ruled out, civil suits would require courts to confront difficult remedial problems. A court may enjoin further collusion, but how does a court enjoin tepid competition by oligopolists? Were it to try, the court would likely find itself second-guessing a firm's pricing decisions, a task courts are ill-equipped to take on.

One solution may be to allow interdependent pricing to pass untouched, but to attack facilitating practices that make it easier for firms to follow one another's prices.[6] For example, a most favored nation clause or price protection agreement offered by the seller—the seller agrees to remit to the buyer any discount in price offered to a subsequent purchaser—may operate to lock in the seller's price. Any temptation to lower price to a would-be buyer would likely be deterred by knowledge that substantial rebates would have to be paid to past purchasers. If price protection agreements are used by all participants in an oligopolistic industry, price competition will be stilled or reduced. In a consent decree entered against General Electric and Westinghouse, the Justice Department forbade the use of such price protection clauses as well as other facilitating practices that allowed the two firms to submit identical bids.[7] In an action against the four member oligopolistic antiknock compound industry, the Federal Trade Commission also aimed its decree at facilitating practices, including devices independently used but that would discourage each of the four from seeking new business by undercutting supracompetitive prices. Among these practices were agreements with customers to reduce their prices if any reduction were given to another buyer and to give advance notice of price increases. But absent evidence that the facilitating practices had been agreed upon, rather than interdependently arrived at, the court of appeals declined to enforce the Commission's decree.[8] Use by oligopolists of a facilitating practice that enables the participants to coordinate prices should be vulnerable under Section 1 even if they are using it interdependently, rather than by explicit agreement. The reason for not treating interdependent pricing as a contract, combination or conspiracy is not that such conduct is not concerted. Such conduct is clearly and willfully concerted, and while it lacks explicit contractual commitment, so do most price conspiracies. Certainly, no horizontal price conspiracy results in enforceable contract obligations. And seldom do such conspiracies entail refined articulation of mutual understanding—often the understanding is no

5. Posner, *Oligopoly and the Antitrust Laws: A Suggested Approach,* 21 STAN. L. REV. 1562 (1969).

6. Hay, *Oligopoly, Shared Monopoly, and Antitrust Law,* 67 CORNELL L. REV. 439 (1982)(suggesting that antitrust analysis focus on "avoidable acts").

7. United States v. General Elec. Co., 1977–2 Trade Cas. (CCH) ¶ 61,659 (E.D. Pa.1977).

8. E.I. Du Pont de Nemours & Co. v. FTC, 729 F.2d 128 (2d Cir.1984).

more than a wink or a nod. The reason for sparing interdependent pricing from Section 1 condemnation is, first, that sellers in a tight oligopoly cannot avoid such conduct without economically irrational behavior (setting nonprofit-maximizing prices) and, second, that no feasible conduct remedy is available. Labeling the interdependent use of a facilitating practice as a contract, combination or conspiracy entails no such dilemmas. First, doing so properly labels such conduct concerted, which it certainly is. Second, there is, in this instance, unlike the instance of interdependent pricing, no policy reason not to do so. Oligopolists *can* avoid interdependent use of facilitating practices without making economically irrational decisions. And, where oligopolists do not avoid but interdependently embrace such conduct, there is an available judicial remedy: their conduct can be enjoined.

5.2b. The Evidentiary Showing of Concerted Conduct

Section 1 of the Sherman Act does not deal with single firm conduct, however anticompetitive it may be. Whenever Section 1 is invoked the question is presented, have two or more parties agreed to coordinate their market conduct? A similar issue arises under Section 2 when conspiracy to monopolize or monopolization resulting from joint conduct is alleged. The existence of a contract, combination or conspiracy seems a straightforward question, one that might be answered within the confines of common law tradition and much the same way at the end of the century as it was at its beginning. Indeed, there has been more stability about how concerted action is distinguished from individual action than there has been about many antitrust issues. This is not to say that development and change is lacking, only that observing it may take a practiced eye. Yet, understanding the developments should help to clarify issues both in counseling and litigation. The Section 1 evidentiary standard has been interpreted differently depending on whether the alleged offense is a horizontal claim, an interbrand vertical claim, or an intrabrand vertical claim. This section explores only a part of that trichotomy: that of an antitrust conspiracy in the horizontal context. Conspiracy in interbrand and intrabrand relationships is addressed in §§ 7.2c, 8.3d3, and 8.4d1.

Change in conspiracy doctrine affecting horizontal restraints has been slow, almost glacial, but it has occurred. Courts began with the proposition that an agreement can be implied from conduct and circumstances. Courts soon recognized that firms in tightly structured markets will often be mutually aware of the advantages of cooperation. Also, courts developed an understanding of the factors that encourage cooperative market conduct by making it more profitable, more feasible, or both. Courts recognized, too, that direct evidence of conspiracy may not be available because conspirators will seek to avoid leaving a paper trail or other direct evidence. In time the law stabilized around three related propositions: (1) that evidence of consciously parallel conduct by ostensibly competing firms is not alone sufficient to warrant an inference of agreement, regardless of how tightly structured the market may be; (2)

that such evidence, if accompanied by additional evidence tending to show deliberate coordination of conduct (some "plus factor" as it has sometimes been called), is sufficient to warrant the critical inference of conspiracy; and (3) that the parties themselves need not have entered into an express agreement but merely have inferred, each from the conduct of the others, that a commitment was being made. On these three propositions consensus remained intact during a long period from the Supreme Court's *Interstate Circuit*[9] decision in the late 1930s, to its *Matsushita*[10] decision in the mid–1980s, which seemed to alter the doctrine.

In *Interstate Circuit,* a movie theater chain sent to eight distributors identical letters which disclosed the names of all other addressees; each letter demanded that the distributor refuse to supply first-run films to exhibitors that either refused to meet the schedule of minimum prices, or that showed first-run films as part of a "double feature" program. There was also evidence that each addressee would gain if all accepted the proposal, but lose if it alone accepted. Each distributor finally responded to the proposal with the same, fairly complex counteroffer. On this evidence, the Supreme Court affirmed the district court's finding of concerted action, noting additionally that no defendant witness denied the conspiracy. The Court also noted that direct evidence of an unlawful conspiracy is the exception rather than the rule. It ruled that the circumstantial evidence in this case not only warranted but virtually demanded a finding of conspiracy, saying:

> It taxes credulity * * * that the several distributors would * * * have accepted and put into operation with substantial unanimity such far-reaching changes in their business methods without some understanding that all were to join * * *.[11]

Three other Supreme Court cases illustrate the scope of discretion to infer conspiracy based upon consciously parallel conduct. American Tobacco Co. v. United States held that evidence that the list prices charged and the discounts allowed by the three dominant tobacco companies were practically identical (1923 until about 1940) and absolutely identical (1928 until about 1940) warranted the jury's inference of a conspiracy.[12] In United States v. Paramount Pictures, Inc.,[13] findings of conspiracy were predicated on evidence that in their dealings with nonintegrated distributors, five vertically integrated companies that made, distributed and exhibited movies, specified the same minimum admission prices in licenses, used the same clearances between first-and second-run theaters, applied the same "block booking" practices, and imposed substantially identical terms with reference to a variety of complex matters. This evidence was held sufficient to warrant the conclusion that concert of

9. Interstate Circuit, Inc. v. United States, 306 U.S. 208, 59 S.Ct. 467, 83 L.Ed. 610 (1939).

10. Matsushita Elec. Indus. Co. v. Zenith Radio Corp., 475 U.S. 574, 106 S.Ct. 1348, 89 L.Ed.2d 538 (1986).

11. *Interstate Circuit*, 306 U.S. at 223.

12. 328 U.S. 781, 66 S.Ct. 1125, 90 L.Ed. 1575 (1946).

13. 334 U.S. 131, 68 S.Ct. 915, 92 L.Ed. 1260 (1948).

action was both contemplated and effected by the five firms. In FTC v. Cement Institute,[14] the Court upheld the Commission's finding of an unlawful conspiracy based upon cooperative conduct in the use of a basing point pricing system—specifically calculating transportation charges to the customer's place of business based on an assumed, common geographic point of shipment, regardless of where the goods were produced and shipment originated. The Commission had found not just that this system was universally used, but that sealed bids submitted by competing cement producers were identical to the fractional part of a penny.[15] But in another case the Court also suggested limits to this doctrine that conscious parallelism can be a basis for inferring conspiracy. In Theatre Enterprises, Inc. v. Paramount Film Distributing Corp.,[16] the Court held that proof of parallel business behavior by movie distributors in restricting "first runs" dates for local theaters was insufficient to show an unlawful conspiracy. There was little evidence of interdependence and considerable evidence tending to show that the restrictions were rational steps for each individual firm, regardless of whether rivals followed suit.

A more substantial—indeed, a law-changing limitation on a jury's discretion to infer conspiracy from circumstantial evidence—came in Matsushita Electric Industrial Co. v. Zenith Radio Corp.[17] For one thing, the Court stressed what perhaps should have been apparent all along, that the plaintiff must be able to specify with reasonable detail what the defendants agreed to do, and that the plaintiff's "plus factor" evidence must in logic tend to show that the defendants acted pursuant to that agreement.[18] For another, the Court indicated that if the plaintiff's inference of conspiracy is implausible as a matter of deductive theory, then the plaintiff's evidentiary burden increases.[19] In that event the plaintiff may not rely solely on circumstantial evidence, but must produce direct evidence of a conspiracy in order to avoid summary judgment and reach a jury.

In *Matsushita*, the plaintiffs—manufacturers of television sets in the United States—alleged that Japanese rivals conspired to price at predatory levels in the U. S. market to injure or vanquish U.S. rivals. Following lengthy pretrial discovery the district court granted summary judgment to the defendants. The Third Circuit reversed. The Supreme Court, in a 5–4 decision, restored summary judgment for the defendants. In so doing, the Court put into question a long-standing practice of allowing juries to find conspiracy solely based upon circumstantial evidence. It did so on the basis of a deductive, economic analysis that it thought convincing. First, it assumed that the Japanese firms must have used short-or mid-term profit-maximizing goals. On this assumption, it

---

14. 333 U.S. 683, 68 S.Ct. 793, 92 L.Ed. 1010 (1948).

15. Id. at 713 n.15 (citing sealed bids submitted by eleven firms offering an identical per barrel price—calculated to six decimal places).

16. 346 U.S. 537, 74 S.Ct. 257, 98 L.Ed. 273 (1954).

17. 475 U.S. 574, 106 S.Ct. 1348, 89 L.Ed.2d 538 (1986).

18. Id. at 588.

19. Id. at 596–97.

inferred that the Japanese industrialists would not persist for years in unyielding predation. Because this theoretical deduction made the jury's contrary inference from circumstantial evidence implausible, the Court reversed. Borrowing language from a vertical restraints case,[20] the majority stated that to survive summary judgment (at least where, as here, the plaintiff's case was bottomed on circumstantial evidence), the plaintiff must present evidence "that tends to exclude the possibility" that the defendants acted independently. In a conclusion vigorously challenged by the dissent, the Court inferred that the Japanese companies "had no motive to enter into the alleged conspiracy."[21] The Court did so, moreover, without much in the way of theoretical justification. Blatantly unlawful conspiracies are seldom provable by direct evidence, at least unless one of the participants discloses and testifies. To say that theoretical plausibility is an essential standard in such a context may seem, on its face, to increase rationality and avoid risk of jury errors. But those gains depend enormously on the power, generality or specificity of the deductions used by the court to segregate "plausible" from "implausible" theories of conspiracy. To pass over the experience, judgment and, yes, intuition of a jury—and to substitute judicial application of the narrow aridities of Chicago microtheory—is hardly a conspicuous application of wisdom and common sense. Chicago theory tells us, perhaps, what most (certainly not all) profit-maximizing entrepreneurs sharing the time frame and cultural goals of an individualistic United States entrepreneur would likely do in a given hypothetical situation. Is that kind of guidance a sufficient basis for withholding from a jury conflicting circumstantial evidence about what particular Japanese entrepreneurs in fact did in a particular context? The motivation they were responding to may well have been collective, not individual, and linked to a national culture that downplayed short or medium term profit-maximizing and firm-oriented conduct in favor of much longer time parameters and collective, national, status-oriented goals.

While few horizontal conspiracy cases allege below cost pricing, *Matsushita* substantially narrowed the jury's discretion to find conspiracy and expanded the summary judgment discretion of the district judge whenever, as is often the case, the conspiracy claim is based on circumstantial evidence. In a later monopoly leveraging and tie-in case, Eastman Kodak Co. v. Image Technical Services, Inc.,[22] the Court appeared to retreat from this broad shift of power from the jury to the district judge. The *Kodak* case, which involved both Section 1 and Section 2 issues, was factually and theoretically complex. The most significant contribution of the majority opinion is that the Court recognized this complexity and assigned to the fact finder, not to its own favorite microtheorist, the tasks of finding the basic facts and perceiving their implications. Although the contentious issue upon which theory was brought to bear

20. Monsanto Co. v. Spray–Rite Serv. Corp., 465 U.S. 752, 764, 104 S.Ct. 1464, 79 L.Ed.2d 775 (1984). The Court's treatment of price predation is addressed in Chapter 4.

21. *Matsushita*, 475 U.S. at 595.

22. 504 U.S. 451, 112 S.Ct. 2072, 119 L.Ed.2d 265 (1992).

entailed market power, not whether the agreement could be inferred as in *Matsushita*, the case contrasts so sharply with *Matsushita* that further exposition is warranted.

Kodak made and marketed photocopiers and micrographic equipment, serviced such equipment and made or purchased and stocked replacement parts for it. The plaintiffs were independent service organizations (ISOs). When Kodak refused to sell them parts needed to service Kodak equipment, the plaintiffs sued under the Sherman Act alleging that Kodak monopolized aftermarket parts for its equipment and leveraged its power in that market to gain power in the service market, thus monopolizing in violation of Section 2 and tying in violation of Section 1. Because the plaintiffs did not allege that Kodak had power in either the photocopier or the micrographic equipment markets, the district court granted summary judgment even before completion of discovery about whether Kodak had power in its own parts or service. The district court thought that refusing to sell parts to a competing service provider was not a tie and that whether or not Kodak had power in the market for its own parts, it had no duty to sell those parts to a competitor.[23] On appeal to the Ninth Circuit, which reversed the district court in a split decision, and before the Supreme Court on certiorari, Kodak contended that the district court was right not for the reasons it adopted but because, as a matter of microtheory, it would be implausible to conclude that Kodak could have power in the aftermarket for parts or service when it lacked power in the equipment market. It was essentially this issue, relevant to both the monopolization and Section 1 tying claims, that was the subject of the two engaging Supreme Court opinions, Justice Blackmun for the six-member majority, and Justice Scalia for the three-member dissent.

Kodak theorized that, regardless of market share for either parts or service, it could exercise no power because if it raised prices for parts or service above competitive levels, buyers would abandon Kodak in the primary market for equipment. The majority was unpersuaded:

> Kodak does not present any actual data on the equipment, service, or parts markets. Instead, it urges the adoption of a substantive legal rule that "equipment competition precludes any finding of monopoly power in derivative aftermarkets." * * *

> [But l]egal presumptions that rest on formalistic distinctions rather than actual market realities are generally disfavored in antitrust law. This court has preferred to resolve antitrust claims on a case-by-case basis, focusing on the "particular facts disclosed by the record." In determining the existence of market power, and specifically the 'responsiveness of the sales of one product to price changes of the other,' this Court has examined closely the economic reality of the market at issue.[24]

---

23. Image Technical Servs., Inc. v. Eastman Kodak Co., 1989–1 Trade Cas. (CCH) ¶ 68,402 (N.D. Cal.1988), rev'd, 903 F.2d 612 (9th Cir.1990).

24. *Kodak*, 504 U.S. at 466–67 (citations omitted).

The Court, moreover, went on to discourage some of the excessive interpretations to which *Matsushita* has sometimes been subject:

> [*Matsushita*] did not hold that if the moving party enunciates any economic theory supporting its behavior, regardless of its accuracy in reflecting the actual market, it is entitled to summary judgment. *Matsushita* demands only that the nonmoving party's inferences be reasonable in order to reach the jury, a requirement that was not invented, but merely articulated, in that decision.[25]

Interestingly enough, the Scalia dissent did not stress or even assert inconsistency with *Matsushita*. Rather, the dissent embraced Kodak's theoretical assertions and chided the majority for trying to counter them "with a theory of its own", namely, a reference by the majority to the information costs and inconvenience to consumers of "acquiring and processing life-cycle pricing data."[26]

In sum, we must conclude that *Matsushita* retains some potency. If the plaintiff relies on circumstances to infer conspiracy, that inference should not be inconsistent with widely credited microtheory. If it is, plaintiff must prove specific facts that differentiate its claim from the assumptions in the model to which the widely credited theory applies.[27] The lesson to be drawn from all of these cases is that the nature of the antitrust claim will influence the latitude allowed the judge or jury to find a conspiracy. At least in a predation context and perhaps in others where the plaintiff's theory strains against the assumptions and deductions of microeconomics, a jury's reading of circumstantial evidence will have to square with what the court finds to be plausible.

Quite apart from the *Matsushita* holding concerning circumstantial evidence, the imprecision of the norms about conspiracy leave immense discretion to the trial level fact finder, whether judge or jury. And, given the complexity of antitrust litigation, the judge can be influential on factual references even in a jury case. A judge who thinks that concerted price setting is nasty conduct can base his own findings of conspiracy, or encourage jury findings, on quite minimal evidence of collusion. If, by contrast, a different judge regards the antitrust laws as institutionalized paranoia, that judge can refuse to infer a conspiracy or could discourage a jury inference except on compelling proof. The pitfalls of this discretion, and the resulting uncertainty in the law, are demonstrated by two court of appeals cases involving alleged cartel activity in the corn products industry.

During the 1990s, the Justice Department pursued investigations of cartel activity in a number of markets for corn derivative products, including lysine, citric acid, and high fructose corn syrup. The investigation and subsequent indictment of firms participating in the lysine and

---

25. Id. at 468 (emphasis omitted).

26. Id. at 496 (Scalia, J., dissenting).

27. Consider also Brooke Group Ltd. v. Brown & Williamson Tobacco Corp., 509 U.S. 209, 113 S.Ct. 2578, 125 L.Ed.2d 168 (1993), which might be viewed as having reenforced the case for broad, district court discretion concerning antitrust summary judgment.

citric acid cartels was highly publicized, in part because of the controversial role of an Archer Daniels Midland (ADM) informant who worked with the FBI to make recordings of many of the lysine cartel meetings.[28] The Justice Department indicted ADM and other firms involved in the lysine and citric acid cartels and obtained large criminal fines against major participants.[29] In addition, three ADM officials served prison time for their leadership roles in the cartels.[30]

The litigation in the Seventh and the Ninth Circuits was brought by private claimants seeking damages for the cartel activity in corn derivative markets. The litigated issues involved products or parties that were not subject to the Department's criminal prosecutions. In the citric acid litigation, the Ninth Circuit affirmed the district court's decision granting summary judgment to one of the alleged participants (Cargill).[31] In the high fructose corp syrup (HFCS) litigation, the Seventh Circuit reversed (and remanded for trial) the district court's decision granting summary judgment to four of the defendants (including Cargill).[32]

In *Citric Acid*, the Ninth Circuit was dealing with a well-established cartel. Four of the participants had been indicted and each of these four had reached a settlement with the plaintiffs in the class action seeking damages.[33] These four firms apparently represented roughly 2/3 of the annual world-wide production of citric acid.[34] Cargill had not been indicted by the Justice Department, yet the firm was a growing presence in the market. Starting with an initial annual production capacity of 56 million pounds, Cargill increased that capacity to 80 million pounds in 1992 and later announced an increase to 120 million pounds.[35] Its share of the U.S. market was said to be 22 percent in 1995.[36] It seemed difficult to explain how a cartel would have functioned without Cargill's participation or at least its tacit cooperation. The class action plaintiffs named Cargill as a co-defendant in their suit to recover damages caused by the cartel, alleging Cargill's participation during the period 1993–1995.[37]

28. Mark Whitacre was an ADM Vice President in charge of the Corn Products Division. The story of the FBI Investigation and Whiticare's controversial role as an informant is told in KURT EICHENWALD, THE INFORMANT: A TRUE STORY (2000) and in JAMES B. LIEBER, RATS IN THE GRAIN: THE DIRTY TRICKS AND TRIALS OF ARCHER DANIELS MIDLAND (2000).

29. According to Justice Department records, ADM paid a fine of $100 million based on its participation in the lysine and citric acid cartels. Ajinomoto Co. and Kyowa Kakko Kogyo Co. of Japan each were fined $10 million for their participation in the lysine cartel. Aside from ADM, the other indicted citric acid conspirators were Haarmann & Reimer Corp. ($50 million fine), F. Hoffmann–La Roche, Ltd. ($14 million fine) and Jungbunzlauer International AG ($11 million fine). Antitrust Division, Department of Justice, Sherman Act Violations Yielding a Fine of $10 Million or More (June 2002).

30. This story is told in United States v. Andreas, 216 F.3d 645 (7th Cir. 2000).

31. In re Citric Acid Litigation, 191 F.3d 1090 (9th Cir. 1999).

32. In re High Fructose Corn Syrup Antitrust Litigation, 295 F.3d 651, 653–54, 665–66 (7th Cir. 2002).

33. The four indicted firms that had reached a settlement with the class action plaintiffs were ADM, Haarman & Reimer Corp., F. Hoffman–LaRoche, Ltd., and Jungbunzlauer International AG. *Citric Acid*, 191 F.3d at 1092.

34. United States v. Andreas, 216 F.3d at 656–57.

35. *Citric Acid,* 191 F.3d at 1100.

36. Id. at 1102–03.

37. Apparently, ADM participated in volume and price allocations in citric acid cartel activity for at least four years (1991–

Cargill did not dispute the existence of the cartel, but contended that it had not been a participant. The district court granted Cargill's motion for summary judgment, concluding that plaintiffs' evidence did not "tend[ ] to exclude the possibility that [Cargill] acted independently."[38] The court rejected plaintiffs' "voluminous" circumstantial evidence because it found it to be "weak" and no substitute for "quality" evidence.[39]

In a unanimous panel opinion by Judge O'Scannlain, the Ninth Circuit affirmed the summary dismissal. The panel relied heavily on *Matsushita*, repeatedly citing the Supreme Court's statement that the plaintiff must supply evidence "that tends to exclude the possibility that the alleged conspirators acted independently."[40] The focus on this language may be misplaced, particularly given the high Court's view, mistaken or not, that the *Matsushita* conspiracy was implausible as a matter of economic theory. There was nothing implausible about the citric acid cartel that had been successfully prosecuted by the Government. The only issue was whether Cargill was a participant in this cartel. Plaintiffs had relied on the following: evidence that list prices for citric acid were virtually identical; Cargill's failure to increase its market share between 1993 and 1995; Cargill's decision to curtail planned expansion of its production capacity; Cargill's failure to enter the European market earlier than it did; and extensive contacts between Cargill and other citric acid producers, including Cargill's participation in the citric acid trade association. The court quite correctly noted that each of these circumstances, while consistent with Cargill's participation in the cartel, was also consistent with more benign behavior. For example, the virtual identity in citric acid prices might be explained by the fungible nature of the product (citric acid), making "price" the overwhelming determinant in most purchase decisions and creating strong competitive pressures for each seller to match the market price.[41]

The court then used this same "tend to exclude" language in rejecting plaintiffs' argument that, although each individual circumstantial evidentiary offerings might be insufficient, taken collectively, the evidence allowed a reasonable fact-finder to find a conspiracy. "Considered as a whole," the court concluded, "the record ... does not tend to exclude the possibility that Cargill acted independently."[42] But this test, in isolation, is not the proper test for granting a defendant summary

1995). United States v. Andreas, 216 F.3d at 656. The plaintiffs alleged Cargill's participation only during the period 1993–1995.

38. Id. at 1093 (quoting language from the district court's opinion). The district court relied on language from Matsushita Elec. Indus. Co. v. Zenith Radio Corp., 475 U.S. 574, 588, 106 S.Ct. 1348, 89 L.Ed.2d 538 (1986).

39. Id.

40. In rejecting specific evidentiary offerings, the court either quoted or paraphrased the "tend to exclude" language in at least 7 instances: 191 F.3d at 1096, 1098, 1099, 1103 (in 2 instances), 1104, 1106.

41. Id. at 1102 (suggesting that identity of prices is insufficient evidence from which to infer a Section 1 violation). The court also suggested that evidence of uniform pricing was negated by other evidence that large buyers had obtained discounts. Id. For a discussion of this point, see notes 58–59, *infra*, and accompanying text.

42. Id. at 1106.

judgment on the conspiracy issue. Even if all of the evidence collectively viewed does tend to exclude benign explanations for a defendant's conduct, a reasonable fact finder might still conclude that the facts demonstrated that the defendant was more likely than not a participant in the cartel. Cargill offered a variety of reasons for various conduct that the plaintiffs advanced as circumstantial evidence of Cargill's participation in the cartel. The court accepted these explanations individually as credible, but if the jury disbelieved even one of them, it could reasonably have given credence to a simple unifying explanation for all of this behavior: that Cargill was a cartel participant.

In *High Fructose Corn Syrup*, the Seventh Circuit was faced with alleged cartel activity in a corn derivative products market. The Justice Department had investigated the high fructose corn syrup market, but limited its prosecutions to the lysine and citric acid markets. This class action suit for damages produced an out of court settlement (CPC International), but the remaining four defendants had obtained summary dismissal because the district judge had deemed the plaintiffs' evidence of a conspiracy insufficient.[43] The unanimous panel reversed and remanded the case for trial.

The court reviewed the nature of the evidence which plaintiffs must offer to establish a conspiracy. In cases (such as this one) in which the non-economic evidence of an actual agreement is suggestive rather than conclusive, the court suggests that economic evidence will be important. That evidence will be of two types: (1) evidence showing that the market was conducive to cartel activity; and (2) evidence of actual anticompetitive effects.[44]

The court cautions that a district judge deciding a summary judgment motion must avoid three traps that defendants can lay: (1) weighing conflicting evidence (a task that must be left for the fact finder at trial); (2) concluding that because no single piece of evidence "points unequivocally to conspiracy", the evidence as a whole cannot defeat summary judgment; and (3) concluding that because the cartel's efficacy was limited, there is no actionable cartel violation.[45]

In reviewing the evidence, the court notes initially that the structure of the HFCS industry was "favorable" to secret price fixing.[46] The five major producers named as defendants made up 90 percent of the industry (making communication among them relatively easy), the product was standardized (with only two commonly sold grades, HFCS 42 and HFCS 55), there were no close substitutes for HFCS that could exercise price discipline on sellers of HFCS, and there was a great deal of excess capacity among producers (increasing the incentive to conspire to limit output and raise price).[47] The court also found that industry

43. The five firms named in the complaint were ADM, A.E. Staley, Cargill, American Maize–Products, and CPC International. *HFCS*, 295 F.3d at 653–54.

44. Id. at 654–55.

45. Id. at 655–56.

46. Id. at 656.

47. The court's analysis of excess capacity was sophisticated. The court noted that the significance of excess capacity will vary

characteristics that might make price-fixing less likely were not compelling. In particular, sales to large buyers (such as Coca Cola and Pepsi Cola) at discounts from the list price did not negate the probability of price fixing because the sellers may well have chosen to tolerate price discrimination that favored large buyers while enforcing cartel prices against smaller buyers.[48]

The court also examined actual evidence of non-competitive behavior. ADM raised the price of HFCS 42 to 90 percent of the price for HFCS 55. The other defendants quickly followed. The defendants argued, against some record evidence, that HFCS 42 is 90 percent as sweet as HFCS 55, and this justified the pricing decision. Judge Posner correctly recognized that in a competitive market, the price of each grade would be determined by its cost, not by its value. The available evidence suggested that the cost of producing HFCS 42 was around 65 percent of the cost of producing HFCS 55, so cost factors could not explain the 90 percent pricing rule that the defendants imposed in lock-step.[49]

The court took note of evidence that the defendants bought HFCS from one another even when the buyer could have produced additional HFCS at a cost lower than the purchase price. These cross-producer sales can be a means of maintaining each cartel participant's market share. If one member exceeds its allotted share, it can make purchases from another whose market share was not maintained, in this manner keeping peace among the participants. The cross-purchases among the defendants, the court observed, abruptly ceased with the end of the alleged conspiracy.[50] That these measures may have achieved their desired end is suggested, the court concluded, by the relative stability of the market shares of the defendants, notwithstanding growth in the market for HFCS that might tend to foster changes in relative market share.[51]

The court then applied these facts (viewed in a light favorable to the non-moving party) to the standard for granting summary judgment. As the court saw it, the issue was whether "there is enough evidence for a reasonable jury to find that there was an explicit agreement, not merely a tacit one." Put another way, the plaintiffs "must present evidence that would enable a reasonable jury to reject the hypothesis that defendants foreswore price competition without actually agreeing to do so."[52] The court concluded that the district court erred in granting summary judgment. The lower court was correct in determining that no single piece of evidence was "sufficient in itself to prove a price-fixing conspiracy." The critical question, however, was whether the "evidence, consid-

---

depending on the relative size of fixed costs when measured against variable costs. The greater the proportion of fixed costs, the greater the incentive to cartelize. The court found that this issue was so far unexplored in the litigation. Id. at 657.

48. Id. at 658.

49. Id. at 658–59.

50. Id. at 659.

51. Id. at 659–60.

52. Id. at 661 (citing Matsushita Electric Industrial Co. v. Zenith Radio Corp., 475 U.S. 574, 588, 106 S.Ct. 1348, 89 L.Ed.2d 538 (1986)).

ered as a whole and in combination with the economic evidence, is sufficient to defeat summary judgment." In making this determination, the district court could consider ambiguous or indirect evidence, the core of virtually every case that goes to trial (because cases in which direct evidence disposes of the issues will usually be resolved short of trial).

The differing results in *Citric Acid* and *High Fructose Corn Syrup* can be reconciled. But the tone and the mode of analysis cannot be. Each of the three summary judgment pitfalls that Judge Posner described are relevant to (and perhaps were directed at) the Ninth Circuit's analysis in *Citric Acid*. The Ninth Circuit affirmed a decision in which the trial judge weighed conflicting evidence in favor of the defendant, a task that should have been reserved for the jury.[53] In addition, despite statements to the contrary, the trial and appellate courts may have failed to give sufficient weight to the possibility that individual actions, each of which might have benign explanations, may collectively persuade a reasonable fact finder that a cartel existed. Finally, the Ninth Circuit gave credence to arguments that Cargill could not have been a participant in the cartel because of evidence that it discounted sales of citric acid to its five largest customers (who purchased a majority of Cargill's product).[54] This testimony may show a less effective or far reaching cartel, but it does not demonstrate that Cargill did not participate in a cartel that injured less powerful or less informed buyers. Indeed, as Judge Posner points out, price discrimination practiced in favor of the largest and most knowledgeable customers is often a tolerated cartel practice.[55]

Price fixing is carried out secretly, often with extensive precautions to ensure that the conduct cannot be discovered. As Judge Posner recognized, "most cases are constructed out of a tissue of such [ambiguous] statements and other circumstantial evidence, since an outright confession will ordinarily obviate the need for a trial."[56] Not only inference, but also "conjecture has its place in building a case out of circumstantial evidence."[57] It is on this point that the Ninth Circuit's treatment of conspiracy claims differs most striking from the Seventh Circuit's approach.

---

53. Another court that may have been entrapped by this pitfall is the Eighth Circuit in its *en banc* holding in Blomkest Fertilizer, Inc. v. Potash Corp. of Sask., Inc., 203 F.3d 1028 (8th Cir. 2000). The majority in this case chastises the plaintiffs for assuming a conspiracy "and then explaining the evidence accordingly." Id. at 1033. Of course, both plaintiffs and defendants will place their own spin on the evidence. As long as a reasonable fact finder could agree with either party, the court must not engage in its own pre-trial weighing of the evidence, but leave this matter for development in evidentiary proceedings.

Blomkest Fertilizer can illustrates the risk that courts give too much weight to *Matsushita*, too little weight to the corrective in *Kodak* and ignore that, as a matter of analysis, *Interstate Circuit, American Tobacco* and *Paramount Pictures* (all controlling precedents) plainly warrant the inference of conspiracy from conduct, including communicative market moves by alleged conspirators.

54. *Citric Acid*, 191 F.3d at 1102–03.

55. *High Fructose Corn Syrup*, 295 F.3d at 658.

56. *HFCS*, 295 F.3d at 662.

57. Id. at 660.

The Ninth Circuit's holding in *Citric Acid* also suggests another unresolved issue. What if a major industry participant (Cargill reportedly had 22 percent of the citric acid market in 1995) is not a direct participant in the cartel, but has knowledge of it and takes steps not to challenge its output limiting and price raising hegemony? Is such a firm immune from antitrust challenge simply because it never participated in a cartel meeting or directly assented to the cartel's leadership? Without this firm's tacit cooperation, the cartel could not exist. With the tacit cooperation, the major industry participant may receive all of the benefits of the cartel.

The preferred result is that a major industry participant that has knowledge of a cartel and makes decisions consistent with the goals of the cartel should be liable for a Section 1 violation, notwithstanding the lack of express agreement or direct participation in the cartel. Liability for "tacit agreement and participation" is consistent with antitrust policy and the wording of Sherman Section 1. This case is easily distinguishable from one in which an entire industry, without formal cartel trappings, tacitly agrees to a parallel pricing strategy. In the latter case, if such a tacit agreement were found to violate Section 1, troubling issues would be raised for the conduct of a firm in any industry in which fungible products force firms to match the prices of their rivals.[58]

5.2c. Intra–Enterprise Conspiracy

The question of when an agreement among affiliated entities will be characterized as a "contract, combination or conspiracy" was addressed in Copperweld Corp. v. Independence Tube Corp.[59] Copperweld acquired Regal, a steel tubing maker, from Lear Siegler, and also obtained from Lear a covenant not to compete. A former Regal executive who had been employed by Copperweld before the acquisition of Regal, left Copperweld after the acquisition and formed Independence Tube to compete with Regal. Although advised by counsel that the Regal covenant did not bind Independence Tube or its principal, Copperweld and Regal concertedly sought to thwart the entry by threatening Independence Tube and its customers with litigation. It was this conduct that Independence Tube challenged as a Section 1 violation. The Supreme Court pruned away a thicket of earlier intra-enterprise conspiracy cases[60] to hold that concerted action by a corporation and its wholly owned subsidiary was *per se* lawful under Section 1, regardless of whether that conduct restrained market competition and hurt other firms.[61] The Court rejected the view,

---

58. For further discussion of this hypothetical and of the holdings in *Citric Acid* and *High Fructose Corn Syrup*, see Grimes, *Conspiracies and Summary Judgment in Sherman Section 1 Cases: Judge Posner Takes on the Ninth Circuit,* 11 COMPETITION 15 (2003).

59. 467 U.S. 752, 104 S.Ct. 2731, 81 L.Ed.2d 628 (1984).

60. Id. at 760–66 (citing Perma Life Mufflers, Inc. v. International Parts Corp.,

392 U.S. 134, 88 S.Ct. 1981, 20 L.Ed.2d 982 (1968); Timken Roller Bearing Co. v. United States, 341 U.S. 593, 71 S.Ct. 971, 95 L.Ed. 1199 (1951); Kiefer–Stewart Co. v. Joseph E. Seagram & Sons, Inc., 340 U.S. 211, 71 S.Ct. 259, 95 L.Ed. 219 (1951); United States v. Yellow Cab Co., 332 U.S. 218, 67 S.Ct. 1560, 91 L.Ed. 2010 (1947)).

61. *Copperweld*, 467 U.S. at 777.

articulated in Justice Stevens' dissent, that an intra-enterprise conspiracy doctrine based on a rule of reason analysis should be used in order to correct, in part, the Sherman Act's failure to forbid even blatantly anticompetitive single firm conduct that does not threaten monopoly. The *Copperweld* majority did not expressly resolve the case in which an affiliate is less than wholly owned. But the majority's language suggests reliance on a control test—is there common control of a firm and its partially owned affiliate?[62] This is the approach most lower courts have been taking.[63]

The majority in *Copperweld* hued closely to the statutory language. It increased simplicity in antitrust analysis but at the expense of consistency with earlier precedents and more comprehensive coverage of conduct that can cause conventional antitrust harms. Conduct that limits output or fixes prices will create competitive injury regardless of whether it is deemed single firm conduct or that of a conspiracy. The extended tolerance for anticompetitive conduct resulting from the majority's tight statutory construction would not inhibit effective enforcement if the attempted monopoly offense under Section 2 was construed to forbid all blatantly anticompetitive single firm conduct.[64] One result of *Copperweld* may be renewed emphasis on the use of the attempted monopolization offense under Section 2.[65]

Imaginative advocates have attempted on occasion, usually without success, to expand the single entity concept derived from *Copperweld* by applying it to corporations separately owned and controlled but cooperating together in some joint venture.[66] Such broad readings of *Copperweld* have been quite consistently and correctly rejected,[67] both in sports league[68] and other cases.[69] By contrast, in one problematic case involving an electric cooperative a similar effort to treat separate but cooperating units as one entity incapable of concerted action was successful.[70] As addressed in § 5.7, the existence of cooperative activity yielding integration between two or more entities is substantively relevant under

---

62. *Copperweld*, 467 U.S. at 771–74.

63. See, e.g., Caribe BMW, Inc. v. Bayerische Motoren Werke Aktiengesellschaft, 19 F.3d 745, 749–51 (1st Cir.1994); Oksanen v. Page Memorial Hosp., 945 F.2d 696, 703–04 (4th Cir.1991), cert. denied, 502 U.S. 1074, 112 S.Ct. 973, 117 L.Ed.2d 137 (1992); Hood v. Tenneco Texas Life Ins. Co., 739 F.2d 1012, 1015–16 (5th Cir.1984); Russ' Kwik Car Wash, Inc. v. Marathon Petroleum Co., 772 F.2d 214, 216 (6th Cir. 1985) (per curiam).

64. United States v. American Airlines, Inc., 743 F.2d 1114 (5th Cir.1984), cert. dismissed, 474 U.S. 1001, 106 S.Ct. 420, 88 L.Ed.2d 370 (1985).

65. Id.

66. See Calkins, Copperweld *in the Courts: The Road to* Caribe, 63 ANTITRUST L.J. 345, 358–63 (1995).

67. See, e.g., Sullivan v. NFL, 34 F.3d 1091, 1099 (1st Cir.1994), cert. denied, 513 U.S. 1190 (1995); McNeil v. NFL, 790 F.Supp. 871, 880 (D.Minn.1992).

68. *McNeil*, 790 F.Supp. at 880; see *Sullivan*, 34 F.3d at 1099. But see Chicago Professional Sports Ltd. Partnership v. National Basketball Ass'n, 95 F.3d 593, 598–600 (7th Cir.1996).

69. Rothery Storage & Van Co. v. Atlas Van Lines, Inc. 792 F.2d 210, 214–15 (D.C.Cir.1986), cert. denied, 479 U.S. 1033, 107 S.Ct. 880, 93 L.Ed.2d 834 (1987).

70. City of Mt. Pleasant v. Associated Elec. Coop., Inc., 838 F.2d 268 (8th Cir. 1988); cf. Williams v. I.B. Fischer Nevada, 794 F.Supp. 1026 (D.Nev.1992), aff'd per curiam, 999 F.2d 445 (9th Cir.1993).

Section 1. It bears on whether *per se* or rule of reason responses are appropriate and, in rule of reason cases, upon whether a restraint is reasonable. But to allow the existence *vel non* of cooperation among separately controlled units to foreclose the application of Section 1 would be errant, indeed.

§ 5.3 Historical Overview of Law Precluding Horizontal Restraints

Any survey of competition law shows change. Few of the nubs of concern about which the law was woven at earlier stages of industrial development still draw great energy and attention. But an overview[1] suggests something of import. In any economy at any given time, there are a variety of industrial, economic, social and political trends as well as legal ones. However distinct, these trends are inexorably linked. Public policy about matters so comprehensive as industrial structure and conduct will be in dynamic interrelationship with processes of development and change both in the way goods and services are produced and in social and political attitudes about these and related activities. Much of what is valued—and thus, much of what is sought through competition policy—will change with time and circumstance. There will usually be contention about important economic issues; any social consensus will have elements of instability. To all of these dynamics the law, in its season and in its fashion, will respond.[2]

5.3a. Common Law Cases

English common law displays no cohesive policy toward restraint of trade. The line of development changed considerably over time. Until perhaps the seventeenth century, the industrial structure in England was energized and integrated by institutions and attitudes markedly different from those which prevailed in the nineteenth and twentieth centuries. Individuals' roles in productive processes were primarily related, as was much else in their lives, to status. Economic roles were governed in part by custom and in part by the regulations of municipalities and guilds.[3] There was no sense of market hegemony, and little sense of social, economic or geographic mobility or of power or potential to alter existing modes through private arrangements.[4] Adam Smith had not yet offered the broad vision of how individual competitors, by pursuing their own profit, furthered the common good.

---

§ 5.3

1. This section draws from two excellent histories: W. Letwin, Law and Economic Policy in America: The evolution of the Sherman Antitrust Act (1965); H. Thorelli, The Federal Antitrust Policy: Origination of an American Tradition (1955).

2. Hofstadter, *What Happened to the Antitrust Movement*, in The Business Establishment 113 (E. Cheit ed., 1964). One can see such dynamic developments in American antitrust history through the present day.

3. See National Industrial Conference Board, Inc., Mergers and the Law 4–25 (1929).

4. These realities are discussed in H. Maine, Ancient Law (5th ed. 1888).

In the *Schoolmasters' Case* of 1410,[5] the court declined to allow an action against a new schoolmaster who had diminished the profits of the sole existing grammar school, said to have been run "since a time beyond which memory does not run." One can find in this holding a commitment to competition—a recognition of the right of a person to open a new business, even if it should diminish the profits of existing businesses. But there is no evidence of an economic commitment in the comments of the judges. They viewed the private dispute in terms of the existing order. Exclusive operations are well and good, but they are based on a grant from proper authority.

In this private law context there also were suits involving agreements by tradesmen not to compete with a rival for a specified period of time. In *Dyer's Case*, the plaintiff alleged that the defendant, a dyer, had violated the obligation of a bond by which he had undertaken not to carry on his trade in a designated town for a period of six months.[6] The court sustained the defendant's demurrer on the ground that an undertaking by an individual not to carry on his customary trade was void. This result flowed not so much from concern for the unemployed dyer, but from a sense that altering the economic status of a tradesman through private arrangement was not a proper mode of assigning tasks and status. By 1711, the view had changed. A similar restriction linked to the lease of a bakery was upheld as a reasonable restraint in Mitchel v. Reynolds.[7] One can find in that case the genesis of the "rule of reason" as an approach to restraint of trade. But the holding was hardly a statement of that doctrine, nor did it anticipate the broad coverage of the law of restraint of trade to come later.

An early English case often viewed with better reason as an antecedent of today's law involved a price fixing conspiracy. The 1758 holding in King v. Norris[8] struck down an agreement among local producers not to sell salt below a specified price—an agreement which raised the then prevailing rate. The court declared that all such agreements involving a "necessary of life" were "of bad consequence, and ought to be discountenanced." The condemnation applied at "what rate soever the price was fixed." Although apparently limited to goods considered necessities, the case is a fairly accurate precursor to an antitrust policy that condemns cartel activity. But the process of common law growth and change did not end at this point, at least in England. Laissez-faire theory eventually gained such ascendancy that the courts backed away from the notion that an agreement among competing traders not to sell except at specified prices or to divide territories was unlawful. Where no element of coercion was involved, these transactions were, by the second half of the nineteenth century, generally held lawful. This unqualified trust that freedom of contract would protect the public was reflected also in the

5. Y.B. 11 Hen. 4, f. 47, pl. 21 (1410).

6. Y.B., 2 Hen. V, f. 5, pl. 26 (1415).

7. 1 P. Wms. 181, 24 Eng. Rep. 347 (K.B. 1711).

8. 2 Kenyon 300, 96 Eng. Rep. 1189 (K.B. 1758).

wide scope then being given to agreements by which a craftsman or trader bound himself not to practice his trade.[9]

By the time the Sherman Act was passed in this country, the English were relying very largely on the market. The only constraining policy developed during the long common law history that did not erode was the view that grants of exclusive prerogatives are not in the public interest. The accommodation reached in England at that time was consonant with the views then generally prevailing among economists. As most of them saw the matter, the main threats to consumer interests came not from private arrangements but from government. If firms acting together set prices too high, others would enter attracted by the profits. But government interventions such as tariffs and exclusive licenses could protect positions of private power from the threat of entry from outside.

U.S. common law during the nineteenth century evolved differently. For one thing, the doctrine of restraint of trade embodied in *Mitchel v. Reynolds* seems to have been given a more rigorous application in some U.S. jurisdictions than ever it had in England.[10] For another, most U.S. decisions treated agreements fixing prices or dividing territories among producers as contrary to public policy.[11] Very few U.S. cases hewed to the line that ultimately prevailed in England, which discriminated between contracts limiting competition between the contracting parties and those which either suppressed the competitive efforts of outsiders or monopolized the bulk of supply in a market.[12]

This, in a very general way, was the status of U.S. law when the Sherman Act was passed. Doctrinal links to the distant past were vague and indirect. But for a century or so there had been a discernible commitment, however general in its expression and multifaceted in its policy bases, to the encouragement of competition. Little was fixed, much was open to development, and there were forces favoring total laissez-

9. See, e.g., Mogul S.S. Co. v. McGregor Gow & Co. [1892] App.Cas. 25 (1891); Hearn v. Griffin, 2 Chitty 407 (1815); Wickens v. Evans, 148 Eng. Rep. 1201 (Ex. 1829); Jones v. North, Eq. 426 (1875); Collins v. Locke [1878–79] App.Cas. 674 (P.C. 1879); Urmston v. Whitelegg, 7 T.L.R. 295 (C.A. 1891). Att'y Gen. of Australia v. Adelaide SS. Co., [1913] App.Cas. 781 (P.C. 1913).

10. See, e.g., Wright v. Ryder, 36 Cal. 342 (1868); Alger v. Thacher, 36 Mass. (19 Pick.) 51 (1837); Duffy v. Shockey, 11 Ind. 70 (1858); Hubbard v. Miller, 27 Mich. 15 (1873).

11. See, e.g., Stanton v. Allen, 5 Denio 434 (N.Y.Sup.Ct.1848); Sayre v. Louisville Union Benevolent Ass'n, 62 Ky. (1 Duv.) 143 (1863); Morris Run Coal Co. v. Barclay Coal Co., 68 Pa. 173 (1871); Gibbs v. Smith, 115 Mass. 592 (1874); Craft v. McConoughy, 79 Ill. 346 (1875); Santa Clara Val-

ley Mill & Lumber Co. v. Hayes, 76 Cal. 387 (1888).

12. See, e.g., Ontario Salt Co. v. Merchants' Salt Co., 18 Grant Ch. (U.C.) 540 (1871); Skrainka v. Scharringhausen, 8 Mo. App. 522 (1880); Dolph v. Troy Laundry Mach. Co., 28 Fed. 553 (N.D.N.Y.1886); Central Shade–Roller Co. v. Cushman, 143 Mass. 353 (1887); Leslie v. Lorillard, 110 N.Y. 519 (1888); Herriman v. Menzies, 115 Cal. 16 (1896). This was the view, quite permissive of cartelization so long as no coercion was used to exclude entrants attracted by the cartels' increase in price, that Justice Holmes seemed to favor and to think the appropriate standard for combinations in restraint of trade under the Sherman Act. See Holmes' dissent in Northern Sec. Co. v. United States, 193 U.S. 197, 402–09, 24 S.Ct. 436, 48 L.Ed. 679 (1904).

faire which were as extreme, if not in the end as forceful, as any favoring the regulation of conduct that restricted competition.

5.3b. Early Section 1 Cases

The first cases in which the scope of Section 1 was considered by the Supreme Court were United States v. Trans–Missouri Freight Ass'n,[13] and United States v. Joint–Traffic Ass'n.[14] Each involved a cartel of railroads, one operating west of the Mississippi (*Trans-Missouri*), the other between Chicago and the East Coast (*Joint-Traffic*). Each delegated to a committee of participants the power to promulgate a rate structure. Market shares were not allocated—participants were free to engage in nonprice competition to win business.

As an industry, railroading displays some characteristics that facilitate cartelization. The number of firms in any competitive segment will be small and cost structures tend to be similar. The incentive for cartelization is strong because the variable costs of carrying any given volume of business are small relative to fixed costs. When supply exceeds demand, railroads would be tempted to reduce rates to the point where variable costs are covered and some contribution is made to fixed costs. Unless pressures for prices to fall below total costs are controlled, the economic health of the industry can be threatened. The other side of high fixed costs is that they create a substantial incentive to cheat if an agreement to maintain rates is achieved. To discourage cheating, participating railroads required a tightly organized cartel. A secret cartel would not be adequate for railroads. Consequently, they acted boldly and sought, in face of the new Act, to assert the legality of their conduct.

The railroads contended that their cartels responded to the industry's special circumstances and were essential to the health of the railroad industry and other industries dependent upon it. Moreover, they contended the cartel rates were reasonable. The Department of Justice rejected any temptation to analyze the economics of the industry or justify the cartel on the basis of high fixed cost. It flatly contended in both cases that the arrangement was a "restraint of trade" that significantly limited the commercial freedom of the members in violation of the Act. In the first of the two cases—*Trans-Missouri*—the Court, in a terse opinion by Justice Peckham, said it was unnecessary to consider whether arrangements such as this one would be invalid at common law. Congress had condemned in Section 1 "every" restraint of trade without exception.

In *Joint-Traffic*, the defendants urged the Court to reconsider this conclusion. They argued that socially beneficial agreements would otherwise be illegal and that without a cartel, cutthroat competition would eliminate all but one competitor, with the surviving monopolist then raising rates to excessive levels. The Court persisted in its view that the cartel was unlawful. It said that "[a]n agreement of the nature of this

---

13. 166 U.S. 290, 17 S.Ct. 540, 41 L.Ed. 1007 (1897).

14. 171 U.S. 505, 19 S.Ct. 25, 43 L.Ed. 259 (1898).

one, which directly and effectively stifles competition, must be regarded under the statute as one in restraint of trade * * *."[15] Cartelization, while capable of protecting railroads against cutthroat competition, entailed an inevitable pressure to establish rates not at the minimum reasonable level which would yield a fair return, but at an unreasonably high level yielding supracompetitive returns. And if the public interest were in fact threatened when railroad rates fell too low, there was an alternative to cartelization—rate regulation by a government agency.[16] The Court found the harm from the cartel (increased rates) immediate, but the fancied danger of ultimate monopoly speculative and, in any event, dependent upon the manner in which the defendants competed. Was the Court, perhaps, implying that the railroads could interdependently, yet lawfully, keep rates from falling below cost?

The Court in *Joint-Traffic* stood by its earlier holding of an unlawful cartel but backed away from the sweeping statement of its rule that "every" restraint of trade was condemned under Section 1 of the Sherman Act. First, it distinguished between arrangements that "directly" and "immediately" reduce competition, as would a rate agreement among competitors, and arrangements that had only indirect or incidental effects. Second, it stated that some arrangements affecting competition, such as "the sale of a good will of a business with an accompanying agreement not to engage in a similar business," were not restraints of trade at all.[17] Still, arrangements that purposefully and explicitly stifled competition between independently operated firms in the same market were unlawful, regardless of whether the terms imposed were reasonable, and regardless of arguments that, as the result of peculiarities of the market, a regime other than competition would better serve the public.

These differing yet complementary lines of analysis in *Joint-Traffic* provide a rich jurisprudence which courts since 1898 have been developing and elaborating. Justice Peckham's opinion provided an embryonic statement of the *per se* doctrine, invalidating without further inquiry arrangements that directly stifle competition. Here, also in embryo, is one way of expressing the rule of reason: where an arrangement does not obviously stifle competition, but may adversely affect it, analysis of the arrangement must be pursued to gauge its purpose and effect. Here also, quite matured, is a unifying feature of both branches of Section 1: that the section mandates competition as the rule of trade regardless of whether the rule of reason or *per se* rule applies.

Despite these values, *Joint-Traffic* failed to provide a systematic approach for distinguishing cases that violated the Act from those that did not. The following year, the Court affirmed the opinion of Judge (later Chief Justice) Taft in Addyston Pipe & Steel Co. v. United States,[18]

---

15. Id. at 577.

16. The Interstate Commerce Act, passed in 1887, did not authorize the Commission to regulate rates and, as the Court read it, did not exempt the railroads from Section 1 of the Sherman Act.

17. *Joint-Traffic*, 171 U.S. at 568.

18. 175 U.S. 211, 20 S.Ct. 96, 44 L.Ed. 136 (1899), modifying and aff'g 85 F. 271 (6th Cir.1898).

a case where the six leading iron pipe producers with 65 percent of the national capacity had fixed prices and divided business among themselves. Judge Taft's circuit court opinion, the most analytical of the early Sherman opinions, suggests a distinction between naked and ancillary restraints of trade, a notion that has come into even greater prominence in modern Section 1 analysis. The arrangement in *Addyston Pipe*, unlike the railroad cartels, was secret: the members collusively submitted supposedly competitive bids. The defendants again asserted the classic cartel defense—that the members were avoiding ruinous price competition and replacing it with reasonable rates. Judge Taft rejected this defense, noting that the defendants had established what economists might call an entry-discouraging price; it was above competitive levels and thus harmful to consumers, but not so high as to encourage distant producers to invade the market. It was, therefore, unreasonable.[19] But reasonableness was in any event not a defense to cartelization. "[W]here the sole object of both parties in making the contract * * * is merely to restrain competition, and enhance or maintain prices, it would seem that there was nothing to justify or excuse the restraint * * *."[20] Judge Taft's opinion, which predated the Supreme Court's opinion in *Joint-Traffic*, is perhaps the true precursor of the *per se* rule so far as price fixing is concerned.

Judge Taft's analysis of ancillary restraints also provides a rational and useful way of distinguishing lawful and unlawful restraints. All restraints on competition are unlawful except those that: (1) are "merely ancillary to the main purpose of a lawful contract" (such as the agreement of the seller of a business not to compete with the buyer, of a buyer of a business not to compete with the seller's retained business, or of a partner, employee or agent not to compete with the firm); (2) are "necessary to protect" the promisee in the enjoyment of the fruits of the contract; and (3) do not contain any restraint that "exceeds the necessity presented."[21] The implication of these three foundation cases is that conduct at odds with competition violates the Act. The only analysis needed is to determine the purpose of the arrangement and its effect on competition; if the competitive restraint is blatant, this process is perfunctory.

5.3c. Development of the Rule of Reason

The *Standard Oil* decision, an antitrust classic, was rendered in 1911, a year after Justice White became Chief Justice.[22] *Standard Oil* announced what has come to be known as the "rule of reason." Justice White, in his *Trans-Missouri* dissent, asserted that Congress intended to invalidate only unreasonable restraints. White's majority opinion in *Standard Oil*, because it also made "reasonableness" the fulcrum, is

19. United States v. Addyston Pipe & Steel Co., 85 Fed. 271, 292–93 (6th Cir. 1898).

20. Id. at 282–83.

21. Id. at 282.

22. Standard Oil Co. v. United States, 221 U.S. 1, 31 S.Ct. 502, 55 L.Ed. 619 (1911).

sometimes said to have retreated from holdings in *Trans-Missouri* and *Joint-Traffic*. But despite confusion arising from Justice White's use of language borrowed from his dissent in the earlier case, *Standard Oil* announces a rigorous rule of reason, a rule which is more in keeping with the majority holdings in earlier cases than with his own earlier dissent. The Court's new rule of reason announced in *Standard Oil* differs from the earlier White dissent calling for reason to govern in precisely this: Under the new rule of reason competition remains the rule of trade, even when it appears reasonable in a particular instance to put competition aside. Reasonableness comes into the analysis only to evaluate whether, on balance, competition is being injured.

Standard Oil involved Rockefeller's Standard Oil trust, a close knit combination of 37 oil corporations which were brought under common management and control through a holding company. The case was more like one in which merger or consolidation was used as a path to power than one in which firms operated separately but collusively. But the clandestine activity of the defendants gave their activities the flavor of the worst cartels. Among the strategies that Rockefeller and his group employed were industrial espionage, threats of predatory local price-cutting aimed at rivals that resisted joining the scheme, and secret rebates paid by the railroads that shipped the Rockefeller group's oil to trust participants but not other oil producers. The defendants ultimately had the power to force the railroads to rebate a percentage not only of their own payments, but to pay to the defendants a percentage of rates paid by rivals for shipments to the East (drawbacks).[23] The Government argued that this conduct violated both Sections 1 and 2 of the Sherman Act and the Supreme Court agreed.

Chief Justice White found that the term "restraint of trade" took its "rudimentary meaning" from the common law, but the statute did not limit the Court to any narrow common law conception. The statute was seen as directed at both static and dynamic concerns—the existence of power to fix prices or limit production, and the danger that quality will deteriorate over time when the spur of competition is withdrawn. As understood by the Supreme Court the common law saw any "undue limitation on competitive conditions" as threatening and, for this reason, made illegal "all contracts or acts which were unreasonably restrictive of competitive conditions." Growing out of this tradition, Section 1 was an "all-embracing enumeration to make sure that no form of contract or combination" affecting an undue restraint "could save such restraint from condemnation." It reached all "undue restraints" on competition whether imposed by methods new or old.[24]

---

23. These and other anticompetitive practices used by Standard Oil trust are described in M. JOSEPHSON, THE ROBBER BARONS 112–19, 161–63 (1962).

It has been argued that Standard Oil's ability to force rivals to sell out at below market prices arose because the railroads encouraged and supported Standard Oil's role

as an enforcer of a railroad cartel that shared cartel profits with Standard Oil. Granitz & Klein, *Monopolization by "Raising Rivals' Costs": The Standard Oil Case,* 39 J.L. & ECON. 1 (1996).

24. *Standard Oil,* 221 U.S. at 58–60.

The Chief Justice's prolix opinion nonetheless stresses the salient points. It notes that although *Trans-Missouri* and *Joint-Traffic* had failed to announce the concept of undue restraint and the test of reasonableness which was now being established, those cases had been correctly decided. The agreements in the earlier cases called for the fixing of rates among competitors. Thus, their nature, character and "necessary effect" was irreconcilable with competition. This was enough to give rise to a "conclusive presumption which brought them within the statute." Agreements having that necessary effect would cause the injury to competition that the statute forbids irrespective of any predatory, abusive or unfair practices. In such instances, "resort to reason was not permissible in order to allow that to be done which the statute prohibited." The Court stated that where the necessary effect of particular contracts is undue restraint on competition, "they could not be taken out of that category by indulging in general reasoning as to the expediency or nonexpediency of * * * [these particular] contracts, or the wisdom or want of wisdom of the statute which prohibited their being made."[25]

Standard Oil thus accepts and reiterates the embryonic *per se* rule, as well as expressing in more complete form a rule of reason. It also reinforces the crucial teaching of the earlier cases. When it appears, either on the face of the matter or after analysis, that competition is interfered with to any significant degree, the law has been violated. As the 1955 Attorney General's Committee stated, the standard of reasonableness announced in *Standard Oil*

> permits the courts to decide whether conduct is significantly and unreasonably anticompetitive in character or effect; it makes obsolete once prevalent arguments, such as, whether monopoly arrangements would be socially preferable to competition in a particular industry * * *.[26]

Contrast the task of a court if it were required not only to judge whether a particular arrangement adversely affected competition but also, if it did, to decide whether in the particular circumstance the public interest was thereby advanced or injured. Such choices are not traditionally judicial, but legislative in nature. Still, the history of adjudication under the Act is marked by repeated efforts to broaden the rule. Time and again, litigants have argued expressly or *sub rosa* that a particular arrangement is reasonable because it advances the public interest even though it substitutes some concerted private regulation of economic affairs for the objective forces of competition. Although the Supreme Court has never expressly endorsed this broad reading of reasonableness, there are two now dated opinions that gave considerable credence to it. They represent an alternative model for the rule of reason that, although authoritatively rejected, from time to time still tempts some courts.

---

25. Id. at 65.

26. REPORT OF THE ATTORNEY GENERAL'S NATIONAL COMMITTEE TO STUDY THE ANTITRUST LAWS 11 (1955).

The first of these decisions is *Chicago Board of Trade v. United States*.[27] The Board operated the nation's leading organized market for grain trading. It adopted rules governing the trading of various types of contracts, including contracts for future delivery ("futures") or for grain already in transit to Chicago ("to arrive sales"). In 1906 the Board adopted its "call" rule. The rule forbade exchange members during hours the exchange was not in operation to purchase or offer to purchase any "to arrive" grain at any price other than the closing bid price at the last call session before the exchange closed. The Court saw this rule as salutary: it limited the hours of trading, reduced the market power of the few warehousemen who by trading at night or holidays gained the advantage of information not accessible to others. It also rendered the daytime market more like the model of perfect competition by channeling all demand and supply into it. Justice Brandeis wrote for the Court upholding the rule against the government's challenge. His opinion contains this classic statement of the rule of reason:

> [T]he legality of an agreement or regulation cannot be determined by so simple a test, as whether it restrains competition. Every agreement concerning trade, every regulation of trade, restrains. * * * The true test of legality is whether the restraint imposed is such as merely regulates and perhaps thereby promotes competition or whether it is such as may suppress or even destroy competition. To determine that question the court must ordinarily consider the facts peculiar to the business * * *; its condition before and after the restraint was imposed; the nature of the restraint and its effect, actual or probable. The history of the restraint, the evil believed to exist, the reason for adopting the particular remedy, the purpose or end sought to be attained, are all relevant facts. This is not because a good intention will save an otherwise objectionable regulation or the reverse; but because knowledge of intent may help the court to interpret facts and to predict consequences.[28]

The Brandeis language appears to revolve around harm to competition—and is in this sense no extension or modification of *Standard Oil*. The catalogue of relevant facts, although it goes beyond an exclusive focus on competition, could, in cases where injury to competition is not clear on the face of the matter, throw light on whether or not a particular arrangement tends to suppress or destroy competition. Indeed, this extension of prior commentary can be viewed as a distinct and useful advance. But the narrow holding of *Chicago Board of Trade* is harder to square with earlier case law. The arrangement was a concerted one that, subject to commercial sanctions, fixed the price that was to prevail on transactions during nonmarket hours. Perhaps the arrangement tended to fix trading hours, rather than prices, and this was its real purpose and effect. But a concerted arrangement that deprives

27. 246 U.S. 231, 38 S.Ct. 242, 62 L.Ed.   **28.** Id. at 238.
683 (1918).

individual traders of freedom of choice as to their hours of trade does restrain competition.

Candidly assessed, *Chicago Board of Trade* holds that arrangements that suppress competition can be lawful so long as there is an adequate justification. The restraint might be regarded as modest—forbidding trading only during the period the market is closed. The countervailing social advantages include: (1) increasing rest and leisure for members; (2) limiting the market power of those positioned to conduct business at night; and (3) making the market during regular trading hours more perfectly competitive. The first of these perceived advantages has no place in an analysis restricted to competitive concerns. The last two are relevant to competition, but may not present a full picture of the competitive consequences of the Board's rule.

It is possible that night warehousemen had some market power during off-hours. This would be true, however, only if they were few in number and if there were barriers that would preclude traders on the organized daytime market from trading at night. But the opinion does not even explore such questions. If night warehousemen had power the rule would prevent them from unfairly exploiting during exchange off-hours any informational advantages they held. But requiring such traders to offer the price at which the grain closed would limit this type of exploitation, not prevent it. If a warehouseman realized the price of grain was likely to go up when the exchange reopened, he might still take unfair advantage of sellers offering their grain "to arrive" during exchange off-hours. Moreover, if buyers and sellers both thought market price was falling, by pegging off market transactions at the higher closing price the rule effectively precluded sellers from liquidating their positions as soon as they wished in order to avoid further loss. Finally, although the record does not resolve this issue, it is possible that the off-exchange trades were made at reduced brokerage fees. The Board's rule may have been an effort to eliminate such fee discounting, thus enforcing a cartel rate on all commissions.

A more complete record might have allowed a more satisfactory competitive analysis of the effect of the Board's rule. But Brandeis' broader embrace of the social advantage of limiting business hours is difficult to justify whatever inference a tight analysis would warrant. To hold as it did, the Court must have felt competent to judge all that could rationally be said about the social advantages of this restraint of trade. Perhaps there are restraints so blatant and severe as to be beyond redemption. But at least for this restraint, the Court appears to be asking whether the arrangement has purposes and effects other than restricting competition and, if so, whether these validate the arrangement when weighed against any resulting competitive injury.

Appalachian Coals, Inc. v. United States[29] is, if anything, even more difficult to square with the classic construction of Section 1 that focuses solely on competitive effects and eschews other, possibly offsetting, social

---

29. 288 U.S. 344, 53 S.Ct. 471, 77 L.Ed. 825 (1933).

values. In the late 1920s and early 1930s, bituminous coal mining was threatened by substitute fuels. Overcapacity was chronic, earnings were low or even negative, and bankruptcies were common. Faced with these conditions, 137 producers accounting for 12 percent of production nationally and between 54 and 75 percent of regional production (depending on market definition) joined to organize the defendant, Appalachian. As the defendants' exclusive selling agent, Appalachian was to sell their coal at "the best prices obtainable and, if all cannot be sold, to apportion orders upon a stated basis."[30] The Justice Department challenged the arrangement on the ground that it eliminated competition among the members of the group and gave the selling agency power to substantially affect or control market prices.

The Supreme Court found the arrangement reasonable in light of the deplorable economic conditions in the industry. The opinion by Chief Justice Hughes stated that under the standard of reasonableness, "[r]ealities must dominate the judgment. The mere fact that the parties to an agreement eliminate competition between themselves is not enough to condemn it."[31] While implying that if either purpose or effect was to fix market prices, the arrangement would be illegal, the Court accepted the defendants' statements that their *intent* was not to do this and felt unable to predict that a common sales agency for these producers, which had only 12 percent of the market nationally, would have the effect of fixing prices.

Appalachian Coals reminds us that antitrust is no more insulated from the deeper currents of American social, political and economic life than is any other aspect of public law. The relationship between competition and phenomena like depression or inflation is complex, but in times of crisis the nation may invest heavily in a policy that takes strong positions with modest regard for their consistency with longer term goals. In the early years of the New Deal, national policy expressed in the industrial recovery legislation—eventually declared unconstitutional[32]—identified competitive excesses as a cause of the Depression and encouraged cartelization as a means toward fuller employment of national resources. Posner has suggested that "[f]aith in the policy of competition was deeply shaken," and that "this more than anything may explain the outcome" in *Appalachian Coals.*[33] The relationship between national attitudes and judicial conduct is rarely so direct as this quote suggests that it was on this occasion. Yet, the relationship can show itself at any juncture where relevant national attitudes alter in response to widely shared economic or social perception. Certainly here, though the New Deal legislation had no direct application to the cartel arrangement in question, it is not unreasonable to assume that the Hughes Court shared and responded to a national mood.

30. Id. at 358.

31. Id. at 360.

32. A. L. A. Schechter Poultry Corp. v. United States, 295 U.S. 495, 55 S.Ct. 837, 79 L.Ed. 1570 (1935).

33. R. Posner, Antitrust: Cases, Economic Notes, and Other Materials 75 (1974).

One can attempt, of course, to read *Appalachian Coals* in a manner consistent with the classic statement of the rule of reason, which tests an arrangement by its impact on competition. The arrangement of coal producers was prospective. The evidence, if subjected to microeconomic analysis, invited expectation of future dampening of competition. But since the arrangement was not yet in operation, the evidence failed to prove accomplished harm. And a court might view the theoretical basis for inferring future harm as lacking the sufficient certitude to warrant immediate current judicial intervention. Another argument, however, for placing *Appalachian Coals* within the mainstream would focus upon the distinction between a selling agency and a cartel. A cartel typically fixes price and may allocate output. It is a "naked" restraint. Because it entails no integration of productive or distributive functions it cannot add to efficiency. The Court assumed that the agency arrangement in *Appalachian Coals* had some integration benefits. It found that the agency provided potential for "better methods of distribution, intensive advertising and research, to achieve economies in marketing."[34] Such efficiencies, the possible effects of integration, were not at issue in the earlier cartel cases. They might reasonably place a higher burden on the Government to prove competitive injury.

Unhappily, such *post hoc* rationalizations of *Appalachian Coals* leave out the tone of the Hughes opinion. The Chief Justice suggested that at least some degree of restraint upon competition is permissible under the Act. Restraints are appropriate not merely when ancillary to an integration which generates efficiencies, but also when the purpose is to eliminate "destructive practices" associated with competitive excess. The Court appeared to be embracing fears of ruinous competition very much like those that fell on deaf ears in the early cartel cases. Among the competitive practices that the selling agency was intended to eliminate were downward pressures on the market resulting from "distress coal" (coal of a size and grade in excess of demand and produced as a by-product when coal of a different size or grade is produced on order), and "pyramiding" of coal (which occurs when several agents all authorized to sell the same lot of coal "bid" against each other to make a sale, thus causing a single supply of coal to " 'compete against itself' "). The selling agency was also seen as a countervailing force to deal with "organized buying agencies, and large consumers" that " 'constitute unfavorable forces.' " Given the industry's distress, concerted action to remedy these practices was to be tolerated. The Court said that the "essential standard of reasonableness" calls for "vigilance in the detection and frustration of all efforts unduly to restrain the free course of interstate commerce."[35] But the Act did not "seek to establish a mere delusive liberty either by making impossible the normal and fair expansion of that commerce or the adoption of reasonable measures to protect it from

---

34. *Appalachian Coals*, 288 U.S. at 359.   **35.** Id. at 362–64.

injurious and destructive practices and to promote competition upon a sound basis."[36]

Although the Court has never done so, it is also possible, probably more plausible, to rationalize *Appalachian Coals* as creating a narrow, crisis cartel exception to Section 1 of the Sherman Act. Merger law now recognizes a failing company and even a failing division defense.[37] For similar policy reasons, one might justify a limited exception to the anticartel prohibition in the Act that would allow an industry to regroup and moderate or slow the impact of a rapid, adverse change in market conditions. Social benefits may flow from saving jobs, or at least phasing them out in a fashion that allows workers to cope more adequately with unemployment. The EC and the German antitrust laws are among those that allow for crisis cartels when an industry is confronted with worsening chronic or abrupt overcapacity problems. Any crisis cartel exception of course raises a difficult definitional problem: At what point should an industry's economic misfortune allow it to operate outside the fundamental rule of competition? Given the dire economic woes confronting bituminous coal, *Appalachian Coals* may well have satisfied even a strict version of such a definition.[38]

Chicago Board of Trade and *Appalachian Coals* are cases discordant to the theme that the rule of reason allows inquiry only into the single issue of whether an arrangement significantly decreases competition. They can be read to suggest the appropriateness of a wide inquiry, one that invites a balance to be struck between alternative social goals without more explicit guidance than the concept of the public interest. The primary theme sounded here—that courts should refuse to validate any private arrangement restricting competition on the basis of a claim that the arrangement advances other social goals—remains the better judicial rule. It is a rule to which the Court has returned in all of its modern restatements of the rule of reason.[39]

5.3d. Development of the *Per Se* Doctrine

The embryonic development of the *per se* doctrine began with *Joint-Traffic* (arrangements like price fixing, which have a "direct and immediate effect * * * upon interstate commerce" are invalid)[40] and *Standard Oil* (the fixing of rates among competitors is in "nature and character" adverse to competition and, therefore, subject to a "conclusive presumption" of invalidity).[41] The next case in the line of development of the *per se* rule was United States v. Trenton Potteries Co.[42] The defendant

---

36. Id. at 360.

37. See §§ 11.2h4–h5.

38. Another case possibly implying judicial readiness to justify some crisis cartels is the earlier National Ass'n of Window Glass Mfrs. v. United States, 263 U.S. 403, 44 S.Ct. 148, 68 L.Ed. 358 (1923), discussed in § 5.5a.

39. See generally §§ 5.3e, 5.3f.

40. United States v. Joint–Traffic Ass'n, 171 U.S. 505, 568, 19 S.Ct. 25, 43 L.Ed. 259 (1898).

41. Standard Oil Co. v. United States, 221 U.S. 1, 65, 31 S.Ct. 502, 55 L.Ed. 619 (1911).

42. 273 U.S. 392, 47 S.Ct. 377, 71 L.Ed. 700 (1927).

corporations engaged in manufacturing vitreous pottery. In the aggregate the defendants had about 82 percent of that market. They formed a secret cartel which fixed prices and limited sales to specified jobbers and were convicted in a criminal case on instructions that if price fixing was found, the reasonableness of the prices should not be considered by the jury. The court of appeals reversed, holding this instruction incorrect, but the Supreme Court reversed and reinstated the verdict. Writing for the Court, Justice Stone said:

> The aim and result of every price-fixing agreement, if effective, is the elimination of one form of competition. * * * The reasonable price fixed today may through economic and business changes become the unreasonable price of to-morrow. Once established, it may be maintained unchanged because of the absence of competition secured by the agreement * * *. Agreements which create such potential power may well be held to be in themselves unreasonable or unlawful restraints, without the necessity of minute inquiry whether a particular price is reasonable or unreasonable * * *.[43]

The opinion thus puts squarely to rest the defense recurrently attempted in earlier cases that a cartel's fixed prices are reasonable prices. But it leaves open two questions concerning the *per se* rule.

First, the Court asserts that competition is eliminated by every "effective" price fixing agreement; it marks out the harm resulting from the persistence of prices fixed by agreements which "create such potential power" as may be needed to resist market discipline. In sum, the opinion addresses itself to price fixing by defendants with market power—like the pottery makers with 82 percent of the national market. It thus leaves open the question whether the plaintiff can win its case merely by showing the agreement or must also prove from structural or other evidence that the defendants, once combined, possess sufficient market power to make their effort to fix prices effective. Second, the Court was not faced with any contention that, given the particulars of this industry, price fixing was more conducive to social well-being than competition. The only defense to price fixing addressed in *Trenton Potteries* was that the prices fixed were reasonable. Thus, the case is not a holding that prices may not be agreed upon where the danger of social injury is diminished or offset by other considerations.

As to the first of these points, *Appalachian Coals*,[44] decided after *Trenton Potteries*, validated a joint sales agency in part because it could not be predicted that the agency would have power to affect prices. From that case, a showing of actual effects on prices, or the market power to work such effects, would seem requisite. In *Addyston Pipe*,[45] market prices had actually been increased by the combination. And in *Trenton Potteries*, though actual market effects were not established, the Court

---

43. Id. at 397.

44. Appalachian Coals, Inc. v. United States, 288 U.S. 344, 53 S.Ct. 471, 77 L.Ed. 825 (1933).

45. United States v. Addyston Pipe & Steel Co., 85 Fed. 271 (6th Cir.1898), modified and aff'd, 175 U.S. 211, 20 S.Ct. 96, 44 L.Ed. 136 (1899).

viewed the combination as possessing power to control price in a " 'substantial part of an industry.' "[46] The Court soon had more to say on this issue. The second open question—whether social gains may be metered against the harm to competition—is the same issue that has arisen in applying the rule of reason. If the rule of reason does not allow inquiry into potential social gains, then surely the same restriction should apply in *per se* cases. If, on the other hand, the rule of reason allows for this open-ended inquiry, then, perhaps a social inquiry might also be pursued in *per se* cases. Indeed, if the social inquiry were pursued under the rule of reason but not under the *per se* rule, the two approaches would no longer be alternative modes for implementing the same statutory standard, but embodiments of alternative standards.

Both of these open questions were addressed thirteen years later in United States v. Socony–Vacuum Oil Co.,[47] a classic opinion which stands in relation to the *per se* doctrine as *Standard Oil* stands to the rule of reason. Oil refining was a depressed industry during the 1930s. Major refiners were fully integrated to the retail level, with ample production, storage and distribution capacity. But independent refiners were not integrated and had limited storage capacity. When such refiners had more gasoline than they could store, the industry labeled it "distressed gasoline," because it was offered on the spot market for immediate delivery to retailers and could force spot market prices to fall below full production cost. Spot market prices in turn affected all prices throughout the industry. In order to hold spot prices to a level viewed as consistent with overall levels of supply and demand, the majors entered into a concerted program of bidding for and buying distressed gas, which they were capable of storing and bringing onto the market in a less sudden, more orderly manner. The Justice Department challenged this arrangement. The Court found that Section 1 had been violated. The Court labeled this concerted arrangement for buying spot market gasoline to keep market prices up as price fixing. This characterization made it easy for the Court to reject predictable defenses. Thus, as in *Trenton Potteries*, the reasonableness of prices was not a defense, even if the resulting prices were no higher than those a healthy competitive market would yield. Going beyond *Trenton Potteries*, and turning away from *Appalachian Coals*, the Court rejected the notion that an industry crisis was relevant to the antitrust analysis. It held that price fixing could not be justified on the ground that it diminished competitive evils. Any contrary implication in *Appalachian Coals* was left to be reconciled either as irrelevant to a naked cartel which entailed no integration or as irrelevant to a price fixing agreement—a species of restraint that can be analyzed in summary fashion. Using the now classic phrase *"per se"* for the first time, the Court said:

> Congress * * * has not permitted the age-old cry of ruinous competition and competitive evils to be a defense to price-fixing

46. *Trenton Potteries*, 273 U.S. at 396.   **47.** 310 U.S. 150, 60 S.Ct. 811, 84 L.Ed. 1129 (1940).

conspiracies. It has no more allowed genuine or fancied competitive abuses as a legal justification for such schemes than it has the good intentions of the members of the combination. * * *

Under the Sherman Act a combination formed for the purpose and with the effect of raising, depressing, fixing, pegging, or stabilizing the price of a commodity in interstate * * * commerce is illegal per se.[48]

Finally, in an elaborate dictum, *Socony-Vacuum* went well beyond *Trenton Potteries* to flatly state that a price fixing agreement violated Section 1 regardless of whether the conspirators possessed power to affect prices or have any effect on the price prevailing in the market.

[We do] not mean that both a purpose and a power to fix prices are necessary for the establishment of a conspiracy under § 1 of the Sherman Act. That would be true if power or ability to commit an offense was necessary in order to convict a person of conspiring to commit it. But * * * conspiracies under the Sherman Act are not dependent on any overt act other than the act of conspiring. * * * In view of these considerations a conspiracy to fix prices violates § 1 of the Act * * * though it is not established that the conspirators had the means available for accomplishment of their objective * * *.[49]

By putting aside both the question of reasonableness of prices and the question of market power, the Court vastly simplified cartel litigation. If power had to be proven, virtually all of the structural and behavioral evidence which is canvassed in a monopoly case could be brought to bear. True, the plaintiff's burden might be simplified—for example, by holding that a prima facie case of power is made out by evidence that the defendants in the aggregate controlled a substantial percentage of the production of a specified product in a particular geographic area. But the defendants could seek to overcome the presumption by evidence that the single product was part of a larger product market or that ease of shipping called for a national market. A court would in the end be forced to delve nearly as fully into the power issue as in a monopoly case.

5.3e. The Rule of Reason and the *Per Se* Doctrine from 1940–1978

Between the early 1940s and the mid–1970s, a Janus-like stability reigned in horizontal restraint law—the prevailing compromise took a rule-oriented *per se* approach in preidentified circumstances and an open-ended rule of reason approach in all others. According to Justice Black, the *per se* category included price fixing, division of markets, group boycotts and tying arrangements.[50] *Socony-Vacuum*[51] dominated

---

48. Id. at 221–23.

49. Id. at 224 n.59.

50. Northern Pacific Ry. v. United States, 356 U.S. 1, 5, 78 S.Ct. 514, 2 L.Ed.2d 545 (1958).

51. United States v. Socony–Vacuum Oil Co., 310 U.S. 150, 60 S.Ct. 811, 84 L.Ed. 1129 (1940), is discussed in § 5.3d.

horizontal restraint cases for almost four decades after it was decided. During this period, the domain of the *per se* rule was extended[52] as plaintiffs strained to bring their antitrust claims within the bounds of *per se* theories. Courts, perhaps because they disfavored the more unwieldy rule of reason, probably abetted these plaintiffs' efforts. During this period, a judge's broad authority to dispose of an antitrust claim at a pretrial stage was not well established. Confronting a trial, a judge might consciously or unconsciously favor a substantive rule that offered a more confined rather than an open-ended trial.

The rationale for a *per se* doctrine was perhaps best stated in a case involving application of Section 1 to a tie-in. In *Northern Pacific Ry. v. United States,* the Court said:

> [T]here are certain agreements or practices which because of their pernicious effect on competition and lack of any redeeming virtue are conclusively presumed to be unreasonable and therefore illegal without elaborate inquiry as to the precise harm they have caused or the business excuse for their use. This principle of *per se* unreasonableness not only makes the type of restraints which are proscribed by the Sherman Act more certain to the benefit of everyone concerned, but it also avoids the necessity for an incredibly complicated and prolonged economic investigation into the entire history of the industry involved, as well as related industries, in an effort to determine at large whether a particular restraint has been unreasonable—an inquiry so often wholly fruitless when undertaken.[53]

It is this simplifying effect of the *per se* rule that has endeared it to those who support strong antitrust enforcement. The *per se* rule can convert antitrust attorneys into an adjunct of the enforcement agencies. If the violation turns on market power, counsel must say so and must, in the client's interest, explore the possibility that a defense can be made on the basis of a broad market definition and apparently modest market shares. If, by contrast, the *per se* rule assigns liability to proof, say, of price fixing alone, antitrust counsel must say so, focusing in all likelihood on the risks of criminal sanctions and treble damages. Also, the difference between a *per se* rule and a rule of reason could have a significant impact, perhaps a profound one, on the effectiveness of the private remedy as a deterrent. Many treble damage actions, especially class actions, that are managerially and economically feasible with a *per se* rule, would cease to be so if the market had to be defined and market power had to be shown as a predicate to proving an offense like price fixing. Moreover, for an offense like price fixing there is little if any social cost to balance against this enhanced deterrence. As a generalization, price fixing does not become socially beneficial when power is lacking; it simply becomes ineffective. A *per se* rule significantly reduces

---

52. For example, horizontal divisions of markets were enveloped within the *per se* rule in United States v. Topco Assocs., Inc., 405 U.S. 596, 92 S.Ct. 1126, 31 L.Ed.2d 515 (1972).

53. 356 U.S. 1, 5, 78 S.Ct. 514, 2 L.Ed.2d 545 (1958).

the cost and increases the effectiveness of enforcement, and even if this leads to overenforcement (in the sense that it discourages efforts to fix prices that would not have worked for lack of power, or even punishes attempts to fix prices that failed), the "overenforcement" would not inhibit any socially valuable conduct; it merely inhibits ineffective attempts to do something both harmful and unlawful.

From 1940–1978 the *per se* rule may sometimes have been applied more widely than its rationale, however powerful, warranted. During that period economic analysis by the courts was often unsophisticated and sometimes poorly crafted. Even with these flaws, mostly since corrected, the *per se* rule was a boon to judicial efficiency, avoiding a costly, complex, and uncertain inquiry. Although on occasion, it was applied too broadly, most applications attacked competitively harmful conduct, and the rule's availability both discouraged such conduct and facilitated enforcement where it was used. The *per se* doctrine avoided another pitfall. Even if a particular inquiry might show a concerted arrangement to be reasonable at the time of suit, it might well become unreasonable later as conditions changed. An alternative rule might often require continuous judicial supervision.

In contrast to the perceived advantages of the *per se* doctrine, some uncertainty still clouded application of the rule of reason during the three decades we are discussing here. As a result of decisions such as *Chicago Board of Trade*[54] and *Appalachian Coals*,[55] the rule of reason has not always been contained within historic limits—balancing tendencies to enhance competition against tendencies to injure competition. At times, courts have asked whether the adverse effects on competition are offset by other public benefits attributable to the restraint. Ambiguity about the content of the rule of reason thus may exacerbate issues about the scope of the *per se* doctrine and induce its expansion beyond the limits of its logic. Judges concerned with being mired in an analytical swamp when rule of reason analysis is held to apply might favor a *per se* rule. On the other hand, if the rule of reason is confined to its historic limits, manageable analytical techniques become available to separate the lawful from the competitively harmful.

5.3f. The Modern Synthesis of *Per Se* and Rule of Reason Analysis

During the 1970s the economic sophistication of antitrust litigators and antitrust courts increased considerably. In part this occurred through the efforts and influence of Chicago School theorists.[56] With this development there was some tendency for *per se* and rule of reason analysis to merge. The modern synthesis begins with National Society of

---

54. Chicago Bd. of Trade v. United States, 246 U.S. 231, 38 S.Ct. 242, 62 L.Ed. 683 (1918).

55. Appalachian Coals, Inc. v. United States, 288 U.S. 344, 53 S.Ct. 471, 77 L.Ed. 825 (1933).

56. See the discussion of the role of Chicago theorists in § 1.5b. Their impact on the law governing price predation, vertical restraints, and vertical mergers has been substantial and is discussed throughout this book.

Professional Engineers v. United States.[57] Implicitly a rule of reason decision, the case teaches that a court may consider only limited factors in antitrust analysis; any matter not bearing on whether an alleged restraint increases or decreases competition is for legislative, not judicial attention. Implications of earlier cases like *Trenton Potteries* and *Socony-Vacuum*, both *per se* cases, are clearly adopted and applied across the whole antitrust spectrum. For the first time, a real structure is imposed upon the undisciplined shopping list—nature of the business, history of the restraint, and all the rest—that Justice Brandeis had tendered to juries in *Chicago Board of Trade*.[58] More than this, the Court, as some scholars had urged, rejected *Chicago Board of Trade's* implication that courts applying the rule of reason could treat a range of social betterments, such as the quietude achieved by concerted agreements limiting trade during market off-hours, as a benefit offsetting competitive harm.[59] This narrowing of the concept of benefit greatly reduces the distance between *per se* and rule of reason analysis. *Professional Engineers* ended fear that the rule of reason would allow courts to evaluate any and all social betterments against adverse competitive impact—a task more legislative than judicial in character. The decision confines judicial inquiry solely to the effect of a practice on competition, and characterizes conventional *per se* offenses not as separate species of restraints, but as clear illustrations of conduct that injures competition.

A number of issues remain. When is competition hurt? Depending on which antitrust goals are embraced, the answer may vary. At a minimum, the injuries from market power are relevant. These cause misallocations of resources and wealth transfers (including transfers due to x-inefficiencies which may increase consumer costs without increasing the return to the monopolist or cartelists and due to rent-seeking expenses). Harm to individual competitors may still be relevant at the margin, as may coercion.[60] Another question left open is what constitutes an offsetting benefit to competition. Efficiencies are certainly relevant; we discuss them below. First, consider this conundrum. The minimal teaching of *Professional Engineers* is that public health and welfare cannot be counted as independent benefit categories, for the Court there rejected a defense that elimination of competition among engineers was necessary to ensure public safety.[61] By contrast, when concerted conduct ends or reduces market failure, these effects should be counted as benefits; limiting the effect of a market failure would tend to improve competition. This being so, the relevance of a particular fact may turn on how it is seen, how it is characterized. As an instance, standard-setting activity often involves a safety component. Suppose, then, that toy manufacturers concertedly agree not to use lead in small toys. Should

---

57. 435 U.S. 679, 98 S.Ct. 1355, 55 L.Ed.2d 637 (1978).

58. Chicago Bd. of Trade v. United States, 246 U.S. 231, 38 S.Ct. 242, 62 L.Ed. 683 (1918).

59. *Professional Eng'rs*, 435 U.S. at 690–92 & n.18 (The Court cited, among other sources, L. SULLIVAN, HANDBOOK OF THE LAW OF ANTITRUST § 72 (1977)).

60. See the discussion of antitrust goals in Chapter 1.

61. *Professional Eng'rs*, 435 U.S. at 693–94.

this be characterized as a public health defense, impermissible under *Professional Engineers*, or as a legitimate response to a market failure, a lack by consumers of sufficient information? One could argue that any information problem can be addressed by supplying information alone—that only the government, not interested industry participants, should be able to exclude market access entirely on the grounds of public safety. But so long as a standard-setting response to an information problem is measured and objective, it can leave ample room for competition.[62] At least in a context like the lead paint on toys hypothetical, the case for labeling the concert as an agreement to tame a market failure resulting from limited consumer information is plausible—perhaps even strong. In an era of deregulation where government interventions are few, perhaps any concerted activity intended to correct consumer information failures should be evaluated under the reason analysis.[63] If so, judicial analysis would address the question whether the restraint was objective and measured—in sum, whether there was an information problem, whether the response was well calculated to correct it, and whether it was more restrictive than necessary to attain the benefit sought.

Even the offsetting benefit that surely counts—enhanced efficiency—can present difficult application problems. Should cost reduction achieved through concertedly developed technology trump cost increases and income transfers due to resulting market power?[64] A strict Chicago analysis would say it depends on whether the efficiency is greater than the deadweight loss from the market power increase. If it is, then gross domestic product is increased; and though they describe themselves as seeking consumer welfare, some Chicagoans assert indifference to the way in which the benefits of an efficiency are shared between consumers and producers.[65] But a more conventional analysis would ask, does the practice lead, on the average, to higher or lower prices?[66] When an antitrust issue is analyzed in this conventional way, if consumers are hurt by higher prices the efficiency, even if it benefits producers more than it hurts consumers, does not constitute a defense.

Another question is whether market power must be proven, or whether it is sufficient that an arrangement, if it has any effect at all, will hurt competition. To the extent conventional *per se* analysis applies,

62. See Allied Tube & Conduit Corp. v. Indian Head, Inc., 486 U.S. 492, 108 S.Ct. 1931, 100 L.Ed.2d 497 (1988) (discussing the merits of standard-setting activity in the course of deciding the scope of the application of the Sherman Act to conduct arguably within the protection of the First Amendment).

63. A broad reading of California Dental Ass'n v. FTC, 526 U.S. 756, 119 S.Ct. 1604, 143 L.Ed.2d 935 (1999), might suggest this result. The case is addressed in this Section, infra. See the discussion in L. Sullivan, *The Viability of the Current Law on Horizontal Restraints*, 75 CAL. L. REV. 835, 839 (1987).

64. Compare Williamson, *Economies as an Antitrust Defense: The Welfare Trade-offs*, 58 AM. ECON. REV. 18 (1968), with Fisher & Lande, *Efficiency Considerations in Merger Enforcement*, 71 CAL. L. REV. 1580 (1983).

65. An influential proponent of this view was R. BORK, THE ANTITRUST PARADOX: A POLICY AT WAR WITH ITSELF 111 (1978). For an overview of the controversy surrounding this point, see Lande, *The Rise and (Coming) Fall of Efficiency as the Ruler of Antitrust*, 33 ANTITRUST BULL. 429 (1988).

66. See Lande, supra note 64 and authorities there cited.

power analysis is not needed. But suppose some degree of integration has resulted so some possible benefits might result. Is full-fledged power analysis always mandatory in such instances? In *NCAA v. Board of Regents of University of Oklahoma*, the Supreme Court determined that an output-reducing scheme, when assessed under the rule of reason, could be condemned without requiring a showing of market power.[67] A different conclusion might follow if the arrangement does not constitute a clear limitation on output. Finally, *Professional Engineers* leaves unanswered questions about who has the burden of proving what, and when these burdens shift.

Supreme Court decisions following *Professional Engineers* are essays on some of these questions. Each attempts to fine-tune the emerging integration of discretion and rule. Yet, seldom is an issue fully clarified; nor should we expect that it will be.

Broadcast Music, Inc. v. CBS, Inc.,[68] models one important proposition. If a practice "facially appears to be one that would * * * almost always tend to restrict competition and decrease output," it is unlawful.[69] The restraint is thus *"per se"* wrong whenever, *given its particulars and its setting*, those adverse characteristics appear on its face. If not, then a fuller analysis—either an analysis of power or perhaps only of whether the benefits sought could be obtained less restrictively—will be required to determine whether a competitive injury is occurring or an efficiency is being attained (or, if both are resulting, whether the net effect is consumer injury in either the conventional or the Chicago School sense). Put in functional terms, *Broadcast Music* teaches that the trial court must do a facial analysis—must take at least a quick look at context and likely effects—before it assigns the case either to the *per se* or rule of reason category. In *Broadcast Music* each defendant held nonexclusive licenses to copyrights entitling them to market rights to use the musical compositions covered by the copyrights that were owned by numerous authors and publishers. Because each defendant granted such performance licenses only to its total library at a package price and refused to license on any other basis, CBS charged each defendant with acting as a sales agent fixing the prices on works in its library, thereby stomping out competition between the works of the numerous copyright holders that had licensed the defendants. Given the obvious transactional efficiencies achieved through joint marketing of these copyright packages and the continued (if somewhat threatened) availability of individual licenses from the owners of individual copyrights, the Court held that the restraint in *Broadcast Music* was not facially invalid.[70] The arrangement opened a whole new sphere of marketing activity—in a sense creating a new product. Moreover, this was achieved without ousting the old product, individual copyright licensing; this old way of doing business remained available to buyers and sellers whenever both preferred it.

67. 468 U.S. 85, 109–10, 104 S.Ct. 2948, 82 L.Ed.2d 70 (1984).

68. 441 U.S. 1, 99 S.Ct. 1551, 60 L.Ed.2d 1 (1979).

69. Id. at 19–20.

70. Id. at 23–24.

Apparently, too, the arrangement was free of coercion; no seller was obliged to come into a packaged songs market, nor to stay out of the individual song market.[71] And if any copyright holder was willing to negotiate individually, buyers would be free to make individual deals, not just packaged ones. For these reasons the Court remanded for rule of reason analysis in the lower court.

In his dissent, Justice Stevens did not disagree with the majority's analysis so much as with its stopping point.[72] Like the majority, Stevens would have rejected a *per se* characterization. A quick look showed some efficiencies that took the case out of the *per se* category. But Stevens would not have remanded the case; he would have resolved the rule of reason inquiry on the basis of the facts already before the Court. He thought that the defendants were liable because even the limited facts plainly showed a less restrictive means available for attaining the efficiencies that had so impressed the majority.[73] The defendants already monitored the frequency of use of individual compositions in order to divide license revenues equitably among copyright owners. Justice Stevens thought this could be done, too, in determining how high a license fee any licensee should pay. If a licensee like CBS used songs in the package that were much in demand it would pay a higher fee than if it limited its use to the songs for which there was a lower demand. He argued that such less restrictive alternatives might have allowed new or less known composers to market their work at lower prices, thus easing the task of entry or market penetration. Though the majority did not accept this argument in this context, a focus on less restrictive alternatives is well rooted in antitrust interpretation, dating back at least to Judge Taft's decision in *Addyston Pipe*.[74] As we shall show, the Court later turned to it.[75]

Both the majority and dissenting opinions in *Broadcast Music* signal a further narrowing of the distinction between rule of reason and *per se* analysis—of discretion and self-executing rule. Both identify circumstances in which a court should decide a case on the basis of a mid-level norm and a truncated record. The majority would never countenance that response when the facial inquiry concerning a restraint suggests not only injury to competition, but offsetting efficiencies as well. The majority would require full inquiry whenever both injury to competition and increased efficiency are possible effects of the defendant's conduct. The majority gives little guidance for balancing efficiency and harm once the record is expanded. Apparently it was content, at least for the present, to leave each district court a free hand in determining whether an efficiency is apparent and how much weight it carries. Justice Stevens would go a step further, arguing that a violation should be adjudicated even when

71. Id.

72. Id. at 25–26 (Stevens, J., dissenting).

73. Id. at 33 (Stevens, J., dissenting).

74. United States v. Addyston Pipe & Steel Co., 85 Fed. 271 (6th Cir.1898), modified and aff'd, 175 U.S. 211, 20 S.Ct. 96, 44 L.Ed. 136 (1899).

75. See the discussion of Arizona v. Maricopa County Medical Soc'y, 457 U.S. 332, 102 S.Ct. 2466, 73 L.Ed.2d 48 (1982), in this section infra.

both benefit and harm are suggested if it is facially apparent that the efficiencies could be obtained by less restrictive means. In his view, it wastes resources and confuses the legal norms to remand such a case for more elaborate factual inquiry.[76] The majority opinion, shunting the case to the trial court, leaves unresolved whether the "less restrictive" alternative approach followed by Justice Stevens is to have a large role, a limited one, or none at all. Perhaps the majority simply wanted a full record before itself attempting to meter efficiency and competitive injury and to balance the one against the other.[77]

Confining the territory for application of the *per se* doctrine, *Broadcast Music* asserted that while *per se* analysis can yield greater simplicity and certainty, it should not be permitted to do so at too great a cost in economic efficiency. The dissent agreed, but insisted that while the rule of reason can yield precision and accuracy, it should not be permitted to do so at too great a cost in delay, uncertainty and litigation.[78] Not long thereafter the Court decided Arizona v. Maricopa County Medical Society,[79] which evidenced a tilt toward the Stevens end of the continuum between rule and discretion. About 1,750 doctors, 70 percent of the practitioners in an Arizona county, were members of a foundation that established a maximum fee schedule which members agreed to accept for services for patients insured under policies approved by the foundation. The *Maricopa* majority opinion by Justice Stevens indicates that once a price agreement (maximum or minimum) among competitors has been shown without integration of any other aspect of their operations, the facial inquiry is over and the *per se* characterization applies.[80] But the specific reasoning of the majority is not draconian in tone and may be as significant as the holding.

The defendants in *Maricopa* argued that their arrangement had an adequate procompetitive benefit; maximum charges for particular medical services limit a physician's charges and allow insurers to calculate their exposure more accurately and thus set lower insurance rates. The majority found the argument unpersuasive on the facts at hand, but did not reject it as a matter of principle. It found there were less restrictive ways, at least nearly as efficient, that insurers could have used to fix a maximum—ways that threatened no competitive injury. Thus, while stressing the possible harms of maximum price fixing, the majority implicitly recognized its possible competitive benefits. Given that the majority gave heed to possible benefits and rejected them not in principle but in this particular context, its decision in *Maricopa* looks not like a knee-jerk *per se* reaction, but like an analytically enhanced approach to

---

76. *Broadcast Music*, 441 U.S. at 26 & n.4 (Stevens, J., dissenting).

77. Concerning the difficulties of comparing an efficiency gain with an increase in market power that might yield x-inefficiencies, a deadweight loss, and an income transfer from consumers to firms, see Fisher & Lande, *supra* note 64; see also A. Fisher et al., Mergers, Market Power, and Property Rights: When Will Efficiencies

Prevent Price Increases? (FTC, Bureau of Econ. Working Paper No. 130, 1985).

78. *Broadcast Music*, 441 U.S. at 26 & n.4 (Stevens, J., dissenting).

79. 457 U.S. 332, 102 S.Ct. 2466, 73 L.Ed.2d 48 (1982).

80. Id. at 351.

facial illegality. Indeed, it much resembles the truncated rule of reason analysis Justice Stevens urged on the Court in *Broadcast Music.*

The *Maricopa* majority saw danger in allowing physicians to control the setting of their own rates. The potential power abuse lays in allowing physician-set rates to supplant those of the marketplace. With the benefit of more than a decade of hindsight, the majority's reading of the facts may seem questionable. It is apparent, for example, that consumers are ill-equipped to second-guess the need for or the cost of medical procedures and medications. Moreover, any incentive consumers might have to exercise cost discipline is undermined by third party payor systems that cover the bulk of consumer medical expenses. Hindsight suggests that any cost cutting discipline is more likely to come from the third party payors, such as government-subsidized medical care programs, private insurance companies, or other private medical care providers. Thus, the defendants' arguments in *Maricopa*, that they were imposing a cost discipline on physicians, might well have been given greater weight were the case decided today.

To be sure, one can argue, as did the minority, that if health insurers want doctors to compute a group maximum price, a presumption of efficiency should attach to their market-dictated choice; price fixing must be the low cost solution to providing health insurance, or it would not be done. Spinning this web farther, one could argue that the burden should be on the plaintiffs to prove precisely what competitive harms, if any, result from the practice and to show that these harms outweigh any cost reduction to the insurers. But this line of reasoning—implicitly rejected by the *Maricopa* majority—would give all the weight to efficiency, and scant attention to competitive abuses associated with market power, including misallocations, wealth transfers, and x-inefficiencies. In any event, the *Maricopa* result seems correct on the record upon which it was decided. Combined, fee-for-services physicians enjoyed a relative position of power. Far fewer doctors were employees of health maintenance organizations (HMOs). Indeed, 70 percent of the Maricopa County physicians, apparently all in private, fee-for-service practice, had joined the price-setting organization that the Court found to have contravened Section 1. Given the changes that have been occurring in the delivery of medical services, the dissenting analysis in *Maricopa* might seem more credible today. In the current market, physicians who are members of similar preferred provider, fee-for-service organizations would likely enjoy less leverage. Such organizations are losing market share to large health care providers as doctors sign with HMOs and find their incomes dependent on capitation arrangements. Pricing by members of today's preferred provider organizations (PPOs) is far more likely to be disciplined by the rates charged by such competing HMOs and like entities.

The Court's next horizontal restraint decision, NCAA v. Board of Regents of University of Oklahoma,[81] further illuminates the nature of

---

81. 468 U.S. 85, 104 S.Ct. 2948, 82 L.Ed.2d 70 (1984).

the balancing inquiry confronting a court under the truncated rule of reason. In particular, *NCAA* addresses what constitutes a competitive injury and what may be considered an offsetting benefit. The plaintiffs, colleges with popular and generally successful football teams, challenged the NCAA's control over football broadcasting. Faced with elaborate and long-standing NCAA regulations of all aspects of intercollegiate sports, including mandatory joint television marketing of NCAA football, the Court rejected a *per se* conclusion. Because some degree of cooperation was needed to market the product at all, a rule of reason analysis was appropriate. But much as *per se* or facial inquiry was enhanced in *Maricopa*, so here rule of reason inquiry was narrowed and constrained. Given the need for some restraints, no particular restraint within the package ought to be labeled *per se* unlawful; nonetheless, when an inquiry has proceeded far enough to show that one or more of the restraints unnecessarily injures competition, all inquiry should end.[82] The rule of reason no longer need signify endless inquiry into market definition and shares, cross-elasticities, supply substitutability, scale economies, transaction costs and learning curves.

The *NCAA* Court appropriately focused primarily on consumer welfare in its truncated rule of reason analysis. But coercion and reduced mobility were also significant factors. The Court found the restraints illegal because: (1) the NCAA plan reduced the total number of games televised and increased the prices paid for games[83]; (2) the plan prevented colleges producing games with mass appeal from either obtaining a share of joint revenues commensurate with their market attractiveness or (because of threats of NCAA discipline in other, unrelated areas) leaving the association and marketing on their own[84]; and (3) the plan prevented small colleges from independently marketing local games, thus depriving them of a market opportunity and precluding local stations from entry into college football broadcasting.[85]

The Court's refusal to apply a *per se* rule to joint pricing was anything but revolutionary. The record showed no conventional price fixing agreement; the NCAA is no conventional cartel. Some integration had taken place—integration of a fairly complex kind.[86] Ever since *Appalachian Coals, Inc. v. United States*,[87] analysts giving any credence to judicial method have known that integration going beyond mere agreement on price requires at least a truncated inquiry to determine whether benefits are attained and, if so, whether they exceed harms.[88] Such an inquiry would encompass, at the truncated stage, whether the

---

82. Id. at 103.

83. Id. at 105 & n.29.

84. Id. at 94–95.

85. Id. at 118 n.62.

86. League teams work together in developing rules and schedules, coordinating the recruiting process, hiring and assigning referees, etc.

87. 288 U.S. 344, 53 S.Ct. 471, 77 L.Ed. 825 (1933).

88. Indeed, though expressing doubt about the ultimate conclusion in *Appalachian Coals*, Justice Stevens' opinion in *Professional Engineers* underscores the doctrinal wisdom of that very aspect of the case. National Soc'y of Professional Eng'rs v. United States, 435 U.S. 679, 681–99, 98 S.Ct. 1355, 55 L.Ed.2d 637 (1978).

integration promises efficiencies, whether joint price setting is necessary to achieve the efficiencies, and whether market participants are being coerced to participate. If the first two questions are answered affirmatively and the last one negatively, a fuller analysis is needed to determine whether there will be adverse resource allocation and wealth transfer effects that outweigh the apparent efficiencies.

Integration among firms should preclude an automatic characterization of conduct as price fixing, but it does not follow that a showing of market power is then essential to warrant inference of anticompetitive effect. For one thing power may be implicit in the nature of the limitation—in *NCAA*, limitations on the output of televised college football games. Justice Stevens put it this way: as a matter of law, the absence of proof of market power does not justify a naked restriction on price or output. To the contrary, when there is an agreement not to compete in terms of price or output, " 'no elaborate industry analysis is required to demonstrate the anticompetitive character of such an agreement.' "[89] For another thing, truncated inquiry may show that there are no resulting efficiencies, or that if they are there, they can be attained without the restraint.

The Stevens opinion for the majority in *NCAA* and the Stevens dissent in *Broadcast Music* are very similar. In both he applied a truncated rule of reason and identified a violation even without a full structural analysis showing market power. In both he saw the harm as outweighing the claimed benefits because the benefits could be achieved in a less restrictive way. In both he saw and emphasized that the restraint distorted the price system—some participants got more and some got less than their products would bring in a competitive market. Two things differentiate the cases, and explain why Stevens had six Justices with him in *NCAA* and none in *Broadcast Music*. First, the resulting efficiencies that in *Broadcast Music* were vivid and large were at least somewhat speculative in *NCAA*. Second, in *Broadcast Music* the copyright licensors came into the concert of their own choice, and remained free to trade outside it as well. The rights of the composer as well as of the licensee were protected. Indeed, Justice White stressed that the two composer-copyright organizations (BMI and ASCAP) promoted the aims of copyright law through the "integration of sales,

---

89. *NCAA*, 468 U.S. at 109 (quoting *Professional Eng'rs*, 435 U.S. at 692). Evidence gathered after *NCAA* was decided tends to support the conclusion that the NCAA's output limitations on TV broadcasts of major college football games produced a higher revenue pool for the participating schools. Indeed, even powerful football schools with the ability to contract for the commercial telecast of most or all of their individual games often found their revenues were reduced after increased output limitations produced a plethora of telecast games on any given football weekend.

M. SPERBER, COLLEGE SPORTS, INC., 52–53 (1990). Sperber states that the NCAA had negotiated TV contracts for $74 million for the 1984 season. After the Supreme Court's decision was announced in July 1984, individual schools were able to sign TV contracts that collectively produced only $30 million. Id. This is precisely the result that cartel theory would predict, and one that benefits consumers, albeit at the expense of virtually all football programs, including the powerful College Football Association members that had instituted the *NCAA* litigation.

monitoring, and enforcement against unauthorized copyright use."[90] The NCAA's licensing arrangements, by contrast, protected the proprietary interests of some football producers at the expense of others that wanted to act independently but were forced into the scheme by coercive threats of sweeping NCAA discipline. A school had to be an NCAA member not only to play football but to participate in numerous other intercollegiate sports. Once in, it was forbidden from marketing its football product independently at the threat of expulsion. Whereas the scheme in *Broadcast Music* enhanced the proprietary control of composers with less obvious impact on total output, the scheme in *NCAA* coercively reduced the colleges' control of their own games, and far more effectively reduced the output of televised games.

Justice White, the only member of the Court to have participated in a college football game, dissented in *NCAA*. In part, this dissent rested on the argument that exclusively televised college football games were "a new product" more valuable than any individual football school could market on its own. The district court had failed to determine whether total viewership in the exclusively broadcasted games might be higher than total viewership for a larger number of nonexclusively broadcasted games. The implicit contention by Justice White that the NCAA marketing process would increase overall viewers seems counterintuitive; the much larger number of televised games surely produced lower individual game TV ratings, but would seem unlikely to lower total viewership unless a flooded market made the public devalue college football games. Moreover, if accepted, the argument may place an impossible burden on the plaintiff in such cases—proving the public reaction to an unshackled output that has never before been tried.

Justice White's final point was that noneconomic benefits attended NCAA's self-regulation of college athletics and that these outweighed any harmful competitive effect.[91] By bringing in asserted social welfare benefits to weigh against competitive harms this contention by Justice White resurrects the open-ended and unwieldy rule of reason suggested in *Chicago Board of Trade* and *Appalachian Coals*; it is flatly inconsistent with the holding in *Professional Engineers*. One could, of course, argue that the Sherman Act was never intended to apply at all to college sports because of their noncommercial aspects. But the litigants in *NCAA* would have been hard pressed to convince a trier of fact that college football programs, at least those involving the College Football Association members, were not substantial participants in the entertainment industry. They generated millions of dollars in ticket and television revenues.

Another example of truncated rule of reason analysis is found in FTC v. Indiana Federation of Dentists.[92] In a case that will be discussed

---

90. Broadcast Music, Inc. v. CBS, Inc., 441 U.S. 1, 20, 99 S.Ct. 1551, 60 L.Ed.2d 1 (1979).

91. *NCAA*, 468 U.S. at 134–35 (White, J., dissenting).

92. 476 U.S. 447, 106 S.Ct. 2009, 90 L.Ed.2d 445 (1986).

later for its treatment of boycotts,[93] the Court unanimously ruled that, absent evidence of an offsetting procompetitive effect, proof that a group of dentists concertedly withheld a particular service from the market was sufficient to show a violation. Given a manifestly harmful purpose and the lack of a credible possibility of benefit, a violation under the rule of reason may be shown without proof of market power.

Slightly more than a decade after deciding *Indiana Dentists,* the Supreme Court confronted what seems a far more straightforward case of concerted action by health professionals in *California Dental Association v. Federal Trade Commission.*[94] California dentists that were members of the Association were obliged to comply with a code of ethics that included restrictions on advertising. The code was implemented through advisory opinions, guidelines, and other enforcement initiatives at a state and local level. The FTC filed a complaint against the Association alleging that it violated Section 5 by applying its guidelines in a manner that restricted truthful, nondeceptive advertising. The administrative law judge (and subsequently the Commission) found that as implemented, the Association's policy restricted truthful and nondeceptive advertising of low prices, across-the-board discounts, and service quality. The Commission found that the Association had market power and that its restrictions on discount advertising were *per se* unlawful and, alternatively, that restrictions on both price and nonprice advertising were unlawful under an abbreviated rule of reason analysis. In a split panel decision, the court of appeals held that the *per se* rule did not apply, but affirmed the Commission's order under a "quick look" analysis.[95]

The Supreme Court agreed with the court of appeals that the nonprofit dental association was subject to the FTC's jurisdiction but vacated and remanded, holding that the quick look analysis applied by the court of appeals was insufficient. The Association had mounted a defense based on patient difficulties in evaluating the quality of medical services and the risk that even truthful disclosure in advertising could be misleading or deceptive to patients. Justice Souter wrote for the five-member majority that the Association's claim of information imperfections raised non-trivial issues and that "the likelihood of anticompetitive effects" was not "comparably obvious" to prior decisions (such as *NCAA, Professional Engineers,* and *Indiana Dentists*) in which a curtailed rule of reason analysis had been applied.[96]

The majority offered generalities but no clear guidance for determining when a truncated analysis would be appropriate:

> [T]here is generally no categorical line to be drawn between restraints that give rise to an intuitively obvious inference of anticom-

---

93. § 5.8b.

94. 526 U.S. 756, 119 S.Ct. 1604, 143 L.Ed.2d 935 (1999).

95. 128 F.3d 720 (9th Cir.1997). Judge Real dissented, arguing in part that a full-blown rule of reason analysis was required.

96. 119 S.Ct. at 1613. On a second issue addressed by the Supreme Court, all nine justices agreed that the FTC had jurisdiction over non-profit associations engaged in the regulation of advertising for its professional members.

petitive effect and those that call for more detailed treatment. What is required, rather, is an enquiry meet for the case, looking to the circumstances, details and logic of a restraint. The object is to see whether the experience of the market has been so clear, or necessarily will be, that a confident conclusion about the principal tendency of a restriction will follow from a quick (or at least a quicker) look, in place of a more sedulous one. * * * For now, at least, a less quick look was required for the initial assessment of the tendency of these professional advertising restrictions.[97]

The majority is of course correct that information imperfections are a relevant touchstone for the consumer welfare analysis integral to application of antitrust law.[98] The issue, then, as Justice Breyer wrote for the four dissenters, is not whether such issues may be considered, but rather the "allocation of the burdens of persuasion" in a horizontal restraints case.[99]

As the dissent stressed, the allocation of those burdens

reflects a gradual evolution within the courts over a period of many years. That evolution represents an effort carefully to blend the procompetitive objectives of the law of antitrust with administrative necessity. It represents a considerable advance, both from the days when the Commission had to present and/or refute every possible fact and theory, and from antitrust theories so abbreviated as to prevent proper analysis. The former prevented cases from ever reaching a conclusion * * * and the latter called forth the criticism that the "Government always wins."[100]

For the four dissenters, the court of appeals use of quick look analysis to affirm the Commission's order was unexceptional and more straightforward than it had been in *Indiana Dentists*.[101] In view of the Commission's findings (which are valid if supported by "substantial evidence") that the Dental Association's rule in practice precluded all advertising that rates were "low, reasonable, or affordable", all advertising of across the board discounts, and all quality claims, the Commission's holding that these restraints unreasonably restrained trade should have been upheld.[102]

Read broadly, *Dental Association* could confuse the careful and incremental building blocks for truncated analysis that the Supreme Court has put together over the past half century. A narrower and less disruptive reading of the case is that the court of appeals was simply too

---

97. Id. at 1618.

98. The Court began paying attention to information imperfections as early as in Chicago Board of Trade v. United States, 246 U.S. 231, 38 S.Ct. 242, 62 L.Ed. 683 (1918) and strongly reaffirmed their relevance to an antitrust analysis in Eastman Kodak Co. v. Image Technical Servs., Inc., 504 U.S. 451, 112 S.Ct. 2072, 119 L.Ed.2d 265 (1992).

99. *Dental Ass'n*, 119 S.Ct. at 1624 (Breyer, J., dissenting).

100. Id. (citing United States v. Von's Grocery Co., 384 U.S. 270, 301, 86 S.Ct. 1478, 16 L.Ed.2d 555 (1966))(Stewart, J., dissenting).

101. Id. at 1623.

102. Id. at 1618.

perfunctory and insufficiently methodical in its quick look analysis. The majority hints at such a construction by suggesting that the inadequacies of the court of appeals holding lie not in the record before it but in the opinion itself. Justice Souter wrote: "Had the Court of Appeals engaged in a painstaking discussion in a league with Justice Breyer's (compare his 14 pages with the Ninth Circuit's 8), and had it confronted the comparability of these restrictions to bars on clearly verifiable advertising, its reasoning might have sufficed to justify its conclusions."[103] Indeed, the Breyer opinion can serve as a checklist for the points that a court or agency should address in explaining why it concludes that truncated analysis is sufficient: how the restraint can hurt competition; why any offsetting benefit claims are deficient; and why an inference of sufficient power to do market harm is warranted.

Although *Dental Association* may create doubt about when and how much truncated analysis is appropriate, the majority decision explicitly recognizes that truncated analysis is sometimes appropriate and did not question the wisdom of the view that in applying a truncated rule of reason, a court should not reach noneconomic social welfare considerations. *Professional Engineers, NCAA* and *Indiana Dentists* are consistent with this view. But this was apparently not the view of the Third Circuit in United States v. Brown University.[104] The United States brought a Section 1 claim against the Massachusetts Institute of Technology (MIT) and eight Ivy League colleges and universities. The schools were alleged to have violated Section 1 by agreeing to distribute financial aid exclusively on the basis of need and by collectively determining the amount of financial assistance students commonly admitted would be awarded. The eight Ivy League participants signed a consent decree. MIT went to trial. Rejecting *per se* analysis, the district court held that under truncated rule of reason analysis, the agreement violated Section 1. The court of appeals reversed and remanded, holding that the district court failed adequately to consider MIT's proffered procompetitive and social welfare justifications for the arrangement.[105] This holding resonates with those aspects of *Chicago Board of Trade* and *Appalachian Coals* that permitted social benefits to be weighed against competitive injury. For example, the appellate court was sympathetic to an MIT argument that the arrangement, by limiting financial aid to the most talented students, made a limited pool of financial aid available to a wider universe of applicants.[106] MIT also argued that by limiting price competition, beneficial nonprice competition might be promoted. Both arguments are inconsistent with the line of Supreme Court cases beginning with *Professional Engineers*. So, too, is the notion implicitly embraced by the Third Circuit, that, in addition to the truncated rule of reason followed in these cases, there still exists a "full-scale rule of

103. Id. at 1617.

104. 5 F.3d 658 (3d Cir.1993).

105. Id. at 661.

106. Id. at 675–77.

reason analysis" that permits the court to weigh social gains against competitive injury.[107]

When the Justice Department first announced its investigation of the financial aid practices of the Ivy League schools, some critics questioned the wisdom of this use of prosecutorial discretion. Assuming the antitrust laws apply to nonprofit educational institutions, this particular application of limited government enforcement resources seemed difficult to justify. In the *Brown University* case, the dissenting opinion argues that the antitrust laws do not apply to financial aid activities of nonprofit educational institutions. Although it is clear that the commercial activities of nonprofit groups are subject to the antitrust laws,[108] there is some room to contend that financial aid to the purely educational mission of such schools is beyond the intent of the Sherman and Clayton Acts. Relatedly, one might reason that if two or more charities devoted to feeding the hungry were to divide territories for benefit distribution in order to assure reasonable uniform regional coverage, the antitrust laws should be irrelevant. If the majority had accepted such a noncoverage argument it might have disposed of the case without undermining the sound doctrine of *Professional Engineers*.

The tension between a tightly structured *per se* rule and a rule focused on reasonableness that invites open-ended, fact intensive inquiry and broad, value laden judicial discretion is not found only in antitrust[109] but also in constitutional law.[110] A celebrated scholar-advocate has observed that in First Amendment analysis, the Court's recent tendency has been to abjure rules of reason for *per se* responses based on the constitutional text, a momentum in the opposite direction from that occurring in antitrust. Reconciliation lies, perhaps, in differences between the level of theoretical development in the two areas. Rules of reason are feasible and can function adequately only when there is a broad enough consensus supporting an adequate body of theory which can be brought to bear on the issue of reasonableness with the expectation that the relevant factual issues will be apparent and that, once the facts are determined, likely outcomes will be predictable and coherent. Otherwise, rules of reason transcend judicial capacity, invite courts to legislate and can lead to *ad hoc*, irreconcilable outcomes. In recent years the Supreme Court has grown more confident about the capacity of federal courts to identify and manipulate a consensus body of relevant antitrust theory. Perhaps it is less capable of identifying or precipitating consensus about theoretical tools for addressing First Amendment issues. In the one instance, opening the analysis produces greater refinement without excessive risk of incoherent outcomes; in the other, mov-

---

107. Id. at 678.

108. Nonprofits were expressly held subject to the FTC Act in *Dental Association* and were deemed within the reach of the Sherman Act in *NCAA*.

109. *Sullivan*, supra note 63; Halverson, *The Future of Horizontal Restraints*

Analysis, 57 ANTITRUST L.J. 33 (1988); Kauper, *Antitrust in 1992: The Year of the Storyteller*, 61 ANTITRUST L.J. 347 (1993).

110. L. Tribe, Address at Harvard Law School, October 26, 1996.

ing away from tightly based rules might risk a norm-barren episodic outcome.

Brown University and some other recent antitrust developments show that the status quo is always vulnerable and that there are risks in moving away from *per se* responses even where good theory is available. Microtheory can tame the discretion invoked by the antitrust rule of reason only if there is a rock-solid consensus that the things relevant to reasonableness are the economic concerns comprehended by the theory and nothing more. When matters of educational policy, public health or any alternative policy concern are invited in, cohesion and predictability are jeopardized and courts are invited to exercise legislative functions. Recent FTC statements about pricing policies of health care providers entail such risks and invite such concerns.[111] For enforcement agencies to dilute a vintage *per se* rule like that against price fixing even in limited (and arguably special) fields like medical practice is to put at risk the valued and reliable certainties. There are, to be sure, issues of buying power and countervailing power that underlie health care enforcement issues that may warrant reconsideration. These issues are addressed in § 13.4a1.

Although truncated rule of reason analysis lessens the distance between rule of reason and *per se* analysis, the distinction remains a critical one. The process of determining which standard will apply is likely to be similar, regardless of the nature of the restraint. Because it is the most basic form of cartel restraint, the delineation between *per se* and rule of reason analysis is examined first in the context of horizontal price restraints. Subsequent sections examine the approach toward other horizontal restraints.

§ 5.4   Pricing Restraints

The evolution of the law precluding horizontal restraints has been shaped by the understanding that limitations on output and price, when instituted by rival firms, are the core elements of cartel conduct. Early Sherman Act Section 1 cases addressed in § 5.3b, such as United States v. Trans–Missouri Freight Ass'n[1] and Addyston Pipe & Steel Co. v. United States[2] involved straightforward and undisguised cartel conduct. Perhaps in part because the Sherman Act's condemnation of such conduct is now widely understood, modern horizontal restraints come in many variations, some of them at least partially obscuring the purpose and intent to limit output and price. One might postulate that once such an intent or effect to limit output or increase price became clear, the practice would be subject to *per se* condemnation. Cases such as *FTC v. Superior Court Trial Lawyers Ass'n*[3] and *Catalano, Inc. v. Target Sales, Inc.*[4] lend support to this hypothesis.

111. See § 13.4.

§ 5.4

1. 166 U.S. 290, 17 S.Ct. 540, 41 L.Ed. 1007 (1897).

2. 175 U.S. 211, 20 S.Ct. 96, 44 L.Ed. 136 (1899), *modifying and aff'g* 85 F. 271 (6th Cir. 1898).

3. 493 U.S. 411, 110 S.Ct. 768, 107 L.Ed.2d 851 (1990).

4. 446 U.S. 643, 100 S.Ct. 1925, 64 L.Ed.2d 580 (1980).

But the hypothesis cannot be sustained. That is apparent from modern Supreme Court cases involving obvious output limitation and pricing controls that were nonetheless addressed under the truncated rule of reason. *NCAA v. Board of Regents of University of Oklahoma,*[5] addressed in § 5.3f, is illustrative. An antitrust analyst addressing a horizontal restraint that will affect price confronts the task of discerning which rule will apply.

5.4a. Distinguishing Rule of Reason from *Per Se* Cases

Despite truncated rule of reason analysis, the Supreme Court has continued to apply the *per se* rule to many forms of price fixing and other hardcore horizontal restraints. In modern cases such as FTC v. Superior Court Trial Lawyers Ass'n,[6] Palmer v. BRG of Georgia, Inc.,[7] and Catalano, Inc. v. Target Sales, Inc.,[8] the Court found a Section 1 violation under the classic *per se* rule. In light of the current trend toward truncated rule of reason analysis one might question whether the distinction between *per se* rule and rule of reason continues to be of great import. After all, the Court has indicated on more than one occasion that a showing of market power is not required to establish a rule of reason violation. To the extent that recent developments blur the line between *per se* and rule of reason, the simplifying effects and consequent enhancement of deterrence associated with the *per se* rule may be shared to a degree by the rule of reason. But the distinction still matters. So long as some courts like the Third Circuit may broaden the scope of a rule of reason inquiry by some uncertain dimension, the distinction can determine outcome. Moreover, there continues to be at least a possibility and in many instances a likelihood that a market power showing will be required in many rule of reason cases, even though not all.

Much commentary celebrates the balanced vision displayed by the Supreme Court in recent decades. But the Court has done nothing to suggest that it would countenance giving up or weakening the *per se* rule in special situations. The modern Court holds firmly to the *per se* tradition applying the rule to traditional categories when the challenged conduct offers no benefit that could not be gained by less restrictive means. In the *Trial Lawyers* case, District of Columbia attorneys who served as court-appointed criminal lawyers concertedly withdrew their services in an effort to force the District government to increase the fees paid for such services. Justice Stevens for the Court called this conduct a "naked restraint" on price and output that required application of the

---

5. 468 U.S. 85, 104 S.Ct. 2948, 82 L.Ed.2d 70 (1984).

6. 493 U.S. 411, 110 S.Ct. 768, 107 L.Ed.2d 851 (1990).

7. 498 U.S. 46, 111 S.Ct. 401, 112 L.Ed.2d 349 (1990) (per curiam).

8. 446 U.S. 643, 100 S.Ct. 1925, 64 L.Ed.2d 580 (1980) (per curiam).

per se rule.[9] In *Palmer* two firms had been competing to sell training services and materials in the same geographic market. In the challenged transaction, one granted the other an exclusive license to market its materials, the licensee paid the licensor a percentage of gross revenue, the licensor withdrew from the market and the licensee increased its charges. In perfunctory fashion, the per curiam opinion labeled this territorial allocation among competitors a "classic" example of a *per se* violation.[10] It is important for deterrent purposes that the *per se* rule remain viably available. If the *per se* threat disappeared or significantly narrowed, the risk of criminal sanctions for blatantly anticompetitive conduct would be considerably abated, the incentives for treble actions, especially class actions against price fixing, would be reduced, and antitrust counsel might turn their skills to the task of rationalizing and justifying anticompetitive action, not counseling against it. Nonetheless, the rapid application of conclusory characterizations like "price fixing" or "market division" may at times obscure deep, troubling issues about the purposes of commercial arrangements.

On the other hand, the fact that challenged conduct bears some surface similarities to a *per se* wrong need not end the inquiry. At least a modicum of analytical thought relating the salient facts to antitrust theory is essential before conduct can be characterized in either *per se* or rule of reason terms. If the facts evoke a traditional *per se* category— whether price fixing, market division, output suppression or boycott— the conduct will be vulnerable *per se* unless the category is being applied more broadly than the compelling theory and logic of *per se* analysis will warrant. If so, to call the conduct price fixing or by some other *per se* term is to mischaracterize it, despite surface resemblances. If a brief, characterization analysis suggests that in context the challenged conduct either threatens no competitive harm or may yield significant benefits that could outweigh any possible harm, the issue should be assigned to the rule of reason. The modern Supreme Court has clearly signaled this analytical course. Trial courts should be alert to the judicial and enforcement efficiencies of the *per se* rule, but should apply it to its purpose: to quickly condemn conduct that risks significant harm and can yield no significant benefits. When suspect conduct escapes *per se* characterization, full structural analysis is not always required. If a *per se* judgment is withheld not because no harm is threatened, but because offsetting benefits are possible, the next question is whether there are less restrictive ways to attain those benefits. If there are, and this is immediately evident, judgment need not be withheld pending inquiry into power. Defendants should lose not *per se*, but because summary (or "quick look") application of the rule of reason shows that their conduct threatens serious harm and cannot be justified as essential to attain offsetting benefits. *California Dental Association* suggests that there may be disagreement about what types of concerted behavior are suited for quick look analysis and how extensive that analysis should be, but it does not

---

9. *Trial Lawyers*, 493 U.S. at 423.   **10.** *Palmer*, 498 U.S. at 49.

question the appropriateness of quick look analysis as the Court had applied it in prior cases.[11]

The balanced solution is to continue to recognize the *per se* rules, as the Court is doing, but to concede the possibility that in some limited instances it may be possible to see even on a quick look that the purpose and likely effect of the challenged conduct is not the cartel-like competitive harm at which the *per se* rule is aimed. In such instances a court need not characterize the conduct in *per se* terms, but may characterize it in terms that more accurately reflect its purpose and effect. For example, if three or four retail stores with trivial shares of a large metropolitan retail grocery market were to agree on prices in order to place a joint ad in a medium that would be uneconomical for them to use individually, a court might characterize their conduct not as price fixing, and thus *per se* unlawful, but as a partial integration aimed at advertising efficiencies, and thus subject to the rule of reason.

Being open to such characterization defenses to conduct which, on superficial examination, might appear to include *per se* elements would not put the values of the *per se* rule in significant jeopardy. The *Maricopa* doctors, the *Catalano* retailers, the *Palmer* bar review marketers, and the Superior Court lawyers would all remain *per se* vulnerable. None of them could show on a quick look that they utterly lacked power and were integrating some aspect of operations to attain an efficiency. Similarly, the conduct of the engineers in *Professional Engineers*, the dentists in *Indiana Dentists* and the colleges in *NCAA*[12] all escaped *per se* characterization, yet were summarily found to be liable under the rule of reason. Their conduct raised competitive risks and any advantage it promised could have been attained without raising these risks.

The modern *per se* case that has stirred the most debate is *Trial Lawyers*. Despite the earlier *Catalano* and *Maricopa* results, one could read recent decisions as signifying that the *per se* rule was moribund or should be filtered through market power screens in all save perhaps blatant cartel cases. Such a view might find support in Judge Ginsburg's court of appeals opinion which called for balancing even in the case of seemingly *per se* violations and even when the weight placed on the other side of the scale was not a possible competitive benefit but a serious First Amendment claim.[13] Moreover, the FTC itself had relied not solely on the *per se* rule but also on a truncated rule of reason analysis. Thus, several avenues were available by which the Supreme Court could have affirmed, yet avoided the question whether the *per se* rule governed. The Court chose none of them. It embraced *per se* analysis to rule unlawful a "strike" by court-appointed criminal lawyers widely conceded to be underpaid and to be subsidizing the vulnerable finances of the District of Columbia. This was something of a surprise. Still, the case

---

11. 526 U.S. 756, 119 S.Ct. 1604, 143 L.Ed.2d 935 (1999). See the discussion of *Dental Association* in § 5.3f.

12. *Professional Engineers, Indiana Dentists,* and *NCAA* are discussed in § 5.3f.

13. Superior Court Trial Lawyers Ass'n v. FTC, 856 F.2d 226, 233–34 (D.C.Cir. 1988), rev'd, 493 U.S. 411, 110 S.Ct. 768, 107 L.Ed.2d 851 (1990).

was not wrongly decided. On the existing tradition the only real choice was *per se* or truncated rule of reason analysis, either of which signified a violation.

Contemporary criticism of *Trial Lawyers* focused on the apparent lack or power and low compensation received by the attorneys who instituted the boycott. Some questioned the FTC's decision to pursue this case, a matter which had provoked dissent by Commissioner Pertschuk.[14] Congress has recognized an exemption from antitrust law for employee unions and the policy behind such an exemption might easily support an interpretive rule that excludes application of the antitrust laws. But there was no readily available interpretive rule and creation of one could easily effect much mischief. For example, one might envision a countervailing power defense that would allow exploration of the full implications of the lawyers' efforts to meet the District's apparent buying power by collectivizing supply. For a century, the Court has declined to open that avenue.

Meanwhile, the teaching of *Trial Lawyers*—that the *per se* rule still applies to naked restraints on price and output—may offer some basis for attorneys to frame their arguments about whether to apply the *per se* rule or the rule of reason. Sometimes the outcome of these arguments may be difficult to predict. At least in some contexts, one judge's naked restraint may be another's ancillary restraint, defensible, perhaps, if shown to be reasonably necessary for a greater competitive good. Still, preserving the *per se* rule largely intact gives a measure of certainty and lawyers in price restraint cases may prepare for trial with at least the assurance that, however characterization is resolved, no wide-open balancing of social benefits against competitive injury will be countenanced.

5.4b. The New Paradigm in the Agencies and Lower Courts

The Federal Trade Commission had an opportunity to apply the new paradigm in a case involving distribution of recordings of three famous tenors who had performed in concerts at the 1990, 1994, and 1998 soccer World Cup.[15] PolyGram had distribution rights for the recordings of the 1990 concert. Warner Communications had distribution rights for the 1994 concert. The two firms, each among the world's largest music companies, formed a joint venture to distribute recordings for the 1998 concert. They agreed to a moratorium on advertising and discounting of the 1990 and 1994 recordings deemed necessary to prevent either of them from free riding on the release of the 1998 recordings.

This case allowed the FTC an opportunity to make a characterization decision that incorporated the learning of the Supreme Court's 2000 *Dental Association* holding. One option was for the Commission to

14. Commissioner Pertschuk argued that the complaint was an unwise use of the Commission's limited resources. In re Superior Court Trial Lawyers Ass'n, 107 F.T.C. 510, 512–13 (1986).

15. Matter of Polygram Holding, Inc., 5 CCH Trade Reg. Rep. ¶ 15,453 (FTC 2003), Commission order enforced, Polygram Holding, Inc. v. FTC, 416 F.3d 29 (D.C. Cir. 2005).

declare the moratorium on discounting to be per se unlawful. At the other extreme, if the respondents arguments were accepted, the joint venture might have been viewed as an efficient instrument to create new products that could be condemned, if at all, only after a full scale rule of reason analysis. In an opinion authored by Chairman Murris, the Commission chose a bifurcated course. Conducting an abbreviated analysis that, in a pre-*Dental Association* world, might be described as "quick-look" analysis, the Commission agreed with its administrative law judge that the moratorium on discounting was "simply a form of price fixing" and "presumptively anticompetitive." As to the proffered justification of preventing free-riding, the Commission said:

> Respondents are not asserting that restraints on the joint venture activities are reasonably necessary to achieve efficiencies in its operations, nor even that expansion of the joint venture is reasonably necessary to achieve such efficiencies. Rather, they are arguing that competitors may agree to restrict competition by products wholly *outside* a joint venture, to increase profits for the products of the joint venture itself. "Such a claim is nothing less than a frontal assault on the basic policy of the Sherman Act." *Professional Engineers*, 435 U.S. at 695, for it displaces market-based outcomes regarding the mix of products to be offered with collusive determinations that certain new products will be offered under a shield from direct competition.[16]

The Commission also found the agreement to suspend advertising on the 1990 and 1994 recordings to be "presumptively anticompetitive", citing *Dental Association* language that complete bans on truthful advertising are likely to be anticompetitive in ordinary markets.[17] The "presumptively anticompetitive" mantel is one that is very much in the antitrust mainstream and seems consistent with Justice Breyer's dissent in *Dental Association*. Cognizant of the result in *Dental Association*, the Commission did not rest solely on this abbreviated analysis. It offered a more detailed factual analysis as a basis for concluding that the agreement unreasonably restrained trade.

On a petition for review, the D.C. Circuit upheld the Commission's ruling.[18] The court agreed with the Commission that, having made an initial determination that the agreement appeared facially anticompetitive, the burden fell on respondents to show a procompetitive justification for their conduct. This approach, the court held, was consistent with the Supreme Court's sliding scale analysis in *California Dental*. The court agreed with the Commission that the "free-rider" justification was faulty and that Polygram had failed to offer "any competitive justification for its agreement."[19] The court of appeals found it unnecessary to review the Commission's more detailed factual findings. *Polygram*, then, is an encouraging sign that truncated analysis is still appropriate when

16. Matter of Polygram Holding, Inc., 5 CCH Trade Reg. Rep. ¶ 15,453.

17. Id.

18. Polygram Holding, Inc. v. FTC, supra note 15.

19. Id. at 37–38.

conduct is presumptively anticompetitive, although determining when the presumption applies may pose a challenge.

While the modern Supreme Court cases suggest truncated approaches and point in modified (if not distinctly new) directions, the analytical tools they provide leave much to the lower courts. Concerted activity is a major part of modern entrepreneurship and technology. Network industries are everywhere: telecommunications, air, railroad and truck transportation, electric power. Hardware and software for the Internet and proprietary nets of large or interlinked businesses abound. In such an environment, where more and more of the economy is being digitalized each day, some cooperation in setting standards and even in executing transactions is essential to keep the economy functioning. But even where cooperation is inevitable, there can be overreaching. Much about the developing digital economy will reduce both scale and scope economies at the horizontal level and will invite more vertical disaggregation. The task of analysis is to determine when the market adequately disciplines firms interacting cooperatively and when antitrust intervention is needed.

An instructive example of the modern approach is the credit card litigation challenging the joint venture through which financial institutions issued and controlled the terms of use of VISA and Mastercard. The first of these cases, National Bancard Corp. (NaBanco) v. VISA U.S.A., Inc.,[20] typifies networking issues[21] in the context of a joint credit card system. Visa cards were issued by individual banks that cooperate to offer a branded credit service. Each issuing bank may charge each of its cardholders an annual fee plus interest at a specified rate on unpaid balances. The issuer also charges merchants who accept the card a fee on each transaction when the card is used. While each Visa bank sets its own charges to cardholders, the participants agree on the charge to merchants, 1.5 percent of each transaction at the time of the litigation. When this arrangement was challenged, the court held it to be legal. Because some cooperation was necessary to market a branded, nationwide credit product at all, the rule of reason applied.[22] Agreeing upon the charge to merchants made the joint product efficient; each merchant knew the cost of accepting a Visa card and could advertise its readiness to do so.[23]

---

20. 779 F.2d 592 (11th Cir.), cert. denied, 479 U.S. 923, 107 S.Ct. 329, 93 L.Ed.2d 301 (1986); see also SCFC ILC, Inc. v. Visa USA, Inc., 36 F.3d 958 (10th Cir. 1994), cert. denied, 515 U.S. 1152, 115 S.Ct. 2600, 132 L.Ed.2d 846 (1995).

21. For discussion and debate on these issues, see Carlton & Frankel, *The Antitrust Economics of Credit Card Networks*, 63 ANTITRUST L.J. 643 (1995); Evans & Schmalensee, *Economic Aspects of Payment Card Systems and Antitrust Policy Toward Joint*

Ventures, 63 ANTITRUST L.J. 861 (1995); Carlton & Frankel, *The Antitrust Economics of Credit Card Networks: Reply to Evans and Schmalensee Comment,* 63 ANTITRUST L.J. 903 (1995).

22. Cf. NCAA v. Board of Regents of Univ. of Okla., 468 U.S. 85, 104 S.Ct. 2948, 82 L.Ed.2d 70 (1984).

23. Cf. Broadcast Music, Inc. v. CBS, Inc., 441 U.S. 1, 99 S.Ct. 1551, 60 L.Ed.2d 1 (1979).

In a second case, Sears, the owner of the Discover credit card, challenged VISA's rules that limited participation in the joint venture to financial institutions. In SCFC ILC, Inc. v. Visa USA, Inc., the court of appeals reversed a jury verdict and trial court judgment that had found a Section 1 Sherman Act violation.[24] Sears had argued that it could not aggressively market its Discover Card except through financial institutions that were members of the joint venture. The court of appeals saw it differently. The court rejected the district court's finding that the joint venture controlled 67% of all credit cards issued in the United States because, in its view, there was competition among the individual joint venture members in issuing VISA and Mastercards. As a part of its expansive rule of reason analysis, the court also gave weight to VISA's argument that there was "system" competition between credit cards issued by the joint venture (VISA and Mastercard) and Discover and American Express, marketed through alternate channels. VISA needed to prevent Sears from free riding on the joint venture's system of issuing credit cards.

The Justice Department obtained a different result when it challenged the joint venture's exclusionary practices. In United States v. Visa U.S.A., Inc., the focus was on the rules that prevented members of the association from issuing cards for competing credit card networks.[25] Under its rule of reason analysis, the court accepted a market of general credit cards and that the joint venture had market power within this market. The inability of American Express and Discover to use the joint venture members as issuing institutions weakened competition and harmed consumers.

Collectively, what do the credit card cases say about the contemporary court's classification decision? On one level, there is consistency: all three decisions recognized that the potential efficiencies of a joint venture required analysis under the rule of reason. But the rule of reason analysis proceeded differently and produced different outcomes. A cynic might draw two conclusions: that courts are loose cannons resting on the foundation of an unpredictable relatively open-ended rule of reason analysis; and that only the Government, with its more substantial resources and powers of persuasion, has respectable odds of prevailing under a rule of reason standard. Both conclusions are overdrawn. In the face of technologically complex industries with network efficiencies and rapid change, courts do face substantial challenges in reaching sound antitrust decisions. There is a risk that courts, lacking the simplicity and security of per se analysis, will seize upon the any decision point within grasp to reach an outcome most in sync with the judge's world view. But good lawyering and economic analysis can keep courts grounded in fundamentals. The government initiated suit against Visa produced a decision which focused on anticompetitive effects, the building block for any sound rule of reason analysis.

24. 36 F.3d 958 (10th Cir. 1994).   **25.** 163 F. Supp.2d 322 (S.D.N.Y. 2001), aff'd, 344 F.3d 229 (2d Cir. 2003).

§ 5.5   Division of Markets and Other Supply and Output Restrictions

5.5a. Introduction

Conventional cartelization—fixing price and controlling and allocating output—presupposes that competitors encounter each other in the same product and geographic market. But competition can also be reduced, perhaps snuffed out entirely, if a market is successfully segmented. In National Ass'n of Window Glass Mfrs. v. United States,[1] an early market division case to reach the Supreme Court, the government's challenge to such an arrangement was unsuccessful. The defendants included manufacturers of handblown window glass and the union representing their workers. The union bargained with the manufacturers as a single unit. The collective agreement set a wage scale and assigned the work to one group of manufacturers during one part of the year and to another group for the remaining part of the year. The Supreme Court, in an opinion by Justice Holmes, reversed the district court's finding of a Section 1 violation. It stressed that the participating manufacturers competed with factories making comparable glass by machine, that the machine input was cheaper than labor, and that handblown glass manufacturers survived only by locating where cheap natural gas was available and were, in any event, going to be displaced entirely by more mechanized competitors before very long. The Court also inferred that qualified laborers were abandoning the field and that, in the circumstances, the arrangement amounted to a reasonable effort to share (rather than to bid against each other for) a scarce resource. The opinion, citing *Chicago Board of Trade*,[2] reflects a readiness to bring into the analysis sociopolitical concerns about the effects of technological development on workers and small employers. Like *Appalachian Coals* it also suggests readiness to accommodate a crisis cartel. In these respects it is utterly out of harmony with *Professional Engineers* and many modern Supreme Court cases.

It was not until after mid-century, in Timkin Roller Bearing Co. v. United States,[3] that the Court expressed misgivings about market division. In that case the challenged conduct was part of a congeries of restraints including price fixing. The government alleged a conspiracy among the Timkin family of firms to stifle competition among themselves in international markets for antifriction bearings.[4] The evidence showed allocation of territories, price fixing on certain products sold by one participant in a territory allocated to another, cooperation to limit

1. 263 U.S. 403, 44 S.Ct. 148, 68 L.Ed. 358 (1923).

2. Id. at 411–12 (citing Chicago Bd. of Trade v. United States, 246 U.S. 231, 38 S.Ct. 242, 62 L.Ed. 683 (1918)).

3. 341 U.S. 593, 71 S.Ct. 971, 95 L.Ed. 1199 (1951).

4. Id. at 594–96, 599. The conspiracy alleged was among firms some in partial and some in total common ownership. The Court treated them as capable of conspiring in violation of Section 1. That outcome would not be obvious today. See § 5.2c.

outside competition, as well as cartel-like participation with outsiders to restrict imports into and exports from the United States. Rejecting the claim that a trademark license and a production joint venture warranted the restraints, the Court ruled that the "aggregation of trade restraints" was illegal regardless of purpose or proof of effect.[5] Because territorial division was central to the arrangement and the price fixing was supportive of that, the holding is often read to imply a *per se* rule against horizontal market division analogous to that long in place for price fixing. But a clear holding to that effect was not yet at hand.[6]

United States v. Topco Associates, Inc., was the first case that the Court treated as raising the issue of the legality of horizontal market division in pure form.[7] In fact the case had a vertical dimension that might well have, though it did not, significantly altered the way the issue was perceived. Twenty-five small and medium-sized regional supermarket chains (with market shares varying from 1.5 to 16 percent and averaging 6 percent) organized Topco, a cooperative association, which purchased food and related items (canned, dairy, frozen foods, packaged produce, etc.), and distributed these to members under Topco's "private label" brand names for sale by members in their stores. Members' stores competed with other stores and Topco products competed both with brand name products (sold at members' and other stores) and with private label products of large chains (like A & P's "Anne Page," sold only at the stores of the chain that was the proprietor of the label). The alleged offense was an ancillary agreement by members that each would sell the Topco branded products only in the geographic territory assigned to it by Topco. The trial court found the arrangement reasonable and lawful: because of the success of major supermarket chains with their private labels, it concluded that any small chain seeking to compete must also offer private label products. It regarded the member chains of Topco as too small for each to be able to develop its own private label. Thus, cooperation to produce such a label made effective competition among themselves and large chains feasible. Moreover, it saw the territorial restraints imposed through trademark licenses as reasonable, ancillary restraints; they were needed to encourage members to invest to bring the cooperative private label into operation. In essence, the lower court regarded the arrangement as one in which some possible (but thus far not actual) intrabrand competition between Topco firms was being

---

5. *Timkin Roller*, 341 U.S. at 598.

6. Id. at 596.

7. 405 U.S. 596, 92 S.Ct. 1126, 31 L.Ed.2d 515 (1972). Two cases in the 1960s also signaled hostility to horizontal market division though falling short of clear *per se* holdings. In United States v. General Motors Corp., 384 U.S. 127, 86 S.Ct. 1321, 16 L.Ed.2d 415 (1966), Chevy car dealers acted concertedly to induce GM to stop dealers who sold to discounters for resale by enforcing GM's vertical location clause. The horizontal conspiracy among dealers was found

unlawful. In United States v. Sealy, Inc., 388 U.S. 350, 87 S.Ct. 1847, 18 L.Ed.2d 1238 (1967), bedding manufacturers combined to market a uniform and consistent product under the Sealy name and market. The Court held their agreement fixing prices and assigning territories *per se* unlawful. In both of these cases, horizontal action caused or induced a supplier to impose a vertical intrabrand restraint. The potential complexity of the vertical element, and the limit of the restraint to a single brand, was not explored.

sacrificed to facilitate more interbrand competition between Topco stores and major chains.

The Supreme Court reversed. Justice Marshall, for the Court, regarded the reasonableness defense that succeeded below as an invitation to "ramble through the wilds of economic theory."[8] As he put it, "[o]ne of the classic examples of a *per se* violation of Section 1 is an agreement between competitors at the same level of the market structure to allocate territories in order to minimize competition."[9] The Court characterized the restraint in *Topco* as horizontal, just as it had earlier so characterized a restraint on Chevy dealers imposed by GM in response to complaints by some dealers of too aggressive same brand competition from others.[10] The Court also characterized as horizontal the "same brand" restraint in *Sealy,*[11] which had a vertical dimension quite analogous to that in *Topco*. In both of those cases only intrabrand competition was affected, and in both the restraint was formally imposed vertically— in the one case by GM, in the other by the cooperative association that members had organized to develop their mattress brand.

The *Topco* court raised no question about the relevance of the vertical dimension or the "same brand" limitation upon the restraint. Given the date that the case reached the Court, and its resulting place in the sequence of vertical restraint developments, this is not surprising. There had, as yet, been no implosion integrating *per se* and rule of reason analysis. The *per se* rule was still unyielding and its field of application wide. The Court had already decided United States v. Arnold, Schwinn & Co.,[12] which labeled vertical territorial restraints *per se* unlawful, and as noted above, had decided several cases implying, if not flatly holding, that horizontal market division was also *per se* unlawful. Unless the holding of *Schwinn* was to be revisited (as a decade later it in fact was in *Sylvania*),[13] to ponder the significance of the vertical and same brand elements presented in *Topco* would have reinforced, not brought into question, the *per se* conclusion. In the event, the Court did not see *Topco* as a complex and challenging opportunity to work out a balanced rule of reason relationship between a reduction in intrabrand competition and an increase in intrabrand competition. It saw the case, rather, as a chance to complete a four-pronged structure based on two propositions: market division is like price fixing; and vertical restraints are like horizontal ones. By 1972 when *Topco* reached the Court, three of the elements of that structure were in place: (1) horizontal price fixing was *per se* unlawful; (2) vertical price fixing was *per se* unlawful; and (3) vertical territorial restraints were *per se* unlawful. The fourth leg would deal with horizontal territorial division. While clearly adumbrated in *Timkin, Sealy* and *General Motors*, this leg was yet to be completed. The

---

8. *Topco*, 405 U.S. at 610 n.10.

9. Id. at 608.

10. *General Motors,* 384 U.S. at 139–40.

11. *Sealy,* 388 U.S. at 352–53.

12. 388 U.S. 365, 87 S.Ct. 1856, 18 L.Ed.2d 1249 (1967).

13. Continental T. V., Inc. v. GTE Sylvania Inc., 433 U.S. 36, 97 S.Ct. 2549, 53 L.Ed.2d 568 (1977).

Court used *Topco* to finish the edifice: Horizontal market division was now *per se* unlawful too.

A decade later, of course, *Sylvania* radically altered the attitude of the Court about the significance of intrabrand competition and its relationship to interbrand competition. Also, in the 1970s and 1980s the Court developed its penchant for truncated analysis as the distinction between the rule of reason and the *per se* rule became less sharp. How the *Topco* case and the *per se* rule against market division have fared in this new environment will be considered in the next subsection.

5.5b. Horizontal Market Division, Intrabrand Cases and Truncated Analysis: The Characterization Defense to *Per Se* Analysis

Topco comports well with the *per se* holdings in *Socony-Vacuum* and *Schwinn*.[14] It is, however, in some tension with *Sylvania*[15]; and in the current era of truncated analysis signaled by *Professional Engineers*, *Broadcast Music*, *NCAA* and even *Maricopa*, it might be anomalous to apply the *Topco* market division *per se* rule over a wide and complex range of situations. Doing so might, in some instances, cost more in efficiency than it would gain in legal certainty and protection against the exploitation of power. This section explores the possibility that recent cases may open a "characterization defense" to the *per se* rule against horizontal market division.[16]

Recent cases put *Topco* under pressure in two distinguishable ways. First, if the market division, though affecting interbrand rivalry, seems to yield efficiencies but not to yield power, the dichotomy between *Topco's per se* response and *Broadcast Music's* analytical initiative must be addressed. Second, if (as in *Topco* itself) the market division pertains only to a single brand, the *Topco-Sylvania* tension must be reckoned with.

Topco and *Broadcast Music*: The first of these tensions may be illustrated by a hypothetical. Assume that three small firms each make a full range of the machine tools needed in a particular industry. They agree that each will specialize in a specified subset of these tools, and that each will supply those it makes to the others at wholesale prices. Suppose further that this enables each of the participants to gain scale economies not available previously, that these efficiencies are the purpose of the agreement, and that the three firms, among them, aggregated only a modest share of the relevant interbrand market, and gain no capacity for output reduction or price enhancement.

---

14. United States v. Arnold, Schwinn & Co., 388 U.S. 365, 87 S.Ct. 1856, 18 L.Ed.2d 1249 (1967).

15. Continental T.V., Inc. v. GTE Sylvania Inc., 433 U.S. 36, 97 S.Ct. 2549, 53 L.Ed.2d 568 (1977).

16. *Topco's* continual force, at least in the context of cooperative associates, has

also been brought into question by Copperweld Corp. v. Independence Tube Corp., 467 U.S. 752, 104 S.Ct. 2731, 81 L.Ed.2d 628 (1984), discussed in § 5.2c. See City of Mt. Pleasant v. Associated Elec. Coop., Inc., 838 F.2d 268 (8th Cir.1988).

This hypothetical arrangement would clearly be vulnerable under *Topco*. Should it be? The European Union has long treated such agreements as lawful when they do more good than harm.[17] Today, might a U.S. court in light of *Professional Engineers, Broadcast Music* and *NCAA* avoid the *Topco per se* rule on the basis of a truncated analysis, much as the *Broadcast Music* Court avoided the *Socony-Vacuum per se* rule? Such a result could be articulated this way: These three small firms were not dividing markets; that is neither their purpose nor the effect of their conduct. "Market division" is more than just a choice about what markets to serve. The concept implies an effort to stifle or at least reduce competition in order to reduce output and increase price. Here, even a quick look discloses that these three firms were not doing that. They manifestly lack power, facing, as they do, competition from large firms each of which has accessible scale economies not available to any of the small three acting alone. That is why the three cooperate; to gain scale efficiencies so that they can compete more effectively with their larger rivals. The *per se* rule therefore does not apply.

Appealing as this result may sound on the facts supposed, allowing such a characterization defense would entail substantial risks. A district court would be responsible for the truncated analysis. Individual judges, let alone different juries, may see relevant issues—whether power is being wielded or whether a particular free rider justification is valid or pretextual—in very different ways. Whether the *per se* rule applied or a characterization defense—i.e., "these defendants are not dividing markets because it is not plausible to assume that output restraint or price enhancement is their intent"—was available might become a speculative matter resolved by the judicial assignment "lottery." Even judges sophisticated in antitrust analysis (and usually viewed as having the same theoretical orientation) might approach similar cases in different ways. This is suggested, indeed, by two post-*Topco* opinions, one written by Judge Posner, the other by Judge Bork.

In General Leaseways, Inc. v. National Truck Leasing Ass'n[18] Judge Posner recognized that in light of *Broadcast Music* and *NCAA* it may no longer be possible confidently to assert that, regardless of circumstances, when firms in the same line of business agree not to enter each other's territories they violate Section 1.[19] In that case, 130 small, truck rental companies acted reciprocally to provide repair service to each others' rented vehicles in order to be able to compete effectively with companies that had their own nationwide service facilities. Although recognizing that recent Supreme Court cases raised some question about *Topco's* disclaimer of judicial capacity to weigh harms and benefits, Judge Posner's opinion first applied the *per se* rule to an ancillary agreement by association members not to enter others' territories. But the court went on to find that the attempted "free rider" justification would in any event fail under the rule of reason. The contrasting opinion by Judge

---

17.   Comm. Reg. No. 417/85, O.J.L. 53/1.   **19.**   Id. at 594–95.
18.   744 F.2d 588 (7th Cir.1984).

Bork in Rothery Storage & Van Co. v. Atlas Van Lines, Inc.,[20] involved not a market division but a refusal to deal. Yet the opinion's approach is distinctly different from the approach by Judge Posner. Difference in attitude both about the continued significance to *Topco* and about the possibility of a free rider defense is apparent. As Judge Bork put it:

> [R]ecent Supreme Court decisions * * * demonstrate[] * * * that, to the extent that *Topco* and *Sealy* stand for the proposition that all horizontal restraints are illegal per se, they must be regarded as effectively overruled.[21]

At least as yet, the Supreme Court has not validated the Bork inferences. In Palmer v. BRG of Georgia, Inc.,[22] the Court had an opportunity to modify *Topco*, but unceremoniously declined to do so. BRG marketed bar review courses and materials in Georgia. In 1976 HBJ, which previously marketed such materials in contiguous states, entered Georgia. From 1977 to 1979 the two companies competed there. In 1980 HBJ granted BRG an exclusive license to market HBJ's material in Georgia and to use HBJ's well-advertised Bar/Bri name, effectively committing itself to withdraw from Georgia. For the license BRG paid HBJ, per student, $100 plus 40 percent of any per student gross over $350. HBJ then withdrew from Georgia and BRG raised prices. When the arrangement was challenged under Section 1, the defendants contended that the restraint was ancillary to the intellectual property license and reasonable. On this ground the defendants moved for and obtained a summary judgment. That the Court reversed this summary judgment is hardly surprising. If HBJ had never entered Georgia and granted the same license on the same terms, a rule of reason issue would have been presented, for HBJ was clearly a potential entrant into Georgia. Analysis would then have required defining the market, examining the extent of concentration and evaluating whether the purpose and effect of the license was so anticompetitive that the restraint on HBJ's operating in Georgia could not be justified as ancillary to the conveyance of the intellectual property license. Certainly no less was required here. The rule of reason issues were intensified because for a few years the two firms were in actual competition. Summary judgment for the defendants was thus blatantly inappropriate. But the Supreme Court did not merely reverse and remand, leaving it to the courts below to sort out whether the rule of reason applied, whether a truncated analysis suggested violation, or whether the *Topco* (or, for that matter, the *Socony-Vacuum*) *per se* rule applied. Instead, it made that critical call itself:

> The revenue-sharing formula * * * coupled with the price increase that took place immediately after the parties agreed to cease

20. 792 F.2d 210 (D.C.Cir.1986), cert. denied, 479 U.S. 1033, 107 S.Ct. 880, 93 L.Ed.2d 834 (1987).

21. Id. at 226.

22. 498 U.S. 46, 111 S.Ct. 401, 112 L.Ed.2d 349 (1990) (per curiam).

competing * * * indicates that this agreement was "formed for the purpose and with the effect of raising" the price * * *.

* * *

In [*Topco*], we held that agreements between competitors to allocate territories to minimize competition are illegal: "[They are] [o]ne of the classic examples of a *per se* violation * * *."[23]

One must conclude that Judge Posner's *General Leaseways* opinion anticipated Supreme Court attitudes better than did Judge Bork's *Rothery* opinion. At least when interbrand competition is at all dampened by market sharing, the recent implosion of *per se* and rule of reason analysis does not and should not result in any weakening of the *per se* rule against horizontal market division that *Topco* solidified. Certainly trivial or pretextual claims based on intellectual property licenses will not trump the *Topco per se* rule.[24] Neither should claims about "specialization economies" imported from European industrial culture where governmental involvement through planning and by encouraging some and discouraging other activities through various forms of inducements have long been traditional.

Topco and *Sylvania*: The second tension is that suggested by the contrast between *Topco* and *Sylvania,* which can itself be subdivided. First, suppose that all the Sylvania TV dealers in California form a trade association that assigns exclusive sales territories for Sylvania products to all participants. The only conceivable defense against application of the *per se* rule to the market division would be the claim that Sylvania dealers, facing competition from other brands, cannot do much harm. There is little, if anything, to be put on the beneficial side of the scale. In that context the market division *per se* rule fulfills the classic *per se* role. Sylvania's demand curve is downward sloping, however, slightly. These dealers, when acting together, have some power with respect of customers who regard the Sylvania product as preferable to other brands. Given that their agreement yields no efficiency benefit, there is no credible reason to allow them to exploit customers who prefer Sylvania and who could benefit from intrabrand competition. *Topco* should govern; *Sylvania* is irrelevant.

The second aspect of the *Topco-Sylvania* dilemma is not solved as easily. One can make consequential arguments against a *per se* rule applied against a single brand market division ancillary to a significant integration. For example, if the Sylvania brand had a trivial share of the appliance market and a group of Sylvania dealers in the San Francisco area acquired a joint warehouse where they stored a complete line of Sylvania products from which they made deliveries to participating stores or to customers of such stores, an ancillary territorial division might do little harm, and might be needed to encourage an efficient

---

23. Id. at 49 (citation omitted).

24. See also United States v. Pilkington Plc, 1994–2 Trade Cas. (CCH) ¶ 70,842 (D. Ariz. Dec. 22, 1994).

integration. Yet, at least for now, this restraint, too, is probably disposed of by *Palmer* and other post-*Sylvania* cases which cite *Topco* as authoritative. The Supreme Court has had its opportunities to modify, qualify or limit the scope of *Topco*. As yet, it has not decided to do so. Surely it is not the appropriate role of lower courts to carve out an exception to *Topco*—indeed, an exception that would swallow up the facts of *Topco* itself. In this, too, Judge Posner was right.

5.5c. Characterization in Market Divisions Ancillary to Capital Transactions

Palmer v. BRG of Georgia, Inc., like *Topco* itself, shows that the ancillary restraint concept may not blunt the *Topco* rule when the attempted justification is based on an assignment of intellectual property.[25] By contrast, the lawfulness of reasonable restraints ancillary to capital transactions that are no more severe than needed to facilitate the transaction is deeply rooted in the common law; and found its place in the antitrust tradition as early as *Addyston Pipe Steel*.[26] Thus, one that sells a business can agree not to compete with the purchaser within a territory and for a time reasonably necessary to protect the capital value of the assets sold from undue erosion. The rule enables sellers to cash out the reasonable value of the good will in a business and protects buyers from the risk of paying for something that soon disappears. Even as common law doctrine the concept had a built-in rule of reason. Were there values in the main transaction that warranted protection? Was the agreement really ancillary to the main purpose of the agreement? Was the time reasonable? Were the territory and activities covered reasonably related to the values being protected? These were the issues to be explored.

There is, of course, an anomaly in limiting the application of the doctrine to capital transactions of a kind that would be protected under the common law. But if it is to be applied very widely beyond those limits, *Palmer* shows that care must be taken to avoid confusion in areas where the basis for *per se* analysis is well established. For example, an ancillary restraint justification might be attempted to validate single brand resale price constraints. But doing so would run up against the *Dr. Miles*[27] rule. There is, perhaps, room for development of and experimentation with the ancillary restraint doctrine and its scope. But not where it collides with settled and well-grounded *per se* analysis.

5.5d. Other Supply and Output Restraints

The effect of a market division that warrants condemnation is that it reduces available supply and thereby increases price by giving each

25. 498 U.S. 46, 111 S.Ct. 401, 112 L.Ed.2d 349 (1990) (per curiam). See the discussion of intellectual property and horizontal restraints in § 15.9a.

26. United States v. Addyston Pipe & Steel Co., 85 Fed. 271 (6th Cir.1898), aff'd, 175 U.S. 211, 20 S.Ct. 96, 44 L.Ed. 136

(1899). See also Maple Flooring Mfrs.' Ass'n v. United States, 268 U.S. 563, 45 S.Ct. 578, 69 L.Ed. 1093 (1925).

27. Dr. Miles Medical Co. v. John D. Park & Sons Co., 220 U.S. 373, 31 S.Ct. 376, 55 L.Ed. 502 (1911).

participant a market segment to itself. Supply can also be concertedly reduced more directly, with all competitors remaining in the same market segments. For example, competitors might agree to run only one or two shifts a day, or not to operate on weekends. Such arrangements, too, can result in price enhancement and supracompetitive returns. When such practices are identified, they should be held unlawful for the same reason that market division is held unlawful,[28] and under a norm fully as unyielding.

While there is little case law articulating a rule against concerted supply reduction, many cases are distinctly on point. Most notably, the element that renders many boycotts vulnerable on *per se* or truncated analysis is their effect on supply. The recent salient cases are discussed in § 5.8. United States v. Socony–Vacuum Oil Co.[29] is also indicative. Though the Court characterized the conduct in terms of its effect on price, the conduct there was an agreement among competing refiners to buy gasoline, store it, and keep it off the market. Hartford–Empire Co. v. United States,[30] also included a concerted supply restraint; among the congeries of restraints held unlawful was an agreement among competing glass producers not to increase their production in a territory served by one of them. Some of the information exchange cases, like *American Column & Lumber*[31] discussed in § 5.6b, also turned at least in part on output reduction. *Per se* responses were appropriately used in all those cases and a *per se* rule ought surely to apply today to any blatant suppression of supply. Yet, the movement toward quick look analysis before applying a *per se* rule, toward truncated or foreshorten rule of reason inquiry, and toward the concept of characterization defenses will presumably influence courts when supply suppression is alleged, much as it does where the focus is on price.

To test whether concerted conduct to reduce supply remains *per se* unlawful today, consider this hypothetical: Assume that each leading cigarette manufacturer has developed its own process to increase the nicotine delivery of a cigarette and that all producers use these processes because market surveys show that not doing so while competitors do results in loss of market share. Because they fear adverse legislative responses if they continue on this course, and in the hope of reducing exposure to cancer lawsuits, these manufacturers agree that all will stop using nicotine delivery enhancement processes.

This agreement reduces output in the sense that it takes off the market entirely or greatly reduces the supply of a still lawful consumer product for which there is substantial demand. Should it therefore be *per*

---

28. The most salient Supreme Court case, National Ass'n of Window Glass Mfrs. v. United States, 263 U.S. 403, 44 S.Ct. 148, 68 L.Ed. 358 (1923), discussed in § 5.5a, is adverse to this conclusion. But as the discussion in that section shows, *Window Glass* holds little if any influence as a precedent today.

29. 310 U.S. 150, 60 S.Ct. 811, 84 L.Ed. 1129 (1940).

30. 323 U.S. 386, 406–07, 65 S.Ct. 373, 89 L.Ed. 322 (1945), clarified, 324 U.S. 570, 65 S.Ct. 815, 89 L.Ed. 1198 (1945).

31. American Column & Lumber Co. v. United States, 257 U.S. 377, 42 S.Ct. 114, 66 L.Ed. 284 (1921).

se unlawful? If even a truncated analysis is available, a characterization defense might be established. The purpose of the manufacturers is not to reduce supply in order to increase price. Although their overall cigarette sales may go down, so will demand; profits are not likely to go up. Given the new paradigm arising from the integration of *per se* and rule of reason analysis, perhaps the agreement should not be characterized as a supply or output restriction because neither the purpose nor the likely effect is to enhance price or gain or increase supracompetitive returns. Moreover, the agreement may mitigate a significant market failure—a disparity of information between producers and consumers on facts relevant to product safety. Over time it may also have a collateral public health effect—reducing addiction to cigarettes.

Allowing room for such a characterization defense would not make the *per se* approach superfluous. Recently the Department of Justice challenged a number of arrangements amenable to supply or output reduction analysis and in each case the defendant consented to effective relief. In *United States v. Association of Retail Travel Agents*, some defendants acted concertedly to withhold services from travel providers that did not meet association minimum commission goals. A consent decree prohibits such conduct.[32] In another consent degree, *United States v. Steinhardt Management Co.*, two investment fund management firms agreed to pay seventy-six million dollars ($25 million to the U.S., $16 million to the SEC, and $35 million to a fund for victims) to settle the charge that they concertedly cornered two-year Treasury notes issued in April and withheld supply in order to raise prices.[33] *United States v. Greyhound Lines, Inc.*, involved the defendant's practice of forbidding competitors that lease Greyhound-owned terminal space from selling tickets within 25 miles of the terminal. DOJ challenged the practice as depriving consumers of additional bus service and inhibiting increased supply of bus services through new terminals. The defendant consented to injunctive relief.[34] While neither the cases nor the literature comprehensively develop the concept, the antitrust vulnerability of concerted conduct to reduce supply or output is adequately established in the case law and seems to be an integral part of enforcement activity.

§ 5.6 Information Exchange

5.6a. Introduction

Information is a key factor in strategic decision making and the exchange of information is an important antitrust topic. Most challenges to an information exchange arise in the context of trade association activities. Despite Adam Smith's disclosure that those in the same trade "seldom meet together, even in merriment and diversion, but the con-

---

32. 1995–1 Trade Cas. (CCH) ¶ 70,957 (D.D.C.1995). For a description of the consent decrees described in this paragraph, see U.S. Dept. of Justice, Antitrust Division, Description of Civil and International Cases, 1993–1996, 16–20.

33. 1995–1 Trade Cas. (CCH) ¶ 70,983 (S.D.N.Y.1995).

34. 1996–1 Trade Cas. (CCH) ¶ 71,334 (D.D.C. Feb. 27, 1996).

versation ends in a conspiracy against the public,"[1] trade associations engage in much activity that is both legal and useful, especially if they employ and attend the advice of knowledgeable antitrust counsel. Routine activities include publications containing useful general information about the industry and about technological and governmental developments affecting it, lobbying activities, standard setting, safety and other "seal of approval" programs, providing media for arbitration, intra-industry promotion and advertising, and the publication of industry statistics. Some such programs are almost always competitively harmless and possibly beneficial to the public as well as industry participants. Others may be efficiency yielding, yet competitively problematic in some contexts. The social effect of lobbying activities, specifically, not only depends on particular content and context, but evokes analysis under the *Noerr* exemption.[2]

Some concerted information collection and dissemination is competitively helpful or neutral. Producers and marketers, as well as consumers, need information to act rationally, and there may be scale efficiencies in the development and dissemination of information, as well as in other functions. If the costs of information are high, market actors may proceed without enough of it. This may be especially so in dynamic markets where information, once gathered, can become quickly obsolete. If scale efficiencies can be gained by cooperation in information gathering, that is a competitive plus. But concerted conduct in gathering and deploying information can also have negative effects. Such conduct is competitively harmful if done to facilitate cartelization or interdependent pricing. Whenever it occurs in an oligopolistic market this is a particular risk. Obviously, information, especially about current price and output, will be helpful or even essential to conspirators seeking to agree on a profit-maximizing price or seeking to allocate a reduced industry output to assure opportunity for supracompetitive pricing. Information of these and related kinds will also be essential to efforts to police a cartel. A related concern is that information exchanges may be able to facilitate the interdependent achievement of supracompetitive prices, even though agreement on a price or output is scrupulously avoided. Such prices (and related reduced outputs) can be achieved without agreement only in an oligopolistic market and only if the oligopolists have essential information at hand. Information can also be harmful even in a competitively structured market if participation in the concerted information program yields significant cost reductions, and some competitors are unreasonably excluded. Concerted information programs and the cases evaluating them are addressed in the following subsections. There is also—or has been at times—a third concern, based on the supposition that competitors ought to guard their secrets and not cooperate with each other. From this vantage point any fulsome exchange of information is suspect.

§ 5.6

1. A. SMITH, AN INQUIRY INTO THE NATURE AND CAUSES OF THE WEALTH OF NATIONS 145 (R.H. Campbell et al. eds., 1976).

2. These activities are discussed in § 14.4.

Undue, perhaps harmful, enforcement responses can result. Concerted information programs should be challenged when analysis suggests that they are, on balance, competitively harmful; not otherwise.

The early antitrust cases dealing with information exchanges (discussed in § 5.6b) turn more on distinctions in conduct than on structure. Concern about the relationship between structure, information and interdependence arose later.[3] When overt cartelization is charged, exchange of information is inevitably involved. This has been evident since cases like *Trans-Missouri*[4] and *Joint-Traffic*.[5] But the more precise question—to what extent can the exchange of information serve as the primary evidence from which cartelization is inferred—was not specifically articulated in those earlier cases. While this question is anticipated in § 5.2b, a more pointed reexploration is warranted.

5.6b. Intent Analysis in the Early Cases

During the early decades of the twentieth century there was a widely deployed conviction that the solution to the century's major industrial problems was to be found in rationalization of production. For some, no doubt, this mainly meant consolidation to attain scale efficiencies. Others, however, had great hope that owners and managers of smaller units, if they could obtain needed information and learn new, improved techniques, would also be able to perform efficiently; if so, the free flow of needed information would preserve small firm capitalism, a form of economic organization which many valued for the political and social benefits resulting from widespread participation in entrepreneurial activity. Still others saw the problem as one concerned with how human activity was organized. It was self-destructive for firms to struggle against each other like jungle animals. Had not social development reached the stage where the benefits of cooperation were evident? Out of this confluence of ideas and attitudes came a rather broadly supported, yet hotly debated, movement for "open price" or "open competition" plans. As these plans, implemented through industry committees or associations, became more common, the Department of Justice proceeded under the Sherman Act.

The first case, American Column & Lumber Co. v. United States[6] challenged the "open competition plan" of the American Hardwood Manufacturers' Association.[7] Although only 365 association members, representing 5 percent of all mills engaged in hardwood manufacture, participated in the plan, these mills produced 1/3 of the output in the United States. Firms provided to the association and it distributed to other participants: (1) daily reports on sales by participants, identifying

---

3. See § 5.6c.

4. United States v. Trans–Missouri Freight Ass'n, 166 U.S. 290, 17 S.Ct. 540, 41 L.Ed. 1007 (1897).

5. United States v. Joint–Traffic Ass'n, 171 U.S. 505, 19 S.Ct. 25, 43 L.Ed. 259 (1898).

6. 257 U.S. 377, 42 S.Ct. 114, 66 L.Ed. 284 (1921).

7. Id. At 402.

the quantity, grade, price, terms and buyer; (2) a monthly report on production and inventory; and (3) a summary of the price lists of all members. The association inspected all operations of participants and sent an inspection report, describing each members grading and related practice to all participants. There were also meetings at which speakers analyzed industry data and trends and gave advice such as "No man is safe in increasing his production * * * the demand won't come" and it is "suicidal to run mills night and day."

The Court found a violation without addressing the question of power nor did it discuss structure except to state basic facts about the number of participants and their aggregate share. Rather, it focused on purpose. It saw in the above and related facts evidence of intent "to suppress competition by production,"[8] and a "persistent purpose to encourage members to unite in pressing for higher and higher prices, without regard to cost."[9] It also concluded from the data that prices were in fact advancing during the relevant period—that the goal of higher price "was fully realized,"[10] and that "prices of the grades of hardwood in most general use were increased to an unprecedented extent."[11] The opinion does not directly indicate whether the inference that the anti-competitive purpose had been, in part, achieved was essential to the outcome, but its tone suggests otherwise. Acting cooperatively in a manner intended to threaten price and output is itself the offense.

Dissents were written by Justices Holmes and Brandeis. The Brandeis dissent is most relevant today. He saw either dominance or coercion as essential to any restraint on competition. Both were lacking. He found no fault in a purpose that competitors be fully informed about industry conditions when they were making competitive decisions, even, presumably, when this might lead to interdependent action yielding lower output and higher prices. His great concern was that economic rationality might be inevitable, and achieved through far worse means—namely by consolidation, toward which the Court was permissive, rather than cooperation, toward which the Court was severe:

> The refusal to permit a multitude of small rivals to co-operate, as they have done here, in order to protect themselves and the public from the chaos and havoc wrought in their trade by ignorance, may result in suppressing competition in the hardwood industry. These keen business rivals * * * produce in the aggregate about one-third of the hardwood * * *. This court held * * * that it was not unlawful [to aggregate as much as 50 percent] in a single corporation * * *.[12]

8. Id. at 402.

9. Id. at 407.

10. Id.

11. Id. at 409.

12. Id. at 418–19 (Brandeis, J., dissenting)(citing United States v. United States Steel Corp., 251 U.S. 417, 40 S.Ct. 293, 64 L.Ed. 343 (1920)). This dissent also cites United States v. United Shoe Mach. Co., 247 U.S. 32, 38 S.Ct. 473, 62 L.Ed. 968 (1918), where the Court found no violation despite a consolidation clearly leading to dominance.

Today, one can identify with the Brandeis concern without fully sharing it. Certainly the Court at that stage was treating consolidation too softly. Surely there was, in this industry, doubt about whether these backwoods traders had enough power to have serious and lasting adverse effect. Yet, there is little doubt that the goal of their program—not just the data exchange, but the exhortations—was to induce participants to hold production down in order to keep prices up. It was a conspicuous effort to suppress supply. Despite this, the Brandeis admonition can have relevance today. Joint activities are always at least ambiguous if they could yield benefits. A wider distribution of information can yield benefit. When coercion is not involved, if any real benefits are evident, the power issue should at least be relevant and, unless the anticompetitive purpose is clamorously obvious, should probably loom large.

This "hardwood decision," in any event, did not end the open price movement, though it lead to revisions. Proponents of open pricing developed revised programs aimed at making shared information more generally available and to encourage caution about price and output admonitions. In Maple Flooring Mfrs.' Ass'n v. United States,[13] such a sanitized open price program was challenged and found lawful. There are anomalies in the outcomes in *Maple Flooring* and in *American Column & Lumber*. The *Maple Flooring* association members had a much larger market share and also engaged in at least some ancillary activities which, looked at critically, seem suspect.[14] Nevertheless, *Maple Flooring* stands for the proposition that circulating industrywide summaries of data on prices, current inventories and sales, as well as holding meetings to discuss industry conditions in comparable general terms, does not violate Section 1—at least, not on its face.

Perhaps the most provocative trade association case during this early era was Cement Mfrs.' Protective Ass'n v. United States.[15] Here, monthly reports on production, shipments and stocks on hand of each member were distributed to other members. The majority concluded, in effect, that exchanging even this detailed data did not violate the Act where there was a legitimate business justification for doing so. The justification offered and accepted by the Court was this: the industry custom was for cement producers to bid to supply contractors at a specified price for a specific job. Contractors bidding on construction projects routinely obtained several such bids. In a rising market, contractors often accepted the bids of several suppliers for the job, using the overage on other jobs or reselling it on the current market. The Court saw these tactics by contractors as unethical and the detailed data exchange as a reasonable way for cement manufacturers to police against them.

---

13. 268 U.S. 563, 45 S.Ct. 578, 69 L.Ed. 1093 (1925).

14. It circulated "average cost" data, a possible surrogate for a member's actual cost, and a base against which to apply a standard markup. It also circulated a freight book, which could have been used to standardize delivered prices from identified basing points. Id. at 566–67.

15. 268 U.S. 588, 45 S.Ct. 586, 69 L.Ed. 1104 (1925).

The last significant case in this early sequence was Sugar Institute, Inc. v. United States,[16] decided more than a decade after *Maple Flooring*. Participating sugar companies supplied over 70 percent of the United States' sugar. Price increases were publicly announced and buyers were given a grace period within which they could purchase at the old price. The Institute was organized in the late twenties to fight secret discounting from announced prices, a practice that was widespread (indicating, it might be inferred, that either a cartel or a system of interdependent pricing achieved through leadership was under stress from cheating). To stifle secret discounting members agreed with each other to sell only on prices and terms openly announced. Discriminatory secret reductions were forbidden. The Institute also standardized the existing practice of public announcement and grace periods. The Supreme Court held that the concerted decision to adhere without deviation to prices publicly announced violated Section 1. In doing so, the Court emphasized the high aggregate market share of firms participating. This was the first time that the Court, in discussing information exchange, seemed to think that market structure might be relevant to the outcome. However, maintaining the practice of public price announcements and cooperation in circulating information about these announcements was held to be a safeguarding of "the just interests of competition"[17] The Court seemed not to think that either the percentage participation in the Institute or the oligopolistic character of the sugar market was relevant to the effect of public price announcements with "grace periods" during which the old price would hold. In this, the Court may have missed something that most judges would perceive today. Assuming the practice could be shown to be concerted, the preannouncement and grace period pattern looks much like a facilitating practice making oligopolistic price leadership possible or more effective. It might well be vulnerable under modern law.

While these early cases can no longer be cited with confidence to exonerate conduct they approved, at least when being used today in an oligopolistic market, they do suggest certain clear lines that cannot be safely crossed in disseminating trade statistics. Detailed information about the production, sales, customers, prices and terms of particular trades by specified traders should not be circulated. Neither should calculations of "average" production costs for standard products of the industry. Absent other incriminating factors, general price level information may be circulated for past transactions, though not future ones. Certainly no commitments should be made to avoid future deviations from announced prices. Exhortations about output and prices must surely be avoided. Any information made available to industry participants should be made available, also, to customers and to the public on reasonable terms, and the fact that it is available, as well as information about the nature and character of the data, should be brought to customer and public attention. As the next section suggests, compliance

---

16. 297 U.S. 553, 56 S.Ct. 629, 80 L.Ed.   **17.** Id. at 602.
859 (1936).

with norms like these may not prevent all risk of violation, but failure to follow such norms is to invite risk.

5.6c. The Modern Structural Approach

The early data cases, instructive as some of them are, miss the analytical depth that structural analysis introduced into antitrust. That deficiency was corrected in United States v. Container Corp. of America.[18] The defendants were 18 to 51 producers that accounted for about 90 percent of the shipments of corrugated containers from plants in the Southeastern States. The six largest accounted for 60 percent. They developed and adhered to a custom: When one defendant asked another for information about the most recent price it had charged or about a recent price quote it had given to a customer the inquiry was promptly and accurately answered. The Court found the practice to be concerted[19] and unlawful. It regarded it as similar to the information exchange in *Cement Manufacturers'*,[20] but lacking the defense of any "controlling circumstance," like the Cement Manufacturers' need to counter fraud by contractors. More importantly, the Court, while noting that "[p]rice information exchanged in some markets may have no effect * * *,"[21] stressed the structural conditions that enhanced the risk that this exchange among these container manufacturers would tend to keep output from increasing and prices stable. In addition to the rather loose oligopolistic structure, these facts were relevant: Buyers shopped for and bought on price. Because containers were a small part of the buyers' total viable costs, demand for containers was inelastic. But because containers were a homogeneous product, the elasticity of the demand for any one producer's product was very high; if A sold at one price and B undercut A, A's customers would quickly switch. Moreover, despite overcapacity and downward trending prices that had gone on for some years, significant new entry was occurring. Based on these facts the Court concluded:

> The result of this reciprocal exchange of prices was to stabilize prices though at a downward level. Knowledge of a competitor's price usually meant matching that price. The continuation of some price competition is not fatal to the Government's case. The limitation or reduction of price competition brings the case within the ban * * * [.] [I]nterference with the setting of price by free market forces is unlawful *per se*. * * * [A] lower price does not mean a larger share of the available business but a sharing of the existing business at a lower return. * * * [Given industry conditions,] [t]he inferences are irresistible that the exchange of price information has had an anticompetitive effect * * *, chilling the vigor of price competition.[22]

---

18. 393 U.S. 333, 89 S.Ct. 510, 21 L.Ed.2d 526 (1969).

19. Its analysis of the issue of concert was utterly perfunctory. Id. at 335–38.

20. Cement Mfrs.' Protective Ass'n v. United States, 268 U.S. 588, 45 S.Ct. 586, 69 L.Ed. 1104 (1925), is discussed in § 5.6b.

21. *Container Corp.*, 393 U.S. at 337.

22. Id. at 336–37 (citing United States v. Socony–Vacuum Oil Co., 310 U.S. 150,

Justice Fortas joined in the majority opinion, but wrote separately to stress that the case did not render exchanges of price information *per se* unlawful; the question is whether, on the evidence, the exchange will tend to raise or stabilize prices.[23] Justice Marshall wrote for three dissenters. They did not quarrel with the proposition, implicit in the majority opinion and expressly stated in the concurrence, that the likely effect of a price exchange must be evaluated on the structural data, but with the outcome of that analysis on these structural facts. The dissent suggests that the degree of concentration, though not insignificant, should be discounted in light of the ease of entry and the fact that 30 of the 51 firms in the market had entered in the last eight years.[24] None of the opinions searched out the significance of the rather curious fact that entry was occurring in the face of overcapacity and despite falling prices. A possible inference—perhaps the one drawn by the majority—is that producers were still earning supracompetitive returns; if prices had fallen to cost the parade of entrants would cease.

The importance of *Container Corp.* far transcends its individual facts and, indeed, whether the Court's analysis of likely effects was, on those facts, wholly warranted. It has long been assumed that oligopolistic interdependence, without collusion, is not unlawful, even in instances where the effect is supracompetitive prices and returns. This proposition remains the law, as the Supreme Court expressly stated quite recently.[25] To ban interdependent pricing would be to criminalize rational market conduct without providing firms in a tight oligopoly any policy guidance about how to lawfully price their product.[26] It would also leave courts without any evident remedy other than a criminal sanction.[27] But one can infer from *Container Corp.* a complementary generalization, a proposition that avoids the guidelines and remedial dilemmas, yet promises to inhibit interdependent, supracompetitive pricing in a significant subset of cases: In instances of interdependent pricing in which the oligopolists act concertedly *to bring about or maintain the industry conditions which make interdependent pricing feasible*, there is no inhibition to the application of Section 1. This is the vital principle of *Container Corp.* When the concerted exchange of price information facilitates interdependent pricing, the concerted exchange is itself unlawful, not because it constitutes price fixing (which, in reason, it does not) but because, given the structural conditions of the market, it makes it possible or easier for the oligopolists to engage in interdependent pricing, conduct which is lawful if it occurs without concerted facilitation, but which is always harmful to competition. From this teaching a more general principle can be inferred. Precisely because interdependent pricing hurts competition,

224 n. 59, 60 S.Ct. 811, 84 L.Ed. 1129 (1940)).

23. *Container Corp.*, 393 U.S. at 338–40 (Fortas, J., concurring).

24. Id. at 342 (Marshall, J., dissenting).

25. Brooke Group Ltd. v. Brown & Williamson Tobacco Corp., 509 U.S. 209, 227–28, 113 S.Ct. 2578, 125 L.Ed.2d 168 (1993).

26. See Clamp–All Corp. v. Cast Iron Soil Pipe Inst., 851 F.2d 478, 484 (1st Cir. 1988), cert. denied, 488 U.S. 1007, 109 S.Ct. 789, 102 L.Ed.2d 780 (1989).

27. Id.

much as does cartelization, any concerted conduct by competitors that facilities such pricing also hurts competition. And unlike interdependent pricing itself, such facilitating conduct is both avoidable by oligopolists and remediable by courts. For this reason, any such concerted practice violates Section 1. This principle is brought to bear in analyzing most of the cooperation activities discussed in § 5.7.

The Supreme Court again addressed the exchange of price information by oligopolists in United States v. United States Gypsum Co.[28] The opinion reaffirmed that information exchanges (including those involving price) are not *per se* unlawful and that "factors including most prominently the structure of the industry involved and the nature of the information exchanged"[29] are relevant to the analysis. *Container Corp.* and *Gypsum*, together, place information exchanges within the mainstream of antitrust analysis. They should be evaluated in the same way as are other nonprice concerted practices, such as standardization of product, services or nonprice terms. All such arrangements, including exchange of information about current prices, facilitate more rational decision making. In a competitively structured market, better information and resulting rational conduct by sellers is likely to reduce the spread of prices; they will cluster more closely around the mean than if less information is available. But in markets so structured unless there is some concerted action on price other than merely circulating information, the mean price itself will remain at the competitive level—a level covering costs and yielding no more than a sufficient return to hold the investment in the industry. By contrast, in a tightly structured oligopoly, interdependent profit maximizing may be the rational course for sellers. In such a context the exchange of price information alone may lead to industry-maximizing prices that yield supracompetitive returns.[30]

Container and *Gypsum* were applied by Second Circuit in Todd v. Exxon Corp.[31] Plaintiff brought the action on behalf of managerial, professional and technical (MPT) employees of 14 integrated oil and petrochemical companies. The firms were alleged to have conspired to collect data and detailed information on the compensation paid to MPT employees, using the information to set salaries at artificially low levels. The district court granted defendants motion to dismiss for failure to state a claim. The second circuit reversed concluding that the complaint alleged "a plausible product market, a market structure that is susceptible to collusive activity, a data exchange with anticompetitive potential, and antitrust injury."[32] The opinion is significant because of its substantial discussion of cartel or conspiratorial activity by buyers, providing economic analysis and theory that is the basis for buyer power abuses. In determining that there was substantial potential for anticompetitive abuse, the court paid particular attention to industry structure, noting that the 14 firms involved were sufficiently numerous to require data exchange for coordination of salary levels. The court stressed that labor

---

28. 438 U.S. 422, 98 S.Ct. 2864, 57 L.Ed.2d 854 (1978).

29. Id. at 441 n.16.

30. See the discussion in § 2.4d.

31. 275 F.3d 191 (2d Cir. 2001).

32. Id. at 195.

is "an extremely perishable commodity–an hour not worked today can never be recovered."[33] After examining additional risk factors, the court concluded that the data exchange in this case evidenced characteristics "precisely those that arouse suspicion of anticompetitive activity under the rule of reason."[34]

5.6d. Inferring Price Fixing from the Exchange of Price Information

Explicit price fixing is *per se* unlawful; exchanging price information is subject to the rule of reason, with legality turning largely on structural analysis of effects on price and output. Is it ever possible to avoid the structural analysis modeled by *Container Corp.* and *Gypsum* and to invoke the *per se* rule on the ground that the exchange of price information is, itself, sufficient evidence of explicit price fixing?

Cases discussed in § 5.2a suggest a negative response to that question. But there may be exceptions. In Goldfarb v. Virginia State Bar,[35] the county bar, a voluntary professional association, published a schedule of fees for title searches and opinions. While this association lacked power to enforce adherence to its schedule, the Virginia State Bar, the agency through which the state supreme court regulated practice, condoned such schedules and opined that lawyers may not ignore them. Because the market was fragmented, structural evidence might not have warranted a facilitating practice analysis. But overt collusion was feasible, despite the fragmented structure, because of the State Bar regulation and its disciplinary powers. On these facts the Supreme Court concluded that "agreement was clearly shown" rendering the conduct *per se* unlawful.[36] There is no implication here that an exchange of price information can alone warrant an inference of price fixing, but certainly such an exchange can serve as the one vital fact which, with other contextual facts, supports a price fixing inference.

United States v. Citizens & Southern National Bank[37] provides an instructive contrast. The defendant bank (C & S), a large city bank, encouraged the organization of a number of suburban banks in which C & S held a 5 percent interest. C & S treated these suburban banks much as *de facto* branches. It consulted with them about the banking business and regularly notified them of its interest rates and service charges, though stamping the notification "for information only." Because the suburban banks rather routinely followed the C & S's price leads of which C & S notified them, the government charged a *per se* violation of Section 1. The Supreme Court's reaction is telling in two significant respects. First, the Court indicated that an exchange of price information along with business consultation could not only warrant an inference of price fixing but, absent special circumstances, could compel it:

---

33. Id. at 211 (Citing Blair & Harrison, *Antitrust Policy and Monopsony*, 76 CORNELL L. REV. 297, 314 (1991)).

34. Id. at 213.

35. 421 U.S. 773, 95 S.Ct. 2004, 44 L.Ed.2d 572 (1975).

36. Id. at 782.

37. 422 U.S. 86, 95 S.Ct. 2099, 45 L.Ed.2d 41 (1975).

Were we dealing with independent competitors having no permissible reason for intimate and continuous cooperation and consultation as to almost every facet of doing business, the evidence adduced here might well preclude a finding that the parties were not engaged in a conspiracy to affect prices.[38]

Second, the Court indicated that a business justification indicative of an effort by the defendants to increase market competition could foreclose the adverse inference. The evidence showed that C & S wanted to branch into suburban markets, thus increasing competition there; that this goal was frustrated by state law which forbade such branching to protect suburban banks from city bank competition; and that C & S organized the 5 percent suburban banks as its next best alternative. Noting that if the 5 percent banks had been *de jure* rather than *de facto* branches, the Sherman Act would not be violated, the Court, in light of the justification, rejected the *per se* analysis.

Citizens & Southern invites a perplexing question. Is the Court saying that the business purpose (trying to compete more aggressively than state law permitted) offsets any inference that circulating and consistently following price suggestions in the context of a pervasive consulting relationship implies agreement on price? This is a possible way to characterize the Court's conclusions, but not a wholly satisfactory one. The fact that C & S saw the 5 percent banks as media through which it could compete in the suburbs seems logically to reinforce, not impeach, the inference that C & S participated with the branches in fixing price. An alternative explanation is that the Court was, in effect, anticipating the *Copperweld* principle. Because of C & S's 5 percent investments, its sponsorship which facilitated starting the banks, its consulting advice and its overriding purpose to use these banks as its only possible means of entering the suburban markets, C & S and the 5 percent banks should be characterized as a single enterprise. The Court did not say this. Yet, an analysis along these lines probably best explains the outcome. Of course, such an explanation answers one question but raises others. *Copperweld,* decided almost a decade later,[39] established that a parent and wholly owned subsidiary should be treated as a single enterprise under Section 1; that holding apparently extends to less complete interests so long as they are controlling.[40] But should a mere 5 percent interest be enough, if the minority owner acts paternalistically and has procompetitive intent?

§ 5.7 Cooperation in Research, Standardization, Procurement, Output or Distribution

Cooperation among rivals may take the form of a joint venture addressed in Chapter XIII. Although a joint venture cannot be precisely

38. Id. at 113–14.

39. Copperweld Corp. v. Independence Tube Corp., 467 U.S. 752, 104 S.Ct. 2731, 81 L.Ed.2d 628 (1984).

40. See § 5.2c.

defined, the term suggests more rather than less structure, intensity, and scope in the cooperative endeavor. Fortunately, the antitrust measure is not likely to turn on whether the cooperative conduct among rivals is or is not called a joint venture. A pivotal question in either case is whether the cooperative conduct is of a nature to take it outside the rule of *per se* unlawfulness. That is a key issue addressed in the U.S. Department of Justice and Federal Trade Commission Antitrust Guidelines for Collaborations Among Competitors, issued in 2000.[41] The Guidelines represent the agencies' effort to provide a broader set of principles for evaluating rival cooperative conduct that had already been addressed in separate guidelines governing intellectual property and healthcare. As with other agency guidelines, the Collaboration Guidelines are not binding on the courts, offering instead an approach for agency evaluation of cooperative conduct and guidance as to whether the agencies are likely to challenge the conduct.

The Collaboration Guidelines do not break new ground, but offer examples of conduct that would or would not be subject to per se condemnation. They also offer a description of the rule of reason analysis that will apply to cooperative conduct that is not subject to the *per se* rule. Section 3.34 of the Guidelines highlights six factors relevant to whether the rivals have the ability or the incentive to compete or collude. These factors include

> "(a) the extent to which the relevant agreement is non-exclusive in that participants are likely to continue to compete independently outside the collaboration in the market in which the collaboration operates; (b) the extent to which participants retain independent control of assets necessary to compete; (c) the nature and extent of participants' financial interests in the collaboration or in each other; (d) the control of the collaboration's competitively significant decision making; (e) the likelihood of anticompetitive information sharing; and (f) the duration of the collaboration."

5.7a.   Cooperative Research

Industrial research is essential to innovation and thus to commercial and industrial progress. Various national policies, including the patent laws and a number of subsidy programs, recognize the importance to national welfare of both innovation and the commercialization of innovative ideas. Research is a process that requires investment, initiative and time. Product research, as an example, begins with an idea, proceeds by identifying possible paths, entails selection among these to the point where a prototype can be built, then making sequential prototypes based on refinements from production, marketing and consumption perspectives, and finally product production. Indeed the process of refinement and modification often continues with production experience, marketing

41. The Collaboration Guidelines are available at <www.ftc.gov/os/2000/04/ftcdojguidelines.pdf>.

experience, use of the product at downstream production or distribution levels, and consumer reactions.

Research is expensive and research investment is aleatory. Neither the cost over time nor the value of outcomes can be predicted with levels of confidence commensurate with those for investments in production. Sometimes research synergies may be yielded by bringing together inputs from firms drawn from different or related industries, firms at different vertical levels, or firms with differing production capacities or experience. For all of these reasons joint research activity may be indicated. Participants may want to reduce risk by sharing it. They may be seeking efficiencies by proceeding jointly on a scale that none of them would risk alone. They may also want to bring together complementary resources, experience, personnel or needs.

The fear that antitrust poses an excessive threat to joint research has frequently been heard. In 1984, Congressional concern led to the National Cooperative Research Act[1] in which two protections were provided: joint research was made subject to the rule of reason; and if the Department of Justice is notified of a joint research project, only actual (nontrebled) damages may be awarded, should the project thereafter be held to violate the antitrust laws. There was in the early 1980s some entrepreneurial concern that antitrust risks to joint research were high. But this concern itself was excessive. The rule of reason has always been the applicable norm for evaluating any significant integration, certainly including joint research. Thus, that provision of the 1984 Act was superfluous. Detrebling in this particular application is probably not very harmful, because treble damage lawsuits are not a very likely response to joint research. But altering the trebling mechanism or other aspects of private remedies in piecemeal fashion is troubling, particularly when it is done in response to lobbyists that lack hard evidence of the benefits of the change.

Rule of Reason—The rule of reason is the appropriate approach to joint research. It presents no undue risk to ventures that entail no competitive threat and, for that matter, little or no threat to most such ventures. A summary of the way the rule applies will be indicative. There are two possible concerns. One is the effect of the venture on the research market: Does the venture result in an increase in concentration that threatens to harm performance in the relevant research market? The other concern is the impact of the venture on the product market or markets from which the participants are drawn: If the ventures are vertically related, will it result in foreclosure? If they are horizontal competitors will product market competition among them or between them and nonparticipants in the market be dampened? We will first consider research market analysis, then product market concerns.

§ 5.7

1. The National Cooperative Research Act of 1984, Pub. L. No. 98–462, 98 Stat. 1815 (codified in 15 U.S.C.A. §§ 4301–4306). See also § 13.5a on research joint ventures.

Research Market Definition—First, the research market must be defined.[2] If participants are horizontal competitors in the same product market and venture outputs are expected to be utilized mainly in that market, that product market would seem an appropriate surrogate for the research market. However, if the research comprehends areas of wider interest spanning a number of product markets (as it likely would if the venturers are from unrelated markets or markets related only vertically and as it might even if the venturers are horizontal competitors), the relevant research market ought to be defined widely enough to comprehend all firms engaging (or likely soon to engage) in relevant research. Next, the effect of the venture on performance in the research market must be evaluated. If the participants hold in the aggregate only a small share of the research market, concern about research market harm from the venture can be dismissed on that ground. The venture involves integration which may yield benefits. Where an integration does not increase concentration to significant levels it is presumptively lawful. This basis for ending the inquiry about research market effects will likely be available if the participants are unrelated, vertically related, or if, though they are horizontal competitors, the research market as defined transcends their product market. It will also be available even if they are horizontal competitors and the product market serves as a surrogate for the research market, in those cases where the venturers hold only a modest share of their product market.

Research Market Harms and Benefits—If the venturers hold in the aggregate a substantial share of the research market as defined, the analysis moves to the next step—identifying and comparing possible harms and benefits. As to the benefits the inquiry includes: possible research scale economies that individual participants could not attain; the potential of the combination to explore paths that are beyond the capacity of participants acting alone; and possible complementary research skills or resources that may yield synergies that participants alone could not duplicate. Potential harms to be examined include: the likely effect of the increased concentration on research market performance; whether aggregate research expenditures and/or alternative research paths increase, decrease or stay about the same; whether any paths will be concertedly avoided; and whether research output will go up or down as measured by the numbers of innovations or patents or as subjectively evaluated for significance.

The imponderability of both the market definition and the harm-benefit issues both tend to reduce the antitrust risk from research market impacts. The burden of proof is on the party asserting violation. Rare, indeed, will be the situation where a convincing case of harm to the research market will be possible absent collateral restraints, such as commitments by venturers not to do independent research. Ancillary

2. See Gilbert & Sunshine, *Incorporating Dynamic Efficiency Concerns in Merger Analysis: The Use of Innovation Markets*, 63 ANTITRUST L.J. 569 (1995). For critique of this approach, see the articles in *Symposium: A Critical Appraisal of the "Innovation Market" Approach*, 64 ANTITRUST L.J. 1–73 (1995).

agreements constraining research by the participants beyond the scope of the venture are and should be vulnerable if the venturers hold a substantial share of the research market. Such commitments, nonetheless, are probably not *per se* violations. If the venturers' share of the research market is modest, so that significant research competition could come from other sources, such a commitment between venturers might be justified as a reasonable ancillary restraint facilitating entry into the venture and increasing its potential by giving each participant confidence that co-venturers had no direct conflict of interest.

Product Market Effects—The remaining concern under the rule of reason is the effect of the venture on the product market or markets. If the participants are not related horizontally or vertically, this concern can be dismissed, save perhaps for the remote possibility that participation in the research venture by competitors in one of the relevant product markets is essential to success in that market and has been unreasonably denied.[3] If participants are vertically related it can be dismissed unless (1) a participant at one level or the other possesses such a large share of the market at that level that foreclosure could be a problem, and (2) provisions in the venture agreement suggest that venture outputs will be exploited by the venturer (or venturers) with a dominant share exclusively through venture participants at the other level. Only if the venturers are horizontal competitors with a large aggregate share of their product market is the risk of product market harm likely to be salient.

Product Market Spillover Effects—In research ventures among horizontal competitors with large shares, two types of issues could emerge. First, horizontal competitors engaged jointly in research relevant to their product market may have intimate connections and widespread communication. They must scrupulously avoid interaction bearing on or that could directly influence product price, territory or output.[4] Certainly they must stay away from ancillary agreements touching on such matters. More than that, they must protect against venture interactions becoming occasions for antitrust offense, much in the way that trade association participants must take steps to sanitize their interchanges. The safest course, and the one often used if the venture is large enough to sustain the expense, is to build a Chinese wall insulating research venture personnel from product market operating personnel. This tends to ensure that interactions between the competing firms about the venture are limited to upper management levels where they can be monitored and that personnel who are directly involved in the venture operations lack antitrust sensitive information about product market costs, prices or processes. If this course is not feasible, a well designed compliance program, including education and monitoring must be put in place. Management owes scrupulous care against tainted interactions to stockholders, to its employees and to itself. All are vulnerable if a blatant antitrust violation should occur.

3. See § 5.7b.   **4.** See § 5.6c.

Essential Facility Issues—A second issue that may arise when a venture includes most but not all of the horizontal competitors in a market is its potential damage to the market position of nonparticipants. This risk is greater when the venture yields research outputs that significantly reduce the production costs or significantly improve the quality of the output product of the venturers. Of course, successful research always has the potential to advantage the entity doing the research and to disadvantage its competition. Normally, no antitrust issue is presented. But where the research is done collectively by a group of dominant firms, and when nondominant firms in the same market are systematically excluded both from participation in the venture and from access on reasonable terms to its successful output, an antitrust problem may be presented under the essential facility doctrine (a doctrine more fully discussed in § 5.7b).

When a serious essential facility issue seems a potential risk in a joint research context, it should be possible to avoid the risk in either of two ways. First, the venture might provide open access to all product market participants that are willing both to contribute their share to the venture pursuant to reasonable, objective, nondiscriminatory standards, and to commit to reasonable norms about protecting the intellectual property or other vulnerable assets of the venture. Alternatively, the participants might commit at the outset to license venture outputs to all applicants on reasonable, nondiscriminatory terms.

As this review indicates, antitrust is not hostile but is accommodating to joint research. Indeed, in the century and more since the passage of the Sherman Act enforcement officials have challenged joint research in only one case. It involved an agreement among the firms dominating the U.S. automobile market as then defined to proceed jointly (rather than competitively) to do research on ways to reduce air pollution from internal combustion engines. The government's theory was this: Under present technology automobiles externalize, or pass on to society, a significant cost through pollution. In consequence, owners pay less for cars, the cost of manufacturing cars is lower and the general public bears part of the cost of automobiles in the form of reduced air quality. If technologies were used that reduced pollution they would internalize these costs in part. It would then cost more to manufacture cars and more to buy them, as some of the pollution cost now borne by the public were shifted to the industry and thence the driving public. So long as pollution research by car manufacturers remains competitive, each manufacturer will have an incentive to succeed and will compete aggressively. Though success would mean internalizing now externalized costs, all manufacturers will be forced by public opinion and legislation to use the new technology, and the successful researcher will earn patent license fees that will tend to compensate for the cost shift. Moreover (as each manufacturer would see it), if another manufacturer succeeded first that manufacturer would collect the royalties; other manufacturers would incur both new costs—the internalization of pollution costs and the royalty costs. Hence, individual research should be pursued aggressively.

By contrast, joint research in this context reduces the incentive to the vanishing point. All participants would gain royalty free access upon any success, so there is no incentive to be successful in order to gain royalty revenues and avoid royalty costs. Yet the disincentive—that success leads to internalizing currently externalized costs—remains in full force. Therefore, joint activity would reduce performance in the research market. The case was disposed of by consent decree which limited joint research.[5]

5.7b. The Essential Facility Doctrine

In § 3.4b3, the use of the essential facility concept to identify monopolizing conduct is discussed. Although most extensions of the doctrine in recent years are in the context of monopolization and leveraging theory, the essential facility doctrine arose initially under Section 1 of the Sherman Act, where, when it operates, it does not forbid cooperation among competitors but requires that it be broadened.

The foundation case is United States v. Terminal R.R. Ass'n of St. Louis.[6] At St. Louis, a major rail center, the Mississippi River was a costly barrier to east-west traffic. Several but (not all) of the competing railroads formed the defendant, Terminal, that acquired, developed and made available to the participating railroads bridges and terminal facilities that facilitated rail traffic across the river. On the theory that reasonable, nondiscriminatory access to these facilities should be available to all railroads serving St. Louis, the government sued to dissolve the defendant and to require it to place the facilities with an owner not vertically integrated with any railroad. The Supreme Court accepted the government's basic theory—in essence, that the facilities in question amounted to a natural monopoly that could not be duplicated. However, instead of the Government's proposed remedy, the Court required that the facilities be shared with other railroads on a reasonable, nondiscriminatory basis. In Associated Press v. United States[7] the Court applied this doctrine again. The association (AP), formed by 1200 newspapers, distributed to its members news gathered by members, foreign sources and its own employees. Under its rules a member could block the association application of any newspaper that directly competed with it, thus assuring each participant exclusive access to the association's services in its own market. Although there was no showing that AP membership was essential to effective newspaper competition, there was no question that in metropolitan markets membership conferred a significant advantage over competitors. The Court held that the association had to be open to all newspapers on a nondiscriminatory basis. Explaining that conclusion, it said that the Sherman Act was "intended to prohibit independent businesses from becoming 'associates' in a common plan which is bound

---

5. United States v. Motor Vehicle Mfrs. Ass'n of the United States, Inc., 47 F.R. 39748 (1982)(consent).

6. 224 U.S. 383, 32 S.Ct. 507, 56 L.Ed. 810 (1912).

7. 326 U.S. 1, 65 S.Ct. 1416, 89 L.Ed. 2013 (1945).

to reduce" other opportunity to compete.[8] Access did not have to be indispensable in order to bring the rule into force. Competitors engaged in joint initiatives do not earn the same right to freely choose their associates that is accorded to "individual 'enterprise[s].' "[9]

Subsequent developments suggest the likelihood of more rigor in the application of this doctrine even to jointly developed facilities. A plaintiff seeking access must define a market and show that the defendants, acting cooperatively, have sufficient power, by withholding access to the facility, to do competitive harm in that market. Once the market is defined, the rule of reason applies in a conventional way: Possible harms and benefits are identified and compared, and judgment made about which outweighs the other.[10] The discussion in § 5.7a about applying the essential facility doctrine to a joint research project is illustrative of the type of analysis required. Here, we use another hypothetical example. Assume that in the U.S. banking industry there are three types of institutions: metropolitan banks, regional banks, and local banks. Years ago the three types related both horizontally and vertically. While banks within each category competed, relationships across these category lines were not intensively competitive. All did "retail" business with depositors and borrowers, but the metropolitan banks tended to deal with large national firms, the regional banks with midsized regional firms and the local banks with small local firms. Their vertical relationships, by contrast, were important. Local banks would deposit excess funds with regionals and would perhaps buy through them investments in secured portfolios of mortgages, and would borrow from regionals when local loan opportunities exceeded locally generated deposits. Regional banks had similar relations with metropolitan banks, which also did international business, including syndicating with other metropolitan and foreign banks to make large loans to foreign firms and governments. In the last few decades, the distinctions between the market functions of metropolitan, regional and local banks have been fading rapidly. Regional banks have grown in size and influence, started relying on each other as well as metropolitan banks both as depositories for excess funds and as sources of funds, and have also started entering into syndicates to make foreign loans. Local banks also cease to be as confined as they once were. Moreover, mergers among banks are blurring the classification.

Assume that a number of regional banks through an association develop an on-line service that would keep all participants informed of (1) available data concerning interbank borrowing and loan opportunities (including firm offers to borrow or to lend at specified rates up to specified amounts), (2) syndicated foreign loan opportunities, and (3) business conditions influencing both. The expenses of the association are

---

8. Id. at 15.

9. Id. (emphasis omitted).

10. See Consolidated Metal Prods., Inc. v. American Petroleum Inst., 846 F.2d 284 (5th Cir.1988); Phil Tolkan Datsun, Inc. v. Greater Milwaukee Datsun Dealers' Adver-

tising Ass'n, Inc., 672 F.2d 1280 (7th Cir. 1982); Alaska Airlines, Inc. v. United Airlines, Inc., 948 F.2d 536 (9th Cir.1991), cert. denied, 503 U.S. 977, 112 S.Ct. 1603, 118 L.Ed.2d 316 (1992).

shared in proportion to aggregate reserves. Next, assume that the membership application of one regional, Southwest National, generally known as an aggressive competitor, is denied on the stated ground that its reserves, evaluated pursuant to a methodology validated by an international accord, were a significantly lower percentage of its assets than were those of participating regionals. Also assume that after the association was in operation for a year Empire City National applied for membership. Its application was denied because it is a metropolitan, not a regional bank.

Whether such an association could lawfully exclude Southwest National or Empire City National presents an essential facility issue to be evaluated under the rule of reason. How should the market be defined and what share of it is held by association members? In product terms the market appears to be an organized market for interbank loans and for the provision of information relevant to such transactions and to syndicated foreign loans. Conceivably there is a relevant submarket: such transactions and information from and for regional banks. Assuming the broader, more inclusive market, what share do the participants hold? A straightforward approach would be to measure their share of aggregate interbank loan transactions. Given that metropolitan banks still remain major participants in the market, the share of association members would presumably be substantially less than 50 percent. If it were—say, 30 percent or less—an essential facility claim on behalf of Empire City National, at least, might well fail on the ground that this bank has ample other alternatives both to trade on the interbank loan market and to get information. Southwest National could perhaps make a stronger claim. Suppose it could show that regional banks that are cut off by other regional banks, though having a theoretical access to metropolitan banks, would be at a significant disadvantage trading with them. Then exclusion might threaten Southwest National's continued viability in the national market. If it did and if the exclusion was arbitrarily imposed, an essential facility claim might still be warranted.

Note, however, that the market might be defined more narrowly—an organized market for interbank loans to and from regional banks. This narrower definition might be justified, for example, by evidence that regional banks deal with and rely mainly on each other as trading partners, and do so for objectively valid business reasons (such as that doing so reduces their aggregated costs, because metropolitan banks do not treat them as equal trading partners, but as correspondents—that is, as profit centers for metropolitans). On this definition, Empire City National's claim clearly fails. It is not a participant in the relevant market and is excluded for objective, nondiscriminatory reasons. Southwest National's claim, however, becomes stronger. On the assumptions that justify defining the narrower market, to effectively exclude any regional bank from the market would be to concertedly impose on it a significant disadvantage. Also, the exclusion appears arbitrary. The asserted justification (that Southwest National's reserves are low) sounds pretextual. For one thing, Southwest National meets and probably exceeds regulatory standards for reserves, even if its reserves are not as far in excess of minimum as other regionals. For another, there is no need for a consolidated decision about whether it is safe to deal with Southwest National. Each regional bank can decide this for itself. If the concern is that some regionals will not know Southwest National's reserve position (an unlikely assumption), there is a manifestly less restrictive alternative than concerted exclusion. The association could supply the regionals with the relevant information. The remaining question, then, is whether by being excluded from this concerted on-line service puts Southwest National at a significant disadvantage. What percentage of the regionals are members? Do they all tend to deal only with other members? If Southwest National makes offers or invites them does it get responses? Are there sufficient nonmember regionals so that Southwest National can find trading partners without membership, or even start a new, alternative association?

Whether the exclusion, even if arbitrary, warrants a holding of an essential facility violation raises significant issues of both fact and law. In the present antitrust climate the broad language of *Associated Press* cannot be taken too literally. When firms that lack significant market power, even when acting concertedly, combine to create a facility they are not likely to be forced to accept unwelcome participants. A modern case effectively demonstrating this is Northwest Wholesale Stationers, Inc. v. Pacific Stationery & Printing Co.[11] Retail stationers formed a cooperative to purchase supplies for participants. When one of the participants that sold at wholesale as well as retail was excluded, that participant sued, alleging a boycott. It sought a ruling of *per se* illegality. The Court dismissed the *per se* boycott claim, a matter discussed in § 5.8a. It applied the rule of reason and held that on the facts established expulsion was not shown to be competitively hurtful:

> Unless the cooperative possesses market power or exclusive access to an element essential to effective competition, the conclusion that expulsion is virtually always likely to have an anticompetitive effect is not warranted.[12]

To prevail on an essential facility theory a plaintiff must prove harm to competition in a defined market. In essence there are two analytical issues. The first has two factual subparts: (1) does the essential facility yield so great a price or quality advantage to participants that the facility threatens the viability of excluded competitors; (2) would the withdrawal from the market of the excluded firms transform a competitive structure into an oligopolistic structure or a loose oligopoly into a tighter oligopoly, thereby facilitating cartelization or interdependence that could reduce output and increase prices to a supracompetitive level. If both these factual conclusions are warranted, a core antitrust harm occurs—a harm condemned by a broad consensus of pre-Chicago, Chicago and post-Chicago analysts and by consistent antitrust tradition. Such conduct,

11. 472 U.S. 284, 105 S.Ct. 2613, 86 L.Ed.2d 202 (1985).   **12.** Id. at 296.

once identified, is unlawful. On this aspect of the essential facility doctrine there should remain a broad judicial and scholarly consensus.

The second analytical issue, by contrast, could divide both judges and commentators along Chicago vs. pre-Chicago or post-Chicago lines. Suppose the essential facility yielded sufficient price or quality advantages so that the continued viability of some excluded firms was threatened, that the exclusion lacked any justification relevant to attainment of efficiencies, but that the exclusion did not convert a competitive structure into an oligopolistic one because there remained a large number of viable firms, none individually holding an overwhelming share. On these facts a Chicago analysis would suggest no violation because the exclusion does not threaten output limitation and price enhancement. But if the exclusion was not made on the basis of neutral standards relevant to the capacity of the joint facility to attain its efficiency goals, an eclectic analysis would challenge the exclusion as an antitrust violation. Such an exclusion would have most of the elements of a classic boycott. It would be a joint conduct by horizontal competitors. It would target competitors in that horizontal market and would threaten their continued participation. Once these conditions are identified through analysis, the conduct should be condemned for the same reasons that a classic boycott is *per se* unlawful.[13]

Returning to Southwest National's exclusion from the facility created by regional banks, if the market is regional interbank transactions and the exclusion is arbitrary (as it appears to be), threatens Southwest National's continued viability in the market (as it might), changes the market structure by creating or tightening an oligopoly in a way significantly increasing the risk of cartelization or interdependence, then Southwest National would have a strong essential facility claim by consensus analysis.[14] If, by contrast, the market definition, arbitrary exclusion and threatened viability are established, but the market even after Southwest National is driven out would remain competitive, then pre-and post-Chicago thinking, antitrust tradition and consistency with boycott analysis would indicate a violation, but pure Chicago analysis would probably conclude that the exclusion was lawful. There is one additional element that in general and on the hypothetical facts, might influence the outcome—intent or purpose. In the hypothetical Southwest National is said to be known as an aggressive competitor. The stated reason for its exclusion appears to be pretextual. If the market as defined is oligopolistic, even if loosely so, and if the excluded firm has been a price-cutter in this or an adjacent market, and if prices in this market have indicia of interdependence and appear to exceed competitive levels, there is warrant for inferring a concerted intent to exclude Southwest National in order to protect a system of interdependent supracompetitive

13. See § 5.8.

14. When the consensus harm—adverse structural change creating reduced output and increased price—is being asserted, issues will arise about the standards that should govern judgments about the likely consequence of the structural change. The standards applied under the horizontal merger guidelines are certainly suggestive and useful.

pricing. On that inference the conduct is one more example of a facilitating practice analogous to that condemned in *Container Corp.*[15]

5.7c. Cooperation in Setting Standards for Products or Trade Terms

There are many reasons why competitors might agree on standards for a product or on standardized terms upon which they will market a product. Standardization can be competitively helpful, competitively harmful, or can have both kinds of effects, which must then be balanced against each other. The effect will depend on the structure of the market, the particulars that are being standardized, and other market and transaction details. Standardization is likely to have little competitive effect if firms participating in the program have, in the aggregate, a modest share of the relevant product or service market. If the rule of reason applies, as often it does, such programs are not under threat from the Sherman Act. But as will be seen, some standardization programs could be characterized in *per se* terms, rendering market definition and share irrelevant. Though there are similarities in analysis between product or service standardization and standardization of trade terms, the former category is the more complex and interesting, especially in dynamic, high tech markets. We will discuss product and service standardization first.

5.7c1. *Product Standardization*

There can be very significant benefits from product standardization, whether the standards deal with quality, safety, interface or user experience and familiarity. Quality and safety standards can always be important. Interface standards are particularly important both in network industries and other industries in which consumers may link into larger systems with compatible products and/or parts supplied by different manufacturers. A network industry is one in which the product or service links consumers to each other, as does a communications network. The value to each consumer of such a product or service increases as the number of other consumers accessible through it increases. Standardization that enabled the competing networks of two or more suppliers to interlink would enhance the value to consumers of the product or service offered by each of the competitors. It could also reduce any first entrant advantage enjoyed by any industry participant. It could yield scale economies to suppliers of related products. Standardization in industries, where different products link into systems—say, lamps and light bulbs—decrease the risk of lock-in through an installed base, a phenomenon that might distort both future competition for additional units and aftermarket competition for parts or service. Such standardization may make scale economies available to producers on both sides of the link. Standardizations built on minimum safety needs can also be beneficial, especially when relevant information is not easily accessible to consumers.

15. *Container Corp.* is discussed in § 5.6c.

Standardization can also yield competitive harms. When products are standardized product variety and consumer choice are reduced, product quality competition is discouraged and the incentive to innovate dampened. Such effects can injure marketing competition. Also, increased price transparency through standardization might facilitate cartelization. Transparency will make it easier to agree on price and easier to detect cheating. In an oligopolistic market price transparency could facilitate interdependent pricing; the industry-maximizing price may become evident and deviation from it obvious. Also, standardization may tend to exclude the innovator that comes to market with a different, perhaps better, product. If such a maverick confronts a standard entrenched by familiarity among distributors, retailers, repair personnel and customers—perhaps confronting even a standard-setting body or governmental rule—this person is less likely to attempt or to succeed with innovation.

Regardless of market structure, standard setting in aid of cartelization is also manifestly unlawful. It falls under the price fixing *per se* rule, but as part of the broader pattern of price fixing conduct. The critical element, in such a case, would not be the standardization, but the goal—the express or implicit agreement to fix prices. Once that is inferred from all the evidence, the harm from the facilitating standardization program would be manifest.

Sometimes a standardization program may be part of a pattern of conduct that can be characterized as a concerted refusal to deal. For example, producers might standardize around a potential technology and agree that new entrants would not be licensed. Again, producers might agree that all would offer certain standardized items, as well as that none would deal in any differentiated products. Each of these examples involved a refusal to deal that might constitute a boycott. In each case, the first part of the agreement—to standardize—could produce competitive benefits as well as harms. The agreement should not be subject to a *per se* rule.[16] By contrast, part of both examples—in the one case, the undertaking not to license new entrants, in the other not to deal in differentiated products—is more restrictive than needed to attain any possible benefits. This part of the first example has the key elements of a classic boycott. It should be *per se* unlawful or, if the rule of reason is applied, found unlawful on the basis of a truncated analysis, in the manner of *NCAA*[17]. Standardization programs of both kinds have elements in common with concerted refusals to deal. See § 5.8. Standards in high tech markets are discussed in § 13.5b.

16. There are at least two Supreme Court cases, predating the structural consensus of the 1940s through 1970s and long before the more recent integration of *per se* and rule of reason analysis that reacted to cases much like the hypothetical in a *per se* manner: Paramount Famous Lasky Corp. v. United States, 282 U.S. 30, 51 S.Ct. 42, 75 L.Ed. 145 (1930); United States v. First Nat'l Pictures, Inc., 282 U.S. 44, 51 S.Ct. 45, 75 L.Ed. 151 (1930). While probably correct in outcome, both seem out of phase with recent cases enlarging the scope of *per se* analysis. See § 5.3f.

17. NCAA v. Board of Regents of the University of Oklahoma, 468 U.S. 85, 104 S.Ct. 2948, 82 L.Ed.2d 70 (1984).

Standardization programs that are not in aid of cartelization and that do not evoke a refusal to deal analysis are subject to the rule of reason. They are likely to be beneficial or neutral in most settings. Nevertheless, they should be looked at critically in oligopolistic markets where they could reduce rivalry through product differentiation or could facilitate interdependent pricing. For example, if the most salient component of competition among an industry of oligopolists is product differences, any standardization that greatly reduces opportunity to differentiate would be suspect. If, for example, cigarette makers standardized tar and nicotine content there would be little left to differentiate and little basis for envisaging any offsetting benefit. Such a move could lead to more price competition. But given a long history of lockstep price moves, that seems unlikely. By contrast, if it were agreed by auto manufacturers that the turn blinker would always be mounted to the right of the steering wheel and the headlight control always placed on the left, ease of product use might be facilitated and brand lock-in reduced, without significant reduction of competition through product differentiation.

5.7c2. *Standardization of Nonprice Contract Terms*

Standardization of nonprice contract terms can also have either harmful or beneficial effects on competition. (To agree on price terms would, of course, constitute a *per se* violation.)[18] In an oligopolistic market, standardizing terms, like standardizing product, reduces competition through differentiation and could facilitate interdependent pricing. If only a few of a wide range of differentiated contract terms are standardized so that competition through differentiation can continue largely unabated, the risk of harm is reduced. If a substantial part of industry production is in the hands of nonparticipating firms, the risk is also reduced. So too, if those that participate in standardizing are willing to differentiate their terms when a buyer negotiates for such a change. Regardless of the extent or scope of the risk, benefits are also possible. In product or service markets where transactions are inevitably complex, standardization, by switching the focus of competition away from differentiation toward price, might enhance competition by reducing the effect of asymmetrically deployed information. In some markets standardizing terms could have another effect—whether for good or ill—that of facilitating the calculation of future costs by competing industry participants. Absent blatantly anticompetitive ancillary arrangements, any agreement among competitors to standardize terms should be evaluated under the rule of reason. Only by considering a particular arrangement in the context of market structure, apparent purposes and likely effects can a sound judgment be reached.[19]

Nevertheless, courts sometimes oversimplify. There are, for example, two cases in which the Supreme Court used embryonic *per se*

18. See §§ 5.3d and 5.3e.

19. Analysis of standardization of nonprice terms can be complex and should not be oversimplified. For example, as noted in § 5.8b, a concert on nonprice terms should not be analyzed as a boycott.

responses to concerted refusals to deal except on specified terms. Unfortunately, these cases (though probably rightly decided on their merits) have both been categorized by scholars[20] and cited by courts as boycott cases,[21] thus adding to the confusion about whether boycotts are *per se* unlawful. The most frequently cited of these decisions is *Paramount Famous Lasky Corp. v. United States.*[22] Ten producers and their distributors representing 60 percent of the national film market agreed to license films to exhibitors only under a standard form of contract which included an arbitration clause. The government's antitrust challenge focused on the concerted requirement of arbitration. The Court, citing *Eastern States*, a real boycott case, saw that concerted requirement was incapable of being classed as " 'normal and usual,' " despite six years of industry discussion and experimentation to develop it. For this reason the concerted contracts were labeled "unusual arrangements which unreasonably suppress normal competition."[23] Whether the fatal flaw was that the Court did not like arbitration or that any form contract covering 60 percent of the market constrains too much was not clarified. In either event there was no inquiry about whether adverse price or output effects were likely. United States v. First National Pictures, Inc.,[24] a companion case, shed little or no additional light. The offense was concert by distributors not to make films available to purchasers of existing theaters unless they assumed any unmet contractual obligations of the exhibitor they were replacing and posted security deposits in an amount determined by a joint credit committee of distributors. While these terms could well have reduced price competition, the Court did not stress the competitive significance of the particular standardized terms. It reiterated the formulaic holding of *Famous Lasky*.

A hypothetical can illustrate the rule of reason analysis that best suits many examples of standardization of contract terms. Consider a common type of service—say, electronic plus guard response alarm service. Suppose that in a region—say, California—there are about 200 firms offering such service, that the four-firm concentration ratio is about 20 percent, and that the HHI is about 250. Such an unconcentrated market would be expected to be competitive. Suppose that it is, and that the competition takes the form of product differentiation through differences in equipment, response time and variations in price. Next, suppose that the competitors acting through an association decide to standardize equipment and service terms. This step could have some

20. See, e.g., Coughlin, *Losing McCarran Act Protection Through "Boycott, Coercion, or Intimidation,"* 54 Antitrust L.J. 1281 (1986); Haddon, *Three Exceptions to the Per Se Rule Against Boycotts,* 65 B.U. L. Rev. 165 (1985); Kissam, *Antitrust Boycott Doctrine,* 69 Iowa L. Rev. 1165 (1984).

21. See, e.g., Hartford Fire Ins. Co. v. California, 509 U.S. 764, 113 S.Ct. 2891, 125 L.Ed.2d 612 (1993); St. Paul Fire & Marine Ins. Co. v. Barry, 438 U.S. 531, 98 S.Ct. 2923, 57 L.Ed.2d 932 (1978); Apex

Hosiery Co. v. Leader, 310 U.S. 469, 60 S.Ct. 982, 84 L.Ed. 1311 (1940).

22. 282 U.S. 30, 51 S.Ct. 42, 75 L.Ed. 145 (1930).

23. Id. at 43 (citing Eastern States Retail Lumber Dealers' Ass'n v. United States, 234 U.S. 600, 612, 34 S.Ct. 951, 58 L.Ed. 1490 (1914)).

24. 282 U.S. 44, 51 S.Ct. 45, 75 L.Ed. 151 (1930).

beneficial effects. First, it would make comparison shopping easier. No longer needing to try to evaluate complex service differences and to integrate this comparison with price comparisons, buyers will be able to do straightforward price comparisons. Now change the hypothetical. There are twelve firms offering these services in California, the four largest hold 76 percent of the market and the HHI is 1528. Standardization will again make it easier for buyers to do comparison shopping. But now it will also be feasible for the twelve firms in the market to price interdependently by following the leads of one or more of the four largest firms. Of course, price and service competition might continue even if the market were oligopolistic. But the risk that interdependent pricing will be facilitated would be great. At times it will be possible to observe whether competition persists despite standardization. If in a given market the change from differentiated to standardized terms has, in fact, occurred, and there is a record of experience in the market under both systems, performance in the market after the change can be compared with performance before the change. Have prices become standardized along with product terms? Have market shares stabilized? Has entry and exit become less volatile? Have company profits increased? Has aggregate coverage gone down?

Sometimes it may be facially clear that an agreement among competitors not to deal with customers on certain terms could yield no efficiency and is intended for an anticompetitive purpose. Given the new paradigm arising from *Professional Engineers, Broadcast Music, NCAA* and like cases,[25] truncated analysis may well be sufficient in such situations. This is demonstrated by FTC v. Indiana Federation of Dentists.[26] A number of dentists agreed that they would not comply with requirements by their patients' insurers to submit x-rays when they submitted claims for payment. After the Commission found a violation of Section 5 of the FTC Act, the court of appeals vacated the cease and desist order because the Commission failed to show that participating dentists had power or that output was reduced and prices increased. The Supreme Court reversed. It said that findings of "collective refusal to cooperate with insurers' requests * * * constitutes an 'unreasonable' restraint"[27] and are "legally sufficient to establish a violation of § 1 of the Sherman Act."[28] However, citing *Professional Engineers* and *Broadcast Music*,[29] the Court "decline[d] to resolve this case by forcing the [defendant's] policy into the 'boycott' pigeonhole and invoking the *per se* rule."[30] Thus, the rule of reason applied. But recalling *NCAA's* holding that "the absence of proof of market power does not justify a naked restriction on price or output,"[31] the Court utilized a truncated analysis to find a violation without remanding for findings about power, and price

25. See § 5.4b.

26. 476 U.S. 447, 106 S.Ct. 2009, 90 L.Ed.2d 445 (1986).

27. Id. at 457.

28. Id.

29. National Soc'y of Professional Eng'rs v. United States, 435 U.S. 679, 98 S.Ct. 1355, 55 L.Ed.2d 637 (1978); Broadcast Music, Inc. v. CBS, Inc., 441 U.S. 1, 99 S.Ct. 1551, 60 L.Ed.2d 1 (1979).

30. *Indiana Dentists,* 476 U.S. at 458.

31. *NCAA,* 468 U.S. at 86.

and output effects. Although the practice here was not a naked restraint warranting the *per se* label, the Commission's finding that participating dentists were a majority in a few localities was enough to show "potential for genuine adverse effects on competition."[32]

5.7d. Cooperation in Obtaining Inputs

In some industries joint or cooperative buying is quite frequent. It can be a way for relatively small firms to gain scale economies or quantity discounts available individually to their larger competitors but not to the small participants. These cases should be distinguished from buyer cartels described in § 5.1b5. Unless the market is concentrated or there are unduly anticompetitive ancillary restraints, such arrangements are lawful. An example from Supreme Court jurisprudence is Northwest Wholesale Stationers, Inc. v. Pacific Stationery & Printing Co.[33] Applying the rule of reason, the Court held that absent aggregate shares large enough to signify market power, a joint purchasing group could lawfully exclude a competitor seeking to participate. In *Topco*,[34] a similar arrangement fell afoul of Section 1 because of ancillary market division. Given the lack of concentration, *Topco* is illustrative of an arrangement which, if devoid of market power and purged of restrictive ancillary terms, would be lawful under the rule of reason. Joint buying entails integration that could yield efficiencies. Such arrangements are not vulnerable under the Sherman Act when neither the risk of gaining and using market power nor unduly restrictive ancillary restraints are evident.

Next, suppose that two or more of twenty competing firms each with about 5 percent of a market should start concertedly buying one or more inputs. How would the rule of reason analysis proceed? If there were purchase price reductions that comes from scale, or cost savings from reducing the aggregate amount of personnel and other resources committed to the purchasing function, these would be efficiencies. Either or both should be appropriately weighed as benefits. Suppose that the purchase price reduction came from gaining and using countervailing power to force supracompetitive input prices closer to cost. This serves to improve allocation, and might also count as a benefit: If the concerted buyers gain no power in the market where they sell, competition in that market should oblige that such savings be passed on to consumer. Next, suppose the purchase price reduction comes from using buying power to force input prices below competitive levels—as well it might if, say, ten or more of the 5 percent firms participated. Such a buyers' cartel effect would be blatantly anticompetitive. The arrangement would entail no measurable benefit. If unchecked buying power is evident, gains attributable to it are a harm, not a benefit.

Note, also, that each of the first three examples, although yielding benefits, could also yield competitive harm—perhaps severe enough to

---

32. *Indiana Dentists,* 476 U.S. at 460.

33. 472 U.S. 284, 105 S.Ct. 2613, 86 L.Ed.2d 202 (1985).

34. United States v. Topco Assocs., Inc., 405 U.S. 596, 92 S.Ct. 1126, 31 L.Ed.2d 515 (1972).

overwhelm the benefit. For one thing, among all firms participating in joint buying there would be an end to competition in the performance of the relevant purchasing function. That could tend toward product standardization (with effects positive and negative, short-term and dynamic, like those reviewed in the prior section). An immediate effect might be reduction of output product variety and lessened consumer choice. A dynamic consequence might be reduced innovation. Also to be factored in would be any increase in rational decision-making that standardization facilitated. On the plus side price terms might be more transparent, making output product price shopping easier. The negative side could be an increased tendency toward interdependence (or even cartel facilitation), although with twenty equal-sized firms the risk of facilitating interdependence might be small. These hypotheticals assume that only one input is cooperatively acquired. If this were but one of several needed inputs, and others were still being purchased competitively, the possible harms might be minimized. Significant purchasing competition would presumably continue and would leave areas open for product variety and innovation. If the joint purchasing covered all or many inputs the risks (and possibly some of the benefits) would be intensified. As the hypothetical is manipulated to increase or to reduce the number of firms participating and their aggregate share of the market, the significance of both harms and benefits would also change. Where, as here, legality turns on a full analysis of power, purpose and effect, the trier of the facts must work through the analytical and balancing process. Usually this will mean choosing which of two competing expert analyses seems best to explain all of the relevant basic facts. There are always alternative analytical stories. The trier of fact must listen to them, listen to argument about them, and draw such conclusions as seem most sensible.[35]

Note that the existence of buying power is not necessarily resolved solely by determining what percentage of the output market participants represent. Even if they represent 100 percent of that market—say, all twenty of the 5 percent firms in an industry—they may not gain power as buyers. The question would be what percentage of the buying market for the input in question is represented by firms in this output industry. If the input were used in a variety of other products, even if all purchases by a particular output product market were consolidated, little or no buying power might be attained. For example, if a number of airplane manufacturers consolidated their purchases in a joint program to buy a given input they might gain great power, or little or no power as buyers. If the only use for the input was in producing airplanes, the extent to which the cooperation yielded buying power would turn on the percentage of the airplane market output that was represented by the firms participating. By contrast, if the input in question was purchased and used not only in making airplanes, but also in making cars, trucks,

35. See L. Sullivan, *Post-Chicago Economics: Economists, Lawyers, Judges, and Enforcement Officials in a Less Determinate*   *Theoretical World*, 63 ANTITRUST L.J. 669 (1995).

and numerous household appliances, whether joint purchases, even by all makers of airplanes, would yield buying power would depend on the percentage of purchases for that input that was represented by these purchasers.

The direct attainment of monopsony through the consolidation of purchases is not the only monopsonistic risk. Even if the percentage of purchases consolidated falls below a threshold where power could be directly anticipated, the joint activity, by aggregating a significant share of purchases, might facilitate cartelization or interdependence between those participating and other purchasers of the input. For example, if there were already two large firms in output industry X whose individual purchases aggregated two-thirds of all purchases of the input and the jointly acting firms from industry Y aggregated all or most of the remaining third, the risk of cartelized or interdependent bidding on the input price would seem significant. The standards in the horizontal merger guidelines[36] might be utilized in evaluating whether buying power was threatened or the risk of cartelization or interdependence was too high.

Exclusion of some industry participants from a joint buying program is another possible source of harm. If the concerted program yields cost reduction through efficiencies, and if firms representing a large share of the output market participate, but some of their competitors are excluded, this exclusion might threaten the continued viability of the excluded firms because of the resulting cost disadvantage to them. The issue presented falls under the essential facility doctrine. See § 5.7b. If withdrawal from the output market of the excluded firms would change the structure of that market from competitive to oligopolistic, thus threatening interdependent or collusive increases in output prices, there would be a violation. If the firms participating were numerous enough so that the structure of the output market remained competitive even if firms excluded were forced to withdraw, legality might turn on whether the court relied on Chicago thinking or used traditional boycott analysis. See § 5.8a.

Competitor cooperation in acquiring inputs can entail conduct different from or in addition to joint buying. If so, the competitive implication of that conduct, too, must be noted and the conduct first characterized and then judged under *per se* rule or rule of reason standards. Some programs affecting inputs entail refusals to deal. A prominent example is Eastern States Retail Lumber Dealers' Ass'n v. United States.[37] When the defendant retail lumber dealers conspired not to buy inputs from wholesale lumber dealers that also sold at retail, the Court held the conduct unlawful *per se*. Participants were acting concertedly to exclude competitors from their own horizontal level. Since no efficiency could be obtained there was no need to consider whether the conduct threatened output reduction and price enhancement. The conduct was either hurtful

---

36. The 1992 Horizontal Merger Guidelines are set forth in Appendix C.

37. 234 U.S. 600, 34 S.Ct. 951, 58 L.Ed. 1490 (1914).

to competition or abortive. It had all the essential elements of a classic boycott. The facts in Silver v. New York Stock Exchange[38] were similar, save that the industry was self-regulated pursuant to statute. Through the self-regulatory program plaintiff, a broker, was concertedly excluded by industry competitors from access to telephone connections essential for him to do business. Because Congress authorized self-regulation, the Court applied the rule of reason. But even under the rule of reason the Court found the conduct unlawful despite the lack of any showing of risk to consumers from a price increase or an output reduction. Because the classic boycott elements were present, to gain protection the defendants, when imposing discipline under the self-regulatory statute, had to proceed with scrupulous procedural regularity. A firm being disciplined had to be notified clearly of the improper conduct charged and given a chance to defend itself. Since the defendants had failed to do these things, their boycott was unlawful. Smith v. Pro Football, Inc.[39] makes an interesting companion case. NFL football teams concertedly declined to deal with would-be players before the draft, or with any player after he was drafted by another team. No classic boycott was involved for the targets of the action were not horizontal competitors, they were players—that is, input suppliers. But the manifest purpose and effect was to dampen bidding for players—inputs—coming onto the market in order to keep input costs below competitive levels. On a rather truncated analysis the court found a violation under the rule of reason.[40]

5.7e. Output Cooperation: Joint Promotion, Sales, Distribution and Production

Competitors may cooperate with respect to outputs in a variety of ways, including: (1) jointly supporting public relations activity and product promotions beneficial to the industry as a whole; (2) establishing a joint sales agency, or teaming to jointly bid on specific contracts; (3) obtaining joint distribution services or facilities; or (4) actually engaging in joint production. We link these somewhat different forms of output cooperation. All of them entail integration that may yield cost savings, and, therefore, are evaluated under the rule of reason.

5.7e1. Cooperative Promotion

Joint promotion of the industry as a whole, which surely is capable of yielding benefits to participants through scale efficiencies and through minimizing free rider concerns, is the least problematical of the joint activities discussed in § 5.7e. Industrywide promotion will seldom if ever entail significant antitrust issues. Such promotions can help the industry as a whole by increasing demand for its products, and thus increase the sales of every firm in the industry. Because of the free rider problem, promotion of this kind may not be feasible at all unless firms that, in the

---

38. 373 U.S. 341, 83 S.Ct. 1246, 10 L.Ed.2d 389 (1963).

39. 593 F.2d 1173 (D.C.Cir.1978).

40. See United States v. Classic Care Network, Inc., 59 F.R. 67719 (E.D.N.Y. 1994) (case involving concerted constraint of input prices, settled by consent decree).

aggregate, represent a significant share participate in meeting the cost. This makes a trade association an ideal vehicle to sponsor such promotion. There may be some tendency for industry members to modify products or services to increase the accord of their own products with jointly advertised elements, and this might marginally reduce product variety. Yet, this effect will seldom if ever be significant enough to be more than a blip on the rule of reason analytical screen.

Joint promotion of their branded products or services by identified industry competitors, by contrast, could entail more significant issues. If the participants had in the aggregate a small market share and were advertising jointly to gain scale efficiencies yielding cost savings or access to media they could not individually afford, the benefits might be significant and notable competitive harm unlikely. Here, too, participants might standardize to facilitate joint ads. If their share was small and the structure effectively competitive, ample room for competition through product variety and innovation would remain. If these firms, lacking power and facing effective competition, agreed on prices to facilitate the ads, analysis might again indicate that no competitive harm resulted. But, unless a characterization defense was accepted (and it might not be, for fear of opening too wide a range of price fixing cases to broad, structural/performance analysis), this conduct would violate the horizontal price fixing *per se* rule. See § 5.4.

Joint promotion of their own branded products by firms that hold in the aggregate a large share of a defined market is highly unlikely to occur. If it did occur it should be vulnerable under the rule of reason. For example IBM and one or more of its major competitors would not likely join in jointly advertising their functionally interchangeable desk top units. If they did, enforcers should suspiciously ask why. Such firms would likely be large enough individually to gain all or most promotional scale efficiencies. Their joint promotion would invite greater price uniformity and product standardization, even though they did not specifically agree on prices or product standards. Given their large aggregate share these harms would be weighty. The joint promotion might appropriately be characterized as facilitating interdependence or cartelization. Indeed, given the anomalous nature of the conduct and the weakness of any efficiency justification, the conduct might well be viewed as one step in a deliberate effort to cartelize. While the rule of reason applies, once it is determined that participating firms have a large share of a market, the inquiry should end and joint promotion focusing on specific products directly competing with each other should be held unlawful.

5.7e2.   *Joint Sales Agencies and Teaming to Bid*

As *Appalachian Coals*[41] held in the early 1930s, joint sales agencies are subject to the rule of reason. Whatever the Court's reason may have

41. Appalachian Coals, Inc. v. United States, 288 U.S. 344, 53 S.Ct. 471, 77 L.Ed. 825 (1933).

been in that case,[42] the rule of reason is applied today because competitors utilizing the agency may hold, in the aggregate, only a small share of the relevant market and continue to face effective competition from others. In such instances: (1) the integration accomplished through the joint agency may reduce aggregate selling costs; and (2) may not reduce output, raise price or significantly stifle product variety competition.

The profound competitive risk in joint sales agencies is cartel facilitation. This risk is present whether the joint agent becomes the exclusive selling agent, or participants remain free to also sell themselves or through other agents. In all instances the joint agent will either set or will strongly influence price, and will either allocate aggregate agency sales among participants or strongly influence how they are allocated. If any appreciable market share is involved and if the agent is exclusive, the arrangement is tantamount to cartelization as soon as the agent sets a price.[43] Indeed, an exclusive joint agency covering a large market share is perilously close to cartelization even if participants set their own prices, since the tendency to standardize, and at a supracompetitive level, will be forceful.

Since *Appalachian Coals*, the Supreme Court has revisited joint sales only once—in *Broadcast Music*.[44] Because as a practical matter it is not feasible for owners of copyright on musical compositions to license their individual properties for the varied and ephemeral uses of these products for which demand exists, copyright holders license clearinghouses like Broadcast Music and ASCAP to license their works. These joint licensing agents do not license individual works, but grant blanket licenses covering all works in their respective libraries for fees that vary with length of time and the type of use authorized. Individual copyright owners remain free to license their own works but, as a practical matter, rarely do so. CBS challenged this arrangement as tantamount to cartelization and *per se* unlawful. The Court rejected the challenge because of the important efficiency achieved through reduction in transaction costs. It remanded for the lower court to evaluate harms and benefits. Justice Stevens, by contrast, would have found the arrangement unlawful under the rule of reason because less restrictive alternatives were available for obtaining the perceived efficiencies. See § 5.3f.

Presumably, the outcome in *Broadcast Music* would have been different if the licensing agencies had the exclusive right to license. That would manifestly have been more restrictive than necessary to attain the marketing efficiencies. Also, given the massive transaction costs avoided only by blanket licensing through a joint agent, the efficiencies attained on these facts were well-nigh overwhelming. Absent that unique feature a joint sales agent, with a share as massive as that involved in *Broadcast*

---

42. See § 5.3c.

43. See, e.g., United States v. American Smelting & Ref. Co., 182 F.Supp. 834, 858 (S.D.N.Y.1960).

44. Broadcast Music, Inc. v. CBS, Inc., 441 U.S. 1, 99 S.Ct. 1551, 60 L.Ed.2d 1 (1979). For a fuller discussion of this case, see § 5.4a.

Music, would be unreasonable, despite the attainment of some efficiency, and regardless of whether the agent's right to sell was exclusive.[45]

Joint selling through teaming to respond to invitations to bid presents rather different issues. These arrangements normally occur when the project on which bids are invited is too big or risky for team participants to be willing to bid alone, or where the team members have complementary skills or resources, or both. Most frequently teams are put together to respond to bid invitations from foreign or domestic governments in high technology products that demand intensive design, engineering and innovation. Many of these arrangements are found in defense industries.

A risk of direct competitive harm is present when team participants are actual or potential competitors that might bid individually or that might each bid with a different associate, not itself a potential bidder. If each of the participants (alone or with another not now bidding) would have bid, the team directly stifles that competition. The seriousness of that harmful effect depends on whether there are many or few other firms capable of and interested in bidding. At one extreme, there might be, say, twenty bids from other competent bidders. If so the teaming arrangement, at worst, reduces the bidders from twenty-two to twenty-one. At the other extreme, there may have been two or three bids without the team, but only one or two with it. The potential for direct benefit is also present. If neither participant would have bid either alone or with another not capable of bidding alone, the team assures a competitive bid that would not have occurred but for the team. Again, the significance depends on the likely number of other bidders. The loss of this team bid might be very significant if there were none or few others; it would not be of great moment if there were several other bidders.

Because integration is entailed, an antitrust challenge to team bidding should evoke the rule of reason. This analysis also focuses on potential competition. It would draw on potential competition merger cases[46] and on the DOJ/FTC merger guidelines. Perhaps, the single bid invitation could be taken as the relevant market or as a surrogate for it, although it is arguable that the market must be defined to include all contracts of similar character, or indeed, the entire industry of suppliers that might be able to respond to the invitation. If such a wider market is appropriate, the fact that the team affects only one contract might diminish harmful effect, perhaps to the vanishing point. Assuming the single invitation to be the relevant market (and this would be justified for any large, nonrecurrent government contract for which few firms could bid), a teaming arrangement would be suspect. A likelihood of further reduction of an already small number of potential bidders might

---

45. See Virginia Excelsior Mills, Inc. v. FTC, 256 F.2d 538, 541 (4th Cir.1958).

46. See United States v. El Paso Natural Gas Co., 376 U.S. 651, 84 S.Ct. 1044, 12 L.Ed.2d 12 (1964); United States v. Falstaff

Brewing Corp., 410 U.S. 526, 93 S.Ct. 1096, 35 L.Ed.2d 475 (1973); United States v. Penn–Olin Chem. Co., 378 U.S. 158, 84 S.Ct. 1710, 12 L.Ed.2d 775 (1964).

well warrant the conclusion of unreasonableness, unless the efficiencies potential in the arrangement were very great, objectively demonstrable, and not capable of being obtained in a less restrictive way (such as teaming with another firm unlikely or less likely to bid).

Here, potential harms and conceivably benefits might also be appropriate for analysis. The team will bring together participants that are horizontal competitors or potential competitors not only on this contract but also others. This could create spillover risks. Will discussion between them about dividing work and responsibility on this contract imply or serve as a model for interdependent division of markets beyond the contract? Will discussion about pricing for this project imply or suggest pricing or markup approaches or conventions to be followed by parties on projects where the participants compete? What arrangements are being made about access to and ownership of relevant intellectual property, and what are the competitive implications? Have the parties built fire walls or implemented need-to-know protocols or taken other steps to isolate and contain the effects of teaming activity? Factors such as these could have significance in the outcome, especially if the potential competition analysis seemed indeterminate. Recent enforcement history suggests that issues like these can and do arrest the attention of enforcement agencies and can lead to regulatory consent decrees intended to minimize the problems.[47] A better response would be for the cooperating firms to identify the risks and build their own adequate fire walls.

5.7e3. Cooperation in Distribution

Cooperation in distribution can take forms as varied as joint development of a parcel delivery service by all or most competing department stores in a city to joint negotiation with a delivery agent by two or three small competing sellers in order to obtain a quantity discount. Because integration is achieved, the rule of reason should apply. Moreover, since joint delivery would (in all save one context) be a relatively weak vehicle for cartelization, cost savings or other efficiencies are the likely purpose and indicated effect. Therefore, such ventures should be presumptively lawful, unless there are restrictive ancillary terms, or unless the efficiencies are very great and some competitors are arbitrarily excluded from participation.[48]

The context in which cartelization or interdependence might be a risk is where all or most participants in an industry jointly negotiate with an outsider for delivery services. If the suppliers of the service do not have sufficient alternative customers in other industries the cooperating buyers, through their concert, may gain and be able to exploit

47. See the discussion of regulatory decrees in merger cases in § 12.4.

48. The exclusion of one or more competitors from joint delivery might be competitively hurtful if access assured significant cost savings to participants. The analysis would be an essential facility analysis exemplified in § 5.7b.

monopsony power. This possibility would require analysis like that for cooperative buying of inputs, discussed in § 5.7d.

5.7e4.   Cooperation in Production

When firms positioned to compete directly pool investment, entrepreneurial effort and other inputs, competition among them is ended. The significance of that for market competition generally will depend on market structure and other available evidence of the purpose and likely effect of their cooperation. If the participants, among them, hold a large market share, combining production *inter se* could significantly hurt market competition. Even were their shares modest other questions are presented. Might the venture increase entry barriers (for example, by filling the most attractive open market niche)? Might it serve as a medium for wider collusion between the venture participants (and perhaps others) or otherwise dampen the competitive energy of the participants in areas not covered by the venture? Involving, as it does, significant integration, any production joint venture will evoke the rule of reason; many, no doubt, will require full analysis, including careful definition of the market and submarket, and evaluation of the way the venture is structured, the extent to which the joint activities are kept administratively separated from competitive activities (such as through separate bureaucratic organizations, need-to-know constraints on information, especially price information, and other fire walls). Typically, when competitors integrate for production they do so by merger. A horizontal merger analysis under Section 7 of the Clayton Act as well as Section 1 of the Sherman Act would be the appropriate response. The best example of such an analysis in the case literature is *In re General Motors Corp.*[49] dealing with the GM–Toyota small car production venture.[50] Such ventures are treated more fully in Chapter 13.

Under the National Cooperative Research and Production Act of 1993[51] some antitrust risks in some joint production ventures are reduced. That statute, conceived as an amendment to and extension of the National Cooperative Research Act of 1984,[52] states, in substance, that if a joint research venture moves into joint production, with principal production facilities in the United States, then, upon notification to the enforcement agency, the production venture is (1) protected from treble damages, (2) assured that it will be evaluated under the rule of reason, and (3) entitled to recover attorneys' fees in some instances of successful defense against an antitrust attack upon the venture. The protection against treble damages and the provision for defendants' attorneys' fees may reduce deterrence excessively. The statutory mandate for rule of reason analysis is declaratory of existing law. Compare § 5.7a, dealing with cooperative research.

---

49. 103 F.T.C. 374 (1984).

50. See also United States v. Penn–Olin Chem. Co., 378 U.S. 158, 84 S.Ct. 1710, 12 L.Ed.2d 775 (1964) (dealing with a production joint venture between potential competitors).

51. Codified in 15 U.S.C.A. §§ 4301–4306.

52. Pub. L. No. 98–462, 98 Stat. 1815 (codified in 15 U.S.C.A. §§ 4301–4306).

5.7f. Business to Business Electronic Marketplaces

Business to business (B2B) electronic marketplaces are a creature of the Internet. Specialized software allows buyers and sellers to find one another on designated web sites, often established by rivals in a particular industry. For example, major automobile producers have established a joint venture that operates a web site on which they can place orders for parts and other needed input. Antitrust agencies in the U.S. and abroad have addressed these B2B marketplaces.[53]

B2B maketplaces increase transparency and can lessen both the buyer and the seller's cost in the exchange. They do, however, raise significant antitrust issues, among them whether the exchange of information facilitates coordination in prices by either buyers or sellers and whether the B2B is an essential facilities or a tool for strategic anticompetitive conduct by which an excluded rival is denied a cost-efficient way of marketing or purchasing. The issues themselves are not new, but the their analysis in this unique Internet setting creates new challenges for antitrust.

§ 5.8 Boycotts and Other Concerted Refusals to Deal

The material examined in this section is anticipated to a degree in the sections on exclusions associated with essential facilities (§ 5.7b) and standard setting (§ 5.7c). Here, the law applicable to boycotts and other refusals is covered more comprehensively, with emphasis on its historical development, its current status, and its significance to the ongoing debate about antitrust values.

5.8a. Concerted Action by Horizontal Competitors to Exclude or Discipline Other Competitors: A *Per Se* Rule for Competitor Exclusion Through Boycotts?

There is a still hardy, though often challenged, theme in the antitrust tradition: Blatantly anticompetitive concert among horizontal competitors violates Section 1 if it forces even one competitor out of the market regardless of whether market competition overall is affected. That proposition was first articulated in Eastern States Retail Lumber Dealers' Ass'n v. United States.[1] Retail lumber dealers through an association exchanged information about lumber wholesalers that were making retail sales. When an association member encountered retail competition from a wholesaler the member reported to the association which notified all members of the wholesaler's name in the implicit expectation that those notified would withhold trade from the offending wholesaler. Seeing the program as a attempt by retailers to arrogate to themselves an "exclusive right to [the retail] trade,"[2] the Court condemned the conduct under Section 1:

---

53. For example, the FTC issued a report in 2000: Entering the 21st Century: Competition Policy in the World of B2B Marketplaces, available at <www.ftc.gov/os/ 2000/ 10/ b2breport.htm >

§ 5.8

1. 234 U.S. 600, 34 S.Ct. 951, 58 L.Ed. 1490 (1914).

2. Id. at 611.

[While a] retail dealer has the unquestioned right to stop dealing with a wholesaler for reasons sufficient to himself * * * [,] "when [such dealers] * * * combine and agree that no one of them will trade with any producer or wholesaler who shall sell to a consumer * * * quite another case is presented. An act harmless when done by one may become a public wrong when done by many acting in concert * * * and may be prohibited or punished, if the result be hurtful to the public *or to the individual against whom the concerted action is directed.*"[3]

This is sweeping language, but the facts and the context limit its implication to a degree. The defendants were horizontal competitors. They acted concertedly to exclude others from competing with them at their horizontal level. They did so not to gain any efficiency or even to introduce or preserve any product or service standard. They concertedly tried to exclude competitors solely to spare themselves from unwanted competitive pressure. Doing so, they injured targets by inhibiting their competitive efforts. On these facts, the defendants' conduct was manifestly unfair to targets (they were being concertedly excluded without any justification whatsoever, save the defendants' anticompetitive animus). It was also either harmful or neutral in its social effects. There was nothing about the conduct that could yield efficiency. If the defendants, acting concertedly, possessed some market power (certainly a possibility) the conduct could raise price, reduce output and distort allocation. It could also reduce efficiency by discouraging wholesalers from integrating vertically in search of efficiencies. It might deprive consumers of the price reduction these efficiencies could yield. Taking account of these implications of the *Eastern States* facts, its generalization can be restated like this:

Though any individual trader can decline to trade with any other trader for any reason, horizontal competitors may not act concertedly to inhibit market access to any other trader solely because they want to be spared its competition. If they take such action, and the target of the restraint is injured, Section 1 is violated and either enforcement agencies or the target can redress the violation.

Viewed this way, the principle of *Eastern States* is hardy and resilient. It matters little whether or not it is called a *per se* rule. It does not comprehend all concerted refusals to deal.[4] It covers only concerted conduct by horizontal competitors aimed at excluding others from their market or disciplining their competitive conduct when doing so is without plausible efficiency or other public interest justification. Conduct meeting these specifications, labeled a "classic boycott" in the original treatise by one of the authors, has been repeatedly and consistently

3. Id. at 614 (emphasis added) (citation omitted).

4. See Northwest Wholesale Stationers, Inc. v. Pacific Stationery & Printing Co.,

472 U.S. 284, 105 S.Ct. 2613, 86 L.Ed.2d 202 (1985)(declining to impose a *per se* analysis on concerted activity by retailers).

condemned by the Supreme Court and others, without need of a showing of market power or allocative or price effect.[5]

In *Fashion Originators' Guild* designers and manufacturers of high fashion women's dresses and fabrics acted concertedly to combat "style pirates" that copied their uncopyrighted designs and sold them at lower prices.[6] Their tactic was to induce retailers not to handle dresses or fabrics with pirated designs by threatening that they would stop selling their original branded, high fashion products to retailers that handled pirated copies. This conduct had ingredients of the classic boycott, exemplified in *Eastern States,* because the defendants were horizontal competitors that acted concertedly to discipline unwanted competitors by depriving them of outlets. The possibly significant difference from *Eastern States* was that the defendants asserted as a justification that they were combating free riding by style pirates that threatened to discourage investment in producing original dress and fabric designs—conduct that the defendants claimed was both tortious and injurious to the public. The Court rejected this justification. It noted that the designs were protected neither by copyright nor patent and that if they were protected by unfair competition law the defendants had a less restricted means of enforcing their rights: suing to enjoin the copying. Then, the merits of the copying claims would be evaluated disinterestedly by courts, not by the defendants acting as prosecutors and judges of their own claim.

Is *Fashion Originators' Guild* a *per se* response? The Court did not evaluate market definition at all or examine market shares with any rigor. But it did take note of the defendants' potency at the high end of the high style dress and fabrics markets.[7] It did not use the term *per se* (first applied a year earlier in *Socony-Vacuum*)[8] and did evaluate (though it rejected) the defendants' asserted piracy justification. Again, it does not matter greatly whether the case is regarded as employing a *per se* response to the classic boycott or as entailing what today might be labeled "quick look" analysis or a truncated rule of reason.[9] The *Eastern States* message of protection for concertedly targeted competitors regardless of allocative effects was enough to outweigh any justification based on free riding by style pirates.

Silver v. New York Stock Exchange[10] also had all the classic boycott elements. But the defendants that, through the Exchange, cut off Silver's wire connection to other brokers—a connection essential to Silver's

5.   E.g., Fashion Originators' Guild of Am., Inc. v. FTC, 312 U.S. 457, 61 S.Ct. 703, 85 L.Ed. 949 (1941); American Medical Ass'n v. United States, 317 U.S. 519, 63 S.Ct. 326, 87 L.Ed. 434 (1943); cf. Radiant Burners, Inc. v. Peoples Gas Light & Coke Co., 364 U.S. 656, 81 S.Ct. 365, 5 L.Ed.2d 358 (1961) (per curiam); Silver v. New York Stock Exch., 373 U.S. 341, 83 S.Ct. 1246, 10 L.Ed.2d 389 (1963); Hartford Fire Ins. Co. v. California, 509 U.S. 764, 113 S.Ct. 2891, 125 L.Ed.2d 612 (1993).

6.   Fashion Originators' Guild of Am., Inc. v. FTC, 312 U.S. 457, 61 S.Ct. 703, 85 L.Ed. 949 (1941).

7.   Id. at 462.

8.   United States v. Socony–Vacuum Oil Co., 310 U.S. 150, 60 S.Ct. 811, 84 L.Ed. 1129 (1940).

9.   See § 5.4a.

10.   373 U.S. 341, 83 S.Ct. 1246, 10 L.Ed.2d 389 (1963).

business—asserted a justification, namely, that the Exchange had disciplined Silver for improper conduct under a statute authorizing industry self-regulation through the Exchange. The Court emphasized the boycott elements, and found that the exclusion violated Section 1. It stated that the conduct would have been *per se* unlawful but for the self-regulatory statute. The tendered justification under that statute failed because the Exchange acted without notifying Silver of the charges against him or giving him an opportunity to defend himself.

Competitors may not concertedly exclude another from their market because they want to keep it for themselves. This is not an archaic antitrust principle. In *Silver,* as in virtually every case where the basic elements of the classic boycott are present, a violation is found whether or not there is basis for inferring that consumers are hurt and resource allocation distorted. Certainly the exclusion of one broker in *Silver* could not have changed the performance characteristic of the competitively structured stock market. The Court's reaction here, as in *Eastern States* and *Fashion Originators' Guild,* was to the unfairness and inappropriateness of the exclusion itself. Freedom of entry is independently an antitrust value. It is entitled to protection irrespective of allocative consequences or impact on output and prices. When firms at the same horizontal level act concertedly to exclude competitors, an adverse presumption arises. Unless the defendants carry the weight of justifying that exclusion by overbearing proof of efficiencies or other statutorily sanctioned interests, the inquiry is over. Call this *per se,* or truncated analysis, as you like. If serious defenses are asserted then power and allocative consequences may come into the analysis. But the plaintiff has no need to show injury to market competition unless the defendants come forward with a credible efficiency or other statutorily validated defense. Even then, as in *Fashion Originators' Guild,* the defendants' justification can be dismissed on a quick look if it is pretextual or if less restrictive ways of achieving the benefit are apparent. This is sound policy. It is also consistent with the trend of eighty years of Supreme Court decisions and with the analytical refinements implicit in the implosion of *per se* and rule of reason analysis that has occurred during recent decades in price fixing and related fields.

Recent lower court cases applying the classic boycott principle are legion,[11] and one strains to find any case where a court has held that as a matter of law allocative distortion and consumer harm must be shown by the plaintiff even though the elements of a classic boycott are apparent. Moreover, though in *Hartford Fire,* a 1993 decision, members of the Court disagreed about whether the McCarron–Ferguson Act protected a particular pattern of refusals to deal in the insurance industry, every member was of the view that concerted tactics taken by some horizontal competitors to force other target competitors to desist from ways of competing that the defendants disapproved would be a boycott violating Section 1.[12]

---

11. E.g., Alvord–Polk, Inc. v. F. Schumacher & Co., 37 F.3d 996 (3d Cir.1994).

12. Hartford Fire Ins. Co. v. California, 509 U.S. 764, 113 S.Ct. 2891, 125 L.Ed.2d

5.8b. Refusals to Deal with Suppliers or Customers Who Reject Concertedly Established Nonprice Terms

Classic boycotts, as that term was used in the this book's precursor[13] and adopted by some courts,[14] differ significantly from many other concerted refusals that are also often called boycotts. The classic boycott involved concert by competitors to protect their own turf. In its pure form the only apparent reason is that participants would like to be spared unwelcome competition. Concerted refusals also occur in contexts that evoke quite different policy questions. Defendants, rather than protecting their own market from entry or unwelcome forms of aggressive competition, may be seeking to impose terms they concertedly favor on vertically related buyers or sellers. For example, competitors might agree to refuse to deal except pursuant to a standard form contract, or without an arbitration clause, or some other desired protection. Doing this does not keep anyone out of their own market; indeed, it may create a new niche for entry for a competitor ready to offer different terms. Competitive harm may or may not arise from such a refusal to deal, but there is no risk of the kind of harm that comes from a classic boycott.

Horizontal agreements that standardize terms can be problematic. If the terms concertedly insisted upon directly implicate price—say, standardize list prices,[15] or credit terms,[16] the conduct can be characterized as price fixing and held *per se* unlawful. But if the terms being standardized are far enough removed from price, whether the concerted refusal will help or hurt competition turns on the market structure, the extent of the market affected and other factors evaluated in § 5.7c2; for the issues are very similar to those in product or service standardization. The question is whether, given the market structure, the level of standardization accomplished will facilitate cartelization or interdependence or, indeed, have the dramatically different effect of facilitating price shopping. This issue is of its very nature quite different from those arising in a classic boycott. This kind of refusal to deal raises problems like those in standardization that are dealt with under the rule of reason. Such conduct should not be labeled a boycott because using that label does not clarify analysis and can confuse it.

The Supreme Court dealt with a concerted refusal to deal except on specified terms in FTC v. Indiana Federation of Dentists.[17] Indiana dentists from several counties had concertedly agreed not to submit x-

612 (1993).

13. L. SULLIVAN, HANDBOOK OF THE LAW OF ANTITRUST 257 (1977).

14. See, e.g., *Hartford,* 509 U.S. at 808 & n.6; U.S. Healthcare, Inc. v. Healthsource, Inc., 986 F.2d 589, 593 (1st Cir. 1993); Fuentes v. South Hills Cardiology, 946 F.2d 196, 202 (3d Cir.1991); In re Workers' Compensation Ins. Antitrust Litig., 867 F.2d 1552, 1561 n. 14 (8th Cir.), cert. denied, 492 U.S. 920, 109 S.Ct. 3247, 106 L.Ed.2d 593 (1989).

15. United States v. Socony–Vacuum Oil Co., 310 U.S. 150, 60 S.Ct. 811, 84 L.Ed. 1129 (1940).

16. Catalano, Inc. v. Target Sales, Inc., 446 U.S. 643, 100 S.Ct. 1925, 64 L.Ed.2d 580 (1980) (per curiam).

17. 476 U.S. 447, 106 S.Ct. 2009, 90 L.Ed.2d 445 (1986). See the discussion of this case in § 5.7c2.

rays to dental insurers that sought the x-rays as a low cost method of confirming the patient's need for the dentist's treatment. The court of appeals had overturned a FTC finding that this conduct constituted a violation of Section 5 of the FTC Act. The Supreme Court reversed, concluding that the dentists' concerted conduct constituted an unreasonable restraint sufficient to violate Section 1 of the Sherman Act (and therefore implicitly within the reach of Section 5).[18] The Court acknowledged that the dentists' conduct "resembles practices that have been labeled 'group boycotts.' "But it nonetheless declined to force the dentists' conduct "into the 'boycott' pigeonhole and invok[e] the *per se* rule."[19] Justice White wrote for the Court:

> [T]he category of restraints classed as group boycotts is not to be expanded indiscriminately, and the *per se* approach has generally been limited to cases in which firms with market power boycott suppliers or customers in order to discourage them from doing business with a competitor—a situation obviously not present here.[20]

The Court nonetheless found a violation of Section 1 under a truncated rule of reason analysis (discussed in § 5.3f). "A refusal to compete with respect to the package of services offered to customers, no less than a refusal to compete * * * [on] price * * * impairs the ability of the market to advance social welfare by ensuring the provision of desired goods and services to consumers at a price approximating the marginal cost of providing them."[21] Absent a countervailing procompetitive virtue (and the Court found none), such conduct violated the rule of reason.

Although the Court did not fully develop this theme, the dentists' power over price was linked to the market imperfections associated with dental care. Patients, who themselves could not competently judge the need for or adequacy of treatment prescribed by the dentist, and who were in any event less motivated to contest overcharges or excessive treatment because insurance would cover dental care costs, could rely on their health insurer to monitor excesses (or even outright fraud) on the part of a dentist who might have an incentive to overcharge or prescribe unnecessary treatment.[22] Of course, the dentists' power to carry out their refusal to supply x-rays was also dependent upon concerted action within the local markets for dental services. Had significant numbers of dentists in these regions provided x-rays to the insurers, noncooperating dentists would have been vulnerable to action by an insurer that terminated a dentist's status as an approved dental care provider eligible for insurance reimbursement. Given the effectiveness of the concerted action in the relevant Indiana counties, the Court could comfortably conclude

---

18. *Indiana Dentists*, 476 U.S. at 457–61.

19. Id. at 458.

20. Id. (citing Northwest Wholesale Stationers, Inc. v. Pacific Stationery & Printing Co., 472 U.S. 284, 105 S.Ct. 2613, 86 L.Ed.2d 202 (1985)).

21. Id. at 459.

22. Although not developing the market imperfection issue, the Supreme Court assumed that customers were denied "a particular service that they desire"—the forwarding of their x-rays to the health insurer. Id.

under its truncated analysis that this particular concerted refusal to deal except on specified terms had the requisite anticompetitive effect.

In Smith v. Pro Football, Inc.,[23] the court of appeals, citing the earlier Sullivan treatise,[24] drew a sharp distinction between classic boycotts and concerted refusals to deal except on specified terms. There, the challenge was the concerted refusal by NFL teams to negotiate with a college player before the draft or after the player had been drafted by another team. The court appropriately applied the rule of reason. The conduct was not a *per se* illegal boycott because the defendant teams were not excluding competitors from their market. It was unreasonable, however, and therefore unlawful because it had the purpose and effect of exercising monopsonistic power to depress player salaries, a needed input. In Hartford Fire Insurance Co. v. California,[25] the Supreme Court majority also distinguished between concerted refusals giving rise to cartel issues and boycotts by which competitors blockade their own market from unwanted competition.[26]

It is safe to conclude that concerted refusals by competitors to deal with suppliers or customers except on specified terms—whether or not they are labeled boycotts—evoke no hard and fast rule of liability. If, on the basis of either full-fledged or truncated analysis they appear to threaten price and output either in the market occupied by the concerting competitors, or in vertically related upstream or downstream markets, Section 1 is violated. Otherwise it is not. This conclusion is suggested both by *Indiana Dentists* and *Hartford Fire* and by the analytical style of most of the cases reviewed in §§ 5.7c, 5.7d and 5.7e.

5.8c. Concerted Refusals to Deal Prompted by a Single Buyer or Seller

If two or more competitors concertedly induce suppliers or customers not to deal with their horizontal competitors their conduct is a classic boycott and probably *per se* unlawful, as *Fashion Originators' Guild*[27] shows. Suppose only one firm acts in that way. If the firm has significant market power the conduct may amount to monopolization or attempt to monopolize.[28] But, if the firm that induces its suppliers or customers to withdraw from a competitor lacks market power, should the conduct be unlawful without reference to price or output effects? In Klor's, Inc. v. Broadway–Hale Stores, Inc.,[29] the Supreme Court labeled conduct much

---

23. 593 F.2d 1173 (D.C.Cir.1978).

24. The Sullivan treatise emphasized that this and like cases in which competitors concertedly insist on certain terms have little in common with classic boycotts and much in common with cartel law—in particular, with cases involving standardization information exchanges or other practices that may, in some structural conditions, facilitate cartelization or interdependence. L. SULLIVAN, HANDBOOK OF THE LAW OF ANTITRUST 257 (1977).

25. 509 U.S. 764, 113 S.Ct. 2891, 125 L.Ed.2d 612 (1993).

26. Id. at 801–02 (also citing the 1977 Sullivan treatise).

27. Fashion Originators' Guild of Am., Inc. v. FTC, 312 U.S. 457, 61 S.Ct. 703, 85 L.Ed. 949 (1941). See § 5.8a for a full discussion.

28. Monopolization and attempted monopolization are discussed in Chapter 3.

29. 359 U.S. 207, 79 S.Ct. 705, 3 L.Ed.2d 741 (1959).

like that a boycott and held it to be a *per se* violation of Section 1. There was in that case an allegation of concert among the appliance suppliers that had been selling to both Broadway–Hale and Klor's and that allegedly cut off Klor's at Broadway–Hale's demand. Because the holding was based on the assumption that the as yet untried allegations were true, *Klor's* does not hold that if a single firm persuades several individual, nonconspiring suppliers to cut off its competitor that conduct is *per se* unlawful. But if there is a basis for inferring that each of two or more cooperating suppliers cared whether others complied also, the *Klor's* holding would apply. The legality of concert among suppliers to exclude even a single firm from a downstream market does not depend on whether "the opportunities for customers to buy in a competitive market are reduced."[30] Even though "unchallenged affidavits * * * showed * * * hundreds of * * * [competitors] some within a few blocks,"[31] it is a violation for even a single competitor that induces a number of suppliers to "act in concert to deprive [even] a single [competing] merchant * * * of the goods he needs to compete effectively [with the instigator]."[32] Such conduct violates Section 1 even if, as in *Klor's*, the horizontal concert was not taken to achieve goals of the firms participating but was invoked by a single customer competing in a downstream market.

Without any effort at market definition or share analysis, *Klor's* presupposed that the suppliers responding to the request of the instigator were "powerful" because they were ten manufacturers of appliances. To overrule the dismissal on summary judgment, the Court must also have supposed on the basis of a conclusionary allegation to that effect that the ten upstream suppliers responded concertedly to Broadway Hale's approach and did so without any basis in the allegation for inferring interdependence among them. The case gives profound emphasis to the significance the Court places on keeping markets open to access. Manifestly, any <u>concerted</u> exclusion, even if evoked by one competitor without any market power, is unlawful. The Court ignored the vertical element, presupposed an upstream concert (the rational basis for which is hard to fathom) on the basis of a conclusionary allegation, and required no showing of output reduction or price enhancement. *Klor's* has been much criticized. The Court has limited the breadth of, but not backed away from, this holding which gives added significance to the Court's often evident concern for open entry.[33]

Klor's does not mean that anytime a single firm induces more than one supplier to cut off a competitor a *per se* rule comes into play. Any doubt as to this issue was resolved in NYNEX Corp. v. Discon, Inc.[34]

---

30. Id. at 210.

31. Id. at 209–10.

32. Id. at 210.

33. See, e.g., Radiant Burners, Inc. v. Peoples Gas Light & Coke Co., 364 U.S. 656, 659–60, 81 S.Ct. 365, 5 L.Ed.2d 358 (1961) (per curiam) (cites *Klor's* as authori-

tative); cf. Allied Tube & Conduit Corp. v. Indian Head, Inc., 486 U.S. 492, 108 S.Ct. 1931, 100 L.Ed.2d 497 (1988), which also cites *Klor's*.

34. 525 U.S. 128, 119 S.Ct. 493, 142 L.Ed.2d 510 (1998).

Discon was a service company that salvaged and disposed of obsolete central office equipment for telephone companies, a business that developed after the AT & T monopoly was broken up by a consent decree.[35] NYNEX, one of the local Bell operating companies emerging from that divestiture, and its affiliate, NYTel, the rate-regulated incumbent local telephone network in most of New York State, were dominant purchasers of such removal services in the geographic area. ME Co., another NYNEX affiliate, made purchases for NYNEX and for its affiliates including NYTel. AT & T Technologies, (unaffiliated with NYNEX or NYTel), offered a salvage and disposal service in competition with Discon. Discon brought a Section 1 antitrust action alleging that, in a conspiracy to defraud NYTel ratepayers, NYNEX and ME Co. conspired with AT & T Technologies to exclude Discon from the market and award all removal contracts to AT & T Technologies because Discon refused, and AT & T Technologies agreed, to inflate rates for the services, thus increasing the capital costs upon which NYTel's regulated rates would be based.[36]

The district court dismissed Discon's complaint for failure to state a claim. It thought that a vertical agreement between one buyer (NYNEX and its affiliates) and one seller (AT & T Technologies) to exclude other bidders lacked the needed horizontal element to bring it under the *per se* boycott rule. The Second Circuit reversed, however, finding that Discon had adequately alleged a horizontal restraint of trade under Section 1.[37] Distinguishing one of its own earlier precedents that rejected a boycott analysis for a two-firm vertical conspiracy to exclude the competitor of one of them,[38] the Circuit held that an agreement between two firms vertically related as buyer and seller "may be characterized as a horizontal restraint of trade if the agreement seeks to disadvantage the direct competitor * * * of one of the conspiring firms." The court concluded that *Klor's* applied a boycott theory to the vertical arrangements in that case "because it found that the intent and effect * * * was a horizontal market impact."[39] It recognized that some courts had resisted extending the *Klor's* principle to two-firm group boycotts because such arrangements often resemble an exclusive distributorship, a decision to favor one supplier over another that may have a procompetitive intent and effect. But it found the allegations here to be different. They indicated an anticompetitive purpose—a determination to exclude a competing

35. United States v. AT & T Co., 552 F.Supp. 131 (D.D.C.1982), aff'd sub nom. Maryland v. United States, 460 U.S. 1001, 103 S.Ct. 1240, 75 L.Ed.2d 472 (1983).

36. The FCC in unrelated regulatory proceedings concluded that NYNEX's treatment of ME Co. as an "outsider" profit center violated the Communications Act. Without admitting any violation, NYTel agreed to refund over $35 million for " 'unreasonable rates reflecting improper capital costs and expense charges.' "In re New

York Tel. Co., 5 FCC Rcd. 5892, 5893 (1990) (citation omitted) (consent decree).

37. Discon, Inc. v. NYNEX Corp., 93 F.3d 1055 (2d Cir.1996).

38. Oreck Corp. v. Whirlpool Corp., 579 F.2d 126 (2d Cir.) (en banc), cert. denied, 439 U.S. 946, 99 S.Ct. 340, 58 L.Ed.2d 338 (1978).

39. *Discon*, 93 F.3d at 1060–61. The court cited among other authorities the 1977 Sullivan treatise. Sullivan, supra note 23, at 230–31 & n.1.

supplier in order to raise consumer prices and earn supracompetitive profits by evading regulatory constraints against exploiting a natural monopoly.

The Supreme Court vacated the Circuit's ruling. The Circuit had allowed nothing to turn on the one distinction between its facts and those of *Klor's* that might have been used to blunt the vertical implication of *Klor's*—namely that the *Klor's* plaintiff alleged (albeit in conclusionary terms) that upstream manufacturers conspired horizontally. For Justice Breyer, in writing for a unanimous Court, this distinction was critical. The opinion noted that the Court had previously described *Klor's* as involving not only a vertical agreement but also a horizontal agreement among competitors.[40] Because the Court viewed NYTel's decision to drop one supplier in favor of another to be a part of a vertical relationship, because the Court viewed "the freedom to switch suppliers" as "close to the heart of the competitive process that the antitrust laws seek to encourage,"[41] and because prior precedent dictated a rule of reason treatment of nonprice vertical restraints, it concluded that "no boycott-related *per se* rule applies." To prevail, "the plaintiff here must allege and prove harm, not just to a single competitor, but to the competitive process, *i.e.*, to competition itself."[42]

Discon, of course, does not preclude a plaintiff from pursuing Section 2 claims against defendants in a position comparable to NYTel and AT & T. The Court remanded the case for further consideration of Discon's Section 2 claim of a conspiracy to monopolize. And, although a *per se* boycott analysis is precluded, the Court's holding expressly allows the plaintiff to proceed with a vertical conspiracy claim under Section 1 upon a proper showing of harm to competition. The nature of such a required showing is uncertain. But a showing of market power in NYTel (as the dominant buyer of removal services in its geographic region) or in AT & T (as the long-established and largest removal service provider) would be a first step to establishing that abusive conduct could injure competition. The complaint also alleged that the defendants' conduct resulted in injury to Discon and to the higher rates for users of NYTel's telephone service. There is language in the opinion that suggests that whatever abuse the defendants may have committed was directed primarily at the regulatory process (describing a "deception worked upon the regulatory agency that prevented the agency from controlling [NYTel's] exercise of its monopoly power").[43] But monopolization abuses have been linked to monopoly rate regulation in antitrust cases involving Section 2[44] and there is no apparent reason why similar abusive exercise of market power should not be actionable under Section 1.

40. 525 U.S. 128, 119 S.Ct. 493, 498, 142 L.Ed.2d 510 (1998) (citing Business Elecs. Corp. v. Sharp Elecs. Corp., 485 U.S. 717, 734, 108 S.Ct. 1515, 99 L.Ed.2d 808 (1988)).

41. *Discon,* 119 S.Ct. at 499.

42. Id. at 498.

43. Id.

44. See the discussion of related monopolization claims in §§ 3.4b3—b4.

An important ruling in a case involving a single powerful firm's conduct to limit dealings between suppliers and the firm's rivals is Toys R Us, Inc. v. FTC.[45] Toys R Us (TRU) was found to have violated the Sherman Act and the FTC Act through its efforts to organize toy manufacturers to limit sales to the warehouse clubs, perceived by TRU as a threat to its leading position as a low price toy retailer. Although TRU sold more than forty percent of the toys sold in some urban markets, its overall share of retail sales of toys in the U.S. was only about 20 percent.[46] But the court of appeals was unconcerned with this relatively small market share because of the demonstrated anticompetitive effects of the defendant's conduct. On the market share issue, Judge Wood wrote for the court:

> TRU seems to think that anticompetitive effects in a market cannot be shown unless the plaintiff, or here the Commission, first proves that it has a large market share. This, however, has things backwards. As we have explained elsewhere, the share a firm has in a properly defined relevant market is only a way of estimating market power, which is the ultimate consideration. The Supreme Court has made it clear that there are two ways of proving market power. One is through direct evidence of anticompetitive effects.[47]

Even the largest toy manufacturers were persuaded to cooperate with TRU in limiting the availability of certain products to warehouse clubs because of the suppliers' fear of losing access to a substantial chunk of the retail market. There was evidence in the record that after several years of rapid increases in warehouse clubs' share of the toy market, this growth was stifled or reversed after TRU persuaded toy manufacturers to limit sales to clubs.[48] The court of appeals rejected TRU's arguments that the restrictions imposed upon suppliers were needed to prevent its retail rivals from taking a free ride on services provided by TRU. Any extra services provided by TRU were not sought by the toy manufacturers. This was deemed critical because free rider theory postulates that the manufacturer and consumer interests would be aligned against the interest of the retailer. The court also noted the FTC's plausible argument that, in any event, there were few opportunities for free riding in retail sales of toys.[49]

TRU was brought under both horizontal and vertical theories. As in *Klor's*, the large retailer was the instigator of conduct by suppliers, but these suppliers were held to have cooperated with TRU only upon being assured that their fellow suppliers would follow the same rules in limiting sales to warehouse stores. This horizontal dimension to the case would be absent if TRU had sought to limit sales to retail rivals only by a single large supplier. These altered facts would leave the plaintiff with only a vertical claim, a circumstance addressed in § 7.4b5.

45. 221 F.3d 928 (7th Cir. 2000).

46. Id. at 930.

47. Id. at 937 (citations omitted).

48. Id. at 933.

49. Id. at 937–38.

5.8d. Concerted Exclusions in the Context of Industry Self–Regulation: Can Even Classic Boycotts Be Justified?

5.8d1. The Dilemma: Industry Self–Regulators Have Conflicting Incentives

As shown in § 5.8a, the Supreme Court has twice rejected out of hand a self-regulatory justification for concert to exclude targeted competitors.[50] An unyielding attitude toward self-regulatory justification for classic boycotts can be defended. Open access to markets by those willing to risk their capital on their entrepreneurial skills is a basic and important value. And given the manifest conflicts of interest often faced by self-regulators, trusting regulation of an industry to the industry itself is not a surefire technique for protecting the public. Perhaps the risk that the industry self "regulation" would protect incumbents' profits rather than the interests of the public could be controlled by antitrust law. The antitrust rule might be that horizontal self-regulation that reduces or excludes competition is unlawful unless the regulations, objectively evaluated, are effectively designed to attain a legitimate end and are not more restrictive than reasonably necessary for that purpose. Such a substantive review of the regulations could be done in the antitrust litigation, with burdens assigned as appropriate. Such an approach would likely deter blatant overreaching by self-regulators, but there are more insidious risks. Industry self-regulation could be tuned to some appropriate public interest goal, but made more restrictive than reasonably needed. This could be done in ways that are not obvious and that burdened disfavored competitors more than favored ones. Also, fair sounding, publicly oriented industry rules could be skewed in their application. Conduct of such kinds would be difficult to police.

Excessive or too aggressively applied self-regulation can hurt competition. It can distort resource allocation, reduce output, raise costs and yield supracompetitive returns to the favored industry participants. This would occur if the rules were successfully designed or applied so as to raise the costs of entrants or disfavored incumbents disproportionally higher than the costs of favored firms.[51] When targets of such a tactic (whether incumbent competitors or likely entrants) are discernible, and when the goal of the regulation is either to keep the targets out of the market or to force them to substitute away from effective ways of competing at disproportionally higher costs than proponents themselves must incur, the tactic should be *per se* unlawful. But it does not follow

---

50. Fashion Originators' Guild of Am., Inc. v. FTC, 312 U.S. 457, 61 S.Ct. 703, 85 L.Ed. 949 (1941) (where defendants labeled targets' tactics piratical.); Silver v. New York Stock Exch., 373 U.S. 341, 83 S.Ct. 1246, 10 L.Ed.2d 389 (1963) (where statute sanctioned self-regulatory justification but defendants ignored implicit procedural constraints).

51. The analysis in Salop and Scheffman, *Raising Rivals' Costs*, 73 Am. Econ.

Rev. 267 (1983), convincingly establishes that price increases by any tactic that raises a competitor's marginal costs to a greater extent than the proponent's own average costs will be profitable to the proponent. See also Krattenmaker & Salop, *Anticompetitive Exclusion: Raising Rivals' Costs to Achieve Power over Price*, 96 Yale L.J. 209 (1986).

that concerted sponsorship of industry self-regulation should always be vulnerable. There are two categories of cases where resistance to industry self-regulation might be overdrawn. First, there will be circumstances where cooperation among industry competitors will be essential for obtaining accessible efficiencies and some self-regulation may be needed to manage that cooperation. Second, there may be circumstances in which self-regulation would mitigate market failures and where antitrust resistance to it would hurt, not help, consumers. As deregulation continues it will be increasingly important to signify ways to accommodate such self-regulation within the antitrust laws. In the following subsections, we examine judicial response to self-regulatory programs that are arguably lawful despite exclusionary effects.

5.8d2.   Industry Self–Regulation Where Cooperation Is Essential to Attain Accessible Efficiencies

This category in which self-regulation might be justified, notwithstanding exclusion of some competitors or constraint on the ways in which they may compete, can be illustrated by cases involving sports leagues. As *NCAA*[52] implies, when sports teams jointly present entertainment productions such as football games, parameters about how the teams will compete are essential. For example, one baseball team could not decide to give all of its three outs in each inning to its three best batters on the ground that by doing so, it could draw bigger crowds than those competitors that shared outs among nine players. The member teams of a league are economic competitors as well as competitors on the field, but they must cooperate. Sufficient integration to agree jointly on the rules of the game, scheduling and the like is essential to have a league at all. Because of this, it would be excessive to find a violation whenever participants act concertedly to exclude a competitor or to force it to modify its activities. Yet, the situations where concerted impingement on competitive style can be justified must be limited. In Molinas v. NBA,[53] the league suspended a player for betting on his own team in league games. For discipline the league forbade the player's employment by any member team. It was the player, not a league team seeking to employ him and use him in competition, that sued the league. Without questioning standing, and after noting that the player admitted the infraction (thus mitigating any possible due process issue), the court rejected the antitrust claim, calling the rule against gambling by players "as reasonable a rule as could be imagined."[54] In Neeld v. National Hockey League,[55] the court approved a league rule precluding teams from employing a player blind in one eye, a practice it thought justified in the interest of the safety of other players. By contrast, rules preventing midseason hiring of players from a defunct competing league,[56] forbidding employment of players during their first four years after high

52. NCAA v. Board of Regents of Univ. of Okla., 468 U.S. 85, 104 S.Ct. 2948, 82 L.Ed.2d 70 (1984).

53. 190 F.Supp. 241 (S.D.N.Y.1961).

54. Id. at 244.

55. 594 F.2d 1297 (9th Cir.1979).

56. Bowman v. NFL, 402 F.Supp. 754 (D.Minn.1975).

school,[57] requiring compensation to be paid to another team in the league upon employment of its former player,[58] or requiring approval of three-fourths of all teams in the league before a team could move to a new city,[59] were all held to be antitrust vulnerable. The essence of the matter is this: rules needed to assure a sufficiently uniform joint entertainment product and which do not regulate economic competition among league members more than necessary for that end are lawful despite their inevitable, though often minimal, effect on how members compete economically. However, rules violate Section 1 if they exceed that reasonable minimum: they have the purpose or effect of impeding economic competition among teams more than required to offer the jointly produced entertainment product.

Similar issues can arise in any field where cooperation among competitors is needed to attain available efficiencies. The health industry, which is going through rapid transformation, gives rise to many such issues in contexts like HMO practice. Actions by insurance companies to hold down fees of health service providers have regularly been upheld.[60] Arizona v. Maricopa County Medical Society,[61] by contrast, teaches that health professionals may not fix maximums for themselves, even when encouraged by insurers to do so. But today's provider-managed HMOs are developing out of provider cooperation. Will not provider-owned HMOs be forced by market pressure into competing with other HMOs to keep down service costs, and hence the providers' own fees? Could the use of maximums in this context be justified?

The Antitrust Enforcement Policy Statements in the Health Care Area issued by the FTC and approved by the DOJ speak to this and related issues.[62] The revision, which deals with physician networks (as well as multiprovider networks) is particularly interesting. Physician networks are physician groups that jointly price services offered by participating physicians to patients who are subscribers to the network's managed care program. The Policy Statement implicitly assumes that by setting up and participating in the network the physicians may achieve integration efficiencies, that attaining such efficiencies may be the reason for forming the network, and that the network and its participating physicians may be in a market for physician services which is sufficiently competitive so that, by forming the network, the physicians do not attain power to raise prices above competitive levels. These implicit assumptions are analytically straightforward and probably reasonable. An integration of some kind is occurring. It could yield efficiencies. It might or

57. Denver Rockets v. All–Pro Management, Inc., 325 F.Supp. 1049 (C.D.Cal. 1971).

58. Mackey v. NFL, 543 F.2d 606 (8th Cir.1976), cert. dismissed, 434 U.S. 801, 98 S.Ct. 28, 54 L.Ed.2d 59 (1977)

59. Los Angeles Memorial Coliseum Comm'n v. National Football League, 726 F.2d 1381 (9th Cir.), cert. denied, 469 U.S. 990, 105 S.Ct. 397, 83 L.Ed.2d 331 (1984).

60. See, e.g., Brillhart v. Mutual Medical Ins., Inc., 768 F.2d 196 (7th Cir.1985).

61. 457 U.S. 332, 102 S.Ct. 2466, 73 L.Ed.2d 48 (1982).

62. FTC/DoJ, Statements of Antitrust Enforcement Policy in Health Care, August 28, 1996, available at <www.ftc.gov/reports/hlth3s.htm>. These topics are more fully addressed in § 13.4, on health care joint ventures.

might not yield power. If it yields efficiencies but does not yield power, the benefits of the efficiencies should be passed on to consumers.

To separate the risky from the nonrisky cases the statement establishes "safety zones." If a network falls within such a zone it will not be challenged, absent extraordinary circumstances. To be in a safety zone the network must meet several criteria. There must be a sharing of financial risk by participating physicians. The percentage of the qualified hospital-affiliated physicians practicing in the relevant geographic market who are network members in each specialty for which the network sets fees is relevant. If network physicians practice only through the network and share financial risk and do not exceed 30 percent of those in the market as defined, they may jointly set fees without risk of enforcement agency challenge. If network physicians practice outside the network as well as within it, the maximum percentage falls to 20 percent.

These recent revisions are more permissive than an earlier version in two respects. First, the Policy Statement now stresses the lack of implication that joint fee-setting arrangements not falling within a safety zone are unlawful. Missing the safety zone means only that an arrangement may be evaluated under the antitrust laws by one of the agencies. If they are evaluated, and the agency has concerns, the network, presumably, may still persuade the agency with its data and analysis that the arrangement does yield efficiency and does not result in output limitation and price enhancement. Second, availability of rule of reason analysis by the agency is apparently widened. The 1994 version assumed rule of reason treatment outside of the guidelines only when providers either (1) shared substantial financial risk (implicitly, much as do individuals forming a firm or firms forming a joint venture), or (2) offered a new product yielding significant efficiencies (implicitly comparable to those discerned by the Court in *Broadcast Music*). The revised statement stresses both that the agencies are aware that there are numerous ways in which physicians can share financial risk sufficiently and that the agencies will be flexible in evaluating this. It also stresses that rule of reason analysis will be available even if the providers do not share financial risk, so long as they integrated sufficiently to produce meaningful efficiencies.

This last assurance is rather startling. If doctors agree on fees when not integrated in an ownership-like, risk-bearing sense, existing case law would seem to call for a *per se* response. Of course, the statement deals only with physician (and certain multiprovider) networks. And it states no more than agency enforcement intention; it does not operate as a regulation or otherwise directly affect the governing law, for which there could be private or state enforcers with different views about the extent to which the law had evolved. Yet, the statement is significant. If it is consistently applied, could the agency justify applying the rule of reason in evaluating provider networks in other professions or industries, if they, too, could offer credible efficiency justifications for joint rate setting?

The market reality is, of course, that doctors are combining not primarily to obtain efficiencies (although this may be an ancillary benefit), but to obtain countervailing market power in dealing with powerful buyers of their services. A more soundly based exception to the per se rule would, then, not be based on ephemeral showings of efficiencies but on the need to equalize bargaining power with powerful HMOs or insurance plans that purchase doctors services.[63]

5.8d3.   Industry Self–Regulation Where Common Conduct Is Essential to Mitigate a Market Failure

A second category where self-regulation might be justified despite some resulting exclusion is where the regulation mitigates a market failure. Much public regulation is aimed at mitigating market failures. For example, environmental regulations seek to make producers internalize their environmental externalities; and professional and other licensing requirements are often justified as needed to assure competence for consumers ill-equipped to evaluate available market information. Here we explore the extent to which self-regulation can be used to attain similar goals.

Consider this hypothetical: Most manufacturers of lawn mowers incur expenses to reduce the pollution produced by mower engines. A few manufacturers, however, save costs by not doing so. Objective tests show that the first group of mowers do substantially less environmental damage than the second group. Could manufacturers producing the benign mowers concertedly refuse to sell to retailers that handle pollution-prone mowers? Or suppose a voluntary bar association certified tax specialists on the basis of objective and reasonable standards. Could the association exact from each certified specialist a commitment not to deal on any tax matter with a lawyer not so certified? Could either of the programs be successfully defended if challenged under classic boycott doctrine—the first on the ground that it mitigated a negative environmental externality, the second on the ground that it mitigated a market failure resulting from asymmetrical deployment of market information?

These hypotheticals both involve manifest, market-blockading concerted restraints. *Fashion Originators' Guild* and *Silver*[64] teach that, absent legislative authorization, industry participants may not effectively deny market access to competitors that fail to meet the industry's self-regulatory norms. These forceful expressions of the rule against classic boycotts should not give way even on an objective showing that a market failure is being mitigated. There are many less restrictive ways that industry participants acting either alone or concertedly could seek to rectify the market failures the hypotheticals assume. If there is a social consensus that lockstep exclusion of offending competitors is essential, then governmental regulation should mandate it. Without such a consensus, industry self-regulators—activated by commercial interests of their

63. See the discussion in § 13.4a1.   **64.** Discussed in § 5.8a.

own—ought not to be free to decide what choices are to be available in the market.

There remains, however, considerable room for self-regulatory industry activity that falls short of concert to exclude. In the lawn mower hypothetical, some consumers may be willing to pollute the air if by doing so they can reduce the cost paid for a lawn mower. But, in an environmentally conscious age, many consumers may be willing to pay more in order to pollute less if given the market information needed to make an intelligent choice. The manufacturers of benign mowers might provide this information, and might act concertedly to do so. They might create and advertise an environmental seal of approval for mowers, awarding the seal only to mowers that meet objective, reasonable pollution standards. Such conduct should be lawful despite some exclusionary effects. True, the seal, in time, may gain some market power. If it was denied arbitrarily, or if the standards for its award were themselves arbitrary, so that the seal did not provide objectively valid information to consumers, the fact that denial might inhibit market access to a competitor would strengthen the analogy between seal denial and a classic boycott. But on the facts in the hypothetical, the seal provides an appropriate informational response, not a coercive response, to a real and perhaps significant market problem that is, at least in part, an information problem. Similarly, the lawyer group having identified an information problem could respond by supplying information. It could grant certification, notify both other lawyers and the public about the standards for certification and about the significance of the standards to the quality of service.

When industry self-regulators are addressing real market failures by objectively reasonable and measured means that respond pointedly to the problem, their conduct should not be swept under a boycott analogy merely because industry members act concertedly and will gain commercially if their effort is successful.[65] They act concertedly because it is efficient to do so. All who meet its standards will gain from a successful seal of approval program. All should bear its costs; none would be motivated to invest maximally if other beneficiaries could free ride on that investment. And so long as excesses are avoided the fact that sponsors expect to gain should not impeach the program. If they did not so expect they would not invest in providing information that could mitigate the market failure.

Yet limits must be drawn. A seal of approval or like program could be a means for deliberately and arbitrarily excluding competitors or significantly and differentially raising their costs relative to the returns they can expect. If it is so used, an antitrust court should be ready to

---

65. Cf. Radiant Burners, Inc. v. Peoples Gas Light & Coke Co., 364 U.S. 656, 81 S.Ct. 365, 5 L.Ed.2d 358 (1961) (per curiam); see Structural Laminates, Inc. v. Douglas Fir Plywood Ass'n, 399 F.2d 155 (9th Cir.1968) (per curiam), cert. denied, 393 U.S. 1024, 89 S.Ct. 636, 21 L.Ed.2d 569 (1969); Eliason Corp. v. National Sanitation Found., 614 F.2d 126 (6th Cir.), cert. denied, 449 U.S. 826, 101 S.Ct. 89, 66 L.Ed.2d 29 (1980).

intervene. Standards must be objectively related to relevant performance characteristics and administered objectively and fairly. If they are not, the concert unreasonably restrains the competition of the noncomplying firms.[66] Much of this is implied in the opinion for the Court in Allied Tube & Conduit Corp. v. Indian Head, Inc.[67] There commercially interested parties enlisted, paid the membership fees and expenses for, and brought in to vote as instructed at a meeting of a standard-setting organization, new members who would provide the necessary majority to enact a rule that would exclude a competitor. This practice was held not to gain *Noerr* state action immunity[68] notwithstanding that the standard approved at the meeting would be routinely incorporated into building codes.

5.8e. Boycotts by Consumers to Achieve Political, Social or Economic Goals

To speak of consumer boycotts as a category can be an oversimplification. Concerted refusals to deal may be organized by consumer, religious, social, political or other interest groups in an effort to induce firms to alter marketing or other economic policies in ways that advance the goals of the sponsor, either by changing the way the market responds to demand and supply, or, through changing the market, influencing political responses. Often such boycotts pursue nonpocketbook interests of the participating consumers or of the sponsoring group. Examples of these boycotts—which we might label "pure consumer boycotts"—might include church, racial or gender groups encouraging consumers to withdraw patronage from, for example, theaters showing movies (or advertisers sponsoring TV shows) that the group finds insensitive to its interests, issues, tastes or goals.[69] At least in this pure form—concerted action by consumers who cohere around a religious, moral, social or political issue not directly related to their pocketbooks—consumer boycotts appear to have First Amendment protection.[70]

Quite aside from constitutional limits, whether such a boycott is covered by the Sherman Act is doubtful. Its objective is social, religious or political, not commercial; no pocketbook interest is at stake for participating consumers. But the means used to attain noncommercial ends is to deprive producers of access to the atomistic consumer market envisaged in the competitive model. Moreover, if successful the consumer boycott will adversely limit the market choices open to other consumers

---

66. This was a concern of the Court in *Radiant Burners*, 364 U.S. 656, 81 S.Ct. 365, 5 L.Ed.2d 358.

67. 486 U.S. 492, 108 S.Ct. 1931, 100 L.Ed.2d 497 (1988).

68. The *Noerr* state action doctrine is discussed in § 14.4.

69. Another example would be an environmental group urging consumers not to buy products made by polluters. The distinction between such a consumer boycott and some of the industry self-regulatory issues discussed in § 5.8d is in the noncommercial status and goal of the proponent. This distinction becomes blurred when a market interest supports the nonmarket sponsor.

70. NAACP v. Claiborne Hardware Co., 458 U.S. 886, 102 S.Ct. 3409, 73 L.Ed.2d 1215 (1982) (holding that an NAACP-encouraged boycott of local merchants that discriminated on racial grounds was constitutionally protected).

who do not share the sponsor's objectives. Perhaps the strongest argument that consumer action is exempt under the Sherman Act would be to turn again to the First Amendment. Even if such conduct were not directly protected by the Amendment (as *Claiborne* suggests it is) all or most consumer boycotts would be well within the Amendment's value ambit. That being so, where Congress has not spoken its intent unambiguously (as it has not about the application of the Sherman Act to such boycotts) the Court should assume that Congress did not intend to push its power as far as it constitutionally might go. Just as the policies of the First Amendment became the source for the petitioning exemption granted in *Noerr*,[71] so they might be used to justify an exemption for consumer action, if not by constitutional mandate then by construction of the Sherman Act.

Sometimes a "consumer boycott" raises the issue in a somewhat adulterated form. Suppose a consumer organization boycotts all grocery stores for three days to protest rising food prices. This is a pocketbook boycott, not a social policy boycott. Or suppose consumers boycott grapes in sympathy with farmworkers to protest the low wages these workers are paid. Each of these withdrawals of patronage is a consumer boycott, but neither is "pure" in the sense of being devoid of either a consumer pocketbook interest or a consumer effort to alter competitive outcomes. Contentions that the Sherman Act was not intended to apply will be attenuated in these situations. Such a contention could prevail only if a court concluded that consumers, the ultimate beneficiaries of competition, are always immune from the Sherman Act, so long as they act solely as consumers, even when their conduct affects resource allocation or competitive interaction—a position with, perhaps, some intuitive, but little rational, appeal.[72]

There are several possible analytical approaches to Sherman Act application to consumer activity. Although the Supreme Court has spoken[73] it has, as yet, said nothing definitive. Modern court of appeals cases, however, have not been sympathetic to efforts to bring the Sherman Act to bear on conduct that, in one sense or another, might be labeled "consumer boycotts." The Eighth Circuit[74] held that a state challenge to a boycott of convention facilities sponsored by a women's organization aimed at inducing the state to validate the Equal Rights Amendment was beyond the reach of the Sherman Act. A like result was reached by the First Circuit when longshoremen refused to unload ships trading with the Soviet Union because that country had invaded Afghan-

71. Eastern R.R. Presidents Conference v. Noerr Motor Freight, Inc., 365 U.S. 127, 81 S.Ct. 523, 5 L.Ed.2d 464 (1961).

72. *Cf.* NOW v. Scheidler, 968 F.2d 612 (7th Cir. 1992), rev'd on other grounds, 510 U.S. 249, 114 S.Ct. 798, 127 L.Ed.2d 99 (1994). Consumers supporting a noncommercial boycott may act for varied reasons. Such a boycott may be supported by those who deeply believe in a principle, by those

who are tired of being left out, and by those who will profit if the boycott has an economic impact.

73. *NAACP*, 458 U.S. 886, 102 S.Ct. 3409, 73 L.Ed.2d 1215.

74. Missouri v. NOW, Inc., 620 F.2d 1301 (8th Cir.), cert. denied, 449 U.S. 842, 101 S.Ct. 122, 66 L.Ed.2d 49 (1980).

istan.[75] Of course, to hold that some or all consumer boycotts are subject to the Sherman Act is not necessarily to say that they are illegal. Consumer-centered activity (even if it fails to gain First Amendment protection or a comprehensive *Noerr*-like exemption) might be spared from *per se* structures on the ground that proximity to First Amendment interest warrants at least this adjustment.[76] Some consumer boycotts may well exercise market power, some even in national markets. Consumer boycotts by major racial, ethnic or religious groups are clear examples; if any such group was, in fact, a cohesive group ready to go to the wall on one of its issues, it would have formidable economic power. If boycott participants did exercise power and consumer boycotts were unlawful, participants would be vulnerable under Section 1. But many consumer boycotts—say a small church group seeking to affect script decisions of major moviemakers—would be powerless; the small group's efforts, however valuable to it as an expressive exercise, would be futile in economic terms. Indeed, this fact would give added strength to the contention that the activity is within the ambit of the First Amendment. If boycott participants will have no economic effect and they know it, does not that suggest noneconomic—that is, social, political or religious—objectives?

Trial Lawyers[77] suggests a limit upon the constitutional protection for the consumer boycott. It was not a "pure" consumer boycott, as we use those terms. The defendants were marketplace actors—criminal defense lawyers—seeking a direct market goal: higher hourly rates. They concertedly withheld service in order to gain that goal. But, they needed to induce a political response in order to gain their end because the District of Columbia paid their fees and was the target of their activity. Also, there were manifest social and political interests involved. Indeed, the district government would not have been bearing the legal expense if there were not. But neither the social importance of the policy question nor the fact that the question had to be resolved by local legislative action overbore the defendants concerted withholding of services to force their own fees to higher levels. *Claiborne* was distinguished on the ground that boycott participants there were trying to challenge all discrimination against blacks, not just discrimination that lined their own pocketbooks. *NOW* and *International Longshoremen* can stand consistently with *Trial Lawyers*. In both those cases the concerted market action advanced political, not economic, interests of the proponents. But *Trial Lawyers* certainly withdraws warrant for a broad reading of either of the earlier opinions.

After *Trial Lawyers*, what would a court say about a pocketbook boycott by ultimate consumers—say, a commitment signed by numerous

---

75. Allied Int'l, Inc. v. International Longshoremen's Ass'n, 640 F.2d 1368 (1st Cir.1981), aff'd, 456 U.S. 212, 102 S.Ct. 1656, 72 L.Ed.2d 21 (1982).

76. But cf. Judge Ginsburg's opinion in Superior Court Trial Lawyers Ass'n v. FTC, 856 F.2d 226 (D.C.Cir.1988), rev'd on other grounds, 493 U.S. 411, 110 S.Ct. 768, 107 L.Ed.2d 851 (1990).

77. FTC v. Superior Court Trial Lawyers Ass'n, 493 U.S. 411, 110 S.Ct. 768, 107 L.Ed.2d 851 (1990).

consumers in response to a call from Ralph Nader to protest an upward trend in car prices by not buying any new car for a year. The intuitive notion, apparently widely held, that ultimate consumers ought to be free to act concertedly even to advance their own marketplace goals as consumers encounters analytical resistance when one thinks about the role and function of consumers in the competitive scheme. Under the competitive ideal, consumers as well as producers are supposed to act independently, each assuming his or her powerlessness to affect market prices by decisions about whether or not to buy. Workers have legislative sanction to act concertedly in their economic interest. But like the lawyers in *Trial Lawyers*, consumers do not unless a court finds such sanction in the interstices of the Sherman Act.

Chapter VI

THE ECONOMICS OF DISTRIBUTION RESTRAINTS

Table of Sections

§ 6.1 Introduction

Most products move through a number of production and distribution stages before reaching the consumer. Starting with the mining of raw materials or the growing of an agricultural commodity, a product may be processed several times, manufactured, assembled into a more complex whole, and passed along successively to a distributor, wholesaler, retailer and finally a consumer. Along the way, ownership of the product may change many times. The links from raw materials to final sale are said to form a vertical or distribution chain. A manufacturer may condition a dealer's purchase in a manner that limits use, distribution or resale of the product. Or a dealer may gain a concession from the manufacturer not to sell similar products to rival dealers. Such restraints are often called vertical restraints because they involve players in a buyer-seller relationship and are distinguished from horizontal restraints, or those imposed among direct rivals. See Chapter V.

Of course, all power abuses are vertical in the sense that a powerful seller (monopolist) or powerful buyer (monopsonist) exercises its power in transactions with customers or suppliers. Horizontal restraints of all types are designed to give the participants power in a vertical context: either in sales or purchases. What distinguishes a purely vertical restraint addressed in Section 1 of the Sherman Act is that it involves a single player–either a buyer or seller–who exercises power within the distribution chain independent of any rivals. If that player is dominant, its conduct can be challenged under Sherman Section 2. If, however, the player lacks monopoly power, there is still the possibility that the abusive conduct is actionable as a restraint of trade. The restraint may be imposed only on the supplier or on the customer. Thus, there may be only two players involved in the distribution restraint: an upstream supplier and a downstream purchaser.

Distribution restraints are usually linked to the sale of branded products. Indeed, the use of vertical restraints as we know them was probably unusual before the proliferation of branded products in the late nineteenth century. Strong brands create an inelasticity of demand among consumers that allows a seller to demand a premium above the price for a generic, yet brand differentiated, item. Such distribution restraints are designed to promote the sale of a particular brand. Whether a particular restraints does so without undue harm to competition becomes a pivotal issue in the antitrust analysis.

A careful analysis must address competition among participants in the distribution chain. Competition occurs not only among rival sellers or rival buyers, but also in vertical relationships. Thus, a supplier and a retailer may compete to determine who can make the largest chunk of the consumer dollar that purchases everything from apples to computers. Because of the overall constraints of the marketplace, a consumer may be willing to pay only 50 cents for each apple. How will the retailer and the upstream suppliers divide up this amount? The answer will lie in the relative power or leverage possessed by the retailer and upstream suppliers. Thus, a key question for all distribution restraints is: who has the relative power in this vertical relationship? Answering that question is fundamental and will assist in analyzing the competitive effects, positive and negative, of the restraint.

This chapter addresses the economics of distribution restraints. The law governing distribution restraints is addressed in Chapter VII (Downstream Power Distribution Restraints) and Chapter VIII (Upstream Power Distribution Restraints). Although there will be exceptions, certain types of restraints, such as vertical minimum price fixing, territorial restraints, or customer allocations among dealers, tend to be associated with downstream or retailer power. Other restraints, such as vertical maximum price fixing, tie-ins, and exclusive selling (a dealer agrees to carry only the supplier's brand) tend to be associated with upstream or supplier power.

6.1a. Contending Economic Views of Distribution Restraints

Distribution restraints matter. They are widely used in the promotion and sale of branded goods. But in fostering downstream promotion, such restraints are likely to raise the price of branded goods and services purchased by consumers.[1] Thus, a key question, and one on which theorists have yet to find consensus, is whether this surcharge to

---

§ 6.1

1. Even some theorists who believe distribution restraints are generally procompetitive acknowledge that they tend to raise consumer prices. As Judge Easterbrook explains, "the manufacturer can't get the dealer to do more without increasing the dealer's margin." Easterbrook, *Vertical Arrangements and the Rule of Reason*, 53 AN-

TITRUST L.J. 135, 156 (1984). Of course, as Judge Easterbrook's comment suggests, if a distribution restraint is an efficient way of encouraging the dealer to deliver valued services, it may result in an overall product-service package at a lower aggregate price than might be possible without the distribution restraint.

consumers provides a unique and critical incentive for valued promotional services that outweighs any antitrust injury. The controversial nature of the law governing distribution restraints is demonstrated by abrupt policy reversals of the Justice Department (issuing Vertical Restraint Guidelines in 1985 and then withdrawing those Guidelines in 1993)[2] and of the United States Supreme Court (issuing three decisions during the years 1963–1977, the first declining to set a standard governing nonprice distribution restraints, the second adopting a *per se* rule, and the third discarding the *per se* rule and opting for a presumptive validity under a so-called rule of reason).[3] These policy shifts by the Executive and Judicial branches (to some extent mirrored in shifts in the federal and state legislatures) reflect an ongoing theoretical debate about the competitive merits of distribution restraints.

Economic arguments concerning distribution restraints can be roughly divided into four categories. Theorists sympathetic to distribution restraints stress that they create valuable incentives for promotion and are an important tool for reducing transaction costs. Theorists less sympathetic counter that distribution restraints tend to facilitate collusive or cartel behavior and undercut the allocative and dynamic benefits of downstream intrabrand competition. Each of these four points of view has some legitimacy. These cross currents of economic analysis, along with the non-economic arguments, are described below and in § 6.1b. These concerns are integrated in § 6.1c, which describes the emerging economic view of distribution restraints. The challenge is to obtain a cohesive and empirically valid understanding of distribution restraints that provides a sound platform for antitrust decisions and counseling. The evolution of brand marketing and vertical restraints is presented in § 6.2. The procompetitive and anticompetitive elements that need attention in a balancing analysis are described in § 6.3.

6.1a1. *Promotional Benefits of Distribution Restraints*

Theorists allied with the Chicago School tend to examine distribution restraints from a producer's perspective, albeit one that they contend is largely consistent with consumer interests.[4] The Supreme Court's *Sylvania* decision[5] viewed distribution restraints from this perspective, bringing a modicum of order and clarity to court decisions said to have

---

2. U.S. Dept. of Justice, Vertical Restraint Guidelines (Jan. 4, 1985), *reprinted in* 4 Trade Reg. Rep. (CCH) ¶ 13,105. The Guidelines were withdrawn on August 10, 1993. Speech of Assistant Attorney General Bingamon, announcing withdrawal of the Guidelines, 65 ANTITRUST & TRADE REG. REP. (BNA) 250 (Aug. 12, 1993).

3. The three cases are White Motor Co. v. United States, 372 U.S. 253, 83 S.Ct. 696, 9 L.Ed.2d 738 (1963); United States v. Arnold, Schwinn & Co., 388 U.S. 365, 87 S.Ct. 1856, 18 L.Ed.2d 1249 (1967); and Conti-

nental T. V., Inc. v. GTE Sylvania Inc., 433 U.S. 36, 97 S.Ct. 2549, 53 L.Ed.2d 568 (1977).

4. R. BORK, THE ANTITRUST PARADOX: A POLICY AT WAR WITH ITSELF 288–98 (1978); Posner, *The Rule of Reason and the Economic Approach: Reflections on the* Sylvania *Decision*, 45 U. CHI. L. REV. 1 (1977); Easterbrook, *supra* note 1, at 156–57.

5. Continental T. V., Inc. v. GTE Sylvania Inc., 433 U.S. 36, 97 S.Ct. 2549, 53 L.Ed.2d 568 (1977).

been in disarray.[6] Although incomplete, the Chicago view has contributed substantially and constructively to the evolving debate.

Chicago theorists stress the procompetitive benefits of distribution restraints and the costs of antitrust intervention as arguments for laissez-faire. Producers want distribution restraints because they are an effective method of winning and maintaining dealer loyalty at relatively low cost to producers. The Chicago view is that by enhancing brand promotion, such restraints increase competition among producers (interbrand competition). A premise of Chicago thinking has been that producers will act in a manner that protects consumer interests. Producers that want to maximize sales at any given producer price have no interest, it is argued, in protecting downstream participants so that they can charge higher retail prices that will lessen consumer demand. If producers countenance higher downstream prices, it must be because these markups pay for marketing services by retailers that consumers value. Taking this logic one step further, some Chicago theorists argue that any distribution restraint that increases output should be presumed procompetitive.[7] The higher output is said to indicate that consumers value the product with added promotional services, even if the price is higher. Other literature defending the use of distribution restraints has argued that the buyer surcharges occasioned by such restraints serve to prevent free-riding on full-service retailers,[8] are a needed payment used in tandem with contract provisions to ensure that dealer services are provided,[9] or are a method of inventory control that allows a manufacturer to deal more efficiently with demand uncertainty.[10]

6.1a2. Transaction Cost Benefits

An alternative or supplement to the Chicago theory that deserves separate mention is the transaction cost approach popularized in the economic writings of Williamson. Transaction cost analysis has evolved from the theory of the firm, which seeks to explain organizational choices by examining the relative efficiencies of organizational forms. Under this view, vertical integration, franchising or distribution restraints are organizational options, each to be chosen when it maximizes efficiency benefits for the firm. Thus, for Williamson, the key to under-

---

6. Burns, *Vertical Restraints, Efficiency, and the Real World*, 62 FORDHAM L. REV. 597, 604 (1993)(describing pre-*Sylvania* Supreme Court holdings as achieving a "wobbly, sometimes inconsistent, accommodation of competing interests").

7. BORK, *supra* note 4, at 295–96; Posner, supra note 4, at 18–19; Easterbrook, *supra* note 1, at 154.

8. The free-rider argument is widely attributed to Telser, *Why Should Manufacturers Want Free Trade?*, 3 J.L. & ECON. 86 (1960). Such arguments can be traced to Brandeis and Holmes. Grimes, *The Seven Myths of Vertical Price Fixing: The Politics*

and Economics of a Century–Long Debate, 21 SW. U. L. REV. 1285, 1295–96 (1992). For recent and expanded interpretations of the free-rider rationale, see Marvel, *The Resale Price Maintenance Controversy: Beyond the Conventional Wisdom,* 63 ANTITRUST L.J. 59, 62–73 (1994); Klein, *Distribution Restrictions Operate By Creating Dealer Profits: Explaining the Use of Maximum Resale Price Maintenance in* State Oil v. Khan, 7 S.CT. ECON.REV. 1 (1999).

9. Klein & Murphy, *Vertical Restraints as Contract Enforcement Mechanisms*, 31 J.L. & ECON. 265 (1988).

10. Marvel, *supra* note 8, at 73–77.

standing distribution restraints is their potential for saving transaction costs.[11] A firm that wants to market its products effectively may need to promote downstream marketing, a step that could require some downstream control over distributors and retailers. Forward vertical integration—the purchasing of downstream distributors and retailers—is one method of achieving this benefit. But, compared to distribution restraints, a vertically integrated firm may be less effective in controlling costs and may require greater resources for management and control.[12] The most efficient way for a producer to exert downstream control may, in some cases, be through contractual mechanisms or distribution restraints short of integration. Although Williamson supposes that distribution restraints are likely to be procompetitive, he recognizes that distribution restraints could still be harmful when associated with market power.[13]

6.1a3. Facilitating Cartel or Collusive Behavior

A third economic approach to distribution restraints focuses on their potential for facilitating cartel or collusive behavior.[14] The collusive behavior might occur at an upstream level (e.g., among producers), at a downstream level (e.g., among dealers), or at both levels. Downstream dealers have an incentive to urge the adoption of distribution restraints in order to eliminate competition with rivals (for example, by eliminating price cutting on the brand). Theorists point out that distribution restraints may in various ways facilitate such pricing coordination that

---

11. Williamson, *Assessing Vertical Market Restrictions: Antitrust Ramifications of the Transaction Cost Approach*, 127 U. Pa. L. Rev. 953, 958–60 (1979). A Chicago theorist had a similar view. Baxter, *The Viability of Vertical Restraints Doctrine*, 75 Cal. L. Rev. 933, 947–48 (1987).

12. E.g., Kaufmann & Lafontaine, *Costs of Control: The Source of Economic Rents for McDonald's Franchisees*, 37 J.L. & Econ. 417, 447–48 (1994) (discussing reasons why McDonald's-owned retail outlets often proved less efficient than franchisee-owned outlets).

13. Williamson, *supra* note 11, at 993 (arguing that distribution restraints are of concern primarily in the case of a dominant firm or a tight oligopoly).

The Justice Department's now withdrawn 1985 Vertical Restraint Guidelines appear to have been influenced by Chicago theorists, and perhaps also by Williamson's transaction cost approach. The Guidelines used market share as a screening test, creating safe harbors if the firm or firms imposing the distribution restraint fell below certain market share thresholds. For example, the Guidelines provided that a restraint would not be challenged if it were imposed by a participant with less than 10 percent of the market, or, if more than one competing firm imposed the restraint, if their collective market share fell below a specified market share measure. Vertical Restraint Guidelines, supra note 2, at § 4.1.

14. The Supreme Court may have anticipated the collusion argument in Dr. Miles Medical Co. v. John D. Park & Sons Co., 220 U.S. 373, 31 S.Ct. 376, 55 L.Ed. 502 (1911). Although there was no allegation in *Dr. Miles* that the dealers initiated the agreements, the Court concluded that Dr. Miles could fare no better than the dealers themselves "if they formed a combination and endeavored to establish the same restrictions." Id. at 408. Collusion arguments have been refined and presented, among others, by Bowman, *The Prerequisites and Effects of Resale Price Maintenance*, 22 U. Chi. L. Rev. 825, 832–48 (1955); Pitofsky, Commentary, *In Defense of Discounters: The No–Frills Case for a* Per Se *Rule Against Vertical Price Fixing*, 71 Geo. L.J. 1487, 1490–91 (1983); and Carstensen & Dahlson, *Vertical Restraints in Beer Distribution: A Study of the Business Justifications for and Legal Analysis of Restricting Competition*, 1986 Wis. L. Rev. 1, 40–59. Collusion theories are strongest when the brand is very strong or many brands are under like restraints.

does not rise to the level of a direct price conspiracy among resellers. Widespread use of distribution restraints in an industry may also insulate producers from dealer pressure to lower producer prices because dealers will have their own relatively high margins protected by the restraints.[15] Although collusion may occasionally be facilitated by distribution restraints, it is probably not the primary motivation for imposing them.[16] Instead, producers are probably looking toward promotional gains when they impose distribution restraints. Indeed, for reasons explored later,[17] from the producer's point of view, the dealer incentive created by a distribution restraint may work more effectively when such restraints are *not* widely used in an industry. Moreover, enhanced promotion of a particular brand may increase brand differentiation, lessening the producer's incentive and ability to engage in collusive behavior. Thus, although collusion is still possible and may occur, particularly among downstream dealers seeking to avoid competition,[18] the danger from distribution restraints may come less from collusion and more from the circumstance that, as effective promotional tools, such restraints are likely to be copied by competitors. If this leads to an industry-wide pattern, the allocative harms resulting may be similar to those produced by a cartel or collusive behavior. The risk of emulation is explored more fully in § 6.3c3.

6.1a4. Benefits of Downstream Intrabrand Competition

The last of the four approaches to distribution restraints emphasizes the importance of downstream distribution to efficient allocation of vital goods and services. Both Chicago theory and the transaction cost approach view distribution restraints from the standpoint of the producer or upstream market participant. Those upstream interests are assumed to be consistent with those of the consumer. But economists as far back as Alfred Marshall recognized that competition at all levels of the

---

15. It has also been argued that producers' use of common retailers, such as supermarkets that sell multiple brands, enhances the risk of collusion. White, *Black and White Thinking in the Gray Areas of Antitrust: The Dismantling of Vertical Restraints Regulation*, 60 Geo. Wash. L. Rev. 1, 44–47 (1991). The argument is that such common retailers will act "as a buffer between different manufacturers, mitigating price competition among them." Id. at 44–45. A retailer's incentive to gain advantage by lowering prices on popular brands would be stifled by widespread use of distribution restraints. Id. at 45–46. This theory would not apply when the distribution restraint is isolated in the industry. The producer's incentive to use a common retailer as a tool for facilitating collusion would also be less forceful when consumers perceive industry brands as highly differentiated. Id. at 44–46 & n.282.

16. See Ippolito, *Resale Price Maintenance: Empirical Evidence from Litigation*,

34 J.L. & Econ. 263, 292–93 (1991)(based upon a litigation sample, concluding that collusion theories do not explain most uses of resale price maintenance).

17. See § 6.3c3.

18. An early example of downstream players colluding to control a manufacturers' distribution in a manner that would limit downstream competition is W. W. Montague & Co. v. Lowry, 193 U.S. 38, 24 S.Ct. 307, 48 L.Ed. 608 (1904). One can find similar overtones in a more recent Supreme Court case in which a dealer was allegedly expelled from a buyer's cooperative as the result of a concerted action by its rivals. Northwest Wholesale Stationers, Inc. v. Pacific Stationery & Printing Co., 472 U.S. 284, 105 S.Ct. 2613, 86 L.Ed.2d 202 (1985)(declining to apply a *per se* rule against boycotts and remanding for consideration under the rule of reason).

distribution system is beneficial to the efficient allocation of goods and services.[19] This view informs arguments that most distribution restraints are harmful and should be *per se* unlawful or at least presumptively unlawful. Arguments for per se unlawfulness, fashionable at the time of *White Motor* in 1963,[20] are now usually confined to core vertical restraints such as vertical minimum price fixing. But more recent scholarship has brought to the fore recognition that intrabrand competition provides a critical competitive check to maintain discipline on the suppliers of strong branded products. This view is also informed by recognition that retailers are not simply a passive instrument of manufacturers, but often (and increasingly with the growth of large multibrand retailers) are the controlling party in the vertical relationship. Competition among retailers, including competition for new and efficient methods of retailing, has been constant over the past 150 years and is a vital part of a free market system for distribution of goods and services. This scholarship is discussed in § 6.1d.

6.1b. The Noneconomic Arguments

Aside from the four described economic approaches to distribution restraints, there are noneconomic arguments for proscribing or permitting distribution restraints. For much of the early twentieth century, Brandeis championed the contention that retail price maintenance was needed to protect small business.[21] Another view invoked in support of distribution restraints is based on the producer's property rights.[22] An owner of a trademarked brand has a right not to sell at all, therefore, it is argued, must have a lesser and included right to sell subject to a restriction on the buyer's resale of the product. This argument has occasionally resonated in the courts. In United States v. Colgate & Co.,[23] the Supreme Court recognized the right of a seller unilaterally to refuse to deal with a customer that did not agree to comply with resale conditions. Of course, a contrary concept of property law—the right of free alienation of property duly purchased—has also been invoked by the

19. See Steiner, Sylvania *Economics—A Critique*, 60 Antitrust L.J. 41, 59 (1991) (tracing the roots of distribution economics to the early twentieth century work of Alfred Marshall).

20. White Motor Co. v. United States, 372 U.S. 253, 83 S.Ct. 696, 9 L.Ed.2d 738 (1963).
In 1949, the Department of Justice took the position that territorial and customer restrictions, like vertical price restraints, were *per se* illegal. See Rifkind, *Division of Territories, in* How to Comply with the Antitrust Laws 127–39 (Van Cise & Dunn eds., 1954). Beginning at that time and extending through 1963, there were at least sixteen Justice Department prosecutions of such activity, each ending in a consent decree that allowed the use of primary territories but prohibited the use of exclusive territories. Stewart, *Franchise or Protected*

Territory Distribution, 8 Antitrust Bull. 447, 470 n.51 (1963). The Supreme Court's 1963 decision in *White Motor* involved the first of these cases to be litigated.

21. Grimes, *supra* note 8, at 1288, 1294 (detailing Brandeis' arguments for resale price maintenance).

22. Krugman, *Soap, Cream of Wheat, and Bakeries: The Intellectual Origins of the* Colgate *Doctrine*, 65 St. John's L. Rev. 827 (1991)(suggesting that *Monsanto's* revitalization of the *Colgate* doctrine is an appropriate recognition of producer property rights). See the discussion of property law arguments in Grimes, supra note 8, at 1293–94.

23. 250 U.S. 300, 39 S.Ct. 465, 63 L.Ed. 992 (1919).

Court in decisions less favorable to distribution restraints.[24] Property law arguments on either side can easily become a smoke screen for ignoring the economic effects of use of a distribution restraint. In the distribution context, neither an absolute seller's right to refuse to deal nor an absolute buyer's right of free alienation has been recognized as a principle of property law. Unadorned, neither principle is sensitive to the many variations in economic effect produced by distribution restraints.

To some extent, these noneconomic arguments still reflect underlying economic policy choices. Protecting small business, or protecting resellers from undue restrictions on the resale of their property, may serve important economic goals, such as ensuring efficient allocation, encouraging dynamic growth in the economy, or preventing undue wealth transfer. But there are cases in which either the desire to protect an individual firm or the desire to recognize a seller's right to select customers will be inconsistent with consensus antitrust goals such as enhancing allocative efficiency.

Another noneconomic argument is that antitrust law should be sensitive to fairness to individual competitors. One theorist points out that failure to show such concern in antitrust cases may simply move reactions to unfairness to other areas of trade regulation law, such as state unfair trade laws, state laws designed to protect the interests of franchisees or dealers, or common law.[25] Under this view, pushing fairness concerns out of the antitrust sector will not eliminate them and may result in unnecessary fragmentation of the law governing distribution, with fewer national and more conflicting or inconsistent state trade law norms. At least in all cases in which other antitrust values are also implicated, fairness disputes involving trade regulation matters might more efficiently and justly be resolved under a single, comprehensive antitrust umbrella.

Consistency, clarity and sound policy results are probably all furthered by an analysis that assumes the primacy of economic goals in determining antitrust policy.[26] Given the off-setting complexities of the competing economic concerns, clarity might be enhanced by per se or presumptive rules whether in one direction or the other. Nevertheless, economic primacy creates an antitrust law that is both discernable and logically consistent. Fairness goals will, in any event, often be encompassed within economic goals. For example, antitrust may properly address elimination of an individual competitor if there is harm to allocative efficiency or the market dynamics that promise innovation and

---

24. Dr. Miles Med. Co. v. John D. Park & Sons Co., 220 U.S. 373, 404, 31 S.Ct. 376, 55 L.Ed. 502 (1911). The right of alienation argument was revived in United States v. Arnold, Schwinn & Co., 388 U.S. 365, 87 S.Ct. 1856, 18 L.Ed.2d 1249 (1967), only to be rejected summarily when the Court overturned *Schwinn*, Continental T. V., Inc. v. GTE Sylvania Inc., 433 U.S. 36, 53 n. 21, 56–57, 97 S.Ct. 2549, 53 L.Ed.2d 568 (1977).

25. Burns, supra note 6, at 600, 617–30 (exploring the adoption of fairness values in state statutes governing franchise and dealer relationships).

26. See the discussion of the goals of antitrust in § 1.5.

future economic growth. But when no such harms are demonstrated, antitrust should not be implicated.[27]

6.1c. The Emerging Economic Assessment of Distribution Restraints

One of the most prescient critics of the *Sylvania* model that sees vertical restraints through the eyes of the producer alone has been the economist Robert Steiner.[28] A key point in Steiner's writings is recognition of competition among the players in a distribution chain. Every seller, whether a provider of raw materials, a producer, a wholesaler, or a retailer, strives to maximize its profits. A producer, for example, attempts to cut the cost of input products needed for manufacture and simultaneously to raise the price charged for outputs. As Steiner recognizes, however, power within the distribution chain will affect any player's ability to affect input or output prices. A key example for Steiner is the comparison between a prominent branded item sold in the supermarket as compared to the supermarket's own house brand. The producer with a prominently branded product can command a fairly high mark up on the sale of its product to retailers. Supermarkets must carry this brand because consumers expect to find it on the shelves. Retailers must also maintain a relatively small mark up on these products because consumers may decide to shop elsewhere if their favorite brand is not competitively priced.

The tables are turned, however, when the supermarket contracts with a food producer to provide a product that will be sold under the supermarket's house brand. The supermarket chain can shop around for a food producer that will provide this product at the best possible price, usually substantially lower than the price for the well-known brand. Because of its low input costs, the supermarket can mark up its house brand much more than the branded product, and still sell it to consumers at a lower price. Steiner calls this the inverse association between markups: when the producer's mark up is high (as will occur with a prominent brand), the retailer's mark up tends to be low; when the producer's mark up is low (as will occur with contracted production of a house brand), the retailer's mark up is high.[29]

This inverse association is an example of the competition that occurs within the distributional chain. When the producer of a prominent brand sells, it is in a relative position of power allowing it to dictate terms to the downstream sellers that would not be acceptable from the purveyor

27. This view does not preclude the use of noneconomic factors as tie-breakers in close cases. Pitofsky, *The Political Content of Antitrust*, 127 U. Pa. L. Rev. 1051, 1074–75 (1979); Burns, *supra* note 6, at 650.

28. Among Steiner's key contributions to vertical restraints literature are: Robert Steiner, *The Inverse Association Between the Margins of Manufacturers and Retailers*, 8 Rev. Indus. Org. 717 (1993); Robert Steiner, *Manufacturers' Promotional Allowances, Free Riders and Vertical Restraints*, 36 Antitrust Bull. 383 (1991); Robert Steiner, *Sylvania Economics—A Critique*, 60 Antitrust L. J. 41 (1991); Robert Steiner, *The Nature of Vertical Restraints*, 30 Antitrust Bull. 143 (1985).

29. Steiner, Inverse Association, supra note 28, at 723–27, 729.

of a weak brand. That this vertical competition occurs is neither unnatural nor undesirable, but its recognition is critical to understanding both beneficial and harmful effects of vertical restraints. Understanding which party possesses the power in a vertical relationship should be a starting point for analysis of any vertical restraint.

6.1c1. The Locus of Vertically Exercised Power

When power is roughly equally distributed between an upstream and a downstream player, as in some cases involving requirements contracts or exclusive dealing,[30] many forms of abusive conduct are less likely. There are exceptions to this rule. For example, if a power buyer is dealing with oligopsonist sellers, there may be enhanced risk of non-cost-justified discounting that excludes smaller buyers. Such exceptions aside, most harmful vertical restraints will evidence a dominant player as either the supplier or the customer. Identifying the locus of this power will allow a quicker and more accurate identification of anticompetitive risks.

The *Sylvania* Court drew no distinction between vertical restraints that are a response to downstream power and those that are a response to upstream power. Although many restraints are nominally imposed by the brand-owner, the power in the vertical relationship may rest with the retailer or other downstream purchaser. Indeed, many of the most common restraints are imposed when there is a weak brand and relatively powerful downstream resellers. Faced with these realities, an insecure brand holder may consider a range of vertical restraints designed to make its product more attractive to downstream resellers. Examples include minimum resale price maintenance, location clauses or exclusive territories for dealers, or customer allocations for dealers. These restraints may or may not have substantial anticompetitive effect, but each is intended to entice downstream dealers to carry and promote the seller's product. Downstream power becomes more problematic when it is exercised by one downstream player to eliminate, or raise the costs of, a rival.

In contrast, other vertical restraints are clear examples of upstream power. Such power is exercised not to provide dealers with promotion incentives, but to enforce desirable dealer behavior (a procompetitive result) or to exploit the power advantage over a rival supplier, the downstream dealer or consumer (an anticompetitive result). Tie-ins, maximum resale price maintenance, exclusive selling (a dealer agrees to carry only the upstream seller's brand), and dual distribution are examples of restraints in which upstream power is usually present. Unfortunately, the Supreme Court has yet to explore and describe the significance of the locus of vertically exercised power. Once grasped, it is, for example, easy to understand that maximum resale price maintenance

---

30. *Cf.* Tampa Elec. Co. v. Nashville Coal Co., 365 U.S. 320, 81 S.Ct. 623, 5 L.Ed.2d 580 (1961).

and tie-ins are close cousins (and frequently arise in the same commercial relationship).[31]

Depending on the locus of power, the application of the rule of reason should proceed quite differently in vertical restraint cases.

6.1c2. Economic Analysis of Downstream Power Restraints

All *downstream power* vertical restraints limit intrabrand competition to some degree. Some may allow a new or weak brand to penetrate the market with relatively few anticompetitive effects. Some, such as exclusive territories, may substantially undermine intrabrand competition, but tend to be self-limiting; at the retail level, exclusive territories may restrict the brand-owner's access to markets and, accordingly, may be incompatible with the goal of maximum market penetration. Still others (such as resale price maintenance) threaten more comprehensive anticompetitive effects with few offsetting benefits that could not be obtained by less anticompetitive means. And some nonprice restraints (i.e., those that would eliminate or raise the costs of rivals) may have similar effects to resale price maintenance.

For *downstream power* restraints, a key issue that courts often overlook is the relative importance of intrabrand competition. Even an amateur student of marketing can perceive distinctions that suggest when intrabrand competition would be more or less important. For example, if brands are relatively undifferentiated and consumers do not demonstrate strong brand preferences, intrabrand competition may be less important. On the other hand, strong brands or highly differentiated products will create potential seller power over price. Under these circumstances, intrabrand competition arises naturally and is a healthy and needed response to maintain retail competition that allows consumers to shop for price and amenities. If particular products enjoy a monopoly, as would be the case with copyrighted books or recordings, competition among retailers is particularly important in giving consumers price alternatives and pressuring the producer to keep prices low.[32]

Intrabrand competition is vital in another less obvious but equally important way, in maintaining competition and innovation in multi-brand retailing. Efficient multi-brand retailers offer consumers one stop shopping, the ability to compare various brands (interbrand competition at the retail level), and sometimes useful advice on which product best suits a consumer's needs. A major attraction for these efficient retailers is the ability to offer a consumer's favorite brand at a discounted price, an ability that can be thwarted by certain vertical restraints (resale price

---

31. For example, in overturning the per se rule applicable to vertical maximum price fixing, the Supreme Court made no mention of the common precondition (upstream seller power) for tie-ins and maximum price fixing. *State Oil v. Khan*, 522 U.S. 3, 118 S.Ct. 275, 139 L.Ed.2d 199 (1997).

32. See the FTC analysis of the proposed consent order of May 10, 2000, available at <www.ftc.gov /os/2000/05/ mapanalysis.htm> (prohibiting five major sound recording firms from using minimum advertised prices for retail sales of compact discs).

maintenance being an obvious example). There seems little doubt that innovation and efficiency in multi-brand retailing is promoted by intra-brand competition that allows the consumer to obtain a favorite brand for less.[33]

It is also important to recognize that large multi-brand retailers that may have 10 percent or less of the retail market for a product may have substantial leverage over suppliers of even the strongest brands. This leverage exists because there are economies of scale in retailing that are difficult for an upstream firm to duplicate and because of the gatekeeper role of such multi-brand sellers. If consumers have strong loyalty to a particular retailer, that retailer will enjoy a relative power advantage over the brand seller. Should the retailer stop carrying the strong brand, both the retailer and the supplier may lose rents, but when, as will be likely if there is strong consumer loyalty to the retailer, the larger loss is suffered by the supplier, the retailer holds the power in this vertical relationship. The special power of large multi-brand retailers is discussed in § 2.7c.

Even relatively small retailers may engage in strategic conduct to raise the costs of smaller retail rivals. The key here is to recognize the local nature of the market power being exercised. Thus, Klor's v. Broadway Hale[34] presents a picture of a city-wide department store chain exercising its leverage over suppliers to disadvantage a small retail rival. Broadway–Hale probably had an insignificant share of the overall national retail market, but in the head to head neighborhood battle with its smaller rival, it held the leverage in negotiations with suppliers.

6.1c3. *Economic Analysis of Upstream Power Restraints*

An upstream seller may possess power because it is a monopolist or simply because it has long term economic relationships with dealers that make the dealers dependent on the seller. These circumstances may be demonstrated in many tie-in or vertical maximum price fixing claims. For example, in some franchising relationships, the franchisor has power over franchisees that, because of non-recoverable or sunk investments, are locked into the franchise relationship. Franchisees can be exploited by a relatively powerful franchisor in a number of ways, including the setting of low maximum resale prices or tie-ins that force the franchisee to pay supracompetitive prices for the tied product.

For *upstream power* vertical restraints, a rule of reason inquiry would usually not focus on intrabrand competition. Once the upstream power has been identified, the key consideration is whether the upstream firm is exercising its power abusively, in a manner that undermines competition. Competitive abuse by upstream sellers has long been subject to an inconsistent patchwork of laws. If that upstream abuse can be classified as tying behavior, a modified per se rule applies to the

---

33. The importance of intrabrand competition for efficient multi-brand retailing is discussed in § 6.3c2.

34. Klor's, Inc. v. Broadway–Hale Stores, Inc., 359 U.S. 207, 79 S.Ct. 705, 3 L.Ed.2d 741 (1959).

conduct. If, on the other hand, the abuse is to limit the maximum resale price of the downstream dealer, a rule of reason will apply, with substantial obstacles standing in the way of a would-be plaintiff (including the market share screening test often applied in vertical rule of reason cases). See the discussion of the law in Chapter VIII.

Buyers who are locked into a commercial relationship have had difficulty establishing Sherman 1 claims of late, whether those claims are for vertical maximum price fixing or for tying. But Eastman Kodak Co. v. Image Technical Services, Inc.[35] seems to vindicate such tie-in claims when a lock-in effect is demonstrated. Many lower courts have interpreted *Kodak* incorrectly to require that the tying seller change its policy after sale of the tying product (or, in the franchising context, that the franchisor change its policies after the franchisee has signed the franchise contract).[36] This interpretation narrows *Kodak's* application, but will still allow many franchisees to claim tying violations. Contrast this legal standard with the more onerous standard for proving unlawful maximum resale price maintenance (in many circuits, a showing that the seller has interbrand market power may be a prerequisite). Sound antitrust policy would allow a claimant to prevail against genuine anticompetitive abuse by upstream sellers, regardless of the particular form that the abuse might take.

§ 6.2 Historical Overview of Brand Marketing and Intrabrand Competition

6.2a. The Evolution of Brand Marketing

Brand merchandising has become an accepted feature of marketing. It was not always this way. Americans living in the first half of the nineteenth century—in a predominantly rural society—went to the general store to purchase generic cotton cloth and tenpenny nails as well as brandless sugar, flour and whiskey.[1] Such stores may have carried only one producer's line. Geographic dispersion of stores may have further limited consumer options. At the retail level, consumers, although surely recognizing the superiority of some suppliers' products, had limited opportunities to shop among manufacturers' lines or among shops selling the same line.

The power in nineteenth-century retailing is said to have been with wholesalers that purchased manufacturers' products and took the lead in marketing.[2] Without direct access to the buying public, a producer of a generic product had little or no leverage to raise its price. For example, if

---

35. 504 U.S. 451, 112 S.Ct. 2072, 119 L.Ed.2d 265 (1992).

36. Warren S. Grimes, *Antitrust and the Systemic Bias Against Small Business:* Kodak, *Strategic Conduct, and Leverage Theory,* 52 CASE W. RES. L. REV. 231, 272–281 (2001).

§ 6.2

1. See S. STRASSER, SATISFACTION GUARANTEED: THE MAKING OF THE AMERICAN MASS MARKET 18–19, 29–32 (1989)(describing nineteenth-century marketing patterns and the gradual evolution of brand marketing).

2. Id. at 19.

molasses is sold undifferentiated by brand, a wholesaler could search out the cheapest molasses, regardless of its source. Under such conditions, a producer may find it difficult to sell above the prevailing market price, even if it is selling a superior product.

Brand merchandising was made possible—probably inevitable—by key features of twentieth-century urban life such as an ability to mass-produce products, an efficient transportation system, and sophisticated print (and later electronic) media that transmit information on buying choices to potential customers. To escape their dependence on the wholesaler, some late-nineteenth-century manufacturers took their cue from patent and copyright holders that had marketed their products directly to the public. By using brand names and advertising to support these names, manufacturers gained direct access to the public and could charge wholesale prices reflecting the brand's newfound consumer clout.[3] Although manufacturers had begun putting their name on products as early as the 1850s,[4] the real boom in brand marketing probably began in the 1880s.[5]

The benefits of brand differentiation were substantial. Brands enable a consumer to identify easily the source of a product, increase a producer's incentives to maintain or improve product quality and features and, through the promotion associated with use of brands, expand sales to achieve large-scale, cost-efficient production and distribution.[6] But the product differentiation flowing from brand promotion, while creating strong brands that consumers preferred, also placed limits on interbrand competition. As consumer loyalty to a particular brand increases, demand for that product becomes more inelastic—consumers are willing to tolerate higher prices for that brand without switching to rivals' offerings. Even when earned through a quality product consistently satisfying consumers, this inelasticity is an indicator of market power.[7]

6.2b. The Growth of Intrabrand Competition and Efforts to Restraint It

As sellers were successful in differentiating brands, they were able to raise prices above the levels of competing products. Downstream

---

3. Id.

4. Strasser notes that the manufacturer's name was stamped on Singer sewing machines and McCormick reapers in the 1850s. Id. at 30.

5. Artemas Ward wrote in 1900: " 'It is wonderful to note the volume of package trading in food products, groceries, and patent medicines * * *. * * * Nobody ever thinks of buying liquors or wines except in bottles, showing where they come from, and who is responsible for their condition and character. The same thing is true of tobacco and cigars, of shoe polish, of baking soda, of stove blacking, of pins and needles, of sewing silk and cotton thread and hairpins.

There has been a revolution in the methods of American trade within the past twenty years.' " Id. at 29.

6. Id. at 30–31 ("By marking their products, manufacturers took responsibility for them, and therefore presumably for the conditions under which they were produced."). The economic arguments for brand marketing are also described in Steiner, *Judging the Welfare Performance of Manufacturers' Advertising*, 10(3) J. Advertising 3, 10 (1981), and Economides, *The Economics of Trademarks*, 78 Trademark Rep. 523, 525–27 (1988).

7. Market power is addressed in Chapter II.

market players responded with intrabrand competition. Such players—often retailers—saw opportunities to increase sales by offering a highly valued brand at a price that was attractive at the prevailing market level. Intrabrand competition provided a modicum of downstream discipline on prices and other competitive terms of highly valued brands. As intrabrand competition began to flourish, so too did efforts to limit it. The tandem development of intrabrand competition and distribution restraints on that competition, both tied to the aggressive promotion of branded goods, can be traced to the last quarter of the nineteenth century.[8]

When brands are highly differentiated, intrabrand competition provides a natural market response. Intrabrand competition, measured by antitrust's economic goals, is less beneficial than rigorous interbrand competition.[9] But interbrand competition recedes as brands become more differentiated—consumer demand for a particular maker's product becomes less elastic than in the absence of branded products. As this occurs, intrabrand competition becomes more important as a disciplining mechanism. Of course, one way that a producer can promote a brand distinction is through a distribution restraint. This gives rise to a paradox: the greater the success of a distribution restraint in promoting brand differentiation, the greater the potential disciplining benefits of intrabrand competition; yet distribution restraints tend to decrease intrabrand competition. Intrabrand competition is probably most important at the retail level, where the risk is highest that a supplier, perhaps under pressure from relatively powerful retailers, will seek to increase demand through means that do not enhance competition on the merits, such as through the exploitation of consumer information gaps.[10]

6.2c. The Growth of Power Retailers

Power in retailing probably always existed in local markets where competition was limited. In the nineteenth century, even if a local retailer enjoyed a monopoly power, it probably enjoyed little buying power, but instead may have been dependent on the few wholesalers that served its territory. The situation is quite different today. Large multibrand retailers with 10 percent or less of the input market may enjoy substantial buying power in relationships with suppliers. See the discussion in § 2.7c. This concern was probably a major impetus behind enactment of the Robinson Patman Act, designed to curtail or prohibit

---

8. Early instances of the use of vertical price fixing—establishing a minimum price for a dealer's resale of a product—can be traced to the 1870s. Price Maintenance, A Policy Beneficent in Results, and Worthy of the Support of All Manufacturers, Jobbers and Retailers, 1909 (remarks of R.E. Shanahan of the Bissel Carpet Sweeper Company, reporting his firm's use of resale price maintenance beginning in 1876), reprinted in *Fair Trade, Hearings Before the Subcomm. on Monopolies and Commercial Law,*

House Comm. on the Judiciary, 94th Cong., 1st Sess. 24 (1975); Bowman, *The Prerequisites and Effects of Resale Price Maintenance,* 22 U. Chi. L. Rev. 825, 826 (1955)(reporting the drug industry's organized use of resale price maintenance in 1876).

9. For example, price discrimination by the producer will be more difficult if there is active arbitrage among resellers. See the discussion of arbitrage in § 6.3a1.

10. See the discussion in § 6.3c2.

non-cost-justified discounts for such power buyers. The Act has done little to limit such discriminatory discounts, in part because of the defense for meeting competition. If the large buyer has power over one large supplier, that power will doubtless also exist with respect to rivals of the large supplier. Each can than use the other rival's offers as a defense for its own non-cost-justified discount.

Although distributional restraints law is underdeveloped in this area, a rival of the power buyer may be able to bring a vertical restraints claim based on the discriminatory non-cost-justified discount. See the discussion in § 7.5b.

§ 6.3 Downstream Power Restraints: The Competitive Effects of Intrabrand Competition

Although intrabrand competition can occur at any level of the distribution chain, it is especially important at the retail level. A key competitive strategy for a retailer is to sell a name brand at a lower price than its retail rivals. If all intrabrand competition at the retail level were stifled, competition among retailers would be severely undercut. Retailers could still compete by offering their own house brand at a lower price than a rival's house brand, but such brands may or may not be a significant presence in the overall market, and small retailers may have difficulty offering a house brand. Intrabrand competition at the retail level is most likely to be curtailed when a distribution restraint is prompted by the downstream power of a retailer; hence the importance of understanding intrabrand competition in analyzing downstream power restraints.

There are three additional preliminary observations. First, distribution restraints occur within the framework of ongoing rivalry among producers, distributors and retailers, each seeking the maximum share of the consumer dollar. An analysis of distribution restraints that assesses their impact only from the point of view of the producer, or only from the point of view of the retailer, is incomplete. Even a two-level analysis is a simplification, for distribution systems may involve many levels leading to the consumer. Yet, a two-level analysis is appropriate for most distribution restraints operating between a buyer and reseller. Second, in applying the two-level approach to a particular restraint, it is critical to identify both possible benefits (catalogued in § 6.3b) and possible harms (catalogued in § 6.3c). Only if both are identified, and their relative strength evaluated, can a balanced and sound competitive assessment be made. Third, the relative power of retailers and distributors is usually measured in the inverse relationship of markups of the two players, described in § 6.1c. As long as this inverse association holds, retailers or producers may be injured, but consumers may pay no increased price. If there is competitive injury, that injury must lie in the stifling of new entry or innovation in distribution. On the other hand, if use of a distribution restraint increases the end price charged to a consumer, the restraint may undercut efficient allocation or wealth transfer goals of competition. This might occur, for example, if the restraint facilitated parallel or oligopolistic practices, or if the restraint exploited consumer information gaps. But the result may also be procompetitive, as when the increased margin encourages and pays for the increased costs of providing valued promotional services.

6.3a.　Understanding the Benefits of Intrabrand Competition

An understanding of the potential benefits of intrabrand competition is vital to making a balanced competitive assessment of a distribution restraint that constrains that form of competition. Intrabrand competition is a downstream market response to upstream market power. The power may arise from a producer that is a classic monopolist or simply from the inelastic demand associated with brand loyalty. When a producer enjoys this power, it may tolerate or even welcome intrabrand competition as a way of limiting resale margins. Limited resale margins ensure the producer the largest share of the profit to be made from available consumer demand. Whatever benefits may flow to the producer, intrabrand competition also serves competition goals in a number of ways discussed below.

6.3a1.　The Arbitrage Function

If consumer demand is focused on a particular brand, arbitragers— those that buy for quick resale at a profit—play a key role in any market response. The producer whose brand enjoys market power may extract any monopoly rent associated with that power, but downstream players will scramble to buy and sell the product in a manner responsive to conditions in the resale market. This arbitrage role of intrabrand competition involves taking products once sold and reselling them under unshackled competitive conditions that adjust to supply and demand.

Popular usage of the word arbitrage has focused on the securities markets, where arbitrage is often associated with securities traders that buy and sell seeking short-term gain by taking advantage of apparent discrepancies between price and market value. Using information (sometimes improperly obtained) as a path to profitability, these arbitragers may bid the price of a stock up or down. Despite the potential for abuse—any market mechanism can be abused—arbitrage in the securities markets is widely recognized as a beneficial mechanism that allows the spreading of risk and brings the price of an issue into a range appropriate to the best available market information.[1] In like manner, a

---

§ 6.3

1. Booth, *The Problem with Federal Tender Offer Law*, 77 CAL. L. REV. 707, 717–18 (1989)(arguing that arbitrage helps solve information and coordination problems in connection with a tender offer); Macey et al., *Restrictions on Short Sales: An Analysis of the Uptick Rule and Its Role in View of the October 1987 Stock Market Crash*, 74 CORNELL L. REV. 799, 800 (1989)(commenting on the efficiency-enhancing role of various forms of arbitrage); Bebchuk, *Toward Undistorted Choice and Equal Treatment in Corporate Takeovers*, 98 HARV. L. REV. 1693, 1779–80 (1985)(explaining the socially beneficial role of arbitrage in enabling risk averse shareholders to sell their shares during the pen-

dealer may resell branded goods to take advantage of discrepancies in price among various buyer markets.

This arbitrage function contributes to efficient allocation of a desired brand. If a popular brand is in short supply, retailers may demand higher prices for it. For example, an automobile dealer may increase its markup above the customary level on a popular model when demand exceeds supply.[2] On the other hand, if a popular brand is in abundant supply, efficient retailers will drive down the retail margin toward the retailer's marginal cost. This mechanism will efficiently allocate the desired brand to consumers. Efficient retailers that provide the lowest consumer prices will be rewarded with more business. Consumers will benefit from the lowest possible prices on the brands they most demand.[3] This arbitrage role of intrabrand competition would operate when a producer is a monopolist, or, in a circumstance more relevant to typical distribution restraints, when the producer has succeeded in differentiating its product from the competition.

Arbitrage tends to limit the use of price discrimination. Suppliers facing inelastic demand for a product often seek to discriminate in price in order to maximize their returns. Often, the discrimination targets the less powerful or less knowledgeable buyers. Arbitrage makes it difficult for suppliers to discriminate in price because a buyer whom the supplier wishes to charge a higher price may be able to procure the product at a lower price from other buyers who have excess inventory purchased at a lower price. Suppliers may use vertical restraints in an effort to prevent or limit arbitrage and more effectively implement a price discrimination scheme.[4]

6.3a2. *Preserving Efficiency and Innovation in Retailing*

Intrabrand competition will contribute to efficient allocation among retailers. Efficient retailers that can sell the desired brand most cheaply will be rewarded with more business; less efficient retailers will tend to

---

dency of a takeover attempt); Gilson & Kraakman, *The Mechanisms of Market Efficiency*, 70 Va. L. Rev. 549, 571 (1984)(activity of arbitragers and other professional traders is an important mechanism of market efficiency).

2. This feature of arbitrage at the retail level is potentially limited by maximum price restraints imposed by upstream players.

3. Steiner's work suggests that the removal of distribution restraints on a highly demanded brand can lower the consumer price even if the producer raises its price after the restraints are removed. The producer's price hike can be more than offset by the retailer's reduced margin, a response to heightened intrabrand retail competition. Steiner, *Intrabrand Competition–Stepchild*

of Antitrust, 36 Antitrust Bull. 155, 196–97 (1991); Steiner, Sylvania *Economics–A Critique*, 60 Antitrust L.J. 41, 56 (1991). Mueller found the same result when distribution restraints on the sale of Sealy mattresses were lifted. Mueller, *The Sealy Restraints: Restrictions on Free Riding or Output?* 1989 Wis. L. Rev. 1255, 1293–96.

4. An alleged price discrimination scheme implemented through a distribution restraint is described in In re Brand Name Prescription Drugs Antitrust Litigation, 123 F.3d 599, 603 (7th Cir.1997)(Posner, J.), cert. denied, 522 U.S. 1153 & 523 U.S. 1040, 118 S.Ct. 1178 & 1336, 140 L.Ed.2d 186 & 148 (1998). See the discussion of customer allocation schemes to further price discrimination schemes in § 7.5b.

be replaced.[5] Active intrabrand competition is also inconsistent with collusion or parallel behavior among downstream players that might create market power. Even greater distribution benefits may flow from creative methods of retailing. Downstream entrepreneurs provide more than a static channel to consumers, as manufacturer-centered vertical analysis implicitly supposes. For example, over the past century, each of the following retailing methods has flourished, in some cases only to be supplanted by more efficient methods: the department store, mail order catalogues and catalogue stores, the specialty boutique, the drive-in, the supermarket, the specialty discount store, the warehouse discount store, and computerized Internet sales. Preserving entry opportunities for new retailers and new retailing approaches is a critical component to the dynamic growth of our economy. Intrabrand competition serves this goal by preserving one of the new entrant's most potent competitive tools: the ability to discount popular branded items that draw customers.

6.3a3. Upstream Benefits of Intrabrand Competition

Intrabrand competition downstream may foster upstream competitive discipline. For example, the arbitrage features of downstream intrabrand competition will make it difficult for producers exercising market power to discriminate in price. And, although the risk of producer collusion diminishes as producers differentiate their products through brand merchandising,[6] comfortable parallel pricing patterns are facilitated if producers can suppress downstream intrabrand competition. In contrast, if downstream intrabrand competition is vigorous, producers will have to compete for distribution outlets through low prices or through brand loyalty won through advertising or other information exchange.

Of course, the suppression of intrabrand competition may still serve important efficiency goals, as, for example, when the suppression fosters more effective brand promotion. These potential efficiencies are explored below in § 6.3b.

6.3a4. Reducing the Risk of Exploitation of Information Asymmetries

Intrabrand competition tends to equalize retailer margins on popular brands, lessening the risk that a multibrand retailer will have a hidden incentive to push one brand over another.[7] As described more fully in § 6.3c2, certain distribution restraints, by creating a high dealer margin that motivates promotion of the favored brand, will increase the

---

5. Interbrand competition will contribute to these allocative goals as well, but, as noted in § 6.3c3, interbrand competition becomes less effective as use of distribution restraints proliferates.

6. The same view is advanced in 2A P. AREEDA ET AL., ANTITRUST LAW: AN ANALYSIS OF ANTITRUST PRINCIPLES AND THEIR APPLICATION ¶ 404, at 13–14 (1995).

7. The benefits from this margin-equalizing tendency of intrabrand competition are explained in Grimes, *Spiff, Polish, and Consumer Demand Quality: Vertical Price Restraints Revisited*, 80 CAL. L. REV. 815, 829 n.43, 836 (1992).

risk that dealers will exploit consumer information gaps. Intrabrand competition lessens this risk because aggressive retailers will tend to discount margins that are higher than those on competing brands.

A related point is that as arbitragers of previously sold goods, independent retailers will tend to eliminate any price discrimination practiced by a producer. Systematic price discrimination is a key indicator of market power.[8] Although price discrimination may be beneficial in some applications, it can be applied to the disadvantage of less informed or less powerful buyers.[9] Retailers that can obtain favorable prices will often act as arbitragers, reselling to buyers that might otherwise be unaware of, or unable to avoid, the discrimination.[10]

6.3b. Promotional and Other Benefits from Intrabrand Distribution Restraints

By limiting intrabrand competition through distribution restraints, a producer provides an incentive for a downstream player to carry and promote the producer's brand. This promotional advantage and a related benefit—enhanced inventory control for the producer—are explored in this section. Finally, this section examines a more narrowly applicable but forceful justification for some distribution restraints: as an inducement for substantial downstream investment in the producer's business.

6.3b1. Distribution Restraints as an Incentive for Promotion

The widespread use of distribution restraints suggests that they are highly effective promotional tools. Of course, they may be effective for the wrong reasons, as when they distort buying decisions.[11] Still, one can easily see the problem confronting a producer of a new or unestablished brand. The brand may offer unique advantages to buyers, yet the producer may have difficulty obtaining distributors and dealers that will carry and promote it. Indeed, even if some dealers are willing to stock the item, it may not sell without active, on-site dealer promotion. To solve this problem, a producer wishing to promote its product—and build and maintain a reliable dealer network—could choose among the following options:

—Beat the competition on price (a low price strategy could allow dealers to carry the product and still sell it at an attractive margin);

—Institute producer-sponsored advertising that will build consumer brand loyalty;

---

8. F. M. Scherer & D. Ross, Industrial Market Structure and Economic Performance 489 (3d ed. 1990); 2A Areeda et al., supra note 7, ¶ 522; R. Posner, Antitrust Law: An Economic Perspective 62–63 (1976).

9. See § 8.3c3 (discussing the use of tieins to affect price discrimination against less powerful or less informed buyers).

10. Where services are sold, intrabrand competition will not operate as effectively to undermine discrimination because services, once performed, cannot be resold. For a discussion of the use of a distribution restraint to prevent arbitrage and foster price discrimination, see § 7.5b.

11. See the discussion in § 6.3c2.

—Send producer representatives to retail outlets to perform promotional services;

—Provide for a producer buyback of a retailer's unsold inventory, lessening the retailer's risk in carrying the brand;

—Use promotional allowances to reward retailers for any of a variety of dealer-performed promotional services, including local advertising, on-site demonstrations, or prominent displays;

—Institute a distribution restraint that ensures the dealer a high margin for selling the product;

—Establish a franchise network of retail outlets; and

—Purchase retail outlets (vertical integration).

The listed alternatives are not equals. Depending on the circumstances, some will work better than others. For example, a producer agreement to buy back the retailer's unsold inventory might reduce the dealer's risk in carrying the product, but it will not necessarily prompt the retailer to promote sales of the product. Sending a manufacturer's representative to the retail outlet would seem feasible only if the volume of sales induced by the representative's presence offsets the manufacturer's cost. Vertical integration, even through less intrusive contractual forms, can be expensive and can be less efficient than relying on owner-operated outlets.

One of the most effective vertical devices is the promotional allowance, which can be contractually tailored to require dealer performance of the services that the producer deems most critical.[12] Any promotional activity that can be rewarded through the use of distribution restraints can also be rewarded through a promotional allowance. Of course, a producer may need to monitor and enforce the dealer's provision of services to consumers, but this is true, also, if the source of the dealer's reward is a distribution restraint. Looking only at enforcement, promotional allowances tied to contractual provisions may be the superior tool for assuring performance and avoiding free-riding. Distribution restraints could operate more effectively to spur dealer performance of services if the downstream dealer carries only the producer's line (exclusive selling), as may occur with many franchisees. Under this circumstance, the success of the downstream dealer is tightly bound with its performance in selling the producer's line; the dealer has no other product to sell. But even in the franchise context, cost-cutting incentives may drive the dealer to free ride on the franchise's reputation, creating substantial monitoring costs for the franchisor.[13]

---

12. The potential advantages of promotional allowances are discussed in Steiner, *Manufacturers' Promotional Allowances, Free Riders and Vertical Restraints,* 36 ANTITRUST BULL. 383 (1991).

13. Klein & Saft, *The Law and Economics of Franchise Tying Contracts,* 28 J.L. & ECON. 345, 349–51 (1985).

Notwithstanding judicial recognition of the free-rider justification,[14] most distribution restraints cannot be justified as a tool for eliminating free-riding. Unless a distribution restraint ends all intrabrand competition (as would occur with an airtight exclusive territory), a rival retailer may simply pocket the added margin without providing the hoped for services. Dealers need have no free-riding concern on postsale services (because dealers may charge for such services). Dealers also have a built-in incentive to provide many presale amenities because they translate directly into increased sales. For example, features such as attractive shelf displays and courteous sales staff will be provided by most retailers regardless of whether a distribution restraint is imposed. If a retailer chooses not to provide these amenities, use of a distribution restraint, unless tied to contractual commitments, will not assure any change in the retailer's performance.[15] Indeed, if retailers can survive without such amenities, the market evidence is that some consumers both discover the product without retailer promotions and value the product in its core form; these are the consumers who might be closed out (and who would certainly not choose to pay for services or enticements of no value to them) if restraints drove such retailers out of the market.

If most distribution restraints do not ensure the elimination of free-riding, why are they used? A distribution restraint can purchase dealer loyalty and performance, reflected in the dealer's decision to carry a particular brand, to display it prominently in the store, or to provide encouraging sales advice to customers. Vertical restraints can be attractive to any upstream seller, particularly sellers of weak brands that are not in a position to dictate to downstream dealers. And the very lack of monitoring associated with many distribution restraints may make them attractive to some retailers. The retailer may chose its own methods to promote the manufacturer's brand, perhaps using means that the manufacturer does not know (and may not approve). Further, the distribution restraint can pass the risk and cost burden for promotion to the retailer (that in turn can pass it to the consumer in the form of a higher price). For example, without lowering its price to the retailer, the producer, by guaranteeing the retailer a higher margin, may induce the retailer to work harder at selling the producer's brand. The higher overall price (including the cost of the promotion) is then paid by the consumer.

A manufacturer's cost in underwriting the promotion on an unestablished brand could be substantial. For a small firm lacking deep pockets

---

14. The Supreme Court has approvingly acknowledged the free-rider argument in Continental T. V., Inc. v. GTE Sylvania Inc., 433 U.S. 36, 55, 97 S.Ct. 2549, 53 L.Ed.2d 568 (1977), and Business Electronics Corp. v. Sharp Electronics Corp., 485 U.S. 717, 728, 731, 108 S.Ct. 1515, 99 L.Ed.2d 808 (1988).

15. Grimes, *Vertical Price Restraints*, supra note 7, at 841 & n.77. Klein and Murphy also argue that distribution restraints, by themselves, will not necessarily induce better dealer services. Klein & Murphy, *Vertical Restraints as Contract Enforcement Mechanisms*, 31 J.L. & ECON. 265, 266 (1988) ("retailers may merely take the additional money created by the vertical restraint and continue to free ride"). But see Marvel, *The Resale Price Maintenance Controversy: Beyond the Conventional Wisdom*, 63 ANTITRUST L.J. 59, 62–73 (1994)(arguing that the free-rider defense should be interpreted as a broader promotional services defense).

and the financial standing to raise capital, the distribution restraint may be the only readily available option for supporting the promotion. A capital-starved entrant could use the distribution restraint to pass some of the promotional risks to dealers, in effect making them joint venturers in the marketing of the new product. This factual setting presents a strong case for use of a distribution restraint because anticompetitive risks are low and alternative promotional techniques may be unattractive or unavailable. In this instance, the distribution restraint is not an exercise in downstream retailer power, but an unencumbered decision by an upstream supplier to use the restraint as a promotion tool. But as the supplier succeeds in building a stronger brand image, intrabrand competition becomes more important in providing this preferred brand at a competitive price. The risk of an abusive exercise of downstream retailer power is increased.

6.3b2.　*Distribution Restraints as an Incentive for Maintaining Inventory*

There is a corollary to the general proposition that distribution restraints create dealer incentives to stock and promote a brand: Such restraints can also provide a valuable tool for ensuring that retailers maintain a constant inventory of the producer's brand. A retailer might be reluctant to stock the brand because of seasonal demand, demand that cannot be anticipated (as in the case of a new product), or price discounting that undercuts the retailer's margin.[16]

Consider a product such as ice skates, where the demand tends to fluctuate predictably based on the season. A retailer's incentive not to forego sales opportunities may resolve the inventory problem without use of a distribution restraint. Where demand is less predictable, the unwillingness of a dealer to stock an item might be addressed through alternatives to distribution restraints, such as a promotional allowance or a commitment to repurchase a dealer's unsold inventory.[17] These alternatives require the producer to bear more of the risk of unsuccessful promotion, but they preserve the benefits of intrabrand retail competition.

It can be argued that distribution restraints are, in general, the most efficient and least anticompetitive way to achieve the promotional goals of the producer, as evidenced by their widespread use in the marketplace.[18] Alternatives to distribution restraints, in this view, may

---

16. Marvel, *supra* note 15, at 73–77. Brandeis anticipated this argument in his 1913 essay on resale price maintenance. Grimes, *The Seven Myths of Vertical Price Fixing: The Politics and Economics of a Century–Long Debate,* 21 Sw. U. L. Rev. 1285, 1296 (1992).

17. Marvel, *supra* note 15, at 77–78. In the grocery trade, promotional allowances paid to grocery stores are called "slotting allowances, payments for what is essentially a rental of retailer shelf space." Id. at 77.

18. Id. at 77–80. Marvel is especially critical of vertical integration, which he suggests has been forced on producers and retailers as a less efficient and more anticompetitive substitute for resale price maintenance. Id. at 78–79. But the fundamental restructuring required for vertical integration, with its attendant capital requirements and monitoring problems, make it an unlikely choice as an alternative to resale price maintenance. More likely alternatives include the use of promotional allowances

occasionally be chosen because they are more efficient; the law should stand aside to let efficiency alone govern the producer's choice of promotional incentives. Antitrust proscriptions on distribution restraints may force second-best solutions on producers. But this argument rests on the premise that distribution restraints have few serious anticompetitive risks.[19] That premise may be credible for some distribution restraints, but as the analysis in the next section demonstrates, it is difficult to sustain as a blanket proposition. The nature and extent of anticompetitive effects will vary with the particular distribution restraint, as will the superior efficiency (if any) of the restraint over the next best promotional tool.

Producers may also perceive themselves as victims of a retailer's loss leader promotions—a retailer's advertisement for a well-known brand below the retailer's cost in order to bring customers into a store. The concern of some manufacturers is that such promotions by an aggressive dealer may make other dealers unwilling to stock the brand because they cannot sell it at a sufficiently high margin.[20] Resale price maintenance could be an answer to the manufacturer's problem.

The loss leader problem can easily be overstated. Even aggressive discounters are unlikely to sell high-demand goods at a loss, particularly if they are big-ticket items. Of course, a particular dealer that has efficiency advantages or that benefits from arbitrage may sell below other dealers' costs. But neither of these circumstances justifies the use of a distribution restraint to prevent below cost selling. An efficient dealer should be permitted to reap its associated gains. And a dealer benefitting from arbitrage is also exercising a natural market tool of intrabrand competition. The most likely explanation for arbitrage is that the manufacturer is selling more of its goods than consumer demand sustains (forcing some dealers to unload inventory at a loss) or is engaging in price discrimination, allowing the aggressive dealer an opportunity for reselling at a profit goods that were purchased at a lower price.[21] In either case, the problem is not beyond the supplier's resolution. If there is a temporary overabundance of the producer's brand in distribution channels, players that were forced to unload the brand at a loss will not continue to purchase it. If the problem is due to price discrimination, the producer can end (or reduce the margin of) the price discrimination. It is still possible that an aggressive discounter, while not selling at a loss, will offer to sell a popular brand at a price that makes

(with fewer anticompetitive effects and performance commitments enforced through contract law) and the use of exclusive territories (with fewer anticompetitive effects on multibrand retailing and lower monitoring costs). It is not clear that these alternatives are less efficient promotional devices than vertical price restraints that, at least in some instances, involve substantial monitoring and enforcement costs. Grimes, *Vertical Price Restraints*, *supra* note 7, at 846–48.

19. Marvel, supra note 15, at 77–80.

20. Id. at 73.

21. This is the situation, for example, with parallel imports: If the manufacturer sets a higher price for a product in one country than another, downstream players may import the good into the high-priced country at a profit, undercutting the manufacturer's established distributors.

less efficient retailers reluctant to carry the product. Although this may make rival retailers and the manufacturer unhappy, this is a beneficial result of competition. The market winners are those that respond most efficiently to consumer demand. Those that cannot meet these conditions may face lost sales or extinction, a harsh but necessary result of the competitive process.

In any event, not all manufacturers will be threatened by such discounting. Those producers with a strong brand—one that consumers will seek when they enter a multibrand retail outlet—are less likely to be threatened by discounting. Retailers will be pressured by consumer demand to carry the strong brand, even if they must do so at narrow margins. Low-cost producers are also less likely to be affected by aggressive discounting. Even if such low-cost producers have weak brands, retailers may purchase their offerings, perhaps in order to sell them as house brands at relatively high margins. Manufacturers most likely to be injured by discounting are those with weak brands that are not the most efficient producers. But even these producers are not powerless to deal with the adverse effects of discounting. They might, for example, embark on a campaign of national advertising to strengthen brand loyalty; they might pay promotional allowances to key retailers that are willing to promote their products; and they might decide to limit distribution through a system of primary or even exclusive territories. The last option involves use of a distribution restraint, but it may, for reasons discussed in § 7.5c, pose relatively few risks to competition.

6.3b3. Distribution Restraints as an Incentive for Downstream Capital Investment

A manufacturer may use a distribution restraint such as an exclusive territory as an inducement for a substantial financial investment by a dealer, as may occur in franchising. Franchising may offer substantial efficiencies because it creates a capital risk incentive for the franchisee to work hard in the interest of a common enterprise, lessening the need for, and cost of, monitoring by the manufacturer.[22] Thus, although most distribution restraints do not offer significant vertical integration benefits, some may be closely linked to such benefits. For example, territorial limitations of various types may provide important inducements to the downstream firm to invest in the business of the upstream firm and join in promoting its product. A balanced distribution restraints policy should accommodate these constructively employed restraints.

6.3c. Competitive Injury from Intrabrand Distribution Restraints

6.3c1. Costs to Innovative and Procompetitive Distribution

Imposition and enforcement of a distribution restraint can undercut innovative and procompetitive distribution. Many distribution restraints are litigated because a supplier terminates one dealer in favor of anoth-

---

22. Distribution restraints in franchising are discussed in § 8.9.

er. Terminations or threats of termination associated with use of a distribution restraint may make it more difficult for a downstream marketer to enter the market or maintain current sales levels. A distribution restraint may prevent a discounter from selling at a discount, or may prevent a downstream marketer from selling a manufacturer's line at all. Dealer terminations associated with distribution restraints that would limit competition among dealers underlay two 1980s Supreme Court cases involving vertical price restraints.[23]

Of course, such injuries to downstream competitors do not necessarily result in misallocation of resources or wealth transfer injuries of the type the antitrust laws should address. A producer may have legitimate, procompetitive reasons for terminating a distributor. In such instances, the loss incurred by the terminated distributor should not be actionable under antitrust law. The Supreme Court nonetheless has held injury to a terminated competitor to be actionable under some circumstances. In Klor's, Inc. v. Broadway–Hale Stores, Inc.,[24] the Supreme Court found that the plaintiff had stated a valid boycott claim against producers that concertedly terminated Klor's at the behest of Broadway–Hale, a Klor's retail competitor. The harm done to the single, terminated retailer would also have injured competition if Klor's was an efficient downstream competitor providing price or service options not otherwise available.

Because injuries to firms are an everyday occurrence of competition, these injuries, by themselves, do not establish an actionable antitrust violation. The phrase that antitrust protects "competition, not competitors"[25] captures this concern. But injury to a downstream competitor is nonetheless relevant to an antitrust analysis of a distribution restraint. One of the forms in which antitrust injury may occur is by making it more difficult for an efficient or innovative downstream firm to survive. As an evidentiary matter, injury to a downstream marketer may be persuasive to a court in demonstrating that this test has been met. In Klor's, for example, the tangible injury from termination of Klor's as a retailer was self-evident. What is implicit but not express in the Supreme Court's opinion is that this termination may have impaired an efficient downstream marketer.

Had Klor's not been an existing retail dealer, but merely a potential entrant denied distribution, the issue would be the same, at least theoretically. If producers refuse to sell to a potential entrant and that refusal tends to preclude efficient downstream marketing, competition is injured. But as a practical matter, the evidentiary hurdle confronting the potential entrant would be very high because its procompetitive impact on distribution would be speculative rather than established. Moreover,

23. Monsanto Co. v. Spray–Rite Serv. Corp., 465 U.S. 752, 104 S.Ct. 1464, 79 L.Ed.2d 775 (1984); Business Elecs. Corp. v. Sharp Elecs. Corp., 485 U.S. 717, 108 S.Ct. 1515, 99 L.Ed.2d 808 (1988).

24. 359 U.S. 207, 79 S.Ct. 705, 3 L.Ed.2d 741 (1959).

25. Brown Shoe Co. v. United States, 370 U.S. 294, 320, 82 S.Ct. 1502, 8 L.Ed.2d 510 (1962) (emphasis omitted).

the injury to the potential entrant would be less substantial than that suffered by a committed market participant such as Klor's.

Costs to third parties such as Klor's do not establish an injury to competition. Still, such costs are, as a practical matter, likely to be a factor in how courts resolve distribution restraint cases, if only because their presence demonstrates a tangible injury, not merely a conjectural or speculative harm. To guard against improper use of such third party harm, courts should ensure that it is connected to an injury to the competitive process, not merely a side effect of legitimate competition.

6.3c2. *Multibrand Retailing: Exploitation of Consumer Information Gaps*

With a markup-enhancing distribution restraint in place, a multibrand retailer has incentive to sell the relevant brand, steering consumers away from rival brands that offer the retailer a lower margin, even if those brands, measured by price and quality, are competitively superior. The on-site conversion of the customer creates a sort of instant brand loyalty for reasons that may be unrelated to the merits of the relevant brand.[26] A retailer's promotion may take the form of a favored display of the high-margin brand, or it may take more active forms—the retail staff may affirmatively promote the favored brand (even disparage rival products). Sales staff may be rewarded with an increased commission when they sell the favored, high-margin brand. In this sense, retail interbrand competition on the merits has now been undermined. Instead of an equal playing field, competitors that have not used the distribution restraint are at a disadvantage in selling through the multibrand retailer that now has a bias, probably hidden from consumers, to favor the high margin brand. Such practices by retailers, even if constrained by laws other than the antitrust laws, are difficult to monitor and control.[27]

The exploitation risk described above does not apply equally to all distribution restraints. It is most relevant to distribution restraints imposed by manufacturers on multibrand retailers, especially when that retailer is selling complex or image products that are typically sold with sales advice.[28] Upstream restraints that do not constrain retailers (such as exclusive territories granted to a distributor) may raise fewer information concerns because retailers, in contrast to consumers, are repeat buyers that gain sophistication. Even some distribution restraints that

---

26. Most dealers would presumably resist pushing the sale of shoddy merchandise because of concern with their reputation. But there are limits to reputation as a market-disciplining device. If the product promoted by the dealer is competitively inferior (based on quality and price) to rival products but still performs satisfactorily, the consumer may never realize that competitively superior options were available, and the dealer will suffer no reputation damage.

27. Grimes, *Vertical Price Restraints*, supra note 7, at 832 (explaining why consumer protection laws and industry self-regulation are unlikely to reach such conduct).

28. Id. at 837–38 (describing the frequency of vertical restraint cases involving complex products); Grimes, *Seven Myths*, supra note 16, at 1313 & n.149 (describing the widespread use of distribution restraints in the consumer electronics industry).

operate at the retail level are unlikely to exploit consumers. For example, creating dealers that sell one brand exclusively (as is common in retail franchising) poses fewer informational risks—consumers entering a single brand franchise outlet expect the seller to promote its brand over the competition.

Retailers are in a powerful position to promote because of their direct contact with potential buyers. Of course, misleading brand promotion is an everyday occurrence and could not be completely eliminated even if all vertical restrains were prohibited. But antitrust can take account of exploitation risks associated with distribution restraints. Buyers unaware that a multibrand retailer has self-interest in promoting a particular brand may be easy targets for the on-site promotion. Indeed, many buyers may actively solicit the advice of a salesclerk before purchasing. The higher sales generated by promotion may, as some Chicago theorists suggest, be a better allocation of society's resources because consumers are now buying a product that, given the additional information provided in the promotion, they prefer.[29] But if biased dealers exploit information gaps, consumers may end up purchasing the wrong product, or the right product at the wrong price. The allocative and wealth transfer injuries occasioned by this conduct (generally beyond the reach of traditional fraud and consumer protection remedies)[30] are common to other antitrust offenses (such as monopolization or cartelization). Preserving intrabrand competition will not end informational abuses. But as § 6.3a describes, intrabrand competition will tend to equalize retailer margins on popular brands, decreasing retailer incentives for hidden promotional biases.[31]

Justice Scalia has questioned whether misallocations prompted by exploitation of buyer information deficiencies belong in antitrust analysis.[32] Market distortions are ubiquitous. A seller may frequently be the passive beneficiary of consumer misinformation that favors the seller's brand. Antitrust has no readily evident answer to such information problems. But antitrust can and should respond to distortions when caused by conduct of a kind long within the domain of antitrust because that conduct poses other anticompetitive risks. Distortions fostered by harmful distribution restraints can be identified and deterred. These

---

29. This is the argument, for example, in Easterbrook, *Vertical Arrangements and the Rule of Reason,* 53 ANTITRUST L.J. 135, 155–56 (1984).

30. Grimes, *Vertical Price Restraints,* supra note 7, at 832.

Marvel describes the risk of consumer exploitation as an argument that resale price maintenance is "too powerful" or "works too well." Marvel, supra note 15, at 71 (emphasis omitted). The point is that certain distribution restraints, including some price restraints, will induce additional sales through noninformational or even misleading means, leading consumers to make poor competitive choices.

31. Of course, if all sellers of popular brands were to impose similar distribution restraints, higher retail margins would tend to cancel one another out, diminishing the risk of biased sales advice. But, as discussed in the next section, the cost increases occasioned by widespread use of distribution restraints would create heightened allocative and wealth transfer injuries.

32. Eastman Kodak Co. v. Image Technical Servs., Inc., 504 U.S. 451, 493–97, 112 S.Ct. 2072, 119 L.Ed.2d 265 (1992)(Scalia, J., dissenting).

distortions are not adventitious, but the result of a conscious decision by a seller to impose a distribution restraint that distorts competition.

6.3c3. *Injury from Emulation of a Distribution Restraint*

To understand the economic injury caused by the use of the distribution restraints directed to a multibrand retailer, it may be helpful to consider how competition would be distorted if a producer pays a bribe to a retailer's agent to induce the purchase of the producer's brand.[33] The bribe, just as the distribution restraint, can distort allocation by causing a retailer to stock and promote a brand that might not otherwise have been selected. An isolated allocation distortion may be modest in and of itself. But the success of a commercial bribe or distribution restraint may pressure rivals to adopt similar devices. Unlike commercial bribes, widespread use of distribution restraints in a producer industry may not significantly raise producer costs (because some distribution restraints are inexpensive to administer). But consumer prices are still likely to rise as efficient retailers are prevented from discounting and as producers fall into comfortable patterns of high-margin pricing.

Initially, a distribution restraint may be imposed by a single competitor, anxious to bolster its network of loyal dealers and provide those dealers an incentive to promote the relevant brand. But the isolation may not endure. If the distribution restraint is unsuccessful as a promotional device, it is likely to be dropped. If it is successful, rivals are pressed to copy it. Emulation can quickly bring the expanded allocative and wealth transfer injuries described here.

When most or all rivals in an industry have adopted similar distribution restraints, the retailer will have an expanded margin on all affected products, and presumably will have no disproportionate incentive to promote one over the other. It is possible that widespread use of a distribution restraint in an industry will shift the demand curve outward, increasing overall consumption of the product in question. But this is unlikely if, as would seem intuitively correct, the retailer brand promotion works primarily to shift consumers among brands and, when used by all producers, to neutralize those effects. With or without distribution restraints, retailers will push potential buyers to buy one brand or another. So a distribution restraint widely used may confer few promotional benefits to a supplier, but may be forced on that supplier in order to maintain its dealer network.[34]

---

33. When bribes paid to retail buyers are isolated, the injury to consumers may be insubstantial. The cost of the bribe may be absorbed by the manufacturer and, even if it is not, will affect only those customers who purchase the brand subject to the bribe. But commercial bribery may not be unusual. Although such bribes are illegal, they are thought to be widespread in some segments of retailing, costing consumers millions of dollars annually. WALL ST. J., Feb. 7, 1995, at A1. The CEO of Wal–Mart Stores has implemented what is said to be the toughest conflict of interest policy in the retail industry. This policy is said to be a factor in helping Wal–Mart keep costs down. Id.

34. For a discussion of the welfare effects of industrywide use of a distribution restraint, see Scherer, *The Economics of Vertical Restraints*, 52 ANTITRUST L.J. 687, 702–04 (1983).

Indeed, when manufacturers in an industry that sell through multibrand outlets are all using restraints that increase dealer margin, these manufacturers are caught up in a market failure of their own making, much as were grocery chains when all offered loyalty stamps that could be redeemed for merchandise. All are using a marketing device that raises costs, and thus prices to consumers, leading to lower aggregate industry output. Although the device is of no competitive advantage when all rivals are using it, none can risk a unilateral move to abandon it.

The more effective a restraint is in diverting buyers to the favored brand, the greater the incentive other dealers will have to copy that restraint. The greatest risk of emulation may occur when a restraint exploits consumer information gaps. For example, when retail price maintenance is imposed on multibrand retailers selling a complex product, the risk of exploitation is high because consumers will likely seek the advice of sales staff—not knowing their hidden incentives. On the other hand, some distribution restraints pose fewer risks of emulation. For example, granting a multibrand retailer exclusive rights to sell a particular brand may create incentives for exploiting information asymmetries, but it may also limit output of the relevant brand and present less of a threat to competing producers. Market structure may also affect the risk of emulation. If strong brands dominate the market, the imposition of a distribution restraint by a marginal producer is less likely to be imitated.

6.3c4. *Injury from Higher Prices to the Inframarginal Consumer*

Some theorists point out that distribution restraints raise the costs of products and services to the inframarginal consumer—a consumer who would have purchased the product without the promotion and does not desire to pay the surcharge to cover the costs of the distribution restraint. The inframarginal consumer is denied the choice of purchasing a lower cost, unpromoted version of the brand.[35] Others dispute the premise of this reasoning, suggesting that distribution restraints may not raise the price of goods. Under this view, although the retailer's margin is increased, the demand for the affected brand will decline if its end price is increased, forcing the manufacturer to lower its price to the retailer sufficiently to offset the increase in the dealer's margin.[36]

In some cases, it is possible that the use of a vertical price restraint may be associated with a reduced producer price.[37] But the assumption

---

35. Comanor, *Vertical Price–Fixing, Vertical Market Restrictions, and the New Antitrust Policy*, 98 Harv. L. Rev. 983, 990–1000 (1985); Scherer & Ross, supra note 8, at 547–48. The inframarginal consumer argument is favorably cited in National Association of Attorneys General, Vertical Restraints Guidelines § 4.2 (March 27, 1995), *reprinted in* 4 Trade Reg. Rep. (CCH) ¶ 13,-400.

36. Marvel, *supra* note 16, at 67–69.

37. There are, for example, reported instances of a manufacturer raising its price after it was forced to drop resale price maintenance. Steiner reports an increase in producer toy prices and in the producer prices for Levi jeans following the elimination of resale price maintenance. Steiner, *Sylvania Economics, supra* note 3, at 55–58. This behavior is consistent with Marvel's

that this behavior is the norm is counterintuitive in instances in which the distribution restraint is associated with a manufacturer's premium offerings.[38] Conventional marketing wisdom holds that such lines are the most profitable for the producer. For example, one seldom sees a vertical price restraint on a low-end item for which the producer's profit is likely to be squeezed.

To be convincing, any argument that a vertical price restraint reduces consumer prices must also explain empirical evidence that prices of any given brand were higher in states that allowed resale price maintenance than in states that did not.[39] The argument must also explain why manufacturers would lower their prices on products subject to vertically imposed prices when, to do so, destroys one of the key advantages of a distribution restraint over alternative promotional tools. Distribution restraints allow a producer to pass the cost and risk of the promotion to downstream dealers. If the manufacturer lowers its price to offset the higher margin created by the distribution restraint, this advantage is lost. The manufacturer may be forced to lower its price to pay for the higher dealer margin if the product in question faces an elastic demand curve—the propensity of consumers to switch brands in the face of a small price increase. But that too is unlikely, particularly if the distribution restraint is an effective promotional tool. The promotion of a brand will tend to increase its differentiation from rival brands, making the demand curve less elastic—consumers will be less likely to switch to another brand in the face of a price increase. Even if a certain segment of price-conscious consumers cease buying an item because of a price increase occasioned by the distribution restraint, that market loss

assumption, but it is also consistent with other assumptions. For example, when resale price maintenance is abandoned, the manufacturer may raise its price in response to increased demand that is sparked by lower retail prices (because without fixed prices, retailers begin driving down retail prices). Another possible explanation for the increased producer price is that the producer wishes to discourage low-end outlets from carrying its brand in order to maintain a high-image brand. If the brand has high image, it is unlikely that the producer was selling it at a low margin. Indeed, it seems quite possible that the manufacturer raised its own price at the time it instituted resale price maintenance as a part of the high-image campaign. The use of vertical price fixing to promote the image of a brand may or may not suggest net welfare benefits. See Grimes, *Vertical Price Restraints*, *supra* note 7, at 844–46.

38. United States v. Canstar Sports USA, Inc., 1993–2 Trade Cas. (CCH) ¶ 70,-372 (D. Vt. Sept. 17, 1993)(consent decree prohibiting vertical price maintenance for high-performance ice hockey skates); see also Marvel & McCafferty, *Resale Price Maintenance and Quality Certification*, 15

Rand J. Econ. 346 (1984)(discussing the use of vertical price restraints to enhance the image of a brand).

39. Marvel attempts this explanation, arguing that producers that impose resale price maintenance wish to discriminate in prices, charging lower prices on price-fixed goods to those retailers that adhered to the pricing regimen, and higher prices to those that do not. According to Marvel, the lower prices in states that did not permit vertical price fixing might be the result of retailer-to-retailer transactions flowing from states where resale price maintenance was permitted to retailers in states where it was prohibited. Marvel, *supra* note 16, at 70. Marvel offers no empirical evidence that such price discrimination occurred. It seems more likely that any price discrimination that occurred was based on the volume of the retailers sales, not on the legal regime that was in place in a particular state. In any event, for reasons explored in the text, it seems unlikely that sellers would reduce prices to retailers as a part of a resale price maintenance scheme.

may be more than offset by new consumers won over as the result of increased retailer promotion.

Thus, distribution restraints surely do raise consumer prices in most instances, forcing the inframarginal consumer to pay more. But the inframarginal consumer will be harmed by any form of promotion, the cost of which is reflected in the final price. For example, a producer-initiated national advertising campaign will tend to raise the price a consumer pays for the promoted brand. Society tolerates such price increases because of the substantial benefits of promotion, which could lead to scale economies from increased production and distribution.[40] There is no injury to the inframarginal consumer if the increased sales occasioned by the promotion produce economies of scale that keep the consumer price down. Should harm to the inframarginal consumer be the basis for forbidding a distribution restraint, at least in instances in which there are no evident scale economies or efficiency benefits associated with the use of the restraint? Although Comanor's analysis and the policy it implies are forceful,[41] one might rationally choose not to proscribe distribution restraints based on injury to inframarginal consumers unless that injury is shown to be substantially higher than the injury caused by other methods of promotion. Such a showing would be difficult to make in the context of litigated distribution restraint cases.[42]

The debate about the inframarginal consumer focuses attention on the higher price that the consumer usually pays for items subject to distribution restraints. The higher price may not in and of itself be a ground for proscribing the restraint. But when the restraint also results in less perfect allocation of society's resources, or an increase in barriers to entry or innovation, that added cost becomes objectionable.

6.3d. Summary of Downstream Power and Intrabrand Distribution Restraints

The overall picture of distribution restraints suggests that a blanket condemnation or approval of all such restraints would be unwise. Distribution restraints are an effective way of providing downstream incentives for promoting a manufacturer's brands. And they allow a producer to transfer the risk and cost of this promotion to the downstream player. Finally, some distribution restraints may constructively promote downstream investment and risk-taking that goes beyond mere purchase of the seller's inventory. On the other hand, the promotional benefits of restraints tend to increase the producer's market power through a reduction in both intrabrand and interbrand competition. Even this double-barreled impact should be tolerated (indeed, welcomed) if the producer's increase in market power is attributable to the competitive

40. Of course, deceptive or misleading promotion is regulated under federal and state consumer protection laws.

41. Comanor, *supra* note 35.

42. It would be difficult to make a comparative showing of the costs of distribution restraints and alternate forms of brand promotion, and further show what percentage of these costs would be reflected in the consumer price.

superiority of its product or service. But, as this section has described, some distribution restraints, especially those applicable to multibrand retailers, are likely to result in exploitation of consumer information gaps. Allocative and wealth transfer injuries flow from such exploitation. And the very success of one producer that has used a distribution restraint can increase pressure on rivals to emulate it. The result can be widespread use of distribution restraints, with multiplied allocative and wealth transfer injuries and heightened barriers to entry and innovation.

§ 6.4 Upstream Power Restraints: The Nature of the Power and How It Injures Competition

When an upstream player holds the leverage in a vertical relationship, the power that the player holds may be based on monopoly or oligopoly power, with downstream buyers unable to procure the product from any competitive source. But this power may not be the common case. Instead, the downstream buyer may be bound to the upstream supplier by sunk costs that preclude the buyer from looking elsewhere for supply. Two common scenarios are evident from the litigation: consumers and other small buyers may be locked into aftermarkets for parts and services because of their sunk investment in a relatively expensive piece of original equipment; and franchisees who have a committed investment in a franchise outlet and are bound to the franchisor (or the franchisor's chosen suppliers) in purchases of required inputs. These downstream buyers may be subject to abuses from tie-ins, from exclusive dealing arrangements, or from vertical maximum price fixing.

6.4a. Lock-ins in Aftermarkets for Parts and Services

Consumers and small buyers generally are free to adjust buying decisions freely based on the competitiveness of a seller's offer. This stands in contrast to small or atomistic sellers, who are more likely to have sunk costs that may be lost if they cannot make a timely sale (See § 2.7b). Buyers, however, also may have sunk costs in a particular line that limit their freedom in making a purchase decision. Information costs can be significant. A buyer may be familiar with a particular vendor's product and reluctant to make a change. More substantial sunk costs arise if the buyer has purchased an expensive product that requires aftermarket parts or service. This gives rise to abuses that some economists label installment base opportunism. Consider a consumer that has purchased an automobile. Many of the aftermarket parts needed to repair the car may be available only through the manufacturer's dealer network at inflated prices. The car owner cannot abandon or sell the vehicle without incurring substantial costs, so demand for these parts may be inelastic, an indicator of market power. Where the manufacturer or its dealers have employed strategic conduct to enforce or extend this market power, antitrust claims may lie.

The Supreme Court dealt with tie-in and monopolization claims involving installment base opportunism in Eastman Kodak Co. v. Image

Technical Services, Inc.[1] There are natural market constraints on the extent to which a seller can abusively treat buyers that have sunk costs. For example, a seller might undermine its reputation through opportunistic conduct in the sale of aftermarket products or service, with the result that consumers will no longer wish to buy that seller's original equipment. On the other hand, if all or most sellers selling in the relevant market charge inflated prices for aftermarket parts and service, the consumer may have little choice but to acquiesce in the overcharges. See the discussion of the issues in the context of franchising claims in § 6.4c.

6.4b. Franchising Lock–Ins

Antitrust problems of all types can occur in a franchising context. The most frequently occurring ones are those related to franchisor market power arising from a continuing vertical relationship. This relational market power, described in § 2.4e2iv, gives rise to antitrust claims associated with seller power, including tie-ins, forced exclusive dealing, vertical maximum price fixing and monopolization. The nature of franchisor market power and the most frequently challenged practices arising from that market power are the central focus of this section.

Franchising plays a substantial role in the distribution of goods and services in the United States. More than one of every three dollars spent on retail transactions is said to be paid to franchisees that include car dealers, gas stations, restaurants, fast-food outlets and motels.[2] For many areas of distribution, franchising has proven an efficient choice, producing high returns and smiling faces among franchisors and franchisees alike. But the rapid growth in franchising has not been untroubled. On the darker side is the high failure rate among both franchisors and franchisees. According to one study, fewer than 25 percent of the new franchisors that began business in 1983 remained in business ten years later.[3] For franchisees, another study found that the failure rate is higher (and the rate of return lower) than for nonfranchised small businesses in comparable lines of business.[4]

Franchising is a contractual relationship, usually among firms that stand in a vertical relationship to one another. Because the choice of contractual terms is limitless, there is great variety among franchise relationships. What distinguishes franchising from other customer-supplier contracts are two pivotal features: (1) the franchisee makes a substantial investment in producing or distributing the trademarked product or service of the franchisor; and (2) the franchisor retains and

§ **6.4**

1. 504 U.S. 451, 112 S.Ct. 2072, 119 L.Ed.2d 265 (1992).

2. 1995 FRANCHISE ANNUAL H5.

3. SHANE, DIFFERENCES BETWEEN SUCCESSFUL AND UNSUCCESSFUL FRANCHISORS 15 (rev. Oct. 1, 1995) (unpublished report prepared for the Office of Advocacy, U.S. Business Administration)(noting that the high-

est failure rate for new franchisors was in the first four years after they began business).

4. BATES, SURVIVAL PATTERNS AMONG FRANCHISEE AND NONFRANCHISEE FIRMS STARTED IN 1986 AND 1987 at 3 (Feb. 1996) (unpublished report prepared for the U.S. Small Business Administration).

exercises a significant degree of control over the trademarked product and the operations of the franchisee. The franchisee may pay the franchisor a royalty usually ranging from 1 to 10 percent of gross sales of the franchisor's trademarked product.

Exclusivity of various types may be associated with franchising. The franchisee may commit to selling only the products of the franchisor. (exclusive dealing discussed in § 8.4). The franchisor may agree to limit the issuance of licenses for outlets that might compete with the franchisee, a form of exclusive territory or location clause discussed in § 7.5c.

Economists have sometimes described franchising as occupying a middle ground in a continuum of distribution forms.[5] At one end of the continuum is an ad hoc sales transaction (such as a one-time sale of a producer's goods to a dealer). At the other end is vertical integration (such as a producer's ownership and operation of its own retail outlets). Franchising contracts usually involve a continuing and close vertical relation between franchisee and franchisor that is easily distinguished from an isolated sales transaction, but also does not constitute true vertical integration (because the franchisor has little or no ownership interest in a franchised outlet).

The model of a distribution continuum is useful in highlighting certain features of franchising. It suggests, for example, that for many producers, franchising may be an intermediate choice between owning their own outlets (vertical integration) and dealing on an ad hoc basis with downstream dealers. But this intermediate position on the continuum can be misleading to the extent it suggests that a franchise contract is the equivalent of partial vertical integration. Because the franchisee risks its own capital and labor to purchase and operate the franchise outlet, the incentives that drive the franchisee's behavior are closer to those of an independent business owner than they are to those of a company manager of a vertically integrated outlet. The independent ownership of a franchise outlet creates powerful incentives for the franchisee to work tirelessly for the success of the outlet. The franchisor, however, may assert substantial control over commercial decisions of the franchisee. The franchisor's control over business assets that it does not own is a source of both competitive strength and anticompetitive risk in the franchise relationship. The franchisor may exercise this control to ensure uniform quality standards, enhancing the goodwill of the franchise and increasing the output of the franchise system. But the franchisor may also act as a disloyal agent, selfishly binding the franchisee to competition-distorting choices that threaten injury to the franchisee, to the consumer, and to efficient outside suppliers of goods and services to the franchisee.

A growing body of state and federal laws and regulations, as well as judicial decisions interpreting venerable common law principles of con-

---

5. Rubin, *The Theory of the Firm and the Structure of the Franchise Contract*, 21 J.L. & Econ. 223, 223–24 (1978); Hadfield, *Problematic Relations: Franchising and the Law of Incomplete Contracts*, 42 Stan. L. Rev. 927, 931 (1990).

tracts and torts, have evolved to deal with franchising abuses. Recent laws and regulations have sought to reduce injury to franchisee investors by mandating minimum disclosure by the franchisor before a franchise contract is signed. Thus, for example, the Federal Trade Commission's 1978 franchise rule requires such minimum disclosure.[6] Legislation in a number of states supplements this protection by requiring franchisors to provide a prospective franchisee with a Uniform Franchise Offering Circular.[7]

Although such prophylactic measures may have reduced the number and severity of misrepresentations, disputes between franchisor and franchisee have by no means been eliminated. Indeed, the separation of ownership and control is a breeding ground for conflicts, many of which end up being litigated. The antitrust claims described in § 8.9. have played a significant role in addressing potential abuses that occur in franchising. The next section examines the economics of franchising, a necessary platform for sound antitrust analysis.

6.4c. The Economics of Franchising

Courts confronting antitrust litigation of franchise claims have increasingly turned to economic analysis to better understand the competitive consequences of franchise relationships. Economic theory offers two relevant descriptions of the incentives underlying franchising behavior: (1) franchising enhances efficiencies that benefit consumers as well as both franchisors and franchisees; and (2) some franchisor gains occur through creation or exploitation of market power that can be abused to the detriment of the franchisee, upstream suppliers and downstream consumers. Franchisor abuse of market power is sometimes referred to as franchisor opportunism. These two models of franchising behavior, which are not mutually exclusive, are explored below.

6.4c1. Market Efficiency Theories

The efficiency premise is straightforward: Franchising flourishes in many areas of distribution—therefore it must be efficient. From the franchisor perspective, two potential efficiencies have been identified: (1) the ability to raise capital to build a network of dealer outlets, perhaps more quickly or at lower cost than would be possible in a vertically integrated business; and (2) the ability to harvest the entrepreneurial energy and dedication that flows from investor-owned and operated outlets.

---

6. 16 C.F.R. § 436.1 (1978).

7. According to one source, 16 states, Puerto Rico and the Virgin Islands have enacted general legislation regulating franchising. Many states have also enacted automobile dealer laws (49 states), alcoholic beverage dealer laws (30 states), petroleum dealer laws (25 states), and farm equipment dealer laws (21 states). ABA ANTITRUST SECTION: MONOGRAPH NO. 17, FRANCHISE PROTECTION: LAWS AGAINST TERMINATION AND THE ESTABLISHMENT OF ADDITIONAL FRANCHISES 16–19 (1990).

Some early analysts of franchising assumed the franchisor's primary advantage from franchising was in raising capital.[8] A small business with a successful product and/or marketing approach may lack the capital to build a dealer network. Franchising offers an alternative to raising that capital directly: Individual franchisees, attracted by the franchisor's offering and any goodwill associated with the franchise system, might put up the bulk of the capital for the dealer network. Because franchisees assume the primary risk for an outlet, finding willing franchisees for an uncertain venture may be difficult but, under some circumstances, perhaps easier than directly raising capital for an equally risky vertically integrated dealer network. The franchisor may be able to expand its operations more quickly and with less risk than through vertical integration, perhaps offering an entrepreneur expansion opportunities that would be unavailable by other means.

The primacy of the capital-raising incentive for a franchisor was challenged by Rubin,[9] who saw as a more important gain for the franchisor the harvesting of initiative and loyalty from a chain of owner-managed outlets.[10] Contrasted with employee-managed outlets, owner-managed ones may benefit from greater initiative, loyalty and dedication. A successful franchisor such as McDonald's could easily purchase and operate all of its outlets, yet has limited company-owned stores to 25 percent.[11] McDonald's apparently has documented better performance (especially among low-volume outlets), a lower turnover of managers, and significantly lower supervisory costs for franchisee-owned restaurants than for company-owned outlets.[12] Still, most franchisors own some outlets, often the most remunerative (and least risky),[13] indicating that a franchisor's desire to harvest franchisee initiative may operate most strongly in outlets that do not promise high-margin returns.

There are also substantial potential efficiency gains from the franchisee's perspective. When investing in an established franchise system, the franchisee may buy risk reduction through the trademarks, standards and associated goodwill; the franchisee may also receive training,

---

8. See the sources cited in Rubin, *The Theory of the Firm and the Structure of the Franchise Contract,* 21 J.L. & Econ. 223, 225 n.6 (1978).

9. Id. at 225–26.

10. Id. at 226–30; see also Klein & Saft, *The Law and Economics of Franchise Tying Contracts,* 28 J.L. & Econ. 345, 350 n.20 (1985) ("[T]he incentive for workers to supply effort that is not explicitly specified and measurable by the employer * * * is harnessed by franchising managements.").

11. Kaufmann & Lafontaine, *Costs of Control: The Source of Economic Rents for McDonald's Franchisees,* 37 J.L. & Econ. 417, 447–48 (1994). Apparently to bolster franchisee performance, McDonald's shuns applications from professionals, such as doctors and lawyers, and requires that franchisees give up any other job. Id. at 441.

12. Id. at 447–48. The authors do not explain what is meant by the statement that low-volume, company-owned outlets do not "do as well" as franchisee outlets. Id. The statement might mean (1) that franchisees tend to achieve greater financial success, measured by higher sales, by lower costs, or both; or (2) that franchisees are willing to operate outlets at low levels of profitability that the franchisor would not tolerate in a company-owned outlet.

13. Hadfield, *Problematic Relations: Franchising and the Law of Incomplete Contracts,* 42 Stan. L. Rev. 927, 936–37 (1990). Hadfield cites a 1971 Senate Report that found sales in 1970 in company-owned, fast-food outlets were, on average, 81 percent higher than for franchised outlets. Id. at 937 n.44.

advice and support.[14] Obtaining a franchised outlet from a reputable and successful franchisor can be a virtual guarantee of success. On the other hand, these advantages are reduced or nonexistent if the franchisor is new or, although established, has yet to win or succeed in holding substantial goodwill for its name. Indeed, more often than not, franchisees that sign up with a start-up franchisor have climbed aboard a sinking ship.[15]

6.4c1i. Benefits of Franchisor Control

One of the keys to franchising efficiency lies in the control that the franchisor exercises over the system. If a standard quality level is not maintained, consumers who have a negative experience in a single outlet may shun the entire chain.[16] The ownership incentives that drive a franchisee to be a dedicated promoter of the franchisor's product also drive the franchisee to cut costs. In pursuit of lower costs, a franchisee may attempt to benefit from the franchisor's reputation without doing its part to maintain standards. This potential free-riding activity by franchisees is thought to be most prevalent when any given franchisee outlet has few repeat customers.[17] For example, a fast-food restaurant located at a rest stop on an interstate highway may have a captive market consisting largely of travelers. Such an outlet might be able to relax its quality standards without suffering a significant loss of business, counting on franchise-loyal travelers who have not previously visited this location.

A franchisee's incentive to engage in free-riding activity at the expense of the franchise system is, however, limited. For example, a fast-food outlet offering poor quality or service may suffer a decline in its own business, regardless of the impact on the franchise system. Thus, high quality standards are consistent with both the franchisee's interest in maintaining high returns for its own outlet and the franchisor's broader interest (shared with the franchisee) in maintaining the goodwill associated with the franchisor's trademark. The franchisor's need to maintain standards may be less driven by the franchisee's incentive to engage in free riding and more by the occasional incompetent or short-sighted franchisee, whose actions injure itself as well as the franchise system more broadly.

---

14. 1995 FRANCHISE ANNUAL H4. Rubin, supra note 5, at 224, 230 (discussing the benefits obtained by the franchisee). Hadfield recites anecdotal evidence that some franchisors seek franchisees with no prior business experience. Hadfield, supra note 5, at 961–62.

15. Shane's study, which found that more than 3/4 of the studied group of new franchisors had failed within ten years, also found that new franchisors are more likely to succeed if they own and operate a minimal number of outlets before initiating franchising. SHANE, DIFFERENCES BETWEEN SUCCESSFUL AND UNSUCCESSFUL FRANCHISORS 14 (rev. Oct. 1, 1995) (unpublished report prepared for the Office of Advocacy, U.S. Small Business Administration) (franchisors that survived the first ten years owned an average of 11 outlets, compared to an average of 1 outlet for franchisors that failed during the first ten years).

16. Rubin, supra note 5, at 227–28.

17. Klein & Saft, supra note 10, at 349–51 (describing the free-rider problem).

There are also substantial negatives to the franchisor's exercise of control. Even well-motivated requirements imposed by the franchisor can stifle the franchisee's creative initiative that could benefit the franchise's reputation. For example, a franchisee may provide products or service not mandated by the franchisor that increase the customer appeal of the outlet and enhance the reputation of the system. But by far the most substantial anticompetitive risk to franchisor control is that the franchisor (like the free riding franchisee) has an inherent conflict of interest. The franchisor controls business assets that it does not own and, as described in § 6.4c1ii, may selfishly assert that control in a manner that does not protect the goodwill or intellectual property of the franchise system.

While an entrepreneur may choose franchising among organizational forms because of its efficiencies, the entrepreneur must also reckon with franchising's inefficiencies. Two potential inefficiencies are the cost of exercising control over a large number of franchisees and the cost of resolving disputes arising from these control efforts. In a vertically integrated firm, internal disputes usually do not generate expensive litigation. In contrast, franchising involves separation of ownership (the franchisee's) and control (shared between the franchisor and franchisee), an arrangement that invites disputes. Resolving them may require litigation or some other sophisticated dispute resolution mechanism.[18] The potential for conflicts is enhanced because a franchisee makes an investment in a franchise outlet with expectations based upon given market conditions, the past record of the franchisor, and the existing management of the franchisor. But all of these conditions may change. Fluctuating market conditions may dictate a change in the franchisor's offerings or market strategy. Decisions to expand the number of outlets may undercut the revenue of existing franchisees, an injury known as encroachment. See the discussion in § 8.9g2.

One way of minimizing the franchisor's cost of exercising control is through corporate franchising, in which large blocks of franchised outlets are owned and operated by a single corporate franchisee. A corporate franchisee is likely to have substantial leverage in negotiations with a franchisor, but the franchisor may view this as an acceptable trade-off for centralized contact with a single corporate entity with a record for solid performance, reducing the franchisor's burdens of communication and dispute resolution.[19] A trend toward fewer franchisees holding a

---

18. McDonald's maintains an ombudsman office to promote resolution of disputes with its franchisees. In a one-year sample of litigated franchise disputes cited in the *Antitrust & Trade Regulation Report (BNA)*(one-year period beginning July 6, 1995), the most frequently arising issues were: termination of the franchise (25 cases); transfer or renewal restrictions (13 cases); territorial or other forms of encroachment (12 cases); venue or choice of law (10 cases); franchisor-imposed system-

wide changes (7 cases); sourcing controls by the franchisor (5 cases); sale of the franchise (4 cases); and franchisor misrepresentations (4 cases).

19. Corporate franchising is not new. For example, a single corporate franchisee was reported to own 48 of the 1099 independently owned Holiday Inns in operation in December 1972. American Motor Inns, Inc. v. Holiday Inns, Inc., 521 F.2d 1230, 1235 (3d Cir.1975).

larger number of outlets may be accelerating.[20] Some of the entrepreneurial energy and efficiency of the small, owner-managed outlets may be lost when a large corporate franchisee must install management systems of its own. But a well-managed corporate franchisee may minimize this efficiency loss, and any such loss may be offset by the experience advantages and the scale economies associated with the corporate franchisee's large, multi-outlet operation, and the franchisor's reduced communication and dispute resolution burdens in dealing with the corporate franchisee.

6.4c1ii.   Control Without Ownership: The Franchisor's Incentives to Distort Competition

The franchisor's control of local franchisees without any significant ownership interest in those local outlets creates franchisor incentives to distort competition. The relational market power enjoyed by many franchisors and the systemic nature of the franchisor's incentives to abuse this power, similar to a monopolist's incentives to enrich itself through exercise of its monopoly power, are central to antitrust analysis in this area.

Although a franchisor usually invests heavily in the franchise system, it is most often the franchisee alone whose capital is invested in individual franchised outlets. But much of the control of that outlet remains in the franchisor's hands. This assignment may offer benefits in the context of franchising (see § 6.4c1i), but it runs counter to one norm of a free enterprise system: Ownership begets control. In support of this tenet, Easterbrook and Fischel make the point that "people who are backing their beliefs with cash are correct; they have every reason to avoid mistakes * * *."[21] Although directed at regulators and scholars who second-guess entrepreneurial behavior, the comment has special relevance for franchisors that have conflicting financial incentives in attempting to control the behavior of franchised outlets that they do not own.

When a franchising system operates smoothly, a franchisor works harmoniously with the franchisee to increase the outlet's returns for their mutual benefit. Typically, a franchisee pays a royalty, usually between 5 and 10 percent, on revenues from the products or services sold under the franchise name. The royalty helps to align the financial interests of the franchisor and franchisee. The more revenue flowing into the franchisee's hands, the higher the royalty earned by the franchisor.

---

20. Tannenbaum, *Broiling Pace: Chicken and Burgers Create Hot New Class: Powerful Franchisees*, Wall St. J., May 21, 1996, at A1 (noting that 5 Burger King franchisees now own 50 or more outlets and that the top 100 restaurant franchisees own about 9100 units, up from 7000 in 1992). According to the *Wall Street Journal* article, "franchisors find it speeds their growth and simplifies their work to place multiple units in the hand of * * * giants who have proved themselves. Indeed, some new franchisers shun mom-and-pop franchisees entirely."

21. F. Easterbrook & D. Fischel, The Economic Structure of Corporate Law 31 (1991).

Despite its capacity to create common incentives, the royalty cannot wholly align the financial interests of a franchisor, whose primary investment is in an upstream enterprise, and a franchisee, whose sole investment is usually in a downstream outlet. The royalty received by the franchisor is more like a commission paid to an agent that renders certain services in return for a percentage of the principal's sales. Franchisor-agents that are in a position to profit without putting additional capital of their own at risk may act in a manner that is inconsistent with the interests of their principals (the franchisees), undermining allocative efficiency and transferring wealth into the franchisor's pockets.

The royalty may be ineffective as an incentive to prevent the franchisor from imposing anticompetitive sourcing requirements on the franchisee. Consider a franchisor that requires a franchisee to purchase an input product only from a selected supplier. The franchisor may receive a rebate from this supplier based on the value of the franchisee's purchases.[22] The cost of this rebate may be passed on to the franchisee in the form of a supracompetitive price for the input product. As a buying agent for the franchisee, the franchisor should be sensitive to the franchisee's interests, but the rebate received by the franchisor can easily create a disloyal agent. The rebate may overwhelm any procompetitive incentive based on a sales royalty paid by the franchisee to the franchisor. Bear in mind that the franchisee's royalty payments are likely to be based on the franchisee's sales. The franchisee's level of sales may be unaffected, or only marginally affected, by the supracompetitive price that the franchisee must pay for the input product. So the royalty is unlikely to deter the franchisor's behavior. See the discussion of the potential anticompetitive effects of such sourcing requirements in § 8.9d1.

One of the most forceful reasons for keeping marketing decisions under the control of the primary risk-taker is that this approach will minimize corruption and related market distortions that undermine competition.[23] Shifting inventory, pricing and marketing decisions into the hands of a person who is not the primary risk-taker increases the incentives for such competition distorting conduct. But a franchisor cannot dictate any competition distorting conduct unless it has market power. The next section examines the nature and extent of the power that a franchisor may possess.

6.4c2. *Franchisor Relational Market Power*

The behavior of parties to a franchising agreement may be explained not only by the efficiencies inherent in franchising, but also by opportun-

---

22. For examples of cases in which rebates were paid, see § 8.9d1iii.

23. Although frequently overlooked, a major concern that underlay passage of the Sherman Act was the corrupting effects of monopoly power, both in the sense of distorting competition and of corrupting firm management, civil servants and legislators. See generally Letwin, *Congress and the Sherman Antitrust Law: 1887–1890*, 23 U. Chi. L. Rev. 221, 225–26 (1956).

istic behavior possible when a franchisor abuses market power. The franchisor may have market power as the result of the franchisor's dominant position among rival sellers of goods or services (the franchisor may be a monopolist). But such interbrand market power has no relevance to most cases of abuse. Indeed, most classic producer-monopolists may have little reason to set up a franchise system, preferring to allow competition in the distribution system to drive down distribution margins such that monopoly profits flow more heavily to the producer.[24] Instead, abuse of franchisees is more likely to arise when a franchisor has relational market power,[25] linked to the difficulty many franchisees have in extricating themselves from the franchise investment. This gives rise to the franchisor's power to impose costs or confer benefits in day-to-day transactions with the franchisee.

6.4c2i. *Market Power Defined as Power over Price*

As explained in § 2.2, market power is the seller's ability to raise and sustain its price above the competitive level without losing revenues that would make the price increase unprofitable. A franchisor has market power if it can, without losing substantial sales, raise a price on a good or service sold to a franchisee above the level at which an equivalent good or service is available from other suppliers.[26]

As described in § 2.4e2iv, three interrelated sources may give a franchisor relational market power over franchisees: (1) the franchisee's sunk costs (nonrecoverable fixed costs) reasonably invested in carrying the supplier's line; (2) the franchisor's ability to impose additional costs on a disfavored or terminated franchisee; and (3) a franchisor's ability to deny profitable business opportunities to a disfavored franchisee. Collectively, these features of franchising can result in the franchisor power over price, or market power over the franchisee.

Although the nuances of this economic analysis have yet to appear in a judicial opinion, the courts have long recognized the potentially coercive power of some franchising relationships. In FTC v. Texaco, Inc.,[27] the Supreme Court affirmed the FTC's holding that Texaco had

---

24. There will be exceptions. When a producer-monopolist sells a product that is most efficiently distributed through a monopolist at the distribution level, the producer-monopolist might choose franchising as a method of gaining control of distribution and minimizing the distributor's take on monopoly profits. See the discussion of successive monopoly in § 8.7d4.

For a discussion of the relation between interbrand and intrabrand competition, see § 6.3a; Steiner, *The Inverse Association Between the Margins of Manufacturers and Retailers,* 8 REV. INDUS. ORG. 717 (1993).

25. The discussion of relational market power tracks the analysis presented in Grimes, *Market Definition in Franchise An-*

titrust Claims: Relational Market Power and the Franchisor's Conflict of Interest, 67 ANTITRUST L.J. (1999). For an opposing view, see Klein, *Market Power in Franchise Cases in the Wake of Kodak: Applying Post–Contract Hold-up Analysis to Vertical Relationships,* 67 ANTITRUST L. J. (1999).

26. A franchisor's market power might also be demonstrated through its ability to force a franchisee to perform additional services without compensation, to purchase additional goods or services that the franchisee would not freely choose to purchase, or to accept a narrower margin based upon an imposed maximum resale price.

27. 393 U.S. 223, 89 S.Ct. 429, 21 L.Ed.2d 394 (1968). The FTC had success-

violated Section 5 of the Federal Trade Commission Act by designating Goodrich as the favored supplier of tires, batteries and accessories for all Texaco dealers. The Court concluded that this arrangement was "inherently coercive" to the dealers, noting that the 10 percent rebate paid by Goodrich to Texaco for all dealer purchases would have been pointless unless Texaco could effectively influence dealer purchases.[28]

In 1971, in Milsen Co. v. Southland Corp.,[29] the Seventh Circuit concluded that a franchisee could be "locked in" to its franchise contract by threats to impose additional costs on a disfavored franchisee. The plaintiff franchisees operated convenience stores subject to requirements ties and maximum resale prices imposed by the franchisor, Open Pantry. In explaining how Open Pantry used uncollected franchise fees to compel compliance by franchisees, the court said:

> The franchisor then allowed the store owners to fall farther and farther behind in their payments of franchise fees. Open Pantry tried to collect fees only when a store owner began buying a different brand of dairy products or raised the resale price above the franchisor's maximum. Open Pantry's practice in effect *locked plaintiffs into* a situation where their franchises were safe as long as they cooperated with the franchisor's merchandising program. A single deviation brought the threat that the franchise would be terminated because of the unpaid fees.[30]

As *Milsen* recognizes, a franchisor can use selectively enforced literal compliance to raise the franchisee's costs and bring home the threat of termination, a threat that is ominous because of the franchisee's fear of losing a substantial sunk investment.

Selectively enforced compliance has come up in other cases. In Blanton v. Mobil Oil Corp.,[31] service station dealers alleged that Mobil coerced them into purchases of motor oil, tires, batteries and accessories (a tie-in) and into lowering the retail price on gasoline (vertical maximum price fixing). In affirming a jury verdict for the franchisee, the Ninth Circuit gave cryptic treatment to the vertical maximum price fixing claim, but explained the nature of the franchisor's market power in its treatment of the tie-in claim. The court focused on evidence of the franchisor's arbitrary and discriminatory enforcement, recounting a dealer's testimony that, after refusing to make a large purchase of Mobil tires, "Mobil representatives made an inspection of his station and cited him for lease violations that included placement of trash in the trash enclosure, an unauthorized handle guard on the bathroom door that had been affixed to avoid vandalism, and damage to his personally owned desk."[32]

---

fully attacked a similar tie-in involving Goodyear and Atlantic. Atlantic Ref. Co. v. FTC, 381 U.S. 357, 85 S.Ct. 1498, 14 L.Ed.2d 443 (1965).

28. 393 U.S. at 229.

29. 454 F.2d 363 (7th Cir.1971).

30. Id. at 368 (emphasis added).

31. 721 F.2d 1207 (9th Cir.1983), cert. denied, 471 U.S. 1007, 105 S.Ct. 1874, 85 L.Ed.2d 166 (1985).

32. Id. at 1210–11. Other dealers testified that they were threatened with loss of

Recognition that a franchisor often has relational market power over franchisees is of course a recognition of market power confined to the franchisor's line.[33] Although some theorists have harshly criticized single brand market power, the Supreme Court in *Eastman Kodak Co. v. Image Technical Services, Inc.* expressly acknowledged that valid antitrust claims can be based on power of this kind.[34] Well before *Kodak*, venerable antitrust precedents in areas such as vertical restraints and tie-ins had established that market abuses based on a seller's power over a single brand could violate the Sherman Act. This history is summarized in § 2.4e. Criticism of single brand market power as a basis for antitrust relief persists, and is addressed in § 2.2b. The question of market definition in the franchise context is addressed in § 8.9c.

Although relational market power of the type described above may be common in many franchise relationships, the mere presence of such market power, in and of itself, is not an antitrust violation. The market power must be linked to competitively hurtful abuse, such as a harmful tie-in, coerced exclusive dealing, or vertical maximum price fixing. The market power requirement remains a meaningful screen. Market power would not be demonstrated if the seller's power over price is a short-term or ephemeral result of market conditions, such as a seasonal shortfall of a highly demanded item. A showing of market power should not be the basis of an antitrust violation if the franchisee has offsetting leverage that makes it unlikely that the defendant could effectively exercise its power. For example, the franchisor may be disciplined (and therefore lack relational market power) in transactions with a corporate franchisee that owns a large number of outlets whose success is critical to the success of the franchisor and the franchise system.

6.4c2ii. Postcontractual Nature of Franchisor Relational Market Power

Any precontractual abuse of the franchisee is likely to be based on the deception and hucksterism sometimes associated with the marketing of franchises. This is primarily a consumer protection problem not well suited to antitrust relief. The franchisee's precontractual informational problems are nonetheless relevant to postcontractual abuse claims. The franchisee is unable at the precontractual stage to engage in accurate life-cycle assessments of costs and benefits of a franchise that may endure for the business life of the investor. The impossibility of making accurate, precontractual projections explains why the precontractual market for investment opportunities is often irrelevant to postcontractual market abuses. See the discussion in § 8.9c.

their lease if they refused to buy tires or other Mobil products. Id. at 1211.

33. The concept of relational market power is not unknown in the competition laws of other countries. For example, the German competition law governing the behavior of dominant firms specifically includes in that category a business that sells to or purchases from "small or medium-sized enterprises * * * in such a way that sufficient or reasonable possibilities of resorting to other undertakings do not exist." German Act Against Restraints of Competition, Art. 20, ¶ 2.

34. 504 U.S. 451, 463–64, 112 S.Ct. 2072, 119 L.Ed.2d 265 (1992).

Once the franchisee has committed its investment to the franchise, the franchisee may be locked into the relationship by high sunk costs and by the franchisor's control over the franchisee's operating costs and benefits. Because of this lock-in, most franchisees will be disinclined to abandon their investment in the face of higher prices or squeezed resale price margins imposed by the franchisor. In contrast, an investor free of this lock-in would more quickly abandon an underperforming business in favor of a more lucrative use of its capital.

Types of potential franchisor abuse include encroachment (dilution of the franchisee's territorial market through competing outlets), misuse of advertising funds collected from franchisees, forcing the franchisee to bear the risk of expansion, innovation or the liquidation of unwanted inventory, and squeezing the franchisee's resale price margin below a competitive level. Some of these abuses may fit the parameters of traditional antitrust claims, such as tie-ins, vertical maximum price fixing, or attempted monopolization as discussed in § 8.9.

6.4c3. *Constraints on Franchisor Abuse of Market Power*

Although some franchisor leverage over franchisees is widely conceded, some theorists object to use of this leverage as a basis for antitrust intervention. Klein and Saft call the franchisor's leverage "economic power," arguing that it should not be equated with market power required for antitrust intervention.[35] Under this view, the leverage possessed by a franchisor is unlikely to be abused because the franchisor is constrained by the freedom of contract (exercised at the point any new franchisee signs a franchise contract) and, once the contract is signed, by the franchisor's need to maintain its reputation (to preserve the goodwill of current franchisees and the ability to recruit new franchisees).[36] If, as the result of antitrust or other legal constraints, the cost of franchising becomes too high, some critics argue that the franchisor will abandon an efficient organizational form in favor of vertical integration or some other less efficient organizational form, with a net allocative loss to society.[37]

---

35. Klein & Saft, supra note 3, at 357–58. The authors cite Justice Stevens' comment in *Jefferson Parish Hospital District No. 2 v. Hyde*, 466 U.S. 2, 27, 104 S.Ct. 1551, 80 L.Ed.2d 2 (1984), that a seller's power based on market imperfections "may generate market power in some abstract sense," but not the sort "that justifies condemnation of tying." Justice Stevens' remark seems inconsistent with a footnote in which he appeared to recognize the anticompetitive potential of tie-ins linked to market imperfections, id. at 15 n.24, and with the Court's subsequent and express consideration of market imperfections as a basis for market power in *Kodak*. Indeed, the Klein–Saft argument has much in common with the dissent by Justice Scalia to

Justice Blackmun's opinion for the Court in *Kodak* in which Justice Stevens joined.

36. Another theorist offering a variation on these arguments is Hay, *Is the Glass Half–Empty or Half–Full?: Reflections on the* Kodak *Case*, 62 ANTITRUST L.J. 177, 185–88 (1993).

37. Brickley et al. found evidence that states with franchise regulatory laws had a slightly higher percentage of company-owned outlets for those franchises associated with a high percentage of nonrepeat customers, but not for franchises in general. The authors concluded that these and other findings were "consistent with the model that predicts that the laws increase the costs of franchising relative to company ownership by making quality control among

The critics do not directly address franchisors' inherent incentives to exploit market power in their dealings with franchisees. See the discussion in § 6.4c2. The existence of these incentives undermines the view that franchisor exploitation of franchisees will be rare. And although a franchisee's freedom of contract and a franchisor's need to protect its reputation will mitigate or reduce the potential for franchisor abuse, for reasons discussed in the following sections, these mitigating circumstances may not fully compensate for the distorted incentives arising from an owner-franchisee's loss of control over vital business decisions.

6.4c3i. The Franchisee's Freedom to Negotiate Contractual Protection

It is argued that freedom of contract and a competitive market for franchises—a franchisee's ability to choose among many franchises—will adequately control franchisors' behavior.[38] Hay writes that "[t]here are literally thousands of franchise opportunities available to prospective investors" and disclosure laws "to help them make an informed choice."[39] There is no question that a contractual negotiation provides a meaningful tool by which experienced or well-represented franchisees might protect themselves from foreseeable risks of exploitation by franchisors possessing market power. In a world of well-informed franchisees, franchisor abuse would be less frequent.

Any person about to undertake a substantial investment in a business is likely to check into the matter with some care. Some, because of experience, knowledgeable and effective professional guidance or some economic leverage of their own, will be able to protect their own interests reasonably well. Even if a franchisee has little leverage to negotiate a contract with a particular franchisor, the franchisee can compare one franchisor's offer with others. Franchisors, anxious to recruit new franchisees, may offer attractive packages to would-be investors and may negotiate some provisions in order to win highly valued recruits. But as arguments for displacing antitrust, these contentions are overbroad. That some—even most—franchisors will be unable to overreach does not militate against appropriate remedies when some franchisors can and do.

franchises more expensive." Brickley et al., *The Economic Effects of Franchise Termination Laws*, 34 J. L. & Econ. 101, 130 (1991). The authors apparently made no attempt to study whether the state laws in question decreased franchisor opportunism and thereby rendered society a net allocative gain. Of course, it is possible that the state laws, although producing allocative gains, are heavy-handed; better laws might achieve the same or greater allocative benefits with fewer costs imposed on franchising.

38. Rubin, supra note 5, at 231–32.

39. Hay, supra note 36, at 188. Rubin states: "Arguments which rely on the ignorance of the franchisee or the bargaining-power advantage of the franchisor are as valid here as in any other context (which is to say, not very valid)." Rubin, supra note 5, at 232. Similarly Brickley et al. argues that widespread disclosure of the rates of termination and nonrenewal makes it unlikely that a franchisee would overpay in purchasing a franchise. Brickley et al., supra note 37, at 111.

Klein asserts that "[c]ontract law is superior to antitrust law" in dealing with franchisor abuses because "it explicitly takes account of the contractual environment."[40] But people negotiate contracts, not some perfectly informed automaton springing from the pages of an economic treatise. Some are experienced and informed, others not. Even a detailed and accurate disclosure document can be no better than the potential franchisee's comprehension of it.

The Supreme Court has recognized that franchisees that sign anticompetitive clauses in franchise agreements can still challenge those clauses if they demonstrate that they acceded to the clauses only to obtain a valuable business opportunity. In Perma Life Mufflers, Inc. v. International Parts Corp.,[41] franchisees in the Midas muffler system alleged unlawful distribution restraints based in part on clauses in the franchise agreement that each franchisee had signed. In explaining why their acquiescence to the agreement would not bar recovery, Justice Black wrote for the Court:

> [The franchisees] sought the franchises enthusiastically but they did not actively seek each and every clause of the agreement. Rather, many of the clauses were quite clearly detrimental to their interests, and they alleged that they had continually objected to them. [The franchisees] apparently accepted many of these restraints solely because their acquiescence was necessary to obtain an otherwise attractive business opportunity.[42]

But one need not go that far to justify well constructed franchise antitrust claims. Although the Court did not elaborate on this issue in *Perma Life,* most franchise antitrust claims involve postcontractual opportunism, often in the context of changed circumstances anticipated by neither franchisor nor franchisee. Because most franchise contracts give broad powers to the franchisor to change a business' products, service or method of doing business, the contract, rather than being a vehicle to protect the franchisee, can become a tool of oppression. Even with the best negotiating skills, a franchisee will have difficulty negotiating protections against unknown future developments. At best, a franchisee may seek to shift risks of uncertainties to the franchisor, or seek to negotiate a voice in future decisions. But these protections may be successfully resisted by franchisors that offer standard contract language on a "take it or leave it" basis.

For most franchisees, freedom of contract means the ability to pick among a variety of marginal franchise opportunities. Under these circumstances, the investor will usually choose the outlet deemed to offer the best potential return on investment. If an opportunity with a well-

40. Klein, *Market Power in Aftermarkets,* 17 MANAGERIAL & DECISION ECON. 143, 151 (1996).

41. 392 U.S. 134, 88 S.Ct. 1981, 20 L.Ed.2d 982 (1968). In Siegel v. Chicken Delight, Inc., 448 F.2d 43, 52–53 (9th Cir. 1971), cert. denied, 405 U.S. 955, 92 S.Ct. 1172, 31 L.Ed.2d 232 (1972), the court employed similar reasoning in explaining why the franchisee's signature of the franchise contract did not authorize the sourcing requirements that were the subject of the franchisee's antitrust claims.

42. *Perma Life,* 392 U.S. at 139.

established franchisor arises, there are usually many other would-be investors waiting in line to seize that opportunity. This exacerbates the "take it or leave it" bargaining climate in which the franchisee must accept the standard contract language put forward by the franchisor or risk losing the investment opportunity altogether. This reality, recognized by the Supreme Court in *Perma Life,* renders the freedom of contract principle an insubstantial protection for many franchise investors, once the unpredictable postcontractual environment is factored in.

6.4c3ii. The Franchisor's Need to Maintain Reputation

The franchisor's concern with its long-term reputation is regarded by some theorists as sufficient to force the franchisor to act in the interests of the franchisee, or at least not to tread heavily on those interests.[43] Again, the inference drawn is that antitrust remedies are not needed. The fear that a franchisor will exploit a franchisee by a threat of nonrenewal or by taking advantage of high franchisee sunk costs is overstated, in this view, because the franchisor whose reputation is tarnished must reckon with difficulties in recruiting new and replacement franchisees.[44] Most franchisors have substantial sunk costs of their own: investments in research and marketing schemes, product development or the goodwill associated with a brand name. These franchisor investments will encourage franchisors to treat their franchisees fairly, lest they lose the loyalty and commitment of their franchise network.

The market discipline afforded by the franchisor's need to maintain reputation is real, but its significance, too, can be overstated. Reputation is a far less direct incentive for maintaining competitive conduct than is the direct discipline of competition. A seller may lose the bulk of its market if its price is 10 percent above the prevailing market level. But forcing the sale of an input product to the franchisee at 10 percent above the prevailing market level may have little or no impact on the franchisor's royalty. Franchisees may be forced to absorb the part of the higher cost they cannot pass along to their customers. The franchisor's reputation with its franchisees will suffer. But this loss of reputation hardly replaces the direct discipline on the input supplier market that a franchisee can exercise if it is free to cast off an inadequately performing supplier. The franchisor, which may be under pressure from stockholders to increase its profits, often receives a direct rebate by forcing franchisees to pay more for an input product and this gain may more than offset any concern the franchisor has with its diminished reputation.

43. The analysis in this subsection tracks closely that presented in Grimes, *When Do Franchisors Have Market Power? Antitrust Remedies for Franchisor Opportunism,* 65 Antitrust L. J. 105, 129–36 (1996).

44. A "franchisor is not likely to terminate franchisees merely to confiscate their sunk investments opportunistically because franchisors must be concerned about their reputations when attempting to sell additional franchise locations." Klein & Saft, supra note 10, at 356. Other theorists taking a similar position include Epstein, *Unconscionability: A Critical Reappraisal,* 18 J.L. & Econ. 293, 315 (1975), and Lockerby, *Franchise Termination Restrictions: A Guide for Practitioners and Policy Makers,* 30 Antitrust Bull. 791, 846, 859–60 (1985).

To put the significance of reputation into perspective, consider the likely response of a vertically integrated company to signals that shoddy performance is damaging its reputation. Beginning in the 1960s, U.S. automobile manufacturers responded lethargically when many consumers began purchasing foreign-made automobiles. Compared to automobile manufacturers, most franchisors may be in a line of business that requires a more supple competitive response to survive changing market conditions. But the risk incentive that drives a franchisor is less powerful than that driving a vertically integrated company. A vertically integrated firm risks its own capital by damaging its reputation. In contrast, a franchisor is gambling to a substantial degree with the franchisee's money.[45] The franchisor's reputation *will* suffer if many franchisees fail. But, when compared with a vertically integrated firm, the smaller percentage of capital at risk will make a franchisor less responsive to the indirect injury from a franchisee's poor performance or failure.

As addressed below, there are several recurrent circumstances linked to franchising that can further dampen the disciplining effect of reputational losses.[46]

The Myth of High Profitability—A myth of high profitability may surround franchising, or a particular type of franchising, that leads inexperienced investors to misapprehend their investment prospects. This myth may be propagated, sustained or reinforced by the franchisor's own marketing. Franchise investments have paid off handsomely for many soft drink bottlers, beer distributors, car dealers and gas station operators.[47] But the rainbow myth, fostered in part by franchisor salesmanship,[48] has, at best, brought meager returns for the bulk of investors. Most new franchise outlets are in areas of marginal return, with high failure rates. The least successful 90 percent of franchising systems are said to share only 26 cents out of every $1 of franchise sales.[49]

---

45. Franchise investments may be most risky when the franchisor has invested little or no capital of its own in downstream outlets. This is consistent with Shane's finding that new franchisors are more likely to fail if they own no outlets, or only a small number of outlets. Shane, supra note 15, at 14.

46. This list is illustrative, and may omit other circumstances under which a franchisor might behave opportunistically. In this discussion of the limits of reputational discipline, we borrow extensively from Borenstein et al., *Antitrust Policy in Aftermarkets*, 63 Antitrust L.J. 455 (1995). The Borenstein paper discusses reasons why reputation will not constrain a supplier that has control over aftermarkets for replacement parts or service. For an opposing view, see Shapiro, *Aftermarkets and Consumer Welfare: Making Sense of* Kodak, 63 Antitrust L.J. 483 (1995).

47. Serwer, *Trouble in Franchise Nation*, Fortune, Mar. 6, 1995, at 115, 116.

48. For example, the 1995 Franchise Annual, supra note 2, at H4, boasts that franchisees buy "risk reduction." In light of statistics showing that franchisees fail at a rate at or above that for small business generally, that statement should be viewed skeptically. See the discussion of failure rates in § 6.4c1.

49. *Franchise Nation*, supra note 47, at 116. The same source quotes Ann Dugan, the Director of the Small Business Development Center at the University of Pittsburgh: " 'Most people think of franchising as some kind of bonanza[.] * * * The reality today is if you get a solid operation, work damn hard, and you're making $40,000 a year after four years, that's good.' " Id.

An investor's options to choose among franchise offerings will be limited if a threshold level of franchisor opportunism is endemic in franchising, or at least in those segments of franchising open to the novice investor. Over time, and with the help of mandated franchisor disclosure, the "gold mine" myth of franchising may be gradually debunked. But the myth still retains power. Even the most detailed and accurate disclosure may be pushed aside by investors prone to believe the franchisor's undocumented predictions of future riches. As one observer puts it, "as the litany of franchisor abuses has mounted, franchising observers have come to recognize that the danger of abuse is inherent in the structure of franchising."[50]

Countering Reputational Damage by Lowering the Franchise Fee- Even if the franchisor is confronting reputational damage that may undermine its ability to recruit new franchisees, the franchisor might counter this loss of reputation by lowering its franchise and royalty fees, the payments made to obtain and maintain a license to operate an outlet. If the market works well, these fees would be discounted by an amount that compensates a new franchisee for the full value of the franchisee's future lost rents as a result of franchisor opportunism. Of course, neither party to a franchise contract can know in advance what the future rent losses might be, but by lowering the initial franchise fee sufficiently, a franchisor should be able to offset a degree of reputational damage.[51] The franchisor might accept a lower franchise fee in return for shifting market risks for unanticipated future events to the franchisee.[52]

One can argue that there is little damage to efficient allocation if high opportunism costs are offset by low franchise fees.[53] Of course, there is damage to current franchisees that did not benefit from the low fees charged to new franchisees. And all generations of franchisees end up bearing much of the risk of the franchisor's loss of reputation. If the franchisor's exploitative behavior toward franchisees drives down the market value of franchise outlets, it is the franchisee that must bear this

---

50. Hadfield, supra note13, at 969.

51. If a franchisor has acted with total disregard for its franchisees, no lowering of the franchise fee could offset this damage. Legitimate franchisors are unlikely to engage in such suicidal behavior, but might well engage in more limited forms of opportunistic behavior.

52. There is some evidence that franchisors discount franchise and royalty fees. Kaufmann and Lafontaine studied the McDonald's franchise system and found that the franchisee's fee is substantially less than the present value of projected rents that will flow from the operation of the outlet. Kaufmann & Lafontaine, supra note 11, at 427–31. These low fees may well, as the authors deduce, provide a valuable economic incentive for franchisees to dedicate their continuing energies to the franchise, knowing that rents are to be won based on

the discounted franchise fee. But this thesis is by no means inconsistent with the use of low fees to offset the franchisor's reputational damage.

Subway, one of the more successful franchisors of the 1980s, generated adverse publicity for its relatively high failure rate, the minimal returns earned by many franchisees, and its shortcomings in providing advice on the location of franchisees. Marsh, *Franchise Realities*, WALL ST. J., Sept. 16, 1992, at A1. Yet Subway expanded very rapidly, apparently with the help of low, upfront starting costs (the franchisor reportedly charged an investor only $10,000 to start a new Subway outlet). Id.

53. Klein makes a similar argument with respect to the sale of original equipment and aftermarket products or services. Klein, supra note 40, at 151–53.

loss when the franchise is sold at a lower price. Indeed, if the franchisor has control over the identity of the purchaser and the terms of the sale, the franchisor may force the price below market value, thus easing the task of marketing the franchise at the expense of the departing franchisee.

In a world of perfect information, newly investing franchisees might adjust their offering price to account for these exploitation risks. But many prospective franchisees, excited to be undertaking a new venture, may find it difficult to focus on the terms of a withdrawal from the business that they may regard as a distant prospect. Even if the franchisee adjusts the offering price to account for these risks, allocative injury is likely. High prices for goods and services forced on a franchisee may result in higher consumer prices or reduced offerings of services that consumers might prefer.[54] If prices for opening a franchise are too low, this may increase the proliferation of franchised outlets beyond the point of efficient allocation, particularly among less savvy investors that do not adequately weigh the lost future rents against the low franchise fee.[55]

Targeting Less Informed Franchisees—The franchisor can also avoid the impact of reputational damage by targeting the sale of future franchises to less informed investors. If all investors perceived a high level of opportunism in franchising, franchising might cease altogether. On the other hand, as long as a significant percentage of potential franchisees perceive franchising as a positive form of investment, the franchisors can continue to market new franchises successfully. A successful marketing strategy may well involve the targeting of unsophisticated investors that are less likely to be aware of information suggesting widespread franchisor opportunism.[56] Indeed, advertising by some new franchisors overtly zeros in on investors most likely to accept myths about franchising and least likely to protect themselves contractually. The opening appeal is: "own your own business; no experience necessary; we'll provide all the help you need."

If such behavior is widespread or extreme, it will damage the franchisor's reputation. But discrimination carefully practiced may bring little or no reputational damage. If a high risk location fails, the franchisor can gloss over the failure by pointing to the unfavorable location or to the franchisee's deficiencies. Even a well-motivated and

---

54. If the franchisee is operating in a competitive market, consumers would presumably shun the franchisee's offerings if prices were increased. But the vigor of interbrand competition will vary and may be substantially dampened by heavy brand promotion associated with many franchise offerings, increasing the likelihood that the higher cost will be passed on to consumers.

55. This may have occurred with Subway franchisees. See *Franchise Realities*,

supra note 52 (discussing failures and low profitability among Subway franchisees). For a parallel analysis of distorted allocation in the aftermarket context, see Borenstein et al., supra note 46, at 469–73.

56. Hadfield, supra note 13, at 961–63 (discussing the propensity of some franchisors to recruit relatively inexperienced investors).

careful investor may have difficulty learning the real reasons for failed outlets.

Targeted discrimination will not end after the franchise contract is signed. In the day-to-day interaction of franchisor and franchisee, there are countless ways that a franchisor may exploit the less knowledgeable or more vulnerable franchisee. The franchisor may pressure a particular franchisee to take excess inventory off the franchisor's hands, bear disproportionate costs of promotion, or bear disproportionate risk of experimentation on a new product. Most franchisors may try to be evenhanded in assigning burdens and benefits to franchisees. But the rules for these assignments are generally within the franchisor's discretion, and frequently subject to more than one interpretation. For example, a franchise located on the fringe of a metropolitan area might be expected to bear its full share of an area promotional campaign notwithstanding a customer base less likely to be reached by the campaign.

Short–Term Franchisor Perspective—The franchisor may also have a short-term perspective that leads it to disregard any reputational damage. In the extreme, a would-be franchisor might be a con artist who collects a down payment on a franchise and disappears. Under less extreme and more likely circumstances, the franchisor may be earning large fees through a program of accelerated franchise growth, a circumstance that might lead it to disregard concerns about long-term reputation.[57] A start-up franchisor, anxious to gain momentum, may discount long-term reputational concerns in favor of action to promote short-term growth, such as deceptively optimistic growth projections offered as a part of a franchise promotion. A rational franchisor facing declining demand might exploit current franchisees to a greater degree because the franchisor anticipates a reduced need to recruit new franchisees.[58] Even more extreme behavior by the franchisor might be anticipated if the franchisor is confronting business failure, as often occurs with start-up franchisors. Under such circumstances, the franchisor may disregard long-term reputation in an effort to stay solvent in the short term.

Management Miscalculation—The franchisor may simply misapprehend the extent of reputational damage as a result of a management error. Well-meaning but mistaken behavior by franchisors might be more common among start-up franchisors that make generous but unrealistic promises to potential franchisees. Such behavior might also be expected if a franchisor achieves initial success in prime locations and,

---

57. The Subway franchisor, one of the most rapid growing of the 1990s, earned a $10,000 fee each time a new outlet was opened. Although the accelerated growth in Subway franchisees is said to have caused many problems, *Franchise Realities*, supra note 52, the franchisor may have discounted reputational concerns in favor of the short-term earnings from new outlets.

58. Borenstein et al., supra note 39, at 465–67 (discussing financial incentives of a producer to raise aftermarket prices in the face of declining demand for the producer's original equipment); see also Klein, supra note 40, at 149 (describing an original equipment seller's incentive to "hold up" the buyer by charging a high price on aftermarket parts when an unanticipated event makes the franchisor's original pricing strategy less profitable).

bolstered by this success, overestimates the potential for less promising locations. Of course, left on this course, such practices could bring self-destruction. The irrational behavior of a business is generally not the concern of competition policy (the competitive process, not the survival of individual firms, is the proper goal of antitrust). But irrational behavior by a franchisor affects not only the franchisor's own survival; it threatens a misallocation of capital and serious economic injury or insolvency to a large class of franchisees.

Management miscalculation is probably less a concern in isolation than in combination with other franchisor incentives for disregarding reputation. A franchisor with a substantial incentive to act opportunistically may do so in part because it has miscalculated the reputational damage, but also for other reasons, such as that it is in financial difficulty, that it can limit the extent of reputational damage through discriminatory targeting of its opportunistic actions, or that it can entice future franchisees with discounted franchise fees.

Chapter VII

DISTRIBUTION RESTRAINTS BASED ON DOWNSTREAM POWER: VERTICAL MINIMUM PRICE AND OTHER DISTRIBUTION RESTRAINTS

Table of Sections

---

§ 7.1   Introduction

This chapter addresses distribution restraints that benefit down-stream players, often retailers. Although these downstream power restraints may be imposed by upstream suppliers, they are imposed in response to the relative position of power enjoyed by the downstream player. In most of these cases, the power that is wielded by the downstream player is buyer power, as described in § 2.7. Consider the supplier's imposition of a minimum retail price, known as minimum vertical price fixing or resale price maintenance. The supplier has an interest in maximizing its sales to all sorts of retailers whether they be no-frills discounters or full-service, higher priced dealers. If the supplier's product is in demand, all retailers will want to carry it, so the supplier may be able to sell its product and let the downstream retailers resell at a any price they wish. Not all suppliers, however, are in this enviable position. If the supplier faces difficulty in finding retailers who will carry and promote its product, the supplier may be forced to offer incentives to retailers. One type of incentive is a guaranteed minimum retail price that will offer dealers an incentive to carry and promote the supplier's product. When this occurs, a retailer is in a relative position of power and exercises buyer power over the supplier. The retailer may pick and chose among various suppliers, looking for the most favorable terms. Vertical minimum price fixing should be contrasted with vertical maximum price fixing. When the supplier imposes a maximum retail price on the dealer, the dealer may not welcome this limit on its pricing discretion and, if it could do so, might choose to discontinue carrying the supplier's product. Thus, the supplier will not dare to impose such a maximum price unless it possesses upstream power. The distinction between downstream and upstream power restraints is explored more fully in Chapter VI.

This chapter considers a variety of distribution restraints consistent with the downstream power condition. Among them are vertical minimum price fixing, various types of customer allocations, location clauses that limit a dealer's place of business, and exclusive selling or exclusive distributorships. The relative power enjoyed by the downstream player does not require that it impose the restraint on the upstream supplier. More often, these downstream power restraints are imposed by the supplier in order to win the loyalty and support of the relatively powerful downstream buyer. The relative power position of the downstream player also does not necessarily signify that the supplier lacks power. For example, the supplier of copyrighted books, DVDs, or sheet music is selling a unique product that, if it is in demand, can command a price premium. Yet suppliers of these products may seek to impose a downstream power restraint such as vertical minimum price fixing if the supplier is dependent upon a downstream retailing system or if the supplier benefits by being able to charge a higher price when selling within that retailing system. Under these circumstances, the restraint may operate to benefit both the downstream retailer and the upstream supplier.

7.1a. Summary of the Law

Antitrust law governing downstream power distribution restraints has evolved primarily from interpretations of Section 1 of the Sherman Act. Of course, the Federal Trade Commission may also proceed against such restraints under Section 5 of the FTC Act. Currently the Supreme Court treats some price restraints more severely than nonprice restraints. An intrabrand price restraint, sometimes called vertical price fixing or resale price maintenance, is *per se* unlawful if it involves an agreement to fix a minimum resale price. Once a showing is made that vertical minimum price fixing has occurred, it is unlawful without further inquiry into its effects. On the other hand, nonprice intrabrand distribution restraints, conduct short of agreement on specified minimum prices, even conduct by which an upstream firm may discourage aggressive downstream pricing and even vertical maximum price agreements, are dealt with under the rule of reason, a more open-ended standard that allows a court to inquire into the competitive effects of the practice in its context. Such restraints are unlawful only if this analysis shows them to unreasonably restrain competition. The boundaries between price and nonprice restraints and between maximum and minimum price limits are not always clear and have been subject to varying interpretations. During the 1980s, the Supreme Court defined the field of nonprice restraints broadly, narrowing the area for application of the *per se* rule against vertical minimum price fixing but continuing to pay homage to it.[1] In Business Electronics Corp. v. Sharp Electronics Corp., the Court required a specific agreement as to price or price levels as a prerequisite for applying the *per se* rule.[2] In State Oil Co. v. Khan, the Supreme Court in 1997 further narrowed use of the *per se* rule, substituting the rule of reason in claims of vertical maximum price fixing.[3]

The decisions of the 1980s also made the conspiracy requirement for applying Section 1 of the Sherman Act to vertical restraints more rigorous than it had previously been. Decisions such as *Monsanto* and *Sharp* appear to use that requirement as a surrogate for substantive policy limits on the law's reach and as a vehicle for enhancing defendants' prospects for obtaining summary judgment on such claims.[4] It is unclear to what extent the conspiracy requirements in *Monsanto* and *Sharp* will be extended beyond the context of those cases (vertical minimum price fixing) to other types of distribution restraints. At least

---

§ 7.1

1. Business Elecs. Corp. v. Sharp Elecs. Corp., 485 U.S. 717, 724, 108 S.Ct. 1515, 99 L.Ed.2d 808 (1988); Monsanto Co. v. Spray-Rite Serv. Corp., 465 U.S. 752, 761, 104 S.Ct. 1464, 79 L.Ed.2d 775 (1984).

2. 485 U.S. at 735–36.

3. 522 U.S. 3, 17, 118 S.Ct. 275, 139 L.Ed.2d 199 (1997).

4. See the discussion of the conspiracy requirement in § 7.4a.

for some forms of distribution restraints, when a downstream dealer is coerced into accepting the restraint, this coerced action may satisfy the conspiracy requirement.[5]

§ 7.2   Evolution of the Law

Evolution of a sustainable and coherent policy framework for assessing distribution restraints began late, proceeded haltingly, and even today remains an elusive goal. The law governing vertical price restraints began its development somewhat earlier, but has vacillated widely over the past century. The law governing nonprice distribution restraints, also subject to vacillation, did not begin to take shape until the 1960s.

7.2a.   The Law Governing Intrabrand Price Restraints

By 1900, manufacturers' use of distribution restraints began to spawn litigation, albeit involving issues of state law.[1] The Supreme Court's first antitrust case involving a classic distribution restraint came in 1911. In Dr. Miles Medical Co. v. John D. Park & Sons Co.,[2] over Justice Holmes dissent, the Court declared that producer contracts fixing retail prices on a brand name, over the counter medicine violated the Sherman Act. The Court recognized that the direct competitive harm from this distribution restraint occurred at the downstream retail level ("competition between retailers, who supply the public, is made impossible").[3] When minimum retail prices are set, the consumer will pay a higher price for the brand subject to the price restraint, raising the specter of misallocated resources or wealth transfers injurious to consumers. But higher prices for the brand in question could be an incentive for widening the dealer network or increasing promotional efforts by existing dealers, circumstances that could potentially benefit interbrand competition. Neither this argument nor its limitations were addressed in Dr. Miles. The Court did offer an important additional insight: that vertical price restraints benefit, and are often sought by, dealers.[4] Whether or not accompanied by dealer cartel conduct, distribution restraints of a variety of types may enhance the margin at which retailers sell their wares. The higher price that the consumer pays for a product subject to a distribution restraint is likely to flow at least in part to the retailer. And, even if consumers receive some additional product information or service valued by some of them, that price premium may cause an anticompetitive misallocation of resources or wealth transfer.

---

5. See the discussion in §§ 7.4a and 8.3d3.

§ 7.2

1. Commonwealth v. Grinstead, 63 S.W. 427 (Ky.1901); Garst v. Harris, 58 N.E. 174 (Mass.1900)(Holmes, J.); Walsh v. Dwight, 58 N.Y.S. 91 (1899).

2. 220 U.S. 373, 31 S.Ct. 376, 55 L.Ed. 502 (1911). Similar issues had arisen earlier in the context of a patented product. Bement v. National Harrow Co., 186 U.S. 70, 22 S.Ct. 747, 46 L.Ed.2d 1058 (1902).

3. Id. at 400.

4. See id. at 407.

Distribution restraints were probably widely used by the time of *Dr. Miles*, but refinement of antitrust analysis still languished. The immediate impact of *Dr. Miles* was limited by the prevailing interpretation of the commerce requirement in the Sherman Act. When a distribution restraint involved a local producer, state courts could ignore the Sherman Act in favor of more lenient state law.[5] In addition, the Court soon recognized two exceptions to the application of Section 1 of the Sherman Act that allowed many distribution restraints to escape antitrust scrutiny. In its 1919 decision in United States v. Colgate & Co.,[6] the Supreme Court said no conspiracy within the reach of Section 1 of the Sherman Act existed when a producer unilaterally refused to do business with a discounter (without the participation of other players in the distribution network). *Colgate* was the progenitor of a line of cases that limited application of the Sherman Act to distribution restraints based on a perceived failure to satisfy the conspiracy requirement of Section 1 of the Sherman Act. In a separate development in 1926 the Court further limited *Dr. Miles'* reach. In United States v. General Electric Co.,[7] it allowed a producer to fix the prices on goods delivered to a retailer on consignment (title to the goods remained with the producer).

By the time that courts began interpreting the Sherman Act's commerce language more broadly, many states (beginning with California in 1933) had passed fair trade laws that allowed a producer to set retail prices. Congress followed suit, enacting the Miller–Tydings Act in 1937 to create an antitrust exemption for vertical price restraints authorized by state fair trade laws.[8]

Even during this period when state and federal law seemed relatively favorable to vertical minimum price fixing, the course for suppliers that imposed minimum resale prices could be difficult. Legal problems still remained in those states that had not adopted fair trade laws or that would not allow enforcement against a dealer that had not agreed to be bound by the resale price limit. The incentive for a dealer to cheat on price limits can be substantial and this made monitoring and enforcement expensive for widely distributed brands. By the 1950s, the tide had turned against fair trade laws and minimum resale prices. In 1951, the Supreme Court refused to extend Miller–Tydings immunity to an enforcement of a retail price limit against a nonsigning dealer.[9] Congress responded in 1952 with the McGuire Act, granting antitrust immunity to such state fair trade laws.[10] Even this legislative success did not stem the tide of challenges to such laws. Some state courts construed enforcement

---

5. See the cases cited in Grimes, *The Seven Myths of Vertical Price Fixing: The Politics and Economics of a Century–Long Debate*, 21 Sw. U. L. Rev. 1285, 1288 nn.7–8 (1992).

6. 250 U.S. 300, 39 S.Ct. 465, 63 L.Ed. 992 (1919).

7. 272 U.S. 476, 47 S.Ct. 192, 71 L.Ed. 362 (1926).

8. Miller–Tydings Resale Price Maintenance Act, ch. 690, tit. VIII, 50 Stat. 693 (1937) (repealed 1975).

9. Schwegmann Bros. v. Calvert Distillers Corp., 341 U.S. 384, 71 S.Ct. 745, 95 L.Ed. 1035 (1951).

10. McGuire Resale Price Maintenance Act Amendments, ch. 745, 66 Stat. 631 (1952) (repealed 1975).

against nonsigning dealers as a violation of the state constitution.[11] Other states repealed their fair trade laws. In the U.S. Supreme Court, decisions limiting the consignment exception to *Dr. Miles*[12] and interpreting narrowly the *Colgate* conspiracy requirement[13] made it increasingly difficult to defend claims of unlawful vertical price fixing. Sentiment in Congress had also shifted. In 1975, Congress enacted legislation repealing all antitrust exemptions for state fair trade laws. This legislation left standing *Dr. Miles,* which the Congress understood to state a controlling *per se* rule against vertical minimum price fixing. In 1980, the FTC took a further step, seeking to overturn the *Colgate* conspiracy exception. That effort was unsuccessful,[14] and marked the beginning of yet another shift in federal law and policy.

The major developments of the 1980s were the Supreme Court's decisions in Monsanto Co. v. Spray–Rite Service Corp.[15] and Business Electronics Corp. v. Sharp Electronics Corp.[16] Both *Monsanto* and *Sharp* were influenced by the Supreme Court's 1977 landmark decision governing nonprice restraints in Continental T. V., Inc. v. GTE Sylvania Inc.,[17] which found procompetitive benefits for nonprice distribution restraints and required their legality to be measured under the rule of reason. In *Monsanto,* the Court upheld a jury verdict that Monsanto was guilty of vertical price fixing in terminating a discounting herbicide dealer. But the Court revitalized the *Colgate* decision by announcing a stiffer burden on the plaintiff to show that the supplier's action in terminating a dealer was not the unilateral act of the supplier. Justice Powell wrote for the Court:

> The correct standard is that there must be evidence that tends to exclude the possibility of independent action by the manufacturer and distributor. That is, there must be direct or circumstantial evidence that reasonably tends to prove that the manufacturer and others had a conscious commitment to a common scheme designed to achieve an unlawful objective.[18]

The consequence of *Monsanto* was to require a terminated dealer to come to court with something more than evidence that rival dealers had complained about the plaintiff's price cutting before the plaintiff was terminated. Without other evidence indicating manufacturer-dealer con-

---

11. For example, in Bissell Carpet Sweeper Co. v. Shane Co.,143 N.E.2d 415 (Ind.1957), the Indiana Supreme Court declared the state's fair trade law an unconstitutional delegation of legislative powers because it allowed private parties, by contract, to bind nonsigning parties to a fixed price. Ten other state supreme courts had, by 1957, declared nonsigner enforcement provisions unconstitutional. Bates, *Constitutionality of State Fair Trade Acts,* 32 IND. L.J. 127, 134–37 (1957).

12. Simpson v. Union Oil Co., 377 U.S. 13, 84 S.Ct. 1051, 12 L.Ed.2d 98 (1964).

13. United States v. Parke, Davis & Co., 362 U.S. 29, 80 S.Ct. 503, 4 L.Ed.2d 505 (1960).

14. Russell Stover Candies, Inc. v. FTC, 718 F.2d 256 (8th Cir.1983).

15. 465 U.S. 752, 104 S.Ct. 1464, 79 L.Ed.2d 775 (1984).

16. 485 U.S. 717, 108 S.Ct. 1515, 99 L.Ed.2d 808 (1988).

17. 433 U.S. 36, 97 S.Ct. 2549, 53 L.Ed.2d 568 (1977). *Sylvania* is discussed in § 6.4b.

18. *Monsanto,* 465 U.S. at 768.

cert, the defendant would likely be granted summary judgement based on the plaintiff's failure to demonstrate a conspiracy under Section 1 of the Sherman Act.

In *Sharp,* the Court affirmed the Fifth Circuit's decision overturning a vertical minimum price fixing verdict against Sharp based on the termination of Business Electronics as a Sharp dealer. Sharp had acted after Hartwell, a dealer competing with Business Electronics, warned Sharp that it would drop the Sharp line unless Business Electronics were terminated. Although the record showed some evidence that Business Electronics was a discounter, there was no evidence that Sharp had attempted to enforce a program of minimum resale prices. The Court held that the plaintiff had failed to demonstrate a conspiracy between the supplier and one or more dealers encompassing an "agreement on price or price levels."[19] Writing for the Court, Justice Scalia viewed *Sylvania* as an untouchable testimonial to the benefits of nonprice distribution restraints that should not be narrowed by a broad construction of the *per se* rule against vertical price fixing. Unless there was a manufacturer-dealer agreement specifying a specific retail price to be maintained, even an agreement between the manufacturer and a price-sustaining dealer to terminate a discounting dealer would be characterized as a nonprice restraint.

By emphasizing the conspiracy doctrine, the Court's opinions in *Monsanto* and *Sharp* revitalized a measure that has no bearing on the economic or competitive aspects of the defendants' underlying behavior. It is difficult to see how the competitive consequences of the defendants' behavior would have been any different had they actually agreed on price or price level for resale to the consumer.[20] In his dissent in *Sharp,* Justice Stevens saw the retailer ultimatum as tantamount to the alleged boycotts instrumented by a powerful rival retailer (with the assistance of multiple suppliers) in Klor's, Inc. v. Broadway–Hale Stores, Inc.[21] or to a cartel of rival dealers in United States v. General Motors Corp.[22] Although Justice Scalia's majority opinion can at least conventionally distinguish these precedents as involving horizontal restraints, it is more difficult to distinguish the economic injury suffered in these cases from that which Business Electronics alleged. *Monsanto* and *Sharp* rely on broad language in *Sylvania* that goes well beyond that decision's holding that a location clause and other nonprice distribution restraints should be subject to the rule reason. These decisions present an imbalanced and incomplete picture of the benefits of intrabrand competition as a discipline for brand-specific market power.[23]

19. *Sharp,* 485 U.S. at 735–36.

20. The Court's emphasis on the conspiracy doctrine has been criticized by scholars with varying perspectives on distribution restraints. See § 7.2c.

21. 359 U.S. 207, 79 S.Ct. 705, 3 L.Ed.2d 741 (1959).

22. 384 U.S. 127, 86 S.Ct. 1321, 16 L.Ed.2d 415 (1966).

23. See the discussion of intrabrand competition in § 6.3a.

The Supreme Court's most recent pronouncement on vertical price restraints, State Oil Co. v. Khan,[24] involved maximum resale price limits. This subject is addressed in Chapter VIII. The Court's decision in *Khan* extends the domain of the rule of reason into the area of price restraints, and suggests a continuation of the trend to narrow the area of application for the *per se* rule against vertical price fixing. The conceptual distinctions between minimum and maximum limits,[25] however, suggest caution in reading *Khan* as an indicator in future treatment of vertical minimum price fixing.

7.2b. The Law Governing Intrabrand Nonprice Restraints

The law governing vertical price restraints, although vacillating widely in the face of judicial and legislative reversals, had achieved some clarity by 1950. That clarity was lacking for the law governing nonprice restraints. One reason for the confusion was that private plaintiffs and government enforcers strained to bring themselves within horizontal conspiracy theories, hoping to benefit from an established *per se* rule that greatly reduced the required evidentiary showing. By advancing horizontal rather than vertical theories, plaintiffs perhaps sought to avoid the exemption created by the Miller–Tydings Act.[26] Apparently seeing no sharp demarcation between harm from horizontal and vertical restraints, the Supreme Court did not resist such horizontal characterization. In consequence, significant Supreme Court precedents involving distribution restraints were analyzed as horizontal issues. For example, United States v. Topco Associates, Inc.,[27] Northwest Wholesale Stationers, Inc. v. Pacific Stationery & Printing Co.,[28] United States v. General Motors Corp.,[29] and Klor's, Inc. v. Broadway–Hale Stores, Inc.,[30] each involved facts that allowed the Court to characterize the combination as a boycott or a horizontal restraint, although the challenged conduct was distributional at its core. Failure to recognize the distributional character of restraints tends to distort policy analysis and probably has delayed a more realistic and coherent approach to nonprice distribution restraints.

In 1949, the Department of Justice took the position that territorial and customer restrictions, like vertical price restraints, were *per se* illegal.[31] Beginning at that time and extending through 1963, there were at least sixteen Justice Department prosecutions of such activity, each ending in a consent decree that allowed the use of primary territories

24. 522 U.S. 3, 118 S.Ct. 275, 139 L.Ed.2d 199 (1997).

25. True vertical maximum price fixing involves coercion by a seller and probably has more in common with unlawful tie-ins than it does with vertical minimum price fixing. See the discussion in § 8.7.

26. The Miller Tydings Act is described in § 7.2a.

27. 405 U.S. 596, 92 S.Ct. 1126, 31 L.Ed.2d 515 (1972).

28. 472 U.S. 284, 105 S.Ct. 2613, 86 L.Ed.2d 202 (1985).

29. 384 U.S. 127, 86 S.Ct. 1321, 16 L.Ed.2d 415 (1966).

30. 359 U.S. 207, 79 S.Ct. 705, 3 L.Ed.2d 741 (1959).

31. See Rifkind, *Division of Territories*, *in* HOW TO COMPLY WITH THE ANTITRUST LAWS 127–39 (Van Cise & Dunn eds., 1954).

but prohibited the use of exclusive territories.[32] The Supreme Court's 1963 decision in *White Motor* involved the first of these cases to be litigated.[33] It was also the first high court decision to use the term "vertical" to describe distribution restraints. In a cautious opinion by Justice Douglas, the Court concluded that it knew too little about the competitive effects of a manufacturer's territorial limits on its dealers to endorse either a *per se* or rule of reason approach. But White Motor chose not to continue litigating on remand. It, like other defendants, signed a consent agreement that prohibited the use of exclusive territories.[34]

Despite the uncertainty generated by *White Motor*, the Justice Department continued to press for a *per se* rule to govern nonprice restraints. Four years later, in United States v. Arnold, Schwinn & Co.,[35] the Court apparently felt it had gained sufficient knowledge to announce a *per se* rule for nonprice distribution restraints. Speaking for the Court, Justice Fortas wrote an opinion in which ownership, title or dominion over the product was pivotal in determining the legality of a distribution restraint: "Under the Sherman Act, it is unreasonable without more for a manufacturer to seek to restrict and confine areas or persons with whom an article may be traded after the manufacturer has parted with dominion over it."[36] On the other hand, "[w]here the manufacturer retains title, dominion, and risk with respect to the product and the position and function of the dealer in question are, in fact, indistinguishable from those of an agent or salesman of the manufacturer," the rule of reason applies in the absence of culpable price fixing.[37]

Schwinn, too, proved short lived. In 1977, the Court overruled it in Continental T. V., Inc. v. GTE Sylvania Inc.[38] In a case in which a producer of television sets with a very small share of the U.S. market had sought to enforce a location clause against a dealer, the Court refused to find this conduct *per se* unlawful. Read narrowly, *Sylvania* was simply an opportunity to restore the cautious approach to nonprice distribution restraints that prevailed before *Schwinn*. But *Sylvania* has had far greater impact because the Court used broad language about the procompetitive effects of nonprice distribution restraints. The case offers a key recognition about the potential procompetitive impact of such restraints. A distribution restraint, by enlarging the dealer network or enhancing dealer performance, may increase the market share of a producer's line. *Sylvania* also touted the value of interbrand competition, suggesting that it was the primary engine driving competition. In effect, such restraints became presumptively lawful, for an antitrust challenger

32. Stewart, *Franchise or Protected Territory Distribution*, 8 ANTITRUST BULL. 447, 470 n.51 (1963).

33. White Motor Co. v. United States, 372 U.S. 253, 83 S.Ct. 696, 9 L.Ed.2d 738 (1963).

34. United States v. White Motor Co., 1964 Trade Cas. (CCH) ¶ 71,195 (N.D. Ohio Sept. 8, 1964).

35. 388 U.S. 365, 87 S.Ct. 1856, 18 L.Ed.2d 1249 (1967).

36. Id. at 379.

37. Id. at 380.

38. 433 U.S. 36, 97 S.Ct. 2549, 53 L.Ed.2d 568 (1977). One of the authors (Prof. Sullivan) represented appellant in this case.

would have to prove that competitive harm at the intrabrand level outweighed the presumed benefit to interbrand competition. See § 7.5 below. Following *Sylvania*, the Department of Justice's now withdrawn 1985 Vertical Restraint Guidelines assumed the primacy of competition at the producer level and discounted concerns that price or nonprice distribution restraints would undermine competition at the retail level.

Although *Sylvania* adopted very useful teachings of the Chicago School, the decision has obvious shortcomings. The Court was on solid ground when it found that distribution restraints can provide an effective tool for promoting a producer brand. But the Court's assertion that distribution restraints "promote interbrand competition by allowing the manufacturer to achieve certain efficiencies in the distribution of his products"[39] is incorrect. Distribution restraints promote the sale of the supplier's brand, but they do not promote interbrand competition. Instead, distribution restraints *reduce interbrand competition by making consumer demand for a supplier's brand more inelastic.*[40] Whether this diminution in interbrand competition is a benefit or loss to society depends on the nature of the promotion fostered by the restraint. For example, promotion fostered by distribution restraints can allow a supplier to attain scale efficiencies in production and distribution. But these benefits, which usually can be attained through means other than distribution restraints, may or may not be consistent with antitrust goals of efficient allocation and avoiding transfer of wealth to those possessing market power. To determine the net competitive effect of a distribution restraint, one must go beyond the restraint's ability to increase sales of a particular brand. Key questions are whether the restraint increases sales by exploiting information asymmetries, whether the restraint undermines efficient and innovative competition in distribution, and whether the restraint's effectiveness will encourage parallel behavior by rival suppliers that causes price increases in the interbrand market.

The *Sylvania* Court also said that interbrand competition "provides a significant check on the exploitation of intrabrand market power."[41] Again, this statement fails to recognize that the more effective a distribution restraint is in differentiating a brand, the greater the reduction in interbrand competition. Assuming that a particular restraint does enhance informed consumer buying, the *Sylvania* Court failed to support

39.　Id. at 54.

40.　See the discussion of the benefits of intrabrand competition in § 6.3a.

41.　The full text of the relevant passage is as follows:

The degree of intrabrand competition is wholly independent of the level of interbrand competition confronting the manufacturer. Thus, there may be fierce intrabrand competition among the distributors of a product produced by a monopolist and no intrabrand competition among the distributors of a product produced by a firm in a highly competitive industry. But when interbrand competition exists, * * * it provides a significant check on the exploitation of intrabrand market power because of the ability of consumers to substitute a different brand of the same product.

Sylvania, 433 U.S. at 52 n.19.

Steiner has criticized at some length the assumptions underlying this footnote. Steiner, *Sylvania Economics—A Critique,* 60 ANTITRUST L.J. 41, 42–45 (1991).

its unstated premise that such promotional benefits are uniformly more important to efficient allocation and other antitrust goals than the downstream intrabrand competition that can promote efficient retailing and the efficient allocation of a highly desired brand. Consider a highly popular book, movie or song that is subject to copyright protection. The copyright holder has exclusive rights to market its work and may be able to sell it through a variety of distribution channels. Intrabrand competition among retailers may benefit consumers who want a particular book or movie at the lowest possible price. If the copyright holder seeks to limit this competition, it is not likely that it does so to inform the public about this popular work. Nor is it likely that interbrand competition will provide much of a check for those consumers who want only a particular book or movie. There may be possible procompetitive benefits to the restraint (such as rewarding retailers who promote the copyright holder's other works), but the Sylvania Court's conclusion that interbrand competition will check intrabrand market power seems overdrawn.

Whatever *Sylvania's* shortcomings, it dominated the Court's reasoning in all 1980s distribution restraint cases. This broadened the application of the rule of reason and confined the *per se* rule against vertical price fixing to ever narrower ground. Quite clearly, there is tension in the existing case law between *Dr. Miles'* implicit recognition of the importance of maintaining intrabrand competition at the retail level and, on the other hand, *Colgate's* emphasis on the freedom of business contract and *Sylvania's* focus on the producer's need to foster a loyal dealer network as a prerequisite to effective competition among producers. The Court's express recognition, in Eastman Kodak Co. v. Image Technical Services, Inc.,[42] that informational market imperfections could be a source of power in the sale of a single line of goods also appears to run counter to some of the premises of *Colgate* and *Sylvania*. Building an antitrust framework that minimizes the points of tension and, where necessary, sets priorities among them, is critical if an enduring and coherent law of distribution restraints is to evolve.

7.2c. The Conspiracy Doctrine in Distribution Restraint Cases

The exclusion for unilateral conduct first recognized in United States v. Colgate & Co.[43] remains central to applying Section 1 of the Sherman Act to distribution restraints. The rigidity of this conspiracy doctrine, just as the substantive standards governing distribution restraints, has ebbed and flowed with changing economic condition, evolving economic theory, and shifts in the political climate. A series of cases that relaxed the conspiracy requirement culminated in the 1960 decision in United States v. Parke, Davis & Co.[44] As a result of that decision, the Supreme Court appeared to have left only the narrowest of openings for

42. 504 U.S. 451, 112 S.Ct. 2072, 119 L.Ed.2d 265 (1992).

43. 250 U.S. 300, 39 S.Ct. 465, 63 L.Ed. 992 (1919).

44. 362 U.S. 29, 80 S.Ct. 503, 4 L.Ed.2d 505 (1960).

a *Colgate* exception: A manufacturer could seek to achieve resale price maintenance or any other unlawful distribution restraint through a prior announcement of policy and the exercise of its right to refuse to deal with a noncomplying dealer. But the exception could be lost if the manufacturer took any step beyond announcement of policy and withdrawal of trade from violators. Thus, use of other dealers to police resale price maintenance, or receipt of assurances from a recalcitrant dealer that it would comply in the future, probably took the manufacturer outside the *Colgate* exception. The *Parke, Davis* line of decisions has been undercut by *Monsanto* and *Sharp*, but the Court has not overruled these earlier cases.

In Monsanto Co. v. Spray–Rite Service Corp.,[45] the Supreme Court held that an agreement could not be inferred merely from the existence of complaints made by competing dealers about pricing practices of a dealer whom the manufacturer had terminated. To find an agreement, the Court required evidence of "a conscious commitment to a common scheme designed to achieve an unlawful objective."[46] In *Monsanto,* the Court did find such evidence in the record. But the revitalization of *Colgate* worked by this holding has made it more difficult for plaintiffs to establish an agreement, even in cases in which the anticompetitive effects of producer-imposed resale price maintenance are self-evident.

The reach of *Colgate* was apparently extended yet again in Business Electronics Corp. v. Sharp Electronics Corp.[47] The Court's opinion seems driven by a desire to expand the range of the *Sylvania* holding that vertical nonprice restraints are to be subject to the rule of reason. To confine the *per se* rule to a narrow domain, the *Sharp* Court held that the rule would only apply when an agreement had been shown about "price or price levels."[48] Although the application of these words is unclear, the direction in which the Court sought to move the law is evident.

An unresolved issue in the *Monsanto* and *Sharp* decisions is the extent to which the holdings apply to conspiracies in nonprice distribution restraints. In each of these cases, the plaintiffs invoked the *per se* rule against vertical price fixing. In both cases, the Court seems to have sought to limit the application of the *per se* rule in deference to a wide application of *Sylvania's* rule of reason. But the logic of *Colgate* would appear to apply to *any* Section 1 claim involving a distribution restraint, regardless of whether the rule of reason or the *per se* rule is the measure of liability. Indeed, *Colgate* was decided before the Court had developed a well-defined *per se* rule in either horizontal or vertical cases. If "unilateral" conduct is deemed beyond the reach of Section 1 of the Sherman Act for a *per se* claim, the same result would logically follow for a rule of reason claim. In light of *Monsanto* and *Sharp*, are the stricter evidentiary burdens for showing an agreement now meant to apply to rule of

---

45. 465 U.S. 752, 104 S.Ct. 1464, 79 L.Ed.2d 775 (1984).

46. Id. at 768.

47. 485 U.S. 717, 108 S.Ct. 1515, 99 L.Ed.2d 808 (1988).

48. Id. at 735–36.

reason cases including nonprice distribution restraints? For tie-ins and exclusive dealing? At least with respect to tie-ins, the Court has not strictly applied the *Colgate* doctrine and, in the 1992 *Kodak* decision, found an agreement based solely on the acquiescence of a Kodak customer to the tie-in arrangement.[49]

The *Colgate* case remains pivotal in modern interpretations of the Section 1 conspiracy requirement in vertical Sherman Act cases. By nature, distribution restraints are often imposed by a single supplier. If the conspiracy can be found in the relationship between the buyer and seller, a court is free to deal with the competitive restraint on its merits. If, on the other hand, the *Colgate* case is aggressively applied, courts will reach inconsistent results in cases with identical competitive injuries. A premium would be placed upon a plaintiff's ability to make an evidentiary showing that does not further analysis of the injury caused by the restraint. A sound policy approach to distribution restraints emphasizes economic policy, not a sterile debate over whether a conspiracy or agreement exists. Theorists with varying views on distribution restraints appear to join in criticizing the recent emphasis on conspiracy generated by *Monsanto* and *Sharp*. The primary basis of this criticism is that the existence of an agreement has no bearing on whether the distribution restraint has worked any economic injury or benefit.[50] A de-emphasis of the conspiracy requirement is consistent with the trend in court decisions prior to *Monsanto*[51] and could bring a welcome focus on economic issues into court decisions on distribution restraints.

The Court's flirtation with a more rigid conspiracy doctrine may be nurtured by a desire to curtail open-ended litigation and provide defendants a basis for seeking dismissal of ill-founded complaints before trial. But substantive screening tests and a structured rule of reason offer a more principled basis for culling out ill-founded claims and more expeditiously litigating meritorious ones. Some defendants have successfully relied on the plaintiff's failure to establish a conspiracy as a basis for obtaining summary judgment.[52] However, a few recent cases suggest

49. 504 U.S. at 463 n.8. See the discussion in § 8.3d3.

50. Marvel, *The Resale Price Maintenance Controversy: Beyond the Conventional Wisdom,* 63 ANTITRUST L.J. 59, 61–62 & n.5 (1994)(lack of principle in the unilateral action defense is "an absence of economics in what is an inherently economic question"); Robinson, *Explaining Vertical Agreements: The* Colgate *Puzzle and Antitrust Method,* 80 VA. L. REV. 577, 620 (1994); Grimes, *Brand Marketing, Intrabrand Competition, and the Multibrand Retailer: The Antitrust Law of Vertical Restraints,* 64 ANTITRUST L.J. 83, 124–25 (1995); Hay, *Observations:* Sylvania *in Retrospect,* 60 ANTITRUST L.J. 61, 66 (1991); Burns, *Rethinking the "Agreement" Element in Vertical Antitrust Restraints,* 51

OHIO ST. L.J. 1, 18–19 (1990); Piraino, *The Case for Presuming the Legality of Quality Motivated Restrictions on Distribution,* 63 NOTRE DAME L. REV. 1, 10–11 (1988). The role of the conspiracy doctrine was being questioned even before *Monsanto* and *Sharp.* Turner, *The Definition of Agreement Under the Sherman Act: Conscious Parallelism and Refusals to Deal,* 75 HARV. L. REV. 655, 686–87 (1962)(a distinction between vertical price fixing effected by contract and vertical price fixing effected by threats of refusal to deal "is wholly untenable").

51. L. SULLIVAN, HANDBOOK OF THE LAW OF ANTITRUST 393–95 (1977).

52. Euromodas, Inc. v. Zanella, Ltd., 368 F.3d 11 (1st Cir. 2004)(agreement to terminate a price cutter in favor of a larger

some erosion in hard-line application of the conspiracy requirement. In *Ezzo's Investments, Inc. v. Royal Beauty Supply, Inc.,* the district court granted summary judgment for the defendants, dismissing a dealer's complaint that it had been terminated as a part of an unlawful conspiracy to fix minimum resale prices. The Sixth Circuit reversed, finding sufficient evidence of an unlawful conspiracy to submit the case to the jury.[53] The defendants had argued that the dealer was dismissed for failure to comply with a "professional salon policy" that required each dealer to earn 50 percent or more of its revenues from hair care services (as distinguished from sale of products). The court of appeals found that this defense may have been pretextual given evidence that the defendants' representatives had warned the plaintiff-dealer that continued supply of the defendants' line of products was contingent upon the plaintiff raising its prices and corroborative evidence of another dealer that it had been similarly pressured to raise its prices.[54]

A plaintiffs may also avoid the constraints of the *Colgate* line of cases if it can establish that a refusal to deal or termination is the result of a horizontal conspiracy or boycott. See the discussion in § 7.6.

§ 7.3　A Structured Rule of Reason for Downstream Power Restraints

Downstream power restraints can be a potent tool for inducing promotional efforts by downstream marketers. They can be used to promote the sale of quality goods and services at competitive prices, or for selling shoddy or overpriced merchandise. The promotional gains can be achieved either by conveying valuable information to consumers, or by exploiting consumer information gaps. The gains may be achieved at the expense of arbitrage, anticollusion, and other beneficial effects of market-stimulated intrabrand competition. For some downstream power restraints, however, the loss of intrabrand competition may be minimal, the risk of exploitation small, and the promotional gain based on valuable information or service substantial. Except for vertical minimum price fixing, where a *per se* rule still obtains, the law now applies a rule of reason to such conduct. But neither courts nor commentators have as yet provided much guidance about the analysis needed to enable a court applying that rule of reason to distinguish competitively harmful from

---

volume retailer does not establish that "manufacturer and others had a conscious commitment to a common scheme designed to achieve an unlawful objective"); Glacier Optical, Inc. v. Optique du Monde, 46 F.3d 1141, 1995–1 Trade Cas. (CCH) ¶ 70,878, at 73,855 (9th Cir.1995) (per curiam) (unpublished opinion affirming summary judgment for defendants because evidence of complaints that wholesaler was reselling to discounters, meetings with dealers, and monitoring was "insufficient to establish concerted action.").

53.　94 F.3d 1032 (6th Cir.1996).

54.　Id. at 1036. see also Isaksen v. Vermont Castings, Inc., 825 F.2d 1158 (7th Cir.1987)(judgment notwithstanding verdict for defendant reversed–agreement may be implicit in conduct), cert. denied, 486 U.S. 1005, 108 S.Ct. 1728, 100 L.Ed.2d 193 (1988); Sportmart, Inc. v. No Fear, Inc., 1996–2 Trade Cas. (CCH) ¶ 71,513 (N.D. Ill. June 3, 1996)(denying summary judgment for the defendant on terminated dealer's claims that the defendant supplier (1) had coerced plaintiff to agree to fix resale prices, and (2) had conspired with rival dealers to fix resale prices).

beneficial or benign restraints. Over time, a structured rule of reason should evolve to achieve a rationale policy with minimal counseling and litigation costs.[1] Such a rule, which could integrate analysis of both price and nonprice restraints by encompassing both, would focus the courts on the salient points that determine antitrust injury, but would eliminate the risk of an overinclusiveness associated with a *per se* rule.[2] At the root of this structured rule of reason would be recognition that market power is the source of antitrust injury of all types, including downstream power distribution restraints.

A well-conceived rule of reason would proceed through two levels. The first level would consist of screening tests. The screening tests are designed to eliminate those distribution restraints that are unlikely to have significant anticompetitive impact. The tests should be useful to defendants in obtaining pretrial dismissal of claims challenging such restraints (and in counseling clients concerning relatively unproblematic restraints). These tests are described in § 7.3a. Those claims that were not eliminated under the screening tests would be measured under a more comprehensive, but still structured, balancing test addressed in § 7.3b.

7.3a. Screening Tests for Downstream Power Restraints

7.3a1. Market Power

The first screening test is *whether the defendant, alone or in the context of other downstream players benefitting from the restraint,* have sufficient market power to injure competition. Establishing a rational policy toward distribution restraints requires careful attention to this question, for this test is not easily applied. Antitrust is concerned with the power of market participants to distort the competitive process. This distortion can misallocate resources, transfer wealth from consumers and other protected groups to power-wielding market participants, or stifle initiative, new entry or innovation. Without power, a market participant can do none of these things and is, instead, itself subject to the discipline of competition.

As described in Chapter 2, market power is the seller's ability to raise price or reduce output. This power is measured by the elasticity of demand faced by a seller. A seller has market power if it faces a downward sloping demand curve—demand decreases (but does not disap-

---

§ 7.3

1. Theorists with a variety of perspectives on distribution restraints have called for adoption of a structured rule of reason. See Robinson, *Explaining Vertical Agreements: The* Colgate *Puzzle and Antitrust Method,* 80 Va. L. Rev. 577, 604–19 (1994)(arguing for a structured rule of reason from a point of view generally accommodating to distribution restraints); Grimes, *Brand Marketing, Intrabrand Competition, and the Multibrand Retailer: The*

Antitrust Law of Vertical Restraints, 64 Antitrust L.J. 83, 114 (1995)(arguing for a structured rule of reason from a point of view that perceives some distribution restraints as anticompetitive).

2. After *Monsanto* and *Sharp,* the risk of an overinclusive *per se* rule may seem small. But that risk was an authentic concern in the days before *Sylvania,* and still has salience for price restraints.

pear as the model for perfect competition would dictate) as the seller increases its price. The more steeply the demand curve is sloped (a steeply sloped demand curve is called *inelastic*), the more market power the seller possesses.[3] A market in which each product is sold subject to brand differentiation may give each producer substantial latitude to limit output and raise prices.[4] Such a market involves what is called "monopolistic competition."[5] For downstream power restraints, the power exercised by a relatively powerful dealer may be exercised as buyer power. The dealer may be in a position to distort the flow of goods in the distribution system, possibly suppressing competition from more efficient rival dealers. The market power of downstream players should not by itself be the basis for condemning a distribution restraint. On the other hand, some form of market power, whether it emanates from a monopolist, a cartel, parallel behavior or brand differentiation, should be a prerequisite for finding a downstream power distribution restraint unlawful.[6]

Antitrust has long recognized that market power is possessed by a monopolist or a cartel that controls output and pricing for an entire market. Such marketwide power has been a focus of antitrust enforcement, including cases in which the power is exercised in a vertical context to affect distribution.[7] As a matter of definition, it is clear that

---

3. Landes & Posner, *Market Power in Antitrust Cases,* 94 Harv. L. Rev. 937, 940–41 (1981)(setting forth an equation that defines market power and "asserts the dependence of the firm's market power on the elasticity of demand that faces it").

4. Schmalensee, *Another Look at Market Power,* 95 Harv. L. Rev. 1789, 1800 (1982)("If substantial differentiation can be demonstrated, market share computation is unlikely to yield reliable information" concerning market power).

5. F. M. Scherer & D. Ross, Industrial Market Structure and Economic Performance 17 (3d ed. 1990). The term "monopolistic competition" was initially used in the 1930s to describe what theorists felt was the state of competition in most markets. See Keppler, Monopolistic Competition Theory: Origins, Results, and Implications 78–89 (1994) (describing the work of Edward Chamberlin and Joan Robinson who first developed monopolistic competition theory). Monopolistic competition theory has enjoyed a resurgence through more recent economic endeavors such as game theory, which assume the strategic power of market players to control price and output. See the discussion of monopolistic competition in § 2.4e.

6. Some theorists who have suggested that market power is a prerequisite for establishing a harmful distribution restraint would apparently exclude the power arising

from brand differentiation from their analysis. Easterbrook, *Vertical Arrangements and the Rule of Reason,* 53 Antitrust L.J. 135, 159–61 (1984); Liebeler, *Intrabrand "Cartels" Under* GTE Sylvania, 30 UCLA L. Rev. 1, 26–27 (1982); Baxter, *The Viability of Vertical Restraints Doctrine,* 75 Cal. L. Rev. 933, 947–49 (1987). This Chicago School contention assumes that the market power at issue is that of the supplier imposing the restraint. For downstream power restraints, however, the primary competition distorting effects, if any, arise from the power of the downstream actor or actors. Injuries to consumers often flow from having to pay more for a preferred brand or unique product (such as a copyrighted or patented product) or being subject to hidden sales tactics that distort consumer choice. This narrow view of the market power requirement for downstream restraints also ignores the definition of market power (proposed by scholars often viewed as Chicago adherents, Landes & Posner, supra note 3) and the holding in Eastman Kodak Co. v. Image Technical Services, Inc., 504 U.S. 451, 112 S.Ct. 2072, 119 L.Ed.2d 265 (1992).

7. In W. W. Montague & Co. v. Lowry, 193 U.S. 38, 24 S.Ct. 307, 48 L.Ed. 608 (1904), wholesale dealers of tile banded together and apparently pressured manufacturers not to deal with the plaintiff, a competing wholesale dealer. Although treated by the Court as an unlawful boycott, the

sellers of brand-differentiated products often possess market power. They, like the monopolist or cartel, can increase price by decreasing output. But recognition of the market power associated with brand differentiation, while not novel to antitrust, has remained largely implicit in most litigated cases. One can find such recognition as early as 1911, when the Supreme Court condemned a defendant's promotion of a single brand of patent medicine through vertical price restraints in Dr. Miles Medical Co. v. John D. Park & Sons Co.[8] These early cases did not discuss market power, yet recognized that significant injury to the public, not simply to individual competitors, could flow from distribution restraints.[9]

For over 80 years, that implicit acknowledgment has continued.[10] In Eastman Kodak Co. v. Image Technical Services, Inc.,[11] the Court expressly recognized the potential market power residing in aftermarket products and services for the defendant's single brand of micrographic equipment. Still, the Court has yet to offer a systematic basis for analyzing the market power flowing from brand differentiation. Indeed, even the question whether it should do so is disputed by some commentators.[12] Theorists who oppose recognizing brand-differentiated market

case is an early example of the condemnation of marketwide (cartel) power to restrain manufacturers' distribution. See also United States v. General Motors Corp., 348 U.S. 127, 86 S.Ct. 1321,16 L.Ed.2d 415 (1966).

8. 220 U.S. 373, 31 S.Ct. 376, 55 L.Ed. 502 (1911).

9. The early cases focused on the need for competition at the retail level. But it is clear that the courts saw themselves protecting a broad societal interest in competition, not simply the interests of a single competitor. In *Dr. Miles, id.* at 399–400, the Supreme Court quoted with approval the reasoning in a related circuit court case, John D. Park & Sons Co. v. Hartman, 153 F. 24, 42 (6th Cir.1907)(as the result of the price maintenance agreements, " 'all room for competition between retailers, who supply the public, is made impossible' "), cert. dismissed, 212 U.S. 588, 29 S.Ct. 689, 53 L.Ed. 662 (1908). Thus, the Supreme Court concluded in *Dr. Miles* that the price maintenance agreements, "having for their sole purpose the destruction of competition and the fixing of prices, are injurious to the public interest and void." 220 U.S. at 408. The Court also said that once Dr. Miles had sold its product to distributors, "the public is entitled to whatever advantage may be derived from competition in the subsequent traffic." Id. at 409. Similar policy concerns were voiced in FTC v. Beech–Nut Packing Co., 257 U.S. 441, 454–55, 42 S.Ct. 150, 66 L.Ed. 307 (1922).

10. For example, in Monsanto Co. v. Spray–Rite Service Corp., 465 U.S. 752, 104 S.Ct. 1464, 79 L.Ed.2d 775 (1984), and in United States v. Parke, Davis & Co., 362 U.S. 29, 80 S.Ct. 503, 4 L.Ed.2d 505 (1960), the Court's holdings were directed at a single manufacturer's line of branded merchandise, thus implicitly accepting that antitrust injury could be generated from distribution restraints involving a single brand.

11. 504 U.S. 451, 112 S.Ct. 2072, 119 L.Ed.2d 265 (1992).

12. For example, Bork argues that any market power arising from product differentiation fostered by distribution restraints is common to all promotion and advertising efforts and not a basis for condemning such restraints. R. BORK, THE ANTITRUST PARADOX: A POLICY AT WAR WITH ITSELF 291 (1978). See also Justice Scalia's dissent in *Kodak*, 504 U.S. at 489 (arguing that allowing courts to define a single product as a market will cause a "torrent of litigation and a flood of commercial intimidation"). A post-*Kodak* statement of this argument is offered in Arthur, *The Costly Quest for Perfect Competition: Kodak and Nonstructural Market Power*, 69 N.Y.U. L. REV. 1, 32–38 (1994)(arguing that the market power generated by brand differentiation and information gaps is "nonstructural" and too insubstantial to be considered by antitrust law).

A more qualified statement of concerns with recognizing market power inherent in

power do not deny its existence. Rather, without empirical support or the use of theoretical tools to measure power they assume its insignificance and assert that it lacks manageable boundaries for application to antitrust cases.[13] But questions of manageability have been partially answered as the result of 80 years of distribution restraints' precedents that have culled out harmful (such as resale price restraints) from benign or procompetitive restraints (such as most location clauses). Meanwhile, market power associated with brand differentiation is now being recognized outside the distribution restraints context, as, for example, in the Justice Department/FTC 1992 Horizontal Merger Guidelines.[14] If brand-differentiated market power is to be a determinant in distribution restraint cases, attorneys must be able to isolate those distribution restraints that create and abuse this power so that courts can reach consistent decisions and clients can be meaningfully counseled. Unfortunately, the most widely used market power measure in antitrust litigation—defining the relevant market and determining the defendant's share of the interbrand market—is only a surrogate for direct analysis of power. In theory, a more direct way of assessing market power is to examine the difference between a seller's price and its marginal cost—the cost of one additional unit of output. A high markup over marginal cost suggests competition is not effective—workable competition would drive prices closer to marginal cost. This method, known as the Lerner Index, is discussed in § 2.6a. It has yet to be widely used in antitrust cases, probably because of the difficulty in establishing marginal cost.[15]

Behavioral indicators may be more useful in assessing downstream power restraints. Evidence of persistent price discrimination in the sale of the same brand, or in the sale of two brands from the same producer that are identical except for brand image, may signal the presence of the requisite market power.[16] Such price discrimination may not indicate the degree of market power, but it may be useful in distribution restraints litigation to show a minimum threshold has been met. Another behavioral indicator of market power may be the use of a downstream power distribution restraint in a manner likely to exploit consumer information gaps. As described in § 6.3c2, the use of such distribution restraints may create "on-site" market power as a result of a dealer's promotion of the relevant brand, particularly when the restraint applies to sales by multibrand retailers.

brand differentiation is offered by Hovenkamp, *Market Power in Aftermarkets: Antitrust Policy and the Kodak Case,* 40 UCLA L. Rev. 1447, 1450–51 (1993)("antitrust policy does not generally recognize small amounts of market power that result from differentiated products as sufficient to warrant intervention").

13. See the views described in supra note 12.

14. The 1992 Horizontal Merger Guidelines call for adjustment in product market definitions based upon the degree to which products are differentiated or the closeness of products as substitutes in a differentiated market. U.S. Dept. of Justice/FTC Horizontal Merger Guidelines §§ 2.21, 2.211 (1992), reprinted in Appendix C. Outside the merger context, similar analytical tools are available for evaluating market power. See the discussion of such tools in § 2.6c.

15. Landes & Posner, supra note 3, at 941–43.

16. See § 2.6c.

Although a showing of market power may be difficult in some contexts, as courts and policy-makers become more experienced with the use of intrabrand distribution restraints in circumstances that create the greatest risk of injury, precedent will guide both the counselor and the judge in determining which restraints are linked to market power. The circumstance that a retailer has a relatively small market share may not be determinative if that locally exercised power is employed to exclude an even smaller rival retailer. A fact intensive inquiry is needed to determine the relative power possessed by the retailer and its targeted rivals. A defendant should be able to obtain dismissal of any claim of an unlawful distribution restraint if the plaintiff lacks evidence to warrant an inference that, acting alone or with others employing the restraint, the defendant exercised market power sufficient to distort competition.

All distribution restraints are designed to foster promotion and, to this extent, may increase the brand-differentiated market power of a producer. Thus, application of this screening test will require some qualitative and quantitative distinctions be drawn among distribution restraints. A seller with a high market share of an interbrand market will generally not be exculpated, nor will a seller, no matter how small its market share, that has a strong brand as measured by the inelasticity of its demand curve. But a small market share producer with a weak brand would be exculpated under this screening test. If such a producer grants distributors (or perhaps its retailers) exclusive territories, some market power may evolve as the result of the promotional incentives produced by this restraint. But the opportunities for substantial competitive injury are limited here, both because of the producer's small market share and the weakness of its brand. If demand inelasticity continues to increase, the producer will at some point fall outside the protective umbrella of this screening test.

There is one likely exception to the protected status of a small market share supplier with a weak brand: If the restraint is likely to skew allocation by exploiting consumer information gaps, the supplier will gain an instant, on-site market power for its brand. This market power creates pressure for rivals to emulate the restraint. For example, if the producer of a weak brand imposes vertical price restraints on multibrand retailers, the exploitation fostered by this restraint could create substantial brand-differentiated market power accompanied by a high risk of exploitation of consumer information gaps. When clearly identified, the qualitative and quantitative reach of these competitive risks should remove this restraint from the protected area of this market power screen.

7.3a2. The Restraint Will Not Significantly Impair Intrabrand Competition

A second useful screening test is *whether a distribution restraint significantly impairs intrabrand competition*. Mild distribution restraints such as location clauses or primary territory allocations often allow significant intrabrand competition to continue, or maintain the threat of such competition should a particular downstream player raise price or let service lapse below competitive levels. Of course, even if these relatively mild distribution restraints fall outside this screening test, they may still be lawful because of the promotional benefits they confer. See §§ 8.3b2—8.3b3. On the other hand, exclusive distributorships and price restraints will usually fail this test because they eliminate or greatly reduce meaningful intrabrand competition.

7.3a3.   *Dealers Bear Little or No Risk of Loss in Marketing a Brand*

The third screening test is *whether the downstream power restraint affects dealers that bear little or no risk of loss for the marketing of the relevant brand.* Antitrust should not restrict a producer's right to dictate downstream terms of sale if the producer owns its downstream outlets, or otherwise maintains title, risk of loss and the cost of promotion downstream, as when the dealer acts not as an independent entrepreneur, but as an agent for the supplier. This screening test would operate to exculpate a supplier that distributes products on consignment, with the supplier bearing the risk of loss should the products be lost, damaged or stolen.[17] The initiative and drive of an entrepreneur with capital at risk provide an incentive to manage the enterprise in a manner to maximize return and—disciplined by competitive forces—to achieve maximum allocation benefits. Competition works best when those that risk capital, reputation and livelihood can make the critical marketing decisions.[18] Of course, this distinction is not always neat. An independent downstream player must still negotiate with its suppliers, accepting many contractually imposed limits on competitive freedom. Similarly, a vertically integrated firm does not enjoy unlimited discretion in setting the terms of downstream sales. But the general proposition remains valid: those that bear the primary risk should also have primary marketing control.

7.3b.   The Second Level: A Balancing Test

7.3b1.   *Assessing Competitive Harms*

If a downstream power distribution restraint is not exculpated under any of the three screening tests, a second level of inquiry will be

17. The Supreme Court recognized a consignment exception in United States v. General Electric Co., 272 U.S. 476, 47 S.Ct. 192, 71 L.Ed. 362 (1926). Although interpreted narrowly in Simpson v. Union Oil Co., 377 U.S. 13, 84 S.Ct. 1051, 12 L.Ed.2d 98 (1964), the exception is still being applied in lower court decisions. E.g., Ryko Mfg. Co. v. Eden Servs., 823 F.2d 1215, 1223–27 (8th Cir.1987), cert. denied, 484 U.S. 1026, 108 S.Ct. 751, 98 L.Ed.2d 763 (1988); Illinois Corporate Travel, Inc. v. American Airlines, Inc., 806 F.2d 722, 725–26 (7th Cir.1986). Consignment case law is more fully reviewed in § 7.4b6.

18. The Supreme Court recognized the value in placing pricing discretion in the hands of the market player whose capital is primarily at risk in United States v. Arnold, Schwinn & Co., 388 U.S. 365, 87 S.Ct. 1856, 18 L.Ed.2d 1249 (1967), and in Albrecht v. Herald Co., 390 U.S. 145, 88 S.Ct. 869, 19 L.Ed.2d 998 (1968). Key holdings in *Schwinn* and *Albrecht* were overturned in subsequent decisions, but these subsequent decisions did not challenge the reasoning of the Court with respect to consignments and the value of placing pricing decisions in hands of the market player that bears the primary risk.

required—weighing the anticompetitive risks against any procompetitive gains that the restraint might offer. Because such a balancing could become subjective and open-ended if not carefully structured, it is vital that the inquiry is focused on features of distribution restraints most relevant to their competitive status. The approach assumes that the plaintiff must initially come forward with evidence that indicates that a restraint raises significant anticompetitive risks. Such risks are raised if the restraint is likely to injure antitrust's primary goals by misallocating resources, transferring wealth to those abusing market power, or harming the dynamic component of competition through increased barriers to innovation or entry. Four factors that can guide a court in assessing the anticompetitive risk are set forth below.

Whether the downstream power restraint will limit the competitive freedom of multibrand retailers—Consumers spend much of their disposable income at multibrand retail outlets selling everything from groceries, over-the-counter drugs, and clothing to major appliances and automobile parts. It is the multibrand retailer that has direct contact with, and often the greatest influence upon, the consumer. Such retailers have been a strong force for innovation in retailing methods over the last century. Any distribution restraint that restricts the freedom of the multibrand retailer poses heightened competitive risks.

Whether the restraint is likely to increase the risk of exploitation of information asymmetries—As described in § 6.3c2, the risk of exploitative retailer promotion increases with high retail margins that are undisciplined by intrabrand competition. Downstream power restraints may increase the risk of exploitative promotion if they apply to complex products, limit the competitive options of multibrand retailers, and operate in an industry in which sales advice is likely to influence purchase decisions. It is true that distribution restraints may have their maximum effectiveness as promotional tools in such situations. But they pose the greatest risk of exploitative promotion in this area as well.[19] The risk of this exploitative injury may be reduced as more and more upstream players in an industry introduce similar restraints. But as use of a restraint becomes widespread, the likelihood and extent of anticompetitive injury increases in part because the limitations on efficient and innovative retailers become more onerous.[20]

Whether the restraint is widespread or likely to be widely emulated in an industry—What is initially an isolated use of a distribution restraint may quickly become widespread if it places rival producers at a disadvantage for reasons unrelated to the competitive merits of their products. The likelihood of emulation increases as the restraint tends to displace rival brands. The conditions likely to foster emulation of a restraint were discussed above in § 6.3c3. Although the control afforded by widespread use of distribution restraints may make actual collusion easier, substan-

---

19. Distribution restraints may achieve maximum effectiveness in the sale of complex products in large part because of their propensity to exploit information gaps.

20. See the discussion in § 6.3c3.

tial injury to antitrust goals is likely even in the absence of collusion. For example, widespread use of distribution restraints may make entry at the retail level more difficult. An efficient new retailer could be denied its most potent competitive weapon: the ability to offer low prices on popular brands.

Whether the restraint is likely to eliminate efficient downstream arbitrage—Even an isolated distribution restraint, if associated with strong brand differentiation, might cause misallocations through injury to an efficient downstream market participant, possibly driving it from the market.[21] Such a restraint could also be used to facilitate price discrimination against less powerful or less knowledgeable buyers. For example, a terminated downstream distributor may have been acting as a buyer's cooperative for small retailers, buying in bulk to obtain favorable rates and then reselling to dealers who, by themselves, could not obtain the favorable rates.[22] This natural market response to price discrimination should be favored over any of the more costly and incomplete remedies afforded by the Robinson–Patman Act.[23]

7.3b2. Assessing Competitive Benefits

If the plaintiff succeeds in showing significant anticompetitive injury, the defendant may respond by showing strong promotional gains associated with use of the restraint. For example, the defendant might make a strong showing that the restraint promotes downstream investment going beyond the purchase of inventory. In franchising, the franchisor may agree to territorial restrictions as an incentive for the franchisee's investment in a retail outlet. The franchisor obtains a substantial investment from the franchisee, and a high degree of loyalty, but may offer something in return, in this case the right to an exclusive territory. But note that when the investment is confined to inventory, the retailer is making much less of a commitment. Many of the efficiencies of the franchise relationship are probably absent. And, the producer often has other reasonable means of inducing a retailer to stock and promote its inventory.

7.3b3. Weighing Harms Against Benefits

If a second-level inquiry demonstrates a probability of antitrust injury, but strong evidence is offered for the promotional benefits of the distribution restraint, a court should examine whether less anticompetitive means, such as promotional allowances, may be available to achieve the same marketing benefits.[24] That the producer or dealer may prefer a

---

21. Examples of cases in which a distribution restraint may have threatened an efficient downstream competitor include Business Electronics Corp. v. Sharp Electronics Corp., 485 U.S. 717, 108 S.Ct. 1515, 99 L.Ed.2d 808 (1988), and Klor's, Inc. v. Broadway–Hale Stores, Inc., 359 U.S. 207, 79 S.Ct. 705, 3 L.Ed.2d 741 (1959).

22. See the discussion of exclusive selling in § 7.5d.

23. Section 2a of the Clayton Act, 15 U.S.C.A. § 13a. The use of Section 2(a) as a tool to challenge predatory pricing practices is discussed in Chapter IV.

24. A catalogue of promotional options was presented in § 6.3b1.

particular distribution restraint is not enough to justify its use because the preference may be based on anticompetitive gains from the restraint. The loss in intrabrand competition should be tolerated only if alternative promotional methods would not reasonably achieve the producer's legitimate goals.

In close cases, a court may also wish to examine the cost of administering the distribution restraint. If there are significant anticompetitive risks associated with use of a distribution restraint, the cost of implementing that restraint may well be rent-seeking—a resource expended to maintain a higher profit margin associated with market power. That cost may be substantial, as for example when an intrabrand price restraint applies to a large number of retailers, requiring a major enforcement effort.[25] Of course, the high cost of implementing a distribution restraint may also be justified because the restraint efficiently delivers substantial promotional benefits. But the higher the implementation costs, the less likely it is that use of the restraint can be explained solely by legitimate promotional gains. These promotional gains must exceed the promotional gains from a competitively less risky promotional alternative (such as a promotional allowance) by an amount that exceeds the cost of administering the distribution restraint. If not, there is rent-seeking behavior associated with anticompetitive gains from the restraint. If these costs and promotional gains could be precisely measured, the competitive effect of a distribution restraint could be determined. Because accurate measurement is not possible, a court should probably use the costs of administering a distribution restraint more as a burden-shifting device: the higher the costs of administering a distribution restraint, the greater the burden on the defendant to show substantial promotional benefits that could not be attained by less anticompetitive means.

§ 7.4 Minimum Price Restraints

Vertical price fixing occurs when an upstream seller attempts to control the price at which downstream marketers resell a product or service. This section addresses vertical *minimum* price fixing, when the supplier will not allow resale below a specified price. Vertical maximum price fixing, when the supplier imposes a maximum resale price, is addressed in § 8.7. Often called resale price maintenance, vertical minimum price fixing was probably the first distribution restraint that the

---

25. Grimes, *Spiff, Polish, and Consumer Demand Quality: Vertical Price Restraints Revisited*, 80 CAL. L. REV. 815, 846–48 (1992). A recent example of the substantial administrative costs associated with some distribution restraints may be their alleged use by the Fuji Photo Film Company of distribution restraints to prevent discounting by Japanese film distributors and dealers. WALL ST. J., June 30, 1995, at A3. According to Kodak, the scheme, apparently designed to maintain high margins to ensure distributor and dealer loyalty, required close monitoring of film dealers all over the country. Kodak alleged that Fuji relied on spot checks by market research firms, specially trained homemakers known as Fuji Color Ladies, and, in remote areas, deputized postal carriers. Chandler & Blustein, *Kodak Finds Barriers to Film Sales in Japan*, LOS ANGELES TIMES, July 3, 1995, at D1.

Supreme Court found to violate Section 1 of the Sherman Act.[1] Beginning with the 1911 decision in *Dr. Miles*,[2] the debate about resale price maintenance has produced passionate but vacillating intervention by the Congress, the Executive branch, and the Supreme Court. Although a *per se* prohibition on vertical price fixing remains in place, the Supreme Court has narrowed the reach of that prohibition in decisions during the 1980s. See § 7.2a. For example, under the Supreme Court's holding in Business Electronics Corp. v. Sharp Electronics Corp.[3], the *per se* rule will not apply unless the plaintiff demonstrates that the defendants reached an agreement on price or price level. Absent such a showing, the claim will be judged under the rule of reason, a standard that places a more difficult burden on the plaintiff.

When the Supreme Court decided *Sylvania* in 1977, it adopted the rule of reason for nonprice distribution restraints, but expressly preserved the *per se* rule against vertical price fixing.[4] Under the *per se* rule, once an agreement to set a retail price is established, it is deemed illegal without any further evidentiary showing. The *per se* rule offers a degree of clarity in the law and a manageable litigation burden for plaintiffs. The rule, or something approaching it, can be justified if vertical minimum price fixing is consistently anticompetitive. But the rule has been under attack because not all applications of vertical minimum price fixing may be anticompetitive. In addition, as Justice White's concurrence in *Sylvania* noted, many nonprice distribution restraints involve similar or, potentially, even greater anticompetitive impact than does vertical minimum price fixing.[5]

Perhaps in response to these criticisms, the *per se* rule has been narrowed, but has endured. In the 1980s, the Supreme Court decided two vertical price fixing cases narrowing the scope of the *per se* rule against vertical minimum price fixing but reaffirming that the rule stands.[6] Will the next step be abrogation of the *per se* rule in all distribution restraint cases? Whether the Court broadens, narrows or abrogates the *per se* rule, a priority for the future evolution of antitrust law is to provide greater structure to rule of reason analysis. Certainly refusing to credit significant evidence of concerted conduct and anticompetitive effect, as in *Monsanto* and *Sharp,* is not an adequate response. Indeed, because these decisions narrowed the area of application for the *per se* rule, there is greater urgency to the task of providing more structured rule of reason analysis for courts and counselors grappling with distribution restraints.

§ 7.4

1. W. W. Montague & Co. v. Lowry, 193 U.S. 38, 24 S.Ct. 307, 48 L.Ed. 608 (1904), involved a distribution restraint enforced by a boycott, but the facts suggested a horizontal dimension to the conspiracy.

2. Dr. Miles Med. Co. v. John D. Park & Sons Co., 220 U.S. 373, 31 S.Ct. 376, 55 L.Ed. 502 (1911).

3. 485 U.S. 717, 108 S.Ct. 1515, 99 L.Ed.2d 808 (1988).

4. Continental T. V., Inc. v. GTE Sylvania Inc. 433 U.S. 36, 51 n. 18, 97 S.Ct. 2549, 53 L.Ed.2d 568 (1977)

5. Id. at 69–70 (White, J., concurring).

6. Monsanto Co. v. Spray–Rite Serv. Corp., 465 U.S. 752, 104 S.Ct. 1464, 79 L.Ed.2d 775 (1984); *Sharp*, 485 U.S. 717, 108 S.Ct. 1515, 99 L.Ed.2d 808. In State Oil Co. v. Khan, 522 U.S. 3, 118 S.Ct. 275, 139 L.Ed.2d 199 (1997), the Court excluded vertical maximum price fixing from the coverage of the *per se* rule. Under these decisions, it is apparent that some conduct that has the same effects as vertical minimum price fixing may be assessed under a rule of reason.

The procompetitive benefits of distribution restraints identified in *Sylvania, Monsanto* and *Sharp* must be recognized. But the unidimensional economic analysis of these cases must be supplemented. For example, in *Sharp*, the Court recognized that any procompetitive promotional benefits of distribution restraints arise because the dealer is guaranteed a higher margin.[7] But procompetitive promotion is only one possible consequence of a higher margin, and not necessarily the most likely. The Court showed no sensitivity to the possibility that this higher margin could be associated with anticompetitive behavior by retailers that sought to limit the vigor of retail competition or to exploit consumer information voids. *Sharp* and *Monsanto* appear to assume that competition at the retail level is either unimportant or will flow naturally from interbrand competition at the producer level. Neither proposition can be routinely sustained. See §§ 6.3b–6.3c.

Looking at a sample of circuit decisions involving allegations of unlawful vertical price fixing, it appears that a large percentage of these cases involved complex consumer products in which the advice of sales staff may be influential.[8] The consumer electronics industry appears to have defended more than its share of vertical price fixing cases.[9] With lower courts following or even expanding on the analysis of *Monsanto* and *Sharp*, defendants have won a large percentage of these decisions.[10] Many reflect the imbalanced economic analysis and the rigid interpretation of the conspiracy requirement that characterizes those Supreme Court precedents. More recently, some plaintiffs have survived pretrial motions so that vertical minimum price fixing claims could be heard by a jury.[11] In addition, state and federal enforcers have brought a number of vertical minimum price fixing cases,[12] some of which appear to extend the law in modest ways.[13]

---

7. 485 U.S. at 728.

8. Grimes, *Spiff, Polish, and Consumer Demand Quality: Vertical Price Restraints Revisited*, 80 Cal. L. Rev. 815, 838 & n.69 (1992).

9. Grimes, *The Seven Myths of Vertical Price Fixing: The Politics and Economics of a Century–Long Debate*, 21 Sw. U. L. Rev. 1285, 1313–14 & n.149 (1992).

10. E.g., Glacier Optical, Inc. v. Optique Du Monde, Ltd., 1995–1 Trade Cas. (CCH) ¶ 70,878 (9th Cir.1995)(per curiam)(unpublished opinion affirming summary judgment for the defendants); Jala v. Western Auto Supply Co., 1995–2 Trade Cas. (CCH) ¶ 71,173 (D.Me.1995)(motion to dismiss granted because acquiescence by dealer insufficient to establish an agreement). For a list of lower court cases in which defendants prevailed, see Ginsburg, *The Effect of GTE Sylvania on Antitrust Jurisprudence: Vertical Restraints: De Facto Legality Under the Rule of Reason*, 60 Antitrust L.J. 67, App. A & B (1991).

11. Pace Elec., Inc. v. Canon Computer Sys., Inc., 213 F.3d 118 (3d Cir.2000)(reversal of trial court's dismissal for lack of antitrust injury); Ezzo's Invs., Inc. v. Royal Beauty Supply, Inc., 94 F.3d 1032 (6th Cir.1996)(reversal of trial court's grant of summary judgment for defendants); Sportmart, Inc. v. No Fear, Inc., 1996–2 Trade Cas. (CCH) ¶ 71,513 (N.D. Ill. 1996)(defendants motion to dismiss denied).

12. United States v. Canstar Sports USA, Inc., 1993–2 Trade Cas. (CCH) ¶ 70,372 (D. Vt. Sept. 17, 1993)(consent decree prohibiting vertical price fixing on high-performance ice hockey skates); Nintendo of Am., Inc., 56 Fed. Reg. 15,883 (FTC 1991)(proposed consent order involving price maintenance on home video game hardware); Maryland v. Mitsubishi Elecs. of Am., Inc., 60 Antitrust & Trade Reg. Rep. (BNA) 446 (D. Md. 1991)(state case involving price maintenance on TV sets).

13. American Cyanamid, File No. 951–0106 (FTC, Jan. 30, 1997)(see the discus-

7.4a. The Conspiracy Requirement in Vertical Minimum Price Fixing Cases

In most privately initiated suits, the claim of vertical minimum price fixing is raised by a terminated dealer that alleges that the termination occurred as part of an unlawful price fixing scheme. Under the line of cases beginning with United States v. Colgate & Co.,[14] unilateral action by the supplier to terminate a dealer is beyond the reach of Section 1 of the Sherman Act because there is no required showing of a contract, combination or conspiracy. As described in § 6.4c, the *Colgate* case received new life after Monsanto Co. v. Spray–Rite Service Corp.[15] required a plaintiff to establish a conspiracy with evidence going beyond termination of the dealer after the supplier received one or more complaints from rival dealers. A plaintiff must make a further showing of conduct by the supplier or rival dealers that tends to exclude the possibility of independent action by the supplier.[16] On the other hand, a plaintiff need not produce a written contract between supplier and seller specifying a minimum resale price. An agreement to fix price may be implicit or signified by conduct.[17] Although establishing that the termination was pursuant to an agreement remains a significant hurdle for the terminated dealer, some plaintiffs have successfully met this burden in recent lower court cases.[18]

Of course, minimum resale prices may be enforced by means other than a threat to terminate. Government agencies have challenged other enforcement schemes. For example, in a 1997 consent agreement (*American Cyanamid*),[19] the FTC prohibited a supplier of agricultural chemicals from making a rebate to the dealer contingent upon the dealer's compliance with a specified minimum resale price. In this case, the minimum resale price imposed by the supplier was the same as the price the dealer paid to the supplier. Without the rebate, a dealer attempting to sell below the minimum price would lose money. The case may be read broadly as signifying that any supplier-imposed discipline short of termination will establish an unlawful price fixing agreement. The combined impact of this decision and the *Colgate-Monsanto* line of cases would appear to place a supplier that continues to deal with a discounter on discriminatory terms at greater risk than a supplier that, without discussion, negotiation or cajoling, quickly and cleanly terminates a discounting dealer. A sound competition policy would reject this distinc-

---

sion of *American Cyanamid* in § 7.4a); In re Toys "R" Us, Inc., FTC No. 9278 (Oct. 13, 1998) (see the discussion of *Toys "R" Us* in § 7.6).

14. 250 U.S. 300, 39 S.Ct. 465, 63 L.Ed. 992 (1919).

15. 465 U.S. 752, 104 S.Ct. 1464, 79 L.Ed.2d 775 (1984).

16. This emphasis on the conspiracy doctrine is criticized in § 7.2c.

17. Isaksen v. Vermont Castings, Inc., 825 F.2d 1158 (7th Cir.1987), cert. denied, 486 U.S. 1005, 108 S.Ct. 1728, 100 L.Ed.2d 193 (1988).

18. See the cases discussed in § 7.2c.

19. American Cyanamid, File No. 951–0106 (FTC, Jan. 30, 1997).

tion and favor an outcome that is based on injury to competition. Lower courts should recognize that the conspiracy analysis in *Monsanto* and *Sharp* was focused and purposeful. The Supreme Court, for the analytical reasons expressed in those cases, did not want to apply the *per se* price fixing rule. But the cases need not and should not be read to require the use of some excessively attenuated conspiracy analysis when facts similar to those in *Monsanto* or *Sharp* are challenged under the rule of reason applicable to nonprice vertical restraints.

7.4b. Variations on Minimum Price Restraints

7.4b1. *Minimum Price Restraints in Multibrand Retailing*

Vertical price restraints imposed on multibrand retailers are likely to threaten competitive harm. If vertical minimum price fixing (or a comparable distribution restraint) is imposed only by producers that have a small percentage of the market, the risk to efficient multibrand retailers is less. But the risk of information exploitation is probably at its peak. See the discussion in § 6.3c2. The higher margin offered to retailers on the relevant brands creates a strong incentive for disguised, self-interested promotion that can distort resource allocation and transfer wealth from consumers to sellers. This circumstance may pressure other producers to institute price fixing, so that the percentage of resale price maintenance users will grow.

What is the impact when most or all of the suppliers in an interbrand market use minimum resale prices? In such circumstances, efficient multibrand retailers may lose the opportunity to compete on price and pass along the benefits of their more efficient operations not just for a single brand, but for a range of competing brands. See the discussion in § 6.3c3.

Parallel use of resale price maintenance, or comparable distribution restraints, could lead to, or be the result of, outright cartel conduct at the buyer or seller level. The cartel theory of resale price maintenance has been widely acknowledged, but probably is not the most common cause or effect of resale price maintenance. The pressure to institute resale price maintenance comes from downstream dealers that want protected margins. In most cases, no concerted action by the dealers is required to prompt a producer to institute resale price maintenance. A unilateral threat by a single dealer may push an insecure producer to institute price fixing. In *Sharp*,[20] the ultimatum of one large dealer caused Sharp to terminate a smaller, apparently discounting dealer. In *Klor's*,[21] a department store chain's leverage apparently was sufficient to cause a number of appliance producers to stop dealing with a smaller, retail competitor located next to one of the chain's department stores. More recently, in the FTC proceeding against *Toys "R" Us*,[22] the

---

20. Business Elecs. Corp. v. Sharp Elecs. Corp., 485 U.S. 717, 108 S.Ct. 1515, 99 L.Ed.2d 808 (1988).

21. Klor's, Inc. v. Broadway–Hale Stores, Inc., 359 U.S. 207, 79 S.Ct. 705, 3 L.Ed.2d 741 (1959).

22. Toys "R" Us, Inc. v. FTC, 221 F.3d 928 (7th Cir. 2000).

leverage of a large retail chain was exercised to force suppliers to stop selling popular toys to discounting warehouse stores.

When vertical price fixing is imposed against the multibrand retailers, the cost of its administration and enforcement can be substantial, particularly when the resale price limit is imposed on a large number of dealers. That the supplier is willing to bear these high costs may indicate the high promotional value of the restraint or anticompetitive rent-seeking behavior. Because many of the promotional gains may be attained through means less threatening to competition and less costly to administer (supplier advertising, promotional allowances, etc.), a high administrative cost, although it is not dispositive of the existence of competitive injury, increases the probability that such anticompetitive injury is present. See the discussion in § 7.3b3.

7.4b2. Minimum Price Restraints on Premium or High–Image Products

There have been a number of cases involving imposition of minimum resale prices on premium or high-image products.[23] A manufacturer may decide to market a high-image brand through a particular class of retail outlets that will promote the products and maintain a high retail price that is profitable to the retailer and also allows the manufacturer to maintain a high price. Or the manufacturer may have a premium line that is sold to its established dealers but at a higher markup than is maintained for other products in the line. In either case, the manufacturer's markup may be threatened if dealers begin discounting the high-image or high-end product. A dealer's incentive to promote such a high-priced product is dependent on the dealer's ability to capture a high resale markup.

A minimum resale price could maintain the dealers' high markup and thereby protect the manufacturer's own high profit margin. But there is serious doubt whether antitrust policy should encourage suppliers to maintain such high-image and high-markup marketing schemes if the cost of doing so is the anticompetitive consequences associated with vertical minimum price fixing. In search of other procompetitive justifications for the use of minimum resale prices, it has been argued that minimum resale prices can provide an incentive for a high-end retail outlet to carry a particular line, thereby providing the supplier a "quality certification" that enhances the strength of the brand.[24] A separated but perhaps related justification for the use of minimum resale price

23. Ezzo's Invs., Inc. v. Royal Beauty Supply, Inc., 94 F.3d 1032 (6th Cir. 1996)(alleged price fixing of beauty products to be sold only by retailers that obtain half or more of their revenue from hair care services); United States v. Canstar Sports USA, Inc., 1993–2 Trade Cas. (CCH) ¶ 70,-372 (D. Vt. Sept. 17, 1993)(consent decree against supplier of high-performance ice hockey skates); In re Germaine Monteil Cosmetiques Corp., 100 F.T.C. 543 (1982)(consent order against supplier of cosmetics).

24. Marvel & McCafferty, *Resale Price Maintenance and Quality Certification*, 15 RAND J. ECON. 346 (1984)(discussing the use of vertical price restraints to enhance the image of a brand).

limits on premium lines is to prevent their use as a loss leader in a manner that would discourage full-price retailers from carrying the line.

For example, tire manufacturers might impose resale price maintenance only on their most expensive, heavily advertised tires. If the fixed retail price creates a higher margin than for less expensive tires, retailers will have an incentive to carry and promote the expensive tires. Without the fixed minimum resale price, manufacturers may be fearful that some nondiscounting retailers will be unwilling to carry their premium line. But whether the resale price limit is designed to provide a quality certification or prevent loss leaders that might discourage retailers from carrying the product, there would seem other less anticompetitive tools that could achieve the desired promotional goals. A promotional allowance, for example, might be used to reward a high-end outlet that provides special displays or valued promotion. Promotional allowances might also reward a dealer that carries the supplier's full line, thereby negating the impact of loss leaders. Premium lines could be (and often are) heavily advertised by the manufacturers, creating increased demand for these products that would encourage retailers to carry them.

The anticompetitive impact of a minimum resale price restraint does not disappear simply because the restraint is used only on premium lines. For example, minimum resale price limits could enhance the risk of information exploitation by dealers whose advice consumers respect. Resale price maintenance, even when limited to premium lines, will significantly limit the efficient retailer's ability to pass along cost savings to consumers, probably on the brands that consumers most desire. Efficient or innovative retailers can no longer attract customers by advertising low prices on the premium lines. The effect is amplified if the practice is widespread among tire producers that sell premium lines in this manner. These concerns may have been persuasive to the Department of Justice in a case in which it acted to halt minimum resale price limits on high-performance ice skates.[25]

What if the retail margin on heavily advertised brands sinks below the margin on unadvertised goods? This may occur if heavily advertised brands become the focus of intensive intrabrand price competition among retailers seeking to attract customers. This result is also consistent with the complaints of some manufacturers that their premium lines are subject to some retailers' lowball or even loss leader advertising intended to draw customers into the store. Such pricing may undercut profits of other retailers, making them less willing to carry or promote the premium merchandise. Often, these premium lines are the source of the highest profits for the manufacturer. But the desire to protect a high-profit margin hardly seems an adequate justification for thwarting intrabrand competition at the retail level. Moreover, intensive intrabrand competition could lower the retail price of the premium line and

---

25. United States v. Canstar Sports USA, Inc., 1993–2 Trade Cas. (CCH) ¶ 70,-372 (D. Vt. Sept. 17, 1993)(consent decree prohibiting vertical price maintenance for high-performance ice hockey skates).

produce additional sales. The bottom line could still be increased profitability for the manufacturer, even if the manufacturer has to spend some of its own resources for promotional allowances or other devices to provide reluctant retailers an incentive to continue to promote premium line products.

7.4b3. *Minimum Advertised Prices*

A minimum advertised price (MAP) operates to limit intrabrand price competition among retailers, but need not eliminate it entirely. With a MAP in place, a retailer may still advertise a brand at "a price too low to quote" or attempt to convey to consumers that a bargain price is available. Still, a MAP will operate to limit intrabrand competition among downstream dealers by preventing advertisements of a popular brand at a discount price. In 2000, the FTC negotiated a consent order to prohibit five major industry participants from using minimum advertised price restrictions on the retail sale of recordings.[26] It is unclear whether the FTC would have taken action had the practice only been implemented by recording firms that only had a small percentage of the market. The impact on retail competition is self-evidently greater when the practice is industry-wide.

Assume that an appliance producer provides advertising allowances to its dealers but requires, as a condition of receiving the allowance, that dealers advertise prices at or above a minimum level. The producer actively implements its restraint, going beyond the simple act of terminating non-complying dealers most likely to be protected under the *Monsanto-Colgate* line of cases.[27] Other major producers follow suit, adopting similar programs as part of promotional allowances to dealers. Under this scheme, a dealer could forego the promotional allowance in order to advertise low prices, but to do so would require it to give a cost advantage to less efficient and less aggressive rival dealers.

This restraint creates a high risk of anticompetitive impact and, by analogy to the FTC's consent order in *American Cyanamid*, may be condemned as a violation of Section 1 of the Sherman Act.[28] The restraint affects multibrand retailing. It also involves a complex product often sold with sales assistance, factors which increase the risk of exploiting information gaps. Conceptually, a MAP has the same anticompetitive risk as a fixed, minimum retail price. The mode of analysis should not vary except that the impact of the restraint may be less. If a MAP creates a higher retailer margin, but does so less effectively than a fixed minimum price, one would expect that both the procompetitive and anticompetitive impacts of the restraint would be dampened. Still, this widely emulated MAP will broadly limit the competitive freedom of efficient downstream marketers. Appliance producers seeking to bolster dealer loyalty should have other, less anticompetitive alternatives—such

---

26. See the FTC analysis of the proposed consent order of May 10, 2000, available at <www. ftc.gov/ os/2000/05/ mapanalysis.htm>.

27. See § 7.2c.

28. See the discussion of *American Cyanamid* in § 7.4a.

as a national advertising campaign or a promotional allowance. At least in cases in which MAPs target multibrand retailers, the burden should be on the seller to show that less anticompetitive methods of gaining dealer loyalty will be ineffective.[29]

Although the case law addressing required MAPs is sparse, any supplier imposing restrictions on the minimum price that can be advertised obviously runs a substantial risk. The law with respect to minimum price restrictions in cooperative advertising is more favorable to those imposing the restrictions, probably because cooperative advertising is viewed as a procompetitive undertaking that might not be possible without some agreement on the pricing of the advertised item.[30]

7.4b4. Minimum Price Restraints Imposed at the Distributor Level

Company M has set up a network of distributors, assigning each the task of promoting Company M's products within its geographic territory. Such primary territory assignments are generally lawful.[31] But now suppose that the distributors begin complaining that one of their number is aggressively marketing within other distributors' primary territories. From an antitrust point of view, the safest way to resolve this problem might be to levy a reasonable fee on out-of-territory sales to cover the local distributor's promotional costs. Company M, however, decides to impose a minimum price on the distributors' out-of-territory sales, perhaps because it is easier to administer and enforce than the fee arrangement.

In a case involving similar facts, the First Circuit has held that this arrangement was not subject to the *per se* rule, reasoning that if all competition among distributors could be constrained, this looser arrangement, which still allows for nonprice competition among distributors, should be viewed sympathetically.[32] When subject to a rule of reason analysis, such a restraint may pass muster. Indeed, if the fixed price is set at a sufficiently low level, the effect of this arrangement may be to discipline distributors to match the lowest price that out-of-territory distributors would be permitted to charge under the price fixing arrangement. From a competitive standpoint, this is less satisfactory than outright competition among distributors, but it is better than a strict

---

29. The analysis presented here is not intended to suggest that all MAPs will be anticompetitive. A MAP imposed on a product sold through a network of exclusive dealers or franchisees could pose fewer anticompetitive risks because the consumer would expect the seller to promote the product for which it has an exclusive dealership. A MAP imposed on a less complex product, generally not sold with the help of sales advice, might also pose fewer competitive risks.

30. Interco, Inc., [FTC Complaints and Orders 1993–1997 Transfer Binder] Trade

Reg. Rep. (CCH) ¶ 23,791 (Mar. 27, 1995)(advertising restrictions permitted); Clinique Lab., Inc., [FTC Complaints and Orders 1987–1993 Transfer Binder] Trade Reg. Rep. (CCH) ¶ 23,330 (Feb. 8, 1993)(restrictions permitted).

31. See § 7.5c discussing location clauses.

32. Eastern Scientific Co. v. Wild Heerbrugg Instruments, Inc., 572 F.2d 883, 885–86 (1st Cir.), cert. denied, 439 U.S. 833, 99 S.Ct. 112, 58 L.Ed.2d 128 (1978).

allocation scheme that prevents even nonprice competition among distributors, a scheme that itself has sometimes been considered lawful.[33]

7.4b5. Termination of a Discounter in the Absence of Minimum Resale Price Limits

A powerful retailer may exercise its buying power by threatening to discontinue a manufacturer's line unless the manufacturer ceases dealing with a discounting rival retailer. The manufacturer, in response, may terminate the discounting dealer. A significant number of litigated vertical cases involve such dealer terminations. Although it is the manufacturer that terminates the dealer, one force behind these terminations often is the complaining retailer. For example, in Business Electronics Corp. v. Sharp Electronics Corp.,[34] Hartwell, a Sharp dealer, apparently issued an ultimatum to Sharp, threatening to drop the Sharp line unless Sharp terminated Hartwell's rival dealer, Business Electronics. Sharp bowed to the pressure and terminated Business Electronics. Klor's, Inc. v. Broadway–Hale Stores, Inc.,[35] where Broadway–Hale apparently exercised its leverage with respect to more than one supplier of appliances, is analogous. Typically, the dealer issuing the ultimatum does so only if it believes it has the economic leverage to force the supplier to choose it over the smaller, rival dealer. This is a form of buyer power addressed in § 2.7c.

Although perhaps confined to a narrow geographic market, the buyer power possessed by the dealer issuing the ultimatum allows it to dictate the terms of retail competition in the local market. The harm to intrabrand competition is also significant: A rival dealer is being eliminated from competing in the sales of the producer's brand. The elimination of local dealer competition, perhaps from a discounter or more competitive new entrant, creates a genuine competitive injury in that local market.[36]

In contrast to the dealer with local market power, the producer may have no significant distribution in this market and be solicitous of the dealer that offers the producer the maximum chance to penetrate that market. The producer may have been coerced by the more powerful of the two dealers, each of whom might seek exclusive rights to sell the manufacturer's brand. As long as the producer has no policy of imposing an unlawful distribution restraint, the terminated dealer's discounting activity should not be the basis of a finding that the producer violated

---

33. See § 7.5d.

34. 485 U.S. 717, 108 S.Ct. 1515, 99 L.Ed.2d 808 (1988).

35. 359 U.S. 207, 79 S.Ct. 705, 3 L.Ed.2d 741 (1959). The Court treated this case as a group boycott subject to a *per se* condemnation. The case, accordingly, did not appear to turn on whether or not Klor's was a discounter. It is apparent, however, that Broadway–Hale did not wish to have Klor's compete from a next door location because it was depriving the department store of sales, either because of Klor's lower prices or other attractive features of Klor's offerings.

36. Even if the terminated dealer is a free rider on the services of the nonterminated dealer, there are usually less anticompetitive steps that the supplier may take to compensate a full service dealer—such as promotional allowances.

Section 1 of the Sherman Act. Sanctions should be imposed only against the offending dealer.[37] The challenge for the terminated dealer is in finding a post-*Sharp* theory that will allow recovery. *Sharp* held that the use of an ultimatum, in the absence of an agreement to set prices or price level, will not suffice to establish a *per se* violation. Language in *Sharp* stressing the procompetitive virtues of distribution restraints is not conducive to a plaintiff's winning a rule of reason case, but need not be fatal. If the plaintiff can survive summary judgment based on the alleged lack of a conspiracy, it may have sympathetic facts to present to the judge and jury, particularly if it seeks relief not from the supplier but from the rival dealer that is the true source of abusive market power in this situation. Finding a single defendant to have violated Section 1 would not be unique even if its coconspirator (in this case the supplier) was coerced.

The Supreme Court has been willing to find the conspiracy requirement satisfied when an unwilling buyer is coerced to comply with a vertical restraint or to purchase a tied product. In Perma Life Mufflers, Inc. v. International Parts Corp.,[38] the Court confronted the question whether individual dealers of the Midas line could establish a conspiracy with their supplier based on their unwilling compliance with the terms of the franchise agreement, which obliged dealers to purchase mufflers only from Midas, sell only from the location specified by Midas, resell only at prices set by Midas, and honor the Midas guarantee on sold mufflers. The Court concluded that "each petitioner can clearly charge a combination between Midas and himself, as of the day he unwillingly complied with the restrictive franchise agreements."[39] In his concurring opinion, Justice White wrote that the Court had as early as 1927 "recognized that participation in an unlawful course of conduct would not bar recovery where the defendant's superior bargaining power led to plaintiff's participation in the unlawful arrangement."[40] These cases involved a claim that the plaintiff dealer was coerced, not the supplier. But the finding of a conspiracy should be the same if it is the supplier that is coerced by a large rival dealer. Indeed, courts may find less

37. Even if a supplier terminates more than one retailer, as long as each termination was coerced, the supplier should not be held to have violated antitrust law. A supplier's liability would be triggered by active cooperation with, or instigation of, a plan to limit retail price competition. United States v. Parke, Davis & Co., 362 U.S. 29, 80 S.Ct. 503, 4 L.Ed.2d 505 (1960). In *Parke, Davis*, the distributor was found to have violated Section 1 of the Sherman Act because it was actively orchestrating with various dealers a mutually acceptable retail price maintenance scheme.

38. 392 U.S. 134, 88 S.Ct. 1981, 20 L.Ed.2d 982 (1968).

39. Id. at 142. This holding in *Perma Life* was cited with approval in a recent tie-in case. Systemcare, Inc. v. Wang Labs. Corp., 117 F.3d 1137, 1140 (10th Cir.1997). See the discussion in § 8.3d3. In a recent lower court decision involving a vertical minimum price fixing claim, the defendant unsuccessfully sought summary judgment based on the argument that the supplier's coercion of the dealer to accept minimum resale prices was not a sufficient showing of conspiracy. Sportmart, Inc. v. No Fear, Inc., 1996–2 Trade Cas. (CCH) ¶ 71,513 (N.D. Ill. 1996).

40. *Perma Life,* 392 U.S. at 142–43 (White, J., concurring)(citing Eastman Kodak Co. v. Southern Photo Materials Co., 273 U.S. 359, 47 S.Ct. 400, 71 L.Ed. 684 (1927)).

tension in recognizing a conspiracy based on coercion when the unwilling participant is not the plaintiff dealer—there will be no argument that the plaintiff should be denied recovery because of its participation in the unlawful conspiracy (the *in pari delicto* defense).[41]

Sharp also leaves open various horizontal and attempted monopoly claims that could afford a terminated dealer relief. There are at least two ways in which the plaintiff might attempt to establish a horizontal claim under Section 1. First, it might try to show that the powerful dealer acted as the hub in a "hub and spoke" conspiracy with a number of suppliers, each of which is convinced to terminate the plaintiff.[42] Second, it might try to show that more than one rival dealer pressured the supplier to terminate the plaintiff.[43] Finally, a theory of local monopoly power on the part of the rival dealer might succeed as an attempted monopoly claim (either based on the local power arising from a single strong brand or in the interbrand market).[44]

Granting relief to discounters victimized by a rival dealer's ultimatum delivered to a supplier would not prevent powerful retailers from influencing the suppliers' marketing decisions. For example, a retailer could still press a supplier not to begin selling to rivals or to provide a promotional allowance to cover the cost of services not provided by rival dealers. But the availability of such relief would discourage the most blatant use of retail buyer power to limit competition. And it would place the blame for such terminations where it belongs: not on the supplier that was willing to deal with all interested retailers, but on the reseller that wishes to thwart competition in its geographic market.

7.4b6.   *The Consignment Exception*

In its 1926 holding in United States v. General Electric Co.,[45] the Supreme Court held that an upstream seller was not in violation of the rule against vertical price fixing when it prescribed the sale price for light bulbs consigned to independent merchants. The Court stressed that the independent merchants never had title to the bulbs. Almost forty years later, in Simpson v. Union Oil Co.,[46] the Court backed away from *General Electric* on facts that are difficult to distinguish. Union supplied gasoline to gas station operators under consignment contracts which, like the General Electric contracts, made the consignee responsible for

---

41. The *in pari delicto* defense was rejected in *Perma Life,* 392 U.S. at 135–41.

42. This was essentially the claim in *Klor's* and was also a basis for the Commission's decision in Toys "R" Us, Inc. v. FTC, 221 F.3d 928 (7th Cir. 2000). See also Interstate Circuit, Inc. v. United States, 306 U.S. 208, 59 S.Ct. 467, 83 L.Ed. 610 (1939).

43. United States v. General Motors Corp., 384 U.S. 127, 86 S.Ct. 1321, 16 L.Ed.2d 415 (1966). This case is discussed in § 5.5a.

44. A local monopoly theory was successful in Aspen Skiing Co. v. Aspen High-

lands Skiing Corp., 472 U.S. 585, 105 S.Ct. 2847, 86 L.Ed.2d 467 (1985). See § 3.4b4. A franchisor's localized market power was also the basis of a successful attempted monopoly claim in Photovest Corp. v. Fotomat Corp., 606 F.2d 704 (7th Cir.1979), cert. denied, 445 U.S. 917, 100 S.Ct. 1278, 63 L.Ed.2d 601 (1980). See § 8.9g2.

45. 272 U.S. 476, 47 S.Ct. 192, 71 L.Ed. 362 (1926).

46. 377 U.S. 13, 84 S.Ct. 1051, 12 L.Ed.2d 98 (1964).

stock losses other than those caused by catastrophe, and which authorized the consignor to establish the resale price. The Court viewed the distribution system in *Simpson* as a clever manipulation masking a coercive device "for administering prices on a vast scale."[47]

The *General Electric* decision was significantly limited in *Simpson*. Application of the rule against vertical price fixing ought not to turn on a formalism such as the passage of title, but rather on meaningful discernment of which party bears the primary economic risk. *Simpson* properly referred to the risk of loss. If the dealer bears little or no risk of loss in selling the merchandise, the distribution mechanism becomes more in the nature of an agency relationship in which the consigning supplier is the principal and the dealer acts as an agent. In such agency relationships, the principal should have the power to set downstream prices. Assigning pricing discretion to the party bearing the economic risk is efficient because the risk bearer, disciplined by competition, has a strong incentive to price the product in a manner that maximizes profits and ensures an efficient allocation.

In 1967, in addressing nonprice territorial restraints, the Supreme Court in United States v. Arnold, Schwinn & Co.[48] revisited and reaffirmed the consignment exception. The Court again acknowledged that a consignment or agency relation properly accorded the risk-bearing supplier the authority to set both price and nonprice terms of sale. Although other aspects of *Schwinn* were overturned in 1977,[49] the consignment holding in *Schwinn* remains untouched.[50] *Schwinn* did not appear to rest on another ground that was cited in *Simpson,* where the Court stressed that the marketwide nature of the arrangement would take it outside the consignment exception. If a consignment arrangement is limited to a specified carload of goods, it is true that the anticompetitive potential for downstream competition is limited. The logic of this limitation seems stretched if the supplier is maintaining a pure agency relationship. Some courts have applied the consignment exception despite a marketwide impact. The Seventh Circuit held that a travel agent falls within the consignment exception for the sale of airline tickets, notwithstanding the marketwide nature of the arrangement.[51] Because travel agents bore no risk for nonsale of airplane seats, their downstream contribution to the airline business might be seen as that of an agent who adds little or nothing to the service being sold. But the Seventh Circuit's holding seems questionable because travel agents contribute substantially to the airline business as effective marketers of airline tickets. Because they are multibrand retailers (i.e., they sell tickets from more than one airline), travel agents can serve as a consumer agent for buyers unaware of the

47. Id. at 22.

48. 388 U.S. 365, 87 S.Ct. 1856, 18 L.Ed.2d 1249 (1967).

49. Continental T. V., Inc. v. GTE Sylvania, Inc., 433 U.S. 36, 97 S.Ct. 2549, 53 L.Ed.2d 568 (1977).

50. Ryko Mfg. Co. v. Eden Servs., 823 F.2d 1215 (8th Cir.1987) (citing *Simpson*), cert. denied, 484 U.S. 1026, 108 S.Ct. 751, 98 L.Ed.2d 763 (1988).

51. Illinois Corporate Travel, Inc. v. American Airlines, Inc., 806 F.2d 722, 725–26 (7th Cir.1986).

full range of travel options. If one travel agent can sell tickets at a lower cost than its competitors, why should it be prevented from rebating a portion of its commission to buyers of airline tickets? The rebate would seem consistent with a major goal of competition: to discipline sellers to provide more quality for less money. The result reached by the Seventh Circuit may have stifled an innovative and efficient mode of retailing. At least insofar as a travel agent seeks to rebate only that portion of an airline ticket price that is allocable to its distribution function, the consignment exception should not have applied.

§ 7.5 Nonprice Downstream Power Distribution Restraints

Nonprice downstream power distribution restraints generally operate to instill dealer loyalty in the same manner as price restraints: by ensuring dealers a higher resale margin. Yet, for purposes of a competitive analysis, there are critical distinctions between price and nonprice restraints, just as there are among the various types of nonprice restraints. Three types of nonprice restraints are discussed here: customer allocation schemes (based on territory or customer type), location clauses, and exclusive selling or exclusive distributorships. Distribution restraints that are based on upstream power, such as exclusive dealing and tie-ins, are addressed in Chapter VII.

Customer allocation schemes operate to limit the customers to whom a downstream marketer may sell. This may be done by delimiting the customers by territory, by market level (wholesalers, retailers, etc.) or in some other manner. For instance, some suppliers prohibit their dealers from selling to large-volume customers or customers with "national accounts." Location clauses, on the other hand, need not limit the class of customers to whom the dealer may sell, but merely the location from which the dealer sells. Exclusive selling differs from other price and nonprice restraints in that the restraint operates against the supplier: The supplier makes a commitment not to sell to any downstream marketer in direct competition with the favored marketer.

What all of these restraints have in common is the presence of downstream or buyer power that pressures a supplier to limit downstream competition in order to win dealer loyalty. Of course, these restraints may be combined or altered in various ways. For example, customer allocation schemes may be subject to exceptions. A downstream marketer may be allowed to sell outside a designated territory on specified conditions, such as adherence to a minimum resale price or payment of an allowance to the marketer in whose territory the sale is made. Or an exclusive selling commitment by a producer may be linked to a location clause limiting the place in which the exclusive dealer operates.

Nonprice upstream power restraints may be analyzed using the structured rule of reason described in § 7.3, employing screening tests to eliminate relatively harmless restraints and a balancing test for more problematic restraints. The courts, however, have yet to evolve a consistent approach to nonprice distribution restraints. In some circuits, a market power screening test is used, although the focus is often erroneously placed on whether the supplier has market power.[1] Failure to establish market power may be grounds for summary judgment against the plaintiff.[2] Whether or not the use of a market power screen will produce sound policy results depends on the definition of market power that is employed and whether the focus is on the presence of downstream power. See the discussion of a market power screening test in § 7.3a1.

An example of a case in which the court used a market power test that focused on the market share of the supplier is *Valley Liquors, Inc. v. Renfield Importers, Ltd.* The plaintiff challenged an exclusive selling arrangement for the wholesaling of liquor and wine in certain Northern Illinois counties. In affirming the district court's denial of a preliminary injunction that would have restored the plaintiff as a wholesaler, Judge Posner wrote that "[a] firm that has no market power is unlikely to adopt policies that disserve its customers * * *."[3] Judge Posner defined market power as the "power to raise prices significantly above the competitive level without losing all of one's business,"[4] a definition that would allow a plaintiff to establish market power based on the defendant's strong brand or market niche. But Judge Posner retreated from this definition on the grounds that market power so defined could rarely be measured by methods of litigation, and embraced a more traditional measurement based on market share in a carefully defined interbrand market.[5] If there was harm to competition in this exclusive selling system, it probably arose from the buying power of favored wholesalers and that power's exercise to suppress competition among wholesalers, some of whom may have operated more efficiently and sold at lower prices than the favored wholesaler. When market power is defined solely from the supplier's point of view, many potentially harmful distribution restraints are placed beyond the reach of the antitrust laws. A more cautiously implemented market power screen, as outlined in § 7.3a1, will produce results consistent with sound competition policy. The complex analysis needed may be beyond the means of a particular plaintiff, but if

---

§ 7.5

1. Examples of circuit cases in which a market power screen was employed include: Assam Drug Co. v. Miller Brewing Co., 798 F.2d 311, 316 (8th Cir.1986); JBL Enters., Inc. v. Jhirmack Enters., Inc., 698 F.2d 1011, 1017 (9th Cir.), cert. denied, 464 U.S. 829, 104 S.Ct. 106, 78 L.Ed.2d 109 (1983); Muenster Butane, Inc. v. Stewart Co., 651 F.2d 292, 298 (5th Cir.1981); Oreck Corp. v. Whirlpool Corp., 579 F.2d 126, 130 n. 5 (2d Cir.)(en banc), cert. denied, 439 U.S. 946, 99 S.Ct. 340, 58 L.Ed.2d 338 (1978).

2. *Assam Drug*, 798 F.2d at 317.

3. 678 F.2d 742, 745 (7th Cir.1982).

4. Id.

5. Id. In a decision in which retail pharmacies challenged the allegedly discriminatory pricing of drug producers, Judge Posner returned to the economically correct definition of market power. In re Brand Name Prescription Drugs Antitrust Litig., 123 F.3d 599, 603 (7th Cir.1997)(market power or monopoly power is "the power to raise price above cost without losing so many sales as to make the price rise unsustainable"), cert. denied, 522 U.S. 1153 & 523 U.S. 1040, 118 S.Ct. 1178 & 1336, 140 L.Ed.2d 186 & 498 (1998). See the discussion of use of this definition consistently for all antitrust claims in § 2.2.

the plaintiff does base the case on a structured rule of reason, the normal methods of litigation are adequate to the task.

Not all courts have employed a market power screen. Eiberger v. Sony Corp. of America[6] is one of a relatively small number of cases in which the plaintiff has prevailed in a post-*Sylvania* claim based on a downstream power restraint. In that case, Sony had introduced a warranty fee plan under which dealers that sold dictation equipment outside their assigned territory would be assessed a warranty fee that eliminated the dealer's profit on that sale. Citing the negative impact on intrabrand competition and the availability of less anticompetitive alternatives to ensure that dealers selling outside their territories bore the fair cost of warranty service for those sales, the Second Circuit affirmed the district court's holding that the plan was an unreasonable restraint of trade.[7]

7.5a. Customer Allocations

Customer allocations may be an indication that a supplier offers a weak brand and must take strong measures to find a loyal distributor. These allocations are potentially far more restrictive of downstream, intrabrand competition than are forms of vertical price fixing. When an upstream participant fixes the minimum resale price at which downstream marketers may sell, these marketers may still compete with one another by offering more or better service, free delivery, or by including extra goods along with the item for which resale price is fixed. But when a customer allocation scheme assigns each downstream marketer a nonoverlapping group of customers, *all* intrabrand competition ceases. The downstream marketer is free to set price and terms for this brand without fear that other distributors or dealers will offer better terms. Nevertheless, customer allocation schemes may not severely threaten efficient downstream methods of distribution. One reason for this is that customer allocation tends to limit a supplier's access to the market, creating a built-in incentive for the supplier to limit their use. If there is only a single downstream marketer that may sell a manufacturer's brand to a customer, the manufacturer has, in a sense, bet all marketing chips on a single player. If that player is not an aggressive or effective marketer, the manufacturer will lose sales. For widely sold consumer products, most manufacturers cannot afford to limit retail access in this manner. Exclusive customer allocations are more likely to be found at the distributor level, where the manufacturer has more direct control over the distributor's behavior to ensure that marketing access is maintained. Even when applied at the retail level, however, customer allocation schemes may have few anticompetitive effects on downstream, multibrand retailers. As long as the manufacturer's decision is isolated and is not likely to lead to an industrywide practice, downstream marketers will still have access to a variety of rival products that will allow competition among dealers that fosters effective and innovative downstream marketing. Under a structured rule of reason as outlined in

---

6. 622 F.2d 1068 (2d Cir.1980).   **7.** Id. at 1081.

§ 7.3, customer allocation schemes that do not curtail all competition among dealers are likely to fare well.

Another reason for the relatively generous treatment of customer allocation schemes is that they, in contrast to minimum price restraints, seem less likely to raise the risk of exploitation of information asymmetries. Allocation schemes that operate at the retail level will still raise these risks. But consumers may be more likely to recognize the self-interest of a marketer that has the exclusive right to sell a product.

Customer allocation schemes are more troubling when their use is widespread in a particular industry. Under such circumstances, they may lead to cartel-like behavior that undermines interbrand as well as intrabrand competition. For example, if most producers in an industry institute customer allocation schemes at the retail level, multibrand retailing may be severely undercut. In Matsushita Electric Industrial Co. v. Zenith Radio Corp.,[8] the plaintiffs alleged that Japanese electronic goods producers agreed among themselves to limit the number of distributors each would use and to allocate retail customers among themselves in an effort to limit interbrand competition. Because the allocation scheme did not include American and non-Japanese foreign producers, its anticompetitive impact may have been limited.

In Eiberger v. Sony Corp. of America,[9] a customer allocation scheme was imposed on Sony dealers of dictation equipment by charging each a warranty fee for out-of-territory sales that eliminated any profit for the selling dealer. The restraint in *Sony,* which potentially ended all competition among dealers, would likely have survived a rule of reason analysis if it had been narrowed to simply require dealers making out-of-territory sales to pay the costs of repairs for those customers. In post-*Sylvania* cases, *most* customer restrictions that do not eliminate all competition among dealers have survived rule of reason analysis. For example, in O.S.C. Corp. v. Apple Computer, Inc.,[10] a prohibition on dealer mail-order sales, said to have been instituted because of rival dealer complaints of price cutting, was upheld under the rule of reason.

7.5b. Customer Allocation Schemes as a Tool for Price Discrimination

Customer allocation schemes, even if they occur upstream from the retail level, may prevent small retailers from access to secondary distributors that function as buyers' cooperatives. A small retailer that cannot buy in bulk may lack the leverage to obtain favorable prices from producers, but may gain some of that leverage through a secondary distributor that buys in bulk in order to resell to small retailer buyers. A customer allocation scheme that prevents distributors from reselling to secondary distributors that function as dealer cooperatives may eliminate this efficient marketing method. This could be considered an

---

8. 475 U.S. 574, 106 S.Ct. 1348, 89 L.Ed.2d 538 (1986).

9. 622 F.2d 1068 (2d Cir.1980).

10. 792 F.2d 1464 (9th Cir.1986).

example of "midstream" power because it is the powerful distributor, operating between the supplier and downstream dealers, that wields power in a potentially anticompetitive manner.

Small dealers denied access to a dealers' cooperative still enjoy protection from price discrimination under the Robinson–Patman Act.[11] Compared to the complexities and costs associated with enforcement of that Act, protecting the role of the secondary distributor may be a more efficient way of ensuring that small retailers continue to receive the best possible prices and the most efficient service. But secondary distributors may not survive in an antitrust climate that allows manufacturers to freely allocate customers and assign exclusive distributors. The manufacturer and the exclusive seller will have an incentive to discriminate in favor of powerful buyers. The incentive is dampened by interbrand competition, but less so if such discriminatory practices are widespread among major brands in an industry or if the brand has a high consumer loyalty.

An example of use of a distribution restraint to limit arbitrage and better maintain a system of price discrimination is *In re Brand Name Prescription Drugs Antitrust Litigation*.[12] Retail pharmacies brought a series of individual and class action suits against drug producers and wholesalers alleging a violation of Section 1 of the Sherman Act in the defendants' alleged schemes to deny retail pharmacists the discounts on brand name drugs that were available to favored classes of customers such as hospitals, nursing homes, health maintenance organizations, and mail-order companies. The alleged method of implementing the price discrimination was not through a direct allocation of customers by the drug producers, but by a "chargeback" system under which producers would contract directly with favored customers authorizing them to buy drugs from the wholesalers at discounted prices not available to other customers. The producer would then allow the wholesaler to "chargeback" the amount of the discount to the producer. This system allegedly allowed the producers to maintain direct control over which buyers received a discount and, in this way, to control arbitrage that might undermine the system of discriminatory prices.

Although an initial favorable ruling allowed the plaintiffs to settle against some drug manufacturers, the plaintiffs' claims were largely dismissed against the remaining defendants because, according to Judge Posner's opinion, there was insufficient evidence of a conspiracy among drug manufacturers to deny discounts to the plaintiff pharmacies.[13] The price discrimination linked to the market power that manufacturers possessed in brand name drugs was undisputed, but the court reasoned that manufacturers could unilaterally engage in such price discrimina-

---

11. Section 2(a) of the Clayton Act, 15 U.S.C.A. § 13(a).

12. 123 F.3d 599 (7th Cir.1997), cert. denied, 522 U.S. 1153 & 523 U.S. 1040, 118 S.Ct. 1178 & 1336, 140 L.Ed.2d 186 & 498 (1998).

13. In re Brand Name Prescription Drugs Antitrust Litigation, 186 F.3d 781, 784–85 (7th Cir. 1999).

tion, and the chargeback system in which the wholesalers cooperated, although collusive at the wholesaler level, would not violate the Sherman Act because it was in pursuit of an end that the manufacturer could unilaterally seek.

Judge Posner is of course correct that brand-specific market power that allows price discrimination is not an antitrust violation. But does the Sherman Act permit a manufacturer to collude with a downstream distributor to implement such price discrimination? And if the downstream distributors collude among themselves to make the price discrimination apply to an entire industry, how is this result different in anticompetitive effect than if the manufacturers had colluded among themselves to implement the discrimination? The Posner opinion concedes that such manufacturer collusion would be unlawful, so it is difficult to explain why either downstream horizontal collusion among wholesalers or vertical collusion between manufacturer and wholesaler to effect the same systemwide price discrimination should be lawful. At issue here is the viability of a class of entrepreneurs (retail pharmacies) that provide offerings valued by consumers (as reflected in centuries of patronage). The higher prices that a pharmacist must pay because of price discrimination can injure consumers in a variety of ways—through higher consumer prices, through reduced pharmacy services, or by driving pharmacists from the market altogether.

Some economists may see the jockeying between secondary distributors and small retailers, on the one hand, and producers and favored distributors, on the other hand, as of little or no concern to antitrust. Arguably, that jockeying involves allocation of revenues among participants but will have little or no impact on consumer prices. One response is that, from the point of view of fairness to competitors, the secondary distributors and small retailers should be protected from oppressive use of customer allocations and exclusive selling. But the case for antitrust intervention rests on more than equity among market participants. Significant resource allocations are altered when secondary distributors are eliminated. These distributors may be the most efficient way of collecting and delivering goods to the small retailer. The retailer may be able to place a large, single order with the secondary distributor and have it delivered in a single truck. If secondary distributors are unable to obtain branded merchandise, the retailer may have to place separate orders with the manufacturers' favored distributors to obtain the same merchandise. The disadvantaged position of small retailers may limit their ability to maintain their market position, not to mention to innovate and gain ground, against the large retailers. Consumers that prefer the service offered by the small retailer are discouraged or prevented from receiving it because of the price differential. These are true resource misallocations.

7.5c. Location Clauses

A location clause is a classic downstream power restraint that limits only the location from which a downstream marketer may operate. The restriction could be imposed at the distributor or retailer level. Although the restriction substantially limits the downstream marketer's freedom to compete, it does not end intrabrand competition at the downstream level. Downstream marketers remain free to compete against one another to the extent they can do so from their established locations. Location clauses may be linked to commitments not to sell outside the designated territory, in which case airtight customer allocation becomes the dominant antitrust concern. By themselves, location clauses present no major threat to intrabrand competition as long as the manufacturer ensures that some intrabrand competition is preserved. For example, if there are ten Ford dealerships in a large metropolitan area, that number probably ensures vigorous intrabrand competition, even if each dealer is required to operate at a specified location. In such instances, an antitrust challenge would probably not survive the second screening test (see § 7.2b)—there would be no substantial lessening of intrabrand competition.

The Supreme Court held that a location clause imposed upon a retailer in *Sylvania*[14] would be subject to the rule of reason. Although the broad sweep of *Sylvania's* language is suspect, the result was probably correct. On the record before the Supreme Court, there was no evidence that use of such location clauses threatened multibrand retailing or other efficient methods of marketing. Sylvania's market share was small (the Court said 1 to 2 percent),[15] a concern that is relevant to an assessment of a distribution restraint's impact. There was no record evidence that Sylvania's location clauses were adopted to favor a powerful retailer who wished to suppress retail competition from less powerful rivals. On remand, the district court found that the location clauses were reasonable as a matter of law. The Ninth Circuit affirmed, holding that the plaintiff has the burden of proving that a nonprice distribution restraint is unreasonable, taking account both of interbrand and intrabrand competition. Showing an adverse effect on intrabrand competition does not shift the burden of justification to the defendant.[16] In instances where market wide competitive harm results, a structured rule of reason could make proof of that fact feasible.

7.5d.   Exclusive Selling (Exclusive Distributorships)

A form of customer allocation will occur if a manufacturer promises a distributor not to authorize any competing distributor in the same territory. This arrangement seems more likely when the purveyor of a weak brand needs to offer strong incentives to the distributor to promote the product. The distributor becomes the exclusive seller for the manufacturer in the relevant territory. The agreement may be implement along with a location clause—agreements discussed in § 7.5c. Suppliers can grant an exclusive distributorship as an incentive for the distributor

---

14. Continental T. V., Inc. v. GTE Sylvania Inc., 433 U.S. 36, 97 S.Ct. 2549, 53 L.Ed.2d 568 (1977). One of the authors represented petitioner in this case.

15. Id. at 38.

16. Continental T.V., Inc. v. G.T.E. Sylvania Inc., 694 F.2d 1132 (9th Cir.1982).

to invest in the supplier's line and to promote it. The favored distributor, knowing that the benefits of its promotional activity will be retained and not shared with rival distributors, is more likely to invest its own resources in promotion. Like customer allocation schemes, exclusive selling arrangements are more often found at the distribution level and will limit a manufacturer's access to the downstream market. Information asymmetries are less likely to be a problem if exclusive selling does not operate at the retail level.

Like location clauses, bare-bones exclusive distributorships have generally fared well in the courts.[17] But anticompetitive effects could be likely if the same distributor serves as the exclusive supplier for most producers,[18] or if exclusive selling is used to undercut efficient, secondary distributors that serve as buying cooperatives for smaller retail customers. See § 7.5b, discussing an allocation scheme that fosters price discrimination against smaller retail buyers.

Exclusive dealing is relatively easy to implement, and with low legal risks, when it is part of the original distribution plan of a producer. Legal risks mount when, in order to implement exclusive selling, the producer must terminate one or more existing distributors. A terminated distributor, particularly if it has substantial investment sunk in carrying the producer's line, is more likely to seek relief under the state or federal antitrust laws, unfair competition law, or any other available remedy. For possible antitrust remedies open to such a distributor, see the discussion in §§ 7.4b5 and 7.5.

§ 7.6 Boycotts and Refusals to Deal Used to Enforce Distribution Restraints

Boycotts and refusals to deal are a common tool for enforcing distribution restraints. For example, retailers confronted with unwanted competition may press a supplier to terminate the unwanted competitor, or limit the competitor's access to supplies. Much litigation involving distribution restraints has its genesis in a supplier's decision to terminate or limit sales to a retailer in response to complaints from one or more competitors. *Sharp, Klor's, Eastern States Lumber*, and *Montague* are representative of almost a century of Supreme Court antitrust cases that fit this general pattern.[1]

---

17. Electronics Communications Corp. v. Toshiba Am. Consumer Prods., Inc., 129 F.3d 240, 245 (2d Cir.1997)(exclusive distributorships are "presumptively legal"); Packard Motor Car Co. v. Webster Motor Car Co., 243 F.2d 418 (D.C.Cir.), cert. denied, 355 U.S. 822, 78 S.Ct. 29, 2 L.Ed.2d 38 (1957). See also Valley Liquors, Inc. v. Renfield Importers, Ltd., 678 F.2d 742 (7th Cir.1982).

18. United States v. Topa Equities (V.I.), Ltd., 1995–2 Trade Cas. (CCH) ¶ 71,-061 (D.V.I.1995)(consent order against distributor of liquor that had exclusive rights to sell most producers' brands in the Virgin Islands).

§ 7.6

1. Business Elecs. Corp. v. Sharp Elecs. Corp., 485 U.S. 717, 108 S.Ct. 1515, 99 L.Ed.2d 808 (1988); Klor's, Inc. v. Broadway–Hale Stores, Inc., 359 U.S. 207, 79 S.Ct. 705, 3 L.Ed.2d 741 (1959); Eastern States Retail Lumber Dealers' Ass'n v. United States, 234 U.S. 600, 34 S.Ct. 951, 58 L.Ed. 1490 (1914). W. W. Montague & Co. v. Lowry, 193 U.S. 38, 24 S.Ct. 307, 48 L.Ed. 608 (1904). See also United States v.

Sometimes the instigator is a single, large dealer that has the leverage to force a supplier (or suppliers) to terminate a smaller dealer, as alleged in *Sharp* and *Klor's*. At other times, retailers have joined forces to gain the leverage to exclude an unwanted competitor, as alleged in *Eastern States Lumber* and *Montague*. The result, in terms of the economic analysis, should not differ based on the source of the complaining retailer's leverage. The bottom line is that a supplier terminates a retailer or grants the dealer unfavorable terms not because of the interests of the consumer or even the direct interests of the supplier, but because the supplier is deferring to the economic clout of one or more competing retailers. The law, however, may make it easier for a terminated dealer to obtain relief if it can demonstrate a conspiracy among competing retailers. A classic case is United States v. General Motors Corp.[2] General Motors, in response to a flood of complaints from local Chevrolet dealers and the local Chevrolet dealers association, took steps to prevent Chevrolet dealers from selling new cars to a number of discount houses that were reselling the cars to consumers at low prices. The Supreme Court deemed this a "classic conspiracy in restraint of trade."[3] In condemning an arrangement in which General Motors may be seen as a cartel enforcer, the Court took care not to pass judgment on individual action that General Motors might take to enforce its dealer location clauses without the participation of rival dealers. In a more recent case involving an alleged conspiracy of retail wallpaper dealers to pressure manufacturers to take action against discounting dealers that sold through "1–800" numbers, the Third Circuit in Alvord–Polk, Inc. v. F. Schumacher & Co.[4] followed similar logic in reversing a grant of summary judgment for the defendants. The *Polk* case presents an interesting wrinkle because the plaintiff discounters apparently conceded their role as free riders that sought customers that had already viewed wallpaper sample books at nondiscounting retailers. Although this solution might not have fully satisfied the nondiscounting retailers, the wallpaper producers might have eliminated the free-rider problem by providing a promotional allowance to any dealer that displayed the producer's sample books at its retail facility, offsetting the cost of that presale service.

A different set of boycott cases arises when a powerful retailer delivers an ultimatum to a supplier threatening to drop the supplier's line unless the supplier stops selling to one or more rival retailers. There is no horizontal action that might constitute a boycott if the ultimatum is delivered to a single supplier, but the boycott argument may arise if two or more suppliers are contacted by the powerful retailer. In what may be called a hub and spoke conspiracy, the powerful retailer may pressure each supplier individually or collectively to stop dealing with

General Motors Corp., 384 U.S. 127, 86 S.Ct. 1321, 16 L.Ed.2d 415 (1966).

2. 384 U.S. 127, 86 S.Ct. 1321, 16 L.Ed.2d 415 (1966).

3. Id. at 140.

4. 37 F.3d 996 (3d Cir.1994), cert. denied, 514 U.S. 1063, 115 S.Ct. 1691, 131 L.Ed.2d 556 (1995).

rival retailers. In Klor's, Inc. v. Broadway–Hale Stores, Inc.,[5] a retail appliance store alleged an unlawful concerted refusal to deal by appliance manufacturers acting at the behest of Broadway–Hale, which operated a major department store next door to the plaintiff's appliance store. Rejecting arguments that this was a purely private dispute between Broadway–Hale and Klor's, the Supreme Court reversed a grant of summary judgment for the defendants. *Klor's* does not present facts that support an inference of a hub (Broadway–Hale) and spoke (appliance manufacturers) conspiracy because it is quite possible that each manufacturer succumbed to Broadway–Hale's pressure not to deal with Klor's without any knowledge of the actions of rival dealers. The case is more easily explained as a series of vertical conspiracies between Broadway–Hale and individual appliance manufacturers. This view of *Klor's* was favored by the dissent in *Sharp,* but speaking for the majority, Justice Scalia insisted on viewing *Klor's* as a horizontal boycott case.[6]

Two more recent cases offer variations on the theme of a powerful retailer dictating that suppliers cease dealing with rival retailers. In an FTC proceeding against *Toys "R" Us (TRU),* the once powerful toy retailer was found to have pressured toy producers not to sell certain popular toys to warehouse discounters. The Commission found that TRU had initiated a hub and spoke conspiracy among manufacturers, with manufacturers agreeing not to sell their most popular toys to warehouse stores on the understanding that rival manufacturers would likewise withhold their most popular toys from such stores.[7] Although the manufacturers were critical players in this scheme, the power that was being wielded was TRU's retail power. Without that power, the manufacturers could not have been persuaded to act against interest to limit their sales to the high volume warehouse discounters. Another variation on this theme is *In re Brand Name Prescription Drugs Antitrust Litigation,*[8] a series of individual and class actions brought by retail pharmacists alleging that powerful buyers such as hospitals, health maintenance organizations, and mail-order drug suppliers were receiving large discounts from drug manufacturers and wholesalers that were not being offered to the pharmacists. Unlike in the TRU litigation, where the FTC named TRU as the primary respondent, the plaintiffs in this case did not name the powerful buyers as defendants, instead framing their claim as an unlawful conspiracy by the drug manufacturers and wholesalers to maintain discriminatory pricing that caused competitive injury to the pharmacists. The court of appeals affirmed the dismissal of the plaintiffs' core claims, concluding that a necessary showing of collusion among the drug manufacturers was not made. See the discussion in § 7.5b.

5. 359 U.S. 207, 79 S.Ct. 705, 3 L.Ed.2d 741 (1959).

6. Business Elecs. Corp. v. Sharp Elecs. Corp., 485 U.S. 717, 734, 108 S.Ct. 1515, 99 L.Ed.2d 808 (1988).

7. In re Toys "R" Us, Inc., FTC No. 9278 (Oct. 13, 1998). The Commission also found that Toys R Us had engaged in a classic vertical conspiracy in violation of Section 5 of the FTC Act. The Commission's decision was upheld in Toys "R" Us, Inc. v. FTC, 221 F.3d 928 (7th Cir. 2000).

8. 186 F.3d 781 (7th Cir.1999).

Chapter VIII

DISTRIBUTION RESTRAINTS BASED ON UPSTREAM POWER: FORECLOSURE AND VERTICAL MAXIMUM PRICE RESTRAINTS; FRANCHISING ABUSES

Table of Sections

---

§ 8.1 Introduction

Distribution restraints based on upstream power (foreclosure restraints such as tie-ins and exclusive dealing and vertical maximum price fixing) are considered distribution or vertical restraints because they operate as restraints that the seller imposes on the buyer. A distinguishing feature is that they are an exercise of seller power. Although sellers are most often the instigators of all types of distribution restraints, many such restraints are instituted in response to buyer preference. Vertical minimum price fixing, for example, may be instituted by the seller in order to induce dealers to market the seller's product more aggressively. All such downstream power restraints are considered in Chapter 7. Tie-ins, in contrast, are a coercive exercise of seller power, the same sort of power that gives rise to maximum (*but not minimum*) resale prices. Indeed, if a seller responds affirmatively to buyers that seek the bundled purchase of goods or services or exclusive dealing, the seller's conduct is usually not a restraint but a procompetitive response to demand.

Some of these restraints, such as tie-ins and exclusive dealing, are foreclosure restraints that directly preclude competitors from making sales to a buyer, who is required not to deal in certain products of rival sellers as a condition of sale. Some portion of the market is foreclosed for competitors. Although this preclusion is not necessarily anticompetitive, its presence suggests a distinguishing and potentially injurious effect of foreclosure restraints.

This chapter begins by examining foreclosure restraints, including tying and exclusive dealing. It also examines vertical maximum price fixing and national accounts and dual distribution, two other potential abuses associated with upstream power. Finally, it examines a variety of claims that can be brought by franchisees subject to abuses by powerful upstream franchisors.

§ 8.2 Foreclosure Restraints

The common characteristic of foreclosure restraints is that they preclude a downstream buyer or dealer from dealing in the products of a rival to the supplier imposing the restraint. These restraints, including tie-ins, forced exclusive dealing, forced reciprocal dealing, and most favored nation clauses, are unlikely to be anticompetitive unless they are imposed by a powerful upstream supplier.

8.2a. Summary of the Law

Foreclosure restraints are governed by Supreme Court interpretations of Sections 1 and 2 of the Sherman Act, by Section 3 of the Clayton Act, and, when actions are initiated by the FTC, by Section 5 of the Federal Trade Commission Act. The role of Section 2 of the Sherman Act in addressing foreclosure restraints imposed by a defendant accused of monopolization or attempted monopolization is addressed in § 3.4b5.

Section 3 of the Clayton Act deals directly with foreclosure restraints. It prohibits sales or leases of products on the condition that the buyer or lessor not deal in the goods of competitors, where the effect may be to substantially lessen competition or tend to create a monopoly. This more pointed language might have usurped the role of Section 1 of the Sherman Act in dealing with foreclosure restraints but for the failure of Section 3 to include foreclosure restraints involving services. Because many foreclosure restraints involve services, many of the Supreme Court's important tie-in cases were brought solely under Section 1 of the Sherman Act.

The language and legislative history of Section 3 of the Clayton Act suggest that it was intended to provide a stricter standard for dealing with foreclosure restraints than is required under Section 1 of the Sherman Act.[1] But recent Supreme Court tie-in precedents appear to have minimized any differences in the standard to be applied. Given the Court's greater discretion in interpreting the general language of Section 1 of the Sherman Act, it may be appropriate for the Court to adjust its interpretations of Section 1 in a manner consistent with Section 3 of the Clayton Act. More troublesome questions of statutory interpretation are raised if the Court, in disregard of express language of Section 3, sought to interpret that Section in a manner to make it consistent with less stringent interpretations of Section 1 of the Sherman Act.

For tie-ins, the Court has applied a form of *per se* rule—the conduct is deemed unlawful without a further showing once the prerequisites for application of the rule are established. But the prerequisites for establishing a *per se* unlawful tie are more extensive than, for example, those that apply to *per se* unlawful horizontal price or nonprice restraints. Therefore, the term "modified *per se* rule" or "structured rule of reason" might be more apt. As set forth by the Supreme Court in *Jefferson Parish Hospital District No. 2 v. Hyde*, a tie-in is *per se* unlawful when the plaintiff establishes: (1) a tying arrangement exists between two products (the term "product" is used here and throughout this Chapter to include services unless otherwise indicated); (2) the "seller has some special ability—usually called 'market power'—to force a purchaser to do something that he would not do in a competitive market"; and (3) the tying arrangement forecloses a substantial volume of commerce.[2]

The black letter law governing exclusive dealing and reciprocal dealing is less clear. The Supreme Court has said that reciprocal dealing is unlawful if it is shown that competition is "foreclosed in a substantial share of the line of commerce affected."[3] But, in contrast to tying, the Court has engaged in a somewhat more extensive economic analysis in determining whether an exclusive dealing arrangement violates Section 3 of the Clayton Act.[4] The Supreme Court has yet to announce a clear rule for addressing reciprocal dealing and most-favored-nation clauses, leaving the lower courts to chart a course based on treatment of tie-ins and exclusive dealing. Whether a modified *per se* rule or rule of reason is applied to reciprocal dealing and most-favored-nation clauses, it is clear that the courts are free to engage in economic analysis to determine whether there are anticompetitive effects from these forms of conduct.

§ 8.2

1. Kramer, *The Supreme Court and Tying Arrangements: Antitrust as History,* 69 Minn. L. Rev. 1013, 1023 (1985).

2. 466 U.S. 2, 12–18, 104 S.Ct. 1551, 80 L.Ed.2d 2 (1984).

3. Standard Oil Co. v. United States, 337 U.S. 293, 314, 69 S.Ct. 1051, 93 L.Ed. 1371 (1949).

4. Tampa Elec. Co. v. Nashville Coal Co., 365 U.S. 320, 81 S.Ct. 623, 5 L.Ed.2d 580 (1961).

8.2b. Contending Views of Foreclosure Restraints

As in the case of intrabrand distribution restraints, the law governing tie-ins and other foreclosure restraints has been controversial. The major schools include advocates of the traditional "leverage" school of ties, who believe that market power in the tying product can be leveraged into market power in the tied product, and Chicago theorists, who largely reject the leverage theory and argue that ties are likely to have procompetitive purposes and effects.

In terms of numbers of antitrust claims brought and litigated, tie-ins have been the dominant form of foreclosure restraint. The law governing all forms of foreclosure restraints has accordingly been influenced by the judicial approach to tie-ins. The leverage approach to ties dominated Supreme Court opinions through the 1970s. Briefly stated, leverage theory provides that a seller with market power in a tying product could extend that power into another product or line through a tie-in. For example, in a 1931 case, the Supreme Court indicated that tying a patented product to unpatented supplies might allow the patentholder to "secure a partial monopoly on the unpatented supplies."[5] As it developed, leverage theory also stressed the foreclosure effect of a tie-in: a seller with market power in the tying product might, through use of a tie, foreclose access of rival sellers to the tied product market. Perhaps because foreclosure was likely to be a problem only if the tying seller had a substantial share of the market for the tying product, the Court appears to have accepted the view that leverage can exist only if the tying seller has market power in the tying product as reflected in a high market share.[6]

Although traditional leverage theory of ties reflected at best an incomplete understanding of the impact of ties, the theory offered the dominant objection to ties when Bowman wrote a seminal article in 1957.[7] A critical point in Bowman's analysis was that in most cases a legally possessed monopoly could not be extended by tying in the sale of an additional item for which no market power existed. The consumer always had the choice of buying the tied product at a competitive price from another source. Accordingly, the consumer, if assumed to know these facts, would pay no more for the bundled products than the sum of the monopoly price for the tying product and the competitive price for the tied product. Under this "fixed sum argument,"[8] the seller could vary the individual prices of the tying and tied product, but maximum revenue could be attained only at a total price equal to the sum of these two values.

---

5. Carbice Corp. of Am. v. American Patents Dev. Corp., 283 U.S. 27, 32, 51 S.Ct. 334, 75 L.Ed. 819 (1931).

6. See *Jefferson Parish,* 466 U.S. at 7–8 (addressing the defendant's market share in the hospital market).

7. Bowman, *Tying Arrangements and the Leverage Problem,* 67 YALE L.J. 19 (1957).

8. The term "fixed sum argument" is used by Kaplow in an article critical of Bowman's analysis. Kaplow, *Extension of Monopoly Power Through Leverage,* 85 COLUM. L. REV. 515, 517–19 (1985).

If most tying could not be explained by the anticompetitive advantage gained from leveraging, Bowman, and others who followed, stressed that ties must have procompetitive benefits that account for their use.[9] Expanding on Bowman's analysis, Chicago theorists have argued that a monopolist may use a tie to attain more efficient allocation of the monopoly product by discriminating in price among buyers. For example, a monopolist might tie its monopoly product, say a sophisticated medical diagnostic device, to a variable use tied product, such as special chart paper used to record the device's measurements. In order to achieve more efficient allocation, Chicago theorists argue that the monopolist would lower its price on the medical device, but make up this lost revenue in higher charges for the specialty paper used in the machine. In theory, this arrangement might invite more users to purchase the machine; low intensity users, who might be unwilling to purchase the machine at the non-tying price, might find it attractive to do so when the machine is discounted as a part of the tying arrangement. Other procompetitive uses of ties are envisioned, such as a seller's use of a tie as a way to finance the buyer's purchase. The tying seller might offer the tying product at an unprofitably low price that is attractive to the buyer (in effect, a downpayment), but then impose higher charges on the tied product subsequently purchased by the buyer (in effect, installment payments with interest added). Taking a step that Bowman never expressly took, Bork concludes that "there is no viable theory of a means by which tying arrangements injure competition" and "a number of plausible theories of the good they may do."[10] Thus, Bork and other theorists conclude that tie-ins should be pre se or presumptively legal.[11]

The view that foreclosure restraints could offer substantial efficiencies was given support in the work of Oliver Williamson, who pointed out that a firm's choice of distribution strategy would be influenced by the relative efficiency of alternative strategies.[12] For example, in obtaining a needed input product, a manufacturer might chose among three possible approaches: (1) an open market strategy in which the input product is simply purchased for the best available terms for short-run needs; (2) partial vertical integration achieved through long-term supply contracts that foreclose the access of rival suppliers; and (3) total vertical integration through the acquisition of an input supplier. The manufacturer's choice will be influenced by which approach is more efficient. For example, long-term supply contracts (that involve a foreclosure restraint) might be more efficient than open market purchases because the manu-

---

9. Bowman, supra note 7; Burstein, *A Theory of Full–Line Forcing*, 55 Nw. U. L. Rev. 62 (1960); R. Bork, The Antitrust Paradox: A Policy at War with Itself 372–75 (1978); Larson, *Antitrust Tie–In Analysis After* Kodak*: A Comment*, 63 Antitrust L.J. 239 (1994).

10. Bork, supra note 9, at 372, 381.

11. Id. at 380–81; Wollenberg, *An Economic Analysis of Tie–In Sales: Re-examining the Leverage Theory*, 39 Stan. L. Rev.

737, 756–59 (1987). Posner would limit the rule against ties to those employed "for purposes of discriminating." R. Posner, Antitrust Law: An Economic Perspective 183 (1976).

12. O. Williamson, Markets and Hierarchies: Analysis and Antitrust Implications (1975); Williamson, *The Economics of Antitrust: Transaction Cost Considerations*, 122 U. Pa. L. Rev. 1439 (1974).

facturer can make business plans with greater certainty of the availability and pricing of the input product. Vertical integration would offer these same savings, but might involve some inefficiencies, requiring the manufacturer to bear risks and management responsibility in an area in which it might have little or no experience. Transactional cost analysis would not lead to a conclusion that all foreclosure restraints are procompetitive, but it would aid understanding of why many foreclosure restraints are beneficial.[13]

The Bowman critique of leverage theory has made substantial headway, gaining the votes of four concurring Justices in the 1984 *Jefferson Parish* opinion[14] and the endorsement of the Justice Department in the 1985 Vertical Restraint Guidelines. Some of that ground seems to have been lost in the Court's 1992 opinion in Eastman Kodak Co. v. Image Technical Services, Inc., and the decision of the Justice Department to withdraw the Vertical Restraint Guidelines in 1993. Indeed, the theoretical basis of leverage theory, if modified in some degree, remains alive and well. As explained more fully in § 8.3c1, Bowman's critique of leverage theory is based on a number of premises that have little or no relevance in real markets. The view that a monopolist cannot extend its market power through use of a tie-in is, for example, premised on the assumption that there are monopolists that enjoy the "perfect" market power ascribed in the theoretical model. No such perfect monopolist exists. In real markets, sellers that enjoy some market power in the tying product may be dissatisfied with their ability to exploit that power through sales of the tying product alone. By imposing a tie-in that complicates the buyer's transaction and, in effect, increases the buyer's demand for the tied product without substantial loss in demand for the tying product, such a seller may enhance its ability to exploit buyers. Increasing buyer demand for the tied product may, of course, be a procompetitive exercise. But, as new literature on tie-ins points out, when a tie-in complicates the buyer's transaction, the tie-in allows the seller to exploit the buyer's informational or motivational deficiencies. An increase in demand based on deception or exploitation is an anticompetitive result that may not be attained through the sale of the tying product alone.[15]

13.   Thus, Williamson agrees that partial vertical integration may be undertaken because it is efficient, but may also be employed for strategic reasons, such as to impede entry. Williamson, *Economics of Antitrust, supra* note 12, at 1461.

14.   Jefferson Parish Hosp. Dist. No. 2 v. Hyde, 466 U.S. 2, 32–47 & n. 9, 104 S.Ct. 1551, 80 L.Ed.2d 2 (1984) (O'Connor, J., concurring). The dissenting opinion in *Kodak* also followed Bowman's analysis. Eastman Kodak Co. v. Image Technical Servs., Inc., 504 U.S. 451, 494–96 & n. 2, 112 S.Ct. 2072, 119 L.Ed.2d 265 (1992)(Scalia, J., dissenting).

15.   Borenstein et al., *Antitrust Policy in Aftermarkets,* 63 ANTITRUST L.J. 455, 467 (1995) (although the ability to exercise market power in tie-ins of aftermarket products does not depend on market imperfections, "the greater the imperfections and the higher the cost of obtaining information, the greater the manufacturer's incentive to exploit aftermarket power"). Other theorists offering analysis of the role of market imperfections in tie-ins include Grimes, *Antitrust Tie–In Analysis After* Kodak: *Understanding the Role of Market Imperfections,* 62 ANTITRUST L.J. 263, 272–82 (1994); Kaplow, *supra* note 8, at 536–39; Craswell, *Tying Requirements in Competitive Mar-*

The view expressed in this Chapter borrows from traditional leverage theory, the Chicago critique of that theory, and recent literature connecting ties and other foreclosure restraints to the exploitation of the buyer's informational deficiencies. Foreclosure restraints, perhaps more than any other restraint subject to antitrust enforcement, lend themselves to exploitation of these deficiencies. Although many anticompetitive uses of ties are linked to high market share in an interbrand market, there is consistently an additional informational component that explains why a seller gains supracompetitive profits from a harmful tie.

§ 8.3   Tie–Ins

Tie-ins occur when the seller conditionally or absolutely denies access to a product or service (the tying product) unless the buyer also purchases another product or service (the tied product). A tie-in also may occur when the tying product is sold on the condition that the buyer not purchase the tied product from a competitor. Tie-ins have been attacked as violations of Section 1 or Section 2 of the Sherman Act,[1] of Section 3 of the Clayton Act (although Section 3 does not apply to tie-ins involving a service as either the tying or tied product) and of Section 5 of the Federal Trade Commission Act.

The fundamentals of tie-ins are straightforward. A tie-in is a particular type of bundled sale that constitutes an abuse of seller power. Sellers bundle the sale of products that might be sold separately as a business strategy—*to make money*. If the decision to bundle is disciplined by competition, the seller's offering cannot harm competition goals: either the seller's bundled offering will be profitable (if consumers want the bundled offering) or it will be a business failure (if consumers reject the offering).[2] In neither case is antitrust implicated. Anticompetitive bundled sales are limited to instances in which competitive discipline is lacking (the seller can force the tied sale) *and* the seller's conduct is abusive (the seller creates, maintains, or extends market power). This subset of bundled sales, known as tie-ins, is the target of antitrust law.

A true tie-in can have two effects that may cause harm: (1) it complicates a buyer's purchase decision, making it more difficult for a buyer to gather information needed to make the most beneficial purchasing choice and, in some cases, also undermining the buyer's incentives for cost-conscious behavior; and (2) it forecloses to some degree market opportunities for competing sellers of the tied product. A tie can also be

---

kets: The Consumer Protection Issues, 62 B.U. L. Rev. 661, 671–700 (1982).

§ 8.3

1. In Section 2 claims, tie-ins can be attacked as abusive conduct of a monopolist. See § 3.4b5.

2. Kaplow has suggested that firms may impose tie-ins or related restrictive practices: (1) under mistaken assumptions about the medium-or long-term profitability of such practices; or (2) to obtain market share even at the expense of profitability (because some managers may value market share and size over profitability). Kaplow, *Extension of Monopoly Power Through Leverage,* 85 Colum. L. Rev. 515, 548–52 (1985). The motives or mistaken assumptions of the seller in imposing a tie-in, while important to a policy analysis, do not alter assessments of the impact of these restraints.

a vehicle for facilitating cartel practices at the buyer or seller level or evading maximum price regulation. As explored below, there will be cases in which none of these effects creates significant competitive injury. On the other hand, each of these characteristics can produce strong (but differing) anticompetitive effects.

Tie-ins are an exercise of seller power. If such seller power cannot be found, the bundled sale of goods is almost always procompetitive. The seller's power to coerce the buyer may be that of a monopolist, but, more often, may be generated in part by the tie itself: the tie may complicate the buyer's transaction and allow the seller to exploit the buyer's informational or motivational deficiencies. Intrabrand distribution restraints can also exploit such market imperfections. See the discussion in § 6.3c2. But a tie is a likely choice of a seller bent on exploitation. A major reason for this is that ties can be designed to require the buyer to make an advance commitment to purchase the seller's products (or not to purchase a competitor's products) well before those products are actually needed. In this manner, ties can force the buyer to decide on the purchase of a tied product before all information about competitive alternatives or even about the nature and extent of the buyer's own need is available. Indeed, one of the goals of a seller that imposes a tie may be to prevent the entry or penetration of rival suppliers of the tied product.

Still, tying is a subset of a much larger group of bundled sales. Most bundled sales are likely to be procompetitive when properly disciplined by competition. Bundling occurs when a seller markets one or more products as a package. As long as the seller's bundling decision is competitively disciplined, there is no reason to suspect anticompetitive consequences. For example, most customers, for reasons of efficiency, convenience and tradition, expect to purchase an automobile with its tires, steering wheel and other necessary parts included. Most customers would not want to purchase the automobile part by part, and if they attempted to do so, could not be nearly as efficient as the manufacturer in assembling the finished product. Thus, a difficult threshold problem is distinguishing the subset of harmful bundlings (anticompetitive tie-ins) from the larger group of procompetitive or benign bundlings.

Until the *Kodak* decision in 1992,[3] the expressed logic of the Supreme Court's tie-in decisions focused on leverage theory: the ability of a seller with market power over the tying product to extend that power in sales of the tied product. *Kodak* brought into the open what many courts had long been tacitly or subconsciously following—a competitive analysis that includes examination of the impact of informational or motivational market imperfections that undermine the buyer's purchase decision. Focusing on all manifestations of market power should enable the courts to make a more balanced and thorough competitive assessment of a tie and, ultimately, to bring greater clarity and certainty to the law.

---

3. Eastman Kodak Co. v. Image Technical Servs., Inc., 504 U.S. 451, 112 S.Ct. 2072, 119 L.Ed.2d 265 (1992).

8.3a. Historical Overview of the Law Governing Tie–Ins

Early tie-in cases brought under the Sherman Act provide a backdrop for the enactment of Section 3 of the Clayton Act in 1914. Among these is the Supreme Court's opinion in Henry v. A. B. Dick Co.[4] A. B. Dick sold its patented stencil-duplicating machine with a restriction that the machine must be used only with paper, ink and other supplies made by A. B. Dick. In a patent infringement action brought by A.B. Dick, Justice Lurton wrote a majority opinion that upheld the restriction as a legitimate condition on the use of a patented machine. The Sherman Act was mentioned only obliquely as not constituting a defense to the patent infringement action. The *A. B. Dick* case was a four-to-three decision. It was prominently cited in support of the need for further legislation to strengthen antitrust law prohibitions of tying arrangements. Although proposed versions of Section 3 would have directly countered the *A. B. Dick* holding, the final version of that Section was a compromise, prohibiting ties and other foreclosure restraints only when their effect "may be to substantially lessen competition or tend to create a monopoly."[5]

Three years after the enactment of Section 3, the Supreme Court overruled *A. B. Dick*. In Motion Picture Patents Co. v. Universal Film Manufacturing Co.,[6] the Supreme Court held unlawful licensing restrictions that required the seller of a motion picture company's patented film projector to permit the projectors to be used only with films that were also patented by the company. The majority opinion concluded that the holding in *A. B. Dick* was a violation of public policy, but cited enactment of Section 3 as a "persuasive expression" of that public policy.[7] The Court soon made it clear that, notwithstanding the enactment of Section 3, not all ties were unlawful. In 1922, the Court upheld a lower court holding that United Shoe had violated Section 3 through the use of certain leasing restrictions on its shoe-manufacturing machinery,[8] but in the following year held that the Sinclair Oil Company had not violated Section 3 or the FTC Act when it required that service station lessees of Sinclair's gasoline tanks and pumps use only Sinclair fuel.[9]

Although occasional private actions were brought to enforce Section 3,[10] the majority of Supreme Court cases involving foreclosure restraints were initiated by the Government. In the 1930s, the Justice Department

4. 224 U.S. 1, 32 S.Ct. 364, 56 L.Ed. 645 (1912). A careful summary of the history leading up to the enactment of Section 3 of the Clayton Act is offered in Kramer, *The Supreme Court and Tying Arrangements: Antitrust as History*, 69 Minn. L. Rev. 1013 (1985).

5. Kramer, supra note 4, at 1035 (quoting IBM Corp. v. United States, 298 U.S. 131, 136, 56 S.Ct. 701, 80 L.Ed. 1085 (1936)).

6. 243 U.S. 502, 518, 37 S.Ct. 416, 61 L.Ed. 871 (1917).

7. Id. at 517–18.

8. United Shoe Mach. Corp. v. United States, 258 U.S. 451, 42 S.Ct. 363, 66 L.Ed. 708 (1922).

9. FTC v. Sinclair Ref. Co., 261 U.S. 463, 43 S.Ct. 450, 67 L.Ed. 746 (1923).

10. Pick Mfg. Co. v. General Motors Corp., 299 U.S. 3, 57 S.Ct. 1, 81 L.Ed. 4 (1936)(per curiam), aff'g 80 F.2d 641 (7th Cir.1935).

successfully prosecuted IBM for tying the sale of its calculating machines to cards manufactured or supplied by IBM.[11] IBM had discriminated in applying the tie, granting the U.S. Government an exception in return for a 15 percent higher lease payment for the machines. In ruling against IBM, the Court rejected the argument that use of its cards was necessary to protect the goodwill of its calculating machines.

Starting with *International Salt* in 1947, the Court has decided seven cases in which tie-ins were a prominent issue.[12] The Justice Department brought the first four of these cases and was successful in three of them.[13] Private plaintiffs brought each of the last three of these cases and achieved a favorable result in one of them.[14]

8.3b. Procompetitive Bundling and Tie–Ins

Five potential procompetitive effects of bundled sales are examined here. The first and predominant benefit of bundled sales is that they can be efficient ways of producing and marketing many goods and services. As explained below, bundled sales driven solely by competition are usually efficient responses to the market and are not characterized as ties, but as sales of a single product. But even when distinct products, each with its own demand curve, are tied, there are potential procompetitive benefits that are addressed here: (1) a tie may be a tool for the seller to implement an efficient form of price discrimination; (2) a tie may enhance the seller's ability to gain entry or market penetration in an otherwise impenetrable market; (3) a tie may aid a producer in maintaining a quality reputation by ensuring that buyers purchase appropriate input products and spare parts; (4) a tie may allow an innovator to increase its reward for innovation; and (5) a tie may enhance the producer's informational flow on technologically sophisticated products.

8.3b1. *Distinguishing Ties from Efficient Bundling*

A seller disciplined by competition will bundle the sale of goods and services only when it is efficient to do so. Producers can, far more efficiently than a consumer, gather and assemble all the necessary products to produce a car or an appliance. Marketing costs for the

---

11. IBM Corp. v. United States, 298 U.S. 131, 56 S.Ct. 701, 80 L.Ed. 1085 (1936).

12. See the cases discussed in § 8.3d5.

13. The Justice Department was successful in United States v. Loew's, Inc., 371 U.S. 38, 83 S.Ct. 97, 9 L.Ed.2d 11 (1962); Northern Pacific Railway Co. v. United States, 356 U.S. 1, 78 S.Ct. 514, 2 L.Ed.2d 545 (1958); and International Salt Co. v. United States, 332 U.S. 392, 68 S.Ct. 12, 92 L.Ed. 20 (1947). The Department lost in Times–Picayune Publishing Co. v. United States, 345 U.S. 594, 73 S.Ct. 872, 97 L.Ed. 1277 (1953).

14. Private plaintiffs achieved a favorable result in Eastman Kodak Co. v. Image Technical Services, Inc., 504 U.S. 451, 112 S.Ct. 2072, 119 L.Ed.2d 265 (1992). After initially achieving a favorable result in Fortner Enterprises, Inc. v. United States Steel Corp., 394 U.S. 495, 89 S.Ct. 1252, 22 L.Ed.2d 495 (1969), the private plaintiff lost in the second round, United States Steel Corp. v. Fortner Enterprises, Inc., 429 U.S. 610, 97 S.Ct. 861, 51 L.Ed.2d 80 (1977). The plaintiff also failed in Jefferson Parish Hospital District No. 2 v. Hyde, 466 U.S. 2, 104 S.Ct. 1551, 80 L.Ed.2d 2 (1984).

bundled product may also be significantly lower than the cost of selling component parts. The same may be true for bundled services. A law school can efficiently put together and market a balanced curriculum needed to train a lawyer. Were the consumer to assemble these packages by purchasing individual items, the result might be a more expensive or qualitatively less desirable package. A seller may engage in a practice known as mixed bundling: The seller offers a product both separately and in bundled fashion, leaving the consumer to choose in which form to buy. For example, a consumer seeking an over-the-counter medication for the common cold can buy separately a decongestant, an antihistamine, a pain reliever and a cough suppressant. Or the consumer can choose from a variety of products that combine some or all of these medications. As long as there is effective competitive discipline, the seller's decision to sell a product solely in bundled or simultaneously in bundled and unbundled fashion should not be considered a tie. Sellers that offer products both in bundled and unbundled fashion may still be engaging in a tie-in, however, if the terms on which two products are sold separately are much less favorable than for a bundled sale–reflecting a lack of competitive discipline in the pricing of the unbundled or separate sales.[15]

Distinguishing a tie from a procompetitive bundling can sometimes be difficult, particularly if the seller has recently changed from separate to bundled sales. The Supreme Court has said that whether "one or two products are involved turns not on the functional relation between them, but rather on the character of the demand for the two items."[16] Two products are considered distinct if there exists "sufficient consumer demand so that it is efficient for a firm to provide" the two products separately.[17] The key question is whether the choice to purchase the items in bundled fashion is market driven—a matter of buyer preference uninhibited by any exercise of market power that the seller might possess.

In making a determination whether two distinct products are involved, courts should be cognizant of the information possessed by those that make purchasing decisions. Thus, the demand of *informed* consumers seems most relevant in separating ties from procompetitive bundling. If the vast majority of informed consumers prefer the bundled sale of a product, as with the sale of a fully assembled automobile, for example, there is no tie. The seller's ability to provide bundled products more efficiently than separate components is an indication that informed consumers might prefer the package, particularly if most consumers have need for all, or at least the most expensive, products included in the package. On the other hand, if there is reason to suspect that the bundling decision is inadequately disciplined by competition, the bundling practice should probably be considered a tie. For example, if a

---

15. Advance Bus. Sys. & Supply Co. v. SCM Corp., 415 F.2d 55 (4th Cir.1969), cert. denied, 397 U.S. 920, 90 S.Ct. 928, 25 L.Ed.2d 101 (1970).

16. *Jefferson Parish,* 466 U.S. at 19.

17. *Kodak,* 504 U.S. at 462 (citing *Jefferson Parish,* 466 U.S. at 21–22).

bundled sale is likely to exploit the buyer's informational deficiencies, or if the seller has a large share of the market for the tying product and there is no manifest efficiency in unmixed bundling, giving no option may push the court toward finding a tie.

In Town Sound & Custom Tops, Inc. v. Chrysler Motors Corp.,[18] the court of appeals struggled in determining that a Chrysler dealer's sale of a sound system with an automobile should be considered a tie. There were probable efficiencies involved in this bundling—it was apparently more efficient for Chrysler to install sound systems at the time of a vehicle's manufacture than for dealers or aftermarket suppliers to add such sound systems at a later time. But Chrysler had earlier addressed this problem by instructing its dealers to remove sound systems and credit customers with the price of the sound system minus a fee that covered the cost of its removal. Under this earlier practice, roughly a third of the buyers apparently opted to have the Chrysler-installed sound system removed, suggesting that a significant body of consumers preferred to purchase their sound systems elsewhere, or to do without them entirely. Chrysler's decision to discontinue the prior practice may suggest a desire to cut off the competition, particularly if the efficiency gains from the coupled sale are minimal.

When a supplier imposes a tie-in by integrating two formerly separate products, this *product integration tying* can raise special problems for the court. Part of this problem is remedial. If a court finds a product integration tie to be unlawful, it is more difficult for the court, and more expensive for the defendant, to redesign its now integrated product. These problems have been encountered in the Microsoft litigation both in the United States and in Europe. As difficult as these remedial problems are, ignoring anticompetitive ties that are implemented through product integration could create a loophole that drives suppliers to effect ties through product integration (instead of through conventional sales restrictions).

The issue of whether a product integration is an efficient bundling or an anticompetitive tie should be addressed using the same consumer demand criteria that are applied for any bundling. The Supreme Court has said that consumer demand is the key;[19] the inquiry is not a rudderless exercise of judicial whim but a focused exercise to determine the actual state of pre-existing market demand. This task, however, can be challenging because all product integration tie-ins are *first mover* bundlings; the two formerly separate products are, for the first time, being sold as a bundled product. There is no record of past consumer conduct that could shed light on whether the bundling is efficient or anticompetitive. Moreover, in rapidly changing high technology industries, the court should look not only at the efficiencies of production and distribution, but also at innovation efficiency. There may be tension

---

18. 959 F.2d 468 (3d Cir.)(en banc), cert. denied, 506 U.S. 868, 113 S.Ct. 196, 121 L.Ed.2d 139 (1992).

19. See notes 16 & 17, supra.

between these values. For example, if M Corporation sells an operating program separately from an Internet browser program, but abruptly shifts to selling the two as a single bundled product, the result may be production and distribution efficiencies and, perhaps, lower prices to consumers. The difficulty comes when this integration is effected by a player with monopoly power in the operating system market. Now rival producers of innovative Internet browser programs may have difficulty getting their products to market. Innovation, or its marketing, may become more costly and consumers may be deprived of the benefits of a competitive innovation market.

These issues were confronted by the court of appeals in its 2001 decision addressing Microsoft's integration of its operating system with its Internet browser program.[20] The Justice Department's efforts to block the bundled sale of operating software (Windows 98) with the Internet browser program (Explorer) were, in the view of Microsoft's lawyers, an effort to stand in the way of technological progress desired by consumers. The Justice Department's position was that the bundling did not produce substantial efficiencies and would foreclose innovative and efficient competitors from developing and marketing applications software that is now integrated into Microsoft's operating software. Of course, both propositions may be true in part. But the Department also argued that the innovation harm would occur not only in the browser market, but in other applications markets and in the operating system market as well. This result was likely, according to the Department, because Internet browsers functioned as middleware which could link directly to application programs rather than through the operating system; this middleware could also provide a platform that would allow consumers to download operating software, thereby providing an alternative to Microsoft's operating software. The court's resolution of these issues was largely favorable to the government.

The court overturned a lower court holding of a Sherman Act Section 1 tying violation, finding that the court had improperly applied the modified per se rule.[21] In a separate portion of the opinion, however, the court of appeals applied a rule of reason analysis to Microsoft's bundling conduct and, after extensive analysis, concluded that this conduct had violated Section 2 of the Sherman Act. The extensive analysis in this portion of the court's opinion embraced many of the government's key arguments.[22]

In a 1998 opinion addressing bundling involving an earlier version of Microsoft's operating system,[23] the same court of appeals had vacated the preliminary injunction directed at the bundled sale of Windows 95 and Microsoft's Internet browser. The court interpreted a prior consent decree in a manner that accorded great latitude to the seller of a high

---

20. United States v. Microsoft Corp., 253 F.3d 34 (D.C.Cir. 2001)(en banc).

21. Id. at 84. See the discussion of this holding in § 8.3d1.

22. Id. at 50–80. The Section 2 holding of the court is addressed in § 3.4b5.

23. United States v. Microsoft Corp., 147 F.3d 935 (D.C.Cir.1998).

technology product in determining what products can be bundled together without constituting a tie. The court's ruling turned on the language of the consent decree and not directly on the antitrust law governing tie-ins. Rather than focus on consumer demand (as Supreme Court precedents would require), the majority thought it was sufficient that the defendant could make a "plausible claim" that integration "brings some advantage."[24] The majority opinion was driven by concerns of the difficulty in administering a test that required a court to weigh the countervailing efficiencies that might determine consumer demand for separate products. As the majority put it: "Courts are ill equipped to evaluate the benefits of high-tech product design, and even could they place such an evaluation on one side of the balance, the strength of the 'evidence of distinct markets,' proposed for the other side of the scale, seems quite incommensurable."[25] The 2001 *Microsoft* opinion did not follow this script. It engaged in extensive analysis that led it to conclude that Microsoft's bundling conduct did violate Section 2 of the Sherman Act. By clear implication, the court's en banc 2001 holding rejected a rule that would absolve any product integration bundling simply because the defendant offers a plausible claim of economic advantage.

The Microsoft litigation demonstrates the limits of using consumer demand as the exclusive measure of whether or not a bundling constitutes a tie. There is a possibility that a bundling that could bring short-term low prices and allocative benefits to the consumer would be highly welcomed in the marketplace and hence not be considered a tie. But that same bundling might serve to entrench a seller's market dominance in a way that stifles innovation and marketing of new products, dynamic efficiency that could greatly benefit consumers in the long term and far outweigh the short-term benefits of the bundled sale. Even informed consumers cannot be expected to turn away from the immediate benefit of an attractively priced bundled product. Consumer demand is an important initial reference point for separating harmful ties from pro-competitive or benign bundlings, but no inquiry is complete without considering the potential impact of the bundling on innovation.

8.3b2. *Can Requirements Ties Be Efficient Price Discrimination?*

Are there circumstances when even a tie—that is a bundled sale of two separate products not adequately disciplined by competition—may have procompetitive consequences? Although there is a fair amount of theoretical economic literature that would answer this question affirmatively, more recent economic literature has challenged this conclusion.[26] Ties can be a way of discriminating in price among various users of a

---

24. Id. at 950.

25. Id. at 952–53 (footnote omitted).

26. Larson, *Antitrust Tie–In Analysis After* Kodak: *A Comment,* 63 Antitrust L.J. 239, 253–59 (1994)(reviewing theoretical literature that finds procompetitive price discrimination may be a purpose of ties). This literature is questioned in Nalebuff, Department of Trade & Industry Economics Paper No. 1, Bundling, Tying and Portfolio Effects 17, 74–75 (2003); Grimes, Antitrust and the Systemic Bias Against Small Business: Kodak, Strategic Conduct, and Leverage Theory, 52 Case W. Res. L. Rev. 231, 259–261 (2001); Kaplow, supra note 2, at 545–552.

tying product. When the tied product is used in proportion to use of the tying product, the seller may use the tie as a meter to measure the use of the tying product and assess a fee for that use. Metering can work when there is a requirements tie: the buyer must buy all of its supplies of a product needed to operate the tying product. For example, a seller of a copy machine might require that toner used in the machine be purchased only from it. The price for the copy machine could be set at a low level—to encourage purchase of the machine—while the price for the toner could be set at a high level—to give the seller a variable return based on the intensity of the machine's use. In effect, the tie allows the seller to levy a charge based on "metered" use of the copy machine.

This metering might under some circumstances produce a less inefficient allocation of resources. For example, if the seller has a patent monopoly on a machine, the monopoly price set on that machine will reduce to some extent its distribution. But if that same seller ties the patented machine to a variable use product employed in connection with the machine, the price for the patented machine might be lowered, allowing more machines to be sold. Thus, under the theoretical model that some economists embrace, the seller could increase its overall return at the same time that the machine is more widely distributed and more widely used. In effect, the seller would be discriminating in price based on the value that the users placed on the machine.

Even if a tie is successful in discriminating among users in a manner that reduces the allocative injury of a seller's market power in the tying product, the tie will not eliminate the wealth transfer injury associated with price discrimination. See the discussion in § 2.5. Thus, if the underlying market power in the tying product is sufficient to sustain a claim under Section 2 of the Sherman Act, any reduction of the allocative injury through the use of a tie should not be a defense. Protection against wealth transfer injury is a primary goal of antitrust enforcement.[27]

The opportunities for use of a tie as a metering mechanism are, in any event, likely to be quite limited. The mechanism would not work well if the tied product had uses other than in connection with the tying product. In that instance, a high price for the tied product would discourage those other uses, with probable negative effects for allocative efficiency. For example, if a seller of a copy machine places a high price on toner used in the machine, and the toner had other useful applications, those other applications would be discouraged. The metering mechanism would also not work smoothly if it were easy for other producers of the tied product to compete for the aftermarket business. For example, if a high price is set on paper for use in a patented copy machine, other suppliers of paper are sure to sell at a lower price, making it costly and perhaps impossible for the tying seller to enforce the mechanism. The metering mechanism would also not work well if the tied product were a dynamic one, subject to change and improve-

---

27. See § 1.5b2.

ment. For example, software for a computer is occasionally tied to sale of a computer. The software itself is a highly complex product subject to change and improvement, so charging a high price for the software, or upgrades in the software, even if it worked as a meter on use of the underlying computer, could have a negative effect on a user's ability to purchase software improvements that enhanced the computer's efficiency.

The conditions for use of a tie as a metering mechanism may be more likely if the seller can design the tying product in a way that limits competition for the tied product. If limited competition in the tied product market flows naturally from the design of an innovative product, the antitrust laws should tolerate this lack of competition as long as it is not preserved by abusive tactics. But note that the condition necessary to make a tie work well as a meter is the very outcome that antitrust tie-in law has traditionally sought to avoid (the limiting of competition in the product for the tied market).

Consider a producer of a mechanical razor that designs its product so that only its specially crafted blade cartridges will fit the razor. The metering mechanism will not necessarily work to create a more efficient allocation. If the price of the variable-use tied product (the cartridges) were set too high, use of the razor might be discouraged. A prescient seller might be able to set the price on the tying and tied products at just the right point to maximize return and increase the efficiency of resource allocation. This outcome, however, assumes not only an omniscient seller but also a buyer with perfect information. If the buyer purchases the razor without researching the cost of the cartridges, or if the buyer does this research, only to have market conditions change, the metering mechanism may not work to increase allocative efficiency and may instead decrease competition on the merits. For perfect informational conditions to hold, a buyer must anticipate future market conditions and the availability of competitive alternatives for the tied product that might develop in the absence of a tie. These are conditions ripe for the exploitation of informational imperfections, as explained more fully in § 8.3c3, or for discouraging the development of competitive alternatives for delivery of the tied product.

Nalebuff questions the feasability of metering on several grounds mentioned here, but also raises an additional point.[28] To produce an efficient allocation of resources, the metering mechanism must operate efficiently. In many cases, it will not. The tying seller may have to expend resources to enforce a contractual tie (warnings to customers, litigation, etc.). Customers, for their part, may spend additional resources to avoid a tie that forces them to pay supracompetitive prices for the tied product.

Stigler has suggested another possible procompetitive use of ties to discriminate in price based upon the value a user places on a product. Stigler argues that the bundled lease of films to a television station

---

28.   Nalebuff, supra note 26, at 78.

might allow the lessor to charge a higher overall price than could be exacted if the films were priced individually.[29] The lessees have varying reservation prices—the highest price each is willing to pay to receive a film. Stigler assumed that the owner of the movies would have to set a single, nondiscriminatory price for the lease of each film. By forcing the lessee to lease movies from two groups (grade A or popular movies and grade B or less popular movies), the lessor could perhaps average out the different values placed on particular movies and charge the lessee a higher, overall price. Once again, the procompetitive effect of this arrangement is linked to the view that lessees or buyers that value certain movies more highly can be made to pay more for them. But here again, the lessor would have to have a detailed understanding of buyer preferences in order to package just the right films together to increase its return. And it is not clear that movie owners needed to rely upon a tie to set discriminatory leasing prices. Movie owners could, for example, vary their leasing prices based upon the size of the audience that a television station served. Stigler also ignores some of the potential anticompetitive effects of the tie-in making it more difficult for a competing seller of television programming to market its products. See the discussion in § 8.3d5.

Neither the metering hypothesis nor the Stigler variation easily fit the facts of litigated cases. One survey of eight Supreme Court tie-in cases (and a larger sample of 45 appellate cases) found none that cleanly fit a procompetitive, price discrimination hypothesis.[30] A number of the Supreme Court's tying cases have involved a variable use tied product, and thus might fit a metering hypothesis. But these cases also involved discriminatory application of the tie. Thus, Eastman Kodak Co. v. Image Technical Services, Inc., Northern Pacific Railway v. United States, and IBM Corp. v. United States, each involved a variable use tied product, but in each case the tie was not imposed against certain large buyers.[31] When a tie is imposed against most buyers, but exceptions are made for large buyers, this does not establish that these large buyers valued the product less than other buyers. More likely, these large purchasers enjoyed countervailing leverage that could force the seller to abandon the tie. Also, because the ties in the three Supreme Court cases involved deferred sale of the tied product, there was a substantial risk that the seller was exploiting informational market imperfections with respect to smaller buyers that might have lacked the knowledge and consulting resources of large buyers. The overall picture presented by these cases is consistent with price discrimination against less knowledgeable buyers, not with charging higher prices to buyers that valued the tying product more. The welfare implications of a tie imposed in a discriminatory fashion would seem highly ambiguous at best, and certainly not consis-

---

29. *Stigler, United States v. Loew's Inc: A Note on Block–Booking,* 1963 SUP. CT. REV. 152, 153. Stigler's theory was based on the facts in United States v. Loew's, Inc., 371 U.S. 38, 83 S.Ct. 97, 9 L.Ed.2d 11 (1962).

30. Grimes, *Antitrust Tie–In Analysis After* Kodak: *Understanding the Role of Market Imperfections,* 62 ANTITRUST L.J. 263, 298, 312–14 (1994).

31. Id. at 275 n.43.

tent with a hypothetical metering scheme that uses a tie to measure how highly the buyer values the use of the tying product.[32]

The litigation sample does not prove that ties cannot be used to implement procompetitive price discrimination, but it may show that if such procompetitive uses occur, they are unlikely to be the target of antitrust litigation. Some industries involving high economies of scale may find it beneficial to discriminate among classes of users in a manner that maximizes output. Transportation industries may be an example. Franchisors may also have a legitimate interest in metering use of the franchise trade name and method of doing business. But such metering functions can generally be more efficiently implemented (and with fewer anticompetitive results) through mechanisms other than ties. For example, a franchisor can charge a franchise fee linked to the franchisee's total revenue or profits. In some transportation industries, such as ocean carriage, discriminatory rates are still authorized by statute. Ocean and rail carriers often negotiate long-term contracts with high-volume users that effectively discriminate in favor of those users. Airlines have devised elaborate fare categories that discriminate against short-notice, business fliers. Not all of these mechanisms are free of anticompetitive concerns, but price discrimination implemented without the use of tie-ins may avoid or reduce the primary risks of a harmful tie: foreclosure of competitive diversity and opportunity in the tied product market and exploitation of the buyer's informational voids.

8.3b3. *Enhancing Entry or Market Penetration*

The use of a tie-in could aid a firm in gaining entry or penetration in a market impervious to conventional entry methods and, in this manner, increase efficiency.[33] In the face of entry barriers, a manufacturer could use a tie to gain entry into the tying or tied product market. Although competition (and dynamic efficiency) would seem better served by attacking the underlying anticompetitive features of the targeted market, this may not be possible.

A seller might use a tie to enhance entry prospects in at least two ways: (1) the seller might offer a promotional tie to make its unestablished product more attractive to consumers; or (2) the seller might offer a tying product at a very low price and seek to increase return by charging a higher price on a tied product that the buyer must also purchase. Promotional ties are generally short-term efforts to increase sales. To the extent that such promotions allow consumers to purchase at low prices, they are usually unproblematic in antitrust terms, although this may not be the case when the promotional loss is forced on a dealer or franchisee. See the discussion in § 8.9f2. Another variation on a promotional tie might occur when a producer or distributor has an established product and requires retailers to buy other less established

---

32. Grimes, supra note 26, at 259–261.

33. Justice White made essentially this point in Fortner Enterprises, Inc. v. United States Steel Corp., 394 U.S. 495, 514 n. 9, 89 S.Ct. 1252, 22 L.Ed.2d 495 (1969) (White, J., dissenting).

products in order to receive the established product. Such a bundled sale is again unlikely to give rise to legitimate antitrust claims except when the seller has market power over its downstream dealers. The short-term nature of most promotional ties, if coupled with a demonstrated procompetitive value in penetrating the market, would militate strongly against any antitrust claim.

The other way to use a tie-in to gain market penetration would be for the seller to offer a new product at an attractively low price (perhaps below cost), planning to make up that loss through the higher return received on the sale of a complementary tied product. To make a profit, the seller must count on intensive users that will purchase sufficient quantities of the tied product. This mechanism might allow the manufacturer to share with buyers the risk that a product will become outdated or lose its competitive edge.[34] Buyers may continue to purchase the tied product on supracompetitive terms if, for example, they have substantial sunk costs in the tying product. The mechanism is similar to that involved when the seller uses a tie to charge the intensive user a higher price and is subject to many of the same criticisms. See the discussion in § 8.3b2.

This risk-sharing hypothesis seems a doubtful procompetitive justification for most ties. In a world in which informational deficiencies are pervasive and affect the seller as well as the buyer, most manufacturers are probably reluctant to sell the tying product at a below cost price.[35] Even if a seller does so, the welfare effects may be negative: The delayed purchase of the tying product increases the risk of diminished consumer information that could distort consumer purchases. Moreover, particularly with respect to a newly marketed product, a seller may obtain many of the benefits from the sale of the complementary product without the use of an unlawful tie. For example, if a seller plans to market a new and innovative razor with specially designed complementary cartridges, the seller can offer the razor at a low price and, without a tie-in, sell the cartridges at a high price for as long as the razor is not a marketing success that attracts rival aftermarket sellers, and for an additional time thereafter needed for the rival to reverse engineer, produce, and market the complementary cartridges at a lower price. This gives the innovator substantial time to recover the investment and earn an ample profit. Thereafter, no competing seller of the razor cartridges is likely to undercut the cartridge price unless the razor manufacturer is an inefficient producer of cartridges or demands an excessive return. But what if the rival is selling shoddy cartridges or cartridges that cause the razor to perform poorly? Consumer education from a consumer's adverse experience, perhaps supplemented by the razor manufacturer's own literature,

---

34. Wollenberg, *An Economic Analysis of Tie-In Sales: Re-examining the Leverage Theory,* 39 STAN. L. REV. 737, 755–56 (1987)(describing the risk-sharing hypothesis).

35. In *Kodak,* for example, the defendant made no claim that its micrographic equipment was sold at prices below competitive rates. Eastman Kodak Co. v. Image Technical Servs., Inc., 504 U.S. 451, 472, 112 S.Ct. 2072, 119 L.Ed.2d 265 (1992).

may be sufficient to address this problem. Still, as the next subsection suggests, some quality control problems with aftermarket parts may be more difficult to rectify.

8.3b4. *Maintaining Producer's Reputation*

Another potential procompetitive invocation of a tie is its use to ensure that buyers of the tying product purchase the appropriate input product or spare parts to make the tying product function properly. Here, the consumer's informational inadequacies might lead to the purchase of shoddy merchandise that could damage the quality reputation of the manufacturer. Because such consumer informational problems are difficult to eliminate, some theorists claim that a tie used in this way can have procompetitive results.[36] Although the informational problems confronting the consumer seem real enough, a tie that could ameliorate may also exploit the same deficiencies. Assume, for example, that a seller's copy machine will work properly only if the appropriate toner is used in the machine. The copy machine producer can solve this problem by requiring that all buyers purchase toner (the tied product) from the producer. But this means that the buyer is cut off from other toner suppliers that may sell an equal or superior toner at the same or lower price. Indeed, some buyers might be willing to tolerate a lower quality copy in order to pay less for the toner. The tie may solve the seller's quality image problem, but may do so in a manner that slights critical antitrust goals by distorting buying choices away from a competitive outcome, coercing transfer of wealth from the consumer to the seller, and making it more difficult for an efficient and potentially superior toner producer to enter and penetrate the market.

In most instances, a manufacturer confronting a potential quality image problem can adequately address that problem without imposition of a tie. For example, a manufacturer can specify the nature of input products or replacement parts that must be used in order for the product to function well. Indeed, the warranty might even be made conditional on the use of proper input or replacement products. But if the manufacturer, instead of specifying the nature of the replacement part, simply requires that two clearly distinct products must be purchased from it alone, anticompetitive effects are likely.

This is not to say that there will be no cases in which a tie serves procompetitive ends by resolving quality control problems. When the link between the tying and tied product is direct, as when the tied product is complementary to the tying product, the manufacturer may properly bundle their sale. For example, a automobile manufacturer may install the fuel injection device of its choice in an automobile without fear of unlawful tying. But note that this procompetitive bundling will not be considered a tie at all because the automobile will be regarded as a single integrated product. See the discussion in § 8.3b1. Although rare,

---

36. R. Bork, The Antitrust Paradox: A Policy at War with Itself 372–74, 380–81 (1978); H. Hovenkamp, Federal Antitrust Policy: The Law of Competition and Its Practice § 10.7a (3d ed. 2005); Wollenberg, supra note 34, at 756–59.

there may be instances in which distinct products are tied together for legitimate quality control reasons. The Supreme Court has recognized a quality control defense may be invoked for newly introduced products that are tied with component parts. See the discussion in § 8.3d4.

8.3b5. Increased Return for Innovation

Even if a tie-in is not employed to meter the use of the tied product, it could enhance innovation simply by increasing the seller's return on investment. Thus, in the case of a patented tying product, a seller might increase its reward for innovation by selling a tied product at a supra-competitive price. This argument has been advanced in support of legislative proposals to extend the right to tie unpatented products to the sale of a patented product.[37] The economic benefits conferred upon the seller by a tie may, however, have no effect on the seller's incentive to innovate. For example, the additional economic rewards conferred by a patent may, in effect, be a gratuitous gain for the seller at the expense of competition.[38] Even for industries in which the patent monopoly does promote innovation, the tie-in is not a well-aimed vehicle for enhancing the innovator's reward. An inventor who directly exploits the patent monopoly through increased prices on the patented product is gaining a reward that is correlated with the value of the invention to society. But increasing the patent monopolist's return through ties creates arbitrary revenue gains not directly related to the value of the innovation. When the patent-holder uses ties, the amount of increased return is affected by a number of new variables unrelated to the value of the innovation, such as the degree of competition in the market for the tied product, the seller's ability to enforce the tie, and any informational deficiencies associated with the sale of the tying and tied products. For example, assume that the seller of a patented copy machine has a choice between using toner or paper as the tied product to meter the use of the machine. Although use of each product should be directly proportional to use of the copy machine, the amount of additional revenue that the seller can generate by choosing one product over another will vary. If it is harder for the seller to monitor the buyer's source of paper than the buyer's source of toner, the seller will not be able to exact the same premium above competitive price for the sale of paper. In addition, if the market for paper is more competitive than the market for toner (i.e., all

---

37. Klein & Wiley, *Competitive Price Discrimination As An Antitrust Justification for Intellectual Property Refusals to Deal,* 70 ANTITRUST L. J. 599 (2004)(arguing that licensing restrictions and tie-ins involving intellectual property should be treated leniently because of the innovation gains that they bring); *Antitrust Treatment of the Licensing of Certain Intellectual Property: Hearing on H.R. 557 Before the Subcomm. on Monopolies and Commercial Law of the House Comm. on the Judiciary,* 100th Cong., 1st Sess. 25 (1989) (statement of Roger Andewelt, Deputy Assistant Attorney General, arguing that a proposed bill that would remove *per se* treatment of tie-ins and other alleged antitrust violations associated with the licensing of intellectual property would enhance innovation).

38. F.M. SCHERER & D.ROSS, INDUSTRIAL MARKET STRUCTURE AND ECONOMIC PERFORMANCE 628–30 (3d ed. 1990) (concluding that in many industries other incentives for innovation are more important than the patent monopoly). See the discussion in § 15.2a.

participants in the toner industry are earning higher profits), the seller of the copy machine is more likely to impose its tie on the toner.

At issue here is not whether innovation is over- or under-rewarded, but whether ties are a refined tool for conferring that reward. Used for this purpose, ties allow a patent owner to exploit market conditions to increase return, but these conditions usually have no bearing on the underlying value of the invention or the inventor's underlying investment. There are, of course, other more direct ways to provide subsidies for innovation, including direct exploitation of the patent monopoly (the rewards for which would seem more targeted if harmful tied sales are prohibited) and government grants to educational and research institutions.

8.3b6. Increasing the Informational Flow on Technologically Advanced Products

In *Kodak*, Justice Scalia argued that tying the sale of equipment to the servicing of that equipment may increase innovation by providing the producer important feedback (from the servicing employees) on how the product may be improved.[39] As a general matter, economists recognize that vertical integration may confer certain efficiencies in the flow of information up and down the vertical network. The feedback that a producer can get by servicing its own products could be valuable in designing the next generation machine. But this benefit, as with many of the potential gains from ties, could probably have been achieved in less anticompetitive ways. In *Kodak*, for example, the sale of Kodak's spare parts should provide information about how Kodak machines are performing. If Kodak needs more information, it could obtain this through servicing records on machines used in-house or through a competitive service organization that it operates for customers (without the use of a tie).[40] Or Kodak could pay independent service organizations to provide input. Indeed, Kodak might seek input from such service organizations in any event: Kodak presumably would want information about the performance of all competing machines on the market.

8.3c. Anticompetitive Potential of Ties

The anticompetitive effects of ties are directly linked to the tying seller's market power. In some instances, the tying seller's market power arises from a high market share in the tying product, or a high collective market share by tying sellers. Typically, the market power is generated or increased by the complicating features of the tie itself. A tie may allow the seller to increase demand for its sales of the tied product, and thereby increase the price it charges for the tied product without the disciplining effect that competition would provide in the absence of the

---

39. Eastman Kodak Co. v. Image Technical Servs., Inc., 504 U.S. 451, 502, 112 S.Ct. 2072, 119 L.Ed.2d 265 (1992) (Scalia, J., dissenting).

40. Kodak apparently did not feel compelled to service all of its machines to gain technological feedback because it sold spare parts (without tied service) to users that serviced their own machines.

tie. If the increased demand for the tied product is based on the exploitation of the buyer's informational or motivational deficiencies, the tie is a proper target of antitrust enforcement. Of course, in many competitively injurious ties, market power in the seller's tying product exists alongside market power in the tied product that is generated by the tie. Before examining the particulars of potential anticompetitive effects of ties, we first examine the status of traditional leveraging theory of tie-ins.

8.3c1. Leverage Theory After Bowman

Under the traditional leveraging theory of tie-ins, a seller with market power could increase the level of its return through the use of a tie-in. Bowman's enduring contribution to the theory of ties was to show that a monopolist-seller could not increase its return by tying the sale of its monopoly product to the sale of another product over which the seller had no monopoly power.[41] But the accuracy of Bowman's perceptions is linked to theoretical models of pure monopoly and perfect competition, not to real market conditions. For example, Bowman assumed that a monopolist-seller would fit the theoretical model for monopoly and that buyers of the tying and tied products had all relevant information. A true monopolist can fully exploit its monopoly, raising its price to the point that buyers in significant numbers would cease use of the monopoly product altogether. For such a monopolist, Bowman reasoned, linking the sale of its monopoly tying product to a competitive tied product would bring no further gain. This theoretical monopolist already has the purest form of market power in the tying product. Bowman also assumed that most ties did not generate any additional market power. This unstated assumption would be correct if buyers either had adequate information to make an informed buying choice or, alternatively, if a sufficient number of buyers were adequately informed to discipline the market for those lacking such information. The tying seller would be forced to charge the competitive price for the tied product, whether or not it was bundled with a tying product as to which the seller possessed monopoly power.

Real markets are strikingly different from Bowman's model in at least two critical respects: (1) a tying seller does not enjoy the perfect market power in the tying product held by a theoretical monopolist; and (2) ties often generate additional market power by exploiting the buyer's informational and motivational deficiencies that went unrecognized in Bowman's world of near perfect competition. The first point aids our understanding of why a real market seller with some market power will not have the pricing latitude of a pure monopolist and might seek to increase its power to charge a higher price. The second point, however, is also critical in understanding why leverage theory stands up to Bow-

---

41. Bowman, *Tying Arrangements and the Leverage Problem*, 67 YALE L.J. 19 (1957). Bowman's views appear to have been developed from ideas expressed in Di-

rector & Levi, *Law and the Future: Trade Regulation*, 51 Nw. U. L. REV. 281, 290, 292 (1956).

man's critique. For traditional leverage theory, the harm from a tie was not in simply transferring profits from the tying to the tied product. The harm lay in expanding the seller's market power to earn a supracompetitive return that could not be captured without use of the tie.[42]

To illustrate this point, assume that the manufacturer has a patent on an electronic device to measure blood glucose levels for diabetes patients. To use the device, the manufacturer provides disposable measurement strips designed for a single use. The manufacturer may lawfully exploit its patent monopoly by raising the price charged for the machine. But the monopoly power is imperfect because competitors quickly come up with competing technologies to measure glucose levels. To increase its return, the manufacturer decides to impose a tie.[43] The manufacturer sets a low price on the machine, but charges a high price on the strips. Sales of strips are substantial because many diabetes patients need to measure blood glucose levels four or more times each day. Unsophisticated first-time buyers may be attracted by the device's low price and purchase it despite the inflated price for the strips. By the time a buyer realizes the high cost of the strips, the buyer may be locked into the manufacturer's device both because of the comfort level associated with a familiar technology and the cost of replacing it with another. The manufacturer is now in a position to obtain supracompetitive returns that would not have been possible if the tie-in were not in place. This result could, of course, not occur under Bowman's assumption of perfect monopoly power over the measurement device and a perfectly competitive market for the measurement strips.

If the hypothetical is altered to assume that every rival manufacturer of a glucose measurement device engages in a similar tying practice, first-time buyers may still be persuaded to buy a device that they would not have purchased at all if they adequately understood the price of the strips. Once again, Bowman's conclusion that a tie will not increase the seller's return does not hold—each machine manufacturer may be able to earn a higher return through the use of the tie-in than would have been possible without it. Indeed, their parallel use of the tying device may be conducive to further oligopolistic price increases. Although manufacturers could conceivably lower their price on the device sufficiently to offset any allocative losses from high-priced strips, this result is unlikely because the manufacturer will quite naturally seek to raise its price to the maximum extent that the market will bear. Even a hypothetical altruistic seller would, absent an omniscient understanding of market conditions, be unable to set prices on the device and strips in a manner that ensures maximum allocative benefits. See the discussion of this issue in § 8.3b2.

42. See Nalebuff, Bundling as an Entry Deterrent Device, 119 Q.J.Econ. 159 (2004) (questioning the assumptions underlying the Chicago critique of leveraging theory).

43. Of course, the manufacturer can charge a supracompetitive price for the disposable strips without imposing a tie for as long as there is no competing seller of the strips. But charging an inflated price for the strips would increase incentives for rivals to enter the strip market.

Bowman correctly discerned that the leverage theory as traditionally understood does not adequately explain the ability of a seller to exploit buyers through the use of a tie. His critique of leverage theory based on conditions of perfect monopoly and perfect competition forced a needed reexamination of leverage theory. That reexamination is still a work in progress, but has already demonstrated real market conditions under which tie-ins can work true anticompetitive injury. The market conditions under which tie-ins are likely to effect such injury are common—certainly much more so than the conditions of perfect monopoly and perfect competition assumed in Bowman's model. Below, we examine in greater detail the particular anticompetitive harms that a tie-in may cause.

8.3c2. Anticompetitive Injury Associated with High Market Share of Tying Sellers

Assuming there are no informational problems associated with the use of a tie, it still can cause anticompetitive injury if the tie promotes oligopolistic or cartel behavior. For example, in International Salt Co. v. United States,[44] the defendant was accused of tying the lease of its salt machines to the purchase of salt tablets that would be used in the machines. The lessee was required to use the lessor's salt tablets unless the lessor failed to meet a generalized price reduction on tablets that could be used in the machine. This clause could have facilitated oligopolistic or cartel behavior at both the buyer's and seller's level. Other sellers of salt tablets might be discouraged from competing for the lessee's business, knowing that the lessor need only match a lower price to win the business. At the buyer level, a purchaser of salt might feel comfortable with a price that it was confident was also the price paid by the buyer's competitors. Similar behavior enhancing buyer parallel practices may have occurred in Northern Pacific Railway Co. v. United States.[45] These practices that facilitate cartel-like behavior will be more effective if the seller or sellers imposing the tie have a dominant share in the market for the tying product. In *IBM Corp. v. United States,* all three producers of tabulating machines in the market at the outset of the case tied tabulating cards to the sale or lease of their machines.[46]

Even without facilitating parallel or cartel practices, a seller with a dominant share of the tying product market may use a tie to raise the costs of, or eliminate, competing producers of the tied product. For example, IBM tied the lease of its tabulating machines to the lessee's agreement to purchase all tabulating cards from IBM. Because tabulating cards had no other significant uses, foreclosure from this market would eliminate competing producers of the cards. Even if IBM is not the only producer of machines that use tabulating cards, the foreclosure

44. 332 U.S. 392, 68 S.Ct. 12, 92 L.Ed. 20 (1947).

45. 356 U.S. 1, 78 S.Ct. 514, 2 L.Ed.2d 545 (1958). See the discussion of this issue in Grimes, supra note 30, at 300–301.

46. 298 U.S. 131, 132, 56 S.Ct. 701, 80 L.Ed. 1085 (1936).

may be sufficient to reduce economies of scale for the competing producer of cards. This result is less likely if the tied product has other significant uses, allowing the competitor to sell cards in other markets, or if it would be easy for others to enter the market for the tied product (for example if makers of other paper products could easily switch to tabulating cards). The anticompetitive effect is also diluted if the competing seller of the tied product would find it relatively easy to enter the tying product market (presumably not the case in the tabulating machine market of the 1930s).

Although each of these anticompetitive effects can occur if a single seller has a substantial share of the market in the tying product, they can also occur if sellers imposing the tie have a high collective market share. Thus, a complete competitive analysis of the effects of a tie should examine not only the tying seller's market share, but also the collective share of rival sellers that impose similar ties. Of course, if all rivals in a market impose a similar tie, that circumstance is consistent with procompetitive as well as anticompetitive explanations. Universal adoption of a tie may suggest that the tie has procompetitive efficiencies, that the tie is an effective method of creating and exploiting market power, or that the tie has both of these effects.

8.3c3. Buyer's Informational Deficiencies

By its very nature, a tie complicates a buyer's purchase decision by forcing the buyer to focus on the purchase of more than one distinct product in a single transaction. While this is self-evident, the connection between tie-ins and informational market imperfections was long ignored (or assumed) in the jurisprudence of tie-ins. In 1982, Craswell offered a careful analysis of the tying seller's ability to exploit the buyer's informational deficiencies.[47] Two years later, in Jefferson Parish Hospital District No. 2 v. Hyde, the Court declined to consider informational problems in its analysis of a hospital's tie-in of anesthesia services.[48] But the Jefferson Parish Court also made clear that information problems could be the basis of competitive injury. The Court wrote that tying may harm a consumer because "the freedom to select the best bargain in the second market is impaired by his need to purchase the tying product, and perhaps by an inability to evaluate the true cost of either product when they are available as a package."[49] Lower court decisions both before and after *Jefferson Parish* have tacitly recognized the role of informational imperfections.[50] In 1992, the Supreme Court cited Craswell favorably in Eastman Kodak Co. v. Image Technical Services, Inc.,[51] holding that the plaintiffs' theory of tie-in leverage based upon the buyer's informational deficiencies should be tried on its merits.

47. Craswell, *Tying Requirements in Competitive Markets: The Consumer Protection Issues,* 62 B.U. L. Rev. 661, 671–79 (1982).

48. 466 U.S. 2, 31–32, 104 S.Ct. 1551, 80 L.Ed.2d 2 (1984).

49. Id. at 15.

50. See the discussion in § 8.3d5.

51. 504 U.S. 451, 473 & n. 19, 112 S.Ct. 2072, 119 L.Ed.2d 265 (1992).

A "market imperfection" can be understood as any condition that departs from the theoretical model of perfect competition. In this broad sense, all markets are riddled with imperfections. Economies of scale, for example, are a departure from the paradigm of perfect competition. So too is the ubiquitous practice of brand marketing and product differentiation (perfect competition assumes fungible products). In theory, these departures from perfect competition can cause distortions and misallocations of resources. In fact, many such "imperfections" may actually improve resource allocation. Brand marketing, for example, may improve consumer knowledge of the source of products, may encourage a manufacturer to maintain quality control and engage in vital research and development, and may allow the high-volume sales that bring economies of scale. Hence, the term "market imperfections" must be used with caution. Some, but not all imperfections may cause actionable injury to competition.

There are two evident market imperfections that are directly relevant to the anticompetitive potential of tie-ins. They are informational deficiencies or voids that a buyer confronts when making a purchase decision (addressed in this section), and motivational deficiencies or the consumer's lack of incentive to exercise cost-conscious behavior when making a purchase decision (addressed in the next section). Although each is relevant to the competitive analysis of ties, informational deficiencies are probably the most widespread and consequential in determining if a tie has anticompetitive consequences.

The task of determining when a tie-in is likely to exploit the buyer's informational deficiencies is, it turns out, not a particularly difficult one. There are a number of factors whose presence or absence will likely signal whether a tie-in is likely to exploit the buyer's informational deficiencies. They are: (1) whether the tie-in requires a deferred purchase of the tied product; (2) whether the buyer's attention is likely to be focused on the tying product (and not on the tied product); (3) whether the tying and tied products are complex goods or services; and (4) whether the tie-in targets unsophisticated buyers of such goods or services.

8.3c3i. *Deferred Purchase of the Tied Product*

A critical measure of a tie-in's potential exploitation of the consumer's informational voids is whether purchase of the tied product is deferred until some point after the tying product is purchased. Whenever the buyer purchases the tied product at a later date, the buyer may be less sensitive to the cost or quality of the tied product at the time the tying product is purchased. Even if the buyer is concerned about the terms for the deferred purchase of the tied product, the buyer may not know how much (if any) of the tied product will be needed. Nor will the buyer be in a position to know what alternatives to the tied product might exist at the uncertain date in the future when the tied product is required.

For example, many tied products that are used in varied proportion to the tying product are purchased at intervals, often extending long after the initial sale of the tying product. Market conditions may change, new competitors offering the tied product may emerge, and the buyer's own need for the tied product may change. This characteristic fits many of the cases in which the Supreme Court has held that a harmful tie may be present, including *Kodak*,[52] Northern Pacific Railway Co. v. United States,[53] International Salt Co. v. United States,[54] and IBM Corp. v. United States.[55] In *Kodak*, the Court expressly recognized the difficulties in life-cycle pricing involving uncertain future events.[56] The buyer subject to the tie can be subject to the seller's leverage because the buyer has invested substantial sums in the tying product and may be locked into the seller's line.

Informational problems associated with subsequent purchases of a complementary product can occur outside the tying context, as when aftermarket parts can be purchased only from the original equipment manufacturer. If no other source of supply for aftermarket parts is available, the buyer is locked into the seller's parts, regardless of whether the seller has required their purchase. The distinction, however, is that the seller has not directly sought to preclude competitors from supplying the parts. If a large number of buyers purchase the original product, the aftermarket becomes a magnet for new entrants. The seller's ability to charge supracompetitive prices will be limited by the potential and actual entry of other aftermarket suppliers. Antitrust tie-in analysis is usually implicated only when the seller takes additional steps to preclude entry in the market for parts.[57]

8.3c3ii.   *Buyer's Attention Focused on the Tying Product*

The buyer is also more vulnerable to exploitation when less attention is focused on the tied product at the time of purchase of the tying product. This result is more likely when the tied product is deferred (as discussed above). But it can occur even when the tying and tied products are purchased simultaneously. In United States v. Loew's, Inc.,[58] the tied product was grade B films that television stations were required to lease along with grade A films. Because station managers would focus their attention on obtaining grade A films that could increase advertising revenues during the most popular viewing hours, they may have paid relatively little attention to the grade B movies shown at early morning hours or other less attractive times to advertisers. Although a station manager might still make reasonable choices among the grade B movies,

---

52. 504 U.S. 451, 112 S.Ct. 2072, 119 L.Ed.2d 265 (1992).

53. 356 U.S. 1, 78 S.Ct. 514, 2 L.Ed.2d 545 (1958).

54. 332 U.S. 392, 68 S.Ct. 12, 92 L.Ed. 20 (1947).

55. 298 U.S. 131, 56 S.Ct. 701, 80 L.Ed. 1085 (1936).

56. 504 U.S. at 473–74.

57. Section 2 product predation issues may be raised if the seller is designing products for the sole purpose of deterring competition from aftermarket suppliers. See § 3.4b9.

58. 371 U.S. 38, 83 S.Ct. 97, 9 L.Ed.2d 11 (1962).

the manager may have ignored competitive alternatives for programming during those hours in order to obtain the grade A movies of choice.[59] Providers of television programming that would compete with the grade B movies could find entry or penetration into the market more difficult as the result of the tie imposed in *Loew's*.

8.3c3iii.   *The Complexity of the Products Subject to the Tie–In*

Another variable that can affect a tying seller's ability to exploit informational deficiencies is the complexity of the goods being purchased. For some products, often called *search* goods, salient characteristics are self-evident from a buyer's superficial examination of a product displayed in a store. A consumer is less likely to be misled when purchasing a search good such as a greeting card. Other products must be purchased and experienced in order to be evaluated. These *experience* goods may be relatively simple and inexpensive (an apple, a can of shoe polish, or a tube of toothpaste) or highly complex (a computer or an automobile). For expensive experience goods, the cost of a mistaken purchase can be substantial. Highly complex products are likely to have some of the attributes of *credence* goods. For such products, the experience of the consumer may itself be insufficient for full evaluation of the product. In determining the need for medical treatment or repair of an automobile engine, the consumer may need to rely on outsiders that have specialized information and expertise.

Tie-ins involving search goods or relatively simple experience goods are unlikely to involve the exploitation of informational voids. If a package of flour is sold together with a package of sugar, most consumers will know, or can easily calculate, whether the package price represents a bargain.[60] That evaluation becomes more difficult when the package involves a computer sold with software and a printer. Most harmful ties involve relatively more complex goods and services, suggesting the relevance of informational problems to the analysis of those ties. Still, even when bundled sales involve complex products, they may raise relatively few informational problems if, in the circumstances, buyers will likely be or become well informed before the purchase.

8.3c3iv.   *The Tie Excludes Large or Sophisticated Buyers*

Ties that target unsophisticated or inexperienced buyers are more likely to involve informational risks. In consumer goods industries, consumers are more likely to lack sophistication if the bundled products are complex and infrequently purchased. When bundled items are sold to businesses, at least some buyers are likely to be more sophisticated. Their presence in the buyer pool may make it more difficult for the seller to impose the tie, unless the seller can target the tie against a class of buyers likely to be less sophisticated. *Kodak, Northern Pacific* and *IBM* each involved ties that were not applied against some larger, more

---

59. Grimes, supra note 30, at 302–03.

60. The example is from Justice Black's opinion in Northern Pacific Railway Co. v.

United States, 356 U.S. 1, 6–7, 78 S.Ct. 514, 2 L.Ed.2d 545 (1958).

sophisticated buyers.[61] When the seller discriminates in its application of a tie, excepting a class of large or informed buyers, there is a higher risk that the tie is exploiting the informational or motivational deficiencies of a large class of less sophisticated buyers.

8.3c4. Buyer's Motivational Deficiencies

The buyer's motivation to exercise cost-conscious behavior may also be affected when tie-ins are used. Two circumstances in which the buyer's motive is likely to be affected are: (1) when an agent making the purchasing decision for the buyer is disloyal or conflicted; and (2) when the buyer can pass on the cost of the purchase to a third party.

8.3c4i. The Defendant's Control of a Buyer's Purchase Decision

A buyer is motivated to make a purchase on its competitive merits because the buyer's own capital is placed at risk by an unwise purchase. But buyers sometimes delegate purchasing authority to an agent. Because an agent owes a duty of loyalty to the principal, an agent's purchasing decisions would in most instances be consistent with the principal's interests. But an agent sometimes has conflicting interests. Gifts, rebates or bribes paid to a purchasing agent can prompt the agent to make a purchase other than that dictated by the competitive merits of the offering. For example, in restaurants and retailing, corrupting payments made to purchasing agents are apparently widespread and have occasioned strict conflict of interest policies by retailers such as Wal–Mart.[62]

In franchising, a franchisor may tie the continued availability of the franchise to the franchisee's purchase of products from a chosen supplier. Although some control over sourcing may be needed to maintain uniform quality within the franchise system, a supplier may corrupt the franchisor's sourcing decision by paying a rebate or kickback directly to the franchisor in return for a requirement that all franchisees purchase the input product from the supplier. In such instances, both franchisees and consumers may be injured if the input supplier charges the franchisees a supracompetitive price or delivers an inferior product.

8.3c4ii. Buyer Pass On

One circumstance likely to dampen the buyer's price consciousness is the buyer's ability to pass on part or all of the costs of a purchase to a third party. This could occur, for example, in health care, where many Americans rely on an insurer or the Government to cover the bulk of health care expenditures. Of course, if the cost of health care is largely borne by an insurer, the consumer would make health care decisions with dampened cost sensitivity regardless of whether health care products and services are bundled. But a seller offering a product or service

---

61. See the discussion in § 8.3b2.

62. WALL ST. J., Feb. 7, 1995, at A1(describing the widespread occurrence of brib-ery of retailers' purchasing agents and Wal–Mart's stringent conflict of interest policy).

not covered by insurance may be able to exploit the consumer's lack of cost sensitivity by tying its sale to another product that is covered by insurance. For example, a seller attempting to market a sophisticated x-ray machine to a hospital might find it advantageous to sell the machine at a low price, but charge a high price for a variable-use tied product such as x-ray film. This might be attractive to the hospital if it could pass on the cost of x-ray film to patients who are not cost-conscious (because someone else pays their health bills). Or, in cases in which both the tying and tied products are covered by insurance, the seller may exploit the consumer's lack of cost sensitivity by designing a tying product with which only the seller's tied product is compatible, thereby gaining a supracompetitive return on the sale of both tying and tied products.

In Jefferson Parish Hospital District No. 2 v. Hyde, the Supreme Court refused to accept arguments of both informational and motivational market imperfections in a health care market.[63] The Court held that the market imperfections relied upon by the court of appeals were not relevant because neither "forces consumers to take anesthesiological services they would not select in the absence of a tie."[64] The Court's holding cannot fairly be interpreted as a blanket rejection of the relevance of information issues, but only as insistence that a "forcing" be demonstrated. This is made clear earlier in the opinion when, addressing the Sherman Act's treatment of ties, Justice Stevens wrote for the Court that tying may harm a consumer because "the freedom to select the best bargain in the second market is impaired by his need to purchase the tying product, and perhaps by an inability to evaluate the true cost of either product when they are available only as a package."[65] In a footnote, Justice Stevens continued: "Especially where market imperfections exist, purchasers may not be fully sensitive to the price or quality implications of a tying arrangement, and hence it may impede competition on the merits."[66] In any event, a much more direct acknowledgment came eight years later with the Court's extensive and approving discussion of informational market imperfections as a basis for a tie-in claim in Eastman Kodak Co. v. Image Technical Services, Inc.[67] *Still, the controversy surrounding the use of such claims has not been silenced and is addressed in the following section.*

8.3c5. Should Buyer's Informational and Motivational Deficiencies Be Excluded from Antitrust Tie–In Analysis?

Critics of *Eastman Kodak Co. v. Image Technical Services, Inc.*, including Justice Scalia in dissent,[68] have raised a number of objections to the consideration of informational and motivational market imperfections in antitrust tie-in analysis. Indeed, in his influential 1982 analysis,

---

63. 466 U.S. 2, 27–28, 104 S.Ct. 1551, 80 L.Ed.2d 2 (1984).

64. Id. at 28.

65. Id. at 15.

66. Id. at 15, n.24.

67. 504 U.S. 451, 473–76, 112 S.Ct. 2072, 119 L.Ed.2d 265 (1992).

68. 504 U.S. at 494 et seq. (Scalia, J., dissenting).

Craswell suggested that informational concerns should be addressed in consumer protection laws, not as a part of antitrust analysis.[69] But information issues have long been a part of tie-in analysis, as when a seller invokes a quality control defense. See §§ 8.3b4, 8.3d4. Congress has commanded that antitrust address the competitive merits of tie-ins and related practices through the enactment of Section 3 of the Clayton Act and Section 1 of the Sherman Act. Informational issues clearly affect that competitive balance. The anticompetitive effects of a tie that exploits the buyer's informational deficiencies are not different in kind from those associated with monopoly or cartel abuses. In either case, the tie creates misallocations of resources (because the consumer buys one product instead of another) and wealth transfers (because the consumer pays a higher price than would be charged under more competitive conditions). In the final analysis, it would be wasteful for an antitrust court, particularly in an area such as tie-ins, to attempt to carve out informational or motivational issues for resolution as a part of another claim, worse yet if the claim was to be brought in another forum at another time. The analysis of informational issues may change the overall competitive assessment of a tie, forcing the subsequent tribunal to reach a result contrary to that reached by the first tribunal. A seller imposing a tie does so because of its overall market impact, whether that impact is positive or negative. But a tribunal instructed to consider only certain competitive effects (say those related to high market share) would likely reach a sterile and incomplete conclusion about the competitive effects of the tie. For example, a tie-in case involving a buyer, such as a franchisee or consumer, may involve both the seller's interbrand market power evidenced by a high tying product market share and increased seller market power in the tied product (arising from the buyer's informational deficiencies). The injuries caused by these differing types of market power are to some degree distinct. A high interbrand market share for the seller may lead to a greater foreclosure risk. But that foreclosure risk would be exacerbated if informational deficiencies contributed to the tie's effectiveness. It would be a highly theoretical exercise (and probably an impossible one) to separate competitive injury caused by interbrand market power from that caused by exploitation of informational deficiencies.

Consider an automobile manufacturer that requires its franchised dealers to buy spare parts only from manufacturer-authorized sources. Such a tie might produce universal supracompetitive pricing for spare parts acquired from dealers. If the tie of a particular manufacturer is challenged in an antitrust action, the plaintiff may rely on evidence of informational deficiencies (a buyer cannot know or predict the life-cycle pricing of aftermarket parts). However, if the practice is common among all automobile manufacturers, this tends to undercut the plaintiff's argument that a buyer lacked knowledge of the practice. A widely emulated tie among competing manufacturers duplicates the heightened allocative injury of a cartel–the issue now is very much one of interbrand

---

69. Craswell, supra note 47, at 700.

market power. But suppose that the evidence shows that the widespread use of such ties dulled the motivation of dealers to shop for lower cost parts because of an awareness that all rival dealers of the same brand were subject to the same restriction. And suppose that the evidence also shows that the particular manufacturer named as the defendant in the suit charges prices for its captive parts that substantially exceed the industry average and that purchasers of this brand of car are generally unaware of this differential. There is now record evidence of allocative injury arising both from the industry-wide nature of the tie-in (related to an interbrand market power) and from two market imperfections (dealers' blunted motivation to shop for the lowest priced parts and the exploitation of the buyer's informational deficiencies by the manufacturer whose parts' prices substantially exceed those of its rivals). Evidence of both types of market power is relevant to antitrust injury and should be considered by the deciding tribunal. Indeed, any effort to separate the analysis of the two types of market power would leave the court with a skewed assessment that is inconsistent with real market conditions.

An implicit acknowledgment of the need to consider informational issues along with more conventional market power analysis came in the D.C. Circuit's 2001 en banc opinion in United States v. Microsoft Corp.[70] In that opinion, without citing *Kodak* or discussing the propriety of doing so, the court simply addresses the informational issues as a part of its thorough factual analysis of Microsoft's exclusionary bundling behavior.[71]

Of course, informational market imperfections are ubiquitous and not typically the target of antitrust enforcement. Antitrust cannot and should not attempt to prevent consumers from making ill-advised purchases under a broad variety of conditions. But when sellers invoke tie-ins and related practices that have long been the province of antitrust law, an analysis of informational deficiencies is both inevitable and necessary. A seller that uses a tie is acting voluntarily and, in many cases, consciously to exploit these deficiencies. In contrast, a seller that takes no special action to exploit such imperfections is, in effect, a passive beneficiary of additional sales that might arise from informational voids. The broader problems with buyer's informational deficiencies can be addressed to some degree through aggressive consumer education programs and greater accessibility for information relevant to buyer choices. But when tie-ins or other traditional practices involving antitrust are involved, the courts should not be asked to wear blinders concerning informational issues.

It has been suggested that informational market imperfections ought not to be addressed in tie-in analysis because the buyer can contract to avoid any anticompetitive effects of tie-ins. Implicit in this argument are premises that the buyer's informational deficiencies are insubstantial or can be corrected easily by large and knowledgeable

---

70. 253 F.3d 34 (D.C. Cir. 2001)(en banc).

71. See the discussion of the 2001 *Microsoft* decision in § 8.3d1.

buyers.[72] But the buyer's foreknowledge is critical, as is the seller's ability to discriminate selectively against those lacking knowledge or bargaining leverage. In cases such as Northern Pacific Railway Co. v. United States and Kodak,[73] the seller made concessions to certain large and knowledgeable buyers but was able to make the tie stick for the majority of purchasers that apparently lacked either the knowledge or the leverage to negotiate a special deal with the seller. Even if a buyer anticipates some of the problems associated with a tie, short of convincing the seller to abandon the tie, it may be impossible to find a contractual mechanism for avoiding them. For example, no buyer can predict in advance subsequent developments in the market for the tied product. New competitors may emerge with varying quality and price offerings, giving the buyer a constantly shifting but rich variety of choices for purchase of the tied product. A buyer cannot, by contract, adjust for future competitive conditions that cannot be foreseen.[74]

A final attack on recognition of the single brand market power that arises from informational deficiencies comes from theorists who argue that sellers will not be abusive because they must look to their business reputation. These theorists point out that the reputation of a seller will suffer if it becomes known for imposition of abusive tie-ins. Thus, franchisors (that control franchisee purchasing decisions through tie-ins) and original equipment manufacturers (that sell aftermarket parts to captive buyers) are unlikely to abuse buyers.[75] That a concern with business reputation will constrain most sellers' behavior seems beyond dispute. But that constraint will often be insufficient to prevent abuse. Addressing the sale of aftermarket products, Borenstein points out that, although sellers risk damaging their reputation if they charge an unduly high price for aftermarket products, this restraint may be ineffective if the seller is insecure about growth in the original equipment market.[76] For example, a computer manufacturer whose only computer is no longer state of the art, and unlikely to retain a large market, has diminished concerns about maintaining reputation. Under these circumstances, the seller may not be competitively disciplined when it raises prices for aftermarket products for that computer. The Borenstein article also points out that buyers may expect to pay more for aftermarket products, giving the seller yet another incentive to tie such products to the sale of original equipment in order to reap the higher return.[77]

Although the *Kodak* decision has been distinguished or ignored by some lower courts, its empirical approach to tie-ins was followed in the

72. Klein, *Market Power in Aftermarkets,* 17 MANAGERIAL & DECISION ECON. 143 (1996).

73. See the discussion of these cases in § 8.3d5.

74. Borenstein et al., *Antitrust Policy in Aftermarkets,* 63 ANTITRUST L.J. 455, 473–74 (1995).

75. This argument is advanced, among others, by Klein, supra note72, and Arthur, *The Costly Quest for Perfect Competition: Kodak and Nonstructural Market Power,* 69 N.Y.U. L. REV. 1 (1994).

76. Borenstein et al., supra note 74, at 464–67.

77. Id.

2001 en banc decision of the D.C. Circuit in United States v. Microsoft.[78] That decision did not cite *Kodak*, instead relying heavily on Justice O'Connor's concurring opinion in *Jefferson Parish* in which she offered a classic Chicago analysis of tie-ins. Yet the court's careful analysis of Microsoft's exclusionary bundling conduct is consistent with a post-Chicago approach that honors evidence over deductive theory, including evidence of consumer confusion relevant to the need for, or response to, bundling behavior. For example, the government had challenged Microsoft's demand that computer manufacturers not remove the Internet Explorer icon from the boot-up screen. Microsoft responded that manufacturers were free to add a second browser program on the display screen. The court, as did the district court, discounted the significance of this because manufacturers had testified to the costs of consumer confusion if the icons of two competing browsers were included on the screen. The manufacturer, the court noted, might have to spend additional funds on consumer assistance in responding to the confusion that the two icons would generate.[79]

In the case of franchisors, sourcing tie-ins may also be the result of commissions or kickbacks paid to the franchisor. The franchisor's concerns with its reputation will be blunted if it receives direct payments from a favored supplier. A franchisor that is publicly traded responds not only to pressures to maintain reputation with franchisees, but also to maintain high stock prices that reward stockholders and stock-owning management. These and other reasons that may lead a franchisor to discount concerns with its reputation are discussed in § 6.4c3ii.

8.3c6. *Avoiding Price Controls*

A seller confronting a regulated price may be able to raise the price for the product by requiring the buyer to purchase a tied product at a higher price. Bowman points out that the increased return should be no more than that which the seller could obtain from selling the tying product if there had been no price control.[80] That conclusion will not hold, however, if the tie, in addition to shifting profit from the tying to the tied product, also operates to increase the seller's overall market power through exploitation of the buyer's informational deficiencies. In theory, the seller may also be able to use the tied product to undercut a minimum price imposed on the tying product, a result that could be procompetitive. But the latter use of a bundled sale is probably not a tie (because informed buyers would wish it). And even if an upward evasion of a maximum price is not an extension of a seller's monopoly, it is often an evasion of regulatory policy (price control) that is a legitimate response to monopoly power.[81]

78. 253 F.3d 34 (D.C. Cir. 2001)(en banc).

79. Id. at 64. For additional analysis of the en banc court's treatment of information issues, see Grimes, *The Antitrust Tying Law Schism: A Critique of* Microsoft III *and*

A Response to Hylton and Salinger, 70 ANTITURST L. J. 199 (2002).

80. Bowman, supra note 41, at 21–23.

81. Black v. Magnolia Liquor Co., 355 U.S. 24, 78 S.Ct. 106, 2 L.Ed.2d 5 (1957)(wholesaler compelled liquor dealers

8.3d. Tie–Ins in the Courts

Tie-ins are frequently litigated. Cases involving tie-ins have reached the Supreme Court with some regularity—seven since 1945.[82] Moreover, tie-ins often involve cutting-edge, high-tech industries. A sample of cases (all initiated by private plaintiffs) decided by courts of appeals during the years 1984–1992 found that 17 of the 44 cases involved tie-ins in the marketing of health care, computers or automobiles.[83]

8.3d1. *Application of the Modified Per Se Rule*

Although the test for measuring the legality of tie-ins is described as a *per se* rule, the preconditions required to apply the rule render it more of a modified *per se* rule (or a structured rule of reason) in which the inquiry, while limited, allows an economic analysis of the effects of a particular tie. As restated by the Supreme Court in Jefferson Parish Hospital District No. 2 v. Hyde, invocation of the *per se* rule against tie-ins requires the plaintiff to show that (1) a tying arrangement exists between two separate products; (2) the "seller has some special ability— usually called 'market power'—to force a purchaser to do something that he would not do in a competitive market"; and (3) the tying arrangement forecloses a substantial volume of commerce.[84]

The first prong of this test is critical for separating procompetitive bundling practices from ties. If a bundling is reasonably disciplined by competition or otherwise within the confines of informed consumer demand, no tie should be found (i.e., the court may properly consider the sale to involve a single product). See the discussion in § 8.3b1. When informed consumers accept the bundling as the most efficient way for the seller to maintain quality control, the bundling does not constitute a tie-in and a quality control defense (discussed in § 7.2d4) is likely to be superfluous.

The second prong of the test—inquiring whether the seller has economic power to force the buyer to change behavior—has been subject to a variety of Supreme Court interpretations. In Times–Picayune Publishing Co. v. United States, for example, the Court seemed to require market dominance to satisfy the test.[85] A few years later, in Northern Pacific Railway Co. v. United States, the Court appeared to retreat from a market dominance requirement, demanding only that the plaintiff

---

to buy undesired brands as a means of raising prices on desired brands); In re Friedman, 113 F.T.C. 625 (1990) (dialysis provider allegedly used tying practice to circumvent Medicare price controls on dialysis service).

82. The *Fortner* case reached the Supreme Court on two occasions, but is counted only once here. Fortner Enters., Inc. v. United States Steel Corp., 394 U.S. 495, 89 S.Ct. 1252, 22 L.Ed.2d 495 (1969); United States Steel Corp. v. Fortner Enters., Inc.,

429 U.S. 610, 97 S.Ct. 861, 51 L.Ed.2d 80 (1977).

83. Grimes, supra note 30, at 307–08 (reporting that in the sample of 44 courts of appeals tie-in cases, 7 involved automobiles, 5 involved computers, and 5 involved health care).

84. 466 U.S. 2, 12–15, 104 S.Ct. 1551, 80 L.Ed.2d 2 (1984).

85. 345 U.S. 594, 611, 73 S.Ct. 872, 97 L.Ed. 1277 (1953).

show an appreciable restraint on free competition.[86] More recently, in *Jefferson Parish,* the Court, while defining the coercion requirement with expansive language ("some special ability–usually called 'market power'–to force a purchaser to do something that he would not do in a competitive market") seems to have limited its application to a showing of interbrand market power, examining whether the seller had a substantial market share in the tying product (local hospitals in which surgery is performed).[87] As the analysis in § 8.3c suggests, an exclusive focus on the interbrand market share of a tying seller will not cast a sufficiently broad net to catch most competitively harmful ties. For example, a tie may work anticompetitive injury because of the existence of market imperfections, allowing the seller to exploit market power in a single brand market. Addressing this problem, the Court in *Kodak* refused to allow summary dismissal of the plaintiff's theory that buyers of Kodak's spare parts were locked in by their purchase of Kodak's original equipment and, because of buyer life-cycle pricing difficulties, could not adequately predict aftermarket conditions at the time the original equipment was purchased.[88] This approach, which effectively viewed the aftermarket for Kodak parts as a separate market, allowed the Court to consider whether the seller's ability to coerce the buyer arises from the buyer's inability to look beyond the seller's brand.

The third prong of the test set out by the Supreme Court, whether the tie forecloses a not insubstantial volume of commerce, may seem difficult to square with the principles of antitrust. One does not hear, for example, that a cartel or monopoly is lawful simply because the defendants are not large players in the economic system. A cartel of dry cleaners operating in a small town could, for example, work substantial competitive injury on affected consumers despite the relatively small size of the conspiring firms and of the market. Yet the requirement that the plaintiff show the foreclosure of a substantial volume of commerce makes sense in the context of tie-ins and other foreclosure restraints. A party to a contract may make a poor choice and be "held up" by the other side, but this individual contractual failure cannot be an unlawful tie-in unless the "substantial foreclosure" test is met. Properly applied, the test provides a useful rule of judicial administration allowing for summary dismissal of claims involving relatively inconsequential contractual failures.

The court of appeals' 2001 en banc opinion in United States v. Microsoft Corp. will be an influential precedent in tying cases, particularly those arising in high technology industries. The government had challenged certain exclusionary bundling behavior of Microsoft, in particular its integration of its Internet browser program (Explorer) with its operating system (Windows 98). The district court found that this conduct violated Section 1 of the Sherman Act's modified per se rule

86. 356 U.S. 1, 6, 78 S.Ct. 514, 2 L.Ed.2d 545 (1958).

87. 466 U.S. at 13–14.

88. Eastman Kodak Co. v. Image Technical Servs., Inc., 504 U.S. 451, 473–78, 112 S.Ct. 2072, 119 L.Ed.2d 265 (1992).

applicable to tie-ins. On appeal, the en banc court reversed and remanded this holding, concluding that the rule of reason must apply in this case. The court reasoned that this case offered "the first up-close look at the technological integration of added functionality into software that serves as a platform for third-party applications." Because of the "serious risk of harm" in applying the per se rule in such circumstances, the court instructed the district court on remand to apply a rule of reason.[89]

In this aspect of its holding, the *Microsoft* court seemed intent on revisiting the *Jefferson Parish* debate over the appropriate tying standard.[90] The court cites the maxim that per se rules should be adopted only after adequate judicial experience. This approach makes sense when confronting a choice between a naked per se rule and a rule of reason. This stark choice, however, was not the one facing the *Microsoft* court. The modified per se rule, which has evolved gradually from stricter per se treatment, substantially opens the inquiry for a court assessing the legality of a tying arrangement, allowing, for example, careful consideration of whether a product integration bundling should not be considered a tie because it is an efficient response to consumer demand.

Even accepting the court's conclusion that the rule of reason should apply in a Section 1 analysis of the tying claims, there is an apparent inconsistency in the treatment of Microsoft's bundling conduct in the Section 1 and Section 2 portions of the opinion. The court held that this bundling conduct constituted unlawful maintenance of a monopoly in violation of Section 2 of the Sherman Act,[91] yet overturned the district court's judgment that this same conduct constituted a Section 1 tying violation. The court explained that, in order to establish that bundling conduct violated Section 1, the plaintiffs on remand would have to demonstrate harmful effects in the "tied-product market" that outweighed any benefits of the tying arrangement.[92] A focus on harmful effects in the tied-product market is a carryover from leverage theory that finds support in some language from *Jefferson Parish*.[93] But a compelling Chicago critique of leverage theory has been that the tying seller might shift the monopoly gain back and forth between the tying and tied products. A competitive assessment of tying conduct must examine the overall picture, not simply the tied product market in isolation. The court of appeals made this overall competitive assessment in determining that Microsoft's conduct violated Section 2 of the Sherman Act. That assessment, which the court called "a similar balancing approach" to that applied in Section 1 cases under the rule of reason,[94] focused on competitive effects in both the operating software and the browser markets. To require further litigation on the Section 1 issues would either be a sterile and repetitive exercise, or one that improperly

---

89. 253 F.3d 34, 84 (D.C. Cir. 2001)(en banc).

90. In the tying portion of its opinion, the court of appeals approvingly cites the O'Connor concurrence (arguing for overturning the modified per se rule) on four occasions. Id. at 88, 94, 94–95, 97.

91. The court's section 2 holding is described in § 3.4b9.

92. Id. at 96.

93. *Jefferson Parish*, 466 U.S. at 14–15.

94. *Microsoft*, 253 F.3d at 34.

places an unequal evidentiary burden on plaintiffs challenging exclusionary bundling conduct under Section 1 rather than Section 2 of the Sherman Act.

8.3d2. The Defendant's Economic Benefit in the Tied Product

The courts of appeals have shown some propensity to graft additional requirements onto the tie-in test adopted by the Supreme Court. A number of circuits now require that the plaintiff show that the defendant has an economic benefit in the tied product.[95] A requirement that the defendant receive such a financial benefit is not without theoretical grounding. Many ties involve a tying product of one seller and a tied product of a second seller. If there is no financial link between the parties, there is a greater likelihood that the tie was imposed for procompetitive reasons. In franchising, for example, the franchisor may require its franchisees to purchase an input product from a third party supplier approved by the franchisor. If there is no financial link between the franchisor and the third party supplier, it is more likely that the franchisor will have selected the supplier based on the merits of the supplier's offering.[96] If, on the other hand, the franchisor is receiving a rebate based on sales by the supplier to franchisees, there is a greater risk that the franchisor will have chosen the supplier for reasons other than the competitive merits of the offering.

However well intended, the requirement is problematic because it erects an evidentiary hurdle that may bar meritorious antitrust claims. The nature of this evidentiary problem is demonstrated by Directory Sales Management Corp. v. Ohio Bell Telephone Co.,[97] a case in which the court found no tie because the economic benefit test was not satisfied. The court held that the plaintiff had failed to meet its burden notwithstanding that the tying and tied products were sold by subsidiaries of the same parent corporation. Tracing the financial links between the separate subsidiaries could have presented the plaintiff with a formidable task, and one that should be wholly unnecessary if the elements of a harmful tie-in have been demonstrated. There seems, in any event, little doubt of the financial link between a parent corporation and its wholly owned subsidiary. The Tenth Circuit had no difficulty in

---

95. See, e.g., Beard v. Parkview Hosp., 912 F.2d 138 (6th Cir.1990); White v. Rockingham Radiologists, Ltd., 820 F.2d 98, 104 (4th Cir.1987); Carl Sandburg Village Condominium Ass'n No. 1 v. First Condominium Dev. Co., 758 F.2d 203, 207–08 (7th Cir.1985). Noting that the Supreme Court has never adopted this requirement, the Second Circuit declined to impose it in Gonzalez v. St. Margaret's House Housing Development Fund Corp., 880 F.2d 1514 (2d Cir.1989).

96. The possible quality control benefits from franchisor control over the source of franchisee purchases have led one court to conclude that the economic benefit test is

most necessary in franchise cases. Thompson v. Metropolitan Multi–List, Inc., 934 F.2d 1566, 1579 (11th Cir.1991), cert. denied, 506 U.S. 903, 113 S.Ct. 295, 121 L.Ed.2d 219 (1992).

97. 833 F.2d 606 (6th Cir.1987). The Supreme Court has never recognized an economic benefit requirement. Kodak, 504 U.S. at 460–62; Jefferson Parish, 466 U.S. at 13–16. In Jefferson Parish, 466 U.S. at 31–32, the Court found no tying violation, but it did not suggest that the hospital's lack of direct involvement in providing anesthesiology services precluded finding an actionable tie.

finding this financial link in Sports Racing Services, Inc. v. Sports Car Club of America, Inc.[98]

The economic interest requirement is not necessary to protect the legitimate business interests of a tying seller. If the bundling is efficient, there is no unlawful tie-in. Or the seller may invoke the quality control defense. Rigidly applied, the economic benefit test will preclude meritorious claims without enhancing the protection of legitimate bundling practices. There may, however, still be room for a defendant to establish, as a part of a quality control defense, that it receives no direct benefit from the sale of the tied product. Such a showing could buttress the defendant's argument that its tie enhances efficiency and was imposed without improper motive. This approach places the burden on the party most capable of showing the financial relationship between the defendant and the seller of the tied product.

8.3d3.   Failure to Establish a Conspiracy

After the Supreme Court's 1984 decision in Monsanto Co. v. Spray-Rite Service Corp.,[99] a vertical minimum price fixing case, a few courts began incorporating into tie-in law Monsanto's rigid conspiracy requirement.[100] In these lower court decisions, the plaintiff was compelled to show that the defendant conspired with someone other than the buyer in imposing the tie. As noted in § 7. a, this requirement may prevent courts from reaching the competitive merits with respect to many genuinely anticompetitive acts. Most ties are unilaterally imposed by the seller, so finding evidence of a genuine conspiracy with anyone other than the seller may be difficult. In Perma Life Mufflers, Inc. v. International Parts Corp., the Supreme Court gave a relaxed interpretation of the conspiracy requirement in a tying context, finding that a franchisee could demonstrate a conspiracy in either of two ways: (1) by showing the franchisee's unwilling compliance with the tying seller's requirements, or (2) by showing that other franchise dealers were forced to comply with the seller's requirements.[101] In Eastman Kodak Co. v. Image Technical Services, Inc., the Court followed a similar approach in concluding that a conspiracy may be found simply from a forced agreement of a purchaser of the tying product to purchase the tied product exclusively from the tying product's seller.[102] This flexible test for conspiracy is consistent with dealing with ties on their competitive merits. The Tenth Circuit, in an en banc rehearing, reversed its own prior precedents and

---

98.   131 F.3d 874 (10th Cir.1997).

99.   465 U.S. 752, 760–61, 104 S.Ct. 1464, 79 L.Ed.2d 775 (1984).

100.   Service & Training, Inc. v. Data Gen. Corp., 963 F.2d 680, 685–86 (4th Cir. 1992); City of Chanute v. Williams Natural Gas Co., 955 F.2d 641, 650–51 (10th Cir.), cert. denied, 506 U.S. 831, 113 S.Ct. 96, 121 L.Ed.2d 57 (1992); Smith Mach. Co. v. Hesston Corp., 878 F.2d 1290, 1294–95 (10th

Cir.1989), cert. denied, 493 U.S. 1073, 110 S.Ct. 1119, 107 L.Ed.2d 1026 (1990); McKenzie v. Mercy Hosp., 854 F.2d 365, 367–68 (10th Cir.1988); Famous Brands, Inc. v. David Sherman Corp., 814 F.2d 517, 523–24 (8th Cir.1987).

101.   392 U.S. 134, 142, 88 S.Ct. 1981, 20 L.Ed.2d 982 (1968).

102.   504 U.S. at 463 & n.8.

embraced the more flexible test followed by the Supreme Court in *Perma Life* and *Kodak*.[103]

8.3d4. *The Quality Control Defense*

A defendant will prevail against a claim of an unlawful tie-in if the plaintiff fails to establish any of the three requirements for the modified *per se* rule (described in § 8.3d1). In addition, the Supreme Court has recognized a business justification defense for a new entrant that might need a tie to ensure that the aftermarket or input products used in conjunction with the tying product do not undermine the quality reputation of the tying product.[104] This defense has been criticized as "surplusage" because the new entrant is, in any event, unlikely to have the requisite market power to establish an unlawful tie.[105] On the other hand, a tying seller's power to coerce may stem from a lock-in based on informational deficiencies so that such power may still be present for a new entrant.

A defense based on the defendant's ability to demonstrate quality control is consistent with the approach for determining whether a procompetitive bundling or tie-in exists. As described in § 8.3b1, there is no tie if informed consumers recognize through their purchases the efficiencies generated by the packaged marketing of two products. Nonetheless, there still may be circumstances in which distinct products are tied because of quality control considerations. For example, consumers may lack information or motivation to make the right choice (a consumer may be unable to assess the quality of an engine replacement part). In such circumstances, manufacturers may argue the need for a tie to protect their reputation from harm generated by deficient aftermarket parts. The availability of the business justification defense allows a defendant to come forward with evidence to rebut the plaintiff's prima facie case by offering evidence that consumer demand for the unbundled product may itself be misguided by informational deficiencies. In cases in which the quality control defense has been raised, the most troublesome issue is whether the manufacturer might have maintained its quality reputation by means substantially less anticompetitive than the imposition of a tie. Two cases involving Mercedes–Benz and a third involving Subaru were defended in part on the ground that a tie-in requiring dealers to carry spare parts manufactured or approved by the manufacturer was necessary to protect the automaker's quality reputation.[106] But a requirements tie imposed on a dealer may severely intrude on competi-

103. Systemcare, Inc. v. Wang Lab. Corp., 117 F.3d 1137 (10th Cir.1997)(en banc).

104. United States v. Jerrold Elecs. Corp., 187 F.Supp. 545, 556–57 (E.D.Pa. 1960), aff'd per curiam, 365 U.S. 567, 81 S.Ct. 755, 5 L.Ed.2d 806 (1961).

105. E. Fox & L. Sullivan, Cases and Materials on Antitrust 689–90 (1989).

106. Mozart Co. v. Mercedes–Benz of N. Am., Inc. 833 F.2d 1342 (9th Cir.1987), cert. denied, 488 U.S. 870, 109 S.Ct. 179, 102 L.Ed.2d 148 (1988); Metrix Warehouse, Inc. v. Daimler–Benz Aktiengesellschaft, 828 F.2d 1033 (4th Cir.1987), cert. denied, 486 U.S. 1017, 108 S.Ct. 1753, 100 L.Ed.2d 215 (1988); Grappone, Inc. v. Subaru of New England, Inc., 858 F.2d 792 (1st Cir. 1988).

tion for aftermarket parts without imparting any significant reputational gain. For many replacement parts the manufacturer could impose reasonable specifications on suppliers that still permit dealers purchase choices among qualifying vendors, thus preserving a degree of interbrand competition for those parts. As long as the standards are reasonable and competing suppliers are afforded an opportunity to meet the specifications, the anticompetitive effects of this practice are mitigated. Where the spare parts involve patented technology or trade secrets that are critical to the operation of the vehicle, the manufacturer may have a strong case for use of a tie-in to maintain its quality reputation.

8.3d5.   Does Kodak Alter Preexisting Case Law Governing Tie–Ins?

Some critics of Eastman Kodak Co. v. Image Technical Services, Inc., see the case as a potential watershed that could fundamentally alter antitrust law.[107] Does *Kodak* represent a radical departure from prior case law governing tie-ins? Many decisions prior to *Kodak* turned on the market share of the tying seller in an interbrand market, with little or no attention paid to informational market imperfections.[108] Plaintiffs are likely to recast claims in light of *Kodak*, seeking where possible to advance theories based upon informational deficiencies and circumstances that may lock in the buyer of a tying product. But it is incorrect to say that informational deficiencies were not a factor in prior tie-in cases. Most of the Supreme Court's decisions, when revisited in light of *Kodak*, would have come out the same way.

IBM Corp. v. United States[109] involved a tie that required users of IBM's tabulating machines to purchase all tabulating cards from IBM. A number of circumstances suggested the likelihood of the buyer's informational deficiencies. The deferred purchase of the tabulating cards increased the likelihood that some buyers would make a purchase decision without full information about the IBM package and available competing offers. A first-time buyer of a tabulating machine might lack information critical to life-cycle pricing, including the intensity of use of the machine and the cost at which competitors might offer the tabulating cards.

International Salt Co. v. United States[110] also involved a requirements tie that forced lessors of salt-injection machines to use salt tablets provided by International Salt. Because there was deferred purchase of the tied product (salt tablets), it would have been difficult for a purchaser to predict its future needs for salt and to weigh the merits of various market options that might be available in the future for procurement of

107. Arthur, supra note 75; Jacobs, *Market Power Through Imperfect Information: The Staggering Implications of* Eastman Kodak Co. v. Image Technical Services *and a Modest Proposal for Limiting Them,* 52 MD. L. REV. 336 (1993).

108. Town Sound & Custom Tops, Inc. v. Chrysler Motors Corp., 959 F.2d 468, 481 (3d Cir.)(en banc), cert. denied, 506 U.S. 868, 113 S.Ct. 196, 121 L.Ed.2d 139 (1992);

Baxley–DeLamar Monuments, Inc. v. American Cemetery Ass'n, 938 F.2d 846, 850–53 (8th Cir.1991). Other cases are cited in Grimes, supra note 30, at 309 n.138.

109. 298 U.S. 131, 56 S.Ct. 701, 80 L.Ed. 1085 (1936).

110. 332 U.S. 392, 68 S.Ct. 12, 92 L.Ed. 20 (1947).

salt. The pricing clauses written into the lease may also have reduced the buyer's motivation to shop for the lowest price. Knowing that rival buyers will be neither more nor less favorably treated, the buyer may have reduced motivation for cost-conscious behavior.[111]

Northern Pacific Railway Co. v. United States involved the sale or lease of railroad lands on the condition that the purchaser/lessee prefer the railroad in future purchases of transportation services.[112] Market informational imperfections seem evident because of the deferred purchase of transportation services, the potential inexperienced status of many that might buy or lease the land, and the likelihood that a buyer or lessee might focus on the land (the major object of the transaction) to the exclusion of the tied service.[113] This conclusion is consistent with the 390 recorded exceptions granted primarily to large firms, likely to have been the most sophisticated and powerful buyers.[114]

A fourth case in which the Court found an unlawful tie, United States v. Loew's, Inc.,[115] is perhaps the most controversial of the pre-*Kodak* decisions. The Court found unlawful the practice of movie distributors that licensed blocks of films for television programming on the condition that the purchaser include, along with popular films (grade A films) sought for prime time television viewing, a certain number of less popular films (grade B films). Most of the market imperfections typifying other tying cases are absent here. For example, the block sales did not involve a deferred sale (all movies were licensed and paid for at the same time) and the buyers (television stations) were presumably sophisticated purchasers. But there are two possible market imperfections of consequence. The first is the widespread use of block booking in the industry, possibly lowering a purchaser's cost-conscious behavior by facilitating cartel behavior at the buyer or seller level. The second is that a television station booking a block of films would have its eye primarily on the popular films that ensure advertising revenues during the station's high-yield, prime time viewing hours. The station manager's performance will be judged primarily by her ability to maintain advertising revenues for this most lucrative programming. This leaves the door open for the movie companies to influence programming choice during nonprime time hours. The block booking practices may have done this very effectively.

In the absence of block booking, a television manager, at relatively low risk, might experiment with differing programs for nonprime time hours. But having already paid for the B-grade movies as part of a block licensing arrangement, the manager will now take an additional loss if

111. Fox & Sullivan, supra note 105, at 663 (questioning whether competitors of International Salt might have been using similar ties).

112. 356 U.S. 1, 3, 78 S.Ct. 514, 2 L.Ed.2d 545 (1958).

113. S. Ross, Principles of Antitrust Law 294 (1993).

114. Cummings & Ruhter, The Northern Pacific Case, 22 J.L. & Econ. 329, 344–45 (1979).

115. 371 U.S. 38, 83 S.Ct. 97, 9 L.Ed.2d 11 (1962).

the manager decides to pay for alternative programs to be shown instead of the movies. The high collective market share of sellers imposing the tie may have also dulled the television manager's incentive to bargain for a package that does not include the less popular movies: The manager would be aware that competing television stations would be showing the same B-grade movies during nonprime time viewing hours. The manager's choice of these movies would, therefore, be easy to explain to the station's owners.

Perhaps the most troubling aspect of the tie-in *Loew's* was its potential impact on dynamic efficiency. Any seller wishing to offer alternative programs to the television station will have difficulty penetrating the market unless the seller also offers the station popular programs for prime-time hours. If one assumes that entry into the market for popular TV programming would be difficult for small or independent producers, the pervasive block booking practices would substantially raise costs and entry barriers for would-be competitors of the movie producers. Although there are possible efficiency gains from some block booking practices, they do not seem substantial on the facts of *Loew's*. Unlike in Broadcast Music, Inc. v. CBS, Inc. (where the blanket licenses covered thousands of compositions),[116] the package in *Loew's* included a relatively small number of items and was individually negotiated with each buyer.

Looking at Supreme Court tie-in cases in which the defendant prevailed, they too appear likely to have come out the same way under the teaching of *Kodak*. In Times–Picayune Publishing Co. v. United States,[117] the Supreme Court held that requiring buyers of classified advertisements to purchase space in both the morning and evening newspaper owned by the defendant was not an unlawful tie. The Court found that a required showing of market "dominance" in the tying product was not met.[118] In United States Steel Corp. v. Fortner Enterprises, Inc. (Fortner II),[119] the Court held that U.S. Steel's favorable financing terms (the tying product) did not give it any unlawful power to coerce buyers in the market for prefabricated homes (the tied product).

In each of these cases, a key factor raising the risk of exploitation of the buyer's informational deficiencies was lacking: There was no deferred purchase of the tied product.[120] In *Times-Picayune,* a buyer of a classified ad purchased space simultaneously in the morning and evening papers. In *Fortner II,* the contractor purchased a prefabricated home at the same time as it received financing (the tying product) from the seller. Nor was there, in either of these cases, any concern with the tied product being a less valued part of the package that might be overlooked. In *Times-Picayune,* one assumes that the tying and tied products were

---

116. 441 U.S. 1, 99 S.Ct. 1551, 60 L.Ed.2d 1 (1979).

117. 345 U.S. 594, 73 S.Ct. 872, 97 L.Ed. 1277 (1953).

118. Id. at 611.

119. 429 U.S. 610, 97 S.Ct. 861, 51 L.Ed.2d 80 (1977).

120. The factors that raise the risk of exploitation of the buyer's informational deficiencies are discussed in § 8.3c3.

weighted roughly equally. In *Fortner II*, the tied product (a prefabricated home) was the major object of the contractor's purchase. Finally, purchasers of classified advertisements were purchasing a relatively simple product, lessening the risk of informational exploitation. And while the products sold in *Fortner II* were more complex, the contractors that purchased them were likely to be sophisticated buyers.[121]

It is more difficult to reconcile the Court's result in Jefferson Parish Hospital District No. 2 v. Hyde[122] with *Kodak*'s analysis. In *Jefferson Parish,* the Court dealt with a defendant hospital that sold hospital services for surgery (the tying product) coupled with the services of one firm of anesthesiologists (the tied product). Any patient requiring anesthesia at East Jefferson Hospital had to use one of the firm's four anesthesiologists. Noting that 70 percent of the patients in the geographic market entered hospitals other than East Jefferson, the Court found that the hospital lacked the requisite leverage in the market for hospital services, negating a showing of *per se* liability.[123] The Court also found no liability under the rule of reason because there was no "showing of actual adverse effect on competition."[124]

There was no deferred purchase of the tying and tied product in *Jefferson Parish*. This circumstance notwithstanding, it is difficult to imagine an industry in which market imperfections are more self-evident than hospital care. The Court, per Justice Stevens, dismissed two market imperfections relied on by the court of appeals: (1) the prevalence of third party payment for hospital services (a buyer pass on); and (2) the consumer's inability to measure the quality of hospital services (inadequate consumer information).[125] According to the Court, "[w]hile these factors may generate 'market power' in some abstract sense," they do not generate the kind of market power required to invoke the *per se* rule.[126]

Yet, the result in *Jefferson Parish* may still be reconciled with *Kodak* if the bundling of anesthesia services with hospital care is an efficient bundling. In the concurring opinion, Justice O'Connor argued that the exclusive arrangement with anesthesiologists permitted more efficient hospital operation.[127] Anesthesia services must be available on a twenty-four hour basis to serve surgical and obstetrical units. There is a need for a hospital to organize these services carefully to serve these emergency needs. The bundled offering of anesthesia and hospital services could be justified in the same manner that a hospital justifies

121. The result in *Times-Picayune* may still be questioned if it raised competitors' costs. See the discussion in Grimes, supra note 30, at 305.

122. 466 U.S. 2, 104 S.Ct. 1551, 80 L.Ed.2d 2 (1984).

123. Id. at 26–27.

124. Id. at 31.

125. Id. at 27. Third party payment for health services is recognized as one of the root causes for the failure of the competitive mechanism to restrain health care costs. *Wasted Health Care Dollars*, 57 Consumer Rep. 435, 436–38, 445 (July 1992). The countervailing power of large purchasers of health care services may restrain costs but do so at the expense of patient care.

126. 466 U.S. at 27.

127. Id. at 43 (O'Connor, J., concurring).

offering numerous other services (ranging from hospital medicine and food to therapy and radiology procedures) as a part of the hospitalization package. If Justice O'Connor was correct, the bundling of hospital and anesthesia services was not a true tie, but an efficient packaging of services that informed consumers would seek.[128]

If *Kodak* does not dictate a different outcome of the Supreme Court's prior tie-in cases, would it have changed lower court decisions? There is a much larger body of lower court decisions presenting a far less coherent picture of the law of tie-ins. Clearly, the outcome of some pre-*Kodak* decisions would have been altered. In Virtual Maintenance, Inc. v. Prime Computer, Inc., the Sixth Circuit had, prior to the decision in *Kodak,* found no tie based in part on the low market share of the tying seller. Upon remand from the Supreme Court for reconsideration in light of *Kodak*, the Sixth Circuit issued a revised opinion and remanded the case for a new trial.[129]

Although some *pre-Kodak* decisions would have been altered, there was clearly a strand of lower court decisions that anticipated the result in *Kodak*. In Digidyne Corp. v. Data General Corp.,[130] the court upheld a jury verdict that the defendant had unlawfully tied computer software (the tying product) to computer hardware (the tied product). In language that anticipates the majority opinion in *Kodak*, the court of appeals emphasized the unique nature of the software product and the lock-in effect for some purchasers that already relied on the tying software. There was evidence that some of these buyers were pushed to buy Data General's hardware despite a preference for competing hardware.[131]

There is a larger body of pre-*Kodak* cases that, without discussing the buyer's informational deficiencies addressed in *Kodak,* reach results consistent with that sensitivity. An example of such a case is Parts & Electric Motors, Inc. v. Sterling Electric, Inc.[132] In this case, Sterling terminated a distributor that did not meet its quota of selling Sterling motors. The jury found that the termination was based on an unlawful tie requiring the distributor to sell a minimum number of motors as a precondition for receiving Sterling spare parts, for which the distributor had maintained an inventory and made a significant number of sales. Judge Posner dissented from a majority opinion that upheld a verdict for

128. An argument against the efficient bundling hypothesis is that other hospitals have apparently been able to regulate the flow of anesthesia services without the sort of exclusive arrangement that was instituted in *Jefferson Parish*. For example, in Konik v. Champlain Valley Physicians Hospital Medical Center, 733 F.2d 1007 (2d Cir.), cert. denied, 469 U.S. 884, 105 S.Ct. 253, 83 L.Ed.2d 190 (1984), the hospital entered into contractual arrangements with anesthesiologists that required the specialists to agree to sharing emergency duties but did not limit entry.

129. 957 F.2d 1318 (6th Cir.), vacated and remanded, 506 U.S. 910, 113 S.Ct. 314,

121 L.Ed.2d 235 (1992), amended, 11 F.3d 660 (6th Cir.1993), cert. dismissed, 512 U.S. 1216, 114 S.Ct. 2700, 129 L.Ed.2d 829 (1994).

130. 734 F.2d 1336 (9th Cir.1984), cert. denied, 473 U.S. 908, 105 S.Ct. 3534, 87 L.Ed.2d 657 (1985).

131. Id. at 1346 & n.6.

132. 826 F.2d 712 (7th Cir.1987), appeal after remand, 866 F.2d 228 (7th Cir.1988) (Posner, J., dissenting), cert. denied, 493 U.S. 847, 110 S.Ct. 141, 107 L.Ed.2d 100 (1989).

the terminated distributor. In the dissent's view, because Sterling's market shares for both motors and motor parts were less than 1 percent, Sterling's imposition of a tie requiring a minimum number of motors to be sold as a condition of receiving spare parts could not have been anticompetitive.[133] But the majority's affirmance of the jury verdict was consistent with *Kodak*'s reasoning that a buyer may be coerced because of a lock-in and life-cycle pricing difficulties. The market power that Sterling possessed over its distributor probably grew out of its continuing commercial relationship with the distributor. In agreeing to become a Sterling distributor, the plaintiff may have invested substantial time and costs in developing expertise and solid customer relationships. These sunk costs and Sterling's likely ability to impose additional costs or withhold business opportunities by terminating the distributor may have given Sterling substantial market power.[134]

8.3d6. A Post–Kodak Wrinkle—The Timing of Plaintiff's Knowledge of the Tie

The Supreme Court's teaching in *Kodak* was applied by the Ninth Circuit after the remanded case resulted in a substantial jury verdict against Kodak[135] and by the Sixth Circuit after its decision in Virtual Maintenance, Inc. v. Prime Computer, Inc. was remanded for reconsideration in light of *Kodak*.[136] But many of the post-*Kodak* opinions in the courts of appeals have found a basis for distinguishing *Kodak* so that its holding recognizing a separate market for a single brand could be ignored. In many of these circuit decisions, the court read *Kodak* to apply only in instances in which the defendant changed its behavior after the buyers of the defendant's products had incurred sunk costs that locked them into the defendant's line. Thus, *Kodak*'s recognition of market power necessary to coerce a buyer to purchase a tied product would, under this reading, apply only if the defendant imposed the tie after the buyer was contractually committed to purchase the defendant's products.[137] In support of this narrow reading of *Kodak,* one can point to

133. 866 F.2d at 236 (Posner, J., dissenting).

134. See the discussion of market power in continuing vertical relationships in § 2.4e2iv. A similar analysis of *Sterling* is offered in Patterson, *Coercion, Deception, and Other Demand–Increasing Practices in Antitrust Law,* 66 ANTITRUST L.J. 1, 69–70 (1997).

135. After the case was remanded for trial, the plaintiffs abandoned their tie-in claim but obtained a favorable jury verdict on its Section 2 monopolization claim, which, as with the tie-in claim, rested on lock-in and the buyer's informational deficiencies that established Kodak's aftermarket parts as a separate market. The jury verdict was in large part affirmed on appeal. Image Technical Servs., Inc. v. Eastman Kodak Co., 125 F.3d 1195 (9th Cir.

1997), cert. denied, 523 U.S. 1094, 118 S.Ct. 1560, 140 L.Ed.2d 792 (1998).

136. 957 F.2d 1318 (6th Cir.), vacated and remanded, 506 U.S. 910, 113 S.Ct. 314, 121 L.Ed.2d 235 (1992), amended, 11 F.3d 660 (6th Cir.1993), cert. dismissed, 512 U.S. 1216, 114 S.Ct. 2700, 129 L.Ed.2d 829 (1994).

137. Some post-*Kodak* circuit decisions that have interpreted *Kodak* to apply only to the defendant's imposition of a tie after the buyer had incurred sunk costs in conjunction with a preestablished contractual relationship with the defendant are Queen City Pizza, Inc. v. Domino's Pizza, Inc., 124 F.3d 430, 439 (3d Cir.1997), cert. denied, 523 U.S. 1059, 118 S.Ct. 1385, 140 L.Ed.2d 645 (1998); PSI Repair Services, Inc. v. Honeywell, Inc., 104 F.3d 811 (6th Cir.),

the majority opinion in *Kodak,* which notes Kodak's change in marketing strategy after the independent service providers had entered the market.[138] In a footnote, the *Kodak* majority also discusses the importance of whether buyers of Kodak's original equipment knew, at the time of purchase, of Kodak's pricing policies toward aftermarket parts and service.[139] But this footnote stresses the buyer's knowledge, not any change of policy by the defendant. Indeed, a primary concern of the *Kodak* Court was with the inability of a buyer to gain full knowledge of life-cycle pricing, an inability that would likely remain regardless of the timing of the defendant's action in imposing a tie-in. For example, the Court was concerned that a buyer confronts unknown future market developments over the period of the product's life.[140] These developments are likely to remain unknown even if the buyer is aware of the tie at the time it makes a contractual commitment to the defendant's products. Even if some sophisticated buyers can adequately anticipate future market developments, the vast majority of buyers that have less knowledge may still be vulnerable to the seller's exploitation.[141]

A mechanical rule such as that followed in some post-*Kodak* circuit decisions would grant the defendant freedom of contract to undermine competitive outcomes as long as the defendant does not change the terms of the tying arrangement after the buyer is contractually committed to the defendant. Although such contractual freedom is appropriate and likely to serve competition when parties' behavior is adequately disciplined by competition, the central point of Section 1 of the Sherman Act is to outlaw contracts that are in restraint of trade. Thus, the antitrust resolution for tie-in law is one that makes ties unlawful when coercion produces anticompetitive results.

Under some circumstances, even if the buyer knows of the tying arrangement before making a contractual commitment, the coercive nature of that tie should still render it unlawful. The Supreme Court has recognized that franchisees that sign anticompetitive clauses in franchise

cert. denied, 520 U.S. 1265, 117 S.Ct. 2434, 138 L.Ed.2d 195 (1997); Digital Equipment Corp. v. Uniq Digital Technologies, Inc., 73 F.3d 756, 762–63 (7th Cir.1996). An indication that the dust has not entirely settled came in Judge Lay's strong dissent in *Queen City,* 124 F.3d at 444–49, and in Judge Becker's unusual opinion dissenting from the denial of a rehearing in *Queen City,* 129 F.3d 724 (3d Cir.1997)(Judge Becker was one of five judges that voted to grant a rehearing).

138. Eastman Kodak Co. v. Image Technical Servs., Inc., 504 U.S. 451, 457–58, 112 S.Ct. 2072, 119 L.Ed.2d 265 (1992).

139. Id. at 477 n.24.

140. Id. at 473.

141. Kodak may have sought to exploit less knowledgeable buyers by discriminat-

ing in making its spare parts available to large users of its original equipment that did their own maintenance, but denying spare parts to all other users unless they used Kodak servicing. Id. at 475–76. For a lower court case sympathetic to *Kodak* and rejecting the narrow reading discussed above, see Red Lion Med. Safety, Inc. v. Ohmeda, Inc., 63 F. Supp. 2d 1218 (E.D. Cal. 1999). Addressing the argument that a change in policy is necessary to find a tying violation, the court said:

> It is noteworthy that in the [*Kodak*] Court's lengthy discussion of information costs it never once makes reference to Kodak's change in policy. Information costs may be high and a manufacturer may thus have considerable market power in the aftermarket, even in the absence of a change in policy. Id. at 1231.

agreements can still challenge those clauses if they demonstrate that they acceded to the clauses only to obtain a valuable business opportunity.[142] The Court's holding with respect to franchisees is consistent with its treatment of tie-ins in other cases. For many anticompetitive ties, the decision on the purchase of the tied product may be deferred, occurring long after the decision to purchase the tying product. The relevant time frame for determining coercion is the market conditions that exist when the buyer is coerced to purchase the tied product, not when the tying product was purchased (there is usually no coercion at the point at which the buyer commits to the tying product). In Northern Pacific Railway Co. v. United States,[143] the Supreme Court condemned a tie that required purchasers or lessees of land from a railroad to favor that railroad when shipping services were purchased. The purchase of the tied railroad services, in many instances, occurred decades after the land was sold or leased. The Court's analysis suggests that it was concerned with the contemporaneous competitive impact of this arrangement on the market, not with the market power possessed or not possessed by the railroad at the time the land was initially sold or leased. Justice Black wrote for the Court:

> [Tie-ins] deny competitors free access to the market for the tied product, not because the party imposing the tying requirements has a better product or a lower price but because of his power or leverage in another market. At the same time buyers *are* forced to forego their free choice between competing products.[144]

Many if not most plaintiffs are aware of the tie at the time they make a contractual commitment to the defendant's products.[145] But pre-contract knowledge of the existence of the tie is not the pivotal question. Instead, *Northern Pacific* and other Supreme Court precedents properly focus on whether there are likely and substantial anticompetitive effects from use of a tie-in, a requirement that is derived directly from the language of Section 3 of the Clayton Act (and implicitly from Section 1 of the Sherman Act). This requirement will be met if the defendant is opting for a course of conduct that exploits systemic information failures. In *Northern Pacific*, the defendant railroad had consistently inserted the restrictive tying clauses in all but a select few of its land sales and leases, with the result that rival carriers would have increased costs in competing for transportation business from these landholders. A franchisor that routinely inserts a sourcing requirement in all of its franchise contracts may also be consciously exploiting a systemic market power arising from franchisee information problems. On the other hand, individual contract failures or hold-ups are usually not valid targets of tie-in law (unless the

---

142. Perma Life Mufflers, Inc. v. International Parts Corp., 392 U.S. 134, 88 S.Ct. 1981, 20 L.Ed.2d 982 (1968). See the discussion of this issue in § 6.4c2ii.

143. 356 U.S. 1, 78 S.Ct. 514, 2 L.Ed.2d 545 (1958).

144. Id. at 6 (emphasis added).

145. Thus, plaintiffs were presumably aware of the tie-in in cases such as *IBM, International Salt, Loew's,* and *Northern Pacific* discussed in § 8.3d5.

plaintiff demonstrates both likely and substantial anticompetitive effects and the foreclosure of a substantial volume of commerce). See § 8.3d1.

8.3d7. Requirements Ties and Full–Line Ties in Dealer–Supplier Relationships

Requirements ties occur when the buyer of a tying product is forced to purchase a needed product solely from a designated seller or sellers. Usually requirements ties can also be challenged as exclusive dealing arrangements, discussed in § 8.4. Most of the Supreme Court's tie-in cases in which the plaintiff has prevailed have involved requirements ties. See the discussion in § 8.3d5.

Full-line ties occur when a buyer of the tying product is required to purchase other products as a condition for receiving the tying product. Unlike a requirements tie, a full-line tie need not require the buyer to purchase all of its needs for the tied product from the tying seller. This distinction is important because the foreclosure effects on competing sellers of the tied product may be substantially less when a full-line tie does not constitute a requirements tie. But both types of ties may be harmful based on their exploitation of the buyer's informational deficiencies. An example of a full-line tie which the Court found anticompetitive is United States v. Loew's, Inc.,[146] a case that is discussed in § 8.3d5.

Both requirements and full-line ties generate litigation most often in dealer-supplier relationships. Many, although not all, of these cases involve a franchise relationship—a dealer that reaches a contractual arrangement to sell a producer's products, often using the producer's trademark or trade name in the name of the dealer's store. The unique aspects of requirements and full-line ties in franchise relationships are separately addressed in § 8.9d.

8.3d8. Standing to Challenge an Unlawful Tie

A survey of 45 tie-in cases decided by the federal appellate courts between 1984 and 1992 showed that slightly more than half of the plaintiffs were rivals of the tying seller (23 cases) while the remaining plaintiffs were customers (often distributors or dealers) of the tying seller (22 cases).[147] The standing of either of these classes of plaintiffs to bring antitrust tie-in claims seems well established, although the Sixth Circuit has held that a rival of the tying seller could not show the requisite antitrust injury to bring a private claim under Section 4 of the Clayton Act.[148] The plaintiff, a seller of liquid and bar soap to commercial distributors, alleged that it was injured when the defendant, a large franchisor of hotel-motel businesses, began tying franchise rights (the tying product) to the franchisee's purchase of soap products from two suppliers approved by the franchisor (the tied product). The court upheld the district court's dismissal of the plaintiff's claim because it found the

---

146. 371 U.S. 38, 83 S.Ct. 97, 9 L.Ed.2d 11 (1962).

147. Grimes, supra note 30, at 298–99.

148. Valley Prods. Co. v. Landmark, 128 F.3d 398 (6th Cir.1997).

loss to the plaintiff's business was occasioned by the termination of its contract with the franchisor, not the franchisor's decision to favor rival sellers of soap products that paid "access fees" to the franchisor. The court reached its conclusion notwithstanding the franchisor's termination notice to the plaintiff that expressly attributed the termination to the franchisor's decision to favor other suppliers, not to any deficiency in the quality of the plaintiff's product or service.[149]

On this record, a holding that a rival of the tying seller has not established antitrust injury seems at odds with the widespread recognition that a foreclosure restraint, such as a tie-in, can injure competition by foreclosing rivals' access to the tied product market. In many cases, the actual buyers of the tying and tied products may be unwilling or unable to challenge the tie, either because the amount of injury to individual buyers is insubstantial or because (as may occur in franchising relationships) the dealers, although confronting supplier or franchisor market power abuses, dare not risk upsetting a business relationship. In such situations, a rival seller is the only remaining private claimant with sufficient financial interest to vindicate the public interest in enforcing the antitrust laws. Although the Supreme Court has yet to address the question of antitrust injury to a rival of the tying seller, it did not question the standing of such rivals in its two most recent tie-in decisions, each of which was instituted by rival sellers.[150]

In Sports Racing Services, Inc. v. Sports Car Club of America, Inc.,[151] the Tenth Circuit faced a different standing issue: whether the plaintiff had standing when it purchased the tied product from someone other than the tying seller. In order to participate in sports car races sponsored by the Sports Car Club of America (the tying service), the individual plaintiff, a sports car racer, was forced to purchase cars and parts from a wholly owned, for-profit subsidiary of the tying seller. The court rejected the defendant's argument that the plaintiff was an indirect purchaser and therefore barred from maintaining its tie-in claim under Illinois Brick Co. v. Illinois.[152]

8.3d9. Tie–Ins and Intellectual Property

A seller may attempt to license a patent or copyright on the condition that the licensee use additional products or services. Many tie-in cases, beginning with *A. B. Dick* and *Motion Picture Patents* decided early in this century,[153] involve a patented or copyrighted tying product. From a policy point of view, tie-in cases involving a patented tying product raise the same issues as those involving a nonpatented tying

---

149. Id. at 401, 406.

150. Eastman Kodak Co. v. Image Technical Servs., Inc., 504 U.S. 451, 112 S.Ct. 2072, 119 L.Ed.2d 265 (1992); Jefferson Parish Hosp. Dist. No. 2 v. Hyde, 466 U.S. 2, 104 S.Ct. 1551, 80 L.Ed.2d 2 (1984).

151. 131 F.3d 874 (10th Cir.1997).

152. 431 U.S. 720, 97 S.Ct. 2061, 52 L.Ed.2d 707 (1977). The indirect purchaser

limitation on private suits is discussed in § 17.2c.

153. Henry v. A. B. Dick Co., 224 U.S. 1, 32 S.Ct. 364, 56 L.Ed. 645 (1912); Motion Picture Patents Co. v. Universal Film Mfg. Co., 243 U.S. 502, 37 S.Ct. 416, 61 L.Ed. 871 (1917).

product. There are, however, several issues that have been raised in connection with patent licensing and tie-ins that deserve special mention.

The Justice Department during the Reagan Administration argued that tie-ins should be treated with special leniency because of the need to reward innovation.[154] If ties involving patented tying products are allowed, it is indeed likely that the innovator's rewards could be increased.[155] But permitting tie-ins of patented or copyrighted products is an arbitrary and undisciplined way to reward innovation because the innovator's ability to reap profits from such a tie depends upon a great many variables that have nothing to do with the value of the innovation for society. See the discussion in § 8.3b5. The Justice Department's 1995 Antitrust Guidelines for the Licensing of Intellectual Property have restored the more traditional view of the Department that tie-ins involving intellectual property should be judged by the same standards as other tie-ins. The Guidelines are addressed more fully in § 15.7.

Although there is no sound policy basis for treating tie-ins involving intellectual property more leniently than other tie-ins, there is also no basis for treating them more strictly. There is some confusion on this issue because the Supreme Court has said that a patent-holder that uses a patented product as a tying product will be presumed to have the market power required in the tying product for application of the *per se* rule against tie-ins.[156] This presumption has been widely criticized, in particular because the relevant market may be much broader than a single patented product, in which case a patent-holder would have no significant interbrand market power.[157] While most patents may be of little or no value, patented products that are used to implement a tie must have value–without it, the tie itself would be worthless. Moreover, parties are highly unlikely to be litigating over worthless patents. Thus, unless parties are making tying claims for strategic reasons, a circumstance that should be readily discernable from evidence presented by the parties, a rebuttable presumption that a patented tying product has market power is sound.[158] Of course, the absence of interbrand market power in the tying product need not preclude the existence of single brand market power as, for example, when the buyer is forced to purchase the tied product because of a lock-in. See the discussion in § 8.3c4.

---

154. Statement of Deputy Assistant Attorney General Roger Andewelt, supra note 37 (arguing that a proposed bill that would remove *per se* treatment of tie-ins and other alleged antitrust violations associated with the licensing of intellectual property would enhance innovation).

155. Whether innovation is over-or under-rewarded is a controversial and complex matter addressed in § 15.2a. See also F. M. SCHERER & D. ROSS, INDUSTRIAL MARKET STRUCTURE AND ECONOMIC PERFORMANCE 628–30 (3d ed. 1990).

156. See the dicta in *Jefferson Parish*, 466 U.S. at 16–17.

157. HOVENKAMP, supra note 36, § 10.3c; ROSS, supra note 113, at 294–96.

158. The presumption that a patented tying product has market power is before the Supreme Court in Independent Ink, Inc. v. Illinois Tool Works, Inc., 396 F.3d 1342 (Fed. Cir. 2005), cert. granted __ U.S. __, 125 S.Ct. 2937, 162 L.Ed.2d 865 (2005).

8.3d10. Product Integration Tie–Ins

In many cases, the easiest way for a powerful seller to enforce a tie is to integrate the tied product into the tying product, forcing the buyer to purchase both products at the same time. Of course, an integration of two formerly separate products may be a technological improvement welcome to buyers. Market forces should discipline the bundling decision. If consumers don't want to buy the bundled product, they will turn to other suppliers, and the bundling decision will be a business failure. There are, however, two obvious situations in which the product bundling will have anticompetitive effects: (1) when the tying seller has market power in the tying product and, through the bundling, can force buyers to purchase a tied product they otherwise would not have purchased; or (2) when the tying seller, although lacking market power in isolation, acts in a parallel fashion to other suppliers, each of whom effects a similar integration of tying and tied products, leaving consumers with substantially reduced options in obtaining the tied product separately.

Some commentators argue that when bundling is accomplished by the integration of two formerly separate products, there is reduced risk of competitive harm. The argument is that there are often sunk costs associated with integrating two separate products, so that in the event the integration fails, the supplier will face substantial losses.[159] This will discipline the supplier to attempt product integration only when it offers substantial advantages to the consumer.

The stakes are higher when a seller makes an investment in integrating two separate products. Some of the investment costs may be sunk or non-recoverable. If there are networking efficiencies associated with the tied product, the potential benefits and losses may be greater still. A tie-in implemented through product integration may also be more efficient to enforce. But alone or collectively, these distinctions between a tie enforced through contract and one enforced through product integration say little about the competitive effect. The distinctions simply show that *both the costs and the gain from product-integration bundling are likely to be higher.* The higher gain may arise either from an efficiency gain or from an anticompetitive market distortion. Because product integration ties are easier to enforce, the potential for consumer injury is greater, a reality ignored by those who pushed for more relaxed treatment of product integration bundling.

There are substantial remedial problems when a tying seller has integrated two formerly separate products. If a judge finds a tying violation, the court must contemplate whether it will force the tying seller to incur the costs of redesigning the now integrated product. In the European proceedings against Microsoft, the Commission has indicated

---

159. Hylton & Salinger, *Tying Law and Policy: A Decision–Theoretic Approach*, 69 Antitrust L. J. 469, 516–17 (2001). A different view is offered in Grimes, *The antitrust* *Tying Law Schism: A Critique of* Microsoft III *and a Response to Hylton and Salinger*, 70 Antitrust L. J.199, 222–225 (2002).

that Microsoft may continue to offer its operating software bundled with certain applications software, but must also offer the operating software in unbundled fashion. The outcome and efficacy of this form of remedy has yet to be determined.

In the United States, the courts have offered various responses to product integration tying involving high tech products. In the 1998 *Microsoft* decision, the court signaled relaxed treatment of such bundling, exculpating any defendant that offers "a plausible claim that [the integration] brings some advantage."[160] In its 2001 *Microsoft* decision, the same court, acting en banc, ignored its 1998 decision, holding that the product integration tie should be subject to the rule of reason.[161] Neither of these approaches are consistent with the current Supreme Court law governing tie-ins. The en banc court in 2001 justified rejection of the Jefferson Parish modified per se rule on the ground that a tie achieved by a new product integration had possible justifications not available for other ties. In another tying suit against Microsoft, a federal court in Utah applied the traditional modified per se rule to Microsoft's product integration and offered criticism of the holding in the 1998 *Microsoft* decision: "Certainly a company should be allowed to build a better mousetrap, and the courts should not . . . [hinder] technological innovation. Yet, antitrust law has developed for good reason, and just as courts have the potential to stifle technological advancements by second guessing product design, so too can product innovation be stifled if companies are allowed to dampen competition by unlawfully tying products together and escape antitrust liability by simply claiming a 'plausible' technological advancement."[162]

§ 8.4   Forced Exclusive Dealing

A downstream buyer may reach an agreement with a seller to buy exclusively from that seller. Such exclusive dealing arrangements are sometimes called requirements contracts because the buyer agrees to purchase all of the required products from the seller. As a *quid pro quo* for the buyer's commitment to take all its needs from the seller, the seller may make an exclusive selling commitment—an agreement not to sell to competing dealers. Exclusive selling is usually associated with downstream power; thus it is considered together with other such nonprice vertical restraints in Chapter VII, whereas exclusive dealing more often is associated with upstream power and can end *interbrand* competition; thus it is considered here along with other foreclosure restraints with similar effects. Just as tie-ins, exclusive dealing can be challenged under Sections 1 and 2 of the Sherman Act, under Section 3 of the Clayton Act, or under Section 5 of the Federal Trade Commission Act. Section 3 of the Clayton Act applies only to the sale or lease of

160. United States v. Microsoft Corp., 147 F.3d 935, 950 (D.C. Cir. 1998).

161. See the discussion in § 8.3d1.

162. Caldera, Inc. v. Microsoft Corp., 72 F. Supp. 2d 1295, 1322–23 (D. Utah 1999).

products and would not cover an exclusive dealing arrangement involving services.

Some arrangements can be described as either a tie or exclusive dealing. For example, if an automobile dealer agrees to purchase all of its spare parts from a manufacturer as a part of a package that allows the dealer to carry the manufacturer's brand of automobile, this arrangement may constitute both a tie-in (with automobiles as the tying product and spare parts as the tied product) and an exclusive dealing arrangement (the dealer commits to buying all of its spare parts from the manufacturer). But there may be critical distinctions between tie-ins and exclusive dealing. Exclusive dealing usually forecloses all interbrand competition for a given dealer, whereas a tie forecloses such interbrand competition only to the extent that the dealer buys the tying product. Exclusive dealing might require an automobile dealer to purchase and sell only General Motors automobiles and parts. But a tie imposed by the manufacturer requiring the dealer to purchase only General Motors spare parts for General Motors cars sold by the dealer would not preclude the dealer from also marketing a competing line of automobiles and rival spare parts for any non-General Motors automobile repaired by the dealer. On these facts, the foreclosure effect of a tie would be less pervasive than for exclusive dealing. But the competitive impact of each foreclosure arrangement will vary with the facts and each should be separately examined. Many ties cover all of a downstream dealer's needs and would accordingly have the same foreclosure effect as exclusive dealing.

Tie-ins and exclusive dealing are potentially distinguished in another respect. Harmful tie-ins often complicate the buyer's transaction in ways that make it more likely that the buyer's informational or motivational deficiencies can be exploited by the seller. For example, harmful tie-ins often involve a deferred purchase of the tied product, placing an unsought and undesired burden on the buyer to predict its future needs for the tied product and the competitive conditions under which the tied product might be available from rival sellers. Exclusive dealing arrangements can also involve a deferred purchase for the buyer, particularly if the buyer signs a long-term requirements contract. But this deferred purchase is often a desired end for the buyer. Although case-specific analysis is required, an exclusive dealing arrangement may be less likely than a tie-in to exploit the seller's information-based market power.

8.4a. Historical Overview of the Law Governing Exclusive Dealing

After enactment of Section 3 of the Clayton Act in 1914, the FTC undertook to establish that Section as a bar on exclusive dealing.[1] In 1922, the Supreme Court held in Standard Fashion Co. v. Magrane-

§ 8.4

1. FTC v. Standard Elec. Mfg. Co., 5 F.T.C. 376 (1923).

Houston Co. that Section 3 had been violated by a dress pattern manufacturer's exclusive dealing arrangements with 40 percent of available retail outlets. The Court found that Section 3 was designed to address such agreements "in their incipiency", but "was not intended to reach every remote lessening of competition."[2]

More recent Supreme Court cases dealing with exclusive dealing are Standard Oil Co. v. United States[3] and Tampa Electric Co. v. Nashville Coal Co.[4] In *Standard Oil*, the defendant was a West Coast refiner and the largest seller of petroleum products in seven Western States, with about 23 percent of the market. Its subsidiary, Standard Stations, entered into contracts with nearly 6,000 independently owned stations, about 16 percent of all outlets in the western area (but selling only 6.7 percent of the gasoline sold in that area). A common feature of the contracts was an undertaking by the dealer to buy all its requirements of petroleum products from Standard for a stated period, typically one year. Standard's six leading competitors in the area, accounting for 42 percent of all retail sales, also employed exclusive dealing contracts. In affirming a lower court decree that found these exclusive dealing contracts to violate Section 3 of the Clayton Act, Justice Frankfurter announced a rule that Section 3 is violated "by proof that competition has been foreclosed in a substantial share of the line of commerce affected."[5] Before announcing this rule, Justice Frankfurter wrestled with the choice between what he perceived as the unmanageability of a judicial interpretation that required in each case a refined market analysis, on the one hand, and a simple, more easily administrable rule that might, however, strike down some harmless or procompetitive arrangements.[6] The rule Justice Frankfurter announced seemed a nod in the direction of a simple, judicially manageable rule.

Although Justice Frankfurter's opinion in *Standard Oil* sought to acknowledge the procompetitive potential of some exclusive dealing arrangements, the decision was criticized for its quantitative substantiality rule and its failure to account sufficiently for market conditions.[7] The Court revisited exclusive dealing in *Tampa Electric* in 1961. Tampa Electric agreed to buy and Nashville to sell all of Tampa Electric's requirements for coal for a new generator station for a period of twenty years. Over this period, it was anticipated that $128 million worth of coal would be supplied. Interpreting the *Standard Oil* opinion to require only quantitative substantiality, the court of appeals found a violation of Section 3 of the Clayton Act. The Supreme Court, per Justice Clark, reversed, holding that dollar volume was not the test. To determine

---

2. 258 U.S. 346, 356, 357, 42 S.Ct. 360, 66 L.Ed. 653 (1922).

3. 337 U.S. 293, 69 S.Ct. 1051, 93 L.Ed. 1371 (1949).

4. 365 U.S. 320, 81 S.Ct. 623, 5 L.Ed.2d 580 (1961).

5. 337 U.S. at 314.

6. Id. at 311–14.

7. Critics included Lockhart & Sacks, *The Relevance of Economic Factors in Determining Whether Exclusive Arrangements Violate Section 3 of the Clayton Act*, 65 Harv. L. Rev. 913 (1952); McLaren, *Related Problems of "Requirements" Contracts and Acquisitions in Vertical Integration Under the Anti-Trust Laws*, 45 Ill. L. Rev. 141 (1950).

whether the effect of the arrangement might substantially reduce competition, the market had to be defined in product and geographic terms and the extent of the foreclosure estimated. After concluding that the relevant market for coal producers was the entire Appalachian region, the Court found that less than 1 percent of the tonnage produced each year would be foreclosed by the requirements contract. Although the twenty year duration of the contract might be troubling under other circumstances, the Court found the length of the contract was warranted by the needs of the utility for a stable supply at reasonable prices.[8]

The straightforward but meaningful economic analysis of *Tampa Electric* is a welcome departure from the more mechanical rule that Justice Frankfurter announced in *Standard Oil*. Whatever burden may have been added to the decision-making process seems amply repaid in avoiding overreaching attacks on exclusive dealing. But *Tampa Electric* might have been dismissed on the simpler ground that the exclusive dealing contract was not an exercise of seller power. Indeed, it was the seller (Nashville) that sought to use antitrust grounds for avoiding a contract that had turned sour because of a generalized increase in coal prices. Although powerful buyers might commit a reciprocal offense, this was not it; Nashville did not commit to sell its entire output to Tampa Electric for twenty years, but only to meet Tampa Electric's requirements. From all that appears in the record, the requirements contract was carefully negotiated by two powerful and experienced market participants in light of existing conditions of demand.

The Supreme Court revisited exclusive dealing again in FTC v. Brown Shoe Co. in 1966.[9] The decision enforced a Federal Trade Commission cease and desist order that held that Brown Shoe's exclusive dealing arrangements with 650 franchise dealers, committing those dealers to carry " 'no lines conflicting with Brown Division Brands of the Brown Shoe Company,' " were unfair trade practices in violation of Section 5 of the FTC Act.[10] In reversing a court of appeals decision that declined to enforce the Commission's order, the Supreme Court held that the Commission need not prove that the exclusive dealing violated Section 3 of the Clayton Act.[11] Because the decision provides support for the Commission's authority to find a violation of Section 5 even if conduct does not violate provisions of the Sherman or Clayton Acts, it probably has little precedential value for exclusive dealing arrangements attacked under provisions of those Acts. The Commission itself has since required proof of market share and likely anticompetitive effect in conformance with the standards applied under Section 3 of the Clayton Act or Section 1 of the Sherman Act.[12]

The Supreme Court had an opportunity to revise its analysis of exclusive dealing in 1984 in Jefferson Parish Hospital District No. 2 v.

8.   365 U.S. at 334.

9.   384 U.S. 316, 86 S.Ct. 1501, 16 L.Ed.2d 587 (1966).

10.   Id. at 318.

11.   Id. at 322.

12.   In re Beltone Elecs. Corp., 100 F.T.C. 68, 204 (1982).

Hyde,[13] but did not do so when the majority chose to analyze the restraint as a tie-in. The concurring opinion of Justice O'Connor, however, concluded that there was no tie-in and went on to analyze whether the hospital's exclusive supply arrangement for anesthesia services was an unlawful exclusive dealing requirement. The concurring justices concluded that the hospital's 30 percent market share was insufficient to establish unlawful exclusive dealing.[14]

The Court should seize an opportunity to rectify the failure of its past decisions to distinguish between exclusive dealing that is competitively disciplined and forced exclusive dealing, characterized by abuse of seller power. The Court should also clarify, in light of *Kodak*, the nature of seller power that can lead to competitive injury. The seller's high market share, a circumstance addressed in cases such as *Tampa Electric,* is one basis for seller market power, but by no means the only one. Exclusive dealing can be forced on buyers in the same ways that tie-ins can and with identical or very similar anticompetitive injury. A complete competitive analysis should encompass the interbrand foreclosure effects of exclusive dealing as well as the ability of the seller to use exclusive dealing to gain a premium above competitive price based on exploitation of the buyer's informational or motivational deficiencies.

8.4b. Procompetitive Potential of Exclusive Dealing

Exclusive dealing arrangements or requirements contracts are likely to be procompetitive in cases in which adequate competitive discipline exists. The point is illustrated by Sewell Plastics, Inc. v. Coca–Cola Co., a case in which Coca–Cola bottlers banded together with the support of Coca–Cola to form a company to manufacture plastic bottles and agreed to long-term supply contracts with the newly created company.[15] Prior to their entry into this market, Sewell supplied over 90 percent of the bottlers' requirements for 2–liter plastic bottles in the Southeast region of the United States. After the entry of the new manufacturing firm, the price of plastic bottles fell substantially. Sewell sued Coca–Cola and the bottlers for attempted monopolization, boycott and exclusive dealing. The court properly granted summary judgment for the defendants on the plaintiff's claim that the exclusive dealing arrangements were *per se* unlawful. The supply contracts may have been a form of vertical integration that was attractive to the bottlers because of their inability to negotiate a fair price from Sewell. The overall picture painted by evidence in *Sewell* seems more consistent with a restoration of competitive discipline than with an abuse of power by the defendants' exclusive dealing arrangements.

Of course, the benefits of partial vertical integration through exclusive dealing may extend well beyond the revealed facts in *Sewell*. As

13. 466 U.S. 2, 104 S.Ct. 1551, 80 L.Ed.2d 2 (1984).

14. Justice O'Connor's concurring opinion dealt with exclusive dealing in greater detail, but offered little more than a summary of past case law. Id. at 32–47 (O'Connor, J., concurring).

15. 720 F.Supp. 1186 (W.D.N.C.1988).

Justice Frankfurter pointed out, requirements contracts may for the buyer "assure supply, afford protection against rises in price, enable long-term planning on the basis of known costs, and obviate the expense and risk of storage in the quantity necessary for a commodity having a fluctuating demand." For the seller such contracts "may make possible the substantial reduction of selling expenses, give protection against price fluctuations, and * * * offer the possibility of a predictable market."[16] More recent commentary has stressed that exclusive dealing can be a form of partial vertical integration, providing efficiencies that, on the one hand, cannot be attained through open market purchases or sales and, on the other hand, avoid costs and risks that would be incurred through full vertical integration.[17]

Theorists have also postulated that exclusive dealing can be a tool to avoid free-riding by a dealer that might otherwise take advantage of the supplier's strong brand to bring customers into a store and then attempt to shift the buyer to a rival supplier's product. If the dealer is committed to carrying only the supplier's line, the free-riding problem is avoided. Along the same lines, a supplier might use exclusive dealing to prevent dealers from passing off a rival's product for that of the supplier. For example, it has been suggested that Coors allowed bars and restaurants to sell Coors draft beer only if they agreed to sell no other draft beer, and in this way discouraged retailers from passing off as Coors rival beers that were indistinguishable in taste to most beer drinkers.[18] With respect to bottled beer, a similar exclusive dealing arrangement would have been unnecessary to prevent passing off because consumers could read the labels on the bottles and determine the brand for themselves.

Economic analysis has highlighted deficiencies in the case law governing exclusive dealing that need to be addressed. The procompetitive benefits of exclusive dealing and the lack of any perceived significant anticompetitive potential have led some theorists to urge generous treatment of exclusive dealing or even its *per se* legality.[19] As the next section details, however, there are some well-recognized anticompetitive risks when exclusive dealing is coercive.

8.4c. Anticompetitive Potential of Exclusive Dealing

Just as ties are a subset of all bundled sales, so too are forced exclusive dealing contracts a subset of all exclusive dealing. Ties are only those bundled sales that are inadequately disciplined by competition. Similarly, anticompetitive exclusive dealing occurs only when the seller is inadequately disciplined by competition because it possesses significant power in its dealings with buyers. The market power that a seller imposing exclusive dealing may possess is, as in the case of ties, either a

16. Standard Oil Co. v. United States, 337 U.S. 293, 306–07, 69 S.Ct. 1051, 93 L.Ed. 1371 (1949) (footnote omitted).

17. See the discussion of the benefits of tie-ins as a form of partial vertical integration in § 8.3b.

18. D.Carlton & J.Perloff, Modern Industrial Organization 532 (2d ed.1994).

19. Posner, *The Next Step in the Antitrust Treatment of Restricted Distribution: Per Se Legality,* 48 U. Chi. L. Rev. 6 (1981).

market power in an interbrand market or brand-specific market power linked to informational or motivational deficiencies on the part of the buyer.

8.4c1.   The Seller's Interbrand Market Power

The traditional concern with exclusive dealing is that the seller may exercise market power because of its strong position in the interbrand market. This form of market power was directly addressed in Tampa Electric Co. v. Nashville Coal Co.,[20] a case in which the volume of coal sales foreclosed by the exclusive supply arrangement was less than 1 percent of overall sales in the Appalachian market, too small in the Court's view to present a threat to competition. A seller's high market share increases the risk that the seller, by using exclusive dealing, may foreclose downstream market access to rival sellers, but only if entry into the downstream market would be difficult for rival sellers. If downstream entry is costly to rivals, the seller's use of exclusive dealing may raise rivals' costs or eliminate them from the market entirely. A recent case illustrating this anticompetitive effect of exclusive dealing was United States v. Dentsply International, where Dentsply's 75–80 percent share of prefabricated artificial teeth allowed it to force exclusive dealing arrangements on its dealers and made it more difficult for rival suppliers to gain access to the market.[21]

Another related anticompetitive risk to exclusive dealing is that the seller employing this device may be following a pattern that parallels that of rival sellers. Parallel use of exclusive dealing could be oligopolistic behavior that results in foreclosing downstream access for existing or potential rivals that could revitalize competition in the market. Thus, imposition of exclusive dealing by a market leader, if followed by major rivals, could collectively foreclose the bulk of the downstream market for the maverick or new entrant that seeks to win business on the competitive merits of its offering.

8.4c2.   Exploitation of Single Brand Market Power

The various ways in which market imperfections might be exploited to create market power or coercion required to establish an unlawful tie are discussed in § 8.3c3 and § 8.3c4. A likely way in which a seller might use exclusive dealing to exploit buyers is through an information-based lock-in.

The theory under which exclusive dealing may be anticompetitive because of the supplier's relational market power tracks closely the relational market power that can be the basis for a requirements tie. See § 8.3c4i. A supplier may exercise leverage over dealers that are locked into a supply relationship. See the discussion of relational market power

---

20. 365 U.S. 320, 81 S.Ct. 623, 5 L.Ed.2d 580 (1961).

21. 399 F.3d 181 (3d Cir. 2005). *Dentsply* was an application of Section 2 of the Sherman Act and is described in § 3.5.

in § 2.4e2iv. This sort of lock-in may occur in franchising. Requirements contracts in the franchising context are addressed in § 8.9.

Concern with informational problems may underlie the view of some courts that the duration of a requirements contract is relevant to its competitive assessment. It is true that a longer contract will raise more difficult informational problems, but the duration of a contract alone should not be a basis for condemning a requirements contract. The buyer, the seller or each of them may seek the long-term contract in part in order to resolve uncertainties about future markets. If a long-term supply contract turns sour for one of the parties, as it apparently did for the coal supplier in *Tampa Electric,* that party may assert that the other party possessed market power based on informational deficiencies, thereby establishing an unlawful exclusive dealing arrangement. But such claims should be rejected. The coal company in *Tampa Electric* was a seller, not a buyer, so its claim does not fit the model for analyzing foreclosure restraints, which focuses on the *seller's* abuse of market power. Even if the buyer (Tampa Electric) had been victimized by altered market conditions, it could not establish an unlawful exclusive dealing arrangement because the supply contract was not the product of an exploitative exercise of market power by the seller. Any market power that the seller might have would post date to the supply contract itself, a contract which appears to have been fairly negotiated by knowledgeable parties on each side.

A different result may be warranted if the exclusive dealing requirement is not the primary focus of the contract negotiation. For example, in signing a franchise contract, a franchisee may be compelled to agree to an open-ended requirement to purchase all input supplies from a supplier designated by the franchisor. The identity of the goods, the designated supplier and the pricing terms may be subject to change at the discretion of the franchisor. When a seller imposes exclusive dealing on a dealer based on the lock-in involved in a continuing vertical relationship, the seller may function like a disloyal buyer's agent that distorts purchase choice away from the competitive merits. See the discussion of this issue in the franchising context in §§ 8.9d1, 8.9e.

8.4d. Exclusive Dealing in the Courts

Lower court cases suggest a skepticism toward claims of forced exclusive dealing, restricting recovery to cases in which the defendant has foreclosed a substantial percentage of the market. In United States v. Dentsply International, Dentsply had a 75 to 80 percent market share, allowing the Justice Department to successfully attack the exclusive dealing forced on Dentsply dealers under Section 2 of the Sherman Act. The government did not press an exclusive dealing claim under Section 1.[22] For an example of a the difficulties in maintaining a Section 1 claim, see the discussion of Omega Environmental, Inc. v. Gilbarco, Inc.[23] in

---

22. 399 F.3d 181 (3d Cir. 2005), described in § 3.5.

23. 127 F.3d 1157 (9th Cir.1997), cert. denied, 525 U.S. 812, 119 S.Ct. 46, 142 L.Ed.2d 36 (1998).

§ 8.4d2. Other courts have dismissed claims of exclusive dealing because: (1) of a failure to establish an "agreement" under Section 3 of the Clayton Act; or (2) of a failure to demonstrate the requisite foreclosure effects.

8.4d1. Failure to Establish an Agreement Under Section 3 of the Clayton Act

In Roland Machinery Co. v. Dresser Industries, Inc.,[24] a terminated dealer sued its construction equipment supplier for unlawful exclusive dealing under Section 3 of the Clayton Act. Although the contract itself carried no exclusive dealing clause, the plaintiff dealer was terminated after the supplier learned that the dealer had signed a contract to carry construction equipment from a rival firm. The Seventh Circuit (per Judge Posner) reversed the district court's grant of a preliminary injunction. The court of appeals held that the plaintiff failed to establish that there was an "agreement" to require it not to carry a competing line. Section 3 applies when the seller's exclusive dealing requirement is a "condition, agreement, or understanding" in the sale or lease transaction. The Seventh Circuit stated that the agreement need not be explicit, but argued that there must be a "meeting of minds" in order for the agreement requirement to be met.[25]

The court's reasoning, perhaps an outgrowth of the "conspiracy" requirement imposed under Section 1 of the Sherman Act (see the discussion in § 8.3d3), seems misplaced in its application to Section 3 of the Clayton Act. A forced exclusive dealing arrangement is a unilateral act by a seller possessing market power, even if it is written into a contract signed by the buyer. There is no true meeting of the minds when this sort of market power is exercised. To allow a powerful seller to force exclusive dealing on a buyer with impunity simply because the seller does not put its exclusive dealing requirement in writing would create an exception that threatens to swallow the whole of Section 3's proscription on forced exclusive dealing.

Of course, the defendant in *Roland Machinery* may well have acted within the confines of the law if it exercised no abusive market power in terminating the plaintiff dealer. But the issue of market power, which is central to determining the competitive effects of an exclusive dealing arrangement, should have been addressed squarely by the court of appeals.

8.4d2. Failure to Establish the Requisite Foreclosure Effects

In U.S. Healthcare, Inc. v. Healthsource, Inc.,[26] the plaintiff and the defendant were rivals in offering medical services in New Hampshire through health maintenance organizations (HMOs). Healthsource, which had an established base of HMO physicians and patients in the state,

24. 749 F.2d 380 (7th Cir.1984).

25. Id. at 381, 392.

26. 986 F.2d 589 (1st Cir.1993).

adopted a contractual arrangement with its physicians that provided for a higher rate of compensation if they agreed not to work for any rival HMO. U.S. Healthcare sued claiming an unlawful exclusive dealing arrangement. The First Circuit affirmed the trial court's holding that there was no violation. The court found that foreclosure of rivals was not demonstrated because: (1) the extra payments to a physician agreeing to exclusivity were modest (about 14 percent higher than payments to a physician who did not agree to exclusivity); (2) the clause was terminable on thirty days' notice from any physician; and (3) only about 25 percent of all primary care physicians in New Hampshire were said to have been tied to Healthsource.

Another case in which competitive analysis revealed no substantial foreclosure effect is Omega Environmental, Inc. v. Gilbarco, Inc.[27] In this case, the Ninth Circuit began its analysis on the premise that the tendency to foreclose rivals was "[t]he main antitrust objection to exclusive dealing."[28] Gilbarco was the largest manufacturer of petroleum dispensing equipment used by gasoline retailers, holding 55 percent of the market. Gilbarco imposed exclusive dealing requirements on its distributors, a step said to have foreclosed 38 percent of the market for rival sellers.[29] Although the court found this degree of foreclosure "significant," it nonetheless ruled that no violation of Section 3 of the Clayton Act had been shown, citing two factors said to diminish the anticompetitive effect of the foreclosure: (1) exclusive dealing operated at the distributor level and left open other modes of distribution for petroleum dispensing equipment; (2) Gilbarco's contracts with distributors were short term, leaving rival sellers an opportunity to win distributors on relatively short notice (all of the distributors had contracts of one year or less, and many were said to have been terminable on sixty days' notice).

The *Omega* court viewed the market foreclosure test as a "rule of reason." The court rejected the plaintiff's argument that the exclusive dealing was anticompetitive because the Gilbarco product line enjoyed a strong reputation that heightened entry difficulties for rivals. The court also rejected the argument that exclusive dealing by the industry leader might facilitate pricing collusion among rivals, noting that the short-term contracts with distributors left rivals frequent opportunity to make lower bids for the business.[30] Although another court might have drawn other inferences from the facts, the *Omega* decision seems a carefully reasoned application of sound principle.

27. 127 F.3d 1157 (9th Cir.1997), cert. denied,525 U.S. 812, 119 S.Ct. 46, 142 L.Ed.2d 36 (1998).

28. Id. at 1162 (citing Roland Mach. Co. v. Dresser Indus., Inc., 749 F.2d 380, 393 (7th Cir.1984)(Posner, J.)).

29. The Ninth Circuit had held that a 24 percent foreclosure was sufficient to es-

tablish unlawful exclusive dealing in Twin City Sportservice, Inc. v. Charles O. Finley & Co., 676 F.2d 1291, 1298, 1304 (9th Cir.), cert. denied, 459 U.S. 1009, 103 S.Ct. 364, 74 L.Ed.2d 400 (1982).

30. *Omega*, 127 F.3d at 1164.

8.4d3. Toward More Consistent Treatment of Forced Exclusive Dealing and Tie–Ins

The same statutory provisions govern various forms of foreclosure restraints, including tie-ins and exclusive dealing. In particular, Section 3 of the Clayton Act is directed at the sale or lease of products on the condition that the buyer or lessee not deal in the products of a competitor, language that expressly governs both tie-ins and exclusive dealing arrangements. Because many foreclosure restraints can be classified as either tie-ins or exclusive dealing, the case law governing these similar restraints should provide for consistent results. Under either classification, the foreclosure should be deemed unlawful only if it is an abusive exercise of market power, whether that power has its origin in a high market share in the interbrand market or a systemic lock-in arising from the buyer's informational deficiencies, producing competitive injury through the corruption of a buying agent.

After the Supreme Court's decision in *Tampa Electric,* the lower courts have for the most part insisted upon a meaningful competitive analysis before concluding whether exclusive dealing is anticompetitive. In many instances, this has resulted in a judgment that vindicates the seller's use of exclusive dealing.[31] Although this analysis is often described as a "rule of reason," and tie-ins continue to be governed by a modified *per se* rule, the differing labels attached to these standards should not, in either case, preclude a meaningful competitive analysis. Nor should the classification of a foreclosure restraint as a tie-in or as exclusive dealing lead to a different result. To ensure this consistency of result, the more developed case law governing tie-ins, including the Court's holding in Eastman Kodak Co. v. Image Technical Services, Inc.,[32] should be incorporated into the law governing exclusive dealing.

The same objections to incorporating the teachings of *Kodak* into the law of tie-ins can be raised with respect to exclusive dealing. As explored more fully in § 8.3c5, those objections focus on concern that the inclusion of market imperfections in a competitive analysis will turn the antitrust laws into a tool for micromanaging the economy. But the words of Section 3 of the Clayton Act and Section 1 of the Sherman Act, expressly require the examination of individual contracts for anticompetitive effects. Of course, in examining individual tie-ins and exclusive dealing arrangements, the courts should focus on harm to competition, not on the undesired consequences of a contract on one of its signers. The key here as in other areas of antitrust is to focus on whether those consequences are the result of an exercise of market power that distorts allocation and transfers wealth from consumers to the defendant possessing market power. Tie-ins and exclusive dealing that are harmful because of the systemic exploitation of market power are, regardless of

---

31. Id. at 1162–65; Ryko Mfg. Co. v. Eden Servs., 823 F.2d 1215, 1234 (8th Cir. 1987), cert. denied, 484 U.S. 1026, 108 S.Ct. 751, 98 L.Ed.2d 763 (1988); Roland Mach. Co. v. Dresser Indus., Inc., 749 F.2d 380, 393 (7th Cir.1984); Barry Wright Corp. v. ITT Grinnell Corp., 724 F.2d 227, 237–38 (1st Cir.1983).

32. 504 U.S. 451, 112 S.Ct. 2072, 119 L.Ed.2d 265 (1992).

the source of that market power, likely to injure consumers, the direct buyers of the relevant product, and competing sellers foreclosed by the restraint.

§ 8.5   Forced Reciprocal Dealing

Reciprocal dealing occurs when a buyer agrees to purchase product A from the seller on the condition that the seller make a reciprocal purchase from the buyer—product B. A simple form of reciprocal dealing is a bartering transaction—"I'll give you product B if you give me product A." More complex reciprocal dealing involves the transfer of money as well as goods or services. The value of the reciprocal purchases on each side need not be identical.

Reciprocal dealing has many of the consequences of bundling and exclusive dealing. And like bundling and exclusive dealing, reciprocal dealing ought not to be of concern to antitrust unless one party uses its market power to force the transaction.[1] From a competitive perspective, the two potentially troublesome market power abuses that may be associated with forced reciprocal dealing, frequently occurring in tandem, are: (1) market power in the defendant's product that can coerce the other party to participate in the reciprocal transaction; and (2) the complicating features of the reciprocity, which may allow the defendant to exploit the buyer's informational or motivational deficiencies and extract a higher price than could be extracted without reciprocal dealing.

8.5a.   Summary of the Law Governing Reciprocal Dealing

As in the case of other foreclosure restraints, reciprocal dealing can be challenged under Section 3 of the Clayton Act, under Sections 1 and 2 of the Sherman Act, or under Section 5 of the Federal Trade Commission Act. Section 3 of the Clayton Act applies only to products, not to services, so that Section would not apply to a reciprocal arrangement in which the party possessing market power is offering a service.

The Supreme Court has yet to provide a road map for determining the lawfulness of reciprocal dealing. In FTC v. Consolidated Foods Corp., the Court in 1965 condemned a conglomerate merger on the theory that it would facilitate reciprocal dealing.[2] But such conglomerate mergers are seldom if ever challenged under current merger policy. See the discussion in § 11.3. *Consolidated Foods* fails to provide a clear platform for assessing the legality of reciprocal dealing outside the merger context.

§ 8.5

1. Brokerage Concepts, Inc. v. U.S. Healthcare, Inc., 140 F.3d 494, 511 (3d Cir. 1998)(concluding that only "coercive" reciprocal dealing is a basis for a claim under the Sherman Act); Betaseed, Inc. v. U & I Inc., 681 F.2d 1203, 1216–17 (9th Cir.1982) (concluding that "coercive reciprocity" should be deemed unlawful on the same terms as tie-ins).

2. 380 U.S. 592, 85 S.Ct. 1220, 14 L.Ed.2d 95 (1965). Another case in which a merger was deemed unlawful because of actual and potential resort to reciprocity pressures was United States v. General Dynamics Corp., 258 F.Supp. 36 (S.D.N.Y. 1966).

In lower court litigation involving reciprocity, the courts of appeals have debated whether a rule of reason or *per se* analysis applies to reciprocal trading. Most courts end up applying a standard similar to that applied to tie-ins, under which a plaintiff may assert illegality under the modified *per se* rule and, should that analysis not establish a violation, under the rule of reason.[3] Defendants have sought to argue that only the rule of reason should apply to reciprocal dealing, but the issue may be of reduced consequence because under either a modified *per se* rule or a rule of reason, the plaintiff must establish that the reciprocal dealing is coercive, an undertaking that should require an encompassing competitive analysis of the practice. The courts must determine whether one of the parties has power that allows that party to define the terms of the reciprocal deal without adequate competitive discipline. The courts should generally look to the same sorts of indicia used for tie-in analysis (high collective market share among parties to reciprocal deal and/or a high risk of exploitation of the buyer's informational or motivational imperfections—see § 8.3d1). In the reported lower court decisions, competitive analysis has generally focused on whether foreclosure in the interbrand market is substantial,[4] often ignoring the potential anticompetitive injury arising from the complicating features of a reciprocal dealing arrangement. It is true that substantial foreclosure is likely to work anticompetitive injury only if it raises rivals' costs or deters entry, but a defendant may also use forced reciprocity to injure competition if the reciprocity complicates the buyer's transaction in a manner that allows the defendant to gain a supracompetitive premium. See the discussion in § 8.5c.

8.5b. Procompetitive Potential of Reciprocal Dealing

Some reciprocal agreements may be seen as two-way exclusive dealing arrangements, in which each firm agrees to buy all of its requirements from the other firm. When reciprocal dealing takes this form, it is likely to have the same competitive effects as exclusive dealing. In most instances, only one of the two parties will be charged with forced reciprocal dealing, so the competitive analysis will focus on possible market power exercised by the accused party. If reciprocal selling lacks a "requirements" feature—if each party to an agreement is not committed to buying all of its requirements from the other party—the arrangement will generally pose fewer competitive risks (because a smaller portion of the relevant market is being foreclosed).

Reciprocal selling, like exclusive dealing, may have some transactional cost savings for parties on both sides of the transaction (the benefits of exclusive dealing are discussed in § 8.4b). For example, if a steel company agrees to purchase all its requirements of cars and trucks

---

3. *Brokerage Concepts*, 140 F.3d at 511–12 (analyzing reciprocal dealing under the tests applied to tie-ins); *Betaseed*, 681 F.2d at 1216–20 (same).

4. *Brokerage Concepts,* 140 F.3d at 517; Key Enters. of Delaware, Inc. v. Venice Hosp., 919 F.2d 1550, 1562–64 (11th Cir. 1990), vacated per curiam, 979 F.2d 806 (11th Cir.1992), cert. denied, 511 U.S. 1126, 114 S.Ct. 2132, 128 L.Ed.2d 863 (1994).

from a particular automobile company in return for that auto company's commitment to buy all of its steel requirements from the steel company, each side in this transaction may reduce some of its marketing costs and may gain a measure of security for future sales that allows more confident business planning and investment. The arrangement, for its term, amounts to a partial integration of the firms' operations.

Reciprocal dealing may also have procompetitive effects as a means of evading a supracompetitive price set by a cartel or through oligopolistic behavior. When a cartel attempts to set a fixed selling price, a seller may be able to discount its price below the cartel level through a reciprocal deal by which the seller pays a premium above market price on the product that is purchased from the buyer. This is a procompetitive result that undercuts the cartel. It is not forced reciprocal dealing, however, as long as it is sought by a buyer lacking significant market power as a means of undercutting the cartel's exercise of market power.[5] Reciprocal dealing may also be used to evade Government price regulation. When a maximum price is set by Government regulators, the seller may use forced reciprocal dealing to raise that price. The buyer can be charged the regulated price for the purchased product, but may be forced to make a reciprocal sale at a price below market. Similar evasions of regulated prices can occur through the use of a tie-in. See the discussion in § 8.3c6. These evasions may have anticompetitive effects if the underlying price regulation is a response to market power abuses by sellers.

8.5c. Anticompetitive Potential of Reciprocal Dealing

It has been suggested that firms engaging in reciprocity do so nearly always for "competitive and efficient" reasons.[6] There is, however, one major exception: when a party to a transaction uses market power over buyers or sellers to force reciprocal selling. The key issue thus becomes identifying those situations in which a party to the transaction possesses market power. As with tie-ins, the source of the market power that allows a party to coerce a buyer or seller lies in one or both of the following elements: (1) the interbrand market power that the party possesses in the product it sells or buys; and (2) the use of reciprocity to complicate the buyer's transaction, allowing the seller to exploit the buyer's informational or motivational deficiencies. Each of these sources of market power are examined below. Absent such market power, reciprocal dealing is unlikely to be anticompetitive.

5. Hovenkamp argues that reciprocal dealing should be treated more leniently than tying because of the possibility that reciprocal dealing can be a means of subverting cartel prices. H. HOVENKAMP, FEDERAL ANTITRUST POLICY: THE LAW OF COMPETITION AND ITS PRACTICE § 10.7 at 383 (1994). But tie-ins might also be used to subvert cartel prices if a buyer convinces a cartel member to tie the sale of the cartel product with a noncartelized product, and charge a combined price that in effect discounts the cartelized item. In any event, cases in which tie-ins or reciprocal dealing are used to subvert a cartel are unlikely to involve an exercise of market power by the seller and hence should not be unlawful foreclosure restraints.

6. Id. at 382.

An isolated and voluntary barter transaction between two small farmers, say a trade of a cow for a used tractor, would appear to present no anticompetitive risks. But what if the barter transaction, although voluntary, is between two large firms, each with a 30 percent share of its market? Suppose, for example, that the largest U.S. automobile manufacturer agrees to purchase all its steel from the largest U.S. steel-producing firm, in return for which the steel producer agrees to acquire all of its cars and trucks from the auto firm. Even this transaction poses few competitive risks as long as the steel and automobiles purchased as part of the reciprocal dealing represent a relatively small percentage of the overall markets for steel and automobiles. There is a possibility of a lemming effect, in which other large steel and automobile producers would rush to enter into similar reciprocal deals, foreclosing an increasing percentage of the two markets. But unless the foreclosure effects seriously increase rivals' costs or raise entry barriers in one of the industries, substantial anticompetitive effects from such a voluntary transaction seem unlikely. Steel and automobile producers seem likely to agree to such arrangements only if they promote the efficiency of their respective operations.

Forced reciprocal dealing, then, should be the focus of a competitive inquiry. The most obvious form of market power that can be used to force reciprocal dealing is a high market share of a product purchased or sold by the defendant. In Betaseed, Inc. v. U & I Inc.,[7] the defendant allegedly had purchasing power (monopsony power) in the market for sugar beets (the defendant was the only purchaser of sugar beets in the relevant geographic area). The complaint alleged that the defendant engaged in forced reciprocity by compelling farmers to buy seed from the defendant as a condition for purchase of the farmer's sugar beets. In a suit brought by a rival seller of seed, the court of appeals reversed the summary judgment granted in favor of the defendant and remanded for a trial.[8]

If the sugar beet processor was a monopsonist, it should have been able to gain a monopsony premium from the farmer (in the form of a lower price paid for the farmer's sugar beets) without any reciprocal dealing.[9] The practice still may be harmful, however, if it forecloses a substantial percentage of the market for sugar beet seed, raising rivals' costs in selling their seed and raising barriers to entry. But a forced reciprocal dealing requirement might also increase the defendant's overall return by complicating the buyer's transaction and obscuring the price paid for the farmer's sugar beets. Assume, for example, that the defendant in *Betaseed* cannot depress the price paid for sugar beets without risking entry from other processors in neighboring geographic areas. But the price paid to farmers can be kept higher if the defendant

7.   681 F.2d 1203 (9th Cir.1982).

8.   Id. at 1235.

9.   It was Bowman's criticism of leverage theory that a monopolist could not increase its return by tying its sale to a competitive product, but the validity of this critique may be limited to circumstances of perfect monopoly (in the tying product) and perfect competition (in the tied product). See the discussion in § 8.3c1.

can make up the difference by charging farmers a premium above market price for the seed that it sells to them. If rival sellers in other regions use a similar reciprocity arrangement with farmers, the practice takes on the look of a parallel oligopolistic practice, one which processors would find it in their self-interest to maintain.

This sort of forced reciprocity might also be a tool for price discrimination that permits a monopsonist to extract greater profit than could occur without reciprocity. For example, a monopsonist grain elevator may be forced to pay a uniform, per bushel price for the grain it purchases. But by forcing the farmers who use that service to buy fertilizer from the grain elevator, additional supracompetitive profits may be obtained from the farmers. A farmer that uses fertilizer more intensively, or uses fertilizer on crops that are not sold to the grain elevator, would pay a higher premium for fertilizer purchases or, in effect, receive a smaller price for the grain sold to the grain elevator. Farmers might tolerate this discriminatory arrangement because, like a tie-in, reciprocal dealing can complicate the transaction in a manner that obscures pricing policies, making it less likely that farmers would view the reciprocal dealing arrangement as a form of discriminatory pricing by the monopsonist. Aside from allocation injuries to local farmers who have to pay a premium for fertilizer, the reciprocal dealing may dampen competitive workings of the local fertilizer market, causing increases in the price of fertilizer as well. For example, the unit costs of competing fertilizer dealers may be increased as their sales drop, forcing increases in fertilizer prices in the local market.

In the grain elevator example, reciprocal dealing creates an opportunity for a party to exercise market power both because of the local, interbrand monopsony power possessed by the grain elevator and because of the complicating features of reciprocity, making it easier to exploit the buyer's informational deficiencies. A recent case that suggests the interplay in interbrand market power and the complicating features of reciprocity is Brokerage Concepts, Inc. v. U.S. Healthcare, Inc.[10] U.S. Healthcare, a large provider of health care services, conditioned participation in its network of medical prescription providers on the pharmacy purchasing from U.S. Healthcare health insurance services for the pharmacies' employees. "I Got It at Gary's," a small chain of Pennsylvania pharmacies, had chosen to self-insure its employees, but was pressured by U.S. Healthcare to drop the plaintiff as the administrator of the self-insurance plan in favor of a U.S. Healthcare subsidiary.

The arrangement was characterized as a tie-in by the plaintiffs and as reciprocal dealing by the defendants. The Third Circuit overturned a jury verdict that found U.S. Healthcare had violated Section 1 of the Sherman Act, concluding that the arrangement lay "somewhere between the two practices" and was not unlawful because U.S. Healthcare's patients were purchasing somewhere between 3 to 20 percent of the

10.   140 F.3d 494 (3d Cir.1998).

prescriptions sold at various Gary's stores, not enough to establish U.S. Healthcare's market power.[11]

The court's analysis seems sterile in its mechanical reliance on market definitions and market shares. For example, the court mechanically distinguishes Eastman Kodak Co. v. Image Technical Services, Inc.,[12] concluding that a single brand market is not appropriate on the facts before it.[13] But legal maneuvering surrounding market definition disputes often obscures the underlying issue: whether the defendant has the power to raise its price above the competitive level without such a loss in sales so as to make the price increase unprofitable. See the discussion of market power in § 2.2. U.S. Healthcare might more logically be seen as a buyer of prescription-dispensing services for its patients (it reimbursed local pharmacies for this service). If so, its monopsony power would be measured by its ability to lower the price paid for prescription-dispensing below the competitive level without such a decrease in stores willing to supply prescription service as to make the price decrease unprofitable. Each local pharmacy needs to bring a large percentage of neighborhood customers into the store for prescription business, if for no other reason than that such customers, when on the premises, are likely to make other purchases as well. So it is likely that U.S. Healthcare, in a position to cut off the store's access to up to 20 percent of its customers by denying participation in the prescription plan, possessed this form of market power. But U.S. Healthcare's ability to exploit this market power varied widely from pharmacy to pharmacy because of the varying percentage of U.S. Healthcare customers each pharmacy served. U.S. Healthcare had to set standard reimbursement rates for prescriptions based on a statewide market, in many segments of which U.S. Healthcare had no market leverage over pharmacies. For example, if U.S. Healthcare lowered its price paid to Gary's stores below the level paid other Pennsylvania pharmacies—such discrimination could have risked the ire of state regulators or given rise to litigation charging unlawful discrimination. Still, U.S. Healthcare could discriminate against any local pharmacy that purchased health care services for its employees by forcing that pharmacy to purchase those services from U.S. Healthcare (either by enrolling the pharmacy's employees in an HMO or by forcing the pharmacy to purchase administrator services for a self-insurance plan). There was some evidence in the record that the plaintiff's administrative services offered to Gary's were significantly less costly than those forced on Gary's by U.S. Healthcare.[14] The potential competition injuries flowing from the defendant's alleged overcharges were: (1) to the plaintiff, which may have lost an opportunity to sell its competitively superior administrator services; (2) to Gary's, which may have been forced to pay a supracompetitive price for the administrator

---

11. Id. at 511, 508.

12. 504 U.S. 451, 112 S.Ct. 2072, 119 L.Ed.2d 265 (1992).

13. *Brokerage Concepts,* 140 F.3d at 513–15.

14. Id. at 507–10. To the extent that the evidence of the relatively higher cost of U.S. Healthcare's administrator services was contested, that matter should be left for the jury and the trial court to resolve.

services; and (3) to consumers, who may have been denied services Gary's would otherwise have offered or have been overcharged for products or services sold by Gary's. If Gary's were forced out of business by the defendant's conduct, consumers would be deprived of a prescription outlet that was their preferred source of prescriptions and other products sold by the drugstore.

Another example of the way in which a seller's interbrand market power may be combined with the complicating features of reciprocal dealing to exploit consumers is Key Enterprises of Delaware, Inc. v. Venice Hospital.[15] In this case, the defendant hospital referred discharged patients to home care nurses on the condition that the nurses would recommend that the patients purchase durable medical equipment, such as wheelchairs, crutches and walkers, from the hospital's joint venture partner, a retailer of durable medical equipment. Both resource misallocation and wealth transfer injuries were likely from this conduct because of the foreclosure effect on competing durable medical equipment suppliers and because consumers may have made purchase decisions relying on the professional advice of nurses who failed to disclose rival sources. The foreclosure effect here was probably substantial because a large percentage of purchasers learn of their need for durable medical equipment while hospitalized. The defendant hospital's discharged patients apparently generated about 46 percent of the area's purchases of durable medical equipment.

The nurses with whom the reciprocal dealing was arranged were not directly exploited by any informational void. Presumably, the nurses were well aware of alternative sources for durable medical equipment. But their role as neutral advisors was compromised. The opportunity for exploiting the consumer's informational deficiencies in the area of medical products and services is substantial precisely because of the tendency of many patients to obediently follow the advice of medical professionals whom patients view as competent and trustworthy agents of patient interests. Thus, in *Key Enterprises* as in *Brokerage Concepts,* it was not the defendant's high market share alone that created the anticompetitive injury, but a combination of the defendant's high market share and the defendant's ability to complicate the buyer's transaction in a way that made it easier to exploit the buyer's informational or motivational deficiencies.

§ 8.6 Most–Favored–Nation Clauses

Most-favored-nation ("MFN") clauses, sometimes referred to as price protection or antidiscrimination clauses, are contract provisions that promise the buyer the lowest price that the seller offers to any other buyer. These clauses are not in and of themselves unlawful. But they have been attacked under Sections 1 and 2 of the Sherman Act as well as under Section 5 of the Federal Trade Commission Act as devices for

15. 919 F.2d 1550 (11th Cir.1990), va- 1992), cert. denied, 511 U.S. 1126, 114 S.Ct.
cated per curiam, 979 F.2d 806 (11th Cir. 2132, 128 L.Ed.2d 863 (1994).

facilitating cartel behavior or monopolization. They are addressed in this Chapter because MFN clauses can also operate to facilitate or implement foreclosure restraints such as tie-ins or exclusive dealing.

8.6a. Competitive Effects of MFN Clauses

MFN clauses have an obviously procompetitive potential. They may afford the buyer a lower price without the costs associated with seeking information about prices offered to other buyers. They address concerns that any buyer might have that its rival buyers might be obtaining the input product at a lower price, thereby gaining a competitive advantage. But while they may relieve buyer anxiety, MFN clauses may contribute to a climate of comfortable, oligopolistic behavior among buyers, each of whom knows its rivals' costs for a primary input product that is governed by an MFN clause. When subject to an effective MFN clause, even a large volume buyer whose purchases might warrant a cost-based discount would be unable to receive a price any lower than that offered to its smaller rivals.

MFN clauses are unusual in competitive markets. They are more commonly found in markets in which the seller has market power as a monopolist, a niche marketer, or as the result of parallel use of MFN clauses among major rivals in an oligopolistic market. A seller with market power can use the MFN clause as a basis for resisting demands of a high-volume buyer for a discounted price: "We cannot offer you a discount without offering it to everyone else." In this way, MFN clauses may provide the seller with power to price above competitive levels the additional tool that it needs to resist countervailing pressure from a large-volume buyer. A seller lacking market power because of meaningful competition from its rivals would probably not wish to agree to an MFN clause because, in the course of bidding for business, it would desire to retain flexibility to offer an occasional discount price to a large volume purchaser without being bound to offer that discount to all other purchasers.

To summarize, MFN clauses can allow a powerful seller to resist competitive pressures from large-volume buyers. And such clauses can facilitate cartel-like behavior at the seller level. A seller will have an incentive not to lower its price to any buyer, knowing that if it does so, it must make the lower price generally available to all buyers. If all rival sellers have similar MFN clauses, each may be relatively secure that its rivals are not discounting, thereby increasing the comfort level in a tacit or express oligopolistic pricing scheme. It is also possible that MFN clauses may make it easier for buyers to engage in parallel or oligopolistic behavior. If each buyer is assured that it pays the same price for key input products, this may foster a climate in which cooperative or parallel buyer behavior leads to higher output prices.

An MFN clause can be used to facilitate a foreclosure restraint in a similar fashion. In International Salt Co. v. United States,[1] the defen-

§ 8.6
1. 332 U.S. 392, 68 S.Ct. 12, 92 L.Ed. 20 (1947).

dant, the largest producer of salt for industrial purposes, owned patents on two machines used for dissolving or injecting salt for various purposes. The Government's complaint alleged that the defendant leased its patented machines on the condition that lessees use only the defendant's salt products. In the case of one of the machine's (the Saltomat), the contract contained a modified MFN clause, allowing the lessee to benefit from any general price reduction on salt tablets sold for the machine. The defendant argued that this MFN clause (and a more strongly worded price protection clause used in the lease of another salt machine) protected buyers and thereby saved the tie-in provisions from illegality. The Court correctly rejected this defense,[2] concluding that the defendant's conduct constituted an unlawful tie. A more likely role for the MFN clause was that its use made it easier for the defendant to impose the tying arrangement. Without the MFN (or related price protection) clause, buyers might have resisted any agreement that they buy salt exclusively from the defendant. With the clause in place, the defendant could more easily convince buyers to accept and abide by the tying arrangement.

8.6b.   Agency and Private Attacks on MFN Clauses

In *Blue Cross & Blue Shield United v. Marshfield Clinic,* Blue Cross alleged that the defendant clinic attempted to establish a floor on prices charged to Blue Cross patients through the use of an MFN clause that prevented a physician from charging the defendant clinic more than the physician charged other patients.[3] According to Blue Cross, this created an incentive for physicians not to lower their prices to Blue Cross because such a price reduction would also have to be passed along to the defendant clinic. In rejecting a price fixing claim under Section 1 of the Sherman Act, Judge Posner wrote for the Court that the plaintiffs' argument was "ingenious but perverse." The unanimous court concluded that the MFN clause was intended to enhance the ability of the defendant to bargain for lower prices.[4] In another case, the First Circuit also rejected a monopolization claim as a basis for challenging a health insurer's MFN clause claimed to limit physician charges.[5]

Although each of these circuit opinions may have reached the correct result, they are open to criticism because they failed to consider adequately the potential anticompetitive consequences from use of an MFN clause. The Seventh Circuit in *Marshfield* is correct that a buyer might embrace an MFN clause as a way of ensuring that no rival received a lower price. But this observation provides only the most superficial competitive analysis. It is possible, perhaps likely, that an MFN clause embraced by both buyers and sellers will cause substantial

2. Id. at 392–97.

3. 65 F.3d 1406, 1415 (7th Cir.1995), cert. denied, 516 U.S. 1184, 116 S.Ct. 1288, 134 L.Ed.2d 233 (1996).

4. Id.

5. Ocean State Physicians Health Plan, Inc. v. Blue Cross & Blue Shield, 883 F.2d 1101 (1st Cir.1989), cert. denied, 494 U.S. 1027, 110 S.Ct. 1473, 108 L.Ed.2d 610 (1990).

competitive injury by eliminating meaningful price competition and preventing large volume buyers from obtaining a cost-based discount that would benefit such buyers in a truly competitive market.

Notwithstanding the cool reception toward antitrust challenges directed at MFN clauses evidenced in these two private claims, the federal agencies have, over a considerable period and with some success, attacked the use of MFN clauses. During the 1970s, the Department of Justice targeted the use of MFN or price protection clauses in a civil proceeding brought against producers of large turbine generators.[6] In the 1980s, the Federal Trade Commission unsuccessfully challenged under Section 5 of the FTC Act the use of MFN clauses by four producers of antiknock, gasoline additives.[7] More recently, the Justice Department has obtained consent decrees prohibiting the use of MFN clauses in a number of cases in which insurance companies had imposed such clauses on doctors or dentists.[8] In two district court decisions, the Justice Department's authority to pursue MFN clauses was sustained when the courts rejected arguments that such clauses were *per se* lawful and beyond the authority of the Department to investigate or prosecute.[9]

The decision law governing use of MFN clauses remains unsettled. That law should focus on whether the party imposing an MFN clause (usually one or more sellers) possesses market power and is using the MFN clause to facilitate cartel or foreclosure behavior. When such a showing is not made, the use of an MFN clause should be lawful.

§ 8.7   Maximum Price Restraints

Vertical maximum price fixing occurs when an upstream seller dictates the maximum price at which a downstream marketer may sell a product or service. Both maximum and minimum resale price restraints are best understood in the context of the relationship between supplier and dealer. But such price restraints differ fundamentally with respect to who holds the power: when minimum price restraints are imposed, the dealer is typically in a relatively powerful position; when maximum price restraints are imposed, the power rests with the supplier. Thus, a harmful maximum resale price and a harmful tie-in both signify the seller's power to coerce a buyer, a common antecedent not shared by a minimum resale price.

Minimum resale price limits are typically imposed by the supplier to give dealers an incentive to carry or promote the supplier's product. A

6. United States v. General Elec. Co., 1977–2 Trade Cas. (CCH) ¶ 61,660 (E.D.Pa. 1977).

7. E.I. Du Pont de Nemours & Co. v. FTC, 729 F.2d 128 (2d Cir.1984).

8. United States v. Delta Dental Plan, Inc., 1995–1 Trade Cas. (CCH) ¶ 71,048 (D.Ariz.1995); United States v. Oregon Dental Serv., 1995–2 Trade Cas. (CCH) ¶ 71,062 (N.D.Cal.1995); United States v. Vision Serv. Plan, 1996–1 Trade Cas. (CCH) ¶ 71,404 (D.D.C.1996).

9. United States v. Delta Dental, 943 F.Supp. 172 (D.R.I.1996)(denying a motion to dismiss); Blue Cross & Blue Shield v. Bingaman, 1996–2 Trade Cas. (CCH) ¶ 71,-600 (N.D.Ohio 1996)(upholding the Justice Department's civil investigative demand), aff'd mem. sub nom. Blue Cross & Blue Shield v. Klein, 117 F.3d 1420 (6th Cir. 1997).

supplier that has power over its retailers is unlikely to impose minimum resale prices because it has no need to provide dealers with an incentive to carry the product. In contrast, a supplier that lacks power over its retailers is unlikely to impose a maximum resale price restraint on its dealers. To do so would risk losing valued dealers that might turn to other suppliers rather than tolerate a squeezing of the resale margin.

8.7a. The Evolution of the Law Governing Vertical Maximum Price Fixing

Jurisprudence governing application of Section 1 of the Sherman Act to vertical maximum price fixing begins with the Court's condemnation of minimum resale prices in its 1911 *Dr. Miles* decision.[1] As described in § 7.4a, the law governing minimum resale prices has oscillated widely at the hands of judges and legislators. What remains of the *per se* rule today, after the Supreme Court's decisions of the 1980s, is a significantly narrowed but still extant *per se* rule condemning vertical minimum price fixing. Although the Court has recognized that vertical maximum price fixing presents a different question, it too was for almost fifty years condemned under a *per se* rule.

The Supreme Court's *per se* condemnation of vertically imposed maximum prices came in Kiefer–Stewart Co. v. Joseph E. Seagram & Sons, Inc.[2] Kiefer–Stewart, an Indiana liquor wholesaler, alleged that Seagram and its wholly owned subsidiary (Calvert) had conspired to refuse to sell to wholesalers that did not comply with maximum resale prices.[3] Seagram had spent $500,000 advertising against inflated whiskey prices at the time government price regulation was lifted in October 1946. But inflationary pressures were severe, making dealers such as Kiefer–Stewart recalcitrant in complying with Seagram's price ceilings.[4] The Supreme Court (per Justice Black) added to Seagram's difficulties, condemning maximum resale prices because "such agreements, no less than those to fix minimum prices, cripple the freedom of traders and thereby restrain their ability to sell in accordance with their own judgment."[5] Perhaps because the proposition seemed self-evident, the Court offered no further analysis of why a market system might efficiently reserve pricing decisions to those whose capital was primarily at risk.

Kiefer-Stewart provoked relatively little critical comment, perhaps because the complaint alleged a "horizontal conspiracy" among affiliated

§ 8.7

1. Dr. Miles Med. Co. v. John D. Park & Sons Co., 220 U.S. 373, 31 S.Ct. 376, 55 L.Ed. 502 (1911).

2. 340 U.S. 211, 71 S.Ct. 259, 95 L.Ed. 219 (1951).

3. This aspect of the *Kiefer-Stewart* holding would presumably not survive after Copperweld Corp. v. Independence Tube Corp., 467 U.S. 752, 104 S.Ct. 2731, 81 L.Ed.2d 628 (1984), which holds that a con-

spiracy under Section 1 of the Sherman Act cannot be found between a corporation and its wholly owned subsidiary.

4. Background underlying *Kiefer-Stewart* is described in Comments, *The Per Se Illegality of Price-Fixing–Sans Power, Purpose, or Effect,* 19 U. CHI. L. REV. 837, 838–39 (1952). See also the opinion of the court of appeals, Kiefer–Stewart Co. v. Joseph E. Seagram & Sons, Inc., 182 F.2d 228, 230–32 (7th Cir.1950).

5. *Kiefer-Stewart,* 340 U.S. at 213.

companies[6] and a conspiracy between two direct competitors that, although commonly owned, conspired to fix minimum prices.[7] No horizontal issue clouded the holding when *Kiefer-Stewart* was reaffirmed in Justice White's opinion in *Albrecht* seventeen years later. The St. Louis Globe–Democrat, the only morning newspaper in the metropolitan area, but one which competed for advertising revenue with the major evening paper, imposed maximum resale prices on independent carriers who provided home delivery. One of these independent carriers (Albrecht) began charging subscription prices above the ceiling. After the Globe took steps to enforce the price ceiling, Albrecht sued claiming a *per se* violation of Section 1 of the Sherman Act under *Kiefer-Stewart*. One of the Globe's defenses was that *Kiefer-Stewart* did not apply when the upstream seller had created exclusive territories for retailers. This defense was accepted by the court of appeals, but rejected by the Supreme Court. Not surprisingly, Justice White wrote that the legality of the exclusive territories was open to question after United States v. Arnold, Schwinn & Co.,[8] a recently minted opinion which concluded that nonprice distribution restraints were illegal *per se*. But the heart of the *Albrecht* opinion was a reaffirmation of the *Kiefer-Stewart* premise that competition was best served by leaving pricing decisions with the firm whose capital was primarily at risk. Justice White said that "schemes to fix maximum prices, by substituting the perhaps erroneous judgment of a seller for the forces of the competitive market, may severely intrude upon the ability of buyers to compete and survive in that market."[9] He elaborated on the damage that could be caused from the dealer's loss of pricing freedom:

> Maximum prices may be fixed too low for the dealer to furnish services essential to the value which goods have for the consumer or to furnish services and conveniences which consumers desire and for which they are willing to pay. Maximum price fixing may channel distribution through a few large or specifically advantaged dealers who otherwise would be subject to significant nonprice competition.[10]

These concerns may be significant in other cases in which price ceilings are imposed, but there was no obvious support for this sort of injury on

---

6. In his dissent in *Albrecht*, Justice Harlan read *Kiefer-Stewart* as a decision premised on a horizontal conspiracy between two liquor producers, ignoring the circumstance that they were commonly owned. Albrecht v. Herald Co., 390 U.S. 145, 164–65, 88 S.Ct. 869, 19 L.Ed.2d 998 (1968)(Harlan, J., dissenting). Although correct on its face, this reading does not provide a basis for a credible economic analysis of the maximum resale prices imposed in *Kiefer-Stewart*. Because the facts demonstrate no horizontally generated market power, a genuine economic analysis must assume the vertical nature of the price restraints.

7. *Kiefer-Stewart*, 340 U.S. at 214. According to one source, the minimum prices were also likely to operate as maximum prices because wholesalers could not distinguish their offerings from rivals, with the result that retailers would quickly switch if a particular wholesaler's prices were out of line. Comments, supra note 4, at 838–39.

8. 388 U.S. 365, 87 S.Ct. 1856, 18 L.Ed.2d 1249 (1967).

9. *Albrecht*, 390 U.S. at 152.

10. Id. at 152–53.

the record in *Albrecht*. Justice White also noted that a fixed maximum price may end up being a fixed minimum price.[11] But the opinion, relying on the precedent of *Kiefer-Stewart,* fails to make a well-considered policy argument for a *per se* rule on the facts before the Court.

Justices Harlan and Stewart dissented. Justice Harlan made much of the fact that unlike minimum prices, which might be imposed in response to dealer pressure, maximum prices are imposed by a manufacturer "in his own interest." "Since price ceilings[ ] reflect the manufacturer's view that there is insufficient competition to drive prices down to a competitive level, they have the arguable justification that they prevent retailers or wholesalers from reaping monopoly or supracompetitive profits."[12]

The dissent's view that the price ceilings were a procompetitive tool to prevent price gouging had particular force on the facts of *Albrecht*. Because of the unique features of the newspaper business, the price ceilings were probably imposed by a newspaper publisher that faced significant competitive discipline on distributors that were natural monopolists. Newspapers generate revenues from both subscriptions and advertising. To maintain advertising revenue—advertising is usually the newspaper's largest revenue source—the circulation base must be maintained to make it attractive to advertisers. A paper such as the Globe, despite its status as the only morning daily newspaper in the city, is subject to competitive discipline in the setting of its subscription rates. If those rates are too high, it will lose circulation to the evening paper (or perhaps to local papers or other news providers) and undercut its value to advertisers. Newspaper distributors do not face the same competitive discipline. Indeed, because distribution is inefficient when more than one distributor serves the same area, distributors selling the only morning paper in town may be natural monopolists.[13] A price ceiling imposed by the Globe may counter some of the lack of competitive discipline facing monopolist dealers.

After the Supreme Court overturned *Schwinn* in 1977,[14] criticism of the *per se* rule against vertical maximum price fixing increased. Commentators of varying persuasions joined the call for reexamination of the rule.[15] But none of this literature focused on the rather simple but inexorable fact that an upstream supplier cannot comfortably impose

---

11. Id. at 153.

12. Id. at 158, 159 (Harlan, J. dissenting).

13. Justice Stewart's dissent in *Albrecht* described the plaintiff distributor as "the only person who could sell for home delivery the city's only daily morning newspaper," and hence as "a monopolist within his own territory." Id. at 168 (Stewart, J., dissenting).

14. Continental T. V., Inc. v. GTE Sylvania Inc., 433 U.S. 36, 97 S.Ct. 2549, 53 L.Ed.2d 568 (1977).

15. Among those who took this position were Blair & Lang, Albrecht *After* ARCO, *Maximum Resale Price Fixing Moves Toward the Rule of Reason,* 44 VAND. L. REV. 1007 (1991); F. SCHERER & D. ROSS, INDUSTRIAL MARKET STRUCTURE AND ECONOMIC PERFORMANCE 558 (3d ed. 1990); 8 P. AREEDA, ANTITRUST LAW: AN ANALYSIS OF ANTITRUST PRINCIPLES AND THEIR APPLICATION ¶ 1625a, at 294–95 (1989); Easterbrook, *Maximum Price Fixing,* 48 U. CHI. L. REV. 886, 887–90 (1981); R. BORK, THE ANTITRUST PARADOX: A POLICY AT WAR WITH ITSELF 281–82 (1978).

maximum price ceilings on a dealer unless the dealer's demand for the supplier's products is inelastic (i.e., unless the supplier has market power in transactions with the dealer).

The Supreme Court next faced a maximum price fixing claim in the 1990 decision in Atlantic Richfield Co. v. USA Petroleum Co.[16] In *ARCO,* the plaintiffs were non-ARCO service station dealers alleged to have been injured because ARCO imposed price ceilings on the gasoline sold by ARCO dealers. Although the Supreme Court had an opportunity to overturn the *per se* rule, it chose not to, instead dismissing the plaintiff's claims because the plaintiff did not allege antitrust injury (the Court concluded that any injury to the plaintiff from lower prices charged by ARCO dealers was a consequence of competition, not of any anticompetitive conduct). The Court reviewed some of the arguments suggesting procompetitive or anticompetitive effects of price ceilings, but did not directly examine the issue, stating that it assumed "*arguendo,* that *Albrecht* correctly held that vertical, maximum price fixing is subject to the *per se* rule."[17]

In 1997, the Supreme Court, with Justice White no longer on the bench, took the final step and eliminated *per se* treatment of vertical maximum price fixing. In State Oil Co. v. Khan, Barkat Khan had contracted with State Oil to lease and operate a Union Oil service station and convenience store.[18] Under the terms of the lease, Khan was limited to a margin of 3.25 cents per gallon of gasoline. Khan was free to charge a price higher than the suggested retail price—but was required to remit any amount above the prescribed 3.25 cent margin.[19] Khan was also free to lower its retail price, but would have to subtract any price reduction from its margin. About one year after the lease was signed, State Oil commenced a proceeding to terminate the agreement based on Khan's failure to meet lease payments. Khan commenced a separate proceeding in federal court alleging that State Oil violated Section 1 of the Sherman Act by fixing the price at which Khan could sell gas. According to the complaint, but for the agreement, Khan could have adjusted retail prices (as a receiver allegedly had done) and increase sales and profits. After the district court granted summary judgment for State Oil, the Seventh Circuit reversed in an opinion by Judge Posner.[20] The court of appeals found that the contract fixed maximum prices by making it worthless for Khan to attempt to charge more for the gasoline—Khan would be forced to remit to State Oil any amount received above the suggested retail price. The court further found that it was bound to follow the *per se* rule announced in *Albrecht* despite "its increasingly wobbly, moth-eaten foundations." It described *Albrecht* as "unsound when decided, * * *

---

16. 495 U.S. 328, 110 S.Ct. 1884, 109 L.Ed.2d 333 (1990).

17. Id. at 335 n.5.

18. 522 U.S. 3, 118 S.Ct. 275, 139 L.Ed.2d 199 (1997).

19. Id. at 7–8.

20. Khan v. State Oil Co., 93 F.3d 1358 (7th Cir.1996), vac'd, 522 U.S. 3, 118 S.Ct. 275, 139 L.Ed.2d 199 (1997).

inconsistent with later decisions by the Supreme Court[,]" and a decision that "should be overruled."[21]

Accepting Judge Posner's invitation to reconsider *Albrecht*, the Supreme Court granted certiorari. The Justice Department and FTC filed a joint amicus brief that joined hands with manufacturer groups in urging that the *per se* rule should be abandoned for maximum resale price limits. Justice O'Connor's opinion showed the influence of the amicus brief in a number of areas. For example, the Court echoed the government's brief in its treatment of past precedent (focusing on *Albrecht* as an anachronism associated with *Schwinn* and largely ignoring the older *Kiefer-Stewart* case), in its policy discussion generally equating producer interests with those of the consumer, and in its failure to address situations in which a dealer might suffer genuine antitrust injury as the result of a vertically imposed price ceiling.[22] The Court also seemed to follow the government's brief in viewing maximum resale price maintenance as a backwater area for antitrust, noting at one point that "*Albrecht* has little or no relevance to ongoing enforcement of the Sherman Act."[23]

Justice O'Connor argued that injuries from vertical maximum price fixing described in *Albrecht* are "less serious than the Court imagined."[24] Justice O'Connor declared it unlikely that price ceilings might cause dealers to withhold services that consumers wanted. She supposed that the supplier would also be harmed, "making it unlikely that a supplier

21.　Id. at 1363.

22.　The government's brief cites without discussion two economic studies said to explore circumstances in which vertical maximum price fixing might be anticompetitive, but offers no explanation or support for these studies. Amicus Brief at 25 & n.13 (citing O'Brien & Shaffer, *Vertical Control with Bilateral Contracts*, 23 RAND J. ECON. 299 (1992); Perry & Besanko, *Resale Price Maintenance and Manufacturer Competition for Exclusive Dealerships*, 39 J. INDUS. ECON. 517 (1991)).

23.　522 U.S. at 18. The Court goes on to state: "Moreover, neither the parties nor any of the *amici curiae* have called our attention to any cases in which enforcement efforts have been directed solely against the conduct encompassed by *Albrecht's per se* rule." Id. at 18–19. Presumably, the reference to "enforcement efforts" includes only enforcement by federal or state governments, not private claims. In light of *Khan*, *ARCO* and a significant number of lower court decisions decided after *Albrecht*, it is clear that there have been substantial private claims. Among post-*Albrecht* court of appeals decisions arising from private claims of vertical maximum price fixing are: Acquaire v. Canada Dry Bottling Co., 24

F.3d 401 (2d Cir.1994); Caribe BMW, Inc. v. Bayerische Motoren Werke Aktiengesellschaft, 19 F.3d 745 (1st Cir. 1994); Northwest Publications, Inc. v. Crumb, 752 F.2d 473 (9th Cir.1985); Jack Walters & Sons Corp. v. Morton Bldg., Inc., 737 F.2d 698 (7th Cir.), cert. denied, 469 U.S. 1018, 105 S.Ct. 432, 83 L.Ed.2d 359 (1984); Blanton v. Mobil Oil Corp., 721 F.2d 1207 (9th Cir. 1983), cert. denied, 471 U.S. 1007, 105 S.Ct. 1874, 85 L.Ed.2d 166 (1985); Auburn News Co. v. Providence Journal Co., 659 F.2d 273 (1st Cir. 1981), cert. denied, 455 U.S. 921, 102 S.Ct. 1277, 71 L.Ed.2d 461 (1982); Yentsch v. Texaco, Inc., 630 F.2d 46 (2d Cir.1980); Arnott v. American Oil Co., 609 F.2d 873 (8th Cir.1979), cert. denied, 446 U.S. 918, 100 S.Ct. 1852, 64 L.Ed.2d 272 (1980); Knutson v. Daily Review, Inc., 548 F.2d 795 (9th Cir.1976), cert. denied, 433 U.S. 910, 97 S.Ct. 2977, 53 L.Ed.2d 1094 (1977); Bowen v. New York News, Inc., 522 F.2d 1242 (2d Cir.1975), cert. denied, 425 U.S. 936, 96 S.Ct. 1667, 48 L.Ed.2d 177 (1976); Blankenship v. Hearst Corp., 519 F.2d 418 (9th Cir.1975); Greene v. General Foods Corp., 517 F.2d 635 (5th Cir.1975), cert. denied, 424 U.S. 942, 96 S.Ct. 1409, 47 L.Ed.2d 348 (1976); Milsen Co. v. Southland Corp., 454 F.2d 363 (7th Cir.1971).

24.　522 U.S. at 18.

would set such a price as a matter of business judgment."[25] Implicitly, this comment assumes that a supplier's business judgment would be exercised with a prescient understanding of the costs and buyer preferences faced by every dealer in every local market and that the supplier would consistently choose long-term gain over immediate or short-term gain that might be seized through the exercise of market power.

The major argument for overturning the *per se* rule has long been that suppliers can use a vertically imposed price ceiling to prevent price gouging by a dealer with local monopoly power.[26] This dual monopoly argument was honed in criticism of the *Albrecht* case[27] and aptly applies to the newspaper's imposition of price ceilings on its exclusive distributors. In *Khan,* the Court picked up on this argument, stating that "both courts and antitrust scholars have noted that *Albrecht's* rule may actually harm consumers and manufacturers."[28] But whatever the truth of these observations, they had little bearing on the case before the Court. As in the *Albrecht* case thirty years earlier, the Court in *Khan* based its decision on a factual premise inconsistent with the facts before it. The *Khan* premise—that supplier-imposed price ceilings may counter the power of a dealer-monopolist—may be defended as sound policy if the dealer has market power. On the record in *Khan,* there was no evidence that the service station operator, bankrupted before the case was filed, had even the smallest modicum of market power.

8.7b. The Market Power Allowing a Supplier to Impose Maximum Resale Price Limits

Vertical price fixing, both minimum and maximum, is linked to the ongoing battle between supplier and dealer over the size of the dealer's margin. When minimum prices are imposed, the power usually rests with the dealer—the supplier imposes the minimum resale price in order to increase the dealer's margin and make it more attractive for the dealer to carry and promote the supplier's product. When maximum prices are imposed, the power rests with the supplier—the supplier imposes the maximum resale price in order to limit the dealer's margin. If the supplier did not possess market power in its transactions with the dealer, it would not impose the price ceiling lest it lose desired dealer outlets for its product. Market power is the ability of the supplier to raise its price above the competitive level without losing revenues that would make the price increase unprofitable.[29] In the context of vertically imposed maximum price ceilings, that market power can be exercised by

---

25. Id. at 17 (citing Lopatka, *Stephen Breyer and Modern Antitrust: A Snug Fit,* 40 Antitrust Bull. 1, 60 (1995)); Blair & Lang, supra note 15, at 1034.

26. The Supreme Court restated this argument in *Arco:* "When a manufacturer provides a dealer an exclusive area within which to distribute a product, the manufacturer's decision to fix a maximum resale price may actually protect consumers against exploitation by the dealer acting as a local monopolist." 495 U.S. at 343 n.13.

27. Among those who made the argument were 8 Areeda, supra note 15, ¶ 1635, at 395.

28. 522 U.S. at 18.

29. See the discussion of market power in § 2.2.

squeezing the dealer's margin—the supplier charges the dealer a high price and imposes a low ceiling on the dealer's resale price.

The opinion by Judge Posner in Khan v. State Oil Co. recognized that maximum resale prices could be used to "reduce * * * dealers' margin below the competitive price for the dealers' service."[30] Judge Posner also recognized that without market power, a supplier attempting to impose a resale price ceiling "would just drive * * * dealers into the arms of a competing supplier."[31] Still, he reasoned, a supplier lacking this market power might set a price ceiling that fixed a dealer's margin at "a competitive level," thereby preventing dealers "from exploiting a monopoly position."[32] But this strategy would entail substantial risk for a supplier lacking market power. Dealers operate in diverse labor, real estate, regulatory and taxation settings. Their costs will vary accordingly, as may the local demand for their products, or the intensity of competition from rival dealers. To obtain a competitive return, each dealer must set a price that allows for such varying costs, demand and competition. Indeed, even if all of these factors were identical among dealers, each might choose a different marketing strategy. One dealer might set a high margin in order to maintain a plush showroom and an attentive sales staff. Another might operate a low-margin, high-volume warehouse outlet. Unless a maximum retail price is set high enough to satisfy all dealers (in which case the price might be meaningless unless it was a disguised minimum price), a supplier lacking market power would lose dealers that find the margin too low. In short, a supplier could comfortably impose a meaningful maximum price only if it has market power in transactions with its dealers.

The market power that allows a supplier to impose maximum resale prices must be viewed in the context of a supplier-dealer relationship, not the interbrand market power more typically used to analyze horizontal restraints. For example, a supplier may be a monopolist in the sense that it is the only seller of a unique product. Or the supplier may be a monopsonist because it is the sole buyer of a certain type of distribution services. This sort of interbrand market power will distort competition and may give rise to claims under Section 2 of the Sherman Act. But this market power may not permit the supplier to impose maximum resale prices. If the supplier has fully exploited its market power in its sale of a product to the dealer, a dealer facing competition from other dealers would have to resell the product at a competitive markup. If forced to sell below that level, the dealer may simply refuse to carry the supplier's product.[33]

30. 93 F.3d 1358, 1361 (7th Cir.1996), vac'd, 522 U.S. 3, 118 S.Ct. 275, 139 L.Ed.2d 199 (1997).

31. Id. at 1362.

32. Id.

33. Even if the supplier is a monopsonist, a circumstance mentioned in the Court's opinion in *Khan*, 522 U.S. at 15–16, the supplier would still be unable to limit the dealer's resale margin below a competitive level unless the dealer had sunk costs associated with its dealership. See the discussion of sunk costs in this section, infra.

The supplier's power over dealers might stem from any of three sources: (1) the supplier's unexercised market power over the product that it sells to the dealer; (2) market power arising from distribution restraints (such as an exclusive dealer territory) that the supplier grants to the dealer; or (3) the supplier's relational market power: power linked to the dealer's substantial sunk costs or unrecoverable investment in the supplier's line. Vertical maximum price fixing is likely to be anticompetitive only if it is associated with market power of the third type.

8.7b1. A Supplier's Unexercised Market Power

A supplier may possess market power in sales to dealers because of inelastic demand for the supplier's product. Such inelastic demand may result because the supplier is a monopolist, because the seller's brand is strong, or because of temporary shortages or high demand conditions. Such a supplier will have market power to force dealers to accept a maximum resale price only if the supplier has not otherwise fully exercised its power in its sales to dealers. For example, if a monopolist extracts all of the possible monopoly profit by the price it charges to dealers, the monopolist (absent some other form of market power) will lack power to control the dealer's resale price.[34] Competition among dealers would push the dealer's margin down toward a competitive level. If the monopolist-manufacturer attempted to raise its price to the dealer above the optimal monopoly price, the dealer would maintain its margin, setting the resale price at a level that would cause a falloff in sales of the supplier's product. Or, the dealer might simply refuse to carry the product if it felt its retail margin were unduly squeezed.[35] On the other hand, if the manufacturer sells to the dealer at a price that has not fully exploited all of the product's market power, the dealer has the ability to resell the product at a markup that exploits the remainder of the unused market power.

Why would a supplier choose to sell a product to a dealer at a price that has not fully exploited the supplier's market power? Generally, one would expect a rational supplier to seek the highest return consistent with maintaining its business. For example, a monopolist-supplier, or a

---

34. In a landmark article, Spengler used economic theory to demonstrate that even if a monopolist-supplier has extracted maximum profit in sales to a monopoly retailer, the retailer would still impose an additional monopoly markup. Spengler, *Vertical Integration and Antitrust Policy*, 58 J. Pol. Econ. 347 (1950). Although Spengler's model can be questioned (for example, because it does not account for the vertical dimension of competition between a retailer and a supplier), his conclusions have implications for the efficiency inherent in some vertical integration and may justify a manufacturer's imposition of a maximum resale price if a price limit is a reasonable way of limiting the monopolist retailer's exploitation of

market power. See the discussion in § 8.7d4. Spengler's analysis, however, does not reach the important question of the nature of the supplier's market power over the dealer that allows imposition of the resale price restraint. As explained in this section, depending on the nature of the supplier's market power, the supplier's imposition of the price restraint may be procompetitive, competitively benign, or anticompetitive.

35. There might be an exception if the product is a necessity that the dealer must carry in order to bring business into the store. In that case, the dealer might be willing to carry the product at a loss.

supplier selling a strong brand, would generally benefit from wide-open distribution, with vigorous competition among dealers that drives dealer margins down, thereby maximizing the supplier's share of the revenue from retail price.[36] But there will be exceptions in which a supplier might choose not to fully exploit its market power. A newspaper publisher, for example, may choose not to fully exploit its monopoly in newspapers in order to compete for advertising revenue that might flow to non-newspaper advertisers such as radio or television. A supplier might also price below a level that fully exploits market power in order to promote goodwill (perhaps in the face of unusual demand or product shortages), to limit price, or to promote the sale of related products for which no market power is present. In *Kiefer-Stewart*, Seagram announced its program of maximum prices with the following statement: "[I]t is not in our nor the public's interest to raise whiskey prices. By holding the price line we can win the fullest measure of public appreciation and confidence in our industry."[37]

If the supplier has not fully exploited the market power available to it because of a conscious marketing strategy, the supplier could object to the dealer's undercutting that strategy by raising dealer margin to exploit the unused power. To prevent such dealer conduct, the supplier might choose to impose resale price ceilings. The supplier has little or no ability to squeeze dealer margins below competitive levels as long as the dealer is free to walk away if the margin is deemed inadequate. Hence, if the supplier's only source of market power over the dealer is the supplier's unexercised market power in the product that it sells, there is little likelihood that vertical maximum price fixing will injure dealers or produce significant anticompetitive results.

8.7b2. Distribution Restraints that Limit Dealer Intrabrand Competition

A second type of market power that the supplier may possess in transactions with dealers arises from distribution restraints that limit competition among dealers. For example, a dealer might be granted an exclusive right to sell the supplier's product in a given location (an exclusive territory). Operating with some assurance that a higher retail price would not be undercut, the dealer may raise its price and receive a higher resale margin than could occur in the absence of the distribution restraint. Consumer demand for the product may increase as the result of promotional efforts by the retailer. But it is not higher consumer demand, but the retailer's increased margin, that gives the supplier market power in its transactions with the dealer. Because of the dealer's

---

36. If a product is distributed through multibrand retailers, the supplier of a strong brand is less likely to feel a need for distribution restraints as a means of obtaining a dealer network because consumer demand for the brand will make a dealer anxious to carry it. Steiner, *How Manufacturers Deal with the Price–Cutting Retailer:* *When Are Vertical Restraints Efficient?* 65 ANTITRUST L.J. 407, 412 (1997)(noting that "famous advertised brands are sold at very thin [retail] markups over factory price").

37. Kiefer–Stewart Co. v. Joseph E. Seagram & Sons, Inc., 182 F.2d 228, 230 (7th Cir.1950), rev'd, 340 U.S. 211, 71 S.Ct. 259, 95 L.Ed. 219 (1951).

higher margin, the dealer now will have a somewhat inelastic demand for the supplier's product. Put another way, within limits, price increases by the supplier (or attempts to squeeze the retailer's resale margin) will not reduce the dealer's demand for the supplier's product.

When a supplier imposes distribution restraints, those restraints may cause competitive injury that gives rise to an antitrust complaint. But many distribution restraints, including the location clause described above, are likely to be lawful. In furtherance of a marketing strategy that includes lawful use of a distribution restraint, a supplier may find it advantageous to impose a maximum resale price that limits the markup charged by the dealer. The price ceiling, in effect, would limit the dealer's ability to exploit any market power conferred by the distribution restraint. But the supplier cannot squeeze the dealer's margin below a competitive level nor distort the dealer's marketing decisions. The supplier's ability to squeeze the dealer's margin is limited because the dealer can reject further sales of the supplier's product if the dealer deems the margin unacceptably low. The supplier may, through use of the price ceiling, take back some of the market power it conferred by granting the distribution restraint, but the supplier cannot force the dealer to accept a margin that the dealer deems below the market level. As discussed below, the situation changes if, in addition to market power based on the distribution restraint, the supplier also possesses relational market power in its transactions with a dealer.

8.7b3.   A Supplier's Relational Market Power over a Dealer

Relational power is the third type of market power that the supplier may possess over dealers, and that would permit the supplier to impose maximum resale prices. A supplier's relational market power may arise from: sunk costs incurred by a dealer in connection with carrying the supplier's line; (2) additional nonrecoverable costs that the supplier can impose on a nonconforming dealer; or (3) business opportunities that a supplier can deny a nonconforming dealer.[38]

Sunk costs are fixed costs that cannot be recovered if a business is sold or abandoned. Such costs are often substantial when the dealer is engaged in exclusive selling–selling one supplier's line to the exclusion of other suppliers. Suppliers may encourage dealers to make substantial investments in carrying the supplier's line in return for a supplier's grant of an exclusive territory. Substantial sunk dealer investments are also a central feature of franchising. See the discussion in § 6. b. The market power that a supplier possesses as a result of dealer investments already committed to carrying the supplier's line is minimal if that investment has already been lost. But if the investment is in business assets that have a variable value based upon the business performance of the dealer, the dealer will be beholden to the supplier in an effort to gain favors and avoid additional costs that the supplier might otherwise impose. For example, the supplier may intensify inspections or other

---

38. Relational market power is discussed in § 2.4e2iv.

requirements that impose costs on the dealer. Or the supplier may grant favors in the form of new products or products in short supply. Disfavored dealers can expect no such favors and may face costs that the supplier can impose at its discretion. Under these circumstances, the supplier will have power over price in its dealings with the dealer.

Most litigated cases involving vertical maximum price fixing have not focused on a supplier's relational market power. Understandably so, because theorists have been slow to pinpoint the source of this market power even when abusively exercised. But judicial recognition of such abuses and intuitive perception of their anticompetitive effects has in some cases foreshadowed theoretical explanation.

What all examples of relational market power have in common is that the dealer is to some degree locked into its relationship with the supplier. One case that did use the term "lock-in" was Milsen Co. v. Southland Corp.,[39] a 1971 Seventh Circuit case in which the court recognized the role of sunk costs in coercing franchisee behavior. The franchisees operated convenience stores subject to requirements that they purchase specified supplies from a designated supplier and maximum resale prices imposed by the franchisor, Open Pantry. In explaining how Open Pantry used uncollected franchise fees to compel compliance by franchisees, the court said:

> The franchisor then allowed the store owners to fall farther and farther behind in their payments of franchise fees. Open Pantry tried to collect fees only when a store owner began buying a different brand of dairy products or raised the resale price above the franchisor's maximum. Open Pantry's practice in effect *locked plaintiffs into* a situation where their franchises were safe as long as they cooperated with the franchisor's merchandising program. A single deviation brought the threat that the franchise would be terminated because of the unpaid fees. The fee-rebate system became both carrot and stick.[40]

The practice of enforcing the letter of a franchise contract only when the franchisor wishes to force certain behavior from the franchisee is a variant on the sunk costs theme. In such instances, the franchisor's market power over the franchisee arises directly from the franchisee's wish to avoid the financial loss associated with literal compliance with the contract. These additional compliance costs are not themselves sunk costs. But the franchisor's market power is related to the franchisee's sunk costs—if the franchisee had no significant sunk costs, it would terminate its business relations with the franchisor rather than subject itself to the franchisor's literal compliance demands. Moreover, selectively enforced literal compliance can be a tool used by the franchisor to bring home the threat of termination, a threat that is ominous to the franchisee because of substantial sunk costs.

---

39.   454 F.2d 363 (7th Cir.1971).   **40.**   Id. at 368 (emphasis added).

Selectively enforced compliance was an issue in at least one other post-*Albrecht* vertical maximum price fixing case. In Blanton v. Mobil Oil Corp.,[41] service station dealers alleged that Mobil coerced them into purchases of tires, batteries and accessories (a tie-in) and into lowering the retail price on gasoline (vertical maximum price fixing). In affirming a jury verdict for the franchisee, the Ninth Circuit gave cryptic treatment to the vertical maximum price fixing claim, but explained the nature of the franchisor's market power in its treatment of the tie-in claim. The court recounted a dealer's testimony that, after refusing to make a large purchase of Mobil tires, "Mobil representatives made an inspection of his station and cited him for lease violations that included placement of trash in the trash enclosure, an unauthorized handle guard on the bathroom door that had been affixed to avoid vandalism, and damage to his personally owned desk."[42]

8.7c. The Antitrust Injury from Exploitation of Relational Market Power

The Supreme Court has now recognized, in Eastman Kodak Co. v. Image Technical Services, Inc.,[43] that a buyer may be locked into an investment by "switching costs" giving rise to a form of power cognizable under antitrust. In agreeing with the court of appeals that summary judgment had been improperly granted for the defendant, the Court's opinion in *Kodak* considered switching costs as a potential source of market power both for purposes of a tie-in analysis under Section 1 of the Sherman Act and a monopolization analysis under Section 2 of the Sherman Act. There is no reason to assume that this form of market power is irrelevant when addressing other traditional antitrust violations.[44] It has been argued that any market power exercised by a supplier as the result of dealer sunk costs will be negated by the supplier's need to maintain its business reputation. Reputation protection may outweigh other motives for a supplier thinking only of long-term return. It hardly can explain many actual examples of dealer exploitation.[45]

If a supplier is able to impose vertical maximum price fixing on its dealers as a result of dealer sunk costs, there is a substantial likelihood that this exercise of market power will produce allocation distortions. The dealer has risked a substantial amount of its own funds to carry the producer's line. The dealer has firsthand knowledge of its own costs, including those arising from the local entrepreneurial environment (costs associated with labor, regulatory and taxation conditions) as well as any idiosyncracies associated with local demand (local purchaser likes

---

41. 721 F.2d 1207 (9th Cir.1983), cert. denied, 471 U.S. 1007, 105 S.Ct. 1874, 85 L.Ed.2d 166 (1985).

42. Id. at 1210–11. Other dealers testified that they were threatened with loss of their lease if they refused to buy tires or other Mobil products. Id. at 1211.

43. 504 U.S. 451, 112 S.Ct. 2072, 119 L.Ed.2d 265 (1992).

44. See the discussion of the implications of *Kodak* for finding single brand market power and various criticisms of that holding in § 2.4e1.

45. These arguments, particularly relevant in the context of franchising, are discussed in § 6.4c3ii.

and dislikes). With its own capital at risk, the dealer has a substantial incentive to make wise and timely pricing decisions. Indeed, the essence of the free market system is that choices are made by those whose money is on the line.[46] If the dealership fails, the dealer bears most or all of the financial loss.

The premise that the market system functions best when primary risk bearers make pricing decisions was of course at the root of the Supreme Court's holdings establishing the *per se* rule. As Justice White put it in *Albrecht*: "[S]chemes to fix maximum prices, by substituting the perhaps erroneous judgment of a seller for the forces of the competitive market, may severely intrude upon the ability of buyers to compete and survive in that market."[47] Justice White went on to explain that the supplier might set the price too low for the dealer to provide services essential to value placed by consumers in the product sold by the dealer. This, of course, is one of the possible allocative injuries that could be caused by maximum price ceilings, but by no means the only one. A dealer may be driven out of business altogether (as the service station dealer in *Khan* allegedly was) or may be forced to operate over a longer period with an inadequate return. Perhaps the dealer will continue to provide the services considered essential by consumers but will try to make up revenue losses by raising prices on ancillary goods or services.

A supplier-imposed margin squeeze could lead to a distortion in the capital market. The dealer has invested its capital in a business that may be underperforming, earning less than the competitive rate available on other investments. A fortunate dealer may be able to offset the lower investment return by raising its prices on other goods and services that it sells, or by withholding services that consumers might prefer. But market conditions may not permit these adjustments, with the result that the dealer is saddled with an underperforming investment or even financial failure.

Shifting inventory, pricing and marketing decisions away from the player whose capital is primarily at risk also invites corruption and related forms of behavior that undermine competitive performance. Such competition distorting behavior is more likely to occur when purchasing decisions are made by those that have little or no capital at risk. It is often asserted that uninvolved decision-makers, whether in government or business, can be induced to make poor buying choices based upon surreptitious payments, rebates or personal favors. An upstream firm with a locked-in downstream customer may be in a comparable position. If it has power and authority to specify inputs purchased by downstream firms it may accept payments from a supplier of such inputs and then force the unwanted product on a dealer with sunk costs; or it may force

---

46. Investors in stocks and bonds would of course expect to delegate business decisions to the management of the company in which they invest. But these investors have consciously chosen a passive form of investment and usually enjoy a liquidity (the abil- ity to sell stocks and bonds) that a dealer with sunk costs does not enjoy.

47. Albrecht v. Herald Co., 390 U.S. 145, 152, 88 S.Ct. 869, 19 L.Ed.2d 998 (1968).

the dealer to accept a resale margin below a competitive level. This conduct can occur through the use of an unlawful tie-in or through imposition of a maximum resale price. Either way, the competitive injury to the dealer, and to a system of efficient capital and resource allocation, is similar.

8.7d. Post-*Khan*: A Structured Rule of Reason

Judicial treatment of vertical maximum price fixing after *Khan* is uncertain. Some of the discussion in *Khan* suggests hostility to any claim of vertical maximum price fixing.[48] On the other hand, the Court did not declare all such price fixing to be lawful and clearly left room for further development of the law. It is possible to describe a structured rule of reason for vertical maximum price fixing that would incorporate sound economic policy and at the same time provide a standard that is both judicially manageable and susceptible to reasonably precise counseling. Such a rule would include the following three elements: (1) a presumption of legality for any vertically imposed maximum price if the dealer has no reasonably incurred and substantial sunk costs linked to carrying the producer's line; (2) a presumption of illegality if the seller, as the result of the dealer's reasonably incurred and substantial sunk investment in carrying the producer's line, has power over the dealer; and (3) an opportunity to rebut the presumption of illegality if the supplier demonstrates both that the resale price ceiling is imposed in pursuit of a procompetitive marketing strategy *and* that the dealer is a natural monopolist.

8.7d1. *A Presumption of Legality When the Supplier Lacks Significant Relational Market Power*

When a supplier lacks significant market power over a dealer carrying the producer's line, any maximum resale price imposed by the supplier is likely to have minimal anticompetitive effects. In particular, the supplier will have slight ability to squeeze the dealer's margin. If the supplier-imposed maximum price were to force the dealer's margin below a competitive level, the dealer could simply refuse to carry the supplier's product.

The record in *Kiefer-Stewart* suggests facts that may warrant application of this safe harbor. From what is known of the background of that case, it would appear that the wholesaler's inelastic demand for Seagram's line stemmed not from wholesaler sunk investment committed to that line, but to the temporary product shortages and heightened demand during the immediate post-World War II era. Multiline wholesalers carrying products of a number of liquor producers, if subject to Seagram's maximum resale prices, would presumably be able to drop the Seagram's line without suffering substantial economic loss. Even if the wholesaler's survival depended on its ability to carry Seagram's line, if

---

48. Perhaps picking up on this hostility, the Ninth Circuit cited *Khan* in affirming without economic analysis a district court dismissal of maximum price fixing claims in *Mularkey v. Holsum Bakery, Inc.,* 146 F.3d 1064, 1065 n. 1 (9th Cir.1998) (per curiam).

the wholesaler's inventory and warehouse facilities could have been sold at or near cost, the wholesaler's sunk costs might have been insubstantial.

8.7d2. A Presumption of Illegality if the Dealer Possesses Significant Relational Market Power

When a supplier in a continuing relationship can impose nonrecoverable costs on its dealers, the result—an inelastic demand for the supplier's products—allows it to squeeze dealer margins below competitive levels. As the previous analysis suggests, this is likely to produce distortions in the capital market (dealer capital investments that underperform the market) and distortions in the allocation of goods and services (the over- or underpricing of some goods or services, or the denial of services that consumers would prefer to receive).

This presumption is likely to apply widely in franchise systems in which franchisees make substantial unrecoverable investments in their outlets. See the discussion in § 6.4c2ii. Although the plaintiff in *Khan* may or may not fit this description, some service station dealers certainly do. Service station dealers may often be dependent on the franchisor alone for receiving their critical inventory of gasoline, so any threat to terminate the franchisee, to inspect it more vigorously, or deny valuable franchisor-supplied services may give the franchisor substantial market power in transactions with dealers that have a substantial sunk investment at risk.

8.7d3. Is the Defendant's Conduct Lawful if No Market Power Existed When the Maximum Resale Price Was Imposed?

In some instances, an upstream supplier may impose a maximum resale price on a dealer at the time when no market power over the dealer exists. This might occur, for example, in a franchising context when the franchisor imposes specified resale prices at the time the franchisee signs the initial franchise contract. After the contract is signed, the franchisee may be locked in and subject to the franchisor's power over price. But the agreement to set a maximum resale price may have been negotiated before any such power existed. If there were minimal information problems associated with this agreement and both the supplier and the dealer were free to negotiate this provision, a *Kodak* theory based on information problems and subsequent lock-in cannot be sustained. On the other hand, a supplier with a popular franchise negotiating with each franchisee individually may exact maximum-price-setting authority as boilerplate. These circumstances are conducive to information problems on the part of the dealer and a subsequent lock-in, which, under the teaching of *Kodak,* may warrant a finding of an abusive exercise of market power. Some courts, however, read *Kodak* narrowly to require a change of behavior on the part of the defendant after the contract is signed. This reading of *Kodak* seems to ignore the underlying information problems that may exist before the contract was signed and opens the door for widespread abuse of dealers or franchisees based on broadly worded contract boilerplate inserted by suppliers. See the discussion in § 8.3d6.

8.7d4.   Rebutting the Presumption of Anticompetitive Effect

The outpouring of criticism provoked by *Albrecht* rests on the logic that the price ceilings imposed by the newspaper in that case probably benefitted both the publisher (by making its sale of advertising space more competitive) and consumers (by maintaining low rates on newspaper subscriptions). But the circumstances that lead to a procompetitive result for the publisher's resale price ceilings should be carefully examined.

If the publisher had no market power in its dealings with the distributor (an unlikely but possible circumstance),[49] the publisher could squeeze the distributor's margin down to a competitive level, but not below it—all to the benefit of the publisher and consumers. But if a supplier is permitted to use sunk costs as a basis for ratcheting down dealer margins, there is no assurance that the ratcheting will stop at a competitive margin. If dealer margins are forced below a competitive level, allocation distortions are likely—because of the capital the dealer unwisely and unprofitably invested in distribution and perhaps because the dealer has reduced incentive to sell a product subject to a squeezed margin and may cut back on services that consumers desire. Supplier concern about business reputation will provide a countervailing incentive not to abuse their dealers. Still, even with the best of intent, a supplier faces the rather formidable task of determining each and every dealer's local costs, demand characteristics, and marketing strategies. If the supplier cannot or does not do so, there is heightened risk that one or more dealers will be forced to price below a competitive margin.

The risk of anticompetitive margin squeezing may be tolerable if the benefits from allowing a vertically imposed price ceiling are substantial. In particular, if the supplier shows (1) that it is subject to substantial interbrand competitive discipline, and (2) that the dealer is a natural monopolist whose power over the local market cannot be efficiently constrained through means other than the vertically imposed price ceiling, the supplier's vertical maximum price fixing should be lawful. Allowing this exception to the presumption of illegality creates some risk of opportunistic or abusive behavior toward dealers, but it is a risk that may be offset by clear and convincing evidence of the benefits of a maximum resale price.

In *Albrecht*, the first of these preconditions appears to have been satisfied. The publisher was subject to interbrand competitive discipline based upon its need to sell advertising (by keeping subscription rates low and circulation high). The need to compete in the advertising market provided substantial competitive discipline in the sale of newspaper

---

49.   According to Justice Douglas' separate opinion in *Albrecht*, the dealer in that case purchased its route for $11,000 and received: (1) a list of subscribers; (2) a used truck; and (3) a newspaper tying machine. 390 U.S. at 155 (Douglas, J., concurring). This outlay does not suggest major sunk costs.

subscriptions. The second precondition—that the dealer must be a monopolist whose monopoly power cannot be efficiently mitigated through means other than the use of maximum resale price ceilings—may or may not have been met in *Albrecht*. Among the ways in which a dealer's monopoly power might be disciplined are: (1) creating competing dealerships; and (2) integrating vertically. Newspaper distribution would seem most efficient when distributors are granted exclusive territories–it would be markedly less efficient to have competing distributors running trucks over the same routes at the same hours of the day. That exclusive territories are the most efficient means of newspaper distribution is suggested not only by the universality of this practice in the newspaper industry, but also by the response of many newspaper publishers to the *Albrecht* ruling. When faced with a proscription on vertically imposed price ceilings, many publishers apparently chose to integrate forward into newspaper distribution.[50] Once the paper owned its distributors, it could lawfully limit subscription prices in order to better compete in the advertising market.

Is vertical integration an efficient alternative to maximum resale price ceilings? The answer will depend upon the extent to which distributors operate with economies of scope that cannot be duplicated when the newspaper takes over its own distribution. For example, if distributors can operate more efficiently by distributing multiple newspapers and perhaps magazines as well, the newspaper may have difficulty in taking on this broader range of distribution activities in order to maintain an efficient operation. On the other hand, if a newspaper can easily and smoothly implement a delivery system, then vertical integration is likely to be efficient. For example, a newspaper publisher might assume control of the subscription and billing process, but still contract with an independent contractor for delivery of the papers, thereby obtaining the needed control to set maximum price limits but still minimizing risk in running the delivery business.

In *Khan*, the Supreme Court apparently assumed that forced vertical integration associated with a *per se* rule against vertical maximum price fixing would be inefficient. The Court said: " 'the ban on maximum resale price limitations declared in *Albrecht* in the name of "dealer freedom" has actually prompted many suppliers to integrate forward into distribution, thus eliminating the very independent trader for whom *Albrecht* professed solicitude.' "[51] But there is nothing in the record that demonstrates that the form of integration chosen by newspapers was in fact inefficient.

A rule that prohibits some uses of vertical maximum price fixing may also serve as a useful constraint on suppliers that consider granting exclusive territories. Although limited territorial protection such as location clauses may have relatively few anticompetitive effects, when

---

50. Paschall v. Kansas City Star Co., 727 F.2d 692 (8th Cir.), cert. denied, 469 U.S. 872, 105 S.Ct. 222, 83 L.Ed.2d 152 (1984).

51. State Oil Co. v. Khan, 522 U.S. 3, 16–17, 118 S.Ct. 275, 139 L.Ed.2d 199 (1997)(quoting 8 Areeda, supra note 15, ¶ 1635, at 395).

the preclusion of intrabrand competition is substantial, exclusive territories can have substantial anticompetitive effects. Efficient distribution in most industries probably does not compel the use of exclusive territories at the retail level. Immoderate use of exclusive territories can place suppliers at the mercy of an inefficient or indolent dealer and eliminate the significant benefits of intrabrand competition that flow both to the supplier (by limiting dealer margins) and the consumer (by encouraging efficient distribution and lower prices). Indeed, in many heavily franchised industries, franchisors fiercely resist granting exclusive territories to franchisees.[52]

Exclusive territories are, under the teaching of *Sylvania*,[53] to be assessed under the rule of reason. But *Sylvania* does not place exclusive territories on a pedestal of *per se* legality. *Sylvania* involved not exclusive territories but location clauses that permitted intrabrand competition among retailers operating out of prescribed locations. Nor should *Sylvania* be read as requiring approval of vertical maximum price fixing associated with the use of exclusive territories. In the face of reasonable and substantial dealer sunk costs, maximum price ceilings should be tolerated only in cases in which the evidence of the efficiency of exclusive territories is convincing and the unavailability of efficient alternatives (such as vertical integration) has been demonstrated.

8.7e. The Aftermath of *Khan*: Some Pitfalls of Counseling

The major uncertainty after *Khan* concerns the method and result of applying a rule of reason analysis to a resale price ceiling, an issue addressed in § 8.7d. But counseling problems are compounded by other troublesome and unresolved issues. In particular: (1) what is labeled as a maximum resale price might be attacked as a minimum price subject to the *per se* rule; (2) what appears to be a distribution restraint might be attacked under a horizontal theory, again subjecting the restraint to the *per se* rule; (3) legal limitations other than those arising from the Sherman Act could be invoked against a vertically imposed price ceiling; and (4) dealers may seek means of thwarting a vertically imposed price ceiling, raising the supplier's administrative and legal enforcement costs.

8.7e1. Distinguishing Between Maximum and Minimum Resale Prices

As long as both maximum and minimum resale prices were *per se* unlawful, courts could sidestep the issue of resolving which form of vertical price fixing was involved. In either case, a *per se* rule of illegality applied.[54] The possibility that a "maximum" resale price could be a

---

52. See the discussion in § 8.9g2.

53. Continental T.V., Inc. v. GTE Sylvania Inc., 433 U.S. 36, 97 S.Ct. 2549, 53 L.Ed.2d 568 (1977).

54. In Kiefer–Stewart Co. v. Joseph E. Seagram & Sons, Inc., the Court did not

hesitate to label the defendants' conduct as involving maximum price fixing, but the opinion suggests that the prices that were fixed ended up being minimum prices as well. 340 U.S. 211, 214, 71 S.Ct. 259, 95 L.Ed. 219 (1951).

disguised minimum price limit was raised by Justice White in *Albrecht*.[55] But the Court dispatched this issue summarily in *Khan*, stating only that use of maximum price fixing to mask minimum price fixing "can be appropriately recognized and punished under the rule of reason."[56] It is unclear at the outset why a minimum resale price disguised as a "maximum" would be subject to anything other than a *per se* rule. If the "maximum" label is merely a disguise to cover true minimum price fixing, the *per se* rule applicable to other vertical minimum price fixing should govern.

If a vertically imposed price is a maximum, a rule of reason will apply, so distinguishing between minimum and maximum is now pivotal. Indeed, in an effort to avoid the *per se* rule, defendants can be expected to design vertically imposed price limits to appear as maximum limits and routinely assert that the *per se* rule does not apply. Plaintiffs can be expected to routinely counter that every fixed resale price labeled as "maximum" is in fact a "minimum." In most cases, the distinction should be an easy one to make. If the supplier calls the price limit a ceiling, and many dealers actually price under the limit, one might safely conclude that the supplier's label is accurate. But courts should pay close attention to which party has power in the vertical relationship. If market power rests with the supplier, the price limit is likely to be a maximum; if power rests with the dealers, the price limit is likely to be a minimum. Unless the supplier has market power in its dealings with dealers, it will not attempt to impose a margin-squeezing maximum price limit lest it lose valued members of its dealer network. See the discussion in § 8.7b.

There are still potential ambiguities. Consider cases in which all of the downstream dealers set exactly the price described as a maximum, with none pricing above or below it. And what if the downstream dealers have countervailing power in their negotiations with the supplier? Under these circumstances, distinguishing between a maximum and minimum price may be difficult. For example, if a health care provider sets a "maximum" limit on compensation for doctors, but it is clear that the doctors have negotiating leverage and are involved in setting this limit, can it safely be concluded that the price limit is a "maximum"? In the absence of any clear precedent resolving the classification issue, clients cannot be securely counseled that the rule of reason will apply. In the case of the doctors, the issue is further complicated because of the possibility of a horizontal dimension to this price fixing, a circumstance discussed in the next section.

8.7e2. *Attacking Maximum Prices Under a Horizontal Theory*

If more than one supplier is involved in a scheme to set a dealer's maximum resale prices, the arrangement becomes a horizontal conspira-

---

55. Albrecht v. Herald Co., 390 U.S. 145, 153, 88 S.Ct. 869, 19 L.Ed.2d 998 (1968).

56. State Oil Co. v. Khan, 522 U.S. 3, 17, 118 S.Ct. 275, 139 L.Ed.2d 199 (1997). The Court cites discussion of this issue by Easterbrook, supra note, at 901–04, and Pitofsky, *In Defense of Discounters: The No–Frills Case for a* Per Se *Rule Against Vertical Price Fixing,* 71 Geo L.J. 1487, 1490 n.17 (1983).

cy likely subject to the *per se* rule. The same result is likely if more than one dealer is involved in the arrangement. This might occur, for example, if the supplier consults with a number of dealers before imposing a maximum resale price.[57] In Arizona v. Maricopa County Medical Society,[58] doctors and an insurance company were involved in an arrangement to set maximum reimbursable rates for medical procedures and services. The Court held that such an arrangement was subject to the *per se* rule as an unlawful horizontal restraint. Although some of the Court's reasoning in *Khan* might suggest that all maximum price ceilings, whether horizontal or vertical, should be subject to the rule of reason, the Court did not address this issue directly. *Maricopa* thus remains the reigning precedent when there is a horizontal dimension to the conspiracy.

8.7e3. Vulnerability of Maximum Prices to Non–Sherman Act Claims

Much of the litigation between dealers and suppliers, particularly those in a franchise relationship, has moved beyond the federal antitrust domain into areas of state antitrust law, state and federal franchise statutes, and even the law of contracts.[59] No catalogue of these remedies is offered here, except to note that dealers whose sunk costs are at risk are highly motivated to seek relief wherever it might be available.

8.7e4. Other Administrative and Legal Costs

Even if a given application of a vertical price restraint is clearly lawful, its implementation may still require substantial management and legal costs. Imposition of a maximum price is, after all, very much akin to the type of price regulation that governments have sometimes sought to impose, at least since the time of the Roman Emperor Diocletian, usually with markedly mixed results.[60] When demand exceeds available supply, or when a downstream seller perceives that it is being undercompensated for its sales, that seller has a substantial incentive to cheat on

---

57. United States v. General Motors Corp., 384 U.S. 127, 86 S.Ct. 1321, 16 L.Ed.2d 415 (1966) (distribution restraints imposed by General Motors at the behest of a dealers association held to involve a classic horizontal restraint of trade).

58. 457 U.S. 332, 102 S.Ct. 2466, 73 L.Ed.2d 48 (1982).

59. States have enacted a variety of franchise regulation legislation as well as more specific provisions governing automobile dealers, petroleum dealers, alcoholic beverage dealers and farm equipment dealers. ABA SECTION OF ANTITRUST LAW, MONOGRAPH 17, FRANCHISE PROTECTION: LAWS AGAINST TERMINATION AND THE ESTABLISHMENT OF ADDITIONAL FRANCHISES 16–19 (1990). Going beyond the franchisee protections provided by these statutes, a few courts have

granted relief to franchisees based upon the franchisor's implied covenant of good faith linked to the franchise contract. In re Vylene Enters., Inc., 90 F.3d 1472 (9th Cir. 1996); Scheck v. Burger King Corp., 798 F.Supp. 692 (S.D.Fla.1992); Cherick Distribs., Inc. v. Polar Corp., 669 N.E.2d 218 (Mass.App.Ct.1996).

60. The Roman Emperor Diocletian (284–305 A.D.) decreed price ceilings on goods and services such as bread, beer, hair cuts and children's school tuition. Although the death penalty was decreed for violators, the effort apparently was abandoned by Diocletian's successors. For a description of Diocletian's maximum price ceilings, see R. ZIMMERMANN, THE LAW OF OBLIGATION, ROMAN FOUNDATIONS OF THE CIVILIAN TRADITION 260–61 & nn.162–65 (1990).

the price ceiling. Given the likelihood of dealer resistance to supplier-imposed price ceilings, suppliers should reckon with administrative and legal costs associated with enforcing the price ceiling.

All of this suggests the importance of a supplier choosing its conduct toward dealers with sensitivity to the existence of supplier relational market power over dealers. For even if those sunk costs do not become the pivotal point for antitrust analysis in areas such as maximum resale prices, unrecoverable dealer costs will be an important motivation for a dealer to resist adherence to a price ceiling, or to challenge that ceiling as unlawful, using whatever vehicle the law might provide for bringing suit. In contrast, a dealer that has insignificant sunk costs has less incentive to seek circumvention or legal recourse.

§ 8.8 National Accounts and Dual Distribution

A supplier's restrictions on dealer access to large customers, such as retail chains or government units (sometimes referred to as national accounts), is considered here as a downstream power restraint, although its use may be an indication that the supplier has sufficient upstream power to withhold certain accounts from downstream dealers. These restraints have been upheld under rule of reason analysis.[1] The problem with reserving certain accounts for the supplier is that it may create a "dual distribution" system, with the supplier competing with its independent distributors for downstream customers. Once cast as competitors, the relationship between a supplier that also distributes and independent distributors may be characterized as a horizontal relationship subject to the per se rule. The outcome of a case should not turn on whether the relationship is characterized as horizontal or vertical, but on whether the particular practice is harmful to competition.

A supplier that reserves national accounts for itself can argue that there is no dual distribution (and therefore no horizontal relation) as long as independent distributors are absolutely barred from competing for the national accounts. But the distinction is a disquieting formalism because an absolute bar on competition for the national accounts is more harmful to intrabrand competition than a true dual distribution arrangement in which the supplier and independent distributors may compete for the same accounts.

Whether a supplier reserves national accounts for itself or allows competition between the supplier and independent distributors for those accounts (dual distribution), the rule of reason should apply. When these allocations do not operate at the retail level, antitrust policy should probably accord the supplier discretion to set up the distribution system in the manner it deems best suited for its marketing goals. Courts have

§ 8.8

1. White Motor Co. v. United States, 372 U.S. 253, 273–74, 83 S.Ct. 696, 9 L.Ed.2d 738 (1963)(supplier reserves government sales for itself); Wisconsin Music Network, Inc. v. Muzak Ltd. Partnership, 5 F.3d 218, 222 (7th Cir.1993) (multiterritory accounts reserved for supplier); Snap–On Tools Corp. v. FTC, 321 F.2d 825, 835–36 (7th Cir.1963)(supplier reserved certain accounts for itself).

generally tolerated such allocations, including arrangements characterized as dual distribution.[2] There is, however, at least one circumstance in which customer allocations such as national accounts raise troublesome issues. That is when the customer allocation is used as a tool to eliminate arbitrage and foster price discrimination, a circumstance discussed in § 7.5b.

Suppliers that are considering reserving specified accounts for themselves should consider pragmatic as well as legal effects. Removing an account from a distributor that the distributor has long served will raise the ire of that distributor. If the distributor has reasonably invested its own resources in nonrecoverable plant and equipment used to serve that account, the distributor may have a credible sunk cost or lock-in argument that would bolster an antitrust claim against the supplier.[3] Even if a federal antitrust claim were not propitious for the distributor, the financial loss associated with the sunk cost investment might impel the distributor to grasp other possible remedies, such as state antitrust or unfair trade claims. A supplier that wishes to exercise greater control over national accounts may wish to consider alternatives to allocations that terminate the distributor's role. For example, a consignment arrangement could allow the supplier to control the resale price to national accounts but still permit the distributor to earn a commission on sales.

§ 8.9   Franchise Antitrust Claims in the Courts

This section examines franchisee-initiated antitrust claims of tie-ins, forced exclusive dealing, vertical maximum price fixing, monopolization and attempted monopolization. The section separately addresses antitrust claims challenging franchisees' cooperative behavior. Most of these claims arise out of a franchise relationship in which upstream power of the franchisor can be exercised abusively and in a manner that may undermine competition.

8.9a.   Early Precedents

8.9a1.   *Unfocused Scrutiny*

Although use of franchising accelerated after the Second World War, its use in some industries was well established before that time. Soft drink bottlers and car dealers, for example, were often established as franchisees early in the century. Early forms of retail franchising were appearing in the petroleum industry by 1923, when the Supreme Court decided FTC v. Sinclair Refining Co.[1] Against the FTC's challenge of an

---

2. Glacier Optical, Inc. v. Optique du Monde, Ltd., 46 F.3d 1141, 1995–1 Trade Cas. (CCH) ¶ 70,878 (9th Cir.1995)(per curiam)(summary judgment for defendants affirmed notwithstanding dual distribution); Smalley & Co. v. Emerson & Cuming, Inc., 13 F.3d 366 (10th Cir.1993). *But see* Graphic Prods. Distribs., Inc. v. Itek Corp., 717 F.2d 1560 (11th Cir.1983).

3. Such an argument would be based on the lock-in theory approvingly discussed in Eastman Kodak Co. v. Image Technical Services, Inc., 504 U.S. 451, 112 S.Ct. 2072, 119 L.Ed.2d 265 (1992).

§ 8.9

1. 261 U.S. 463, 43 S.Ct. 450, 67 L.Ed. 746 (1923).

unlawful tie under Section 3 of the Clayton Act, the Court upheld Sinclair's requirement that gasoline pumps leased to dealers could be used only to sell Sinclair brand gas. Gasoline, the Court noted, was readily available from other sources and dealers could sell such gasoline using pumps acquired from someone other than Sinclair.[2]

In *Sinclair*, as in other early franchise antitrust cases, judicial assessment was under prevailing antitrust standards without discussion of (or perhaps even awareness of) the unique features of franchising. In Pick Manufacturing Co. v. General Motors Corp.,[3] the Supreme Court upheld lower court rulings that a provision in the GM dealers' contracts requiring dealers to sell only parts manufactured or authorized by General Motors did not violate Section 3 of the Clayton Act. The Seventh Circuit reasoned that exclusive selling was justified as a quality control device that protected the manufacturer's reputation and that competition in the sale of spare parts was growing notwithstanding the contractual restraint imposed upon dealers.[4] Although this reasoning anticipates subsequent economic writings stressing the franchisor's need to maintain quality controls, the analysis is incomplete. No attention is devoted to the relational market power that the manufacturer may exercise over the dealer, to possible less restrictive measures that might have protected the manufacturer's reputation, or to the impact on consumers who (wisely or not) may gravitate to authorized dealers for servicing.

The Supreme Court in 1949 was less tolerant of exclusive dealing in the franchise relationship in Standard Oil Co. v. United States.[5] Standard had entered into exclusive supply contracts with independently owned service stations that constituted about 16 percent of the service stations with almost 7 percent of the gasoline sold in the seven Western States. Justice Frankfurter, writing for the Court, found that these arrangements violated Section 3 of the Clayton Act based on their foreclosure of a substantial share of the market. The Frankfurter opinion shows sensitivity to the efficiency advantages of requirements contracts, rejecting a rule of *per se* condemnation. Yet the majority opinion still paid no attention to the benefits that might flow to both the refiner and dealer from a franchising relationship. In dissent, Justice Jackson, without using the word "franchise," briefly addressed the oil companies need to establish responsible dealers and the desire of both wholesalers and dealers to have regular outlets and supply.[6] *Standard Oil* is indicative of a Court (and an antitrust bar) which is not yet fully awakened to the value of using economic analysis in deciding franchise antitrust claims.

The Supreme Court dealt with another franchise antitrust claim in 1966 when, in FTC v. Brown Shoe Co.,[7] it upheld an FTC order that a

2. Id. at 473–74.

3. 299 U.S. 3, 57 S.Ct. 1, 81 L.Ed. 4 (1936) (per curiam), aff'g 80 F.2d 641 (7th Cir.1935).

4. 80 F.2d at 644.

5. 337 U.S. 293, 69 S.Ct. 1051, 93 L.Ed. 1371 (1949).

6. Id. at 323 (Jackson, J., dissenting).

7. 384 U.S. 316, 86 S.Ct. 1501, 16 L.Ed.2d 587 (1966).

shoe manufacturer's exclusive selling requirements on retail stores violated Section 5 of the Federal Trade Commission Act. Although the restrictions were promoted as the "Brown Franchise Stores Program," the distribution arrangements lacked some of the traits commonly associated with franchising. The case, therefore, did not afford opportunity for full-blown analysis of the competitive risks or advantages of franchising.

8.9a2.   An Analytical Approach Begins

Early recognition of the potential ability of a supplier to use a continuing vertical relationship as a source of market power over a dealer came in FTC v. Texaco, Inc., where the Supreme Court affirmed the FTC's holding that sales commission arrangements between oil company franchisors and selected tire and accessory suppliers were "inherently coercive" to the oil company dealers.[8] The *Texaco* decision, however, still lacked a thorough economic analysis of why such supplier market power might exist. More pointed analysis of the competitive risks and benefits of franchising began later in the lower courts. One of these cases was Siegel v. Chicken Delight, Inc., in which the Ninth Circuit found that a franchisor had unlawfully tied when it required franchisees to purchase disposable buckets and trademark-bearing packaging from the franchisor.[9] What distinguishes this and like cases is analysis of the efficiencies associated with franchising and an occasional (although not consistent) sensitivity to the franchisor's potential leverage over franchisees. The franchisor's need to maintain quality standards is given credence,[10] but franchisors may also be required to show that less anticompetitive controls could not have provided the desired benefits.[11]

The lower court decisions of the 1970s often assumed that the relevant market for antitrust analysis consisted of the franchisor's trademarked line of goods or services. Under this market definition, franchisees were often able to prevail on a variety of antitrust claims. By the late 1980s, however, courts were more likely to accept broader market definitions that tended to preclude antitrust relief. This controversy surrounding the appropriate market definition, addressed in § 8.9c, remains unresolved.

---

8.   393 U.S. 223, 228–29, 89 S.Ct. 429, 21 L.Ed.2d 394 (1968).

9.   448 F.2d 43, 50–51 (9th Cir.1971), cert. denied, 405 U.S. 955, 92 S.Ct. 1172, 31 L.Ed.2d 232 (1972).

10.   E.g., Krehl v. Baskin–Robbins Ice Cream Co., 664 F.2d 1348, 1352–54 (9th Cir.1982)(rejecting the franchisee's claim that an ice cream manufacturer had unlawfully tied the purchase of its ice cream to the license to operate a franchise). See Dehydrating Process Co. v. A. O. Smith Corp., 292 F.2d 653 (1st Cir.) (a nonfranchise case in which customer tie-in claims were reject-

ed because the seller had a proper business reason to bundle the products), cert. denied, 368 U.S. 931, 82 S.Ct. 368, 7 L.Ed.2d 194 (1961).

11.   *Chicken Delight,* 448 F.2d at 51; see Kentucky Fried Chicken Corp. v. Diversified Packaging Corp., 549 F.2d 368 (5th Cir.1977) (a case in which franchisor successfully defended tie-in claims by establishing that it had approved ten sources for the tied product, only one of which was affiliated with the franchisor).

Although the Supreme Court has yet to provide its own full economic analysis of a franchise antitrust claim, the need for such a framework is a policy matter that the Court should not ignore. But many economic precepts applicable to franchising remain controversial, contributing to the unsettled nature of the lower court decisions.

8.9b. Standing and Pretrial Hurdles to Antitrust Franchise Claims

As a growing class of small- and medium-sized businesses, franchisees have solid claim to standing to bring antitrust claims. In many cases (as in tie-ins), the franchisees are either the direct customers of franchisors or are direct purchasers from suppliers designated by the franchisor. As direct purchasers, the standing of a franchisee to raise antitrust claims has generally been recognized. A foreclosed rival supplier that is unable to sell to franchisees also has generally been accorded standing. See § 8.3d8. The Sixth Circuit has, however, affirmed the dismissal on standing grounds of a foreclosed supplier's suit against the franchisor.[12] Although the foreclosure injury seemed self-evident, the court ruled that the termination of the plaintiff's contract was the cause of the injury, not the franchisor's decision to favor rival suppliers that had paid access fees to the franchisor.

Even if standing is established, lower courts have occasionally accepted theories that allow dismissal of franchise antitrust claims without reaching the merits. In tie-in cases, some courts require that the claimant establish that the tying seller has an economic interest in the sale of the tied product, an evidentiary hurdle that may be difficult if the franchisor is not the seller but instead has designated an exclusive supplier. This issue is examined in § 8.9d3.

In Williams v. I.B. Fischer Nevada,[13] the Ninth Circuit affirmed the district court's holding that a franchisee and franchisor could not conspire under Section 1 of the Sherman Act because they shared a unity of economic purpose. Read broadly, this decision could signal the end to Section 1 tie-in claims brought by franchisees because such claims usually involve only a "conspiracy" between the tying franchisor and the franchisee. The court's premise of unity of purpose is strikingly at odds with the separate ownership of franchisors and franchisees and the large number of litigated franchisor-franchisee disputes. *Williams* case may reflect a broader tendency for courts to seek a pretrial basis for dismissing franchise antitrust claims deemed lacking in merit.[14] But even if the franchisee could not have prevailed on the merits of an antitrust suit, the distortion of procedural or substantive principles to achieve a prelim-

---

12. Valley Prods. Co. v. Landmark, 128 F.3d 398 (6th Cir.1997). This decision is criticized in § 8.3d8.

13. 999 F.2d 445 (9th Cir.1993) (per curiam), aff'g 794 F.Supp. 1026, 1030–33 (D.Nev.1992).

14. Another franchise antitrust case dismissed on a Fed. R. Civ. P. 12(b)(6) motion was Queen City Pizza, Inc. v. Domino's Pizza, Inc., 124 F.3d 430 (3d Cir.1997), cert. denied, 523 U.S. 1059, 118 S.Ct. 1385, 140 L.Ed.2d 645 (1998). This ruling is criticized in § 8.9c1.

inary dismissal creates unwarranted obstacles to meritorious claims. If an adequate evidentiary basis for the franchisee's claim is lacking, the court should grant summary judgment at the close of the discovery.

8.9c. Market Definition in Franchise Antitrust Cases

Market definition is pivotal in most franchise antitrust claims. Although defining the market and assigning market shares is merely a surrogate for determining the existence of market power, it is the most commonly used mode of analysis.[15] Market power may be assumed under the *per se* rule governing certain claims under Section 1 of the Sherman Act, but most franchise antitrust claims brought under Section 1 require application of a rule of reason, a modified *per se* rule (tie-ins), or forced exclusive dealing analysis, each of which builds upon a market power analysis. In monopolization or attempted monopolization claims brought under Section 2 of the Sherman Act, a demonstration of market power in the relevant market is again required, as it is for tie-in or forced exclusive dealing claims brought under Section 3 of the Clayton Act.

Case law reflects three competing approaches to market definition: (1) a market that measures the franchisor's relational market power; (2) an interbrand market that consists of all firms that sell the type of input goods required by the franchisee; and (3) a market consisting of all franchise opportunities available to the franchisee at the time the franchisee signed the initial franchise contract. For many franchise antitrust claims, the first of these theories is consistent with Supreme Court precedent and seems most soundly grounded in language of the Sherman and Clayton Acts that focuses on the anticompetitive effects of conduct. But some lower court decisions have embraced the second or third theories, often in a manner that precludes antitrust relief.

8.9c1. A Market That Assesses the Franchisor's Relational Market Power

Although there is an established line of franchise cases in which courts have expressly or implicitly measured the franchisor's relational market power,[16] a sound economic analysis that could justify such a definition is wanting in the case law. The Supreme Court offered the analytical underpinnings in Eastman Kodak Co. v. Image Technical Services, Inc.[17] That case dealt with a tie-in involving the purchase of aftermarket parts and services for original equipment sold by Kodak. The opinion focused on allegations about buyers' difficulty in calculating the life-cycle pricing for a complex piece of micrographic equipment. This difficulty along with costs linked to switching from one brand of equipment to another allegedly created an anticompetitive lock-in. If proved, a

---

15. See § 2.6.

16. See notes 19–20, infra.

17. 504 U.S. 451, 112 S.Ct. 2072, 119 L.Ed.2d 265 (1992). For the decision after trial following remand, see Image Technical Services v. Eastman Kodak Co., 125 F.3d 1195 (9th Cir., 1997), cert. denied, 523 U.S. 1094, 118 S.Ct. 1560, 140 L.Ed.2d 792 (1998).

single brand aftermarket would be appropriate. This logic would appear to apply with even greater urgency to franchising.

The life-cycle pricing difficulties for a buyer of one or several pieces of micrographic equipment, the life cycle of which may be five to ten years, could be substantial. But these difficulties pale by comparison to the uncertainties confronting a franchisee, whose investment in the franchise often is indefinite and may last as long as the working lifetime of the franchise owner. Market uncertainties in evaluating the franchise at the time the franchise contract is signed are far more pervasive than anything facing a buyer of a Kodak micrographic machine. The franchisor may change the product line, the input specifications on products, the marketing image, the number and location of competing outlets under the same flag, and the rules of quality or service. Market conditions beyond the control of either the franchisee or the franchisor will also change: new rivals may enter the market; public tastes will vary; regulatory provisions may change; etc.

If a *Kodak* theory is applied to franchise antitrust cases, a plaintiff may be able to prove a franchisor's relational market power. The franchisee may be locked into the franchisor's network by the franchisor's ability to impose costs or confer benefits on the franchisee. See § 2.4e2iv. Such a franchisee might be subjected to various forms of franchisor opportunism including coerced supra competitive prices for input products, squeezed resale margins, and encroachment of the franchisee's territory.

The *Kodak* approach to market definition is more structured than earlier franchise cases that adopted a market definition limited to the franchisor's trademarked line. Many of the venerable franchise cases of the 1960s and 1970s embraced a market coextensive with the franchisor's trademarked products or services. The Supreme Court implicitly accepted this definition in three franchise cases decided in the 1960s.[18] In Siegel v. Chicken Delight, Inc.,[19] the Ninth Circuit assumed a market limited to the franchisor's line in measuring the anticompetitive effects of the franchisor's sourcing tie that left franchisees no choice but to purchase generic products on competitively inferior terms from the supplier designated by the franchisor. *Chicken Delight* has been justly criticized for its rote assumption that a trademarked product necessarily

---

18. FTC v. Texaco, Inc., 393 U.S. 223, 89 S.Ct. 429, 21 L.Ed.2d 394 (1968)(application of Section 5 of the FTC Act); Perma Life Mufflers, Inc. v. International Parts Corp., 392 U.S. 134, 88 S.Ct. 1981, 20 L.Ed.2d 982 (1968)(application of Section 1 of the Sherman Act); Atlantic Ref. Co. v. FTC, 381 U.S. 357, 85 S.Ct. 1498, 14 L.Ed.2d 443 (1965)(application of Section 5 of the FTC Act).

19. 448 F.2d 43, 51 (9th Cir.1971), cert. denied, 405 U.S. 955, 92 S.Ct. 1172, 31 L.Ed.2d 232 (1972). Other pre-*Kodak* franchise cases implicitly or expressly accepting a market coextensive with the franchisor's line include Parts & Electric Motors, Inc. v. Sterling Electric, Inc., 866 F.2d 228 (7th Cir.1988), cert. denied, 493 U.S. 847, 110 S.Ct. 141, 107 L.Ed.2d 100 (1989); Metrix Warehouse, Inc. v. Daimler–Benz Aktiengesellschaft, 828 F.2d 1033 (4th Cir.1987), cert. denied, 486 U.S. 1017, 108 S.Ct. 1753, 100 L.Ed.2d 215 (1988); Blanton v. Mobil Oil Corp., 721 F.2d 1207 (9th Cir.1983), cert. denied, 471 U.S. 1007, 105 S.Ct. 1874, 85 L.Ed.2d 166 (1985); Milsen Co. v. Southland Corp., 454 F.2d 363 (7th Cir.1971).

carries market power with it. But the result in that case could easily have been sustained under a *Kodak* lock-in theory. Other pre-*Kodak* cases anticipated *Kodak's* "lock-in" terminology in describing the franchisor's power over the franchisee. In Milsen Co. v. Southland Corp., the Seventh Circuit described how the franchisor "locked plaintiffs into" compliance with sourcing and retail pricing requirements by selectively enforcing certain franchise fees against noncomplying franchisees.[20] These older cases, perhaps wanting in economic analysis but sound in result, are more comprehensible in the light cast by *Kodak*.

A number of post-*Kodak* lower court cases have declined to accept a *Kodak* theory for franchise antitrust claims. In Queen City Pizza, Inc. v. Domino's Pizza, Inc., the Third Circuit concluded (in a 2 to 1 panel decision) that *Kodak* did not apply because the franchise contract informed franchisees of the franchisor's power to control input purchases.[21] Other circuits have similarly limited the application of *Kodak* in franchise and nonfranchise antitrust cases.[22] But post-*Kodak* lower court jurisprudence remains restive. The dissent in *Queen City Pizza* contended that the majority failed to properly interpret *Kodak*[23] and a denial of a petition for rehearing en banc (5 judges dissenting) produced an unusual written dissent.[24] A few district courts have interpreted post-*Kodak* law as permitting the franchisee to pursue tie-in and monopolization claims.[25]

8.9c2. A Market Consisting of All Rivals That Could Supply Franchisee Input Products

In Queen City Pizza, Inc. v. Domino's Pizza, Inc., the majority rejected a market definition coextensive with the franchisor's trademarked products and concluded that the market consisted of all provid-

---

20. 454 F.2d at 368. A nonfranchise pre-*Kodak* case that mentions the concept of lock-in is the Ninth Circuit's opinion in Digidyne Corp. v. Data General Corp., 734 F.2d 1336, 1342 (9th Cir.1984), cert. denied, 473 U.S. 908, 105 S.Ct. 3534, 87 L.Ed.2d 657 (1985).

21. 124 F.3d 430, 440 (3d Cir.1997), cert. denied, 523 U.S. 1059, 118 S.Ct. 1385, 140 L.Ed.2d 645 (1998).

22. Valley Prods. Co. v. Landmark, 128 F.3d 398 (6th Cir.1997)(affirming dismissal of tie-in claim against franchisor). Nonfranchise cases in which the court has declined to follow *Kodak* in limiting the market to the seller's line of goods or services include PSI Repair Services, Inc. v. Honeywell, Inc., 104 F.3d 811 (6th Cir.), cert. denied, 520 U.S. 1265, 117 S.Ct. 2434, 138 L.Ed.2d 195 (1997); Digital Equipment Corp. v. Uniq Digital Technologies, Inc., 73 F.3d 756 (7th Cir.1996); Lee v. Life Insurance Co. of North America, 23 F.3d 14 (1st Cir.), cert. denied, 513 U.S. 964, 115 S.Ct. 427, 130 L.Ed.2d 340 (1994).

23. 124 F.3d at 444–49 (Lay., J., dissenting).

24. Queen City Pizza, Inc. v. Domino's Pizza, Inc., 129 F.3d 724 (3d Cir.1997), cert. denied, 523 U.S. 1059, 118 S.Ct. 1385, 140 L.Ed.2d 645 (1998).

25. Collins v. International Dairy Queen, Inc., 939 F.Supp. 875 (M.D.Ga.1996) (defendant's summary judgment motion denied with respect to tie-in claims); Collins v. International Dairy Queen, Inc., 980 F.Supp. 1252 (M.D.Ga.1997)(defendant's summary judgment motion denied with respect to monopolization claims); Campbell v. Irving Oil Corp., 1998–1 Trade Cas. (CCH) ¶ 72,164 (D.Me.1998) (defendant's motion to dismiss denied with respect to tie-in claims). See also Red Lion Med. Safety, Inc. v. Ohmeda, Inc., 63 F. Supp. 2d 1218 (E.D. Cal. 1999)(alleging manufacturer of medical anesthesia equipment tied parts and services).

ers of input products purchased by the franchisee.[26] This interbrand market definition may make some sense in aftermarket cases such as *Kodak,* where a buyer arguably had an opportunity to purchase original equipment from any rival of Kodak in the original equipment market.[27] But, in a franchising context, the reasoning used to arrive at this definition is unclear and the result is difficult to defend. The interbrand market identified by the court, that of wholesale pizza dough, was not available to Domino's franchisees precisely because of the sourcing tie-in that was the target of the franchisees' antitrust complaint. The hard reality for Domino's franchisees was that Domino's, with sole power to control the choice of input products, had power over price in dictating the franchisees' choices of those products.

If the market were assessed before any franchise contract were signed, a market consisting of rival suppliers of input products still makes no sense. Seen in precontractual terms, the investment choices available to the franchisee may be quite extensive, perhaps even more extensive than the interbrand market made up of all suppliers of an input product. See the discussion in § 6.4c2ii. A market definition consisting of rival suppliers of input products could still be useful in assessing the anticompetitive foreclosure effects of a requirements tie imposed by a franchisor. This foreclosure of rival suppliers is a genuine anticompetitive injury that should be actionable, but it does not describe the full extent of competition injuries caused by a requirements tie. Such a tie can cause competitive injury to consumers (by raising prices or distorting product or service choices) and to franchisees (by forcing them to accept a less than competitive rate of return on investment). Suboptimal returns on franchising could produce a reduced and inefficient flow of new investors into franchising.

8.9c3.   A Market Consisting of All Franchisee Precontractual Opportunities

In a case involving franchised accounting firms' claims of an unlawful tie-in, Judge Easterbrook wrote for the Seventh Circuit that the relevant market for assessing the tie was for all accounting positions.[28] This definition makes sense if one examines the choices of an investor before signing the franchise contract. For trained accountants who are considering signing a franchise agreement to operate an accounting franchise, their precontractual opportunities include all employment opportunities in the field of accounting. Based on this logic, Judge Easterbrook concluded that the franchisor had no market power in this overall market for accounting firms and dismissed the franchisees' tie-in claims.

---

26. Id. at 435.

27. In a nonfranchise case, Judge Easterbrook concluded that the original equipment market was the relevant market for assessing a tie-in in Digital Equipment Corp. v. Uniq Digital Technologies, Inc., 73 F.3d 756 (7th Cir.1996).

28. Will v. Comprehensive Accounting Corp., 776 F.2d 665 (7th Cir.1985), cert. denied, 475 U.S. 1129, 106 S.Ct. 1659, 90 L.Ed.2d 201 (1986).

In many franchise antitrust cases, the market for potential franchise investments is far broader than a single profession. In Wilson v. Mobil Oil Corp.,[29] the defendant's economic expert testified that the franchisees of quick lube outlets could have chosen any other franchise investment of comparable worth that did not require specialized knowledge, a market definition that would have given the franchisor a minuscule share of the relevant market. The district judge agreed, concluding that the "defendants' market power should be measured at the precontract stage."[30] Such market definitions would rule out virtually any antitrust claim by a franchisee, no matter how blatantly anticompetitive the defendant's conduct.

Examining the relevant market based on the franchisee's precontractual investment options may have gained impetus after Klein and Saft's article argued that the freedom of contract of any potential franchisee investor prevented postcontractual abuse by the franchisor.[31] Although conceding that the franchisee's sunk costs might permit the franchisor to engage in abusive conduct, the authors argued that the franchisor's long-term interest in maintaining its reputation would discipline franchisor conduct. If the franchisor abused its franchisees, in the longer term it would have difficulty recruiting new franchisees.[32]

However well crafted this deductive logic may seem, it does not always work to prevent the central anticompetitive abuses of franchising. Frequently encountered limitations on the discipline provided by freedom of contract are addressed in § 6.4c3. When an alternative definition is predicated on such market realities, the proper definition becomes a factual issue to be appropriately explored, as it was in Perma Life Mufflers, Inc. v. International Parts Corp., where the Supreme Court observed that the franchisees accepted clauses that they objected to "solely because their acquiescence was necessary to obtain an otherwise attractive business opportunity."[33] Justice Black's words accurately capture many franchise negotiations.[34]

A market definition exercise is one that is undertaken as a surrogate for more direct means of identifying the market power that can produce

---

29. 984 F.Supp. 450, 458–59 (E.D.La. 1997).

30. Id. at 460.

31. Klein & Saft, *The Law and Economics of Franchise Tying Contracts,* 28 J.L. & Econ. 345 (1985). For a more recent defense of this view, see Klein, *Market Power in Franchise Cases in the Wake of Kodak: Applying Post–Contract Hold-up Analysis to Vertical Relationships,* 67 Antitrust L.J. 283 (1999). For criticism of this view, see Grimes, *Market Definition in Franchise Antitrust Claims: Relational Market Power and the Franchisor's Conflict of Interest,* 67 Antitrust L.J. (1999).

32. Professor Areeda is another adherent to the precontractual approach for

measuring the franchisor's market power. 9 P. Areeda, Antitrust Law: An Analysis of Antitrust Principles and Their Application ¶ 1709 (1991).

33. 392 U.S. 134, 139, 88 S.Ct. 1981, 20 L.Ed.2d 982 (1968).

34. *See also* Siegel v. Chicken Delight, Inc., 448 F.2d 43, 52–53 (9th Cir.1971), cert. denied, 405 U.S. 955, 92 S.Ct. 1172, 31 L.Ed.2d 232 (1972), (franchisee's signature on franchise contract not construed as consent to abusive sourcing requirements). An individual applicant offered a popular franchise, unable to bargain collectively, will have little capacity to effect a change.

anticompetitive abuses. In the final analysis, the inadequacy of a market analysis based solely on the franchisee's precontractual choices is that it will virtually eliminate antitrust's role in preventing anticompetitive abuses of franchisees. That failure may produce a loss of investor confidence in franchising, but it may also prompt action by courts (interpreting nonantitrust laws) or by legislatures that is even more oppressive to freedom of contract than the traditional antitrust paradigm.

8.9c4.　The Limits of Relational Market Power: Individual Contract Disputes and Other Matters Outside the Reach of Antitrust Law

A primary objection to recognition of relational market power is that such power is common in franchise relationships and might invite firms to raise antitrust claims in routine contract disputes.[35] To prevent this result, one possible approach is to insist that the plaintiff demonstrate that the franchisor had pre-contract market power in its dealings with the franchisee. As the previous section indicates, this approach would eliminate virtually all franchise antitrust claims, no matter how substantial the competitive injury. A more balanced approach would allow recognition of relational market power to provide antitrust relief for genuine and substantial anticompetitive injury, but would also limit antitrust remedies to cases involving such injury. This section addresses traditional antitrust limits on the invocation of relational market power in franchise antitrust litigation.

A century of jurisprudence has sought to separate those contracts that are appropriately proscribed by the Sherman Act from the much larger number that should be left for the discipline of the market. Perhaps the most basic example is the Supreme Court's reading of Section 1 as proscribing only *unreasonable* restraints of trade. Although the application of this case law to franchising relationships presents unique challenges, recognition of the concept of relational market power should not be read as inviting antitrust claims by any party dissatisfied with the terms of a contract. There are four evident antitrust rules that would limit invocation of relational market power in franchising disputes: (1) a plaintiff must demonstrate the existence of relational market power—the conditions giving rise to this power exist in many but not all franchise relationships; (2) relational market power, even when it exists, may not be a basis for an antitrust remedy when a dispute involves an insubstantial volume of commerce; (3) relational market power gives rise to an antitrust violation only when coupled with an abusive exercise of that power that threatens substantial competitive injury; and (4) the franchisor may invoke any valid defense to forestall the franchisee's antitrust claim, including defenses based on the need to protect the good will of the franchise system.

---

35. Klein, *supra* note 31, at 299 ("Because franchisee sunk investments and imperfect information are almost always present, every franchisor would possess antitrust market power").

8.9c4i. The Absence of Relational Market Power

Relational market power in franchising is linked to the franchisee's sunk investment and the franchisor's ability to control the flow of costs and benefits to the franchisee. These factual predicates are widely met in franchising relationships, but are not universal. The facts of FTC v. Brown Shoe Co.[36] provide an instructive illustration of the absence of relational market power. Shoe retailers that agreed to concentrate their business on the Brown Shoe's lines and not to carry competing lines were given certain merchandising services, group insurance rates, and other benefits from the company. Although the Supreme Court describes this as a franchising relationship, the dealers were permitted to withdraw without penalty. There is no evidence that the dealers had any substantial sunk investment in the Brown line, a circumstance that suggests that Brown possessed no significant relational market power over the dealers.

Even when the preconditions for relational market power are met (substantial franchisee sunk investment and franchisor control over the flow of costs and benefits), that showing may be negated if the franchisee has substantial countervailing power. A corporate franchisee that controls a substantial number of the franchisor's outlets may possess that countervailing leverage because of the franchisee's importance in generating revenue for the franchisor. Similarly, any single franchisee, if it generates a significant percentage of the franchisor's revenues, may possess such countervailing leverage.

8.9c4ii. Insubstantial Volume of Commerce

To demonstrate an unlawful tie-in, the Supreme Court requires a showing that a tie-in forecloses a substantial volume of commerce.[37] This requirement would eliminate many franchisee tie-in claims arising in isolated contractual disputes. Thus, if a contractual restraint is unique to a particular franchisee, or, although included in numerous franchise contracts, is applied in a manner that causes competitive injury only to a single franchisee, the franchisor could seek dismissal on the grounds that an insubstantial volume of commerce is involved.

Although the substantial commerce requirement was generated in the Supreme Court's tie-in cases, the test appears to be based on broader concepts of the substantiality of competitive injury as a requirement for antitrust relief, and hence could be applied in other franchise antitrust claims. For example, Section 3 of the Clayton Act proscribes tying or exclusive dealing conduct only if its effect "may be to substantially

---

36. 384 U.S. 316, 86 S.Ct. 1501, 16 L.Ed.2d 587 (1966). The Supreme Court affirmed the FTC's holding that the franchising arrangement violated Section 5 of the FTC Act. Absent a showing of relational or some other form of market power, it is doubtful that this sort of exclusive dealing arrangement would be deemed unlawful under current law. See the discussion of exclusive dealing in § 8.4.

37. Jefferson Parish Hospital Dist. No. 2 v. Hyde, 466 U.S. 2, 12–18, 104 S.Ct. 1551, 80 L.Ed.2d 2 (1984). The use of this requirement to screen out relatively inconsequential contract disputes is addressed in § 8.3d1.

lessen competition or tend to create a monopoly in any line of commerce." As interpreted by the Supreme Court, Section 1 proscribes only "unreasonable" restraints of trade. Individually and collectively, these concepts allow courts to screen out contract disputes and grievances involving inconsequential volumes of commerce.

8.9c4iii. *Inability to Show a Substantial Threatened Competitive Injury*

The mere possession of market power is not an antitrust violation. If it were, most firms that have established strong brands (and therefore confront relatively inelastic consumer demand) would be Sherman Act violators. Franchisors that possess relational market power violate the antitrust laws only if they abuse their power in a manner recognized in traditional antitrust claims, such as tie-ins, exclusive dealing, or vertical maximum price fixing. Moreover, that abuse must threaten substantial competitive injury (see the discussion in § 8.9c4ii).

An individually negotiated franchise contract often may fail to meet this requirement. To begin with, the theory of relational market power (based on *Kodak*) requires both an information or life-cycle pricing problem and a lock-in. When franchisee and franchisor have meaningful negotiations and give and take on a contract item that is later challenged as anticompetitive, the franchisee will be hard put to demonstrate that it did not consider or was not allowed to modify the provision in question.[38] On the other hand, when a broadly worded sourcing requirement is inserted as boilerplate in a class of franchise agreements, and franchisees have no meaningful opportunity to negotiate alternative language, the *Kodak* preconditions of an information asymmetry and lock-in appear to be met.[39] When boilerplate language is inserted in a class of franchise contracts, the threatened injury is also more likely to meet the requirements of foreclosure of a substantial volume of commerce and of a substantial anticompetitive effect.

8.9c4iv. *Defenses Based on Protecting the Goodwill of the Franchise System*

A franchisor may invoke any valid defense relevant to the particular antitrust claim that is alleged. These defenses vary with the nature of the claim and are described in the following sections addressing tie-ins, exclusive dealing, vertical maximum price fixing, and attempted monopolization. Many of these defenses have a common theme: the franchisor's

---

38. This appears to have been the case, for example, in a non-franchise exclusive dealing case decided for the defendant. Tampa Elec. Co. v. Nashville Coal Co., 365 U.S. 320, 81 S.Ct. 623, 5 L.Ed.2d 580 (1961).

39. Here the facts described are more comparable to Perma Life Mufflers, Inc. v. International Parts Corp., 392 U.S. 134, 88 S.Ct. 1981, 20 L.Ed.2d 982 (1968). In many

such situations a free rider-like problem may undermine franchisee bargaining power. All or most franchisees presented with a contract containing an objectionable clause may resist it. But if the franchise is a desirable one, each potential franchisee with whom the franchisor negotiates alone will feel powerless to resist when told: "Those are the terms. Others are waiting in line to accept them if you do not."

recognized need to protect the good will of the franchise system. The franchisor must be empowered to protect the system's goodwill to forestall selfish or free-riding conduct by franchisees. For example, a franchisor may defend a sourcing requirement from claims of an unlawful tie-in or a forced exclusive dealing arrangement if the requirement is necessary to protect the goodwill of the franchise system. There are, however, limits to these goodwill defenses. The franchisor should not be permitted to impose an anticompetitive restraint when a measure far less threatening to competition is reasonably available to protect the goodwill of the franchise system. See the discussion in § 8.9d1ii.

8.9d. Tie–In Cases

For the most part, franchising tie-in cases present the same issues as tie-ins generally. See the discussion in § 8.3. Tie-ins can distort allocation and cause other antitrust injury when a seller uses its market power to force the purchase of a tied product. Market power may predate the use of a tie—as it would when a franchisor imposes a tie after the franchise contract is signed—or it may be generated or compounded by the complicating features of a tie-in. In franchising, the anticompetitive effects of tie-ins are similar to those for tie-ins generally. But the source of the tying franchisor's coercive power is usually the relational market power arising out of the franchisee's sunk costs and the franchisor's control of the flow of benefits and burdens to the franchisee.

Fairness issues may also arise in franchise tie-in cases. Although sometimes ignored in antitrust decisions, fairness remains an important factor in franchise litigation applying state or common law doctrines.[40] In franchise antitrust cases, fairness is often linked to resource or capital allocation issues. Franchisees fail for many reasons, not the least of which may be the franchisee's own incompetence. But if the franchisor's policies, such as the imposition of an anticompetitive requirements tie-in, are a substantial cause of the poor-performing investment, the franchisee will justifiably perceive this as unfair.

Two types of ties occur with some frequency in franchising: (1) *requirements ties*—sometimes called sourcing controls, these ties require the franchisee to purchase all its requirements for a given input from a franchisor-designated supplier; and (2) *inventory disposition ties*—those that require a franchisee to purchase unwanted inventory from the franchisor as a condition for receiving items that the franchisee wishes to buy. In either case, the tying product may be seen as the franchise license purchased by the franchisee. More properly, the tying product should be the franchisee's right to continue operating under that license. The relational market power that the franchisor may possess would not have existed at the time the franchisee signed the initial franchise contract. But if the franchisee has made a substantial sunk investment and is subject to the franchisor's power to impose costs and withhold

---

40. Burns, *Vertical Restraints, Efficiency, and the Real World,* 62 Fordham L. Rev. 597, 617–30 (1993).

benefits, or terminate the franchise altogether, the franchisor will have the requisite power over price that constitutes market power.

8.9d1.　Requirements Ties

A franchisee required to purchase supplies from a source approved by the franchisor might attack such sourcing control either as forced exclusive dealing or as an unlawful tie. Although the underlying facts and policy issues may be identical, the legal standards for establishing an unlawful forced exclusive dealing arrangement are somewhat different and are addressed in § 8.9e.

Franchisor-imposed requirements ties have been justified on two grounds. The first justification is that tie-ins are an efficient metering mechanism, allowing the franchisor to collect a variable franchise fee based on the intensity of the franchisee's use of the franchisor's trademark.[41] The second justification is that such ties may serve a quality control function. By controlling the source of supply, the franchisor ensures that the product sold by its franchisees is uniform and meets quality standards. In this manner, the franchisor maintains the goodwill of the franchise system.[42] Assessing the validity of these defenses requires understanding both the potential benefits and the potential injury from use of a requirements tie. There is one anticompetitive risk that is a constant for all requirements ties: The franchisee is denied the right to choose the supplier. If the designated input supplier overcharges or provides shoddy merchandise or service, the franchisee cannot invoke the simple but effective expedient of changing suppliers. See § 8.9d1iii.

8.9d1i.　The Tie as an Efficient Metering Device

The benefits that a franchisor gains from using a requirements tie as a metering device for collecting a variable franchise fee are generally more directly attained through a royalty payment based on the franchisee's sales.[43] If total sales correlate directly with the volume of a critical input purchased from the franchisor, a requirements contract may work smoothly as a means of collecting a variable royalty. This might be the case, for example, with ice cream sold by a franchisor to its chain of franchisee ice cream shops. But unless there are important quality control objectives for imposing this tie (to be addressed below), the tie risks allocative and wealth transfer injuries without any evident advantage over a more straightforward royalty based on sales. There will be some enforcement burden no matter how the royalty is collected. The franchisor must monitor and collect on either the franchisee's total sales (in the case of a direct royalty payment) or the franchisee's purchases of ice cream (in the case of a requirements tie).

---

41. Klein, supra note 31, at 308–15; Bowman, *Tying Arrangements and the Leverage Problem*, 67 YALE L.J. 19, 23–24 (1957); H. HOVENKAMP, FEDERAL ANTITRUST POLICY: THE LAW OF COMPETITION AND ITS PRACTICE § 10.6e (3d ed. 2005).

42. Klein & Saft, supra note 31 at 351–54.

43. The metering device argument as a rationale for tie-ins is discussed in § 8.3b2.

The widespread use of sales royalties suggests that most franchisors can effectively monitor and enforce such a royalty. Indeed, most franchisors might desire the information about total franchisee sales of the franchise product regardless of whether the royalty is based on such sales. There may, however, be circumstances in which another type of monitoring of franchisee performance is more efficient. Suppose that a franchisor wants to weight its royalty in a manner that collects a higher fee on higher margin sales. For example, if a fast-food outlet had a higher margin when selling single meals than for family-pack meals, it might collect a differentiated royalty through a requirements tie that placed a surcharge on the packaging used for single meals.[44] Whether this method of collecting a margin-adjusted royalty is more efficient than other available methods is open to question. The franchisor might efficiently (perhaps more efficiently) monitor sales through computerized cash register receipts. Computer-generated records could provide the franchisor a great deal of additional and highly desirable sales information beyond that provided by a requirements tie. Of course, even if a requirements tie proves the most efficient way to charge a margin-sensitive royalty, the anticompetitive effects of the tie must be factored in before concluding that such a tie offers a net competitive gain. See § 8.9d1iii.

It may also be argued that a metering tie will produce an efficient form of price discrimination by allowing low intensity users to purchase a product that otherwise might be priced beyond their means.[45] For example, a sophisticated ice cream-dispensing machine might be offered to franchisees at a low price, allowing the largest possible number of franchisees to acquire the device. The franchisor might require purchasers of the machine to obtain from it all ice cream used in the machine. By charging a high price for the ice cream, the franchisor could extract a higher bundled price from high-intensity users of the dispenser (because they would use more ice cream).

The more likely explanation for such a bundled sale is that the manufacturer believes it will achieve a higher return. It requires a blind leap of faith to equate the manufacturer's higher return with more efficient allocation. The manufacturer cannot know (and probably does not care) whether this bundled pricing scheme produces a more efficient allocation of ice cream. The odds are that it will not. If more dispensers are sold to small franchisees that use them inefficiently (say, a few times a day), society may have too many ice cream dispensers, many of them inefficiently utilized, and too little ice cream (because of its inflated price). Compare this outcome with a nonbundled sale of the dispensers and ice cream, allowing each franchisee to determine whether its use of the dispenser would warrant the up-front investment in its purchase. Under this scenario, dispensers may cost more, but ice cream will cost less. Fewer franchisees may buy the dispensers, but they will have an

---

44. Klein & Saft, supra note 31, at 357–58.

45. Klein, supra note 31, at 359–60.

incentive (and an opportunity) to use them intensively, perhaps even drawing customers from smaller franchisees that do not own the machines. This is likely to be the more efficient allocation because it will lead to wide availability of ice cream at a lower price.

Aside from any allocative injury caused by a requirements tie that enables price discrimination, every price discrimination will result in a transfer of wealth from the buyers that pay the higher price to the seller whose market power allows the imposition of the discriminatory price. In theory, a seller might charge a higher than competitive price to high-value users and a lower than competitive price to low-value users in such a manner that the average sales price would be the competitive price, so that there would be no net wealth transfer loss to buyers. But this theoretical possibility would not occur because the seller would have no gain from the imposition of price discrimination (indeed would suffer a net loss because of the costs associated with implementing and enforcing price discrimination). In real markets, a seller will impose price discrimination only when it increases the seller's profits. Hence, there will always be a wealth transfer loss if price discrimination does not increase output. Preventing that wealth transfer loss is a primary if not the preeminent goal of antitrust.[46]

To sum up, every franchisor sourcing requirement that results in price discrimination will consistently risk two anticompetitive effects: (1) the franchisee will have greater difficulty changing suppliers to address a particular supplier's inflated prices or quality or service deficiencies; and (2) there will be a shift of wealth from franchisees (and possibly consumers as well) to a power-wielding franchisor in contravention of antitrust's wealth transfer goal. In addition, the price discrimination will likely undermine efficient allocation.

8.9d1ii. Maintaining Quality Standards

The stronger argument for a requirements tie in the franchising context may be that it is the most effective way of enforcing quality and protecting a brand name for critical items. These arguments can be forceful if a franchisor sells franchisees the right to market a product, the quality and performance of which are critical to the franchisor's image. For example, if the franchisor has developed a strong brand name for ice cream that it produces, the franchisor will have a strong interest in requiring that the franchisee acquire the ice cream only from it or from a licensed supplier. The success or failure of the franchise may be integrally related to the uniform quality of the ice cream served by all franchisees. The requirements tie may in some circumstances be the most efficient way to monitor quality control.[47] Monitoring outside suppliers may become increasingly difficult and costly as the complexity of the product increases. Indeed, the licensing of outside suppliers may entail unacceptable risks that trade secrets will be disclosed. Of course, if

---

46. See the discussion of the wealth transfer goal in § 1.5b2.

47. Klein & Saft, supra note 31 at 346–48.

trade secrets can be protected, it may be possible to designate more than one approved supplier.[48]

In Sherman Act or Clayton Act cases, the courts have, in two ways, made allowances for situations in which single source supply is required. The first allowance is through the requirement that, to prove an unlawful tie-in, the plaintiff establish that two separate products are tied together.[49] Requiring the franchisee to purchase from the franchisor an input product integrally linked to the franchisor's brand name may be regarded as a properly bundled sale, not a tie of two separate products.[50] The test for whether two products are properly bundled should turn on informed consumer demand, tempered by supply-side considerations. See the discussion in § 8.3b1. For example, it is more efficient for an automobile to be sold as a single product. Most consumers prefer it this way, not wishing to buy either a steering wheel, motor or tires separately from the rest of the car. But even if some consumers prefer to buy certain parts separately (e.g., tires), the overwhelming efficiency from the supply side (it is much more efficient for the manufacturer to design, purchase and assemble the parts than to leave this task to the buyer) should control: the sale should be considered a properly bundled product, not a tie. Similar reasoning should control in the franchise context. If an ice cream recipe or soft drink formula is critical to the identity and reputation of the franchise system, informed franchisees would prefer to buy these items as a part of the franchise, realizing that the franchise's success, and their own individual success, depends on the integrity of the trademark. Even if some franchisees might desire alternate sources for the product, when the franchisor's efficiency gains from a bundled sale are substantial and cannot reasonably be achieved through less anticompetitive means, this circumstance should be controlling.

Some courts have made a determination whether separate products are being tied based on whether the franchisor owns the trademark and produces the product sold under that mark (a bundling not involving a tie-in), or whether the trademark is rented independently of any product produced by the franchisor (a tie-in). The question of whether the

---

48. Klein and Saft argue that if more than one approved supplier is designated, the suppliers will have a free-ride incentive—to cheapen the product in order to gain increased profit. This result will occur because the suppliers no longer have a property interest in the future rents of the franchisee. Id. at 353–54.

This argument may overstate the risk of supplier free riding. Even if free-riding suppliers are a major concern, the franchisor can respond by occasional monitoring of any approved supplier. A supplier has a strong incentive to remain on the approved list, without which its ability to make sales to franchisees is lost.

49. Eastman Kodak Co. v. Image Technical Servs. Inc., 504 U.S. 451, 461–62, 112

S.Ct. 2072, 119 L.Ed.2d 265 (1992); Jefferson Parish Hosp. Dist. No. 2 v. Hyde, 466 U.S. 2, 19–21, 104 S.Ct. 1551, 80 L.Ed.2d 2 (1984).

50. Krehl v. Baskin–Robbins Ice Cream Co., 664 F.2d 1348, 1352–54 (9th Cir.1982) (holding that the franchisor's ice cream trademark could not be regarded as a product that could be tied to the sale of the ice cream itself); see also Principe v. McDonald's Corp., 631 F.2d 303, 308 (4th Cir. 1980)(concluding that the franchise agreement, on the one hand, and lease and security note, on the other hand, "are not separate [tied] products but component parts of the overall franchise package"), cert. denied, 451 U.S. 970, 101 S.Ct. 2047, 68 L.Ed.2d 349 (1981).

trademark is "rented" or "owned" should, however, not be determinative.[51] Properly analyzed, the issue is whether conditions of supply and demand justify bundling these products together.

In the case of a business format franchise, such as a fast-food restaurant, it is possible to argue that a great many input products or services are critical to the franchise image. A fast-food franchisor may argue that the quality of plastic or paper plates, containers or napkins is significant to maintaining the chain's reputation for product and service quality and consistency.[52] But note that if the quality of these products is relatively easy to monitor and if the franchisee's incentive to cheat is limited (because the franchisee will damage its own return business by providing inadequate dinnerware), the requirements tie is simply not needed to maintain quality. The franchisor can address quality control by issuing standards or certifying a number of approved suppliers.

Some courts have addressed this group of issues by applying a quality control defense for tie-ins. The defense is usually superfluous because quality control issues can be addressed in determining whether products are properly bundled. Still, the Supreme Court has recognized this defense, at least for a new and technologically complex product, and a number of courts have applied it.[53] The defense offers a franchisor a second opportunity to vindicate use of a requirements tie based on a need to control quality.

8.9d1iii.   Anticompetitive Aspects of Requirements Ties

When purchasing decisions are made by an agent, a person other than the principal with the primary capital at risk in the transaction, there is a heightened risk of corruption or distorted purchase choices. For example, purchasing agents for government agencies or private firms can be induced to make poor buying choices based upon surreptitious payments, rebates or personal favors to the purchasing agent.[54] This

---

51. Klein & Saft, supra note 31, at 359–61 (making the same point).

52. In Siegel v. Chicken Delight, Inc., 448 F.2d 43, 50–51 (9th Cir.1971), cert. denied, 405 U.S. 955, 92 S.Ct. 1172, 31 L.Ed.2d 232 (1972), the franchisor unsuccessfully argued quality control as a defense for a requirements tie on the disposable buckets and other supplies sold to the franchisees.

53. United States v. Jerrold Elecs. Corp., 187 F.Supp. 545 (E.D.Pa.1960), aff'd per curiam, 365 U.S. 567, 81 S.Ct. 755, 5 L.Ed.2d 806 (1961). In two cases involving the same requirements tie imposed on dealers by Mercedes–Benz of North America, the juries reached opposite conclusions about whether a quality control defense justified use of the tie. Mozart Co. v. Mercedes–Benz of N. Am., Inc., 833 F.2d 1342 (9th Cir.1987)(embracing the quality control defense), cert. denied, 488 U.S. 870, 109

S.Ct. 179, 102 L.Ed.2d 148 (1988); Metrix Warehouse, Inc. v. Daimler–Benz Aktiengesellschaft, 828 F.2d 1033 (4th Cir. 1987)(affirming a jury verdict that rejected the quality control defense), cert. denied, 486 U.S. 1017, 108 S.Ct. 1753, 100 L.Ed.2d 215 (1988). Another case with similar facts is Grappone, Inc. v. Subaru of New England, Inc., 858 F.2d 792, 799 (1st Cir. 1988)(suggesting that an efficiency defense related to quality control may have justified use of a tie on spare parts). The better result is to prohibit requirements ties as long as the manufacturer can adequately control quality by designating a number of approved suppliers. See § 8.3d4.

54. Some of this competition-distorting behavior might constitute a crime (such as offering or accepting a bribe). But the criminal law will reach only egregious instances of this competition-distorting behavior. Even if the criminal law reaches a particu-

conduct can occur in franchising when a franchisor requires franchisees to purchase a product or service from a particular source. That source may be the franchisor itself, an entity controlled by the franchisor, or an outside firm. If the franchisor or an entity owned by the franchisor is the designated supplier, the conflict of interest in this choice is self-evident. But even if the franchisor designates an outside supplier, the franchisor may have an incentive other than the well-being of the franchise system that impels this choice: the supplier may offer a payment to the franchisor in return for being awarded the status as exclusive supplier. The payment may be described as a rebate, an access fee, a franchise fee, or in some other fashion, but its potential anticompetitive effect is always the same: The ability to distort the buying choice away from the competitive merits. The payment will distort the competitive process if it forces the franchisee to purchase a competitively less desirable product and diverts business from suppliers offering competitively more attractive products. Although the potentially corrupting nature of supplier payments to the franchisor often goes unrecognized, it is not difficult to find examples of such payments in reported cases.[55]

The royalty payment received by the franchisor does not substantially deter a franchisor from accepting a rebate from a favored supplier in return for the supplier's exclusive status. Consider a franchisor that receives a rebate of 5 percent on all sales made by a favored supplier to the franchisees. If the supplier passes this 5 percent increase to the franchisee by raising prices on the input product, the franchisee's costs will be increased. But this may not affect a sales-based royalty paid to the franchisor because the franchisee may have to absorb the higher costs.[56] Even if the franchisee raises its prices, that increase in price is unlikely to decrease sales sufficiently to cause a fully offsetting decline in the franchisor's royalty. In all likelihood, the franchisor will gain far more through the rebate received from the favored supplier than it will lose from any decline in franchisee royalty payments.

lar franchisor competition-distorting abuse, the franchisee may be unable to convince a public prosecutor that this matter deserves priority among the many demands on law enforcement resources, or the higher burden of proof in a criminal proceeding may prevent successful prosecution despite obvious anticompetitive effects.

55. See, e.g., FTC v. Texaco, Inc., 393 U.S. 223, 229, 89 S.Ct. 429, 21 L.Ed.2d 394 (1968)(franchisor-selected supplier company paid 10 percent commission to Texaco for all franchisee purchases of tires, batteries and accessories); Atlantic Ref. Co. v. FTC, 381 U.S. 357, 365, 85 S.Ct. 1498, 14 L.Ed.2d 443 (1965)(similar rebate paid by Goodyear to Atlantic); Valley Prods. Co. v. Landmark, 128 F.3d 398, 401 (6th Cir.1997)(two franchisor-selected soap suppliers paid "access" fees to franchisor in return for exclusive

right to sell to franchisees); Milsen Co. v. Southland Corp., 454 F.2d 363, 368 (7th Cir.1971)(franchisor-selected dairy products supplier paid 14 percent rebate to franchisor—described as a rebate that was paid against the franchise fee—on all sales to franchisees); Wilson v. Mobil Oil Corp., 940 F.Supp. 944, 947 (E.D.La.1996)(franchisor-selected petroleum products supplier paid franchisor $650,000, said to be designated for advertising for franchisees but allegedly misappropriated by the franchisor, in return for exclusive supplier status).

56. A franchisor's royalty based on the franchisee's profits rather than the franchisee's sales would be more effective in deterring anticompetitive sourcing decisions by the franchisor. But franchisor royalties are almost always based on sales, not on profits.

Even if the franchisor receives no rebate from the selected supplier, shifting control over input purchases away from the market player that pays for these goods can have anticompetitive consequences. Perhaps for many of the same reasons that late-twentieth-century U.S. automobile manufacturers have found that in-house produced parts are often inferior in quality or price to those produced by outsiders, franchisees may find that what they are getting from the franchisor or its designated supplier is no longer a competitive product. The incentives to correct this problem are weakened in a franchising system. In the case of the vertically integrated company, the risk of inadequate competitive performance falls on the player with control. If General Motors' divisions are producing inferior parts, the firm and its stockholders must directly incur the loss. But if the franchisor is forcing franchisees to purchase inferior or overpriced merchandise, it is the franchisees that are most directly injured. Reputational constraints may discipline franchisor behavior, but are likely to do so far less effectively than if the franchisor owned all of the outlets forced to purchase inadequate input goods or services.

Most franchisors choose a reputable supplier offering competitive prices, the franchisor's dictated choice may have anticompetitive consequences. Once locked into a particular supplier, the franchisee loses its leverage if the supplier raises prices above a competitive level or provides defective goods or inadequate service. Consider a fast-food franchisee obliged by the franchisor to purchase all soft drink supplies and dispensers from a soft drink distributor designated by the franchisor. The franchisor's choice of the soft drink distributor may be based on selfish interests of the franchisor that conflict with the interests of the franchisee. For example, the franchisor or its key employees may receive a rebate from the favored supplier, or there may be cross-ownership of the franchisor and the favored supplier. The franchisee may be required to pay a higher price than is paid by franchisees in competing fast-food chains. But the injury may not stop there. The favored provider may perceive that it is insulated from competition. When a soft drink dispenser provided by the distributor malfunctions, the franchisee may be unable to obtain prompt service, notwithstanding repeated complaints to the soft drink distributor and to representatives of the franchisor. For most firms, an inadequately performing supplier is not a problem—the firm would unceremoniously drop the inattentive supplier in favor of a more reliable rival. The franchisee, however, cannot use this simple and effective market response because of franchisor's control.

The franchisor may also use a tie to force the franchisee to bear the risk of changing market conditions. For example, if a franchisor of accounting services requires its franchisees to purchase all computer services from the franchisor, franchisees must bear the risk that changing market conditions will render obsolete the equipment purchased by the franchisor.[57] Of course, neither franchisees nor franchisors may know

---

57. These facts are roughly those presented in Will v. Comprehensive Accounting Corp., 776 F.2d 665 (7th Cir.1985), cert. denied, 475 U.S. 1129, 106 S.Ct. 1659, 90 L.Ed.2d 201 (1986).

in advance how quickly obsolescence may occur. Shifting the risk of obsolescence to the franchisee may seem relatively inconsequential, yet there are obvious consumer welfare consequences. The ability to modernize rests with the franchisor, but the franchisor may have insufficient incentive to do so. The franchisees are saddled with paying for a service that is no longer competitive, with insufficient leverage to force the franchisor to update the equipment.[58] Efficient rival providers of computer services may be injured and, depending on market conditions, consumers may receive antiquated or overpriced services. If the outdated equipment drives a franchisee out of business, its capital will have been misallocated to the franchise outlet.

A sourcing requirement imposed on a franchisee has, therefore, very substantial competitive risks. The result of a requirements tie may be injury to competition because allocation is distorted away from competition on the merits and because wealth is transferred from the franchisee and consumers into the pockets of franchisors, their corrupted employees, or the favored supplier. The franchisor's incentives to distort the competitive process in dictating input choices are real and systemic, a circumstance that explains and supports an antitrust remedy.

Despite the classic nature of the competitive injury often associated with sourcing tie-ins, some lower courts have dismissed franchisee tying claims on theories that would all but render franchise tie-ins *per se* lawful. In Queen City Pizza, Inc. v. Domino's Pizza, Inc.,[59] the plaintiff franchisees (including one plaintiff representing 40 percent of all Domino's Pizza franchisees in the United States) brought suit alleging that Domino's had violated Sections 1 and 2 of the Sherman Act by depriving franchisees of the opportunity to purchase pizza dough and other ingredients on competitive market terms. The plaintiffs offered evidence that pizza dough prepared by other franchisees in Domino's-approved commissaries was available at a cost from 25 to 40 percent less than the amount franchisees were forced to pay to Domino's. The district court's order dismissing the plaintiff's claim on a Fed. R. Civ. P. 12(b)(6) motion was affirmed in a 2 to 1 decision by the Third Circuit, which reasoned that neither a monopolization nor a tie-in claim could be sustained because Domino's had no demonstrated market power in the interbrand market for pizzas.[60] The court rejected the argument that the market consisted only of pizza dough produced for Domino's franchisees.[61] A

---

58. In *Comprehensive Accounting*, there are indications that the franchisor moved slowly, and perhaps only under the pressure of litigation, to provide franchisees with alternatives to a computer service that franchisees found no longer competitive. Id. at 668–69. In this decision, Judge Easterbrook ignored the franchisees' sunk costs and concluded that the franchisor lacked the requi-site market power to establish an unlawful tie. Id. at 674.

59. 124 F.3d 430 (3d Cir.1997), cert. denied, 523 U.S. 1059, 118 S.Ct. 1385, 140 L.Ed.2d 645 (1998).

60. Id. at 443.

61. The majority's market definition is criticized in § 8.9c2.

dissenting judge disagreed, pointing to the sunk costs of franchisees that locked them into the Domino's network.[62]

As one judge has recognized, tie-in arrangements "are clearly quite onerous to the average franchisee, a relatively small business person whose sunk costs in the franchise represent all or most of his or her assets and who lacks the considerable resources necessary to switch or defranchise."[63] The injury, of course, is not simply to the franchisees, but to the efficient allocation of capital, goods and services. Depending on local competitive conditions, consumers may have to pay more for pizza or other products sold by local franchisees, or may be denied services that the local franchisee would offer if the input costs were kept at competitive levels. The flow of capital into efficient franchise investments may also be reduced.

8.9d2. *Inventory Disposition Ties*

A franchisor with market power may require franchisees to purchase excess or unwanted inventory in order to transfer a loss to the franchisees, much as a, vertically integrated firm, might shift a loss among subsidiaries. Absent vertical restraints, unwanted inventory could not be forced on customers unless the supplier has market power. Franchisors often have sufficient relational market power over franchisees to force them to absorb such losses. A number of litigated cases involve automobile dealers that alleged that they were forced to purchase unwanted models in order to receive models more in demand.[64] In these cases, the plaintiffs alleged that the tying product is not the franchise itself, but popular models that they could not obtain without purchasing unwanted models. The manufacturer's actions are sometimes referred to as "full-line forcing" because they require dealers to carry all products in the line.[65] But the objectionable feature of the manufacturer's actions is not that it requires dealers to carry a full line including unpopular models, but rather from that it requires the purchase of a substantial inventory of such models, absorbing a loss, as a condition for receiving the popular models.

As is the case with a requirements tie, a critical issue is whether the unwanted inventory is a part of one properly bundled product—a full line—or whether it is a separate, tied product. In one case, the dealer had difficulty establishing a separate tied product, in part because the same model was, depending on the time of sale, sometimes classified as

62. 124 F.3d at 446 (Lay, J., dissenting).

63. Queen City Pizza, Inc. v. Domino's Pizza, Inc., 129 F.3d 724, 726 (3d Cir. 1997)(Becker, J., dissenting from order denying rehearing en banc), cert. denied, 523 U.S. 1059, 118 S.Ct. 1385, 140 L.Ed.2d 645 (1998). Four other judges on the Third Circuit voted to grant the rehearing en banc.

64. Southern Pines Chrysler–Plymouth, Inc. v. Chrysler Corp., 826 F.2d 1360 (4th

Cir.1987); Fox Motors, Inc. v. Mazda Distribs. (Gulf), Inc., 806 F.2d 953 (10th Cir. 1986).

65. *Southern Pines Chrysler–Plymouth*, 826 F.2d at 1362 n.3 (using the term "full-line forcing"); Smith Mach. Co. v. Hesston Corp., 878 F.2d 1290, 1297 (10th Cir. 1989)(using the term "line forcing"), cert. denied, 493 U.S. 1073, 110 S.Ct. 1119, 107 L.Ed.2d 1026 (1990).

the tying (popular) product, sometimes as the tied (unpopular) product.[66] The difficulty in separating tying from tied products is puzzling because the manufacturer itself would specify which products must be purchased in order to obtain others. In a Supreme Court case involving full line forcing, the Court found an unlawful tie involving popular movies (the tying product) and less popular movies (the tied product).[67]

Defendants have often avoided antitrust liability for inventory disposition ties.[68] Whether or not the results are sound, the economic analysis has often been deficient. Inventory disposition ties can cause authentic injury to competition when the franchisor possesses market power and the franchisee is forced to sustain the loss from an unpopular product. In defense of such ties, it can be argued that the franchisee's loss is simply a franchise fee—a shifting of the risk of an unpopular product from the franchisor to its independently owned distribution outlets. Still, there are clear allocative injuries from such action. The franchisor decides whether and in what quantities to market a product, and it is the franchisor who should bear the primary market risk. To the extent that a franchisor can use its market power to insulate itself from that risk by forcing unwilling franchisees to take the loss, the franchisor's incentive to take only sound business risks is diluted. The franchisees with little influence on the marketing decision, can be burdened with the direct costs of failure. A franchisor that forces inventory losses on its franchisees will pay an indirect price in terms of lost reputation, but that loss is, for reasons explained in § 6. , likely to be only a partial restraint on the franchisor.

The manufacturer is (and should be) free to use a carrot to persuade reluctant franchisees to sell an unpopular product. For example, a car model that does not sell well can be discounted to dealers, who can reduce retail prices and still sell at a profit. When the manufacturer discounts the product, there is no competitive injury because the loss is properly borne by the manufacturer—the player that controls the decision to produce and market the product.[69]

The analysis may vary when the franchisor asks one or more franchisees to commit to carrying a new product as a condition for retaining the franchise.[70] Such a request differs from the more opportun-

66. *Southern Pines Chrysler–Plymouth,* 826 F.2d at 1362–63.

67. United States v. Loew's, Inc., 371 U.S. 38, 83 S.Ct. 97, 9 L.Ed.2d 11 (1962). See the discussion of *Loew's* in § 8.3d5.

68. In two previously cited cases, the defendant franchisor escaped liability under the antitrust laws, but faced additional issues concerning claims under the Automobile Dealers' Day in Court Act. *Fox Motors,* 806 F.2d at 959–60; *Southern Pines Chrysler–Plymouth,* 826 F.2d 1360.

69. One could also attempt to justify the franchisor's inventory disposition tie in the context of an overall product line, some items of which the franchisee can sell at a high margin and others of which the franchisee must sell at or below cost. This justification may be appealing if the manufacturer has only infrequently and in small doses forced loss items on its franchisees. But the allocation incentives of the market will work better when the manufacturer properly prices both high and low demand items and bears the primary risk for failed products that it introduces.

70. Smith Mach. Co. v. Hesston Corp., 878 F.2d 1290 (10th Cir.1989), cert. denied, 493 U.S. 1073, 110 S.Ct. 1119, 107 L.Ed.2d 1026 (1990).

istic action of forcing a franchisee to dispose of the franchisor's unwanted inventory at the franchisee's expense. The franchisor has a legitimate interest in ensuring that its representative line is carried by franchisees. The franchisee, however, may be locked into the franchise system because of high sunk costs and, in effect, may be forced to accept the new product despite its belief that it will not be profitable. Still, in cases in which the franchisee is contractually committed to carry the franchisor's full line, that commitment, absent unwanted inventory forcing, should be enforced unless the new product, not envisioned when the franchise agreement was signed, would substantially alter the business of the franchisee.

8.9d3. The Economic Benefit Requirement in Franchise Tying Cases

Although the Supreme Court has never imposed such a requirement, some lower court decisions require that a plaintiff establish that the tying seller has some economic benefit in the sale of the tied product. See the discussion in § 8.3d2. Because a financially disinterested franchisor that imposes a sourcing requirement on its franchisees is more likely to do so with an eye to the benefits for the franchise network, at least one court has suggested that the economic benefit test is important in franchising cases.[71] But such a test is unnecessary to protect a franchisor's legitimate interests and can work much mischief.

The franchisor has ample opportunity to vindicate the use of a procompetitive bundling or tie-in without an economic benefit test. For example, if a franchisor imposes a sourcing requirement on its franchisees, forcing them to purchase an input product from a third party supplier, it can defeat an antitrust tie-in claim on a number of grounds. If the sourcing requirement is for a product central to the franchise's operation (such as the ice cream sold through an ice cream franchisor), it may not constitute a tie but will be regarded as a procompetitive bundling. See § 8.3b1. If the bundling is nonetheless regarded as a tie of distinct products, the franchisor may still prevail by demonstrating that its action was a necessary step to maintain quality control. See § 8.3d4. If the franchisor cannot rely on either of these defenses, it can forego use of a tie without losing control over franchisee sourcing decisions: The franchisor can impose reasonable quality requirements and permit qualifying vendors that meet these requirements to compete for sales to franchisees.

The mischief that can be worked by an economic interest requirement is that it can prevent franchisees from challenging genuinely anticompetitive sourcing requirements. Franchisors often receive a payment from a supplier that is awarded exclusive status in selling to the franchisees.[72] Although these payments may be aboveboard and known

---

71. Thompson v. Metropolitan Multi–List, Inc., 934 F.2d 1566, 1579 n. 12 (11th Cir.1991), cert. denied, 506 U.S. 903, 113 S.Ct. 295, 121 L.Ed.2d 219 (1992).

72. The corrupting effect of these pay-

to the franchisees, an economic interest test creates a powerful incentive for a franchisor to keep these payments secret. In some instances, the franchisor itself may be unaware of illicit payments made by the supplier to key franchisor employees that control franchisee relations. In either instance, strict enforcement of an economic interest test imposes a difficult and unnecessary discovery burden on a franchisee that can demonstrate that the tie-in causes genuinely anticompetitive results.

8.9e. Forced Exclusive Dealing

Franchise contracts frequently require the franchisee to market only the products or services produced (or whose trademark is owned) by the franchisor. This practice, called exclusive dealing or a requirements contract, is addressed in § 8.4. In franchising, the competitive analysis of exclusive dealing may be the same as for requirements ties, discussed in § 8.9d1. Indeed, plaintiffs bringing such claims may have a choice whether to characterize the defendant's conduct as a tie-in or as exclusive dealing. For example, under the facts of Standard Oil Co. v. United States,[73] the requirement that a dealer buy only the petroleum products of Standard Oil may be a basis for a claim of unlawful exclusive dealing (as it was) or for a claim of an unlawful sourcing tie (requiring the purchase of Standard Oil gasoline, the tied product, in order to procure the tying product, perhaps the right to operate under the Standard Oil name or to obtain other Standard Oil products).

The reported cases suggest that franchisees have had greater success with tying claims than with exclusive dealing claims. See the cases cited in § 8.9d1. The reason may lie in differences in the substantive law dating to early cases in which the Supreme Court saw tying as inherently anticompetitive and exclusive dealing as capable of both harms and benefits. Tie-ins are still governed by a modified *per se* rule—one that may allow the court to restrict the scope or nature of evidence brought in defense of the practice. See § 8.3d1. For exclusive dealing, the most recent Supreme Court case is Tampa Electric Co. v. Nashville Coal Co.,[74] a 1961 holding in which the Court found that a long-term requirements contract did not violate Section 3 of the Clayton Act. That case, discussed in § 8.4a, requires a careful market analysis as a prerequisite for establishing that the exclusive dealing "will foreclose competition in a substantial share of the line of commerce affected."[75] Despite the historically diverse antecedents for the law governing these two claims, there is no basis in policy or in law for treating the claims differently.

8.9f. Vertical Maximum Price Fixing

Vertical maximum price fixing, discussed in § 8.7, is the seller's imposition of a maximum resale price on the buyer. Franchisors often attempt to assert control over the end prices a franchisee charges. The

ments received by the franchisor is discussed in § 8.9d1iii.

73. 337 U.S. 293, 69 S.Ct. 1051, 93 L.Ed. 1371 (1949).

74. 365 U.S. 320, 81 S.Ct. 623, 5 L.Ed.2d 580 (1961).

75. Id. at 327.

franchisors' interest is no different from that of any upstream supplier that desires to gain for itself the maximum share of a consumer dollar by squeezing the reseller's margin to the lowest possible level. A supplier cannot squeeze a dealer's margin below a competitive level unless the supplier has market power over the dealer. A franchisor often has this relational market power for reasons addressed in § 6.4c2. When the franchisee's margin is squeezed, the franchisee's profits may decrease, but this will not affect the franchisor as long as the royalty paid by the franchisee is based upon sales, not upon profits (this is usually the case). Thus, at least in the short term, a franchisor may have a substantial incentive to squeeze the franchisee's margin through imposition of a maximum resale price.

The resource misallocation associated with franchisor-imposed price ceilings and requirements ties can be similar—in either case, the franchisee can be forced to accept a lower return on its capital investment and may adjust prices or services on other offerings in an attempt to offset this loss. These distortions, although perhaps of marginal importance to consumers in isolation, take on increasing importance in light of the ubiquity of franchising in the United States. Investors and would be entrepreneurs are, by the thousands, joining the ranks of new franchisees each year. These franchisees are a legitimate class of consumers as buyers of the franchisor's offers. Providing antitrust remedies to franchisees and dealers victimized by vertical maximum price fixing is consistent with bedrock principles of antitrust designed to ensure distribution of capital, products and services in a manner that maximizes consumer welfare. It is to be hoped that the rule of reason, applicable under State Oil Co. v. Khan,[76] will facilitate such claims when market power is shown and competitive harm results.

8.9f1.   Franchising as Fertile Ground for Vertical Maximum Price Fixing

Franchisors frequently have both the incentive and the power to impose resale price limits on franchisees. The franchisors' incentives can be procompetitive, anticompetitive or a mixture of both. Because a franchisor's goods or services are often distributed only through its franchised outlets, there is a risk that some franchisees may become price gougers, demanding a high price that undercuts sales and damages the franchisor's reputation. A maximum resale price fixed by the franchisor might be used to prevent such excessive prices. The franchisor may also have a legitimate interest in running promotional events for the entire franchise system. Such promotions might be more effective if the franchisor can limit the maximum resale price and advertise that price as part of the promotion.

The same market power that might enable procompetitive use of a maximum resale price can also allow exploitative price limits set by the franchisor. The franchisor may seek to capture an ever larger share of

---

76. 522 U.S. 3, 118 S.Ct. 275, 139 L.Ed.2d 199 (1997).

the resale price for itself by limiting the franchisee's markup. Outside the franchise relationship, sellers are often unable to enforce a maximum resale price. If a seller attempts to limit the resale margin below a competitive level, the dealer simply declines to carry the seller's line. But, for reasons detailed in § 6.4c2ii, franchisees are often unable to walk away from the franchisor in the face of such a margin squeeze. Faced with substantial sunk investment in its outlet and franchisor power to impose additional costs or confer business benefits, the franchisee must continue to do business with the franchisor notwithstanding an oppressive price squeeze.

This is the same market power that allows a franchisor to impose a requirements or inventory tie on unwilling franchisees. The competitive injury from exploitative resale price limits or exploitative ties is very much the same: a wealth transfer injury (wealth is transferred from the franchisee to the franchisor), a distortion in allocation of goods and services flowing through the franchise system, and distorted incentives for future investment in an efficient franchise method of distribution. The franchisor's incentive to distort or corrupt the competitive process through tie-ins or resale price limits is linked to its control of the franchisee's capital investment.

Most franchise cases involving vertical maximum price fixing have not focused on the franchisor's potential market power over the franchisee. Understandably so, because pre-*Kodak* theorists have been slow to pinpoint sunk costs as the source of abusive exercises of market power. But judicial recognition of the anticompetitive effect of such abuses did not await the theorists' enlightenment. By the mid–1970s, the Supreme Court and a number of lower courts had acknowledged a franchisor's potential power to coerce franchisees.[77] Among these cases were courts of appeals rulings that franchisor-imposed vertical maximum price fixing was unlawful.[78]

Other pre-*Kahn* appellate opinions involving vertical maximum price fixing show sensitivity to the franchisee's sunk costs or locked-in investment. In two cases, the record showed a franchisee that relocated to a different city at the behest of the franchisor, presumably incurring substantial nonrecoverable costs, on the promise of a more profitable outlet in the new location.[79] In other cases, the factual record was not adequately developed to determine whether franchisor market power was a factor. But the background of these cases is consistent with the existence of franchisee sunk costs and substantial franchisor control over

77. See the cases discussed in § 6.4c2i.

78. Blanton v. Mobil Oil Corp., 721 F.2d 1207 (9th Cir.1983), cert. denied, 471 U.S. 1007, 105 S.Ct. 1874, 85 L.Ed.2d 166 (1985); Milsen Co. v. Southland Corp., 454 F.2d 363 (7th Cir.1971). These cases are discussed in § 8.2b1.

79. Arnott v. American Oil Co., 609 F.2d 873, 877 (8th Cir.1979)(service station lessee gave up a station in Minneapolis and relocated in South Dakota on the franchisor's promise of a more lucrative outlet), cert. denied, 446 U.S. 918, 100 S.Ct. 1852, 64 L.Ed.2d 272 (1980); Greene v. General Foods Corp., 517 F.2d 635, 639 (5th Cir. 1975)(food distributor moved from South Carolina to Florida at the request of General Foods to run a different distributorship), cert. denied, 424 U.S. 942, 96 S.Ct. 1409, 47 L.Ed.2d 348 (1976).

franchisee costs and benefits. These cases include Caribe BMW, Inc. v. Bayerische Motoren Werke Aktiengesellschaft[80] (a car dealer that typically would have substantial nonrecoverable investment in the dealership), and Jack Walters & Sons Corp. v. Morton Building, Inc.[81] (a franchised building materials dealer that may have invested significant nonrecoverable funds in its outlet in return for a grant of an exclusive territory).

8.9f2. Maximum Resale Prices Set in Franchisor Promotional Campaigns

A maximum resale price may be imposed as a part of a promotional campaign instituted by the franchisor.[82] The campaign might be more successful if the franchisor advertises a uniform retail price for the promoted item. Perhaps franchisees expect to bear some or all of the burden of such promotions.[83] But the possibility that franchisees may be exploited is real. A uniform price set for all franchisees necessarily hits the high-cost franchisees the hardest. Franchisees may have high costs because they are inefficiently managed, but also because they are located in areas of high taxes, intensive regulation, high labor costs, or high real estate values. In order to sell at a uniform price, the high-cost franchisee must accept a lower margin (or greater loss) than other franchisees. Although the promotion may be limited to "participating outlets," franchisees may feel obliged to participate because of their fear of jeopardizing their relationship with the franchisor.

Because it is the franchisee's capital invested in the local outlet and because the franchisee is most familiar with local costs and marketing conditions, the franchisee should ordinarily retain resale pricing authority. See the discussion in § 6.4c1ii. A short-term and occasional promotion that requires a uniform price may produce few allocation injuries and be consistent with the precontractual expectations of franchisees. On the other hand, as such promotions become constant or continuing occurrences, the potential for distortion and competitive injury increases.

---

80. 19 F.3d 745 (1st Cir.1994).

81. 737 F.2d 698 (7th Cir.), cert. denied, 469 U.S. 1018, 105 S.Ct. 432, 83 L.Ed.2d 359 (1984).

In Acquaire v. Canada Dry Bottling Co., 24 F.3d 401 (2d Cir.1994), the court's recitation of the record reveals no sunk costs, but the soft drink dealers' vigorous challenge to the maximum resale prices is consistent with either or both of two factual settings: (1) margin squeezing by the supplier that can be enforced because the dealer has substantial nonrecoverable investments in carrying the supplier's line; and (2) the supplier's unexercised product market power that was being exploited by the dealer. A dealer confronting such circumstances would be more likely to bear the substantial risks of litigation to contest the supplier's resale price limit.

82. In Jack Walters, 737 F.2d at 706–07, the court held that a plaintiff dealer lacked standing to challenge its termination for failure to adhere to the manufacturer's advertised prices. The decision shows no sensitivity to the dealer's sunk costs or to the possibility that dealer services desired by consumers would be curtailed if the dealer were compelled to adhere to the advertised retail price.

83. If the franchisor lowers its price as a part of a promotion, it may reasonably expect franchisees to pass along the discount to consumers. But the same monitoring that a manufacturer may use to ensure that a retailer passes along a promotional discount may also be used to enforce a maximum resale price. Acquaire, 24 F.3d at 409–11 (discussing this possibility).

The degree of franchisee participation in a decision to institute a promotion can be consequential. The lack of such participation will not, by itself, establish competitive injury. On the other hand, when there is meaningful franchisee participation in a discussion to implement a promotion, this may tend to negate claims that franchisee expectations were injured. Franchisee participation can itself, however, raise issues of a horizontal antitrust violation. See the discussion in § 8.9h.

The surest protection for a franchisor implementing a systemwide promotion is to avoid setting prices as part of the promotion. The franchisor may still offer price reductions ($.50 off the regular price) or franchisor-financed coupons without risking maximum resale pricing violations.

8.9f3. Maximum Resale Prices Set to Counter Price Gouging

A franchisor may impose maximum resale prices on franchisees in an effort to prevent price gouging by individual franchisees. As the Supreme Court noted in *State Oil Co. v. Khan,* it is possible that a local franchisee will possess market power because of the strength of the franchisor's brand and because there are no nearby franchisees that can provide intrabrand price competition.[84] Under these circumstances, the franchisor might opt to limit the resale prices charged by franchisees.

The problem with this approach is twofold. First, by allowing the franchisor to exercise its market power over a franchisee, a court would be making a judgment that the franchisor's market power is more benign or less harmful than the market power exercised by one or more franchisees. There is no empirical evidence to support this premise. Indeed, there is a real possibility that a franchisor that possesses market power over its franchisees will attempt to squeeze the franchisees' resale margin below a competitive level, giving rise to a variety of competition distorting effects. See the discussion in § 6.4c3ii.

A second problem with use of resale price limits to counter price gouging is that there are often less anticompetitive means available to the franchisor. The franchisor might be able to achieve its goal by suggesting maximum prices. Another solution for a franchisor is to license the opening of additional franchised outlets that can provide the intrabrand competition needed to drive down franchisee prices. Some franchisors may also be in a position to sell their products or services outside the franchise network, providing the necessary intrabrand competition in this manner. Franchisors may simply terminate the franchise contracts of price gouging franchisees. Short of termination, a franchisor is usually in a position to bring substantial pressure to bear on any misbehaving franchisee. Of course, any such conduct can raise the issue of whether a franchisor's actions are genuine efforts to deal with

---

84. 522 U.S. 3, 15–16, 118 S.Ct. 275, 139 L.Ed.2d 199 (1997)(quoting with approval the opinion of Judge Posner in the court below, 93 F.3d 1358, 1362 (7th Cir. 1996)).

excessive prices or are an attempt to squeeze a franchisee's margin below a competitive level.

There are situations in which an upstream seller should be allowed to impose a maximum resale price as a counter to price-gouging dealers. For example, if the dealer is a natural monopolist because it would be inefficient to open competing outlets that discipline the dealer's pricing, the seller may lack effective counters (other than vertical maximum price fixing) to control the price-gouging dealer. These circumstances are discussed in § 8.7d4. A franchisee could not be considered a natural monopolist if the franchisor could efficiently open additional competing outlets that can discipline resale pricing. If, however, the franchisor can demonstrate that this and other alternatives to maximum resale prices are inefficient or infeasible, the franchisor should be permitted to impose resale price limits on franchisees possessing local market power.

8.9f4. *Maximum Resale Prices Under a Rule of Reason*

Because the Supreme Court's opinion in *Khan* did not expressly address vertical maximum price fixing in a franchising context, and because the Court's opinion gave little indication of how maximum resale prices would be assessed under the rule of reason, there is considerable uncertainty how future franchisee claims of vertical maximum price fixing will be assessed. A rule of reason claim can be sustained only upon a showing of the defendant's market power, so the relevant market for assessing market power will be an issue. The controversy concerning the appropriate market definition in franchise antitrust cases is addressed in § 8.9c.

8.9g. Monopolization and Attempted Monopolization Claims

Franchisees have at various times challenged franchisor conduct as monopolization or attempted monopolization in violation of Section 2 of the Sherman Act. In some instances, the franchisee attacks sourcing or pricing controls both as a violation of Section 1 of the Sherman Act (and perhaps Section 3 of the Clayton Act) and as abusive conduct that violates Section 2 of the Sherman Act. In other instances, franchisees have claimed that franchisor conduct in encroaching on the franchisee's territory or in wrongfully terminating a franchise constitutes a violation of Section 2.

Chapter III addresses the elements of a claim for monopolization (§ 3.1a) or attempted monopolization (§ 3.6). A key requirement for success of either of these claims is a proper showing of market power in the relevant market. Thus, as with claims brought under Section 1 of the Sherman Act, the franchisee's success often depends upon the market definition. If the defendant establishes a market consisting of all precontractual franchise opportunities available to the franchisee, the franchisee will inevitably lose. If the franchisor's relational market power is evident, the franchisee has an opportunity to establish an antitrust claim. Market definition in franchise antitrust cases is addressed in § 8.9c.

8.9g1.   *Attempted Monopoly Based on Sourcing or Pricing Abuses*

If a franchisee challenges what it perceives as abusive sourcing or resale pricing restraints imposed by a franchisor, the logic of a Section 2 claim gained new recognition after Image Technical Services, Inc. v. Eastman Kodak Co.[85] *Kodak* was a nonfranchise case in which independent service organizations that competed with Kodak in servicing micrographic equipment successfully asserted a market definition limited to aftermarket parts for Kodak machines. The plaintiffs dropped their tie-in claims against Kodak before obtaining a favorable jury verdict, a tactic that may suggest that a monopolization claim may in some instances be established more easily, or with fewer elements that might confuse a jury, than a tie-in claim. The *Kodak* result notwithstanding, franchisee claims of abusive franchisor sourcing control, whether brought as tie-ins, forced exclusive dealing or monopolization claims, will generally succeed or fail based on the market definition adopted.[86]

8.9g2.   *Attempted Monopoly Based on Encroachment or Wrongful Termination*

Franchisors and franchisees frequently are at odds over decisions by the franchisor to expand the number of franchise outlets. Because additional outlets bring the franchisor additional sales, the franchisor may wish to expand even in instances in which a new outlet substantially undermines the profitability of an existing franchisee. Franchisees, on the other hand, have a selfish interest in opposing even the most procompetitive expansion that might incrementally undercut their returns. Neither franchisors nor franchisees, acting alone, may favor an optimal degree of expansion.

To understand why a franchisor has incentives to expand beyond the optimal competitive level, a result known as encroachment, compare a vertically integrated fast-food chain with one that operates through franchised outlets. Assume that the McBurger Company, vertically integrated, owns two fast-food outlets in Small City. McBurger will open an additional outlet only if the profitability of the new outlet would be satisfactory *and* would not be offset by a decrease in profits at the remaining Small City outlets. After weighing these considerations, the vertically integrated McBurger decides to establish one new outlet, making a total of three citywide. This response of the vertically integrat-

---

85. 125 F.3d 1195 (9th Cir.1997), cert. denied, 523 U.S. 1094, 118 S.Ct. 1560, 140 L.Ed.2d 792 (1998).

86. Franchisees were unsuccessful in asserting both tie-in and monopolization claims in Valley Products Co. v. Landmark, 128 F.3d 398 (6th Cir.1997)(assessing only interbrand market power and declining to recognize a *Kodak* lock-in theory); and Queen City Pizza, Inc. v. Domino's Pizza,

Inc., 124 F.3d 430 (3d Cir.1997)(same), cert. denied, 523 U.S. 1059, 118 S.Ct. 1385, 140 L.Ed.2d 645 (1998). In another franchise sourcing case, the court denied the franchisor's motion for summary judgment on the franchisee's monopolization claims. Collins v. International Dairy Queen, Inc., 980 F.Supp. 1252 (M.D.Ga.1997).

ed firm becomes a benchmark for estimating the ideal allocation of capital and resources.[87]

The incentives change significantly if McBurger is considering expansion of franchised outlets. McBurger will still consider whether opening new outlets will increase its overall sales and profitability. But the decrease in revenues and profits for an existing outlet becomes relatively less important, because that loss is no longer borne directly by McBurger. Any increase in overall sales in Small City will increase McBurger's royalties, even if sales of existing outlets decrease below a satisfactory market level for return on their investment. The franchisor's incentive to expand is also enhanced if the franchisor receives up front franchise fees each time a new outlet is established (even if that outlet should quickly fail).

If McBurger Company is well run, its managers will heed the concerns of its existing Small City franchisees in order to maintain good franchisee relations. Still, a decision to expand the number of Small City outlets will increase McBurger's revenues and profits primarily through someone else's capital outlay. The question is, which incentive will control? For some franchisors, the incentive to increase revenues and profits through expansion may be irresistible, particularly if disaffection of current franchisees can be kept to a minimum. One way to reduce disaffection is to offer the new franchise location to the nearest existing franchisee, whose sales would be most heavily diluted by the new outlet. The franchisor presents the matter in this manner: "We have decided to open a new outlet. We are offering you the first chance to purchase and operate this outlet." The franchisee might prefer not to have the new outlet established at all. Operation of the outlet may increase the franchisee's revenues, but not sufficiently to offset the owner-operator's increased costs. Nonetheless, given the franchisee's high sunk costs, it may reluctantly agree to purchase the new location as a way of cutting the reduction in its net profit (or reducing losses) that would occur if someone else purchased the outlet.

Under these circumstances, McBurger Company decides it will open two new outlets in Small City, offering one each to two existing franchisees. There would be four McBurger outlets in Small City, one more than would have been opened had McBurger been a vertically integrated chain. The overall impact of this expansion is increased revenues and profitability for McBurger. But there will be a misallocation of capital to the extent the operation of the new outlet forces down profitability of the Small City outlets below a rate that a franchisee would tolerate absent its high sunk costs. Keep in mind that the franchisor's response to overexpansion will vary depending on whether new outlets are manufac-

---

87. Of course, to the extent that a franchise system can more efficiently do business than a vertically integrated chain, this benchmark would have to be adjusted. Franchising may have significant efficiency advantages over a vertically integrated chain (such as harvesting the entrepreneurial energy of franchisee owners) but may also carry with it certain inefficiencies (such as more frequent and difficult-to-resolve disputes). See the discussion in § 6.4c1.

turer-owned or franchised. If a vertically integrated chain has expanded to the point that its outlets face declining revenues and profits, it will have a direct financial incentive to close one or more of its outlets. But a franchisor may have little incentive to close a franchisee-owned outlet that has insufficient sales and is undercutting the profitability of nearby outlets. As long as the expansion has produced an increase in overall sales, the franchisor benefits in the short run (through increased royalties) by allowing each of the struggling outlets to operate.

In cases challenging encroachment, the appropriate test of antitrust injury should not be a showing by neighboring franchisees that their sales were marginally affected. A merits test is whether a vertically integrated firm would have opened the new outlet. Because that test may be difficult to apply, a court seeking to resolve an encroachment dispute may look to whether the expansion is pursuant to an orderly plan that furthers the franchisor's interests while showing sensitivity to the interests of existing franchises. Although marginal loss of revenue by an existing franchisee should not establish competitive injury, a reduction in the profitability of an existing outlet below the level a reasonable investor without sunk costs would require may establish an allocative injury.

Franchisees have occasionally brought actions under Section 2 of the Sherman Act to challenge encroachment. In Photovest Corp. v. Fotomat Corp.,[88] the plaintiff purchased from the defendant franchisor the right to open fifteen drive-through, film development kiosks in Marion County, Indiana (Indianapolis). The plaintiff alleged that after it had profitably established its outlets, the defendant, in an effort to pressure the plaintiff to sell its interests, established new outlets that undercut the profitability of plaintiff's existing outlets. The Seventh Circuit affirmed the district court's judgment for the plaintiff on an attempted monopoly count, finding market power in a relevant submarket consisting of drive-through, film development kiosks (excluding other providers of film development services such as drugstores or supermarkets).[89]

This definition of the relevant market is strained. The power that the defendant in *Photovest* possessed was directly linked to the franchisor's relational market power (the franchisee's high sunk costs and the franchisor's control over the franchisee's costs and benefits). This power could surely have been exercised regardless of whether the defendant had a large or small share in an interbrand market of film development services.[90] The court reached what seems a sound result, but not on

88. 606 F.2d 704 (7th Cir.1979), cert. denied, 445 U.S. 917, 100 S.Ct. 1278, 63 L.Ed.2d 601 (1980). In Domed Stadium Hotel, Inc. v. Holiday Inns, Inc., 732 F.2d 480, 486–91 (5th Cir.1984), the franchisee brought claims under Sections 1 and 2 of the Sherman Act challenging alleged unlawful encroachment and wrongful termination. The claims were dismissed for failure to satisfy the conspiracy requirement under Section 1 and because the franchisor was not shown to have market power in the interbrand hotel market as required under Section 2. The court did not address any franchisor market power that might have arisen because of the franchisee's sunk costs.

89. 606 F.2d at 711–21.

90. The extent of the defendant's market power in an interbrand setting is relevant to this extent: Without a market niche

grounds that make economic sense. Confronted with the same facts today, the court might have relied on *Kodak* to explain the defendant's relational market power based on the " 'commercial realities' "[91] confronting the franchisee.

The Supreme Court has yet to address a franchise antitrust claim on facts analogous to *Photovest*. But the Court's treatment of an exclusionary practice in Aspen Skiing Co. v. Aspen Highlands Skiing Corp.[92] is instructive. The plaintiff, owner of a ski resort in Aspen, Colorado, brought a monopolization claim against the owner of the remaining three ski resorts in the Aspen area. The defendant refused to continue a cooperative arrangement for the sale of an "all-area" lift ticket, instead offering skiers a ticket for the three areas that it owned. The plaintiff's inability to participate in the all-area ticket brought a substantial drop in its revenues. On this record, the Court upheld a jury verdict that the defendant had violated Section 2 of the Sherman Act.

Eight years after the Court's ruling in *Aspen Skiing*, the defendant announced a plan to purchase the plaintiff's ski resort (by then owned by someone else).[93] This acquisition, which apparently proceeded without antitrust objection, gave the defendant ownership of all four local ski resorts. The result in *Aspen Skiing,* and the subsequent and presumably lawful acquisition of the fourth resort, are difficult to reconcile. Although not suggested by the Court's analysis, the *Aspen Skiing* defendant's power in the local Aspen market might possibly be traced to relational market power.[94] Because the all-area ticket had been the standard arrangement since 1962,[95] the plaintiff may well have invested in maintaining and improving its resort with the expectation that the all-area ticket would continue to be offered. Thus, as in a franchise case, horizontal cooperation among franchisees, or the consolidated ownership of adjacent outlets in a single owner, is generally unobjectionable because of competition in the broader interbrand market. But abusive behavior by the dominant resort owner (or by the franchisor) is anticom-

---

that allowed the franchisor to price profitably the services provided by its kiosks, the defendant would have had no incentive to take over the kiosks operated by the plaintiff franchisee. Put another way, there probably would have been no litigation without some inelasticity of demand in the interbrand market (an ability to price above interbrand rivals without losing substantial sales).

91. Eastman Kodak Co. v. Image Technical Servs., Inc., 504 U.S. 451, 482, 112 S.Ct. 2072, 119 L.Ed.2d 265 (1992).

92. 472 U.S. 585, 105 S.Ct. 2847, 86 L.Ed.2d 467 (1985).

93. *Ski Merger May Perk Up Aspen,* N.Y. Times, Nov. 20, 1993, § 1, at 37.

94. Another explanation, not inconsistent with the plaintiff's sunk costs, is that skiers preferred the convenience and freedom of choice that came with a lift ticket that would allow admission to any of the four Aspen-area resorts. *Aspen Skiing,* 472 U.S. at 605–07. Thus, the allocative injury worked by the defendant's exclusionary conduct would be felt both by the plaintiff competitor and by consumers (skiers). In franchising, franchisor opportunism may also work an allocative injury at two levels, injuring the franchisee and potentially injuring consumers through altered pricing or service offered by the franchisee as the result of the franchisor abuse. For further discussion of *Aspen Skiing,* see § 3.4b4.

95. *Aspen Skiing,* 472 U.S. at 589.

petitive if it exploits the sunk costs or other relational market power of an investor within the intrabrand market.[96]

The result in *Photovest* has not produced a flood of litigation by disgruntled franchisees. Not every franchisee will succeed in showing franchisor market power.[97] Moreover, the mere existence of franchisor market power does not render every decision by a franchisor to expand an unlawful attempted monopolization. The franchisee still must bear the burden of establishing abusive conduct that shows allocative injury, a showing linked to the unreasonableness of the franchisor's expansion. The franchisor may counter allegations of abusive conduct by showing that the acquiring of new outlets was part of an orderly market expansion designed with sensitivity to its existing franchisees.[98]

8.9h. Antitrust Claims Against Franchisees

The antitrust claims discussed in the previous sections are brought by franchisees against franchisors. Franchisor claims against franchisees are less likely, perhaps because franchisees generally do not have the market power that is the root of anticompetitive injury. One question that has arisen is whether franchisees violate Section 1 of the Sherman Act when they band together to increase their bargaining leverage with the franchisor. Even under such circumstances, franchisees may lack intrabrand market power because of the disciplining effect of interbrand competition with rival firms in competition with the franchisor. But the lack of market power will not be a defense if a *per se* rule applies to such horizontal activity.[99]

For example, if franchisees cooperative activity is designed to protect against encroachment, the market division that occurs appears to fall under the *per se* rule announced in United States v. Topco Associates, Inc.[100] Applying *Topco*, the Third Circuit concluded that radius letters sent to franchisees, allowing them to express their views about the opening of a nearby outlet, constituted a violation of Section 1 of the Sherman Act.[101] Use of a *per se* rule to condemn such give-and-take between franchisors and franchisees is unwarranted. As is developed in § 5.5 (discussing the law governing horizontal market divisions), there is doubt about the wisdom of *Topco* as a broad holding condemning all horizontal market divisions under a *per se* rule. Discussions between

---

96. The competitive injury in *Photovest* and *Aspen Skiing* can be traced to the same sort of horizontal abuse. In *Photovest*, the franchisor became a direct competitor of the plaintiff franchisee by establishing encroaching outlets. In *Aspen Skiing,* the defendant and the plaintiff were direct competitors in the operation of Aspen-area ski resorts.

97. See the discussion in § 6.4c3. Even if a franchisor has market power, a corporate franchisee with a large number of outlets may have sufficient leverage to counter the effects of that market power.

98. A franchisor might best protect itself against charges of abusive conduct by consulting franchisees before deciding to expand. But franchisee participation may bring antitrust risks of its own. See the discussion in § 8.9h.

99. For a discussion of these issues, see Emerson, *Franchising and the Collective Rights of Franchisees,* 43 VAND. L. REV. 1503 (1990).

100. 405 U.S. 596, 92 S.Ct. 1126, 31 L.Ed.2d 515 (1972).

101. American Motor Inns, Inc. v. Holiday Inns, Inc., 521 F.2d 1230 (3d Cir.1975).

franchisors and franchisees about territorial expansion have a strong vertical element, and vertical territorial allocations are now clearly subject to the rule of reason. See § 7. Seen in vertical terms, a location clause that protects the territorial integrity of a franchisee's operations is more defensible as a franchisee pours more of its own capital into the operation. Without territorial protection, a franchisee might be unwilling to make that substantial investment—and a major benefit of franchising would be lost. Moreover, under Broadcast Music, Inc. v. CBS, Inc.,[102] even strictly horizontal territorial allocations may be subject to the rule of reason if a substantial efficiency is thereby achieved. In a franchise context, that efficiency might be found in the smoother functioning of a franchise system that provides efficient distribution in many industries.

Despite what may be a fairly wide opening for lawful cooperative activity by franchisees, that window has obvious limits. Where franchisees conspire to prevent the franchisor from dealing directly or indirectly with discounters, that activity will fall within the proscription of United States v. General Motors Corp.[103] In that case, Chevrolet dealers were found to have unlawfully conspired to eliminate sales from the manufacturer to discounting dealers. Clearly, franchisee cooperative activity that operates directly to increase or maintain retail prices, and thereby to reduce output, is vulnerable. But the *General Motors* case can be easily distinguished from one in which the franchisees merely resist participation in a promotion that will set a maximum resale price on the franchisor's product. Under this scenario, retail competition among discounting franchisees is not suppressed.

102. 441 U.S. 1, 99 S.Ct. 1551, 60 L.Ed.2d 1 (1979).

103. 384 U.S. 127, 86 S.Ct. 1321, 16 L.Ed.2d 415 (1966).

Chapter IX

MERGERS: AN OVERVIEW

Table of Sections

§ 9.1 Introduction

Merger enforcement, like other areas of antitrust, is directed at market power. It shares with the law of monopolization a degree of schizophrenia: an aversion to potent power that heightens risk of abuse; and tolerance of that degree of power required to attain economic benefits. Mergers can be harmful—as when they facilitate oligopolistic practices or single firm strategic behavior that brings control over price and output. But most mergers are probably benign or even procompetitive. Mergers help to ensure the relatively free flow of capital and can create scale efficiencies or tie together complementary businesses in a manner that creates economic gain. The most difficult mergers to assess may be those that combine both negative and positive effects: creating market power that increases the risk of oligopolistic pricing while at the same time creating efficiencies that reduce production or marketing costs.

Contemporary merger enforcement dates from 1977 when the premerger notification program was implemented. It has a number of unique aspects that separate it from the rest of antitrust. The first of these is the prophylactic nature of most merger enforcement. Unlike monopolization cases that address abusive exercise of market power, the aim of merger enforcement is to prevent the creation of market power. It anticipates potential market abuses arising from power rather than responding to those that have already occurred. This prophylactic aspect makes merger control at once a powerful and effective enforcement tool, yet one laden with the uncertainties inherent in predicting the future effects of market conduct. The goal of merger enforcement is to stop those combinations with likely anticompetitive consequences that outweigh likely competitive benefits. No matter how well grounded in economic theory and historical experience, there is a speculative dimension to such predictions about future competitive effects.

A second and related unique feature of merger enforcement is its direct concern with oligopolistic power. Many of the means by which oligopolists can achieve supracompetitive returns may be beyond prosecution under existing antitrust statutes. But the prophylactic nature of merger enforcement is well suited to anticipate and forestall the creation of oligopolistic structures that might facilitate interdependent pricing or other harms beyond the reach of the law. At least since the Celler–Kefauver Act of 1950, merger enforcement has focused more on preventing the creation of industry structure conducive to oligopoly power and less on single firm market dominance—perhaps because fewer mergers that could create single firm market dominance have been attempted.

Finally, the enforcement mechanism for mergers is unique. Merger enforcement is now dominated by the federal antitrust agencies, with supplementary roles played by state attorneys general and private plaintiffs. Far more than other areas of antitrust, merger enforcement implicates issues of discretion in the proper functioning of a limited but highly consequential regulatory scheme: the premerger notification system. As much as two-thirds of the enforcement resources of the two federal agencies has been dedicated to reviewing proposed mergers before they occur and challenging a small percentage of them. The prophylactic remedies imposed by the agencies are also unique, and most often implemented without any significant role for the courts. Reported merger decisions have become the exception rather than the rule. Meanwhile, merger enforcement by state attorneys general grew during the 1980s, a period when many regarded federal enforcement as unduly lax. Private enforcement, although severely undercut as the result of a controversial standing decision,[1] retains a significant secondary role.

9.1a. Definitions

The term "merger" in the antitrust context is often used more broadly than that term is understood in state corporations law. In corporations law, a merger is the process by which two separately incorporated entities become a single corporation. In antitrust dialogue, "merger" is sometimes used to include, in addition to the more precise corporate law meaning, any acquisition of the assets or stock of another firm. For example, the premerger notification program administered by the Federal Trade Commission and the Department of Justice applies to acquisitions of another firm's assets or stock. Even acquisitions that involve only a part of a firm's assets (for example, an operating division) or a percentage of a firm's stock (for example, enough for the acquiring firm to influence the conduct of the firm whose stock is acquired) may be subject to antitrust scrutiny. An acquisition of insubstantial assets of a firm (such as a machine or a stock of raw materials) or a small investment portfolio in another firm's stock would generally be beyond the reach of antitrust merger law.

In antitrust analysis, mergers are classified as horizontal (involving direct competitors), vertical (involving firms in a customer-supplier relationship), or conglomerate (involving neither direct competitors nor customer-supplier relationship). There are two types of conglomerate mergers that may reduce potential competition: market extension mergers between firms that make the same product but distribute in distinct geographic markets; and product line extension mergers between firms that make different products but whose production processes or marketing channels are similar. Such mergers are analyzed differently from pure conglomerate mergers, those lacking complementarities warranting concern about potential competition.

9.1b. Summary of the Law

The primary federal antitrust statutes governing mergers are Section 7 and Section 7A of the Clayton Act.[2] Section 7 prohibits mergers (acquisitions of stock or assets of another firm) that, in any line of commerce in any section of the country, may substantially lessen competition or tend to create a monopoly. Invocation of Section 7 requires a showing of market power, but less power than is required for monopolization, or even attempted monopolization, under Section 2 of the Sherman Act. To succeed, a plaintiff need not prove that the merged entity is likely to commit antitrust violations in the future. It is sufficient to show that the merger may substantially lessen competition. Actions to enforce Section 7 may be brought by the Justice Department, by the FTC, by

---

§ 9.1

1. Cargill, Inc. v. Monfort of Colorado, Inc., 479 U.S. 104, 107 S.Ct. 484, 93

L.Ed.2d 427 (1986). See the discussion in § 10.4b.

2. 15 U.S.C.A. §§ 18, 18a.

state attorneys general, or by private litigants. A merger may also be attacked as a violation of Section 1 or Section 2 of the Sherman Act[3] or, in the case of the FTC, as a violation of Section 5 of the FTC Act.[4]

Section 7 remains the heart of merger enforcement. Interpretations of the language—"the effect * * * may be substantially to lessen competition"—have varied, reaching the point of maximum coverage during the 1960s, but more recently according merging firms greater leeway. Interpretations of Section 7 are linked to the type of merger (horizontal, vertical or conglomerate) and, in more recent cases, have been strongly influenced by agency merger guidelines.

Section 7A of the Clayton Act, added by the Hart–Scott–Rodino Act of 1976,[5] requires premerger reporting of certain substantial acquisitions. Under this provision, qualifying mergers must be reported in advance of consummation to both the FTC and the Antitrust Division of the Department of Justice. The merger cannot be lawfully consummated until the requisite waiting period has lapsed or the agencies grant early termination. A substantial body of administrative practice now surrounds Section 7A and the FTC's interpretive regulation governing that section.[6]

§ 9.2 Historical Overview

9.2a. The First Merger Wave and Early Merger Cases

Although merger activity has been continuous throughout the last century, periods of intense activity—merger waves—can be documented from 1887–1904, from 1916–1929, during the mid–1960s, in the 1980s, and again in the late 1990s.[1] Each of these waves has had defining characteristics. The first wave, said to have parallels in Great Britain and Germany, often involved the simultaneous consolidation of five or more firms into a single, market-dominating enterprise. United States Steel, for example, was the result of a combination of combinations: two hundred independent firms were combined into twenty firms, many of them vertically integrated. Thereafter, twelve of these firms were consolidated yet again to create United States Steel.[2] Among the industries that spawned mergers creating dominant or near dominant firms were petroleum, tobacco, steel, copper, lead, railroad cars, explosives, tin cans, electrical equipment, rubber products, paper, farm machinery, brickmaking, chemicals, leather, sugar, business machines, photographic supplies, and shoe machinery.[3] Larger firms had the advantage of better scale

---

3. 15 U.S.C.A. §§ 1, 2.

4. 15 U.S.C.A. § 45.

5. Hart–Scott–Rodino Antitrust Improvements Act of 1976, Pub. L. No. 94–435, Title II, § 201, 90 Stat. 1390 (1976) (codified as amended at 15 U.S.C.A. § 18a).

6. Codified at 16 C.F.R. §§ 801–803.

§ 9.2

1. F.M. Scherer & D. Ross, Industrial Market Structure and Economic Performance 153–59 (3d ed. 1990).

2. Id. at 155.

3. Id. For more detailed descriptions of this early merger wave, see Markham, *Survey of the Evidence and Findings on Merger, in* Business Concentration and Price Poli-

economies in production, transportation and advertising. But even large firms could not control capacity unless they formed a cartel or achieved near market dominance. Cartels were fragile, and legally vulnerable under Section 1 of the Sherman Act,[4] so mergers were an enticing avenue for achieving this desired control over output and price.

Typically, structural imperatives (such as scale economies), conditions in the financial markets, and legal or regulatory developments combine to influence the timing and extent of merger waves. Merger activity declined in 1903 and 1904, probably as the result of a severe economic recession and because the Justice Department began to attack market-dominating mergers under the Sherman Act.[5] Almost from its inception, the Sherman Act has been invoked against extensive consolidation, including early cases involving the distillery industry[6] and the sugar industry.[7] Some of these early cases were setbacks for Government merger enforcement. In United States v. E. C. Knight Co., the Supreme Court held that a series of acquisitions that gave the defendant 98 percent of the sugar-refining capacity in the nation involved only manufacture, not the interstate commerce that "succeeds to manufacture."[8] The *Knight* decision, now long ignored as a legal precedent, left its lasting mark on American industrial market structure by permitting the merger wave to continue after 1904.

The Government prevailed in a major merger case in 1904: Northern Securities Co. v. United States.[9] The case involved a consolidation of major railroads owned by Morgan and Hill (acting in concert) and Harriman. Made into a major showcase by President Theodore Roosevelt and Attorney General Knox, the Government showed that what the defendants characterized as a mere acquisition of stock with incidental market effects was a consolidation of interests that substituted control where competition had once prevailed.[10] The holding of the Court seemed broad, albeit limited by Justice Harlan's inability to command a fifth Justice on his opinion. The opinion implied that the Sherman Act would be violated by *any* merger between previously competing firms, however slight the competitive consequences, and regardless of the purpose that motivated the merger.[11] Accepting this position as the law, the district

---

CY 141, 154–67 (1955); R. Nelson, MERGER MOVEMENTS IN AMERICAN INDUSTRY, 1895–1956 (1959) (counting 3238 acquisitions and consolidations between 1895–1905).

4. See United States v. Addyston Pipe & Steel Co., 85 F. 271 (6th Cir.1898), modified and aff'd, 175 U.S. 211, 20 S.Ct. 96, 44 L.Ed. 136 (1899), and the discussion of the development of the law governing horizontal restraints in § 5.3.

5. SCHERER & ROSS, supra note 1, at 155.

6. See United States v. Greenhut, 50 F. 469 (D.Mass.1892); In re Greene, 52 F. 104 (S.D. Ohio 1892).

7. United States v. E. C. Knight Co., 156 U.S. 1, 15 S.Ct. 249, 39 L.Ed. 325 (1895).

8. Id. at 12.

9. 193 U.S. 197, 24 S.Ct. 436, 48 L.Ed. 679 (1904); see also Loewe v. Lawlor, 208 U.S. 274, 28 S.Ct. 301, 52 L.Ed. 488 (1908).

10. See W. LETWIN, LAW AND ECONOMIC POLICY IN AMERICA 182–237 (1980).

11. *Northern Securities*, 193 U.S. at 331. The opinion perhaps reflects the early conception that Section 1, forbidding "every" restraint, should be construed sweepingly—or construed, at least, to give the enforcement agency broad authority to select targets.

courts in later cases challenging the oil[12] and tobacco trusts[13] held these consolidations unlawful simply because they brought together under common ownership previously competing firms. Thus, while *Knight* facilitated the great merger movement by limiting antitrust enforcement, *Northern Securities* helped to end the wave by restoring an enforcement threat.

When the oil and tobacco trust cases reached the Supreme Court in 1911, Justice White wrote the opinions that embraced a rule of reason standard, a median position between the extremes of *Knight* and *Northern Securities*. Standard Oil Co. v. United States, which yielded the primary opinion, stressed that only "undue restraints" transcended the Sherman Act's limits.[14] Both the oil and tobacco consolidations merged a substantial portion of the proprietary interests of a great national industry, and it was this, as well as the calculated way in which the consolidation was effected—precisely for the purpose of attaining control—that put them beyond the bounds of lawful conduct.[15] The Court put to rest arguments that the form of the merger (for example, an acquisition of assets[16]) might be sufficient to remove a merger from the reach of the Sherman Act: the Act's "all-embracing enumeration" was intended "to make sure that no form of contract or combination * * * could save" an unreasonable restraint.[17]

Although the rule of reason announced in *Standard Oil* provided needed flexibility for dealing with mergers, it failed to provide workable and concrete guidance. Because the rule focused on *conduct*, both pre- and post-merger, it appeared to give little or no weight to the structural considerations that are critical in modern merger analysis. This weakness was confirmed in United States v. United States Steel Corp.[18] in which the Court held that the defendant's conduct, including the acquisitions that led to near dominance, did not violate the Sherman Act. The case is devoid of the structural analysis that characterizes modern merger and monopolization law.

9.2b. The Clayton Act and the Second Merger Wave

Well before *United States Steel* was decided, and notwithstanding the Government's success in the oil and tobacco cases, there was a political response to the perceived inadequacies of antitrust enforcement. Legislative proposals were offered to specify what the law permitted, but also, in a few cases, to turn merger enforcement over to a specialized agency empowered to intervene in transactions with little statutory

12. United States. v. Standard Oil Co., 173 F. 177, 183–86 (E.D. Mo. 1909), modified and aff'd, 221 U.S. 1, 31 S.Ct. 502, 55 L.Ed. 619 (1911).

13. United States v. American Tobacco Co., 164 Fed. 700, 702–07 (S.D.N.Y.1908), rev'd, 221 U.S. 106, 31 S.Ct. 632, 55 L.Ed. 663 (1911).

14. 221 U.S. 1, 60, 62, 31 S.Ct. 502, 55 L.Ed. 619 (1911).

15. Id. at 76–77.

16. Cincinnati, Portsmouth, Big Sandy, & Pomeroy Packet Co. v. Bay, 200 U.S. 179, 26 S.Ct. 208, 50 L.Ed. 428 (1906).

17. 221 U.S. at 59–60.

18. 251 U.S. 417, 40 S.Ct. 293, 64 L.Ed. 343 (1920).

guidance. Still other proposals provided for agency preclearance of specified corporate actions,[19] an early hint of a premerger notification scheme that was not to arrive until 1976. In the 1912 election campaign, Taft, Roosevelt, Wilson and their parties, each in their own way, committed themselves to legislation more rigorous than existing Court interpretations.[20]

The legislative process after Wilson's election yielded both the Federal Trade Commission Act[21] and the Clayton Act.[22] Section 7 of the Clayton Act, later to become the most significant substantive provision of that Act, was born, albeit in a form that initially proved ineffective as a merger enforcement tool. In its original form, the Section expressly applied only to acquisitions of another corporation's stock, not to acquisitions of assets. It forbade such stock acquisitions where the effect might be to lessen substantially competition between the acquiring and the acquired firm, to restrain commerce in any section of the country, or to tend to create a monopoly.[23] But if the intent of some of the framers of the Clayton Act had been to provide more concrete guidance as to the line delineating lawful and unlawful mergers, the Act was a short-term failure. The congressional intent underlying Section 7 might be summarized along these lines: Stock acquisitions of competing firms should be held to violate the law, subject to a competitive effect test about which there is no congressional consensus, but with the admonition that the courts, in interpreting Section 7, should employ a stricter test than that established under the Sherman Act.[24]

The FTC sought to eliminate the loophole left for acquisitions of assets in two ways: by interpreting Section 7 of the Clayton Act to cover asset acquisitions consummated after stock had been unlawfully acquired and, presumptively, in the exercise of power attained by virtue of the stock acquisition.[25] The Commission also took the position that an asset acquisition, without any related stock acquisition, could violate Section 5 of the FTC Act.[26] Initially, the Supreme Court held that the Commission could require the disgorgement of assets acquired after an unlawful stock acquisition that gave the respondent the power to affect the asset acquisition, but only as to assets acquired after the date that the Commission filed its complaint.[27] Soon, the Court rejected flatly the

19. D. MARTIN, MERGERS AND THE CLAYTON ACT 20–56 (1959); LETWIN, supra note 10, at 247–55, 270–78.

20. MARTIN, supra note 19, at 23–29.

21. Act of September 26, 1914, ch. 311, 38 Stat. 717 (codified as amended at 15 U.S.C.A. §§ 41–51).

22. Act of October 15, 1914, ch. 323, 38 Stat. 730 (codified as amended at 15 U.S.C.A. §§ 12–27).

23. The development of the original language of Section 7 is traced in MARTIN, supra note 19, at 32–43.

24. Id. at 20–56.

25. Id. at 62–67. For cases in which the FTC ordered the respondent to dispose of assets acquired from a corporation after an acquisition of controlling stock interest was found to violate Section 7, see, e.g., FTC v. Swift & Co., 5 F.T.C. 143 (1922); FTC v. Armour & Co., 4 F.T.C. 457 (1922); FTC v. Western Meat Co., 5 F.T.C. 417 (1923); FTC v. Thatcher Mfg. Co., 6 F.T.C. 213 (1923).

26. MARTIN, supra note 19, at 93–97.

27. FTC v. Western Meat Co., 272 U.S. 554, 47 S.Ct. 175, 71 L.Ed. 405 (1926).

Commission's assertion of authority to dissolve asset acquisitions under Section 5 of the FTC Act.[28] And in 1934, the Court dissolved its rather contorted construction of the Commission's powers under Section 7, ruling that the Commission was powerless to deal with an asset acquisition under that provision even if the assets were acquired after an unlawful stock acquisition.[29]

The collective result of the *United States Steel* decision (construing the Sherman Act narrowly) and of the narrow construction of the FTC's powers was to leave few antitrust obstacles to the second major merger wave, which reached its peak in the late 1920s, only to be abruptly shut down by the Depression. The number of mergers occurring during this period may have approached that of the first merger wave. But these mergers were less likely to produce a single dominant firm, perhaps because antitrust, despite relaxed interpretations, still discouraged such transactions, or because there were simply fewer opportunities for such consolidations.[30] Instead of mergers for monopoly, the 1920s merger wave has been characterized as "mergers for oligopoly."[31]

9.2c. The Celler–Kefauver Amendment

Merger activity remained measured and increased only modestly toward the end of the Second World War. The leading merger case of the 1940s was United States v. Columbia Steel Co. in 1948.[32] United States Steel, through a wholly owned subsidiary, sought to acquire Consolidated Steel, a large West Coast fabricator of specialty steel products. The Government argued that the acquisition would thwart direct competition between the two companies, but would also have foreclosing vertical effects (by eliminating access to Consolidated Steel for competing producers of rolled steel, a raw material used in producing specialty products). Despite an attempt at structural analysis, the Court permitted United States Steel, the leading firm in an already highly concentrated industry, to acquire this substantial West Coast specialty producer.

This second decision involving United States Steel provided impetus for passage of the Celler–Kefauver Act, effecting a pivotal amendment to Section 7 of the Clayton Act.[33] The Amendment made two major changes: (1) Section 7 was made applicable to all mergers, whether by acquisition of stock or assets; and (2) the statement of requisite competitive effect was broadened to cover any substantial reduction in competition, not just competition between the acquired and acquiring firms, thus capturing the foreclosure or cost-raising effects of a merger on rivals. The legislative history shows an intent to plug what Congress

28. FTC v. Eastman Kodak Co., 274 U.S. 619, 47 S.Ct. 688, 71 L.Ed. 1238 (1927).

29. Arrow–Hart & Hegeman Elec. Co. v. FTC, 291 U.S. 587, 54 S.Ct. 532, 78 L.Ed. 1007 (1934).

30. SCHERER & ROSS, supra note 1, at 156.

31. Stigler, *Monopoly and Oligopoly by Merger*, 40 AM. ECON. REV. 23 (1950).

32. 334 U.S. 495, 68 S.Ct. 1107, 92 L.Ed. 1533 (1948).

33. Celler–Kefauver Act of December 29, 1950, ch. 1184, 64 Stat. 1125 (codified as amended at 15 U.S.C.A. §§ 18, 21).

viewed as a loophole in the original section—the failure to cover asset acquisitions.[34] The legislative history concerning foreclosure effects is more vague. There is little to indicate when vertical foreclosure crosses the line of legality. Still, congressional concern with the economic, social and political effects of increased concentration is clear. Lacking well-formed theories about the changing structure of U.S. industry, Congress wanted the courts to be tougher than they had been since 1911. In what came to be known as the "incipiency" doctrine,[35] Congress wished Section 7 applied prophylactically to stop mergers that are likely, alone or as part of a merger movement, to cause irreversible injury to the competitive process.

9.2d. Populist Enforcement and Inadequate Remedies in the 1950s and 1960s

In the face of a strong congressional statement of alarm, but vague statutory language concerning the effects that made a merger unlawful, the enforcement agencies and courts proceeded to apply Section 7 aggressively during the next two decades. Brown Shoe Co. v. United States was the first decision to reach the Supreme Court under the amended Section 7.[36] In an opinion by Chief Justice Warren, the Court condemned Brown Shoe's acquisition of a rival firm (both firms produced and distributed shoes). Much of the analysis the Court undertook was sound. The Court examined the market shares of the participants, the degree of concentration in the industry, the history of the acquired and acquiring firms, whether there was a trend toward concentration, whether the market shares had special significance in light of industry conditions, and whether third party rivals were left vulnerable as the result of the merger. Yet the Court ended up invalidating a rather small merger in a rather competitive industry on the basis of a modest increase in concentration. In doing so, the Court suggested that an increase in efficiency, even if it led to lower costs to consumers, would not save this merger.[37]

Brown Shoe failed to establish a workable rule for weighing the various factors that determine a merger's legality. That left merger analysis open-ended—and allowed the Court to give determinative weight to any of the listed factors. The *Brown Shoe* Court assigned great importance to stopping a trend toward concentration in its incipiency,[38] a consideration that, if it trumps all others, would prohibit the consolidation of any fragmented industry through mergers, even if such a consolidation would produce substantial economies of scale at little cost to competition. Despite the shortcomings of *Brown Shoe*, it is by no means clear that a merger with the characteristics of the Brown–Kinney consol-

---

34. See the review of the legislative history in Brown Shoe Co. v. United States, 370 U.S. 294, 311–23, 82 S.Ct. 1502, 8 L.Ed.2d 510 (1962).

35. See the discussion of the incipiency doctrine in Rodino, *The Future of Antitrust:*

Ideology vs. Legislative Intent, 35 ANTITRUST BULL. 575, 586–87 (1990).

36. 370 U.S. 294, 82 S.Ct. 1502, 8 L.Ed.2d 510 (1962).

37. Id. at 344.

38. Id. at 332, 343–46.

idation would wholly escape antitrust merger enforcement under modern standards. Focusing on the numerous local markets in which the combined entity would have had more than 30 percent of the market, it is possible that divestitures or spin-offs would have been required before clearing such a merger.[39] But such negotiated spin-offs were not before the Court under the all-or-nothing approach of the 1962 case.

One year after deciding *Brown Shoe,* which had suggested an open-ended analysis, the Court announced a more structured test in United States v. Philadelphia National Bank.[40] The Court acknowledged the need to provide a simpler measure of illegality where possible "without doing violence to the congressional objective."[41] It announced a rule of presumptive illegality for any merger "which produces a firm controlling an undue percentage share of the relevant market, and results in a significant increase in the concentration of firms in that market * * *."[42] Although the precise market share or measure of industry concentration was not specified (here the merger resulted in a 30 percent share of the local market), the opinion provides the basis for subsequently developed agency merger guidelines.

After *Philadelphia National Bank,* the Court generally followed a more closed-end analysis of the possible anticompetitive effects of mergers. This, however, has not prevented controversy. In United States v. Von's Grocery Co., the Court struck down a merger involving two Los Angeles retail grocery chains.[43] The largest firm in the market had 8 percent of market sales and the two merging firms, with 4.7 percent and 4.2 percent respectively, were third and sixth largest. Although industry concentration as measured by the four-firm concentration ratio was only 24.4 percent (28.6 percent after the merger), there had been a noticeable concentration trend in the industry during the previous decade. The Court saw in this decision the execution of congressional intent to protect small businesses that might not survive in a world dominated by large chains. Criticism of *Von's* focused on the merging firms' low market shares, arguably too low to produce a substantial risk of oligopoly power and insufficient to allow a firm to achieve a size that reaps maximum gain from scale economies. Critics also questioned the emphasis placed on the trend toward concentration and whether the Court's desire to save small businesses was furthered by the decision. As Justice Stewart pointed out in dissent, no action by the Court could resurrect "Mom and Pop" stores "run over by the automobile or obliterated by the freeway."[44] Although the obituary for the small store was premature, Justice Stewart's underlying point—that the antitrust laws cannot long block economic trends driven by economies of scale or technology—appears sound, if somewhat overdrawn. If the grocery store merger wave was truly driven by a desire to achieve minimum efficient scale, then

39. S. Ross, Principles of Antitrust Law 325 (1993).

40. 374 U.S. 321, 83 S.Ct. 1715, 10 L.Ed.2d 915 (1963).

41. Id. at 362.

42. Id. at 363.

43. 384 U.S. 270, 86 S.Ct. 1478, 16 L.Ed.2d 555 (1966).

44. Id. at 288 (Stewart, J., dissenting).

Justice Stewart was correct in seeing consolidation of power in fewer hands as inevitable. If, on the other hand, the advantages of a large chain rest less in efficiencies and more in its ability to exercise strategic leverage and buying power unrelated to efficiency, then the majority's decision is cast in a more favorable light. Stopping such a merger wave in its incipiency could indeed have protected the small grocery store from a lemming-like rush to consolidation. But the Court failed to deal with these more complex issues of competitive effect, perhaps because they were not adequately presented on the record.

More recent analysis of supermarket mergers has focused on much more confined geographic markets—while consumers will likely drive, not walk to the market, they are thought unlikely to travel more than a few miles for most grocery shopping. Under this view of grocery store markets—a view that Justice Stewart suggested in 1966—the *Von's* outcome still appears questionable. Von's (operating primarily in the southern and western portions of Los Angeles) and Shopping Bag Food Stores (operating primarily in the northern and eastern portions of Los Angeles) had very little overlap in the small neighborhood markets now deemed relevant for market analysis. Apparently each chain had a few stores in common neighborhoods in central Los Angeles,[45] a circumstance that might warrant a required divestiture of one or more of these stores under today's standards, but not the rigid prohibition sought by the Justice Department and sustained by the Court.

The 1960s are widely perceived as the halcyon days for populist merger enforcers, leading to Justice Stewart's famous remark that the "sole consistency" to be found in merger litigation was that "the Government always wins."[46] In fact, the Government more often lost in the remedial phase of the case. One survey of merger cases brought between 1950 and 1960 showed that the federal agencies obtained no relief (21 cases) or deficient relief (8 cases) in 29 of 39 cases.[47] One example is illustrative. Pabst, the nation's tenth largest brewer, acquired Blatz Brewing Company, the eighteenth largest, in 1958.[48] The Department of Justice filed suit challenging the acquisition in 1959, but did not finally prevail until a 1966 decision of the Supreme Court. The *Pabst* decision has been justly criticized for its undisciplined approach to defining the geographic market.[49] But the history of this litigation also demonstrated the inadequacies of the Government's remedial powers. Following the Supreme Court's decision, the case was remanded to find a buyer for what was left of Blatz. But Blatz as a separate entity no longer existed, and finding a buyer for its brewing plant proved impossible. In 1969, the district court dismissed the complaint.[50] Although the Government had won on the merits, it obtained no relief.

45. Id. at 295 (Stewart, J., dissenting).

46. Id. at 301 (Stewart, J., dissenting).

47. Elzinga, *The Antimerger Law: Pyrrhic Victories?*, 12 J.L. & ECON. 43, 48 (1969).

48. United States v. Pabst Brewing Co., 384 U.S. 546, 86 S.Ct. 1665, 16 L.Ed.2d 765 (1966).

49. Elzinga & Hogarty, *The Problem of Geographic Market Delineation in Antimerger Suits*, 18 ANTITRUST BULL. 45 (1973).

50. United States v. Pabst Brewing Co., 296 F.Supp. 994 (E.D.Wis.1969).

The activism surrounding merger enforcement in the 1950s and 1960s did not prevent another major merger wave. In the 1960s in the course of a stock market boom, acquisition activity surged. But merger enforcement affected the direction of this activity. Acquisitions of this era were more likely to be conglomerate, or diversifying. During the period 1948–1955, 39 percent of acquisitions were horizontal and only 10 percent purely conglomerate. During the surge in mergers between 1964 and 1971, these figures were reversed. Only 12 percent of mergers were horizontal, while 35 percent were purely conglomerate. The average number of lines of business in which leading U.S.-manufacturing enterprises operated more than doubled. But levels of industry concentration did not change markedly during the period 1954 to 1982, a result that may be linked to active horizontal merger enforcement during this era.[51]

9.2e. Merger Guidelines and Premerger Notification

Two of the critical shortcomings of merger enforcement of the 1950s and 1960s—the absence of rigor in many court analyses and the wholesale remedial failures of that era—have now been addressed. A step toward adding rigor to merger analysis came with the issuance of the Department of Justice's 1968 Merger Guidelines.[52] This first version of the Guidelines, as with subsequent versions, was designed not to bind the agency but merely to provide guidance to antitrust lawyers and their clients as to how the agency would analyze a merger. Still, as perhaps was inevitable for Guidelines issued by an agency with substantial expertise in merger enforcement, they grew in influence and became a touchstone for judicial analysis.

Major revisions were made in a new edition of the Guidelines in 1982.[53] The Guidelines were revised yet again in 1984.[54] The current Guidelines governing horizontal mergers were jointly issued by the Department of Justice and the FTC in 1992.[55] Vertical and conglomerate mergers were not addressed by the 1992 Guidelines, and remain governed by the Department of Justice's 1984 guidelines.[56]

The response to the Government's inability to obtain adequate relief for unlawful mergers came in the form of a mandatory premerger notification program, enacted as part of the Hart–Scott–Rodino Act of 1976.[57] Premerger notification, the last major legislative change that has produced today's prophylactic merger enforcement mechanism, allows the federal agencies to investigate major acquisitions before they occur,

51. The figures presented in this paragraph are from SCHERER & ROSS, supra note 1, at 156–58.

52. U.S. Department of Justice, Merger Guidelines (1968), reprinted in 4 TRADE REG. REP. (CCH) ¶ 13,101.

53. U.S. Department of Justice, Merger Guidelines (1982), reprinted in 4 TRADE REG. REP. (CCH) ¶ 13,102.

54. U.S. Department of Justice, Merger Guidelines (1984), reprinted in 4 TRADE REG. REP. (CCH) ¶ 13,103.

55. U.S. Department of Justice and Federal Trade Commission, Merger Guidelines (1992), set forth in Appendix C.

56. 1984 Merger Guidelines § 4.

57. The Act added Section 7A to the Clayton Act (codified as amended at 15 U.S.C.A. § 18a).

and, in the event they are found to raise serious antitrust issues, to seek injunctive relief to preserve the target firm as an independent entity pending a judicial resolution of antitrust issues. Another result of premerger notification was to transform merger enforcement more into the realm of administrative law, with less judicial oversight of the result.

9.2f. The 1980s Merger Wave

Although premerger notification appeared to ensure the preeminence of federal merger enforcement (only the Department of Justice and FTC received premerger notifications), state merger enforcement activity enjoyed a renaissance in the 1980s, in part because of a perceived laxness in federal enforcement of merger law during that period. The states adopted their own set of merger guidelines and worked cooperatively to extend their limited resources. See the discussion in § 10.3.

The 1980s also saw the fourth major merger wave. Mergers during the 1980s were sparked initially by low stock prices (making acquisition of a firm's stock a cheap way to acquire desired assets), but continued during stock market recovery.[58] One defining characteristic of this wave was the prominence of hostile takeovers—acquisitions pursued against the wishes of the target company's management. Although hostile bids often failed, they could push the target company into the arms of a "white knight," an acquiring firm preferred by the target company's management. The hostile takeover was touted by some as an efficient market mechanism—a market for corporate control that would supplant inefficient managers with others who could make more profitable use of the target firm's assets.[59] But others have seen the hostile takeover movement as distracting managements from pursuit of long-term goals and motivated by rent-seeking behavior of the acquiring managements.[60] New financing arrangements ("junk bonds") may also have contributed to the 1980s surge of mergers. Merger activity waned with the collapse of the junk bond market, the increased difficulty in obtaining bank financing, the increased use of defensive tactics such as the "poison pill" and widespread state legislation that made it difficult to pursue a takeover against the wishes of the target company's management.[61]

58. SCHERER & ROSS, supra note 1, at 158–59.

59. This view was forcefully presented in *The Annual Report of the President, February 1985,* published in ECONOMIC REPORT OF THE PRESIDENT, FEBRUARY 1985 187–216 (1985), and in Jensen & Ruback, *The Market for Corporate Control: The Scientific Evidence,* 11 J. FIN. ECON. 5 (1983).

60. For a more skeptical view of corporate takeover activity, describing perceived detrimental effects, among them an undue emphasis on short-term profitability, see the separate testimonies of F. Scherer and W. Law in *Corporate Takeovers: Hearings*

Before the Subcomm. on Telecommunications, Consumer Protection, and Finance of the House Comm. on Energy and Commerce, 99th Cong., 1st Sess. Part I, at 242–255, 258–262 (1986).

61. In 1987, the Supreme Court ruled that an Indiana anti-takeover statute was not preempted by federal law and did not violate the Commerce Clause of the Constitution, sparking many other states to adopt similar legislation. CTS Corp. v. Dynamics Corp. of America, 481 U.S. 69, 107 S.Ct. 1637, 95 L.Ed.2d 67 (1987).

Although the level of antitrust enforcement was not likely a primary cause of the 1980s merger wave, concerns have been raised that enforcement was not sufficiently vigorous during the 1980s. Merger enforcement may have been inadequate, for example, in regulating airline mergers in the newly deregulated airline industry, which allowed a single firm to gain a dominant position in hub cities such as Minneapolis, Detroit and Pittsburgh.[62] These perceived inadequacies of federal enforcement apparently motivated state enforcers to assert a more active merger enforcement presence in the 1980s.

9.2g.   The 1990s Merger Wave

The 1990s began with a relatively low level of merger activity. One observer declared that "[t]he takeover wars are over. Management won."[63] But if hostile takeovers were less likely, negotiated mergers were to gain new impetus. By the mid–1990s, merger activity had picked up and, by late 1996, was at record levels. According to the Assistant Attorney General in charge of the Antitrust Division, the expected merger value for the year 1998 alone would exceed the value of all mergers for the years 1990 through 1995 and the early part of 1996.[64] By 1998, it was clear that this merger wave would exceed that of the 1980s both in terms of the number and the value of transactions.[65]

There was no single cause for the surge in merger activity in the late 1990s. Among the *reasons* cited are deregulation and convergence of markets (as in electric power and telecommunications), the rapid restructuring or downsizing of significant industries (such as defense, health care, and banking), the influence of technological developments (as in communications), and the globalization of markets for many goods and services (such as automobiles, aircraft construction, and banking and investment services). With stock market values in the United States also reaching new highs, low stock prices were not a primary inducement for takeovers, but many companies were able to pay for acquisitions through stock swaps that reduced liquidity needs.

With takeovers back in the hands of corporate management, many acquisitions were now being pursued for strategic reasons. Many of these strategically driven acquisitions raised difficult antitrust questions, taxing the resources of the enforcement agencies and producing record numbers of antitrust challenges. Although most challenged acquisitions

---

62. The possible inadequacies of airline merger enforcement was cited in *Statement of the Federal Trade Commission, Mergers and Corporate Consolidation in the New Economy, Hearings before Senate Comm. on Judiciary*, 105th Cong., 2d Sess. (June 16, 1998) ("More rigorous application of antitrust principles to airline mergers in the 1980's could have prevented the levels of market concentration we now see in certain airline hubs across the country.").

63. Grundfest, *Just Vote No: A Minimalist Strategy for Dealing with Barbarians*

Inside the Gates, 45 Stan. L. Rev. 857, 858 (1993).

64. *Statement of Assistant Attorney General Joel Klein, Mergers and Corporate Consolidation in the New Economy, Hearings before Senate Comm. on Judiciary*, 105th Cong., 2d Sess. (June 16, 1998).

65. The estimated value of transactions for 1998 was $2 trillion compared to $600 billion for the peak year (1989) of the 1980s merger wave. Statement of the Federal Trade Commission, supra note 62.

involved horizontal issues, a significant number involved issues of vertical foreclosure or potential competition. The federal agencies found their resources stretched in conducting premerger review of record numbers of transactions. Perhaps in part in order to extend available resources, federal/state cooperation in conducting merger investigations increased markedly. See the discussion in § 10.3. Many of the mergers subject to the scrutiny of United States officials were also investigated by foreign antitrust authorities, producing a few notable conflicts (as when the FTC approved the McDonnell Douglas/Boeing merger but European antitrust authorities imposed strict conditions on it). See the discussion in § 18.7c. Although most mergers with international reach do not produce conflicting results, the difficulties in meeting various regulatory timetables and rules produced additional burdens and delays on the merging parties.

The jointly issued DOJ/FTC Horizontal Merger Guidelines in 1992 allowed economic evidence that demonstrated the unilateral effects of a combination as a basis for demonstrating a violation of Section 7 of the Clayton Act.[66] Under this doctrine, even if the traditional methods of market definition did not demonstrate a likely threat to competition, that threat could be inferred from economic evidence demonstrating likely anticompetitive pricing effects from the proposed combination. In a 1997 case challenging a merger between the nation's two largest office supply superstore chains, the FTC offered evidence that the firms charged higher prices in cities in which they were not rivals than in cities in which they were rivals, vindicating the market definition that established the proposed combination's market power. The parties abandoned the acquisition after the FTC won a preliminary injunction.[67]

In the first decade of the new century, mergers continued at high levels, albeit short of the record setting pace of the 1990s. There were a number of large mergers in highly concentrated industries, decreasing the number of significant players in the relevant market to 2 or 3 players. Although some of these acquisitions were successfully challenged, the enforcement agencies seemed increasingly willing to permit such transactions.[68]

Overall, this historical survey of merger activity suggests a number of truths. First, antitrust enforcement affects merger activity. In its absence or during periods of lax enforcement, industry concentration has increased rapidly; this occurred during the first and second merger waves (and may have occurred to some extent during the 1980s). In the 1990s, despite (or perhaps because of) record-setting levels of merger activity, antitrust enforcement has left its mark on United States and

66. 1992 Horizontal Merger Guidelines § 4.

67. FTC v. Staples, Inc., 970 F.Supp. 1066 (D.D.C.1997).

68. FTC v. H.J. Heinz Co., 246 F.3d 708 (D.C.Cir. 2001)(FTC successfully challenges a 3 to 2 merger); Statement of the Federal Trade Commission Concerning Royal Caribbean Cruises, Ltd./P & O Princess Cruises plc & Carnival Corporation/P & O Princess Cruises plc, FTC File No. 021 0041 (2002), available at <http://www.ftc.gov/os/2002/10/cruisestatement.htm> (A divided FTC decides not to challenge a 4 firm to 3 firm cruise line merger).

international market structure. Second, merger enforcement has become more effective under the premerger reporting program and more sophisticated as the result of several iterations of agency guidelines. With this sophistication has also come complexity that clouds transparency and threatens the workability of enforcement rules. Still, there seems little doubt that current enforcement is achieving substantial benefits without the overreaching that may have occurred during the 1960s. Finally, the increasing number of mergers that involve international reach poses new challenges for developing coordinated enforcement responses with antitrust enforcers outside the United States.

§ 9.3 The Causes and Effects of Mergers

9.3a. Why Mergers Occur

If mergers are undertaken to make money, there are two obvious explanations as to why they occur. One is that mergers create efficiencies, allowing the merged firm to reap the economic benefits of these efficiencies. This is a socially desirable result. A second explanation, and one that is the primary concern of antitrust, is that mergers create market power that allows the merged entity to exploit less powerful buyers or sellers, in this manner achieving economic gain. One or both of these expectations may partially explain why many mergers occur. Yet these explanations do not fully reflect the range of motives for acquisitions.

Among the other suggested motivations for mergers are economic uncertainty (propelling some managers to seek diversification), tax considerations, the desire to obtain economic and financial power associated with bigness (empire building), and the lemming effect (the follow-the-leader mentality that causes a rash of mergers in a particular industry to follow upon an initial consolidation).[1] Because these various motives often occur in combination, it is difficult to analyze them separately. For example, during the 1990s, a wave of mergers began in the health care industry. The result was a series of consolidations with both horizontal and vertical dimensions. Hospitals merged with one another, but also with providers of nonhospital health care (health maintenance organizations), and firms involved in producing and distributing medical products, such as drugs and diagnostic and treatment hardware. A number of considerations may have sparked this wave, including uncertainty about the direction of government-initiated health reform initiatives, the need to downsize inefficiently managed facilities, and the desire to obtain lower prices from suppliers (either through more efficient procurement in larger scale or through the exercise of buyer power). Once the initial mergers had occurred, the lemming effect probably played a role. Fear that larger rivals might attain some known or unknown benefit that

§ 9.3

1. F. M. SCHERER & D. ROSS, INDUSTRIAL MARKET STRUCTURE AND ECONOMIC PERFORMANCE 162–67 (3d ed. 1990).

would not be available to smaller firms may have been a propellant of this merger activity.

Merger activity may not always be a coldly rational calculation of prescient market players based on projected financial gain. This is suggested by the large number of failures among conglomerate mergers during the 1960s and among the hostile takeovers of the 1980s.[2] Reviewing the studies of mergers more recently, the economist F.M. Scherer concluded that a majority of[3] mergers fail to live up to expectations and may make matters worse rather than better, many muddle through, "a fair number succeed, and a few succeed spectacularly." These considerations bear on antitrust analysis only indirectly. Merger enforcement is concerned most directly with anticompetitive effects and, only indirectly, with the overall outcome of mergers. Still, the overall balance sheet on the benefits and detriments of mergers may influence marginal cases where an analysis of the predicted competitive effects of a merger leads to no clear conclusion.

9.3b.   A Cost–Benefit Analysis

The costs and benefits of merger activity are those generally associated with the increase in size of a firm and with its gain in market share. The internal growth of a firm and its gain in relative market share from such growth, occur gradually. While gradual changes in firm size and market share from internal growth may raise antitrust questions, such changes may be regarded as the natural result of superior skill and foresight and not a proper target for antitrust enforcement. Of course, abuse of market power, however obtained, may be challenged under Section 2 of the Sherman Act. See the discussion in Chapter III. But a gain in market power from a merger may be viewed as objectionable not only because of its abruptness, but also because this gain may eliminate a competitor and is not viewed as a natural or inevitable consequence of a competitive market. Mergers are often the source of both competitive gains and risks. Thus, for example, a horizontal merger may at the same time increase economies of scale and increase risk of market power abuse, such as that associated with oligopolistic conduct.[4]

9.3b1.   Benefits of Mergers

9.3b1i.   Economies of Scale and Other Efficiencies

By creating a larger firm, mergers can create economies of scale. Economies of scale are the economic gains won when larger output allows a firm to lower its costs per item sold. Such economies may occur at the production level or at the distribution level. At the production

2. Id. at 172–74. According to one analysis, roughly one-third of studied acquisitions were viewed as failures by the acquiring firms. D. Ravenscraft & F.M. Scherer, Mergers, Sell-offs, and Economic Efficiency 192–3 (1987).

3. Scherer, *Some Principles for Post-Chicago Antitrust Analysis*, 52 Case W. Res. L. Rev.5, 16–18 (2001).

4. Benefits and costs associated with joint ventures are cataloged in § 13.2. Impacts arising from mergers can be similar and can be analyzed in similar ways.

level, economies may occur in an individual plant—for example, higher output that allows for more efficient use of machines—or at the multiplant level—for example, increased specialization among plants that reduces the need for expensive changeovers of equipment and allows greater worker specialization. At the distribution level, a merger may allow a firm to make more efficient use of a firm's sales, advertising or other distribution resources.

If two firms merge, they can also consolidate their research and development, perhaps eliminating redundant research that would have been done by separate firms. Indeed, the combined resources of a firm may enable it to undertake more expensive research and development beyond the means of either firm by itself. These research, production or distribution economies of scale are most likely to occur when the merger is horizontal—among rivals. Some of these benefits, such as the benefits of joint research, might be attainable through means short of a merger (such as a joint venture).

Some economies might still be attained if firms that do not compete are able to eliminate redundant costs or facilities. A merger between two firms that use aluminum to fabricate wholly different products might still produce some efficiencies—for example, research that seeks new methods of fabricating raw aluminum into finished products might be useful for each of the lines that the two firms produce. Even two wholly unrelated firms, should they merge, may be able to cut certain administrative costs. For example, the cost of arranging an annual meeting or of accounting and tax preparation services may be something less than that incurred by two separately operating firms. But one would expect these gains to be far less than in the case of a horizontal merger in which large production and distribution economies are achieved. The formation of a conglomerate enterprise was also once seen as a way of pooling the risk of business cycles by operating in diverse lines of business. But the experience with conglomerates has shown a darker side: Consolidated entities were often ineffective in managing their diverse enterprises, with the result that capital markets began to regard them as high-risk investments.[5] There may also be inefficiencies associated with large size. See the discussion of costs and risks of mergers in § 9.3b2.

Mergers that allow firms to integrate vertically may also produce significant efficiencies. A company may, for example, be active only in drilling for oil and supplying it to upstream buyers. But it may be more efficient for the company to integrate by owning its own pipelines, refining facilities, distributors and even retail outlets. This vertical integration would not bring economies of scale, but might reduce transaction costs. The firm would have a secure outlet for its petroleum production, perhaps allowing for better long-term planning and investment. The downstream facilities might receive similar benefits from a secure supply of petroleum. The possible benefits of vertical integration are discussed in § 12.3a.

5.   SCHERER & ROSS, supra note 1, at 163.

9.3b1ii. Capital Market Liquidity

During the 1980s, the notion of a market for capital was pushed to new limits. Proponents of this theory argued that the hostile takeover activity is an outgrowth of this market's incentive to place capital in uses with the highest return. Thus, a bidder in a hostile takeover attempt might expect to manage the target company more efficiently, with a net benefit to society from the more productive use of the target firm's assets.[6] Hostile takeovers are doubtlessly undertaken to make money, but it is less clear whether this money was to be made from more efficient management of the target firm or from less desirable trading of corporate equity for corporate debt, short-term profit taking, or payoffs to the new firm management.[7]

Whatever doubts may exist about hostile takeovers, there is a clear interest in the liquidity of investments. An entrepreneur that invests heavily in an enterprise has an interest in being allowed to sell that ownership to recover the often substantially enhanced value of the investment. If all acquisitions of firms were tightly regulated, the sale of an ongoing business with its valuable goodwill might be difficult. On the other hand, this legitimate interest in the free transferability of a firm's ownership is undermined minimally if antitrust prohibits a limited and well-defined category of mergers. For example, under a policy of prohibiting horizontal mergers that substantially increase market share, an entrepreneur may be prohibited from selling to a major competitor, but will still be free to sell to other potential buyers. Any reduction in the sale value of the enterprise might reflect only the buyer's inability to reap an anticompetitive gain associated with a merger that would increase market power.

9.3b1iii. Increased Buying Power

Another possible gain from a merger is the increased buying power of the merged entity. The merger of two hospitals, for example, might allow them to bargain more effectively for the purchase of drugs and expensive technology needed to run a modern hospital. This is unquestionably a gain to the merged firm and its owners, allowing it to compete more effectively against other hospitals. But price discrimination is often involved in the more favorable terms that the buyer receives. Price discrimination in the economic sense is associated with an exercise of market power, so the ability of a merged firm to obtain a lower price is a sign that it possesses market power, the major concern of merger enforcement.

---

6. Economic Report of the President Together with The Annual Report of the Council of Economic Advisers, 187–216 (1985) (describing the "market for corporate control").

7. Wall Street specialists that orchestrated major takeovers often placed relatively little of their own capital at risk, making gains on loan fees and other transactions associated with a takeover. See Hamilton, *Reliance and Liability Standards for Outside Directors*, 24 WAKE FOREST L. REV. 5, 15 (1989) (describing a firm's orchestration of the leveraged buy-out of RJR Nabisco).

The price discrimination may by itself be lawful (for example, when a lower price is attributable to legitimate savings associated with a bulk purchase). But whether or not the lower prices are lawful, the buying power that they reflect does not increase the efficiency of the merged hospitals' operation. What may be occurring is a zero sum game in which wealth is transferred back and forth among powerful buyers and sellers, with little of it reaching the consumer. On the other hand, the consolidations occurring in the health care industry may be an aid in reducing health care costs that will ultimately flow to the benefit of the health care consumer. The merged hospitals' buying power might not be required if the supplier industries were themselves functioning competitively.

Arguments that a merger will increase the buying power of the merged entity are thus a double-edged sword. Buying power is simply another way in which a firm with leverage may exercise its power. Power is at the root of all antitrust concerns and greatly increases the risk of market abuse. On the other hand, when faced with suppliers that themselves exercise power, allowing the creation of powerful buyers may discipline those sellers to some degree. It cannot be a complete answer, however, for sellers with market power will remain free to discriminate against the smaller buyers. Moreover, the newly created powerful buyer may exercise its own market power to extract supracompetitive prices from its buyers, thereby preventing the gains from being passed on to consumers. Once the buyer has obtained market power, it may be abused in ways not wholly predictable.

A partial answer may lie in allowing large buyers to be created without allowing undue market power in the relevant market. For example, mergers may create a national chain of hospitals with enormous buying power, yet that chain might have no more than 25 percent of the market in any local hospital market and hence lack power in such local markets. Price discrimination favoring such a large chain may distort the hospital market, forcing other hospitals to join large chains as well. But under the specified conditions, there is a reasonable prospect that some of these gains will be passed on to consumers because of the competition in local hospital markets.

9.3b1iv.   *Synergies*

It is often said that mergers of compatible firms can create synergies. Like efficiencies, synergies are a financial gain, but the term has been used loosely to describe potential gains that are less certain in their occurrence and reach than other gains (generally called efficiencies). For example, one may read that a proposed merger of a cable television company and a regional telephone company will create "synergies" that may enable the merged company to better compete in providing a full range of entertainment and information services to customers. Certainly, these benefits may occur, but they seem highly uncertain and should not detract from risks that must also be weighed, such as the loss of potential competition in local telephone service that might emerge if the cable company upgraded its lines to accommodate two-way communication. It also appears that these gains—perhaps accomplished through a knowledge transfer—could be obtained in other ways. A limited joint venture or a license to transfer technology, for example, might place one or both firms in the same advantageous position without the need to merge. The 1992 Merger Guidelines do not use the term "synergies." A highly speculative potential gain from a merger is probably entitled to little weight in weighing the benefits and risks of a merger, particularly if the gain might be achieved in other, less anticompetitive ways.

9.3b2. *Costs and Anticompetitive Risks of Mergers*

Potential anticompetitive effects of a merger, as in the case of benefits, will vary with the type of merger. What all anticompetitive mergers have in common is a propensity to increase the merging parties' market power and the potential for abuse of that power. Horizontal mergers have an obvious anticompetitive potential because they can directly create market power by increasing market share. Vertical mergers can also create market power that can be abused—by foreclosing access to a market or increasing a rival's costs, by facilitating collusion or evasion of maximum price regulations, or by reducing potential competition. Some conglomerate mergers, too, may undermine potential competition, thereby increasing market power.

9.3b2i. *Creating Market Power Through Horizontal Mergers*

The creation of market power through horizontal mergers is the core concern of merger enforcement. Mergers at the turn of the century often created market-dominating firms—monopolists. See § 9.2a. Today, mergers of this sort are less frequently attempted. More often, horizontal mergers operate at the fringe, creating market power that is well short of market dominance but may still enhance the risk of oligopolistic behavior. Because oligopoly, though likely to be less stable than monopoly, potentially has the same adverse effects on competition, federal merger policy addresses the creation of undue market power in its incipiency. Precisely what constitutes undue market power is a point of controversy.

The rule of thumb reflected in all iterations of the Merger Guidelines is that the more concentrated an industry, the more likely is oligopolistic behavior by that industry. The rule, which points to tendencies, may not be an accurate clue to any given industry's behavior. For example, an industry with only three participants could be very competitive if one of the firms were an aggressive competitor. On the other hand, an industry with ten participants may operate with minimal competition because of parallel pricing and marketing practices by the participants. Still, the inference that higher concentration increases the risks of oligopolistic conduct seems well grounded.[8] As the number of industry participants becomes smaller, the task of coordinating industry

8. SCHERER & ROSS, supra note 1, at 189–90.

behavior becomes easier. For example, a ten-firm industry is more likely to require some sort of coordination to maintain prices at an oligopoly level, whereas the three-firm industry might more easily maintain prices through parallel behavior without express coordination.

Oligopoly conditions may or may not require collusion that would independently violate Section 1 of the Sherman Act. A supracompetitive price level may be maintained through price leadership (usually the leader is the largest firm), through observance of a well-established trade rule (e.g., a convention of a 50 percent markup in price among competing retailers), or through strategic discipline of nonconforming members of the industry. The most common form of such disciplining action is the price war, instituted to prevent any member from gaining market share at the expense of the others. An industry characterized by two-level pricing—a high level of pricing interrupted by occasional price wars— may be exercising this oligopolistic behavior. The price war is aimed at discouraging industry participants from abandoning price discipline.[9]

To the extent that one or very few members of a concentrated industry have much higher market shares than other members, the opportunities for strategic disciplining may expand. Of course, a large market share participant cannot cut its prices across the board without suffering loss commensurate with its high market share, a consequence that limits the large firm's freedom of action. But in such a structure, strategic price disciplining in a targeted fashion may be very feasible. A larger firm may discipline its smaller rival by cutting prices only in the segment of the market in which the smaller rival is most heavily involved. In this manner, the losses to the larger firm are limited. Its larger resource base gives it an expanded ability to finance such strategic behavior that the smaller industry members will lack. The expanded ability of the larger firm to coerce price discipline is reflected in the Herfindahl–Hirschman Index (HHI), which will assign a high concentration index to an industry with a very large participant. An industry with the same number of participants, each of them roughly equal in size, will have a lower index.[10]

The market power created by a merger may have effects going beyond an oligopolistic pricing scheme. For example, a comfortable oligopoly may reduce its research and development initiatives, decreasing the prospect of innovative products or services being discovered or, if they are discovered, being marketed promptly to consumers. Competition may be the best incentive for aggressive innovation in an industry. Difficult issues arise when research is so expensive that no single member of the industry can afford to undertake it on its own. In such

---

9. The "price war" pattern of oligopolistic conduct is described in Baker & Bresnahan, *Empirical Methods of Identifying and Measuring Market Power*, 61 ANTITRUST L.J. 3, 13–15 (1992). Because such conduct can seriously injure competition and may not be vulnerable under the Sherman Act once the facilitating structure is in place (see § 5.2a), it is important in applying Section 7 to take reasonable steps to inhibit mergers resulting in such structures.

10. See the discussion of the HHI in § 2.6b and § 11.2d.

instances, however, the best solution may be joint research and development, not mergers that create dominating firms. Congress appears to agree, having enacted legislation that lowers the antitrust risks for such joint research and development undertakings.[11]

Horizontal combinations may work competitive injury through either buyer or seller market power, a reality that is recognized in the 1992 Merger Guidelines.[12] The enforcement agencies have reviewed and occasionally challenged mergers that increase buyer power. Concern with such mergers may be heightened when the sellers are fragmented and not in a position to exercise countervailing power in negotiating with powerful buyers.[13]

9.3b2ii. Creating Market Power Through Vertical Mergers

Many mergers involve vertical combinations, firms that are involved in a customer-supplier relationship. Vertical integration through mergers is widely recognized as an efficient way to run some businesses. But vertical combinations may still create market power if, for example, they foreclose rivals from access to a needed input or distribution outlet, if they are likely to raise rivals costs, or if they foster evasion of maximum price regulation. These and other theories under which a vertical combination may generate market power are discussed in § 12.3b and § 13.3c2.

9.3b2iii. Costs Associated with Size

Although a larger size may bring economies of scale, once that size has been reached, further increases in size beyond minimum efficient scale can impose additional bureaucratic costs on a firm. For example, while a firm may gain through a specialized work force, if that specialization becomes too great, productivity may decrease with worker alienation or boredom. The ability to interchange employees may also be reduced as firms specialize too greatly. In addition, if the production of a single plant becomes too large, it may have greater transportation costs in distributing the product to a wider geographic market needed to absorb the large production.[14] Some data suggests that the larger firms in key U.S. industries are already beyond the size needed to attain minimum efficient scale.[15] Further growth in the size of these firms through merger activity may run a high risk of fostering diseconomies of scale. To be sure, firms may be able to counter the effects of some of these diseconomies through decentralized management and production. But some of these diseconomies may be difficult to counteract. Large

---

11. National Cooperative Research Act of 1984, Pub. L. No. 98–462, 98 Stat. 1815 (1984) (codified as amended at 15 U.S.C.A. §§ 4301–4306). See the discussion of high technology joint ventures in § 13.5.

12. 1992 Horizontal Merger Guidelines § 0.1,

13. For a discussion of agency treatment of buyer power issues in merger cases,

see Grimes, *Buyer Power and Retail Gatekeeper Power: Protecting Competition and the Atomistic Seller*, 72 ANTITRUST L. J. 563,570–71, 583–88 (2005).

14. These and other diseconomies of scale are discussed in SCHERER & ROSS, supra note 1, at 102–08.

15. Id. at 111–18.

entities may be inherently less flexible in dealing with changing market conditions. Large U.S. automobile firms ultimately responded to aggressive import competition beginning in the 1960s, but their response does not dazzle by its speed and flexibility. The long term health of large U.S. based automobile manufacturers remains open to question in the first decade of the 21st century.

9.3b2iv. Transaction Costs of Mergers

Every merger costs something to execute. When a small business is sold to another firm, these costs may be insignificant, particularly over the long term. When a large, publicly traded firm is sold, the transaction costs are likely to be substantial, even if proportionate to the size of the enterprise. But these costs are likely to escalate if a takeover is contested by the management of the target firm. Looking only at the fees charged by investment bankers, lawyers, and other merger professionals, these fees appear substantial. For example, in the leveraged buyout of RJR Nabisco during the 1980s, two securities firms received a $200 million fee for their commitment to provide bridge financing of $5 billion, while a separate group of banks received an even larger commitment fee for their loans of $13.3 billion. These fees had to be paid regardless of the success of the takeover bid (in this case the bid was successful).[16] Investment bankers, merger specialists, lawyers and banks unquestionably perform valuable work. But they also become an institutional force to promote mergers, regardless of their efficiencies.

Internal corporation costs may also be substantial both before and after a merger occurs. During the vigorous hostile takeover activity of the 1980s, many firms spent substantial resources devising defensive schemes to takeovers. But the cost measured in terms of corporate resources and merger professionals fees is still incomplete. Mergers cause turnovers, layoffs and other disruptions in the lives of employees and their families. These social costs are addressed in the next section.

9.3b2v. Social Costs of Mergers

The layoffs that result from a merger may be of two types. The first type of layoff is the replacement of an old management employee with one appointed by new management, perhaps to assure loyalty to the new management. Such layoffs might properly be regarded as transition costs. A second type of layoff is that of an employee who is not replaced. This second type of layoff is probably not a transition cost, and may well be a procompetitive response to overcapacity or underutilization of resources. The new management put in place by a takeover can perhaps institute such cost-cutting measures more quickly because new management has fewer loyalties and commitments to the existing work force. But a more drawn-out schedule of layoffs, if less efficient, might have produced fewer social costs. Thus, even when such layoffs do not

---

16. R. HAMILTON, CASES AND MATERIALS ON CORPORATIONS, INCLUDING PARTNERSHIPS AND LIMITED LIABILITY CORPORATIONS 1172–74 (8th ed. 2003).

constitute transition costs, their overall impact cannot be rotely characterized as beneficial.

A related concern with large firms is the social cost or alienation that may come from association with an elephantine and impersonal enterprise. When Congress passed the Celler–Kefauver Act, it arguably opted for a world of small, owner-managed enterprises in which a maximum number of citizens shared in owner-management of the nation's productive enterprises. This concern now appears dated and counterproductive to many antitrust theorists.[17] Yet modern management theories stressing decentralization of large firm management seem a partial vindication of the concerns that underlay populist merger enforcement of an earlier era.

Weighing social costs in determining whether to oppose a merger disrupts the rigor of the analysis. It is often difficult to predict whether the old or new management will produce fewer social costs over the long term. The failure to take necessary cost-cutting steps in a timely fashion could cause more rather than less social disruption if the firm's viability is placed in doubt. Still, when issues of social costs are clearly presented by a merger, an antitrust decision-maker ignores such costs at some political peril. Although such costs do not cleanly fit a market power analysis of a merger, they are clearly a matter of great interest to the electorate and elected officials. The desire of citizens and elected officials of Marathon, Ohio, to maintain Marathon Oil Company's headquarters in that town was a powerful, silent partner in the court's decision to enjoin Mobil's attempted takeover of Marathon.[18] When such issues are clearly presented to the decision-maker, the failure to account for these social costs could undermine the political base for merger enforcement.

9.3c.　Overview of the Costs and Benefits of Mergers

Judges and agency officials who must decide whether or not to permit a particular merger cannot rely on platitudes that mergers are efficient or are a valuable exercise of contractual freedom at the one extreme, or, at the other extreme, that mergers are a prescription for strategic oligopolistic abuses or are likely to undermine a nation of owner-manager enterprises. The truth is a more complicated mix of these and other consequences of mergers. Summing up the available statistical evidence, Scherer and Ross find only weak support for the proposition that profitability and efficiency are the most likely result of a merger. Indeed, particularly when small firms are absorbed by larger firms that have no experience in the target firm's line of business, efficiency is likely to be reduced following the merger. But these authors

17.　A theorist who defends maintaining small firms as a goal of antitrust is Peritz, *Some Realism About Economic Power in a Time of Sectorial Change*, 66 ANTITRUST L.J. 247, 261–72 (1997).

18.　Marathon Oil Co. v. Mobil Corp., 530 F.Supp. 315 (N.D.Ohio), aff'd, 669 F.2d 378 (6th Cir.1981), cert. denied, 455 U.S. 982, 102 S.Ct. 1490, 71 L.Ed.2d 691 (1982).

concede that whatever the overall picture, in individual cases, efficiency benefits or anticompetitive effects will prevail.[19]

The premise of merger enforcement is that when mergers are classified into narrow categories and analyzed for unique factual circumstances, the decision-maker can make intelligent and reasonably accurate predictions about the competitive effects of a merger. This exercise is guided by the separate approaches to horizontal, vertical and conglomerate mergers, discussed in Chapters 11–12. Before addressing these matters, Chapter 10 describes the merger enforcement mechanism.

19. SCHERER & ROSS, supra note 1, at 174; Scherer, supra note 3, at 16–18.

Chapter X

MERGERS: THE ENFORCEMENT MECHANISM

Table of Sections

---

§ 10.1 Introduction

Mergers are well-defined events, often accompanied by substantial publicity. When one or more of the participating firms has publicly traded stock, securities laws may require advance disclosure of the event. Even for closely held firms, state corporation law may require stockholder votes for fundamental structural changes. Thus, unlike ongoing conduct that might be challenged under the antitrust laws—for example, cartel activity or foreclosure restraints such as tie-ins—merger enforcement focuses on a singular event, often well publicized in advance. The enforcement may come from one or more of three sources: (1) federal agencies—either the Antitrust Division of the Justice Department or the Federal Trade Commission; (2) state attorneys general; or (3) private parties, usually rivals, customers or suppliers of the merging parties. If the merger involves a significant antitrust interest outside of the United States, one or more foreign antitrust agencies may also enter the enforcement picture.

For transactions involving no significant foreign interest, this tripartite enforcement mechanism should be measured by its success in attaining three important goals: (1) substantive policy success—prohibiting mergers likely to be anticompetitive while allowing those that are benign or procompetitive; (2) procedural efficiency—keeping enforcement costs down for the enforcer, the merging firms, and any tribunal that resolves disputed issues; and (3) visibility and accountability—permitting the interested public and the Congress to understand the rules and to monitor the enforcement in terms of both substantive and procedural goals. There are, of course, necessary tradeoffs in striving for these objectives. A system that carefully investigates and fully litigates every questionable merger may score high marks for carrying out a substantive merger policy, but may present unacceptably high procedural costs. Achieving visibility of agency investigation and disposition of a merger requires another tradeoff. The most effective oversight of the agency's actions might be achieved if the agency operated in a fishbowl. Yet, forcing the agency to operate in this manner could undercut its efficiency and compromise the confidentiality of sensitive firm information (which in turn might make private parties less willing to cooperate with the agency's investigation).

§ 10.2 Federal Enforcement

The preeminence of federal merger enforcement, although perhaps clear after the Celler–Kefauver Act in 1950,[1] was enhanced by two more recent developments. One was the issuance of agency merger guidelines beginning in 1968.[2] The Guidelines, issued jointly by the FTC and the Justice Department's Antitrust Division in their 1992 iteration,[3] influence the standard for merger enforcement no matter who initiates that enforcement. The second development was the premerger notification program authorized in the Hart–Scott–Rodino Act of 1976.[4] Premerger reporting is designed to give the two federal agencies advance notice of any major merger involving U.S. corporations and, if an investigation uncovers likely anticompetitive effects, to allow either agency to seek injunctive relief to preserve the premerger structure of the industry

§ 10.2

1. Celler–Kefauver Act, ch. 1184, 64 Stat. 1125 (1950)(codified at 15 U.S.C.A. §§ 18, 21).

2. U.S. Dep't of Justice, 1968 Merger Guidelines, *reprinted in* 4 Trade Reg. Rep. (CCH) ¶ 13,101.

3. U.S. Dep't of Justice and Federal Trade Commission, Horizontal Merger Guidelines (April 2, 1992), as amended in 1997, available at <http:// www.usdoj. gov./atr/public/ guidelines/hmg.htm>.

4. Hart–Scott–Rodino Antitrust Improvements Act of 1976, Pub. L. No. 94–435, Title II, 90 Stat. 1390 (1976) (codified as amended at 15 U.S.C.A. § 18a).

pending judicial resolution of disputed issues. The Antitrust Division and the FTC thus have the tools to play a preeminent role in merger enforcement. To carry out this task, however, they have been required to dedicate a major portion (as much as two-thirds) of their limited resources to premerger review.[5]

10.2a. Federal Agency Guidelines

Agency merger guidelines are designed to provide an outline of the analytical process the agency will use to assess a proposed merger and to provide some indication of which mergers are most likely to be challenged. The 1992 Guidelines cover only horizontal mergers. The Antitrust Division's 1984 Guidelines still provide guidance on vertical and conglomerate acquisitions.[6]

The Merger Guidelines provide a structure to merger analysis that was lacking during some of the Supreme Court's merger decisions of the 1960s. Although the Guidelines are frequently cited in support of a challenge to the legality of a merger, they have also been cited against the Department in cases in which the court perceived the Antitrust Division's analysis to have departed from the Guidelines.[7] The Division, finding its own analysis trumped by a rigid interpretation of the Guidelines, responded by including in the 1992 Guidelines a warning against mechanical application and a reservation of the agency's flexibility to depart from a strict reading in dealing with a broad range of circumstances.[8] But citation to the Guidelines by both sides in a litigated case will doubtlessly continue.

There are legitimate concerns about the role that the Guidelines play and the method by which they are adopted. The Guidelines were promulgated without the minimal protections of notice and comment prescribed for informal rulemaking under the Administrative Procedure Act. Accordingly, there was no assured opportunity for public comment before the Guidelines were issued.[9] Of course, as a technical matter the Guidelines are not "rules" because they are not supposed to bind the agency to a particular interpretation. But despite the designation of these policy statements as "Guidelines" intended to describe the agen-

---

5. In 1987, the Department conducted 269 antitrust investigations, 132 of which (49 percent) involved Section 7 of the Clayton Act. Antitrust Division Workload Statistics, *Oversight and Authorization Hearings into the Policies and Enforcement Record of the Antitrust Division (DOJ): Hearings Before the Subcomm. on Monopolies and Commercial Law of the House Comm. on the Judiciary*, 100th Cong., 1st & 2d Sess. 517–524 (letter from John R. Bolton to Peter Rodino) (March 2, 1988).

FTC Chairman Robert Pitofsky reported in 1998 that, in the face of record-setting volume of merger activity, the agency was devoting more than 2/3 of its antitrust enforcement resources to premerger review

and enforcement, compared to about 50 percent a few years earlier. Statement of the Federal Trade Commission on Mergers and Corporate Consolidation in the New Economy. Before the Senate Judiciary Comm., (June 16, 1998).

6. U.S. Dep't of Justice, 1984 Merger Guidelines, *reprinted in* 4 Trade Reg. Rep. (CCH) ¶ 13,103.

7. United States v. Waste Management, Inc., 743 F.2d 976, 983 (2d Cir.1984).

8. 1992 Merger Guidelines § 0.

9. The procedures for informal rulemaking are set forth in 5 U.S.C.A. § 553(b), (c).

cy's internal processes, they tend to have a broad influence outside the agency. This influence is not surprising, given that no outside body—and certainly no court—can hope to match the resources and merger expertise that the two federal agencies possess. Their influence is probably much greater (and their field of application arguably far more important to the public interest) than many rules issued by federal agencies. Although the agencies may have consulted informally with outside experts and have circulated a draft of Guidelines to such persons before they were issued, there has been no assurance that potential critics will have seen a revised iteration of the Guidelines before issuance. These concerns have led some in Congress to consider requiring the agencies to provide public notice and an opportunity to comment prior to issuance of new guidelines. Of course, legislation is not required to resolve this problem if the agencies act on their own to publish draft guidelines for comment before they are issued. The agencies appear to have chosen this course with respect to more recently issued guidelines (such as the proposed joint venture guidelines published for public comment in 1999).

Another criticism of the Guidelines has been that they often do not accurately reflect actual agency policy. By the late 1970s, the 1968 Guidelines were said to have been widely ignored within the Antitrust Division, which failed to challenge many mergers that the Guidelines would have designated as presumptively anticompetitive. Then–Antitrust Division Chief William Baxter cited this as one of the justifications for issuing revised Guidelines in 1982.[10] But even the 1982 Guidelines (revised again in 1984), were said not to have been followed during the Reagan years. An American Bar Association Task Force criticized the Division for not enforcing its own Guidelines with respect to horizontal mergers, the category most likely to create substantial anticompetitive effects.[11]

The Merger Guidelines are a partial response to inadequate public information about enforcement decisions. Although the Guidelines may aid the practitioner in delineating areas in which a merger will not be challenged, their use is limited. In comparison with the 1968 Guidelines, more recent iterations are more complex, leaving more discretion to the enforcement agency (and therefore providing less concrete guidance to the practitioner).[12] For example, under the unilateral effects doctrine first announced in the 1992 Guidelines, traditional methods of defining the market may be discarded in favor of economic evidence showing that a particular acquisition will increase prices. The unilateral effects doctrine is discussed in § 11.2e2. The increased discretionary powers assigned to the agency exacerbate the information vacuum. With greater

---

10. Baxter, *Responding to the Reaction: The Draftsman's View*, 71 CAL. L. REV. 618 (1983) (the revisions were intended "to bring the Guidelines into line with subsequent developments").

11. REPORT OF THE AMERICAN BAR ASSOCIATION, SECTION OF ANTITRUST LAW TASK FORCE ON THE ANTITRUST DIVISION OF THE U.S. DEPARTMENT OF JUSTICE 26–30 (1989).

12. Kauper, *The 1982 Horizontal Merger Guidelines: Of Collusion, Efficiency, and Failure*, 71 CAL. L. REV. 497, 508–09 (1983). Kauper suggests that the complexity and discretion built into the newer Guidelines makes it easier for the merging parties to negotiate a settlement with the Department. Id.

policy discretion comes a need for more, not less, disclosure. Some enforcement decisions may respond to circumstances not addressed by the Guidelines or may simply be inconsistent with the Guidelines. In 1989, a Bar Association Task Force recommended that the Division initiate "some form of generic public reporting" to reveal the Division's overall enforcement record.[13] A study published in 2003 found that the most troubling aspect of the lack of transparency was the FTC and Antitrust Division's failure to release more information about merger cases that were subject to an investigation but resulted in no enforcement action.[14] See the discussion in 10.6b.

10.2b. Premerger Notification

The premerger notification program, authorized in 1976,[15] has survived its formative years and has become an established enforcement tool. Measured by its drafters' objectives,[16] premerger notification has been a prominent success. The legislation responded to the enforcement agencies' inability to obtain sufficient information about many proposed acquisitions before their consummation. Before 1976, the Government frequently was unable to challenge an acquisition until after it had occurred. When the Government won such a suit, the courts were often unwilling to grant an effective structural remedy.[17] Premerger notification allowed the agency to halt a troublesome transaction before it had occurred, thereby preserving the premerger structure of an industry. The statute requires that, for all transactions exceeding specified size thresholds, both the acquiring and the target company file a premerger report with the Federal Trade Commission and the Antitrust Division of the Justice Department. Once the reports are filed, the companies must wait 30 days (15 days if the acquisition is by cash tender offer) before completing the acquisition. Before expiration of this time period, either federal agency may request from the parties additional information. Such a request triggers an additional twenty-day waiting period (ten days if the acquisition is by cash tender offer) that begins to run only after the agency has received the requested information.[18]

Representatives of large corporations opposed enactment of the premerger notification program in 1976.[19] Today they have learned to live with it, even welcoming the opportunity to obtain a prompt and

---

13. ABA REPORT, supra note 11, at 34–36.

14. Grimes, *Transparency in Federal Antitrust Enforcement,* 51 BUFF. L. REV. 937 (2003).

15. Section 7A of the Clayton Act, 15 U.S.C.A. § 18A.

16. The House Report indicates that the premerger notification program would give the government "a meaningful chance to win a premerger injunction—which is often the only effective and realistic remedy against large, illegal mergers." H. Rep. No. 1343, 5 (94th Cong., 2d Sess. 1976). The

Senate Report makes similar points. S. Rep. No. 803, 65, 70 (94th Cong., 2d Sess. 1976).

17. In a study of 39 merger cases brought by the federal agencies in the period 1950–1960, Elzinga found that the Government had been unsuccessful in obtaining relief in 21 cases and had obtained deficient relief in 8 cases. Elzinga, *The Antimerger Law: Pyrrhic Victories?* 12 J.L. & ECON. 43, 48 (1969).

18. 15 U.S.C.A. § 18a(e).

19. *Merger Oversight and H.R. 13131, Providing Premerger Notification and Stay Requirements, Hearings before the Sub-*

definitive premerger ruling from the federal agency.[20] Meanwhile, premerger notification has become something of an international success. Indeed, the proliferation of premerger filing requirements among countries all over the world has produced difficult compliance problems for multinational firms involved in a merger transaction.[21]

Perhaps the most unexpected legacy of premerger notification is the degree to which it has shifted interpretations of merger policy away from the courts and into the hands of the federal agencies. Until 1976, the federal agencies litigated merger cases frequently, with a steady flow of cases reaching the Supreme Court.[22] The proponents of premerger notification apparently assumed that the new law would expedite (but not substantially reduce) the flow of cases to the courts.[23] In operation, the 1976 premerger notification legislation has substantially lessened opportunities for judicial review. Today's cases tend to be settled through largely confidential agency-party negotiation without the benefit of publicly available judicial records and opinions.[24]

Although there are advantages to premerger review for the merging parties, there is little question that it has shifted the balance of power to

comm. on Monopolies and Commercial Law, House Comm. on the Judiciary, 190 (94th Cong., 2d Sess. 1976)(statement of James M. Johnstone, representing the U.S. Chamber of Commerce).

20. In a report for the Federal Trade Commission, Thompson conducted interviews with 13 individuals who represented private parties subject to premerger filing requirements. Although Thompson received critical comments about specific FTC rules implementing premerger notification, he reported an "overwhelming" positive reaction. None of the interviewees urged repeal of the law. Thompson, Evaluation of Premerger Notification Program 80–81 (May 1981) (prepared for the Bureau of Competition, FTC).

21. Japan is said to be the first nation to have adopted a premerger notification program. Haley, *Harmonized Rules, Peculiar Law: Recent Developments in Japanese Competition Law,* in TOWARDS WTO COMPETITION RULES 137, 138 (1999). In the EEC, prenotification is necessary when each of three requirements are met: (1) the combined aggregate worldwide turnover of all undertakings involved in acquisition exceeds ECU (European Currency Unit) 5,000,000; (2) the aggregate Community-wide turnover of each of at least two participants exceeds ECU 250,000; and (3) at least one of the participants achieves more than one-third of its aggregate Community-wide turnover in more than one member state—see the discussion of EC merger law in § 18.6b3.

22. For example, the Supreme Court rendered a number of decisions on the merits of Section 7 cases in 1974 and 1975. United States v. Citizens & S. Nat'l Bank, 422 U.S. 86, 95 S.Ct. 2099, 45 L.Ed.2d 41 (1975); United States v. Connecticut Nat'l Bank, 418 U.S. 656, 94 S.Ct. 2788, 41 L.Ed.2d 1016 (1974); United States v. Marine Bancorp., 418 U.S. 602, 94 S.Ct. 2856, 41 L.Ed.2d 978 (1974); United States v. General Dynamics Corp., 415 U.S. 486, 94 S.Ct. 1186, 39 L.Ed.2d 530 (1974). Since that date, the Court has rendered no decision on the merits of a Section 7 case.

Baker and Blumenthal attribute the Department's failure to seek certiorari to changes in procedural law that make direct appeal to the Supreme Court more difficult and to the Department's relative lack of success before the High Court in the 1974–75 cases. Baker & Blumenthal, *The 1982 Guidelines and Preexisting Law,* 71 CALIF. L. REV. 311, 313 (1983). While these factors may to some degree explain the reduced flow of cases to the Supreme Court, they do not address the reduced flow of cases to the lower courts.

23. H.R. Rep. No. 1343, supra note 16, at 14; S. Rep. No. 803, supra note 16, at 70.

24. Of 51 mergers opposed by the Department of Justice during the period 1982–1987, only 6 resulted in litigated decisions, or an average of one each year. See the chart reproduced in § 10.5a. During 1974–1975, the Department had four litigated decisions in the Supreme Court alone. See cases at note 22, supra.

the enforcement agencies. Before premerger notification, merging parties could face an antitrust challenge propelled by the momentum of a completed transaction and the courts' historic aversion to order divestiture of a merged entity.[25] Today's litigants confront the same high costs of litigation from a far less favorable strategic position—they can no longer rely on the leverage created by an already completed transaction. Faced with a premerger challenge, parties are likely to abandon the transaction or push for a settlement that allows completion of as much of the acquisition as possible without contested litigation.

Judicial review remains an option for litigants that believe the enforcement agency has improperly interpreted and applied the law. Still, because relatively few merger parties force the agency to litigate to stop the merger, courts have had fewer opportunities to influence the development of merger law.[26] Even merging parties that choose to litigate may abandon the transaction if they are unsuccessful in the district court. In another unforeseen consequence of its increased leverage to force settlements, the Government has vastly reduced the flow of cases from which it can choose a favorable case for appellate or Supreme Court review. Those relatively few cases that go to court are selected by the merging parties based on their assessment of prospects for success (and thus may be less favorable to the Government). More fundamentally, the absence of judicial records and information from the agencies deprives practitioners and scholars of information with which to critique enforcement policy. The 1976 legislation drew a tight curtain of secrecy around the agency's enforcement deliberations. Current federal antitrust law does not require disclosure of a premerger filing and strict confidentiality provisions prevent the agency from disclosing the content of the filing.[27] In cases in which the federal agencies decide not to challenge a proposed acquisition, the agencies generally disclose nothing—not even the fact that the merger was closely scrutinized. Ironically, today's critics have lost much of the accessibility to merger enforcement decisions that allowed an earlier generation of scholars to shape today's policy. At its worst, lack of accountability among the enforcement agencies could make it easier to conceal improper influence on decision-makers. See the discussion at § 10.6b. Or it may allow an agency to pursue an enforcement policy at odds with mainstream antitrust views, a result that some believe to have occurred during the 1980s.[28]

25. Elzinga, supra note 17, at 73.

26. During the 1980s, when the federal agencies were substantially relaxing merger controls, there may have been less likelihood of a court intervening on the side of a merging party because the agency was less likely to be perceived as overreaching.

27. Section 7A(h) of the Clayton Act, 15 U.S.C.A. § 18A(h). Under current law, the the statute, subject to agency rules specifying exceptions, requires that a transaction be reported if the acquiring and acquired firms exceed specified size thresholds and if, as the result of the acquisition, the acquir-

ing person would hold: (a) voting securities or assets in excess of 15 percent of the total voting securities or assets of the acquired person; or (b) voting securities or assets of the acquired person that exceed $15 million. 15 U.S.C.A. § 18A(a). Proposed legislation, pending as of January 2000, would raise the $15 million threshold to $35 million and provide for annual inflation adjustments.

28. ABA REPORT, supra note 11, at 26–30 (describing the perception that the Division was not rigorously enforcing its own Guidelines).

10.2b1. Compliance Issues

Determining whether a particular transaction must be reported can involve complex questions about the coverage of the statute and regulations. Under Section 7A(c) of the Clayton Act, various purchases of securities or assets are excepted from reporting requirements.[29] For example, an important exception allows the acquisition of a firm's securities in excess of the threshold amounts when that acquisition is solely for the purpose of investment and does not exceed 10 percent of the outstanding voting securities issued by the firm.[30] The Federal Trade Commission has also from time to time adopted rules that provide for additional filing exemptions. For example, the Commission reported adopting five new rules in 1996 to exempt additional categories of mergers from the reporting requirements, reducing the number of filings by an estimated 7 to 10 percent.[31] The exemptions reduce the amount of filing fees and burdens on firms involved in transactions and also reduce the reviewing demands on agency attorneys. The Federal Trade Commission's rules governing premerger filings are published in the Federal Register and codified in federal regulations.[32]

Some companies may be able to structure transactions to avoid filing requirements, but the Commission has taken steps to address evasion through actual or perceived loopholes.[33] A failure to file a required premerger notification may be relatively infrequent, but some intentional or negligent failures do occur. The statute allows the United States to seek a penalty of up to $11,000 for each day in which a person remains in violation of the premerger reporting requirements.[34] In 1996, the FTC obtained a $3.1 million civil penalty against a firm believed to have deliberately understated the value of the acquired assets in order to avoid a premerger filing.[35] In 1997, the Commission forced parties to an unreported merger to pay civil penalties of $5.6 million (the record so far).[36] The Commission has also pursued penalty actions against firms that fail to make a full disclosure in the premerger report, particularly with respect to a firm's own central decision-making documents.[37] Al-

---

29. 15 U.S.C.A. § 18A(c).

30. 15 U.S.C.A. § 18A(c)(9).

31. Federal Trade Commission & Department of Justice, Twenty–First Annual Report to Congress, Fiscal Year 1998.

32. Codified at 16 C.F.R. pts. 801–803.

33. Pfunder, *Transactions or Devices for Avoidance of Premerger Notification Obligations: Toward an Administrable and Enforceable Interpretation of 16 C.F.R. § 801.90,* 58 ANTITRUST L.J. 1031, 1031–32, 1038–44 (1990).

34. 15 U.S.C.A. § 18A(g)(1). The statute provided for a $10,000 per day penalty that has now been adjusted for inflation. Federal Trade Commission Rule 1.98, 16 C.F.R. § 1.98 (1996).

35. United States v. Sara Lee Corp., 1996–1 Trade Cases ¶ 71301 (D.D.C. 1996);

Sara Lee Corp., FTC Docket No. C–3523 (Consent Order, Aug. 24, 1994).

36. United States v. Mahle GmbH, 1997–2 Trade Cas. (CCH) ¶ 71,868 (D.D.C. 1997). In 1998, the FTC obtained a $500,000 civil penalty against a chain of funeral homes when it failed to file a premerger report for the acquisition of $16 million in voting securities of another chain (exceeding the $15 million size of transaction test). United States v. Loewen Group, Inc., 1998–1 Trade Cas. (CCH) ¶ 72,151 (D.D.C.1998).

37. United States v. Blackstone Capital Partners II Merchant Banking Fund L.P., 1991–1 Trade Cas. (CCH) ¶ 72,484 (D.D.C. 1999).

though the Commission seems unlikely to pursue all such violations, the probability that it will do so increases, as does the amount of the sanction it will seek, when the unreported or inadequately reported transaction raises obvious antitrust concerns.

10.2b2. *The Costs and Burdens of Premerger Notification*

For the agencies the cost of reviewing and evaluating premerger notifications, and for merging parties the burdens and delays of compliance, are significant. Because the vast majority of mergers raise no serious antitrust issues, these costs and delays serve no public purpose other than providing a screening device that is likely to identify the small percentage of transactions that do raise substantial antitrust issues. The agencies have responded with expanded exemptions to the filing requirements and accelerated clearance procedures.[38] Section 7A of the Clayton Act allows the Federal Trade Commission or the Antitrust Division to grant early termination of the 30 day waiting period (15 days for cash tender offers), permitting the parties to proceed immediately with an acquisition.[39] Efforts to expand early termination have borne fruit. In fiscal year 1979, the federal agencies granted 60 of 123 requests for early termination. That was slightly less than 7 percent of all premerger filings for that year.[40] By fiscal year 1987, after a relaxation in the requirements for early termination, the agencies granted 1739 of 2251 such requests. For that year, 69 percent of all reported transactions received early termination.[41] In fiscal year 1997, a year of record-setting merger activity, early termination was granted in 68 percent of all reported transactions or 75 percent of all transactions in which early termination was requested.[42] One risk to increased use of early termination is that it may reflect less than thorough agency review of premerger reports. Although it is difficult for outsiders to assess the thoroughness of this review, there is no available evidence to suggest that agency review has missed large numbers of acquisitions that raise serious antitrust questions.[43]

For those transactions in which possible antitrust issues are identified, the reviewing federal agency is empowered to make a request for additional information from the filing parties. Such requests can also be onerous both in terms of burden and delay. When the Commission or the Justice Department seeks additional information, this automatically triggers an additional 20–day waiting period (10 days for cash tender offers) after the additional information is received. Any additional delay can be costly to firms that have committed major resources to the timely

---

38. The Federal Trade Commission's efforts to close perceived loopholes in premerger notification are described in Pfunder, supra note 33, at 1032, 1038–44.

39. 15 U.S.C.A. § 18a(b)(2).

40. Federal Trade Commission, *Tenth Annual Report to Congress Pursuant to Section 201 of the Hart–Scott–Rodino Antitrust Improvements Act of 1976*, at app. A.

41. Id.

42. 1998 Annual Report to Congress, supra note 31, at app. A.

43. Past concerns that agency enforcement has been inadequate appear more directed to agency policy, not to the failure of the agencies to receive necessary information. ABA REPORT, supra note 11, at 26–32.

completion of an acquisition. Because the agency knows that the additional request is its last premerger opportunity to force the disclosure of information that might shed light on the transaction's competitive consequences, it may frame the additional request broadly. Responding to such a request can be time-consuming. The federal agencies have worked to scale back the scope of additional requests, and, after an additional request is issued,merging parties are usually able to negotiate with agency staff to obtain mutually acceptable further reductions. Still, receipt of an additional request adds substantial expense and delay to a merger transaction. One may hope that such requests are only made when there is objective reason, in addition to the size of the transaction, for concern about its competitive effect.

Given these burdens, the merging parties have an obvious incentive to avoid issuance of an additional request. Fortunately, the agencies have been willing to work with the filing parties to allow them to supply additional information without the agency's triggering the additional request mechanism. There has been a steady decrease in the use of additional requests over the past two decades. For example, in fiscal year 1981, additional requests were made in 10.2 percent of reported transactions; in fiscal year 1987, this rate had fallen to 3.7 percent; and in fiscal year 1998, the rate was 2.7 percent.[44] Although the rate of additional requests may vary from year to year based on the type of mergers being reported, it is clear that the long-term trend is toward reduced use of the additional request, a reflection of the agencies' enhanced ability to obtain needed information on a cooperative basis without filing a formal request[45] and the agencies' greater sophistication in digesting and interpreting the information initially provided in the premerger filing. For fiscal year 1997, almost half of the transactions subject to a request for additional information resulted in agency enforcement action or the parties abandoning the transaction because of the antitrust concerns.[46] The federal agencies have also cooperated in developing a streamlined model request for additional information.[47] Beneficial as this is, it tends to reinforce the nontransparent administrative character of merger enforcement.

44. 1998 Annual Report to Congress, supra note 31, at Exhibit A, Table 1.

45. The FTC, for example, has employed a "quick look" strategy to aid it in obtaining relevant information quickly without the use of the additional request. M. Steptoe, Deputy Director, FTC Bureau of Competition, Remarks before the ABA Section of Antitrust Law, Clayton Act Committee, (March 1990), *reprinted in* [1985–1997 Current Comment Transfer Binder] TRADE REG. REP. (CCH) ¶ 50,033.

46. Federal Trade Commission & Department of Justice, *Twentieth Annual Report to Congress, Fiscal Year 1997*.

47. Id. Despite such efforts, merging parties occasionally are confronted with an additional request because the agency uncovered a potential anticompetitive issue at the last stage of its review. When this occurs, the parties may be saddled with a broadly framed request and the added delay through no fault of their own. Of course, one way for the parties to reduce this risk is to address all substantial competition issues squarely in the initial filing. When nonetheless confronted with the possibility of an eleventh hour request, the parties may be able to convince the agency to allow them to withdraw their premerger filing and refile it, giving the agency more time to examine the transaction without automatically triggering the burdensome additional request.

10.2b3.   Exercise of Control over the To–Be–Acquired Firm During Premerger Review

One purpose of premerger notification was to allow the federal agencies to review a proposed acquisition before it took place. Parties to an acquisition, while delaying the legal takeover until after completion of the premerger review, may transfer beneficial control to the acquiring firm while the premerger review is still underway. This shift of beneficial ownership during the waiting period is properly viewed by the agencies as an unlawful circumvention of the Hart–Scott–Rodino Act. For example, substantial civil penalties have been levied against firms that acquired control before filing a premerger notification[48] or during the waiting period.[49]

A more subtle form of shifting of control may occur during the waiting period and should be avoided. In the negotiations leading up to a decision to go forward with an acquisition, firms often agree to exchange confidential business information. When rival firms are involved in merger discussions, the exchange of information may be guarded (and subject to confidentiality restrictions) for the simple reason that valuable proprietary information may fall into the hands of a rival if the acquisition does not go forward. But reserve in protecting proprietary information may dissipate quickly when a definitive agreement is reached on an acquisition. At this point, managers for the target firm, anxious to establish a cordial and cooperative relationship with officials in the acquiring firm who may soon be their superiors, may rush to accommodate the acquiring firm's information requests. This sharing of information, however, can undermine the viability of the to-be-acquired firm should the federal agencies challenge the transaction.

To address this concern, the federal agencies may require the parties to cease exchanging information during the pendency of a premerger investigation and return documents containing confidential information not needed to complete the transaction. The argument that this information would be helpful in planning for the future integration of the firms is not an adequate response when the sharing of this information undercuts a major goal of premerger notification: maintaining the independence and viability of the to-be-acquired firm until premerger review has been completed.

10.2c.   International Conflict and Cooperation

A significant number of acquisitions reported to the federal agencies involve antitrust issues that cross national borders. This is so even if the acquisition involves two U.S.–chartered companies. A prominent example is the acquisition of the McDonnell Douglas Corporation by the Boeing Corporation in 1997. Although this transaction involved two U.S. based firms, its antitrust implications were subject to premerger review

---

48.   United States v. Loewen Group, Inc. and Loewen Group Int., Inc. 1998–1 Trade Cas. (CCH) ¶ 72,151 (D.D.C. 1998).

49.   United States v. Titan Wheel International, Inc., 1996–1 Trade Cases ¶ 71,406 (D.D.C. 1996).

both by the Federal Trade Commission and by the competition authority of the European Union. The acquisition involved two of the three largest firms in the world that build commercial airliners (the third firm was Airbus Industrie in Europe). Although the potential anticompetitive effects of this horizontal acquisition were obvious, the Federal Trade Commission nonetheless determined not to challenge the transaction because it concluded that McDonnell Douglas would not survive as an independent company without the acquisition. U.S. merger law gives weight to the likely future competitive strength of the merging parties, not to their current market share.[50]

The Competition Directorate of the European Union, however, reached a different conclusion about the legality of the Boeing acquisition under European competition law. That law gives greater weight to the likely effect of an acquisition on competitors. In this case, the only significant remaining competitor after the acquisition was a European firm (Airbus Industrie) and European authorities were concerned that it would have difficulty competing against the combined U.S. firms. As a result, the Directorate imposed conditions on the acquisition requiring that certain Boeing contracts with customer airlines be opened to allow for competition.

Although there is talk of convergence between U.S. and European merger law, conflicts have continued. After the Antitrust Division had cleared GE's proposed acquisition of Honeywell, the European Commission challenged that acquisition in 2001.[51] One of the grounds for the Commission's decision was the risk that General Electric could bundle products at lower aggregate costs at the expense of rivals. This stirred a public debate involving officials and commentators on both sides of the Atlantic, with U.S. officials arguing that the combination was efficient and would bring lower prices to consumers, while European officials saw the combination as enhancing strategic power that could undermine combination.[52]

Despite the attention surrounding the partially conflicting conclusions on the Boeing acquisition reached in Washington D.C. and Brussels, international cooperation among the antitrust authorities appears common in merger investigations. The federal agencies have cooperation and information sharing agreements with the European Union, Australia, Brazil, Canada, Germany and Israel (discussed in § 18.2a4vi). The cooperative discussions among such authorities usually result in a coordinated approach to merger enforcement issues. A recent example is the coordinated response of the European Union and Department of Justice investigations of WorldCom Inc.'s acquisition of MCI Communication's Corp. According to a Justice Department press release, the investigations

50. United States v. General Dynamics Corp., 415 U.S. 486, 94 S.Ct. 1186, 39 L.Ed.2d 530 (1974). The substantive law governing this point is discussed in § 11.2h.

51. Case No. COMP/M.2220, General Electric/Honeywell, 2004 O.J. (L 48) 1 (2001).

52. See the discussion of the Boeing and Honeywell cases in § 18.7.

were coordinated from the outset, information was shared, and final remedial relief was coordinated between the two agencies.[53]

With the proliferation of competition law throughout much of the world, multiparty premerger investigations are likely to be increasingly common. While there remains a risk that different legal regimes will reach conflicting resolutions about likely competitive effects, direct conflicts in remedial provisions will probably remain the exception. Even if one country's antitrust authority imposes conditions on an acquisition approved elsewhere, as occurred in the Boeing case, the parties may still be able to effect their combination.

A major compliance headache for multinational firms is their obligation to make premerger filings in multiple jurisdictions. With the international proliferation of premerger filing requirements, a particular merger may require premerger filings in many countries. Although any individual filing may be relatively straightforward, the difficulty may come in sorting out the differing informational demands for each jurisdiction and then waiting for the clearance periods, which may differ significantly. Multilateral cooperation would be highly beneficial in achieving some uniformity as to the core information to be supplied and the waiting periods. This uniformity could greatly reduce compliance burdens and need not undercut the integrity of any country's enforcement system. See § 18.8.

10.2d. Remedial Issues

10.2d1. *Preliminary Injunction*

When an agency merger investigation reveals substantial competition issues, the agency often negotiates a settlement or forces the parties to the transaction to abandon it. The leverage behind the agency's position is the threat that, should the parties not take satisfactory remedial action, the agency will seek a preliminary injunction to prevent consummation of the transaction. The Department of Justice has authority to seek injunctive relief under Section 15 of the Clayton Act[54]; the Federal Trade Commission's authority is under Section 13(b) of the FTC Act.[55]

Section 15 of the Clayton Act does not specify the standards for obtaining preliminary injunctive relief, leaving the district court to apply the general standards for preliminary equitable relief that prevail in its circuit.[56] In many cases, the parties agree to consolidate the hearing on the preliminary injunction with a hearing on the merits, so the separate standard that might apply to the granting of preliminary relief is no

---

53. Department of Justice Press Release, Justice Department Clears Worldcom/MCI Merger After MCI agrees to Sell Its Internet Business, July 15, 1998.

54. 15 U.S.C.A. § 25.

55. 15 U.S.C.A. § 53(b). The agencies' general injunctive authority is addressed in § 16.2e.

56. United States v. Gillette Co., 828 F.Supp. 78, 80 (D.D.C.1993) (applying the standards for a preliminary injunction established by the D.C. Circuit).

longer relevant.[57] For the Commission, the procedures vary somewhat because the court is asked only for preliminary relief; if preliminary relief is granted, the proceedings switch to the Commission where the administrative complaint proceeding will address the legality of the merger under Section 7 of the Clayton Act. Section 13(b) of the FTC Act also spells out the standard for granting preliminary relief. It provides that "upon a proper showing that, weighing the equities and considering the [FTC]'s likelihood of ultimate success, such action would be in the public interest, and after notice to the defendant, a temporary restraining order or a preliminary injunction may be granted without bond * * *."[58] This standard has been applied by a number of courts, with the unsurprising result that the case usually turns on whether the Commission shows "a reasonable probability that the proposed transaction would substantially lessen competition in the future."[59] If the Commission is successful in obtaining a preliminary injunction, the parties to the transaction generally abandon it, choosing not to litigate further.

10.2d2. Failure to Execute an Agreed upon Divestiture

The Government's ability to confront a proposed acquisition before it occurs has increased both the choices and effectiveness of remedies. For example, with foreknowledge of a proposed merger, the enforcement agency can negotiate a settlement that allows the merger to proceed on the condition that competitively viable units are spun off in order to preserve a more competitive structure for the affected market. Such a remedy was unlikely if the agency could challenge a merger only after consummation. Despite the superior bargaining position that premerger review accords the enforcement agency, abuses still occur, particularly when the reviewing agency allows an acquisition to go forward on the condition that the acquiring firm later divest certain assets.

A case in point is a 1995 supermarket acquisition by Schnuck's Markets. The Federal Trade Commission permitted Schnuck's to acquire National Food Markets on the condition that it divest within one year twenty-four supermarkets in the St. Louis area. The Commission required Schnuck's to maintain the assets of these stores prior to divestiture. According to the Commission, Schnuck's failed to preserve the stores to be divested, closing departments, failing to maintain adequate inventory or staffing, delisting phone numbers, and referring customers to Schnuck's stores that would not be divested. In consequence, as the Commission found, sales in the affected stores fell by 35 percent in the year in which divestiture was to occur. The Commission responded in 1997 by requiring Schnuck's to divest two additional stores and to pay a $3 million civil penalty.[60]

57. United States v. Mercy Health Servs., 902 F.Supp. 968 (N.D.Iowa 1995), vac'd, 107 F.3d 632 (8th Cir.1997) (court decided case on expedited hearing on the merits).

58. 15 U.S.C.A. § 53(b).

59. FTC v. University Health, Inc., 938 F.2d 1206, 1218 (11th Cir.1991); FTC v. Cardinal Health, Inc., 12 F. Supp. 2d 34, 45 (D.D.C.1998); FTC v. Staples, Inc., 970 F.Supp. 1066, 1072 (D.D.C.1997).

60. FTC v. Schnuck Markets, Inc., Civ. No. 01830 (E.D. Mo. 1997).

The sort of compliance problem confronted in *Schnuck's* would not occur if the enforcement agency maintained a "fix it first" policy that required the divestiture of identified assets before the underlying acquisition could be consummated. No matter how clearly the obligation to maintain assets to be spun off may be articulated, and no matter how effective the procedures for reviewing compliance, once a merger is consummated, the surviving firm holds units it must sell that compete with units it will keep. The resulting conflict of interest creates significant market incentives to minimize if not to evade maintenance obligations. But holding back a large acquisition perhaps involving hundreds of millions of dollars because the parties have not yet divested assets worth only a fraction of this amount may be seen as unduly harsh. The agencies frequently do allow major transactions to go forward while requiring divestiture to occur within a stated period. According to a former FTC Bureau of Competition Director, divestitures have often required 15 months or longer after the consummation of an acquisition, leading to many compliance problems. The Commission has responded in a number of ways. One is to urge the parties to identify a buyer at the time they propose a divestiture in response to the agency's competitive concerns. Other steps include requiring the sale of a firm's crown jewel assets if an agreed upon divestiture is not promptly effected, appointing trustees to oversee the to-be-divested entities, and shortening the period allowed for completion of the divestiture. The Commission reports substantial progress in achieving these goals. For example, in recent supermarket mergers, the Commission has required that a buyer for the assets be identified before a settlement is approved, that the divestiture be completed within 20 days, and that all of the stores in a particular firm (either the acquiring or the acquired firm) be spun off as a unit. This approach provides greater assurance that the stores that are spun off will survive as competitively viable units with recognized goodwill.[61] The Federal Trade Commission has concluded that a divestiture of a freestanding business is much more likely to be successful (measured by the viability of the business in selling the overlapping product) than is a divestiture of selected assets. If the divested entity is to remain viable, it may require ancillary lines or services to be spun off along with the directly overlapping lines.

10.2e. Problems with Litigated Cases

Once the premerger notification program was underway, relatively few merger cases were litigated to judgment. Of those that were, the Government was losing a surprisingly large number of them. For example, of eleven litigated merger cases during the period 1982–1990, the Department of Justice scored a clear victory in only three of them. See the discussion in § 10.5a. In a series of hospital merger cases during the 1990s, the FTC and Justice Department failed to obtain a preliminary

---

61. William J. Baer, Director, Bureau of Competition, FTC, Remarks before the ABA   Section of Antitrust Law (April 15, 1999).

injunction to halt a proposed acquisition.[62] These results may reflect a number of factors. Most merging parties, when confronted with Government opposition to a merger transaction, choose to negotiate a spin-off or other relief that will allow the transaction to proceed. When this is not possible, many abandon the merger. Those few that choose to litigate may do so based upon an assessment of their ability to succeed before a court. The Government's relatively low success rate may reflect the skill of opposing counsel in assessing their chances for success.[63] But other factors may also be at work. In the hospital merger cases, for example, the Government may have had difficulty persuading the courts that non-profit mergers should be assessed with the same Section 7 standards that apply to other mergers. In some cases, the bias of local judges, perhaps sympathetic to the concerns of community hospitals involved in a particular transaction, may have increased the burden on the Government. The FTC has continued to monitor the impact of selected hospital mergers and, in 2004, filed an administrative complaint seeking the divestiture of a hospital acquired in earlier merger. The complaint alleges that the acquisition resulted in higher prices for hospital and related services in the Evanston, Illinois area.[64]

§ 10.3 State Enforcement

Although several states brought cases to challenge corporate mergers during the period immediately before and after the enactment of the Sherman Act,[1] states were not a consistent enforcement presence until the 1980s. Beginning at that time, state attorneys general stepped up their merger enforcement efforts in response to a perceived laxness in federal enforcement. In 1987, the states adopted their own merger guidelines suggesting a more activist stance than that described by the Justice Department's 1984 Guidelines.[2] These Guidelines were revised in

62. United States v. Long Island Jewish Med. Ctr., 983 F.Supp. 121 (E.D.N.Y.1997); FTC v. Butterworth Health Corp., 946 F.Supp. 1285 (W.D.Mich.1996), aff'd, 121 F.3d 708 (6th Cir. 1997); FTC v. Freeman Hosp., 911 F.Supp. 1213 (W.D.Mo.), aff'd, 69 F.3d 260 (8th Cir.1995); United States v. Mercy Health Servs., 902 F.Supp. 968 (N.D.Iowa 1995), vacated as moot, 107 F.3d 632 (8th Cir.1997). The FTC obtained a preliminary injunction against a hospital merger in a 1998 case, but the injunction was overturned on appeal. FTC v. Tenet Healthcare Corp., 17 F.Supp.2d 937 (E.D. Mo.1998), rev'd, 186 F.3d 1045 (8th Cir. 1999).

63. More recent examples of government failures to win a preliminary injunction include United States v. Oracle and FTC v. Arch Coal, 329 F. Supp. 2d 109 (D.D.C. 2004) (denying the FTC's application for a preliminary injunction).

64. Evanston Northwestern Healthcare Corp. and ENH Medical Group, Inc., File No. 011 0234, Docket No. 9315 (Complaint filed in 2004).

§ 10.3

1. Richardson v. Buhl, 77 Mich. 632, 43 N.W. 1102 (1889); People v. Chicago Gas Trust Co., 130 Ill. 268, 22 N.E. 798 (1889); People v. North River Sugar Ref. Co., 121 N.Y. 582 (1890); Nebraska v. Neb. Distilling Co., 29 Neb. 700, 46 N.W. 155 (1890); Distilling & Cattle Feeding Co. v. People, 156 Ill. 448, 41 N.E. 188(1895); Merchants' Ice & Cold Storage v. Rohrman, 138 Ky. 530, 128 S.W. 599 (1910).

2. National Ass'n of Attorneys General, Horizontal Merger Guidelines (1987), reprinted in 4 Trade Reg. Rep. (CCH) ¶ 13,-405. See generally, Barnes, Federal and State Philosophies in the Antitrust Law of Mergers, 56 Geo. Wash. L. Rev. 263 (1988).

1993 in a manner that more closely tracks the FTC/DOJ Horizontal Merger Guidelines of 1992.[3]

In their enforcement efforts in the 1980s, state enforcers had difficulty obtaining the premerger data supplied to the federal agencies under the premerger notification program. In the early 1980s, the Federal Trade Commission reversed an earlier policy of providing state enforcers access to FTC investigative files. Two appellate courts agreed with the Commission that it had no authority to give to the states premerger filings received from merging parties.[4] The states responded by adopting a compact intended to invite merging companies to submit voluntarily premerger notification data in return for a time commitment on the closure of any state investigation.[5] If the merging parties do not voluntarily supply the data, the states must rely on a court's compulsory process (after filing suit) or on any existing authority that the state enforcer may possess. Any of these options may be costly, duplicative, and delay completion of the investigation. But because a delayed acquisition imposes substantial costs on the parties, their incentive to cooperate with state investigators is substantial. Problems with obtaining necessary information have receded in the 1990s as cooperation between state and federal agencies has increased. A protocol adopted in 1998 provides for protection of information shared by a federal agency with a state enforcer.

Despite procedural difficulties, state attorneys general were frequently successful in negotiating restructured merger transactions during the 1980s. Suits were brought either under state[6] or federal antitrust law.[7] In *California v. American Stores Co.*, the Supreme Court upheld the authority of a state or private plaintiff to obtain injunctive relief in an antitakeover suit under Section 16 of the Clayton Act.[8] The facts of *American Stores* also suggest the substantial costs of uncoordinated, multitiered enforcement. The merging parties had negotiated a consent settlement with the Federal Trade Commission (approved by a 3–2 vote)[9] and had completed the purchase of stock. The FTC required American Stores to hold the acquired company's assets separately during a 90–day public comment period. At the end of this period, the California Attorney

---

3. National Ass'n of Attorneys General, 1993 Horizontal Merger Guidelines, *reprinted in* 4 Trade Reg. Rep. (CCH) ¶ 13,406.

4. Mattox v. FTC, 752 F.2d 116 (5th Cir.1985); Lieberman v. FTC, 771 F.2d 32 (2d Cir.1985).

5. National Ass'n of Attorneys General, Voluntary Pre–Merger Disclosure Compact, 4 Trade Reg. Rep. (CCH) ¶ 13,410 (incorporating 1994 revisions to the 1987 Compact).

6. The California Supreme Court has ruled that California antitrust law does not permit the state to challenge corporate acquisitions. California ex rel. Van de Kamp v. Texaco, Inc., 46 Cal.3d 1147, 762 P.2d 385, 252 Cal.Rptr. 221 (1988). Other states,

however, do have authority under their state laws to challenge acquisitions. E.g., Maine v. Connors Bros. Ltd., 1988–2 Trade Cas. ¶ 68237 (Me.Super.Ct.1988); Texas v. Coca–Cola Bottling Co. of the Southwest, 697 S.W.2d 677 (Tex. App. 1985).

7. E.g., California v. American Stores Co., 495 U.S. 271, 110 S.Ct. 1853, 109 L.Ed.2d 240 (1990) and Connecticut v. Wyco New Haven, Inc., 1990–1 Trade Cases ¶ 69024, 58 Antitrust & Trade Reg. Rep. (BNA) 809 (D.Conn.1990).

8. 495 U.S. 271, 110 S.Ct. 1853, 109 L.Ed.2d 240 (1990).

9. In re American Stores Co., 111 F.T.C. 80 (1988).

General filed suit challenging the acquisition. The district court granted preliminary injunctive relief to ensure that the acquired assets were held separately, but the court of appeals reversed. The Supreme Court ultimately sustained that injunction. A negotiated settlement followed, but the required divestiture was not completed until over 3 years after the announcement of the acquisition.[10] Although the merging parties share responsibility for these drawn out proceedings,[11] the lack of coordination among enforcement entities was a contributing cause of this delay.

In the 1990s, the states have continued their involvement in merger enforcement. In some cases, the states continue to act without federal involvement.[12] But in contrast to state efforts in the 1980s, state enforcement in the 1990s has frequently been undertaken with extensive cooperation between the responsible federal agency and state enforcers. In particular merger investigations, state and federal agencies have coordinated their efforts, in some cases even sharing personnel.[13] In 1998, a Federal/State Coordination Protocol said to formalize existing approaches for cooperation on merger investigations was signed by the Justice Department, Federal Trade Commission and the National Association of Attorneys General.[14] The Protocol deals with (1) procedures for maintaining the confidentiality of information; (2) procedures under which the FTC and DOJ will provide the states with certain sensitive information; (3) guidelines for joint investigation; and (4) collaboration in the settlement process.

§ 10.4 Private Enforcement

10.4a. The Role of Private Enforcement

Although statutory authority for private antitrust suits of all types was a part of the original Sherman Act, the number of such suits was insignificant before the Second World War. Private antitrust suits of all types grew following the war to a record high of 1400 complaints in

---

10. American Stores publicly announced its takeover attempt on March 21, 1988. California v. American Stores Co., 872 F.2d 837, 839 (9th Cir.1989). Following the Supreme Court's decision, the parties reached a negotiated settlement on May 16, 1990. Los Angeles Times, May 18, 1990, at D1. In April of 1991, American Stores reached agreement to sell its 142 Alpha Beta supermarkets to Yucaipa Cos. of Claremont, Ca. Los Angeles Times, June 18, 1991, at D2.

11. The merging parties could have sought a negotiated settlement with the California Attorney General prior to his filing suit in federal court or at any earlier point in the course of that litigation.

12. An example of this continuing involvement is Bon–Ton Stores, Inc. v. May Department Stores Co., 881 F.Supp. 860

(W.D.N.Y.1994), supplemented 1995–1 Trade Cas. (CCH) ¶ 70,917 (W.D.N.Y.1995), where the New York Attorney General joined with a private plaintiff in obtaining an injunction against a department store acquisition.

13. The Federal Trade Commission, for example, credits state cooperation with assisting its efforts in the *Staples, Shell/Texaco,* and *American Cyanamid* cases. William J. Baer, Director, FTC Bureau of Competition, Prepared Remarks Before the ABA Antitrust Section Spring Meeting (April 2, 1998).

14. Protocol for Coordination in Merger Investigations Between the Federal Enforcement Agencies and State Attorneys General (1998) *reprinted in* 4 Trade Reg. Rep. (CCH) ¶ 13,420.

1978.[1] Increasingly rigid standing requirements[2] and a larger plaintiff's burden for surviving a summary judgment motion[3] may have contributed to recent reductions in private suits.[4]

Private suits to enforce Section 7 have followed this general pattern.[5] Like state-initiated suits, private plaintiffs bring antimerger suits under Section 16 of the Clayton Act.[6] Private plaintiffs mounting a Section 7 suit start from a vastly different strategic position than Government enforcers. A private enforcer may have some advantages. For example, most plaintiffs are competitors or customers of firms involved in an acquisition. The plaintiff's firsthand knowledge of the industry can aid it in presenting a case. On the other hand, a private plaintiff operates under a number of handicaps. A private litigant has no access to compulsory process until suit is filed and discovery becomes available. Unless the court grants preliminary relief, private plaintiffs may lack leverage to negotiate a settlement. Finally, private plaintiffs may have an uphill burden in persuading a court to block an acquisition when neither federal nor state enforcers oppose it. Despite these handicaps, the flow of such private suits continues, perhaps because of the strong self-interest perceived by many plaintiffs.

10.4b. Standing Issues

The growth in number of private suits was curbed after Cargill, Inc. v. Monfort of Colorado, Inc.[7] In *Cargill*, the Supreme Court dismissed a competitor's suit because the nature of the alleged threatened or actual injury was said not to accord the competitor standing under the antitrust laws. This holding grew out of the Court's earlier decision in Brunswick Corp. v. Pueblo Bowl–O–Mat, Inc.,[8] a case in which a plaintiff's suit for damages from an allegedly unlawful acquisition of a competitor was dismissed because the injury to the plaintiff (lost profits) was not an antitrust injury. In *Brunswick*, the Court gave special attention to Section 4 of the Clayton Act, which authorizes private suits for treble

---

§ 10.4 Private Enforcement

1. The 1400 private suits filed in 1978 were 20 times the number of antitrust suits initiated by the federal government. White & Salop, *Private Antitrust Litigation: An Introduction and Framework, in* Private Antitrust Litigation: New Evidence, New Learning, 4 (L. White ed., 1988).

2. Brunswick Corp. v. Pueblo Bowl–O–Mat, Inc., 429 U.S. 477, 97 S.Ct. 690, 50 L.Ed.2d 701 (1977).

3. Matsushita Elec. Indus. Co. v. Zenith Radio Corp., 475 U.S. 574, 106 S.Ct. 1348, 89 L.Ed.2d 538 (1986); Monsanto Co. v. Spray–Rite Serv. Corp., 465 U.S. 752, 104 S.Ct. 1464, 79 L.Ed.2d 775 (1984). The Supreme Court may have relaxed somewhat these rigid requirements for surviving summary judgment in Eastman Kodak Co. v. Image Technical Services, Inc., 504 U.S.

451, 112 S.Ct. 2072, 119 L.Ed.2d 265 (1992). See § 17.3.

4. Private Antitrust Litigation, supra note 1, at 4.

5. There were few private suits to enforce Section 7 of the Clayton Act prior to 1950, probably in part because the loophole for asset acquisitions was not closed until that year.

6. Private plaintiffs may also sue for a threefold recovery of damages caused by an illegal merger under Section 4 of the Clayton Act, 15 U.S.C.A. § 15. A damage recovery is possible only if the plaintiff can establish antitrust injury. See § 17.2a.

7. 479 U.S. 104, 107 S.Ct. 484, 93 L.Ed.2d 427 (1986).

8. 429 U.S. 477, 97 S.Ct. 690, 50 L.Ed.2d 701 (1977).

damages when the plaintiff can show that it was injured in its "business or property by reason of anything forbidden in the antitrust laws."[9]

Because the plaintiff in *Cargill* sought only injunctive relief under Section 16 of the Clayton Act,[10] the special antitrust injury requirement that the Court found in private damage suits did not apply. But the Court cited language in Section 16 that paralleled that in Section 4 (a plaintiff may obtain injunctive relief from "threatened loss or damage by a violation of the antitrust laws"). Justice Brennan's opinion is also laced with a skepticism toward private suits that perhaps spilled over from the treble damage context, notwithstanding the lack of any claim for such damage relief in *Cargill*. Because the merger between the second and third largest firms in the industry would create a larger competitor, but still one slightly smaller than the market leader, Monfort (the fifth largest firm) could not argue that monopoly power would be created by this merger. Accordingly, its strongest argument was that the risk of oligopolistic practices was increased as the result of this acquisition. Such arguments are the heart and soul of agency merger enforcement policy.

The Justice Department, however, challenged the plaintiff's suit in an amicus brief. The Department argued that oligopolistic pricing would benefit the plaintiff to the extent that it shared in supracompetitive returns. Accordingly, no injury would flow to the competing firm as the result of an oligopolistic structure created by the merger.[11] But this response ignores the possibility of the leading firms' strategic behavior designed to discipline and repress competition, the consequence of which may be injury to both the smaller rival and to consumer welfare. For example, if Monfort is discontent with its 5 percent market share, it might seek to win new customers through lower prices. If the leading firms are in a position to discipline a discounting rival through targeted price decreases that undercut those offered by the rival, Monfort may be forced to discontinue such competitive initiatives. Moreover, such price war cuts by Monfort's oligopolistic rivals would not likely be vulnerable to antitrust challenge. The repressed competition resulting from the merger may benefit Monfort to some degree (by giving it an option to take oligopolistic returns on its limited sales, as long as it does not rock the oligopolistic boat). But such strategic behavior can stultify industry structure, assigning Monfort to a passive secondary role inhibiting procompetitive growth initiatives. Consumers are injured by high prices as well as the dampened opportunity for innovative marketing initiatives.

The Supreme Court dealt with possible strategic behavior on the assumption that it would be actionable only if it met the definition of predatory pricing.[12] Predatory pricing, the Court concluded, had not been adequately pleaded, but even if it had, the Court saw no prospect that

9. 15 U.S.C.A. § 15.

10. 15 U.S.C.A. § 26.

11. H. HOVENKAMP, FEDERAL ANTITRUST POLICY: THE LAW OF COMPETITION AND ITS PRAC-

TICE § 16.3a1, at 605–06 (3d ed. 2005)(making the same argument).

12. *Cargill,* 479 U.S. at 117.

Monfort could make out an adequate case for likely price predation. Indeed, under the Court's constricted definition of price predation,[13] this may be so. But the strength of Section 7 of the Clayton Act has been its flexibility in dealing with structural changes in an industry that are likely to increase the risks of oligopolistic behavior, even if that behavior in and of itself would not directly violate the antitrust laws. Section 7 prohibits a merger that "may" substantially reduce competition, regardless of whether potential anticompetitive effects would violate other provisions of the antitrust law.[14] Indeed, Section 7 is the only established useful tool for combatting oligopolistic pricing that is not collusive within the meaning of Section 1 of the Sherman Act. The Court's unfortunate construction of Section 7 and Section 16 of the Clayton Act appears to rule out this constructive role of forestalling oligopolistic injury when suits are brought by private plaintiffs.[15]

In response to *Cargill*, many lower courts have dismissed competitors' Section 7 suits for lack of standing.[16] Some competitors nonetheless continue to bring such challenges. The Court's language in *Cargill* did not absolutely preclude standing for a competitor,[17] and the Second Circuit, citing this flexibility, has ruled that a competitor,[18] including one that is the target of a hostile takeover attempt,[19] can have standing to challenge an acquisition under the antitrust laws.

13. This definition is criticized in § 4.1c.

14. This interpretation of Section 7 is borne out by the 1992 Merger Guidelines, which state that the anticompetitive effects of oligopoly power can be achieved through tacit or express collusion that "may or may not be lawful in and of itself." Dep't of Justice and Federal Trade Commission, Horizontal Merger Guidelines, § 2.1 (1992).

15. The *Cargill* decision may also be inconsistent with the implications of the Court's subsequent holding in California v. American Stores Co., 495 U.S. 271, 110 S.Ct. 1853, 109 L.Ed.2d 240 (1990), where the authority of a state or private enforcer to obtain injunctive relief to stop a merger was expressly upheld.

16. Axis S.p.A. v. Micafil, Inc., 870 F.2d 1105 (6th Cir.1989), cert. denied, 493 U.S. 823, 110 S.Ct. 83, 107 L.Ed.2d 49 (1989); Phototron Corp. v. Eastman Kodak Co., 842 F.2d 95 (5th Cir.1988); Alberta Gas Chem. Ltd. v. E.I. Du Pont de Nemours & Co., 826 F.2d 1235 (3d Cir.1987); Ansell Inc. v. Schmid Laboratories Inc., 757 F.Supp. 467 (D.N.J.1991); Remington Prod. Inc. v. North Am. Philips Corp., 755 F.Supp. 52 (D.Conn.1991); Sewell Plastics, Inc. v. Coca-Cola Co., 720 F.Supp. 1196 (W.D.N.C. 1989), aff'd and remanded, 912 F.2d 463 (4th Cir.1990); Hayden v. Bardes Corp., 1989–1 Trade Cas. (CCH) ¶ 68,477 (W.D. Ky. 1989); Burnup & Sims, Inc. v. Posner,

688 F.Supp. 1532 (S.D. Fla. 1988); O'Neill v. Coca–Cola Co., 669 F.Supp. 217 (N.D.Ill. 1987); Burlington Indus. Inc. v. Edelman, 666 F.Supp. 799 (M.D.N.C. 1987).

17. The Court's opinion appears to leave room for a competitor to obtain standing if the complaint alleges a risk of injury from predatory practices by the merging companies. *Cargill*, 479 U.S. at 110.

18. R.C. Bigelow, Inc. v. Unilever N.V., 867 F.2d 102 (2d Cir.), cert. denied, 493 U.S. 815, 110 S.Ct. 64, 107 L.Ed.2d 31 (1989); Bon–Ton Stores, Inc. v. May Dep't Stores Co., 881 F.Supp. 860 (W.D.N.Y. 1994), supplemented, 1995–1 Trade Cas. (CCH) ¶ 70917, 1995 WL 215307 (1995); Square D Co. v. Schneider S.A., 760 F.Supp. 362 (S.D.N.Y.1991). Other non–Second Circuit cases apparently recognizing a competitor's standing are: International Travel Arrangers v. NWA Inc., 723 F.Supp. 141 (D.Minn.1989) aff'd in part, rev'd in part, 991 F.2d 1389 (8th Cir.), cert. denied, 510 U.S. 932, 114 S.Ct. 345, 126 L.Ed.2d 309 (1993); Tasty Baking Co. v. Ralston Purina, Inc., 653 F.Supp. 1250 (E.D.Pa.1987). Cf. First & First, Inc. v. Dunkin' Donuts, Inc., 1990–1 Trade Cas. (CCH) ¶ 68,989 (E.D.Pa. 1990)(franchisees of acquired company apparently have standing to bring § 7 action).

19. Consolidated Gold Fields, PLC v. Minorco, S.A., 871 F.2d 252 (2d Cir.), cert. denied, 492 U.S. 939, 110 S.Ct. 29, 106

Because a firm ought not to be compelled to participate in an unlawful activity, the case for standing would appear to be at its strongest when a takeover target challenges the acquisition. Indeed, directors of a target company may face shareholder derivative suits if they knowingly participate in an unlawful acquisition. Some theorists disagree, urging that a firm that is a target of a takeover attempt can never have standing.[20] If the merger increases the possibility of collusion, the merged firm (including the shareholders of the formerly independent firm) will benefit through increased profit. But collusion is an antitrust violation that could bring treble damage litigation highly detrimental to the merged firm's shareholders. Even assuming oligopolistic price levels are achieved without any independent violation of the antitrust laws, there is still the possibility that the targeted firm's shareholders will be harmed by the unlawful merger. The management of the targeted firm, if it had remained independent, might have achieved an enhanced role in a competitive industry, one that ultimately could have brought a larger market share and increased shareholder value for the target company.

In the final analysis, a takeover target ought to have standing to challenge the merger if it presents a credible claim that the merger violates Section 7 of the Clayton Act. The view that a target company lacks standing to prevent its own participation in an unlawful merger is, at best, a highly cynical reading of the law. One could equally argue that a firm lacks standing to challenge any unlawful transaction in which it is involved simply because, if unchallenged, the transaction is likely to benefit the corporation and its shareholders. It is true that the management of the targeted company may have selfish motives in mounting an antitrust challenge to a takeover: Management may seek to preserve well-paid positions that would be lost after the takeover. But the selfish motives of management in opposing the takeover should be no more relevant to an antitrust analysis than the selfish motives of the acquiring company management in pursuing the takeover. If the targeted firm can show that a merger increases the risk of oligopolistic behavior, that in itself should be enough to show a violation of Section 7 of the Clayton Act, and to assure it standing to bring the action. If it cannot make this showing—or an equivalent showing of anticompetitive injury—the case should be dismissed.

§ 10.5   An Overview of Merger Enforcement

The preeminence of federal merger enforcement is now well established. But looking at data from the 1980s and 1990s shows that the tripartite enforcement mechanism still is evolving and shifting in re-

L.Ed.2d 639 (1989). Also granting standing were Marathon Oil Co. v. Mobil Corp., 669 F.2d 378, 383–84 (6th Cir.1981)(decided before *Cargill*) and A. Copeland Enters. v. Guste, 1989–2 Trade Cas. (CCH) ¶ 68,713 (E.D. La. 1988). Other courts have denied standing to a takeover target: Anago v. Tecnol Medical Products, 976 F.2d 248 (5th Cir.1992); Moore Corp. v. Wallace Computer Servs. Inc., 907 F.Supp. 1545 (D.Del. 1995); Hayden v. Bardes Corp., 1989–1 Trade Cas. (CCH) ¶ 68,477 (W.D. Ky. 1989).

20. Easterbrook & Fischel, *Antitrust Suits by Targets of Tender Offers*, 80 Mich. L. Rev. 1155 (1982); Hovenkamp, supra note 11, § 16.3a2, at 606–07.

sponse to changes in merger activity and views about the proper level of merger enforcement activity.

10.5a. Merger Enforcement During the 1980s

Despite more relaxed substantive standards imposed by the federal agencies during the 1980s, federal merger enforcement remained preeminent. The opportunity of the federal agencies to conduct a systematic review of all premerger filings is the key to this preeminence. The universe of transactions was large—in fiscal year 1987, 2533 merger transactions were reported to the federal agencies.[1] State and private enforcers did not have access to these filings.

During the six-year period 1982–1987, the Department of Justice and the Federal Trade Commission filed court or administrative complaints challenging 71 corporate acquisitions.[2] This figure does not fully reflect enforcement activity because, in a significant number of cases, merging parties chose to abandon the proposed transaction in the face of anticipated agency opposition. Thus, during the same six-year period, merging parties reportedly abandoned 25 merger transactions at some point in the investigation after the FTC issued a request for additional information.[3] During those same six years, parties abandoned or restructured an estimated 27 transactions in the face of Justice Department investigations.[4] When these abandoned or restructured transactions are counted, a more realistic estimate of federal enforcement initiatives during this period may be 100 or more (roughly 50 by each federal agency).

The Government's high success rate also demonstrates federal preeminence. Looking at the 51 cases during 1982–1987 in which the Justice Department filed a complaint or announced its intention to do so,[5] the

---

§ 10.5

1. Federal Trade Commission, Tenth Annual Report To Congress Pursuant To Section 201 of The Hart–Scott–Rodino Antitrust Improvement Act of 1976, Appendix A.

2. Thirty-six of these suits were filed by the Department of Justice; 35 by the Federal Trade Commission. Subcomm. on Monopolies and Commercial Law of House Comm. on the Judiciary, *Federal Merger Enforcement (1979–1987)*, reprinted in 54 Antitrust & Trade Reg. Rep. (BNA) 476–478 (1988).

3. Id. A few of these transactions may have been abandoned for reasons unrelated to the federal agency's investigation.

4. The Justice Department reports that, during the years 1982–1987, 15 transactions were abandoned or restructured to avoid agency objections prior to the filing of a court complaint. *Authorization for the Antitrust Division of the Department of Justice,* Hearings before the Subcomm. On Monopolies and Commercial Law, House Comm. on the Judiciary, 100th Cong., 1st & 2d Sess.

517–524 (letter from John R. Bolton to Peter Rodino (March 2, 1988)). In a 1989 speech, Assistant Attorney General James Rill offered another example of an acquisition being deterred by the mere announcement to the parties of the Department's opposition. Antitrust Enforcement: An Agenda for the 1990's, Remarks of James F. Rill Before the 23rd Annual New England Antitrust Conference, (Nov. 3, 1989) (describing Eastern Airlines decision to abandon the sale of gates at the Philadelphia Airport to US Air).

It appears that 12 other transactions were abandoned during this period after the Justice Department issued a request for additional information. Tenth Annual Report to the Congress, supra note 1, at app. A. It is unclear how many of these decisions were influenced by the Department's investigation.

5. These figures do not include approximately 12 cases in which the merging parties withdrew the premerger filing after the Department had issued a request for addi-

Department obtained some form of substantial relief (or forced the parties to abandon the transaction) in 43 of these cases (a success rate of 84 percent). These statistics count as a success any transaction in which the Department obtained a significant divestiture (by far the majority of the cases) or a commitment to alter the organization or behavior of the resulting entity. There may be disagreement whether the relief was in each case adequate to address the competitive concerns. Nonetheless, compared to the Government's well-documented failure to obtain structural relief in cases before 1976,[6] these statistics show a high degree of success.

DEPARTMENT OF JUSTICE MERGER ENFORCEMENT RECORD (1982–1987)

Results of 51 investigations in which the Department determined to oppose a proposed acquisition

SIGNIFICANT RELIEF			NO SIGNIFICANT RELIEF	
43			8	
Abandoned By Parties	Consent Judgment	Court Judgment	Consent Judgment	Court Judgment
12	30	1	3	5

In the relatively small number of cases in which the Department was unsuccessful, the Government either lost on the merits or, though successful on the merits or in obtaining a settlement, did not get significant relief.[7] Presumably, the Department failed not because of inadequate authority but because of an inability to persuade the court on the facts or the law.[8] Looking only at cases that went to judgment, the days when "the Government always wins"[9] appear gone. Of eleven litigated cases filed during the period 1982–1990, the Department lost seven of them and obtained only insignificant relief in the eighth,[10]

---

tional information. Federal Merger Enforcement, supra note 2. Withdrawal of the filings suggests either that the transaction was abandoned or that new filings were made for a restructured transaction.

6. Elzinga, *The Antimerger Law: Pyrrhic Victories?* 12 J.L. & ECON. 43 (1969).

7. The Department prevailed on the merits in one of the five cases in which it is recorded as obtaining no significant relief by court judgment.

8. For example, the Justice Department was able to negotiate only a weak consent order after it failed to convince the court of the merits of its case in United States v. Calmar, Inc., 612 F.Supp. 1298 (D.N.J. 1985). Of the 51 cases at issue during 1982–1987, only one appears to have resulted in

ineffective relief because the Government's challenge was not mounted until after the acquisition was effected. United States v. Newell Cos., (D. Conn., filed June 14, 1982), 1988 House Authorization Hearings, supra note 4, at 469–470.

9. United States v. Von's Grocery Co., 384 U.S. 270, 301, 86 S.Ct. 1478, 16 L.Ed.2d 555 (1966)(Stewart, J., dissenting).

10. Of litigated cases initiated in the period 1982–1990, the Department's losses include: United States v. Baker Hughes Inc., 908 F.2d 981 (D.C.Cir.1990)(the Government obtained partial relief); United States v. Syufy Enterprises, 903 F.2d 659 (9th Cir.1990); United States v. Archer–Daniels–Midland, 781 F.Supp. 1400 (S.D.Iowa 1991); United States v. Country

leaving only three clear victories.[11] The Federal Trade Commission's record in litigated cases was better; it won nine of thirteen decided cases.[12] Between 1987–1990, however, the Commission had only a break-even record.[13] Although the Government's spotty success record could have several causes,[14] premerger notification has no doubt played a role. Merging parties facing Government opposition to an acquisition find it unattractive to litigate unless they perceive a substantial chance of success in court.

While challenging a much smaller number of mergers, the states had a high success rate. In a sampling of 12 cases decided or settled from 1981 until 1990, the states obtained a negotiated settlement or favorable court ruling in nine cases (75 percent).[15] In some instances, states have

Lake Foods, Inc., 754 F.Supp. 669 (D. Minn. 1990); United States v. Carilion Health System, 707 F.Supp. 840 (W.D.Va.), aff'd, 892 F.2d 1042 (4th Cir.1989); United States v. Calmar, Inc., 612 F.Supp. 1298 (D.N.J. 1985); United States v. Virginia National Bankshares, Inc., 1982–2 Trade Cas. (CCH) ¶ 64,871 (W.D. Va. 1982). The Department achieved no significant relief in United States v. National Medical Enterprises, Inc., 792 F.2d 906 (9th Cir.1986)(vacating district court dismissal of merger case), consent order entered, 1987–1 Trade Cas. (CCH) ¶ 67,640 (E.D. Cal. 1987). Not included in the list of Department losses are United States v. Central State Bank, 817 F.2d 22 (6th Cir.1987) (Government loses challenge to acquisition based on Section 1 of the Sherman Act) and United States v. Waste Management Inc., 743 F.2d 976 (2d Cir.1984)(case initiated prior to 1982).

11. The Department's only clear successes during this period were: United States v. Rockford Memorial Corp., 898 F.2d 1278 (7th Cir.1990); United States v. Ivaco, Inc., 704 F.Supp. 1409 (W.D.Mich. 1989); United States v. Rice Growers Ass'n, 1986–2 Trade Cas. (CCH) ¶ 67,288 (E.D. Cal.1986).

12. The Commission prevailed in: FTC v. Elders Grain, Inc., 868 F.2d 901 (7th Cir.1989); Hospital Corp. of Am. v. FTC, 807 F.2d 1381 (7th Cir.1986), cert. denied, 481 U.S. 1038, 107 S.Ct. 1975, 95 L.Ed.2d 815 (1987); FTC v. PPG Indus., Inc., 798 F.2d 1500 (D.C.Cir. 1986); FTC v. Warner Communications Inc., 742 F.2d 1156 (9th Cir.1984); FTC v. Harbour Group Investments, 1990–2 Trade Cas. (CCH) ¶ 69,247 (D.D.C. 1990); FTC v. Imo Indus. Inc., 1992–2 Trade Cases ¶ 69943 (D.D.C. 1989); FTC v. Pacific Resources, Inc., No. C–87–1390 (W.D. Wash. Nov. 6, 1987), described in 53 BNA Trade Reg. Rep. 855 (Dec. 3, 1987); FTC v. Coca–Cola Co., 641 F.Supp. 1128 (D.D.C.1986), vacated without opin-

ion, 829 F.2d 191 (D.C.Cir.1987); FTC v. Bass Bros. Enter., Inc., 1984–1 Trade Cas. (CCH) ¶ 66,041 (N.D. Ohio 1984).

The Commission lost in: FTC v. R.R. Donnelley & Sons Co., 1990–2 Trade Cases ¶ 69240 (D.D.C. 1990); FTC v. Promodes S.A., 1989–2 Trade Cas. (CCH) ¶ 68,688 (N.D.Ga. 1989); FTC v. Owens–Illinois, Inc., 681 F.Supp. 27 (D.D.C. 1988), vac'd, 850 F.2d 694 (D.C.Cir.1988); FTC v. Occidental Petroleum Corp., 1986–1 Trade Cas. (CCH) ¶ 67,071 (D.D.C. 1986).

13. As noted in the previous footnote, the Commission lost 3 of the 6 decisions after 1987.

14. Calkins, *Developments in Merger Litigation: The Government Doesn't Always Win*, 56 ANTITRUST L.J. 855 (1988)(arguing that the Antitrust Division's briefing strategy may have contributed to their poor success rate).

15. The sample includes cases disposed of by court order since 1980, either by stipulation of the parties or after judgment by the court. Successful court cases include: North Carolina v. P.I.A. Asheville, Inc., 740 F.2d 274, (4th Cir.1984)(rejecting a state action immunity defense, hospital acquisition ruled unlawful); Ohio v. United Transp., Inc., 506 F.Supp. 1278 (S.D.Ohio 1981)(Ohio Attorney General has standing to challenge acquisition); Texas v. Coca Cola Bottling Co. of the Southwest, 697 S.W.2d 677 (Tex. App. Dist. 1985), appeal dismissed, 478 U.S. 1029, 107 S.Ct. 9, 92 L.Ed.2d 764 (1986)(trial court order dismissing state case on constitutionality grounds reversed). The latter two cases sustained the state's authority to bring suit, placing it in a favorable position to obtain a settlement.

States obtained a negotiated settlement in: California v. American Stores Co., 495 U.S. 271, 110 S.Ct. 1853, 109 L.Ed.2d 240

achieved relief without filing suit.[16] Looking only at documented cases in which states filed suit, filed papers in a federal proceeding, or obtained a nonlitigated settlement, the states were involved in 22 cases during the 1980s, or an average of just over 2 cases each year. In only 3 of these cases was the state's intervention clearly unavailing.[17]

These statistics, while showing a sharp increase in state enforcement presence during the 1980s, probably understate it. There were only a handful of documented state merger cases during the preceding two decades.[18] Although state intervention in the 1980s often involved rela-

(1990); Connecticut v. Wyco, New Haven, Inc., 1990–1 Trade Cases ¶ 69024 58 Trade Reg. Rep. (BNA) 809 (D. Conn. 1990)(defendant agrees to divest New Haven terminal and cancel an underlying lease); Massachusetts v. Campeau Corp., 1988–1 Trade Cas. (CCH) ¶ 68,093 (D. Mass. 1988)(Campeau agrees to divestitures as a condition of acquisition of department store chain); Pittsburgh v. May Dep't Stores Co., 1986–2 Trade Cas. (CCH) ¶ 67,304 (W.D. Pa. 1986); Maine v. Connors Bros., Ltd., 1988–2 Trade Cas. (CCH) ¶ 68,237 (Maine Sup. Ct.1988)(Connors Bros. agrees to divest a herring processing facility); Texas v. Gearhart Indus., Inc., 1988–2 Trade Cas. (CCH) ¶ 68,308, ¶ 68,309 (Texas D. Ct. 1988) (A TRO was issued, then withdrawn, after the parties to the acquisition agree to adhere to preacquisition policies).

The states were unsuccessful in: Palmieri, Inc. v. New York, 779 F.2d 861 (2d Cir. 1985)(New York Attorney General apparently unsuccessful in bid to intervene); Fairlawn Oil Serv., Inc. v. Texaco, Inc., 1984–1 Trade Cas. (CCH) ¶ 65,899 (D.R.I. 1984); California ex. rel. Van de Kamp v. Texaco, Inc., 46 Cal.3d 1147, 762 P.2d 385, 252 Cal.Rptr. 221 (1988)(state antitrust law does not authorize California Attorney General to attack an acquisition).

16. Documented instances during 1981–1990 in which state attorneys general apparently obtained a settlement in connection with a proposed acquisition without filing suit include: United States v. BNS, Inc., 858 F.2d 456, 463 (9th Cir. 1988)(reporting California's separate settlement with the merging parties); North Dakota's 1986 agreement concerning Northwest Airlines' acquisition of Republic Airlines, reported in 57 Antitrust & Trade Reg. Rep. (BNA) 158 (Aug. 3, 1989); California's settlement concerning Von's acquisition of California Safeway supermarkets, Supermarket News, Fairchild Pub., Inc., Sept. 18, 1989; New York State's settlement concerning A & P's acquisition of Waldbaum and Shopwell supermarkets, 55 Antitrust & Trade Reg. Rep. (BNA) 1073

(Dec. 22, 1988); R.H. Macy's unsuccessful takeover bid for Federated Department Stores, 54 Antitrust & Trade Reg. Rep. (BNA) 502 (1988)(New York attorney general negotiated a settlement for the eventuality that the takeover went forward); New York State's settlement concerning U.S. Air's acquisition of Piedmont Aviation, 52 Antitrust & Trade Reg. Rep. (BNA) 1066 (June 4, 1987); Maine's settlement concerning Hannaford Bros.' acquisition of First National's grocery stores, 33 Supermarket News 23 (Aug. 1, 1983).

In another category of cases, the states' opposition or concerns with proposed mergers was communicated to the reviewing federal agency: State of New York filed comments with FTC concerning of West Point–Pepperell's acquisition of J.P. Stevens, 111 FTC 349 (1989); New York and other states had intervened in Department of Transportation proceedings concerning Texas Air Corp.'s acquisition of Eastern Airlines, 58 Antitrust L.J. 221 (1989); on behalf of 22 states, Minnesota Attorney General filed comments in opposition to proposed merger of computer reservation systems of American and Delta Airlines, 56 Antitrust & Trade Reg. Rep. (BNA) 495 (1989).

17. The states lost three litigated cases, supra note 15. In the three cases in which the states intervened informally with federal authorities, it is difficult to determine the impact of the state role. See the cases cited in note 16, supra.

18. A computer search revealed only five reported state-initiated cases during the preceding twenty-one years (1960–1980). The states were successful in Peoples Savings Bank v. Stoddard, 359 Mich. 297, 102 N.W.2d 777, 83 A.L.R. 2d 344 (1960)(Defendant enjoined from obtaining 2/3 ownership in target bank). The states obtained a negotiated settlement in People v. Timberlanes of Redding, Inc., 1979–2 Trade Cas. (CCH) ¶ 62,987 (Cal. Sup. Ct. 1979)(defendant required to divest ownership of bowling facility).

The states were unsuccessful in Oleksy v. Sisters of Mercy of Lansing, 74 Mich.App.

tively small acquisitions,[19] the states challenged two large supermarket mergers in the California market,[20] two major department store acquisitions,[21] and several large airline acquisitions.[22] Predictably, larger states were the most active. California and New York played a major role in 10 of the 22 documented state interventions during the decade.

Competitors mount most private Section 7 challenges. The Georgetown data compiled for the period 1973 through 1983 shows that competitors brought 58 percent of all private Section 7 suits filed in five urban centers; plaintiffs in a downstream relationship with the merged companies (dealers, franchisees or customers) brought 27 percent of these suits.[23] A competitor or a customer that is the target of a hostile takeover attempt has special inducement to sue. A sampling of reported cases during the period 1981–1990 shows that 14 of 39 private plaintiffs (36 percent) were opposing a hostile takeover attempt.[24]

During the period 1981–1990, private plaintiffs brought 39 Section 7 suits (or about 4 each year) that resulted in reported court opinions.[25] Extrapolating from the Georgetown data (showing that roughly 75

374, 253 N.W.2d 772 (1977); City of York v. Pennsylvania Pub. Util. Comm., 295 A.2d 825, 449 Pa. 136 (1972); Kelly v. Michigan Nat'l Bank, 1966 Trade Cas. (CCH) ¶ 71,-741 (S.Ct. Mich. 1966).

19. E.g., Maine v. Connors Bros. Ltd., 1988–2 Trade Cas. (CCH) ¶ 68,237 (Maine Sup. Ct.1988)(challenge to acquisition of fish processing facility); Texas v. Coca Cola Bottling Co. of the Southwest, 697 S.W.2d 677 (Tex. App. Dist. 1985), appeal dismissed, 478 U.S. 1029, 107 S.Ct. 9, 92 L.Ed.2d 764 (1986)(challenge to soft drink bottler's acquisition).

20. Von's acquisition of California Safeway Stores, supra note 16, and American Stores acquisition of Lucky's stores, California v. American Stores, supra note 15.

21. Pittsburgh v. May Department Stores, supra note 15; Massachusetts v. Campeau Corp., supra note 15.

22. See note 16, supra.

23. White & Salop, *Private Antitrust Litigation: An Introduction and Framework*, in PRIVATE ANTITRUST LITIGATION: NEW EVIDENCE, NEW LEARNING Table 1.7 at 9 (L. White ed. 1988). The authors own sampling of 38 reported cases in the period 1981–1990 shows that in 18 of 39 privately initiated Section 7 suits, the plaintiff was a competitor. Fourteen of these suits were initiated by the targets of a hostile takeover bid (in many cases, the target was a competitor of the bidding company). Note 24, infra. In at least one of these cases, the plaintiff had apparently purchased a competing firm at least in part in order to create an antitrust defense against the defendant's hostile takeover attempt. Frank

B. Hall & Co. v. Ryder Sys. Inc., No. 82C0092, slip op. (N.D.Ill. July 12, 1982).

24. In 9 of the 14 cases, the court either denied a preliminary injunction, dismissed the complaint (for lack of standing or on the merits) or took both actions. Central Nat'l Bank v. Rainbolt, 720 F.2d 1183 (10th Cir. 1983); Hayden v. Bardes Corp., 1989–1 Trade Cas. (CCH) ¶ 68,477 (W.D. Ky. 1989); Burnup & Sims, Inc. v. Posner, 688 F.Supp. 1532 (S.D. Fla. 1988); Burlington Indus. Inc. v. Edelman, 666 F.Supp. 799 (M.D.N.C. 1987); Midcon Corp. v. Freeport–McMoran Inc., 625 F.Supp. 1475 (N.D. Ill. 1986); Gearhart Indus. Inc. v. Smith Int'l, 592 F.Supp. 203 (N.D. Tex. 1984)(preliminary injunction issued on non-antitrust grounds); Carter Hawley Hale Stores, Inc. v. The Limited, Inc., 587 F.Supp. 246 (C.D. Cal. 1984); Chem—Nuclear Sys., Inc. v. Waste Management, Inc., 1982–2 Trade Cas. (CCH) ¶ 64,860 (W.D. Wash. 1982); Crane Co. v. Harsco Corp., 509 F.Supp. 115 (D.Del. 1981). The remaining 5 cases are: Consolidated Gold Fields, PLC v. Minorco, *supra* note 19; Marathon Oil Co. v. Mobil Oil Co., 669 F.2d 378 (6th Cir. 1981); Grumman Corp. v. L.T.V. Corp., 665 F.2d 10 (2d Cir. 1981); Laidlaw Acquisition Corp. v. Mayflower Group, Inc., 636 F.Supp. 1513 (S.D.Ind. 1986); Frank B. Hall & Co. v. Ryder Sys. Inc., No. 82 C 0092, slip op. (N.D. Ill., July 12, 1982). The sample does not include cases in which the section 7 issue was clearly secondary to other claims. Whittaker Corp. v. Edgar, 535 F.Supp. 933 (N.D.Ill.1982).

25. See the cases cited in note 24, supra.

percent of all Section 7 cases were settled),[26] private parties may have filed four times as many suits (an estimated 156 suits during the period 1981–1990, or 16 each year). Private plaintiffs' scored some prominent successes during this period. Among them were Marathon Oil's and Grumman's defeat of hostile takeover bids.[27] Nonetheless, measured against cases actually filed, private plaintiffs are far less likely to obtain significant relief than either federal or state enforcers. Private plaintiffs' complaints for injunctive or damage relief failed in 24 of the 39 reported cases.[28] In another 6 cases, although the plaintiffs successfully overcame motions to dismiss,[29] their ultimate success on the merits is unclear.[30] The plaintiffs achieved some form of injunctive relief in 9 of the 39 cases, or 23 percent.[31] Adding cases settled or disposed without court opinion,

26. The 75 percent figure counts dismissals as judgments for the defendant. White & Salop, supra note 23, Table 1.17 at 42.

27. Grumman Corp. v. L.T.V. Corp., 665 F.2d 10 (2d Cir.1981). Marathon Oil Co. v. Mobil Corp., 669 F.2d 378 (6th Cir.1981).

28. In addition to the nine cases cited in footnote 24, the court denied a preliminary injunction, dismissed the complaint (for lack of standing or on the merits), or took both actions in each of the following cases: Cargill, Inc. v. Monfort of Colorado, 479 U.S. 104, 107 S.Ct. 484, 93 L.Ed.2d 427 (1986); Axis S.p.A. v. Micafil, Inc., 870 F.2d 1105 (6th Cir. 1989), cert. denied 493 U.S. 823, 110 S.Ct. 83, 107 L.Ed.2d 49 (1989); Phototron Corp. v. Eastman Kodak Co., 842 F.2d 95 (5th Cir. 1988); Alberta Gas Chems. Ltd. v. E.I. Du Pont de Nemours & Co., 826 F.2d 1235 (3d Cir. 1987); Cable Holdings, Inc. v. Home Video, Inc., 825 F.2d 1559 (11th Cir. 1987); Arthur S. Langenderfer, Inc. v. S.E. Johnson Co., 729 F.2d 1050 (6th Cir. 1984); Bayou Bottling, Inc. v. Dr. Pepper Co., 725 F.2d 300 (5th Cir. 1984); Lektro–Vend Corp. v. Vendo Co., 660 F.2d 255 (7th Cir. 1981); Remington Prods., Inc. v. North Am. Philips Corp., 717 F.Supp. 36 (D.Conn. 1989)(denying summary judgment for plaintiff), vacated, 755 F.Supp. 52 (D. Conn. 1991); First & First, Inc. v. Dunkin' Donuts, Inc., 1990–1 Trade Cas. (CCH) ¶ 68,989 (E.D.Pa. 1990); O'Neill v. Coca–Cola Co., 669 F.Supp. 217 (N.D. Ill. 1987); Frank Saltz & Sons, Inc. v. Hart Schaffner & Marx, 1985–2 Trade Cas. (CCH) ¶ 66,768 (S.D.N.Y. 1985); Joseph Ciccone & Sons, Inc. v. Eastern Indus., Inc., 559 F.Supp. 671 (E.D.Pa. 1983); Turner v. Johnson & Johnson, 549 F.Supp. 807 (D. Mass. 1982), aff'd, 809 F.2d 90 (1st Cir. 1986); Ohio–Sealy Mattress Mfg. Co. v. Kaplan, 545 F.Supp. 765 (N.D. Ill. 1982), aff'd, 712 F.2d 270 (7th Cir. 1983).

This list does not include cases in which the Section 7 claim was secondary. E.g., Sewell Plastics, Inc. v. Coca–Cola Co., 720 F.Supp. 1196 (W.D.N.C. 1989), aff'd mem., 912 F.2d 463 (4th Cir. 1990); Whittaker Corp. v. Edgar, 535 F.Supp. 933 (N.D. Ill. 1982); Zenith Radio Corp. v. Matsushita Elec. Indus. Co., 513 F.Supp. 1100, 1329 (E.D.Pa. 1981), aff'd in part sub nom. In re Japanese Elec. Prods. Antitrust Litig., 723 F.2d 238 (3d Cir. 1983), rev'd sub nom. Matsushita Elec. Indus. Co. v. Zenith Radio Corp., 475 U.S. 574, 106 S.Ct. 1348, 89 L.Ed.2d 538 (1986).

29. A motion to dismiss was denied in: R.C. Bigelow, Inc. v. Unilever N.V., 867 F.2d 102 (2d Cir. 1989); Cia. Petrolera Caribe, Inc. v. Arco Caribbean, Inc., 754 F.2d 404 (1st Cir.1985); International Travel Arrangers v. NWA, Inc., 723 F.Supp. 141 (D.Minn.1989), aff'd in part, 991 F.2d 1389 (8th Cir. 1993); Chrysler Corp. v. General Motors Corp., 589 F.Supp. 1182 (D.D.C. 1984); Mr. Frank Inc. v. Waste Management, Inc., 591 F.Supp. 859 (D.Ill.1984); Arnett v. Gerber Scientific, Inc., 566 F.Supp. 1270 (S.D.N.Y.1983).

30. For example, although Chrysler defeated General Motors motion to dismiss its suit to block the GM–Toyota joint venture, Chrysler, 589 F.Supp. 1182, Chrysler was ultimately unsuccessful in blocking the joint venture.

31. The courts issued some form of injunction in 7 cases: Consolidated Gold Fields PLC v. Minorco, S.A., 871 F.2d 252 (2d Cir.), cert. dismissed, 492 U.S. 939, 110 S.Ct. 29, 106 L.Ed.2d 639 (1989); Christian Schmidt Brewing Co. v. G. Heileman Brewing Co., Inc., 753 F.2d 1354 (6th Cir.), cert. denied, 469 U.S. 1200, 105 S.Ct. 1155, 84 L.Ed.2d 309 (1985); Marathon Oil Co. v. Mobil Corp., 669 F.2d 378 (6th Cir. 1981); Grumman Corp. v. L.T.V. Corp., 665 F.2d 10 (2d Cir. 1981); Tasty Baking Co. v. Ralston Purina, Inc., 653 F.Supp. 1250

the plaintiff's success rate is probably significantly lower (according to the Georgetown data, around 11 percent).[32]

This survey of 1980s cases leaves little doubt about the continued dominance of federal enforcement. While federal enforcers were effectively challenging around 17 acquisitions each year (with a high degree of success), states (also with a high degree of success) were challenging or affecting far fewer transactions (slightly more than 2 documented cases each year). Private plaintiffs were bringing an estimated 16 challenges each year, but far fewer of these (probably less than 20 percent) were able to achieve any significant relief. For reasons examined in § 10.6, private plaintiffs low success rate does not necessarily support a conclusion that such actions are an inappropriate use of the antitrust laws.

10.5b. Merger Enforcement During the 1990s

By the late 1990s, with a record setting merger wave underway, federal enforcement levels grew to unprecedented levels. In fiscal year 1997, there were 3702 premerger filings (compared to 2533 filings ten years earlier).[33] In that year, 59 merger transactions were either challenged by one of the two federal agencies through court or administrative action (52 transactions) or were abandoned before enforcement action was announced (7 transactions).[34] This represents more than a three-fold increase over the average of 17 yearly federal enforcement initiatives during the mid–1980s. See the discussion in § 10.5a. The much higher enforcement numbers in 1997 probably reflect the larger number of acquisitions that were occurring and the higher percentage of acquisitions that raised troublesome antitrust issues. To some degree, the higher numbers in 1997 may also reflect a more aggressive enforcement stance by the federal agencies than was evident during the 1980s.

State involvement in merger enforcement continued during the 1990s, but the emphasis shifted from stand-alone enforcement initiatives undertaken by an individual state or a group of states[35] to cooperative action undertaken with the FTC or the Justice Department. Cooperation between a federal agency and state attorneys general is now common-

---

(E.D.Pa. 1987); McCaw Personal Comm., Inc. v. Pacific Telesis Group, 645 F.Supp. 1166 (N.D.Cal.1986); Laidlaw Acquisition Corp. v. Mayflower Group, Inc., 636 F.Supp. 1513 (S.D.Ind.1986).

In White Consolidated Indus., Inc. v. Whirlpool Corp., 781 F.2d 1224 (6th Cir.1986), the court vacated the preliminary injunction subject to a divestiture requirement. In Frank B. Hall & Co. v. Ryder Sys. Inc., No. 82C0092, slip op. (N.D.Ill. July 12, 1982), the court indicated its intent to issue a preliminary injunction unless the defendant agreed to grant the plaintiff 30–days notice of any attempt to acquire more of the plaintiff's stock.

32. White & Salop, supra note 23, Table 1.17, at 42.

33. Statement of the Federal Trade Commission, Mergers and Corporate Consolidation in the New Economy, Senate Judiciary Comm., June 16, 1998 (reporting the 1997 data and estimating 4500 premerger filings for fiscal year 1998).

34. Id.

35. An example of continued state enforcement undertaken without direct federal involvement is Bon–Ton Stores, Inc. v. The May Department Stores Co., 881 F.Supp. 860 (W.D.N.Y.1994), supplemented 1995–1 Trade Cas. ¶ 70917, 1995 WL 215307 (W.D.N.Y.1995).

place in merger investigations and is governed by the 1998 Protocol governing joint investigations.[36]

Private merger enforcement has continued in the 1990s, albeit apparently at a level substantially less than occurred in the 1980s.[37] To the extent that federal enforcement has been more aggressive in the 1990s, private parties may have had fewer occasions to risk the expense of a private suit to challenge a merger. In addition, with the substantial drop in hostile takeover attempts, there were fewer target firms to mount challenges to takeovers. But the continued resistance to competitor standing may have also contributed to the lower profile for private suits during the 1990s (see the discussion in § 10.4b).

§ 10.6 Unresolved Procedural Issues of Merger Enforcement

How well does the tripartite domestic merger enforcement system work in combination with the increasingly international scope of merger enforcement? Section 10.1 suggested three goals of a merger enforcement system: (1) achieving substantively correct decisions (2) at low procedural cost (3) with adequate visibility and accountability. A more refined examination of whether merger decisions have reached the correct decision on the merits must await the separate examination of horizontal, vertical and conglomerate mergers. Achieving substantively correct merger decisions is also something of a moving target—the goals of merger enforcement are constantly changing. Still, one measure of the merger enforcement system's success is whether any substantive merger policy, whatever it might be, can be carried forward in merger enforcement decisions. Measured in these terms (and in terms of the other stated goals), modern merger enforcement, while flawed, works significantly better than it did before the premerger notification program was implemented.

The premerger notification system has enabled the federal agencies to challenge most questionable mergers before they occur, thus enhancing the prospect of meaningful relief. It has also given the agencies access to information that allows knowledgeable decisions about the lawfulness of a merger. There are, however, a number of lingering issues. The first is the proper role of private enforcement: Should the current strict limits on the standing of private plaintiffs be maintained? A second issue is whether visibility and accountability in the federal merger enforcement can be widened. Finally, assuming that state and

---

36. See § 10.3.

37. Anago, Inc. v. Tecnol Medical Prods., Inc., 976 F.2d 248 (5th Cir. 1992)(denying standing to a takeover target) cert. dismissed, 510 U.S. 985, 114 S.Ct. 491, 126 L.Ed.2d 441 (1993); Moore Corp. v. Wallace Computer Servs., Inc., 907 F.Supp. 1545 (D.Del.1995)(denying standing to a takeover target); Bon–Ton Stores, Inc. v. May Department Stores Co., 881 F.Supp.

860 (W.D.N.Y.1994), supplemented 1995–1 Trade Cas. (CCH) ¶ 70917, 1995 WL 215307 (W.D.N.Y.1995) (rival accorded standing and injunction issued in a suit in which the New York Attorney General was a co-plaintiff); Square D Co. v. Schneider S.A., 760 F.Supp. 362 (S.D.N.Y.1991)(rival accorded standing).

private enforcement suits are to be permitted, are there ways of smoothing the interaction between potential federal, state and private enforcers in the United States and foreign merger enforcement agencies?

10.6a. The Role for Private Enforcement

Private plaintiffs are unlikely to sue at all if a federal or state agency initiates enforcement action against a merger. For a private plaintiff, the costs of an enforcement suit are substantial and the statistical risk of failure is great. Under these circumstances, a private party opposing a merger is far more likely to urge a federal or state enforcement initiative and, if one is undertaken, use its resources to support that initiative. Only as a last resort is a private plaintiff likely to sue on its own to enjoin a merger. Thus, even if no standing requirements were imposed on private plaintiffs, the courts are unlikely to be flooded with a great number of such private suits.

Yet, the availability of a remedy for a private plaintiff is an important enforcement tool. Private suits have occasionally halted very substantial (and presumptively, significantly anticompetitive) mergers.[1] The prophylactic nature of the premerger injunction suit—and the importance of merger enforcement as the sole effective weapon against oligopolistic markets—weigh in favor of a continued role for private enforcement. Given the limited enforcement resources available to federal and state agencies, the private suit could fill a significant enforcement vacuum.

The category of plaintiffs likely to have sufficient incentive to bring such suits is limited—the data suggests that most such plaintiffs are rivals or (less frequently) customers of the merging firms. Of course, the takeover target (often a rival or customer of the acquiring firm) is also likely to have the incentive to sue if it opposes the takeover. Current law makes it very difficult for rivals or takeover targets to obtain standing. For the reasons stated in § 10.4b, that law should be interpreted flexibly to allow this group of most likely and best-informed private plaintiffs to show threatened anticompetitive injury based on a likelihood that a merger will facilitate oligopolistic practices in the industry. In the case of a rival, standing should be established by a credible economic theory that explains how such oligopolistic practices might harm the rival, including harm that flows from limiting the rival's ability to expand its market share. Standing ought to be relatively automatic in the case of a plaintiff that is a takeover target—any firm ought to have standing to challenge its participation in an allegedly unlawful merger based on a credible showing of likely anticompetitive effect. Although substantive screens may have inhibited harmless or even procompetitive mergers in the 1960s, that certainly has not been true since the 1980s.

§ 10.6

1. Grumman Corp. v. LTV Corp., 665 F.2d 10 (2d Cir.1981). Marathon Oil Co. v. Mobil Corp., 669 F.2d 378 (6th Cir.1981).

10.6b. Visibility and Accountability of Merger Enforcement

Few would dispute the importance of openness for fair, responsive, and wise democratic government. There is a compelling case for greater transparency in the merger enforcement decisions of the Justice Department's Antitrust Division and the Federal Trade Commission. Although both agencies disclose a great deal of information through guidelines, opinions, speeches, testimony, and public case filings, their record in publishing information about enforcement decisions is problematic. Neither agency routinely provides any explanation of its decision not to challenge a proposed merger, even if genuine issues were raised, carefully studied, and decided by the agency. Similarly, when agency opposition to a proposed merger results in the would-be participants abandoning the transaction, there is typically no disclosure of the agency's analysis. In merger inquiries in which the agency reaches a negotiated settlement, agency public disclosure is often inadequate, particularly in the case of Justice Department fix-it-first resolutions.

The matter of transparency is especially urgent with respect to merger enforcement because the locus of law and rulemaking power has shifted to the federal agencies, with only sparse judicial review of agency decisions. The virtual vacuum on explanations of decisions to drop substantial merger enforcement investigations, or of agency concerns underlying a decision of the merging parties to abandon the transaction or restructure in a fix-it-first agreement, is highly unsatisfactory. Yet transparency for this vital area is lacking. For example, during the five fiscal year period 1998–2002, a study revealed that the FTC provided minimally adequate disclosure in only 56% of its key merger enforcement decisions; the Antitrust Division's record was worse, providing minimally adequate disclosure in only 21% of its key merger decisions.[2] This interpretation of the agency record is generous. Even among the cases counted as providing "minimally adequate" disclosure, there was a consistent failure to identify and explain agency analysis of "near-miss" issues: competitive concerns that were non-trivial but were nonetheless deemed insufficiently weighty to require agency action.

The lack of meaningful disclosure can mask errors of under enforcement or over enforcement. But the problem is more acute with respect to under enforcement because of the tendency of both agencies to not reveal analysis of issues for cases that are not brought or claims that are not made. Indeed, even if the agency brings an action, the case is usually settled by a consent in which the agency discloses its thinking only with respect to issues that are addressed in the remedy, leaving the public in the dark as to conduct deemed unlawful but not addressed in the remedy or conduct considered borderline but not challenged by the agency. The possibility that enforcement errors are undiscovered is most troublesome at the Antitrust Division because, unlike the FTC where any of five

---

2. Grimes, Transparency in Federal Antitrust Enforcement, 51 Buff. L. Rev. 937, 959–73 (2003).

commissioners can release a statement when there is disagreement about an enforcement decision, the Antitrust Division has no existing mechanism for disclosing agency analysis of disputed or "near-miss" issues.

Reform of agency disclosure policies is needed, but cannot be achieved without a commitment at the highest level. Former FTC Chairman Murris has made helpful initial steps.[3] The dimensions of reform must be framed with an eye to the law of unintended consequences. A disclosure policy that is overly broad or unduly burdensome could lead to unnecessary costs on enforcers and targets alike, and circumvention that conceals instead of disclosing. Congressional oversight would be helpful and some amendments to current law may be needed.

The case for transparency is not that it will be a panacea for all that ails antitrust or the system of competition that antitrust supports. Short-sighted and expedient enforcement decisions will continue to be made. Political influence, often subtle and indirect, will still be a factor. But transparency can support meaningful and timely debate about the cutting edge issues of competition that actually confront contemporary antitrust enforcers. And it can cast sunlight on decisions in a way that can discourage expedient, careless or unprincipled decisions. Transparency will more effectively communicate the law to those who wish to comply with it. Yes, it might in some instances more readily show a path for those who would evade the law, but evasions too may more readily come to light and be remedied if there is openness in enforcement. These are concepts subtle in measurement if not in description. Yet the case for greater openness seems compelling. This is so, in part, because transparency is consistent with fundamental and deeply held values that support a responsive, fair and democratic system of governance.

Achieving transparency reform will be difficult. There are well-meaning and experienced antitrust enforcers who have genuine reservations about moving away from the law-enforcement model of antitrust that has become central to the culture of the Antitrust Division. They have non-trivial concerns about the burdens of greater transparency and a system of voluntary submissions that rests on maintaining the confidentiality of business information. The truth is, however, that in this age of internet communications, antitrust has already moved well beyond the classic model of law-enforcement as a secret process in which the government enforcer alone knows the critical facts. The Federal Trade Commission has demonstrated that antitrust enforcement can be effectively carried out in a more open environment. In a much more emphatic way, so too has the European Commission.

---

3. The Commission issued a statement at the close of its merger investigation involving ocean cruise lines. Statement of the Federal Trade Commission Concerning Royal Caribbean Cruises, Ltd./P & O Princess Cruises plc & Carnival Corporation/P & O Princess Cruises plc., FTC File No. 021 0041 (2002), available at <http://www.ftc.gov/os/2002/10/cruisestatement.htm>.

That more openness is needed, then, is not likely to be the point of contention. The critical questions will be how much, how soon, and how to achieve it at the lowest cost to other enforcement values. The goal of transparency reform should be to achieve adequate public disclosure of all agency enforcement decisions likely to have significant guidance value within or outside the agency. To achieve this goal, substantial change in current disclosure policy will be required. This will require a firm commitment at each agency's highest level. The 2003 study made a number of recommendations to foster merger enforcement transparency, among them that: (1) for all publicly traded firms, each agency should promptly and effectively disclose each critical stage of a civil enforcement investigation, thereby addressing concerns that leaked information is the basis for unfair trading in the firm's stock; (2) the FTC and the Antitrust Division should consider making more efficient use of their web sites to provide information about pending merger investigations and to invite interested outsiders to provide comments about pending mergers; (3) the Antitrust Division and the FTC should immediately begin disclosing all merger enforcement decisions for firms that exceed a minimum size threshold (e.g., the merged firm has at least 200 million in assets and its assets are increased by at least $100 million as the result of the transaction) or that, regardless of size, involve the issuance of a second request. The disclosure of these enforcement decisions should be accompanied by an explanation in each instance in which an extended investigation was conducted, regardless of whether the agency decided to take enforcement action.[4]

Most of these changes would not involve substantial costs to the agency. The exception is the issuance of more detailed explanations at the conclusion of a major investigation. These more detailed statements will not be required in a large number of cases, but the statements will involve nontrivial costs for the agency. Internal decision memoranda may be the basis for the agency's public explanation, but such memoranda would have to be carefully edited to assure no confidential material is released. It is likely, however, that once agency disclosure becomes routine, the process would become more efficient and less resource intensive.

Both the FTC and the Antitrust Division probably have the authority to issue explanatory statements without further legislation. Indeed, both agencies already do so on occasion. To the extent that additional legislation is required to authorize such statements, or to the extent that the agencies do not voluntarily provide these statements, the Congress should act to ensure that transparency is achieved.

10.6c. Coordination Among Enforcers

A third concern is the lack of the limited scope of interaction among enforcers. Cooperation is needed both among the tripartite enforcers within the United States (federal, state and private plaintiffs) and internationally. Within the United States, continued federal primacy in

---

4.   Grimes, supra note 2, at 990–92.

merger enforcement is inevitable and necessary. Resources available for interaction with other enforcers, especially private parties, beyond processing information they provide, is manifestly limited. Nonetheless, federal primacy will be more widely accepted (and more effectively exercised) if state and local governments and even interested private parties feel that they, too, can be heard before an enforcement decision is made. Routine announcements of premerger filings are a constructive step in this direction. In addition, federal enforcers ought to solicit actively the views of state or even local governments when there is reason to believe that a proposed acquisition will seriously affect their interests or those of their constituents.

Often, state intervention in a proposed acquisition has not gone beyond lobbying the responsible federal agency to take enforcement action.[5] Some countries provide a formal mechanism for hearing state or local governments. For example, German law requires that the Federal Cartel Office afford an opportunity to comment to authorities from the states of incorporation for the merging parties before prohibiting a merger.[6] Provided a spirit of cooperation prevails, no new legislation is required to implement an equivalent scheme in the United States.

When states seek an active enforcement role, an ideal system would coordinate the positions of federal and interested state authorities. While state attorneys general have occasionally acted independently of (and inconsistently with) the federal agencies, they have more frequently cooperated with federal enforcers. The states, more so than the Federal Government, lack resources to challenge large numbers of mergers on antitrust grounds. Indeed, some state attorneys general have no experienced antitrust attorneys on their staffs. Although this need not prevent state enforcement action—the Pennsylvania Attorney General engaged the services of a Pittsburgh law firm to bring the state's case against a department store merger[7]—many smaller states may lack the resources to mount a major merger case, either through their own staff attorneys or through an outside law firm. Thus, cooperation between state and federal agencies institutionalized through the 1998 Protocol has substantial benefits for all agencies involved.

To the extent the Protocol simplifies review procedures, it may also benefit the parties whose merger is being reviewed. Lack of coordinated enforcement can substantially increase the costs for the merging parties. In *BNS*, the Justice Department reached a consent settlement with the merging parties that differed from the settlement sought by the California Attorney General.[8] In that instance, the merging parties apparently reached separate agreements with the federal and California agencies

5. Twenty-two state attorneys general are said to have expressed their concern to the U.S. Department of Justice over the proposed merger between American and Delta Airlines. Further action by the states was apparently not necessary. 56 ATRR (BNA) 495 (March 30, 1989).

6. Germany, Act Against Restraints of Competition, Art. 40(4).

7. Pittsburgh v. May Dept. Stores, 1986–2 Trade Cas. (CCH) ¶ 67,304 (W.D. Pa. 1986).

8. United States v. BNS Inc., 858 F.2d 456, 460 (9th Cir. 1988).

without undue delay. However in *American Stores*, the California Attorney General's insistence on substantially greater divestiture than that negotiated by the FTC led to two additional years of litigation at great expense to the parties involved in that transaction.[9] Had the FTC and the California Attorney General been able to coordinate their positions on the appropriate remedy, much cost and delay might have been avoided. Even if there can be no agreement on the appropriate remedy, all parties involved in the enforcement should be encouraged to make timely decisions on their enforcement posture. The California Attorney General delayed his decision on enforcement action until after the FTC had announced its consent agreement with the parties and the agreement had been available for comment for 90 days. Such a delay appears strongly at odds with the goal of the premerger program to provide expeditious enforcement decisions.

Difficult conceptual problems can arise once the federal agency has reached an enforcement decision. For example, if the federal agency has determined not to pursue enforcement action, should it send the premerger filings to a state enforcement official who might reach a contrary conclusion? The answer might logically turn on such matters as the thoroughness of the federal agency's review, whether the federal agency made an affirmative determination that the transaction is procompetitive (or not anticompetitive), or whether the agency simply lacked the interest or resources to pursue the matter further. If the latter, a strong case can be made for the federal agency sharing any available information with the state enforcement officials.

On the international level, cooperation and coordination has also become commonplace. See the discussion in § 18.2a4vi. Although antitrust authorities from various nations may occasionally seek inconsistent remedies, such conflicts can be minimized. In many cases, a merger authority can design the remedy that it imposes in a manner that primarily affects operations or distribution in its home country. Still to be addressed is the timing of premerger review. With competition laws proliferating throughout the world, many with premerger clearance procedures, it would be beneficial to have some standardization of the review periods so that a transaction that might be quickly cleared in one country is not unnecessarily held up merely because another reviewing country has a much longer waiting period for premerger review. Resolution of this problem may require multilateral discussions.

Another fruitful point for multilateral discussion might be efforts to standardize the information included in an initial report filed by the merging parties. To the extent that various antitrust authorities could agree on the content and form in which information is submitted in an initial notification, this might substantially reduce the burdens on filing parties. Each authority may wish to seek additional information relevant to the impact of a merger within its jurisdiction, but this should not preclude reaching agreement on aspects of the basic notification document.

9. 495 U.S. 271, 110 S.Ct. 1853, 109 L.Ed.2d 240 (1990).

Chapter XI

HORIZONTAL AND CONGLOMERATE MERGERS

Table of Sections

§ 11.1 Introduction

Horizontal mergers, long the focus of most merger enforcement, are addressed in this chapter. See § 11.2. A merger is horizontal if it involves firms which compete head-to-head in one or more markets, or market segments. A merger between firms that are in a supplier-customer relationship is a vertical merger, discussed in Chapter 12. Mergers between two firms that are neither rivals nor in a vertical relationship are called conglomerate mergers. See § 11.3. Not all conglomerate mergers involve unrelated firms. For example, though firms may not be rivals, they may be potential rivals. Potential competition issues arise in conglomerate mergers that include two firms that sell the same product or service in differing geographic regions (a market extension merger) or two firms that market related products in the same geographic area (a product extension merger).

The contemporary law governing all types of mergers is largely the product of post–1950 evolution. Although the statutory touchstone for this law, Section 7 of the Clayton Act, was enacted in 1914, its effectiveness as an enforcement tool was established only after the Celler–Kefauver Act in 1950.[1] Beginning in 1962, the Supreme Court took an active part in shaping that law for the next thirteen years. But the Supreme Court has not decided a merger case on substantive grounds since 1975.[2] The vacuum created by the Supreme Court's abstinence has been filled by lower court rulings and, most prominently, by agency-issued merger guidelines, now in their fourth iteration.[3] The major reason for this change (explored in § 9.2e) was a shift of leverage to the enforcement agencies accomplished through implementation of the premerger notification system beginning in 1977. Where once judicial interpretations were dominant, increasingly technical agency interpretations have moved to the forefront.

The influence of agency interpretations of the substantive law is evident, for example, in developments such as the unilateral effects doctrine, first described in the 1992 Guidelines and applied in at least one lower court opinion,[4] but yet to be addressed by the Supreme Court. Another example is the defense based on ease of entry. Since 1982, many mergers have been cleared by the federal agencies (and a few found lawful by the lower courts) on the ground that ease of entry into the relevant market removes the anticompetitive risks of a merger. Yet, the United States Supreme Court, although addressing the issue obliquely in potential competition cases, has never directly ruled on this controversial defense. Another defense that has been invoked to justify mergers

---

§ 11.1

1. The historical evolution of merger law is traced in § 9.2.

2. See § 10.2b n.22.

3. Dep't of Justice and Federal Trade Commission, Horizontal Merger Guidelines

(1992), as amended in 1997, available at <http://www.usdoj.gov/atr/public/guidelines/ hmg.htm>.

4. FTC v. Staples, Inc., 970 F.Supp. 1066, 1088 (D.D.C.1997).

creating high concentration, the efficiencies defense, has likewise been given shape and credence by agency guidelines.

To be sure, judicial review remains a critical control on agency discretion and interpretation. The Supreme Court will doubtless have opportunities over the coming years to leave its mark on evolving interpretations of Section 7. It is likely that the Supreme Court's next Section 7 opinion, although by no means bound by agency guidelines, will revolve around issues developed in the guidelines, which increasingly provide the basis for arguments of both proponents and opponents of a merger. Agency guidelines sprang from judicial interpretations, but those guidelines have now matured and become an independent force in the evolution of the law. Merger law will continue to evolve as a joint enterprise of judicial and agency interpretation, but the initiative and a great deal of power have shifted to the agencies.

§ 11.2   Horizontal Mergers

Federal enforcement has focused on horizontal mergers because they are thought most likely to create or enhance market power. Although horizontal mergers can be an obvious path to monopolization, most merger enforcement is directed at preventing oligopoly conditions that can lead to collusion or coordinated interaction, not at consolidations that have reached monopolization levels.

Horizontal mergers pose the most obvious and substantial competitive risks, yet by no means are all horizontal mergers competitively suspect. Indeed, such mergers probably have greater potential for efficiencies than other types of mergers. The most prominent of these potential efficiencies is the attainment of economies of scale. Mergers can achieve such economies only if the merging firms are sufficiently small so as not to have achieved minimum efficient scale. Firms already large enough to have achieved this scale cannot enhance scale efficiencies by merging, although other efficiency gains are possible.

11.2a.   Some Flash Points of Horizontal Merger Analysis

Mergers are unlawful under Section 7 of the Clayton Act if they may substantially reduce competition or tend to create a monopoly in any market in any section of the country. The central question in any competitive analysis of a merger is whether the combination will create or enhance market power in the merged entity, allowing it (alone or with others) to raise prices above the competitive level without losing sales that would make the price increase unprofitable. To identify this market power, merger analysis proceeds by defining the relevant market, noting its level of concentration, and determining the merging firms' market share in that market.

The analytical task in defining a market ought to be the same whether in a monopolization, merger or tie-in case. This general methodology was discussed in § 2.6b. The particular approach employed in the 1992 Horizontal Merger Guidelines is discussed in the following section

(§ 11.2b). No matter how carefully a market is defined, the description is likely to overlook or ignore circumstances that may increase or reduce the market power that the merging firms might exercise. But the exercise of defining the market, perhaps in default of a more workable approach, remains the standard approach for determining market power in a Section 7 analysis. Mergers almost always offer up facts that are fertile ground for disputes about market definition. These disputes become even more critical if a decision-maker relies mechanically on a market share presumption for deciding a case. The better approach is to regard market definition as the starting point for competitive analysis of a merger. In two mergers in which market definitions produce identical concentration indexes, the competitive effects of the mergers may vary substantially because of circumstances that go beyond market definition. The 1992 Horizontal Merger Guidelines now devote substantial attention to assessing the potential adverse competitive effects of a merger after the market definition is established.[1]

In addition to factual disputes about market definition, there are other points of substantive controversy in the market definition approach. One such area is the point at which a structural presumption of illegality ought to attach to a merger. Beginning with the Justice Department's 1968 Merger Guidelines, and continuing through the 1992 iteration of those Guidelines, the enforcement agencies have gradually relaxed the standards, setting increasingly high measures of concentration that allow mergers creating greater degrees of concentration. Given the extreme complexity of industrial organization, objective standards cannot be precise. Clearly, and probably not inappropriately, ideological and political views influence those who establish the presumptions of illegality. At the same time, there is a need to be attentive to the growing body of empirical data about the effects of increasing industry concentration, which can affect not only pricing patterns, but also the all important dynamic element of competition that leads to innovation. A related point is, assuming the structural presumption applies, how much weight should be accorded to it (see the discussion in § 11.2d).

Another area of change is the recognition that, although a market participant may have a relatively small percentage of the interbrand market, it may nonetheless have power over price. This may occur in oligopolistic markets and even in markets where segments differentiated in the minds of buyers are oligopolistic. Although all automobiles may be a part of a single market, most buyers are likely to purchase an automobile from among one segment of that market. Economy-minded buyers are unlikely to purchase a luxury car, and, conversely, buyers seeking a luxury car will pay little attention to economy cars. The conventional theoretical wisdom is that where products in a market are highly differentiated by brand, cartel-like practices are less likely. But if

§ 11.2

1. United States Dep't of Justice and Federal Trade Comm., Horizontal Merger

Guidelines § 2 (1992), as revised (1997).

any segment of a highly segmented market is oligopolistic, firms in that segment may be able to achieve oligopoly pricing without the need for coordination. Segmentation means fewer products will be in direct competition with one another. When buyers tend to shop only one such segment, tacit or express interaction may become unnecessary or easier to attain. As the 1992 Guidelines now recognize (see the discussion in § 11.2e2), this outcome is relevant when assessing the potential anticompetitive effects of a horizontal merger in a highly segmented market.

Two other flash points for merger analysis involve defenses invoked to justify what otherwise would appear to be anticompetitive mergers. Each of these defenses came to the fore after the issuance of the Justice Department's 1982 Merger Guidelines: (1) the ease of entry defense and (2) the efficiencies defense. In theory, a merger leading to high levels of concentration will have few anticompetitive effects if entry into the relevant market is easy. Ease of entry can be injected into merger analysis at the market definition stage—by widening the market definition to include likely entrants. On the other hand, as a defense, ease of entry can be regarded as a mitigating circumstance that counters the otherwise high competitive risks of a merger creating high concentration. Although most theorists agree that ease of entry will make it difficult for a firm—even one with an apparent high market share—to exercise market power, the controversy has centered on the breadth of the defense and the sort of evidentiary showing that should be required to offset high concentration. During the 1980s, the Department of Justice is said to have permitted a number of mergers with high concentration measurements based upon unsupported assertions that future entry was likely.[2] During this same period, a number of court decisions also recognized a defense based upon presumed ease of entry. See the discussion in § 11.2h1.

The efficiency defense is recognized in the 1992 Guidelines and was the subject of an amendment in 1997. See the discussion in § 11.2h2. But the defense remains controversial both as a matter of theory and in its application. Unlike ease of entry, efficiencies do not eliminate the anticompetitive risks of a merger—but the gains from efficiency may partially or wholly offset those risks. The theoretical controversy surrounding the efficiency defense centers on whether these efficiency gains should be considered only if they are likely to be passed on to consumers. If a merger creates efficiencies that the consolidated firm absorbs as increased profits, as x-inefficiencies, or in rent seeking behavior, should the efficiencies nonetheless be allowed to counter the anticompetitive risks? Even if the theoretical basis for invoking an efficiency defense were clarified, there still might be a question of the evidentiary showing that would suffice to invoke the defense.

---

2. Pitofsky, *Merger Analysis in the '90s: The Guidelines and Beyond—Overview,* 61   Antitrust L.J. 147, 148 (1992).

Yet another flash point in merger analysis is the extent to which social costs of a merger other than competitive harm may be relevant to its legality under Section 7. Theorists and agency guidelines have resisted a transplantation of broader social concerns that could disrupt the rigor of antitrust merger analysis. That position has been eroded to some extent by the failing company defense, recognized by the Supreme Court and included in several iterations of agency guidelines. Major questions surround the legitimacy of this defense and how it should be applied. See the discussion in §§ 11.2h4–.2h5.

11.2b. Defining the Market

To answer the question whether a merger may substantially reduce competition in any line of commerce in any section of the country, the decision-maker must understand the state of competition before the merger as well as sense how the merger may alter that dynamic. A starting point is a general concept of a market as the bounds within which competitive interaction occurs.

The Supreme Court has said that "[t]he outer boundaries of a product market are determined by the reasonable interchangeability of use or the cross-elasticity of demand between the product itself and substitutes for it."[3] If consumers are willing to switch to another related product in the face of a small price increase, cross-elasticity of demand is said to be high. High cross-elasticity of demand suggests that the related product belongs in the same market.

Whether in a merger or monopolization case, all market definition tasks face a common goal—determining whether a market participant can exercise market power. Despite this common goal, market definition in merger cases has developed on a somewhat separate track, both because of specialized judicial interpretations in the merger context and because of agency merger guidelines. Although the concept of cross-elasticity of demand is straightforward enough, applying it to define a market, the 1992 Guidelines suggest, is a complex task. This complexity may add sophistication to merger analysis, but it may or may not contribute to more objective or predictable results. The Guidelines raise a multitude of fringe issues (discussed in the §§ 11.2b1, .2b2, and .2b3) that invite clashes of opinion and factual interpretation in any contested merger case. All of this can add cost to merger investigations and litigated cases. Market definition is, when complete, only a basis for further analysis of the likely competitive effects of a merger.

11.2b1. Product Market

A relevant market has two components: a definition delimiting the products or services in the market (the "product market") and a second definition of the geographic reach of that market (the "geographic

---

3. Brown Shoe Co. v. United States, 370 U.S. 294, 325, 82 S.Ct. 1502, 8 L.Ed.2d 510 (1962).

market"). The 1992 Guidelines provide that market definition "focuses solely on demand substitution factors"—the consumer's willingness to substitute one product or source for another.[4] The ability of a producer to switch its production resources from one product that consumers do not consider a substitute to another that consumers do consider a substitute thus has no bearing on the choice of the market definition, although it may affect the selection of firms in the relevant market.[5] To illustrate this point, assume that two firms that produce machine-made drinking glasses propose to merge. A firm that uses the same raw materials and machinery to produce glass ashtrays might easily switch its production to drinking glasses, perhaps by simply changing a mold on a production machine. The ability of the ashtray-manufacturing machine to easily switch to making drinking glasses does not mean that ashtrays are in the same market as drinking glasses. But the ashtray firm may still be considered a participant in the drinking-glass manufacturing market. See the discussion in § 11.2b4.

In the 1992 Guidelines, the critical concept for measuring cross-elasticity of demand (a consumer's willingness to substitute one product for another) is the "small but significant and nontransitory increase in price (SSNIP)."[6] The agency chooses a narrowly defined hypothetical product market and asks whether consumers would switch to another product in response to the SSNIP. If a hypothetical monopolist would lose a sufficient number of customers to the next best substitute as a result of the SSNIP, this consumer propensity to switch would limit the monopolist's ability to extract a monopoly profit. Accordingly, the next best substitute good would be added to the product market.

The Guidelines indicate that either a "product or group of products" may constitute a relevant market.[7] The phrase "group of products" is an acknowledgement that the market may consist of a "cluster of products." In *United States v. Philadelphia National Bank*, the Supreme Court defined the market to include a cluster of banking services, including checking and savings accounts, loans and related banking services.[8] The Guidelines do not address how one is to determine the extent of such a cluster. The problem of setting the confines of such a market is similar to the problem of determining when a bundled sale of goods should be treated as a single sale, and when such a bundled sale should be regarded as a tie-in subject to antitrust limitations. See the discussion in § 7.2b1. The best guide is probably that of informed consumer demand. If a significant group of the bank's informed customers desire and expect that all banks will offer each of the clustered services, such a cluster would represent a valid starting point for a SSNIP analysis. Of course, what informed consumers desire will in turn be influenced by what a seller can efficiently provide. The clustering of banking services was surely determined in part by a supply-side consid-

---

4. 1992 Merger Guidelines § 1.0.

5. Id.

6. Id. § 1.11.

7. Id.

8. 374 U.S. 321, 356–57, 83 S.Ct. 1715, 10 L.Ed.2d 915 (1963).

eration, namely what a bank could efficiently cluster and what regulatory permission envisaged as a group of services. Still, what consumers demand and come to expect from a bank should dominate the inquiry.[9] Consumer recognition may have been a factor in court decisions recognizing supermarkets,[10] department stores,[11] and office superstores[12] as relevant markets.

If buyers are likely to switch to the next best substitute in response to a SSNIP, the definition process must continue at least one more step. Assuming the same SSNIP for all products under the enlarged definition, the agency again asks how consumers would respond. If a sufficient number would switch to the next best substitute, that substitute is again added to the market. The process stops only when the agency concludes that a sufficient number of consumers would be unlikely to switch to the next best available substitute (and the hypothetical monopolist would therefore be able to extract a monopoly profit without fear of losing significant business). At that point, the product market is set, subject to reconsideration if the hypothetical monopolist might be able to discriminate in price in sales to a particular group of buyers.[13]

The Guidelines specify the base price to which the SSNIP is added (normally prevailing prices), how much the hypothetical price increase would be (usually 5 percent), and how long the price increase should last ("lasting for the foreseeable future"), specifications suggesting a degree of rigor in the process that is misleading.[14] Evidentiary questions are apparent in any application of the Guidelines. For example, how does an interested party establish the consumer response to a hypothetical price increase? Would an affidavit of an economic expert, voicing an opinion about likely consumer response be a sufficient showing? In listing what would be considered by the agency, the 1992 Guidelines suggest that evidence of past behavior of buyers and sellers is relevant to predicting a future consumer response.[15] By omission, the Guidelines imply that unless based on a study of such earlier market responses, an economic or industry expert's opinion testimony about a likely consumer response is not entitled to much weight.

The apparent precision in the SSNIP analysis is perhaps warranted if only to provide a common starting point and framework for market definition analysis. But successive iterations of the Guidelines have been forced to qualify the SSNIP assumptions in response to strong criticisms of earlier versions. For example, in the 1982 Guidelines, the apparent

9. *See* Ayres, *Rationalizing Antitrust Cluster Markets*, 95 YALE L. J. 109 (1985), (discussing the relevance of efficiencies in the definition of cluster markets).

10. California v. American Stores Co., 697 F.Supp. 1125 (C.D.Cal.1988), *rev'd in part on other grounds*, 872 F.2d 837 (9th Cir.1989), rev'd on other grounds, 495 U.S. 271, 110 S.Ct. 1853, 109 L.Ed.2d 240 (1990).

11. Bon–Ton Stores, Inc. v. May Department Stores Co., 881 F.Supp. 860 (W.D.N.Y. 1994), *supplemented*, 1995–1 Trade Cas. (CCH) ¶ 70917, 1995 WL 215307 (W.D.N.Y. 1995).

12. FTC v. Staples, Inc., 970 F.Supp. 1066 (D.D.C.1997).

13. 1992 Merger Guidelines § 1.12.

14. Id. § 1.11.

15. Id.

assumption was that the prevailing price (the starting point for SSNIP analysis) was necessarily a workably competitive price. Yet, if oligopoly power was already being exercised in the market in question, the prevailing price might already have been pushed close to the point of maximum monopoly profit. The assumption that a current price is workably competitive, an assumption apparently made in the *DuPont* monopolization case with respect to the price of cellophane,[16] could lead an unwary analyst falsely to conclude that consumers who switched their funds to alternate uses in response to a hypothetical price increase found these alternate uses as desirable (or nearly as desirable) as the purchase of the primary product. In fact, the substitute goods may be much less desired by consumers, but a hypothetical significant price rise added to a price already at an oligopoly level could push the primary good beyond reach.[17] The 1992 Guidelines address this problem by cautioning that the agency will use prevailing prices as a base "unless premerger circumstances are strongly suggestive of coordinated interaction." In that instance, the agency will choose a price it believes more reflective of the competitive price.[18] The Guidelines are silent as to how the alternative to prevailing price should be determined, but it would seem that profit or other performance evidence might be relevant.

Notwithstanding the outcome of the SSNIP process, the 1992 Guidelines allow the agency to reverse direction and shrink the size of the market if the hypothetical monopolist might be able to discriminate in price with respect to a delimited group of buyers.[19] This new language is an apparent response to the possibility that the prevailing price used for its SSNIP analysis is in fact not the price charged to all buyers. If the seller can discriminate in price, charging a distinct group of buyers a higher price, the seller may have market power with respect to sales to those buyers. Without the separate consideration of buyers subject to this discriminatory higher price, the SSNIP process might falsely indicate that the seller operates only in a larger market (to all buyers) in which no market power is exercised.

The 1992 Guidelines also qualify the use of a 5 percent price increase in the SSNIP process. This too is a response to criticism of earlier, more rigid formulations. The consumer injury from a 5 percent price increase will vary widely depending on the extent of consumer purchases. Thus, a 5 percent increase in the price of a production input representing a very small percentage of total production cost will affect buyers much less than such an increase in the price of an input representing a larger part of total cost. So too, at the level of final consumption. A 5 percent increase in the price of shoe polish will

---

16. United States v. E.I. du Pont de Nemours & Co., 351 U.S. 377, 76 S.Ct. 994, 100 L.Ed. 1264 (1956)(see the discussion of the cellophane market in § 3.3a.).

17. This point is amplified in F. M. Scherer & D. Ross, Industrial Market Structure and Economic Performance 178–79 (3d ed. 1990).

18. 1992 Merger Guidelines § 1.11.

19. Id. § 1.12.

generate far less reaction than a 5 percent increase in the price of gasoline.[20] Responding to this reality, the 1992 Guidelines acknowledge that the percentage increase for SSNIP analysis may be larger or smaller than five percent depending on "the nature of the industry."[21]

Interchangeability of demand is recognized both by the Supreme Court and in agency guidelines as the key to a relevant market definition. And although the Merger Guidelines have influenced the courts in their approach to market definition,[22] courts have not hesitated to look to other measures of a market's limits. In *Brown Shoe Co. v. United States,* the Court spoke of "practical indicia" for determining the confines of a submarket, including "industry or public recognition of the submarket as a separate economic entity, the product's peculiar characteristics and uses, unique production facilities, distinct customers, distinct prices, sensitivity to price changes, and specialized vendors."[23] Although the Court was speaking of a "submarket" in *Brown Shoe,* the criteria it listed also determine *the market* most relevant for measuring the competitive effects of a merger. In *FTC v. Staples, Inc.,* the court looked at evidence that the merging office superstores regarded other office superstores as their primary rivals, that they made price checks of various rivals (but most frequently of other office superstores), that the office superstores had a large size and expanded product line that nonoffice superstores did not have, and that buyers for small businesses and home offices favored office superstores.[24]

In the *Staples* case, the FTC was also able to rely on pricing evidence to establish the relevant market. The Commission introduced evidence to show that each of the merging firms tended to charge significantly higher prices in metropolitan areas in which there was no competing office superstore than in areas in which two or more office superstores competed.[25] Such direct pricing evidence is likely to be persuasive if it is established by a valid sample. Computerized records of past prices may be sought in future merger investigations involving retail firms, but such pricing evidence may sometimes be difficult to gather and analyze. The *Staples* case demonstrates, however, that information about past pricing practices may be another focal point for determining the relevant market.

---

20. The point is elaborated in Scherer & Ross, supra note 17, at 180. In Marathon Oil Co. v. Mobil Corp., 530 F.Supp. 315, 322 (N.D.Ohio 1981), aff'd, 669 F.2d 378 (6th Cir. 1981), a proceeding in which Professor Scherer was an expert witness for Marathon, the court set the significant price increase threshold at one percent.

21. 1992 Merger Guidelines, § 1.11.

22. FTC v. Staples, Inc., 970 F.Supp. 1066, 1076 n.8 (D.D.C.1997) (citing the 1992 Guidelines 5 percent rule and attempting to apply it).

23. 370 U.S. 294, 325, 82 S.Ct. 1502, 8 L.Ed.2d 510 (1962).

24. 970 F.Supp. at 1082. In *FTC v. Cardinal Health, Inc.,* the court similarly was attentive to which firms the merging parties regarded as their rivals. 12 F. Supp. 2d 34, 46 (D.D.C.1998).

25. 970 F.Supp. at 1076 (Staples was said to have charged 13 percent more in one firm markets than in three-firm markets; Office Depot was said to have charged well over 5 percent more in one firm markets than in three-firm markets).

11.2b2. Geographic Market

The second component of a relevant market is its geographic reach (the geographic market). Merging firms may make virtually identical products, yet not be in the same market because their products are sold in entirely different geographic regions (such a merger would be considered a market extension merger, discussed in § 11.3b). Geographic markets are likely to be limited for inexpensive products, the transportation of which is expensive—for example, cement—or for consumer products or services that are purchased frequently—for example, groceries or dry cleaning. On the other hand, high-technology goods that are relatively inexpensive to transport can easily be distributed nationally or even worldwide. Relevant geographic markets can, accordingly, be as small as a city neighborhood (in which consumers do most of their grocery shopping), as large as the United States, or even encompass a global market of all or some subgroup of trading nations. As trade barriers crumble in the face of the WTO, integrations like the EU, and instruments such as the North American Free Trade Agreement, geographic markets that cross national borders are more likely.

The approach for defining geographic market is essentially the same as that used to define the product market: It turns on cross-elasticity of demand—the buyer's capacity and willingness to substitute products from other geographic sources. Thus, the geographic market for a retail grocery store would be the region in which most consumers looked to buy the bulk of their groceries. A manufacturer seeking a source of raw materials might search a much larger area, perhaps one extending beyond national borders. The geographic market for the same product can be vastly different at different levels of distribution. For example, a computer distributor or retailer may search widely for the best source of computers, perhaps extending the search world-wide. But the consumer wishing to buy a computer is more likely to confine a search to dealers in the local area in which the consumer lives or works, although as Internet shopping grows more common even geographic markets for some consumer products may grow much wider.

Like the product market, the geographic market is determined by the buyer's willingness to substitute products—the buyer's cross-elasticity of demand is the final arbiter of the size of the geographic market. This approach is largely consistent with that announced by the Supreme Court. Applying Section 3 of the Clayton Act, the Supreme Court has said that the geographic market is the region "in which the seller operates, and to which the purchaser can practicably turn for supplies."[26] Among the considerations that may influence the buyer are cost considerations (including transportation and outlays needed to overcome trade

---

26. Tampa Elec. Co. v. Nashville Coal Co., 365 U.S. 320, 327, 81 S.Ct. 623, 5 L.Ed.2d 580 (1961). The Eighth Circuit has said that the relevant geographic market is the area "to which consumers can practically turn for alternative sources of the product and in which the antitrust defendants face competition." Morgenstern v. Wilson, 29 F.3d 1291, 1296 (8th Cir.1994), cert. denied, 513 U.S. 1150, 115 S.Ct. 1100, 130 L.Ed.2d 1068 (1995).

barriers) as well as convenience and tradition. But the buyer's willingness to substitute can be affected by either the buyer's or the seller's practices. In some cases, the buyer may extend a search to a wide area of sources. In other cases, the buyer may look only locally, but faraway sellers may extend their marketing efforts to the buyer's local area. In either instance, new sellers may be added to the geographic market.

Although the theory of a relevant geographic market may have been fairly well understood by the time of *Brown Shoe*,[27] rigor of analysis was often lacking in Supreme Court holdings of the 1960s. In United States v. Von's Grocery Co.,[28] the majority stated, without supporting analysis, that the relevant market for a grocery store chain merger was the Los Angeles area. Justice Stewart pointed out in dissent that most consumers were unlikely to search the massive L.A. area for groceries, and that the two merging chains had few stores that overlapped within a short driving radius.[29] In United States v. Pabst Brewing Co.,[30] the merger of two breweries had created the nation's fifth largest brewer (but with only 5 percent of the national market). To show higher market shares, the Government argued that in Wisconsin, the consolidated entity was the largest brewer with 24 percent of the market. Although the Government had not, in the district court's view, shown that Wisconsin was a relevant geographic market in which to judge the economic effects of this merger, the Supreme Court reversed. Justice Black wrote that Section 7 merely requires that "the Government prove the merger may have a substantial anticompetitive effect somewhere in the United States," and that "Congress did not seem to be troubled about the exact spot where competition might be lessened; it simply intended to outlaw mergers which threatened competition in any or all parts of the country."[31] The sort of gerrymandered geographic market accepted in *Pabst* is subject to the same criticism aimed at improvised submarkets. See the discussion in § 11.2b3. There cannot be harm to competition from increased concentration limited to "somewhere" if competitors elsewhere can readily reach the buyers in "somewhere."

United States v. Marine Bancorporation, Inc.[32] may have restored some rigor to geographic market definition. The Court stated flatly that the phrase "section of the country" in Section 7 means relevant geographic market and that the relevant geographic market is one in which the "goods or services at issue are marketed to a significant degree by the acquired firm."[33] Moving well beyond any language of the Supreme Court, agency merger guidelines, beginning with the 1982 version, incorporated for geographic market definition the same rigorous SSNIP

---

27. Brown Shoe Co. v. United States, 370 U.S. 294, 82 S.Ct. 1502, 8 L.Ed.2d 510 (1962).

28. 384 U.S. 270, 86 S.Ct. 1478, 16 L.Ed.2d 555 (1966).

29. Id. at 295–96 (Stewart, J., dissenting).

30. 384 U.S. 546, 86 S.Ct. 1665, 16 L.Ed.2d 765 (1966).

31. Id. at 549–50. *Pabst* was severely criticized in Elzinga and Hogarty, *The Problem of Geographic Market Delineation in Antimerger Suits*, 45 Antitrust Bull. 45 (1973).

32. 418 U.S. 602, 94 S.Ct. 2856, 41 L.Ed.2d 978 (1974).

33. Id. at 620–21.

approach employed for the product market.[34] The agency begins with the location of each merging firm (or each plant of a multiplant firm) and assumes that a hypothetical monopolist imposes a small but significant nontransitory price increase. If the monopolist would be adequately disciplined by a reduction in sales caused by other suppliers moving into the region, the reach of the geographic market is expanded to include the next nearest source. Other more distant sources may also be added to the market if it is concluded that the hypothetical price rise would also bring them into the market. The process stops only when the geographic market is sufficiently broad that the small but significant price rise would no longer bring meaningful competitive discipline from sources outside the geographic area.[35]

The Guidelines follow the same approach for the SSNIP analysis as used in the product market: The base price is normally the prevailing price at the time of the merger; the price increase is typically 5 percent; the duration of the increase is usually the foreseeable future. The agency retains the same flexibility to depart from these standards as in the product market SSNIP analysis. Thus, the agency reserves the right not to use the prevailing price as its base if it concludes that this price is already above competitive levels as the result of "coordinated interaction." The same types of evidence of prevailing buyer and seller behavior will be examined in assessing buyer response to the hypothetical price increase.[36]

Finally, also following the methodology used for product market definition, the Guidelines provide that a geographic market may be shrunk in size in the face of a showing of price discrimination that unfavorably affects a targeted group of buyers in a smaller geographic region.[37] A seller's ability to charge the higher price to buyers in that smaller region suggests that, as to those buyers, the seller possesses market power. The same result could be achieved through the use of a geographic submarket. Although the term "submarkets" is used less frequently with respect to the geographic dimension of a market, courts have recognized that geographic markets can have different definitions depending on the category of customers. For example, in FTC v. Cardinal Health, Inc.,[38] the court recognized that a national market for wholesale drugs existed with respect to certain large buyers such as chain drugstores, but also recognized regional markets of large West Coast cities for many smaller buyers (such as independent pharmacies or group purchasing associations for such pharmacies).[39]

Although insufficient rigor in analysis has in the past led to gerrymandered markets favorable to the government, the more sophisticated analysis suggested by the Guidelines has its own pitfalls, among them the need for evidence against which to measure the indicators of the

---

34. *E.g.,* 1992 Merger Guidelines § 1.2.

35. Id. § 1.21.

36. Id.

37. Id. § 1.22.

38. 12 F. Supp. 2d 34 (D.D.C.1998).

39. Id. at 59–60.

reach of the geographic market. In United States v. Eastman Kodak Co.,[40] the court concluded over the vigorous opposition of the Department of Justice that the geographic market for the sale of film was "worldwide," consisting of the United States, Western Europe, and Japan. The Government offered evidence that wholesale and retail prices for Kodak film were higher in the United States than in non-U.S. markets, and that these premium prices suggested Kodak possessed market power in the U.S., which was inconsistent with a worldwide market definition. The court was unpersuaded that the Government had made a sufficient evidentiary showing.[41] In dissolving prior decrees that had been entered against Kodak, the court may have placed an evidentiary burden on the Government that could not reasonably be met under real market conditions. The decision also may give inappropriate weight to the market definition, which after all is only a means to determining whether market power exists. Direct empirical evidence that the defendant possessed a degree of market power might logically obviate the need to even define the market at all. In any event, the definition process ought not to be applied with a rigidity that compels disregard of hard evidence that market power exists.

11.2b3. Submarkets

To resolve with legal certainty whether a monopoly exists, a court first resolves the question of market definition. Although market definitions pose comparable difficulties in either the merger or the monopolization context, courts may sense less latitude in monopolization cases to acknowledge that more than one alternative market definition has meaning. The language of Section 7 of the Clayton Act, which requires a court to resolve only whether a particular merger "may" substantially reduce competition in "any" market in "any" section of the country, may invite greater flexibility. In Brown Shoe Co. v. United States, Chief Justice Warren acknowledged that interchangeability and cross-elasticity of demand would determine the outer bounds of a market, but stressed that "well-defined submarkets" may exist in any market.[42]

Conceptually, this statement about submarkets appears sound. Depending on the type of customer, different market definitions may be valid. It is possible that two firms might compete generally in the clock market, but also in a segment of that market—for example, clocks modified or specially designed for use on board a ship or boat. Customers interested in a shipboard clock may have no interest in other types of clocks, and purchasers of other types of clocks may have no interest in shipboard clocks. A complete assessment of the competitive effects of a merger between the two firms might require scrutiny of the impact both on the broader and more specialized market. But the *Brown Shoe*

---

40. 63 F.3d 95 (2d Cir.1995). For another decision in which statistical evidence apparently doomed the Government's product market definition, see FTC v. Tenet Healthcare Corp., 186 F.3d 1045 (8th Cir. 1999).

41. Id. at 105–09.

42. 370 U.S. 294, 325–26, 82 S.Ct. 1502, 8 L.Ed.2d 510 (1962).

Court's invitation to use submarkets led to undisciplined market analysis in some subsequent cases.

In United States v. Aluminum Co. of America,[43] the Court acted on the irrational proposition that any combination of submarkets could also constitute a relevant product market. In particular, the Court approved a submarket consisting of both insulated aluminum conductor and bare aluminum conductor without clear evidence that buyers considered these products interchangeable. When the market shares in the separate insulated and bare aluminum conductor were calculated, the merger would not have reached a market share that warranted a presumption of illegality. This principle invited gerrymandering to find the combination of submarkets most likely to show an unlawful concentration. For example, if the ice cream market had three submarkets—chocolate, vanilla and strawberry—an antitrust enforcer could search for any combination of two submarkets that gave two merging firms the highest market share. If merging firms A and B each had a 10 percent share in the ice cream market, but firm A sold a high percentage of strawberry and firm B sold a high percentage of chocolate, a gerrymandered submarket consisting only of strawberry and chocolate ice cream might be improvised in order to establish a market share significantly higher than the combined 20 percent share in the overall ice cream market. If courts place undue emphasis on concentration measurements at the expense of more refined analysis of competitive effects, the use of such speciously constructed submarkets could work much mischief.

Another demonstration of lack of rigor in analysis was United States v. Continental Can Co.,[44] where the Court lumped together two submarkets—glass bottles and cans—to construct a market on which the legality of the merger turned. The inclusion of two products with quite different supply-side characteristics was legitimate if consumers would freely switch between the two. But the Court should have considered whether other containers—such as plastic bottles—were equally a part of this interindustry market. If special demand characteristics warrant the use of some but not all of a group of submarkets in the relevant market, these characteristics should have been expressly addressed in the analysis.

Perhaps in response to these perceived abuses, the Justice Department's 1982 Guidelines abandoned the concept of the submarket, an approach followed in the two more recent iterations of the Guidelines. All versions of the Guidelines since 1982 contain the statement that the agency will consider the relevant market to be "the smallest group of products" that satisfies the test for a market.[45] This language preserves the agency's ability to examine a merger in terms of its impact on the smallest relevant subcategory, but does not expressly permit consider-

---

43. 377 U.S. 271, 84 S.Ct. 1283, 12 L.Ed.2d 314 (1964).

44. 378 U.S. 441, 84 S.Ct. 1738, 12 L.Ed.2d 953 (1964).

45. E.g., 1992 Merger Guidelines § 1.11.

ation of more than one market. The 1992 Guidelines, however, provide that the agency may consider "additional relevant product markets" consisting of a particular use or uses by groups of buyers as to whom the seller could discriminate in price.[46] This latest version appears to make explicit an agency's ability to consider a merger's effect on multiple markets. It does so, however, without inviting the sort of undisciplined gerrymandering that might have been invited under the language of Court decisions of the 1960s.

The courts continue to recognize submarkets as a valid basis for Section 7 analysis. In FTC v. Staples, Inc.,[47] the district court enjoined a proposed acquisition involving the nation's two largest chains of office supply stores. In doing so, the court recognized a market consisting of all sellers of consumable office supplies (in which the merging firms had only a 5.5 percent national share), but found a smaller market relevant for assessing competitive effects: a submarket consisting only of office supply superstores in which the merging firms would have a dominant share in 42 metropolitan geographic markets.[48] Such "submarkets" have been accepted for supermarkets,[49] department stores,[50] and drug wholesalers.[51] But a submarket consisting only of "home centers" has been rejected.[52] Other courts have questioned the use of the term "submarket" as confusing.[53] In *FTC v. Staples*, the court found that the market relevant for the competitive analysis was office supply superstores. Similarly, in FTC v. Cardinal Health, Inc., the court focused on the narrowly defined wholesale drug market.[54] In each of these cases, the *relevant market* for purposes of the competitive analysis was described as a submarket, perhaps because there were some categories of customers for whom a broader market would be relevant. Use of the term may be a legitimate way of signaling that the potential anticompetitive effects

---

46. *Id.* § 1.12. The Guidelines contain a similar provision with respect to the geographic market. Id. § 1.22.

47. 970 F.Supp. 1066 (D.D.C.1997).

48. Id. at 1081 (court concluded that the combined firms would have 100 percent of the market in 15 metropolitan areas and shares ranging from 45 to 94 percent in 27 other areas).

49. California v. American Stores Co., 697 F.Supp. 1125 (C.D.Cal.1988), rev'd in part on other grounds, 872 F.2d 837 (9th Cir.1989), *rev'd on other grounds*, 495 U.S. 271, 110 S.Ct. 1853, 109 L.Ed.2d 240 (1990). The court of appeals did not address the market definition, but noted: "Were we to evaluate independently the evidence of the relevant product market, we might reach a different conclusion." 872 F.2d at 841.

50. Bon–Ton Stores, Inc. v. May Dep't Stores Co., 881 F.Supp. 860 (W.D.N.Y. 1994), supplemented 1995–1 Trade Cas. (CCH) ¶ 70917 (W.D.N.Y.1995) (accepting a market definition of department stores despite the defendants' objection that this definition overlooks other stores that compete with department stores).

51. FTC v. Cardinal Health, Inc., 12 F. Supp. 2d 34 (D.D.C.1998) (accepting an overall market for pharmaceuticals through all distribution channels and a submarket, which was the relevant market for assessing the competitive impact of the merger, consisting of only pharmaceuticals sold through drug wholesalers).

52. Thurman Indus., Inc. v. Pay 'N Pak Stores, Inc., 875 F.2d 1369 (9th Cir.1989).

53. Allen–Myland, Inc. v. IBM Corp., 33 F.3d 194, 208 n. 16 (3d Cir.), cert. denied, 513 U.S. 1066, 115 S.Ct. 684, 130 L.Ed.2d 615 (1994); Olin Corp. v. FTC, 986 F.2d 1295, 1299 (9th Cir.1993)(pointing out that every market that "encompasses less than all products is, in a sense, a submarket"), *cert. denied*, 510 U.S. 1110, 114 S.Ct. 1051, 127 L.Ed.2d 373 (1994).

54. 12 F. Supp. 2d at 50.

within the submarket would not extend to all groups of customers. The term should be reserved for situations in which both a general and subdivided market are relevant in measuring the competitive effects of a merger.

Even if a broad market definition is accepted as the most relevant for competitive analysis, the 1992 Merger Guidelines make clear that, in measuring competitive effects, the agencies will look to the possibility that the merging firms will unilaterally alter their behavior after the merger.[55] In particular, in a merger of firms in a market characterized by differentiated products and in which the merging firms' products are considered close substitutes by buyers, the agency may find likely anticompetitive effects from the merger. See the discussion in § 11.2e2.

11.2b4. Identifying Firms in the Relevant Market

A list of firms participating in the relevant market is evident once the product and geographic components of the relevant market are determined. The 1992 Guidelines provide that the captive production of a vertically integrated firm may be included to the extent that its inclusion accurately reflects its "competitive significance" in the relevant market. Reconditioned or recycled goods may also be included if their sale would be a competitive discipline on a hypothetical monopolist's price increases.[56] But the list may be incomplete because of supply-side responses. In response to a price increase, firms that do not participate in the market still might do so through rapid and low-cost switching of production or marketing resources such that they too should be identified as market participants.

The 1992 Guidelines distinguish for the first time between two levels of supply-side response. An "uncommitted entrant" is a potential entrant that would likely enter the market "within one year and without the expenditure of significant sunk costs of entry and exit, in response to a 'small but significant nontransitory' price increase."[57] Such firms will be included as market participants. In contrast, a "committed entrant" is a potential participant whose entry or exit would require the expenditure of "significant sunk costs." Committed entrants will not be included as market participants, but rather as a part of an entry analysis that can counter otherwise likely anticompetitive effects.[58]

The presence or absence of significant sunk costs, then, are pivotal in determining which firms at the edge should be included in the market. Sunk costs are "the acquisition costs of tangible and intangible assets that cannot be recovered through the redeployment of these assets outside the relevant market, i.e., costs uniquely incurred to supply the relevant product and geographic market."[59] As examples of sunk costs, the Guidelines list market-specific investments "in production facilities, technologies, marketing (including product acceptance), research and

55. 1992 Merger Guidelines § 2.2.

56. Id. § 1.31.

57. Id. § 1.32.

58. Id. § 3.0.

59. Id. § 1.32.

development, regulatory approvals, and testing.''[60] A sunk cost is said to be significant if it would not be recovered within a year of the commencement of the supply response, assuming a small but significant nontransitory price increase in the relevant market.

The bifurcated approach to entry in the 1992 Guidelines adds further complexity to an already intricate analysis. This sophistication may have been needed because entry analysis during the 1980s was often simplistic and insufficiently demanding.[61] Except for a firm selling the self-same product slightly beyond the geographic bound of the market as defined, it is unlikely that many firms will meet the definition of an uncommitted entrant. Most firms entering new markets will have to make a significant investment likely to be considered sunk costs. Any firm that meets the uncommitted entrant definition will have existing production or distribution facilities that can easily be transferred to production or distribution within the relevant market. As the Guidelines recognize, this firm's willingness to transfer its productive resources to a new market will depend on whether those resources are already profitably and fully committed to another market.[62]

However, the 1992 Guidelines fail to address another potential problem with the uncommitted entry. If a firm meets the requirements for that classification it may also be uncommitted to assertive competition. A participation in the market that risks no substantial funds may be tepid or passive, unlikely to bring dynamism and change to the market. Such an entrant might easily be deterred or forced out by strategic behavior of larger market participants—for example, by targeted price cuts that reduce its profits.[63] Having once been disappointed in its entry, such a firm may not boldly enter a second time, even when high prices appear to offer significant profits. In sum, a low-cost entrant may be susceptible to oligopolistic tactics and easily dissuaded from providing meaningful competitive discipline over the medium or long term.

11.2c. Determining Market Shares

Once the relevant market is defined and its participating members identified, there is still the task of determining the market shares of each participant. The extent of a firm's participation in the market is critical not only for the firms involved in a merger, but for each firm in the market: The overall size of the market changes depending on how much of a firm's output is assigned to the relevant market. In some cases, this is simply a matter of identifying a firm's total output and adding it to the relevant market. But the task often becomes more complicated.

A participating firm may not have its entire output counted in the market, such as when the geographic market is the State of California

---

60. Id.

61. Pitofsky, supra note 2, at 148.

62. 1992 Merger Guidelines § 1.321.

63. Pitofsky, supra note 2, at 153 (making a similar point).

but much of the firm's output is produced and sold on the Eastern Seaboard. A firm's outside production may still be included in the market if it is likely to have a significant disciplining effect on sales within the market. Still, even if outside production could be shipped into the relevant market at relatively low cost, it may be unavailable for that purpose if it is already committed or profitably distributed in other markets. A similar problem is encountered in measuring the market share of an uncommitted entrant that is included in the market by virtue of its possible low-risk supply response. Much of the uncommitted entrant's capacity may be unavailable for use in the relevant market because it is profitably committed elsewhere.

The 1992 Guidelines provide that the market shares of foreign firms are generally to be calculated in the same manner as those of domestic firms.[64] Foreign firms that participate in a relevant United States market are likely to have much of their capacity profitably engaged in other national markets. But there are additional limitations on a foreign firm's participation, including exchange rates and governmental trade barriers, or barriers resulting from differences in standards for compatibility among national markets (electric appliances that function only on the electric current used in particular markets). When a nation's shipments to the United States are limited by quota, the Guidelines provide that the total market shares assigned to firms from that nation shall not exceed the amount allowed under the quota.[65] If the participation of foreign firms in the U.S. market is coordinated, all firms involved in that coordination (from one country or a group of countries) may be assigned a single market share.[66] The consequence of assigning a combined market share can be substantial under the Herfindahl–Hirschman Index (where each market share is squared, then added to determine the index) because the concentration index for the industry will increase, perhaps markedly, as a result of the single share approach.

Market share may be calculated in dollars—the Guidelines suggest this to be the more likely measure if firms are distinguished primarily by differentiation of their products—or in unit terms through measurement of output, sales, or capacity.[67]

11.2d. Evaluating Concentration and Applying the Presumption

Once the market is defined, the participants in the market identified, and market shares determined, there remains the task of assessing whether that market, as the result of a merger, is significantly at risk for collusion or other anticompetitive effects. The 1992 Guidelines operate on the premise, expressed in United States v. Philadelphia National Bank,[68] that a more highly concentrated market is at greater risk than a market with low concentration.

---

64. 1992 Merger Guidelines § 1.43.

65. Id.

66. Id.

67. Id. § 1.41.

68. 374 U.S. 321, 83 S.Ct. 1715, 10 L.Ed.2d 915 (1963).

The 1968 version of the Guidelines used a four-figure index as the primary measure of concentration (the sum of the market share of the largest four participants). Beginning with the 1982 revision, the Guidelines have used the Herfindahl–Hirschman Index (HHI), which operates by squaring the market share of each participant, and adding these figures to obtain the index. These methods for measuring concentration are discussed in § 2.6b4. An important feature of the HHI is its heightened sensitivity to large market shares, allowing it to distinguish between two industries with the same number of participants based upon differences between the size of the shares of the largest members of each industry. Thus, using the HHI, a five-member industry will have an index of 2000 if each firm has a 20 percent market share. But another five-member industry would have an index of 4000 if the largest firm has a 60 percent market share, while each of the remaining four firms has a 10 percent share. By way of comparison, if the four figure concentration measure is used, the apparent difference between the two industries is dampened (the first industry has a concentration of 80 percent, the second has a concentration of 90 percent).

Each of the five-member industries described above is capable of collusion or coordinated pricing practices that could be harmful to consumers. But a heightened sensitivity to large market shares makes sense if coordinated pricing is facilitated by price leadership exercised by the largest firm in an industry. Price leadership may also be more easily enforced through strategic behavior when the leading firm has a large market share. A firm wishing to discourage price-cutting may initiate a targeted price war to deny the discounting firm any gain.[69] If the major firms in the industry are all roughly the same size, the deterrent effect of such a price war on competitors may be roughly equal (because each firm suffers losses on a roughly equal sales volume). On the other hand, in an industry in which the leading firm has 60 percent of the market, a price war may have a greater intimidating effect on the smaller participants, which fear the power of the market leader.

If price-cutting affected the entire output of all market participants, each would presumably suffer in proportion to its market share, so predation would not be as attractive to the leading firm in the industry. But most strategic price-cutting is probably selective. If the leading firm has 60 percent of the market, it will target its price cuts to have maximum effect on the intended rival while minimizing its own losses. The leading firm can then use its profits from the bulk of its business to subsidize any losses suffered by the targeted price cuts. Other firms in that market may have fewer resources to use in subsidizing any losses caused by the discounting.

The 1992 Merger Guidelines provide some guidance as to how the agency will respond to various mergers. The agency's response is based

---

69. Baker, *Predatory Pricing After* Antitrust L.J. 585, 590–92 (1994).
Brooke Group: *An Economic Perspective*, 62

on two variables: (1) the postmerger HHI; and (2) the amount of increase in the HHI occasioned by the merger. The Guidelines describe three categories of agency response, depending on these variables.

Unlikely to have adverse competitive effects and ordinarily requiring no further analysis:

—All mergers with postmerger HHIs below 1000;

—All mergers with postmerger HHIs between 1000 and 1800 if the increase in HHI is less than 100 points; and

—All mergers with postmerger HHIs above 1800 if the increase in HHI is less than 50 points.

Raising significant competitive concerns depending on other factors:

—All mergers with postmerger HHIs between 1000 and 1800 if the increase in HHI is more than 100 points; and

—All mergers with postmerger HHIs above 1800 if the increase in HHI is more than 50 points and less than 100 points.

Creating a presumption that market power is created or enhanced or its exercise facilitated:

—All mergers with postmerger HHIs above 1800 if the increase in HHI is more than 100 points.

The thresholds for agency action have been gradually relaxed with each successive iteration of the Guidelines. Despite this relaxation, one could question whether the 1992 thresholds accurately reflect agency practice. For example, although the thresholds create no absolute safe harbor, there is no record of either agency attacking a merger with a postmerger HHI below 1000 since issuance of the 1982 Guidelines. De facto, the first area amounts to a safe harbor. The agencies also appear very unlikely to attack a merger that falls into the second category of risk. In a study of merger enforcement during the mid–1980s, the House Judiciary Committee concluded that the Justice Department attacked no mergers with a postmerger HHI below 1800 (unless the merger also involved a separate market in which the postmerger HHI was above 1800), and allowed many with significantly larger HHIs to proceed unopposed.[70] Indeed, even mergers in the category of highest risk were often allowed during this period. Merger enforcement may have tightened somewhat since the mid–1980's, but data reflecting HHIs of unchallenged mergers is not routinely released by either agency. There is little question but that both agencies exercise considerable discretion that seems only weakly constrained by the Guidelines.

An FTC statistical program to gather data on industrial performance (broken down by line of business) offered some useful data for analyzing the impact of mergers on industrial performance. That program was abandoned during the Reagan years, leaving the setting of

70. Subcomm. on Monopolies and Commercial Law of House Comm. on the Judiciary, *Federal Merger Enforcement (1979–* *1987), reprinted in* 54 Antitrust & Trade Reg. Rep. (BNA) 476–78 (Mar. 17, 1988).

merger standards in something of an empirical vacuum.[71] In the absence of objective evidence to guide enforcers as to where to set concentration thresholds, the drafters of the Guidelines must act somewhat arbitrarily. But the choice of thresholds matters greatly, both as a substantive merger policy and as a device for facilitating business planning. If the agencies allow mergers that enhance the risk of oligopolistic behavior, economic allocation becomes less efficient and consumers pay more. The dynamic component of competition may also be injured as fewer players are available to make aggressive innovative efforts—hence, stultified oligopolistic industries may discourage or slow the pace of innovation.

There is still enough information to show, for example, that most major domestic industries have firms that are more than large enough to meet minimum efficient scale.[72] Thus, mergers among these players seem unlikely to achieve significant scale efficiencies, quite possibly the most important economic gain that a merger may produce. Although such mergers may still achieve other less potent efficiencies, they reduce the number of players that might make bold innovative initiatives, which are the lifeblood of the dynamic component competition. Thus, whether or not mergers involving the larger firms in an industry directly facilitate oligopolistic pricing behavior, they may well be objectionable because of their impact on the dynamic component of competition.

Regardless of where concentration thresholds are set, those thresholds should be taken seriously by the agency. Business planners of acquisitions should be able to rely on the Guidelines in evaluating whether a transaction will be allowed. When the Guidelines are inconsistently utilized, many mergers may be deterred by false expectations that they will be challenged, while insiders with knowledge of the agency's inconsistencies may be able to maneuver nonconforming mergers through the regulatory process.

Whatever questions may exist about the appropriate threshold level for presumptions, it is clear that the courts treat the Guidelines levels as something of a benchmark. The court of appeals for the District of Columbia has said, for example, that the Guidelines are not binding on a court, but do provide "a useful illustration of the application of the HHI."[73] A discussion of the HHI threshold levels from the Guidelines is now common in litigated merger cases.[74]

A more troubling question is how much weight to accord to the presumption. Within the antitrust agencies, it is now more or less standard practice to require a plausible theory for anticompetitive effects before the agency will challenge an acquisition, even when the acquisi-

---

71. The FTC Line of Business Reporting Program is described in § 16.2g.

72. SCHERER & ROSS, supra note 17, at 138–41.

73. FTC v. PPG Indus., Inc., 798 F.2d 1500, 1503 n.4 (D.C.Cir.1986)(citing the 1984 Guidelines).

74. FTC v. Arch Coal, Inc., 329 F. Supp. 2d 109, 123–24 (D.D.C. 2004); FTC v. University Health, Inc., 938 F.2d 1206, 1211 n.12 (11th Cir.1991); FTC v. Staples, Inc., 970 F.Supp. 1066, 1081–82 (D.D.C.1997); FTC v. Cardinal Health, Inc., 12 F. Supp. 2d 34, 53–54, (D.D.C.1998).

tion will significantly increase concentration in an already concentrated market. The major theories of anticompetitive effects are (1) coordinated interaction; (2) unilateral effects; and (3) strategic behavior. If, despite market share increases that would trigger the presumption, agency staff are unable to identify any credible theory for anticompetitive effects, the agency will likely not challenge the acquisition.[75] The agency does not have to have evidence of past anticompetitive conduct in the industry, nor need it possess evidence that anticompetitive effects will happen in a post merger setting. In practice, competitive harms from a proposed merger are speculative. Merger enforcement policy remains a "predictive" exercise, not one in which the results can be demonstrated beyond a reasonable doubt.

In a recent district court case that went against the FTC, the court appears to be requiring the government to prove that anticompetitive effects of the merger will occur, or are extremely likely to occur.[76] This requirement would turn on its head the language of Section 7, which prohibits acquisitions that *may* substantially reduce competition, and the long established presumption of illegality. Neither the Government, nor any other plaintiff, can prove that particular post-merger conduct will occur. The prophylactic benefits of Section 7 of the Clayton Act will be lost if the evidentiary bar is raised too high.

11.2e. Predicting Anticompetitive Effects

The notion that market concentration measures do not tell all has a strong foundation in United States v. General Dynamics Corp.[77] That 1974 case involved a merger of coal mining companies. The high market share of the merged company was found an inaccurate predictor of the competitive effects of the merger because the acquired company lacked the necessary coal reserves to continue its current output level.[78] The decision invited consideration of other factors that might tend to show that market concentration figures overstated the competitive strength of the merged company. While other inputs in a productive process may be capable of being quickly replenished on the market, some assets— perhaps oil or virgin redwood forests—may be incapable of being replenished when current reserves are exhausted. Extending this logic, *General Dynamics* might also be read to suggest that market concentration figures may understate the competitive strength of the merged firm.

75. For a discussion of these points, see Grimes & Kwoka, *A Study in Merger Enforcement Transparency: The FTC's Ocean Cruise Decision and the Presumption Governing High Concentration Mergers*, ANTI-TRUST SOURCE 6–7 (May 2003), available at <www.antitrustsource.com>.

76. FTC v. Arch Coal, Inc. 329 F. Supp. 2d 109, 131 (D.D.C. 2004)(calling the FTC's "output restriction" theory of tacit coordination a "novel theory" and concluding that "the FTC *must* show projected future tacit coordination")(emphasis supplied). See also United States v. Oracle Corp., 331 F. Supp. 2d 1098 (N.D. Cal. 2004)(to establish a unilateral effects theory, the plaintiff must demonstrate that the merging parties would enjoy a post-merger monopoly or dominant position).

77. 415 U.S. 486, 94 S.Ct. 1186, 39 L.Ed.2d 530 (1974).

78. Id. at 508.

That reverse argument has, however, yet to make significant inroads in litigated cases.

Read broadly, *General Dynamics* might be construed to allow a merger creating high levels of concentration merely because of the temporary financial weakness of one of the merged firms. This view may have received impetus from the 1984 version of the Justice Department's Merger Guidelines, which contained a provision entitled the "Financial Condition of Firms in the Relevant Market."[79] But a firm's temporary financial weakness may be corrected through an infusion of capital, obtained in a variety of ways less threatening to competition than a high concentration merger.[80] The 1992 Guidelines, although retaining a failing company defense (discussed in § 11.2h4–.2h5), wisely omitted any reference to financial weakness as a consideration that would reduce anticompetitive risks. Of course, if the financial weakness of a firm is caused by underlying structural conditions, those conditions themselves may be relevant to a competitive analysis.

A feature of the 1992 Guidelines is a new Section 2 dealing with the potential anticompetitive effects of a merger.[81] This section details other market conditions (beyond the measure of market concentration) that may affect the risk that market power is created or its abusive exercise facilitated. The section is a welcome reminder that rote application of a presumption of illegality based upon the HHI or any other concentration index cannot assure a rational result. No index is better than the market definition from which it is calculated, and no market definition should be viewed as more than a starting point for analysis.

On the negative side, this new section is theoretical and complex in its application. It will surely add to uncertainty in discerning and applying the standards of merger law. It is also at the forefront of evolving economic theory about the anticompetitive effects of mergers. Keeping the Guidelines up-to-date with theoretical developments is desirable, yet carries risks. However convincing it may seem, the validity of relatively untested theoretical literature is not always borne out by experience. A catalogue of ways in which mergers can have anticompetitive or procompetitive effects based upon those addressed in such literature may omit some not yet in the literature, or may include others that would not be borne out by empirical study. Economic theory governing antitrust issues often trails behind the wisdom of common law case evolution, profiting from the experience of judicial applications in a litigated case. Antitrust attorneys and economic experts working on a particular case may offer new and constructive theories that advance the evolution of the law. If the Guidelines were used to block an attempt to offer a new theory about competitive effects of a merger, it is by no means clear that merger enforcement would benefit from this reordering.

79. 1984 Merger Guidelines § 3.22.

80. FTC v. University Health, Inc., 938 F.2d 1206, 1221 (11th Cir.1991)(indicating that the acquired firm's financial weakness is a weak ground for justifying a merger).

81. 1992 Merger Guidelines § 2.

Section 2 of the 1992 Guidelines discusses the manner in which a merger may cause adverse competitive effects through coordinated interaction or through unilateral action. If a merger would result in substantial increase in concentration, placing it in the category of highest anticompetitive risk based on HHI levels, must the agency also show that anticompetitive effects are likely under one of the theories listed in Section 2 of the Guidelines? The Guidelines state that before determining whether to challenge a merger, the agency "will assess the other market factors that pertain to competitive effects."[82] The Guidelines do not say what response will follow if none of the listed anticompetitive theories appears decisive. What if a merger, by eliminating an independent player, runs a high risk of undermining innovation and development? This concern is nowhere mentioned in Section 2, yet it may well be the most important of all adverse competitive effects from increased concentration. The next two subsections discuss matters addressed in Section 2 of the Guidelines.

11.2e1. Anticompetitive Effects from Coordinated Interaction

The coordination that can produce adverse effects can be either tacit or express. And such coordination need not be unlawful in and of itself.[83] According to the 1992 Guidelines, to coordinate successfully, firms must (1) reach terms of interaction that are profitable to the firms involved and (2) be able to detect and punish deviations. The conditions likely to facilitate these two elements are discussed separately, although they frequently overlap.

In discussing how firms might reach terms for profitable coordination, the Guidelines avoid using the term "agreement," probably because no agreement or conspiracy within the meaning of Section 1 of the Sherman Act is necessary for the profitable interaction to occur. As examples of such profitable coordination, the Guidelines list "common price, fixed price differentials, stable market shares, or customer or territorial restrictions."[84] Sometimes the facilitating device may be as simple as a tradition or convention in an industry. For example, if there is a convention that market-makers for a stock exchange quote price differentials between selling and buying prices only in intervals of 1/4 point (25 cents) or 1/8 point (12.5 cents), this convention could prevent an aggressive market-maker from offering a lower interval—say 5 or 10 cents—when competitive conditions warranted.[85]

The 1992 Guidelines also stress that adherence to terms of coordination need not be perfect to be effective. Thus, in the stock market example, the fact that some large traders are able to negotiate narrower buy/sell intervals does not mean that the convention is not effective in

82. Id. § 2.0.

83. Id. § 2.1.

84. Id. § 2.11.

85. See United States v. Alex. Brown & Sons, Inc., 169 F.R.D. 532 (S.D.N.Y.1996), aff'd, 153 F.3d 16 (2d Cir.1998) (proposed consent order involving price fixing charges arising out of breadth of margin between buying and selling prices).

extracting supracompetitive premiums from smaller traders. Coordination may be facilitated if products are homogeneous or if key information about rival firms and the market is readily available to market participants. The absence of these conditions, the Guidelines state, may make coordination less likely.[86]

The presence or absence of these conditions (homogeneity of products and the transparency of the market) may also be relevant in determining whether leading firms in an industry can detect and punish deviations from common pricing schemes. The most common way of punishing a noncooperating firm is to abandon the cooperative conduct, punishing the noncompliance through lower returns. Such discipline may be a price war that affects all business of the participating firms, but it may also be a carefully targeted price cut aimed at the business of the noncomplying firm.[87] The Guidelines also mention the presence of a maverick firm as a factor preventing effective coordination. If such a maverick firm were to be acquired in a merger, coordination may become more likely.[88]

A weakness in the 1992 Guidelines is their failure to acknowledge that segmented markets in which products are differentiated by physical characteristics or brand loyalty can be subject to coordinated action.[89] Indeed, the segmentation of a market itself could be the result of tacit interaction. Although homogeneity of products may make the creation and enforcement of a traditional cartel easier, tacit collusion may be easier when products are differentiated. When products are highly differentiated, direct competition between them is limited, in effect creating a smaller number of critical points for tacit interaction. For example, when a market is segmented into low-priced, medium-priced, and premium-priced brands, each category may be relatively insensitive to price changes that occur outside the segments. As a result, tacit interaction, to be successful, may require only that those producers of brands within a given segment follow parallel pricing practices. These may be far fewer in number than the number of firms in the market as a whole. The result may be that highly segmented markets, such as cereals or tobacco, can sustain high profits more effectively than homogeneous markets, such as grain or milk.[90] Because tacit interaction of players in a differentiated market will be difficult to attack under Section 1 of the Sherman Act, prophylactic merger enforcement may be the best defense against such anticompetitive conduct.

The failure of the Guidelines to recognize possibilities for tacit interaction in differentiated markets is partially addressed in the treatment of unilateral action.[91] As the discussion in the following section indicates, the potential for unilateral anticompetitive steps is increased

---

86. 1992 Merger Guidelines § 2.11.

87. Baker, supra note 69, at 590–92.

88. 1992 Merger Guidelines § 2.12.

89. Davidson, *The Competitive Significance of Segmented Markets*, 71 CALIF. L.

REV. 445 (1983) (Arguing for greater enforcement weight on mergers in segmented markets).

90. Id. at 462.

91. 1992 Merger Guidelines § 2.2.

in differentiated markets. But coordinated action among differentiated producers is probably the greater danger in most oligopolistic markets.

11.2e2. Anticompetitive Effects from Unilateral Action

If coordinated interaction is unlikely, as when the products in the market are differentiated and information about a firm's market transactions is not readily available to rivals, the 1992 Guidelines indicate another avenue by which a merger may produce adverse competitive effects—by facilitating unilateral action. The Guidelines point to two conditions under which anticompetitive effects from unilateral action may be likely in a merger creating a firm with 35 percent or more of the market: (1) when the products in the market are differentiated and the merging firms sell products that are close substitutes; and (2) when the products in the market are relatively undifferentiated, but the merged firm is in a position to profitably limit output and raise price because of capacity limitations on other market players.

If the firms involved in a merger make products which are close substitutes likely to be in direct competition with one another, a merger can eliminate a desirable choice for buyers. A merger in the same industry would be less of a concern if the offerings of the merger partners are not close substitutes. For example, a merger between a producer of luxury automobiles and another firm that makes only models that appeal to economy-minded buyers would be less problematic, whereas a merger between two firms that made automobiles that appealed to the same economy-minded buyers would be more troublesome.

The Guidelines state that market share data may be relied upon to show a significant anticompetitive risk when the merger falls outside the safe harbor set by the Guidelines, when the merging firms have at least 35 percent of the market, and the market share of each product is reflective of its appeal as both a first and second choice of buyers (a circumstance that might be demonstrated by market surveys).[92] The Guidelines recognize that depending on the closeness of substitutability of the products, the market share of the merged firm may either understate or overstate these competitive risks. Finally, the Guidelines indicate that even if the underlying conditions for anticompetitive risk in a merger of firms selling differentiated products are met, there should be no anticompetitive effects if a rival not involved in the merger is likely to reposition its lines to offer a close substitute for the goods subject to the merger.[93]

The second type of unilateral action discussed in the Guidelines involves the risk of a limitation in output by the merged firm controlling at least 35 percent of the market. Such a reduction in output might generally be met by the remaining market participants, who would increase their output to restore supply to an effectively competitive level. But this may not occur if rival firms are already operating at full

92. Id. § 2.211.   **93.** Id. § 2.212.

capacity or if the excess capacity of those firms cannot be operated as efficiently as capacity already in use.[94]

11.2e3. Anticompetitive Effects from Strategic Conduct

As the size and market share of a firm increase, so too do its opportunities to engage in strategic conduct that may raise the costs of its rivals. For example, a powerful firm can pressure upstream suppliers or downstream customers to deal on less favorable terms with rivals of the powerful firm. Research has shown the possibility of new types of anticompetitive behavior and re-examined some traditional concerns that had been relegated to the dustbin. The result has been a greater appreciation of the variety of methods by which an aggressive company can secure an advantage over its rivals, ultimately diminishing their competitive force and conferring greater market power on the firm engaging in strategic conduct.[95]

Strategic conduct risks are thought to be a concern in vertical mergers when a powerful firm gains control of an upstream supplier or downstream customer (discussed in § 12.3b). These concerns, however, are not limited to vertical mergers. A large, vertically unintegrated firm may have the power to force suppliers or customers to discriminate against the powerful firm's rivals. These sorts of concerns led the Federal Trade Commission to impose restrictions on Time Warner's acquisition of Turner Broadcasting.[96]

11.2f. Halting a Trend Toward Concentration in Its Incipiency

Beginning with the Senate report on the original Clayton Act in 1914,[97] Congress has at various times and in various ways manifested a concern that market-concentrating mergers that initiate a trend should be halted in their incipiency. The incipiency doctrine was given new impetus by the Temporary National Economic Commission in the 1940s, was restated in various places in the legislative history in 1950,[98] was restated again in the legislative history of the Hart–Scott–Rodino in 1976,[99] and so forth. Of course the doctrine was never stated expressly in the statute. But the changes in the language of Section 7 in 1950 were

---

94. Id. § 2.22.

95. See, e.g., Church & Ware, INDUSTRIAL ORGANIZATION: A STRATEGIC APPROACH (2000); Smith & Sterling, Challenging Competitors' Mergers: A Real Strategic Option, 65 ANTI-TRUST L.J. 57 (1996).

96. Time Warner, Inc., 61 Fed. Reg. 50,-301 (1996). See Beson et al., Vertical and Horizontal Ownership in Cable TV: Time Warner–Turner (1996), in THE ANTITRUST REVOLUTION 452 (Kwoka & White eds., 3d ed. 1999).

97. S. Rep. No. 698, 63d Cong., 2d Sess. 1 (1914).

98. The Supreme Court described this history at some length in Brown Shoe Co. v. United States, 370 U.S. 294, 314–23, 82 S.Ct. 1502, 8 L.Ed.2d 510 (1962).

99. The House Report on the Hart–Scott–Rodino Act, quoting language in the preamble of the original Clayton bill, described the purpose of Section 7 as to "prohibit certain trade practices which * * * singly and in themselves are not covered by the Sherman Act * * * and thus to arrest the creation of trusts, conspiracies and monopolies in their incipiency and before consummation." H. R. Rep. No. 1373, 94th Cong., 2d Sess. 7 (1976).

directly linked (in the legislative history) to a desire to stop trends toward concentration in their incipiency.

The Supreme Court embraced the incipiency doctrine in 1960s decisions beginning with Brown Shoe Co. v. United States.[100] In United States v. Von's Grocery Co.,[101] the Court once again cited this concern in reversing a district court holding for the defendants and ordering divestiture in a grocery store merger in which the combined market share of the merging firms was 7.5 percent. While the Court's description of the doctrine is historically accurate, the opinion is a prime example of improper application of the incipiency concept. The best explanation of *Von's* may be that the majority regarded the Clayton Act as aimed at maintaining small business regardless of the inefficiency of that form of enterprise. The case was decided at a time when the Court gave great weight to the preservation of small business as an antitrust goal, declaring at one point that efficiency effects were irrelevant to an antitrust analysis of a merger.[102]

More properly understood, the incipiency doctrine addresses the "lemming" effect of mergers. As one economist put it, "mergers do beget mergers."[103] When a prominent merger occurs in any industry, rivals may decide to follow suit for a number of reasons. A rival may think or fear that the merger will create efficiencies and desire to achieve similar efficiencies through a similar merger. But the rival may also perceive the merger as giving strategic (perhaps anticompetitive) advantages to the merged firms, and desire to emulate that result or at least facilitate defensive tactics. Or, the CEO of a rival firm may simply not know what the effect of the merger will be, but desire to copy the merger lest the board of directors ask why the CEO is not in-line with the industry trend.

Sometimes, a rival may see a follow-the-leader merger as a way of thwarting the merger of its major rival. When the Coca–Cola Company announced the proposed acquisition of Dr. Pepper, Pepsi quickly announced that it would acquire Seven–Up in a tactical move widely perceived as seeking to reduce the chances that Coca–Cola would receive antitrust clearance for its acquisition. The Federal Trade Commission successfully forestalled both acquisitions.[104] Somewhat more subtle tactical considerations may have underlain the decision of the nation's two largest drug wholesalers, each of whom had a pending acquisition of

---

100. 370 U.S. at 317, 322. This aspect of *Brown Shoe* was cited with approval in United States v. Philadelphia National Bank, 374 U.S. 321, 362, 83 S.Ct. 1715, 10 L.Ed.2d 915 (1963).

101. 384 U.S. 270, 86 S.Ct. 1478, 16 L.Ed.2d 555 (1966).

102. See the discussion of FTC v. Procter & Gamble Co. in § 11.2h2.

103. Testimony of Alan Ferguson, Mergers and Competition in the Airline Industry, Hearings before the Subcomm. On

Monopolies and Commercial Law, House Comm. On the Judiciary, 99th Cong., 2d Sess. 109 (1987).

104. Pepsi–Cola abandoned its proposed acquisition of Seven–Up after the Commission voted to seek a preliminary injunction against the transaction. The Commission subsequently obtained a preliminary injunction against the Coca–Cola acquisition. FTC v. Coca–Cola Co., 641 F.Supp. 1128 (D.D.C. 1986).

another large wholesaler, to allow their proposed acquisitions to be challenged in a consolidated proceeding brought by the Federal Trade Commission.[105] The consolidated proceeding, by focusing attention on the combined impact of the two mergers, might well have reduced the chances that either firm would be allowed to proceed with its acquisition. But the merging firms each may have viewed the worst possible outcome as one in which its merger was disapproved while the other was allowed to go forward, a risk that may have been reduced through the consolidated hearing.

The follow-the-leader effect of mergers need not be a concern of antitrust unless the trend toward concentration threatens injury to the major substantive goals of merger enforcement. If after the dominos fall adequate competition remains, and if each of the mergers in the sequence yields efficiencies, the public is benefitted, not hurt, by the phenomenon. Perhaps a more careful and defensible interpretation of the incipiency doctrine is that it is designed to stop a trend toward concentration at the first point at which the threat of significant anticompetitive effects becomes evident. At a time in which maintaining the viability of small business was considered a goal of antitrust enforcement, it might make sense to stop a merger between two firms holding (when combined) a small percentage of the market simply because of the potential lemming effect of that merger. But that result would be viewed as highly questionable today. If the merger threatened no other substantive antitrust goal, or if it promised economies of scale to the merged firms that outweighed any negative risk, the incipiency doctrine should not preclude the transaction.

Perhaps because of its association with the now less prominent goal of maintaining small business, the incipiency doctrine has been largely ignored in lower court merger decisions of the last twenty years. The moribund status of the doctrine was probably assured when the enforcement agencies no longer relied upon it. The 1992 Merger Guidelines make no mention of a trend toward concentration as a relevant factor in merger analysis. It is possible to see the threshold HHI levels set forth in Section 1.51 of the Guidelines as presupposing the incipiency doctrine. This section provides that mergers to HHI levels between 1000 and 1800, when producing Index increases of 100 points or more, potentially raise significant competitive issues. Yet the agencies rarely challenge mergers at these HHI levels.

The incipiency doctrine remains a powerful reminder to the agencies and the courts that Section 7 of the Clayton Act is a prophylactic statute designed to address a trend toward concentration at the first point at which it threatens significant anticompetitive consequences. The 1992 Merger Guidelines may fall short of this standard in several respects. For example, even at the highest concentration level (above 1800), the Guidelines provide that mergers that increase the HHI less than 50

105. FTC v. Cardinal Health, Inc., 12 F. Supp. 2d 34, 37–39, 43–44 (D.D.C.1998).

points are unlikely to be challenged.[106] This language may be read as granting the largest firms in an already concentrated industry *carte blanche* to continue acquiring ever higher market share levels as long as it can be done in increasingly small, incremental steps. The incipiency doctrine also reminds us that Congress was concerned with all of the threatened anticompetitive consequences of industry concentration, not merely those involving allocative efficiencies, as one might conclude from reading the Guidelines. Thus, a trend toward concentration, even if it does not adversely affect allocation, may have an adverse impact on the dynamic element of competition, as addressed in the next section.

11.2g.   Preventing Injury to Dynamic Competition

The most substantial shortcoming of the 1992 Merger Guidelines is their focus on allocative efficiencies to the exclusion of dynamic efficiency. The Guidelines say little or nothing about the impact that mergers may have on the all-important dynamic element of competition. Allocative efficiency addresses the production and distribution of currently available goods and services to enhance consumer welfare. Dynamic efficiency addresses change in the system—new products, new services, new methods of production, and new distribution approaches. The importance of dynamic efficiency is addressed in § 1.5c. Of course, the mathematical precision that drafters of various versions of the Guidelines may have sought is not possible when looking at matters such as innovation. But there is today a broad consensus supporting the Shumpeterian insight that consumers benefit much more from dynamic efficiency than from allocative efficiency.[107] To ignore the impact of mergers on dynamic efficiency would be a perilous oversight.

It may be allocatively most efficient to have only a single provider of telephone lines into a neighborhood, and no more than two or three supermarkets serving that neighborhood. But recognition of how to maximize allocative efficiency in a local markets should not alone dictate national competition policy toward large acquisitions that concentrate control on a national basis. For example, recognizing that allocative efficiency is served by having one provider of wired telephone service in any local market need not lead to the conclusion that mergers that result in a single national provider of local telephone service will have no anticompetitive effect. Similarly, even if local neighborhoods can usually support only two or three supermarkets, it does not follow that mergers at the national level are of no competitive concern so long as there remain three supermarket chains in the nation and no monopoly in any particular neighborhood. Wholly aside from any monopsony, buying power issues raised by these mergers, they implicate the dynamic element of competition, which is better served by maintaining a larger number of players on the national scene that can inject new ideas, new products, and new distribution techniques into the system. At the

---

106. 1992 Merger Guidelines § 1.51.   **107.** SCHERER & ROSS, supra note 17, at 31.

national level, preserving maverick or fringe firms, or at least their opportunity to exist, is vital to dynamic efficiency.

During the late 1990s, the presence of the Liggett Group, a distant fourth in market share among domestic cigarette producers, sparked a major change in litigation strategy employed in tobacco products liability litigation. Without Liggett's actions in releasing industry documents and negotiating settlements, this change, although perhaps inevitable, might have occurred much later. The Liggett example illustrates that dynamism or change in an industry comes not only from new products, services, or production or distribution methods, but also in the relationship between an industry's firms and executive, legislative or judicial branches of government. When there are fewer firms in an industry, the possibility of a comfortable and consistent relationship with government, or a common position in opposing a government initiative, is enhanced. If the industry concerned is subject to rate regulation, concentration may reduce the prospect of meaningful rate controls because regulators lose the ability to make rate comparisons among firms. For example, a state regulatory agency charged with oversight of local telephone rates might be able to use rate information from other companies in other markets as a benchmark for determining the fairness of rates charged within its jurisdiction. If local telephone companies are owned or operated by a small number of national firms, these comparisons become a less reliable benchmark because concentration increases the risk of tacit coordination among these firms in raising local rates.

The Merger Guidelines failure to address dynamic efficiency is exacerbated because the Guidelines call for assessing the competitive impact of a merger in the smallest market in which anticompetitive effect might be demonstrated.[108] Often the market for research and development must be described in broader geographic (and perhaps product) terms than would be relevant for measuring the likely allocative effects of a merger. The agencies could address these shortcomings in the Guidelines through revisions that highlight the importance of maintaining dynamic efficiency, by fleshing out considerations that will be relevant in assessing the market for research and development, and by providing some examples of the kind of cases in which dynamic efficiency would be pivotal, perhaps even in cases involving HHIs in the 1000 to 1800 range (where enforcement agencies rarely tread). The Guidelines might, for example, select out for analysis of dynamic effects any merger in an industry in which postmerger national participants would be six or fewer, even if no market power in local markets is created. Any such figure would have to be adjusted for the circumstances facing a particular industry (economies of scale, worldwide market, etc.). For example, the construction of large, passenger-carrying airliners presumably would not be efficient with six market participants. But benchmarks for dynamic analysis could fill a critical substantive loophole in the current

---

108. 1992 Merger Guidelines § 1.0 (describing a relevant market as "a group of products and a geographic area that is no bigger than necessary to satisfy this test [for an economically meaningful market]").

guidelines and provide the antitrust bar and potential merging firms with useful guidance.

11.2h. Defenses

A merger that is deemed presumptively anticompetitive because of high levels of concentration or other effects (discussed in § 11.2e) may still be lawful if the merging parties can establish one or more defenses. The defenses discussed in this section are: (1) ease of entry; (2) efficiencies; (3) power buyers; and (4) averting a business failure.

11.2h1. Ease of Entry

Although the origins of this notion are older, the 1982 Guidelines were the first to recognize ease of entry as a defense for a merger creating or increasing unacceptable levels of market concentration. The theory is that even a monopolist will enjoy no significant market power if entry into the relevant market is so easy that the monopolist must keep its price at effectively competitive levels to discourage it. But this defense has been subject to controversy from the outset, both as to its theoretical grounding and in its application.

A merger that falls into a high-risk category usually means the loss of a competitive player in a market already concentrated. In the traditional logic, such a loss would be thought dispositive; in the hunter's wisdom, a bird in the hand is worth two in the bush. Entry theory, however, suggests otherwise. Giving up a captured bird may be of little consequence if capturing others is easy. So too, the loss of a competitor in a concentrated market will not be harmful when entry is easy and likely. Indeed, the mere anticipation of entry is said to counteract ill effects from the loss of the existing competitor.

Notwithstanding its deductive theoretical support, the wisdom of this modified rule is not self-evident. One of the major benefits of a multiplayer industry is that each player is an existent force for competitive pricing. Innovation benefits may also be more likely in a multiplayer industry. Any given market participant may be the one that brings substantial innovation or productive change to the industry. The loss of a single player in a concentrated industry may have indeterminate effects on innovation and change in the industry. Although it is true that easy entry might allow a nonparticipant to enter a market in order to offer an innovative product or service, such an outsider may lack the precommitment to the industry that is most likely to produce innovation.

Another question is whether effective entry will ever be easy in a concentrated market. Most concentrated industries are those most likely to have substantial entry barriers. The classic example of a low entry barrier industry might be one in which an individual with a small amount of capital can enter. Examples might include providing babysitting services, clerical services, local haul trucking, or even opening a retail dry-cleaning business. Such industries are usually relatively unconcentrated. When an industry has remained concentrated over a period of time—say five or fewer major rivals dominate the market—one can infer that entry is difficult, even if economies of scale or other factors that limit participants are not clearly evident. If further consolidation of an industry is necessary to fully achieve economies of scale, this circumstance is properly addressed under the efficiencies defense, but has no relevance to entry analysis.

There is always an element of speculation about whether entry is easy and, should it occur, whether that entry will be a significant competitive discipline on the market. In the 1970s and 1980s, deregulation and consolidation of the domestic airlines industry proceeded against a backdrop of claims by deductive theorists that because airline capital assets were highly mobile, entry barriers were low in the airline industry (airlines were said to be "contestable markets").[109] Numerous studies of airline markets have found that, notwithstanding any perceived ease of entry, airline pricing and profitability depends primarily on the level of actual competition in a city-pair route served by an airline.[110] The flaw here may be that analysts understated the entry barriers in the airline industry. Even low entry barriers may give existing players a certain amount of leverage that would be absent if rival airlines were competing in the same city-pair market.

Another controversy centers on how widely or narrowly entry barriers should be defined. The traditional definition would include any costs of entry that would allow incumbent firms to charge a higher price without inviting entry by new firms.[111] So understood, entry barriers would include the cost of incorporating a new business, the purchase of specialized production machinery, obtaining technical know-how, advertising and marketing campaigns for introducing a product and obtaining a minimum efficient scale for operations, and obtaining any regulatory approvals from local, state or national government. Stigler argued that entry barriers should be defined more narrowly, including only those costs that a new entrant would incur that were not borne by existing firms in the market.[112] Thus, for example, the cost of winning a sufficient share of the market to operate at an efficient level is a cost borne by all firms. So too is the related cost of establishing a brand identity. These costs would not be considered entry barriers under Stigler's definition. The Stigler approach has the advantage of not counting as an entry barrier those costs incurred by an entrant that would dilute the market by creating overcapacity (and perhaps threatening to erode the efficient size level achieved by other firms). Still, as a practical matter, entry into that industry will undeniably be difficult—incumbent firms that might lose their minimum efficient scale will fight to keep any entrant from taking away their business. Moreover, the narrow definition would ignore entry costs that create real market power, allowing the incumbent

109. Peteraf & Reed, *Pricing and Performance in Monopoly Airline Markets*, 37 J.L. & Econ. 193 (1994).

110. Id. at 193 n.2 (citing various studies of airline performance).

111. See the discussion of entry barriers in § 2.6b3.

112. G. Stigler, The Organization of Industry 67–70 (1968).

firm to charge a higher price than competition would permit. These costs might be present even if there was room in the industry for a new entrant to achieve sufficient scale without undercutting the efficiency of incumbent firms. Stigler's definition also ignores the wealth transfer injury that occurs when efficient firms charge higher prices to consumers because competition does not adequately discipline their prices. Finally, the Stigler definition may give inadequate weight to the dynamic benefits of an industry with multiple players. If a merger is justified on the ground that entry barriers are low, the industry has one less potential innovator.

During the 1980s, low entry barriers were successfully offered as a defense to mergers that would produce high concentration. In United States v. Waste Management, Inc.,[113] the Justice Department's challenge to the merger of two waste-hauling firms was rejected, despite the district court's finding that the merged firm would hold almost 49 percent of the relevant market. The court of appeals cited the ease of entry into the waste-hauling market. The district court found that small entry into this market was easy, but that the "majority of new entrants have either remained relatively small or disappeared as independent entities."[114] The district court's finding was significant because the merged firm would be a major force in the Dallas/Fort Worth market, serving many commercial customers whose needs could not be met by small trash haulers. The conclusion that entry on some level was easy may thus have missed the critical point: Was this entry likely to discipline the prices of the merged firm with 50 percent of the market? Particularly if likely entrants were unable to serve key groups of customers, the answer may well have been "no."

Ease of entry as a defense was given a further boost in United States v. Baker Hughes, Inc., in 1990.[115] Although there was some uncertainty about the measurement of market shares in this case, the postmerger HHI was above 4000 and the merged companies may have had a combined market share as high as 76 percent. Although these levels were well above those required to establish a presumption of illegality under the Guidelines, the court held that the defendant had defeated the presumption by showing that ease of entry would counter any tendency toward collusive or oligopolistic pricing. The government argued that the defendants' showing was inadequate because of a failure to demonstrate that entry would be "quick and effective." The court rejected the government's position, holding that Section 7 deals with "probabilities, not certainties," and that it would be anomalous to place a high burden on defendants to show that quick and effective entry is

113. 743 F.2d 976 (2d Cir.1984). Another circuit case criticized for its undisciplined approach to entry analysis is United States v. Syufy Enterprises, 903 F.2d 659 (9th Cir.1990).

114. *Waste Management*, 743 F.2d at 982 (quoting the language of the district court).

115. 908 F.2d 981, 983–87 (D.C.Cir. 1990). Other cases in which the government's merger enforcement was defeated by an entry defense include United States v. Calmar Inc., 612 F.Supp. 1298 (D.N.J. 1985); United States v. Country Lake Foods, Inc., 754 F.Supp. 669 (D.Minn.1990).

likely.[116] But the court's interpretation of Section 7 itself appears anomalous. That Section prohibits mergers that *may* substantially lessen competition, suggesting that once the probability of anticompetitive effects is demonstrated, the burden should be on the defendant to make a clear showing that negates this probability.

Concern with the superficial nature of the "entry" showing made by merger proponents was perhaps a guiding force in shaping the 1992 Merger Guidelines.[117] The Guidelines now bifurcate entry analysis. Uncommitted entry, discussed here in connection with the definition of the market in § 11.2b4, is limited to entry that would occur within a year without the expenditure of significant sunk costs. Committed entry requires the expenditure of significant sunk costs of entry and exit. Committed entry can be a defense only if it "would be timely, likely, and sufficient in its magnitude, character and scope to deter or counteract the competitive effects of concern."[118] In determining entry, the agency will consider all phases of the entry effort, including "planning, design, and management; permitting, licensing, and other approvals; construction, debugging, and operation of production facilities; and promotion (including necessary introductory discounts), marketing, distribution, and satisfaction of customer testing and qualification requirements."[119] The Guidelines reject Stigler's view that entry barriers are only those costs that an incumbent firm did not have to bear. Overall, the Guidelines pose rather formidable obstacles for assertion of the ease of entry defense.

Accepting the wisdom that maintaining an existing competitor is superior to potential competition, the agencies may be justified in drawing a tight circle around the entry defense. But is the defense now little more than a complicated charade that should be discarded altogether? Concentrated industries are almost by definition industries in which entry represents a substantial undertaking. To allow further concentration via merger in such an industry seems counter to a fundamental of merger enforcement—that higher concentration creates greater risks of anticompetitive injury. If this defense now has any role, it might be in justifying a merger that exceeds concentration thresholds but has some significant potential benefits to society. But the major benefits of a merger are efficiencies, and efficiencies are a distinct defense, discussed in the next section.

Ease of entry is routinely asserted by defendants in merger litigation. Whatever may have been the case before the 1992 Guidelines, most courts now appear to impose a substantial burden on the merging firms to show that entry is likely and that it will forestall the likely anticom-

116. *Baker Hughes,* 908 F.2d at 987. For criticism of the *Baker Hughes* holding, see H. HOVENKAMP, FEDERAL ANTITRUST POLICY: THE LAW OF COMPETITION AND ITS PRACTICE § 12.4d, at 526 (3d ed. 2005).

117. See the criticism of the undisciplined standards for entry defenses in Pitof-

sky, *Merger Analysis in the '90s: The Guidelines and Beyond—Panel Discussion/Q & A,* 61 Antitrust L.J. 175, 179 (1992).

118. 1992 Merger Guidelines § 3.0.

119. Id. § 3.1.

petitive effects of the merger. In conformity with past and current versions of Guidelines,[120] a number of courts have paid close attention to the history of entry into the market.[121] In FTC v. Staples, Inc., the district court, after citing *Baker Hughes*, proceeded to carefully weigh and ultimately reject the defendants' arguments that entry into the office supply superstore market was easy and would counter any anticompetitive effects of the proposed merger.[122] The defendants had offered evidence that all entry in the market had been within the preceding 11 years, a circumstance suggesting that the industry was youthful, growing, and receptive to new entry. But the Commission countered by showing that 20 of the 23 entrants had failed, and that many of the urban markets for office superstores were saturated, leaving little or no room for new entrants.[123] In *FTC v. Cardinal Health, Inc.*, the district court again rejected an ease of entry defense, relying on the history of entry (only one small firm had entered the market in the previous decade) and a pattern of consolidation that had substantially reduced the number of firms.[124]

11.2h2. *Efficiencies*

The efficiency defense is invoked for mergers that may increase the risk of oligopolistic conduct but may also enhance efficiencies.[125] The tension between these two goals may be less than first appears. Mergers between firms small enough not to have achieved minimum efficient scale often involve firms that have low market shares, thus raising few risks of oligopolistic behavior. However, this is not uniformly true. In some industries in which demand is limited, achieving minimum efficient scale may require obtaining a large or even dominant share of the market. The classic case of this tension may be a natural monopoly where maximum efficiency can be obtained only by a firm gaining a monopoly in a geographic market.

The controversy surrounding a merger that simultaneously increases risk of anticompetitive behavior and enhances efficiencies exposes a disagreement about the purposes of antitrust law. Is that law meant solely to enhance efficient allocation of resources, or is it intended also to ensure that efficiencies are passed along to consumers in the form of lower prices or higher quality?[126] Throughout this book, the working

---

120. Id. § 3.1.

121. United States v. Baker Hughes, Inc., 908 F.2d 981, 988 (D.C.Cir.1990); United States v. Waste Management, Inc., 743 F.2d 976, 982 (2d Cir.1984); FTC v. Cardinal Health, Inc., 12 F. Supp. 2d 34 (D.D.C.1998); United States v. United Tote, 768 F.Supp. 1064, 1080–82 (D.Del.1991).

122. 970 F.Supp. 1066, 1086–88 (D.D.C. 1997).

123. Id.

124. *Cardinal Health*, 12 F.Supp.2d at 56–58.

125. An early exposition of the economic theory underlying the efficiencies defense was offered in Williamson, *Economies as an Antitrust Defense: The Welfare Trade–Offs*, 58 AM. ECON. REV. 34 (1968). The topic was revisited in Fisher & Lande, *Efficiency Considerations in Merger Enforcement*, 71 CAL. L. REV. 1580 (1983).

126. For example, Williamson took the view that, in applying the efficiency defense, the only anticompetitive risk of concern is the loss of efficient allocation. Williamson, supra note 121. Fisher and Lande, relying on a consistent pattern of concern

assumption is that while antitrust seeks to enhance efficient allocation, that goal must go hand in hand with the goal of encouraging the transfer of efficiency gains to consumers. The 1992 Merger Guidelines appeared to accept this broader view by acknowledging that the result of exercise of market power from a merger "is a transfer of wealth from buyers to sellers or a misallocation of resources."[127] A 1997 amendment to the Guidelines revises the treatment of the efficiencies defense and requires that efficiencies must benefit consumers to be considered a defense. For example, the revised Section 4 of the Guidelines lists the potential benefits of merger-generated efficiencies as "lower prices, improved quality, enhanced service, or new products."[128] None of these benefits to consumers would occur if efficiency gains were simply absorbed by the merged firms as higher profits or x-inefficiency. The view that efficiencies must benefit consumers also appears consistent with the political constituency for antitrust, which assuredly rests on public distaste for market power abuses that enrich the powerful at the public's expense. See the discussion in §§ 1.2, 1.5b. As with government regulation of a natural monopoly (such as an electric or gas utility), the public wants efficient production and distribution, but also wants the benefits of that efficiency to be passed on in the form of low prices.

If both efficient allocation and transfer of the efficiency gain to consumers are goals of antitrust, the dispute over the efficiency defense may be reduced to two questions: (1) are significant efficiencies likely; and (2) will competition require those efficiencies to be passed on to consumers? Both questions should be answered affirmatively to establish a defense to an otherwise high-risk merger. Because a merger that enhances market power by definition makes it easier for the consolidated firm to deny consumers efficiency benefits through oligopolistic pricing, the higher the risk of anticompetitive consequences from a merger, the more difficult it should be to establish an efficiency defense.

This leaves a relatively small window for asserting the efficiency defense. A qualifying transaction would be a merger that is thought only marginally to raise anticompetitive risks, perhaps when the postmerger HHI is barely over the line into a higher risk category. In that instance, a strong showing of efficiency, even in the absence of clear evidence that it would be passed on to consumers, might be rationally thought to tip the balance in favor of allowing the merger. Another theoretical possibil-

about income transfer throughout the legislative history of the antitrust laws, concluded that both efficient allocation and wealth transfer losses should be considered in applying any efficiency defense. Fisher & Lande, supra note 121.

127. 1992 Merger Guidelines § 0.1. See the 1992 comments of FTC Bureau of Competition Director Kevin Arquit, agreeing that wealth transfer is an agency concern with mergers that create or increase high concentration. Arquit, *Perspectives on the 1992 U.S. Government Horizontal Merger*

Guidelines, 61 ANTITRUST L.J. 121, 135 (1992).

128. 1992 Merger Guidelines § 4 (as revised in 1997). Section 4 of the Guidelines also indicates in a footnote that "[d]elayed benefits from efficiencies (due to delay in the achievement of, or the realization of consumer benefits from, the efficiencies) will be given less weight because they are less proximate and more difficult to predict." Id. § 4 n.37.

ity for use of the efficiency defense is a merger creating such substantial efficiency gains that even if the merger would produce a monopoly, the profit-maximizing price would be less than the premerger prices of the much less efficient premerger rivals. Although such instances may be rare, they may occasionally occur, for example, in an industry in which technological change has generated a new natural monopoly. A skeptical attitude toward the efficiency defense is suggested by agency experience that many such defenses appear to be eleventh hour presentations not backed by credible facts that would salvage a suspect merger.[129]

Finally, it has been argued in support of an efficiency defense that if a merger creates a new and efficient firm, that firm may have both the incentive and the ability to destabilize a collusive market.[130] If existing firms could not have attained the efficiencies without merger, then the classic trade-off between efficient operations and consumer welfare is presented. But if the merger creates an efficiency that other firms might emulate without a merger, something of a paradox is created: It seems likely that if other firms could obtain the efficiency without a merger, so too could the original merging parties. By acknowledging the dynamism of competitive responses, the theory moves away from a static analysis of the competitive effects of a merger. That movement toward dynamic analysis is appropriate, but by no means compelling in establishing the credentials of an efficiency defense. A merger, by eliminating one of the market players, may have long term stifling effects on innovation and initiative in the relevant market.

The judicial response to an efficiency defense has varied. In 1967, the Supreme Court in FTC v. Procter & Gamble Co.[131] held that "possible economies cannot be used as a defense to illegality" in Section 7 cases. Weighing possible efficiencies against anticompetitive effects was inappropriate, in the Court's view: "Congress was aware that some mergers which lessen competition may also result in economies but it struck the balance in favor of protecting competition."[132] But attitudes, including those of the enforcement agencies, have changed. Recent lower court cases have entertained efficiency defenses. In *FTC v. University Health, Inc.,* the court held that a defendant "may rebut the government's prima facie case with evidence showing that the intended merger would create significant efficiencies in the relevant market."[133]

In acknowledging that an efficiency defense may be presented, the lower courts, implicitly assuming that today's Supreme Court would not

---

129. Arquit, supra note 127, at 135–36.

130. Stockum, *The Efficiencies Defense for Horizontal Mergers: What is the Government's Standard?* 61 ANTITRUST L.J. 829, 835 (1993).

131. 386 U.S. 568, 580, 87 S.Ct. 1224, 18 L.Ed.2d 303 (1967).

132. Id. The Court also has said that a merger that may substantially lessen competition is not saved because "on some ultimate reckoning of social or economic debits and credits, it may be deemed beneficial." United States v. Philadelphia Nat'l Bank, 374 U.S. 321, 371, 83 S.Ct. 1715, 10 L.Ed.2d 915 (1963).

133. 938 F.2d 1206, 1222 (11th Cir. 1991). Recent cases in which an efficiency defense was entertained but rejected include FTC v. Staples, Inc., 970 F.Supp. 1066, 1088–90 (D.D.C. 1997). FTC v. Cardinal Health,12 F. Supp. 2d 34 (D.D.C.1998).

accept the *Procter & Gamble* pronouncement, have followed the lead of the federal agencies, which have long acknowledged at least the theoretical possibility of an efficiency defense. The 1968 Guidelines were the first to recognize an efficiency defense, but limited its consideration to "exceptional circumstances."[134] In successive iterations, the Guidelines have retreated only marginally from this position. More recent versions of the guidelines have responded to society's interest in efficiency gains by relaxing the concentration thresholds for mergers thought to raise anticompetitive risks. Mergers that exceed these thresholds are less likely to involve substantial efficiency gains and, when they do, those gains are less likely to be passed on to consumers. The 1992 Guidelines, as revised in 1997, do not fundamentally alter earlier versions that treated skeptically efficiency claims for mergers that exceed concentration thresholds.[135] Although eliminating a phrase that required an efficiency showing with "clear and convincing evidence," this change is said to have been a part of a general effort to remove statements of evidentiary burden from the Guidelines, not to relax the standards for establishing an efficiency defense.[136] The Guidelines now provide for a sliding scale, suggesting that cognizable efficiencies must be greater as anticompetitive risks (as measured in Sections 1–3 of the Guidelines) increase.[137] The 1997 Revision provides that "certain types of efficiencies are more likely to be cognizable and substantial than others." As an example of a potentially substantial and verifiable efficiency, the Guidelines offer "shifting production among facilities formerly owned separately." The Guidelines also identify claimed efficiencies relating to "procurement, management, or capital cost" as "less likely to be merger-specific or substantial" or perhaps not cognizable "for other reasons." The revised Guidelines, expanding on earlier versions, also indicate that an efficiency defense will be accepted only if the efficiencies are "likely to be accomplished with the proposed merger and unlikely to be accomplished in the absence of either the proposed merger or another means having comparable anticompetitive effects."[138] Spelling out what was perhaps implicit in earlier versions, the Guidelines provide that other means of attaining the efficiencies will be considered only if they "are practical in the business situation faced by the merging firms."

The case law suggests that while courts may be willing to consider efficiency defenses, they are slow to sustain them.[139] In a number of district court decisions, the defendants' efficiency claims were found to be exaggerated because much of the asserted savings could be achieved without a merger.[140] Even when the court is convinced that efficiencies

---

134. 1968 Merger Guidelines § 10.

135. 1992 Merger Guidelines § 4 (as revised in 1997).

136. Arquit, supra note 127, at 134.

137. 1992 Merger Guidelines § 4 (as revised in 1997).

138. Id.

139. A number of courts have rejected efficiency defenses as inadequately demonstrated or not of a nature to justify a merger. FTC v. University Health, Inc., 938 F.2d 1206, 1223–24 (11th Cir.1991); FTC v. Alliant Techsystems, Inc., 808 F.Supp. 9, 23 (D.D.C.1992).

140. FTC v. Tenet Healthcare Corp., 17 F.Supp.2d 937, 948 (E.D.Mo.1998), *rev'd,*

will be realized by a merger, they may be insufficient to overcome the likely anticompetitive effects.[141] Such cases have led some commentators to lament the slow pace of judicial acceptance of the defense.[142] But there may be sound reason for proceeding slowly in recognizing this defense. In United States v. Carilion Health System,[143] a merger of two local hospitals was allowed to proceed over the challenge of the Justice Department, in part because of claimed efficiencies. At least one post-merger study found postmerger prices to have risen above premerger levels, although the extent to which these increases were caused by market power was unclear.[144] An FTC study of an unchallenged high concentration merger between two titanium dioxide producers—also claimed to have created efficiencies—found substantial postmerger price increases.[145]

A significant decision addressing the efficiencies defense was the D.C. Circuit's holding in FTC v. H.J. Heinz Co.[146] Heinz, the second largest U.S. seller of canned baby food, sought to acquire Beech–Nut, the third largest seller. The firms argued that their combined 32.8% of the U.S. market would have made them a more vigorous competitor of Gerber, which had 65% of the market. The merger would have substantially raised the HHI (by 510 points to 4775) and left only two significant players in the market.[147] In the district court, the merging parties persuaded the court that the merger would have substantial efficiencies and minimal anticompetitive effects (because Beech–Nut and Heinz generally were not competitors in the same retail stores). The parties argued that the combination would allow the closure of Beech–Nut's old and less efficient production facilities in favor of Heinz's underutilized modern plant. The court of appeals gave little weight to this efficiency defense, primarily because of the very high concentration level that this merger would create (leaving only two significant firms). The court said that in such cases, the merging parties would have to show "extraordinary efficiencies."[148]

The court's recognition of a sliding scale test, requiring a stronger showing of efficiencies as the level of industry concentration rises, is sound. Monopolies may potentially be the most efficient production and distribution machines, but monopolies tend to dissipate profits in rent-seeking and x-inefficiencies and are unlikely to pass efficiency gains on

186 F.3d 1045, 1054 (8th Cir.1999) (although district court properly rejected efficiency defense, the court should have considered efficiencies in weighing the anticompetitive effects of the merger). FTC v. Cardinal Health, 12 F.Supp. 2d 34, 62–63 (D.D.C.1998); FTC v. Staples, 970 F.Supp. 1066, 1090.

141. FTC v. Cardinal Health, 12 F. Supp. 2d at 63 (Casting doubt on whether the demonstrated efficiencies "are enough to overcome the evidence that . . . possibly greater benefits can be achieved by the public through existing, continued competition.").

142. Stockum, supra note 130, at 829–30.

143. 892 F.2d 1042 (4th Cir. 1989).

144. *Aftermath of the Carilion Merger,* MODERN HEALTHCARE, Feb. 10, 1992, at 58–64.

145. Arquit, supra note 127, at 136–37.

146. 246 F.3d 708 (D.C.Cir. 2001).

147. *Heinz,* 116 F. Supp. 2d 190, 193–96 (D.D.C. 2000), rev'd, 246 F.3d 708 (D.C. Cir. 2001).

148. *Heinz,* 246 F.3d at 720.

to consumers. There was an additional issue in this case. Assuming that some of the efficiency gains of the merger might be passed on to consumers, was there a less anticompetitive way to achieve these gains? For example, could Beech–Nut have contracted with H.J. Heinz to produce the Beech–Nut baby food at Heinz's modern and efficient facilities, still leaving Beech Nut free to compete in downstream markets?[149]

11.2h3. *Power Buyers or Power Sellers*

Merging parties often claim a defense based on the ability of large buyers to obtain competitive prices even after a merger that would produce a substantial increase in concentration in the relevant market. Large buyers may have sufficient leverage to force participants in even a concentrated industry to discount prices. In addition, large buyers may have the capability of entering the upstream industry themselves (or sponsoring a new entrant) in order to force down prices. If large buyers are able to force down prices for all buyers (including smaller buyers), there should be no short-term adverse effect on pricing as a result of a concentration-enhancing merger in the supplier industry.

There are, however, potential pitfalls to this defense. One is that sellers in a concentrated industry may find a way to discriminate among buyers, charging large buyers a significantly lower price than is charged to small buyers. If a merger increases concentration, and thereby enhances the probability that smaller buyers will pay higher prices, a strong case can be made that the smaller buyers should be protected under Section 7 of the Clayton Act, which addresses mergers that may substantially lessen competition in *any* market in *any* section of the country. If the market is defined to include all buyers large and small, adverse competitive effects on small buyers, a significant group within that market, should still be sufficient to invoke Section 7 of the Clayton Act. By facilitating the discrimination, the merger will have injured competition and threatened increased concentration downstream. The power of a large buyer to force down prices cannot be attributed to efficiency because the capacity to exercise countervailing power is not a scale economy. Alternatively, it would be legitimate to regard the small buyers as a separate market because a seller's ability to discriminate unfavorably in the price charged such buyers is a classic measure of power over price that characterizes a market subject to inadequate competitive discipline.

Another concern with the powerful buyer defense is that, although short-term price increases may be thwarted by such buyers, the long term dynamic effects of a market dominated by a small number of firms could be adverse. Innovation in and new entry into the firms' market may be undercut by tacitly parallel conduct or oligopolistic behavior by these firms as sellers. How great the risk of such anticompetitive effects will be is difficult to predict in particular instances, but the great

---

149. Leary, *An Inside Look at the Heinz Case,* Antitrust, *Spring 2002, at 32, 33.*

importance of the dynamic element of competition (addressed in § 1.5b2) bespeaks caution in allowing mergers in highly concentrated markets even if adverse short-term pricing effects are reduced.

The 1992 Merger Guidelines do not directly address a "powerful buyer" defense, but the second phase of the Guidelines inquiry calls for the agency to consider the likely adverse competitive effects of a merger. In determining whether the merger would facilitate anticompetitive coordination, the Guidelines also call for considering the role of large buyers that purchase through long-term contracts, thereby making deviations from the terms of coordinated interaction less transparent.[150] There is, in any event, nothing in the Guidelines that would preclude merging parties from attempting to demonstrate to the agency that adverse competitive effects are unlikely because of the role of powerful buyers. The Guidelines also allow room for an ease of entry defense in instances in which a powerful buyer would itself be a likely entrant or perhaps sponsor such an entrant.[151] On the other hand, the Guidelines would expressly limit recognition of a powerful buyer defense by providing for a separate geographic or product market when the seller has the ability to discriminate in price against a significant class of buyers.[152] In short, a powerful buyer defense should be unsuccessful under the Guidelines if the sellers retained the ability to discriminate in price.

In the courts, a defense based on powerful buyers has met with mixed success. In United States v. Baker Hughes, the court declined to enjoin a proposed merger because buyers had leverage to thwart higher prices through a procurement system of multiple, confidential bids and because entry into the sellers' market was said to be easy.[153] Powerful buyer defenses were also a factor in other decisions in which the Government failed to obtain injunctive relief against a merger.[154] In other district court decisions, a powerful buyer defense has failed on findings that smaller buyers would not necessarily benefit from discounted prices obtained by powerful buyers.[155] This reasoning is consistent with the Merger Guidelines recognition of separate product or geographic markets based on a seller's ability to discriminate in price.

Although there is as yet little case law addressing the issue of a "power seller" defense, a merger between two large buyers could have fewer anticompetitive effects if those who sell to the merging firms are themselves large firms with substantial market shares. A complete antitrust analysis would have to consider not only the merging firms' impact on the firms that sell to it, but also the impact on downstream markets where the merging firms market their products.

---

150. 1992 Merger Guidelines § 2.12.

151. Id. § 3.0.

152. Id. §§ 1.12, 1.22.

153. 908 F.2d 981, 986 (D.C.Cir.1990). The Baker Hughes reasoning with respect to ease of entry was questioned in § 11.2h1.

154. FTC v. Tenet Healthcare Corp., 186 F.3d 1045, 1054–55 (8th Cir.1999);

United States v. Archer–Daniels–Midland Co., 781 F.Supp. 1400, 1416 (S.D.Iowa 1991); United States v. Country Lake Foods, Inc., 754 F.Supp. 669 (D.Minn.1990).

155. FTC v. Cardinal Health, Inc., 12 F. Supp. 2d 34, 58–61 (D.D.C.1998); United States v. United Tote, 768 F.Supp. 1064, 1085 (D.Del.1991).

11.2h4. Averting a Business Failure

The origin of the failing company defense was a 1930 Supreme Court case applying the pre–Celler–Kefauver version of Section 7 of the Clayton Act.[156] In Citizen Publishing Co. v. United States,[157] the Court offered in dicta a very constricted view of the defense: Its proponents would have to show that the acquired firm was moribund, that all alternative ways of saving it were tried or explored and found wanting, and that no alternative buyer whose purchase might pose fewer competitive risks could be found. These limitations have, in variation, appeared in each iteration of the Merger Guidelines, including the 1992 version.[158]

The policy arguments for recognizing such a defense at all are seldom clearly articulated. If the acquired company were allowed to fail, its assets would still be sold as a part of a bankruptcy liquidation, with many of them perhaps finding productive use in the same industry. But the transaction costs of a failed company can be substantial. Workers are displaced, creditors left unpaid, communities disrupted, and customers and suppliers lose long-standing trading partners. A merger may avoid some or all of these losses, also reducing social costs for families and communities involved.

There is no question that strong political pressures are brought to bear in the case of a potentially failing company. Sensitivity to these interests is not only smart politics, but arguably a sound interpretation of an antitrust law designed to benefit citizens injured by exercises of unrestrained power. Where a considerable body of citizens avoid injury by an extension of economic power, and there is no less anticompetitive alternative to avoiding the injury, the policy rationale underlying the failing company defense is that antitrust should not intervene to the detriment of the affected citizens.

One problem is that this rationale admits merger justifications hard to characterize as competitive benefits; another is that it makes no effort to weigh the benefits against the competitive harms. Furthermore, the argument itself is overbroad. Its logic could apply to any merger in which market power could benefit a group of citizens. Any merger that increases market power may benefit stockholders, employees and other residents of the communities of the consolidating firms. These benefits are real but have little or nothing to do with protecting competition; it would be difficult to weigh them against the broader public interest in maintaining a competitive structure for industry. If a merger could be defended on such a ground, the greater public interest in competitive pricing and innovation would be eviscerated. Furthermore, there is little justification for singling out mergers of failing companies for this favored treatment.

156. International Shoe Co. v. FTC, 280 U.S. 291, 50 S.Ct. 89, 74 L.Ed. 431 (1930).

157. 394 U.S. 131, 89 S.Ct. 927, 22 L.Ed.2d 148 (1969).

158. 1992 Merger Guidelines § 5.

Under the constraint of case law and earlier Guidelines, the 1992 Merger Guidelines recognize a failing company and a failing division defense. However, the Guidelines attempt to explain the defense solely in terms of the competitive effect of the merger, apparently limiting it to cases in which the extracompetitive concerns are most substantial. The defense would be available if one of the merging firms is subject to imminent failure such that its assets would exit the relevant market, with the consequence that the "post-merger performance in the relevant market may be no worse than market performance had the merger been blocked and the assets left the market."[159] The reasoning here is that employed in United States v. General Dynamics Corp., where the Court analyzed a merger in terms of the firms' "probable future ability to compete."[160] The conclusion that future competitive conditions would be no better without the merger is, however, hardly self-evident. For example, if the assets left the market altogether, all remaining firms in the market would be free to compete for the business once held by the exiting firm. The departing firm's assets might end up in the hands of less quiescent or relatively efficient rivals, increasing competitive pressure on the market leaders. If, however, a merger of the financially troubled firm is permitted with a market-leading firm, that market leader has probably captured the goodwill and customer base and achieved a higher market share at the expense of its rivals. The only justification for allowing this merger must be that it has saved substantial social and economic costs that would emanate from a business failure.

The 1992 Guidelines attempt to guard against these concerns by imposing conditions on the application of the failing company defense: (1) that the failing firm would be unable to meet its financial obligations in the near future; (2) that the failing firm cannot reorganize under Chapter 11 of the Bankruptcy Act; (3) that unsuccessful good faith efforts were made to find an alternate acquiring firm with whom a merger would create fewer anticompetitive risks; and (4) absent the acquisition, the assets would exit the market.[161] Except for the Chapter 11 bankruptcy requirement, the same conditions must be met to assert the failing division defense.[162]

11.2h5. *Financial Weakness—The Flailing Company Defense*

Although the reasoning underlying the failing company defense is similar to that employed in *General Dynamics*, the Supreme Court's focus on a firm's future ability to compete (as opposed to its existing market share) can be read more broadly to permit a "weak competitor" defense, sometimes called the *flailing company defense*. Although such a defense is not recognized in the Guidelines, the Seventh Circuit appeared to recognize it in United States v. International Harvester Co., wherein it concluded that the merging firms' market share statistics did not

159. Id. § 5.0.

160. 415 U.S. 486, 503, 94 S.Ct. 1186, 39 L.Ed.2d 530 (1974).

161. 1992 Merger Guidelines § 5.1.

162. Id. § 5.2.

establish a prima facie case because of the acquired firm's "weak financial reserves."[163] Under the Guidelines, the financial status of a firm may be a relevant factor in determining the likely competitive impact of a merger, but allowing financial weakness alone to trump a prima facie showing of anticompetitive effect is troublesome. If the financial weakness is an enduring problem, one would expect that this weakness would already be reflected in the market share statistics of the firm. If financial weakness is not an enduring problem, perhaps because it is due to recent poor management decisions, then the weakness can be corrected by means that do not threaten anticompetitive effects, as for example by replacement of the management. In a subsequent opinion, the Seventh Circuit appeared to limit its view of the significance of weak financial condition, suggesting that it is "one relevant economic factor among many" to be considered in assessing the competitive effects of a merger.[164]

The flailing company defense was rejected in a 1998 hospital merger case in which the parties argued that one of the hospitals was in weak financial condition.[165] The district court cited evidence that suggested the hospital was suffering from market conditions affecting hospitals nationwide (such as shorter hospital stays) and that the hospital was rebounding from a downturn in profitability.[166] The Federal Trade Commission appears to have relied on the weak competitive status of the McDonnell Douglas Corporation in its 1997 decision not to challenge that firm's acquisition by the Boeing Corporation. The Commission focused on the rivalry between the two companies in the manufacture of commercial aircraft. Even though the merger reduced the firms in this global market from three to two, in view, apparently, of McDonnell Douglas' unfavorable prospects for surviving, the Commission decided not to challenge the acquisition. Significantly, the evidence of McDonnell Douglas' weak competitive status could be demonstrated not simply based on financial considerations, but on its declining market share in the sale of commercial aircraft and the viability of its commercial aircraft offerings. The Commission may also have given some weight to a powerful buyer defense.

§ 11.3   Conglomerate Mergers

Conglomerate mergers are a default category, encompassing all mergers that are not horizontal or vertical in nature. Within the category are three distinguishable subcategories: mergers between firms that make or sell the same product in different geographic markets (a market extension merger); mergers between firms that make different products but have similar production or marketing channels (a product-line extension merger); and mergers with neither of these complementarities (a

---

163. 564 F.2d 769, 773 (7th Cir.1977).

164. Kaiser Aluminum & Chemical Corp. v. FTC, 652 F.2d 1324, 1339 (7th Cir.1981).

165. FTC v. Tenet Healthcare Corp., 17 F. Supp. 2d 937, 947 (E.D.Mo.1998), *rev'd on other grounds*, 186 F.3d 1045 (8th Cir. 1999).

166. Id.

pure conglomerate merger). Another way of characterizing conglomerate mergers is based upon whether they involve issues of potential competition. Potential competitors are likely to come from the ranks of firms that make the same or similar products, or that are in a vertical relation with firms in the market. Thus, all product-line and market extension mergers involve potential competition issues. Vertical mergers, treated in Chapter XI, also may involve potential competition issues. Only purely conglomerate mergers ordinarily would not involve potential competition issues.

11.3a. Overview of Conglomerate Mergers

Merger enforcement is responsive to merger activity. In the 1960s, conglomerate mergers reached heretofore unprecedented levels,[1] prompting concern about the potential adverse competitive effects of these mergers. During the period 1964–1971, 35 percent of all reported mergers were conglomerate; the average number of lines of business of leading U.S. manufacturing firms more than doubled.[2] During this period, the federal agencies were pursuing both horizontal and vertical acquisitions. Acquisition-hungry firms may have opted for conglomerate mergers in part because they were a form of acquisition that was relatively unhampered by antitrust restrictions. Conglomerate mergers were also thought to be a form of risk insurance—a firm might be able to even out the peaks and troughs of performance in a particular line of business by diversifying into other fields where business cycles would differ in their timing and intensity.[3] Although conglomerate mergers offered no economies of scale in production, product and market extension mergers may offer some scale economies in advertising and distribution. For example, a market extension merger that allows a firm to expand its sales to a national market may make it more efficient to buy certain forms of national advertising. These efficiencies become less likely if the merger is purely conglomerate, but even such mergers could offer small savings in administrative or other expenses. A larger firm may also be able to purchase input products more cheaply. Lower prices on input products may be due to efficient buying, or it may involve the exercise of buyer power. If buyer power is exercised in transactions with power sellers, it may be little more than a shifting of oligopoly rents among power players in the vertical chain. If, on the other hand, buyer power is exercised against small sellers, genuine anticompetitive effects may ensue. See the discussion in § 2.7.

Whatever may have been the motivations for it, conglomeration has not lived up to high expectations. Managing diversified lines of business requires varying business strategies and expertise. The market activity

---

§ 11.3

1. See the description of merger activity in the 1960s in § 9.2d.

2. F.M. Scherer & D. Ross, Industrial Market Structure and Economic Performance 156–58 (3d ed. 1990). The peak year for conglomerate mergers was 1968, when 4000 were reported. Federal Trade Commission, Bureau of Economics, Current Trends in Merger Activity 1971, Table 6 (1972).

3. Scherer & Ross, supra note 2, at 127–30.

demonstrates that in many conglomerates management has failed in this challenge. Numerous diversification mergers of the 1960s have been reversed, with spin-offs of unrelated and distantly related operations, and a renewed emphasis on a firm's primary lines.[4] Despite these sobering lessons, conglomerate mergers still occur, but now tend to cluster in lines that bear some relation to the firm's primary line of business.

The federal agencies challenged conglomerate mergers during and after the merger wave of the 1960s. First the Federal Trade Commission,[5] and later the Justice Department, began bringing such enforcement actions on various theories and with varying degrees of success. During the period 1964–1977, there were 33 court challenges to conglomerate acquisitions, 11 of them successful. By the end of this period, it became increasingly difficult to win such cases—none were successful after 1974.[6] If there was a common theme running through most of these cases, it was the alleged loss of potential competition—the acquiring firm was said to be a potential competitor of the firm that it had acquired. Broader theories, such as that increases in the aggregate concentration of the economy threatened competition, were uniformly unsuccessful.

Potential competition doctrine can be traced to United States v. El Paso Natural Gas Co.[7] El Paso, the only out-of-state firm that supplied natural gas in California, supplied more than 50 percent of the California market. The Justice Department successfully challenged El Paso's acquisition of Pacific Northwest Pipeline Corp., the only interstate gas pipeline of consequence with a distribution system west of the Rockies. Northwest had large gas reserves accessible to California, operated in adjacent states, and possessed the management and experience that made an entry into the California market feasible. Indeed, Northwest had made previous unsuccessful attempts to enter that market. El Paso had responded in one instance by lowering its gas prices 25 percent to stave off the attempt. Entry barriers in the natural gas market were high, so Northwest was, if not the only potential entrant, one of very few that might have successfully entered the California market.

In FTC v. Procter & Gamble Co.,[8] the Court sustained an FTC order declaring unlawful Procter & Gamble's acquisition of the largest manufacturer of liquid household bleach. The Court apparently concluded that, in the absence of the merger, Procter & Gamble was a likely entrant in the household bleach market. The various brands of liquid household bleach were chemically identical, so manufacturers sought to differentiate their brands through advertising. Clorox was the only national seller, with 50 percent of the U.S. sales. The second firm, selling

4. Id. at 90–91.

5. The Federal Trade Commission's first major success was FTC v. Procter & Gamble Co., 386 U.S. 568, 87 S.Ct. 1224, 18 L.Ed.2d 303 (1967).

6. Bauer, *Challenging Conglomerate Mergers Under Section 7 of the Clayton Act:* *Today's Law and Tomorrow's Legislation,* 58 B.U. L. Rev. 199, 200 nn.8–9 (1978).

7. 376 U.S. 651, 84 S.Ct. 1044, 12 L.Ed.2d 12 (1964).

8. 386 U.S. 568, 87 S.Ct. 1224, 18 L.Ed.2d 303 (1967).

only west of the Mississippi, had 16 percent of national sales. Although P & G did not sell household bleach, it held 50 percent of all sales nationally of household cleaning products such as detergents and soaps. The Court saw liquid bleach as a "natural avenue" for P & G diversification. Neither the FTC nor the Supreme Court found that P & G was more likely than not to enter the bleach market, but the Court labelled P & G the single most likely entrant into the highly concentrated bleach market.

In United States v. Falstaff Brewing Corp.,[9] the Government challenged Falstaff's acquisition of a New England brewer. Falstaff was the country's fourth largest brewer, but the only one of the top four that did not sell nationally—Falstaff sold everywhere but the Northeast. The Government argued that the acquisition of the New England brewer— with 20 percent of that market—violated Section 7 of the Clayton Act because, in the absence of the merger, Falstaff would have entered the northeastern market independently or by a "toehold" acquisition of a company with a small market share. Either of these alternatives, the Government argued, would be more procompetitive than the merger. The Supreme Court reversed and remanded a decision of the district court holding for the defendant. The Court did not challenge the lower court's finding that Falstaff was unlikely to enter independently or by toehold acquisition, instead focusing on the possibility that Falstaff's rivals moderated their conduct because they perceived Falstaff a likely entrant in that region.[10]

The Supreme Court's most recent potential competition opinion is United States v. Marine Bancorporation, Inc.[11] There, the Government challenged a geographic market extension merger between banks on the grounds that the market of the acquired firm (a Spokane, Washington bank) was highly concentrated and that the acquiring firm (a Seattle bank) was a firm whose entry could reduce concentration. Because of regulatory restraints on banking, the Court found untenable an inference that the acquiring bank would enter the acquired bank's market if the merger were blocked. The Court also said that to succeed under the theory of future deconcentration, the Government must prove both the capability of independent (or toehold) entry and that such an entry is likely to produce deconcentration or other procompetitive effects.

The Government's lack of success in *Marine Bancorporation* foreshadowed similar failures in lower court cases.[12] The difficult evidentiary burdens placed upon the government in *Marine Bancorporation* and later cases may explain in part why enforcement against conglomerate

9. 410 U.S. 526, 93 S.Ct. 1096, 35 L.Ed.2d 475 (1973).

10. On remand the district court held that the Government had failed to carry its burden of proving that the entry by merger of Falstaff, "an on-the-fringe potential competitor" in the Northeast, "would probably lead to a substantial lessening of competition." United States v. Falstaff Brewing Corp., 383 F.Supp. 1020, 1028 (D.R.I.1974).

11. 418 U.S. 602, 94 S.Ct. 2856, 41 L.Ed.2d 978 (1974).

12. *E.g.,* Tenneco, Inc. v. FTC, 689 F.2d 346 (2d Cir.1982); BOC Int'l Ltd. v. FTC, 557 F.2d 24 (2d Cir.1977).

mergers slowed to a stop.[13] Yet, the Justice Department's 1982 Guidelines facilitated further potential competition enforcement by clearing away both the doctrinal clutter and unnecessary evidentiary burdens that surrounded these cases.[14] Because the Justice Department ignored any rationale other than potential competition for attacking conglomerate mergers, the 1982 Guidelines were also criticized for taking an unduly narrow approach.[15]

Despite constricting case law, the enforcement agencies continue to consider potential competition issues in merger enforcement. For example, a 1999 consent order involving a pharmaceutical firm's proposed acquisition of a rival raised these concerns because of threatened loss of potential competition in the market for local anesthetics, in which the acquired firm was a major player. The Commission addressed this matter through a consent order that required the acquiring firm, which was not a producer of local anesthetics, to divest its interests in a third firm (and cease cooperation with that firm) that was actively promoting the marketing of a new, long acting local anesthetic.[16]

11.3b.   The Potential Competition Doctrine

During the early years of the Sherman Act, economists saw potential competition as a force which severely limited the market power of firms, however large their market shares. Economists of that age thought that market power was largely the product of government grants and restrictions, such as patents, tariffs, and regulations limiting entry, which protected those in the market from further entry.[17] Government barriers to entry are still seen as a source of market power, but not the only source. No longer do we view the great reservoir of private capital as capable of flowing into any market where incumbents increase prices above competitive levels.

Some firms, although not competitors in a market, are potential entrants in that market. Their status as potential competitors may influence competition, now or in the future. It is this possibility that is the core of the potential competition doctrine. If a potential competitor attempts to merge with a strong incumbent firm in the industry, the doctrine may be invoked to prevent the loss of the potential competitor in that market. If, instead of acquiring the strong incumbent, the potential competitor acquired a small incumbent (toehold acquisition) or

13. *See generally*, Brodley, *Potential Competition Mergers: A Structural Synthesis*, 87 YALE L.J. 1 (1977).

14. Brodley, *Potential Competition Under the Merger Guidelines*, 71 CAL. L.REV. 376 (1983).

15. Bauer, *Government Enforcement Policy of Section 7 of the Clayton Act: Carte Blanche for Conglomerate Mergers?* 71 CAL. L.REV. 348 (1983).

16. Zeneca Group PLC, FTC Dkt. No. C–3880 (June 7, 1999) (consent order).

17. There is still isolated suppport for the turn of the century view. Demsetz, *Two Systems of Belief About Monopoly, in* INDUSTRIAL CONCENTRATION: THE NEW LEARNING 166 (Goldschmid, Mann & Weston eds., 1974). The author revises, restates and reasserts the classic view that unless government shields it, no firm can earn excessive profits without attracting new entry. Demsetz attempts to explain apparently adverse evidence gathered in empirical studies of relationships between concentration and profits.

entered the relevant market on its own (de novo entry), competition in the relevant market would presumably be invigorated.

In a sense, the potential competition doctrine (used to challenge a merger involving potential rivals) is the flip side of the ease of entry doctrine (used defensively in a horizontal merger). The potential competition doctrine is persuasively invoked when the market is oligopolistic and entry barriers are high. The ease of entry defense depends upon a showing that entry barriers are low.

11.3b1.   The Distinction Between Perceived and Actual Likely Entry

Economic theory and much of the case law in this area turns on whether a firm involved in a merger is *perceived to be a likely entrant into the relevant market*.[18] If this perception is widespread, firms in the industry will likely, so the theory goes, engage in limit pricing—they will charge lower prices so as not to give unnecessary inducement to a likely entrant to become a rival. Whether firms already in the market would actually engage in limit pricing has been questioned.[19] There is, however, some empirical evidence in support of limit pricing,[20] and even if consumers do not benefit significantly from limit pricing behavior as the result of a perceived entrant, the greater instability and uncertainty created by that potential entrant may add a valuable dynamic element to an otherwise stultified, oligopolistic market.

Regardless of whether a firm is perceived as an entrant, it might benefit competition if it actually entered the relevant market. This has led some lower courts to apply an *actual potential entrant* theory.[21] On this approach even if a firm were not perceived as likely to enter, evidence such as the firm's internal planning documents might show that it is likely to do so either by de novo entry or by a toehold acquisition. But the timing of such a showing is problematic. Such proof would have to be advanced at the time the actual potential entrant had changed its mind and, instead, chose to acquire a prominent player in the market. Moreover, as a practical matter, the supposed dichotomy between perceived entrant and a nonperceived but likely actual entrant seems unrealistic. If a firm is so involved with entry that it has been doing actual planning, it is probable that its affinities for the market in

18. This seems to have been the core of the policy concern underlying the potential competition doctrine in cases such as United States v. Falstaff Brewing Corp., 410 U.S. 526, 93 S.Ct. 1096, 35 L.Ed.2d 475 (1973) and FTC v. Procter & Gamble Co., 386 U.S. 568, 87 S.Ct. 1224, 18 L.Ed.2d 303 (1967).

19. *See* G. STIGLER, THE ORGANIZATION OF INDUSTRY 19–22 (1968)(arguing that limit pricing theory lacks explanatory power).

20. In his survey of economic arguments on limit pricing, Brodley cites several sources that report finding instances of limit pricing. Brodley, supra note 14, at 383–86, & n. 47. Evidence gathered from the

domestic airline industry suggests that any pricing discipline from potential entrants will not be as effective as head-to-head competition. *See* Peteraf & Reed, *Pricing and Performance in Monopoly Airline Markets*, 37 J. L. & ECON. 193 n.2 (1994)(citing a number of studies that concluded that head-to-head competition produced lower fares than potential competition).

21. Cases applying a potential competition theory include: Tenneco, Inc. v. FTC, 689 F.2d 346 (2d Cir.1982); United States v. Siemens Corp., 621 F.2d 499 (2d Cir.1980); FTC v. Atlantic Richfield Co., 549 F.2d 289 (4th Cir.1977).

question will be perceptible to its competitors, not solely to itself. The actual potential entrant doctrine has never been accepted by the Supreme Court and, because of difficult evidentiary hurdles adopted by the courts, seems moribund. It is, in any event, a doctrine that would rarely be needed if the perceived potential entrant approach is properly applied.

11.3b2. Determining Likely Entrants

The challenge in potential competition is identifying potential entrants. The most likely entrants into any market are those already in markets related to it by product, geographical or distributional affinities. These affinities are, of necessity, either horizontal or vertical in nature. For example, steelmakers, having no link to the bleach business, are less likely to enter it than detergent-makers, chemical companies, or grocery chains, each of which enjoys one or more horizontal or vertical affinities. Firms having some nexus with a market will be more aware of opportunities and more capable of conceptualizing and executing some means to exploit them successfully. Firms considering entry will likely choose a market in which they have information and expertise. The size and reputation of a firm may add to these affinities, making it easier for a firm to raise money on the capital market. One commentator has aptly labelled these factors "proximity."[22] The closer and stronger this proximity, the greater the likelihood that a firm will be perceived as a potential entrant in the relevant market.

11.3b3. The Future of the Potential Competition Doctrine

The doctrine of potential competition has fallen on hard times. Difficult evidentiary obstacles lay in the path of any plaintiff seeking to demonstrate that the loss of potential competition is a threat. Courts require evidence of the subjective mind-set of interested corporate officials to prove that a firm was perceived as a potential entrant and evidence that this perception disciplined the competitive behavior of incumbent firms. Each standard is difficult, if not impossible, to meet.[23]

Where an agency challenge was based on actual potential entry, the standards were, if anything, even more onerous. For example, in BOC International Ltd. v. FTC, the Second Circuit required an evidentiary showing that (1) but for the merger, the acquiring firm would have entered the market by de novo entry or toehold acquisition; and (2) that the alternative means of entry would have had procompetitive effects in the relevant market.[24] A few years later, that same court refused to enforce an FTC cease and desist order directed at a conglomerate merger despite high market shares, oligopolistic markets, and a strong showing of proximity. The court said that the FTC had not demonstrated that the acquiring firm had actually contemplated de novo entry into the relevant market.[25]

---

22. Brodley, supra note 14, at 391–92.

23. *Tenneco*, 689 F.2d at 358; *Siemens*, 621 F.2d at 509.

24. 557 F.2d 24, 26–27 (2d Cir.1977).

25. See Tenneco, Inc. v. FTC, 689 F.2d at 355–58.

One can sympathize with courts wanting stiff evidentiary burdens in the absence of a clear standard by which to separate likely from unlikely entrants.[26] But the evidentiary hurdles courts have erected virtually repeal the potential competition doctrine. The 1984 Guidelines suggest that a workable potential competition standard may lie in a two-step inquiry. The first step would be determining whether the market relevant to the merger inquiry is an oligopolistic one with substantial entry barriers. This will involve the same initial steps required for assessing a horizontal merger: defining a market, determining market shares, and assessing entry barriers. If the market is found not to be oligopolistic, the inquiry ceases—there is no likely competitive injury from a loss of potential competition. If the market is found to be oligopolistic, the second step is to measure the proximity to this market of the party to the merger that is not already in the market. Although proximity, as a measure of likelihood of entry, cannot be determined with the apparent precision of a concentration index, it is an objective standard, not dependent upon the subjective views of officers or employees of any particular firm. In cases such as *Procter & Gamble,* the courts seem not to have experienced great difficulty in assessing a firm's information, experience and structural affinities in entering a related market. Using a similar analytical approach, the Eighth Circuit upheld the FTC's challenge to a joint venture by a Japanese and U.S. firm, both producers of outboard motors for boats.[27]

The need for a well-reasoned rule for addressing potential competition issues is probably greater than ever. Potential competition is a major issue in addressing competition in markets for innovation, as addressed in § 13.5a1. Potential competition is also an issue to be addressed after innovation has occurred. Consider a pharmaceutical firm that holds the patent on an important new drug. In anticipation of expiration of the patent, rival firms may prepare to produce generic versions of the drug. If the patent-holding firm seeks to acquire one or more of these firms before the expiration of the patent, an important source of potential competition has been eliminated. Failure to address the potential competition issue could lead to substantial competitive injury to consumers forced to pay supracompetitive prices for the drug after expiration of the patent.

11.3c. Anticompetitive Effects Related to the Acquiring Firm's Large Size

Although the 1982 and 1984 Merger Guidelines recognize only potential competition as a basis for challenging a conglomerate merger, the Supreme Court has explored a number of other theories that are loosely based on the large size of the acquiring firm. Two such theories are examined here: (1) entrenchment; and (2) enhancing the price leadership or strategic power of a leading firm. Rather than evaluating

26. R. POSNER, ANTITRUST LAW: AN ECONOMIC PERSPECTIVE 122–23 (1976).

27. Yamaha Motor Co. v. FTC, 657 F.2d 971 (8th Cir.1981), *cert. denied,* 456 U.S. 915, 102 S.Ct. 1768, 72 L.Ed.2d 174 (1982).

loss of potential competition, these theories focus on likely adverse effects of a particular acquisition. A precondition for applying either theory is that a very large firm is acquiring a market-leading firm in the relevant market. These theories have usually been applied to market or product extension mergers, but could also be applied to a pure conglomerate transaction.[28]

11.3c1. Entrenchment

Courts have said that size disparity can injure competition by helping to entrench a dominant firm. In FTC v. Procter & Gamble Co.,[29] the acquired firm, Clorox, vastly outsold rivals in the bleach industry. The acquiring firm, Procter & Gamble, had a potential for offering efficiencies in marketing and promotion and had better access to capital markets than rival bleach firms, all of which would tend to discourage others from entering or challenging Clorox's dominance, once acquired by P & G. In consequence, the possibilities of future deconcentration were reduced, or so both the FTC and the Court concluded. The concern in this case centered on P & G's massive advertising budget, but entrenchment could occur for other reasons. The acquiring firm might offer research capacity, management skills, or scale efficiencies other than in advertising and capital accumulation.

The efficiencies that might be achieved in a case such as *Procter & Gamble* could be raised as a defense.[30] But if the entrenchment theory is limited to acquisitions of dominant or market-leading firms in an oligopolistic industry, efficiencies may not be passed on to consumers. A market-leading firm such as Clorox might absorb any efficiency gain as a supracompetitive profit—or spend it through x-inefficiencies or rent-seeking. The opinion in *Procter & Gamble* may be deficient to the extent that it fails to spell out this analysis, but on the facts before it the

---

28. Concern with this type of merger, signaled in cases such as FTC v. Procter & Gamble, 386 U.S. 568, 87 S.Ct. 1224, 18 L.Ed.2d 303 (1967), has been the focus of attention in other countries. The German legislature has amended that nation's antitrust law to create a presumption of anticompetitiveness for a large outside firm (with annual sales of DM 2 billion) from acquiring a firm with 5 percent or more of the market in which small or medium-sized firms have at least 2/3 of the total market share. Gesetz Gegen Wettbewerbsbeschränkungen § 23a(1)1. Note that such legislation has much in common with the congressional concern with protecting small business and resisting a trend toward concentration reflected in the Celler–Kefauver Act of 1950. But unlike the amorphous and difficult to confine incipiency doctrine voiced in *Brown Shoe*, the German law is more structured and targeted in its applica-

tion. This provision of the German law would not apply to horizontal acquisitions which would still be subject to more generalized restrictions of German competition law. Thus it would not forbid rivals merging to achieve economies of scale. The law also would not apply if 1/3 or more of the market share in the relevant industry is already in the hands of large firms. The policy justification for the German law could rest on, in addition to a desire to protect small business, concerns with entrenchment and enhanced strategic power originally voiced by the United States Supreme Court in *FTC v. Procter & Gamble*.

29. 386 U.S. 568, 87 S.Ct. 1224, 18 L.Ed.2d 303 (1967).

30. 1984 Merger Guidelines § 4.135 (indicating that the Department will consider efficiencies in a merger challenged under a potential competition theory).

Court's intuitive rejection of an efficiency defense may have been warranted.

11.3c2. Enhancing Price Leadership or Strategic Power

A concentrated market may perform collusively, interdependently or reasonably competitively. Interdependent conduct may not emerge in the absence of a recognized leader. If in such a market a firm with a large share is acquired by a large outside firm, the acquired firm will enhance its potential for price leadership in its market. Other circumstances may add to this potential. For example, if the outside firm participates in interdependent pricing in other markets, these propensities enhance the risk.

Price leadership alone may not produce an interdependent scheme of pricing. Often, more aggressive strategic moves must be taken to discipline rivals to adhere to an oligopolistic pricing pattern. A common tactic for disciplining a price-cutting rival is to respond with an even lower price that cuts the rival's profits. Such price wars can be sustained if they are relatively infrequent interruptions in longer periods of oligopolistic pricing. If all members of an oligopolistic industry suffer proportionately to their volume, they will all have roughly equal power to coerce others through strategic responses, making it less likely that oligopolistic price levels can be sustained in the face of a maverick that persists with its discounted pricing. But a market-leading firm may be positioned to target its price cuts to hurt a maverick seriously without sustaining substantial reductions in its own larger volume of sales. The keys to strategic power to discipline others are the ability to target price cuts in the maverick's market segment while cross-subsidizing the aggressor's reduced revenues through profits obtained in other segments. If a market leader lacks the ability to effect this cross-subsidization by itself, it may gain the needed additional backing if it is acquired by a large, outside firm. Bear in mind that it may never be necessary for the market-leading firm, under the umbrella of an even larger firm with substantial capital resources, to exercise its strategic powers. The power of that firm, apparent to its rivals, may be enough to deter any breach of price discipline. This in terrorem effect of large size may not only lessen price-cutting activity by rivals but may also deter new entry by firms that might have instilled renewed competition in the market.

The strategic power associated with a conglomerate merger could also lead to predatory pricing. Current case law on predatory pricing (discussed in Chapter IV) may leave little room for a plaintiff's success in a predatory pricing action. But proving a likely violation of predatory pricing law is not necessary to establish a violation of Section 7 of the Clayton Act. That requires only a showing that the merger may substantially reduce competition in the relevant market. A showing that the merger would increase the likelihood that strategic power would be used in ways leading to higher prices for consumers should suffice to establish a Section 7 violation, regardless of whether that likely conduct would constitute a predatory pricing violation.

Ford Motor Co. v. United States[31] also involved strategic power created or enhanced by a conglomerate merger in which the acquiring firm had domineering size. In that case, Ford sought to acquire one of three firms that produced spark plugs in the United States. Although the merger was analyzed as a vertical combination likely to have foreclosure effects, the in terrorem concerns could be seen lurking beneath the surface. A similar undertone is apparent in the Court's condemnation of a horizontal merger in United States v. Aluminum Co. of America.[32]

11.3c3. Reciprocity

Reciprocity—the agreement of two firms to purchase one another's products—may be condemned as a violation of Section 1 of the Sherman Act. See the discussion in § 8.5. That a merger creating a structure conducive to reciprocity can violate Section 7 of the Clayton Act was recognized in FTC v. Consolidated Foods.[33] Consolidated was vertically integrated, engaged in food processing, distribution, and retailing. After acquiring Gentry, a firm that manufactured processed onion and garlic, Consolidated began urging its suppliers of processed food to use Gentry as a source of onion and garlic products. Although the record showed postmerger reciprocity, the Court, in upholding the FTC finding of a Section 7 violation, declined to require such postmerger evidence; it was sufficient to show a probability of such future reciprocity practices.

The federal agencies have not used reciprocity as a ground for attacking a merger in more recent years. Like tying and other interbrand vertical restraints, reciprocity is anticompetitive only if it is forced. Courts have avoided condemning mergers on the basis that they might facilitate the use of interbrand distribution restraints (such as tie-ins) that could have beneficial as well as harmful effects, and should similarly avoid blanket condemnations of mergers that could result in some reciprocity. Although reciprocity may be difficult to detect after a merger (because it is an intrafirm matter), reciprocity is unlikely to work significant competitive harm. When there is a high risk that reciprocity generated by an acquisition will be harmful, the acquisition probably will involve other conditions (high market share and high entry barriers) that should allow corrective action by merger enforcers.

11.3d. The Merger Guidelines and Potential Competition

With the waning of the conglomeration movement in the 1960s and the Government's frequent failures in challenging conglomerate mergers, the incentive for attacking such mergers has also dissipated. The 1982 Merger Guidelines, which mentioned only potential competition as a ground for attacking such mergers, were seen as step toward eliminating conglomerate merger enforcement.[34] Yet those same Guidelines were

---

31. 405 U.S. 562, 92 S.Ct. 1142, 31 L.Ed.2d 492 (1972).

32. 377 U.S. 271, 84 S.Ct. 1283, 12 L.Ed.2d 314 (1964). See also the opinion of

Judge Burger in Reynolds Metals Co. v. FTC, 309 F.2d 223, 229–30 (D.C.Cir.1962).

33. 380 U.S. 902, 85 S.Ct. 881 (1965).

34. Bauer, supra note 15, at 350 (noting that the "practical result" of the 1982

welcomed as restoring a workable rule for asserting potential competition theories.[35]

The 1982 Guidelines treatment of potential competition was carried forward in the 1984 version, which is the most recent agency statement on the doctrine (the 1992 Guidelines deal only with horizontal mergers). The Guidelines' omission of theories other than potential competition deserves a mixed review. The entrenchment theory seems an inadequate basis, by itself, for attacking a merger. On the other hand, theories associated with the very large size of the acquiring firm (entrenchment and increasing strategic power) are legitimate concerns of an antitrust law that is aimed at power abuses. Particularly when entrenchment and enhancement of strategic power occur in tandem with a loss of potential competition, they are properly elements to be weighed in determining a merger's likely competitive effects.

Although the 1984 Guidelines mention both perceived and actual potential competition,[36] they properly treat the potential competition doctrine as a single concern addressed by assessing four factors: (1) the degree of concentration in the market of the acquired firm (the Department is more likely to challenge a merger if the HHI is above 1800)[37]; (2) the ease of entry into the market of the acquired firm (easy entry will usually negate a challenge to the merger)[38]; (3) the acquiring firm's entry advantage (if three or more other firms have an equivalent entry advantage, the Department is unlikely to challenge the merger)[39]; and (4) the market share of the acquired firm (the Department is unlikely to challenge a merger if the acquired firm has a market share of 5 percent or less, but is likely to challenge such a merger if other conditions are met and the acquired firm has a share of 20 percent or more).[40]

The Guidelines fail to define the term "entry advantage." As Professor Brodley has suggested, this term is best understood as a measure of the acquiring firm's proximity to the acquired firm's market—its information, expertise and ability to overcome entry barriers with respect to the acquired firm's market.[41] The other major shortcoming of these Guidelines is their failure to consider the dynamic element of competition. Mergers that raise issues of potential competition may impede dynamic competition that contributes new products and services as well as new methods of manufacture and distribution to our economy. Elimination of a potential competitor, just as elimination of an existing competitor, can undermine the pace of innovation or its commercialization. A merger analysis that accounts for dynamic efficiencies is discussed in § 11.2g.

Guidelines would be that most conglomerate acquisitions would be allowed).

35. Brodley, supra note 14, at 401.

36. 1984 Merger Guidelines, §§ 4.111, 4.112.

37. Id. § 4.131.

38. Id. § 4.132.

39. Id. § 4.133.

40. Id. § 4.134.

41. Brodley, supra note 14, at 389–401.

Chapter XII

VERTICAL MERGERS

Table of Sections

§ 12.1 Overview of Vertical Mergers

Vertical mergers involve the acquisition of a firm that can supply an input product (an upstream acquisition) or purchase an output product (a downstream acquisition). As in the case of horizontal mergers, the same result could occur through internal expansion—a firm could enter an upstream or downstream market without acquiring any existing participant in that market. Whether attained through internal expansion or through acquisition, the result is vertical integration—the integrated firm now operates on more than one level of the distribution system. The terms "forward" and "backward" integration are often used. A firm integrates forward when it initiates a downstream business or acquires a customer; it integrates backward when it initiates an upstream business or acquires a supplier.

Vertical mergers are subject to the same statutory enforcement provisions as any other merger (see § 9.1), but the competitive problems they raise are unique. Measured in terms of allocative efficiencies, vertical mergers may present less acute competitive risks than horizontal mergers. The risk of enhancing coordinated interaction or collusion is less obvious in vertical mergers for the simple reason that such mergers do not directly increase the level of concentration in either the upstream or downstream market. Although vertical mergers can still undercut efficient allocation and may represent a substantial risk to dynamic efficiency (see § 12.3b), during most of this century, vertical integration has not been a prime target of merger enforcement. A significant exception occurred during the enforcement era from the mid–1950s through the mid–1970s. The Celler–Kefauver Act of 1950 provided a mandate for attacking vertical mergers, although not a well-defined one.[1] In 1962, the Supreme Court in Brown Shoe Co. v. United States condemned both the horizontal and vertical aspects of a merger of firms involved in the manufacture and distribution of shoes.[2] The Court suggested that the amount of an upstream or downstream market foreclosed by a vertical merger was the starting point for analysis. The roughly 5 percent foreclosure in *Brown Shoe* was probably insufficient by itself to condemn the vertical aspects of this merger. The Court stressed that the shoe industry was in the midst of a trend toward concentration (horizontal) and integration (vertical) and cited the legislative history of the Celler–Kefauver Act suggesting that such trends were to be stopped in their incipiency.

The Department of Justice's 1968 Merger Guidelines followed. Retreating only modestly from the standard set in *Brown Shoe*, the Guidelines suggested presumptive illegality for an upstream firm with 10 percent of the market acquiring a downstream firm possessing 6 percent of its market.[3] Enforcement against vertical mergers was active—there were 27 federal antitrust complaints challenging vertical combinations between 1960 and 1970.[4] During this period, the major concern was with the foreclosure effect of a vertical merger: The consolidated firm would lock rivals out, preventing them from doing business, or doing business on nondiscriminatory terms, with the acquired upstream or downstream firm. In its most recent vertical merger case the Supreme Court in 1972 upheld the Government's challenge to Ford's acquisition of a spark plug manufacturer.[5] This merger of significant players in vertically related oligopolistic industries would have foreclosed 15 percent of the spark plug market.

After foreclosure theory came under vigorous attack from some theorists (see the discussion in § 12.2), lower courts began to show hostility to agency prosecutions of vertical cases. In Fruehauf Corp. v. FTC,[6] the Second Circuit rejected an FTC order condemning a combination of Fruehauf (the largest truck trailer manufacturer with 25 percent of the market) and Kelsey–Hayes (a manufacturer of heavy-duty truck and trailer wheels with 15 percent of the market). By 1982, when the second iteration of the Guidelines was issued, a substantial retreat

1. For a discussion of the Celler–Kefauver Amendment, see § 9.2c.

2. 370 U.S. 294, 82 S.Ct. 1502, 8 L.Ed.2d 510 (1962).

3. U.S. Department of Justice Merger Guidelines, §§ 12–13 (1968), reprinted in 4 Trade Reg.Rep. (CCH) ¶ 13,101.

4. Fisher & Sciacca, *An Economic Analysis of Vertical Merger Enforcement Policy,* 6 Res. L. & Econ. 1, 59 (1984).

5. Ford Motor Co. v. United States, 405 U.S. 562, 92 S.Ct. 1142, 31 L.Ed.2d 492 (1972).

6. 603 F.2d 345 (2d Cir.1979).

seemed in order. The 1982 Guidelines, changed only modestly in the 1984 revision, abandoned the broad foreclosure rationale and suggested that vertical mergers could be harmful only as the result of their horizontal effects. Three circumstances were described: (1) a vertical merger leaves relatively little unintegrated capacity in the secondary (upstream or downstream) market and simultaneous entry into the primary and secondary market is difficult; (2) a vertical merger facilitates collusion; or (3) a vertical merger allows a regulated firm to evade price regulation.[7] The 1992 joint agency guidelines did not address vertical restraints, so the 1984 Guidelines remain the most recent agency map for dealing with such mergers.

The federal agencies largely ignored vertical merger cases during the 1980s. There were isolated exceptions such as the FTC's challenge to the Goodrich–Diamond Shamrock merger in 1988 (there were horizontal as well as vertical aspects to this merger).[8] The pace of vertical claims picked up in the 1990s.[9] Because vertical enforcement initiatives were resolved through consent orders, the courts played no significant role in this revival. Noteworthy government initiatives included a Justice Department consent order arising out of the investigation of AT & T's acquisition of McCaw, a cellular phone company with franchises nationwide. The order permitted the merger, but sought to limit the interaction between the consolidated companies to ensure against foreclosure effects and to preclude misuse of proprietary information obtained by McCaw through its dealings with AT & T's equipment supplier competitors or obtained by AT & T through its dealings with McCaw's equipment-buying competitors.[10] Another prominent consent resolution was obtained by the FTC in connection with Time Warner's acquisition of Turner Broadcasting, addressing both horizontal and vertical aspects of the combination.[11]

Since the adoption of the 1984 Guidelines, economic literature has provided additional theory as to how vertical mergers can create anticompetitive results.[12] But the root of the controversy surrounding vertical integration boils down to several key questions. Will vertical mergers

---

7. U.S. Department of Justice Merger Guidelines § 4 (1984), reprinted in 4 Trade Reg. Rep. (CCH) ¶ 13,101. The non-horizontal provisions of the 1984 Guidelines are available at <http://www. usdoj.gov/atr/ public/ guidelines/2614.htm>.

8. In the Matter of the B.F. Goodrich Co., 110 F.T.C. 207 (March 15, 1988). During the 1980s, the Justice Department challenged a proposed combination of Showtime and The Movie Channel with a number of film distributors. Again there were horizontal as well as vertical aspects to this combination.

9. Among the agency challenges in the 1990s to mergers involving vertical aspects were: Cadence Design Systems, Inc., FTC No. C–3761 (Aug. 7, 1997); The Boeing Co., FTC No. C–3723 (March 5, 1997); Silicon Graphics, Inc., FTC No. C–3626 (Nov. 14, 1995); Alliant Techsystems, Inc., No. 941–0123 (Nov. 15, 1994); Eli Lilly & Co., No. 941–0102 (Nov. 3, 1994); Martin Marietta Corp., FTC No. C–3500 (June 22, 1994)(Comm'r Owen dissenting); United States v. Tele–Communications, Inc., 1996–2 Trade Cas. (CCH) ¶ 71496 (D.D.C.1994).

10. United States v. AT & T Corp., 59 Fed. Reg. 44,158 (Aug. 26, 1994). See § 12.3b3, infra.

11. Timer Warner Inc., 61 Fed. Reg. 50301 (1996) (proposed consent), 62 Fed. Reg. 11202 (1997) (consent order).

12. Riordan & Salop, *Evaluating Vertical Mergers: A Post–Chicago Approach,* 63 ANTITRUST L. J. 513 (1995).

bring substantial efficiency gains as a matter of course, or are possible inefficiencies associated with vertical integration likely to offset them? Under what circumstances might such mergers create market power that produces anticompetitive injury? Even if vertical mergers are unlikely to create short-term allocative injury, will some of them undermine dynamic efficiency in a manner that undermines technological progress and new or improved methods of distribution?

There seems little doubt that a particular vertical merger can produce procompetitive benefits, anticompetitive injury, or both results. But motivation for vertical integration may be neither procompetitive nor anticompetitive gains. Vertical mergers can be a defensive step taken by a firm that fears more difficult access to suppliers or customers. For example, a firm that fears that its rivals will acquire key suppliers or customers may decide to integrate vertically to forestall this result, not because it believes such integration will be more efficient or produce anticompetitive gains. Or a vertical merger might be undertaken because it was thought to be a sound investment of the firm's resources—perhaps for the same reasons that a pure conglomerate merger is undertaken. A vertical merger may be more attractive to some firms than a purely conglomerate merger because the acquiring firm has some familiarity with the business it is entering. Whatever the motivation, not all vertical acquisitions benefit the firms involved. Vertical integration can be inefficient. For example, a supplier considering integrating forward into retailing may have difficulty offering a full range of diverse brands and, without that range, may have difficulty attracting customers to the store.

§ 12.2   The Chicago Critique of Vertical Enforcement

The foreclosure concern that dominated enforcement initiatives against vertical mergers in the 1960s can easily be overdrawn.[1] Foreclosure of a rival is not an inevitable consequence of a vertical merger. If the upstream and downstream market include a sufficient number of unintegrated rivals, vertical integration of a few market participants, perhaps involving as much as one third of the upstream or downstream market, may cause no significant competitive harm. But neither is this concern frivolous. If a monopolist acquires an upstream or downstream firm, the combination can create immediate problems for competitors of the acquired firm. For example, if a monopolist acquires a supplier, competitors of that supplier may be denied access to the monopolist, or may be forced to deal with the monopolist on less favorable terms. Similarly, if the monopolist acquires a distributor, other distributors may find their supply cut off, or may be forced to procure it at less favorable terms.

---

§ 12.2

1. The limitations of foreclosure theory were, for example, addressed in L. Sullivan,

Handbook of the Law of Antitrust § 210 (1977).

But harm to individual firms (upstream or downstream rivals of the firm acquired by the monopolist) would not necessarily bring harm to consumers. If the acquiring firm was already a monopolist or monopsonist, Chicago theory questioned whether it could attain any additional power by integrating vertically.[2] There is but one monopoly profit to be garnered from a monopoly, these theorists argue, and that profit could not be expanded by the vertical merger of the monopolist with an upstream supplier or downstream distributor. Although the monopolist's rivals might be foreclosed from access to the upstream supplier or downstream distributor, the net amount of trade foreclosed was likely to equal that placed back in play (because the monopolist's exclusive use of the merged firm's output or demand released third party suppliers or distributors that had formerly done business with the monopolist). At most, a realignment of supplier and distributor relationships is required.

Chicago theory also stressed that vertical integration could be an efficient method for dealing with successive monopolists. If an input supplier and its output producing customer each possess market power, each may impose a supracompetitive mark-up so that the consumer may end up paying a price for the output that exceeds the price of an integrated monopolist. Vertical integration of these successive monopolists could result in a lower consumer price because the integrated seller would not price above monopoly level (lest it lose more revenue from lost sales than it gains from imposing a higher price).[3]

Finally, Chicago theory stressed that communication was necessary between suppliers and customers, particularly when the products or services involved highly complex technologies. Vertical integration was seen as an efficient way of enhancing this communication. This led some theorists to conclude that vertical integration was likely to be driven by efficiencies as a matter of course, and perhaps far more than horizontal acquisitions.

These insights were useful in reassessing a vertical merger policy of the 1960s, one that presumed illegality for any significant vertical integration. But if prior applications of vertical theory went too far, so too did the Chicago critique of those applications. The conclusion that a monopolist's power cannot be extended through vertical integration is limited by its assumptions—for example, that a pure monopoly exists in one market, and that workable competition exists in the upstream or downstream market (keeping price at or near marginal cost). These conditions are seldom met in vertical mergers, where one or both of the

2. The Chicago thesis that vertical integration could allow a monopolist to redistribute but not to increase monopoly profits is also relevant to claims of leveraged monopoly (§ 3.4b1) and upstream power distribution restraints (§ 8.3c1). Robert Bork was among the most prominent critiques of vertical foreclosure theory. R. Bork, The Antitrust Paradox: A Policy at War with Itself 225 (1978); Bork et al., *The Goals of Antitrust: A Dialogue on Policy,* 65 Colum.

L. Rev. 363 (1965). For a more recent defense of the Chicago critique of foreclosure theory, see Reiffen & Vita, *Comment: Is There New Thinking on Vertical Mergers?,* 63 Antitrust L. J. 917 (1995).

3. This theory is described in Riordan & Salop, *Evaluating Vertical Mergers: A Post–Chicago Approach,* 63 Antitrust L. J. 513, 526 (1995).

markets may be oligopolistic. If the acquiring firm's power is the limited power of an oligopolist (not the full power predicted by the theoretical model of monopoly), vertical integration may, for reasons addressed in § 12.3b, add to that oligopoly power or make it easier to exploit that power. The conclusion that vertical integration will result in lowering the price by integrating successive monopolists also seems highly questionable when applied to real market conditions, where few market players enjoy the power of the pure monopolist.

Perhaps the most critical deficiency in Chicago theory toward vertical integration is its focus on a static analysis of price effects. If the vertical merger does not immediately create market power that enables a firm to limit output or raise price, the merger is assumed to have no significant anticompetitive effects. This pays insufficient attention to the possibility that vertical integration makes the introduction of technological change or new marketing methods more difficult. Chicago theory addressed dynamic efficiency by arguing that vertical integration can improve communication between upstream and downstream players, leading to better coordination of new competitive initiatives. But it is likely that much of this improved communication might be achieved through means short of consolidation, such as long-term contractual relationships that provide for the sharing of technology. The availability of computers and electronic methods of communication makes it much easier for unintegrated customers and suppliers, even those on opposite sides of the world, to exchange technological information that can lead to coordinated development of new products and processes.

During his tenure as chief of the Antitrust Division of the Justice Department, Professor Baxter was a leading advocate of the relatively benign or even procompetitive effects of most vertical and conglomerate mergers. To illustrate his point, Baxter said that there was no reason to fear a world in which all of the productive assets were owned by only one hundred corporations, as long as each firm controlled only one-percent of each market for goods or services.[4] Under the 1992 Horizontal Merger Guidelines, one can extrapolate that even a world consisting of as few as 5 megafirms, each with 20 percent of every product and service market, would be tolerated.[5] However unattractive this vision may seem, the point was presumably that allocation of resources could proceed on a highly competitive basis as long as the requisite horizontal separation of market players was maintained in all markets.

Professor Baxter's example runs roughshod over a number of traditional values that underlay the Sherman Act. In particular, its focus on static, allocative efficiency leaves unaddressed the important dynamic

---

4. Interview with William F. Baxter, Dun's Review 38 (Aug. 1981) ("There is nothing written in the sky that says the world would not be a perfectly satisfactory place if there were only 100 companies, provided that each one had 1% of every product and service market").

5. Under the Guidelines, each industry would have an HHI of 2000. 1992 Merger Guidelines § 1.5. Although challenges to mergers that create HHIs above the 1200 range are foreseen, in practice the enforcement agencies have seldom intervened in cases in which the post-merger HHI is below 2000.

element of competition that produces innovation and technological progress. There is considerable evidence that large corporations are less flexible in dealing with changing market conditions. As one business expert puts it, large firms appear to make "fewer but bigger errors, tend to continue wrong policies too long, and have the resources to delay until crisis is unmistakable."[6] The difficulty of the U.S. automobile industry in adjusting to foreign competition after 1960 corroborates this insight. See § 12.3a.

The legacy of the Chicago critique of vertical merger enforcement has been constructive to the extent it raised awareness of potential efficiencies in some vertical integration and by demonstrating some of the limitations of foreclosure analysis. But the efficiencies in vertical integration are easily overstated and many can be obtained by other means. See § 12.3a. Although there has been a steady flow of vertical mergers over the past century, there has apparently been an equally strong pattern of divestitures in which vertical integration is abandoned, a pattern that suggests that efficiencies related to vertical integration are either insignificant or are offset by countervailing inefficiencies.

§ 12.3   Benefits and Costs of Vertical Integration

12.3a.   The Efficiencies and Inefficiencies of Vertical Integration

It is widely accepted that vertical integration can produce efficiencies. If one assumes that the market controls decisions to vertically integrate, it follows that a firm will integrate whenever it is likely to achieve some gain—when vertical integration is more efficient than relying on other market mechanisms to supply inputs or distribute output.[1] A firm that owns its suppliers and distribution outlets may be able to operate more efficiently because it has an assured source of supply or regular and certain distribution outlets. Controlling both the upstream and downstream flow, the firm may face fewer business uncertainties and be in a better position to plan future investments and growth. An unintegrated firm may incur bargaining costs to ensure the reliable flow from suppliers to distributors, or because it must hedge against disruptions in this flow.

A strong case for efficiency benefits of vertical integration may occur when a firm needs a specialty product that is not already available on

---

6. Corporate Takeovers: Hearings Before the Subcomm. on Telecommunications, Consumer Protection and Finance of the House Comm. on Energy and Commerce Concerning Corporate Takeovers, (Pt. 1), 99th Cong., 1st Sess. 259 (1986)(statement of Professor Warren Law, Harvard Business School).

§ 12.3

1. The notion that a vertically integrated firm may operate more efficiently than

the existing market mechanism is usually traced to Coase, The Nature of the Firm, 4 *Economica* 386 (1937). More recently, the transactional costs of market transactions has been developed in the work of Professor Williamson. See O. WILLIAMSON, MARKETS AND HIERARCHIES: ANALYSIS AND ANTITRUST IMPLICATIONS (1975).

the market. For example, if a producer of a space shuttle needs a computer suited for onboard use, no such product may be readily available on the market. One solution is to contract with an existing computer producer to design and manufacture such a computer. But the costs of supervising and controlling the design and production of such a computer could be high. For example, the drafting of a detailed contract specifying the requirements for the computer may be costly. Interpreting and enforcing that contract will add to that cost.[2] A related point is that the flow of information between two independent firms in a vertical relationship may be restrained—one or both firms may be reluctant to disclose trade secrets or other confidential information. Once the two firms are merged, the door should be open to the free flow of information between the upstream and downstream divisions.[3]

The space shuttle producer will opt for vertical integration only if these efficiencies are likely to outweigh the inefficiencies inherent in such integration. If there are substantial scope economies involved in becoming a designer and producer of computers, i.e., if computer design and production is efficient only if a market player carries a full-line of computers, the space shuttle producer will face substantial additional capital risk in entering the computer business. Moreover, the exchange of information no longer requires, if it ever did, a vertically integrated company. Although face to face meetings and exchanges can still be more advantageous, detailed, on-going communication between firms in a customer-supplier relationship is easier than ever before thanks to computers and electronic communication methods.

The considerations that influence a space shuttle producer in determining whether upstream or backward vertical integration is an efficient choice are similar to those that apply to any producer considering downstream or forward vertical integration. Consider a newspaper publisher that wishes to control its own distribution. As in the case of backward integration, forward integration is more likely to be attractive if the downstream business does not have significant economies of scope. If a distributor, in order to be efficient, must carry a full line of newspapers and magazines, then substantial scope economies are present that may deter the newspaper publisher from attempting forward integration. If, on the other hand, a newspaper distributor can operate efficiently when selling only the publisher's newspaper, then scope economies are less of a factor and the publisher may more readily contemplate forward vertical integration.

If economies of scope require a distributor to sell a full line of magazines and newspapers, the publisher might still consider forward integration by acquiring one or more existing full-line distributors that

---

2. Hovenkamp offers a summary of these and other potential efficiencies of vertical integration. H. HOVENKAMP, FEDERAL ANTITRUST POLICY: THE LAW OF COMPETITION AND ITS PRACTICE § 9.2b (3d ed.2005).

3. Arrow, *Vertical Integration and Communication*, in 4 COLLECTED PAPERS OF KENNETH J. ARROW 185 (1984); Jorde & Teece, *Innovation and Cooperation: Implications for Competition and Antitrust*, 4 J. ECON. PERSP. 75 (1990).

have already achieved economies of scope. But even forward integration by acquisition may be inefficient if management of a full-line distributorship creates conflicts of interest in dealing with other publishers that sell through the full-line distributor. These outside publishers may withdraw their business if the distributor is acquired by a rival publisher. There may also be management or labor problems associated with forward vertical integration.

The probability that vertical integration does not usually produce a substantial net gain in efficiencies that could not be attained by other less competitively threatening means suggests that other motives drive much vertical integration. The acquiring firm may choose vertical integration simply because the acquired company was underpriced and a sound investment, a circumstance that, by itself, does not raise antitrust issues. But any instance of vertical integration, regardless of its motivation, may raise antitrust issues if the integration contributes to a more rigid distribution system that tends to stifle innovation and change. And some motivations for vertical integration directly raise more traditional competition issues. A firm may integrate vertically because of a trend toward vertical integration that might imperil access to suppliers or distribution outlets, notwithstanding the inefficiencies associated with that integration. Finally, vertical integration may be driven in some instances by the expected financial gain from an ability to develop or exploit market power. These anticompetitive effects of some vertical integration are explored in § 12.3b.

The empirical evidence suggests that while efficiencies may favor vertical integration in some industries, that circumstance is by no means universal. Some industries (such as petroleum) are highly integrated vertically. For a refinery to own oil fields or engage in exploration may be efficient because, despite the obvious scale economies in the petroleum business, there may be few economies of scope involved in oil exploration and production. A refinery-owned oil field does not need to produce other products in order to be efficient.

Other industries, such as the glass bottle-manufacturing industry, show little integration,[4] perhaps because their major raw material (sand) is easily available. One indication that vertical integration may not be uniformly efficient is that despite a relaxed antitrust policy toward vertical integration during most of the century, there has apparently been no clear trend toward additional vertical integration in the United States over the past fifty years.[5]

The automobile industry provides a further instructive lesson on the efficiency claims for vertical integration. U.S. automobile producers tended to be vertically integrated through much of the twentieth century, with General Motors leading the way through its Fisher Body Division that produced parts for GM automobiles. But by the 1960s,

---

4. F.M. Scherer & D. Ross, Industrial Market Structure and Economic Performance 95 (3d ed. 1990).

5. Id. at 95–96.

Japanese automobile producers were operating with greater efficiency and with far less vertical integration, forcing U.S. producers to change their tactics. One of General Motors problems may well have been the inability of the firm to turn quickly to other suppliers when its inhouse production proved inefficient or of poor quality.[6] General Motors owed loyalty to the diverse levels of its elephantine organization, a loyalty that could hamper its ability to respond flexibly and quickly to a new world order. When the shift to independent suppliers came, the necessary exchange of technological information between producers and suppliers apparently continued. The Ford Motor Company, for example, used specially designed software programs to foster the exchange of design information with its suppliers.[7] GM, for many years the least efficient U.S. producer, finally followed suit when it announced plans to divest the Fisher Body Division operations in 1998. The stated reason for the divestiture was to allow GM more freedom in choosing suppliers and to allow Fisher Body greater opportunities to sell parts to other automobile manufacturers that would have been reluctant to deal with a GM-owned subsidiary. Although not publicly stated, labor relations may also have influenced the divestiture decision. As long as GM owned its parts suppliers, GM was subject to pressure from the union to purchase only through the GM-owned and unionized parts suppliers. The union's leverage over the choice of supplier might be reduced once GM no longer owns any suppliers.

None of this suggests that there cannot be substantial efficiencies in individual vertical mergers. It does tend to negate any blanket assumption that all vertical mergers generate substantial efficiencies, or that vertical integration is the only way of obtaining certain efficiencies. If, as seems likely, the potential for economic efficiency in vertical integration has been overstated in much of the literature, antitrust enforcement against vertical mergers poses relatively few risks of producing anticompetitive results. On the other hand, even if proactive merger enforcement against vertical mergers poses relatively few risks of thwarting efficiencies, such aggressive enforcement is still wasteful if it prevents vertical mergers that do not present genuine anticompetitive risks. The potential anticompetitive risks of vertical mergers are addressed in the following section.

12.3b. The Potential Anticompetitive Effects of Vertical Integration

Despite the criticism directed at traditional foreclosure theory, it remains a valid antitrust concern when the degree of foreclosure in an

---

6. For some of the possible reasons for General Motors inflexibility in dealing with changing conditions see id. at 105–06. The authors suggest that Ford responded more quickly than General Motors to foreign competition in part because Ford accomplished its vertical disintegration more rapidly. Id. at 370.

7. The hardware and software used to share design information is described in Virtual Maintenance, Inc. v. Prime Computer, Inc., 957 F.2d 1318 (6th Cir.1992), vacated, 506 U.S. 910, 113 S.Ct. 314, 121 L.Ed.2d 235 (1992), *amended* 11 F.3d 660 (6th Cir. 1993), *cert. dismissed*, 512 U.S. 1216, 114 S.Ct. 2700, 129 L.Ed.2d 829 (1994).

upstream or downstream market is substantial. A number of supplementary or additional theories provide explanations as to how a vertical merger that involves a substantial percentage of an upstream or downstream market may give rise to anticompetitive injury: (1) the merger may facilitate price discrimination that raises rivals, costs; (2) the merger may facilitate cooperative interaction or collusion at the upstream or downstream levels; (3) the merger may allow a regulated entity to evade regulation; or (4) the merger may force potential entrants to make a difficult, dual-level entry. After reviewing traditional foreclosure theory, each of these variations are described below.

12.3b1. Substantial Foreclosure

Although the limitations of foreclosure theory have been pointed out (see the discussion in § 12.2), foreclosure remains a primary concern in vertical merger analysis. In most harmful vertical mergers, it is not true monopoly power that is leveraged, but oligopoly power that is extended. If merging parties possess a large market share in an upstream or downstream secondary market, the result may be increased costs to rivals in the primary market that need access to these secondary markets. Foreclosure may raise entry barriers in the primary market because of the difficulty in obtaining access to supply or distribution, or because supply or distribution is available only on unfavorably discriminatory terms.

The risk of anticompetitive injury flowing from a vertical foreclosure is greater when premerger barriers to entry in the secondary market are high. Thus, if a large automobile producer acquires the largest tire manufacturer (with 1/3 of the total tire market), the risk of anticompetitive injury increases if entry into the tire market is difficult. But some of the anticompetitive consequences of vertical mergers may still occur notwithstanding relatively low entry barriers in the tire market. The mere foreclosure or threatened foreclosure of rival automobile producers may drive them to similar vertical integration even in situations in which vertical integration is not an efficient choice. As vertical integration increases in an industry, flexibility and the dynamic element of competition may be undercut.

A modern application of foreclosure theory was the Federal Trade Commission's consent order that imposed conditions on Time Warner's acquisition of Turner Broadcasting.[8] There were three firms involved in this acquisition because Tele–Communications, Inc. (TCI) owned a 24 percent interest in Turner that would be converted into a significant ownership share in Time Warner after the acquisition. The Commission's consent order addressed two relevant markets: (1) cable television programming and (2) cable television distribution. After the acquisition,

---

8. Time Warner, Inc., 61 Fed. Reg. 50301 (1996). See the Separate Statement of Chairman Pitofsky and Commissioners Steiger and Varney, citing Ash Grove Cement Co. v. FTC, 577 F.2d 1368 (9th Cir. 1978), cert. denied, 439 U.S. 982, 99 S.Ct. 571, 58 L.Ed.2d 653 (1978); Mississippi River Corp. v. FTC, 454 F.2d 1083 (8th Cir. 1972); United States Steel Corp. v. FTC, 426 F.2d 592 (6th Cir.1970).

Time Warner alone would control more than 40 percent of programming assets. For cable distribution, the combination of Time Warner and TCI would control about 44 percent of all cable television households. The Commission was concerned about foreclosure in both directions. Providers of programming might have more difficulty obtaining adequate distribution of their programming through cable and direct satellite broadcast outlets. Time Warner and TCI's control of 44% of cable households was of substantial concern because a new programmer, in order to achieve adequate economies of scale, was said to require access to 40 to 60 percent of all subscribers.[9] After the acquisition, Time Warner (and TCI) would have an incentive to protect their existing programs by denying new programmers access to their distribution network. In the other direction, distributors of television programming (including both cable and direct satellite providers) might be given less favorable terms in obtaining access to Time Warner or TCI programming.

The concern with foreclosure was heightened in Time Warner because potential entrants in either the programming or distribution markets might be forced to undertake a difficult dual entry. See the discussion of dual entry in § 12.3b65 Entry into the programming market by itself might be possible for firms possessing the capital and expertise, but obtaining distribution could be far more difficult. Some cable systems may have a limited number of available channels, increasing the barriers confronting a new entrant. And, although a programming entrant might wish to simultaneously enter the distribution market, as long as cable systems remained local monopolies, the only realistic option might be entry by acquisition of an existing cable distributor. Time Warner and TCI already served 44 percent of all cable households, so acquisition opportunities would be limited. New delivery systems, such as direct satellite broadcast, were more expensive to consumers and had yet to gain substantial market shares against cable providers.

12.3b2. *Facilitating Price Discrimination*

One result of a vertical merger involving a firm with market power in the primary market is an enhanced ability to foster discrimination harmful to rivals in the secondary market. For example, if a manufacturer-monopolist acquires a critical distributor, it can charge a lower price to the acquired distributor, while selling to other distributors at a monopoly price. Or a manufacturer-oligopolist may acquire a critical supplier in an oligopolistic supply industry, after which the supplier might institute discriminatory pricing favorable to the manufacturer and unfavorable to rival manufacturers that may be unaware of the discrimination. By itself, these results might produce neither benefits nor detriments to consumers because the consumer price for end products might remain unchanged in the short term. Under this result, there

---

9. Separate Statement, supra note 8.

would be no short-term allocative injury to competition. But these mergers could allow the favored firm to muscle rivals out of the market, raise entry barriers, and undercut the flow of innovative products, services, and methods of production or distribution.

As the above examples suggest, price discrimination may be more easily facilitated if a vertical merger involves oligopoly at one or both levels. If a large automobile producer acquires a large tire manufacturer, and both industries are oligopolistic, the newly integrated firm may refuse to sell tires to rival car manufacturers. Other tire manufacturers could fill this vacuum. But if, instead of refusing to sell to the rival car manufacturers, the integrated firm simply raises the price of tires sold to other manufacturers, the integrated firm may effectively implement a price discrimination, charging rival car manufacturers a higher price than it charges itself. The consolidated firm can maintain this discriminatory pricing only if the price to other automobile manufacturers is followed by other tire manufacturers. But this condition may be met. Because the tire industry is oligopolistic and subject to price leadership, a higher tire price initiated by the integrated tire company may be followed by other tire manufacturers. If so, rival automobile manufacturers are now faced with higher costs. Misallocations may occur to the extent that the tire prices are supracompetitive. The merged firm's lower automobile manufacturing costs (because it pays less for tires) may not be passed on to consumers if the automobile industry is also oligopolistic. The combination of oligopolistic conditions in the tire industry and the merged firm's incentive to discriminate would allow it to raise rival automobile manufacturers' costs and exercise leverage in the automobile industry.[10]

Of course, rival automobile manufacturers may respond by vertically integrating themselves. In this instance, the follow-on vertical integration appears not to be prompted by efficiencies but by a desire to avoid discriminatory treatment by oligopolistic sellers. Given the concentrated state of both the tire and automobile industries, additional vertical integration probably poses a high risk to dynamic efficiency because it increases the risk of parallel, market-closing conduct and reduces the channels through which new technology and products can be commercialized.

In its consent order addressing the Time Warner acquisition of Turner Broadcasting, the Federal Trade Commission expressly prohibited Time Warner from price discrimination in the sale of cable television programming to rival cable television distributors.[11] The Commission was concerned not only with discrimination against existing cable outlets, but also against firms using other methods of distributing television programming (such as direct broadcast satellite networks).[12]

---

10.   Riordan & Salop, *Evaluating Vertical Mergers: A Post–Chicago Approach,* 63 ANTITRUST L. J. 513 (1995).

11.   Time Warner Inc., et al., supra note 8.

12.   Separate Statement, supra note 8.

12.3b3.   Facilitating Collusion or Cooperative Interaction

A vertical merger may also facilitate price collusion. Using a merger of a large tire firm and a large automobile firm as an example, assume that after the merger the merged company must still solicit bids for tires from outside tire manufacturers. All information about the bids received is then passed on to its tire division, allowing it to see the competitive bidding practices of rival tire manufacturers. This information may be used by the tire division to orchestrate collusive practices among tire manufacturers, or it may be used less overtly to pursue parallel pricing practices. Without the merger, automobile companies soliciting tire bids would have no incentive to share such bidding information with any tire manufacturer, nor would tire manufacturers themselves normally share such information with their rivals (a sharing that might constitute horizontal collusion).

Such a merger can also provide the vertically integrated firm access to confidential information of its rivals. If the large tire manufacturer acquired by the automobile producer is an important supplier of other competing automakers, it will likely pick up in its dealings with such automakers sensitive information about their competitive plans–for example, what their production goals are for various classes of vehicles in the next year. This information could be passed on to the automobile producer with which the tire manufacturer is now integrated.

12.3b4.   Facilitating the Evasion of Price Regulation

Vertical integration may provide a means for the merged company to evade regulation of prices. Prior to 1982, AT & T was an integrated supplier of local telephone services and telephone equipment, including phones and switchboards for customer use and a major portion of the hardware used in the telephone network (cables, switching machines, etc.). Local telephone rates were regulated by utility commissions to maintain reasonable levels. Long-distance rates were regulated by the Federal Communications Commission. But AT & T was generally permitted to set a rate that allowed a minimum return on investment. If AT & T raised the transfer price on manufactured telephone equipment such as cables and switching machines, regulators might find it difficult to second-guess this transfer pricing and maintain competitive discipline on AT & T's purchases and, ultimately, on telephone rates themselves. In the absence of vertical integration, the market would presumably determine the price of these inputs, providing the regulatory body an indication of true cost (and protecting the public against overcharges).

A vertical merger could also facilitate price discrimination that is prohibited by regulation. One of the purposes of regulatory schemes may be to ensure that rates are nondiscriminatory—available to all comers on equal terms. If a regulated entity acquires one of its major customers, the regulated entity may be able to subsidize the operations of that customer in various ways, evading regulations designed to ensure that equal prices are paid by all customers. The cost of these subsidies may be passed on to consumers who pay for the regulated service. Allocative injuries would follow. Increased barriers to entry could stifle innovation or its commercialization.

12.3b5. *High Entry Barriers in the Secondary Market*

A variation on the foreclosure doctrine can occur when a vertical merger forecloses access to suppliers or distributors in a manner that requires new entrants in the primary market to enter both markets simultaneously. Such a result is likely if, as a result of the merger and previously occurring vertical integration, there is insufficient independently owned capacity at either level to allow a new entrant to obtain necessary supplies or outlets. If entry in the secondary market is easy, the anticompetitive effect of the vertical merger may be minimal. On the other hand, if entry into the secondary market requires a firm to generate substantial additional capital or expertise, or overcome regulatory or licensing hurdles, the anticompetitive effect could be substantial. The combination of foreclosure effect and high entry barriers can create substantial market power in the primary market. These circumstances appear to fit the Time Warner acquisition of Turner Broadcasting addressed in an FTC consent order. See the discussion of Time Warner in § 12.3b1.

High entry barriers are also a substantial concern when consideration is given to dynamic efficiency. Participants in a concentrated industry may be lethargic when it comes to spending resources on innovation. Or they may tacitly or overtly conspire to block or slow the commercialization of new products or processes that would substantially enhance consumer welfare.

12.3c. **Relevance of a Trend Toward Vertical Integration**

The legislative history underlying the Celler–Kefauver Act documented a concern with rising concentration and vertical integration among U.S. firms. The concern with halting such trends in their incipiency appeared of controlling proportion in a decision such as *Brown Shoe*,[13] but seems to have all but disappeared from the antitrust decision-making calculus. For horizontal mergers, an incipiency doctrine is defensible when based on pro-competitive goals of antitrust enforcement (see the discussion in § 11.2f). Incipiency does not warrant trying to stop a trend when each merger is efficiency justified.

Similar concerns can be raised with an incipiency doctrine wielded without reference to the other substantive goals of vertical merger enforcement. However legitimate the congressional concern with rising vertical integration, it was stated amorphously, without the benefit of clear analytical vision of how vertical merger enforcement was to proceed. Moreover, as discussed in § 12.3a, the factual premise may simply

---

13. Brown Shoe Co. v. United States, 370 U.S. 294, 82 S.Ct. 1502, 8 L.Ed.2d 510 (1962).

be false: There does not appear to be a trend toward increased vertical integration across the board. Such trends may be occurring, however, in various regulated industries such as telecommunications and cable television. Moreover, if the efficiencies inherent in vertical mergers are likely to be less substantial than those arising from horizontal mergers (see § 12.3a), then the motivation for vertical combinations must lie elsewhere—perhaps in the anticompetitive gains that merging parties hope to reap.

If the case for an incipiency doctrine is somewhat stronger in the vertical context, it is still a doctrine that must be applied in a principled fashion. As the result in *Brown Shoe* may suggest, even the smallest and least problematic vertical merger might be unlawful if the doctrine were broadly invoked. Even if vertical integration does not offer substantial efficiencies for most market players, such efficiencies may exist in individual cases. And if vertical integration has been demonstrated to be efficient in a particular industry, one would expect a trend toward concentration in that industry.

The concern with stopping a trend toward integration in its incipiency seems rational if such a trend is driven not by efficiencies, but by likely anticompetitive gains or by defensive mergers undertaken to assure that supply and outlet channels are not foreclosed by rivals undertaking similar mergers. When a wave of vertically integrating mergers begins, as for example in the health care industry in the 1990s, the participants may be acting out of fear—fear of facing higher costs because market options are foreclosed or rivals have discriminatory buying power—far more than any well-grounded belief that operations may be more efficient. If these facts were clear, stopping such a merger wave "in its incipiency" may be sound antitrust policy, particularly if the incipiency doctrine also serves other antitrust goals, such as maintaining the diversity, flexibility and initiative vital for dynamic efficiency.

The use of an incipiency doctrine in the vertical context, as in the horizontal context, thus comes down to a showing that stopping a trend toward vertical integration serves other valid antitrust goals. If no showing is made that a trend toward vertical integration threatens to undercut ease of entry, innovation, or other valid antitrust goals, the trend itself is no basis for antitrust relief.

§ 12.4   Remedies in Vertical Merger Enforcement

As with agency merger enforcement generally, a high percentage of mergers challenged on vertical grounds are resolved through negotiations that lead to a consent order.[1] The agencies have, however, invoked a wider array of remedial provisions in dealing with vertical issues. Some

---

§ 12.4

1. There remain isolated challenges by private plaintiffs to mergers involving vertical aspects. HTI Health Services, Inc. v. Quorum Health Group, Inc., 960 F.Supp. 1104 (S.D.Miss.1997)(plaintiff hospital unsuccessfully challenged merger involving the combination of a rival hospital and the two largest physician clinics that referred patients to those hospitals).

of these remedies have been regulatory, requiring the merged firm to commit to postmerger behavior subject to actual or potential monitoring by the enforcement agency. In 1994, the Justice Department obtained a conduct-oriented consent decree governing the behavior of AT & T after its acquisition of McCaw Cellular Communications. One goal of the decree was apparently to insulate the long-distance operations of the merged firm to ensure that rivals of McCaw in providing cellular phone service would still receive fair and non-discriminatory treatment in purchasing AT & T's long-distance services. Another was inhibiting the passing on of sensitive competitive information.[2] A Federal Trade Commission consent order in 1997 addressed vertical issues arising out of the Boeing Corporation's acquisition of Rockwell International. Because Rockwell produced space launch vehicle propulsion systems that would be useful to Boeing and to Boeing rivals in bidding on space vehicles, the consent order prohibited Boeing's division responsible for space launch vehicle propulsion systems from sharing any competitor's proprietary information with its space launch vehicle division.

Whether such regulatory provisions can be effective, or whether their effectiveness offsets the costs in imposing and enforcing them, is a matter of some controversy. Monitoring a firm's internal behavior (such as communication between divisions) may be a particularly frustrating and probably impossible task. A more direct way of dealing with anti-competitive risks growing out of a vertical integration is to forbid the merger or require a divestiture. In the FTC consent order involving the Time Warner acquisition of Turner Broadcasting, the Commission was concerned that Time Warner and TCI (which would own a significant percentage of Time Warner upon completion of the transaction) would foreclose rivals access to television programming or to cable television distribution. Apparently not content with conduct provisions, the Commission required TCI to take steps to divest its interest in Time Warner.[3] Although the order also contained conduct provisions, these provisions seem relatively straightforward in their enforcement. For example, Time Warner was prohibited (1) from the bundling of HBO with any Turner programming, or the bundling of CNN, TNT and WTBS with Time Warner programming; (2) from engaging in price discrimination in the sale of programming to cable or direct satellite distributors; and (3) from carrying out an agreement that required TCI to carry Turner programming for the next twenty years at a discount price. The most open-ended provision required Time Warner to commit to conduct and reporting requirements to protect unaffiliated programers in their efforts to obtain access to Time Warner cable distribution.

The Time Warner decree, by imposing divestiture and some relatively straightforward conduct requirements, commendably avoids some of the concerns with regulatory consent decrees. Conduct provisions, when

---

2. United States v. AT & T Corp., 59 Fed. Reg. 44,158 (1994). See § 12.3b3.

3. The divestiture was conditioned upon receipt of a favorable tax ruling from the Internal Revenue Service. Time Warner, Inc., 61 Fed. Reg. 50301 (1996).

narrowly drafted to address concretely identified anticompetitive risks, are a defensible means of antitrust enforcement. In many cases, the alternative to such provisions would be (for the agency) a risky effort to enjoin the merger entirely and (for the merging parties) a substantial risk associated with drawn out litigation.

§ 12.5 The Future of Vertical Merger Enforcement

The last iteration of the guidelines to address vertical mergers was the Department of Justice's 1984 Merger Guidelines. Those Guidelines suggest three limited circumstances under which vertical mergers could create competitive risks: (1) when the merger would force a potential entrant in the primary market to undertake a difficult, dual-level entry; (2) when price collusion would be facilitated; and (3) when evasion of regulation would be facilitated.[1] Although these theories may remain the core of vertical merger enforcement, the Guidelines should be revised to address additional concerns such as the possible facilitation of price discrimination (which may or may not be the result of collusion).

The Guidelines also need to address more forthrightly the concern that vertical integration can create a stultified market structure that undermines the dynamic element of competition. To be sure, by indirection, the 1984 Guidelines touch on dynamic competitive issues (for example, by addressing the possibility of entry barriers that would require a difficult, dual level entry). But the dynamic element of competition is almost certainly of greater importance to long-term consumer welfare than issues of allocative efficiency, the focus of the current Guidelines.

The challenge for policy-makers is to set relatively concrete thresholds in an area in which predictability is low. Innovation in products, processes and distribution cannot be securely charted for the future. But industry structures that are more conducive to this dynamic element must be preserved. The 1984 Guidelines, unlike the 1968 and 1982 versions, contain no measures of concentration at upstream or downstream levels as guides to the presumptive legality or illegality of vertical mergers. Given the formative and rapidly changing base of economic theory addressing vertical integration, the agencies can be forgiven for treading lightly in this area. But the thresholds provided an important guide that could preserve flexibility and dynamism in critical markets. Particularly in industries where vertical integration has not been widely practiced, the efficiencies of vertical integration will often be less substantial than those involving horizontal combinations. Because those efficiencies can usually be attained by other less anticompetitive means, thresholds such as those set by the 1982 Guidelines did not pose significant risks of thwarting allocative efficiencies and could substantially benefit long term dynamic efficiency.

§ 12.5

1. U.S. Department of Justice, Merger Guidelines § 4.2 (1984), available at <http:/ /www. usdoj.gov/ atr /public/ guidelines/ 2614.htm>.

Chapter XIII

JOINT VENTURES

Table of Sections

§ 13.1 Introduction

"Joint venture," when used in an antitrust context, can be taken to imply: (1) an undertaking cooperatively established by two or more parent firms that maintain their own identities separate from that of the venture; (2) integration of resources, operations, and/or management provided by the parents; (3) a constitutive form (whether tight or loose) for the venture entailing more structure than mere contractual arrangements among the parents; and (4) ongoing business activities by the venture as an entity. In today's economy cooperative arrangements among firms, sometimes generically labeled "strategic alliances," vary in structure from joint subsidiaries at one extreme, through incorporated or unincorporated consortia or associations in the mid area, to mid to long term contractual cooperation or mere recurrent consultations by individual firms, at the other extreme. The definition above is intended to draw a line between subsidiaries, consortia or associations—forms that all involve, at a minimum, separate, "letter head" organizations, with officers, staff, and a place of business (all of which are considered to be joint ventures)—and contractual cooperation or recurrent meetings among independent firms, however significant their ongoing effects (none of which are here labeled joint ventures).[1]

§ 13.1

1. A more open-ended conception is used to organize a permissive antitrust analysis in Compton, *Cooperation, Collaboration, and Coalition: A Perspective on the Types and Purposes of Technology Joint Ventures*, 61 Antitrust L.J. 861 (1993); broadly inclusive definitions were used in the now superceded 1988 Antitrust Enforcement Guidelines for International Operations § 3.4 (reprinted in 4 Trade Reg. Rep. (CCH) ¶ 13,109) and in the Federal Trade Commission/Department of Justice, Antitrust Guidelines for Collaborations Among Competitors § 1.1 (2000), available at <www.ftc.gov/OS/2000/04/ftcdojguide-lines.pdf>. A more restrictive definition than the one in this text is used in Brodley, *Joint Ventures and Antitrust Policy*, 95 Harv. L. Rev. 1521 (1982). P. Areeda and L. Kaplow, Antitrust Analysis: Problems, Texts, Cases § 222 (5th ed. 1997), rejects all effort to define, stating that the term, joint venture, lacks "any definite meaning. . . ." id. at 247. The definition used in, "Note on the Antitrust Status of Joint Ventures" in M. Handler et al., Trade Regulation: Cases and Materials, 415, 416 (4th ed. 1997) is consistent with that in this text.

Although, as Areeda and Kaplow point out, labeling an arrangement a joint venture does not invoke any distinctive legal rules

The joint venture concept is of interest to antitrust because whenever two or more firms cooperate in a business activity there may be competitive harm and because whenever there is integration of these firms' activities (one of the hallmarks of a venture), efficiencies may result. Because a venture involves cooperation and may cause harm, Section 1 of the Sherman Act may apply and, if the cooperation entails creating a new joint subsidiary, Section 7 of the Clayton Act may be relevant. But because the integration involved may yield significant efficiencies, joint ventures, as a concept, are not inherently suspect. Because of their variety, ventures may fall almost anywhere on the array of analytical approaches that antitrust affords. Many, raising no discernable or significant competitive threat and entailing possible efficiency gains, may be legal on their face. At the other extreme cooperation labeled a joint venture can violate Section 1 of the Sherman Act *per se* or on the basis of a truncated analysis; a so-called venture could be a sham for a cartel. For many joint ventures, however, analysis will be needed to determine whether competitive harm results; if so, whether there are offsetting efficiencies; and, if both harms and benefits appear, whether the net effect of the venture is harmful or beneficial to competition.

Because a joint venture implies possible benefits as well as harms, the label implies a contrast from a "naked restraint." Hence, proponents of cooperative activities may be quick to claim the venture characterization, hoping to shunt off or blunt antitrust inquiry. It must be stressed at the outset that arrangements called joint ventures do not avoid, but are strictly subject to, conventional antitrust analysis. The joint venture label is no antitrust shield. All such activities, whether or not meeting any scholar's definitional norm, may involve or facilitate collusion, may reduce, discipline or inhibit actual or potential competition, or may foreclose rivals from inputs or outputs. Any activity that has such tendencies should be scrutinized in the conventional way. If harms are manifested and claims of integration benefits are pretextual or trivial, the activity may be condemned—perhaps *per se* or, more likely, after a "quick look."[2] If there is non-trivial integration that yields some bene-

or analytical tools, it is nevertheless appropriate to think about joint venture antitrust issues as a subcategory. To assign arrangements that the business community regards as having special characteristics to the more comprehensive category, horizontal arrangement, without any attention to the integration and continuity aspects of ventures that lead business people to think of them as a species, would risk failing to identify recurrent factual aspects that may have special relevance under conventional legal rules and analytical conventions. The definition in the text seeks to strike a balance. The Compton definition, because of its breadth, would sweep too many largely undifferentiated agreements into the category, while the Brodley definition (although well linked to appropriate analytical tasks

and still useful in "smoke stack" industries) might exclude some limited purpose consortia or associations in high tech, information-oriented markets that, given the special aspects of those markets, partake of characteristics shared with other, more formally structured ventures.

2. Timken Roller Bearing Co. v. United States, 341 U.S. 593, 598, 71 S.Ct. 971, 95 L.Ed. 1199 (1951) (an agreement to suppress competition cannot be justified by the joint venture label); Arizona v. Maricopa County Medical Soc'y, 457 U.S. 332, 102 S.Ct. 2466, 73 L.Ed.2d 48 (1982) (*per se* rule applied to ancillary price restraint although the Court apparently considered the claimed benefits and concluded that they could have been attained without competi-

fits, but the competitive harms are manifestly weightier, a violation can be adjudicated on the basis of a truncated analysis.[3] Legality can also be found on the basis of such an analysis if any harms are outweighed by overwhelming efficiencies.[4] And, of course, there will also be joint venture cases in which a more conventional rule of reason analysis may be needed, focusing, perhaps, on whether the constraint causing harm is reasonably necessary to attain the venture's benefit.[5]

In sum, joint ventures do not present a distinct set of doctrinal problems; whether a venture is loose knit, and so amenable to Section 1 analysis, or involves formation of a corporate entity appropriately evaluated under Section 7 of the Clayton Act, it shares in broadly applicable antitrust doctrinal traditions. Of course, doctrine evolves. During the last two decades when the rule of reason and *per se* standards were imploding, a number of the signal cases involved arrangements fairly called joint ventures.[6] Currently antitrust doctrine seems quite stable both in Section 1 and Section 7 analysis. Yet, there could be change ahead. Such change may develop initially out of joint venture problems. Indeed, there are two areas of venture law that hold particular interest because of their dynamic aspects. First, in provider controlled health care networks rapid, far reaching entrepreneurial change is occurring. Enforcement agency responses, while articulated in conventional terms, seem to be accommodating to countervailing power. This interactive process may be leading to new law, perhaps in health care only, but with a potential for being generalized to other joint activities. Also, as the information based economy thrives, more industries depend on interactive networks. These give rise to externalities that encourage standardization as a means of maximizing value to all network participants. These developments can evoke aggressive competition among proprietors of alternative standards, each attempting to sponsor the de facto industry standard. When this occurs such competition may be short-lived and

tion in pricing). It is the *Timken* case language that Areeda and Kaplow cite in support of the statement that the joint venture label has no antitrust consequence. See note 1, supra. See also United States v. Columbia Pictures Indus. Inc., 507 F.Supp. 412, 429 (S.D.N.Y.1980).

3. National Collegiate Athletic Ass'n v. Board of Regents of Univ. of Oklahoma, 468 U.S. 85, 104 S.Ct. 2948, 82 L.Ed.2d 70 (1984).

4. Broadcast Music, Inc. v. CBS, Inc., 441 U.S. 1, 99 S.Ct. 1551, 60 L.Ed.2d 1 (1979).

5. L.A. Memorial Coliseum Commission v. NFL, 726 F.2d 1381 (9th Cir.1984); National Bancard Corp. v. VISA U.S.A., Inc., 779 F.2d 592 (11th Cir.1986), cert. denied 479 U.S. 923, 107 S.Ct. 329, 93 L.Ed.2d 301 (1986); Rothery Storage & Van Co. v. Atlas Van Lines Inc., 792 F.2d 210 (D.C.Cir.1986)

cert. denied 479 U.S. 1033, 107 S.Ct. 880, 93 L.Ed.2d 834 (1987). The FTC/Department of Justice Draft Antitrust Guidelines for Collaborations Among Competitors, supra note 1, are consistent with the views in text related to this note and notes 2, 3 and 4.

6. See, e.g., National Soc'y of Professional Eng'rs v. United States, 435 U.S. 679, 98 S.Ct. 1355, 55 L.Ed.2d 637 (1978); National Collegiate Athletic Association v. Board of Regents of University of Oklahoma, supra note 3, Broadcast Music v. CBS, supra note 4 and Arizona v. Maricopa County Medical Soc'y, supra note 2. For an analysis of the case law development between the late 1970s and the late 1980s which resulted in the close integration of rule of reason and *per se* analysis common today, see Sullivan, the Viability of the *Current Law on Horizontal Restraints*, 75 Calif. L. Rev. 938 (1987).

result in long lasting market power for the winner. Alternative scenarios include cooperation to achieve and administer industrywide standards and protocols. Because of the complexity of network externalities, which have only recently come under intense study by economists, such cooperative efforts to establish standards can generate novel issues. These, too, may call for doctrinal development and refinement.

The main purpose of this chapter is to illustrate methods of analysis, those warranted by the case law and supported by tradition and scholarship, that should be used for ventures within the definitional parameters suggested above. Section 13.2 shows how ventures can be classified and identifies possible benefits and costs of ventures in major classifications. The ways in which ventures can improve allocative efficiency and enhance consumer welfare are discussed and illustrated, as are the means by which such undertakings can reduce competitive incentives and interactions. Section 13.3 deals with balancing harms and benefits, and illustrates ways ventures within major categories may be analyzed.

The last two sections of the chapter deal with the two dynamic areas referred to above. Section 13.4 discusses the application of joint venture analysis to health care ventures, including provider controlled health care organizations and cooperation and merger by hospitals. It examines the 1996 Statements of Antitrust Enforcement Policy in Health Care issued by the Department of Justice and the Federal Trade Commission and considers whether these guides to enforcement policy are consistent with the case law. Section 13.5 discusses the costs and benefits of cooperative research and standard setting ventures in high tech communication, computer and information industries with significant network externalities. Here, too, dynamism generates pressure to ease some conventional antitrust constraints on cooperation. Section 13.6 considers the remedial problems which competitively harmful joint venture can engender.

§ 13.2   The Benefits and Costs of Joint Ventures

Joint ventures can be classified, much as can mergers, on the basis of how the market in which the venture functions relates to the market or markets in which the parents operate. If the venture and one or more of its parents are competitors, the venture might be labeled horizontal. If the venture and one or more parents relate as buyer and seller, it might be called vertical. If the venture and its parents are in different fields, it may be called conglomerate. In such cases, it should also be determined whether parental and venture markets have affinities that warrant classifying the venture as involving extension of the market or the product line. Ventures should also be examined to determine how the fields in which the parents operate relate to each other. Are the parents competitors? Vertically related? Are there other affinities between their markets? As indicated in §§ 13.2a and 13.2b, such classifications and parental relationships can be relevant both to possible efficiencies and possible competitive harms that a venture can spawn.

13.2a. Competitive Benefits of Joint Ventures

A joint venture may be long term. Such a venture might be carried out through a jointly owned and controlled subsidiary. For example an airline and a steamship company might form such a subsidiary to exploit a sea or air transportation market tangential to those each of them currently serves. Also, a long term venture might be accomplished contractually without any subsidiary. For example, two airlines with interlinking routes might do interline ticketing, integrate frequent flier programs, do maintenance for each other at their hubs, and cooperate in other ways. Alternatively, a venture established by contract among the parents may be relatively short term. For example, a number of banks doing international business might form a syndicate to share the risks and returns of a very large, three year, Eurodollar loan to a newly privatized state enterprise in an emerging country. The forms of these hypothetical ventures may have legal relevance. Section 1 of the Sherman Act might apply to all of them while Section 7 of the Clayton Act might apply only to the first. But the differences in form should have little influence on how competitive effect is analyzed. Whether a venture entails a subsidiary or only a looser contractual relationship, the parents continue to preserve their own identities, share the risks and profits of the venture in agreed upon ways, contribute not only capital but also resources such as management or marketing skills, intellectual property, credit enhancement, input sources or distribution facilities, while the venture takes on an identity of its own as a business undertaking. On the face of it, any such venture entails either horizontal, vertical or conglomerate integration. Therefore, it may yield efficiencies. In the subsection that follows the kinds of efficiencies that may be associated with joint ventures of various classifications are examined.

13.2a1. *Benefits of Horizontal Ventures*

While significant competitive harms may be associated with horizontal ventures (see § 13.2b1), such ventures are not without potential for efficiencies. Below benefit possibilities are cataloged. This enumeration has no definitive implication for the overall competitive effect or the antitrust legality of the horizontal ventures referred to. It merely lists possibilities on the benefit side of the scale. When considering each one of these, the astute reader will also consider whether the exemplary fact situations would or might also yield offsetting competitive harms. In § 13.2b, possible harms from ventures are comprehensively listed. Only after benefits and harms of a particular venture are both identified can a balance be struck and a legal standard applied.

13.2a1i. *Scale and Transaction Cost Economies*

A horizontal venture might enable operations at a scale not possible without the venture. This could yield scale as well as transaction cost economies, or even facilitate the offering of a product or service that could not be offered without the venture. Consider this example: A number of banks, American, European and Asian, compete in making

Eurodollar loans. All are subject to regulatory prudential standards that require diversification of credit risk, country risk and sector or industry risk. The recently privatized zinc mining enterprise of emerging country X needs a $3 billion Eurodollar loan for three years, and country X offers credit guarantees. No single bank can make the loan without excessive exposure to this borrower, to country X and to the mining sector. Several banks form a syndicate to make the loan. Economies result. The venture reduces the exposure of each participant, enabling each to remain sufficiently diversified to meet the prudential standards imposed by its regulators. In addition, there may be a reduction in transaction costs. The lead bank will investigate, evaluate and negotiate the loan. One bank will be designated to manage disbursements and collections. If several banks made individual loans aggregating $3 billion there would be several investigations, evaluations, negotiations and loans, each with its own pattern of disbursement and collection, each needing to be managed. The reduction in transactions, moreover, is experienced not only by the banks through the syndicate, but also by the borrower. It, too, negotiates once and deals with one payment schedule, one payee, and one manager representing all participating lenders. True, scale economics may not be found in horizontal ventures as often as in horizontal mergers. The continued separate operation of the parents might preclude certain efficiencies such as integration of manufacturing operations. But some formidable scale advantages may be accessible within a venture, even one quite limited in time and scope, as in this example. Note, however, that when, as here, a benefit related to transaction costs is identified in a venture, the possibility of offsetting new expenses must also be considered. In this example, the costs of negotiating the syndicate and its terms will tend to offset savings in loan negotiation and loan management expenses.

As Broadcast Music, Inc. v. CBS, Inc.[1] signifies, a horizontal venture can also open the possibility for a new product or market that would not have existed without the venture. In *BMI,* the transaction cost savings resulting from agency marketing of music through blanket copyright licenses were so great that in the Court's view they overshadowed what seemed to constitute price fixing and an increase in market power. Savings in the hypothetical about the Eurodollar loan syndicate would no doubt be more modest. Nonetheless, the development of syndicates for large Eurodollar loans might also result in a new, "large Eurodollar" loan market, one which, if several such syndicates formed and reformed, might effectively compete. As the U.S. banking market continues its pattern of consolidation (which may reduce other valued aspects of competition) an optimally large Eurodollar loan market may develop without such ventures. Banks joining together in a venture to offer national credit cards like Master Charge or Visa are another example. The scale of these joint ventures so vastly exceeds the scale of consumer

§ 13.2

1. 441 U.S. 1, 99 S.Ct. 1551, 60 L.Ed.2d 1 (1979).

lending open to local and even regional banks individually that, quite apart from scale and transaction cost efficiencies, a wholly new service market may be established.

A horizontal joint venture to jointly buy inputs or to market outputs or provide ancillary services such as delivery might also yield scale economies. Examples in the case law where the potential for such efficiencies may be perceived include Appalachian Coals v. United States[2] (joint marketing) and Northwest Wholesale Stationers, Inc. v. Pacific Stationery & Printing Co.[3] (joint purchasing). Although the risks of such arrangements (discussed in § 13.2b) can be substantial, they do have the potential for reducing costs through larger scale in buying and selling.

13.2a1ii. *Complimentary Resources*

Linking complimentary resources is another possible efficiency from a horizontal joint venture. Even though a number of horizontal competitors face each other in an appropriately defined market, two or more of these competitors may fashion their output from differing sets of inputs. This being so, one of the competing firms may have one or more inputs—say, management, facilities or intellectual property—that, if linked with the different inputs of another of the competing firms, would yield outputs either at lower cost (in consequence of process improvements or other operating efficiencies) or of higher value (in consequence of product improvement) than either of the competitors could have achieved alone. If so, a joint venture might be the most feasible means of bringing those complementary and synergetic inputs together. Of course, negotiating and managing the venture has its own costs. These must be offset against gain. Also, there may be possible alternatives: merger; one firm buying the needed resource held by the other; either or both replicating the resource it needs by finding comparable ones elsewhere or (if that resource is proprietary technology) obtaining a license or inventing around. But in some situations the venture might be the surest, least risky and lowest cost means for achieving a real cost or quality improvement.

Any of these potential gains will be more likely if one of the resources being brought together was underutilized by the firm that controlled it. For example, if both firms have significant intellectual property but one has personnel highly skilled and experienced in the strategic exploitation of such property, using the venture to place a wider category of such property under the control of that personnel might achieve a species of scale economy. But underutilization is not a precondition to achieving beneficial efficiencies, especially if the venture is aimed at developing and getting to market a new product or service. Suppose, for example, that of two computer manufacturers one is a

---

2. 288 U.S. 344, 53 S.Ct. 471, 77 L.Ed. 825 (1933).

3. 472 U.S. 284, 105 S.Ct. 2613, 86 L.Ed.2d 202 (1985). See also Arizona v. Maricopa County Medical Soc'y, 457 U.S. 332, 102 S.Ct. 2466, 73 L.Ed.2d 48 (1982), where the Court recognized the potential for economies but thought them to be accessible in less restrictive ways.

leader in designing user interfaces and the other has greater skill and experience both in other aspects of technology such as manufacturing and marketing hardware of the size identified as appropriate for the new product. Linking these skills and resources might result in a better, faster and less expensively developed new product.[4]

13.2a1iii. *Establishing a Standard*

A horizontal joint venture might also achieve efficiency by establishing an industry standard in a network industry. For example, to be attractive to buyers, mobile phones made by different manufacturers must be compatible with each other. As mobile technology has moved from analog to digital, alternative standards have been available and, in Europe, manufacturers such as Ericsson and Nokia opted for one technology while Siemens, Sony and Motorola opted for another, with the consequence that two networks were developing. Mobile phone users had either to choose one or the other, or equip themselves with phones compatible with both. Because the first alternative reduced the value to the user and the second increased consumer expense, the on-going competition to become the standard, so long as it lasted, reduced the value and increased the cost of industry output. With the facilitation of the European Commission, these manufacturers, under the auspices of their industrywide venture, the European Telecommunications Standards Institute, compromised on a hybrid standard, called W–CDMA.[5]

13.2a1iv. *New Entry*

A horizontal venture in which two firms each making the same standardized product organize entry of a jointly owned firm in the same market gains no presumptive credit for new entry. There is a new unit in the market but it is controlled by existing competitors, either or both of which might have expanded their own output. Yet in some situations significant new entry may be made possible or speeded up by a horizontal venture. A clear example is where the scale achieved through the venture offers consumers a distinctly new and different alternative. *BMI*[6] and examples like Master Card and Visa[7] and the Eurobank syndicate hypothetical discussed earlier illustrate possibilities. Significant new entry could also result from a joint venture that combines previously separate, synchronistic resources. For example, if one firm owns a valuable patent and another an improvement patent, combing the two in a joint venture may open a more efficient technology or a better product than the market offered previously. Finally, venture parents may have

---

4. Compare the description of the 1992 venture between Apple and Sharp to develop a "personal digital assistant" in Compton, *Cooperation Collaboration and Coalition: A Perspective on the Types and Purposes of Technology Joint Ventures*, 61 ANTITRUST L.J. 861 at 865–66 (1993).

5. A. Cane and G. McIvor, *Compromise Over Mobile Phone Standards*, FINANCIAL TIMES, January 30, 1998, at C3.

6. Broadcast Music, Inc. v. CBS, Inc., supra note 1.

7. See, e.g., National Bancard Corp. v. VISA U.S.A., Inc., 779 F.2d 592 (11th Cir. 1986), cert. denied 479 U.S. 923, 107 S.Ct. 329, 93 L.Ed.2d 301 (1986).

affinities for different segments of the same market. For example, a United States firm in a global market might hesitate to expand by establishing production facilities in Europe. If so, a venture with a European firm might facilitate scaling that barrier.

13.2a1v. Facilitating Innovation

Some high tech markets may experience special impediments to innovation. As suggested by the Apple–Sharp hypothetical,[8] in such markets ventures between horizontal competitors may facilitate more rapid, less expensive and more useful innovation than might be possible without such a venture. The possible benefits as well as identifiable and possibly offsetting harms will be more fully explored in § 13.5, dealing with ventures in high tech industries.

13.2a2. Benefits of Vertical Ventures

Here, as in § 13.2a.1., possible benefits alone are cataloged. Evaluation of any vertical venture, as with a horizontal venture, must await identification and measurement of both harms and benefits, matters treated in § 13.2b.

13.2a2i. Transaction Costs

Sequential processes must be linked. Vertical joint ventures, like vertical mergers, can substitute hierarchical or managerial integration for market integration, thus substituting the costs associated with managerial decision-making for those of gathering market information and executing purchases and sales. If the cost of managerial integration achieved through a venture are lower than the transaction costs associated with market linkage, the venture yields an efficiency.[9]

13.2a2ii. Design and Flow Coordination

Effective integration across vertical lines requires design compatibilities and product flows that assure timely availability of inputs without undue inventory costs. Achieving effective integration may require interactive flows of relevant services or relevant information about design plans and changes, production scheduling and the like. A vertical venture may be able to achieve these ends more effectively than market interactions.[10]

13.2a2iii. Internalizing Marketing and Promotional Incentives

Some of the benefits of marketing and promotional expenses incurred by firms vertically linked through the market may be externalized. If Intel advertising convinces buyers that its microchip is superior,

---

8. Supra note 4 and accompanying text.

9. Williamson, *The Vertical Integration of Production: Market Failure Considerations*, 61 AM. ECON. REV. 112 (1971). See the discussion of the efficiencies of vertical mergers in § 12.3a.

10. Riordan and Salop, *Evaluating Vertical Mergers: A Post–Chicago Approach*, 63 ANTITRUST L.J. 513, 523–527 (1995).

Intel expenditures benefit IBM and Compaq, known to use Intel chips, as well as Intel. While this externality can be borne or adjusted either contractually or through the market (as witness "Intel inside" sloganeering by some Intel customers), a vertical venture might rationalize incentives more effectively.[11]

13.2a2iv.   Facilitating Marginal Cost Guidance

If one input comes from an oligopolistic market with supracompetitive prices and a substitute from another market at competitive prices, a downstream firm will be guided by market prices and will likely use more of the competitively priced and less of the oligopolistically priced input then is allocatively efficient. Consumers might prefer or be better served by the input from the oligopolistic market but would receive less of that input because of its supracompetitive pricing. A venture linking a downstream firm with one of the upstream oligopolists might allow the downstream firm to acquire the desired input at prices closer to marginal cost and, hence, increase the use of this desired input.[12]

13.2a2v.   Scale Economies

A vertical joint venture might obtain scale economies with respect to services that both vertically related parents obtained through the market.[13] One likely area is in raising capital. As Scherer and Ross stress, scale economies are particularly pervasive in this function.[14] If one of the parents of the venture is large and another small, lower capital cost of the larger may carry to the venture. Also a venture might link a firm producing a product—say widgets—at efficient scale and needing a limited amount of an input—say, transportation—that is subject to large scale economies. If the manufacturer provides widgets to the venture and the transporter provides carriage, both at cost, the venture might yield some scale economies that neither partner could attain on its own.

13.2a2vi.   Synergistic Product or Service Improvement

A vertical joint venture might be capable of providing a product or service improvement significant enough to warrant a claim like that made for the horizontal venture in *BMI*—namely, that the improvement is so significant that it establishes a new market. Alternatively such a venture might yield synergies that, although not creating a new product or service market, are sufficient to be credited as a discernible improvement in market competition.

Consider this hypothetical: Telecommunications has long been divided into local and long distance markets, with ancillary (yet partially competing) markets for cellular and personal communication services. Moreover, each of these markets entail numerous product and service submarkets. Assume (as is widely asserted) that large business custom-

---

11. Id. at 529.

12. Id. at 525–526

13. F.M. Scherer & D. Ross, Industrial Market Structure and Economic Performance, 162–163 (3d ed. 1990).

14. Id. at 163

ers desire "one stop shopping" for all communication services from a single source that will also provide equipment installation and guidance as to alternative communication services and systems. Assume also (as is now apparent) that although carriers in each major market segment have sought to enter the other segment, none has, or appears likely in the near future, to be notably successful. Next, assume that a long distance carrier (say, MCIWorldCom) enters into a joint venture with one or more local carriers (whether incumbents like Bell South or competitive local exchange carriers like Unstar, Nextel or ICG) to provide such one stop service to business customers. Such a venture might establish a new, unified market for a full range of telecom services.

13.2a2vii. New Entry

A vertical joint venture fields a new participant in the market the venture exploits. Whether that effect should be characterized as a new entry may depend on how the parents relate to each other as well as to the form of the venture. A venture between a department store and a delivery service which assigns a given number of trucks and drivers to the department store to meet its delivery needs might add no significant new entrant into either delivery or retailing, yet might enhance the quality of retail service previously available. As in all instances when a venture involves new entry into a market, the significance of that entry to competition will depend on whether, before the entry, the market was concentrated, and (if the claimed benefit is a qualitative improvement) whether there are alternative ways (as in the department store delivery service hypothetical, there clearly would be) in which the improvement could be achieved. Some vertical ventures may add the equivalent of an additional competitor to one of the two vertically related markets by vast service improvement over that available before the venture.

13.2a2viii. Facilitating Innovation

Some vertical ventures may facilitate information flows between people at different levels with different but complementary perspectives on product or process development. In some instances this may facilitate innovation. See § 13.2a2viii.

13.2a3. Benefits of Conglomerate Joint Ventures

A frequent competitive benefit from conglomerate joint ventures is new entry into a market. For example, if a finance company and a manufacturer form a venture to offer local phone service in competition with Ameritech, the venture will not likely facilitate efficiencies in telecom service, but will nonetheless constitute valued new entry into a concentrated market. Of course, a conglomerate venture could also bring synergistic resources together leading to product or service improvement and innovation.

13.2b.   Competitive Harms of Joint Ventures

Joint ventures can cause competitive harms in one or more of five different ways. Each of these can reduce output and raise prices, or can discourage innovation leading to product improvements or cost reduction and widened consumer choice. First, horizontal (or in limited circumstances, even vertical) joint ventures can facilitate collusion between or among competitors through managerial intimacy and information sharing. Also, they can reduce the incentive for and the intensity of competition and encourage collusion by increasing market concentration, or reducing potential competition. Second, if vertical, a joint venture can foreclose competitors from inputs or marketing opportunities. Third, a joint venture of any type can reduce potential competition.[15] Fourth, a joint venture of any type, if one of the participants has market power, can have effects similar to market division or effects analogous to tying or bundling by leveraging power from one market to another. Fifth, any such venture may contain ancillary or even wholly collateral terms that might threaten competition.

13.2b1.   *Managerial Intimacy and Information Sharing*

Collusion is a particular risk in horizontal ventures, but can occur in other ventures, too. The risk is manifest whenever direct competitors collaborate in any aspect of the planning, development, production or marketing activities in which they have been competitively engaged. Any such venture between competitors, however limited in scope, brings them together to plan a joint activity in the market in which they compete. In such planning, they share conceptions about the opportunities and challenges encountered in their market (or some segment of it), and provide to each other information directly or tangentially relevant, perhaps including sensitive price and cost data. As they interact they refine their cooperative parameters. Finally, they act jointly to execute the venture, bringing it to fruition and in doing so may widen the venture in ways that may intensify their interaction, homogenize their conceptions about market conditions, and provide new channels and incentives for explicit collusion, oligopolistic interdependence, or soft, live-and-let live pseudo-rivalry.

These kinds of risks (always present in a horizontal ventures) can appear also when the venturer parents are potential competitors, firms that deal with each other vertically, face each other from adjacent geographical or product markets, or otherwise have affinities, capacities or resources that might lead one or both to seriously consider entry into the market of the other. In limited circumstances a vertical venture might occasion a similar risk even if the vertical relationship does not imply the potential for upstream or downstream entry. Assume that A and B are competitors, that C is a customer of A, and that B and C form a venture in C's downstream market. Because A and C may communi-

---

15. See generally, Brodley, *Joint Ventures and Antitrust Policy,* 95 Harv. L. Rev. 1521 (1982).

cate with each other about future plans in order to share information needed to assure a good market linkage between them, this venture may create a new channel through which A and B can communicate and coordinate. Suppose B, considering the timing of a new generation product, would like to delay for two or three years, but fears falling behind if A precedes it by a significant period. C is in a position to broker the information needed by A and B for an implicit agreement between them about timing. As a customer interested in the output plans of both suppliers, C will talk with each about when they anticipate a new generation product and, unless subject to an explicit fire wall, will likely tell A what B is considering, and vice versa. Indeed, C may directly carry messages back and forth, even though attempting only to advance its own distinct interest as a customer.

Managerial intimacy is not a categorical bad, even among firms in the same market. It may be focused on and essential to some benefit, such as development of a new product through combining synergistic inputs. Ultimately, the question is whether managerial intimacy facilitates output reduction and price enhancement between competitors. The worst scenario is one in which the venture establishes[16] or, over time, transforms itself into, an explicit price or output cartel.[17] This is an obvious, perhaps a nearly inevitable, risk when the venture entails joint marketing of the output of competing parents.[18] But overt cartelization is not essential to collusive, anticompetitive harm. Close, continuing managerial cooperation covering any significant aspects of competitive activity in a tightly structured market tends to invite collaboration, oligopolistic interdependence and price leadership. The closer the venture activity lies to the central pricing and output decisions in the market in which the venture parents compete, the greater the risks of serious competitive harm.

The extent to which venture partners meet together, share information, views and attitudes, and work intimately in an ongoing collaboration can vary depending on the way the venture is structured and its operating rules and protocols. To some extent, the problems discussed in this subsection can be mitigated by antitrust compliance policies deliberately built into the venture itself. Section 13.6, discusses various devices (such as fire walls) that a court or agency might impose to end or reduce collusion dangers after a venture is found unlawful. Such devices could also be introduced into the venture by the parties at the time of formation in order to reduce the risk of an antitrust attack.

16. E.g., Timken Roller Bearing Co. v. United States, 341 U.S. 593, 71 S.Ct. 971, 95 L.Ed. 1199 (1951).

17. United States v. Imperial Chem. Indus., 100 F.Supp. 504 (S.D.N.Y. 1951), opinion supplemented by 105 F.Supp. 215 (S.D.N.Y.1952); United States v. Pilkington, PLC, 1994–2 Trade Cases (CCH) ¶ 70,842 (D. Ariz. 1994).

18. E.g., Virginia Excelsior Mills, Inc. v. FTC, 256 F.2d 538 (4th Cir.1958); but cf. Appalachian Coals v. United States, 288 U.S. 344, 53 S.Ct. 471, 77 L.Ed. 825 (1933), and Broadcast Music, Inc. v. CBS Inc., 441 U.S. 1, 99 S.Ct. 1551, 60 L.Ed.2d 1 (1979).

A recent Second Circuit case demonstrates that managerial intimacy can result in buyer power abuses just as much as seller power abuses. In Todd v. Exxon Corporation, managerial, professional, and technical (MPT) employees of fourteen integrated oil and petrochemical companies brought a Sherman Section 1 action against the firms alleging that they conspired to collect data and detailed information on the compensation paid to these employees, using the information to set salaries at artificially low levels.[19] After the district court dismissed for failure to state a claim, the Second Circuit reversed. The court found that plaintiffs had alleged a credible market consisting of the opportunities for the employees who must sell their services to the oligopsony firms. In determining that there was substantial potential for anticompetitive abuse, the court paid close attention to industry structure, noting that the number of firms involved was sufficient to require data exchange for coordination of salary levels. The court concluded that the supply for MPT services was inelastic, stressing that labor is "an extremely perishable commodity—an hour not worked today can never be recovered."[20]

13.2b2. *Structural Harm*

A joint venture between competitors that will operate a separate business within the market in which the parents already compete is not only fraught with conduct risk arising from intimacy (see § 13.2b1) but will also inevitably alter structure; much or little, it will increase concentration. The venture must set its own prices. If the personnel of two or more parents participate in this activity this concert by competitors of the venture in fixing its prices will inevitably reflect and influence the prices each parent sets for its own "competing" unit. If the industry already is or as a result of the venture becomes highly concentrated, that structural deterioration will reduce competitive incentives and invite overt collusion or follow-the-leader pricing regardless of how effectively the venture seeks to insulate against direct involvement of parent personnel in price setting by the venture and other manifestations of managerial intimacy.[21]

A joint venture involving two or more parents that are potential entrants into the market the venture plans independently to exploit, or a venture involving one or more parents that might enter the market of another parent, also involves structural change that can be competitively harmful. Entry by the venture will likely end any prospect of entry by any of the parents. If the market is highly concentrated and if, but for the venture, two or more parents might have individually entered, the venture entry could be of less competitive value than the previous

19. 275 F.3d 191 (2d Cir. 2001).

20. Id. at 211 (citing Roger D. Blair & Jeffrey Harrison, *Antitrust Policy and Monopsony*, 76 CORNELL L. REV. 297, 314 (1991)).

21. Cf. United States v. Columbia Pictures Corp., 189 F.Supp. 153 (S.D.N.Y. 1960); United States. v. Amer. Smelting & Refining Co., 182 F.Supp. 834 (S.D.N.Y. 1960). See also Brodley, *Joint Ventures and Antitrust Policy*, supra, note 15 and Pitofsky, *Joint Ventures Under the Antitrust Laws: Some Reflection on the Significance of Penn–Olin*, 82 HARV. L. REV. 1007, 1034 (1969).

structure involving two or more potential entrants.[22] This will be especially significant if the parents were the only (or among very few) potential entrants; their joint presence on the market's edge may have constrained collusion or oligopolistic interdependence more than would actual entry by the venture. In instances where one or more parents is a potential entrant into that market of one of the other parents, the risks are like those presented by a horizontal joint venture. After the venture the parent already in the subject market and the potential entrant into that market share a new commonality of interest and new managerial interactions both of which could blunt the incentive of the potential entrant to move against its venture partner. Of course, the significance of any such structural deterioration will depend in large measure upon the extent of concentration, entry barriers and other structural features.

A venture between parents both of which operate in the same horizontal market can also do serious structural harm when the parents, rather than fielding a new, jointly owned entrant into that market, limit their joint activity to cooperation. For example, a joint venture between airlines with intersecting routes might include through-ticketing, integrating frequent flyer programs, and cooperative maintenance. While such a venture could yield some efficiency benefits, it would facilitate not just information sharing but also joint decisions about critical matters like route relationships and schedules, equipment and parts acquisition decisions—indeed even pricing; and it would certainly discourage forays by either into a city pair market important to the other. If the markets served by each venture participant were effectively competitive irrespective of the potential competitive threat either provided to the other, significant identifiable efficiencies might outweigh such harms. But in already concentrated airline markets and often hugely concentrated hub-oriented sub-markets, such competitive harms could result in significant reductions in consumer welfare.

13.2b3. Foreclosure

Where venture parents relate to the venture vertically, whether as input suppliers or output buyers, the most salient competitive risk is that other competitors at the parents' horizontal levels will be foreclosed from needed inputs from upstream suppliers or opportunities to market to downstream customers. Harmful foreclosure of competitors of the parent might occur if the venture enters and prevails in a natural monopoly market or if, by innovation or enterprise, it obtains a monopoly or any significant advantage over its competitors that enables it to gain a substantial share of its market.[23] In any such situation, the venture under the control or influence of its parents may be positioned to do serious competitive harm to up or downstream competitors of the parents. If the venturers relate vertically and one of them independently possesses power at its level, the venture might be structured in a way

---

22. Cf. Yamaha Motor Co. v. F.T.C., 657 F.2d 971, 979 (8th Cir. 1981).

23. Associated Press v. United States, 326 U.S. 1, 65 S.Ct. 1416, 89 L.Ed. 2013 (1945).

that may leverage that power into the vertically related market. Suppose, for example, that one of the venturers has substantial market power in a market for computer operating system software and that the other venturer is one of three or four competitors in a market for important application software. If the venturers agree to bundle the operating system and the proprietary, but competing, application software, or agree to integrate the application software into the operating system, the effect will be to leverage power gained in the operating system market into the application system market, thus foreclosing application software competitors.

13.2b4.   *Ancillary and Collateral Terms*

The parents of a joint venture may be concerned that the venture may invade the market that one or more of them occupies or that the venture may compete with one or more of them unduly. To avoid such a risk venturers may negotiate ancillary or collateral terms intended to protect themselves by limiting the activities in which the venture (or in some cases, the parents) may engage. For example, a venture between Pan Am, an air carrier, and Grace, a steamship line, created Panagra, a steamship line operating in a market that neither parent had entered. But the venture terms included covenants precluding the venture from impinging on parental markets.[24] Consider, also, the *Topco* venture which brought small super market chains together to establish and supply to themselves store brand products, thus strengthening their competition with large chains each big enough to support a store brand alone; the *Topco* venturers collaterally agreed that no parent would sell the venture-developed brand in the territorial area of any other parent.[25] Whether or not such harm was likely on the facts of *Topco*, provisions directly aimed at reducing or even stifling competition may do serious competitive harm if actual or potential competition among the parents is important to the competitive dynamic.

§ 13.3   Evaluating Possible Benefits and Harms of a Joint Venture

Once the possible benefits and harms of a venture have been identified they must be weighed against each other and the legality of the venture evaluated pursuant to conventional antitrust standards. At a general level, the basic legal principles are clear enough. Even loose knit joint ventures entail more than "cooperation, collaboration and coalition" in Compton's title phase;[1] of their very nature all ventures are contracts, combinations or conspiracies. Therefore, if they restrain trade

---

24. United States v. Pan American World Airways, Inc., 193 F.Supp. 18 (S.D.N.Y.1961) rev'd on other grounds 371 U. S296 (1963)

25. United States v. Topco Assoc., Inc., 405 U.S. 596, 92 S.Ct. 1126, 31 L.Ed.2d 515 (1972). See also Arizona v. Maricopa County Medical Soc'y, 457 U.S. 332, 102 S.Ct. 2466, 73 L.Ed.2d 48 (1982).

§ 13.3

1. Compton, *Cooperation, Collaboration, and Coalition: A Perspective on the Types and Purposes of Technology Joint Ventures,* 61 ANTITRUST L.J. 861 (1993).

in the antitrust sense—if, on balance, they are unreasonably harmful to competition—they violate Section 1 of the Sherman Act. Additionally, ventures, when executed though jointly held subsidiaries, are acquisitions by firms engaged in commerce and therefore subject to Section 7 of the Clayton Act. If their "effect may be substantially to lessen competition or to tend to create a monopoly" they violate that act.

The first step is to determine whether the competitive analysis should be carried out under Section 1 of the Sherman Act or whether the prophylactic Clayton Act standards apply; indeed, if concentration is high there may also be an issue under Section 2 of the Sherman Act. Because ancillary or collateral agreements can be *per se* unlawful, regardless of the competitive effect of the other aspects of the venture, a convenient second step is to determine whether there is any ancillary agreement and, if so, whether it raises a competitive concern. If there is and it does (and subject to the possibility of *per se* illegality in a blatant case), the competitive effect of that venture term must be evaluated under the ancillary restraint doctrine. Third, if there is no ancillary agreement (or any that exists is not unlawful) the legality of the venture in its essence must be considered under the Sherman Act, the Clayton Act, or both, as appropriate. Unless the venture is a cloak for a cartel (a possibility in some horizontal ventures), all of the possible competitive benefits and harms of the substantive provisions of the venture itself (the venture in its essence) as well as the competitive impact of any ancillary restraint must be catalogued and evaluated in the context of other relevant facts, including: the structure of the market or markets involved (those occupied by the parents and the venture); whether the venture is horizontal, vertical or conglomerate (and, if conglomerate, whether parent and venture markets have possible market or product extension affinities); how the markets of the parents (if they are in different ones) relate to each other; whether the venture market is concentrated; whether it is protected by entry barriers; whether there are few or many potential entrants; and whether one or more parents are potential entrants.[2] Only then can a legal standard—conceivably *per se* or a quick look, more likely a truncated or full blown rule of reason—be applied to determine legality.

In § 13.3a, the application of ancillary restraint doctrine to ventures is discussed. Section 13.3b comments upon market definition in the venture context. Finally, § 13.3c describes how the rule of reason applies to horizontal, vertical and conglomerate ventures.

13.3a. The Ancillary Restraint Doctrine

Setting up a joint venture, whether a loose knit consortium or a highly structured joint subsidiary, involves contractual undertakings by parents. Some, such as commitments to supply capital, management or resources to the venture, are central to its operation and purpose. These

---

2. As noted in § 13.1, a quick look or truncated analysis may be utilized, if appropriate, but if there are both significant potential harms and benefits, a full rule of reason analysis may be needed.

yield the benefits and harms that go into analysis of the competitive effect and legality of the venture in its essence. There may, however, also be other parental assurances, commitments not intrinsic to the venture, yet given to reassure participants that some defuse or unrelated effect of the venture (which one or more parents regard as harmful) will not occur. Some such commitments—say, that parent A will not enter some market unrelated to the venture that parent B is planning to enter—maybe so far removed from the venture's central purpose as to seem irrelevant to it. Such promises, even if folded into venture negotiations or documentation, are here called unrelated collateral restraints. Such restraints must be evaluated on their own under the antitrust laws. They take neither burden nor advantage by being nested in a venture to which they have little or no functional relationship. But other parental commitments, even though not intrinsic to the venture (i.e. not central to its operation and purpose), may be connected to it in the sense: (1) that they are intended to protect venture parents from defuse, but possible, consequences of the venture, which the parents wish to avoid, and (2) that without such protection the venturers (or some of them) would be unwilling to proceed. Such restraints are here called ancillary to the venture. The pledge by the venturers in United States v. Topco Associates[3] is an example of such an ancillary restraint. At its essence, that venture entailed cooperation among small supermarket chains each functioning in different local markets to produce and supply to themselves a line of house brand products. However, some of the venturers feared that other participants might invade their local territories. Hence, they agreed that each would have an exclusive area for the resale of the venture developed and advertised products. This subsection deals with how such ancillary restraints (related, but not intrinsic, to the venture) are evaluated.

Agreements like that in *Topco* limiting the ability of venture partners to compete with the venture or with each other are not uncommon. When used in a venture which, in its essence, results in significant net competitive benefits, such restraints are often upheld.[4] In some instances, however, the ancillary commitment, even though supportive of an otherwise beneficial venture, may be found unlawful.[5] Ancillary restraint doctrine is fact intensive, thus leaving much discretion to courts. It stems from the common law and has its antitrust genesis in United

3. 405 U.S. 596, 92 S.Ct. 1126, 31 L.Ed.2d 515 (1972).

4. E.g, Rothery Storage & Van Co. v. Atlas Van Lines, Inc., 792 F.2d 210 (D.C.Cir.1986), cert. denied, 479 U.S. 1033, 107 S.Ct. 880, 93 L.Ed.2d 834 (1987); Northrop Corp. v. McDonnell Douglas Corp., 705 F.2d 1030 (9th Cir.1983), cert. denied, 464 U.S. 849, 104 S.Ct. 156, 78 L.Ed.2d 144 (1983); National Bancard Corp. v. VISA, U.S.A., Inc., 779 F.2d 592 (11th Cir.1986), cert. denied, 479 U.S. 923, 107 S.Ct. 329, 93 L.Ed.2d 301 (1986).

5. E.g., United States v. Topco Associates, Inc., 405 U.S. 596, 92 S.Ct. 1126, 31 L.Ed.2d 515 (1972); Arizona v. Maricopa County Medical Soc'y, 457 U.S. 332, 102 S.Ct. 2466, 73 L.Ed.2d 48 (1982); United States v. Sealy, Inc., 388 U.S. 350, 87 S.Ct. 1847, 18 L.Ed.2d 1238 (1967); Palmer v. BRG of Georgia, Inc., 498 U.S. 46, 111 S.Ct. 401, 112 L.Ed.2d 349 (1990); United States v. NFL, 196 F. Sup. 445 (E.D.Pa.1961); United States v. Columbia Pictures Corp., 189 F.Supp. 153 (S.D.N.Y.1960); United States v. Morgan, 118 F.Supp. 621, 689–91, 731, 733–39 (S.D.N.Y.1953).

States v. Addyston Pipe & Steel Co.[6] Rationalizing disparate common law cases, Judge Taft stated that a covenant restraining competition was valid only if "ancillary to the main purpose of a contract [and] * * * reasonably adapted and limited to the necessary protection of a party in the carrying out of such purpose * * * ."[7] It is this discretionary search for a less restrictive alternative that often must be brought to bear when a competitive restraint is used to assuage venture parent concerns about excessive intra-venturer competition. To use this approach,[8] a court must first determine that the venture, in its essence (that is, without the ancillary restraint) has competitive benefits as well as harms and therefore may be lawful under the rule of reason if benefits outweigh harms. Next, the court must find that the ancillary restraint is intended to blunt some effect that the parties anticipate may arise from the venture and that blunting this effect is essential (or reasonably necessary) to assuage parental resistance to venture entry. Lastly, it must conclude that no significantly less restrictive alternative would be as (or approximately as) effective in avoiding the effect that would deter parental entry into the venture. If these standards are met, the court should then add the anticompetitive effects of the ancillary restraint to any anticompetitive effects associated with the venture in its essence and should then evaluate whether aggregate venture benefits outweigh aggregate venture harms. Note, however, that when the restraint, though ancillary, falls in or close to a *per se* category, the Supreme Court has sometimes rejected justification analysis entirely,[9] or found the proposed justification for the ancillary restraint inadequate after a quick look.[10] Ancillary restraint doctrine does not displace the conventional analytical framework for horizontal arrangements. It leaves open possibilities for *per se* or quick look as well as for fuller analysis.

In *Topco*, the parents, small supermarket chains operating in different local markets, joined to package and wholesale to their chains a line of house brand products in order to make each of the parents a more effective competitor against major chains large enough to meet minimum scale for house brands of their own. The Court eschewed ancillary restraint analysis because it resisted a dilution of the *per se* rule against horizontal territorial division.[11] In both *Broadcast Music* and *NCAA*[12] the Court ameliorated the rigor of this earlier insistence on the *per se* approach, allowing efficiencies to be weighed against the harms from venture restraint that might have been challenged *per se*. As a result of

---

6. 85 F. 271 (6th Cir.1897), aff'd, 175 U.S. 211, 20 S.Ct. 96, 44 L.Ed. 136 (1899).

7. 85 F. 271 at 283.

8. See Rothery Storage & Van Co. v. Atlas Van Lines, 792 F.2d 210 (D.C.Cir. 1986) (Bork, J.), cert. denied, 479 U.S. 1033, 107 S.Ct. 880, 93 L.Ed.2d 834 (1987); General Leaseways, Inc. v. National Truck Leasing Ass'n, 744 F.2d 588 (7th Cir.1984) (Posner, J.). Cf. Broadcast Music, Inc. v. CBS, Inc., 441 U.S. 1, 99 S.Ct. 1551, 60 L.Ed.2d 1 (1979).

9. United States v. Topco Associates, 405 U.S. at 607–608.

10. Cf. Arizona v. Maricopa County Medical Soc'y, 457 U.S. at 350–351.

11. United States v. Topco Associates, 405 U.S. at 612.

12. Broadcast Music v. Columbia Broadcasting System, 441 U.S. 1, 99 S.Ct. 1551, 60 L.Ed.2d 1 (1979); NCAA v. Board of Regents of Univ. of Oklahoma, 468 U.S. 85, 104 S.Ct. 2948, 82 L.Ed.2d 70 (1984).

these more recent Supreme Court cases, lower courts are more likely widely to apply the ancillary restraint doctrine.[13]

Do *NCAA* and *BMI* warrant abandoning *per se* analysis for all restraints ancillary to a joint venture having in its essence some benefits? Essentially this issue is before the Supreme Court in Texaco, Inc. v. Dagher,[14] a case in which Texaco and Shell formed a joint venture to produce and distribute gasoline in the Western United States. As a part of this agreement, the companies agreed to set common prices for gasoline sales in the region. The court of appeals reversed a district court decision that dismissed the case and held that the pricing agreement was an ancillary restraint that was per se unlawful. If the Supreme Court reverses this holding, it could heighten the risk to consumer welfare and resource allocation, a risk that can and should be narrowed.[15] First, when a restraint affecting price or territory is said to be ancillary and hence entitled to be integrated into the overall rule of reason analysis of the venture, the court should start with a rebuttable presumption that the restraint is either unrelated (not really intended to encourage the venture, but to gain cover from it) or more restrictive than reasonably necessary to accomplish the goal of making the venture possible. Venture proponents should have a heavy burden of showing that, if there is rejection of direct competition between venture partners or between them and the venture, that rejection is reasonably necessary for the venture is to go forward at all. Second, even if proponents persuade the court or jury, for example, that a territorial restraint is essential to implementation of the venture, the unquestioned and certain harm from such a blatant restraint should be given full weight in the final balancing of harms and benefits. If, apart from the ancillary restraint, the reasonableness of the venture in its essence is a debatable issue, the additional adverse effects of the ancillary restraint should tip the balance. Manifestly, any clear, immediate, negative effect from such a restraint should overwhelm any collection of small, doubtful, speculative, problematic or time-delayed benefits.

13.3b. Market Definition For Rule of Reason Evaluation of Ventures

Whether the venture is being executed by creating a joint subsidiary subject to the Clayton Act, or through a looser consortium or association subject only to the Sherman Act, conventional market definition methodologies apply. In either case merger guideline provisions can model the

---

13. See the cases cited in note 8, supra. Compare some of the cases from the 1950s and 1960s cited in note 5, supra. See also the discussion in §§ 5.4–5.7.

14. 369 F.3d 1108 (9th Cir. 2004), cert. granted ___ U.S. ___, 125 S.Ct. 2957, ___ L.Ed.2d ___ (2005).

15. See Polygram Holding, Inc. v. FTC, 416 F.3d 29 (D.C.Cir. 2005)(court of appeals upholds FTC's truncated analysis of adver-tising restraints on products not a part of the joint venture); Brunswick Corp. 94 F.T.C. 1174 (1979), modified, 96 F.T.C. 151 (1980), aff'd sub. nom, Yamaha Motor Co. v. F.T.C., 657 F.2d 971 (8th Cir.1981), cert. denied, 456 U.S. 915, 102 S.Ct. 1768, 72 L.Ed.2d 174 (1982)(agency indicated that a venture that was probably valid in its essence was marred by an ancillary territorial restraint).

analysis.[16] Product market is first considered. Begin with the product or service the venture will supply. Any substantially identical products or services as well as any differentiated ones that buyers regard as good substitutes are included. The goal is to comprehend all products or services to which buyers would shift if those offering the venture product or service should raise prices significantly above competitive levels and maintain them there for an appreciable time. Supply side constraints must also be factored in by identifying and including producers of any product or service not considered a substitute, but so positioned that they would make adjustments and start to offer the venture product or service if prices for it were raised to and sustained at supracompetitive levels. A comparable analysis must also be done with respect to geographic markets.

13.3c. Balancing Harms and Benefits

The towering concern when a venture is analyzed, whether under Section 1 of Sherman Act or Section 7 of Clayton Act, is that it may threaten output limitation and price enhancement. This question is addressed much as it would be in a merger or in a looser combination.

13.3c1. Horizontal Ventures

After the market is defined, the Merger Guidelines can be used to characterize the degree of concentration, and to characterize the extent to which the venture increases concentration.[17] If concentration is not increased sufficiently to trigger the Guidelines, the venture should be presumed to be lawful.[18] Implication based on concentration, however, can be moderated in light of high or low entry barriers, apparent potential entrants, whether products are differentiated, or a history of coordination on the one hand or aggressive competition on the other. Indeed, any other evidence (including any ancillary agreement) that may help to signify purpose or effect should be considered. If, on the basis of guideline characterizations as so adjusted, significant allocative harm is identified, the venture should be presumed to be anticompetitive and thus regarded as unlawful unless venture specific efficiency benefits can be identified, calibrated, and are found to outweigh the harms.

All possible efficiencies and other benefits identified or claimed must be brought into focus, and an overall evaluation begun. In some instances, the indicated outcome may be quickly evident. A past history of coordination, a vulnerable collateral or ancillary restraint, or claimed benefits that seem pretextual on their face or clearly obtainable in less

---

16. U.S. Dept. of Justice and FTC, Horizontal Merger Guidelines (1992, as amended in 1997), available at <http:// www.us-doj.gov/atr/public / guidelines/hmg.htm>.

17. Horizontal Merger Guidelines § 1.5.

18. The agency Collaboration Guidelines suggest that the nature of the agreement should also be considered in determining whether the agreement falls within a safe harbor ("If the nature of the agreement and the absence of market power together demonstrate the absence of anticompetitive harm, the Agencies do not challenge the agreement."). FTC/DoJ, Antitrust Guidelines for Collaborations Among Competitors § 3.3, available at <http://www.ftc.gov/os/2000/04/ftcdojguidelines.pdf>.

restrictive ways may justify a negative evaluation, perhaps even on the basis of a quick look. Similarly, if market concentration is on the low side of moderate, there are indicia of effective competition and low barriers, and the story of significant efficiencies is convincing, a conclusion of legality may require no elaborate inquiry.

Yet there may be instances—say, moderately high to high concentration, apparent barriers to entry, some indications of past leadership but a persuasive showing of significant scale, scope or affinity advantages— where the likely outcome will not be quickly evident. In such a situation attorneys advising venture parties should be sure that all potentially negative factors and all possible benefits are identified, understood and effectively articulated, that possible risk-reducing adjustments are identified and considered, and that clients are given a clear evaluation of the rules. If the form of the venture is a merger, the enforcement agencies may use premerger notification procedures to develop a wider range of information. If the venture need not be reported, whether it will be noticed by enforcement agencies or challenged by potentially injured parties may not be quickly apparent.

13.3c2.   Vertical Ventures

If venture participants relate vertically the principal concern about output reduction and price enhancement arises from foreclosure possibilities. The norm-oriented, deductive view (dominant in the Antitrust Division during the 1980's) was that vertical integration is seldom anticompetitive except in the context of price regulation and natural monopoly. This view has persisted among some commentators. Nevertheless, modern economic scholarship,[19] antitrust commentary[20] and current enforcement policy[21] all approach vertical integrations with inquiries, not pre-set convictions. See the discussion in § 12.3. The process today is to gather available information and to use post-Chicago thinking to analyze it inductively. The decision maker must gauge the strengths and weaknesses of alternative contentions in order to reach a balanced judgment about competitive harms and benefits.[22] After carefully evaluating all benefits of the kinds reviewed in § 13.2a2, the analyst should be alert to identify significant risks of foreclosure (either of inputs or outputs) and to gauge the likely effect, if any, of any such foreclosure on prices or stifled or significantly reduced incentives for innovation. Where input foreclosure occurs, the critical question is the effect on prices paid by foreclosed competitors for substitute inputs.[23] In the case of output

19. Ordover, *Equilibrium Vertical Foreclosure*, 80 Am. Econ. Rev. 127 (1990); Ordover, Sykes, and Willig, *Nonprice anticompetiive Behavior by Dominant Firms Toward the Producers of Complementary Products in* Antitrust and Regulation: In Memory of John J. McGowan, 115 (F. Fisher, ed, 1985).

20. E.g., Krattenmaker and Salop, *Anticompetitive Exclusion: Raising Rivals' Costs to Achieve Power Over Price*, 96 Yale L.J. 209 (1986).

21. See the Survey in Riordan and Salop, *Evaluating Vertical Mergers: A Post–Chicago Approach*, 63 Antitrust L.J. 513 (1995).

22. Id.

23. Riordan and Salop suggest that prices paid by downstream customers of these foreclosed competitors must also be

foreclosure it is the impact, if any, on prices paid by customers buying in the market where the venture competes as a seller.

In dealing with vertical mergers, Riordan and Salop propose a presumption that unless an appreciable adverse price effect in a consumer market can be inferred, the merger should be presumed lawful, without the need for critical evaluation of possible efficiencies.[24] A better rule would be to apply a presumption of legality only if there is no likely allocative injury from the vertical combination. Because an adverse price effect in an input market can have significantly adverse allocative effects, requiring a consumer market price effect to defeat the presumption of legality could insulate genuinely anticompetitive conduct. If the only apparent price effect is in an intermediate (non-consumer) market, the adverse allocative effect in that market should be balanced against any evident offsetting efficiencies. Nevertheless consumer markets do have special importance. Even if there are offsetting efficiencies these should not outweigh allocative harm when there is a continuing adverse price effect in a consumer market. The proper approach would treat both intermediate effect on competitors and price effects further downstream as relevant. Under neither Section 1 of the Sherman Act nor Section 7 of the Clayton Act should a vertical venture be vulnerable because of foreclosure unless the evidence indicates that it will result in a significant price increase that will be sustained for an appreciable period of time before market responses can neutralize it. If such an adverse price effect is inferred, the venture should be held unlawful unless (1) the allocative benefits from efficiencies that the venture yields (and that could not be attained without the foreclosure) are substantial enough to outweigh the allocative harm from the adverse price effect, and (2) there is no persisting adverse price effect in any consumer market.

In addition to foreclosure concerns, a vertical venture could conceivably result in a structural change that facilitates either express collusion or price or output leadership.[25] This was one of the issues raised in connection with AT & T's acquisition of McCaw Cellular.[26] AT & T (before the Lucent spin-off) was a supplier of equipment to McCaw competitors. Also, McCaw bought cellular equipment from Ericsson, one of AT & T's manufacturing competitors. It was contended that AT & T and Ericsson could collude through McCaw as a channel and that McCaw and its cellular competitors could collude through AT & T as a channel. Also (and to quite the opposite effect) there was a concern that McCaw could disclose sensitive Ericsson information to AT & T and/or AT & T could disclose to McCaw sensitive information about McCaw's cellular competitors to which AT & T became privity as their cellular supplier. Scenarios like these can present no serious concern if the upstream and

---

evaluated and that illegality should be adjudicated only if the adverse price effect carries down to a consumer market. Id. at 563–564.

24. Id. at 522–523.

25. See § 13.2b2.

26. United States v. AT & T, 59 Fed. Reg. 44, 158 (Aug. 26, 1994). One of the authors was a witness for AT & T before the California Public Utilities Commission concerning the competitive effects of this merger.

downstream markets are effectively competitive. At the time the AT & T long distance market was effectively competitive, but McCaw's local cellular markets were duopolies. At any rate, as urged by McCaw's cellular competitors, DOJ challenged the merger and negotiated a regulatory consent decree,[27] later made largely irrelevant by AT & T's spin-off of Lucent and ultimately vacated by the 1996 Telecommunications Act.[28]

13.3c3. *Conglomerate Ventures*

Conglomerate ventures are the least likely to give rise to serious competition problems. The only evident risk is that a product extension or market extension merger in a compacted market could bring an end to potential competition. This would be a serious concern only if the market affected was highly concentrated and there were few potential competitors. Whether the venture is highly or loosely structured, analysis should track that used for conglomerate mergers.[29]

§ 13.4 Health Care Joint Ventures

For a variety of reasons, the health care industry presents some distinctive competition problems and antitrust issues. First, third party payors, including governmental (through subsidies for health care such as Medicare and Medicaid), employer negotiated health plans (subsidized, in part, through business expense tax deductions) and privately purchased health insurance (subsidized, in part, by limited tax deductibility), are omnipresent. Second, demand for many health services tends to be highly inelastic. Third, technological dynamism across the whole spectrum (procedures, devices, drugs) has been accelerating. Fourth, there is considerable governmental subsidy for research of various kinds as well as for hospital construction. Fifth, substantial consumer-information problems make it difficult for consumers to make wise buying decisions without the aid of health professionals. Sixth, significant federal and state regulation influences both conduct and structure in the industry. Seventh, following the abortive legislative restructuring unsuccessfully attempted during the first term of the Clinton administration, there have been aggressive private efforts to control costs through health maintenance organizations (HMOs) and preferred provider organizations (PPOs), which to a large extent have replaced not only conventional fee for service practice, but also previously conventional indemnification through insurance. The first three of these industry characteristics have led to rapid acceleration of annual aggregate health care expenditures. The seventh factor has probably limited aggregate expenditures somewhat, but perhaps at the cost of reduced quality of care.

The private restructuring process has produced horizontal joint ventures among physicians or other health care professionals aimed at

27. Id.

28. Telecommunications   Act,   47 U.S.C.A. § 274 (1996).

29. See § 11.3.

cost reduction and service improvement, but probably in most cases also as a means of developing countervailing power in dealings with third party payors. Such ventures can raise antitrust questions about cooperative price setting (§ 13.4.a1), covenants precluding physicians' participation in more than one venture (§ 13.4a2), covenants forbidding third party payors to contract with competing ventures (§ 13.4a3), and foreclosure of competing suppliers from venture participation (§ 13.4a4). The restructuring has led, also, to horizontal ventures between hospitals, varying from mergers integrating all services to arrangements limited to the co-development only of specialized facilities (§ 13.4b), and has entailed a variety of vertical ventures including arrangements between hospitals and ancillary service providers or between physicians and ancillary service providers (§ 13.4c). These kinds of ventures will be considered in sequence.

13.4a. Horizontal Ventures Among Physicians or Other Professionals

13.4a1. Ventures Involving Cooperative Price Setting

As Havighurst has noted,[1] an HMO can take one of three basic forms. In the familiar "staff model HMO," exemplified by Kaiser Permamente, the HMO hires staff physicians (and may also operate hospitals). It then contracts with employers or individuals to provide service for covered patients who turn to HMO staff members (and HMO facilities, if provided) for service. For a significant period the major alternative, and, indeed, the dominant model, was the "individual practice HMO"—an HMO that contracted with employers and individuals to supply health care and then contracted with a sufficient number of otherwise unaffiliated, independent practitioners (either as individuals or as small partnerships) to provide service to covered members. As fee for service practice waned, HMOs and other third party payors grew stronger and more aggressive both in limiting fees and in constraining choices about procedures and medications by physicians. In response physicians began to establish larger physician-controlled groups that contracted with an HMO to provide service to persons acquiring (through employment or individual contract) a membership in the HMO. It is this newer, but increasingly common, "group model HMO" that tends to raise antitrust issues and, most significantly, issues about how the fees paid by the HMO to the physicians in the physician controlled group are determined.

Doctors and nurses, the soldiers of the healthcare system, are increasingly forced to bargain with large healthcare providers who wield buyer power. As atomistic sellers with a large time and financial investment in their training, doctors and nurses have substantial sunk costs (and perhaps a psychological commitment as well) that make them

§ 13.4

1. Havighurst, *Doctors and Hospitals: An Antitrust Perspective On Traditional Re-*   *lationships,* 1984 DUKE L. J. 1071.

reluctant to change professions and therefore vulnerable to buyer power. These concerns, addressed in § 2.7b, have pushed health professionals toward collaboration in order to obtain countervailing power in bargaining with the large providers. In many instances, the doctors or nurses lack employee status and do not qualify for the labor law exemption from antitrust. Thus, their collaboration on output prices may run squarely up against the per se rule against price fixing.

The antitrust agencies have struggled in developing a coherent strategy for dealing with this collaboration. There are tensions here and their sources are fairly obvious. Physician-employees of a staff model HMO have a Taft–Hartly right to negotiate collectively for their compensation (§ 14.3a). Physician-members of a physician controlled group, though they may have no more (or even less) market power than staff HMO employee-physicians, have no such right. Indeed, if employee physicians of a group model HMO jointly announced a fee schedule or jointly negotiated one with an HMO, they might well be vulnerable under the price fixing *per se* rule.[2] Of course, if the physician controlled group, however large, is a partnership, with all participating physicians sharing in its profits or losses, the partnership could lawfully negotiate its fees;[3] its only antitrust vulnerability would be illegality of the venture in its essence if the group aggregated too high a percentage of a well defined physician service market.[4] But if participating physicians do not as co-principals share the financial risk of the group, conventional analysis would expose them to manifest risk under Section 1 of the Sherman Act. Yet, the countervailing power justification for joint fee negotiation by such groups has had appeal to some authorities.

In United States v. A. Lanoy Alston, DMD,[5] Judge Kozinski addressed a related issue. Three Arizona dentists (the named defendants in the case), noting that third party payor fees in their city had not risen as far as they had in other cities, convened meetings of dentists to discuss the need for higher fees, after which one of the three circulated to several other dentists a statement to the effect that a "minimum acceptable fee schedule" would be established. After a verdict of guilty on a criminal indictment of the three dentists, the district court set aside the verdict, acquitted two of them, and ordered a new trial for the third. On the government's appeal the Ninth circuit vacated the acquittals but affirmed the new trial. In his opinion for the court, Judge Kozinski stated that while scrutiny under the *per se* rule was appropriate, nevertheless:

---

2. Arizona v. Maricopa County Medical Society, 457 U.S. 332, 102 S.Ct. 2466, 73 L.Ed.2d 48 (1982). See also Hahn v. Oregon Physicians' Serv., 868 F.2d 1022 (9th Cir. 1988), cert. denied, 493 U.S. 846, 110 S.Ct. 140, 107 L.Ed.2d 99 (1989). Cf. Hassan v. Independent Practice Associates, 698 F.Supp. 679 (E.D. Mich. 1988), which signifies that a payment mechanism such as capitation that imposes financial risk on doctors will avoid characterizations of the venture as *per se* price fixing.

3. Cf. Rothery Storage & Van Co. v. Atlas Van Lines, Inc. 792 F.2d 210 (D.C.Cir. 1986), cert. denied 479 U.S. 1033, 107 S.Ct. 880, 93 L.Ed.2d 834 (1987)

4. Id.

5. 974 F.2d 1206 (9th Cir.1992).

"[H]ealth care providers who must deal with consumers indirectly through plans such as [that involved] face an unusual situation * * *. Medical plans serve, effectively, as the bargaining agents for large groups of consumers; they use the [resulting] clout * * * to drive down health care service fees. Uniform fee schedules—anathema in a normal, competitive market—are standard operating procedure when medical plans are involved. In light of these departures from a normal competitive market, individual health care providers are entitled to take some joint action (short of price fixing or a group boycott) to level the bargaining imbalance * * *."[6]

In general, courts have been unresponsive to countervailing power defenses to conduct vulnerable under the Sherman Act.[7] The Kozinski dictum, above, is perhaps as accommodating a judicial response as can be identified to claims that power on the other side of the market changes the rules. It does not specify an analytical approach to efforts "short of price fixing" that might be used to level the field, but does specify possible subjects for joint negotiation: payment procedures, documentation, referral protocols and dispute adjustment mechanism.[8] Judge Kozinski also suggested that health care providers might be able, lawfully, to "pool cost data in justifying a request for an increased fee schedule * * *,"[9] implying, perhaps, that independent health professionals can act jointly to prepare their case for increased fees, so long as each participant makes its own decision about how much of an increase to demand and they do not threaten a collective withholding of service if their demands are not met.

The enforcement agencies have become sensitive to these problems, perhaps excessively so. In 1996, the Department of Justice and FTC issued joint statements addressing pricing practices by provider controlled health care ventures.[10] This document revised statements about physician joint ventures contained in guidelines first issued in 1993[11] and revised in 1994.[12] In the 1993 and 1994 versions the guidelines indicated that ventures among and controlled by physician providers are subject to

---

6. Id. at 1214. See also the dissent by Justice Powell in Arizona v. Maricopa County Medical Soc'y, 457 U.S. 332, 357, 102 S.Ct. 2466, 73 L.Ed.2d 48 (1982). Although dissenters asserted that "insurers may be the only parties who have effective power to restrain medical costs," the majority rejected the claim that this countervailing power issue should foreclose application of the *per se* rule against price fixing. Note also that by enacting a specific defense for labor unions, Congress may have impliedly recognized the lack of any general, overarching countervailing power defense.

7. E.g., Arizona v. Maricopa County Medical Soc'y, supra note 6; FTC v. Superior Court Trial Lawyers Association, 493 U.S. 411, 110 S.Ct. 768, 107 L.Ed.2d 851 (1990).

8. United States v. Alson, supra note 6 at 1214.

9. Id.

10. Joint Department of Justice/Federal Trade Commission Statements of Antitrust Enforcement Policy In Health Care, 1996, 14 Trade Reg. Rep. (CCH) ¶ 13,153 (1996) (hereinafter 1996 Enforcement Statements), reprinted in Appendix E.

11. Joint Department of Justice/Federal Trade Commission Statement of Antitrust Enforcement in Health Care, 1993, 4 Trade Reg. Rep. (CCH) ¶ 13,152.

12. Joint Department of Justice/Federal Trade commission Statement of Antitrust Enforcement in Health Care, 1994, 4 Trade Reg. Rep. (CCH) ¶ 13,152.

conventional antitrust law and gain no preferred status in light of structural change that may give third party payers market power over providers, or imbue HMOs with market power physician provider groups cannot match. While it has long been clear that ancillary restraints in ventures yielding efficiencies may be lawful,[13] there was considerable opinion, supported by *Maricopa*,[14] that when a physician controlled venture jointly negotiated with third party payers to establish a fee schedule for otherwise independent fee-for-service physicians, resulting reductions in transaction costs (even when combined with modest utilization reductions), would not yield benefit enough to blunt the *per se* rule against horizontal price fixing.[15] Hence, many attorneys, including a spokesperson for the FTC, advised that physician controlled ventures could not jointly negotiate or set fees for a group, unless their integration included sharing financial risk which would motivate cooperation to control venture costs and would deter efforts by participants to maximize their individual incomes by offering additional service at the expense, in part, of the venture.[16]

The 1993 and 1994 guidelines provided, if not crystal clarity, an understandable standard closely related to antitrust tradition. If actors competing in the same market integrate sufficiently to share profit and loss, they will be motivated to achieve cost cutting efficiencies. If their market remains effectively competitive after such an integration, there is no reason to challenge their venture. It can, and probably will, yield efficiencies and on-going competition should assure that these are passed on to buyers. Physicians combined in a financial risk-sharing venture should be treated the same way. There are many media for sharing risks: capitation; venture acceptance of a percentage of the premium collected by the third party payer; sharing of the fee between the venture and the physician provider; a conditional retention of the fee or a portion of it, subject to profit/loss outcomes, etc. If any such mechanism is effectively used, there is a real integration reflected in the bottom line. Such a venture would warrant critical antitrust evaluation only if it had integrated enough physicians in a local health care market to exercise market power.

By contrast, any reduction of transaction costs associated solely with joint price setting has never been thought sufficient to avoid a *per se* analysis and cartel characterization,[17] a view reflected in the 1993 and 1994 guidelines. Indeed, despite the anomalies involved in *Appalachian*

---

13. See § 13.2b4, supra.

14. Arizona v. Maricopa County Medical Soc'y, 457 U.S. 332, 102 S.Ct. 2466, 73 L.Ed.2d 48 (1982).

15. But cf. Broadcast Music, Inc. v. CBS, Inc., 441 U.S. 1, 99 S.Ct. 1551, 60 L.Ed.2d 1 (1979) which held that the massive transaction cost savings that resulted in what amounted to a new market for a new product—licenses to broad bundles of music copyrights—were sufficient to avoid

per se liabilities for jointly setting price for the bundle.

16. See the comments by M.J. Haraschak, Asst. Director, Bureau of Completion, FTC, "Recent Developments in FTC's Antitrust Program For Health Care", Remarks for National Health Lawyers Ass'n (February 16, 1995).

17. See notes 6 and 7, supra and accompanying text.

Coals,[18] even setting up a separate marketing subsidiary that could reduce selling expense significantly has not generally been regarded as blunting *per se* or quick look illegality when participating independent sellers leave price setting to the subsidiary.[19]

The 1996 Enforcement Statements, however, modify the earlier implication. According to the current statement, neither DOJ nor the FTC will treat shared financial risks as a precondition for rule of reason treatment of a physician controlled health care network in which the venture either establishes a fee for service schedule or negotiates payment terms with third party payers. Specifically, statements 8 and 9 indicate that if "clinical integration" among the venturers is sufficient, price negotiation by the venture may be ancillary and lawful, even without financial risk sharing. If non-financial integration is sufficient and that integration can be shown to generate substantial efficiencies, and if joint negotiation of fees for service is reasonably necessary to attain the efficiencies, the rule of reason will apply. Once the efficiencies and the need for joint pricing to sustain them have been shown, such arrangements will be at risk only if the integration yields power in an appropriately defined market, thus threatening price enhancement and supply reduction. Even then, the efficiencies will presumably be balanced against the possible harms, in a conventional rule of reason analysis.

While "clinical integration" is not expressly defined, the statement provides examples:

> Such integration can be evidenced by the network implementing an active and ongoing program to evaluate and modify practice patterns by * * * physician(s) * * * and [to] create a high degree of interdependence and cooperation among the physicians to control costs and ensure quality. This program may include: (1) * * * mechanisms to monitor and control utilization * * * [which] control costs and assure quality * * *.; (2) * * * [selectivity in granting network membership] to further these efficiency objectives; and (3) the significant investment of capital, both monetary and human, in the necessary infrastructure and capability to realize the claimed efficiencies.[20]

The enforcement judgment is that when physicians participate in a cooperative venture their pocketbooks need not be at risk to assure that they are striving to reduce costs while preserving the quality of care. This goal can come from other (perhaps finer) professional motivations, and if it does there may be ways to demonstrate that it is there.

---

18. Appalachian Coals v. United States, 288 U.S. 344, 53 S.Ct. 471, 77 L.Ed. 825 (1933).

19. Virginia Excelsior Mills, Inc. v. FTC, 256 F.2d 538 (4th Cir.1958).

20. 1996 Enforcement Statements, Statement 8(B)(1), available at <http://www.ftc.gov/reports/hlth3s.htm>. There are illustrative hypothetical examples

following the Statement. For an instructive analysis of the implication of the Statements see Proger & Love, *Current Antitrust Issues for Provider–Payer Networks: The Hospital's Perspective,* in ABA SECTION OF ANTITRUST LAW, ANTITRUST AND HEALTH CARE: NEW APPROACHES AND CHALLENGES 117 (Ross, ed. 1998) (hereinafter "ANTITRUST AND HEALTH").

No doubt such possibilities exist. And no doubt there may be many ventures where little or no significant competitive harm would result even if every participating physician would like, if possible, to maximize her own return at the expense of the venture. If there is effective competition in the relevant health service market the venture may have little or no market power. Nonetheless, moving from the conventional *per se* approach to the Enforcement Statements' approach may diminish protection against competitive harm. Note that under the conventional approach joint price setting required financial integration except in rare situations like that in *BMI* where massive transaction cost gains were manifestly attained and a new market created. Consequentially, unrelated collateral restraints gained no protection from a venture, and ancillary restraints were subject first to a less restrictive alternative test and then integrated into a critical evaluation of all harms and benefits under the rule of reason. As the *Maricopa County* case showed, physician ventures were treated as were other ventures. By contrast, under the 1996 DOJ–FTC Enforcement Statements a physician venture structured to achieve "clinical integration" that may help to protect quality and control cost may be able to engage in joint price setting without financial integration and without losing the benefit of a rule of reason analysis, at least by the enforcement agencies.

If joint price negotiation is contemplated, such a venture will always be structured to meet enforcement guidelines at the surface level, so long as the 1996 Enforcement Statements are not withdrawn. The grave danger is not that of bad faith. Physicians participating in such a venture will expect and intend to act effectively to control costs and will be determined to provide good service. Rarely would a physician enter such a venture with opportunistic free-riding plans. The danger, rather, is that devices designed to police utilization, control costs and assure quality will tend to erode in the interactions of busy, ongoing, active, professional involvements. If no power reposes in the venture, competition may tend to protect against undue deterioration of service quality. But absent any direct pocketbook spur on each participating physician to control costs, erosion in cost control may be inevitable. The doctors' profit motives, concern about malpractice exposure, and patient and political pressure to achieve the highest quality of care will, in combination, tend to erode the best of intentions about complying with rigorous utilization standards. Therefore, if the venture does have market power in a local physician service market, utilizing the rule of reason for ventures not sufficiently integrated to impose bottom line risk on all participants may court significant risk of competitive harm. Of course, the 1996 Statements are not hard law; they are only a statement of enforcement intentions. Presumably private suitors suffering antitrust injury could still sue in reliance on cases like *Maricopa County*.[21] But guidelines can be very influential both on marketplace conduct and on how the law develops. Giving up on the *per se* approach converts the private bar that advises doctors and their groups from tough minded

21. Supra note 6.

parts of the antitrust enforcement system into designers of arrangements that will likely avoid serious scrutiny except when substantial market power is blatant.

The steady flow of price fixing actions brought against physicians and other health care professionals[22] may suggest commendable vigilance on the part of the enforcement agencies. It also may suggest, however, that antitrust policy in this area does not rest upon a sound and stable foundation. Mergers among health care providers have led to concentrated buyer power that is wielded against vulnerable health care professionals. If the sole consequence of this buyer power were to trim excess compensation paid to doctors and nurses, there would be little basis for concern. But few careful observers of the health care system would claim that resources are being soundly allocated. For example, there is a need for physicians willing to serve rural and low income communities and a general need for more trained nurses. One cannot comfortably conclude that these supply distortions can be attributed solely or primarily to excesses in buyer power. Yet the economics and history of competition and antitrust suggest that allocative distortions are a likely result of market power abuses.

A strong case can be made that current antitrust policy is biased against physicians, nurses, and other atomistic sellers.[23] Mergers of buyers of these services can produce and some have produced oligopsony power, while the sellers, for a variety financial and personal reasons may be reluctant to integrate sufficiently to create a countervailing oligopoly power. If the atomistic seller lacks the protection of the labor law exemption, collaborative bargaining units that could exercise countervailing power are considered unlawful price fixing. How should antitrust respond to these realities? A sound first step would be for the agencies to pay more attention to buyer power in passing on mergers that affect industries of atomistic sellers. Mergers of health care providers, for example, should be scrutinized not only for their effects on consumers but also for their impact on atomistic suppliers such as doctors and nurses. Although merger enforcement's greater attention to buyer power will help, it cannot undo a structure of oliopolistic health care providers. A reexamination of antitrust policy toward bargaining collaborations is also needed. In today's world, the primary purpose of doctor and nurse collaborations is to exercise countervailing power, not to achieve greater efficiencies in the delivery of medical services. To assess such collaborations solely on the basis of efficiency or integration of services is to invite the sort artificial constructs designed to appear integrative while clearly aimed at the exercise of bargaining power. Yet that countervailing

---

22. The FTC has been most active in bringing price fixing cases against physician organizations. Most of these cases have been settled by consent. E.g., Piedmont Health Alliance, C–4106 (2004), available at <www.ftc.gov/opa/2004/08/piedmont.htm>; Physicians Integrated Services of Denver, Inc., C–4054 (2002)available at <www.ftc.gov/os/caselist/0110173.htm>.

23. Grimes, *The Sherman Act's Unintended Bias Against Lilliputians: Small Players' Collective Actions as a Counter to Relational Market Power,* 69 ANTITRUST L.J. 195 (2001).

bargaining power may well be needed to prevent allocative injury and to ensure fairness to physicians and nurses, whose support for antitrust is undermined by a skewed policy favoring power buyers. One solution might be to place market share limitations on groups of bargaining physicians, perhaps commensurate with the market shares possessed by the health care providers that buy these services. Antitrust does not require that a merger of health care providers be efficient–only that it not threaten competition. Perhaps the same standard should be applied to bargaining collaborations of health care professionals that confront oligopsony that engenders allocative injury.

13.4a2. Covenants Against Provider Participation in Competing Ventures

Provider controlled groups earn compensation for member doctors by contracting with one or more HMOs which collect fees from employers and individuals on commitment to provide them with health care. Whether it's physician members participate in other such groups may be of interest to a provider controlled group. For one thing (and on the procompetitive side), a physician who is involved with only one such group will have strong incentive to improve the competitive position of that group through high quality and reasonably priced services. For another, a fixed and constant group of physicians regularly participating might facilitate group management and promotion of quality control and usage based on patient need, not physician revenue goals.[24] On the other hand, because groups compete with each other on price and service in seeking contracts with HMOs, such exclusivity could be anticompetitive. If a group were to gain exclusive access to a large percentage of the most competent or best reputed physicians in a local market, it might gain sufficient advantage to attain market power. For one thing, entry by a new HMO might be inhibited. For another, linking large numbers of physicians in stable relationship might result in network advantages both for patients and physicians tending toward "HMO of Choice" status. Given the possibility of advantages and disadvantages that depend on whether market power is being gained, rule of reason analysis, with the possibility of a truncated analysis or even a quick look, should apply.[25]

---

24. See Enders, *An Introduction to Special Antitrust Issues in Health Care Provider Joint Ventures,* 61 ANTITRUST L.J. 805, 823 (1993).

25. If full blown rule of reason analysis were required, a geographic and a service market definition would be essential. The narrowest possible service market would be physician controlled groups on the supply side and HMOs on the demand side. Can such groups be distinguished? Can HMOs be assigned to a different relevant market from fee for service indemnification insurance, etc? Cf. Blue Cross and Blue Shield United of Wisconsin v. Marshfield Clinic, 65

F.3d 1406 (7th Cir.1995), cert. denied, 516 U.S. 1184, 116 S.Ct. 1288, 134 L.Ed.2d 233 (1996). The importance of market definition to the outcome is illustrated by U.S. Healthcare, Inc. v. Healthsource, Inc., 986 F.2d 589 (1st Cir.1993). Where an HMO required participating physicians to deal only with it in order to qualify for maximum reimbursement rates, the market was defined broadly. Twenty-five percent of primary care physicians licensed in New Hampshire were foreclosed by the restrictions. Plaintiff apparently made no effort to prove what number of the remaining 75 per cent were foreclosed by exclusive employ-

13.4a3. Covenants Precluding HMOs from Using Competing Provider Ventures

Provider controlled groups may negotiate to be the exclusive provider organization with which a particular HMO will contract during a given period, thus effectively tying that HMO out of access to other competing provider groups. Such an arrangement should be analyzed much as any other exclusive dealing arrangement. An exclusive relationship can yield some efficiencies. If the HMO in question (or if a series of several HMOs with which a provider controlled group had similar exclusive relationships) controlled a substantial share of demand for service in a well defined market,[26] then the arrangement should be vulnerable; otherwise not.[27]

13.4a4. Foreclosing Competing Individual Providers from Participating

Stationary wholesalers that form a group to buy supplies for resale need not admit competing wholesalers unless access to the group is essential to market entry, or at least gives a significant, competitive advantage.[28] The same rule of reason standard should apply to a physician-controlled group marketing health care services to HMOs. To gain access, an excluded physician would have to start by showing the crucial competitive importance of access. Indeed, even though non-access to such a group foreclosed nonparticipants from, say, as much as 30 percent of a local market, the decision in Jefferson Parish Hospital District No. 2 v. Hyde[29] might be read as suggesting that there is no antitrust basis for compelling access.[30] But realistic evaluation of market options open to excluded physicians or other providers is essential. In a health care structure where most patients are covered by HMOs, the HMOs are linked to provider groups, and provider groups are closed, the effect system wide could be serious foreclosure of individual providers seeking to enter.

Certainly if a particular venture obtained such a share of a well defined market that access to it was essential to compete in that market, rule of reason analysis would require that access to the group be

ment with other HMOs. The court found that plaintiff did not meet its burden under Tampa Electric Co. v. Nashville Coal Co., 365 U.S. 320, 81 S.Ct. 623, 5 L.Ed.2d 580 (1961).

26. See the discussion in note 25, supra.

27. See EGH, Inc. v. Blue Cross and Blue Shield of Oregon, Civil No. 90–1210–JO (D. Or. 1992) cited and discussed in Enders, *An Introduction to Special Antitrust Issues In Health Care Provider Joint Ventures, supra* note 24, at 823–24.

28. Northwest Wholesale Stationers, Inc. v. Pacific Stationery & Printing Co., 472 U.S. 284, 105 S.Ct. 2613, 86 L.Ed.2d 202 (1985); compare United States v. Ter-

minal R.R. Ass'n of St. Louis, 224 U.S. 383, 32 S.Ct. 507, 56 L.Ed. 810 (1912); Associated Press v. United States, 326 U.S. 1, 65 S.Ct. 1416, 89 L.Ed. 2013 (1945), See § 5.7d.

29. 466 U.S. 2, 104 S.Ct. 1551, 80 L.Ed.2d 2 (1984). See also U.S. Healthcare, Inc. v. Healthsource, Inc., 986 F.2d 589 (1st Cir. 1993).

30. See Enders, *An Introduction to Special Antitrust Issues in Health Care Provider Joint Ventures, supra* note 24 at 824. *Cf.* Barry v. Blue Cross of California, 805 F.2d 866, 1986–2 Trade Cas. (CCH) ¶ 67,367 (9th Cir. 1986).

granted, unless there was a reasonable, efficiency related basis for excluding any particular applicant.[31] If, for example, a particular physician were excluded on the ground that he was not adequately qualified, the peer review standards articulated in cases like Patrick v. Burget[32] and Summit Health, Ltd. v. Pinhas[33] should apply.[34]

By contrast, any blatant concerted conduct by health care providers to exclude competitors by depriving them of an essential input can be vulnerable. For example, Nurse Midwifery Associates v. Hibbett[35] teaches that concerted action by physicians to exclude competing midwives by cutting off the malpractice coverage of their supervising physician could violate Section 1 of the Sherman Act.

13.4b.   Horizontal Ventures Among Hospitals

13.4b1.   Substantial Horizontal Integration

There has been a spate of horizontal mergers among hospitals during the last several years, associated, perhaps, with the emphasis on less costly outpatient care and the concomitant reduction in inpatient care[36] or with regulatory constraints on health care facility investment,[37] or both. While some of these mergers might be labeled joint ventures, especially when two or more previously independent units survive in separate corporate form but with wholly or partially integrated ownership, all of them should be conventionally analyzed under Section 7 of the Clayton Act. The 1992 Horizontal Merger Guidelines[38] apply, but a more telling indication of current enforcement attitudes is found in Statement 1 of the 1996 DOJ/FTC Statements of Antitrust Enforcement Policy in Health Care.[39] That statement presages a permissive enforcement attitude toward hospital mergers. Paragraph A of Statement 1 of the 1996 Joint Enforcement Statements establishes a safety zone for mergers of two acute care hospitals. Except in extraordinary circumstances, the agencies will not challenge such a merger if one of the hospitals (1) has an average of fewer than 100 licensed beds over the three most recent years and (2) has an average daily inpatient census of fewer than forty patients during that period. Paragraph B of that Statement announces that the agencies have challenged relatively few

---

31. See § 5.7b.

32. 486 U.S. 94, 108 S.Ct. 1658, 100 L.Ed.2d 83(1988).

33. 500 U.S. 322, 111 S.Ct. 1842, 114 L.Ed.2d 366 (1991).

34. See Flynn, *Antitrust Policy and Health Care Reform*, 39 ANTITRUST BULL. 59, 81 (1994); Ponsoldt, *Refusals to Deal in "Locked–In" Health Care Markets Under § 2 of the Sherman Act After Eastman Kodak v. Image Technical Services*, 1995 UTAH L. REV. 503. See also The Health Care Quality Improvement Act of 1986, 42 USC §§ 11101–52 (1994), which provides a limit-

ed immunity from damage suits in covered peer review cases.

35. 918 F.2d 605 (6th Cir.1990).

36. Cf. Kimball, UCLA Business Forecasting Project, 4 Health Care Policy 29 (BNA, 1996).

37. National Health Planning and Resources Development Act of 1974, 42 (USC § 300K et seq.) (1991).

38. U.S. Dept. of Justice and FTC, Horizontal Merger Guidelines (1992, as amended in 1997), available at <http://www.usdoj.gov/atr/public/guidelines /hmg.htm>.

39. Available at <http://www.usdoj.gov/atr/public/ guidelines/1791.htm>.

hospital mergers. It states that even when the concentration increases exceed merger guideline levels the agencies often conclude that substantial lessening of competition will not occur where there will be strong post merger competition, where the merging firms are sufficiently differentiated, where sufficient cost savings that could not otherwise be realized are attained, or where the merger eliminates a hospital that would likely fail.

Where a proposed merger appears to entail significant efficiencies, yet to create some market power, recent enforcement initiatives suggest agency readiness to explore with participants the possibility of preserving the benefits while minimizing the risks by limiting the integration to comprehend only those aspects promising efficiencies while continuing separate and competitive control of other services.[40] The essence of this approach is to convert a full fledged merger into a more focused joint venture, which leaves separately owned and controlled venture partners operating those aspects of their pre-venture competitive services that can remain unintegrated without an undue sacrifice of possible efficiencies.

Despite these accommodations, mergers thought likely to facilitate cartelization or oligopolistic cooperation continue to be challenged by the agencies. An exemplary decision is United States v. Rockford Memorial Corp.[41] The horizontal merger of two non-profit hospitals (therefore, arguably not subject to Clayton Section 7) was considered by the court of appeals under Sherman Section 1. Judge Posner's opinion accepted the district court's market definition—in patient services in acute care hospitals in Rockford, Illinois and its catchment area. Of course, acute care hospital service is a cluster market concept; such hospitals offer a vast array of services. In accepting that definition the court conceded defendant's contention that a substantial numbers of those clustered services were available from others. But the opinion states that,

> the force of the point eludes us. If a firm has a monopoly of product X, the fact that it produces another product, Y, for which the firm faces competition is irrelevant to its monopoly unless the prices of X and Y are linked.[42]

In short, a hospital can have a monopoly with a market defined in terms of service clusters, so long as it has monopoly power in the supply of one or more of the services in the cluster.[43]

40. See the discussion of *United States v. Marlon Plant Health System, Inc.* in Sunshine, *How Does Antitrust Enforcement Fit In?*, in THE PROBLEM THAT WON'T GO AWAY: REFORMING U.S. HEALTH CARE FINANCING, 207, 213 (H. Aaron, ed., 1996).

41. 898 F.2d 1278 (7th Cir.1990), cert. denied, 498 U.S. 920, 111 S.Ct. 295, 112 L.Ed.2d 249 (1990).

42. Id. At 1284. For another Posner opinion on health care market definition, see Blue Cross and Blue Shield United of Wisconsin v. Marshfield Clinic, 65 F.3d 1406 (7th Cir.1995), cert. denied, 516 U.S.

1184, 116 S.Ct. 1288, 134 L.Ed.2d 233 (1996), where the court rejected a jury finding that HMOs constitute a separate market, concluding that an HMO "is basically a method of pricing medical services," not itself a category of medical service. Id. at 1409. For an informed discussion of market definition in health care facility markets by an enforcement official, see Vastness, *Hospital Mergers and Antitrust Enforcement*, 20 J. HEALTH POL., POL'Y & L. 175 (1995).

43. Hospital merger defendants have sometimes found a court more sympathetic to challenges to agency geographic market

In other respects, the *Rockford Memorial* analysis was straight forward. The merger combined the two largest acute care institutions to yield a hospital with from 64 to 72 percent of a market in which, post merger, the three largest hospitals would have 90 percent. In assessing the effect of this on competition the Posner opinion for the court said:

"Three firms, having 90 percent * * * can raise prices with relatively little fear that the fringe of competitors will be able to defeat the attempt by expanding their own output ... To take away 10 percent of the customers of the three large firms * * *, thus reducing [their] * * * share * * * to 81 percent, the fringe firms would have to increase their own output by 90 percent * * *."

Judge Posner also commented on the conviction, sometimes accepted,[44] that non-profit hospitals are not likely to collude. He thought that if nonprofit managers "may be less prone to engage in profit-maximizing collusion," they would be "by the same token less prone to engage in profit-maximizing competition * * *."[45]

During the 1990s, both the FTC and the Justice Department had difficulty in persuading courts to enjoin hospital mergers that the agencies considered relatively straight forward horizontal violations, well within the high risk area under the merger guidelines. These adverse results,[46] which have been variously attributed to the non-profit status of some hospitals, to the local perspectives of judges who must rule on mergers of hospitals that service the judge's community, or to other factors unique to the health care delivery system, are addressed in § 10.2e.

13.4b2.   Ventures to Share Expensive Equipment or Service

Statement 2 of the 1996 Joint Enforcement Statements addresses collaborative efforts by hospitals to share the cost of obtaining and operating expensive health care equipment. Statement 3 deals in turn with such collaboration for specialized clinical or other services. State-

definition. In United States v. Mercy Health Services, 902 F.Supp. 968 (N.D.Iowa 1995), vac'd, 107 F.3d 632 (8th Cir. 1997), the Justice Department pressed for a market focused on Dubuque County, Iowa which was strongly supported by evidence of where Dubuque area third party payers negotiated coverage, where Dubuque area physicians had privileges and made references, and patient flow data. The court rejected this definition, however because it was static: a snap shot of the present, not a projection of what would happen if the defendants substantially increased prices. In the court's view rural hospitals outside the defined area were expanding their services; doctors' attitudes and references were a weak indicator because patient loyalty to physicians was eroding and because many hospital patients lacked regular primary care physicians; and patients are increas-

ingly disposed to shop on the basis of price as their residual share of medical expenses increases. See also FTC v. Tenet Healthcare Corp., 186 F.3d 1045 (8th Cir. 1999)(FTC's geographic market definition rejected).

44. United States v. Rockford Memorial Group, 898 F.2d, at 1283.

45. Id. at 1285.

46. FTC v. Tenet Healthcare Corp., 186 F.3d 1045 (8th Cir. 1999); FTC v. Freeman Hospital, 69 F.3d 260 (8th Cir.1995), aff'g 911 F.Supp. 1213 (W.D.Mo.1995); United States v. Mercy Health Services, 902 F.Supp. 968 (N.D.Iowa 1995), vacated as moot, 107 F.3d 632 (8th Cir.1997); FTC v. Butterworth Health Corp., 946 F.Supp. 1285 (W.D.Mich.1996), aff'd, 1997-2 Trade Cas. (CCH) ¶ 71,863 (6th Cir.).

ment 2 stresses the potential for procompetitive cost reduction and, in paragraph A, establishes a safety zone. Absent extraordinary reasons, the agencies will not challenge ventures to share the cost of acquiring, operating, and marketing the services of expensive health care equipment "if the venture includes only the number of hospitals where participation is needed to support the equipment * * *." As an example, if two hospitals jointly acquire an MRI the cost of which either, alone, would not likely recover over its useful life, the agencies would not challenge the arrangement. By contrast, if a third hospital, for which an MRI would be financially viable even if it acted alone, were to join the venture, the venture would be outside the safety zone.

Paragraph B calls for rule of reason analysis of ventures outside the safety zone, unless a quick look discloses that the venture presents little likelihood of competitive harm. When fuller analysis is called for the steps are these: define the market and evaluate structure. If many providers would compete with the venture, harm is unlikely. If a viable competing provider was eliminated and few competing providers remain, price coordination between the venture and other providers becomes a concern. Factors facilitating or inhibiting such coordination should be considered. Also, if there are others competing to use the equipment to provide a service (say, MRIs), but few sources other than the venture partner hospitals and physicians affiliated with them that might refer patients needing such services, there may be risk of foreclosure doing competitive harm in the market of those competing to provide MRIs. Factors facilitating or inhibiting this possibility should be considered too. Finally, any collateral agreements associated with the venture must be identified and evaluated. Statement 3 calls for similar analysis of collaboration for specialized clinical or other services.

13.4c. Vertical Health Care Ventures

13.4c1. Hospital Ventures with Equipment or Service Providers

When hospitals enter into vertical ventures, ancillary to hospital care, with providers of equipment or services needed by hospital patients, the resulting vertical integration can raise foreclosure issues. The hospital and its staff and its affiliated doctors can influence choices by hospital patients about where to buy such equipment or service. If patients from the hospital represent a significant portion of a relevant market that competing equipment or service providers can reach, efforts by the hospital through its personnel to steer patients to the hospital's affiliated provider can result in seriously harmful foreclosure. Key Enterprises of Delaware, Inc. v. Venice Hospital[47] is illustrative of the problem as well as the complexities and doubts about how it should be handled.

---

47. 919 F.2d 1550 (11th Cir.1990), rehearing granted and opinion vacated 979 F.2d 806 (11th Cir.1992), order for rehearing vacated and appeal dismissed, 9 F.3d 893 (11th Cir.1993), cert. denied, 511 U.S. 1126, 114 S.Ct. 2132, 128 L.Ed.2d 863 (1994). See also In re Home Oxygen & Medical Equipment Co., FTC File Nos. 901–0109 and 901–0020 (1994), discussed in Thompson, *Provider Joint Ventures* in Antitrust and Health, supra note 20, 106–07.

Plaintiff was a provider of durable medical equipment (wheel chairs, beds, walkers, prophylactic devices, etc.) ("DME") in a Florida city. When the defendant hospital entered that market through a vertical venture, its "referral power"[48] (exercised through hospital employees and perhaps through "pressure" on others who gave advice to patients) damaged plaintiff's business. In the district court, a jury awarded plaintiff substantial damages on Sherman Section 1 and Section 2 theories, which the trial judge set aside. On appeal, a panel of the court of appeals reinstated the verdict. Later, a rehearing *en banc* was granted, but that order was vacated and the appeal dismissed after the parties settled.

Although application may be complex in some settings, the norms that should govern are reasonably clear. Certainly a hospital may lawfully enter an adjacent market such as DME, whether or not the hospital possesses market power in its own market. If it does enter, it is entitled to the benefit of any efficiencies arising from the integration—including any reduction in its marketing costs for DME arising from its relationship with its hospital patients.[49] What it may not do, if it possesses monopoly power, is act in a predatory or exclusionary way.[50] Competitor disparagement, misrepresentation or any other tortious marketing practice should fail under that standard. Perhaps excesses in hospital sales pressured by authoritative hospital personnel (doctors, nurses, physical therapists) should too, given patient vulnerability and their inelastic demand for the product. Providing such personnel with financial rewards for "successful recommendations" certainly should be viewed as exclusionary.[51] By contrast, temperate statements by hospital personnel to the effect that the hospital can provide equipment that meets its own recommended standards ought not to be viewed as exclusionary.[52] More difficult issues arise if hospital staff whom the patient looks to for advice routinely inform patients only of the hospital-affiliated provider.

In situations like these, Sherman Section 1 theories are intrinsically weaker than Section 2 theories.[53] Perhaps a restraint of trade could be found on the basis of an express or implied contract between the hospital involved and the venture committing the hospital to recommend the venture regardless of whether its prices were higher and/or the quality of its services lower than those of competitors. If so, antitrust injury could be predicated on a showing that the services received were in fact priced above or of a quality below that available on the market.

48. Enders, supra note 24, at 813.

49. Berkey Photo, Inc. v. Eastman Kodak Co., 603 F.2d 263, 283 (2d Cir.1979), cert. denied, 444 U.S. 1093, 100 S.Ct. 1061, 62 L.Ed.2d 783 (1980).

50. Id. at 295.

51. Cf. the discussion in Enders, supra note 23 at 817–19 of the unpublished Ninth Circuit opinion in *American Computech v. National Medical Care,*, 959 F.2d 239 (9th Cir. 1992). When a medical professional has a financial conflict of interest that motivates the professional to make recommen-dations to a patient favoring a firm with market power, that conduct should be characterized as exclusionary.

52. See generally, Blue Cross and Blue Shield United of Wisconsin v. Marshfield Clinic, 65 F.3d 1406 (7th Cir.1995), cert. denied, 516 U.S. 1184, 116 S.Ct. 1288, 134 L.Ed.2d 233 (1996) and see the discussion of this case in § 13.4c2.

53. See the discussion of the DME cases in § 3.5.

13.4c2.   *Physician Ventures with Ancillary Service Providers*

Physician owned and operated joint ventures can also raise foreclosure issues. Orthopedic surgeons with an interest in a physical therapy center, cardiologists with a financial stake in a rehabilitation center, and radiologists who own an imaging center are not disinterested when recommending such services. The antitrust issues, nonetheless, are as sticky, or more so, than those encountered in hospital ventures with vertical suppliers.

Blue Cross & Blue Shield v. Marshfield Clinic[54] explores some of these and related problems. Blue Cross and Compcare, a Blue Cross HMO, alleged that Marshfield Clinic, a nonprofit treatment and research center owned and controlled by 400 of its own employee-doctors, unlawfully monopolized and excluded Compcare from a Wisconsin HMO market, a market dominated by Marshfield and its own HMO, Security. As a result, Blue Cross was obliged to pay supracompetitive prices to Security for services to patients covered by Blue Cross. To establish exclusionary conduct Blue Cross had relied upon evidence that the clinic: (1) refused to allow its owner-employees to enter into reciprocal arrangements with other doctors to "cover" for each other when the doctor primarily responsible for a patient was unavailable; (2) discouraged hospitals that its doctors controlled from joining an HMO competing with Security; and (3) restricted staff privileges of non-Marshfield Clinic physicians at those hospitals. The court of appeals reversed a Section 2 jury verdict for plaintiff on grounds not here relevant. Doing so, the court (Posner, C.J.) provided provocative dicta about what kinds of conduct by physicians owning a clinic with an HMO subsidiary would be exclusionary. The court said:

> "[W]e will not conceal our skepticism that [the practices summarized above] are exclusionary in the invidious sense * * *. All [of them] * * * are ambiguous from the standpoint of competition and efficiency. Hospitals are not public utilities, required to grant staff privileges to anyone with a medical license. The Marshfield Clinic's reputation for high quality implies selectivity in the granting of staff privileges at hospitals affiliated with the Clinic. Physicians employed by the Clinic, which has its own HMO, are hardly to be expected to steer their patients to another HMO, as they would be doing if they used their control of hospital staffs to induce the hospital to join another HMO. And given the extensive network constituted by the physicians either employed by or contracting with the Clinic, they would have little occasion to 'cross cover' with other physicians and would be reluctant to do so if, * * * consistent with Compcare's version of the 'essential facilities' doctrine, the Clinic maintains a reputation for high quality by being selective about the physicians to whom it entrusts its customers * * *."[55]

---

54. 65 F.3d 1406 (7th Cir.1995), cert. denied, 516 U.S. 1184, 116 S.Ct. 1288, 134 L.Ed.2d 233 (1996).

55. Id. at 1413–1414.

In essence, the *Marshfield Clinic* opinion indicates that, so far as regulatory constraints permit, health care institutions and providers are to be treated for antitrust purposes much as any other market place actors. For Section 2 purposes, exclusionary conduct must be invidious in some sense. Failure to comply with the highest ethical standards of the medical profession, so long as neither tortuous nor violative of licensing or regulatory constraints, is apparently not invidious enough. Perhaps the principal vulnerability of such institutions, when they have power in a well defined market, will be tortious overreaching that exploits the vulnerability of patients and the authority, stemming from specialized knowledge and patient trust, that health care providers and institutions possess.

§ 13.5   High Technology Joint Ventures

Joint ventures are common in dynamic, high technology industries and claims are sometimes made that, in light of their contributions to dynamic efficiency, such markets should receive permissive antitrust analysis.[1] Most such contentions are overbroad. Credible theory has never suggested that concentration enhances innovation. Quite to the contrary, theory suggests that significant concentration reduces incentives to introduce new products.[2] High tech industries are often marked by network externalities and sometimes by potent first entrant advantages that can distort allocative outcomes. Ventures may have the potential for intensifying such externalities or advantages, reducing the potential for more aggressively competitive development. But ventures may also be so structured that they can reduce or ameliorate externalities and first entrant advantages. Both types of tendencies should be taken into account in evaluating high tech ventures. Also, when one of the venturers possesses market power in a high tech market, a venture may have effects similar to market division or to bundling that effectively leverages the power into an ancillary market. All such tendencies should be identified and evaluated. Some of these issues are discussed more fully in Chapter 15, dealing with antitrust and intellectual property. Two types of ventures are considered below.

13.5a.   Cooperative Research

Industrial research is essential to innovation, thus to commercial and industrial progress. Various national policies, including the patent laws, copyrights for software and a number of subsidy programs, recognize the importance of developing and commercializing innovative ideas. Research is a process that requires investment, initiative and time. Product research, as an example, begins with an idea; proceeds by identifying possible paths; entails selection among these and the pursuit

§ 13.5

1. Jorde and Teese, *Innovation, Cooperation and Antitrust* in ANTITRUST, INNOVATION AND COMPETITIVENESS at 55 (Jorde and Teese, eds., 1992).

2. See Gilbert and Sunshine, *The Use of Innovation Markets: A Reply to Hay, Rapp, and Hoerner,* 64 ANTITRUST L.J. 75, 76–78 (1995) (citing some of the relevant economic literature).

of one or more to the point where a prototype can be built; then, making sequential improvements in the prototype, based on refinements from production, marketing and consumption perspectives; and finally producing and distributing the end product (after which refinement and modification often continues with critiques based on actual experience at production, marketing, distribution and consumption levels).

Research is expensive and research investment is aleatory. Neither the cost over time nor the value of outcomes can be predicted with levels of confidence commensurate with those for investments in production. Sometimes research synergies may be yielded by bringing together inputs from firms drawn from different or related industries, firms at different vertical levels, or firms with differing production capacities or experience. For any of these reasons joint research activity may be desirable. Participants may be seeking efficiencies by proceeding jointly on a scale that none of them would risk alone. They may also want to bring together complimentary resources, experience, personnel or needs.

It is sometimes asserted that antitrust poses an excessive threat to joint research. In 1984, Congressional concern led to the National Cooperative Research Act (later incorporated in a broader cooperative research and production act),[3] in which two protections were provided: joint research is made subject to the rule of reason; and if the Department of Justice is notified of a joint research project, only actual (non-trebled) damages may be awarded, should the project thereafter be held to violate the antitrust laws. There was in the early 1980's entrepreneurial concern that antitrust risks to joint research were high. But this concern itself was excessive. The rule of reason has always been the applicable norm for evaluating any significant integration, certainly including joint research. Thus, that provision of the 1984 Act carried over to the 1993 Act was superfluous. Selective detrebling, although perhaps of some value here to reduce excessive and unneeded entrepreneurial apprehension, weakens antitrust by segmenting it. In this particular instance, the segmentation may not be particularly harmful, because treble damage law suits are not and never were a likely response to joint research. But detrebling in response to overstated concerns expressed by lobbyists is in any instance unfortunate and could be far more disruptive if it became a pattern.

Appropriately, the rule of reason is the mandated approach to joint research. It presents no undue risk to ventures that entail no competitive threat and, for that matter, little or no threat to most such ventures, for few of them are vulnerable under the rule. A summary of the way the rule applies will be indicative. Joint research presents two possible concerns. One is the effect of the venture on the research market: does the venture result in an increase in concentration that threatens to harm performance in a relevant research market? The other concern is the impact of the venture on the product market or markets from which

---

3. Today the provisions of that act are embodied in the National Cooperative Research and Production Act of 1993, which extended similar protection to certain joint production activities developing out of joint research. 15 U.S.C.A. § 4301 (1994).

the participants are drawn: if the venturers are vertically related, will it result in foreclosure? If the venturers are horizontal competitors, will product market competition among them or between them and venture non-participants be dampened?

13.5a1.   Research Market Definition

In R & D ventures, it may be appropriate to define and consider effects upon technology or innovation markets.[4] If participants are horizontal competitors in the same product market and venture outputs are expected to be utilized mainly in that market, that product market would seem an appropriate surrogate for the research market. When the research market, as defined, transcends the product market where the venturers compete, concentration may be low even though the venturers product market is concentrated. Thus, if the research comprehends areas of wider interest spanning a number of product markets (as it likely would if the venturers are from unrelated markets or markets related only vertically, and as it might be even if the venturers are horizontal competitors), the relevant research market should be defined widely enough to comprehend all firms engaging (or likely soon to engage) in relevant research.

Next, the effect of the venture on performance in the research market must be evaluated. If the participants hold in the aggregate only a small share of the research market, concern about harm resulting from the venture can be dismissed on that ground. The venture will involve integration that may yield benefits. Where any integration in research or production does not increase concentration to significant levels, it is presumptively lawful. This absence of significant concentration is likely if the participants are unrelated or vertically related. Lack of concentration will also warrant ending the inquiry when the venturers are horizontal competitors and their product market serves as a surrogate for the research market, where the venturers hold only a modest share of that product market.

Perhaps there will also be high tech ventures other than R & D ventures where credible claims of dynamic effects will be made, and where adequate appraisal of those claims may be facilitated by defining a technology or innovation market. Consider a venture aimed at producing a wholly new product. In such a venture, any effort to identify current competitors and prices, the stuff of conventional product market analysis, will inevitably be fruitless. It may, however, be possible to define a market for a prospective product by addressing the matter from the supply side. The analyst might identify firms both positioned and motivated to imitate or produce a substitute for the venture's output should

---

4. See Antitrust Guidelines For Licensing of Intellectual Property § 3.2 (April 6, 1995), available at <www.usdoj.gov/atr/public/guidelines/0558.htm>. See also Gilbert & Sunshine, *Incorporating Dynamic Efficiency Concerns in Merger Analysis: The* *Use of Innovation Markets,* 63 ANTITRUST L.J. 569 (1995). For comments on the Gilbert and Sunshine see Brunell, *A Critical Appraisal of the Innovation Market Approach,* 64 ANTITRUST L.J. 174 (1995).

the venture be successful. While these firms might include all or many now competing in a related product market with that of the venture, it might also include other firms familiar with relevant technology. Of course, it may also be useful to consider demand even when there is no current product market. Are there firms that could currently be developing products that, once on line, would be valued by consumers as reasonable substitutes for the venture's planned product?

It is argued that because of the social importance of dynamic change, joint ventures to do research or bring new products to market should be presumptively valid and spared critical antitrust analysis at least until such time as the venture has produced and started to market a new product or service.[5] Thus, no effort should be made to define research or innovation markets or otherwise identify and evaluate risks of dynamic harm. In its broadest form, the argument supposes that even if most of the firms in a market—say IBM, Compaq, and other major desktop hardware producers—formed a venture aimed at developing and licensing a non-existent ancillary product or service—say, a significantly faster means of interconnecting—that no antitrust concern should arise until the product or service is produced and protocols agreed upon about how to license and market it.

But this ignores possible current dangers. If the target product or service is the next in sequence in a well developed and predictable cycle of innovation, if the venture participants include most of those most likely to undertake that developmental effort, including some capable of doing it alone or in less comprehensive ventures, the venture may, with the full support of its participants, exercise a considerable constraint on research competition. If so, less may be invested in the developmental effort, fewer research paths attempted, and the prospect for alternative and competitive solutions substantially reduced. Indeed, the venturers may even see a common interest in slowing or discouraging the pace of innovation, perhaps to the point of obstructing the adoption of innovation from their own or others' research efforts. If a credible market can be defined within which to evaluate a research or product development venture, there is no more reason to ignore ventures that stifle competition in these activities than to ignore ventures in a production or marketing activity. Where analysis of the harms and benefits is feasible, it should be done. Anyone challenging the legality of the venture has the burden of proof.[6] If there are scale efficiencies, or other reasons why the research is feasible or is more cost effective only through the venture, these reasons will appear in the benefit analysis.[7] Unless there is credible basis for concluding that harms exceed benefits, the venture is not vulnerable. If convincing proof is not available, no presumption of

---

5. See, e.g., Clapes, *Blinded by the Light: Antitrust Analysis of Computer Industry Alliances*, 61 ANTITRUST L.J. 899 (1993).

6. Indeed, because the rule of reason applies, that burden may be substantial. See the discussion in § 13.3.

7. See § 13.2a.

legality is necessary, and such a presumption would be harmful if such proof is available.

13.5a2. *Research Market Harms and Benefits*

If the venturers hold in the aggregate a substantial share of the research market as defined, the analysis moves to the next step— identifying and comparing possible harms and benefits. As to benefits the inquiry includes: Whether the venture will bring scale economies that individual participants could not attain; whether the combination will explore paths that cannot be explored by participants acting alone; and whether the participants will provide complementary research skills or resources that may yield synergies that participants alone could not duplicate. As to harms, the inquiry includes whether the increased concentration will diminish research market performance; whether some research paths will be concertedly avoided; and whether research output will go up or down as measured by aggregate investment or by numbers of innovations or patents or by a subjective evaluation of their significance.

Both the market definition and the harm-benefit issues may be imponderable. This fact significantly reduces the risk of any antitrust challenge to joint R & D; the burden of proof is on the enforcement agency or other party asserting a violation. Ancillary agreements constraining research by the participants beyond the scope of the venture are and should be vulnerable if the venturers hold a substantial share of the research market. Such commitments, nonetheless, are probably not *per se* violations. If the venturers share of the research market is modest, so that significant research competition could come from other sources, such a commitment between venturers might be justified as a reasonable ancillary restraint facilitating entry into the venture and increasing its potential by giving each participant confidence that co-venturers have no direct conflict of interest and will not be motivated to free ride on the venture while exploring their most promising ideas individually. It should be remembered that when firms interested in the same research market do proceed concertedly, each will have a free rider's incentive and, so far as this is feasible, may concur with strategies to shift costs to others and benefits to themselves. For example, one of several firms asked to participate in a research venture where ideas and resources are to be shared may have intended to explore a research path it regards as promising and that no other firm has considered. Such a firm might conclude that its ideal position would be to keep that idea secret, to do its own work on it, while contributing other ideas and resources in order to participate in the venture. A contractual commitment by participants to disclose all currently known and relevant ideas, though apt to limit such free-riding, would be hard to police and enforce. A covenant against any individual research in the field would be more effective because violation of it would be more transparent. Ancillary restraints of this character should not be vulnerable unless the research market is concentrated.

13.5a3. Product Market Effects

The remaining concern under the rule of reason is the effect of the venture on the product market or markets of the participants. If the participants are not related horizontally or vertically, this concern can be dismissed. If participants are vertically related it can be dismissed unless (1) one (or more) participants at one level or the other possesses such a large share of the market at that level that foreclosure could be a problem, and (2) provisions in the venture agreement suggest that venture outputs will be exploited by the venturer (or venturers) with a dominant share exclusively through venture participants at the other level. Only if the venturers are horizontal competitors with a large aggregate share of their product market is the risk of product market harm a significant concern. This concern is discussed in § 13.5a4, below.

13.5a4. Spill–Over Effects

In research ventures among horizontal competitors with large product market shares, two types of issues can emerge. First, horizontal competitors engaged jointly in research relevant to their product market may have intimate connections and widespread communication. They must scrupulously avoid interaction bearing upon or that could directly influence product price, territory or output.[8] Certainly they must stay away from collateral agreements touching on these matters. More than that, they must protect against venture interactions becoming occasions for antitrust offense, much as trade association participants must take steps to sanitize their interchanges. The safest course, and the one often used if the venture is large enough to sustain the expense, is to build a firewall insulating research venture personnel from product market operating personnel. This tends to insure that interactions between the competing firms about the venture are limited to upper management levels where they can be monitored by antitrust counsel. Personnel directly involved in venture operations may interact freely because they lack antitrust sensitive information about product market costs, prices or processes. If this course is not feasible, a careful compliance program, including education and monitoring, must be put in place. To stockholders, employees and itself, management owes scrupulous care to avoid tainted interactions. All of these constituencies could suffer if a blatant antitrust violation should occur.

Second, a venture that includes most but not all of the horizontal competitors in a market, and which yields research outputs that significantly reduce the production costs or significantly improves the quality of outputs in that market, could seriously damage the product market position of venture nonparticipants. Of course, successful research always has the potential to advantage the entity doing the research and to disadvantage its competition. Normally, no antitrust issue is presented. But where the research is done collectively by a group of dominant firms, and when nondominant firms in the same market are systematically

---

8. See § 13.3c1.

excluded both from participation in the venture and from access on reasonable terms to its successful output, an antitrust problem may be presented under the essential facility doctrine discussed in § 5.7b. When a serious essential facilities issue seems a potential risk in a joint research context, it should be possible to avoid the risk in either of two ways. First, the venture might provide open access to all product market participants who are willing both to contribute their share to the venture pursuant to reasonable, objective and non-discriminatory standards, and to commit to reasonable norms about protecting the intellectual property or other sensitive assets of the venture. Alternatively, the participants might commit at the outset to license venture outputs to all applicants on reasonable, nondiscriminatory terms.

As this review indicates, antitrust is accommodating to joint research. Indeed, in over a century since the passage of the Sherman Act, enforcement officials have rarely challenged joint research One exception involved an agreement among the firms dominating the American automobile market jointly to share information and patents for ways to reduce air pollution from internal combustion engines.[9] The government's theory was this: Under the current technology automobiles externalize a significant industry cost through pollution. In consequence, the cost of manufacturing cars is lower, buyers pay less for cars, and the general public bears part of the cost of automobiles in the form of reduced air quality. If technologies were used that reduced pollution, they would internalize these costs. Cars would become more costly to manufacture and to buy, as some of the pollution costs were shifted to the industry and the motoring public. So long as pollution research by car manufacturers remains competitive, each manufacturer will have an incentive to succeed and will compete aggressively. Though success would mean internalizing now externalized costs, all manufacturers will be forced by public opinion and legislation to use the new technology, and the successful researcher will earn patent license fees that will tend to compensate for the cost shift. Moreover (as each manufacturer would see it), if another manufacturer succeeded first, that manufacturer would collect those royalties; other manufacturers would incur both of the new costs—the internalization of pollution costs and the royalty fees. Hence, individual research provides a strong incentive for an aggressive research effort. By contrast, joint research in this context reduces the incentive for successful research toward the vanishing point. All participants would gain royalty free access upon any success, so there is no incentive to be successful in order to gain royalty revenues or to avoid royalty costs. And success would internalize now externalized costs on all industry participants. For these reasons, joint research would reduce the incentive to do successful research and would evoke oligopolisticly inter-

---

9. United States v. Automobile Mfrs. Assn., 1969 Trade Cas. (CCH) ¶ 72907 (C.D. Cal.) (Consent decree requiring termination of agreement to exchange information and patents respecting pollution control).

dependent obstruction or delay. The automobile case was disposed of by consent decree which limited joint research.[10]

13.5b. High Tech Standard Setting

While standard setting by groups made up of, supported by, or influenced by industry members is common in a number of contexts,[11] this section deals with the special problem of compatibility standards in high tech industries like telecommunications and computers networks where, over time, standards may become almost imperative, and ventures to establish them are common. Such industries experience substantial externalities associated with networks and/or input/output compatibility. Telecommunications input and output devices (phones, fax machines, data transmission devices) must be compatible with a network in order to work at all, and every network (the local phone company, a cellular phone system, a long distance network, the Internet) must be compatible with all other networks in order to maximize value to each subscriber of obtaining network access. In the now fading era of free standing desktop computers, application programs as well as input and output devices had to be compatible with the operating system installed in any computer the marketer of the application system wanted to reach. This, of course, gave a great advantage to the proprietor of the operating system that gained a market share lead because more and more application systems would be designed to be compatible with the leading operating system and, as the advantage of that system to users based on application systems availability increased, the market position held by that system would be reenforced and expanded. Today more and more desktops, even those in private homes, are linked not only with internal corporate (or university) networks, but to the Internet. Hence, the computer industry experiences the full range of compatibility externalities: operating system compatibility with application systems and hardware; software compatibility with input/output devices; and the advantages associated with a larger universe of users linked to a network.

Industries like these are dynamic. The competitive advantage of proprietary control of an industry standard is immense, is obvious to industry participants, and can be secured through software copyrights and through patents. When different standards appear in the market, consumers must make choices. As they do, the early leader gains advantage from network and input/output externalities. These can be crucial to the outcome. If so, a de facto standard may quickly emerge. If not, two or even three alternative standards may gain market acceptance. This outcome is more likely if groups of significant industry participants converge around and support different standards. If that occurs, standard setting competition continues. When it does, positive

10. Id. Could a similar joint venture reduce tobacco industry incentives to produce low risk, non-addictive cigarettes?

11. Quality standards are common where product use results in significant externalities (e.g. auto emission standards) or in safety risks (e.g. appliance safety standards). Industry groups have strong incentives to participate in such standard setting. See § 5.7.

network externalities are reduced and negative input/output externalities are increased. Some of these may be diminished and the period of the contest reduced if firms clustering around one of the standards decide on open access to their standard. They will also be tempered if there is an open-source software product, such as the Linux operating software, competing to become the standard, and significant participants make meaningful commitments to it, as the United States Navy, General Motors and French Telecom have recently considered with Linux.

If a de facto proprietary standard emerges, the inefficiencies associated with incompatibilities are mitigated. Network efficiencies increase and input/output inefficiencies are reduced, but the proprietor gains market power that can distort allocation. Moreover, it may not be the most efficient standard that prevails. Of course, in highly dynamic markets a product generation may be short. If new generation products significantly alter technological patterns the initial standard victory may be short lived; a new standard setting contest may develop for the next product generation. For the above reasons, and also because unresolved standard competition may decelerate overall industry growth, there will be incentives for participants in such industries to agree on an industry standard.

Cost-benefit analysis for standard setting ventures in high tech markets should be done in the conventional manner. Many of the possibilities explored in §§ 13.2 and 13.3 can be relevant. Yet, distinct possibilities for both harm and benefit warrant attention. The possible benefits unique to these markets arise from the motivation for standard setting discussed above. Setting a standard can increase beneficial network externalities and reduce harmful input/output externalities. Industry dynamism can be enhanced. Also, if an open, agreed upon standard prevails, no firm will be in a position to exploit market power based on proprietorship of the standard in the subject market or by leveraging that power into adjacent markets. This will be especially so if that standard is an open source product, such as Apache (important to the Internet), Linux, or BSD Unix (which could also substitute cumulative for duplicative R & D and reduce recurrent upgrading costs common with proprietary standards).

But there are potential competitive harms that should also be considered. Whenever a standard emerges—whether de facto, by agreement, or pursuant to governmental action—firms in the industry will be differentially affected. The standard may impose new (perhaps appreciable) costs on some firms while reducing costs for others. When there is collaboration among firms to establish a standard, the collaborators may include all or most firms in the market or a subset of such firms. The standard they are advancing may be proprietary or not; and, if proprietary, it may be accessible to all who want it without charge, at a modest charge, or at significant charge. The differences in impacts on firms within the market will give a competitive advantage to some firms and competitive disadvantage to others. Depending upon the structure of the market, on the aggregate market shares of the firms collaborating on the standard, and on the share or shares of non-participating firms that are hurt or helped, such impacts on particular firms might adversely affect competition.

Suppose, for example, that at an early stage, three firms each sponsor a proprietary standard that they license competitively, each hoping to prevail as the industry standard setter, but that when, after a time, no victor emerges the three,—or, alternatively, two of the three— agree to support one of the competing standards. Either of these scenarios could have effects that improve market competition. But either scenario could also cause competitive harms. These must be identified, evaluated and measured against the benefits in a rule of reason analysis.

Alternatively, consider this hypothetical. A proprietary operating system becomes dominant for a particular type of computer and is installed by hardware manufacturers for, say, 68 percent of aggregate output of these computers. Most of the remaining 32 percent of computers leave factories with one of three competing proprietary systems, each system having about 10 percent of the market. These three proprietors then combine around a hybrid system that will be compatible with application systems and input/output devices for any of the three previously competing systems. This collaboration has some of the benefits that conventionally motivate standard setting, and also a possible additional benefit. The collaboration may revitalize the standard competition. As long as that competition prevails in a reasonably aggressive form (instead of settling into oligopolistic cooperation), it will tend to reduce the market power of the dominant firm.[12] The collaboration will likely hurt the dominant firm to some extent, but not in any way that interferes with competition. It will also hurt the one or more fringe firms which represent the 2 percent share not held by the dominant firm or the three collaborators. Although the collaboration should not be vulnerable because of possible damage to this small fringe, a less restrictive alternative issue may arise: could the proprietor or proprietors of the remaining two percent have been costlessly incorporated into the collaboration? There is a considerable, suggestive and growing literature relevant to standard setting with which analysts should become familiar.[13] Many of the standard setting agreements involve potential abuse of Intellectual Property rights, matters which are addressed in Chapter XV.

---

12. See the discussion in Brown, *Technology Joint Ventures to Set Standards or Define Interfaces*, 61 ANTITRUST L J. 921, 931–33 (1993).

13. E.g., Farrell and Soloner, *Standardization, Compatibility and Innovation*, 16 RAND J. ECON. 70 (1985); Katz and Shapiro, *Network Externalities, Competition and Compatibility*, 75 AM. ECON. REV. 424 (1985); Katz and Shapiro, *Systems Competition and Network Effects*, 8 J. ECON. PERSP. 93 (1994); Salop and Scheffman, *Raising Rivals'*

Costs, 73 AM. ECON. REV. 267 (1983); Saloner, *Economic Issues in Computer Interface Standardization*, 1 ECON. INNOVATION & NEW TECH. 135 (1990); Farrell & Saloner, *Coordination Through Committees and Markets*, 19 RAND J. ECON. 235 (1988). For one of the few discussions of the present and potential future significance of open source software to standard competition and efficiency, see E. Raymond, THE CATHEDRAL AND THE BAZAAR: MUSINGS ON LINUX AND OPEN SOURCE BY AN ACCIDENTAL REVOLUTIONARY (1999).

§ 13.6   Remedies in Joint Venture Cases

There is little, if any, remedy law that is unique to joint ventures. Venture cases involve issues that can arise in connection with other cooperation and integration, horizontal, vertical or conglomerate. Venture remedies are also affected by developments encountered more generally, such as the increased use of intrusive or regulatory decrees in lieu of structural ones, especially in ventures subject to agency premerger review.

In counseling an attorney must identify harms and benefits of ventures and make predictions about how these will be evaluated by enforcement agencies. But it is also appropriate for two distinct reasons to give consideration to possible remedial responses if an enforcer (or a court) should determine that the venture, on balance, is anticompetitive. First, if remedy possibilities are surveyed at the outset by those representing venture proponents, they will be better prepared to work toward beneficial solutions if and when the venture is challenged. Second, early exploration could facilitate feasible changes in the venture that, by reducing possible harms, can reduce the likelihood of a challenge. In short, if there are means short of prohibition of the venture to mitigate its possible adverse effects, the participants may find it beneficial to build these into the venture at the outset, thus reducing the likelihood of challenge and the possibility of a regulatory consent decree.

Remedies short of prohibition can be considered only when it is feasible to alter the venture to reduce the incentives of participants to act, post venture, in ways thought to threaten competition. Sometimes such remedies may not be possible. For example, pure horizontal ventures where competitors jointly establish another undertaking to operate in their market result in a strong incentive for the venture to collude with or follow the pricing lead of the parents and to become a medium through which the parents may collude with each other. There is little that can be done, short of prohibition, to end the first of these incentives. As has been noted, even adding a separate, outside entity to the ownership and control group, while modifying the incentive to collude with parents, does not end it.[1] Collusion can still increase venture profits to the benefit of the additional owner, even though the original parents may attain advantages through their own horizontally related firms that the independent owner may not share. The outside interest, if it became a constant management presence, could perhaps discourage the horizontally related parents from using the venture as a medium for their own collusion, but even that may not follow as of course.[2]

§ 13.6

1. Brodley, *Joint Ventures and Antitrust Policy*, 95 Harv. L. Rev. 1521 at 1553–54 (1982).

2. There is an exception. If horizontal competitors jointly acquire the provider of an essential input, their incentive to reduce their own output by controlling the availability of that input could be mitigated if an outsider, not capable of profiting from a reduction of output in the other parents' market, were added as an owner with capacity to control or influence venture strategies. Id. at 1565–66.

On the other hand, if the collusion risk associated with the venture is attributable only to managerial intimacy and information sharing—as, for example, in a vertical venture where one or both of the venture partners has market access to proprietary information of a competitor of the other venture partner—it may be possible to mitigate the risk of harm by foreclosing avenues for intimacy, and/or limiting types of information that can be exchanged. If so, requiring the venture to have its own management and staff separated by fire walls from those of the parents, and/or establishing categories of information never to be exchanged and an audit mechanism to assure compliance, might significantly reduce risks.[3] But changes of this kind can have negative effects too—not increases in risk, but reduction in benefits. For example, one of the benefits often associated with vertical integration is an increase in dynamic efficiency that depends on easy and regular interaction between firms developing and firms using or marketing new or improved products. Fire walls could end this benefit.[4]

Foreclosure is another possible harm capable of being mitigated short of terminating the venture. As classic foreclosure cases like *Terminal Railroad*[5] and *Associated Press*[6] signify, the solution to foreclosure problems is to modify access standards to assure that they are reasonable and non-discriminatory. Attorneys advising venture parents should both identify possible foreclosure harms and consider possible mitigation whenever significant harms are identified. If broader access can be implemented without reducing venture benefits (other than those arising from market power resulting from foreclosure), the appropriate changes should be recommended.

---

3. Cf. the AT & T–McCaw merger consent decree, described in § 13.3c2. Compare AT & T's voluntary spin-off of Lucent.

4. The increased flow of information was one of the advantages claimed for the AT & T–McCaw merger. The consent decree could tend to reduce any such benefit. See § 13.3c2.

5. United States v. Terminal Railroad Ass'n of St. Louis, 224 U.S. 383, 32 S.Ct. 507, 56 L.Ed. 810 (1912).

6. Associated Press v. United States, 326 U.S. 1, 65 S.Ct. 1416, 89 L.Ed. 2013 (1945).

Chapter XIV

ANTITRUST AND COMPETITION POLICY IN REGULATED MARKETS

Table of Sections

---

§ 14.1 Introduction

Because its primary policy goal is to encourage and to protect competition, antitrust is the core of competition policy. But national competition policy is broader. It includes aspects of intellectual property law, of trade policy, and many aspects of regulatory regimes. Competition is valued principally because it tends to advance allocative, productive and dynamic efficiency. Effectively competitive markets are consistent with these outcomes as well as with collateral goals like scaling economic rewards to contribution, avoiding discriminatory pricing that targets the less powerful or less informed, product and service variety that enhances consumer choice, economic opportunity, dispersion of economic power, and a reasonable system of resource governance. But failures of various kinds may keep markets from attaining the competitive ideal. Antitrust can challenge monopolization, cartelization and some other failures, but there are also market failures that antitrust cannot address. Hence, there is a role for regulation that is wholly consistent with the values sought through competition. For example, if production by a single firm minimizes cost, public utility regulation may improve performance. Regulation may also be used to deal with externalities not readily addressed by market forces (environmental injury caused by methods of production), or in markets characterized by asymmetric deployments of information (the justification for labeling legislation, drug efficacy control, and banking and securities regulation). In such instances, market failures may distort allocation and regulatory intervention may mitigate that distortion. Yet, all regulation does not deal with allocative problems. Far less likely to comport with antitrust is regulation aimed at abating "excessive" competition (certain regulation of petroleum and airlines), at restricting new sectors in order to protect sectors already regulated (regulation of motor carriers to protect railroads, of cable to protect broadcasters) or at shifting resources from one group of market actors to another (rent control). Moreover, government may use regulation to attain goals ancillary to those associated with competition, such as rules that ease access by disadvantaged persons to public or commercial facilities.

Regulation, like antitrust, is part of a recurrent American political consensus. In general we leave markets alone when they are functioning reasonably well. But we intervene both when they fail badly or when politically approved goals are beyond their reach. Economic regulation is ancient but has its modern roots in the government response to the industrial revolution. State regulation of grain elevator rates was constitutionally validated[1] and the Interstate Commerce Commission (ICC) was established[2] before the Sherman Act was passed in 1890. Of course, politically dominant social and economic views as well as economic conditions change over time. In consequence, the extent, purpose, scope and character of regulation also changes. In the *Lochner* era,[3] the Supreme Court treated much regulation that displaced the competitive market as a violation of substantive due process. As a result, intervention was limited primarily to state regulation of industries identified as public utilities. But broader state and federal programs became common after the Court lifted the due process constraint.[4] The New Deal Congress created the Civil Aeronautic Board (CAB), Federal Communications Commission (FCC), Federal Power Commission (FPC) and the Securities and Exchange Commission (SEC). It also expanded the ICC's jurisdiction, and enacted comprehensive banking legislation. Regulation at the state level also became widespread and spacious in purpose.

In recent decades—as signified by FCC initiatives in the 1970s—there has been a trend toward deregulation. This is most pronounced at

§ 14.1

1. Munn v. Illinois, 94 U.S. (4 Otto) 113, 24 L.Ed. 77 (1877).

2. Act to Regulate Commerce, February 4, 1887, 24 Stat. 379 (1887).

3. Lochner v. New York, 198 U.S. 45, 25 S.Ct. 539, 49 L.Ed. 937 (1905).

4. Nebbia v. New York, 291 U.S. 502, 54 S.Ct. 505, 78 L.Ed. 940 (1934).

the federal level, yet has had echoes in the states. Airlines, railroads, and trucking have been substantially deregulated. Telephone, cable and broadcast deregulation has been going on in various forms since the 1980s, and in 1996, Congress deregulated and reregulated these areas in an as yet largely abortive quest for more competition.[5] In addition, at both the federal and state levels, there is movement toward market friendly regulatory techniques like peak load pricing, franchise bidding, and incentive devices such as price caps and performance standards. All of this has enhanced the significance of competition as a regulator of allocation, prices and performance. It has also enlarged the range for and the potential significance of antitrust.

Competition policy can be expressed in regulated markets in two different ways. First, the regulatory scheme itself may rely in part upon or try to enhance market forces. Second, antitrust may have a role either displacing or complimenting regulation. The first aspect—the manner in which regulatory programs themselves incorporate and utilize competition—varies widely with the purpose of the regulation, with the particular sector involved, and with the extent to which a deregulatory ethos has influenced the process. Market oriented regulation, including new initiatives apparent in many regulatory regimes, cannot be examined thoroughly except by looking at specific programs in particular industries, a task not within the scope of this text. A great deal of regulation, however, focuses on a few conventional public utilities, seeking to make them function better through constraints on entry, services and rates. Because this type of regulation has been so common and because comparable problems are presented and similar solutions or deregulatory steps are attempted by a number of federal and state regulators, in § 14.2 we address utility regulation and some of its techniques that utilize market forces.

Sections 14.3 and 14.4 deal with the role of antitrust in regulated markets. The relation between regulation and antitrust (or ways of articulating it, if not its substance) will differ between federal regulation and state or local regulation. When the regulatory and antitrust statutes are both Congressional products, the question is how that body intended them to interact. The relation between federal antitrust and state regulation is constitutionally more complex. Federal law is constitutionally dominant. In general, the question is whether Congress intended the antitrust law to displace, defer to, or share the terrain with state regulation.[6]

Whether the regulatory scheme is federal or state, another important distinction is between legislation (such as a environmental regulation) which seeks to mitigate a market failure and achieve outcomes closer to those of a more perfect market, and legislation (such as rent control law) intended to change an outcome that a well functioning market might achieve. Federal regulation correcting a market failure

---

5. E.g., Telecommunications Act of 1996, Pub. L. No. 104–104, 110 Stat. 56 (1996).

6. Schwegmann Bros. v. Calvert Distillers Corp., 341 U.S. 384, 71 S.Ct. 745, 95 L.Ed. 1035 (1951).

may leave ample room for antitrust without interfering with regulatory goals. But even for such market oriented regulation, when the state is its author, a federal antitrust court may hesitate to attempt to engineer a refined fit between the two regimes.

When the federal regulatory norms reject pure market goals (e.g., labor law), interpretation does not entail accommodation so much as drawing boundaries. Antitrust applies this far and no further; beyond a specified point, the market values championed by antitrust are displaced. Where the federal regulation intends to make markets work better by muting a particular failure, a different orientation is possible. A court or agency can search out consistencies and devise interpretive cannons that tend to harmonize antitrust and the regulatory program into a unified whole. When state regulation encounters federal antitrust, the policy problems are similar. Nevertheless, most of the issues must be articulated in quite different legal terms. The law's theoretical tools include both preemption and a "preemption doctrine in reverse"—a judicially developed "exemption" from antitrust for state action as well as for some state mandated or approved private action.

The economic and political literature suggests a number of theories of regulation, including normative, capture and public choice theories, some of which will be briefly summarized hereafter. Antitrust scholars have drawn on some of this writing seeking to unify and rationalize decisions about the ways antitrust and regulation relate. Although sometimes helpful, these efforts provide no wholly reliable guide. In all cases where antitrust and regulation interact—whether market failure or market displacement regulation, and whether both systems are federal or the regulation is by a state—particulars control outcomes.

This chapter first discusses regulation of public utilities and focuses on natural monopoly as an economic phenomenon. We explore some of the ways regulation deals with utilities, noting some of the techniques that mimic markets and possible ways of integrating utility regulation and antitrust. The chapter looks briefly at both conventional public utility regulation and some recent variants. A successful integration of antitrust and regulation must be based on understanding of both traditions. After reviewing regulatory basics, the chapter summarizes some explicit statutory exemptions to antitrust that Congress has articulated. Later, the chapter addresses some of the developments in telecommunications and in ocean shipping as illustrations of ways in which regulation and antitrust can interact either to improve or to impede market performance. Finally, the role of antitrust in markets with important governmental participants will be appraised.

§ 14.2 Public Utilities and the Natural Monopoly Concept

14.2a. Economic Theory About Natural Monopoly

Some industries, usually called public utilities, are comprehensively regulated. Industries where entry, rate and service have conventionally been regulated include communications, water, power and transportation. The common rationale for such regulation is that these industries are natural monopolies—that is, industries in which production by a single firm minimizes costs. If the long run average cost for any product or service declines continuously with increases in output, monopoly will yield the lowest per unit cost irrespective of the size of the output. Traditional price theory further supposes that for any such market, monopoly must result. Expansion, even in the face of competition, will lower cost and enable lower prices. Such a market is not contestable. A first entrant will not likely be challenged. If there is a challenge, the winner will take all.[1] Regulation is justified because in such a market, the goals of productive efficiency and allocative efficiency collide. To minimize cost, there must be a monopolist. But if the market is not regulated, the natural monopoly, even if producing efficiently, will reduce output and charge supracompetitive prices, producing monopoly returns, a deadweight loss from shrinkage of consumer surplus and an income transfer from consumers to the monopolist. Monopoly will also reduce dynamic efficiency by dampening incentives to innovate. These negatives are taken to justify the usual regulatory response: allow entry only by a single firm, then regulate that firm to assure prudent investment, adequate service, and prices appropriately related to cost.

One problem with the rationale for public utility regulation is that the natural monopoly assumption may not accurately describe the regulated market.[2] Oligopoly, not monopoly, is typical, for example, in many transportation sectors where marginal cost may not continue to fall with increasing output. Indeed, considerable competition prevails in some such sectors. Though natural monopoly may in fact exist in some communications and some power segments, it clearly does not in all, and technological advances may erode natural monopoly where it does exist. Even where monopoly prevails for a given utility technology, there often is or could be competition with other technologies: gas vs. electric power; broadcast vs. satellite vs. cable TV; copper wire vs. fiber vs. cellular vs. cable telephone. Also, monopoly and protective regulatory regimes may extend beyond the natural monopoly segment (as it did for years in telephone where a natural monopoly for local service was assumed to extend to equipment, always potentially rivalrous, and to long distance, which became open for competition once microwave transmission was developed).

§ 14.2

1. W. Viscusi, J. Vernon & J. Harrington, Economics of Regulation and Antitrust, Ch.11 (1992) (hereinafter, Viscusi et al.). There are many texts on the economics of regulation, this one explores in depth the relationships between antitrust and regulatory policies. Chapter 11 thoroughly reviews the theory of natural monopoly and Chapter 12 reviews a number of the policy solutions. Regulation or socialization as al-

ternative responses to natural monopoly are discussed in Sullivan, *The U.S. the EU, the WTO, and Telecom Competition* in Festchaift Für Wolfgang Fikentscher (Mohr Síebeck 1998). This section draws directly on both sources.

2. F.M. Sherer & D. Ross, Industrial Market Structure and Economic Performance, 80–81 (3d ed. 1990).

For two reasons, even manifest natural monopolies need not be permanent. First, long run average costs, even if falling over all outputs now likely or foreseeable, might level out or rise if in the future output grows beyond currently foreseeable levels. Over a sufficient time span such a future may arrive, perhaps unnoticed. Multifirm participation may become possible without any cost penalty through demand growth even if technology remains almost constant. Second, technology may change in ways that bring a rapid and perhaps previously unexpected end to natural monopoly, as it did when microwave became a substitute for wire in long distance telecommunications.

Flaws in the natural monopoly rationale—both recognition that a number of utility markets are rivalrous oligopolies, and that changes in demand and technological can reduce or eradicate scale economies—have helped to stimulate deregulation. So, too, has theory about "regulatory failure," sometimes regarded as more harmful than the market defects that regulation is supposed to mitigate. Capture theory, associated with Stigler,[3] posits that private interests (usually the participants in the industry subject to regulation) affect and may ultimately control regulation by influencing the legislature that enacts, amends and funds the regulation or the officials that implement it. By "capturing" the regulatory apparatus, industry participants may convert the regulatory agency into a cartel enforcement agent that sets supracompetitive prices and shields incumbents from unwelcome entry. Whether or not capture occurs, public choice theory posits self-serving rather than consumer-serving motivations of legislators who enact regulation or agency personnel who apply it.[4]

The popular appeal of capture and public choice theory stems from a cynical, populist strain in American culture. In the 1940s, populists worried about the movement of power from Main Street to Wall Street and about removing faceless corporate bureaucracies from people's backs. Today's populists worry about the movement of power from the town hall and state capital to Washington and about checking faceless government bureaucracies. But capture and public choice theory also stand on intellectual legs. Capture theory, for example, gains support from observation that some industries with no natural monopoly characteristics (e.g. motor carriers) are regulated, that industries sometimes support regulation, and that regulation may increase, not diminish, profitability.[5] It can also be hypothesized that there is a "free-rider" problem that distorts regulatory politics: none of the supposed beneficiaries—members of the consuming public—will have a sufficient stake to invest in identifying the right course and urging the legislature or the agency to follow it. Industry members, by contrast, being greatly affected

---

3. Stigler, *The Theory of Economic Regulation*, 2 Bell J. of Econ. 3 (1971).

4. D. Faber & P. Frickey, Law and Public Choice: A Critical Introduction (1991).

5. Jordan, *Producer Protection, Prior Market Structure and the Effects of Government Regulation*, 15 J.L. & Econ. 151 (1972). *See also* the discussion in H. Hovenkamp, Federal Antitrust Policy, The Law of Competition and Its Practice § 19.2b (3d ed. 2005).

by legislative and agency policies and outcomes, will lobby to protect themselves.[6] Yet, much observation and some data confront capture theory. Within an industry there may be participants whose interests conflict and who lobby and litigate against each other about regulation. Moreover, the consuming public may be represented, perhaps quite effectively, by consumer groups that lobby and litigate. Finally, many market and political events cannot be explained by capture theory. Regulation is often opposed by industry and supported by consumers; cross-subsidization is frequent in regulated markets, as is preference for small producers; deregulation occurs, sometimes supported and sometimes opposed by industry members; and many tight oligopolies lack sentiment favoring regulation although regulatory cartelization could yield large gains to the participants.[7] At least as plausible as capture theory are these propositions: subject to the drag of political inertia, regulation occurs when the legislature, influenced by its members' observations, public perception and input, current theory, and the current political ethos, becomes persuaded that regulation will benefit the public. Similarly, regulation is modified or withdrawn when, under the same influences, the legislature concludes that change will increase the public benefit. Legislators and regulators both engage in "satisficing" behavior.[8] Legislatures are not constantly monitoring and reacting to market activities or swings in political sentiment. Regulators, in turn, work out regimes consistent with the current legislative mandate, relying no doubt on vicarious experience where other regulators in other jurisdictions have previously tread similar paths. Once a statute, regulatory approach and technique are in place, these are followed, unless serious perturbations demand fresh evaluation of particular aspects or issues. This is the context in which regulators seek peace with the regulated, their legislative overseers and the public.

14.2b. Regulatory Approaches to Public Utilities

14.2b1. *Rate of Return Regulation*

Once a single firm receives its certificate to operate, the primary goal of conventional public utility regulation is to reduce the allocative efficiency loss that would result from that firm's monopoly pricing. Within a specified geographic area,[9] an exclusive franchise is granted to a utility which commits to provide service at rates and of a quality approved or specified from time to time by a regulatory commission. The statute speaks in broad language.[10] The conventional regulatory focus is

---

6. Public choice theory attempts to add theoretical rigor to capture analysis. Policy makers select policies to maximize political support, votes and contributions. Relevant variables include the numerosity, the intensity of interest and the resources of groups with alternative or conflicting interests.

7. A number of those theoretical problems are noted and some of the literature is cited in H. HOVENKAMP, *supra* note 5, § 19.2b.

8. *Cf.* Simon, *A Behavioral Model of Rational Choice*, 69 Q.J. ECON. 99 (1955); Morris & Mueller, *The Corporation, Competition and the Invisible Hand*, 118 J. ECON. LIT. 32 at 58–59 (1980).

9. Often the territory is state-wide.

10. E.g. CAL PUB. UTILITY CODE, Ch. 3, Art. 1, § 451 (Deering 1990) (requiring Public Utilities to charge reasonable and fair rates for products and services).

on "rate of return."[11] The utility proposes a tariff which sets forth services and rates. The commission reviews this tariff in a complex and lengthy hearing. Once approved, rates remain stable for a considerable period.[12] The regulatory goal is to bring investment into line with need and rates into line with costs, allowing the utility no more than a reasonable return on prudently invested capital. The commission determines what capital is to be recognized as an appropriate part of the rate base. It also determines the portions of the rate base appropriately supported, respectively, by equity and by bonded investment, estimates the rate of return needed on each segment to attract the needed investment, and calculates a composite rate of return on the aggregate. Relying on recent past experience, adjusted as deemed appropriate for inflation or other identifiable dynamics, the commission also estimates the expenses that will necessarily be incurred to provide the specified services. These data—that is, the expenses plus the rate base multiplied by the rate of return—give the total revenue that must be yielded by the rates.

To evaluate rate levels regulators rely on the utility's past experience. Past expenses, appropriately adjusted, are taken as an appropriate basis for predicting future expenses. Past expenses are seldom critically evaluated unless some aspect—say, executive salaries or labor costs—become politically salient. Past and planned capital investment usually passes muster, too, without harsh critique, except in instances of politically lively concerns like dam or nuclear power plant construction, which raise contentious environmental issues. From time to time, there may be debate about the way existing capital equipment is evaluated. Yet, once a method—say, original cost less depreciation—has been adopted, inertial forces come into play. Occasionally, the needed rate of return on investment may also become contentious. Theoretically, it is the rate the investor could obtain elsewhere at comparable risk. While many capitalization techniques are available, there is no automatically correct answer to capitalization questions. Again, once an issue is disputed and resolved, the momentum is with that resolution.

In addition to determining the aggregate allowable revenue needed to cover expenses and attract capital, the commission must approve a rate structure—that is, a set of rates for the various services offered. The various rates for different services must be appropriately interrelated (there must not be inappropriate discrimination) and all rates must, in the aggregate, yield the target return. To avoid discrimination, the regulators might seek to assure prices for all services and to all groups of customers that exceed incremental cost by the same percentage. Such an ideal is elusive. Myriad common costs for many or all services often make

11. See Viscusi, et al., *supra* note 1, at Ch. 12 (economic analysis of natural monopoly regulatory methods). See also T. Morgan, J. Harrison & P. Verkuil, Economic Regulation of Business: Cases and Materials, Chap. 3, Regulation of Rates (2d Ed. 1985)

(exposition of the process of cost of service regulation and the issues encountered in determining operating costs and allowable return).

12. Id. at 379.

allocation a costly process and, in the end, largely a matter of judgment, not calculation. Also, discrimination favoring customers with high demand elasticities over those with low elasticities may be sought by utilities, and discriminations favoring politically preferred groups—usually households over businesses—may be supported by regulators. In addition, ancillary social goals either built or read into the legislation—goals captured in phrases like "universal service" or "life line service"—may lead to rate structures that subsidize the initial link between customer premises and the utility. This, of course, favors low volume users at the expense of high volume users.[13]

Even when the industry clearly remains a natural monopoly, conventional regulation can adversely affect incentives. Not only is there a reduced incentive to control costs (a matter discussed hereafter); there may also be a distortion in decisions about the mix of inputs. If the allowed rate of return always equaled the actual cost of capital, regulation would yield the same mix of capital, labor and other inputs as would an unregulated market. But selecting the rate of return is an inexact process that depends significantly on information provided by the utility. If the rate is set above actual capital costs—perhaps not an infrequent eventuality[14]—the utility not only earns more on its investment than other opportunities of similar risks would yield, but it also has the incentive to exceed the efficient level of investment. The efficient mix of capital and other inputs such as labor would be achieved if returns could not be increased by substituting one for another. In a competitive market the returns to all factors are market validated. Therefore, market forces encourage an efficient mix. But if the utility's capital were earning an excessive return, the utility would have the incentive to substitute capital for labor and other inputs beyond the point of allocative efficiency. Whatever method the regulator uses to decide what capital belongs in the rate base, it can make mistakes that shift the cost of inefficient investment in capital equipment from stockholders to rate payers.

Despite this tendency (known as the Averch–Johnson effect),[15] conventional utility regulation can work reasonably well when the utility is, in fact, a natural monopoly. The aggregate of allocative costs of regulation plus the transaction costs of regulatory supervision, though by no means insignificant, may nevertheless be lower than the allocative distortion plus the x-inefficiencies from natural monopoly that regula-

---

13. For an insightful discussion of the inefficiencies usually associated with utility pricing. See Kahn, *The Road to More Intelligent Telephone Pricing*, 1 YALE J. ON REG. 139 (1984).

14. Setting the rate of return involves judgment and recognizable risk. If the rate of return remained lower than the cost of capital the utility would presumably founder and eventually fail. For this reason, although regulators will not want to see the utility earn an excessive return they as well

as the utility may be more adverse to the risk of setting too low a figure than too high a figure. Given this and the utility itself as a major source of data, there may be a systematic bias toward a generous rate of return.

15. The seminal article noting the incentive to inefficiently increase capital is Averch & Johnson, *Behavior of the Firm Under Regulatory Constraint* 52 AM. ECON. REV. 1052 (1962).

tion avoids or reduces. There are serious questions, however, about whether rate of return regulation is worthwhile in oligopoly segments of utility markets; perhaps so, if the segment is marked by interdependent pricing[16] or other significant distortions; surely not if effective competition prevails, as it may in some utility oligopolies.[17] Unneeded regulation not only distorts allocative outcomes but entails significant bureaucratic cost. In some areas, deregulation has probably not progressed as far as it profitably could. On the other hand, some deregulation may be excessive. Generalizations are not reliable. One must examine particular markets before venturing judgment.

There is also concern that rate of return regulation does little or nothing to reduce the negative effect of natural monopoly on dynamic efficiency. While there is no consensus about whether competition or oligopoly most encourages innovation,[18] there is reason to suspect that market dominance leads to a level of research and development (R & D) sufficient only to discourage entry. Dominance also provides a much reduced incentive to commercialize such innovations as are achieved. A natural monopolist subject to rate of return regulation will likely have inadequate incentive either to invest in innovation or to bring its innovations promptly to market. AT & T possessed a monopoly on local telephone service in most communities throughout most of the twentieth century. Although AT & T had formidable resources for R & D, the firm was often slow to introduce major technological improvements. For example, the automatic switching machine that replaced most telephone operators for connecting local (and later long distance) calls was introduced first by independent telephone companies and only later by the Bell System.

14.2b2. *Competitive Values within the Regulation Scheme*

The classic rationale for rate of return regulation is that when competition is not attainable, regulation must be used to foreclose supra competitive returns. Two major problems are encountered. First, regulators must find an acceptable substitute for marginal cost pricing, the competitive ideal. Second, natural monopolists, even more than other monopolists, lack incentive to control their costs, and rate of return regulation does not provide such an incentive. In addition to these ever salient problems, regulators may encounter a variety of other structural or conduct issues in which competitive analysis may have value. In the subsections following, these problems are considered.

---

16. Interdependent pricing may be difficult or impossible to challenge under existing antitrust constraints.

17. Long distance telephone service is an example. See Sullivan, *Elusive Goals Under the Telecommunications Act: Preserving Long Distance Competition Upon Baby Bell Entry and Attaining Local Exchange Competition: We'll Not Preserve the One Unless We Attain the Other*, 25 Sw. U. L. Rev. 487 (1996) (hereinafter, "Elusive Goals").

18. See Anticipating the 21st Century: Competition Policy in the New High–Tech Global Market Place, Vol. I, Chaps. 6–10 (Report by Federal Trade Commission Staff, 1996).

14.2b2i.   Average, Marginal or Peak Load Pricing

A natural monopoly's average total costs continue to fall over the full range of its possible outputs. Because marginal cost is below average cost when average cost is falling, there is no output at which marginal cost pricing would cover full costs. A frequent regulatory response is to authorize two separate charges, one for connecting customers to the utility's infrastructure so that they can be served and another for the provision of service, the later charge to vary with quality and quantity of service used. If the charge for getting on line is large enough to cover the gap between marginal and full costs, it will then be possible for the service charge to be related to incremental cost, a reasonable surrogate for marginal cost. When this system is used, connection charges are usually constant, rather than varied with the cost of providing the connection. Alfred Kahn, a preeminent scholar and regulatory practitioner, proposes that connection charges be set at the marginal cost of providing connection and service charges at the marginal cost of service.[19] But the practical difficulties in implementing this ideal would be formidable because of cost accountants' discretion and uncertainties in calculating marginal costs.

An alternative is to allow or encourage price discrimination that imposes the burden of "closing the gap" between average and marginal cost disproportionately on users who have relatively low demand elasticities for the utility's service. In effect, those whose need for the service is most intense would subsidize those whose need is less intense. Although some cross-subsidies may fairly be called "taxation by regulation,"[20] higher prices to low elasticity customers than to high elasticity customers is not one of them. Such a subsidy can result in fuller use of the utility's infrastructure. If some users have no close substitutes while others have market options, discrimination can add additional users that pay their own variable cost plus something additional that will reduce the fixed cost burden on those who cannot substitute.[21] Note, also, that in situations where the utility faces competition sufficient to result in identifiable customer groups with different demand elasticities, the natural monopoly may already be eroding. If the market were deregulated,

19. Kahn, supra note 13.

20. Posner, *Taxation by Regulation*, 2 BELL J. ECON. 22 (1971). Then Professor Posner applied the term to cross-subsidies resulting in services that are offered at lower rates and in higher quantities under regulation than they would be in an unregulated market.

21. Charging low-demand elasticity users a higher rate and high-demand elasticity users a lower rate will always result in higher use of the utility's infrastructure. This may increase allocative efficiency. The "Ramsey pricing" theory teaches that when prices for products with common costs marketed to different customer groups must

vary from marginal cost to constrain the utility's aggregate revenue, the most efficient outcome is to see that the price for each product deviates from marginal cost in inverse proportion to its elasticity of demand. Baumol & Bradford, *Optimal Departures from Marginal Cost Pricing*, 60 AM. ECON. REV. 265 (1970) formally demonstrates that Ramsey pricing would maximize aggregate social welfare. But regulators cannot know the elasticity of demand for each product or customer group. Consequently, even if regulators attempt to impose a Ramsey pricing rule high elasticity users may end up over-using the utility, which would diminish allocative efficiency.

such discrimination, if feasible, would be the profit maximizing choice. Avoidance of discrimination, nonetheless, is often a specified goal of regulatory programs. Accordingly, average cost pricing may at times be mandated. Such a course, abandoning both the marginal cost concept and the allocative efficiency goal,[22] leaves no gap to be filled either by charges for connection or by discrimination.

Aggregate demand for many utility services varies from season to season and from hour to hour in the course of a day, while some capital costs and all variable costs, such as fuel, vary with the level of output. Peak load pricing attempts to allocate the additional capital and increased variable costs that must be incurred in meeting peak loads to those customers that consume service during peak periods. It is claimed that, if properly done, the resulting rate structure will be closer to marginal cost. While that may be questionable,[23] peak load pricing should tend to induce shifting of usage as cost-conscious consumers seek to substitute service during non-peak hours for peak hour service. This will have the effect of spreading loads more evenly, lowering the capacity needed for peaks times, and thus lowering aggregate capital costs.

Peak load pricing is inevitably experimental and inexact. For example, it is never suggested that off peak customers should pay almost none of the capital costs because the additional capital cost of carrying any additional unit of gas during any off-peak period approximates zero; any allocation must involve pragmatic judgments. Because of this, peak load pricing schemes may be challenged as inequitable discrimination. Courts, however, have accepted such practices—indeed, given regulators considerable discretion. Both efforts to initiate[24] and to reduce[25] peak load burdens have been found just and reasonable.

14.2b2ii.   Regulatory Incentives to Control Costs

Cost control is the second problem associated with rate of return regulation. Natural monopolists, by definition, possess monopoly power. A monopolist—even one facing the possibility of competition—can enjoy its power in one or more of several ways. It can earn monopoly returns (controlling cost but setting supracompetitive prices). It can indulge factor providers such as management and labor through excessive payments. It can enjoy the quiet life, by not adequately and aggressively controlling costs, thereby letting "x-inefficiencies" creep in. It can reduce the threat of future entry by limit pricing or other "rent-seeking" activities. Natural monopolists in public utility markets may have some of these options. Regulation may foreclose monopoly returns and limit pricing, but it may or may not successfully inhibit rent-seeking.[26] Any firm capable, as is the rate regulated utility, of passing on all costs to

---

22. Id.

23. See T. Morgan, J. Harrison & P. Verknil, Economic Regulation of Business: Cases and Materials, supra note 11 at 381–383.

24. Metropolitan Washington Board of Trade v. PSC of D.C., 432 A.2d 343 (App. D.C.1981).

25. Consolidated Gas Supply Corp. v. FPC, 520 F.2d 1176 (D.C.Cir.1975).

26. See § 2.3b.

consumers with inelastic demand and then adding a mark up for profit will have little incentive to manage costs aggressively. Conventional rate of return regulation is quite likely to leave room for such inefficiency. The usual regulatory devices for dealing with this problem address outcomes, not causes. In the course of a rate case, any cost can be compared with the past experience of the regulated firm. Also, other utilities can be used as bench marks. Payments to affiliates, intrafirm transfers, depreciation, salaries and some other expenses or capital investments may be scrutinized. But utilities have resources to placate the regulators and incentives to ignore them, so such reviews will not stimulate cost cutting passion. What, then, might regulators do?

14.2b2iii. Allowing Entry

Competition, if feasible, is the most powerful incentive for productive efficiency. Regulators should be empowered to reduce entry constraints when actual or potential rivalry begins to encroach on a public utility's supposed natural monopoly market. For example, United States law governing international ocean carriage permits carriers to form conferences (cartels) to set rates, but requires that conferences remain open to entry and exit. New carriers may form and enter the conferences, and existing conference members may at any time leave the conference without penalty. Closed conferences, which still exist in some ocean trades not affecting the United States, might more effectively limit output, and may be more efficient (because they can eliminate wasteful excess capacity). But United States maritime law has for some time operated under the policy premise that open entry promotes beneficial competitive discipline of the conferences.

Of course an agency decision must be within the bounds of the discretion it possesses under the statute. In *RCA Communications* the Supreme Court rejected an agency's general panegyric to competition as a sufficient justification for allowing entry, but said that " * * * reasonable expectation that competition may have some beneficial effect would be enough."[27] If a true natural monopoly exists and persists, the incumbent's scale economies ought to deter entrants without the need for regulatory barriers. Yet, caution is warranted and analysis of likely consequences needed. If the incumbent successfully discriminates, high demand customers may subsidize low demand customers and this may be responsive to the legislature's regulatory goal. If so, allowing an entrant to "cherry pick" may be disruptive to the regulatory plan.[28]

---

27. FCC v. RCA Communications, Inc., 346 U.S. 86, 97, 73 S.Ct. 998, 97 L.Ed. 1470 (1953). But *cf.* Bowman Transportation Inc. v. Arkansas–Best Freight System, Inc., 419 U.S. 281, 95 S.Ct. 438, 42 L.Ed.2d 447 (1974). For an example of a successful decision by regulators to open a market to competitive entry, see In re Use of Carterfone Device in Message Toll Telephone Service, 13 F.C.C.2d 420 (1968). In MCI Telecommunications Corp. v. FCC, 561 F.2d 365 (D.C. Cir. 1977), cert. denied, 434 U.S. 1040 (1978) the court prompted further deregulation by the Commission.

28. For an interesting, and appropriately unsuccessful, effort to challenge a 1970s FCC decision to allow entry of specialized private communications service carriers into interstate telephone, see Washington Utilities & Transport Comm. v. FCC, 513 F.2d 1142 (9th Cir.1975). Petitioner noted

The critical question is whether the natural monopoly is eroding due to technological change, demand growth, or both.[29] But saying "no" to all entry embraces the risk that a potentially rivalrous market will be treated as though it were not contestable—clearly not an outcome consistent with the public interest. Attitudes about whether entry should be permitted experimentally have varied over time[30] and, it seems, among forums.[31] Some of the issues will be addressed more fully in the discussion of deregulation in § 14.2b3.

14.2b2iv. Regulatory Lag

Where entry cannot be used as a cost control incentive, other means may be attempted. A common one is "regulatory lag." When a rate case ends, the rates established on the basis of predictions about costs apply in the future. If the utility succeeds in reducing its cost below the anticipated level, it increases its return. That cost experience will be reflected in the next rate case, but in the interim, there are profits to be made from cost control. If the period between rate cases is relatively short, this incentive will be weak. Cost predictions based on last years experience will likely be quite accurate through the coming year. There is little time for management to change enough to have a significant impact on the bottom line. But if the next rate case is delayed—say, three years—the incentive to reduce cost to increase current returns may be significant. But a long regulatory lag has its risks for the utility. Unless on-going inflationary rates were accurately predicted and built into the rate calculation, a long wait before the next rate determination could be devastating to a utility confronting high inflation.

14.2b2v. Price Caps

An incentive device now widely discussed is the use of "price caps."[32] A price cap, rather than rate of return regulation, enables the utility to share in gains from its own efficiency. As currently used by the FCC the method has two features: First, the price is set for the future to reflect expected costs, adjusted upward for any expected inflation and downward for any expected increases in productivity not attributable to

---

that because common facilities were used by incumbent telephone companies to provide both interstate service, regulated by the FCC, and intrastate service, regulated by petitioner, it had an interest in objecting to the FCC's order because entry, by reducing the interstate business of incumbents, would decrease their use of common facilities and that this, in turn, would require allocation of a larger share of service and equipment costs to intrastate carriage, compelling a rate increase.

29. Bowman Transportation Inc. v. Arkansas–Best Freight Systems, Inc., 429 U.S. 281, 95 S.Ct. 438, 42 L.Ed.2d 447 (1974).

30. Compare Idaho Power & Light Co. v. Blomquist, 26 Idaho 222 (1914) with In re Application of MCI, 18 FCC2d 953 (1969). See the cases cited in note 27, supra.

31. Compare Application of MCI, supra note 30 with Hawaiian Tel. Co. v. FCC, 498 F.2d 771 (D.C.Cir.1974).

32. P. Brenner, Law and Regulation of Common Carriers in the Communications Industry, Ch.6 (2d ed. 1996) contains a useful summary.

special management effort. For example, if a productivity increase of 2 percent is normal in the industry and inflation of 4 percent is anticipated, a "productivity index" of 2 percent will be subtracted from anticipated inflation and the utility authorized to raise prices only 2 percent per year. Second, services are grouped into "baskets" and the utility is free to adjust prices of individual services within a basket so long as the average price of the basket of services stays within the price cap. The inflationary index (and, if thought essential, the productivity index) can be adjusted from time to time—indeed, as often as annually if thought necessary and wise. Also cost reductions resulting from matters the utility cannot control might, when identified, be passed on to consumers. The utility must reduce costs as much as the productivity index to earn the allowed return. If it succeeds in reducing them more, it shares in the benefit of increased productivity. The freedom to make price adjustments within the basket of services enables the utility to adjust prices with reference to demand elasticities and competition.

As a practical matter, the influence of price caps in encouraging efficiency improvements may be no greater than that of regulatory lag. Price caps are nonetheless conceptually sound in markets where one firm dominates but some competition is encountered. The "basket," giving the utility some discretion as to particular rates, may facilitate some discrimination. But this may not be a vice in contexts where the natural monopoly has been or may be eroding. A range of discretion for the incumbent confronts entrants with market realities. It reduces the risk that the utility, obliged to subsidize high cost users through uniform rates covering all average costs, will suffer diversion to higher cost entrants that are able to undercut the incumbent's prices only for low cost customers.

Requiring the utility to meet normal productivity standards to earn a normal return can, if effectively used, be a "stick" that substitutes for market pressure to avoid x-inefficiency. The opportunity to earn greater than normal productivity is the carrot. But the carrot could provide an advance over regulatory lag only if the productivity index, once established, remained stable for a substantial number of years. The problem, of course, is that "normal" productivity is itself a historic trend that might alter, perhaps significantly, at any time. Given the opportunity for frequent adjustments in the productivity index as well as the inflation index, the difference between the regulatory lag incentive and the price cap incentive may be quite modest. When the utility reduces costs more than the productivity index predicted, the regulator does not know for sure whether the cause is management efficiency or a change in the trend. So long as the productivity index remains adjustable, the utility operates under the risk of annual "excess profit" renegotiations with the regulator.[33]

33. The FCC adopted price Cap Regulation for dominant carriers in 1989. In re   Policy & Rules Concerning Rates for Dominant Carriers, 4 FCC Rcd 2873 (1989).

14.2b2vi. Franchise Bidding

Franchise bidding, first proposed by Demsetz,[34] might also be used to get closer to market outcomes in some natural monopoly industries. Only one entrant is permitted to facilitate scale economies. The regulator specifies the price level and monitors quality. The franchise is awarded to the firm bidding the lowest price for supplying the required service for a specified period of time. If service is homogeneous, the quality tightly specified and enforceable, and there is sufficient competition in bidding, then average cost prices and normal profits could be expected to result. The practical problems are numerous, however, as is shown by bids to municipalities for licenses to supply cable service. Unanticipated delay is common, there are differences in facilities and service offerings as well as in price, and renegotiation after award is well neigh inevitable. Also, limited numbers of bidders meeting in different auctions at different places may seek to share franchises interdependently or may use game theory strategies that raise prices above average cost.[35]

Subject to some qualifications, under current law the FCC is using franchise bidding to award available communications wave spectrum not only for personal communications system (PCS) licenses but even for commercial broadcast service, previously awarded after comparative hearings.[36] On economic grounds, the case for turning to an auction to license spectrum rather than using comparative hearings, status rules (such as those resulting in cellular service licenses issuing to local telephone companies) or a lottery (also used for some cellular phone licenses) is compelling. Even if bidders use game theory strategies to keep bids down, the auction will reduce if not obliterate the donations of capital value of franchises which, until recently, were not marketed but awarded. If the system works well, licenses will end up in the hands of those bidders who will be able to put them to the highest economic use. Perhaps this experience with bidding for spectrum will lead to wider use of bidding in other areas.

14.2b2vii. Competitive Values in Structural and Behavioral Controls Imposed by Regulators

Antitrust rules may apply to particular structural or conduct issues in regulated markets. Here, we put that observation aside and ask whether the regulatory agency in performing its duties can and should consider competition in making judgments about structure.

Often, regulatory agencies must approve transactions such as mergers that will affect the structure of the regulated market.[37] Competitive

34. Demsetz, *Why Regulate Utilities*, 11 J.L. & Econ. 55, 56 (April 1968).

35. For a pointed discussion see Viscusi et al., *supra* note 1, at 399–415.

36. See First Report and Order Re: Implementation of Section 309(J) of the Communications Act—Competitive Bidding for Commercial Broadcast and Instructional Television Fixed Service Licenses, MM Dkt. No. 97–234; GC Dkt. No. 92–52, GEN Dkt. No. 90–264 (Release Number FCC 98–194).

37. See, e.g., Section 5(2) of the Interstate Commerce Act.

concerns can come into play in the exercise of such power. In *McLean Trucking Co. v. United States*,[38] the Supreme Court held that the ICC, under its broad public interest mandate, should consider any risks of competitive injury. In doing so, however, the agency was not compelled to apply antitrust standards. Rather, it was obligated to consider all relevant public interest factors and to weigh possible competitive harm in the balance with all other factors.[39] While significant rail mergers have been approved under *McLean* despite apparent competitive risk,[40] competition may not be ignored. The evaluation of competitive effects must be a rational exercise, not the pro forma recitation of a formula.[41] The *McLean* principle is applied not just to the ICC, but when other federal regulatory agencies must decide whether a transaction affecting market structure is in the public interest.[42] It may also be fair to assume, if Congress through use of a public interest standard has in other provisions of the regulatory statute shown a commitment to making competition work, that antitrust values will be given a forceful role.[43] Many state regulatory decisions also take account of competitive concerns in reviewing structural change under broad standards like the public interest.[44]

Competitive values may also inform some regulatory decisions about conduct. A notable example, discussed more fully hereafter, is the effort of the FCC to constrain cross-subsidy and self dealing by AT & T (before the antitrust decree that broke up that company) and more recently by the baby Bells, the post-decree telephone monopolists.[45] Today both the FCC and state commissioners audit transactions between regulated utilities and vertically related affiliates. The effectiveness of such conduct constraints is uncertain. Discovering violations can be difficult where regulated and unregulated activities share joint costs.[46] It is appropriate, therefore, that regulators be vigilant and that sanctions for violations be significant.

14.2b3. *Deregulation*

The January 1989 Economic Report to the President[47] marks the "deregulation wave" as beginning in 1971 with an FCC decision showing

---

38. 321 U.S. 67, 64 S.Ct. 370, 88 L.Ed. 544 (1944).

39. When the FCC is asked to approve the transfer of spectrum licenses upon acquisition of the license in the course of a merger, it must operate under the McClean principle. In Re Application of Craig O. McCaw, Transferor, 9 F.C.C. 5836 (1994) (transfer of McCan Cellular Communications, Inc. to AT & T approved), *aff'd sub nom.*, SBC Communications, Inc. v. FCC, 56 F.3d 1484 (D.C.Cir.1995). It is this requirement that mandates FCC evaluation in addition to antitrust agency evaluation of the competitive effects of mergers such as World Com–MCI.

40. E.g., In re Penn Central Transp. Co., 458 F.Supp. 1234 (E.D.Pa.1978).

41. See, Denver & Rio Grande W.R.R. v. United States, 387 U.S. 485, 87 S.Ct. 1754, 18 L.Ed.2d 905 (1967).

42. See, Application of Craig O. McCaw, *supra* note 39.

43. See, Sullivan, *Elusive Goals*, supra note 17, at 534.

44. E.g., In re American Telephone and Telegraph Company 54 Cal. P.U.C.2d at 58 (1994) (AT & T–McCaw merger approved).

45. See § 14.7a, infra. See also Sullivan, *Elusive Goals*, supra note 17, at 518–527 (cross-subsidy in telephone).

46. Sullivan, *Elusive Goals*, supra note 17, at 518–531(telephone cross-subsidization and self-preference).

47. COUNCIL OF ECONOMIC ADVISERS' ECON. REPT TO THE PRESIDENT (1989).

a new openness to competition,[48] about the time capture theory was being fully articulated and not long after Peter Drucker coined the term, "privatization."[49] There were earlier soundings. President Kennedy's 1962 message on transportation called for more competition and less regulation.[50] Indeed, important economic literature critical of airline regulation dates to 1962.[51]

Whatever the sources, the deregulation movement continues, albeit not without occasional criticism that it has reached too far. Often in the face of opposition from regulated firms (as capture theory would predict), sometimes with their support, deregulation moved from administrative efforts to facilitate entry and to regulate in ways that mimic markets to comprehensive legislative change mainly at the federal but also at the state level. True, there are glaring exceptions, usually at the municipal level (e.g., taxis). But most surface and air transportation businesses are largely deregulated except for safety, and telephone, gas and electric are being deregulated, albeit slowly, as is cable.[52] Deregulation sentiment continues to influence regulatory responses even where legislative change has not occurred.[53] Courts, by and large, have construed deregulatory legislation broadly.[54]

Yet, the deregulatory agenda is not complete. Deregulation of international transportation, requiring multilateral support, has proceeded slowly. For example, international ocean carriage, although undergoing some deregulation, continues to operate under a system of government-sanctioned cartels. Also, telephone deregulation at the local level is being successfully resisted or decelerated, and further deregulation in other transportation sectors is needed.[55]

§ 14.3   Statutory Exemptions to the Antitrust Laws

Congress has explicitly modified or displaced the application of antitrust in some areas (e.g., securities markets, energy) where it concluded that the success of a federal regulatory scheme might be frustrated if antitrust fully applied. Congress has also, in a few instances (e.g. agricultural collectives, joint newspaper operating agreements) expressly modified the application of antitrust not to accommodate conventional regulation but to facilitate a particular market outcome that Congress

---

48. Specialized Common Carrier Services, 29 F.C.C.2d 870 (1971).

49. Druker, *The Sickness of Government*, 14 THE PUB. INT. 31 (1969).

50. President J. Kennedy, Transportation Message, 1962.

51. R. CAVES, AIR TRANSPORTATION AND ITS REGULATION: AN INDUSTRY STUDY (1962).

52. See VISCUSI ET AL., *supra* note 1, at 303, Table 10.2. Since that work was published the ICC has been abolished, and deregulation has occurred in telecommunications. See Sullivan, *Elusive Goals*, supra note 17.

53. Most prominently, the FCC has wholly or partially deregulated domestic satellites, satellite earth stations, cable television, and customer premises equipment; the FCC has also eliminated the fairness doctrine, freed some carriers from rate filing obligations and adopted price caps.

54. E.g., Morales v. Trans World Airlines, 504 U.S. 374, 112 S.Ct. 2031, 119 L.Ed.2d 157 (1992) (giving broad interpretation of airline deregulation Act to preempt states from enforcing state deceptive practice laws against newly deregulated airlines).

55. See § 14.7c.

approved and thought might be inhibited by antitrust. In one instance (insurance), antitrust has been displaced in part to facilitate state regulation, at least where a meaningful state regulatory scheme is in place. In connection with another matter (resale price maintenance), Congress, for a period of years, displaced antitrust to accommodate not state regulatory policy, but state legislative and judicial decisions that antitrust should be abated. In one instance (the labor-exemption), the Court has, by its own construction of the reach of the Sherman Act, extended a statutory exemption beyond the point to which the statute, as long construed, had carried it. Although this extension is not an explicit statutory exemption, we discuss it here along with the associated labor exemption that is statutorily based.

The most important of the specific exemptions are the labor exemption and the insurance exemption. They are discussed, respectively, in §§ 14.3a and 14.3b. In § 14.3c other exemptions enacted by Congress are described.

14.3a. The Labor Exemption

In recent years, unions have not played a particularly prominent role in the economy or in the development of antitrust. It was not always so, nor need it be so in the future, given successes of unions in bargaining, in industrial action, and in organizing white collar and professional employees. In this section we proceed chronologically.

A significant feature of both pre-Sherman Act common law of restraint of trade[1] and early Sherman Act Section 1 enforcement[2] was the use of conspiracy theory by employers to challenge the legality of labor union activities. Pre–Sherman common law cases were sometimes but not always successful[3] and, although the Sherman Act's legislative history does not suggest union activity as a target of the statute, early Sherman Act cases often were successful.[4] In *Loewe v. Lawlor*,[5] the Supreme Court sanctioned the use of Section 1 to challenge union activity. This is not surprising because such activity is unquestionably concerted. Its aim often is to "cartelize" the labor supply for an activity in or affecting commerce. Thus, much union activity falls within the broad language of Section 1. The judicial culture of early Sherman Act

§ 14.3

1. Commonwealth v. Pullis, Mayor's Court of Philadelphia (1806), reprinted in J. R. Commons, Documentary History of American Industrial Society 61–248 (1958); People v. Fisher, 14 Wend. 9 (N.Y.1835); See also Nockelby, *Two Theories of Competition in the early 19th Century Labor Cases*, 38 Am. J. Legal Hist. 452 (1994). Material in § 14.3a appeared in L. Sullivan Antitrust Law (1977); it is updated.

2. United States v. Cassidy, 67 Fed. 698 (N.D.Cal.1895); United States v. Agler 62 Fed. 824 (C.C.D.Ind.1894); Loewe v. Law-

lor, 208 U.S. 274, 28 S.Ct. 301, 52 L.Ed. 488 (1908).

3. People v. Fisher, supra note 1; H. Hovenkamp, Enterprise and American Law, 1836–1937 (1991).

4. Hovenkamp, *Labor Conspiracies in American Law*, 1880–1930, 66 Tex. L. Rev. 919, 950 (April 1988) (predominance of labor related cases involving the Sherman Act during the first seven years after its enactment).

5. 208 U.S. 274, 28 S.Ct. 301, 52 L.Ed. 488 (1908).

years was one of market-oriented liberalism.[6] One can assimilate the Court's decision in *Lawlor* to the view expressed about industrial combination a few years later in *Standard Oil*.[7] Far reaching and aggressive union activity, like trustification by industrialists, was not, in the lexicon of the liberal jurist of the era, a "normal" method of "attaining dominance."[8]

Union influence grew politically as well as in the marketplace, and Congress, after a time, reacted to these developments. The labor exemption is the product of two statutes. Section 6 of the Clayton Act,[9] enacted in 1914, states that labor is not an article of commerce and that the antitrust laws should not forbid labor organizations. Section 20 of that Act[10] limits the power of federal courts to grant injunctions in labor disputes and lists certain labor activities that should not be held to violate any law of the United States. These activities include conventional labor activities such as ceasing to perform work or urging that others cease to perform work or to employ any party to urge others to cease to perform work. The Norris–La Guardia Act,[11] passed in 1932, contains a declaration of policy favoring freedom of employees to organize and further limits the jurisdiction of federal courts to grant injunctions in labor disputes. Because it is so directly related in purpose and effect to Section 20 of the Clayton Act, the two statutes have been construed to exempt from the antitrust laws the practices that Norris–La Guardia protects from injunctions. Read together, the two provisions thus grant antitrust exemption to a broad range of conduct of the kind traditionally engaged in by unions.

The National Labor Relations Act[12] and the Labor Management Relations Act[13] affect antitrust less directly but are the basic sources of the non-statutory labor exemption. These statutes establish a national policy favoring collective bargaining. They set forth methods and procedures for the determination of bargaining units and the certification of bargaining representatives, and, where employees are represented, impose a duty to bargain collectively about wages, hours and terms and conditions of employment both on the employer and the bargaining representative. These acts also regulate the bargaining process in various particulars and, in addition to mandatory bargaining, identify various employer and labor practices as unfair. The National Labor Relations Board is established as the enforcement agency. Although neither act contains any explicit antitrust exemption, there may be conduct that seems to be required or permitted by these acts but forbidden by

---

6. Hovenkamp, supra note 4, at 950.

7. Standard Oil of New Jersey v. United States, 221 U.S. 1, 75, 31 S.Ct. 502, 55 L.Ed. 619 (1911) (maintaining dominance not as a result of normal methods of industrial development, but by means of combination violates the Act).

8. Loewe v. Lawlor, 208 U.S. 274, 301, 28 S.Ct. 301, 52 L.Ed. 488 (1908).

9. 15 U.S.C.A. § 17.

10. 29 U.S.C.A. § 52.

11. 29 U.S.C.A. §§ 101–10, 113–15.

12. Act of July 5, 1935, ch. 372, 49 Stat. 449.

13. Act of June 23, 1947 (Taft–Hartley), ch. 120, 61 Stat. 136, codified as 29 U.S.C.A. § 141 *et. seq.*

antitrust; hence, a proper accommodation between labor policy and antitrust policy may require that policies of one act or the other be altered or give way.

The Court's effort to integrate labor and antitrust has a tortured history. The modern era begins with *United States v. Hutcheson*[14] or, perhaps, with the enforcement program which led to that decision: Thurmond Arnold's determination, as head of the Antitrust Division, that various "unreasonable" restraints imposed by labor (such as prevention of the use of cheap materials, more efficient methods or labor saving equipment, feather-bedding, price-fixing beyond the labor market, and disruption of established collective bargaining relationships) would be challenged under the antitrust laws.[15] *Hutcheson*, one of the cases brought to advance that policy, involved a jurisdictional dispute and union resistance to the installation of new equipment. The union's activity was challenged as a criminal conspiracy under the Sherman Act. The Supreme Court affirmed a dismissal of the complaint holding that, so long as a labor organization does not combine with non-labor groups, all activities of the general kind described in Section 20 of the Clayton Act are exempt. As the Court held, this statutory exemption was broad enough to include even secondary picketing and boycotts; the "right and the wrong, the selfish and the unselfish" were not to be distinguished. If the conduct by the union and its members acting without others fell within the language of Section 20, there was, in essence, a *per se* antitrust exemption. If the challenged activity was conventional labor activity by a labor organization alone, that ended the inquiry.

But in *Allen Bradley*,[16] a case decided a few years later, the Court began to work out limits to the exemption. In the interest of obtaining better wages, hours and working conditions, a union induced electrical contractors to agree to use only equipment manufactured by firms having contracts with the union. Although the union was the prime mover, this arrangement, unlike *Hutcheson*, combined the union with employers in a common cause. The Supreme Court rejected the view taken by the Second Circuit that so long as the union was acting solely in its own self-interest and by means sanctioned by the Clayton Act's Section 20, the conduct escaped antitrust liability. Rather, the Court adopted another *per se* rule, an alternative to that in *Hutcheson*: immunity is lost when a labor group is acting to "aid and abet businessmen" in conduct that, if carried out by businessmen alone, would violate the Act. Given the primacy of the union's interest and initiative, the case seemed to make clear that immunity was not achieved merely because the union, acting for its own ends, was the architect of an employer-union combination; if manufacturers agreed, even though unwillingly and under union pressure, to a scheme of joint action that would violate

14. 312 U.S. 219, 61 S.Ct. 463, 85 L.Ed. 788 (1941).

15. See, C. SUMMERS & H. WELLINGTON, LABOR LAW; CASES AND MATERIALS 195 (1968).

16. Allen Bradley Co. v. Electrical Workers Local 3, 325 U.S. 797, 65 S.Ct. 1533, 89 L.Ed. 1939 (1945).

the law if undertaken by non-labor conspirators, then the union, and presumably the manufacturers, were in violation.

So the matter stood until *Pennington*[17] reached the Court in 1965. An antitrust agreement was negotiated between the United Mine Workers and an association which represented large mine operators. These operators made substantial wage and other concessions, and the union agreed to abandon its previously vehement opposition to increased mechanization. But the union also agreed that it would impose the same wage and other terms of employment on small operators who were not members of the association. The anticipated consequence was that wages would be improved, jobs reduced, and marginal mine operators forced out of the market. A small mining company, allegedly forced out of business by the agreement, challenged the agreement under the Sherman Act. In a treble damage action, it alleged that the agreement constituted a conspiracy by the union and large companies to foreclose the small mining companies. Six justices voted to reverse a judgment below for the defendants but divided in three ways on why the union's conduct was not exempt from antitrust liability. Justice White's opinion for three justices gave voice to the goal of accommodation. The courts should, where possible, resolve apparent conflicts between antitrust and labor policy in ways that avoided the need to give full scope to one policy at the cost of stifling the other. Given what was explicit in the labor law, where a multi-employer bargaining unit was appropriate, a union could lawfully negotiate with a representative of several companies even though this took wages (and skill at negotiating with unions) out of the area in which competition would be effective between the companies.[18] Moreover, a union, acting independently and not in concert with employers, can determine that all employers will have to meet the rate set in its negotiations with the most efficient employer. A union need not set its wage demands with the problems of marginal producers uppermost in mind; it may take action of the kinds listed in Clayton Section 20 and in Norris–La Guardia to gain its ends even if marginal producers are driven from the market. When it acts alone, all such conduct is exempt.

17. United Mine Workers v. Pennington, 381 U.S. 657, 85 S.Ct. 1585, 14 L.Ed.2d 626 (1965).

18. The opinion does not address important issues that lurk in the background. But for the national labor policy, concerted action by employers to negotiate wage rates would involve serious antitrust jeopardy. Such conduct might be characterized as price fixing and held to be unlawful *per se*. Alternatively, if it were concluded that significant scale efficiencies were feasible, it might be tested under the rule of reason; in this event it would nevertheless be unlawful where, as in *Pennington*, the arrangement brought a substantial part of the market under common control and yielded power to affect market price. Since the national labor policy purports to sanction multi-employer bargaining only where the multi-employer unit is the "appropriate" unit, in terms of the goals of national labor policy, it appears that, should a multi-employer unit in any instance be held not to be appropriate, bargaining for that unit would not be exempt conduct. Also unexplored are whether the national policy of maintaining competition among employers is entitled to weight where a decision is made about whether in any industry a multi-employer unit is appropriate and whether appropriateness of the unit can be considered by the court in an antitrust case or only initially by the Labor Board.

But this opinion also insists that when a union agrees with one employer about the wages it will exact from another employer not involved in the negotiation, the union has forfeited its antitrust exemption. Nothing in the national labor policy suggests exemption for concerted action between a union and one or more employers about the labor terms which competing employers will be forced to meet. Antitrust policy stands forcefully against such concerted action. There is, then, no conflict between the application of antitrust policy and the demands of labor policy. Consequently, on such facts the antitrust prohibition should prevail. That response was seen, indeed, as particularly appropriate where one group of employers was conspiring with the union on a course of conduct designed to eliminate other employers from the market. The opinion analogized what occurred in an agreement between the union and the companies about the price at which coal would be sold, an agreement which, as the three justices saw it, would be clearly illegal.

An opinion by Justice Douglas,[19] with whom two justices concurred, agreed that no labor exemption was warranted in this case. But Douglas implied that the labor exemption was exceeded only because the union and employers agreed upon a particular wage scale to be enforced against all employers, knowing that some could not meet it and with the intent of driving those employers out of business. As he saw it, such a labor-management conspiracy to drive competitors out of the market would both make the conduct illegal under antitrust and de-energize the labor exemption. Nonetheless, some of the Douglas language came close as a practical matter to the more sweeping view expressed by Justice White, in a third opinion—one that construed *Interstate Circuit*[20] to mean that any industry-wide agreement which, in fact, exceeded the ability of some operators to pay would be sufficient evidence to reach a jury on the conspiracy issue. The three remaining justices dissented in a single opinion for this case and *Jewel Tea*, to be discussed next.[21]

The most significant thing in *Pennington* was the view developed in the White opinion that the Court does not merely determine whether the specific activities challenged are cataloged in Clayton Section 20 or in Norris–La Guardia and, if so, assume exemption; nor does it mechanically conclude, where a labor-management combination is accomplished, that exemption is gone, as *Allen Bradley* might have implied. Two important national economic policies are interacting; the appropriate response is to determine whether there is, on the face of the matter, some conflict and, if so, whether it can be rationally reconciled in terms of the deeper goals of the policies involved. Only if reconciliation is not possible need a choice be made between the conflicting policies; and when choice cannot be avoided, the Court must gauge the force of the competing policies as they apply in the particular context. Although one

19. 381 U.S. 657, 672, 85 S.Ct. 1585, 14 L.Ed.2d 626 (1965).

20. Interstate Circuit v. United States, 306 U.S. 208, 59 S.Ct. 467, 83 L.Ed. 610 (1939).

21. Meat Cutters Local 189 v. Jewel Tea Co., 381 U.S. 676, 85 S.Ct. 1596, 14 L.Ed.2d 640 (1965).

might quarrel with the way in which labor and antitrust policies were assessed in *Pennington*, it is hard to oppose the White manner of structuring the problem. Anything else would be unduly simplistic and mechanical. Despite the contrary and conflicting implications of *Hutcheson* and *Allen Bradley*, this is not an area where the Court can hope to fashion simple, workable, self-administering *per se* rules.

Jewel Tea,[22] a companion case, reinforces the notion that the Court must balance conflicting policies. The case grew out of an industry-wide agreement between the meat cutters union and Chicago butchers that restricted store hours from 9:00 a.m. to 6:00 p.m, an agreement that Jewel Tea accepted under threat of a strike. After signing, Jewel Tea sued under Section 1 of the Sherman Act, alleging that the union and the employers who negotiated the agreement had conspired to prevent Jewel Tea from marketing at such hours as it, as an individual competitor, chose for itself. The district court found that the union's sole motive was to gain desirable working conditions for members and held the arrangement within the labor exemption. The Seventh Circuit reversed and the Supreme Court, *on certiorari*, reinstated the trial court's judgment. But in explaining the law, the justices split in the same three-three-three pattern that marked *Pennington*, with six Justices voting to hold that Jewel Tea had no cause of action.

The White opinion concluded that on these facts, unlike those in *Pennington*, accommodation required that antitrust give way to labor policy. These justices viewed the collective bargaining agreement as a "combination" between union and employers to affect a matter of competitive concern. The lack of an intent or motive to inhibit competition as to hours did not require a different characterization since that was the clear effect. Hence, under the approach of *Allen Bradley*, mechanically applied, the conduct would be unlawful; since the agreement involved a combination of labor and employers, the Clayton/Norris–La Guardia exemption was gone. But even though such a combination existed, there could be, as the opinion indicated, an exemption implied by the statutes setting forth the national labor policy. The problem was not a simple one; it involved accommodating labor and antitrust policy. There are subjects, such as wages, hours and working conditions, that are mandatory subjects of collective bargaining. Where a union and employers in a bargaining relationship agree on these, no antitrust violation occurs even though a combination of a labor group and several competing employers is achieved through industry-wide bargaining. But should a union and employers agree on things such as product or service prices, which are not mandatory bargaining subjects, the protection of the implicit exemption derived from the National Labor Relations Act (NLRA) and Taft–Hartley would be gone. In this instance, hours of operation had been a historic concern of the butchers' union and there were indications that night operations alter the character of

22. Meat Cutters Local 189 v. Jewel Tea Co., 381 U.S. 676, 85 S.Ct. 1596, 14 L.Ed.2d 640 (1965).

the work itself. In that context, hours of operation are sufficiently related to wages, hours and working conditions, to fall within the proper scope of collective bargaining for the multi-employer unit; thus the agreement is exempt.

Justice Goldberg's opinion, which expressed his view on *Jewel Tea* and *Pennington*, concurred that Jewel Tea was exempt but dissented from the *Pennington* conclusion that the mine workers were not. The opinion harkens back to the *Hutcheson* case. As Justice Goldberg saw the matter, hours of operation were clearly a matter of working conditions and, that being so, a mandatory subject of collective bargaining. Any agreement between a union and employers on such a subject is antitrust exempt, as was *Pennington*. Discussion of wage rates naturally involves discussion of the impact of the wage demanded upon the employer's business and this, in turn, inevitably involves discussion of the wages to be demanded from competitors. To deny the right to consider such matters in bargaining is frustrating to the collective bargaining process.[23] The opinion by Justice Douglas expressed his *Jewel Tea* dissent. Since the employers could not themselves agree on hours of operation, the union, by joining with them, exceeded the *Allen Bradley* rule and lost its exemption. This mechanical response is hardly satisfactory. Employers alone could not agree, for example, on the wages they would pay their employees; yet it is obvious that in a multi-employer unit permitted under the labor laws, a union and employers may join in fixing that element and in taking it out of the competitive struggle.[24]

In their totality this series of labor cases suggest both an analytical stance and an objective: to reconcile labor and antitrust policy where possible and, where not, to weigh claims of each and give way to the stronger. The difficulty of this task was reemphasized in *Connell Construction Co. v. Plumbers and Steamfitters Local 100*.[25] A union for one of the construction industry sub-trades had successfully used picketing to

23. *Pennington*, in indicating the illegality of an agreement between a union and an employer about the terms the union will insist upon in bargaining with others, places in jeopardy additional common arrangements. A common event is for an employer, in signing with a union, to seek and obtain a "most favored nation" clause, providing that if the union later grants more favorable terms to any other employer those terms will apply to the earlier signing employer also. At least in the situation where that clause is entered into between a union and a dominant employer or group of employers, so that all parties will realize that the union will as a practical matter concede no less onerous terms later, that arrangement is no different in effect from an explicit arrangement such as that in *Pennington*. Therefore one cannot confidently assume its legality.

24. In Ramsey v. United Mine Workers, 401 U.S. 302, 91 S.Ct. 658, 28 L.Ed.2d 64

(1971), another case arising out of a coal agreement, the lower court, citing *Pennington*, held that the jury must be instructed that "clear proof" of an employer-union conspiracy to drive out competing employers had to be shown to warrant a plaintiff's verdict. The majority of the Court disagreed and, in opinion by Justice White, held that a plaintiff suing on a *Pennington* theory need establish his case only by a preponderance of the evidence. Although Justice Douglas' *Pennington* and *Jewel Tea* opinions were even less hospitable to the labor exemption than the White opinions, in this instance Justice Douglas dissented. As he viewed it, bargaining with a multi-employer unit was itself no violation. He would therefore insist on clear proof of the conspiratorial animus before finding an antitrust violation.

25. 421 U.S. 616, 95 S.Ct. 1830, 44 L.Ed.2d 418 (1975).

force a number of general contractors to agree to subcontract work in the trade only to subcontractors that had current collective bargaining agreements with the union. Connell, one of these contractors, wanted to let subcontract work by competitive bidding to any qualified subcontractor and had signed the agreement under the duress of job site picketing which caused its own employees, represented by a different union, to walk off the job. Connell asserted in its suit against the union that the contract it was obliged to sign violated Section 1 of the Sherman Act. Justice Powell, writing for the majority, held that the statutory exemption of the Clayton Act's Section 20 was not available because the arrangement involved both labor and non-labor groups and that the "non statutory" exemption which can arise by implication from the NLRA or Labor Management Relations Act (LMRA) was not available for two reasons: first, because the union did not represent or seek to represent Connell's employees; second, because the "construction industry proviso" to Section 8(e) of the NLRA,[26] which authorizes secondary activity of the kind here involved, was, as the syllabus tersely put it, "not intended to authorize subcontracting agreements that are neither within the context of a collective bargaining relationship nor limited to a particular job site."[27] Justice Stewart, joined by Justices Douglas, Brennan and Marshall, dissented, first on the ground that secondary activity is subject to detailed and comprehensive regulation under Section 8(b)(4) of the NLRA,[28] and Section 303 of the LMRA,[29] which gives a cause of action for single damages in the event of a violation and because secondary activity of the kind involved was specifically authorized by Section 8(e).[30]

The most important issue of general, theoretical importance which *Connell Construction* seems to resolve is whether the antitrust exemption implied from the NLRA and LMRA applies whenever an activity, otherwise violative of antitrust, is of a kind that is dealt with in detail by the labor statutes, or only when the activity is in some sense authorized or approved by the labor statutes. There is no question but that the labor statute regulates in considerable detail secondary activity of the genus involved in this case; NLRA Section 8(b)(4) makes that activity an unfair labor practice, except insofar as it is shielded by other provisions. Section 8(e) shields some secondary activity of the general kind involved, but not all. Section 303 of the LMRA gives cause of action for single damages for 8(b)(4) violations, among others. The majority, held that NLRA Section 8(e) did not protect this particular secondary activity from the prohibition of Section 8(e)(4), and that LMRA Section 303, by giving a single damage cause of action for violations of 8(b)(4), did not imply the absence of a treble damage action under the antitrust laws. Thus, the majority impliedly held that an antitrust exemption does not apply to all activities of a class regulated by labor law but only to activities

26.   29 U.S.C.A. § 158(e).

27.   Connell Construction Co. v. Plumbers and Steamfillers Local 100, 421 U.S. at 617.

28.   29 U.S.C.A. § 158(b)(4).

29.   29 U.S.C.A. § 187.

30.   29 U.S.C.A. § 158(e).

approved and protected by labor law. Although the minority opinion argued vehemently that even assuming the majority to be right on the more specific statutory issues, the various strands of regulation constituted a sort of "occupation of the field" by the labor statutes to the exclusion of the antitrust laws, the majority assumed almost without discussion that unless a particular practice is affirmatively sanctioned by labor law, it is entitled to no exemption. That need not be so. Although the minority's "occupancy" concept seems unduly mechanical, it is surely possible that in some instances there is sufficient importance in allowing unions to push the edges of labor policy, subject only to correction under the labor laws, to warrant holding that any conduct within the ambit of the labor law should be free from antitrust attack whether that conduct is mandated, tolerated or forbidden by labor law. The particular conduct in *Connell* may not be in an area where labor policy demands such deference from antitrust; but that matter is one to be decided after consideration, not blithely assumed.[31]

Note also that whenever a union negotiates with a group of employers in a multi-employer bargaining arrangement, it is agreeing with each about the wage rates of the others. Where the multi-employer unit is the appropriate unit for collective bargaining within the meaning of the NLRA, the union would, of course, have an exemption based on the implication of the NLRA. But if the multi-employer unit should not be held appropriate, *Connell Construction* may imply union and employer liability for jointly agreeing on wages. If the unit is not appropriate, then labor policy may not call for any exemption. And if there is no exemption, antitrust policy has full sway.[32] If the union's goal is to induce an employer not to alter its own union policy, but to change a supplier's policy, the conduct cannot be sheltered under Section 20 of the Clayton Act.

31. The specific statutory issues in the *Connell* case, although of less general importance, are not devoid of interest. Section 8(e), literally construed, would shield the union-employer contract from the prohibition of 8(b)(4) as "an agreement between a labor organization and an employer in the construction industry relating to * * * subcontracting of work to be done at the site of the construction * * * "; and it is not particularly clear that the majority got the better of the argument about the limit upon the meaning of the phrase emanating from its legislative history. Yet the minority also overlooked a significant question. The minority assumed without discussion that if Section 8(e) saved the activity involved from being an unfair labor practice forbidden by Section 8(b)(4), it must also save it from being an antitrust violation. That surely does not follow as a necessity. To say that a particular activity falls barely within the scope of a proviso which thus barely keeps it from being an unfair labor practice is not to make a strong case for protecting

the activity from antitrust prohibition because of the activity's importance to labor policy. If, as the majority holds, an exemption applies only when there is a greater interest under the labor law in allowing the conduct than there is under the antitrust law in forbidding it, unless there were some positive reason under labor policy for encouraging a practice, any significant antitrust policy against it ought to suffice to make it unlawful.

32. See note 18 supra. Note that if industry-wide bargaining is not carried on, but employers act concertedly in agreeing on the position each will take in bargaining with the union, there is after *Connell* virtually no room left for employers to claim a labor exemption. The lawfulness of such joint employer activity must therefore be determined under normal antitrust principles. *But see*, Brown v. Pro Football, Inc., 518 U.S. 231, 116 S.Ct. 2116, 135 L.Ed.2d 521 (1996), discussed in the text accompanying note 33, *infra.*.

Brown v. Pro Football, Inc.,[33] the most recent Supreme Court labor exemption decision, addresses a related issue. The case involved the National Football League's long-term labor dispute. League teams had for years been recognized as the appropriate multi-player bargaining unit. As the representative of its members the league recognized the union and bargained in good faith to an impasse, after which bargaining broke off. The players then dismissed the union as their bargaining agent. Despite this change in status, the employers agreed among themselves that each would implement their last joint offer to the union. The theory of the Sherman Act claim was that once the bargaining process had ended, the league lost its status as an appropriate bargaining agent under the Taft–Hartley Act. Therefore, when employers acted concertedly to fix employee wages, they were not protected by the non-statutory exemption and their conduct was a *per se* violation of Section 1. The Court held that in implementing unilaterally its last good faith offer made in a bargaining context, the employers remained protected even though the bargaining relation that was sanctioned by the Act had terminated. In so holding, the Court gave the non-statutory labor exemption greater capacity to fill interstices in a statutory scheme than it has customarily given to other exemptions implied from regulatory statutes. In that respect the opinion seems inconsistent with the notion of balancing labor and antitrust interests inherent in the opinions of Justice White, which until *Brown* had represented the central tendency of the Court's work in this area. Indeed, the opinion suggests unwillingness to invite lower courts to engage in such balancing even though the alternative is a far reaching and mechanical rule that might reduce the influence of competition policy in many situations in which, under Justice White's approach, concerns about competition might have played a significant role.

It is from the line of cases beginning with *Jewel Tea*[34] and running through *Brown v. Pro Football*[35] that the lower courts must now construct the so-called non-statutory labor exemption.[36] Although these cases rely, in part, on the NLRB and Taft–Hartley when working out the significance of the Clayton and Norris La Guardia exemptions, they might well be seen as a judicial effort to rework the parameters of these statutory exemptions, rather than as reflecting a judicial narrowing of the Sherman Act. The more interesting question today is not the source of the exemption, but its continuing significance.

What, then, is the meaning of this dual statutory, non-statutory labor exemption in today's commercial and industrial context? The economic significance of craft and industrial unionism has waned. When

---

33. 518 U.S. 231, 116 S.Ct. 2116, 135 L.Ed.2d 521 (1996).

34. Meat Cutters Local 189 v. Jewel Tea Co., 381 U.S. 676, 85 S.Ct. 1596, 14 L.Ed.2d 640 (1965).

35. *Brown v. Pro Football, Inc., supra* note 33.

36. Continental Maritime of S.F., Inc. v. Pacific Coast Metal Trades, 817 F.2d 1391, 1393 (9th Cir.1987); Mackey v. NFL, 543 F.2d 606, 614 (8th Cir.1976), *cert. denied*, 434 U.S. 801, 98 S.Ct. 28, 54 L.Ed.2d 59 (1977); Utilities Serv. Engg. v. Colorado Bldg. & Constr. Trades Council, 549 F.2d 173 (10th Cir.1977).

new organizational efforts by unions now gain public attention, they are likely to be aimed at doctors or other professionals. Moreover, as outsourcing grows common, both skilled and unskilled people are turning for help not to unions but to agents or agencies. In such a context, the significance of the exemption must turn at least in part upon the scope of the concept "labor group." The Court has already broadened the concept to comprehend self-employed theatrical agents working with performers to attain employment for them on acceptable terms—certainly a considerable extension beyond the conventional concept of the union as a bargaining agent.[37] By slight additional extension, the concept would cover any entity—say, an outsourcing agency—that seeks to aggregate groups of salaried employees and to place them with an employer. Indeed, so long as the entity is negotiating terms of employment for employees, might it not qualify for an exemption even if its own interests were involved in the dispute, perhaps even in conflict with those of another party (such as an employer that might seek, in competition with the agent, to find employees for itself)?[38]

Another question that may gain salience concerns what disputes affecting parties being collectively represented in negotiations about compensation should be characterized as disputes about "labor." The Court has thus far refused to analogize to the labor exemption when evaluating concerted action by independent contractors that have combined in an effort to influence their contract terms.[39] Need this matter inevitably turn on common law concepts fashioned for other purposes with other issues in mind? Today, doctors and other health professionals (often asserting a need to gain countervailing power to deal successfully with a healthcare maintenance organization that possess market power) are forming unions and seeking collective representatives. Would it be inappropriate to bring to bear considerations other than those drawn from common law concepts about the tort liability of employers in deciding whether activities and disputes to which such an organization is a party are entitled to a labor exemption?

14.3b. The Insurance Exemption

Much insurance industry activity, including the development and evaluation of loss data and reinsurance of certain risks, requires collaboration to attain needed scale. When the Supreme Court in 1944 first held that the business of insurance was within the regulatory power of

---

37. H.A. Artists & Associates v. Actors' Equity Ass'n, 451 U.S. 704, 101 S.Ct. 2102, 68 L.Ed.2d 558 (1981).

38. Compare American Fed. of Musicians v. Carroll, 391 U.S. 99, 88 S.Ct. 1562, 20 L.Ed.2d 460 (1968).

39. FTC v. Superior Court Trial Lawyers Ass'n, 493 U.S. 411, 110 S.Ct. 768, 107 L.Ed.2d 851 (1990). Recent efforts to collectively bargain for independent physicians may signify the next area for debate. In

Mesa County Physicians Independent Practice Ass'n, Dkt. No. 9284 (February 1998) the FTC obtained a consent against an IPA representing 85% of physicians in private practice in a county that forbade the IPA from collectively bargaining with HMOs on behalf of its members. However, such arrangements may not be challenged at lower levels of concentration. Cf. United States et al. v. Health Care Partners, 1996–1 Trade Cases (CCH) ¶ 71,337.

Congress under the commerce clause,[40] Congress responded to industry fears of excessive antitrust constraint on cooperation by enacting the McCarran–Ferguson Act.[41] Section 2 of the Act exempts the "business of insurance" from the antitrust laws when and to the extent the business is regulated by state law,[42] and subject to an exception to the exemption for conduct amounting to "boycott, coercion or intimidation," which cannot avoid the application of antitrust statutes regardless of whether the state regulates. The statute thereby raises three distinct and sometimes troublesome issues: what constitutes the business of insurance, what state involvement constitutes regulation by state law, and what conduct constitutes "boycott, coercion or intimidation." There is considerable case law on each of these issues.

14.3b1.   The Business of Insurance

In SEC v. Variable Annuity Life Ins. Co.,[43] an important limiting principle was established. The essential element of the exempt business is the "underwriting of risks" for a premium. Activities that significantly lacked this element, including the sale of variable-annuity contracts, which, though traditionally regarded as appropriate activity for insurance companies, did not transfer sufficient risk from the policyholder to the company, did not qualify. Similarly, arrangements collateral to the business of insurance, such as the financing of payments for premiums[44] or contracts, with providers like drug stores or health professionals for covered services at low rates—that is, activities aimed at reducing costs when covered risks occur[45]—are not the business of insurance. Most recently, in Federal Trade Commission v. Ticor Title Insurance Co.[46] the Court held that title searches done by title insurance companies were collateral to and not part of the business of insuring titles. On the other hand, activities essential to underwriting, such as the specification of covered risks and the determination of rates, are part of underwriting risks, and are thus the business of insurance.[47] So, too, are contracts of reinsurance that spread among others large risks assumed by one insurer.[48]

In *Union Labor Life Ins. Co. v. Pireno*,[49] the Court added two additional factors that can aid evaluation. To be part of the business of insurance, the activity should be "an integral part of the policy relation-

40. United States v. South–Eastern Underwriters Ass'n, 322 U.S. 533, 64 S.Ct. 1162, 88 L.Ed. 1440 (1944).

41. 15 U.S.C.A. § 1011–1015.

42. Id. § 1011.

43. 359 U.S. 65, 79 S.Ct. 618, 3 L.Ed.2d 640 (1959).

44. Perry v. Fidelity Union Life Ins. Co., 606 F.2d 468 (5th Cir. 1979), *cert. denied*, 446 U.S. 987, 100 S.Ct. 2973, 64 L.Ed.2d 845 (1980); Cody v. Community Loan Corp., 606 F.2d 499 (5th Cir. 1979) *cert. denied*, 446 U.S. 988, 100 S.Ct. 2973, 64 L.Ed.2d 846 (1980).

45. Group Life & Health v. Royal Drug Co., 440 U.S. 205, 99 S.Ct. 1067, 59 L.Ed.2d 261 (1979).

46. 504 U.S. 621, 112 S.Ct. 2169, 119 L.Ed.2d 410 (1992).

47. Lowe v. Aarco–American Inc., 536 F.2d 1160 (7th Cir.1976).

48. Hartford Fire Ins. Co. v. California, 509 U.S. 764, 113 S.Ct. 2891, 125 L.Ed.2d 612 (1993).

49. 458 U.S. 119, 102 S.Ct. 3002, 73 L.Ed.2d 647 (1982).

ship" and should be "limited to entities within the insurance industry." Consequently, and in consideration of all three factors, peer review of medical claims to determine their reasonableness is not part of the business of insurance. This, like contracting to reduce the cost of medicine, is a strategy for controlling the costs of transferred risks, and thus only collateral to defining and underwriting the risk and determining the premium for which it will be transferred from the insured to the insurer.

The scope of the business of insurance discerned from the primary criterion, initially expressed in *Variable Annuity Life*,[50] may be narrowed if the additional factors added by *Perino* are applied. This is evident in cases in which health care policies limit coverage to providers with specified credentials and exclude others—for example, a policy insuring against the risk that the insured will require psychotherapy, but providing for coverage only in the event of treatment by a medical doctor, not a clinical psychologist or other qualified professional. If the underwriting standard were applied alone, such a limit on coverage might be viewed as defining the risk, and thus part of the underwriting process. But such a policy distinction draws on entities beyond the insurance industry as sources for the policy distinction. Like peer review, it is in essence a cost control device that, under *Perino*, does not constitute part of the business of insurance.[51] This case teaches this distinction: when an insurer decides whether or not to cover a particular risk—e.g., in a health care policy, the need for psychotherapeutic intervention; in a automobile collision policy, the rental of a substitute vehicle while the covered vehicle is repaired—and when it sets a dollar maximum to its exposure on any given risk it assumes, the insurer is engaged in the business of insurance. But when the insurer goes beyond this and specifies to the insured the providers to whom he or she may turn for service, it is utilizing cost control measures that do not qualify as part of the business of insurance. Hence, activities of the latter kind gain no McCarran–Ferguson exemption.

Section 14.6 discusses the "state action" exemption, a judicially fashioned exemption that can protect private parties from antitrust liability for conduct authorized and activity supervised by the state under a state program intended to displace competition with regulation. There is a distinct affinity between that judicial exemption and the one Congress fashioned in McCarran–Ferguson. How do the two interact? Could conduct, such as writing a health insurance policy that covers drugs only if sold by a pre-approved retailer, be protected under the state action doctrine but not under McCarran–Ferguson? In the first place, the state action exemption has limits of its own, not found in McCarran–

---

50. SEC v. Variable Annuity Life Ins. Co., supra note 43.

51. Health Care Equalization Comm. v. Iowa Medical Soc'y, 851 F.2d 1020 (8th Cir.1988); Hahn v. Oregon Phys. Serv., 689 F.2d 840 (9th Cir.1982), *cert. denied*, 462 U.S. 1133, 103 S.Ct. 3115, 77 L.Ed.2d 1369 (1983); Virginia Academy of Clinical Psychologists v. Blue Shield of Va., 624 F.2d 476 (4th Cir.1980), *cert. denied*, 450 U.S. 916, 101 S.Ct. 1360, 67 L.Ed.2d 342 (1981); Dana Corp. v. Blue Cross & Blue Shield Mutual of N. Ohio, 900 F.2d 882 (6th Cir. 1990).

Ferguson.[52] If the state "regulates" and the conduct is part of the business of insurance it can qualify for the statutory exemption. There is no test focusing on the intensity of state involvement. By contrast, the state action exemption does test the intensity of the states' regulation. That exemption becomes available only if and to the extent that the state intends to displace competition with regulation and actively supervises the conduct for which exemption is claimed. A general program of insurance rate regulation, for example, would probably not afford state action exemption to a policy term limiting supply sources. It is unfortunate that the Court has construed the state law standard of McCarran–Ferguson so broadly. It might have read into it norms like those the Court has worked out under the state action doctrine, but the broader reading of the statute was in place before the state action doctrine was developed. There continues to be sentiment for repealing McCarran–Ferguson. If that occurs state regulation of insurance would be treated on a parity with other regulatory regimes pursuant to the state action doctrine.

Suppose a state did intend to displace competition between, for example, psychiatrists and clinical psychologists in the provision of psychotherapy covered by insurance, and did actively supervise that state policy. Would the conduct, not exempt under McCarran–Ferguson, gain state action exemption? If it fully meets state action exemption standards, that exemption is available.[53]

14.3b2.   Regulation by State Law

McCarran–Ferguson exempts only conduct "regulated by state law" and provides no guidance about what degree or extent of state involvement meets that standard. The Court has been permissive. If a state statute can be read as directly or indirectly regulating an aspect of the "business of insurance," this second requirement is met.[54] Thus, states can perfunctorily exempt all activities that constitute the business of insurance simply by passing a statute which requires a filing or gives an agency authority to regulate whether or not that authority is exercised. In consequence, even blatant cartelization such as joint rate making or market division by insurers can be similarly exempted by state legislation.[55] There are, however, limits. The law of a state cannot exempt a foreign resident, an insurance company that is beyond its jurisdictional

---

52. In FTC v. Ticor Title Ins. Co., 504 U.S. 621, 112 S.Ct. 2169, 119 L.Ed.2d 410 (1992) the defendants, charged with violation of Section 5 of the FTC Act, unsuccessfully asserted a McCarran–Ferguson defense for state authorized conduct found to be collateral to the business of insurance. They also asserted a broader "state action" defense. On this they lost because their conduct, although state authorized, was not adequately supervised by the state (a requirement for state action, but not McCarran–Ferguson, protection).

53. This is implicit in FTC v. Ticor Insurance Co., id., because the court held that in those states where there was *adequate* supervision, the state action deference was successful.

54. St. Paul Fire & Marine Ins. v. Barry, 438 U.S. 531, 98 S.Ct. 2923, 57 L.Ed.2d 932 (1978); FTC v. National Casualty Co., 357 U.S. 560, 78 S.Ct. 1260, 2 L.Ed.2d 1540 (1958). See also Feinstein v. Nettleship Co., 714 F.2d 928 (9th Cir. 1983).

55. Id.

reach. Moreover, in-state insurers lose their exemption merely because non-protected foreign firms join in their conspiracy.[56]

14.3b3. Boycott, Coercion or Intimidation

Although the Court has read the state regulation requirement permissively, it has been rigorous not only in identifying the "business of insurance" but also in defining the scope of the Section 3 exception[57]that precludes exemption for acts of boycott, coercion or intimidation.[58] It is no overstatement to say that, if a refusal to deal would be vulnerable under the Sherman Act but for McCarran–Ferguson, that refusal seriously risks being characterized as a boycott not protected by the statutory exemption.[59] The leading case is *Hartford Insurance* where a five to four majority held, in effect, that the limiting case to the scope of the boycott exception is cartelization.[60] The lower court treated as a boycott an agreement among liability insurers not to cover medical malpractice unless the tortuously vulnerable event and the assertion of the claim both occurred during the policy period. Under the lower court's view, the statutory concept, boycott, was spacious enough to cover at least some agreements not to deal except on specified terms. Yet, it was still generally assumed that a price fixing cartel among insurers would not be called a boycott; if it were, the exception would have swallowed up the entire statutory exception.[61] But where the line between a cartel and a boycott was to be drawn was unclear—indeed, it had been shrouded by *St. Paul*,[62] for the restraint there amounted to nothing more than a cartel-like agreement not to deal except upon concertedly determined terms.

Although the Supreme Court opinion in *Hartford Insurance* does not purport to overrule *St. Paul,* it is discernibly inconsistent with the earlier case. In *Hartford Insurance*, the majority drew a sharp distinction between a cartel and a boycott, as the latter term is used in McCarran–Ferguson. In doing so, it cited and quoted from the Sullivan treatise in which, not in the context of McCarran–Ferguson but in the context of the scope of the boycott *per se* rule, such a distinction was drawn.[63] Thus, the Scalia majority opinion (concurred in by four other justices) said that a concerted agreement on terms is a cartel, not a boycott, because participants "Are not coercing anyone at least in the usual sense . . . [but] merely (though concertedly) saying 'we will deal with you only on

56. *In re* Insurance Antitrust Litigation, 938 F.2d 919 at 927–28 (9th Cir.1991), *aff'd in part, rev'd in part sub nom.,* Hartford Fire Ins. v. California, 509 U.S. 764, 113 S.Ct. 2891, 125 L.Ed.2d 612 (1993). The Supreme Court remanded to the Ninth Circuit for a finding on whether the foreign insurers were within state's regulatory jurisdiction.

57. 15 U.S.C.A. § 1013(b).

58. E.g., St. Paul Fire & Marine Ins. Co. v. Barry, 438 U.S. 531, 98 S.Ct. 2923, 57 L.Ed.2d 932 (1978); Hartford Fire Ins. v. California, *supra* note 56.

59. Id. *See also* Nurse Midwifery Assoc. v. Hibbett, 549 F.Supp. 1185, 1191–92 (M.D.Tenn.1982).

60. *Hartford,* 509 U.S. at 801–82.

61. Id. at 809–11.

62. Id. at 802.

63. L. SULLIVAN, HANDBOOK OF THE LAW OF ANTITRUST 257 (1977).

the following trade terms.' "[64] Hence, if insurers agree on policy terms that are within the business of insurance and refuse to deal in a manner directly related to their concerted effort to establish those terms, and if the practice is regulated by state law, their conduct is exempt from antitrust constraint. The boycott exception to the exemption is not triggered. To the four dissenters the term boycott need not be a "unitary" concept, meaning the same thing in every context. Specifically, the dissenters would include within the concept as used in McCarran–Ferguson if not any cartel, then at least any cartel "enforcement activity," such as disparaging the services of insurers not participating in the cartel and threats to withdraw relationships with persons who purchased from nonparticipants.

If the record would support findings of such enforcement activity, the minority position would seem more consistent with the overall tenor of McCarran–Ferguson than that of the majority. The most compelling thing to be said for the majority view is that the term boycott ought to have a unitary meaning wherever found in an antitrust context. But this goal need not lead to rejection of the position taken by the minority in *Hartford Insurance*. Enforcement conduct of the kind eluded to by the minority goes beyond agreement as to the terms on which participants would deal. Such enforcement *conduct* exceeds the cartel *agreement* and is separate and distinct from it. To label cartel enforcement conduct as a boycott should not dilute the concept excessively or imply that it comprehends an agreement not to deal except on specified terms.

Regardless of how broadly the statutory term boycott is construed, *Hartford Insurance* establishes that the boycott exception is exceeded when insurers bring noninsurers into the arrangement.[65] There, evidence indicated an agreement between cartelizing insurers and a statistical information service provider that agreed to stop gathering data needed by insurers writing the policies the boycotters wanted to end. The Court unanimously held that such an agreement would be an unprotected boycott.[66]

There is, or ought to be, another limiting case, on a matter that the Supreme Court has not yet considered and upon which there are inconsistent lower court decisions. Some courts have held properly that when an insurance company agrees with a newly recruited agent that it will assign the agent to replace an existing agent, this conduct does not constitute a boycott by the insurer and the new agency against the old.[67] But at least one court of appeals has taken the contrary view.[68] Such a vertical decision by an insurer about how to market its policies entails none of the elements characteristic of a classic boycott.[69]

---

64. *Hartford,* 509 U.S. at 802.

65. Id. at 780–784.

66. Id. at 784.

67. E.g., Card v. National Life Ins. Co., 603 F.2d 828 (10th Cir.1979).

68. Malley–Duff & Associates v. Crown Life Ins. Co., 734 F.2d 133 (3d Cir.1984).

69. See § 5.8a.

14.3c. Miscellaneous Express Exemptions

There are a number of statutory provisions that expressly grant limited exemption from the antitrust laws for various regulated activities. Agricultural cooperatives[70] and fishery associations[71] both have such exemptions, as do jointly owned export trading companies,[72] small businesses,[73] newspapers,[74] banking,[75] professional athletes,[76] ocean carriers,[77] and securities and future markets.[78] None of these exemptions are as comprehensive as the labor or insurance exemptions discussed above. Indeed, none of them entails any cohesive legislative policy about the proper offices of competition and regulation within the industries they affect. The business referred to and these limited statutory exemptions give rise to many issues discussed in § 14.5 for federal regulatory regimes and in § 14.6 for state regulatory regimes.

§ 14.4 Petitioning Government to Interfere with Competition: The *Noerr-Pennington* Immunity

Governments, both state and federal, intervene in markets to the advantage of some participants and to the disadvantage of others. This occurs when Congress or state legislatures establish regulatory regimes which directly implicate price and output and on other occasions when legislative, administrative or judicial action establishes or changes the legal ground rules which regulate central or even peripheral aspects of the competitive process. Such impacts may be economy-wide (e.g., price control), or in specific markets or sectors (e.g. telecom reregulation; deregulation of electric power; administrative decisions implementing regulatory or deregulatory statutes; zoning or environmental law changes). These and countless other governmental acts can grant competitive advantage that the market previously denied or can withdraw advantage that the market previously granted. No wonder, then, that governmental relationships and efforts to influence government decisions—whether by lobbying, by litigating or by less conventional means—can be important parts of any competitive strategy. Such business conduct, categorically referred to as petitioning, can and, if successful, does change the tilt of the competitive playing field.

Deciding whether petitioning conduct can be vulnerable under the antitrust laws and, if so, when, can be complex. A governmental intervention may be directed toward any one or more of a wide range of possible goals: promoting economic efficiency by inhibiting monopoly pricing or by internalizing some externality; promoting equity or fairness

---

70. Capper–Volstead Agricultural Producers Association Act, 7 U.S.C.A. § 291.

71. Fishers Cooperative Marketing Act, 15 U.S.C.A. § 521.

72. 15 U.S.C.A. §§ 4001–03.

73. 15 U.S.C.A. § 640.

74. 15 U.S.C.A. §§ 1802–03.

75. Bank Holding Company Act of 1956, as amended by the Merger Act of 1966, 80

Stat 7 (1966), codified as 12 U.S.C.A. § 1828(c).

76. 15 U.S.C.A. § 1291.

77. Section 7 of the Shipping Act of 1984, 46 U.S.C.A. § 1706.

78. Securities Exchange Act of 1934, 15 U.S.C.A. § 78(a).

by altering market outcomes (e.g. truth in advertising, favoring labor over management, the physically handicapped or other disadvantaged people over others); fostering public safety or, even aesthetic objectives (e.g., drug or zoning regulation). If the governmental action petitioned for is granted, the resulting governmental intervention may itself be lawful (e.g., state law disrupting competition but exempt from antitrust under the "state action doctrine") (addressed in § 14.6) or may be invalid (e.g., state action directly conflicting with and preempted by federal law). Finally, the means utilized to petition may be honest and truthful (e.g. a good faith law suit or on-the-merits lobbying) or dishonest and unfair (e.g. misleading campaign tactics or bribery). Antitrust issues about petitioning invite thought about all such concerns as well as about First Amendment values.

Petitioning conduct was first challenged as an antitrust violation in Eastern Railroad Presidents Conference v. Noerr Motor Freight Co.[1] Railroads, under competitive threat from truckers on long-haul freight, retained a public relations firm through a trade association and initiated a comprehensive lobbying effort to foster and gain public support for laws and enforcement programs adverse to the trucking industry. Truck operators and their trade association sought to enjoin such conduct under the Sherman Act. On evidence of lobbying excesses (especially use of the so-called "third party technique," making lobbyist-planted statements seem to be spontaneous expressions of independent opinion), the district court found a violation and the court of appeals affirmed. In an opinion by Justice Black, the Supreme Court reversed. It acted not on First Amendment grounds but because "no violation of the [Sherman] Act can be predicated upon mere attempts to influence the passage or enforcement of laws"[2] and because "use of the third-party technique was, so far as the Sherman Act is concerned, legally irrelevant."[3] The Court found a crucial dissimilarity between combinations aimed at gaining legislative or executive action and those combinations normally held to violate the Act. It noted, too, that a contrary holding would impair the power of government which, in a representative democracy, depends on the ability of people to provide information and make their wishes known. Only if a purported petitioning actively is a mere "sham" used not to gain government action but to cloak direct interference with the business of a competitor might the antitrust laws apply.[4]

The opinion is rich in implication: legislation, regardless of its effect on competition, should be taken to serve the public interest. Antitrust is no shield against state action, anymore than it would protect against new Congressional legislation inconsistent with the Sherman Act.[5] The

---

§ 14.4

1. 365 U.S. 127, 81 S.Ct. 523, 5 L.Ed.2d 464 (1961). *See also* United Mine Workers v. Pennington, 381 U.S. 657, 85 S.Ct. 1585, 14 L.Ed.2d 626 (1965) which implied applicability of the doctrine to petitioning for administrative action and has, ever since, been memorialized as the *Noerr* immunity.

2. Id. at 134.

3. Id. at 142.

4. Id. at 144.

5. The "state action" exemption from the antitrust laws, which the *Noerr-Pennington* immunity complements, is examined in § 14.6.

right to petition, vital to democracy, is unconstrained for a collective as it is for an individual; a purpose to gain ends that would be unlawful if achieved by direct private action does not corrupt it. Even unfair means—inferentially, lying, for that is what the third party technique involved—at least unless violative of a separate, constitutionally valid legal constraint on petitioning practices, do not put petitioning within reach of the antitrust laws. Over the years since *Noerr* these implications have been reinforced or expanded.

The Courts' dictum putting sham conduct outside of the immunity became law in California Motor Transport Co. v. Trucking Unlimited.[6] Plaintiff truckers that needed agency-granted operating rights to compete with defendants sued under the Sherman Act alleging that defendants conspired to bring lawsuits and administrative proceedings in order to create barriers to plaintiff's efforts to obtain such rights. The court of appeals reversed a district court dismissal based on *Noerr* and the Supreme Court affirmed. In distinguishing *Noerr*, the Supreme Court emphasized allegations of conspiratorial intent to drive plaintiffs from the market and an initiation of litigation, with or without probable cause, not to persuade courts or agencies on facts or law, but in order to "harass and deter respondents in their use of administrative and judicial proceeding so as to deny them 'free and unlimited access' to those tribunals * * *."[7]

Despite rather sweeping prose, *Noerr* and *California Motor Transport* left some questions open. Is there no means test whatsoever when petitioning conduct is challenged under the Sherman Act? Perhaps lines could be drawn based on the nature of the forum. Executive departments and legislative committees no doubt expect exaggeration and excess and have experience in discounting it. Courts and agencies performing adjudicative functions may be more vulnerable. Although petitioning immunity resonates with the First Amendment, the Constitution leaves room for some, perhaps considerable, regulation of the petitioning process. Certainly there is no constitutional right to commit perjury. If there is any social reason to protect deceitful lobbying or litigation aimed at damaging competition from antitrust challenge, it cannot be found in the government's need for information.[8] Perhaps the justification for the Court's apparent indifference to means is the assumption that appropriate general norms applying to such conduct should be worked out legislatively and judicially, not patched together episodically by antitrust

---

6. 404 U.S. 508, 92 S.Ct. 609, 30 L.Ed.2d 642 (1972). See also MCI Communications Corp. v. AT & T, 708 F.2d 1081 (7th Cir.), *cert. denied*, 464 U.S. 891, 104 S.Ct. 234, 78 L.Ed.2d 226 (1983) (filing tariffs with numerous state utility commissions while knowing that jurisdiction reposed solely in the FCC supports sham characterization).

7. Id. at 511.

8. Columbia v. Omni Outdoor Advertising, Inc., 499 U.S. 365, 111 S.Ct. 1344, 113 L.Ed.2d 382 (1991), if read broadly, may imply that the sole question under *Noerr* is whether petitioner *really* wants the governmental response, regardless of how unfair or illegal may be the petitioning conduct. But cf. FTC v. Superior Court Trial Lawyers Ass'n, 493 U.S. 411, 110 S.Ct. 768, 107 L.Ed.2d 851 (1990) (conspiratorial boycott not defensible under *Noerr*).

courts and applicable only when the offense occurs in an antitrust context.

Nor is the scope of the sham concept manifest.[9] In Professional Real Estate Investors v. Columbia Pictures,[10] the Court sought to clarify its breadth, but was not entirely successful. PRE, which operated a hotel, installed videodisc players in rooms and rented disks to occupants for viewing. Columbia held copyrights to the movies on the disks and sued for infringement. PRE then counter-claimed under the Sherman Act, alleging that the infringement suit was a sham aimed at driving PRE out of the market. When summary dismissal of Columbia's copyright claim was affirmed on appeal, PRE's antitrust claim was remanded to the district court which dismissed summarily on the ground that the copyright suit was not a sham, and thus was protected by _Noerr_. Concluding that the copyright claim did not lack probable cause, the court of appeals affirmed as did the Supreme Court _on certiorari_.

The Court's opinion by Justice Thomas denies sham status to a lawsuit, even a suit brought to harass and thereby inhibit market access, unless the suit is also "objectively baseless."[11] Subjective intent of the kind _California Motor Transport_ focused upon is irrelevant if, objectively evaluated, there is a reasonable basis for the suit. A purpose to disrupt competition by inhibiting access is still essential before petitioning can be labeled "sham", but where the "petition" is a claim of right asserted in a lawsuit, there is a prior threshold test: that "no reasonable litigant could realistically expect success on the merits."[12]

The concurrence in the judgment by Justice Stevens, in which Justice O'Connor joined, found problems with the Court's opinion. These Justices agree that an "objectively reasonable effort to litigate cannot be sham regardless of subjective intent,"[13] but disagreed with the equation in the majority opinion between "objectively baseless" and the answer to the question of whether any "reasonable litigant could realistically expect success." Justice Stevens thought that such efforts at specificity did not help. The test demanded a choice between characterizing a suit as "abusing the judicial process to restrain competition [or as] prosecuting a lawsuit that, if successful, will restrain competition."[14] Many elements might influence such a characterization. Justice Stevens would, in short, have allowed subjective intent as well as objective factors to guide the classification.

Questions remain. Could the majority opinion in _PRE_ be limited to the context of a single suit or proceeding? Under _PRE,_ what percentage chance of winning a lawsuit is enough? Should that vary with the relationship between the likely cost and the value of the relief if

---

9. See Clipper Exxpress v. Rocky Mountain Motor Tariff Bureau, Inc., 690 F.2d 1240, 1252, 1263–64 (9th Cir. 1982), _cert. denied_, 459 U.S. 1227, 103 S.Ct. 1234, 75 L.Ed.2d 468 (1983) (Single false protest to protect cartel could be a sham—summary judgment for defendants reversed).

10. 508 U.S. 49, 113 S.Ct. 1920, 123 L.Ed.2d 611 (1993).

11. Id. at 51.

12. Id. at 50.

13. Id. at 57.

14. Id. at 68.

successful? For example, could an expectation of a one in ten chance of winning a modest recovery in a expensive lawsuit constitute a realistic expectation of success by a reasonable litigant? Furthermore, does *PRE* apply to sequential litigation? Might a series of cases that in the aggregate made economic sense for petitioners only because they disrupted competition be labeled sham, even if each, viewed in isolation, might not seem objectively baseless? Yet again, does *PRE* have application in a non-litigation context? Suppose a vast lobbying campaign were initiated with the purpose and effect of directly disrupting competition: would it avoid the possibility of being labeled sham if there were some chance it might gain helpful legislation?

There are simply too many open-ended terms embodied in the *PRE* standard to provide more than an invitation to debate. The petitioner must be acting reasonably, his expectations must be success, and that expectation must be realistic. No doubt a better than fifty-fifty chance of winning a single lawsuit that will predictably cost less than ten percent of the likely recovery would meet that standard. But suppose that after factoring in chance of recovery, likely amount of recovery and likely cost of the suit, the activity could not be defended as a reasonable business strategy. Would such a suit fail the reasonable litigant part of the standard? The realistic expectation of success part? Does it depend on whether the economic imprudence of the suit is attributable, in part, to a small likelihood of winning, or could a suit fail the *PRE* test despite a plausible hope of winning if the expected cost would greatly exceed the expected value of the remedy?[15]

A guide to such questions is available: conventional rule of reason analysis about whether challenged petitioning conduct is predatory. Courts should use this methodology when dealing with the *PRE* standard. If on all the facts the parties bringing an allegedly sham lawsuit (or series of suits) must have realized that the suit was economically imprudent except for its capacity to raise competitors' costs and thereby inhibit their entry or expansion, then the so-called "petitioning activity" is presumptively aimed not at exercising legal rights but at frustrating competition. On such facts, the petitioning should be labeled sham unless defendant carried a heavy burden of proving a non-economic motive for seeking to vindicate a legal principle. If, by contrast, the suit or suits could plausibly be regarded as reasonable business policy regardless of any stifling effect arising from the litigation itself, then the petitioning is not a sham even if it has, of itself, an adverse effect on competition.

Allied Tube & Conduit Corp. v. Indian Head, Inc.[16] raised a question about when a petition is properly characterized as directed to government. Allied and other petitioners made steel conduit to carry electrical wires in building construction, a product approved in the model code of a

---

15. See the discussion in Premier Electrical Constr. Co. v. National Elec. Contractors Ass'n, 814 F.2d 358, 372 (7th Cir. 1987) (Easterbrook, J.).

16. 486 U.S. 492, 108 S.Ct. 1931, 100 L.Ed.2d 497 (1988).

private standards organization, which in turn was routinely enacted into law by many state and local governments. When, at Indian Head's initiative, a professional panel of the standards organization examined plastic tubing of a kind made by Indian Head and recommended code approval, petitioners, fearing competition, agreed to pack the meeting at which the panel's proposal would be accepted or rejected by vote of the membership. They recruited 230 voters, whose membership, registration and attendance expenses they paid, and the proposal was rejected.

Indian Head sued under Section 1 of the Sherman Act. It prevailed before a jury that, under rule of reason instructions and on the basis of answers to special interrogatories, awarded substantial damages based upon the marketplace effect of exclusion of plastic conduit from the code and not based upon the adoption of the code by governmental entities. The district court, relying on *Noerr*, set aside the verdict and dismissed the complaint. The court of appeals reversed and the Supreme Court, on certiorari, also concluded, with two dissents, that *Noerr* did not preclude the verdict. Because damages were limited to those arising from the association's adoption of the standard, not from governmental action to incorporate the standard in binding codes, the conduct to be evaluated was private standard-setting by an association that included members having horizontal and vertical business connections and economic incentives to influence standards to restrain competition. Such concerted standard-setting activity is subject to antitrust scrutiny.[17] And even if its output often becomes law, lobbying to influence such a private standard association "does not enjoy the immunity accorded to those who merely urge the government to restrain trade."[18]

The distinction drawn in *Indian Head* is sound theoretically, but could give rise to perplexing problems in application. Can a code authority, not itself government sponsored, ever be closely enough linked with state or local governments so that petitioning the code group is tantamount to petitioning government? How, as a practical matter, is the trier of fact to distinguish between losses arising from adoption of the code and losses arising from governmental enactment of it when, as in *Indian Head*, the code once adopted by the authority is routinely enacted by government?

§ 14.5 Balancing Between Antitrust and Agency Control in Federally Regulated Markets

From the 1920s through the 1980s, there were at least twenty significant Supreme Court decisions about the application of antitrust to

17. Radiant Burners, Inc. v. Peoples Gas Light & Coke Co., 364 U.S. 656, 81 S.Ct. 365, 5 L.Ed.2d 358 (1961); American Soc'y of Mechanical Eng'rs, Inc. v. Hydrolevel Corp., 456 U.S. 556, 102 S.Ct. 1935, 72 L.Ed.2d 330 (1982).

18. *Allied Tube*, 486 U.S. at 501. Compare Sessions Tank Liners, Inc. v. Joor Manufacturing, Inc., 17 F.3d 295 (9th Cir. 1994) distinguishing *Allied Tube* where the damages claimed resulted from governmental enactment of a standard recommended by an association of fire chiefs.

issues of conduct and of structure in federally regulated industries.[1] All of them arose either in industries for which Congress had granted a specific but limited exemption or in industries where there was a federal regulatory scheme and Congressional silence about the role of antitrust. These decisions do not provide a body of solid law. In the labor area, courts have attempted to fashion a structured, non-statutory companion exemption to the one Congress put in place. In every other instance where Congress gave an express exemption, judicial extensions and constraints on the scope of the exemption have varied with shifts in regulatory and industrial context and with time. Where there is no express exemption but defendants seek to imply one on the basis of a comprehensive legislative scheme, judicial responses have also lacked cohesion. Despite this, cases in these areas can have value in addressing current problems.

So long as any significant federal regulation remains or may occur, issues like those dealt with earlier may recur. In a market oriented, deregulatory era, it is tempting to circumscribe the teaching of these cases as possessing only historical interest. But there are areas, most notably the environment, in which current levels of federal regulation are probably modest, compared with what the future development may demand. Also, the U.S. is likely to enter additional, perhaps more comprehensive, multilateral and bilateral economic arrangements that will influence the role of regulation on global aspects of the U.S. economy. These, too, will have to interact with U.S. antitrust. Major banking and securities markets are increasingly international and subject to multilateral regulatory accords.[2] Also, intellectual property licensing is rapidly becoming an internationalized service market both in practice and in aspects of governance.[3] Goods markets continue to

§ 14.5

1. Keogh v. Chicago & Northwest R. Co., 260 U.S. 156, 43 S.Ct. 47, 67 L.Ed. 183 (1922); U.S. Navigation Co. v. Cunard Steamship Co., 284 U.S. 474, 52 S.Ct. 247, 76 L.Ed. 408 (1932); United States v. Borden Co., 308 U.S. 188, 60 S.Ct. 182, 84 L.Ed. 181 (1939); McLean Trucking Co. v. U.S., 321 U.S. 67, 64 S.Ct. 370, 88 L.Ed. 544 (1944); Far East Conference v. U.S., 342 U.S. 570, 72 S.Ct. 492, 96 L.Ed. 576 (1952); United States v. RCA, 358 U.S. 334, 79 S.Ct. 457, 3 L.Ed.2d 354 (1959); California v. FPC, 369 U.S. 482, 82 S.Ct. 901, 8 L.Ed.2d 54 (1962); Pan American World Airways, Inc. v. U.S., 371 U.S. 296, 83 S.Ct. 476, 9 L.Ed.2d 325 (1963); Silver v. New York Stock Exchange, 373 U.S. 341, 83 S.Ct. 1246, 10 L.Ed.2d 389 (1963); United States v. Philadelphia Nat. Bank, 374 U.S. 321, 83 S.Ct. 1715, 10 L.Ed.2d 915 (1963); Carnation Co. v. Pacific Westbound Conference, 383 U.S. 213, 86 S.Ct. 781, 15 L.Ed.2d 709 (1966); Denver & Rio Grande W.R.R. v. United States, 387 U.S. 485, 87 S.Ct. 1754, 18 L.Ed.2d 905 (1967); Hughes Tool Co. v. TWA, 409 U.S. 363, 93 S.Ct. 647, 34 L.Ed.2d 577 (1973); Chicago Mercantile Exchange v. Deaktor, 414 U.S. 113, 94 S.Ct. 466, 38 L.Ed.2d 344 (1973); Ricci v. Chicago Mercantile Exchange, 409 U.S. 289, 93 S.Ct. 573, 34 L.Ed.2d 525 (1973); Otter Tail Power Co. v. United States, 410 U.S. 366, 93 S.Ct. 1022, 35 L.Ed.2d 359 (1973); Gordon v. New York Stock Exchange, 422 U.S. 659, 95 S.Ct. 2598, 45 L.Ed.2d 463 (1975); United States v. NASD, 422 U.S. 694, 95 S.Ct. 2427, 45 L.Ed.2d 486 (1975); Maryland v. United States, 460 U.S. 1001, 103 S.Ct. 1240, 75 L.Ed.2d 472 (1983); Square D Co. v. Niagara Frontier Tariff Bureau, Inc., 476 U.S. 409, 106 S.Ct. 1922, 90 L.Ed.2d 413 (1986).

2. See Waller, *The Internationalization of Antitrust Enforcement,* 77 B.U. L. Rev. 343, 348–349 (1997), but cf. Hachigian, *Essential Mutual Assistance in International Antitrust Enforcement,* 29 INT'L LAWYER 117, 150 (1995).

3. See Gurry, *The Evolution of Technology and Markets and the Management of Intellectual Property Rights,* 72 CHI-KENT L. REV. 369 (1996).

integrate at an accelerating pace. Despite globalization and vaunted deregulatory rhetoric, economies in Asia remain managed and somewhat unstable, and most of Europe wears a social democratic complexion (with the EU's social charter now accepted even by the UK and the asperities of the single currency program being tempered). All of this bespeaks revival of the view that government's job is to smooth capitalism's rough edges. Whether or not the "middle" of the U.S. consensus on the role of government in the economy shifts in a social-democratic direction (which, indeed, it may, if severities of maldistribution become more painful), inevitable concessions to comity, whether bilateral or unilateral, may move U.S. antitrust involvement in the world market into interaction with regulatory cultures from other countries. Questions which courts have struggled with since 1922 in the context of the well integrated federalist system, may be confronted anew and in more complex forms in the context of a less well integrated global market.[4] If such issues arise out of U.S. environmental or labor standards, other regulation or out of a felt need to integrate U.S. antitrust and foreign regulatory concerns, then cases dealing with U.S. or state regulation and antitrust may be suggestive. Here is a catalog of the issues that can arise when an antitrust claim is made in a context involving regulation:

> Has the legislature specifically addressed the matter of competition in the regulatory statute? If so, how clearly related are issues it addressed to questions raised in this dispute? Has the legislature given any explicit antitrust exemption? If so, is it broadly stated or highly specific? Does it cover the conduct now being challenged or any like conduct? Has the legislature been more explicit on related issues in this or other regulatory statutes? Were there relevant judicial precedents that the legislature did not disturb?

> What factual and policy questions that might arise in this antitrust claim could be raised in an administrative proceeding under the regulatory statute? Is the antitrust court or the regulatory agency better equipped to resolve these questions? How important is uniformity of outcome if recurrent cases occur?

> Are the substantive concerns or the regulatory scheme consistent, conflicting, complementary, or unrelated to the allocative and other goals of antitrust? To the antitrust remedies sought?

> Is there any policy implied by the statute or the context that might depend on whether the antitrust plaintiff is the Government, a private party, or a state? On whether the remedy sought is damages, an injunction, or a criminal sanction? On whether any injunctive relief seeks to affect only market conduct or market structure also? Should the outcome turn on whether the regulator is insulated from conflict of interest? Should it be influenced by the breadth of the agency's discretion? By whether the agency is active or passive in exercising its relevant jurisdiction? By the availability and procedural adequacy of the administrative hearing? By whether the antitrust

---

4. See generally, Chapter XVIII.

plaintiff or only other possible parties could evoke agency consideration?

No one theory nor factor is an adequate guide to outcomes. Although it has its exponents, capture theory does not yield confident predictions about results.[5] Focus upon whether the regulatory decision-maker faces conflicting interests is more useful,[6] although not talismatic. Given the variety of regulatory arrangements, changes over time of theoretical views and political attitudes about the proper roles of regulation and competition, and the frequent lack of Congressional specificity, lack of doctrinal clarity is hardly surprising. In each case, a court must fathom what Congress wanted, must respect Supreme Court precedents, and must integrate antitrust and regulatory values as currently understood. From a modern vantage point one can challenge a number of earlier outcomes including a recent and important one.[7] Yet, the Supreme Court has performed this difficult task at least tolerably well. In what follows we discuss several significant Supreme Court cases. The more complex and varied involve antitrust challenges to anticompetitive conduct by regulated firms; we discuss these in §§ 14.5a through 14.5c.[8] In § 14.5d we turn to the interaction of antitrust and regulatory norms where the regulator makes decisions about market structure.

14.5a. Antitrust Challenges to Conduct in Federally Regulated Transportation Markets

The Sherman Act had been on the books some thirty years and the Interstate Commerce Act regulating interstate rail transportation a decade longer when the Supreme Court first considered the relationship between regulation and antitrust. The ICC Act was predicated on conventional public utility theory. Railroads were assumed to be natural monopolies. Entry and rates should be regulated in the public interest. Keogh, a shipper, sued under the Sherman Act seeking treble damages when parallel railroads concertedly set freight rates,[9] a practice the Court had condemned as a *per se* Sherman Act violation over two decades earlier.[10] Defendants responded that the rates complained of had been filed with, investigated and approved by the ICC. Ignoring the possibility that the agency may not have even known that these were concertedly set rates, let alone decided that concert on prices would serve the public interest, the Court ruled that ICC approval of the rates

---

5. See § 14.2a.

6. E. Elhauge, *The Scope of Antitrust Process,* 104 HARV. L. REV. 668, 682–96 (1991).

7. Square D v. Niagara Frontier Tariff Bureau Inc., 476 U.S. 409, 106 S.Ct. 1922, 90 L.Ed.2d 413 (1986).

8. First, we discuss transportation industries, a convenient if somewhat artificial category. §§ 14.5a–5b. Then we discuss conduct cases in other regulated industries § 14.5c.

9. Keogh v. Chicago & Northwestern R. Co., 260 U.S. 156, 43 S.Ct. 47, 67 L.Ed. 183 (1922).

10. United States v. Trans–Missouri Freight Ass'n, 166 U.S. 290, 17 S.Ct. 540, 41 L.Ed. 1007 (1897). In that case the Court had rejected the contention that, being subject to the Interstate Commerce Act, railroads were exempted from the Sherman Act.

"settled" that the rates were "reasonable and non-discriminatory."[11] The Court noted that concerted prices violate the Sherman Act and opined that ICC approval "would not, it seems, bar proceedings by the Government."[12] Yet, Keogh, a private suitor, could not recover the excess it paid over "rates still lower, which, but for the conspiracy, he would have enjoyed."[13] Enigmatically, the Court reasoned that a "rate is not necessarily illegal because it is the result of a[n illegal] conspiracy * * * in violation of [the Sherman Act]."[14] Moreover, the Court thought that if Keogh were given an antitrust claim for damages, it would be compelled to prove not only that in the absence of the conspiracy a lower rate would have prevailed, but also that the lower rate would have been approved by the ICC as reasonable and non-discriminatory, a matter bringing the carriers' entire rate structures under scrutiny. This would entail an inquiry that neither the plaintiff nor the antitrust court would be well-equipped to undertake.[15]

Justice Brandeis' opinion is a pastiche of concerns. It stresses agency expertise and capacity to deal with complexity, the availability of agency relief for related wrongs, and a distinction between the antitrust standing of a private party and that of the Department of Justice. The opinion does not identify—indeed, seems to negate the existence of—residual room for any private response to price conspiracy in a price regulated industry. It is conceivable that when concerted rates were initially filed, a shipper might complain to the ICC which might then reject those rates, directing each carrier to set its own, before the agency would evaluate justness and reasonableness. But such agency relief was not likely because the ICC had no mandate to pass upon rate agreements. Thus, only on a showing that the rate is excessive or discriminatory could a shipper gain relief under the regulatory statute. Justice Brandeis anticipated by more than a decade the judicial respect for regulatory competence that became common during the 1930s and 1940s, a deference that has eroded greatly in recent years.[16] Yet, Keogh cannot be dismissed as quixotic or time bound. Although some of its themes are seldom sounded today, its specific holding remains law.[17]

United States Navigation Co. v. Cunard Steamship Co.[18] was decided at the beginning of the regulatory wave of the 1930s. The Court

---

11. *Keogh*, 260 U.S. at 161, *citing* Interstate Commerce Commission v. Atchison, T. & S. F. R. Co., 234 U.S. 294, 34 S.Ct. 814, 58 L.Ed. 1319 (1914).

12. Id. at 162.

13. Id.

14. Id.

15. Id. at 163–64. Eluding to the since rejected "passing on" defense (that the victim of a conspiratorial overcharge that passed the overcharge on to its customers has no cause of actions) (see § 17.2c1), the Court also noted that Keogh may not itself have been injured (since it may have passed on any overcharge to its customers) (Id. at

165) and that for unjust or discriminatory rates the ICC can award damages. Id. at 164.

16. Aman, *Administrative Law in a Global Era: Progress, Deregulatory Change, and The Rise of the Administrative Presidency,* 73 CORNELL L. REV. 1101, 1153 (1988).

17. Square D Co. v. Niagara Frontier Tariff Bureau, Inc., 476 U.S. 409, 106 S.Ct. 1922, 90 L.Ed.2d 413 (1986) relied upon *Keogh* and discussed more fully in § 14.5b, infra.

18. 284 U.S. 474, 52 S.Ct. 247, 76 L.Ed. 408 (1932).

broadened and applied to ocean transportation[19] the *Keogh* proposition that shippers could not obtain antitrust relief for concerted rate-making once the rates were approved by the cognate regulator.[20] The plaintiff in *Cunard* sought to enjoin a concerted agreement by which a group of water carriers discounted tariff rates only for shippers committed to deal exclusively with members of the group. The tariff rates had, but the concerted discount scheme had not, been approved by the Shipping Board. The Court cited *Keogh,* emphasizing not only agency expertise but also that the Shipping Act, like the ICC Act, is a "comprehensive measure" giving broad power to the Board, including, by inference, power on complaint or on its own initiative to investigate conduct such as that alleged in the antitrust suit.[21] But, as in *Keogh,* the Court ignored the fact that the agency had given no consideration to whether concert by steamship lines was needed to attain the regulatory goals of the statute. The tenor of the opinion is trustful and supportive of regulation—perhaps naively so and to a degree uncommon in a deregulatory era. For this 1930s era Court, if an industry is subject to (or has itself successfully obtained) comprehensive regulation, the agency replaces the market as the arbiter of the public interest.

Keogh had supposed that a government suit remained possible; *Cunard* is silent about this. Whether any antitrust defense akin to that in *Cunard* would apply upon a government antitrust suit involving shipping arose explicitly in Far East Conference v. United States.[22] Under a conference agreement a number of competing carriers established a dual rate system, giving lower rates to shippers that agreed to ship only with conference members and higher rates to shippers free to use competing carriers. This conference agreement was approved by the Shipping Board in 1922. When, years later, the Government challenged the system under the Sherman Act, the Federal Maritime Board, successor to the Shipping Board, joined the conference members to defend. They successfully contended that the Government must first resort to the Maritime Board before asserting an antitrust claim. Presumably the Government could seek to persuade the Board that competitive concerns overwhelmed others relevant to its decision and, if it failed in that, could seek court review of the Board's decision. In any event, the *Far East Conference* Court read *Cunard* as validating the agency's primary jurisdiction. The implication seems to be that even a Justice Department antitrust action would be appropriate only if the agency first forbade concerted rate conduct. In support of its conclusion the Court stressed

19. Id. at 486–87.

20. The regulation of ocean shipping is discussed more fully in § 14.7c.

21. *Cunard*, 284 U.S. at 480. The Court ignored the implication of Section 16 of the Clayton Act which withdrew antitrust jurisdiction for private injunction suits in industries like railroads regulated by the ICC but not in the steamship industry regulated by the Shipping Board. It also made no effort

to determine the significance, if any, of the different purposes of the contrasting railroad *(Keogh)* and ocean carriage *(Cunard)* regulatory regimes. Railroads were regulated because they were natural monopolies, steamships because they were threatened by excessive competition, especially from subsidized foreign carriers.

22. 342 U.S. 570, 72 S.Ct. 492, 96 L.Ed. 576 (1952).

agency expertise and the breadth of agency regulatory jurisdiction. The Court held that the case should be dismissed subject to refilling if after final agency action there appeared to be any basis for it.

Far East Conference broadened the *Keogh-Cunard* principle. *Keogh* implied that antitrust courts had jurisdiction upon a government complaint irrespective of whether the relevant agency, by approving a rate, might effectively shield carriers from a challenge by shippers. *Cunard* seemed to concur. *Far East Conference* aborts that implication in the instance of water carriage and probably whenever the regulatory scheme is pervasive. Perhaps some question remained for rail carriage. The *Keogh* dictum implying that the government could sue for an injunction despite ICC expertise was reinforced by the Clayton Act, which in Section 16 expressly withdraws equitable jurisdiction for private, but not for government, suits.[23]

The next transportation case in sequence was Pan American World Airways, Inc. v. United States.[24] Pan Am, an airline serving eastern parts of South America, and Grace, a steamship line serving that continent, formed a jointly owned subsidiary, Panagra, to provide air service on the west coast of South America. An ancillary agreement provided that neither Pan Am nor Panagra would challenge the territory of the other. Also, Pan Am successfully suppressed Panagra's efforts to extend its routes to the United States. Although the Civil Aeronautics Board (CAB) had jurisdiction under the Civil Aeronautics Act to challenge "unfair practices" and "unfair methods of competition" by air carriers—language paralleling Section 5 of the FTC Act—the CAB had never used the Act as an antitrust weapon and apparently regarded the Justice Department and the antitrust court as better equipped to deal with competition issues than it was itself. The CAB therefore asked the Department to challenge the Pan Am–Panagra arrangement under the Sherman Act. The Department did so, seeking injunctive relief.

The Supreme Court, while "hesitat[ing] * * *, as in comparable situations, to hold that the new regulatory scheme was designed completely to displace the antitrust laws,"[25] found that the acts alleged to be antitrust violations "are precise ingredients of the Board's authority in granting, qualifying, or denying certification to air carriers * * *."[26] It would therefore be "strange, indeed, if a division of territories or an allocation of routes which met the requirements of the 'public interest'

---

23. Four years before *Far East Conference*, Congress had enacted the Reed–Bullwinkle Act *expressly* authorizing the ICC to grant approval to agreements establishing rate bureaus for the establishment of joint rates, and granting antitrust exemption to agreements so approved. This statute had no like provision for agreements approved by the Maritime Board. A few years after *Far East Conference*, the Maritime Board considered a dual rate system upon complaint of a shipper and approved it. Contract rates—Japan/Atlantic–Gulf Freight Conf., 4FMB 706 (1955). Although the Board gave little if any weight to antitrust values, the Supreme Court ultimately approved this order. Federal Maritime Board v. Isbrandtsen Co., 356 U.S. 481, 78 S.Ct. 851, 2 L.Ed.2d 926 (1958).

24. 371 U.S. 296, 83 S.Ct. 476, 9 L.Ed.2d 325 (1963).

25. Id. at 304–05.

26. Id. at 305.

as defined in * * * [the Act] were held to be antitrust violations."[27] Stating that all questions of injunctive relief as to route allocations and territorial divisions were encompassed by the Act, the Court, with two justices dissenting, remanded the case to be dismissed so that the Government could proceed under the Act to seek relief from the Board. While the *Pan Am* opinion rejects the implication that any comprehensive regulatory program impliedly repeals antitrust entirely, it ceded to exclusive agency action much of the disputed ground that earlier transportation opinions stated or implied might be subject to antitrust challenge by the Government or even by private parties after primary agency jurisdiction was exercised. On matters bearing upon CAB regulation, the Court expressly assigns to the Board all matters of injunctive relief and negates the possibility of damages or criminal sanctions; it impugns the very idea that matters central to regulatory analysis might be controlled through antitrust.

Given the CAB's disinclination to undertake antitrust-like enforcement under its own statute[28] and its readiness to invite the Justice Department's antitrust involvement, *Pan Am* might have been the occasion for a change from the direction the Court initiated in *Cunard* and *Far East Conference*. By the 1960s, there seemed less sentiment for rate and entry regulation as means for controlling power and greater readiness to rely on markets subject to activist antitrust intervention.[29] Yet, the New Deal Justices who had fashioned the earlier, regulatory-centric opinions were still a working majority of the Court, and the law did not shift direction. Indeed, *Pan Am* represents a high point in Supreme Court reliance upon agency action to resolve competition questions in regulated markets.

Change did come a few years later, although it ultimately proved not to be as extensive as first appeared. Carnation Co. v. Pacific Westbound Conference[30] raised the broad question whether the Shipping Act, as amended,[31] exempts the industry entirely from antitrust. The plaintiffs, shippers seeking treble damages under the Sherman Act, alleged rate fixing between conferences that had never been approved by the Commission. The district court dismissed the suit on motion, and the court of appeals affirmed. Both courts held that the matter had to be passed on by the regulatory agency. Perhaps surprisingly, given *Cunard* and *Far East Conference*, the Supreme Court reversed. It held "that the implementation of rate-making agreements which have not been approved by the FMC [Federal Maritime Commission] is subject to the antitrust

---

27. Id. at 309.

28. Federal Aviation Act of 1958, 49 U.S.C.A. § 1381.

29. See, e.g., California v. FPC, 369 U.S. 482, 82 S.Ct. 901, 8 L.Ed.2d 54 (1962); Silver v. New York Stock Exchange, 373 U.S. 341, 83 S.Ct. 1246, 10 L.Ed.2d 389 (1963); and Otter Tail Power Co. v. United States, 410 U.S. 366, 93 S.Ct. 1022, 35 L.Ed.2d 359 (1973).

30. 383 U.S. 213, 86 S.Ct. 781, 15 L.Ed.2d 709 (1966).

31. Congress revised the Act creating the Federal Maritime Commission as successor to the Board and articulating the Commission's powers with greater specificity than those of the Maritime Board.

laws."[32] The Court emphasized that this regulatory statute (unlike those before the court in the earlier ocean carrier cases) expressly exempted FMB approved rate agreements among carriers. From this fact, the Court inferred that "unlawful [that is, unapproved] rate making activities are not exempt."[33] This result was reached despite the *Keogh* distinction between the lawfulness of the rates and of the conspiracy, despite the *Cunard* concept of going to the agency before the antitrust court and the implication of *Pan Am* that comprehensive regulation might wholly shield an industry from antitrust. Although those cases suggested a different outcome, the Court, by the mid-sixties, was apparently more responsive to antitrust values and less deferential to regulatory expertise.[34]

Both *Far East Conference* and *Cunard* were narrowed in *Carnation,* seemingly with deliberation. Both were distinguished as merely precluding antitrust sanctions for conduct of debatable legality under the Shipping Act and only until after the agency had considered them. By contrast, when as in *Carnation* the conduct charged could not be defended under that Act, an antitrust court needed no expert agency advice before passing on its legality under the Sherman Act and fashioning a remedy if appropriate. *Carnation* thus moved the law. Yet, one could not assert that after *Carnation* the law was clear even in ocean shipping let alone in transportation segments regulated by other agencies. For one thing, the standard to be applied by the antitrust court—whether a credible argument could be made before the agency for an antitrust shield—was hardly self-executing. Secondly, *Carnation* teaches little if anything about whether an antitrust action could proceed if, in anticipation of it, potential antitrust defendants sought agency approval of their agreement. Would the antitrust court then have to wait, even if it found no "debatable legality" in the Shipping Act? Third, might the *Carnation* approach be limited only to actions for damages, leaving private equitable and perhaps even government enforcement subject to the seemingly more restrictive *Far East Conference* norms?

In Hughes Tool Co. v. TWA,[35] the Court had the opportunity to carry revisionism into the airline industry by narrowing *Pan Am* much as *Carnation* had narrowed the *Cunard* and *Far East Conference* cases. That opportunity was rejected. The case raised vertical antitrust issues. TWA, the plaintiff, alleged that Hughes Tool used its control of the airline to foreclose competition for the sale of aircraft and the provision of financing to TWA, thus injuring competition in those input markets

---

32. Carnation Co. v. Pacific Westbound Conference, 383 U.S. 213, 216, 86 S.Ct. 781, 15 L.Ed.2d 709 (1966).

33. Id. at 217. A similar holding was reached in United States v. Borden, 308 U.S. 188, 60 S.Ct. 182, 84 L.Ed. 181 (1939).

34. Of course, although deregulation was not yet a national movement, *Carnation* was decided at the height of the Warren Court antitrust epoch.

35. 409 U.S. 363, 93 S.Ct. 647, 34 L.Ed.2d 577 (1973). The decision not only failed to modify *Pan Am* but became a new symbol for the proposition—never fully accepted by the Supreme Court, but nevertheless influential in many lower court cases— that if an industry was pervasively regulated activities routine to it were presumptively exempt from antitrust.

and causing TWA to pay excessive prices. In an opinion by Justice Douglas (who had authored *Pan Am*), the challenged transactions were held immune from antitrust attack. The Civil Aeronautics Board (CAB) had power under the Act to control the TWA transactions with Hughes Tool. Although review of the transactions was not a requisite CAB function, and although TWA, while under Hughes' control, would not likely complain to the Board about the way Hughes operated, Hughes had needed and obtained Board approval of its initial acquisition of control. At that time, as the Court majority saw it, the CAB (under a norm reflective of the *McLean* principle)[36] had to have considered the competitive effects of Hughes' control in deciding that Hughes' acquisition of TWA was in the public interest. Moreover, the CAB had ongoing jurisdiction to look into whether control was misused. For these reasons, and despite alleged competitive injuries to aircraft and financial markets, not to the airline industry (the only industry that the CAB regulated and the industry on which any CAB inquiry into the effects of Hughes' control would focus), the majority found the *Pan Am* decision controlling. Despite *Carnation*, the role of antitrust was to remain modest in a comprehensively regulated industry, at least in this one.

As a group, the transportation cases do not yield any solid, generally reliable legal principles. They do suggest themes that must be considered in evaluating the relationships between federal economic regulation and federal antitrust: deference to administrative expertise, reliance upon the scope of administrative inquiry, and the adequacy of administrative procedure. These regulator-centric themes are reflected in the earliest cases and resound throughout the development here traced. Contrapuntal sub-themes include the capacity to draw sharp analytical distinctions (as in *Carnation*, which narrowed *Cunard* and *Far East Conference*) and loyalty to precedent (as in the refusal in *Hughes Tool* to engage in analytical refinement of *Pan Am* implications). Relevant throughout, of course, is just what the statute says. Although significant in *Carnation*, this factor has seldom proved controlling because statutory guidance has seldom been precise. Evident early on, but only occasionally thereafter, is the possible significance of the status of the antitrust plaintiff and the nature of the remedy it seeks. These, perhaps, are factors which could again be brought to the foreground. Agency passivity has thus far been a non-factor. Usually the agency asserted itself. In *Pan Am*, the one case where the agency sought to defer to antitrust, the Court foisted the burden of decision back upon the agency.

14.5b. Interstate Transportation and Antitrust Today

With the Railroad Revitalization and Reform Act of 1976,[37] the Air Cargo Deregulation Act[38] and Airline Deregulation Act of 1978,[39] the

---

36. Id. at 368. The *Hughes Tool* Court did not cite *McLean Trucking Co. v. U.S.,* 321 U.S. 67, 64 S.Ct. 370, 88 L.Ed. 544 (1944), but adopted the same approach as did the *McLean* Court. See § 14.5d.

37. 45 U.S.C.A. §§ 801 *et. seq.*

38. Pub. L. No. 95–163, 91 Stat. 1228 (1977) (codified in scattered sections of 49 U.S.C.A.).

Motor Carrier Reform Act[40] and the Staggers Rail Act of 1980,[41] the Shipping Act of 1984,[42] and finally the abolition of the ICC,[43] there has been massive federal deregulation of transportation. As a practical matter, air transportation and much of motor carrier transportation is now unregulated except as to safety. Indeed, little railroad regulation of any kind remains. Most concerted conduct by carriers should now be fully subject to the antitrust laws.[44] Despite these developments, when any federal rate regulation does remain, the *Keogh* case is still the law. In Square D Co. v. Niagara Frontier Tariff Bureau, Inc.[45] shippers sued motor carriers for concertedly fixing freight rates. Although the rates were filed with and approved by the ICC, the agreement establishing them had never been filed or approved under the Reed–Bullwinkle Act.[46] The Court granted certiorari to determine whether the conduct alleged was protected by *Keogh*. It found that under "the plain language" of the Sherman Act, petitioners have alleged a violation and that Reed–Bullwinkle "strictly limits [its] exemption to actions that conform to the terms of 'an approved joint rate agreement.' " In light of failure to comply with the specific Reed–Bullwinkle exemption, *Keogh* could unquestionably have been distinguished on the strength of *Carnation*. After all, *Carnation* had held that a narrow, specific statutory exemption impliedly negated a broader, more general implicit exemption. Not only that, the *Keogh* reasoning—strained even when adopted—grows increasingly anomalous in a deregulatory era, and the Solicitor General, at the urging of the Antitrust Division, urged the Court to overrule *Keogh* outright. Nevertheless, in an opinion by Justice Stevens with Justice Marshall alone dissenting, the Court affirmed dismissal of the claim. It concluded "that the developments in the six decades since *Keogh* ... are insufficient to overcome the strong presumption of continued validity that adheres in the judicial interpretation of a statute."[47] An earlier holding about the same industry and statutes, even though one statute had been amended in a relevant respect, outweighed both the inference to be drawn from a narrow express antitrust exemption and the policy implication of broad and growing deregulatory sentiment. *Keogh* thus applied with full force to ICC rate regulation and presumably could continue to apply today whenever rates are subject to federal regulation and approved by a cognate agency.[48] In ocean shipping, where deregula-

39. 49 U.S.C.A. §§ 1301, 1302 *et seq.*

40. 49 U.S.C.A. §§ 10101, 10927.

41. 49 U.S.C.A. § 10101.

42. 46 U.S.C.A. ppx. §§ 1701, 1702 *et. seq.*

43. 49 U.S.C.A. § 101.

44. Cf., e.g., United States v. American Airlines, Inc., 743 F.2d 1114 (5th Cir.1984), *cert. dismissed*, 474 U.S. 1001, 106 S.Ct. 420, 88 L.Ed.2d 370 (1985); Rothery Storage Van Co. v. Atlas Van Lines, Inc., 792 F.2d 210 (D.C.Cir.1986), *cert. denied*, 479 U.S. 1033, 107 S.Ct. 880, 93 L.Ed.2d 834 (1987).

45. 476 U.S. 409, 106 S.Ct. 1922, 90 L.Ed.2d 413 (1986).

46. Id. at 413, 414.

47. Id. at 424.

48. There is, however, a debate about whether it should apply to all filings where the regulator can reject a filed rate only if the carrier is dominant, (cf. Litton Sys. v. AT & T, 700 F.2d 785, 820 (2d Cir.1983), *cert. denied*, 464 U.S. 1073, 104 S.Ct. 984, 79 L.Ed.2d 220 (1984)) or to a rate challenged not as excessive but as predatorily low. See In re Wheat Rail Freight Rate Antitrust Litigation, 759 F.2d 1305 (7th

tory efforts have thus far been limited and agency protected cartelization remains in place, elements of *Cunard* undoubtedly survive under the Shipping Act of 1984,[49] which granted antitrust immunity in sweeping terms.[50] Only if implemented without being filed or after being filed and rejected would a joint rate be vulnerable to antitrust attack. It may, indeed, be that *Square D* has also weakened the force or narrowed the scope of *Carnation*.[51]

14.5c. Antitrust Challenges to Conduct in Other Federally Regulated Markets

Although few other federal regulatory programs have involved as many antitrust issues as transportation, antitrust exemption has frequently been claimed on the basis of other federal regulatory schemes. Sometimes an issue of jurisdictional primacy is presented. We discuss significant Supreme Court decisions in agriculture, organized markets, and electrical power.

14.5c1. Agriculture

United States v. Borden Co.[52] reached the Court during a decade long wave of New Deal regulation. Members of an agriculture cooperative and others were indicted under Sherman for price fixing. The Capper–Volstead Act[53] exempted members of agriculture cooperatives (but not others) from specified (but not all) antitrust violations. The Agriculture Marketing Agreement Act granted the Secretary of Agriculture power to regulate interstate marketing of agriculture products including milk and conferred an antitrust exemption for transactions made pursuant to such regulations. Although no relevant regulation had been issued under the latter Act, the district court dismissed the indictment in *Borden* on the grounds that the Act, in and of itself, exempted interstate agriculture marketing from the antitrust laws. The Supreme Court rejected this "grant of immunity by virtue of [the Secretary's] inaction,"[54] stating that "repeals by implication are not favored."[55] It stressed that when there are two acts on the same subject appropriate effect should be given to each.[56] Because *Cunard* (decided earlier) exempted jointly set rates that had not been filed with or approved by the Maritime Board, *Cunard* might have been thought to lend support to the district court dismissal. But the Court did not cite *Cunard* nor discuss a

Cir.1985), *cert. denied*, 476 U.S. 1158, 106 S.Ct. 2275, 90 L.Ed.2d 718 (1986).

49. Compare Pinney Dock & Transport Co. v. Penn Central Corp., 838 F.2d 1445 (6th Cir.), *cert. denied*, 488 U.S. 880, 109 S.Ct. 196, 102 L.Ed.2d 166 (1988) with Barnes v. Arden Mayfair, 759 F.2d 676 (9th Cir.1985).

50. See the discussion in § 14.7c3.

51. For a recent interpretation of the reach of the 1984 Shipping Act's immunity, *see* American Association of Cruise Passengers v. Cunard Line, Ltd., 31 F.3d 1184 (D.C.Cir.1994) (holding that an antitrust claim involving non-common carriage could proceed despite parallel FMC proceeding involving common carriage).

52. 308 U.S. 188, 60 S.Ct. 182, 84 L.Ed. 181 (1939).

53. 7 U.S.C.A. §§ 291, 292.

54. *Borden*, 308 U.S. at 198.

55. Id.

56. Id.

possible distinction: the Maritime Board's power was focused and it regularly reviewed rate filings while the Secretary's power was sweeping and he left many transactions within his jurisdiction unattended. *Borden* has not been widely influential, perhaps because such broad regulatory grants to executive officials were a time-limited legislative practice. The opinion was cited in *Carnation*[57] for the proposition that an explicit exemption negates a broader implied exemption—a proposition that still may invite confidence, although the Court was not impressed by it in *Square D.*[58]

14.5c2. Organized Markets

Silver v. New York Stock Exchange[59] is a provocative conduct case involving the interplay of antitrust and stock market regulation. Under the Securities Exchange Act of 1934, the New York Stock Exchange, as a private, self regulatory exchange, had statutory power to regulate members and to approve and cancel private wires connecting member firms and other traders. Silver, a nonmember dealer-broker, had wire connection with member firms which Silver used for over-the-counter trading. Without an explanation of the charges and without notice or hearing, the Exchange, presumably to sanction conduct by Silver of which the Exchange disapproved, caused member firms to cut off Silver's wire connection, thus disrupting Silver's operations. The Court regarded this collective action as an unlawful boycott. It held that the statutory self-regulatory authority of the Exchange "affords no justification for anti-competitive collective action taken without fair procedure."[60] The case is the first in which the Court gave warning that a regulatory shield against the antitrust laws will weaken when the regulatory judgment could be influenced by a possible conflict of interest. Despite the specific statutory grant to the Exchange, the competitive relationship between Exchange members and Silver infused that power with competitive risk. The Court thought that procedural niceties affording a reviewing court some chance to evaluate whether the Exchange acted for legitimate regulatory or for anticompetitive reasons were essential. Given the potential conflict of interest, the statute's pervasive regulatory scheme did not dissuade the Court from requiring procedural fairness.

Ricci v. Chicago Mercantile Exchange[61] decided a decade later confirms that possible conflict of interest in a statutory self-regulator can affect whether procedural defenses against it may be significant in evaluating the scope of a regulatory exemption. Ricci had purchased a mercantile exchange membership with borrowed funds. His Sherman Act suit alleged that the Exchange conspired with the lender to transfer

---

57. *Carnation*, 383 U.S. 213 at 216, 217, 86 S.Ct. 781, 15 L.Ed.2d 709.

58. See, e.g., FMC v. Seatrain Lines, 411 U.S. 726, 733, 93 S.Ct. 1773, 36 L.Ed.2d 620 (1973).

59. 373 U.S. 341, 83 S.Ct. 1246, 10 L.Ed.2d 389 (1963).

60. Id. at 364. In 1975 the 1934 Act was amended giving the SEC specific power to review disciplinary action by the Exchange and to affirm, modify or set aside any sanction. 15 U.S.C.A. § 78(c), (f).

61. 409 U.S. 289, 93 S.Ct. 573, 34 L.Ed.2d 525 (1973).

Ricci's membership to another without notice or hearing. The case was like *Silver* in that the Exchange asserted it was acting within statutory self-regulatory powers. It differed, however, in two respects. For one, if the Exchange was exercising statutory self-regulatory powers, the scheme of the Commodity Exchange Act gave review powers to a federal agency, the Commodity Exchange Commission. For another, the Court was unclear whether the Exchange action was within the ambit of its self-regulatory powers. Because the available adjudication of the dispute by the Commission would be of material aid in resolving the immunity question, the Court affirmed the lower court's stay of the antitrust action pending an administrative hearing.[62]

The primary jurisdiction mechanism, which first surfaced in an antitrust context in *Keogh,* is seen again in dealing with an organized exchange. In *Silver,* there was no avenue to an agency hearing. In *Ricci* there was. It made a difference in the outcome. Two years after Ricci in Gordon v. New York Stock Exchange,[63] the agency had already acted before the antitrust suit was brought. Concertedly fixed rates for broker-age services, already approved by the SEC under specific statutory authority, insulated concerted rate making from a later antitrust attack. In United States v. National Association of Securities Dealers,[64] the majority found that mutual fund marketing practices challenged under the Sherman Act, both by DOJ and private plaintiffs, were authorized by and subject to SEC regulations, even though as a practical matter that agency paid these practices scant attention. In the aggregate, then, the cases appear to accord antitrust immunity (as in *Gordon* and *NASD*) to statutorily authorized self-regulatory action of an organized exchange, so long as there is clear statutory provision for agency review, but to deny immunity (as in *Silver*) when there is potential conflict of interest and no opportunity for independent review, and to accord primary jurisdiction to the agency (as in *Ricci*) only when at the time of the antitrust suit it is not clear whether the conduct challenged is or is not protectable self-regulation. Overall, there is general consistency with the transportation cases. *Gordon* comports directly with *Keogh, Cunard, Far East Conference* and *Square D; Silver* comports tangentially with *Borden* and *Carnation.* All seem consistent with the implication of the airline cases that more comprehensive regulation accords wider immunity, although even pervasive regulation is likely to leave interstices for antitrust. Beyond concepts developed in the transportation cases, there is in this array of organized market cases one new and apparently powerful notion: regulatory responsibility sufficient to trigger immunity when in the hands of an administrative agency may not be sufficient when conferred on an industry organ as a self-regulatory regime. This is the implication of *Silver.*

62. See also, Chicago Mercantile Exchange v. Deaktor, 414 U.S. 113, 94 S.Ct. 466, 38 L.Ed.2d 344 (1973), reaching a similar result.

63. 422 U.S. 659, 95 S.Ct. 2598, 45 L.Ed.2d 463 (1975).

64. 422 U.S. 694, 95 S.Ct. 2427, 45 L.Ed.2d 486 (1975).

14.5c3. Electric Power

Otter Tail Power Co. v. United States[65] was decided the same year as *Ricci*. The opinion, difficult to square with the above summary, marks a transition from the conduct issues in this section to the structural issues in the next. *Otter Tail* was a vertically integrated producer, transporter ("wheeler"), wholesaler and retail distributor of electric power. In order to force independent municipal power retailers within reach of its lines to merge with it, Otter Tail refused to wheel power to their systems. It defended against the government's challenge under Section 2 of the Sherman Act on the ground that the Federal Power Commission's jurisdiction to order interconnection gave Otter Tail antitrust immunity. The relevant statute granted no explicit immunity and the Court refused to imply one. The Court thought the major thrust of the statute was to encourage voluntary interconnection and that the antitrust concerns, though relevant, would not be determinative under the public interest standard the FPC would apply if asked to order interconnection. Although it recognized the possibility of an antitrust-regulatory conflict (the FPC denying interconnection while the antitrust court ordered one), the majority declined to defer to the agency, as it had in *Pan Am* and *Hughes Tool*, or to grant that agency primary jurisdiction as in *Far East Conference* and *Ricci*. The alleged conduct by Otter Tail was raw—the brazen kind of aggression from a position of power that characterized some of the excesses during turn of the century trust busting. At this Warren Court stage of antitrust development, doubt about the zeal of the FPC for competition may have generated a reluctance to move such a contest out of the judicial antitrust forum. Perhaps the Justice Department has greater credibility than other plaintiffs, but the Department's involvement is no sure ticket to success, as demonstrated by cases such as *Borden* and *National Association of Securities Dealers*, discussed above.

14.5c4. Telecommunications

Verizon Communications v. Trinko[66] is the Court's most recent holding on the application of antitrust in a regulated industry and, for that reason alone, worthy of attention. The plaintiff was a law firm that claimed that Verizon, the dominant local telephone exchange carrier (LEC), had failed to provide prompt access to the local network for rival LECs that sought to offer local service to the plaintiff and other class members. As the three dissenters pointed out, the case could have been disposed of on antitrust standing grounds. However, the Court chose to offer sweeping language on the interaction of antitrust and regulation and to address the plaintiff's claims on the merits.[67]

The court began by dismissing arguments of implied antitrust immunity, holding that any such immunity was precluded because there

---

65. 410 U.S. 366, 93 S.Ct. 1022, 35 L.Ed.2d 359 (1973).

66. 540 U.S. 398, 124 S.Ct. 872, 157 L.Ed.2d 823 (2004).

67. The Court's Sherman Section 2 discussion is addressed in § 3.4b3.

was an express anti-immunity provision or savings clause in the underlying legislation.[68] The Court ruled out any application of the essential facilities doctrine to Verizon's conduct, but in reaching this conclusion, Part IV of the Court's opinion suggests that antitrust analysis should be sensitive to the regulatory context. In the Court's words, " 'antitrust analysis must sensitively recognize and reflect the distinctive economic and legal setting of the regulated industry to which it applies.' "[69] Here, Verizon was subject to an array of requirements from 1996 federal legislation governing local exchange carriers' entry into the long distance market. The Court saw these requirements as reducing the likelihood of an antitrust violation and reasoned that the FCC was an effective enforcer of the antitrust function.

The holding in *Trinko* is less controversial than some of the language the Court employs in getting there. The Court finds satisfaction in the need to lessen the impact of "false positives" or faulty condemnations of a monopolist's conduct that are genuinely benign or procompetitive.[70] Erroneous condemnations of a defendant's conduct are indeed troublesome, but so too are false negatives, or rulings that excuse genuinely anticompetitive conduct. The Court's discussion of false positives is devoid of any empirical assessment of the costs of these errors or any comparison of the relative costs of too much versus too little enforcement.[71]

Trinko may be read broadly as a basis for implied antitrust immunity whenever a regulatory agency has some competition-related responsibility. This reading would be unfortunate and a substantial departure from prior rulings. Many agencies with a public interest or competition-protecting charge have little expertise and incentive to pursue that role. To take one example, the Federal Energy Regulatory Commission (FERC), in the deregulatory spirit that permeated the 1990s, granted wholesale sellers of electric power broad "market-based rate" authority without first ascertaining whether the sellers seeking such authority could, either individually or in concert, exercise market power. As the former FERC Chairman has conceded, the agency gave out its deregulatory certificates without an honest inquiry into whether a competitive market existed.[72] The reality is that the regulatory agencies, when they operate without a guiding hand from the antitrust agencies, have a very uneven record in protecting competition interests.

A narrower reading of *Trinko*, that the Court described and relied upon the regulatory setting primarily as a means of limiting the essential facilities doctrine under Sherman Section 2, would appear sound, more

68. 540 U.S. at 406, citing 110 Stat. 143, 47 U.S.C. § 152, note.

69. Id. at 411, quoting Town of Concord, Ma. v. Boston Edison Co., 915 F.2d 17 (1st Cir. 1990).

70. 540 U.S. at 414.

71. For criticism of the Court's focus on false positives to the exclusion of false nega-

tives, see Gavil, *Dominant Firm Distribution: Striking A Better Balance,* 72 ANTITRUST L. J. 3, 30–51 (2004).

72. FERC Chairman Pat Wood, final press conference, June 22, 2005, as reported by *Energy Daily,* June 23, 2005.

consistent with past Supreme Court precedent, and beneficial to competition.

14.5d. Federal Structural Regulation and Antitrust

The power granted by Congress to federal regulatory agencies to deal with mergers and other structural events must also be accommodated to antitrust. Many of the themes evident in the last three sections are present here, too; for example, the primary jurisdiction issues have frequently been raised. The range of judicial responses, however, has not been as wide in antitrust cases raising structural issues as in conduct cases. Recent structural cases have involved more focused judicial attention upon the specific provisions of the regulatory statute. It was not always so. In Northern Securities Co. v. United States,[73] the Court gave scant attention to the Interstate Commerce Act when it found that integration of the Great Northern and the Northern Pacific Railroads violated the Sherman Act by ending competition between them. United States v. Union Pacific Railroad Co.[74] and United States v. Southern Pacific Co.[75] decided within the next twenty years, also applied antitrust rules without adjustment attributable to regulation. But later regulatory statutes (including Interstate Commerce Act amendments) typically give the cognate agency explicit power to evaluate structural change under a public interest standard. At times explicit antitrust exemption has been granted for structural change approved by the agency. The Interstate Commerce Act, for example, exempted trucking mergers approved by the ICC from antitrust challenge. But even without explicit exemption, a grant to an agency of power to evaluate structural change under a broad public interest conception may blunt antitrust. In McLean Trucking v. United States,[76] a merger approved by the ICC was challenged on the ground that the Commission failed to apply the antitrust standard for evaluating competitive effect. The Court ruled that the Commission must evaluate the competitive effects of the merger and that it must factor these, along with other relevant effects, into its overall evaluation of whether the merger is in the public interest. Competition becomes a public interest factor to be considered; this is implicit in the very fact that Congress enacted the antitrust laws. But the public interest standard in the regulatory statute is not controlled by those laws. Competitive effects must be evaluated, and given weight commensurate with the other goals of the regulatory scheme.[77] When such balancing is done by the agency, its conclusions are, if not invulnerable, to be given great weight.[78]

73. 193 U.S. 197, 24 S.Ct. 436, 48 L.Ed. 679 (1904).

74. 226 U.S. 61, 33 S.Ct. 53, 57 L.Ed. 124 (1912).

75. 259 U.S. 214, 42 S.Ct. 496, 66 L.Ed. 907 (1922).

76. 321 U.S. 67, 64 S.Ct. 370, 88 L.Ed. 544 (1944).

77. Denver & Rio Grande W.R.R. v. U.S., 387 U.S. 485, 87 S.Ct. 1754, 18 L.Ed.2d 905 (1967).

78. Id. See also, Gulf States Utilities Co. v. FPC, 411 U.S. 747, 93 S.Ct. 1870, 36 L.Ed.2d 635 (1973); United States v. ICC, 396 U.S. 491, 90 S.Ct. 708, 24 L.Ed.2d 700 (1970); Minneapolis & St. Louis Ry. v. United States, 361 U.S. 173, 80 S.Ct. 229, 4

Pan Am,[79] discussed above because of its ancillary conduct restraints, also involved a Department of Justice challenge to a structural change—the Pan American and Grace Line joint venture. Because the CAB had explicit statutory power to evaluate the competitive aspects, the Department found itself out of court. United States v. Radio Corporation of America,[80] by contrast, emphasizes the limits of the *McLean* principle. The Justice Department sued RCA and its subsidiary, the National Broadcasting Company, under the Sherman Act to challenge their exchange with others of certain TV licenses, with the alleged purpose and effect of increasing RCA–NBC dominance. Under its regulatory jurisdiction, the Federal Communications Commission (FCC) had found these exchanges to serve the public interest and approved them. The FCC had before it all of the information that the Department relied upon in its suit and, although it had the opportunity, the Department did not appear before the Commission.

The Court rejected defendants' contention that under these circumstances, the regulatory scheme displaced the Sherman Act or at least gave the Commission jurisdiction and that, by failing to challenge before the agency, the Department was collaterally estopped. Noting that the Communications Act did not give the FCC authority to decide antitrust issues "as such," the Court held that Commission action "was not intended to prevent enforcement of the antitrust law."[81] License transfer evaluations by the FCC differed from rate regulation in the common carrier industries. TV licensees set their own rates and make related business decisions. Because there is no "rate structure to throw out of balance, sporadic action by federal courts can work no mischief." True, the FCC must factor competition into its more broadly oriented public interest judgments about licensing, and sometimes these might even be determinative.[82] But when, as here, they are not, there is no antitrust court need for administrative guidance, nor is there any regulatory interest in assuring uniformity of outcomes sufficient to warrant forbidding the antitrust court to go forward.

The *RCA* opinion, it will be seen, distinguishes the concerted practices cases in carrier markets in two quite different ways. One distinction pertains to the character of regulation. In the Court's view, transportation regulation on the natural monopoly model is considerably more pervasive than is the regime of public interest and comparative evaluation used by the FCC to decide which applicants will receive TV licenses.

L.Ed.2d 223 (1959); Seaboard Air Line R.R. v. United States, 382 U.S. 154, 86 S.Ct. 277, 15 L.Ed.2d 223 (1965). All of these cases emphasized agency discretion in integrating competition concerns with other public interest factors.

79. Pan American World Airways Inc. v. United States, 371 U.S. 296, 83 S.Ct. 476, 9 L.Ed.2d 325 (1963).

80. 358 U.S. 334, 79 S.Ct. 457, 3 L.Ed.2d 354 (1959).

81. Id.

82. The Court mentions the case of a publisher of a markets' sole newspaper applying for its sole radio, TV licenses. Id. at 350. Antitrust could also come into TV licensing decisions in a different way. In comparative hearings among competing applicants for a license the character of the applicants can be given weight. Greater Boston Television Corp. v. FCC, 444 F.2d 841 (D.C.Cir.1970), *cert. denied*, 403 U.S. 923, 91 S.Ct. 2229, 29 L.Ed.2d 701 (1971).

The other pertains to the character of the event under scrutiny. Every rate is related to every other rate. Uniformity of treatment is needed and sporadic interference is to be avoided. But structural events like license trades or mergers are contained, one time events. If a court decision in one case differs from that of the agency in another, no ball of twine will unravel. This latter distinction would presumably be entitled to some weight in reference to structural change in any industry, including common carrier markets. Perhaps it could be brought to bear on some conduct issues, too, although not on concerted rate-fixing. Indeed, the Court in *Otter Tail* might well have cited *RCA*. Although power generation is more pervasively regulated than television, no antitrust court response to a single acquisition could send shock waves through the regulatory system. A major reason for precluding antitrust interference with regulation that was present in most of the transportation common carrier conduct cases was prominently lacking in *Otter Tail* as well as in *RCA*.

For reasons like those evident in *RCA*, the Court has preserved antitrust jurisdiction over particular mergers even in the face of strong implications that Congress might have anticipated a dispositive regulatory decision. The most pronounced example is United States v. Philadelphia Nat. Bank.[83] The decision was significant on the substantive law of mergers and perhaps the Court's only 1960s merger decision that has retained great influence,[84] but the result was somewhat startling at the time it was decided for the way it parceled out merger review authority between antitrust court and regulatory agency. The Justice Department challenged the merger of a national (PNB) and a state chartered (Gerard) bank under the antitrust laws. In the Bank Merger Act of 1960, Congress granted the banking agencies authority to approve mergers, directing them to consider competitive factors among others. The statute also stated that "[in] the interest of uniform standards" the agency required a report on competitive factors from the attorney general. That statute, however, did not grant express immunity from antitrust. Although some legislative history suggested that, in light of the critical importance of banking structure to the economy, competitive effect was not to dominate bank merger decisions, the Court held that the Act did not impliedly exempt such mergers from the antitrust laws. At least if the legislative history is put aside, that holding, although in some tension with cases like *Rocci*, *NASD* and *Hughes Tool*, was not a great stretch beyond *Carnation* (which refused to find a wide implied exemption from regulatory responsibilities when Congress had created a specific but narrow one). But the Court's accommodation to antitrust did not stop there. Given the limits of the then apparent Sherman Act merger standards,[85] a substantively critical question remained—whether the

---

83. 374 U.S. 321, 83 S.Ct. 1715, 10 L.Ed.2d 915 (1963).

84. See, e.g., the opinion by Judge Posner in Hospital Corp. of America v. FTC,

807 F.2d 1381 (7th Cir.1986) *cert. denied*, 481 (1987).

85. See, United States v. Columbia Steel Co., 334 U.S. 495, 68 S.Ct. 1107, 92 L.Ed. 1533 (1948). The decision in United States

stricter standards of Section 7 of the Clayton Act, as amended in 1950, applied to bank mergers. The strict standards of Section 7 applied to all stock acquisition, but to asset acquisitions only by corporations "subject to the jurisdiction by the FTC"—which banks, being subject to the banking agencies, were not. The PNB–Gerard consolidation was structured as an asset acquisition. Gerard assets were turned over to PNB. PNB stockholders retained their original share certificates. The court, however, characterized the transaction as ambiguous, apparently because Gerard stockholders were not only issued PNB shares but surrendered their old Gerard shares, too. It then resolved the ambiguity by applying Section 7 and invalidating the merger, on the basis of the canon: immunity from the antitrust laws is not to be implied lightly.[86]

Responding to *Philadelphia National Bank*, Congress passed the Bank Merger Act in 1966 which compromised between antitrust and any competing public interests that bank regulators might evaluate. First, it enhanced the significance of antitrust in agency evaluations by obliging agency application of Sherman Act and Clayton Act tests.[87] To the extent that a bank regulator is capable of being an aggressive antitrust enforcer, antitrust plainly gets the preferred position over other regulatory concerns.[88] Second, the Act imposes a thirty day statute of limitations on any Justice Department challenge to agency-approved bank mergers.[89] If the merger gets by agency scrutiny and is unchallenged by the Department on antitrust grounds for thirty days, it becomes effectively exempt from antitrust.[90]

California v. FPC,[91] entails a unique application of primary jurisdiction doctrine in a gas industry merger context. It is another instance where the Court reached out to protect a structural antitrust inquiry from interference by regulatory action. El Paso Natural Gas Co. acquired stock of Pacific Northwest Pipeline Corp (PNP). The Justice Department brought suit under Section 7of the Clayton Act. When, pursuant to the requirements of the Natural Gas Act, El Paso sought Federal Power

v. First Nat. Bank & Trust Co., 376 U.S. 665, 84 S.Ct. 1033, 12 L.Ed.2d 1 (1964), only a year after *United States v. Philadelphia National Bank*, 374 U.S. 321, 83 S.Ct. 1715, 10 L.Ed.2d 915 (1963), suggests that the expectation, still then current, that Sherman merger standards would be much more permissive than Clayton Act Section 7 standards may also have been erroneous.

86. 374 U.S. 321, 348, 83 S.Ct. 1715, 10 L.Ed.2d 915; *see also* Georgia v. Pennsylvania R. Co., 324 U.S. 439, 456–457, 65 S.Ct. 716, 89 L.Ed. 1051 (1945).

87. No merger resulting in monopoly or furthering a conspiracy or attempt to monopolize banking, or the effect of which may be to substantially lessen competition or tend to create a monopoly shall be approved. 12 U.S.C.A. § 1828(c).

88. The Act requires prior regulatory approval for any merger, consolidation or purchase of assets with assumption of liabilities. Authority to administer the Act is divided among "responsive agencies" (the FDIC for transactions between an insured and non-insured bank), the comptroller of the currency for transactions between insured banks if the resulting bank will be national, the Federal Reserve Board if it will be a state bank. Id. In 1989 the FDIC's authority was broadened slightly and the Director of the Office of Thrift Supervision was assigned responsibility if the resulting institution was a savings association.

89. Id.

90. *See generally,* 2 M.P. Malloy, The Corporate Law of Banks 819–827 (1988 and 1990 Cum. Supp.)

91. 369 U.S. 482, 82 S.Ct. 901, 8 L.Ed.2d 54 (1962).

Commission (FPC) authority to acquire PNP's assets,[92] California intervened in opposition to the merger and supported a request by the Justice Department that the FPC stay its proceedings pending the antitrust suit. The Department's request was denied and the FPC proceeding went to hearing. On application of the merging parties, the antitrust court then stayed its proceedings pending decision by the FPC. In due course, the FPC approved the merger and it was consummated. California appealed unsuccessfully to the court of appeals. The Supreme Court, however, granted California's certiorari petition to consider a single question: whether the FPC should have deferred to the antitrust court. It held that for two "practical reasons" the FPC should have waited until the court had acted. First, agency approval enabled the merger to go ahead; if the court later found it illegal, complex unscrambling would be necessary. By contrast, even if the court found no antitrust violation, the merger would be unable to proceed until approved by the agency on the broader grounds open to its consideration. Second, although FPC approval under a public interest standard yields no antitrust exemption, the "prospect of [the antitrust court] undoing what was done [by the agency] raises a powerful inference" that could affect the outcome of the antitrust litigation. Either the Justice Department or the antitrust court, as the Supreme Court viewed it, were at risk of being pressured. The Court also noted that the FPC characterized the adverse competitive effect of the merger as insubstantial, thus treading on the domain occupied by the antitrust court in a pending case.[93] After the Supreme Court's decision, the merger was found unlawful.[94]

The Courts' retroactive application of the primary jurisdiction doctrine to protect the antitrust court in *California v. FPC* seems extreme. For one thing, the antitrust court had the capacity to protect itself. When asked to litigate the antitrust claim it could have proceeded without delay: it didn't; it decided to defer to the agency. Indeed, if the court thought its independence or remedial capacity would be compromised by the FPC decision not to defer to the court, it could have enjoined the merging parties from altering the status quo until further order of the court. An explanation sometimes proposed—that the Supreme Court did not trust the FPC[95]—seems inverted or incomplete. The district court and Justice Department earned no more deference than did the FPC. Also, the Court's apparent criticism of the FPC not just for getting its competitive evaluation wrong but for doing its own evaluation at all is beyond justification. Under the *McLean* principle (applied also in *Hughes Tool*), an agency evaluating a public utility merger under a public interest standard *must* factor competitive concerns into the balance.

The Federal Communications Commission has exercised a *McLean* responsibility to consider competitive effects when evaluating telecom-

---

92. 369 U.S. 482, 82 S.Ct. 901, 8 L.Ed.2d 54 (1962).

93. Id. at 490.

94. United States v. El Paso Natural Gas Co., 376 U.S. 651, 84 S.Ct. 1044, 12 L.Ed.2d 12 (1964).

95. Id.

munication regulatory issues and, since the late 1960s, has accorded the competitive interest considerable weight.[96] This FCC competence has never been found to displace or limit the jurisdiction of antitrust courts.[97]

§ 14.6 Federal Protection for Competition in State Regulated Markets

14.6a. An Analytical Framework for the State Action (*Parker*) Exemption

Intergovernmental relationships within a federal system are inevitably complex. For federalism to remain vital, they must also be dynamic. Beyond the two cardinal principles upon which American federal cohesion is based—the supremacy of constitutionally sanctioned national policy and the Supreme Court as the ultimate arbiter of conflict—changes, responsive to economic and social development and to shifts in political attitudes, are essential and inevitable. There are many media for orderly development of federal relationships. The commerce clause mediates between federal and state power, thereby assigning to the courts, ultimately the Supreme Court, the duty to demarcate separate and shared terrains of state and national responsibility. The Due Process clause and Bill of Rights also impose constraints that can put some efforts to regulate out of bounds both for the nation and the states. From these sources, the Court has developed a preemption doctrine, including a negative commerce clause and occupancy of the field doctrine, with sufficient generality to resolve most conflicts between state and national power. The Court also developed procedural due process norms that once did, and commercial free speech doctrine that can today, inhibit both state and federal interference with competition. The negative commerce clause constrains state regulation regardless of any Congressional action if the state regulates in a way that disproportionately burdens commercial interests not having access to state political organs. By contrast, occupancy of the field analysis, in its application to state economic regulation, depends upon implication from policy expressed by Congress, as in the antitrust laws.

The Court has not relied solely on constitutional limits and preemption analysis to arbitrate between federal antitrust and state regulation. The state action doctrine, something unique in the jurisprudence of federalism, entails a set of judge-made rules that exempt from the antitrust laws certain conduct compelled or authorized by state law. Because this doctrine fashions an exemption from antitrust, a state action analysis logically precedes a preemption analysis. If the antitrust laws do not apply, they cannot preempt; within constitutional bounds, state law will prevail. Nevertheless, preemption analysis can still be relevant in antitrust cases. Sometimes the Court turns to the state

---

96. Carterphone, 13 F.C.C.2d 420 (1968); MCI, 18 F.C.C.2d 953 (1969).

97. E.g., Maryland v. United States, 460 U.S. 1001, 103 S.Ct. 1240, 75 L.Ed.2d 472 (1983).

action doctrine and seems to ignore preemption, but other times it makes no mention of the state action doctrine and uses conventional, constitutionally based preemption analysis.

If the cases do not show comprehensive order, they do display discernible patterns. When state law compels or authorizes conduct that facially violates antitrust norms, the Court regularly applies the state action doctrine. If the conduct in question is protected under that doctrine, state law governs and federal antitrust gives way, even though a conventional preemption analysis might have invited the opposite result. The state action doctrine is used, in short, when antitrust clearly could override state law and when the antitrust statutes do not in terms defer, but the court thinks state policy warrants greater deference than Congress has expressly granted. On the other hand, if the conduct (arguably violative of antitrust) is not protected by the state action doctrine, the antitrust laws fully apply. Because of this pattern, the state action doctrine discussed in §§ 14.6a through 14.6d is of major significance. Preemption doctrine, discussed in § 14.6e, although logically applicable, usually stands in the background.

14.6b. Protecting the State and Protecting Private Parties: Two Aspects of the State Action Exemption

Here are two black letter propositions that encapsulate the state action doctrine: First, conduct by state or municipal officials that facially violates the antitrust law is exempt if compelled or clearly authorized pursuant to clearly articulated state law. Second, conduct by private parties is also exempt if it is both so compelled or authorized and, in addition, is actively supervised by the state. Although distinct from preemption, this doctrine can best be understood against the context of preemption analysis. When state or local policy conflicts with an act of Congress within an area delegated to Congress, federal displacement of state or local policy "flows directly from the substantive source of power of the Congressional action coupled with the supremacy clause * * *."[1] As the Court first said in Gibbons v. Ogden,[2] state acts, even if otherwise lawful, must yield if they "interfere with, or are contrary to * * * any [valid] law of Congress * * *."[3] The inquiry is confined. What does each enactment mandate? Does that by the state interfere with that by Congress? If so, the inquiry ends. Such conflict can occur when federal and state legislation blatantly conflict, as when one requires what the other forbids.[4] Such conflict can also occur when the state law forbids or discourages conduct that federal law seeks to encourage.[5] Conflict could

§ 14.6

1. L. Tribe, American Constitutional Law § 6–25 (2d ed. 1988). The summary in this text draws on the Tribe analysis.

2. 22 U.S. (9 Wheat.) 1, 6 L.Ed. 23 (1824).

3. Id. at 209.

4. McDermott v. Wisconsin, 228 U.S. 115, 33 S.Ct. 431, 57 L.Ed. 754 (1913);

Southland Corp. v. Keating et al., 465 U.S. 1, 104 S.Ct. 852, 79 L.Ed.2d 1 (1984).

5. E.g., Nash v. Florida Industrial Comm., 389 U.S. 235, 88 S.Ct. 362, 19 L.Ed.2d 438 (1967) (state law denying unemployment compensation to applicants because they filed an unfair labor practice charge with the NLRB is invalid.)

occur, too, when state law pushes in the same general direction as federal law, but pushes further; the question here is whether the federal line was drawn with deliberation to strike a balance between competing interests or policies, so that allowing the state to go further might distort a desired and uniform federal policy.[6] Indeed, preemption can occur even without facial conflict as, for example, when allowing even limited state entry to establish its specific goals would unduly limit the flexibility of a broader, more general federal policy.[7]

Given the scope and breadth of the antitrust commitment to competition, conventional preemption analysis might impinge heavily on state regulation of economic activity. For example, all state regulatory statutes encouraging or protecting concerted price making or other clear antitrust violations would plainly conflict with antitrust, as might any number of state statutes that draw materially different lines between permitted and forbidden economic cooperation than do the antitrust laws. In light of this and in the interest of a better balanced federalism, the Court fashioned the state action doctrine. When dealing with the relation between federal regulation and federal antitrust, the Court is able to fine tune.[8] Conventional preemption analysis, by contrast, offers only a binary choice. It asks only whether conflict exists: when it does federal policy controls. But some judicial refinement becomes feasible when the issue is reframed as it is under the state action doctrine. In the interest of a well balanced federalism, how far should federal competition law intrude on this particular state regulatory regime? The state action doctrine, then, must be frankly recognized as judicial law-making. The Supreme Court, custodian of the antitrust tradition, fashions substantive antitrust doctrine case by case, working much as would a common law court. In the exercise of this function and in the interest of widening the states' power to impose economic norms even when they impinge on competition further than conventional preemption analysis would validate, the Court has developed a substantive antitrust exemption which conditions the relationship between state law and federal antitrust by factoring into the analysis a public interest other than competitive effect: namely, the states' interest in such non-competitive goals as its regulation seeks to attain. In an important sense, federal supremacy prevails: judicially fashioned federal law mediates between the federal interest in competition and in the conflicting state interests. A federal antitrust court does the mediating. This judicial activism gives operative content to the state action doctrine. Its complexities, the factors that have and may yet influence its development, and its abiding uncertainties can best be fathomed by tracing the main lines of case law evolution.

The state action doctrine has its genesis in Parker v. Brown,[9] a case that can be adequately explained on preemption principles, but which

---

6. Cf., Edgar v. MITE Corp., 457 U.S. 624, 102 S.Ct. 2629, 73 L.Ed.2d 269 (1982).

7. E.g., Burbank v. Lockheed Air Terminal, Inc., 411 U.S. 624, 93 S.Ct. 1854, 36 L.Ed.2d 547 (1973).

8. FMC v. Seatrain Lines, Inc., 411 U.S. 726, 733, 93 S.Ct. 1773, 36 L.Ed.2d 620 (1973); Square D Co. v. Niagara Frontier Tariff Bureau, Inc., 476 U.S. 409, 106 S.Ct. 1922, 90 L.Ed.2d 413 (1986).

9. 317 U.S. 341, 63 S.Ct. 307, 87 L.Ed. 315 (1943).

nevertheless became the source book for an approach that displaces preemption analysis for most state law-antitrust interaction. When *Parker v. Brown* arose, the economy, including agriculture, was in depression. Over 90 percent of the nation's raisin crop was grown in California. Prices for that product (like those for most farm products at the time) were very low. A California statute imposed a stabilization program "among growers [to] maintain prices * * * to conserve agricultural wealth * * * and to prevent economic waste."[10] The statute created a commission that selected a committee (largely from nominees of growers) which prepared a marketing program. The commission, after a public hearing, could approve that program; it would then be instituted and enforced by law if consented to by a specified percent of producers owning a requisite share of the acreage producing raisins. The statute—essentially a state supported cartelization program for raisins—was challenged under the Sherman Act by growers that wanted to market free of its constraints.

Because the California statute in *Parker* encouraged concerted price fixing and output allocation controlled by producers, there was a facial violation of Section 1 of the Sherman Act. Plaintiffs argued that the Sherman Act both preempted the California law and rendered conduct under the marketing scheme a violation. They also argued that Congress had occupied the field by the Agriculture Marketing Act of 1937. That statute authorized the Secretary of Agriculture to set up stabilization programs for raisins—a power the Secretary had refrained from exercising. The Court rejected occupation of the field by the federal agricultural program. It did not read the Secretary's failure to act as implying a judgment that action was unnecessary or would be harmful.[11] It also rejected Sherman Act preemption. Because Congress had expressed itself not only in the Sherman Act but also in the Agriculture Marketing Act, in light of the very conditions to which the California statute was a response, Congress had shown its willingness that the Sherman Act be displaced. By empowering federal officials to establish a federal marketing program Congress impliedly authorized a comparable state program, at least until the federal authorities acted.

If the *Parker* Court had simply articulated these propositions negating preemption and stopped, the impact of the case might have been modest. But the opinion by Chief Justice Stone ranged more broadly:

"* * * The Sherman Act makes no mention of the state as such, and gives no hint that it was intended to restrain state action or official action directed by the state * * *.

"* * * [The authority the state gave] to the Commission and to the program committee * * * is not rendered unlawful by the Sherman

---

10. Id. at 346.

11. Compare, United States v. Borden Co., 308 U.S. 188, 60 S.Ct. 182, 84 L.Ed. 181 (1939).

Act since, in view of the latter's words and history, it must be taken to be a prohibition of individual and not state action."[12]

This second ground for the *Parker* holding, that the Sherman Act was not aimed at state action, was rich in potential. Nevertheless, it was not further examined by the Court until some years later. The court passed over an opportunity to do so in Schwegmann Bros. v. Calvert Distillers Corp.[13] There, Congress, by statute, had specifically exempted from the antitrust laws contracts between certain sellers and buyers that specified the price at which the buyers would resell, when such contracts were authorized by a state statute. Several states, however, passed statutes purporting to make the resale price specified in any such contract enforceable not only against buyers who agreed to be bound by it, but also by their competitors. When enforcement against these "non-signers" was challenged under the Sherman Act, the Court did not turn to the state action concept in *Parker* for guidance. It used conventional preemption analysis and ruled that a state may not authorize restraints of interstate commerce that violate the Sherman Act.[14]

Parker came back into view, however, two decades later and has been a prominent aspect of antitrust federalism ever since. In Goldfarb v. Virginia State Bar,[15] private parties—lawyers, not acting under any statute and exercising no state function—concertedly established minimum fees. Once such minimums were established, however, a lawyer who habitually ignored them could be disciplined by the State Bar. When this program was challenged under the Sherman Act the Court ignored preemption doctrine and turned to the state action language in *Parker*. But because it viewed the nexus between this lawyer cartel and Virginia as more tenuous than that between California and raisin cartel in *Parker*, the Court imposed a strict substantive test. To gain a state action exemption from the Sherman Act, conduct by private parties "must be compelled by the state acting as sovereign."[16] Because there

---

12. Id. at 352. A knowledgeable commentator has labeled the Court's reliance on the silence of Congress about regulating state activities "fictional" history. HOVENKAMP, FEDERAL ANTITRUST POLICY § 20.2a, at 724 (2d ed.1999). See also Hovenkamp & Mackerran, *Municipal Regulation and Federal Antitrust Policy*, 32 UCLA L. REV. 719, 725–28 (1985); Jorde, *Antitrust and the State Action Doctrine: A Return to Deferential Economic Federalism*, 75 Calif. L. Rev. 227, 229. The constitutional position was very different when the Sherman Act was enacted than it was when *Parker* was decided. In 1890 there was no federal competence to regulate the intrastate transactions to which state regulatory regimes were directed. Wickard v. Filburn, 317 U.S. 111, 63 S.Ct. 82, 87 L.Ed. 122 (1942). But by 1943 Congress was competent to regulate intrastate activities affecting interstate commerce.

13. 341 U.S. 384, 71 S.Ct. 745, 95 L.Ed. 1035 (1951).

14. See, Northern Securities Co. v. United States, 193 U.S. 197, 24 S.Ct. 436, 48 L.Ed. 679 (1904), where the Court first said much the same thing.

15. 421 U.S. 773, 95 S.Ct. 2004, 44 L.Ed.2d 572 (1975).

16. Id. at 791. In Bates v. State Bar of Arizona, 433 U.S. 350, 97 S.Ct. 2691, 53 L.Ed.2d 810 (1977) *Parker* was held to preclude antitrust liability for restrictions on lawyer advertising sanctioned by the State Supreme Court. In Hoover v. Ronwin, 466 U.S. 558, 104 S.Ct. 1989, 80 L.Ed.2d 590 (1984), *Parker* protected state bar examiners working under State Supreme Court supervision. As both cases suggest, the state can act as a sovereign through its courts as well as its legislature and executive.

was no such compulsion in *Goldfarb*, the lawyer cartel was not protected. But, by using this analytical route, *Goldfarb* established two significant points. First, it confirmed the existence of a state action exemption—the second ground for decision in *Parker*—which until *Goldfarb* might have been viewed as dictum, or an awkward discussion of preemption, rather than the judicial creation of a new, substantive antitrust exemption. Second, it signaled that in some circumstances private parties as well as state officials might be protected by *Parker*.

With *Goldfarb*, the state action doctrine became firmly planted in the modern law. But there remain two questions: when is the state itself acting, and thus entitled to immunity; and under what circumstances may a private party shelter under the wing of the state.

14.6c. Identifying State Action for *Parker* Exemption Purposes

When problems arise under *Parker*, they usually concern whether a private party is protected, not whether the state itself is protected. But whoever seeks protection must show state action. This section looks at cases suggesting the scope and limits of the concept "state action" as a basis for an antitrust exemption.

The minimum *Parker* teaching is that the state is not itself liable for its own anti-competitive conduct. When is it the state itself acting? That inquiry is pertinent both to whether the actor can be liable (if it is the state, it cannot be) and to whether one acting in the manner that some state-linked agency requires or suggests can be liable (if the agency is itself "the state", others may be able to shelter because they act as it requires or encourages). In *Parker*, the state acted through a commission established by statute. Action by the commission was state action. But so, too, was action by members of a committee selected by the commission to prepare the marketing program mandated by the statute, even though those chosen were nominated by growers who had an interest in the committee's actions. While a state itself typically acts through its legislature, its executive, or an agency established by law to perform regulatory functions, action by courts within their constitutional, legal authority can also be state action.[17] Thus, regulation of the bar may be in part or even primarily a judicial function; yet, as such, state action.[18]

Municipal action, by contrast, is not action by the state, whether that action is commercial or governmental in nature[19] and whether or not the city has "home rule" powers—that is a grant from the state of the full scope of the state's sovereignty.[20] A city may be able to shelter under the wing of the state[21] (as may a private party in appropriate

---

17. Bates v. State Bar of Arizona, 433 U.S. 350, 97 S.Ct. 2691, 53 L.Ed.2d 810 (1977).

18. Id.

19. City of Lafayette v. Louisiana Power & Light Co., 435 U.S. 389, 98 S.Ct. 1123, 55 L.Ed.2d 364 (1978).

20. Community Communications Co. v. City of Boulder, 455 U.S. 40, 102 S.Ct. 835, 70 L.Ed.2d 810 (1982).

21. City of Lafayette v. Louisiana Power & Light Co., 435 U.S. 389, 412–13, 98 S.Ct. 1123, 55 L.Ed.2d 364 (1978). This proposi-

circumstances)[22] but it has no antitrust defense predicated on its own governmental status. The same is true for special districts and other such governmental subdivisions.[23] It follows that a private party gains no exemption for doing what a city directs or authorizes unless, in giving that direction, the city is acting for the state (much as did the commission and committee in *Parker*) in which case the private party may succeed in sheltering under the state's *Parker* immunity.

It does not follow that municipal action not attributable to the state violates the antitrust laws whenever the action is adverse to competition. Such action, even though injuring competition (as, for example, might a rent control ordinance) may involve neither monopolization nor concerted conduct restraining trade; substantive antitrust provisions may not touch it.[24] Has the city or others with its aid monopolized or attempted to monopolize a defined market? Has it, with others, conspired to restrain trade? Unless the city's conduct can be characterized in conventional Sherman Act terms the city is not violating the Act regardless of adverse competitive effects from its action.[25]

14.6d. Determining When Private Parties Can Shelter Under *Parker*

The law about private party protection under the *Parker* exemption begins with *Goldfarb v. Virginia Bar*.[26] That case not only confirmed and reinforced the existence of the state action exemption; by stressing sovereign compulsion as the basis for private party protection, *Goldfarb* also began the process of confining the new immunity lest it cut too wide a swath through federal policy. In so doing, the case moved most of the federalism debate about competition policy from the constitutional issue of preemption to the judge-made statutory arena of state action. This made possible judicial fine tuning of state-federal policy of the kind already feasible when two seemingly inconsistent policies both stem from federal statutes, but constitutionally awkward when statutes by separate sovereigns are in contention. It also increased private incentives to seek to capture state policy and opened possibilities for states to advance parochial economic interests at the expense of out of state interests.[27]

A year after *Goldfarb*, the Court experimented with the state action doctrine in an interesting way. Not since the days of Lochner v. New

---

tion is now confirmed by statutes. 15 U.S.C.A. §§ 34–36.

22. Parker v. Brown, 317 U.S. 341, 350–52, 63 S.Ct. 307, 87 L.Ed. 315 (1943); *see also*, Cantor v. Detroit Edison, 428 U.S. 579, 623, 96 S.Ct. 3110, 49 L.Ed.2d 1141 (1976).

23. City of Lafayette v. Louisiana Power & Light Co., 435 U.S. 389, 408–09, 98 S.Ct. 1123, 55 L.Ed.2d 364 (1978).

24. Fisher v. City of Berkeley, 475 U.S. 260, 106 S.Ct. 1045, 89 L.Ed.2d 206 (1986).

25. Id. Nonetheless, it is conceivable (however unlikely) that municipal action authorized by the state could be so blatantly inconsistent with antitrust goals as to be preempted by the antitrust laws. *See* § 14.6g.

26. 421 U.S. 773, 95 S.Ct. 2004, 44 L.Ed.2d 572 (1975).

27. See, Wiley, *A Capture Theory of Antitrust Federalism*, 99 Harv. L. Rev. 713, 728 (1986).

York[28] had the Court undertaken broad substantive evaluation of state legislation against a free market. In the *Lochner* era, the source of the federal critique was constitutional. In Cantor v. Detroit Edison,[29] the Court drew upon antitrust as a statutory warrant for a review of state law to determine whether it constrained the free market too aggressively. The defendant, an electric utility, filed a tariff for electrical service to residential customers that bundled the provision of power and the provision of light bulbs under a single charge based on the amount of electricity used. Cantor, who sold light bulbs at retail, alleged that the defendant was leveraging monopoly power in electricity distribution to foreclose competition in light bulbs in violation of the Sherman Act. Once the tariff was filed and accepted by the PUC, Detroit Edison was "compelled" by state law to comply with it. For this reason the district court, citing *Parker* and *Goldfarb*, dismissed the complaint. The Supreme Court reversed. It was apparent that the PUC had no strong interest in the light bulb market. As Justice Stevens noted, the utility fashioned its tying scheme on its own initiative; the PUC did not care one way or the other. The Court should fashion an antitrust exemption based on state action only when "necessary in order to make the regulatory act work," and even then only to "the minimum extent necessary."[30] As if to emphasize the appropriateness of a substantive review of state law, in order to assure that it fit with antitrust into a cohesive system, the opinion analogized to the retro-fitting of antitrust and federal regulation and remarked that in the outcome of Cantor's antitrust suit, "Michigan's interest in regulating its utilities' distribution of electricity" will not be compromised.[31] Justice Blackmun, concurring, went even further in articulating a *Lochner*-like (though statutorily based) analysis. In an opinion directly reminiscent of *Lochner*-era due process review of state legislation, he proposed a balancing test to determine whether the benefits of a state's regulation outweighed the anticompetitive harm to the national economy. This approach, one might suppose, would seldom grant exemption. It would probably lead to results generally consistent with those which would be reached under preemption analysis with no state action doctrine to intermediate.

Cantor was the Court's boldest effort to develop doctrine that frankly claimed for courts the same responsibility for shaping state regulation and antitrust that the Court exercises in shaping federal regulation and antitrust. For good or ill, *Cantor* analysis has not been further developed or much explored. The next year, in Bates v. State Bar of Arizona,[32] the Court narrowed the significance of both *Goldfarb* and *Cantor*, while opting for a bright line approach to the meaning of *Parker*. Attorneys running a legal clinic were disciplined by Arizona for advertising their services in violation of an ethical rule. The Court found that the anti-advertising rule (although vulnerable under the First Amend-

28. 198 U.S. 45, 25 S.Ct. 539, 49 L.Ed. 937 (1905).

29. 428 U.S. 579, 96 S.Ct. 3110, 49 L.Ed.2d 1141 (1976).

30. Id. at 597.

31. Id. at 598.

32. 433 U.S. 350, 97 S.Ct. 2691, 53 L.Ed.2d 810 (1977).

ment) was immune from antitrust challenge. *Goldfarb* was distinguished on the ground that the Virginia Supreme Court did not require the anticompetitive conduct challenged in *Goldfarb*, whereas the anti-advertising rule involved in *Bates* was "the affirmative command of the Arizona Supreme Court * * * ."[33] *Cantor* was found unpersuasive because the state in that case had no independent regulatory interest in light bulbs, whereas Arizona clearly did have such an interest in the practice of law. Both *Goldfarb* and *Cantor* suggested a balancing test: Could the states' interest in assuring ethical conduct by lawyers be adequately met without a total ban on advertising? But the *Bates* Court addressed the problem as presenting only an issue of characterization: Did the state, acting as a sovereign, forbid lawyer advertising? If so, the Sherman Act does not apply; no retro-fitting was done to strike a proper balance between the state interest in constraining excessive lawyer commercialism and the federal interest in preserving competition.

Perhaps because the bright line substantive test that the *Bates* Court derived would countenance even severe intrusions on federal competition policy if an industry successfully captured the support of state policy makers, the Court soon began to erect process limits upon the scope of its new, bright-line, substantive state action rule. This process-oriented development began in 1980,[34] but there were earlier intimations.

Lafayette v. Louisiana Power & Light Co.,[35] a Sherman Act suit by a private utility against a municipal utility for the allegedly anticompetitive business conduct of the latter, presented the question whether municipalities or other political subdivisions are themselves fully protected by the *Parker* immunity. If so, the risks of capture might be enhanced. Intensified, too, would be the risk of economic parochialism; municipalities might have both the incentive and the opportunity to confiscate economic benefits within the city while exporting economic costs to other parts of the state or to other states. Five Justices voted not to extend the *Parker* exemption to a city, four on the ground that municipal action should never be protected by the state action doctrine and one on the ground that this municipal power company was performing commercial, not governmental, functions, and that *Parker* should never protect such a function. The opinion by Justice Brennan for the four stressed that to warrant *Parker* immunity a policy should be "actively supervised" by the state itself. Although this process-oriented proposition was used in support of a norm that would exclude municipalities, as such, from *Parker* protection, the language was later grasped upon as a conditional basis for extending *Parker* protection not only to a governmental subdivision like a municipality but to private parties too.[36]

---

33. Id. at 360.

34. See, California Retail Liquor Dealers Ass'n. v. Midcal Aluminum, Inc., 445 U.S. 97, 100 S.Ct. 937, 63 L.Ed.2d 233 (1980), discussed infra.

35. 435 U.S. 389, 98 S.Ct. 1123, 55 L.Ed.2d 364 (1978).

36. Id. at 410.

In the same year, the Court decided New Motor Vehicle Board of Calif. v. Orrin W. Fox Co.[37] In rejecting a Sherman Act preemption challenge to a state statute the Court for the first time signaled the character of the relationship between preemption and the rapidly developing *Parker* immunity. It also used language that was later adopted to refine the process limitation announced in *Bates* upon the *Parker* substantive rule. The California statute was intended to protect auto dealers from intrabrand competition. If a manufacturer authorized a new dealership, an existing dealer in the same territory could complain to a state board. If such a complaint were filed, the new dealership could not be established without approval of the board. On the face of it, the California statute, devoid as it was of explicit standards, gave the state board a sweeping discretion. It seems clear that the statute would not survive either a conventional preemption analysis or a *Parker* test predicated on balancing the state and federal interest in the manner invited by *Cantor*. Nevertheless, the Court rejected the preemption challenge, holding that the state policy was within the scope of *Parker* protection. It also turned away from the balancing approach in *Cantor*. It held that *Parker* applied because the state had established "a system of regulation, clearly articulated and affirmatively expressed, designed to displace unfettered business freedom."[38]

The elements for a comprehensive restatement of *Parker,* substantively very permissive to states, but scrupulous about the reality of state involvement, were now in place. They were drawn together in California Retail Liquor Dealers Assn. v. Midcal Aluminum, Inc.[39] A California statute required wine producers or wholesalers to file a price schedule with the state and required resellers to adhere to these posted prices. Midcal allegedly resold for less. On the strength of Schwegmann Brothers v. Calvert Distillers[40] (and without noting any tension between that case and *Orrin Fox*), the Court recognized an inconsistency between the California statute and the Sherman Act. But a preemption analysis was not warranted because *Parker* established that the Sherman Act had "no purpose to nullify" all such competitive intrusions by the state.[41] It was necessary, therefore, to apply both substantive and procedural norms to determine whether the California statute passed muster under *Parker*. Clearly, it met the substantive test formulated in *Goldfarb* and applied again in *Bates*, a test based on compulsion. Unquestionably, both wholesalers and retailers of wine were under state compulsion. But there remained a process test first suggested in *Bates* which concerned the relevant language from the recent *Lafayette* and the *Orrin Fox* cases. Drawing on these cases, the Court made clear that there are now "two standards for antitrust immunity under *Parker v. Brown*. First, the challenged restraint must be 'one clearly articulated and affirmatively

37. 439 U.S. 96, 99 S.Ct. 403, 58 L.Ed.2d 361 (1978).

38. Id. at 109.

39. 445 U.S. 97, 100 S.Ct. 937, 63 L.Ed.2d 233 (1980).

40. 341 U.S. 384, 71 S.Ct. 745, 95 L.Ed. 1035 (1951).

41. Midcal, 445 U.S. at 104.

expressed as state policy'; second, the policy must be 'actively supervised' by the state itself."[42]

California's resale price maintenance scheme for wine met the first standard. No question: California wanted upstream firms to set downstream prices. But the program failed to satisfy the second, the process, standard. "The state neither establishes prices nor reviews the reasonableness of [the prices set by private parties]."[43] This critical second requirement suggests movement away from *Parker v. Brown*, a case in which that requirement might well not have been met (because the marketing board was little more than industry self-regulation).

The elements of *Bates*, *Lafayette* and *Orrin Fox* were thus brought together to create a new antitrust federalism. Apparently, a state could run roughshod over antitrust values if it scrupulously exercised power to do so on its own behalf. But no state may delegate to private parties its power to displace the Sherman Act. In this, at least, the much earlier *Schwegmann* decision had been right. There have been interesting decisions since *Midcal*; that case did not answer all possible questions, and more recent developments are noted in the next two subsection. But post-*Midcal* developments are not revisions but refinements of the two-tiered test the Court announced in *Midcal*.

14.6d1. The Substantive Criterion of Midcal: Has the State Itself Compelled or Authorized the Conduct?

After *Midcal*, there are two quite distinct state action issues: Has the state itself acted to displace competition? Has the state involved itself sufficiently to affect that outcome, rather than simply deferring judgments to private actors? Before *Midcal* there were polar cases. *Parker* itself entailed significant but superficial state involvement. *Schwegmann* taught that the state cannot simply identify an area in which federal antitrust norms are not to apply. *Bates* emphasized that when the state insists on conduct forbidden by antitrust, the private party is protected. *Midcal* raised state compulsion to a necessity for private party shelter. But, the Court soon held that the compulsion requirement is purposive, not formulaic.

Southern Motor Carriers Rate Conference v. United States[44] involved state statutes that authorized rate bureaus of motor common carriers to engage in concerted rate making, but did not compel them to do so. Rates, whether individually or collectively proposed, had to be filed with a state agency. They become effective if the state took no action within a specified time. If the agency scheduled a hearing, the rates become effective only if specifically approved.

The Justice Department challenged this system. The district court rendered summary judgment in the Department's favor and the court of appeals affirmed. In an opinion by Justice Powell, the majority of the

---

42. Id. at 105.

43. Id. at 105.

44. 471 U.S. 48, 105 S.Ct. 1721, 85 L.Ed.2d 36 (1985).

Supreme Court reversed holding that the *Midcal* test does not include an inflexible compulsion requirement. *Parker* is aimed at resolving federalism conflicts. Compulsion can be an important signifier of state involvement. But to insist upon compulsion would foreclose to the state other regulatory alternatives adequate in particular contexts to meet its regulatory objective. Properly construed, *Midcal* had two elements. One of these, adequate state supervision, was found below to be met. The other, at its essence, concerned whether anticompetitive action was taken pursuant to a clearly articulated state policy. Here, the carriers are entitled to *Parker* immunity because collective rate making is both clearly sanctioned and adequately supervised by the State.

Southern Motor Carriers gives the *Parker* exemption about as wide a reading as the *Midcal* formulation would permit. It authorized state displacement of competition well beyond terrain that preemption analysis would tolerate and well beyond what a *Cantor*-like balancing approach might sanction. As the dissent insisted, collective rate making by potentially competitive motor carriers will have an upward thrust on rates despite state approval and capacity to review. Indeed, carriers have little motive save cartel-like price objectives for engaging in the collective process. Collective conduct may reduce agency costs by reducing the number of filings to be reviewed and may reduce filing and review costs of participants, too, but only at the expense of alternative transaction costs: The processes for reaching agreement on price are not costless either for classic cartels or common carrier rate-making bureaus.

The *Southern Motor Carrier* norm, as contrasted with the compulsion norm of *Bates*, will increase counseling and litigation uncertainty. It moves the integrated federal-state economic system away from the competitive area where theory can be a guide to outcomes. There may be a new source of certainty of course—not economic analysis, but broad deference to state legislative responses, whether in the public interest or the interest of politically potent industries. *Cantor* reinvigorated the free market concept that once underlay substantive due process, not as a constitutional matter, but subject to the possibility of congressional deference to alternative federal or state approaches. *Southern Motor Carrier* firmly blocks that path; it takes the system to the point where states seem free to ignore the implication of federal competition policy, so long as they do so deliberately and keep an eye on outcomes.

14.6d2.   The Process Criterion of Midcal: Has The State Actively Supervised?

Midcal itself turned on California's lack of involvement, beyond indicating it did not want competitive market outcomes to control retail liquor prices. *Southern Motor Carriers* not only read *Midcal's* firm expression policy rather loosely, but it also left unquestioned immunity for a rate-making system over which state supervision might be a matter of opportunity, not actuality. Rates had to be filed but the state agency was under no compulsion to hold a hearing or even to review them actively. Unless it acted—and often it did not—the rate became effective.

Southern Motor Carriers, however, appears to have been a low point in this process of dilution, with reference to supervision, of the process criterion. Patrick v. Burget,[45] decided three years later, marks a limit. That case arose in an Oregon locality where most doctors that staffed the only hospital were associated in a group practice. Plaintiff, a surgeon, first a staff member of the hospital and an employee of the group, was invited to become a partner in that practice. He refused, left the group's employ and entered into competition with it. Group members thereafter refused to deal with him. Sometime later a member of the group initiated peer review proceedings to challenge plaintiff's hospital privilege. Plaintiff was awarded antitrust treble damages. The Ninth Circuit reversed, holding that an articulated state policy favoring peer review in Oregon hospitals was sufficient to shield plaintiff despite evidence that the peers used the review procedure in bad faith. The Supreme Court reversed. *Parker* applies, it ruled, only when anticompetitive acts are true products of state regulation. Here the "active supervision" prong of the "rigorous" *Midcal* procedural test is not met. In the Oregon system, the state does nothing to assure that the authorized anticompetitive acts advance the state's interest, not the interest of private actors.[46] Lacking any procedure for disinterested administrative review of self interested peer evaluations, the Oregon system gave no such assurance.

Patrick v. Burget is not facially inconsistent with *Southern Motor Carriers*. A significant, plainly influential and perhaps controlling distinction is that in the hospital privilege case all participants in the review were self-interested. In the carrier rate case, by contrast, the decision makers were state bureaucrats, who, however passively they might respond, had no interest of their own in the outcome. Nevertheless, the tone of the latter case—for instance, its insistence that *Midcal* creates a rigorous test—raises doubt that adequate supervision can now be as casual as *Southern Motor Carriers* seemed to imply it might be, even when no conflict of interest is entailed.

The Court's most recent active supervision decision is even harder to square with the permissive approach of Southern Motor Carriers. FTC v. Ticor Insurance Co.[47] held that title insurers violated Section 5 of the FTC Act when they concertedly fixed charges for title searches, a service not within the "business of insurance" and, thus, not protected by the *McCarran–Ferguson* antitrust exemption. The FTC had found insurers to have acted concertedly on these rates. While it granted *Parker* defenses to insurers in some states based on review of the rates by a state agency, it rejected that defense for insurers in four of the states involved because these states used a negative option system: charges filed became effective after a specified number of days unless the state objected. The court of appeals reversed, ruling that a state program that is staffed, funded and grants power to review sufficiently meets the

45. 486 U.S. 94, 108 S.Ct. 1658, 100 L.Ed.2d 83 (1988).

46. Id. at 101.

47. 504 U.S. 621, 112 S.Ct. 2169, 119 L.Ed.2d 410 (1992).

Midcal supervision requirement. The Supreme Court thought this court of appeals standard too permissive. Exploring the record itself, it concluded that in two of the four states, the evidence showed that state supervision was inadequate. The state agency, being staffed and funded, might be assumed to have reviewed the rates, found them appropriate and allowed them to become effective. But the detailed findings by the FTC "demonstrated that the potential for state supervision was not realized in fact * * *. [A]t most the rates were checked for mathematical accuracy. Some were unchecked altogether. * * *. [On one occasion] a filing became effective despite the failure of the rating bureau to provide additional requested information * * *. [On another] information was provided after a lapse of seven years, during which time the rate remained in effect. These findings * * * [show lack of] active supervision."[48]

Southern Motor Carriers and *Ticor Insurance* can be reconciled in the following manner. If there is a disinterested state agency with power, opportunity and resources to review state authorized private action to assure that the action serves state and not merely private interests, the state's supervisory involvement is presumptively adequate. But if the antitrust plaintiff adduces evidence to show that the state agency does not, in fact, exercise a disinterested review function, that presumption can be overcome.

In 2003, the Federal Trade Commission staff issued a report that found substantial problems with application of the state action doctrine.[49] One of the problems mentioned in the report is that some courts have rested a grant of state action immunity on broad statutory language conferring authority to act.[50] Followed blindly, this line of analysis could lead to the conclusion that any market foreclosure by a city is a foreseeable result of a city's broadly delegated authority. The report also expressed a concern that courts have ignored the purpose of the statute, focusing instead on whether it confers a general authority to act. For example, a deregulatory statute may leave some regulation in place while attempting to move a market toward a more competitive status, a purpose that is consistent with application of the antitrust laws.[51]

14.6e. Determining When Municipalities Can Shelter under *Parker*

Given that the *Boulder* case settled that municipalities, unlike states, cannot confer on other parties *Parker* protection for anticompetitive conduct,[52] after *Midcal* one might infer that a municipality itself, like a private party, could shelter under *Parker* only if it met both

---

48. Id. at 638.

49. Federal Trade Commission Staff, Report of the State Action Task Force (Sept. 2003), available at <http://www.ftc.gov /os/ 2003/09/stateactionreport.pdf>.

50. See, e.g., Independent Taxicab Drivers' Employees v. Greater Houston Transportation Co., 760 F.2d 607 (5th Cir. 1985).

51. See, e.g., California ex rel. Lockyer v. Dynegy, Inc., 375 F.3d 831, 852–53 (9th Cir. 2004).

52. See §§ 14.6d1 and 14.6d2.

Midcal tests—that is, only if the municipality acted with clear state authorization and adequate state supervision. Town of Hallie et al v. City of Eau Claire[53] relieves municipalities of some of the rigor in the first *Midcal* requirement and frees them entirely from the second. Eau Claire offered access to its sewage treatment facility to other municipalities only on condition that Eau Claire be hired to collect the refuse and deliver it to the facility. The Town of Hallie challenged this as monopolistic leveraging and illegal tying. The Court confirmed a state action defense for Eau Claire because the state had authorized cities to refuse to collect refuse beyond their borders without regard to any anticompetitive consequence this might have. In the context, this was a weak application of the "clear articulation" requirement of *Midcal*. The state did authorize a municipal choice whether to take on extra-municipal refuse duties, but did nothing to suggest indifference to, let alone authorization of, anticompetitive leveraging. When the challenged conduct is that of a municipality, the *Eau Claire* holding is an unqualified abandonment of the active state supervision prong of *Midcal*.

City of Columbia v. Omni Outdoor Advertising, Inc.[54] reinforces the conclusion that municipalities do have special status under *Parker* even if they do not have the same status as states. As the contrast between *Southern Motor Carriers* and *Patrick v. Burget* shows, conflict of interest is a significant concern in sorting out whether private action is adequately supervised. But *Omni* suggests that even grave risk of self-interested action by a municipality or those who act for it does not foreclose municipal capacity to escape antitrust liability by showing that the state gave it general authority to engage in the action being challenged. Columbia Outdoor, an outdoor billboard company, dominated that market in Columbia, South Carolina. The company also had close personal relations with city officials (to whom it donated political advertising space at election time). When Omni, a competitor, entered the market, the city enacted zoning ordinances protecting Columbia's near monopoly. Despite evidence of a conspiracy between municipal officials and Columbia Outdoor, all acting for self-interested motives, and in the face of a jury verdict for Omni on that evidence, the Supreme Court reversed. The state action defense precluded recovery. The general zoning statute gave the city authority to regulate—and thereby, to suppress—competition. That was sufficient state involvement to shield the municipal action, without regard either to the lack of state supervision or to whether the municipal decision was interested and conspiratorial (as the jury found) or a disinterested expression of a policy, which, one must assume, is all that the state authorized the municipality to exercise.

14.6f. Limiting Municipal Damages: The Local Government Antitrust Act

Although Congress has not directly interfered with the Supreme Court's line of cases applying *Parker v. Brown* to municipal action,

---

53. 471 U.S. 34, 105 S.Ct. 1713, 85 L.Ed.2d 24 (1985).

54. 499 U.S. 365, 111 S.Ct. 1344, 113 L.Ed.2d 382 (1991).

pressure from local governments produced legislation in 1984 that should sharply curtail damage recoveries in such cases. The Local Government Antitrust Act of 1984[55] eliminates damage recoveries (as well as costs or attorney's fees) under Section 4, 4A or 4C of the Clayton Act for local governments, officials or employees acting in "an official capacity."[56] This immunity extends to suits against any person for conduct "based on any official action directed by a local government, or official or employee thereof acting in an official capacity."[57] The Act leaves untouched the ability of a plaintiff (including private plaintiffs) to seek injunctive relief for antitrust violations involving local government.[58] Except that the Justice Department may no longer sue for damages to the business or property of the United States under Section 4A of the Clayton Act, the federal antitrust agencies retain their full panoply of civil and criminal remedies for antitrust violations.

The 1984 Act was Congress' response to cries from local government that the costs of defending an increasing number of treble damage suits were excessive and, even if local government should engage in unlawful conduct, local taxpayers should not be burdened with payment of treble damage judgments. But the impact of the 1984 Act remains unclear because of questions about the Act's coverage. For example, a corrupt conspiracy between a government official and a private firm to exclude the firm's rivals may enjoy no effective immunity. Under the 1984 Act, local government officials or employees are protected from damage suits only if they are "acting in an official capacity."[59] A person claiming exemption from damages because the person acted on the direction of local government would presumably lose protection if: (1) the local government's conduct were not "official action;" (2) if the local officials directing the conduct were not acting in "an official capacity"; or (3) the conduct was *permitted* but not *directed* by the local government.[60] The case law interpreting the 1984 Act is growing.[61]

14.6g. Antitrust and Classic Preemption

Given the *Parker* exemption, a judicial accretion upon the antitrust statutes, preemption analysis has a role in antitrust only when the claim of a state action exemption fails. Given the breadth of application of the

---

55. 15 U.S.C.A. A §§ 34–36.

56. Id.

57. 15 U.S.C.A. § 36.

58. A study in 2000 found that courts issued injunctions in only two of 116 cases involving application of the Local Government Antitrust Act. This suggests that courts have misinterpreted the Act to limit the availability of injunctive relief. E. T. Sullivan, *Antitrust Regulation of Land Use: Federalism's Triumph Over Competition, The Last Fifty Years*, 3 Wash. U. J. L. & Pol'y 473, 511 n. 196 (2000).

59. Id. *See*, H. Rep. No. 965, 98th Cong., 2d Sess. 20 (1984) (discussing the limits of "official conduct").

60. 15 U.S.C.A. § 35.

61. See e.g., Crosby v. Hospital Authority of Valdosta, 93 F.3d 1515 (11th Cir. 1996); Sandcrest Outpatient Services, PA. v. Cumberland County Hospital System, 853 F.2d 1139 (4th Cir.1988); Kane, McKenna & Assocs. v. Remcorp. Inc., 1988 WL 9108 (N.D.Ill.1988); Huron Valley Hospital, Inc. v. City of Pontiac, 612 F.Supp. 654 (1985); Miami International Realty v. Town of Mt. Crested Butte, 607 F.Supp. 448 (1985).

judge-made state action exemption, preemption issues have only a narrow field remaining. There are only three logically possible preemption situations. The first is where the state law flatly and directly collides with antitrust and is not protected by the *Parker* doctrine. The second is where the state policy does not, on its face, conflict with antitrust, but is anticompetitive to a degree arguably excessive of what federal antitrust policy can tolerate. The third is where the state law is more aggressively pro-competitive than is federal antitrust.

14.6g1. *Preemption Due to Direct Conflict*

In the first class of cases, there is a significant conflict between state policy and antitrust. In some instances, the state action exemption protects such state policy. But if the state policy is not executed by state officials or if the anticompetitive private action it authorizes does not meet the *Midcal* supervision test, the state action doctrine does not protect it. Therefore, if the state law must yield to federal antitrust, it must be on the basis of traditional, constitutionally based, preemption analysis. The classic case is Schwegmann Brothers v. Calvert Distillers.[62] Federal antitrust made resale price maintenance *per se* illegal, but excepted instances where a state statute authorized upstream and downstream firms to agree on resale prices. But the state statute in *Schwegmann* purported to make it lawful for an upstream firm to fix resale prices of all downstream firms, so long as one reseller agreed to such a contract. The federal law preempted this state statute which "demands private conduct the Sherman Act forbids."[63] *Midcal*[64] is to the same effect. The California statute obliged resale at prices set by upstream sellers (clearly a Sherman violation if there were not state involvement). The statute failed the test the Court articulated for the *Parker* exemption. Because the state statute purported to validate conduct that directly conflicted with Sherman (and was not protected by *Parker*), it was preempted.[65] Any state statute that demands private conduct unlawful under the antitrust laws will be preempted if there is insufficient state involvement to assure a *Parker* exemption pursuant to the *Midcal* test. Preemption analysis, although logically involved in cases like *Midcal,* is not always openly discussed. If there is direct collision between state law and antitrust and the *Parker* defense fails, the Court tends silently to assume preemption; it simply applies the antitrust rule without discussing the constitutional reason for doing so—federal supremacy leading to preemption of state law directly conflicting with valid federal law.

14.6g2. *Anticompetitive State Law Not in Direct Conflict*

In the second class of cases, state law authorizes or compels anticompetitive conduct that would not, on its face, be vulnerable under

62. 341 U.S. 384, 71 S.Ct. 745, 95 L.Ed. 1035 (1951).

63. Id. at 388.

64. California Retail Liquor Dealers Ass'n v. Midcal Aliminum, Inc., 445 U.S. 97, 106, 100 S.Ct. 937, 63 L.Ed.2d 233 (1980). *See also,* FTC v. Ticor Title Ins. Co., 504 U.S. 621, 112 S.Ct. 2169, 119 L.Ed.2d 410 (1992) where the same analysis governs.

65. See also, 324 Liquor Corp. v. Duffy, 479 U.S. 335, 107 S.Ct. 720, 93 L.Ed.2d 667 (1987).

Sherman. The preemption argument—that such conduct, being in conflict with federal competition policy should be displaced—now routinely fails. The Sherman Act is no greater protection against state anticompetitive legislation than is substantive due process. Rice v. Norman Williams Co.[66] is suggestive. The state statute authorized liquor manufacturers to stifle intrabrand competition in the state by permitting some wholesalers but not others to import the manufacturer's brands. When the statute was challenged as inconsistent with the competition policy embodied in the Sherman Act, the Court rejected the contention not because the anticompetitive effect of the statute was minimal. It ruled that a state statute is not preempted "simply because * * * [it] may have an anticompetitive effect."[67] The Court explained that preemption occurs only when the state law, without supervision in the interest of achieving state policy, either "mandates or authorizes conduct that necessarily constitutes a violation of the antitrust laws in all cases, or * * * places irresistible pressure on a private party to violate the antitrust laws."[68] Fisher v. Berkeley[69] makes the same points. However much a rent control ordinance (authorized under state law) interferes with competition, it cannot be challenged on antitrust grounds because it does not directly conflict with Sherman. It is not a conspiracy by renters or by their legislators nor is it a monopoly; it is an ordinance. Thus for the reasons announced in *Rice v. Norman Williams*, it is not preempted.

14.6g3.   Non–Preemption of Procompetitive State Law

Preemption claims on the ground that state law goes further than federal in protecting competition also routinely fail. Exxon Corp. v. Governor of Maryland[70] is an example. On the basis of judgments about what is necessary to protect competition against leverage, federal monopoly and merger law places some constraints on vertical integration and on market conduct by some vertically integrated firms. The Maryland statute involved in *Exxon* forbade refiners to integrate vertically at all, thus totally inhibiting their engaging in retail competition. Refusing to construe the lines drawn by the federal law as implying a Congressional intent to encourage or at least positively authorize integration not constrained, the Court rejected a preemption challenge. California v. ARC America Corp.[71] also signifies the extent to which state antitrust can extend beyond federal law without triggering preemption. Federal antitrust confines treble damage awards to first purchasers from the violating monopolist or cartelists. Violators may not defend against first purchasers by showing that the plaintiff passed on the overcharge to its customers and that its recovery would be a windfall.[72] Buyers further

66. 458 U.S. 654, 102 S.Ct. 3294, 73 L.Ed.2d 1042 (1982).

67. Id. at 659.

68. Id. at 661.

69. 475 U.S. 260, 106 S.Ct. 1045, 89 L.Ed.2d 206 (1986).

70. 437 U.S. 117, 98 S.Ct. 2207, 57 L.Ed.2d 91, *reh'g denied*, 439 U.S. 884, 99 S.Ct. 232, 58 L.Ed.2d 200 (1978).

71. 490 U.S. 93, 109 S.Ct. 1661, 104 L.Ed.2d 86 (1989).

72. Hanover Shoe, Inc. v. United Shoe Machinery Corp., 392 U.S. 481, 88 S.Ct.

downstream may not recover from the violators by showing that the overcharge was passed on to them.[73] The Court thought tracing the overcharge too complex a judicial task and outcomes too uncertain; thus, maximum deterrence would be achieved by confirming to each first purchaser the right to recover the full overcharge, despite possible windfalls.[74] This result was controversial.[75] A number of states responded to *Illinois Brick* by enacting statutes to confer upon downstream purchasers a state cause of action for treble damages. In *ARC America*, the Court upheld these statutes against a preemption challenge, even though doing so subjected defendants to the risk of suffering duplicative treble damage awards for all overcharge. They could be liable under federal law to first purchasers for three times any overcharge; additionally, under state law, they could be liable to downstream purchasers, to whom first purchasers had passed on all or part of the overcharge, for three times the passed-on overcharge. If one concedes that overdeterrence can hurt competition by inhibiting aggressive but lawful competitive conduct, the potential for these state laws to interfere with federal interest in competition is manifest. Yet, they are not preempted.[76]

§ 14.7 Tripartite Competition Policy: Antitrust, Regulation and Deregulation in Concert

One theme of this chapter is that the policy underlying some regulation and most deregulation is, like the predominant antitrust policy, to improve performance by moving both structure and conduct closer to the competitive ideal. Antitrust can be potentially available whenever structure or conduct varies significantly from the competitive norm. Rate of return regulation is often invoked in the presence (real or assumed) of natural monopoly; when it is used, subject to the possibility that exemption might be inferred from the regulatory scheme, antitrust will fill interstices and reinforce the regulatory goal. Deregulation (and sometimes reregulation) is an appropriate response to dynamism; when a natural monopoly is eroding, termination or modification of regulation may improve performance. Change of this kind will enlarge the realm of antitrust. At decision points—whether to regulate and in what manner, whether to extend an antitrust exemption, whether and to what extent to deregulate—judgment calls must be made, initially by legislatures and also by regulators, antitrust enforcers and courts. Sometimes these decisions are well made and yield good results, but not always. This section summarizes major developments in the application of tripartite

2224, 20 L.Ed.2d 1231 (1968); addressed in § 17.2c.

73. Illinois Brick Co. v. Illinois, 431 U.S. 720, 97 S.Ct. 2061, 52 L.Ed.2d 707 (1977).

74. Id. at 730.

75. § 17.2c3.

76. The EU response makes interesting contrast. Member state antitrust law may not directly conflict with community law. If a state and the community both proceed against the same conduct each may proceed unless conflict appears. However, if both challenge the same conduct, the second to do so must take into account the sanction imposed by the other when fixing its remedy. Case 14/68, Wilhelm v. Bundeskartellamt, [1969] ECR I, [1969] CMLR 100.

competition policy to telecommunications and to transportation industries (with a particular focus on ocean shipping).

14.7a. The Interplay of Regulation, Deregulation and Antitrust in Telecommunications

14.7a1. *The 1949 Antitrust Case*

The early history of telephone begins before antitrust and extends into the early post Sherman years, an era when cartels were challenged but integrations leading to power were often tolerated. Telephone is a paradigm network industry. It quickly displayed horizontal power, vertical integration and single firm dominance.[1] The Bell patent dates to 1876. AT & T, which held it, had constructed local loops in major cities by 1880 and soon linked them to establish long distance service. In 1881, it acquired Western Electric, which served thereafter as its exclusive equipment supplier. By the end of 1890s, AT & T had built or acquired loops in most cities nationwide. It also acquired Western Union, a telegram monopolist. In 1913, in response to an antitrust threat, it divested Western Union and stopped acquiring local phone companies. In these years, hardwired local loops were natural monopolies and hardwired long lines likely were natural monopolies. Yet, the manufacture of telephone equipment, which AT & T had linked vertically with its local loop and long line monopolies, could have been a rivalrous market, although scale economies might have limited entry for the manufacturer of switching and some other equipment.

In 1949, the Justice Department brought an antitrust action seeking divestiture of Western Electric.[2] The government relied on leveraging theory developed in *Griffith*[3] and the essential facilities concept implicit in cases like *Terminal Railroad*[4] and *Associated Press*.[5] AT & T's case against divestiture was straightforward: true, AT & T is not faced with rivalry as a telephone carrier because its markets are natural monopolies. Scale economies limit entry; there are no artificial barriers. But, AT & T's intrastate rates and services are effectively regulated on a cost of service basis by state PUCs and its interstate rates and services are effectively regulated by the FCC. These agencies are alert to preclude cross-subsidy or self-preference between the equipment and the telephone service market, and the presence of such comprehensive state and federal regulation results in a regulatory exemption. Antitrust interven-

§ 14.7

1. See, W.G. Shepherd, *Long Distance Telephone Service: Dominance in Decline?* in L. DUETSCH, INDUSTRY STUDIES at 342–363 (1993) and Rosenblum, *The Antitrust Rationale for the MFJ's Line of Business Restrictions and a Policy Proposal For Revising Them*, 25 Sw. L. REV. 605 (1996).

2. United States v. Western Elec. Co., 1956 Trade Cas (CCH) ¶ 68,246 (D.N.J. Jan. 24, 1956).

3. *See e.g.*, United States v. Griffith, 334 U.S. 100, 68 S.Ct. 941, 92 L.Ed. 1236 (1948).

4. United States v. Terminal Railroad Ass'n of St. Louis, 224 U.S. 383, 32 S.Ct. 507, 56 L.Ed. 810 (1912).

5. Associated Press v. United States, 326 U.S. 1, 65 S.Ct. 1416, 89 L.Ed. 2013 (1945). *See also* Otter Tail Power Co. v. United States, 410 U.S. 366, 93 S.Ct. 1022, 35 L.Ed.2d 359 (1973).

tion would be not just superfluous but disruptive. The real test of the public interest is service quality and consumer satisfaction. The U.S. has both the best and the least expensive phone service in the world.

At this 1949–1956 stage of antitrust development, the government case seemed potent, although not without risk given the 1952 holding in *Far East Conference*[6] and the later 1960s–1970s holdings in *Pan Am*[7] and *Hughes Tool*,[8] which might have been read to support the broad regulatory exemption for which AT & T argued. AT & T, facing a major antitrust challenge, lobbied effectively with the Commerce Department, the Department of Defense, and significant governmental consumers of communications. Having induced key agencies to support its view, AT & T succeeded in settling the case in 1956 on the basis of a consent decree that, by excluding AT & T from unregulated areas, limited some of AT & T's collateral activities while leaving its vertically integrated structure intact.[9] AT & T's claim that all risk of cross-subsidy and self-preference between equipment and telephone service can be handled by regulators was accepted as a basis for this limited decree.

14.7a2. The 1974 Case and the Modified Final Judgment

Long line telephone service was clearly a monopoly at the time of the 1949 suit and its 1956 settlement. Whether or not it was still a natural monopoly is debatable. If it was, that condition unquestionably ended soon thereafter when microwave technology began to replace hardwired intercity connections. MCI, using microwave, began offering lower cost long line service to some customers. AT & T vigorously resisted accommodating MCI connections with its system. There was also growing market pressure on AT & T rules about equipment. The company offered packages of service with Western Electric equipment provided on a rental basis. Claiming the need to assure quality of service and the integrity of its network, AT & T also banned interconnection of equipment owned by customers but manufactured by someone other than Western Electric.

The FCC, the federal regulator (perhaps mindful of the 1956 decree), decided to facilitate competitive developments and took regulatory steps against AT & T efforts to inhibit entry.[10] Nevertheless, aware of the limits of and the costs and delays associated with regulatory responses to cross-subsidy and self-preference, and in light of the dramatic technological possibilities associated with microwave, the Department of Justice brought another antitrust action in 1974 which was finally terminated by consent to a modified final judgment (MFJ) amending the

---

6. Far East Conference v. United States, 342 U.S. 570, 72 S.Ct. 492, 96 L.Ed. 576 (1952).

7. Pan American World Airways, Inc. v. United States, 371 U.S. 296, 83 S.Ct. 476, 9 L.Ed.2d 325 (1963).

8. Hughes Tool Co. v. Trans World Airlines, Inc., 409 U.S. 363, 93 S.Ct. 647, 34 L.Ed.2d 577 (1973).

9. United States v. Western Elec. Co., supra note 2.

10. *E.g.* Carterphone, 13 F.C.C.2d 420 (1968); *MCI*, 18 F.C.C.2d 953 (1969). See also Carter v. AT & T, 250 F.Supp. 188 (N.D. Texas 1966), *aff'd*, 365 F.2d 486 (5th Cir.1966).

1956 consent decree issued in the 1949 case.[11] The 1974 complaint alleged that combining the potentially competitive long distance service with local exchange natural monopolies encouraged cross-subsidy, self-preference and the use of local power to foreclose long distance competition. Although the Justice Department vacillated to some extent about what remedy it wanted, it ultimately pressed for divestiture of the local service monopolies, structural relief that would end the incentive and opportunity to cross-subsidize or self-prefer between local and long distance service and would reduce the risk and opportunity for such leverage between telephone service and equipment.[12]

AT & T defended against this suit much as it had against the earlier one. But this time its contention that pervasive regulation gained it antitrust immunity was twice rejected in the district court.[13] The company also petitioned the executive branch, as it had successfully done in the 1950s, and, in addition, aggressively lobbied for Congressional intervention.[14] In Congress, lobbying efforts were almost successful. In the end, that they were not is attributed in significant degree to William Baxter, then head of the Antitrust Division, Judge Harold Greene, to whom the pending case was assigned, and AT & T Chairman Harold Brown.[15] Due to the determination of Baxter and to the vigilance of Judge Greene and his no-nonsense style of courtroom administration, extensive discovery was completed in orderly fashion and the case went to hearing on the merits.

In support of its prayer for structural relief, the government presented evidence of (1) monopoly power in local service, long distance and equipment markets; (2) exclusionary interference by AT & T with interconnection between competitive long distance services and its monopoly local subsidiaries; (3) exclusion from local service markets of competitive equipment manufacturers; and (4) exclusionary intercity pricing without relation to cost by which AT & T set supracompetitive rates for services facing no competition and discriminatorily low rates for certain long distance services for which some competition was available. To blunt AT & T's defense that regulatory intervention yielded antitrust immunity (or, at a minimum, precluded the need for structural relief),

---

11. United States v. AT & T, 427 F.Supp. 57 (D.D.C. 1976), (hereinafter "AT & T"). *See also*, United States v. AT & T, 552 F.Supp. 131 (D.D.C.1982), *aff'd sub nom.* Maryland v. United States, 460 U.S. 1001, 103 S.Ct. 1240, 75 L.Ed.2d 472 (1983).

12. Leverage between local service and equipment would be ended but, unless manufacturing were also separated from long lines, leverage between long lines and manufacturing might remain possible until AT & T's long distance power eroded.

13. *AT & T*, 427 F.Supp. at 61, *cert. denied*, 429 U.S. 1071, 97 S.Ct. 824, 50 L.Ed.2d 799 (1977), and *United States v. AT & T*, 461 F.Supp. 1314, 1320–30 (D.D.C. 1978).

14. *See* P. Temin, The Fall of the Bell System (1987); (hereinafter Tamin); F.W. Henck and B. Strassburg, Slippery Slope: The Long Road to the Breakup of AT & T (1988) (hereinafter Henck & Strassburg); R. Noll & B. Owen, *The Anticompetitive Use of Regulation*: United States v. AT & T in the Antitrust Revolution 290 (J. Kwoka & L. White, eds., 1989).

15. The story of the political machinations at this stage is instructive about the relationships between antitrust enforcement, competitive values, the law and politics. Temin, at 217–235.

the Government also presented evidence that the local network is so complex, technologically dynamic and replete with costs shared jointly with long distance that it is impossible for regulators to control effectively against inefficient cross-subsidy and self-preference. After Judge Greene denied AT & T's motion for summary judgment,[16] the courtroom battle soon ended. The parties negotiated a structural consent decree and presented it to the court as a modification of the 1956 decree. With certain modifications upon which Judge Greene conditioned his Tunney Act approval, the negotiated settlement became the modified final judgment (MFJ) that controlled the industry from 1982 until 1996[17] when the Telecommunications Act of 1996 became law.[18]

The MFJ ordered AT & T to spin off or divest itself of its local exchange (LX) monopolies, the Bell operating companies (BOCs). Also, in order to end any future incentive for them to self-prefer or cross-subsidize, they were enjoined from entering long distance, manufacturing and certain other fields vertically related to the local network. In their local service business, the BOCs remained subject to state regulation. AT & T would retain the long distance or interexchange (IX) business where it was facing competition from MCI and Sprint. AT & T would also retain Western Electric, the manufacturing arm. The BOCs would be free to buy AT & T equipment but not to discriminate in favor of any manufacturer. They were also obliged to provide links to their local network to all long distance carriers on nondiscriminatory terms for access charges subject to FCC control. The decree was expected not to end the BOC's LX power but to end any incentive to use LX power to self-prefer or to prefer AT & T or any other firm in either IX, manufacturing or other markets. It was recognized that AT & T as an IX carrier would still have an incentive to prefer Western Electric, but it was expected that separating the BOCs from Western Electric would encourage more vigorous competition in manufacturing, and that AT & T, now facing increasingly vigorous IX competition, would be forced by that competition to cut its equipment costs. It would thus have an incentive to turn away from Western Electric when alternative suppliers could offer better or cheaper equipment.

14.7a3.   *The Effects of the MFJ: Long Distance and Manufacturing*

Until legislatively terminated in 1996, the impact of the decree on the IX and manufacturing markets was dramatic. It is no exaggeration to acknowledge the AT & T decree as the most impressive success story of the Sherman Act. Before the MFJ, AT & T stood virtually alone in the IX market. The shares of MCI and Sprint remained from trivial to modest even after FCC efforts to facilitate their entry. By 1983, AT &

16. United States v. AT & T, 524 F.Supp. 1336 (D.D.C. 1981).

17. United States v. AT & T, 552 F.Supp. 131 (D.D.C.1982), *aff'd* sub nom. Maryland v. United States, 460 U.S. 1001, 103 S.Ct. 1240, 75 L.Ed.2d 472 (1983). *See*

also, United States v. Western Electric Co., 673 F.Supp. 525 (D.D.C.1987) which provides a summary of the judicial events leading to the 1982 decree.

18. Pub. L. No. 104, 110 Stat. 56 (1996).

T's percentage of revenues had dropped but still was in the mid 80s. Between 1984 and 1993 AT & T's share fell about 20 percent more. During that period MCI and Sprint both grew rapidly, reaching about 12 percent and 8.5 percent respectively by 1993. There was also significant entry by other facility-based carriers, both national and regional, and entry by numerous resellers who brought back to the market those parts of the increasing fiber capacity not used by customers of facility-based firms.

The competitive contest continued apace. As of August, 1997 AT & T had 47.9 percent of the IX market, MCI had 20 percent, Sprint had 9.7 percent, WorldCom had 5.5 percent, Frontier and Ecel (with Telco, which Ecel is acquiring) each had 1.9 percent.[19] Part of this 86.9 percent, and almost all of the remaining 13 percent of IX—a total of about 17 percent—is carried on the lines leased by facility-based carriers to resellers. Demand characteristics have added to competitive pressure. Business customers, sensitive to quality and price differences and facing no significant switching costs, shopped aggressively, often using knowledgeable brokers and dealing with more than one provider to monitor outcome. The result was increasingly competitive performance. By the time of the passage of the Telecommunications Act of 1996, AT & T's share of LX was between 50 and 60 percent. There was aggressive price cutting in all submarkets and switching by consumers among carriers was rampant. There has also been persistent, rapid technological development, particularly for enhancing the amount of traffic accommodated on a line. New services have been rapidly developed, competitively priced, and rapidly deployed. Marketplace conduct reflected all of this. Participating firms invest for growth and rapidly develop and expand new services. Prices dropped substantially, and new products and reduced prices were promoted prominently.[20] As competitive conditions developed, the FCC responded. It attempted (ultimately unsuccessfully) to free IX carriers other than AT & T from rate regulation and subjected AT & T only to price cap regulation, thus giving the market considerable discretion about how prices were structured.[21]

Post-decree competitive developments in manufacturing were similar, although not as dramatic. There are four major markets: customer

---

19. S. Schiesel, *Watch 800 Companies Stuff Themselves Into One Phone Booth: In the Long–Distance Market, Lean and Mean Just Gets the Door Open*, NY Times, August 4, 1997. The data on shares reported in the article came from the FCC.

20. For a more comprehensive review of these developments see L. Sullivan, *Elusive Goals Under the Telecommunications Act: Preserving Long Distance Competition Upon Baby Bell Entry and Attaining Local Exchange Competition: We'll Not Preserve the One Unless We Attain the Other*, 25 Sw U. L. Rev. 487, 494–509 (1996) [hereinafter "*Elusive Goals*"].

21. The FCC sought to modify its rules in response to changes in the industry resulting from the decree. It classified carriers in terms of market power, subjecting firms with power to full regulation and subjecting firms without power to no regulation or limited non-intensive regulation. Ultimately, the Supreme Court found these changes unauthorized by the statute. *MCI Telecommunications Corp. v. AT & T*, 510 U.S. 1107, 114 S.Ct. 1045, 127 L.Ed.2d 369 (1994). This history is traced in greater detail in D. Brenner, Law and Regulation of Consumer Carriers in the Communication Industry, ch.5 (2d ed. 1996) (hereinafter "Brenner").

premises equipment (CPE), transmission equipment, central office equipment, and cellular systems equipment. There are narrower submarkets for particular products and groups within each market. In each of these markets and submarkets, concentration has fallen significantly. Before the decree, AT & T domination of equipment sales in America was intact and, though innovation occurred, commercialization of developments was slow. This, too, changed after the MFJ. Before long most CPE submarkets (call processors, key systems, handsets, voice messaging, fax machines, answering machines, etc.) approached the classic competitive model. The market for transmission equipment was occupied by numerous suppliers, most of them large and technologically advanced; AT & T had about 38 percent, Alcotel, Northern Telecom., Siecar and NEC aggregate about 22 percent and about twenty other firms, including Motorola, Hughes, Fujitsu and General Cable, held the balance. Often, markets were competitive or rivalrous oligopolies. The market for much central office equipment also became competitive under the decree. In the most concentrated equipment market—central office switches, where scale economies in software development were high—concentration reduced notably. AT & T held about 80 percent from 1973 to 1980. By 1993, its share was below 50 percent. By the early to mid 1990s, the cellular systems market, which had grown rapidly since the decree, was also rivalrous. AT & T had about 31 percent, Ericsson about 24 percent, Motorola over 16 percent and Northern Telecom over 10 percent. Postdecree performance improved impressively, too. Equipment market prices fell, and markets became more dynamic.[22]

In sum, the MFJ removed most of the local exchange's power to cross-subsidize and self-prefer in both the interexchange and manufacturing markets. In consequence, single firm dominance of these markets erroded and effectively rivalrous conditions and performance emerged. All of this was directly attributable to the MFJ, an antitrust consent decree.

14.7a4. Developments in Local Exchange Markets Under the MFJ

The MFJ was not intended to and did not improve local exchange (LX) markets, which were assumed to remain natural monopolies in which good performance could be achieved only by regulation. But even natural monopolies need not last forever. As other aspects of telecommunications became rivalrous and dynamic, change became evident in LX markets, too. Although technological, economic and regulatory barriers remained high until the Telecommunication Act of 1996, there were three areas of dynamic development which implied the potential for weakening the hegemony of Bell operating companies (BOCs) and other LX incumbents. First, competitive access providers (CAPs) began to run fiber lines through high density business areas of cities to provide to

22. *See,* Chap. J, § I–1, Economic Overlook and Industry Overview (1993/1994), NATA Telecommunication Market Review & Forecast; The Post–Divestiture US Telecommunication Equipment Manufacturing Market: the Benefits of Competition (collaboration study by IDCMA, NATA, and Telecommunication Industry Ass'n) (1990).

large business users alternatives competitive with BOCs for access from the customer's premises to its interexchange (IX) carrier. This mode of entry was feasible at least in part because (even after the break up of AT & T) a long distance subsidy to local service continued in the form of charges in excess of costs, which the FCC authorized the LX carrier to exact from IX carriers to gain access to their customers through the local loop.[23] These services grew and some CAPs began providing other wireline services. The more effective of them, although limiting activities to dense business areas, sought interconnection with local exchange carriers (LECs) and began to style themselves competitive local exchange carriers (CLECs). By the end of 1995, these services had reduced IX dependence on the LX monopolist only minimally. All residential users and most business users remained entirely dependent on their regulated LX carrier. LX monopolists earned roughly 95 percent of non-switched revenues and an even larger share of switched revenues from access services, and virtually all other services, including the needed local termination service on IX calls, remained monopolized.[24] Second, beginning before the decree and accelerating in post-decree years, American homes were being wired for cable. Although American cable systems (unlike some in Europe) were non-switched, one directional, tree and branch configurations that could not support two-way communications, it appeared possible to convert them for two-way communication and some companies began to experiment to test technological and economic feasibility.[25] Third, in the years after the MFJ, cellular service came into its own and burgeoned as a higher cost, lower quality compliment to fiber line telephone that made it possible to link into LX and IX networks when on the move. As prices began to fall and service improve, and as new, low power digital transceivers providing mobile service over small areas—the so-called personal communication services (PCS)—were developed and licenses auctioned, the possibility that cellular connections might ultimately be used to provide competitive alternatives to the hardwired LX local loop came fully into view.[26]

By the end of 1995, all of these possible alternatives remained just that. Save for the extremely limited IX access service achieved through CAPs, none had as yet been shown to be either a technologically or economically feasible LX substitute that could meet the price and quality standards achieved through the regulated local monopolies. Moreover, although some state PUCs were interested in facilitating competitive LX service to the extent possible,[27] state regulatory barriers to LX competition were high and largely intact, and the LX monopolists—traditionally,

---

23. For a fuller discussion see BRENNER, supra note 21, Ch. 9.

24. *Elusive Goals,* supra note 20 at 501–503.

25. Id. at 504–05; For a discussion of technological possibilities and problems see Botein, *Cable/Telco Mergers and Acquisitions: An Antitrust Analysis,* 25 Sw U. L. REV. 569 at 577–591.

26. *Elusive Goals,* supra note 20, at 506–507.

27. In the Matter of Alternative Regulatory Frameworks For Local Exchange Carriers, 51 CPUC 2d 32 (1993) (Decision 93–09–076 which was designed to facilitate local telephone exchange competition).

very effective lobbyists in state capitols where they presented themselves as the "home team" in the telephone wars—displayed little readiness to see them dismantled.[28]

14.7a5.   The Telecommunications Act of 1996

The Telecommunications Act of 1996 emerged out of the context described above. Arguing that their local monopolies were eroding and would soon be gone, the BOCs had for years attempted (unsuccessfully except for small adjustments), to persuade the decree court to modify the MFJ to allow their entry into IX and manufacturing. The decree court was responsive to the position of the Justice Department and the IX carriers: the time for the BOCS to enter IX is after their LX monopolies erode, not before. Uncertain predictions that local monopolies will disappear overtime were insufficient. While the BOCs pursued their efforts in the decree court, they also carried their case to Congress. In 1994 and 1995 when Congress considered omnibus telecommunications legislation, lobbying from all quarters was intense. The act that became law in early 1996[29] was intended to open local and long distance markets, facilitate video service by telephone companies and telephone service by cable companies, reduce constraints on media concentration and impose time limits on cable rate regulations.

The provisions concerning LX and IX entry can be summarized briefly. The MFJ is displaced.[30] Every telecommunications carrier is now obliged to interconnect with other carriers[31] and not to initiate network features, functions or capabilities that frustrate interconnection.[32] All LX carriers are obligated, in addition, not to prohibit or inhibit resale of their services by others who acquire them;[33] to provide number portability when subscribers switch;[34] to assure dealing parity to interconnection;[35] to provide right of way access to competitors;[36] and to establish reciprocal compensation arrangements for origination and termination of calls.[37] Incumbent LX carriers—the LX monopolists entrenched in local markets at the time the law was enacted—have these additional duties: to negotiate in good faith agreements to fulfill their duties to resell and to provide portability, parity, rights of way; to meet the interconnections obligation by providing access to its local network for transmission, routing and access at any technically feasible point that is at least equal in quality to that it provides to itself; to unbundle its services and provide non-discriminatory access to all network elements; and to resell at wholesale rates any service it provides at resale.[38] The Act establishes

---

28.   Chen, *The Legal Process and Political Economy of Telecommunications Reform,* 97 COLUM. L. REV. 835, 867–69 (1997).

29.   Pub L. No. 104, 110 Stat. 56 was signed by the President, February 8, 1996.

30.   Id. § 601.

31.   Id. § 101(a), adding 47 U.S.C.A. § 251(a)(1).

32.   Id. § 251(a)(2).

33.   Id. § 251(b)(1).

34.   Id. § 251(b)(2).

35.   Id. § 251(b)(3).

36.   Id. § 251(b)(4).

37.   Id. § 251(b)(5).

38.   Id. § 251(c)(1) through (4).

procedure for approval of the agreements mandated,[39] calls for FCC regulations, presupposes supportive involvement by both the FCC and state PUCs,[40] and also assures that the new federal law preempts conflicting state law or policy.[41]

The 1996 Act also provides that a BOC, through a separate affiliate,[42] may gain access to the IX market, even where it is the incumbent LX carrier, if it unbundles its services and opens its network subject to several conditions. It must provide access and interconnection to one or more competing local carriers or stand ready to do so.[43] It must meet the requirements of a competitive checklist: (1) unbundling of loop, transmissions, switching and transport elements of the network,[44] and (2) providing non-discriminatory access for competitors to poles, ducts, conduits, rights of way, directory assistance, operator and 911 services, white pages, data pages, and signaling,[45] all at wholesale prices reasonably related to cost.[46] In addition, after consulting with the Justice Department, the FCC must determine that allowing the BOCs to enter long distance would be in the public interest.[47]

Effectiveness of both the local access and long distance access provisions will depend on how they are interpreted and administered. The tone of the published FCC regulations indicate that this agency wants to do what can be done to make local competition work under the new framework. The Supreme Court has clarified the broad scope of the Commission's authority under the regulations and, while requiring some changes, has upheld existing regulations in material respects and has left ample room for effective, pro-competitive requirements.[48] In consequence, BOC long distance entry should be conditioned on complete, effective unbundling with open, prompt, timely and cost based access. If all this occurs, IX carriers, CLECs (the post 1996 Act designation for CAPs), PCP carriers and (if current efforts of AT & T to gain local access through mergers and ventures with cable companies are technologically and financially successful) cable companies and others will enter local markets, partly with their new facilities, partly with upgraded cable capable of providing interactive broadband voice, data and video service, and partly by reselling unbundled LX services. There will be opportunity for market tests to determine whether entrants will be able to economically replace parts of the local loop with their own substitute facilities in order to reduce the supracompetitive access charges they pay to LX

---

39. Id. § 252.

40. Id.   § 253(b),   (c);   § 261(a)-(c); §§ 160–161.

41. Id. § 253(a), (d). The extent of the preemptive effect of this provision as well as of a Section of the Cable Act (47 U.S.C.A. § 556(c)) which also contains preemptive language may be resolved in AT & T v. City of Portland, 43 F.Supp.2d 1146 (D. Ore. 1999), appeal pending in the Ninth Circuit.

42. Id. § 271(e)

43. Id. § 251.

44. Id. § 271.

45. Id.

46. Id. § 252(d).

47. Id. §§ 251(c)(1)-(4).

48. AT & T v. Iowa Utilities Board, 525 U.S. 366, 119 S.Ct. 721, 142 L.Ed.2d 835 (1999). See also SBC Communications Inc. v. FCC, 138 F.3d 410 (D.C. Cir. 1998) (rejecting permissive state agency and accepting strict FCC construction of the requirements of § 271, supra, n. 44).

carriers. It may be that one or more entrants will be able to use digital cellular (PCS) for local connection while relying on the BOC for switching or other services. It may be that one or more entrants—i.e. IX carriers—will be able to do their own switching while using the local loop to initiate and terminate calls. It may be that cable companies interlinked with IX carriers will find a mix which maximizes their potential, perhaps by emphasizing the speed potential of cable modems for Internet browsing. The types of strategies being used to enter the LX market vary. Many entrants may rely in part on resale of significant parts of incumbent LEC local loop and switching facilities. Except to say that each of them hopes to offer one stop integrated, LX–IX–Internet voice and data service, partly on their own and partly on leased facilities, the strategies of major long distance carriers as well as of CLECs for getting into local markets are still being in fkux.

A new contentious issue has arisen. In the process of upgrading cable lines to provide high speed Internet access (vastly faster than dial-up modems available over copper phone lines) AT & T and other cable companies have limited direct connection to their cable modem platforms to affiliated Internet service providers (ISP's) such as @Home. America On Line (before seeking cable modem access control through merger) as well as other unintegrated ISPs (relying on slower LX ISDN lines for connecting customers to the Internet) and some municipalities have proposed (or are considering) cable ordinances requiring that unaffiliated ISPs be allowed access to high speed cable connections. Unaffiliated ISPs argue that high speed cable modem platforms are an essential facility and that to allow cable companies to limit access to affiliates would undermine ISP competition. AT & T and other cable companies, stressing that massive investments must be made in order to upgrade cable lines, contend that compulsory interconnection would discourage such investment. They also assert that there is nothing essential about direct connection to cable modem platforms. In addition to ISDN lines local telephone companies (and others) can now provide DSL connections, comparable in speed to those available through cable. ISPs can also connect through telephone, regular or cellular, and will likely soon have a high speed fixed radio option.[49]

14.7b. Transportation Industries and Common Carriage

Transportation industries, like telecommunications, have been subject to varying federal regulatory regimes. Railroads were the first industry to be subject to pervasive federal regulation in 1887.[50] Federal statutes regulating ocean shipping (1916),[51] truck transportation (1935),[52]

49. *See* AT & T Corp. v. City of Portland, 43 F.Supp. 2d 1146 (D.Or. 1999), reversed, 216 F.3d 871 (9th Cir. 2000).

50. The Interstate Commerce Act of 1887 created a regulatory commission charged with investigating and maintaining access to railroads and the reasonableness of railroad rates.

51. The Shipping Act of 1916.

52. Motor Carrier Act of 1935.

and airlines (1938),[53] were to follow. To varying degrees and using differing methods, all of these regulatory regimes were charged with protecting the common law principle of common carriage. At common law, a common carrier was one whose services were open to all in a nondiscriminatory fashion. Like innkeepers obliged to provide room and board to travelers, providers of transportation services were seen as public servants obliged to take all comers, subject only to carriage availability and to payment of reasonable, nondiscriminatory charges.[54] The duties of a common carrier stand in contrast to the freedom of contract enjoyed by other businesses.

In a well functioning competitive market, universal and nondiscriminatory access are by-products of competition. Numerous firms compete to win business by striving for all available customers at a nondiscriminatory rate that competition pushes down toward the industry's marginal cost. No regulation (other than perhaps occasional antitrust intervention to maintain competitive structure and conduct) is necessary. As an alternative to antitrust (but in large part to address the same policy concerns), Congress chose regulation for many forms of transportation of people and goods. Some transportation providers may experience high scale economies. Many may experience high fixed costs and relatively low variable costs. This invites discrimination. A ship, train, or plane that is nearly empty costs almost as much to run as one that is full. This creates a substantial incentive for any carrier to fill its vehicle, even if it must discount rates to do so. Large shippers that could fill a substantial portion of the carrier's capacity on a regular basis are highly sought customers. To win them, many carriers provide heavily discounted and discriminatory rates. If overcapacity is general and ongoing, high fixed and low variable costs can also generate what some call "cut-throat" competition, with prices above variable but below full costs.

Price discrimination in transportation rates can be a market power abuse. As the above discussion indicates, power may rest with large shippers who exploit the carrier's high fixed costs, to the detriment of smaller or less knowledgeable shippers who do not receive discounted rates. In a classic nineteenth century demonstration of this power, the Standard Oil Company was able to negotiate favorable railroad rates for itself (and discriminatorily high rates for its competitors, including a drawback paid to the railroad and turned over to Standard Oil). The result was a monopoly for the Standard Oil trust and cartel profits for the railroads. One view of this arrangement is that it was sought and maintained by the rail carriers, who used Standard Oil as a cartel enforcer.[55] Whatever the original motive may have been, Nelson Rockefeller used the arrangement to create an oil industry juggernaut that was

53. Civil Aeronautics Act of 1938.

54. *See* Holmes, *Common Carriers and the Common Law,* 13 Am. L. Rev. 611 (1879).

55. Granitz & Klein, *Monopolization By "Raising Rivals Costs": The Standard Oil Case,* 39 J.L. & Econ. 1 (1996)

to become the subject of the most important monopolization case brought during the first 80 years of the Sherman Act.[56]

Price discrimination of the type practiced by Standard Oil and the railroads was a major impetus for transportation regulation designed to guarantee common carriage—equal access for all users, large or small. In economic terms, true discrimination occurs only through the exercise of market power. If a shipper is able to negotiate a lower rate simply because it is a high volume user that generates lower per unit costs to the carrier, no true discrimination occurs. If, on the other hand, a large shipper is able to negotiate rates below the carrier's average total cost, smaller rivals may be forced to subsidize the carrier and, indirectly, their larger rivals. This is a true allocation injury. The large shipper is in a position to raise its rivals' costs and deter entry or vigorous competition by those unable to attain transportation on nondiscriminatory terms.

During the era in which transportation regulatory schemes were adopted, regulation was seen as the best method of maintaining common carriage, open to all on nondiscriminatory terms. Although details varied, most statutes provided for tariffs to be published and enforced by the regulatory agency. Usually the agency had power to reject a tariff thought to be too high, although high tariffs were probably less a political hot spot than tariffs perceived as discriminatory.

By 1980, many transportation industries had been deregulated to a considerable degree. During the Carter Administration, Congress enacted the Air Cargo Deregulation Act of 1977, the Airline Deregulation Act of 1978, the Motor Carrier Act of 1980, and the Staggers Rail Act of 1980. All of these initiatives involved significant (but not total) deregulation. For example, after airline deregulation, fares for domestic airlines no longer had to be filed with any regulatory body (although safety regulation of airlines continued in full force). Deregulatory initiatives increased the contractual freedom of carriers and their large customers to negotiate individualized contracts for transportation services, known as service contracts. As the example of ocean shipping (discussed below) illustrates, the freedom to negotiate service contracts carries with it significant potential efficiencies but also serious anticompetitive risks.

14.7c.   The Example of International Ocean Carriage

International ocean shipping illustrates a number of issues about the relationship between competition policy and regulation. Some are common to other transportation industries, others not. For example, the high percentage of fixed costs relative to variable costs and the concomitant leverage of large buyers of transportation services are found in many transportation industries. Less common features of ocean transportation are the chronic overcapacity, the widespread use of interna-

---

56. Standard Oil Co. of New Jersey v. United States, 221 U.S. 1, 31 S.Ct. 502, 55 L.Ed. 619 (1911).

tional cartel organizations known as conferences, and the complexity of multilateral regulation by many nations.

Well before federal regulation of ocean shipping commenced, ocean carriers had joined conferences that functioned as rate-setting and output limiting cartels. The conferences were organized by trade—for example, the first to be organized was for carriers operating between Calcutta and England (in 1875).[57] National policies of many nations led them to foster (often through subsidies) the development of a national flag fleet. The result was overcapacity and rate wars, which were said to have pushed revenues below profitable levels. By setting common tariffs and attempting to schedule sailings (and thereby limiting output), the conferences sought to enhance profitability. They constituted what today might be called a crisis cartel, except that the crisis, fueled by continuing subsidies for national flag fleets, was enduring.

14.7c1. *The Shipping Act of 1916*

Because ocean carriage cartels were tolerated under the laws of other nations, including the most important trading partners of the United States, the Congress in 1916 perceived only limited options for ocean carriage regulation. An investigation by the House Merchant Marine Committee (headed by Congressman Alexander) concluded in 1914 that conferences improved service (through regular scheduling) and provided greater stability of rates. But that Committee also noted negative effects to the conference system, including the possibility of excess profits and conference retaliation and discrimination against shippers.[58] Drawing on the Alexander Report, the 1916 Act provided for toleration of conferences under regulatory supervision. Among the 1916 Act's major features were: (1) a requirement that all conference agreements be filed with the U.S. Shipping Board (a predecessor to the Federal Maritime Commission); (2) antitrust immunity for all conference agreements approved by the Board; (3) a required open conference system, which allowed free entry and exit from a conference by any carrier; (4) a prohibition of discriminatory rates or services; (5) a prohibition of deferred rebates (used by conferences to bind shippers to use of conference carriers); (6) a prohibition of "fighting ships" (used predatorily by conferences to shadow and undercut the prices offered by vessels of a non-conference carrier).[59]

Under the Shipping Act's regulatory scheme, conferences continued to set common tariffs and to fight independent carriers through the use of dual rate contracts. Shippers who contracted to ship exclusively with conference carriers were provided a lower rate (often 15 percent lower). In 1958, the Supreme Court held that dual rate contracts were unlawful under Section 14 of the Shipping Act because they were designed to stifle

---

57. Report of the Advisory Commission on Conferences in Ocean Shipping 5 (April 1992).

58. Id. at 5–6.

59. The original 1916 act is set forth in 46 USCS Appx. § 812, at 4 (1997).

competition from non-conference carriers.[60] Congress responded in 1961 by authorizing dual rate contracts unless the FMC found them detrimental to U.S. commerce, contrary to the public interest or unjustly discriminatory or unfair as between certain entities.[61] The 1961 amendments also added a public interest standard to the FMC's review of agreements between carriers.[62] In 1968, the Supreme Court concluded that the public interest standard required the FMC to consider the policies of the antitrust laws.[63] The Court there stated that any conference agreement in violation of the antitrust laws was presumptively invalid and could be approved only if the restraint was required by "a serious transportation need, necessary to secure important public benefits, or in furtherance of a valid regulatory purpose of the Shipping Act."[64] Carriers complained that the resulting prolonged hearings before the FMC (with intervention by the Justice Department a possibility) greatly increased the time and expense of regulatory approval and deterred carriers from submitting even beneficial cost saving agreements to rationalize sailing schedules. Carriers also complained of the uncertain antitrust status of intermodal rate agreements—agreements that provided for a combination of land and sea transportation between two points. Intermodal shipping became an efficient alternative after carriers began using containerized ships with especially designed containers that could be quickly transferred between ships and trucks or trains. The estimated 157 hours of average in-port handling time for a non-containerized ship was reduced to 31 hours for a containerized ship.[65]

In 1979, the Justice Department indicted major European and American carriers serving the North Atlantic trades, alleging that they fixed prices and restricted competition through secret, non-filed agreements. The criminal charges were resolved through nolo contendere pleas and payment of several million dollars in fines. Subsequent private litigation forced the carriers to pay an additional $51 million.[66] This litigation increased the pressure from carriers for new legislation that decreased regulatory burdens and clarified antitrust immunity. Shippers groups, especially those representing large shippers, also sought deregulatory legislation, but they had a different agenda: they sought to eliminate or modify tariff filing to provide greater freedom to negotiate individual transportation contracts, an agenda that threatened traditional principles of common carriage.

14.7c2. The Shipping Act of 1984

Ocean shipping was one of the last transportation industries to undergo deregulation. When deregulation came it was less comprehen-

---

60. Federal Maritime Board v. Isbrandtsen Co., 356 U.S. 481, 78 S.Ct. 851, 2 L.Ed.2d 926 (1958).

61. 46 USCS Appx § 812, at 4 (1997).

62. 5 USCS Appx § 706, at 87 (1997).

63. Federal Maritime Commission v. Aktiebolaget Svenska Amerika Linien, 390

U.S. 238, 88 S.Ct. 1005, 19 L.Ed.2d 1071 (1968).

64. Id. at 243.

65. REPORT OF THE ADVISORY COMMISSION, *supra* note 57, at 9.

66. 42 ANTITRUST & TRADE REG. REP. (BNA) No. 1052, at 370 (Feb. 18, 1982).

sive than for other transportation forms. Both domestic and international carriers made strong pushes for legislation in 1980 and again in 1982, but disagreements among carriers and shippers, and disagreements about the reach of antitrust immunity in Congress and the Executive Branch slowed progress. When the carriers and large shippers reached their own private understanding about major features of the legislation, and the House Merchant Marine Committee reached an accommodation with the House Judiciary Committee, the path was cleared for enactment of new legislation in 1984.[67] Its major features are described below.

Expedited handling of agreements submitted to the FMC—Although other deregulatory initiatives failed (such as the House Judiciary Committee's effort to end tariff filing), the 1984 Act took a meaningful step in expediting review of agreements filed with the FMC. Prior to 1984, the FMC occasionally took years to approve carrier agreements submitted to it. The 1984 Act instituted a negative clearance review—an agreement filed with the FMC takes effect within 45 days of filing unless the Commission takes affirmative action to reject it because it does not meet filing requirements or to enjoin its operation because it is deemed likely to be substantially anticompetitive.[68]

Extension and clarification of antitrust immunity—In a step that ran counter to the trend of deregulation, the 1984 Act extended antitrust immunity to all agreements filed with the FMC and effective, or exempt from filing, pursuant to FMC order or rule. The immunity also extended to any agreement or activity within the scope of the Act "undertaken * * * with a reasonable basis to conclude" that it is covered by an agreement that is filed and effective, or exempt from filing. Finally, private damage or injunction suits under the antitrust laws may not be maintained for any conduct that is prohibited by the Act, a provision designed to force an injured party to rely on remedies that the Act itself provides.[69]

This comprehensive antitrust immunity leaves only a limited role for the antitrust laws. Mergers and acquisitions are still subject to antitrust, as is conduct not reasonably covered by a filed and effective agreement or not exempt from filing. The position that ocean shipping activity should not be simultaneously subject to FMC regulation and the antitrust laws carried the day in this 1984 enactment. To some extent, this outcome may be regarded as an implicit rejection of capture theory. Congress placed virtual complete responsibility for protecting the public interest in a specialized agency that some regard as highly susceptible to control by the interests that it is charged with regulating. That view is at best an oversimplification. Although the FMC may not directly represent the interests of consumers, the constituencies of the FMC include not only carriers, but also big and small shippers, freight forwarders, agents,

---

67. The Shipping Act of 1984, P.L. 98–237, 97 Stat. 67, codified in 46 U.S.C.A. §§ 1701 et seq.

68. Section 6(b), (h) of the Shipping Act of 1984, 46 U.S.C.A. §§ 1705(b), (h).

69. Section 7 of the Shipping Act of 1984, 46 U.S.C.A. § 1706.

and port authorities, a constituency with diverse and often conflicting points of view. At the same time, a number of other features of the 1984 Act suggest that Congress remains concerned with protecting and fostering competition in ocean shipping. Among these are: (1) inclusion of an FMC standard for rejection of substantially anticompetitive agreements; (2) a fairly comprehensive list of prohibited acts, including unjustly discriminatory practices, deferred rebates, and dual rate contracts that violate the antitrust laws; (3) continuation of an open conference requirement and an additional guaranteed right of independent action for members of a conference; and (4) validation of individually tailored service contracts between shippers and conferences.

Substantially anticompetitive agreements—Early versions of the 1984 legislation conferred broad antitrust immunity and removed the general public interest standard that would allow the FMC to reject anticompetitive agreements. When the legislation was reviewed by the House Judiciary Committee, it reinstated language that would allow the FMC to reject substantially anticompetitive agreements.[70] As modified by the conference committee prior to final passage, that language instructs the Commission, at any time after the filing of an agreement, to seek injunctive relief with respect to any agreement that it determines is likely, "by a reduction in competition, to produce an unreasonable reduction in transportation service or an unreasonable increase in transportation cost."[71] The wording of this section was a compromise between those who sought a flexible competition standard that would allow the FMC to respond to anticompetitive conduct not foreseen in the laundry list of prohibited acts and those who feared that an open-ended standard would result in uncertainty, delay, and costly litigation similar to that generated under the general standard that was reviewed by the Supreme Court in *Svenska*.

The Conference report suggests that both groups had their way. Section 6(g) is described as a "flexible standard" that reaches beyond the list of prohibited acts listed elsewhere in the Act, but a standard that is distinguished from the "vague and unworkable" public interest test in the old law.[72] The language also indicates that the burden is on the FMC to establish substantial anticompetitive effects and that these anticompetitive effects are to be balanced against procompetitive effects of the agreement. Finally, although the a showing of anticompetitive effects does not switch the burden to the parties to the agreement to show no less anticompetitive alternative was available, the FMC "need not wear blinders" in considering the availability of reasonable and less anticompetitive courses.[73]

Prohibited acts—The prohibited acts listed in Section 10 of the Shipping Act carry forward prohibitions from preexisting law. Among

---

70. H. Rep. No. 53, Pt. 2, 98th Cong., 1st Sess. 13–21 (1983).

71. Section 6(g) of the Shipping Act of 1984, 46 U.S.C.A. § 1705(g).

72. H.R.REP. No. 600, 98th Cong., 2d Sess. 31–31 (1984).

73. Id. at 36.

these are prohibitions on the use of fighting ships, deferred rebates, or unjustly discriminatory rates. A significant new forbidden act is the use of loyalty contracts that violate the antitrust laws. To the extent conferences are denied the ability to offer discounts to large shippers, they are under added pressure to sign individual service contracts as a means of retaining the trade of large volume shippers.

Open conferences and a member's right to take independent action— The 1984 Act continued the requirement that any carrier be allowed to enter or leave a conference without penalty. This policy choice was made despite criticism that open conferences undercut the conference's ability to operated more efficiently by reducing excess capacity. Instead of moving toward closed conferences, the 1984 Act added a new right of independent action that may have further undermined conference authority.[74] Any member of a conference, by giving ten days notice to the conference, could set a tariff that differs from the tariff adopted by the conference. As a practical matter, when a carrier notified the conference of an intent to adopt an independent tariff, members of the conference usually negotiated with that member to maintain a common conference tariff. But the guaranteed right of independent action gave substantial leverage to individual conference members and, in this way, tended to weaken the conference's authority.

Service contracts—Long-term transportation contracts with large shippers were used before the 1984 Act, but always at the risk that they would be deemed unjustly discriminatory. Such long-term contracts may benefit shippers by fixing (and lowering) their transportation costs and facilitating business planning. Carriers may also benefit to the extent such contracts guarantee that their vessels will operate at greater capacity. The risk associated with such contracts is that they will facilitate market power abuses associated with the leverage large shippers enjoy over a carrier. Experience suggests that a carrier with high fixed costs may be all too willing to reduce overcapacity through discriminatory rates that are below average total costs and, hence, lower than any efficiency associated with large volume would justify.

After railroad deregulation legislation gave express approval to service contracts, large shippers pressed for similar recognition in the 1984 Act. This recognition was provided in Section 8(c) of the new Act, which authorized carriers or conferences to enter into service contracts with shippers or shippers associations. The service contract could be filed "confidentially", but a concise statement of essential terms had to be simultaneously filed and made available to the general public. The carrier or conference then had to make these essential terms available to all shippers "similarly situated."

The Act permitted individual conference members to enter into service contracts, but the conferences were allowed to limit this right.

---

74. Section 5(b)(8) of the Shipping Act of 1984, 46 U.S.C.A. § 1704(b)(8). This sec- tion was amended in 1998. See § 14.7c3.

Perhaps not surprisingly, conferences, with few exceptions, prohibited members from individually negotiating service contracts. A conference member's right of independent action did not extend to service contracts, although a member could still announce an intent to take independent action on a general tariff as a lever for starting conference negotiations leading up to a conference service contract. Although obviously beneficial to large shippers, service contracts heightened the risk of discriminatory rates that could place small shippers at a competitive disadvantage and could force them to subsidize a carrier's operations. In an effort to lessen these risks, the 1984 Act, in addition to the filing, publication, and non-discrimination requirements, offered small shippers the opportunity to negotiate service contracts through shippers associations.

14.7c3. The Ocean Shipping Reform Act of 1998

Service contracts continued to be a friction point after 1984. Large shippers protested that the publication of essential terms of such contracts revealed confidential information and was a disincentive for them to negotiate such contracts. These same shippers also complained of the bureaucracy associated with negotiating a service contract with a conference and asked that the law be amended to stop conferences from impeding individual carriers from negotiating such contracts. Carriers vigorously resisted this change, arguing that service contracts were primarily a vehicle for negotiating discriminatory lower rates for large shippers, with few volume guarantees that would benefit the carriers.[75] But carriers were fighting a losing battle. By the early 1990s, service contracts had grown to cover as much as 76 percent of the cargo in a given trade.[76]

In the Ocean Shipping Reform Act of 1998,[77] Congress expanded the contractual freedom of carriers and customers to enter into service contracts. The new Act shortens from ten to five days the notice that a carrier is required to give a conference before taking independent action. The act now gives each carrier the right to take independent action on a service contract, eliminating the conference's right to prevent a carrier from individually negotiating such a contract. The 1998 Act also relaxed the publication requirements for service contracts, making it easier for the parties to maintain the confidentiality of vital terms.

14.7c4. The Impact of the 1984 Act and the 1998 Amendment

The Shipping Act of 1984 was a complex compromise involving the interests of carriers and large shippers, and (to a less obvious extent) the interests of small shippers and the general public. The mantel of deregulation fits somewhat uncomfortably on this legislation. For while the Act clearly lessened the regulatory burdens associated with filing agreements and increased the freedom of large shippers to contract with individual

75. Report of the Advisory Commission, *supra* note 57, at 144–52 (discussing the views of shippers and carriers toward service contracting).

76. Id. at 137.

77. P.L. 105–258, 112 Stat. 1902, codified in 46 U.S.C.A. §§ 1701 et seq.

ocean carriers, it failed to eliminate tariff filing and virtually eliminated the antitrust enforcement common to most unregulated or deregulated industries.

The balance sheet on the 1984 Act, already modified by a substantial amendment in 1998, is still being compiled. But a few tentative observations about the effects of the legislation can be offered.

Carriers gained expanded antitrust immunity and lessened regulatory burdens but ceded power to their largest customers. Conferences began to lose their authority with increased use of the right of independent action and the emergence of the individually negotiated service contract as the dominant mechanism for setting the terms of carriage. In some trades, discussion agreements, which allow carriers to discuss rates without actually fixing them, have replaced conference agreements as the vehicle for pricing discussions.[78] As conferences have lost their authority, the trend toward consolidation and cooperative agreements among carriers has increased. Some observers think that the 1984 Act, by permitting and facilitating operational alliances, has given carriers an option short of merger for obtaining efficiencies and, in this respect, has lessened the pressure toward concentration.[79]

The clear winners in this legislation were the large shippers who, subject to now reduced disclosure requirements, won the right to negotiate individual service contracts. That such service contracts allow large shippers to gain lower rates and greater business certainty is clear. The service contract may also force carriers to adopt more quickly to the needs of their large customers, speeding the adoption of innovative and efficient services. The bottom line appears to be better shipping services at lower cost. But it is unclear to what extent large shippers, often operating in oligopolistic industries, pass these benefits on to consumers. And, as addressed below, service contracts raise the risk of anticompetitive rate discrimination that can entrench powerful firms at the expense of new and innovative smaller firms in the same industry.

14.7c4i. Rate Discrimination as a Tool for Entrenchment

If service contracts become a tool for large shippers to obtain rates below the carrier's average total costs, the effect is to force smaller users to subsidize the large shippers. The power to force costs on rivals becomes a tool by which a powerful incumbent buyer of transportation services can deter new entry or market penetration by smaller, more innovative rivals. New entrants and efficient small businesses may be saddled with higher transportation costs that prevent them from competing on equal terms with larger incumbent firms. To be sure, small shippers, although lacking the leverage to negotiate individual service contracts, can benefit from the terms of such a contract by forming an association or employing the services of a freight forwarder or middle-

78. Statement of the Honorable Harold J. Creel, Jr., Chairman, Federal Maritime Commission, Hearings before the House   Committee on the Judiciary, 106th Cong., 1st Sess. (May 5, 1999).

79. Id.

man. To some extent, this has occurred. Of the service contracts filed with the FMC between June of 1984 and May of 1991, 4 percent were with freight forwarders known as NVOCCs (non-vessel operating common carriers) and 1 percent were with shippers' associations. But these figures probably should be larger if the service contract is a meaningful protection against discrimination. Moreover, the mere existence of service contracts that serve the small shipper does not end the risk of harmful discrimination. If large shippers negotiate rates that are much more favorable than those available to NVOCCs or shippers' associations, anticompetitive discrimination may still occur. The needed scrutiny to determine whether large shippers are able to obtain discriminatorily favorable transportation rates may be more difficult after the 1998 amendment that strengthens the confidentiality of individual service contracts.

The re-emergence of the discrimination issue brings the transportation-regulation cycle back to the days before regulation began. The abuses associated with discrimination in access and rates of transportation were a major impetus behind the movement to regulate transportation a century ago. A great deal has changed since then. The technology of transportation and the information available to shippers are vastly improved over conditions one hundred years ago. This will aid particularly the large and well-managed shipper that can shop among a variety of carriers for the most favorable rates. Compared to a century ago, the percentage of commerce that is generated by large corporations may be significantly larger, and these firms are unlikely victims of grossly discriminatory practices. This changes the politics of common carriage regulation. The small shipper who might push for a common carriage agenda has a voice that carries less economic clout and diminished political weight. But economic incentives have not changed. The overcapacity generated by national flag subsidies continues to plague carriers, and this overcapacity will serve the large and well-informed shipper, but also place in that shipper's hands the leverage to negotiate harshly discriminatory rates.

According to some economists, the potential for harmful price discrimination is limited by the ease with which information is transmitted (although this condition may be undercut by the increased confidentiality permitted under the 1998 Act) and the ability of shippers to negotiate most-favored-nation clauses that ensure they will receive equal treatment with their rivals.[80] Such protections against discrimination may work reasonably well among business rivals of roughly comparable size and resources. Whether these self-regulating mechanisms effectively protect new entrants or small rivals in shipper industries is doubtful. Secret rebates, although unlawful, may exacerbate injury to small shippers.

80. *See generally*, Advisory Commission Report, *supra* note 57, at 154–55.

14.7c4ii. Competition Safeguards

With the antitrust agencies jurisdiction largely limited to control over carrier mergers and acquisitions and private antitrust enforcement all but eliminated, the task of ensuring competition for ocean carriage falls squarely on the FMC. The FMC has come to rely on its authority to seek an injunction against anticompetitive agreements in Section 6(g) of the 1984 Act as leverage to persuade carriers to abandon or change cooperative agreements that may unduly harm competition. The mere threat of the FMC seeking an injunction appears to suffice to persuade most carriers to modify provisions that the FMC finds objectionable. The FMC's authority was bolstered by language in the Senate Committee Report on the 1998 legislation that made clear the agency's authority to act to prevent threatened anticompetitive abuses before they occur.[81]

The FMC also has broad investigatory powers and the ability to bring actions to enforce the substantial list of prohibited acts. At least in theory, these powers can be exercised to prevent unfair and discriminatory actions against small shippers. The vulnerability of small shippers was highlighted in late 1998 when, according to preliminary findings released by the FMC, a shortage of available carrier capacity in the Eastbound Asia–North America trade led carriers to disregard service agreements and encourage a bidding war for available capacity. Service agreements with shipper's associations or NVOCCs were apparently the first to be abandoned, and some small shippers were forced to pay much higher rates for available space.[82]

§ 14.8   Antitrust and Federal Commercial Activity

We have examined the interaction of antitrust with conduct by a state,[1] with the conduct of private parties responding to state regulatory activities[2] and with the conduct of parties responding to federal regulation.[3] Does antitrust have any application where the federal government enters a market and takes commercial action through its own instrumentality?

Several cases have held that particular federal instrumentalities may not be sued under the antitrust laws.[4] Each of these cases dealt with a different instrumentality—a Federal Reserve Bank, a federally owned transportation system, Army post exchanges, the Rural Electrification Administration and a federally owned power generating facility (TVA)—and each examined the instrumentality's own mix of governmental and

---

81. Statement of FMC Chairman Creel, supra note 78.

82. Id.

§ 14.8

1. See § 14.6.

2. See id.

3. See id.

4. Jet Courier Serv. v. Fed'l Reserve Bank of Atl., 713 F.2d 1221 (6th Cir.1983);

Sea–Land Service, Inc. v. Alaska R.R., 659 F.2d 243, 244 (D.C.Cir. 1981), *cert. denied*, 455 U.S. 919, 102 S.Ct. 1274, 71 L.Ed.2d 459 (1982); Champaign–Urbana News Agency, Inc. v. Cummins News Co., 632 F.2d 680 (7th Cir.1980); Alabama Power Co. v. Alabama Elec. Coop., 394 F.2d 672 (5th Cir.1968); Webster County Coal Corp. v. TVA, 476 F.Supp. 529 (W.D.Ky.1979).

commercial functions and its own statutory context. Distinctions are possible. Refined analysis might, for example, suggest reasons why units of the Federal Reserve System ought to be antitrust immune while these same reasons would not apply to a PX outlet or a federal railroad. Yet the cases in the aggregate constitute well reasoned, convincing authorities suggesting exemption for federal instrumentalities performing a wide range of commercial or quasi-commercial activities. There is also a telling policy concern that supports all of these outcomes: the seeming inappropriateness of subjecting a federal instrumentality to the risk of treble damages.

There is, nonetheless, one holding (and one partial dissent) that sounds a warning about possible limits. *Hecht v. Pro–Football, Inc.*[5] held that a congressionally authorized board that operated a stadium in the District of Columbia was subject to antitrust liability unless Congress "knowingly adopted a policy contrary to or inconsistent with" the antitrust laws.[6] In *Alaska Railroad*, a different panel of the same court differentiated the board involved in *Hecht* from that operating a regional railroad system; it characterized the stadium board as "municipal" and said that "*Hecht* does not supply analysis appropriate in a case in which the activities of a United States instrumentality are at issue," as they were in *Alaska Railroad*.[7] The dissent that does not resonate well with most of the cases is that of Judge Swygert in *Champaign-Urbana News*,[8] the post exchange case. It suggests that where Congress authorizes a federal instrumentality to perform a narrow, routine, commercial function, it may be taken to have expected the instrumentality to have done so in compliance with antitrust norms.[9]

Note that a court could give ample weight to policy concerns mentioned in *Hecht* and in the Swygert *Champaign-Urbana* dissent without subjecting a federal instrumentality to antitrust liability. The *McLean* principle[10] requires federal regulators to factor competitive concerns into the public interest standard that governs their activities. That principle might be brought to bear here. It seems reasonable to say that a federal instrumentality engaged in conventional commercial activity should comply with any standard expressed or implied in the federal statute that grants its powers. Its market powers are likely granted in broad and general terms, much as are the regulatory powers of a federal regulatory agency. A court, in construing the scope of those market powers, might avoid tension with competition policy by construing them in ways that reduce the risk of conflict. In light of this, the instrumentality, in exercising the powers granted, should give appropriate weight to

---

5. 444 F.2d 931 (D.C.Cir.), *cert. denied,* 404 U.S. 1047, 92 S.Ct. 701, 30 L.Ed.2d 736 (1972).

6. Id. at 934.

7. Supra note 4.

8. Champaign–Urbana News Agency, Inc. v. J.L. Cummins News Co., Inc., 632 F.2d 680, 693 (7th Cir.1980).

9. Id. at 695. Compare the treatment of foreign sovereigns performing commercial functions. § 18.5.

10. McLean Trucking Co. v. United States, 321 U.S. 67, 64 S.Ct. 370, 88 L.Ed. 544 (1944). See also § 14.2bii, discussing competitive values in structural and behavioral controls imposed by regulators.

federal competition policy much as it should to other cognate federal policies, for example, those dealing with the environment. If, by inappropriately ignoring competition policy, it does harm to competition, a court could hold that it was acting beyond its powers. Appropriate remedies may be available without imposing antitrust treble damages.

At times a federal instrumentality with market functions may act in concert with other private market actors. Suppose, for example, that TVA or a federal power marketing agency acted cooperatively with private power suppliers to package power resources in ways that neither the private nor federal marketer could achieve alone and which made the resources attractive to buyers for long term commitments. In such a situation, the antitrust laws would very likely apply to the private actors, even if not to the federal instrumentality. There is little if any basis for implying any private exemption.[11] For that reason alone, the federal instrumentality should be motivated to see to it that the joint program, on its face and in execution, is consistent with antitrust norms. If it does not, the entire program may be vulnerable to an antitrust challenge against the cooperating private marketer. Once again, the *McLean* principle could and should be read to limit the manner in which the federal instrumentality exercises its powers.

---

11. Courts are not responsive to claims of implied exemption and, in general, they have been granted only when a clear repugnance exists between antitrust and an alternative federal regulatory scheme as when a federal regulatory agency requires regulated firms to engage in conduct that would violate antitrust laws if done voluntarily.

Compare, e.g., National Gerimedical Hosp. & Gerontology Center v. Blue Cross of Kansas City, 452 U.S. 378, 388, 101 S.Ct. 2415, 69 L.Ed.2d 89 (1981) (exemption available) with Northrop Corp. v. McDonnell Douglas Corp., 705 F.2d 1030, 1056 (9th Cir.1983) (no exemption available). See generally § 14.5, especially § 14.5a.

Chapter XV

ANTITRUST AND INTELLECTUAL PROPERTY

Table of Sections

§ 15.1 Introduction

Intellectual property (IP) is a core element in United States competition policy. In today's technologically sophisticated and highly dynamic markets much competitive interaction revolves around efforts to stay abreast or ahead of competitors in the realm of information and ideas. In this atmosphere firms are frequently involved in IP issues, either asserting IP rights as a strategic weapon or arguing that such rights claimed by their competitors are non-existent or invalid. Nor is any firm in a dynamic, high tech market likely to find itself constantly championing or constantly challenging IP claims. The interests of most firms in most dynamic markets will sometimes be served by strong, spacious IP, sometimes by IP that leaves room for refinement, development, variation and thus, rivalry.

Because of IP's practical link to strategy, IP issues and antitrust issues sometimes (indeed, in high tech markets, often) interact. These two bodies of law are often perceived as conflicting. Antitrust responds to market power abuses. IP tolerates or even fosters the creation of market power (although not its abuse). There may be circumstances in which the two systems cannot be reconciled, but a premise of this chapter is that IP and antitrust can and should be complementary; Apparent conflicts can usually be reconciled or mitigated. Only where values underlying two legal regimes markedly differ should conflict be irreconcilable. This seldom occurs between antitrust and IP. While both antitrust and IP can be multi-valued systems, a key goal of each is the same: consumer welfare resulting from efficient resource allocation. Beyond allocative efficiency, both systems support the all important goal of dynamic efficiency: the fostering of changes, innovations, and technological progress. This commonality is the key to accommodation.

Although theoretical accord between the two systems will usually be within reach, there may be a few situations where one system or the other is responding strongly to a non-efficiency value and ignoring or rejecting a salient efficiency concern to which the other system responds. For example, a moral rights statute, one form of IP, might point to a result which an antitrust efficiency analysis would reject; or an antitrust rule based on fairness or access, despite lack of allocative harm, might point to a result inconsistent with an efficiency analysis supported by IP. More frequently commitment to the primacy of allocative and dynamic efficiency prevails in both systems. Even when it does some conflict may occur because the efficiency problems addressed by the two systems differ and neither system routinely identifies, nor makes effort to evaluate, the efficiency issue addressed by the other. But there are ways in which such conflicts can either be reduced (in the application of IP concepts) or reconciled (in the course of antitrust analysis).

The allocative problem with which IP deals is that markets may generate inadequate investment in innovation because, without IP, "free riding" is often feasible and innovators are unable to internalize some of the rewards from their investments. IP seeks optimum resource allocation and consumer welfare by striking a balance between, on the one hand, granting sufficient exclusivity to provide the incentive needed to encourage innovation and, on the other hand, assuring adequate access and deployment of existing intellectual output by avoiding gratuitous or excessive protection, providing information about innovations, and protecting the public domain. Seen in dynamic terms, IP strives for a balance that encourages investment leading to innovation, but avoids limiting the use of this innovation such that future innovation is stymied. For example, copyright law strives for this balance by denying protection to ideas, facts, processes, methods of operation, etc., and through the fair use and a series of other exceptions to exclusive rights (including several compulsory licensing provisions). Also, copyright law does not unqualifiedly forbid copying of protected materials; the infringement question is whether defendant took too much.[1] Similarly, patent law strikes the balance by requiring that the patentee give the public useful information about what the invention is, how it is constructed and how it operates; by the utility, novelty, originality, and non-obviousness requirements; by a limited right of repair, a misuse doctrine, and a limited experimental use defense; and by an emphasis on limiting the scope of protection to the metes and bounds of the claims, thus effectively emphasizing what remains in the public domain.

While antitrust can and often should take dynamic factors into account, the major allocative problem antitrust routinely addresses is that once a technology is on line it may be exploited by strategies that expand, reinforce or abuse market power. Antitrust seeks to optimize resource allocation by prohibiting conduct having the purpose and effect

---

§ 15.1

1. E.g., Dawson v. Hinshaw Music, Inc., 905 F.2d 731 (4th Cir.), *cert. denied,* 498 U.S. 981, 111 S.Ct. 511, 112 L.Ed.2d 523 (1990).

of foreclosing market access unless that conduct can be justified as yielding offsetting efficiencies, and by foreclosing cartelization among competitive or potentially competitive firms. These prohibitions tend to assure prices closely related to costs, except where power is earned by innovation or efficiency. Antitrust restraints also tend to facilitate rapid commercialization and wide deployment of innovations.

Despite the common concern with efficiency, conflict can occur because of the timing of the analysis. IP analysis looks at the adequacy of innovation incentives, thus addressing the "ex ante" problem—the problem apparent before the innovation occurs: When incentives are inadequate, something should be done now to increase them. This ex ante view contrasts with the "ex post" prospective embodied in many antitrust questions. The antitrust analyst looks at the situation that exists after the innovation is on line and asks, now that we have this technology, is it being exploited through strategies that cause undue allocative distortions?

In judicial construction of IP laws the potential for such conflict can be reduced, at least marginally, by awareness that in an ideal economy the exclusivity (and hence, the market power) conferred by the IP would be no greater than needed to encourage the investment that leads to such innovation. True, in much IP litigation the room for allocative fine tuning by courts is limited. In important areas major ex-ante allocative judgments are made legislatively. Congress passes "one-size-fits-all" rules for all patents and all copyrights, regardless of their individual contributions. As applied to some IP these rules may either under or over reward. Yet, in the judicial application of categorical legislative rules there will be lines to draw—occasions in which fact situations could plausibly be characterized either as falling within or outside of a protected category. Suppose, for example, that a court must decide whether a menu command hierarchy which had become an industry standard is a "work of authorship," and thus copyright protectable, or a "method of operation" and thus in the public domain. A court sensitive to the amplifications of the IP reward associated with an industry standard in a market displaying network externalties might be more inclined to make this judgment call against protection than would a court paying no heed to ex ante (post development) allocative consequences.[2] Issues entailing

2. Lotus Development Corp. v. Borland International, Inc. 49 F.3d 807 (1st Cir. 1995), aff'd by equally divided court, 516 U.S. 233, 116 S.Ct. 804, 133 L.Ed.2d 610 (1996). Accord, MiTek Holdings, Inc. v. Arce Eng'g Co., Inc., 89 F.3d 1548 (11th Cir.1996); Mitel, Inc. v. Iqtel, Inc., 896 F.Supp. 1050 (D.Colo.1995). There is also support for the *Lotus* view in the House Report, H.R. Rep. No. 1476, 94th Cong. 2d Sess. 571 (1976). See also Lemley, *Convergence in the Law of Software Copyright?*, 10 HIGH TECH. L. J. 1 (1995); Menell, *The Challenges of Reforming Intellectual Property Protection For Computer Software*, 94 CO-

LUM. L. REV. 2644, 2653 (1994). But see Autoskill Inc. v. National Educational Support Sys., Inc., 994 F.2d 1476, 1495 n. 23 (10th Cir.1993), *cert. denied,* 510 U.S. 916, 114 S.Ct. 307, 126 L.Ed.2d 254 (1993); Brown Bag Software v. Symantec Corp., 960 F.2d 1465, 1477 (9th Cir.1992); Engineering Dynamics, Inc. v. Structural Software, Inc., 26 F.3d 1335 (5th Cir.1994), supplemented 46 F.3d 408 (5th Cir.1995). In recent years courts have often recognized that IP and antitrust laws are not irreconcilable and that the judicial task is to reconcile them by striking a balance be-

"close calls" occur in many contexts: an independent service organization (ISO) transfers IP protected diagnostic software from a licensee's permanent storage to random access memory in the licensee's computer in order to service the licensee's computer; is the ISO "copying" the software?[3] Can any or all of the elements of a graphic user interface claimed as authorship be filtered out by doctrines such as originality, functionality, standardization, scenes à faire, or merger?[4] In answering such questions information may be available relevant to the innovation markets involved and to the incentives needed to encourage innovation of the kind the IP might protect. Such information (and argument related to it) might help the court reach judgments that reflect a proper balance between adequate and excessive innovation incentives. Furthermore, some IP with important effects on market access and competition is entirely or largely judge made. The misappropriation tort is one example,[5] the right of publicity another.[6] In applying and developing legal norms for such areas courts are free to balance consumer interests in open, competitive markets against their interests in adequate incentives for innovation. Indeed, fealty to the ancient common law commitment to open market access[7] as well as to the balanced consumer welfare policy implicit in the federal constitution and in IP and antitrust statutes may demand nothing less.[8] This view of the matter, central to the thesis of this chapter, is effectively expressed by Judge Kozinski in his *Samsung Electronics* dissent:

tween unfettered ex post competition and the encouragement of innovation which requires sufficient protection for the IP innovation. E.g., Atari Games Corp. v. Nintendo of Am., Inc., 897 F.2d 1572, 1576 (Fed.Cir. 1990); Data General Corp. v. Grumman Sys. Support Corp., 36 F.3d 1147, 1185 (1st Cir.1994). See the discussion in the introduction to Vermut, *A Synthesis of Intellectual Property and Antitrust Law: A Look at Refusals to License Computer Software*, 22 COLUM.-VLA J.L. & ARTS 27, 27–31 (1997).

3. MAI Systems Corp. v. Peak Computer, Inc., 991 F.2d 511 (9th Cir.1993). *MAI* holds, in effect, that any *use in a computer* of any application program (which necessarily entails making a temporary "copy" in the RAM) constitutes copying of the program. But cf. NLFC, Inc. v. Devcom Mid-America, Inc., 45 F.3d 231 (7th Cir.1995). In *MAI* the issue had competitive significance because of the context: A licensee with a right to use copyrighted diagnostic software to service its own computer provided the software for that use to a service company that competed with the holder of the copyright, the manufacturer of the computer. *MAI* was followed in Triad Systems Corp. v. Southeastern Express Co., 64 F.3d 1330 (9th Cir.1995), *cert. denied,* 516 U.S. 1145, 116 S.Ct. 1015, 134 L.Ed.2d 96 (1996), another case in which the question,

copying or not, had competitive significance. Commentary tends to be critical of *MAI*; (e.g., Johnson, *The Uncertain Future of Computer Software Users' Rights in the Aftermath of MAI Systems*, 44 DUKE L. J. 327 (1994); Lemley, *Intellectual Property and Shrink Wrap Licenses*, 68 S. CAL. L. REV. 1239, 1280 n.184 (1995)).

4. Apple Computer, Inc. v. Microsoft Corp., 35 F.3d 1435 (9th Cir.1994), *cert. denied,* 513 U.S. 1184, 115 S.Ct. 1176, 130 L.Ed.2d 1129 (1995) held that all such elements should be filtered out.

5. International News Service v. Associated Press, 248 U.S. 215, 39 S.Ct. 68, 63 L.Ed. 211 (1918); United States Golf Ass'n v. St. Andrews Systems, 749 F.2d 1028 (3d Cir.1984). See Raskind, *The Misappropriation Doctrine as a Competitive Norm of Intellectual Property Law,* 75 MINN. L. REV. 875 (1991).

6. Midler v. Ford Motor Co., 849 F.2d 460 (9th Cir.1988).

7. The Schoolmaster Case, 11 Hen. IV, F.47, pl.21 (1410).

8. White v. Samsung Electronics America, Inc., 989 F.2d 1512 (9th Cir.1993) (Kozinski, J., dissenting from order rejecting the suggestion for rehearing *en banc*).

" * * * Overprotecting intellectual property is as harmful as under-protecting it. Creativity is impossible without a rich public domain. Nothing today, likely nothing since we tamed fire, is genuinely new: Culture, like science and technology, grows by accretion * * *. Overprotection stifles the very creative force it's supposed to nurture."[9]

Antitrust analysis affords greater leeway for integrating the ex ante allocative concerns of IP with antitrust's conventional ex post concerns because antitrust often requires a specific, fact-focused analysis of allocative issues. While antitrust does have categorical *per se* rules, most antitrust issues fall under a full or truncated rule of reason, or at least the analytically enhanced presumption-approach that increasingly displaces cut and dried *per se*. In many instances, therefore, an antitrust court must do more than assign an event to a legislatively specified category; it must do a fact specific allocative analysis. However, this necessity does not of itself assure integration of the IP ex ante and the antitrust ex post allocative perspectives. To the contrary, just as courts in IP cases often ignore whether the uses to which IP is being put can do allocative harm that outweighs the efficiency benefit of having encouraged the innovation, so too antitrust courts may focus so sharply on an allegedly exploitive use of technology that they ignore whether the opportunity for this particular use (for example, the right to exclude competitors from a repair or service market may have been essential to bring about the innovation and its commercialization). When a particular use of IP is challenged as sufficiently exploitive to constitute an antitrust violation (or a misuse of the IP) the outcome would, ideally, turn not solely on whether the use initiated ex ante competition, but also on whether the expectation that this use would be available was a necessary incentive to the R & D investment that produced the IP.

Take this hypothetical: Assume that a software company (call it MS) has an IP based monopoly in a well-defined market for computer operating systems. Assume, too, that there is a separate, distinct and different market for another product, say an application software or an Internet browser, in which MS and others compete. Assume, finally, that MS uses its operating system power to gain power in the application or browser market by refusing to license its operating system to hardware manufacturers that install competing application software or browsers in their hardware.[10] On these assumptions the antitrust contention that this conduct is unlawful is a conventional tying or monopoly leveraging claim. That analysis need not even mention IP, save in rejoinder to an IP defense. The IP defense may be equally one sided. It will cite the IP holder's statutory right to refuse to deal and assert that this right trumps the alleged antitrust violation. But such conflicts could be dealt with by doing a deeper analysis of the undergirding allocative issues

9. Id. at 1513.

10. The allegations in United States v. Microsoft Corp., 253 F.3d 34 (D.C.Cir. 2001)(en banc) are more comprehensive and complex than this sparse hypothetical. That case will be discussed in § 15.8c4.

than either conventional antitrust or conventional IP, used alone, might require. Based on appropriate evidence submitted by the parties, the antitrust court could do an allocative analysis not just of the leveraging, but also of whether being able to exploit the IP in this manner in this particular market was an expectation reasonably necessary to encourage the IP innovation and its commercialization. If an expectation of being able to exploit the operating system IP by leveraging into, say, the browser market was essential to encourage the R & D investment yielding the operating system, then denying that right might lead to a less than optimum investment in software innovation. If so, that ex ante allocative loss might be weighed against the ex post allocative loss resulting from stifling competition in the browser market. But if, on the other hand, the R & D investment that produced the operating system would have been made in any event—for example, if at the time the operating system was developed no one involved was even thinking about browsers—then allowing operating system power to be leveraged into the browser market would be to tolerate allocative harm in the browser market. That harm, on its face, violates antitrust norms without any allocative benefit of the kind the IP laws are intended to encourage.

A balancing inquiry of the kind here suggested could be complex. How serious is the allocative harm done by the leveraging in the market as now structured, and what structural developments does it threaten (or promise) for the future? Is there evidence that the expectation of an IP shield for this conduct was needed to encourage the innovation or its commercialization, or that such a shield is needed to encourage further investment, innovation, refinement and exploitation in the relevant and adjacent markets? Again, what is the risk that granting such a shield will discourage adaptation and further development of the innovation in question by limiting its deployment? Will it stifle competition, discourage entry or inhibit ongoing innovation and commercialization in these markets? After the significance of identifiable negative and positive allocative effects, both ex ante and ex post, have been gauged, they must be placed on the scale. On balance, will the allocative consequence of allowing such leveraging conduct be negative or positive? The factual issues and questions of judgment involved in applying such an integrative rule of reason may not be easy. But when relevant information about affected markets has been gathered and sifted, they are matters post-Chicago economics is equipped to address inductively and which should not tax judicial patience much more than does any complex, full blown rule of reason analysis.[11]

In this chapter evaluation and criticism of existing case law will reflect the policy proposition stated above. The chapter provides grounding in intellectual property thinking, a brief introduction to salient aspects of patent and copyright law, and a more comprehensive explora-

---

11. Cf. Eastman Kodak Co. v. Image Technical Services, Inc., 504 U.S. 451, 112 S.Ct. 2072, 119 L.Ed.2d 265 (1992). See also Sullivan, *Post-Chicago Economics: Econo-* *mists, Lawyers, Judges and Enforcement Officials in a Less Determinate Theoretical World*, 63 ANTITRUST L.J. 683 (1995).

tion of the ways in which antitrust rules may apply to certain strategic uses of IP. Section 15.2 summarizes major strands of theory that underlie intellectual property regimes and the values these regimes seek to advance. In doing so, it notes similarities to and differences from antitrust. The section is general, claiming application to all or most significant aspects of IP, both the three federal statutory systems and the major common law or state statutory systems.

Drawing on theory from § 15.2, § 15.3 examines the relationship between patent law and competitive values. Section 15.4 describes and evaluates copyright law from that perspective.[12] Section 15.5 provides a brief overview of the intersection of trademark and competition law. Section 15.6 then sets the stage for integrating antitrust and intellectual property analysis. It summarizes the variety of ways in which IP can be used strategically to protect, enhance or exploit market power, identifying situations in which uses of IP can give rise to significant antitrust issues. Also, when such activities are evaluated from the vantage point of intellectual property theory, the reasons for accommodation between antitrust and IP law become evident. Section 15.7 deals with the ways in which information technology can be protected by IP. Section 15.8 reviews the Department of Justice and Federal Trade Commission Antitrust, Intellectual Property Guidelines. These guidelines state at a general level and explain with examples the current attitude of the federal enforcement agencies about the application of antitrust to intellectual property licensing.

After discussion of the guidelines, specific antitrust areas are addressed. Section 15.9 deals with an area of considerable current interest, the application of Section 2 of the Sherman Act to the strategic use of intellectual property to monopolize or attempt to monopolize a well defined economic market through either horizontal restraints (e.g. patent pooling) or vertical restraints (e.g. tying). Section 15.10 discusses the use of IP licenses to impose horizontal restraints on competing firms and § 15.11 deals in a similar way with IP and vertical issues. Both sections invoke both Sherman Section 1 and the Clayton Act. These three sections utilize both the guidelines and the case law (much of it now fairly old) to illuminate the current interaction between antitrust and IP, and also examine recent antitrust challenges by enforcers and private claimants to strategic uses of IP that might threaten allocative harm. From §§ 15.9 through 15.11, the primary goal is to describe current law and enforcement policy. Excessively protective aspects of current IP

---

12. This Chapter makes no effort to summarize trademark, trade secrets or other branches of intellectual property law. However, some of the issues and approaches developed in here apply also to such other regimes as well as to patent and copyright law. For example, software companies often rely on trade secret law to exclude competitors and would-be entrants from access to application system file formats, thus inhibiting compatibility of competing systems with installed base and reducing the likelihood of after-market innovations, add-ons and improvements. See Garfinkel, *Let My Data Go!* (Jan. 1, 1998), available at <http:www.wired.com/news/technology/01,1282,9482,00.html>

doctrine are criticized, as is overbroad antitrust doctrine that may unnecessarily inhibit competitive uses of intellectual property.

§ 15.2 Theoretical Justifications for and Explanations of Intellectual Property

The term, intellectual property, comprehends all law that fosters "human creativity without unduly restricting its fruits."[1] The field is a spacious miscellany of federal and state statutory and common law materials—patents, copyright, trademarks, trade secrets, misappropriation of trade values, right of publicity and the law of ideas.[2] A major strand of theory sees all IP systems as in service to two goals, encouraging and rewarding innovation, but doing so without unduly limiting access to the ideas, technology, information or art that the innovation produces. A core problem is that from the social point of view every recognition of proprietary rights in intellectual output creates both harms and benefits. To the extent that such recognition stimulates innovation that would not have occurred without it, IP law enriches the public. It corrects a market failure by internalizing a hurtful externality, thus enhancing the resources available to the public in the marketplace. But to the extent that recognizing a property right gives the innovator proprietary control over an innovation which, but for IP law, would have been produced anyway and have become a free good available in the public domain, that law facilitates output reduction and price enhancement. Whether, on balance, the public is benefitted or harmed depends on whether the innovation would have occurred if there were no (or a lesser) IP incentive. To the extent that an IP system seeks to strike a balance that maximizes the public benefit and reduces the harm from conferring property rights in intellectual output, IP is consistent with antitrust. As has been recognized, the federal statutory IP systems have goals essentially consistent with those of antitrust.[3]

Note that each of the many legal systems that protect intellectual property try to strike this balance. They circumscribe the subject matter

---

§ 15.2

1. D. CHISUM & M. JACOBS, UNDERSTANDING INTELLECTUAL PROPERTY 1–2 (1992).

2. Protection under the Patent Act, 35 U.S.C.A. §§ 1–376 (1996) and the Copyright Act of 1976, 17 U.S.C.A. § 101–1101 (1996) have a common constitutional base, U.S. CONST. Art. I § 8, cl.8. Trademarks, 15 U.S.C.A. §§ 1051–1128 (1996), and marks 17 U.S.C.A. §§ 901–914 (1996) are also subject to federal statutory protection under the commerce clause. There are numerous state statutes as well as state common law bases for IP protection. See, e.g., UNIF. TRADE SECRET ACT.

3. Atari Games Corp. v. Nintendo of Am., Inc., 897 F.2d 1572 (Fed.Cir.1990); International Wood Processors v. Power Dry, Inc., 792 F.2d 416 (4th Cir.1986); Data Gen. Corp. v. Grumman Sys. Support Corp., 36 F.3d 1147, 1185 (1st Cir.1994); National Cable Television Ass'n v. Broadcast Music, Inc., 772 F.Supp. 614, 645 (D.D.C.1991); but see SCM Corp. v. Xerox Corp., 645 F.2d 1195 (2d Cir. 1981). Views about the relationship between IP and antitrust have varied over time. See, e.g., Simpson v. Union Oil Co. of California, 377 U.S. 13, 24, 84 S.Ct. 1051, 12 L.Ed.2d 98 (1964) (patent law modifies antitrust law pro tanto); American Hoist & Derrick Co. v. Sowa & Sons, Inc., 725 F.2d 1350, 1367 (Fed.Cir. 1984) (patent system, which preceded antitrust, is not an exception to antitrust). See Reynolds, *Antitrust and Patent Licensing: Cycles of Enforcement and Current Policy*, 37 JURIMETRICS J. 129 (1997).

that can be protected, establish substantive preconditions for protection, and delimit both the scope of and term for which protection is granted. For systems, such as trade secrets law, in which the rules are largely derived from common law, courts have considerable discretion to do such balancing on a case by case basis. By contrast, for the two major statutory systems—patent and copyright—most of this balancing is done by the legislature. For example, utility patents are available for processes, machines, manufacturers and compositions of matter, while copyrights are available for works of authorship embodied in a tangible medium of expression. To warrant a patent the qualifying subject matter must be new, useful and non-obvious; for a copyright the qualifying subject matter must be an original work of authorship. A patentee gains the right to exclude others from making, using or selling, while the copyright holder gains the right to prevent others from copying the expression embodied in the protected work. As can be seen, the legislatively established standard for patent protection (new, useful, non-obvious) is relatively high, while that for copyright (originality, in the sense of not having been copied and showing some trivial degree of creativity, not a qualitative advance over prior work) is relatively low. Commensurately, a patent protects not just against imitators but also later inventors, while a copyright protects only expression, not facts, information or ideas, and only against those who copy, not from belated originators who did not have access to the protected work.

Even under these legislative systems courts must do some balancing at borderlines. Each intellectual property regime has its own complexities and its own unsettled, fact intensive, or problematic issues. It is in filling such statutory interstices, resolving such factual issues and addressing such doctrinal problems that IP courts have the opportunity to integrate ex ante IP allocative concerns with the ex post concerns to which antitrust responds. In seeking to resolve such issues courts respond to the values implicit in intellectual property theory. There are two major theoretical sources for such values. First, and most important, is economic theory. It invites striking a balance between granting incentives to generate and commercialize innovations, versus the goal to promote wide accessibility of innovations once produced, both to maximize their current utility and to facilitate their use as stepping stones to refinement, improvement and further innovation. From this perspective, the ideal balance would provide the minimum reward needed to encourage sufficient innovations, thus assuring the highest possible accessibility consistent with encouraging such production. Insufficient incentives would distort resource allocation and exact a social cost: insufficient investment in innovation. But excessive incentives would yield another social cost: returns on protected IP gratuitously higher than needed to generate the innovation, thus resulting in reduced output, and increased prices for that output. To the extent the proper balance is struck, the tensions between IP and antitrust are minimized.

The second major category of intellectual property theory is less cohesive and has many subcategories. It is a concept of moral, natural or civil rights. Viewed in this way an innovation is an expression of the innovator's creativity, an aspect of his or her personality. No utilitarian justification is needed to warrant proprietary control of that which one has created. As a matter of natural justice, property in the innovation belongs to the innovator. In the subsections following we examine both of these perspectives. The first is generally consistent with and the second is quite out of accord with antitrust.[4]

15.2a. Economic Theory Supporting Intellectual Property

For IP regimes that grant innovators proprietary rights (such as patents or copyright) the validating economic ideas concern the public goods concept and the need for incentives. For IP regimes that focus on risks of consumer confusion about source (trademark and related doctrines, including aspects of the right of publicity), validating economic theory considers these but also takes account of information asymmetry between producers and consumers and its influence on the incentives of both.

All intellectual property has a public good or free good aspect. Unlike tangible property IP, like the air we breath, can be used by infinite numbers of people at once. My use of your intellectual output need not exclude your's or anyone else's concurrent use of it. Firm A's use of a new and inventive process need not preclude firm B through D from using it simultaneously. That musician X is playing a newly created song does not keep other musicians Y and Z from doing so, too. This aspect of intellectual output gives rise to an incentive problem. If firm A invented the process and its competitors are using it too, firm A will have invested time, effort and money that benefits competitors as well as itself. If X composed the song, she will have invested her time, talent and resources to enrich not only herself, but Y and Z also. Often, the cost of creating is high. By contrast, the cost to other firms to imitate A's process or to other musicians to mimic X's song will be much lower, perhaps trivial, once the imitator has access to the needed information. This is so whether the invented thing is a product or a process and whether the created expression is a novel, a song, a painting, or anything else. The originator incurs all the costs of the inventive or creative effort plus the costs of producing and marketing the output. Unless the originator gains an intellectual property right in the invention or creation, imitators may compete with the originator with a substantial cost advantage. Imitators, like originators, face production and distribution costs. They will also incur some costs in gaining access to the relevant

---

4. There is, indeed, a third theoretical attitude about IP, the view that all intellectual output should be freely available to everyone, that none should have possessory rights in thought, expression and ideas. This conception, which has long subsisted in an intellectual "underground," emerges to justify third world decisions not to recognize first world IP claims and in defense of free access to ideas and information accessi-ble on the Internet. This third attitude, in a more balanced and structured form, can also be found reflected in the "Open Source Software" movement, which has generated BSD Unix, Linux, the Perl language and other open source products. See, e.g. Barlow, *The Economy of Ideas: a framework for rethinking copyright and patent in the digital age,* 2 WIRED 84 (1994).

information. In some cases access cost may be substantial: e.g., industrial espionage to pierce secrecy; time and cost to reverse-engineer. But access costs to others' innovations are often small, and probably seldom approach, let alone equal or exceed, the cost of the innovation. Most creations and much invention discloses itself as soon as it is used. In consequence, unless there is a protective regime of intellectual property law, the innovator will not be able to capture all of the benefits of the innovation. Some benefits—perhaps even most of them—will be accessible to imitators, free riders who made no investment in innovation and perhaps little in copying.

An investment in innovation is socially efficient whenever the total return on the innovation exceeds its cost. Because of this, the public good aspect of innovation constitutes a serious market failure. From a social perspective, no socially efficient investment in innovation should be discouraged. But in deciding whether to invest, the innovator ignores advantages to others which she cannot internalize. She will invest to achieve the innovation only if the anticipated benefit to herself exceeds the anticipated cost, a very different test from the one that signifies social efficiency.

Of course, considerable innovation would likely go on regardless of whether a legal regime entitled the innovator to capture all or most of the benefits. There are considerable non-economic incentives to create and innovate. Down through the ages, troubadours, songsters, storytellers, musicians, artists, writers and inventors were driven to create without the incentive of copyright or patent protection. The inward satisfaction and outward recognition that flows to a creator are not dependent upon IP legal protections. And some economic benefits would go to creators with or without IP systems. Innovators have some lead time when they enter the market. They will be first to cut costs, improve product, or offer something entirely new. Such "first to market" advantages may be both substantial and long lasting.[5] Many innovations could be protected by secrecy, perhaps for a substantial time, even if patent, trade secrets, and other legal IP protection were unavailable. This could be true, for example, for software file formats or for innovative production processes. Whenever the gains the innovator can anticipate garnering for itself exceed anticipated innovation costs, there will be an incentive to innovate, regardless of secondary benefits to others. After all, externalized benefits, omnipresent to some extent in virtually all markets, do not bring markets to a halt. If one real estate owner improves his vacant lot, other adjacent landowners may also realize increased property value. The law need not give the improver a lien on adjacent land for those secondary increases in order to provide sufficient incentive for an owner to improve its own real estate. Some externalities are inevitable. They are anticipated and accepted parts of market interactions. So here, competition and profit incentives would motivate con-

---

5. Breyer, *The Uneasy Case for Copyright: A Study of Copyright in Books, Photocopies and Computer Programs*, 84 HARV. L. Rev. 281 (1970) (discussing the economic advantage that naturally flow to the "first to market").

siderable innovation regardless of the existence or scope of protective IP law.

Note, also, the aggregate effects of a legal regime allowing the innovator to capture all or most of the benefits of innovation. Such a regime benefits the innovator unqualifiedly. But the effect on social welfare is mixed. Assume that all innovations yield some social gain. If the market were not altered by intellectual property law, all those gains not captured by the innovator through first entrant or like effects would be free goods readily available to the public. This would maximize social welfare in every instance in which the innovation would have occurred without an intellectual property regime. But without a legal basis for internalizing more of the gain, the innovator might not invest in making the innovation. Social welfare would thus be maximized overall if the innovation took place, was commercialized and the innovator was able to internalize no more than the minimum percentage of the benefit that would have been sufficient to induce the innovative investment. It is socially beneficial to allow the innovator to internalize enough of the gain that a wholly free market would externalize to assure that the innovation will be made and commercialized. But it is not socially beneficial to allow the innovator to capture any greater part of the benefit that a market without IP would assign to others. To do so would gratuitously shift to the innovator benefits that a free market would treat as a public good accessible to all, and would do so despite the lack of any social return.

Conferring gratuitous benefits on innovators in the form of greater proprietary control of new information, ideas or authorship can distort the socially optimal resource deployment in another important respect. Viewed dynamically, proprietary control of information can reduce future innovation, both in technology and in the arts. Innovation is always cumulative. It is a social process. No innovator starts from scratch. All build upon what others have already done: before the computer, the calculator; before that, the abacus; before the chip, the transistor; before that, the vacuum tube. Most new things are expansions, contractions, alterations, convolutions or other reactions to identifiable and usually not very remote predecessors. In short, they are built upon and dependent on information accessible to the innovator. To assure ongoing dynamic innovation today and tomorrow, access to what was novel yesterday should not be blockaded too aggressively. To the extent that IP grants more extensive rewards than needed to stimulate current innovation, future innovation is decelerated by removing building blocks from the public domain. Would-be-innovators scanning the market today would lose access to the needed raw materials of tomorrow's innovation.

The above observations have relevance to trademark and analogous regimes as well as to patent, copyright, trade secrets and other regimes that directly stimulate innovation. A firm that uses a new mark, like one that generates a patentable idea, can plausibly ask protection from free riding. But because trademark and related regimes aim to facilitate consumer identification of the source of a product or service, there is for this kind of IP an additional concern upon which economic thinking can be brought to bear. In most markets—virtually all consumer markets and many intermediate ones—information is asymmetrically deployed. In general, sellers know more than buyers about product characteristics. Products of competing producers differ from each other. Breads, for example, do not all taste alike. But unless buyer information about differences between the products of different bakers can be efficiently deployed, buyers will have no alternative except to shop generically. A bread buyer unable to differentiate among products might know he usually enjoys the taste of bread, some more than others. For every purchase of bread, he'll be hoping for a positive, or at least an average, experience. But if he has efficient ways to differentiate—for example, by brand mark and name—a consumer can discover which producer or producers make bread that satisfy him, and which do not. As consumers become better informed, producers will have higher incentives to learn themselves about consumer tastes, to bake products that meet these tastes, to improve product where possible, and to assure product consistency. These effects all tend to increase efficiency, resource allocation and consumer welfare. Trademark and other intellectual property regimes facilitate these beneficial effects.

But note, too, that in oligopolistic markets IP protection can have offsetting harms. Product differentiation, facilitated by trademark and related rules, may become the major, even the only source of rivalry. See the discussion of brand marketing in § 6.2. Incentives to compete on price can be displaced, thus facilitating interdependent, supracompetitive pricing. Also, where first entrant advantages are strong and the first entrant gains a big early lead, brand name property rights and significant advertising and in-store promotional budgets can be used to raise entry barriers high enough to protect dominant firm supracompetitive prices.[6] This will be especially true if there are network externalities or if the product is an important but relatively inexpensive input into an output.

15.2b.   "Moral Imperative" Theories

There is a conception that attributes moral character to intellectual creativity. Authorship and other expressions of creativity are expressions of the self. Because the law should respond to the "intimate bond"[7] between the intellectual output and the author's personality, granting the creator legal control over self expression is a moral imperative. These views have long been influential in France and other Mediterranean countries where a moral rights copyright tradition flowers. They also have old and respected, although contentious, philosophical underpin-

---

6. Cf. Borden, Inc. v. FTC (ReaLemon) 674 F.2d 498 (6th Cir. 1982), *judgment vac'd*, 461 U.S. 940, 103 S.Ct. 2115, 77 L.Ed.2d 1298 (1983). See the discussion in Schmalensee, *On the Uses of Economic Models in Antitrust: The Realemon Case*, 127 U. Pa. L. Rev. 994 (1979).

7. Saurraute, *Current Theory on the Moral Right of Authors and Artists Under French Law,* 16 Am. J. Comp. L. 465, 480 (1968).

nings, as well as other links to significant aspects of Western cultural development. Exponents of moral rights, personhood, and natural law theories for intellectual property have found support in Locke's labor theory of property and in Hegelian conceptions of autonomy.[8] It may be that such theories can also be linked to the ideology of authorship that initially arose in England in the seventeenth century[9] and to "possessive idealism," more a cultural than a philosophical development, which led to romanticism as an artistic movement.[10]

If any of these conceptions are given full credit, the property claim of the artist or inventor does not turn upon effects on the public—on incentives, efficiency, or resource allocation. It is merely necessary to identify what, precisely, was the unique contribution of the innovator. This is hers as a matter of natural, moral or civil right. Like all natural law contentions, imperative theories supporting IP are also linked to the Judeo–Christian underpinning of Western culture. While direct appeals to Judeo–Christian source books are seldom heard in legal discussion today, such appeals might be fitting here. It was the creative spirit that hovered over the void in Genesis before the first day. It was the creative spirit, the word, the logos, that the fourth gospel, too, identifies with primary being. When that creative spirit expresses itself in the works of man should it not be revered and appropriately acknowledged?

Of course, under a more utilitarian view, all expressions of moral rights can be seen as efforts to gain support for the most beneficial social outcome. Under this view, moral rights are expressions of a society's drive to achieve a desirable social benefit. The moral right of a creator should be recognized only to the extent it provides a net gain to the society that sustains the artist or inventor. To the extent that a moral right oversteps and establishes legal norms that undermine a goal such as consumer welfare, they have lost their legitimacy.

§ 15.3   Patent Law and Resource Allocation

Patent protection stands on the constitutional authorization to Congress to "promote the Progress of Science and Useful Arts, by Securing for limited Times to * * * Inventors the exclusive Right to their * * * Discoveries * * *."[1] This clause seems utilitarian, intended to advance the public interest, not to recognize in inventors a natural right. Congress has consistently so responded. The patent statutes strike a bargain between the government, representing the public interest, and the inventor. The bargain encourages investment in innovation by

---

8. Hettinger, *Justifying Intellectual Property,* 18 Phil. & Pub. Aff. 31 (1989); Gordon, *A Property Right in Self-Expression: Equality and Individualism in the Natural Law of Intellectual Property,* 102 Yale L.J. 1533 (1993). Radin, *Property and Personhood,* 34 Stan. L. Rev. 957 (1982). See P. Mergers, P.Menell, M. Lemley and T. Jorde, Intellectual Property in the New Technological Age 3–12 (1997).

9. Joyce et al., Copyright Law 4–5 (2d ed. 1991).

10. Id. (citing MacPherson, The Political Theory of Possessive Individualism: Hobbes to Locke (1962)).

§ 15.3

1. U.S. Const. Art. I, § 8, cl. 8.

enabling the inventor to internalize benefits of a qualifying invention. If the invention is patent-worthy, the inventor must disclose it to the public. In return he gains a proprietary interest in it for a period, currently twenty years from the date of application. At the end of the term the invention enters the public domain. This tradeoff enriches the public to the extent that it encourages investment leading to innovation. Whether or not resulting innovations are patentable, the benefit to the public from any innovation that would not have occurred but for the patent statute constitutes an efficiency attributable to the patent system. But the statutory trade off also imposes costs on the public. No doubt some inventions for which valid patents are issued would have occurred even if there were no patent system or if that system gave less copious rights then in fact it confers. Any enhancement in the cost of a product resulting from patent protection is an allocative loss if the invention would have occurred without the patent. The patent system encourages investment in innovation and by doing so may correct or reduce a market failure, bringing investment in innovation closer to the optimum. But this is done, perhaps inevitably, in a rough and imprecise way. Every patent can yield harms—gratuitously excessive protection—as well as benefits.

Taking the pharmaceutical industry as an example, one might expect that patent protection afforded new drugs would serve as an incentive for drug companies to concentrate their research and development on diseases or ailments that cause the most illness and death. But critics of the drug industry believe that the industry devotes relatively little to basic research on diseases such as AIDS or cancer, instead focusing on copy-cat designer drugs that sell well and represent a relatively low developmental challenge. It is reported, for example, that most of the new drugs pharmaceutical firms have brought to the market are versions of drugs previously marketed.[2] After the 1987 introduction of Mevacor, a statin drug that lowers cholesterol, pharmaceutical manufacturers responded by introducing five other statins. The wide use of these drugs suggests a genuine need is being addressed, but it is unclear whether the sums spent on developing and promoting variations on a successful drug might better be spent on basic research that could lead to breakthroughs in heretofore unaddressed areas. The patent reward system, it would seem, provides a substantial incentive to bring to market variations on a successful formula precisely because much of the underlying work has been done and the marketing potential has already been proven. Patent rewards, however, may work far less effectively in promoting basic research when the marketing potential of any new ideas is highly uncertain.

A related point is that the monetary rewards from the exclusivity conferred by IP law provide an incentive for an IP holder to obtain, retain and extend those rights for the longest possible period. The IP holder may spend substantial funds to these ends. Thus, for example, an

---

2. Marcia Angell, The Truth About the Drug Companies 74–93 (2004).

IP holder might engage in any of the following conduct that would not enhance (and may injure) competition:[3]

1) Lobby legislative bodies to enact legislation that retains or extends a particular patent monopoly;

2) Engage in litigation that increases a rival's costs in producing or selling a competing product (for example, litigation designed to delay or block the introduction of a generic drug that is identical to a drug with expiring patent protection);

3) Use patents to block a rival's access to technology, or raise the rival's costs (these patents may be validly issued, but may also be patents that have been issued because of loopholes or deficiencies in the patent issuance process);[4]

4) File patent applications that would control possible improvements or modifications in the original invention, possibly extending the effective period of protection;

5) File repeated amendments to a patent application, preserving the opportunity to restructure patent application to raise rivals' costs and extend the date that exclusivity would terminate; or

6) Use grant back licenses or cross licenses to establish a cartel-like arrangement that limits competition among rivals.

There are troubling indications that patent rewards have fostered a great deal of rent-seeking behavior. Among these indications is the increased attention paid by the enforcement agencies to IP-related abuses.[5] Again using the pharmaceutical industry as an example, critics of that industry charge that excessive amounts are spent in promoting patent-protected drugs precisely because of the high profits associated with exclusive patent rights. Effective but no-longer patent-protected drugs are not promoted. An example is the promotion of patent-protected hypertension drugs to lower blood pressure. These drugs were new on the market and assumed by physicians to be superior to diuretics, an older type of drug prescribed to reduce high blood pressure. Hypertension drugs were widely prescribed for high blood pressure until a 2002 study showed that diuretics were equally effective in reducing blood pressure and superior in preventing some of high blood pressure's complications.[6] All of this suggests that the patent rewards currently

3. Many of these abusive tactics are described in Report of the Federal Trade Commission, To Promote Innovation: The Proper Balance of Competition and Patent Law Policy (2003), available at <http://www.ftc.gov/os/2003/10/innovationrpt.pdf>

4. A variation on this theme may be Unocal Corp's alleged conduct in defrauding California air pollution regulators into adopting air quality standards for gasoline that required the use of Unocal patents that would result in hundreds of millions of dollars of royalties for the firm. In the Matter of Union Oil Co. of California, FTC Docket No. 9305 (July 7, 2004)(Decision of the FTC reinstating administrative complaint against Unocal), available at <http://www.ftc.gov/os/adjpro/d9305/040706commissionopinion.pdf>

5. Report of the Federal Trade Commission on Patent Policy, supra note 3.

6. Angell, supra note 2, at 95–99.

available for drug manufacturers may generate behavior that not only won't help consumers but may actually harm them.

To qualify for a patent, the subject matter must be a process, machine, manufacture, composition of matter or improvement thereon.[7] Protection can be earned only if the invention exceeds significant standards of utility,[8] novelty[9] and non-obviousness.[10] There must be disclosure sufficient to enable the invention to be practiced.[11] The scope of the protection is limited to what appears in the applicant's valid claims.[12] To the extent all these requirement's are met, the patentee, for the term, gains the right to exclude others from "making, using, offering for sale, or selling the invention * * *."[13] Inferentially, the right to suppress is included, for nothing in the statute obliges the patentee either to use or to license.

If statutory subject matter is involved and all statutory standards are met, the patentee gains sweeping rights. Some judgment about the social importance and significance of the claimed invention can be and sometimes is exercised in deciding whether a particular subject matter (say, a mathematical algorithm) falls within the language of Section 101 and whether the standards of Sections 101, 102 and 103 are met. If some standards are met but one or more fails, by however small a margin, no rights at all are gained. There are no tradeoffs, such as less protection, or protection for a shorter time, for a lesser contribution. Neither is there any inquiry about whether the invention would have occurred without the statute or with a lower level of statutory protection. Congress in striking a bargain with inventors uses a "form contract" that applies to all innovations in all industries.

Although issues about subject matter and qualification are initially raised and resolved in an ex parte administrative proceeding before the Patent and Trademark Office,[14] they can be and often are relitigated in court when a patentee sues to enforce. Enforcement claims can also give rise to contentious issues about the scope of the valid claims and whether the accused device infringes them. In evaluating whether a particular invention falls within the subject matter and meets these high, general standards, the agency and the courts do have a balancing role to play. They also have some discretion—in some contexts, significant discretion—in making decisions about infringement. To the extent that such discretion exists, a court may exercise it to protect only what needs protection in order to encourage innovation, thereby avoiding gratuitous over-protection which depletes the public domain. Only through perspectives that balance encouraging new innovations with assuring adequate access to technological knowledge already achieved

---

7. 35 U.S.C.A. § 101 (1994).

8. 35 U.S.C.A. § 101 (1994).

9. 35 U.S.C.A. § 101, 102 (1994).

10. 35 U.S.C.A. § 103 (1994).

11. 35 U.S.C.A. § 112 (1994).

12. 35 U.S.C.A. §§ 111, 112, 113, 115 (1994).

13. 35 U.S.C.A. § 154.

14. 35 U.S.C.A. § 114.

will the constitutional and statutory goal of promoting science and the useful arts be achieved.

There are many unresolved or debated issues about patentability and about infringement concerning which it might be useful for courts to evaluate the extent and scope of protection needed to encourage successful innovation. Here are a few examples: Should the innovator who first purified a natural product to a "commercially and therapeutically" useful level[15] be entitled to a product patent? Only a process patent? Only trade secrets protection? Should the discovery of genes or other substances that have research uses that may yield therapeutic outcomes meet the utility test?[16] When an applicant attempts to limit the use of an algorithm sufficiently to gain patent protection for the claimed use, how and where should the line be drawn to avoid granting more protection than needed to stimulate the innovation.[17] In sum, the most important problem may not concern how patent law and antitrust interact, but the extent to which the overall efficiency benefits from patent law could be enhanced by integrating an ex post prospective into the evaluation of patent issues that seem debatable when examined solely from an ex ante, statutory perspective.

§ 15.4   Copyright Law and Resource Allocation

15.4a.   Copyright Basics

Federal copyright, like a patent, stems from Article I, Section 8, of the Constitution, which invites an instrumental analysis. The constitutional mandate is to promote progress in the arts by protecting "writings" of "authors" for "limited times."[1] To comply Congress must balance incentives to authors to produce new writings against deterrence to the production of such work resulting from excessive restraints on access to writings already completed.[2] The 1790 Copyright Act granted protection only to books, and for a renewable term of 14 years.[3] It was amended from time to time to widen coverage.[4] In 1909 copyright act protection was broadened further and expanded to a 28 year renewable

---

15.   Parke–Davis & Co. v. H.K. Mulford Co., 189 F. 95 (C.C.S.D.N.Y.1911), *aff'd in part, rev'd in part*, 196 F. 496 (2d Cir. 1912).

16.   Cf. Amgen, Inc. v. Chugai Pharmaceutical Co., Ltd., 927 F.2d 1200 (Fed.Cir. 1991).

17.   See State Street Bank & Trust Co. v. Signature Financial Group, Inc., 149 F.3d 1368 (Fed.Cir.1998). Cf. In re Alappat, 33 F.3d 1526 (Fed.Cir.1994).

§ 15.4

1.   The constitutional terms that justify copyright, "writings" and "authors," have both been given wide reading.

2.   See Sony Corp. of Am. v. Universal City Studios, Inc., 464 U.S. 417, 429, 104 S.Ct. 774, 78 L.Ed.2d 574 (1984).

3.   Act of May 31, 1790, 1 Stat. 124.

4.   For example, prints, musical compositions, dramatic works, photographs, artistic works and sculpture were covered as writings of authors. See, Act of April 29, 1802, 2 Stat. 171; Act of February 3, 1831 4 Stat. 436; Act of August 18, 1856 11 Stat. 138; Act of March 3, 1865, 13 Stat. 540; Act of July 8, 1870, ch. 230, 16 Stat. 198.

term.[5] Both scope and term of protection were expanded by passage of the 1976 Act and yet again in 1996.[6]

The standards for copyright are considerably lower than those for patents, although the term of protection is longer. Authorship is required, but broadly construed.[7] Originality is needed, but only a modicum: Beyond that the author may not copy the work from another (the "independent selection" requirement), only minimal, almost trivial, creativity suffices.[8] The work must be fixed in a tangible medium, but even quite ephemeral media have sometimes met this standard,[9] and under present law protection reposes without need for formalities as soon as the work is fixed.[10] But in two important ways the scope of statutory protection is lower than that which a patent procures. First, copyright protects the author's expression, not her ideas nor the facts, information, procedures, processes, systems, methods of operation, concepts, principles or discoveries set forth in her work, however new or useful these may be, and regardless of the form in which they are presented.[11] In most instances any copyrightable expression will, of itself, disclose any underlying and unprotectable facts or ideas adhering in the protectable mode of expression. These, being in the public domain, will be available to all others so long as expressed by them in different, non-infringing ways. But copy-rightable expression in machine readable software does not, of itself, disclose the underlying and unprotectable idea. Hence, patent-like protection—not for the expression but for the idea itself—can be obtained by such a copyright unless competitors

---

5. Copyright Act of 1909, ch. 320, § 9, 35 Stat. 1077.

6. Copyright Act of 1976, Pub. L. No. 94–553, 90 Stat. 2541. This act extended the maximum term from 56 years to the life of the author plus 50 years, or 75 years from the date of publication, or, in the case of works for hire, anonymous, or pseudonymous works, 100 years from creation. Recent amendments, ostensibly to bring the law into accord with European law, have extended the basic term to life plus 70 years and extended other terms comparably. It has been common wisdom at least since Macaulay's speech in 1841: (1) that copyright does both good (the incentive) and evil (the monopoly), and (2) that the evil is proportionate to the length of protection, while the good is manifestly "front loaded." As Macaulay put it, a "monopoly of sixty years produces twice as much evil as a monopoly of thirty years, and thrice as much evil as a monopoly of twenty years. But it is by no means the fact that a posthumous monopoly of sixty years gives an author thrice as much pleasure and thrice as strong a motive as a posthumous monopoly of twenty years. On the contrary, the difference is so small as to be hardly perceptible." MACAULAY, PROSE AND POETRY, 731 (Yancy ed., 1967). Despite the common recognition of these facts the information industries have persistently and successfully lobbied for longer and longer terms.

7. 17 U.S.C.A. § 102 (1994); see Feist Publications, Inc. v. Rural Telephone Service Co., Inc., 499 U.S. 340, 111 S.Ct. 1282, 113 L.Ed.2d 358 (1991).

8. 17 U.S.C.A. §§ 101, 102 (1994); see Feist Publications, Inc. v. Rural Telephone Service, Inc., 499 U.S. 340, 111 S.Ct. 1282, 113 L.Ed.2d 358 (1991).

9. 17 U.S.C.A. § 102. See Williams Electronics, Inc. v. Arctic Intern., Inc., 685 F.2d 870 (3d Cir.1982); Triad Systems Corp. v. Southeastern Express Co., 64 F.3d 1330 (9th Cir.1995), cert. denied, 516 U.S. 1145, 116 S.Ct. 1015, 134 L.Ed.2d 96 (1996).

10. 17 U.S.C.A. § 102; see, Pacific & Southern Co. Inc. v. Duncan, 744 F.2d 1490 (11th Cir.1984), cert. denied, 471 U.S. 1004, 105 S.Ct. 1867, 85 L.Ed.2d 161 (1985).; Apple Computer, Inc. v. Microsoft Corp., 35 F.3d 1435 (9th Cir.1994), cert. denied, 513 U.S. 1184, 115 S.Ct. 1176, 130 L.Ed.2d 1129 (1995).

11. 17 U.S.C.A. § 102(b) (1994); see, Kepner–Tregoe, Inc. v. Leadership Software, Inc., 12 F.3d 527 (5th Cir.1994), cert. denied, 513 U.S. 820, 115 S.Ct. 82, 130 L.Ed.2d 35 (1994); Gund, Inc. v. Applause, Inc., 809 F.Supp. 304 (S.D.N.Y.1993).

remain free to "copy" for the purpose of reverse engineering. Second, copyright protects only against copying, not against independent production of the protected expression.[12]

While the instrumental thrust of the Constitution and the copyright statute are both reasonably clear, courts have, at times, drifted to other philosophical rationales. For example, finessing questions about what constitutes authorship and what degree of originality is needed, considerable case law developed which justified protection of non-creative works like databases on "sweat of the brow" theories.[13] In *Feist*,[14] the Supreme Court rejected this approach, though its opinion does not clearly signify how much originality is prerequisite. Of course, one can offer instrumental and labor theory of value justifications for protecting data bases (or other accumulations of facts) which require investment that might be unduly discouraged if not protected against free riders.[15] But these justifications, which might warrant legislative protection based on the commerce clause, do not fit comfortably under the phrasing of the copyright clause of the constitution.

Unresolved or debatable issues occur in copyright law as they do in patent law and here, too, courts, when drawing relevant lines, could usefully consider the extent and scope of protection needed to encourage the innovation for which protection is being claimed. The originality requirement, as an example, is replete with difficult issues: Does the existence or non-existence of utility affect the degree of originality required?[16] Should 'scenes a faire' be protectable "arrangements" when presented in sequences; should they be protected as a "series" when presented in an audio visual sequence?[17] Should derivative works be subjected to a higher originality standard?[18] So, too, the lines delimiting protectable subject matter. For example, what is the proper test for protection for a character in a play or a film? Who is entitled to protection when the character is delineated in part by the script writer and in part by the actor—indeed not only under copyright law, but also under the right of publicity?[19] Here too, as in respect to patent law, the constitutional and statutory goals call for judgment and balance between incentives for innovation and access to available information. Inevitably, courts must resolve such issues. The most sensible way of doing so is to strike a reasonable balance between the ex ante interest (giving suffi-

---

12. Gund, Inc. v. Smile International, Inc., 691 F.Supp. 642 (E.D.N.Y.1988), *aff'd* 872 F.2d 1021 (2d Cir. 1989).

13. Jeweler's Circular Pub. Co. v. Keystone Pub. Co., 281 Fed. 83, 88 (2d Cir. 1922).

14. Feist Publications, Inc. v. Rural Telephone Service Co., Inc., 499 U.S. 340, 111 S.Ct. 1282, 113 L.Ed.2d 358 (1991).

15. There have been proposals for federal statutory protection of data bases under the commerce clause. H.R. 1476, 94th Cong., 2nd Sess. at 54, *reprinted in* U.S. Code Cong. & Ad. News 5659, 5667 (1976).

16. Oddzon Products v. Oman, 16 U.S.P.Q.2d 1225, 1989 WL 214479 (D.D.C. 1989).

17. Atari Games Corp. v. Oman, 979 F.2d 242 (D.C.Cir.1992).

18. Gracen v. Bradford Exch., 698 F.2d 300 (7th Cir.1983); Entertainment Research Group, Inc. v. Genesis Creative Group, Inc., 122 F.3d 1211 (9th Cir.1997), *cert. denied*, 523 U.S. 1021, 118 S.Ct. 1302, 140 L.Ed.2d 468 (1998).

19. Cf. Anderson v. Stallone, 11 U.S. P.Q.2d (BNA) 1161 (C.D.Cal.1989).

cient protection to encourage innovation) and the ex post concern (not depleting the public domain and conferring market power by gratuitously granting more protection than needed to attain an optimum level of innovation).

15.4b. Computers and the Integration of IP and Competition Policy: The Judicial Role

Section 15.1 stresses that IP aimed, as it is, at encouraging R & D by internalizing a greater portion of IP benefits, is an aspect of competition policy, though one that looks only at the allocative problem as it appears ex ante—that is, before the innovation has been brought online. That introductory section also noted that in any IP system there is some room for judicial fine tuning of legislative decisions and that resulting judicial discretion could be used to some extent to bring ex ante and ex post allocative concerns into balance. IP litigation in the computer industry is illustrative. The modern computer utilizes several hardware and software elements. Hardware includes (1) a central processing unit (CPU), (2) three kinds of memory storage—random access chips (RAM) on to which data can be entered and erased, read only chips (ROM) with information permanently embedded, and disk space for storing data; (3) disk drives for transferring data and programs in and out of RAM; (4) an external keyboard and printer; and (5) connections to form networks with other computers.[20] Software provides basic computer management through an operating system that assigns data among the CPU, memory chips, drives, keyboard, printer, and application programs (including interface protocols designed to simplify and facilitate use) that perform desired processing tasks like word processing, bookkeeping, and linking to the Internet and the world wide web.[21]

A program is written in a source code, one of several high level languages in which programmers are literate, and then is translated by an assembler into machine readable binary language, the object code that the computer can read.[22] Programs may also be expressed in microcode. Finally, programs, of a sort, can be built into computer hardware: Functions are hardwired in the processor.

Markets for computer hardware and software are complex and dynamic. Virtually every organization interacting in the modern economy has data processing needs. Increasingly individual consumer households recognize that they have such needs (or wants), too. Hardware and chip manufacturers, software developers, assemblers and vendors, some operating at a single vertical level, others more fully integrated, respond to the resulting demands.[23] Dynamism in the hardware market has led to

---

20. P. MERGERS, P.MENELL, M. LEMLEY AND T. JORDE, INTELLECTUAL PROPERTY IN THE NEW TECHNOLOGICAL AGE 831 (1997). While most IP case books describe computer basics, the section Overview of Computer Technology and the Economics of Computer Markets (Id. at 830–850) is particularly well organized and lucid.

21. Id. at 833. See State Street Bank & Trust Co. v. Signature Financial Group, Inc., 149 F.3d 1368 (Fed.Cir. 1998).

22. Id. at 836–837.

23. Id. at 843–845.

rapid evolutions from an industry dominated by mainframes to one dominated by desktops and a responsive software evolution from a world of custom programs designed and sold after careful negotiation for specialized commercial purposes to a world of pre-packed general purpose applications marketed through shrink-wrap licenses.[24] Nor is there reason to suppose that the "winds of creative destruction" have blown themselves out.

Any of the elements involved in computers may be the subject of IP claims based on copyright, patent, trade secrets or trademarks. While copyright and contract (often in the form of shrink-wrap license claims) are nearly universal bases for claiming software protection, patents or trade secrets are often asserted to protect hardware and, with increasing frequency in recent years, as bases for protecting software.[25]

Consider copyright first.[26] The contrast between Whelan Associates, Inc. v. Jaslow Dental Lab., Inc.[27] and Computer Associates International v. Altai,[28] is a starting point. The *Whelan* opinion noted that while the idea of a conventional literary work is unprotected, its structure does gain protection. Thus, without comment on the breadth and elasticity of the concepts—idea, on the one hand, and structure on the other—it selected the software's ultimate purpose, management of a dental lab, as the unprotected idea, and regarded virtually everything at a lower level of generality as protectable parts of structure. *Altai*, by contrast, though recognizing that non-literal elements warrant some protection, meticulously broke the copyrighted program down into its various levels of abstraction, extracted unprotectable elements at each level (for example elements dictated by hardware or relevant industry constraints), and then compared the residual protected material with the structure of the allegedly infringing material.[29] On the face of it, *Whelan* is overbroad. Its gross response and simplistic analogies protect far more material than needs to be taken out of the public domain in order to fully meet the goal and purpose of copyright protection for software—namely, encourage software development. In consequence the *Whelan* opinion gratuitously facilitates proprietary power over ranges of material that ought to be open to competitive use, development and further improvement. Fortunately, abstraction-filtration-comparison, the approach initiated in *Altai*, is becoming standard.[30]

24. Id. at 844–45.

25. Id. at 833.

26. See generally, id., at 829–955.

27. Whelan Associates, Inc. v. Jaslow Dental Lab., Inc., 797 F.2d 1222 (3d Cir. 1986), *cert. denied*, 479 U.S. 1031, 107 S.Ct. 877, 93 L.Ed.2d 831 (1987).

28. Computer Associates International v. Altai, Inc., 982 F.2d 693 (2d Cir.1992).

29. Accord, Gates Rubber Co. v. Bando Chem. Indus., Ltd., 9 F.3d 823 (10th Cir. 1993); Engineering Dynamics, Inc. v. Structural Software, Inc., 26 F.3d 1335 (5th Cir.

1994), supplemented on denial of rehearing, 46 F.3d 408 (5th Cir.1995). See Samuelson, *The Nature of Copyright Analysis for Computer Programs: Copyright Law Professors' Brief Amicus Curiae in* Lotus v. Borland, 16 HASTINGS COMM. & ENT. L J. 657 (1994).

30. Id. See also Apple Computer, Inc. v. Microsoft Corp., 35 F.3d 1435 (9th Cir. 1994), *cert. denied*, 513 U.S. 1184, 115 S.Ct. 1176, 130 L.Ed.2d 1129 (1995), which filter out licensed and unprotected material before evaluating whether residual protectable material was infringed and called for a "virtual identity" standard of substantial

Another lively issue concerns intermediate copying of protected software in order to gain access to the unprotected ideas and principles that the code contains. Such copying was necessarily involved in *Altai*, though not separately challenged or discussed. *Sega Enteprises Ltd. v. Accolade, Inc.* involved disassembling protected machine readable software into human readable form in order to gain access to the unprotected ideas and principles. The court said that such reverse engineering was copying but was protected as fair use.[31] MAI Systems Corp. v. Peak Computer, Inc.,[32] by contrast, found infringement when an independent service provider made an unlicenced transfer of a diagnostic program from floppy disk storage to the computer's RAM at the request of a licensee of the software who owned the computer. The *Sega* court considered the competitive context and the effect on ex post competition before making its judgment call. *Sega* clearly resulted in the right substantive outcome, although one might have doubted that any infringement occurred at all or concluded that the effort to extend protection from expression to idea was a copyright misuse. It would be perverse to give copyright protection to machine readable expression if the consequence were assuring proprietary protection of unprotectable ideas. Nor does the *Sega* outcome wholly avoid the competition problems that can be associated with blocking reverse engineering. Even if a software copyright does not preclude reverse engineering, a contract might. Once a particular software product gains wide use or becomes an industry standard, its proprietor may license it subject either to a shrink wrap or click wrap license that precludes reverse engineering. If such a provision were valid and enforceable, the proprietor could protect not just his expression but his software idea—even dispute that only the expression and not the embodied idea has earned protection. Whether mass marketed shrink or click wrap restraints are enforceable is a matter of dispute.[33] One possibility is denial of enforcement under state

similarity for utilitarian works with a narrow range of protectable material.

31. Sega Enterprises Ltd. v. Accolade, Inc., 977 F.2d 1510 (9th Cir.1992). But cf. Walt Disney Productions v. Filmation Assoc., 628 F.Supp. 871 (C.D.Cal.1986). See also Sony Comp. Entertainment Inc. v. Connectix Corp., 48 F.Supp.2d 1212 (1999) (narrow *Saga* construction); L. A. News Service v. Reuters Television International, 942 F.Supp. 1265 (C.D.Cal.1996), *aff'd in part, rev'd in part*, 149 F.3d 987 (9th Cir. 1998). See the discussion in Lande & Sobin, *Reversal Engineering of Computer Software and the U.S. Antitrust Law*, 9 Harv. J. Law & Tech., 237 (1996). Despite theoretical issues and doubts about intermediate copying in other areas, most courts in software cases have approved reverse engineering. E.g., Vault Corp. v. Quaid Software Ltd., 847

F.2d 255, 270 (5th Cir.1988); DSC Communications v. DGI Technologies, 81 F.3d 597, 601 (5th Cir. 1996); Atari Games Corp. v. Nintendo of America, Inc., 975 F.2d 832 (Fed.Cir.1992). See also Digital Millennium Act of 1998 § 1201f(4) (reverse engineering exception to technology access constraint).

32. MAI Systems Corp. v. Peak Computer, Inc., 991 F.2d 511 (9th Cir.1993). But see 17 U.S.C.A. § 117(c) as amended in 1998 which makes such transfers for purpose of machine maintenance.

33. Compare Step–Saver Data Systems, Inc. v. Wyse Technology, 939 F.2d 91 (3d Cir. 1991); Vault Corp. v. Quaid Software Ltd., 847 F.2d 255, 268–70 (5th Cir.1988); and Arizona Retail Systems, Inc. v. Software Link, Inc., 831 F.Supp. 759 (D.Ariz. 1993) with ProCD, Inc. v. Zeidenberg, 86 F.3d 1447 (7th Cir.1996).

law as adhesion contracts,[34] or, if not, vulnerability on the ground that the state contract law is preempted by federal copyright law.[35]

MAI Systems[36] raises another problematic issue. An independent service provider made an unlicenced transfer of diagnostic software licensed to its customer from floppy disk storage to the RAM of the customer's computer in order to service the computer at the customer's request. The court held this to be an infringement, implying that whenever any computer is used to access any application program, however ephemerally and for whatever purpose, there is a copying infringement unless protected by one of the statutory limitations upon the exclusive rights. For example, suppose that A's program, X, is protected, and that B, a competitor, transfers X to the RAM of her computer and scans it on her screen in order to identify more precisely its unprotected idea and any unprotected elements. *MAI* suggests that B is infringing. Indeed, *MAI* underlies the position taken in the Clinton administration white paper that any downloading from the Internet constitutes infringement.[37] Whether any use of a computer involves "copying" the software that is temporarily transferred to the RAM raises a discrete legal question, one that should be answered in a consistent way in every context. Nevertheless, recognition that in some contexts an affirmative answer might lead to blatantly anticompetitive outcomes should be a factor in deciding what that consistent answer should be. If the floppy disk is not itself an infringing copy of the protected software, and the transfer to RAM is not the first step toward printing out and distributing protected material (both of which are independently infringing acts), there is only a remote relationship between such a transfer and the kind of copying that misappropriates copyright values. This fact, together with the risk of competitively adverse outcomes in some situations, argues against treating such a transfer as copying. For this reason the result in *MAI* seems wrong.

Problems of possibly gratuitous protection also occur with patent protection of software. In State Street Bank & Trust Co. v. Signature Financial Group, Inc.[38] a patent was used successfully to protect application software. The case serves to show why courts in software cases should consider the public interest in access and competition when deciding borderline issues about whether a claim is within protectable subject matter or deciding about the scope of protection. The Signature patent claimed to protect software for a data processing system. The system facilitated joint management of separate mutual funds, thus enabling scale economies to be attained. The essence of the claim was an algorithm that calculated the effects on the separate funds of transactions in the combined corpus. The district court had found the patent invalid, holding that the claim based on a mathematical algorithm was

---

34. Step–Saver Data Systems, supra, n. 33. But see ProCD, Inc. supra, n. 33, which flatly rejects adhesion analysis.

35. Vault Corp., supra, n. 33. But see ProCD, Inc. supra, n. 33, which also finds that copyright law does not preempt a broadly used shrink-wrap retail marketing scheme.

36. 991 F.2d 511.

37. White Paper: Intellectual Property and the National Information Infrastructure, Part IV.A. 4. a., Working Group Report, available at <http://www.uspto.gov/web/ offices/com/doc/ipnii/ipnii.txt>.

38. 149 F.3d 1368 (Fed.Cir.1998).

not protectable subject matter. The court of appeals reversed. It ruled that a "transformation of data representing discrete dollar amounts by a machine through a series of mathematical calculations into a final share price constitutes a practical application of * * * [the algorithm] because it produces 'a useful, concrete and tangible result'—a final share price."[39] In so doing, the court rejected the concept of a business method exception to subject matter and, seemingly eschewing earlier cases,[40] held that any application of a mathematical algorithm that achieved a practical outcome was patentable if it met the new, useful and non-obvious requirements.

The spacious language of Section 101's subject matter description,[41] the Supreme Court's emphasis of its breadth,[42] and the fact that there is no theoretical difference between an algorithm hard wired into a machine and an algorithm embodied in software that commands a machine's performance, all tend to support this court of appeals decision. Yet, the prior case law made Section 101 a barrier to overbroad patent protection for application programs—protection that might preempt the result achieved by the patented application even when attained through software using different expressive elements. For example, a patent to the first producer of spread sheet software or word processing software might have established an overbroad patent monopoly on such applications. Indeed, the originator of an operating system that used a mouse and screen icons to interface with users might have attained protection against any other such operating system. Protections of such vast scope seem greatly excessive of what is needed to motivate sufficient investment in software development, especially given first user advantages and network effects which amplify those advantages. Perhaps such breadth could be constrained by more parsimonious construction in software patents of the new, useful and non-obvious standards[43] than those terms now receive in evaluating other machine or process patents. But to develop a case law which treated these Sections 101, 102, and 103 standards differently depending on field of application would produce its own tensions and uncertainties. For these reasons, *State Street Trust* seems a threat to adequate continuing software development. Perhaps ongoing experience will teach the Court of Appeals, the Supreme Court or Congress that some means of containing the breadth of software

39. Id. at 1373.

40. While this outcome may find some support in In re Lowry, 32 F.3d 1579 (Fed. Cir.1994), the decision not only seems to abandon the implications of Diamond v. Diehr, 450 U.S. 175, 101 S.Ct. 1048, 67 L.Ed.2d 155 (1981) but also the teaching of In re Freeman, 573 F.2d 1237 (CCPA 1978), In re Walter, 618 F.2d 758 (CCPA 1980) and In re Abele, 684 F.2d 902 (CCPA 1982), all widely regarded as showing that an invention utilizing an algorithm built into software can be patentable subject matter only when the invention as a whole showed

a physical relationship between the software's algorithm and the claims. In effect, an algorithm could be covered only when embodied in a machine or linked as a step in a physical process. See Chisum, *The Patentability of Algorithm*, 47 U. Pɪᴛᴛ. L. Rᴇᴠ. 959 (1986).

41. 35 U.S.C.A. § 101.

42. E.g., Diamond v. Chakrabarty, 447 U.S. 303, 100 S.Ct. 2204, 65 L.Ed.2d 144 (1980).

43. 35 U.S.C.A. §§ 101, 102 and 103.

patents is essential to achieving the constitutional purpose of patent law.[44]

§ 15.5 Trademark Law and Resource Allocation

Trademarks facilitate brand marketing that is central to modern distribution. Brand marketing has substantial benefits detailed in § 6.2, but its use can create single brand market power addressed in § 2.4e. Abuses of such power, usually vertical restraints, can be antitrust vulnerable as noted in § 6.3a, 6.3c, 7.2c and 15.2. See also § 3.3c.

§ 15.6 Strategic Use of Intellectual Property in Competition

In today's dynamic economy, gaining an advantage in the realm of ideas and information is a step toward competitive success. Each competing firm in a dynamic market must work out for itself the ways it will use ideas and information to improve and differentiate its product or service. All firms in such markets will inevitably dip into numerous information sources. They will, in part, use material drawn from the public domain. But they may also draw, in part, on material recently originated by others, and/or on in-house creativity. A competitor that utilizes elements originated by others, may be—or may not be—vulnerable to an intellectual property claim. And where a competitor uses elements originated in-house, it may—or may not—gain, or be in a position to gain, proprietary control of those elements. Because competitors are prospecting a range of sources and processing what they find in search of advantage, and because intellectual property law may do service either as a weapon or as a shield, it is not surprising that both proprietary claims to intellectual output and conflicting claims that such materials are already owned by others or are in the public domain are important parts of competitive strategy.

Aggressive competition alone does not violate the Sherman Act. Hence, most strategic uses of intellectual property do not give rise to antitrust issues. A routine assertion of statutory proprietary rights under patent or copyright statutes may distort resource allocation to the extent that, in the given context, the rights these statutes grant are either too narrow or overbroad. But where Congress has clearly struck the balance, no court has a credential to fine tune statutory outcomes either in IP cases or antitrust cases. For example, a "breakthrough" patent might yield to the patentee an economic monopoly. Regardless of how broad the area of protection afforded by a valid patent, the patentee may lawfully occupy that market or market segment alone, excluding all others, and charging such prices as the market will bear; even if an economic monopoly is the result, doing these things are within the patentee's statutory right.[1] When an intellectual property right is based

---

44. U.S. Const. Art. 1, § 8.

§ 15.6

1. See, e.g., Datagate, Inc. v. Hewlett–Packard Co., 60 F.3d 1421, 1427 (9th Cir.

on trade secret, trademark, trade dress or other interest bottomed on state law, federal antitrust could preempt as a matter of constitutional theory. But as shown in Chapter XIV, the state action exemption might preclude antitrust liability.[2] But where an IP plaintiff turns to state law sources for protection, it can face another serious preemption problem. If the state right is equivalent to one of the exclusive rights within the general scope of copyright, and two other requirements are met, Section 301(a) of the copyright law can result in preemption of the state claim, thereby widening the possible range for antitrust enforcement by displacing the statutory exemption.[3] In any event, use of intellectual property to attack competitors can give rise to an antitrust issue if the IP is used in ways that exceed the bounds of the IP proprietary grant. If doing this reduces output (and thus raises prices and distorts allocation) and if the particular strategic conduct was chosen by the proprietor because of its anticompetitive potential, antitrust may come strongly into play.[4]

Antitrust issues can arise in an IP context either when two firms act concertedly in a way that gives rise to and exploits IP-based market power or when one firm possesses such market power and uses it in exclusionary ways. Issues involving concerted conduct can arise out of horizontal or vertical relationships established or implicated through licensing relationships. These issues are examined in §§ 15.9 and 15.10. Single firm issues can arise whenever IP alone or with other market factors confers substantial market power. In the current economy power based wholly or in part on IP is not uncommon. Hence, antitrust issues based on the conduct of a single firm IP exploitation are encountered. These issues are examined in § 15.8.

In any market, first entry advantages can be significant. Sometimes they can be bolstered and extended by IP. In markets for products or services characterized by significant network externalities, the advantages of a first entrant protected by IP will be greatly amplified. If the first entrant's IP protected product or service falls anywhere on a quality spectrum from excellent to good-enough, significant network externalities may raise high entry barriers against later entrants. One recent manifestation of this is the Windows operating system. This IP protected, user-friendly software has many advantages. As it thrived in the market and application system developers zeroed in on the exploding market for desktops, the Windows operating system, the best of few good systems, quickly became dominant and the network advantages associated with it multiplied. Today, Windows is found in about 95 percent of desktop computers, leaving about 5 percent accessible for competitors.

1995), *cert. denied*, 517 U.S. 1115, 116 S.Ct. 1344, 134 L.Ed.2d 492 (1996); Service & Training, Inc. v. Data General Corp., 963 F.2d 680, 686 (4th Cir.1992). See Vermut, *A Synthesis of the Intellectual Property and Antitrust Laws: A Look At Refusal to License Computer Software*, 22 Colum.-VLA J.L. & Arts, 27–31 (1997).

2. See § 14.6.

3. 17 U.S.C.A. § 301(a). See 3 P. Goldberg, Copyright (2d ed. 1996)

4. Of course a violation of Sherman Section 2 requires a sufficient showing of power or an attempt or conspiracy to monopolize and a violation of Section 1 requires concerted conduct.

It is no antitrust violation to gain even monopoly power by an effective entry with a quality product or service into an IP protected market yielding network externalities. But when a firm possesses substantial power in any such market, the law may narrow its otherwise very broad strategic options. Some of its conduct options could protect or reinforce its power, or expand that power into other, different but related markets. Also, some of those options may enable it to block off innovating paths that could transform the market by generating new and different alternatives to the currently dominant product. Conduct chosen by a monopolist because it may have effects such as these can do significant competitive harm—harm that is in no sense an inevitable development from the monopolist's market position and harm that is neither earned, nor justified by the monopolist's innovation or initial entry. Even though an outgrowth of legitimate, IP advantages, strategically based expansion or reinforcement of power does not flow from innovation and first entry alone, it is a consequence also of deliberate choices about what tactics to bring to bear on other market actors. Therefore, if such tactics harm competition and stifle innovation more than they yield in efficiency, and if they can be identified and rectified by judicial process and judicial remedies, they should be subject to antitrust constraint.

Lorain Journal Co. v. United States[5] is a classic example of deliberate, strategic conduct chosen to protect or reinforce a position of power. Defendant dominated the daily newspaper market in Lorain by consequence of initial entry, absorbing a competitor, and the provision of a product in this thin market on a quality spectrum sufficiently high to discourage entry by another daily paper. But even by the late 1940s information technologies were not wholly stable. Radio was a partial substitute capable of drawing off some of Lorain Journal's advertising revenue. When a new station was licensed in the area in 1948 defendant developed a strategy to forestall erosion of its power. It refused to accept advertising from Lorain merchants that advertised with the radio station. The court rejected the Journal's defense, a claim of a right to select its customers on terms it thought appropriate. When used strategically "as a purposeful means of monopolizing interstate commerce" such conduct violates Sherman Section 2.[6] This act of monopolizing, take note, was not an effort to expand power from the newspaper to the local radio market, much less to use newspaper power to monopolize radio. The essence of the offense was taking strategic action to inhibit erosion of power in the monopolized newspaper market by stifling partial competition from a different medium. That conduct effectively increased the costs and reduced the revenue of the partial competitor, apparently at relatively little cost to the defendant. On the face of it, this strategy stifled the choices open to advertisers and narrowed the sources of commercial information available to ultimate consumers.

---

5. 342 U.S. 143, 72 S.Ct. 181, 96 L.Ed.   **6.** Id. at 155.
162 (1951).

Power can be protected or reinforced by any strategy putting rivals at significant relative disadvantage. For example, practices that require customers to deal solely with the monopolist if they wish to deal with it at all can foreclose current competitors, discourage entry and inhibit innovation. Classic devices include exclusive dealing and requirements contracts. IP licenses committing licensees to use the licensed IP exclusively or for all requirements for a period of time approaching, equal to, or longer than the product cycle of the IP would clearly have such an effect. Less direct methods may achieve similar results. Suppose, for example, a patentee of a micro-processor or the holder of an operating system copyright were to license OEMs to use the protected IP on price terms requiring payment based on the number of computers they made (rather than on the number in which the proprietary product or IP is used). OEMs wishing to use that microprocessor or IP in most of their output but wanting a competitive alternative in some of their output would need to pay two license fees for computers using the alternative— one for the alternative, and one for the microprocessor or IP used in the OEM's other units.[7] Predatory pricing, selectively used, can also protect and reinforce power.

Strategies, such as raising rivals costs or leveraging, can be used to bring power in one market to bear in a separate, but related market. Doing this can injure competition in, or even threaten monopoly in, the second market. Tying is a direct method of leveraging. To refuse to license an IP protected software product unless the licensee accepts another software or hardware product would be an example. If the licensor had power in the market for the first product that power could distort competition in the second. If several markets are linked to the first market (as, for example, application systems, browsers, and other devices are linked to an operating system), such tactics might be used to expand operating system power into several or even all of the linked markets, thereby reducing consumer choice, increasing competitor's costs and discouraging entry in the linked markets. Worse still, such a tactic might inhibit innovation in the linked markets; because no innovator, whatever the quality of his advance, would be able to exploit a linked market innovation without the cooperation of the firm dominating the first market, there would be little or no incentive for independent innovation in any linked market. A dominant firm might become a gatekeeper capable of influencing, perhaps even controlling, the rate, direction and agents of further development.[8]

Nor would leveraging have to be achieved through tying in order to harm competition. Pricing strategies, such as bundling products at a single price, or even product integration strategies, such as linking an

---

7. Prior to 1995, Microsoft used a "per processor" licensing fee for its Windows operating systems that was similar to that hypothesized in this text. This method of pricing licenses for Microsoft's Windows software was prohibited in a consent decree in United States v. Microsoft Corp., 1995–2 Trade Cases ¶ 71,096 (D.D.C. 1995).

8. This type of argument was persuasive in United States v. Microsoft Corp., 253 F.3d 34 (D.C.Cir.2001)(en banc), a case discussed in § 15.8c4.

operating system with an application system or with a device like a browser, might be designed to achieve similar purposes and effects. If blatant tying is used, the cost-benefit analysis is not likely to be complex. If two products with separate demand functions are involved and power is evident in one, tying can do significant harm and the possibility of benefit may be remote. When indirect leveraging strategies are used, analysis may be complex because bundling and product design strategies may yield efficiencies or other consumer benefits that may offset any resulting harms. For example, integration of a spread sheet or even a browser into an operating system might yield efficiencies such as fewer lines of code to accomplish the two functions. The marginal cost of the integrated product might be less than the aggregate marginal costs of the two previously separate products. Moreover, these users who would have selected the monopolist's version of each of the integrated items even if they were marketed separately would suffer no injury. But benefits are not the only competitive effects. There are also harms. Some users might prefer to use the monopolist's operating system, but a spreadsheet or browser produced by a competitor. Integration could narrow their choices. Also, by amplifying the network externalities which already favor a dominant operating system, integration might preempt market share, discourage entry, raise costs of remaining rivals and reduce incentives to innovate in the previously separate, but now integrated product market.

When network externalities are derived from dominant software or hardware a net competitive harm may be the consequence of any of the strategies summarized above that tend either to protect or to leverage power. In any such market there are also other miscellaneous strategies open to the dominant firm that might disrupt the functionality of other products. Such disruption might result, for example, from manipulating interfaces to inhibit inter-operability by withholding technological information about such matters as file formats, by favoring links to selectively preferred products or Internet content, or by manipulating compatibility test reports.

A foreclosure strategy similar to some of those outlined above was alleged in an Advanced Micro Device's (AMD's) suit against Intel.[9] Intel's then current micro processor chip was dominant and the company was developing an improvement. In order to forestall market gains being made by AMD against Intel's current chip, Intel allegedly threatened to deny its upcoming advanced chip to customers who purchased the AMD chip.[10] Such conduct, not a conventional tie but an exercise of power by refusal to deal in the future with customers currently turning to competitors, also has the elements of anti-competitive, exclusionary behavior. Assuming the requisite market power, Section 2 would be violated.

9. Fogt & Gotts, *The Antitrust and Technology Transfer Licensing Interface: A Comparative Analysis of Current Developments,* 13 INT'L TAX & BUS. LAW 1, 39 (1995) (noting the prospect of more active anti- trust enforcement involving intellectual property).

10. See Advanced Micro Devices, Inc. v. Intel Corp., 9 Cal.4th 362, 368 (Cal. 1994).

Even when no single firm has dominant power, intellectual property rights, used cooperatively, can give rise to Sherman Act issues. For example, a patentee might grant licenses but condition them on licensees following the licensor's pricing leads. Or it might use the licenses to divide markets. Also, suppose two or three competitors claim proprietary rights to technologies that could substitute for each other. If these technologies are pooled and managed jointly, power may result.[11] Would such pooling be justified if, say, each of the three proprietors had been asserting the validity of its own rights and challenging the validity of the claims of the other two and the pool arose as a settlement device?[12] Alternatively, suppose that two or three of the leading manufacturers of desktop computer hardware, tired of paying supracompetitive operating system license fees to a dominant software firm, set up and funded a joint subsidiary to develop, license and market a new desktop computer using the subsidiary's own, new, proprietary operating system. The venture might lead to power in a desktop computer hardware market. It might also reduce dominant firm power in desktop operating systems. Would the venture be vulnerable under Sherman Act Section 1 or Clayton Act Section 7?[13] Would harm in one market be weighed against increased competition in the other?

Finally, intellectual property could be used to impose license restraints that reduce not the competition faced by the IP proprietor but downstream competition among its licensees. Resale price, territorial or field of use restraints in licensees are all possible examples. Sections 15.8 through 15.10 will discuss monopolization, horizontal restraint and vertical restraint issues in which intellectual property is a strategic element. Before that, § 15.7 will examine antitrust guidelines on licensing IP expressing the enforcement intentions of the federal enforcement agencies.

§ 15.7 Antitrust Guidelines for the Licensing of Intellectual Property

In 1995 the Antitrust Division and the FTC published joint guidelines for intellectual property licensing[1] which state broad general principles about intellectual property protection and the antitrust laws. Using instructive examples, these Guidelines identify major concerns about anticompetitive uses of intellectual property, articulate relevant norms, and apply these to restraints such as tying, exclusive dealing, cross-

11. Whether power resulted would depend on whether there were other available substitute technologies.

12. Cf. Standard Oil Co. (Indiana) v. United States, 283 U.S. 163, 51 S.Ct. 421, 75 L.Ed. 926 (1931).

13. Cf. United States v. Borland International, Inc., 1992 WL 101767 (N.D.Cal. 1992) (court approved consent decree allowing Borland to acquire Ashton–Tate, subject

to Borland's agreement not to enforce certain intellectual property rights).

§ 15.7

1. Department of Justice and Federal Trade Commission, Antitrust Guidelines For the Licensing of Intellectual Property (1995), available at <http://www.usdoj.gov/atr/public/ guidelines/0558.htm> [hereinafter the IP–Antitrust Guidelines or, where clear from the context, the Guidelines].

licensing, pooling, grant backs, intellectual property acquisition programs, and enforcement of invalid intellectual property rights. The overriding principles as well as some specific points will be stressed here because they reflect current enforcement attitudes and are consistent with the trend of case law. First, the agencies, while not blind to distinctions between IP and other species of property, regard IP as basically similar to other property. The essence of all property is power to exclude. It is this capacity which, if misused, can have adverse competitive effects. While there can be differences in the significance of this power between one species of property and another (and when there are, the difference could have antitrust significance),[2] there can also be differences between one example of a particular species—say IP—and another example. As the ABA Antitrust Section Commentary on the Guidelines points out, where a process could be more easily reverse-engineered than invented around, a patent would confer far more power than a trade secret, but the reverse would be true for a process more easily invented around than reverse-engineered.[3]

Second, turning away from important older[4] as well as some more recent[5] case law, the Guidelines insist that no presumption of market power will be based on the mere existence of an intellectual property right. In theory, this is sound policy and consistent with the first principle. Capacity to do harm to competition may or may not be associated with possession of any such right to exclude; it depends entirely upon whether the right is broad enough to confer market power. This will turn upon whether unprotected close substitutes are accessible.[6] At the same time, it should be recognized that when a patent is genuinely the subject of litigation (as distinguished from a claim related to a patent advanced primarily to gain strategic advantage in a dispute not closely related to the IP), there is a very high probability that the patent confers market power. Although most patents confer little or no market power, those that are worth litigating about are those in which the exclusive rights have value: they allow the holder to generate profits that would not be available in the competitive market absent the exclusive rights. Unless acting for strategic reasons, a rational litigant would not spend a nickel litigating a worthless patent. Thus, as a method of structuring litigation so that it is both efficient and fair, a

---

2. For example, a real property interest is probably much less likely to confer economic market power than are intellectual property interest.

3. ABA Commentary on Draft Antitrust Guidelines For the Licensing and Acquisition of Intellectual Property, October 13, 1994, 14–15 [hereinafter ABA Guidelines Commentary].

4. Unites States v. Loew's, Inc., 371 U.S. 38, 83 S.Ct. 97, 9 L.Ed.2d 11 (1962).

5. Jefferson Parish Hospital Dist. No. 2 v. Hyde, 466 U.S. 2, 104 S.Ct. 1551, 80 L.Ed.2d 2 (1984).

6. The Supreme Court has recognized this when applying Sherman Section 2 (Walker Process Equipment, Inc. v. Food Machinery and Chemical Corp., 382 U.S. 172, 86 S.Ct. 347, 15 L.Ed.2d 247 (1965)), but not always when applying Sherman Section 1. United States v. Loew's, Inc., 371 U.S. 38, 45–47, 83 S.Ct. 97, 9 L.Ed.2d 11 (1962); Jefferson Parish Hospital Dist. No. 2 v. Hyde, 466 U.S. 2, 16, 104 S.Ct. 1551, 80 L.Ed.2d 2 (1984).

rebuttable presumption of market power may be sound, at least for some types of intellectual property. Placing the burden on the defendant to show that there are reasonable substitutes for its product may be both the fairest and most efficient way to order the litigation.[7]

Third, the Guidelines recognize that licensing is often efficiency producing and procompetitive. Although the Guidelines have been read to assert that licensing is "generally procompetitive,"[8] the guideline text does not say this, nor would it be sound to presume that any given license helps competition. The competitive effect of licensing will always depend on context and particulars.[9] True, any unconditional license may be more competitive than no license at all; even one competitor is better than none. But licenses may not be unconditional. The purpose and effect of any condition must be evaluated in the structural context in which it is utilized.

The potential benefits of licensing are clear enough. By deploying the relevant technology more broadly, licensing (with or without restrictions) may lead to more competition during the IP term. More extensive deployment may increase the likelihood or rapidity of improvement, which will maximize the chance that when the technology enters the public domain its value will be more widely appreciated and more quickly exploited (and perhaps still further developed). But when the way in which the licensee exploits the license is controlled by the licensor, either interdependently (as where a patentee with an economic monopoly grants a short term license with the unexpressed expectation that the license will follow the licensor's pricing lead for fear of non-renewal), or by explicit license restrictions, there may also be negative competitive effects that may offset or even overwhelm the advantages. If so, these must be placed on the scale. After all, the licensor grants the license not to serve the public interest, but because the licensor thinks the license will maximize it's own return. What the licensor does for itself may reduce licensor-licensee competition not only with respect to the subject matter under license, but even beyond it. The Guidelines, quite appropriately, recognize all of this. The analytical task they identify is to determine whether the license will inhibit competition that would have taken place if no license had been given.[10] For example, if the licensee would have entered the licensor's market by introducing a substitute, inventing around, or successfully challenging the licensor's IP claim (for example, by showing that a licensor's patent is invalid), the competition facilitated by the license is not a net gain.[11] There is also a loss of competition that would partially or even wholly offset any gain from the license. The Guidelines invite this basic analytical approach: if there does not appear to be any competition that the license discourages

---

7. The validity of the presumption of market power for IP goods is before the Supreme Court in Illinois Tool Works Inc., v. Independent Ink, Inc., *cert. granted*, 125 S. Ct. 2937, 162 L. Ed. 865 (2005).

8. ABA Guideline Commentary supra note 3, at p.19.

9. See § 15.8.

10. IP–Antitrust Guidelines § 4.1.2.

11. See, e.g., United States v. S.C. Johnson & Son, 1995–1 CCH Trade Cas. ¶ 70, 884 (N.D. Ill. 1994).

or precludes, the license has no competitive cost. Its effect on competition is beneficial or neutral and the inquiry ends. But if a possible adverse competitive effect can be inferred the negative and the positive consequences should be identified, evaluated and compared.

Balancing harms and benefits will often call for rule of reason analysis, but the guidelines do not foreclose use of the *per se* rule or truncated analysis, where appropriate.[12] Hence, there may be instances— say, where the benefits plainly overwhelm possible harms, or conversely—where the inquiry need not entail elaborate economic evidence. Also, there is a safe harbor: the agency will not normally challenge an IP license that is not facially anticompetitive when the licensor and licensees account for no more than 20 percent of any affected market.[13]

§ 15.8 Intellectual Property and Monopolization

There are three intellectual property strategies that could result in or threaten single firm monopolization and which might be vulnerable under Section 2. First, an IP right powerful enough to confer or threaten dominance in an economic market might be wrongfully obtained or two or more such rights collectively conferring such power might be wrongfully combined. Second, the lawful holder of IP giving substantial power in a market might exploit that IP in a manner that expands or protects the power by injuring competitors in a manner not efficiency justified. Third, the holder of IP yielding monopoly power might, by conduct not efficiency justified, lever that power to gain or threaten monopoly or substantial competitive injury in an adjacent aftermarket or a market for a complimentary product. Section 2 violations based on concerted conduct also constitute unreasonable restraints violating Section 1, or violations of Clayton Section 7, and are addressed in § 15.9 dealing with horizontal restraints.

Most IP antitrust cases arising under Sherman Section 2 have been patent cases. Indeed, IP other than patents, secret know how or software copyrights, is unlikely to yield sufficient economic power to gave rise to serious Section 2 issues. In this section, therefore, references to patents are sometimes intended generically to connote power-yielding patents or other IP. Throughout, this section accepts the Guidelines principle[1] that economic power should not be presumed from intellectual property, although a more limited presumption may be warranted. If the plaintiff establishes that an antitrust claim relating to tying or other abusive conduct of an IP holder is not advanced for strategic reasons and is genuinely the core of the economic dispute between the parties, it is very

---

12. IP–Antitrust Guidelines § 3.4; see also id. § 5.2, anticipating application of the *per se* rule for resale price maintenance.

13. Id. at § 4.1 ("Antitrust 'safety zone' ").

§ 15.8

1. Department of Justice and Federal Trade Commission, Antitrust Guidelines

For the Licensing of Intellectual Property § 2.2 (1995), available at <http://www.usdoj.gov/atr/public/guidelines/0558.htm> [hereinafter the IP–Antitrust Guidelines or, where clear from the context, the Guidelines].

likely that the IP right does confer market power. A more limited presumption recognizing this reality would be warranted. The Supreme Court has accepted certiorari in a case that will likely determine the future of the presumption.[2]

Section 15.8a. discusses market definition in IP-based cases, always an issue under Section 2 and sometimes an issue in other claims challenging IP strategies. Section 15.8b considers challenges under Section 2 to patent acquisitions. Thereafter, § 15.8c discusses Section 2 law applicable to using IP in ways that protect or expand market power by disadvantaging rivals, as by exclusive dealing, leveraging or refusal to deal.

15.8a. Market Definition in Cases Involving Intellectual Property

Conduct by a single firm cannot violate Section 2 unless it yields or threatens power in a well defined relevant market.[3] For example, a monopolist might by conduct allegedly violating Section 2 obtain, or exploit a patent or patents that gave it control of a significant product or several product markets. While a single patent or copyright, when combined with other advantages like network externalities, first entry and an appealing product, might give dominance over an industry, where only one species of IP is involved the relevant product market may well be narrow, specialized and small. Of course, all viable substitutes should be included and analyzed in accordance with the merger guidelines and conventional case law. Picture, for example, the scope of a market for ultra-high pressure waterjet intensifier pumps.[4] Also, as the IP–Antitrust Guidelines now suggest, it is possible to define either a technology or an R & D market that could be narrower still. Assume the following facts (variations on those in *Flow International*): One of the two firms researching a significant area used conduct vulnerable under Section 2 to gain a patent that blocked the only research path still open to the other. The result would be monopolization of a defined innovation market. Assuming the market definition would withstand judicial scrutiny and assuming the conduct sufficiently exceeded the "honestly industrial," and could not be efficiency justified, monopolization would result.[5]

Market definition can determine outcome in an antitrust-IP dispute, just as it can in other antitrust situations. The Guidelines call for analysis using broad norms that allow the agencies ample room to challenge any license regarded as a significant competitive threat. At a theoretical level the relevant market in which to gauge the effect of an IP restraint will always be the market in which that IP competes against

---

2. Illinois Tool Works Inc. v. Independent Ink, Inc., ___ U.S. ___, 125 S.Ct. 2937, 162 L.Ed.2d 865 (2005).

3. Id. at 177.

4. Cf. United States v. Flow International Corp., CA. No. 94–71320 (E.D. Mich. Filed Apr. 4, 1994).

5. In recent merger cases enforcement agencies have alleged similarly narrow innovation markets. E.g., Sensormatic Electronic Corp., FTC File No. 941–0126 (complaint).

other technologies. Often—indeed, typically—an affected market for goods will serve as a surrogate for this market. When this is true, merger guideline standards will be used by the enforcement agencies.[6] If A holds a patent on a new widget and licenses B, the effect of the license can be measured in the widget market; so, too, if A holds and licenses IP in a cost saving process for manufacturing widgets. Again, if gizmos are inputs essential to widget manufacture and A's proprietary technology pertains to gizmos, the widget market may be appropriate.[7]

At times, however, no surrogate goods market will adequately reflect the market power derived from the IP. In such instances analysis may require the definition of a market for the proprietary technology and any alternative technologies that might be substituted for it in order to produce the same goods or services or to produce other goods or services that are close substitutes for these.[8] On still other occasions there may be no surrogate goods market because the problem arises from the competitive effect of the license on research and development for products or processes yet to be developed. In such a case, the guidelines propose defining an "innovation market" consisting of "research and development directed to particular new or improved goods or process, and close substitutes for that research and development."[9] Suppose, for example, that a given product market is competitive, and that several alternative technologies for making the product are available and used, but that two firms in it are especially well positioned to do research and they alone are exploring a significant R & D area which, if successful, could yield significant advantage. If the two were to merge there might be little change in product market concentration. Nevertheless, a relevant R & D market could change from a two firm to a one firm market. This could reduce the research incentive, the aggregate research investment, and the number of research paths being simultaneously explored; it could also inhibit future development of a more diverse and competitive product market.[10]

15.8b. Intellectual Property Acquisitions and Sherman Act Section 2

15.8b1. Enforcing a Fraudulently Obtained, Or Otherwise Invalid, Patent

IP monopoly cases are governed by the standard Section 2 conduct test. If the monopolist acts to protect, expand or leverage monopoly power, or eliminate or injure competition in the monopolized market,

---

6. IP–Antitrust Guidelines at § 3.2.1.

7. Id.

8. Id. § 3.2.2.

9. Id. § 3.2.3.

10. Cf. United States v. Flow International Corp., C.A. No. 94–71320 (E.D. Mich. filed April 4, 1994), discussed in Dunlap, *A Practical Guide to Innovation Markets*, 9 ANTITRUST 21 (1995). See also Gilbert, *Defining the Crossroads of IP and the Antitrust*

Law: The 1995 Antitrust Guidelines for Licensing IP, 9 ANTITRUST 6, 7–8 (1995). The Guidelines use several examples to illustrate both market definition and *per se* and rule of reason analysis. This text will draw on these in discussing the ramifications of monopolization, horizontal restraint and vertical restraint law on intellectual property.

that conduct can violate Section 2. In *Walker Process* the Court held that a deliberate, knowingly false statement to the patent office committed to procure a patent followed by a suit to enforce against a competitor is antitrust-vulnerable. Such conduct will violate Section 2 if the other elements of that section's violation are established. Such a fraud, followed by a suit against a competitor knowingly to enforce the invalid patent, can, in and of itself, and without any other action, meet the Section 2 conduct requirement.[11] If the patent alone yields monopoly power in an economic market, the violation is established because the fraud followed by the suit to enforce meets the exclusionary test and is devoid of any efficiency justification. In an attempt case such a fraud could be a significant factor in proving the requisite intent. If the patent would yield sufficient power to threaten monopoly, the fraud plus an enforcement suit would make out the attempt violation. This kind of conduct independently violates the patent law and other criminal statutes and fails of any credible justification. Suppose that before a fraudulent acquisition the defendant has significant power but does not threaten dominance, that the patent in other hands would not threaten dominance, but that, given the defendant's pre-existing position in the market, adding the patent yields or threatens monopoly. Given defendant's market situation the power test for Section 2 is met and defendant's fraud meets the conduct requirement.

Next, suppose that a defendant did not obtain its patent by fraud, but nevertheless knows that the patent is invalid. If this defendant sues to enforce and, in so doing, threatens to obtain monopoly power, Section 2 is violated.[12] The essence of the violation in *Walker Process* is using a fraudulently gained patent to obtain or protect monopoly power by

11. Walker Process Equipment v. Food Machinery & Chemical Corp., 382 U.S. 172, 86 S.Ct. 347, 15 L.Ed.2d 247 (1965); see also Charles Pfizer & Co. v. FTC, 401 F.2d 574 (6th Cir.1968), *cert. denied*, 394 U.S. 920, 89 S.Ct. 1195, 22 L.Ed.2d 453 (1969) (submitting false information to patent office violates § 5 of FTC); cf. Handgards, Inc. v. Ethicon, Inc., 743 F.2d 1282 (9th Cir.1984). In *Walker Process* there was no Section 2 violation because the fraudulently obtained patent did not confer power. In *Handgard* a firm with 90 percent of a market sued to enforce a patent it knew to be invalid; the court held this conduct constituted attempt to monopolize. See also American Cyanamid Co. v. FTC, 363 F.2d 757 (6th Cir.1966); Brunswick Corp. v. Riegel Textile, 752 F.2d 261 (7th Cir.1984), cert. denied, 472 U.S. 1018, 105 S.Ct. 3480, 87 L.Ed.2d 615 (1985). There has been debate about whether *Walker Process* is limited to instances of deliberate, false statements to the patent office, or whether (assuming power were so obtained) it would apply to a fraudulent failure to disclose prior art which, had it

been disclosed, would have precluded issuance of the patent for lack of novelty or non-obviousness. In Nobelpharma AB v. Implant Innovations, Inc., 129 F.3d 1463 (Fed. Cir. 1997), superseded 141 F.3d 1059 (Fed. Cir. 1998), a panel of the Federal Circuit first held, in November, 1997, that affirmative misrepresentation was necessary to trigger the *Walker Process* fraud rule. In March, 1998 (1998) WL 122399 (Fed. Cir.), the same panel withdrew the earlier opinion and held that fraudulent non-disclosure to the patent office, followed by suit to enforce the patent, known to be invalid because of the fraud, was sufficient to establish monopolizing conduct. The second opinion is correct. Where there is a duty to disclose, a knowing fraudulent failure to do so can not be credibly distinguished from an active fraud. In either case the patentee is suing to enforce a patent known to have been fraudulently obtained.

12. Handgards Inc. v. Ethican, supra note 12 (Suit by firm with dominant market share based on a patent known to be invalid violates Section 2).

bringing a lawsuit aimed at excluding a competitor. *Handgard* extends that holding by teaching that if a patent is invalid and the patentee, though knowing it to be, seeks to obtain, expand or protect a monopoly by suing on the patent, the basis for the patent's invalidity is not critical to the Section 2 claim. Both *Walker Process* and *Handgard* can raise issues under the *Noerr-Pennington* doctrine, discussed in § 14.4. This suggests that a suit to enforce a patent claim known to be invalid is not conduct vulnerable under Section 2, unless the suit is a sham within the meaning of California Motor Transport,[13] as clarified by *Professional Real Estate Investors (PRE)*.[14] The critical case is *PRE*. After *PRE*, a patent infringement suit would be vulnerable on either a *Walker Process* or a *Handgard* theory only if the suit is objectively baseless and is brought to interfere directly with the business activities of a competitor. If a patent is clearly invalid and known by the patentee so to be, any suit to enforce it would seem to meet the objectively baseless standard of PRE. While the precise content of the subjective element in *PRE* is not entirely clear, there seems no reason to doubt that trying to enforce a patent known to have been obtained by fraud would meet the test. If some other basis for invalidity is relied upon, the *PRE* test should require convincing evidence that defendant knew of the invalidity and by the suit would frustrate plaintiff's effort to compete.[15]

A serious fraud issue could be particularly vexing where an interference is declared in the patent office and the parties settle. Suppose, for example, that of two contending parties in an interference, one can prove that the other engaged in a fraud on the patent office but, fearing loss because of a weakness in its own claim, concedes priority to the other in return for a license.[16] Or suppose the applicant that defers had information which, whether or not known also to the prevailing party, would have foreclosed issuance if the proceeding had continued and the deferring party had disclosed this information. Would later enforcement of the patent be vulnerable under Section 2?[17] Would its vulnerability depend on whether the deferring party expressly or inferentially bargained to withhold relevant information in return for the license? In this context, *Noerr-Pennington, California Motor Transport* and *Professional Real Estate Investors (PRE)*, all discussed immediately above, would be relevant, and whether the subjective test in *PRE* were met might well turn on whether there was a consciously made bargain to suppress. Yet, in dealing with such issues the analyst should be mindful that the goal is not to use antitrust to police patent application processes, but to apply

---

13. 404 U.S. 508, 92 S.Ct. 609, 30 L.Ed.2d 642 (1972).

14. 508 U.S. 49, 113 S.Ct. 1920, 123 L.Ed.2d 611 (1993).

15. See Kobak, *Professional Real Estate Investors and the Future of Patent–Antitrust Litigation: Walker Process and Handgards Meet Noerr–Pennington*, 63 ANTITRUST L.J. 185 (1994).

16. American Cyanamid Co. v. FTC and Brunswick Corp. v. Riegel Textile, supra note 11. See also United States v. Singer Mfg. Co., 374 U.S. 174, 83 S.Ct. 1773, 10 L.Ed.2d 823 (1963).

17. Cf. United States v. Singer Mfg. Co., supra note 17.

established antitrust norms about conduct and power in a fair, objective manner to competition issues arising in a patent context.

Walker Process should have implications for the application of Section 2 not only to fraudulently invalid patents but also to enforcing patents acquired by other blatantly criminal or tortious conduct. Suppose an inventor is about to assign a significant patent to a small but aggressive challenger in a market dominated by Firm A, but that by fraud or other tortious conduct, Firm A persuades the inventor to assign to it instead of to the aggressive challenger. If the patent solidifies monopoly power for Firm A in a well defined market, that tortious conduct should make a patent enforcement suit by Firm A vulnerable to a Section 2 claim. Suppose, next, that a patent is obtained by an inventor by fraud, that Firm B is a stranger to the fraud, that the inventor comes directly to Firm B as the most likely buyer and Firm B pays inventor a price for an assignment that reflects the monopoly power the patent will yield. Without question the patent remains vulnerable to cancellation; an assignee's good faith does not absolve the patentee's fraud. But suppose that for two years until the patent is challenged and the fraud brought out, Firm B exercises its monopoly power by enforcing the patent without knowledge of the fraud. Has Firm B monopolized in violation of Section 2? In our judgment Firm B is not violating Section 2 so long as it remains scrupulously innocent of information that would invite inquiry about the fraud. But as the holder and exploiter of a patent in a field it dominates, Firm B's state of innocence would not likely last very long. It should be held to be monopolizing during any period in which it exploits monopoly power from a fraudulently obtained patent while in possession of information that would put it on notice that the patent was, or likely was, fraudulently obtained.

Of course, fraud can occur not only in connection with the issuance of a patent but also in how it is employed. An example is the FTC's case against Unocal Corp., alleging that the firm defrauded California air pollution regulators into adopting air quality standards for gasoline that required the use of Unocal patents resulting in hundreds of millions of dollars of royalties for the firm and higher gasoline prices for consumers.[18]

15.8b2. *Acquisition by a Market Transaction*

The Supreme Court's mid-century dictum that the "mere accumulation of patents, no matter how many, is not in and of itself illegal * * * "[19] is unquestionably sound law today, as applied to patents acquired as the result of research sponsored and supported by the firm that holds the patent. Patents encourage efficient investment in innova-

---

18. In the Matter of Union Oil Co. of California, FTC Docket No. 9305 (July 7, 2004)(Decision of the FTC reinstating administrative complaint against Unocal), available at <http://www.ftc.gov/os/adjpro/d9305/040706commissionopinion.pdf>

19. Automatic Radio Mfg. Co. v. Hazeltine Research, 339 U.S. 827, 834, 70 S.Ct. 894, 94 L.Ed. 1312 (1950).

tion. These are the prizes that Congress has designated for those entering and prevailing in the R & D race. Section 2 does not unseat the R & D winners,[20] even if they fail to exploit and merely stockpile their IP rights. By contrast, there is no constraint that shields from balanced antitrust review the acquisition through a market transaction of IP from the innovator who earned it. A predatory acquisition of any productive resource can be vulnerable under Section 2 if the purpose and effect of the acquisition is exclusionary. For example, Section 2 can be violated by buying and stockpiling scarce resources far in excess of anticipated need when this conduct is deliberately and successfully done to deny competitors essential resources and cannot be efficiency justified.[21] There is no reason why the norm should differ for predatory purchase and stockpiling of excessive, unneeded and unused IP the strategic function of which is to discourage entry into an already concentrated market.[22]

A counter argument is that innovation is encouraged if the patentee—rewarded for having won the R & D race—can collect the full reward her innovation can yield, including any premiums that any assignee will pay because the patent would reinforce the assignee's power. True, if her patent is, of itself, the sole source of monopoly power the patentee would be inadequately rewarded could she not either exercise or sell her monopoly at her own election. But patent accumulations by an existing monopolist present a different issue. Assume defendant, dominant in a significant market, sets out to acquire all new technology that might alone or when combined with other technology serve to enhance the barriers that protect its power. To such a defendant any relevant patent has two elements of value: first, the intrinsic market value of the patented technology; second, the additional value the patent would provide only to the dominant firm and solely because it heightens entry barriers that protect that firm's pre-existing dominance. The inventor receives the full reward to which the patent system entitles him when he receives in full the first element of value—the intrinsic value of the technology he invented. When the dominant firm and the holder of the new patent meet to negotiate, they face each other, in a sense, as bilateral monopolists. The inventor alone has the new patent that will make the dominant firm's monopoly position more impregnable. But that firm alone holds the position of market power which vests the inventor's patent with its additional value. Assume the intrinsic value of the patent technology is 10 and that its value to the dominant firm is 20. The bargain will concern the point between 10 and 20 at which resolution can be reached—about how the supracompetitive return of 10 is to be divided between these bilateral monopolists. It would be logical and consistent with the resource allocation goals of both the patent and

20. See § 15.8.

21. See § 3.4b9. Acquisition of intellectual property by purchase can, of course, raise issues under Sherman § 1 and under Clayton section 7. See IP–Antitrust Guidelines § 5.7. Discussion here is limited to issues under Sherman section 2.

22. Cf. Kobe, Inc. v. Dempsey Pump Co., 198 F.2d 416 (10th Cir.1952), *cert. denied*, 344 U.S. 837, 73 S.Ct. 46, 97 L.Ed. 651 (1952).

antitrust laws to rule that the inventor earns the full reward to which the patent system entitles him when he receives the intrinsic value of his IP protected technology. He could gain this by a sale or auction that excludes the dominant firm from bidding.[23] On these supposed facts the remedial issue would be complex, but the basic principle is not. The patentee should gain the value of his invention, not that value plus the externality attached to it because of the dominant firm's desire to make its position of power less vulnerable.

As Areeda and Kaplow have stressed, Judge Wyzanski's *United Shoe* decision can be cited in support of the above analysis.[24] United Shoe had accumulated over 2000 patents, about 5 percent from outsiders. The government asserted that this acquisition practice along with other conduct constituted monopolization. While Judge Wyzanski bottomed his holding of a Section 2 violation on other conduct, his opinion criticized these acquisitions too. He rejected the company's business justifications—that the acquisitions occurred in the process of settling patent disputes or were made to avoid the risk that United Shoe would itself be foreclosed from useful technology; non-exclusive licenses would have served both of these purposes.[25]

A market acquisition of IP may be predatory not only because excessive numbers of IP rights are stockpiled and not used. Predation might also be found in the consideration utilized to exact the conveyance of the IP. Intergraph Corporation vs. Intel Corporation[26] found a violation on the basis of evidence that Intel cut off the flow of product information needed by its customer, Intergraph, in order to force Intergraph to convey certain Intergraph patents to Intel. An FTC consent order against Intel (terminating in ten years) was also based upon this conduct affecting Intergraph and allegedly similar Intel conduct that forced Digital Equipment Corp. and Compaq Computer Corp to turn over patent rights.[27] Some of the allegations in The Government's Section 2 case against Microsoft had a similar tenor.[28]

When a firm possessing monopoly power indiscriminately or inappropriately acquires additional IP it runs a Section 2 risk. In *Transparent-Wrap* the Supreme Court emphasized that as "patents are added to patents a whole industry may be regimented. The owner of a basic

---

23. It would not help to allow the dominant firm to buy later lower in the chain of title. That would merely put the monopoly windfall into hands other than those of the inventor. Neither would it be appropriate to let the dominant firm buy the patent but at intrinsic value. That would give the monopoly windfall to the monopolist.

24. See Areeda and Kaplow, Antitrust Analysis ¶ 332 (5th ed. 1997).

25. United States v. United Shoe Machinery Corp., 110 F.Supp. 295, 333 (D.Mass.1953), *aff'd per curiam*, 347 U.S.

521, 74 S.Ct. 699, 98 L.Ed. 910 (1954). See also United States v. Singer Mfg. Co., 374 U.S. 174, 83 S.Ct. 1773, 10 L.Ed.2d 823 (1963), where the court said that "Singer cannot ... contend that it sought the assignment [to assure its own access], since the ... cross license agreement had assured that result." Id. at 195.

26. 3 F.Supp.2d 1255 (N.D.Ala.1998).

27. FTC Dkt. No. 9288 (Consent Order, March 17, 1999).

28. See § 15.8c4.

patent might thus perpetrate his control over an industry * * *."[29] While we know of no flat holding of violation based solely on excessive accumulation with the intent and purpose of attaining or protecting monopoly, Kobe v. Dempsey Pump[30] comes close. Although not one of the three is a recent case, *Kobe, Transparent–Wrap* and *United Shoe,* taken together, sound a warning against any assumption that IP accumulation by purchase is never vulnerable. Interestingly, this view of the law, dismissed as obsolete by some IP exponents, accords with principles championed by both Chicago and post-Chicago theorists. Chicagoans insist that the policy underpinnings of both intellectual property and antitrust are rational resource allocation and consumer welfare.[31] Post Chicagoans[32] share this conviction and the related one that in doing resource allocation analysis, intellectual property should be treated much as any other property right conferring power to exclude.[33] If these interlinked principles are taken at face value, accumulations of intellectual property have no shield against Section 2 scrutiny. Excessive, unneeded accumulation of any species of property can violate the Sherman Act or Section 7 of Clayton when it reaches the point where foreclosure of competitors threatens competition in a well-defined market.

To test the contention that a patentee has a right to assign to the highest bidder even if, by the acquisition, the bidder gains or protects monopoly, try the same contention in another context. Consider, for example, the acquisition of operating businesses—aggregations of capital—by merger. One would hardly argue that antitrust merger enforcement should be stayed even though concentration exceeds safe levels because capital market rewards are part of the incentive that induce entrepreneurs to build successful business in the first place. Yet, it is only a directly analogous and equally spurious argument, both economically and in terms of fairness, that would spare from antitrust scrutiny

29. Transparent–Wrap v. Stokes & Smith, 329 U.S. 637, 646–47, 67 S.Ct. 610, 91 L.Ed. 563 (1947). See also Hartford–Empire Co. v. United States, 323 U.S. 386, 417, 65 S.Ct. 373, 89 L.Ed. 322 (1945), supplemented, 324 U.S. 570, 65 S.Ct. 815, 89 L.Ed. 1198 (1945). And see Kobe v. Dempsey Pump, 198 F.2d 416 (10th Cir.), cert. denied, 344 U.S. 837, 73 S.Ct. 46, 97 L.Ed. 651 (1952). But cf. In re E.I. duPont de Nemours & Co., 3 Trade Reg. Rep. (CCH) ¶ 21,770 (FTC Oct. 20, 1980) (rejecting contention that plant expansion was exclusionary when it might meet anticipated demand).

30. Kobe v. Dempsey Pump, supra note 22.

31. See e.g., USM Corp. v. SPS Tech., 694 F.2d 505 (7th Cir.1982) (Posner, J.), *cert. denied*, 462 U.S. 1107, 103 S.Ct. 2455, 77 L.Ed.2d 1334 (1983).

32. The terminology "Post Chicago Economics" is taken from a 1994 symposium co-sponsored by the U.S. Department of Justice (Antitrust Division), the Federal Trade Commission, Georgetown University, and the ABA. See *Royall Symposium: Post–Chicago Economics, Editors Note,* 63 ABA ANTITRUST J. 445 (1995). Many of the scholars represented in the symposium were staff members of the federal enforcement agencies which in recent years have generally adopted approaches consistent with the Post–Chicago effort to show "that the Chicago School's simplified economic models are of limited usefulness in understanding the complex economic forces that operate in the real world." A recent judicial example of Post–Chicago thinking is found in the majority opinion from Eastman Kodak v. Image Technical Services, 504 U.S. 451, 112 S.Ct. 2072, 119 L.Ed.2d 265 (1992).

33. IP–Antitrust Guidelines § 2.1.

an excessive accumulation by purchase of patents that successfully blockade a market.

It does not follow that large firms need to be timid about buying desired patents. The point where monopoly power is reached or threatened will never be trivial, whether in a goods, research or innovation market. Nor should the analysis oversimplify market definition or overreact to HHI's or share percentages. Also, even when some degree of power is gained or protected, offsetting efficiencies must be considered. For example, having access to a number of patents may enable product improvements or cost reductions that could not be attained without the accumulation. If so, and if taking an assignment is the only way to access the protected technology, this efficiency should be weighed against any possible competitive harm. Of course, as in capital market merger analysis,[34] offsetting efficiencies should be weighted only when they could not be obtained in less restrictive ways. For IP this will often be a stumbling block. As *United Shoe* and *Singer* emphasize, nonexclusive licensing is possible; a firm need not control two patents to be able to practice both.[35]

Does this analysis suggest that an established monopolist, though warranted in doing R & D, may never acquire by assignment a significant patent in its field, because doing so will inevitably extend and protect its monopoly? The problem need not be addressed at so abstract a level. When specifics are considered there are complex permutations. First, consider a difficult hypothetical: M holds monopoly power. X invents and patents a new, groundbreaking technology that would produce a far better product than M's at a lower price, tending to render M's technology obsolete. X has put the patent up for sale and Z, a powerful, deep pocket firm in a related market, is seeking to buy it. M's options are limited. If it does nothing it may soon be displaced by a new monopolist. There will be no improvement in market structure. If M outbids Z, M will protect its monopoly and make it less vulnerable at the cost of sharing some of the value of the strengthened monopoly with X, the patentee. Of course, M could urge X to grant M a non-exclusive license. This would open the market to competition. But as a profit-maximizer the patentee might reject this proposal. It will want the full value of its innovation, including any enhancement attributable to market power associated with the invention itself.[36] One might gather case support for asserting that if M were to win the bidding contest, the

---

34. United States Department of Justice and Federal Trade Commission Horizontal Merger Guidelines § 4 (1992 as revised, April 8, 1997), available at <http://www.usdoj.gov/ atr/public/ guidelines/hmg.htm>.

35. See United States v. United Shoe Machinery, 110 F.Supp. 295 (D.Mass.1953), *aff'd per curiam*, 347 U.S. 521, 74 S.Ct. 699, 98 L.Ed. 910 (1954); United States v. Singer Mfg. Co., 374 U.S. 174, 83 S.Ct. 1773, 10 L.Ed.2d 823 (1963).

36. Our assumptions suggest that any single holder of the patent can exact monopoly profits. If capital and information markets were perfect, the patentee could extract this full return by licensing to enough licensees to generate a competitive goods market. But such markets are not perfect. The easy and probably most prudent way for the patentee to maximize is probably to let would-be goods monopolists bid against each other.

patent, in M's hand, should be treated as an essential facility and M be required to make it available to others at reasonable cost.[37] But there is no basis whatsoever for saying that the patentee itself holds an essential facility, nor for saying that Z or any other buyer than M holds an essential facility. That being so, the only effect of applying the essential facility rule upon M's successful bid would be to keep M from bidding. This would leave Z in a position to garner the monopoly, while sharing less with X. It appears, then, that M should be free to outbid Z, if so disposed. M is not accumulating patents to protect its existing dominance. Rather, it has identified a single patent, in the patentee's hands, that alone will give dominance to the firm that practices it. The patentee is entitled to harvest the full reward of the power of its invention, whether from M or another bidder.

Second, an easy hypothetical: M holds a product market monopoly based on patented technology. P has a patent on a new technology that is better than other alternatives but not as good as M's. M fears that others, by using the new technology, might force M to lower its limit price or, by improving the new technology further, might cause M's power to erode substantially. To avoid these risks M acquires P's patent by assignment and suppresses it. On conventional principles this acquisition should violate Section 2. The clear purpose and effect of M's conduct is to diminish the information available in the market place in order to preserve M's monopoly returns. Competitive harm is done. M gains no efficiency. Nor does P need to be able to sell to M in order to gain the intrinsic value of its patent. On the face of the matter, to the extent that P can gain more by assigning to M than by exploiting the patent in other ways, this bonus would represent part of the value that suppression of this promising but less efficient technology adds to M's already existing monopoly.[38]

In sum, whether a dominant firm takes an assignment of a single patent or engages in a series of acquisitions, the essential question is whether the conduct has the purpose and effect of distorting resource allocation by reducing available information below, or taxing consumers above, the levels that arise naturally out of the bargain struck between the patentee and the government upon issuance of the patent. If so, the acquisition or acquisitions are vulnerable unless there are justifications yielding offsetting efficiencies. The factors that the 1955 Attorney General's Antitrust Committee said were relevant remain cogent today.[39] They include the nature and value of the patents, the effect of the acquisition on whether and how the patent is used, whether a patent dispute is being resolved, and the likely effect of the acquisition on market structure and conduct.

---

37. See § 3.4b3.

38. Interesting acquisition hypotheticals appear in P. AREEDA & L. KAPLOW, ANTITRUST ANALYSIS, §§ 333 and 334 (5th ed. 1997).

39. Report, Attorney General's National Committee to Study Antitrust Law 277 (1955).

15.8b3. Acquisition by Grant Back

Patent licenses sometimes oblige the licensee to assign or license to the licensor any patent or new "know how" obtained by the licensee that improves the licensed invention. In Transparent–Wrap Machine Corp. v. Stokes & Smith Co., the Court rejected the contention that such clauses are intrinsically anticompetitive because they insulate the patent holder's position from erosion under market forces and discourage innovation by the license.[40] But the Court's opinion notes that a grant back "could be employed" with a purpose and effect that violates the antitrust laws, stressing that by patent accumulations "a whole industry may be regimented."[41]

In any event, since the *Transparent-Wrap* decision grant backs have seldom, if ever, been the main target of an antitrust challenge. There are, nonetheless, a number of cases in which grant backs, along with other patent-related conduct, have been found to be antitrust vulnerable and subject to remediation.[42] This is consistent with, and perhaps a direct outcome of, the recognition in *Transparent-Wrap* both that grant backs can be wrongly used and that patent accumulations can regiment an industry. When power is evident and other aggressive strategies are also used, grant back clauses can present serious antitrust risks.[43]

15.8b4. Improper Extension of the Life of a Patent

Just as fraudulent conduct leading to the issuance of a patent is subject to antitrust attack, so too is similar conduct that leads the extension of the life of a patent. This issue has come to light as a result of investigations of the FTC that established practices of certain pharmaceutical firms that abused the FDA regulatory process (improperly listing a patent on the FDA's Orange Book), resulting in 30 month or longer delays in the entry of generic drugs that would compete with the patented drug. The FTC has obtained consent settlements to preclude such behavior[44]

15.8c. Exclusive Dealing and Leveraging to Protect or Expand Markets Monopolized Through Intellectual Property

By exclusive dealing arrangements, express or implicit, a monopolist bolsters its power by resisting its erosion, sometimes at the cost of

40. 329 U.S. 637, 67 S.Ct. 610, 91 L.Ed. 563 (1947).

41. Id. at 646.

42. Hartford–Empire v. United States, 323 U.S. 386, 65 S.Ct. 373, 89 L.Ed. 322 (1945), supplemented, 324 U.S. 570, 65 S.Ct. 815, 89 L.Ed. 1198 (1945); United States v. E.I. Du Pont De Nemours & Co., 118 F.Supp. 41, 224–25 (D.Del.1953); United States v. G.E. (Carboloy), 80 F.Supp. 989, 1005–06 (S.D.N.Y. 1948); United States v. G.E. (Lamps), 82 F.Supp. 753, 815–16 (D.N.J.1949).9

43. See the discussion in § 15.8f.

44. Biovail Corporation, C–4060 (Oct. 2, 2002), available at www.ftc.gov/opa/2002/04/biovailtiazac.htm.; Bristo–Myers Squibb Company, C–4076 (April 14, 2003), available at www.ftc.gov/opa/2003/bms.htm. See FTC, Generic Drug Entry Prior to Patent Expiration: An FTC Study (July 2004), available at www.ftc.gov/os/2002/07/genericdrugstudy.pdf.

discouraging some buyers at its selected monopoly or limit price. The tactic is analogous to a single firm boycott. In effect, the monopolist says to customers, if you want my product, you may have it, but only if you do not use any of my competitors' products. Current power is being used (or, in part, expended) to protect against an even greater reduction of the power in the future by blockading the market against entry or expansion by current fringe firms. The tactic distorts allocation, hurts consumers and, absent any counterbalancing efficiency justification, violates Section 2.[45]

It has long been settled law that Section 2 prohibits leveraging monopoly power held in one market to create, threaten or protect monopoly in a second market.[46] Doing this monopolizes (or attempts to monopolize or injure competition in) a separate competitive market. It therefore distorts allocation and injures consumers in markets beyond that where power was lawfully obtained—and it does so by conduct which, more often than not, may be utterly lacking in offsetting efficiency justifications.[47] In its 2004 decision in Verizon Communications v. Trinko, the Supreme Court cast some doubt on these past leveraging holdings. In a footnote, Justice Scalia wrote for the Court that leverage theory is valid only if the plaintiff establishes a threat to monopolize the new market.[48] This view allows power in one market to be deliberately used to hurt competition elsewhere, so long as the intended and resulting harm does not approach a monopoly level. If indeed the Court intended to reverse a great deal of past precedent Other claims, such as exclusive dealing, raising rivals costs or monopoly maintenance may be invoked to attack conduct that in an earlier era might have been attacked as leveraging.

---

45. Lorain Journal Co. v. United States, 342 U.S. 143, 72 S.Ct. 181, 96 L.Ed. 162 (1951); United States v. Standard Oil Co. of California, 362 F.Supp. 1331 (N.D.Cal. 1972), *affirmed,* 412 U.S. 924, 93 S.Ct. 2750, 37 L.Ed.2d 152 (1973); United States v. United Shoe Mach., 110 F.Supp. 295, 344–45 (D.Mass.1953); *aff'd per curiam,* 347 U.S. 521, 74 S.Ct. 699, 98 L.Ed. 910 (1954) (lease only discussion); Standard Oil of California v. United States, 337 U.S. 293, 69 S.Ct. 1051, 93 L.Ed. 1371 (1949); Eastman Kodak of New York v. Southern Photo Materials Co., 273 U.S. 359, 47 S.Ct. 400, 71 L.Ed. 684 (1927); United States v. Microsoft Corp., 56 F.3d 1448 (D.C.Cir.1995) (consent decree enforcing contract terms requiring OEM to pay Microsoft a royalty for operating system license for each computer the OEM sells whether or not the OEM has included Microsoft operating system).

46. Eastman Kodak Co. v. Image Technical Serv., Inc., 504 U.S. 451, 112 S.Ct. 2072, 119 L.Ed.2d 265 (1992); United States v. Griffith, 334 U.S. 100, 68 S.Ct. 941, 92 L.Ed. 1236 (1948); Eastman Kodak of New York v. Southern Photo Materials

Co., 273 U.S. 359, 47 S.Ct. 400, 71 L.Ed. 684 (1927); Lorain Journal Co. v. United States, 342 U.S. 143, 72 S.Ct. 181, 96 L.Ed. 162 (1951); MCI Communications v. AT & T, 708 F.2d 1081 (7th Cir.1983), *cert. denied,* 464 U.S. 891, 104 S.Ct. 234, 78 L.Ed.2d 226 (1983); Otter Tail Power v. United States, 410 U.S. 366, 93 S.Ct. 1022, 35 L.Ed.2d 359 (1973). See § 3.4b1.

47. This analysis, properly, is based on the rule of reason, not *per se.* If under particular circumstances a justification is offered that results in an offsetting efficiency that improves allocation and consumer welfare, that business justification should be considered and evaluated. Aspen Skiing Co. v. Aspen Highlands, 472 U.S. 585, 105 S.Ct. 2847, 86 L.Ed.2d 467 (1985); Sullivan, *Section 2 of the Sherman Act and Vertical Strategies By Dominant Firms,* 21 Sw. U. L. Rev. 1227 (1992).

48. 540 U.S. 398, 415 n.4, 124 S.Ct. 872, 157 L.Ed.2d 823 (2004). See the discussion of this case in § 3.4b.

The similarity between exclusive dealing and leveraging is sharply focused where, as in *Lorain Journal*,[49] the monopolist is seeking to protect its power from erosion caused by a partial substitute produced in a different market by the target at which the conduct is aimed. In *Lorain Journal*, defendant was a newspaper monopolist that feared the loss of advertising revenue to a new radio station, as advertisers started to divide their advertising budgets between the old medium and the new. Defendant's exclusive dealing requirement forced its advertisers to abandon radio. In consequence, there was competitive harm in the radio market, but the gravamen of the offense was doing injury elsewhere in order to protect the monopoly power already held in the newspaper market. The *Verizon* footnote would have no application to such a case. Similarly, in the 2001 Microsoft decision, the Government prevailed in its monopoly maintenance claim that Microsoft's exclusionary conduct limited the ability of Netscape and Sun Microsystems to compete in ancillary markets that might have undermined Microsoft's monopoly over operating system software.[50] When the monopolist acts to protect its own power in the monopolized market, the standard Section 2 conduct test inevitably governs. Did the monopolist's conduct have the purpose and effect of injuring competition? If so, can it be business justified by showing offsetting efficiency gains? If not, and the facts can be sorted out and a remedy fashioned in a judicial proceeding, Section 2 is violated.

Does anything in the analysis of exclusive dealing or leverage change when the power lawfully held and exploited through exclusive dealing or leveraging derives from intellectual property? That is the issue pursued in the next two subsections.

15.8c1.   *Exclusive Dealing with Intellectual Property*

Consider this hypothetical: Assume Net Co. has an IP based monopoly (say, 90 percent of installed base and current sales of Internet browsers, a well defined relevant market), but knows that MS, a software firm with a strong position in operating systems and some applications, is about to enter the browser market. Desk top users obtain browsers mainly through two distribution channels. Either a browser is installed by the computer manufacturer (OEM) before marketing the computer or the browser is provided by the Internet service providers (ISPs) with which the desktop user deals. Net Co. initiates the following tactics in order to inhibit MS's entry and expansion in browsers. First, Net Co. authorizes an OEM to pre-install its browser only upon the OEM's commitment not to pre-install any other browser in any desktop manufactured by it. Second, Net Co. provides its browsers to an ISP for provision to its customers only upon a commitment by the ISP to distribute and promote Net Co. browsers exclusively.[51] In this way Net

---

49. 342 U.S. 143, 72 S.Ct. 181, 96 L.Ed. 162 (1951).

50. United States v. Microsoft Corp., 253 F.3d 34 (D.C. Cir. 2001)(en banc). The case is discussed in § 15.8c4.

51. The facts in this hypothetical constitute an inversion of some of the facts alleged in the complaint in the two government cases against Microsoft. United States v. Microsoft Corporation, 147 F.3d 935

Co. extracts from major participants in both browser distribution channels commitments foreclosing MS and other browser competitors from these channels. This strategy raises the costs of Net Co.'s browser rivals and reduces the utility and value of their offerings. It accomplishes this by using some of Net Co.'s current power in the browser market to foreclose the future erosion of that power. Whether or not this conduct reduces Net Co.'s current monopoly return (it probably does, though conceivably not),[52] it is inefficient in the same way that other "rent chasing" strategies and expenditures are inefficient. It protects allocatively inefficient monopoly power from erosion by normal market forces. Nor is there any ex ante justification for this ex post social cost. Certainly Net Co. did not need the legal right to exploit its power in this manner in order to be motivated to produce its browser. Nor is there any other efficiency justification evident, even a pretextual one. Nothing in the case law or in either the antitrust or relevant IP statutes need be read as precluding normal application of Section 2 analysis merely because the source of power is intellectual property. Power from IP has, over the years, been routinely integrated into conventional antitrust analysis.[53] The Supreme Court specifically affirmed this view in Eastman Kodak v. Image Technical Services.[54]

Now compare this hypothetical: MS has monopoly power in desktop operating systems and develops a copyrighted diagnostic tool which it intends to use in offering to service computers using its operating system. This tool reduces service costs significantly and gives MS power in the service market. Competing service providers seek licenses from MS to use the proprietary diagnostic tool in order to compete with MS

(D.C. Cir. 1998); United States v. Microsoft Corporation, 253 F.3d 34 (D.C. Cir. 2001)(en banc). In those complaints it is alleged that Microsoft used some of its power in the desktop operating system market to induce firms in the two browser distribution chains to favor Microsoft over others. Those allegations described a strategy involving both exclusivity, and leveraging. The hypothetical is intended to delete the leveraging element and present only an exclusive dealing issue. Compare Problem 8–4 in P. Mergers, P. Menell, M. Lemley and T. Jorde, Intellectual Property in the New Technological Age 1084 (1996).

52. Kaplow, *The Patent—Antitrust Intersection: A Reappraisal*, 97 Harv. L. Rev. 1813 (1984); Sullivan, *Section 2 of the Sherman Act and Vertical Strategies By Dominant Firms*, supra note 46; Sullivan and Jones, *Monopoly Conduct, Especially Leveraging Power From One Product or Market to Another*, in Antitrust, Innovation and Competitiveness, (T.M. Jorde & D.J. Teece, eds. 1991).

53. Walker Process Equipment, Inc. v. Food Machinery and Chemical Corp., 382 U.S. 172, 86 S.Ct. 347, 15 L.Ed.2d 247

(1965); LaPeyre v. Federal Trade Commission, 366 F.2d 117 (5th Cir.1966); United States v. Line Material Co., 333 U.S. 287, 68 S.Ct. 550, 92 L.Ed. 701 (1948); Hartford–Empire Co. v. United States, 323 U.S. 386, 65 S.Ct. 373, 89 L.Ed. 322 (1945), supplemented, 324 U.S. 570, 65 S.Ct. 815, 89 L.Ed. 1198 (1945); United States v. New Wrinkle, Inc., 342 U.S. 371, 72 S.Ct. 350, 96 L.Ed. 417 (1952); Service & Training, Inc. v. Data General Corp., 963 F.2d 680 (4th Cir.1992).

54. Eastman Kodak v. Image Technical Services, 504 U.S. 451 at 479, note 29, 112 S.Ct. 2072, 119 L.Ed.2d 265. See also § 15.8c3, which discusses the implications of this case in greater detail. While 35 U.S.C.A. § 271(d)(4) (refusal to license is not misuse) could be read to suggest otherwise, such a reading is strained. See the discussion in § 15.8c3. For recent examples about using leveraging theory to evaluate the legality under Section 2 of the use of intellectual property, see United States v. Microsoft, 147 F.3d 935 (D.C. Cir.1998) and Intergraph Corp. v. Intel Corp., 3 F. Supp. 2d 1255 (N.D.Ala.1998), *vacated*, 195 F.3d 1346 (Fed. Cir.1999).

more effectively in the service market. MS refuses. M.S., like Net Co., is protecting existing power (this time in the service market, not the operating system market) by refusing to license to competitors the IP on which its service market power is, in part, based. But there are two distinctions between these facts and those of the Net Co. hypothetical. First, the Net Co. did not unconditionally refuse to license. Rather, its refusal had a secondary target. It conditioned its licenses on collateral agreement by licensees (not themselves Net Co. competitors) not to deal in other, separate transactions with Net Co. competitors. By contrast, in the diagnostic tool hypo, MS simply reserves its own software for its sole use, by refusing to license its direct competitors in the repair market. Second, in the diagnostic tool hypothetical the IP may well have been explicitly developed to advance MS's position as a competitor in the service market where its use by others is being restricted. Perhaps MS would not have made the R & D investment to develop the repair tool absent expectation of capacity to exploit exclusively in the intended market.

Data General[55] establishes that these distinctions between the two hypotheticals are relevant. It suggests a strong presumption that a copyright holder may refuse to license competitors intending to compete in the very market where the copyright is being exploited by its owner. In *Data General*, a computer manufacturer sued for misappropriation of copyrighted trouble shooting software which was used to sell computer maintenance services. The defendant responded with a counterclaim that the manufacturer's refusal to license the software constituted an antitrust violation. The Court first noted that one objective of copyright law is to encourage investment in "functional works of expression." The court then reconciled the Sherman Act and Copyright Acts by reasoning that each is "designed ultimately to improve the welfare of consumers in our free market system."[56] The court ultimately held that "while exclusionary conduct can include a monopolist's unilateral refusal to license a copyright, an author's desire to exclude others [from a copyrighted work] ... is a presumptively valid business justification for any immediate harm to consumers."[57] *Data General*, of course, is a far easier case for the IP holder than is the MS hypothetical. *Data General* involved an effort to appropriate IP—to use it without paying for it and then to defend this free ride on antitrust grounds, not an effort to obtain and pay for a license to use IP at fair market value. Antitrust contentions in the context of such blatant free riding ought always to fall on unresponsive ears. In the context of the MS hypothetical, by contrast, the question is whether the IP owner needed the expectation of exclusivity in order to encourage the relevant R & D investment. For this reason the *Data General* presumption should not be taken as conclusive—perhaps it

55. Data General Corp. v. Grumman Systems Support Corp., 36 F.3d 1147 (1st Cir.1994).

56. Id. at 1187. The court, in footnote 64, also qualified its ruling by adding "we do not hold that an antitrust plaintiff can never rebut this presumption, for there may be rare cases in which imposing antitrust liability is unlikely to frustrate the objectives of the Copyright Act."

57. Id.

should not even be taken as particularly strong—unless the monopolist shows that its expectation of exclusive use of the IP in the monopolized market was an important incentive for the R & D that yielded the protected IP. On such facts, allowing the IP proprietor to withhold access may increase allocative efficiency. But if protecting the IP in the monopolized market would be an unanticipated (and in that sense a gratuitous) reward, the monopolist's refusal of access to its IP should be evaluated much as would its refusal to grant access to any other species of property. Ultimately the issue is whether the monopolist acted for good business reasons that enhance efficiency or with the purpose and effect of stifling competition.[58]

15.8c2. Leveraging with Intellectual Property

Leveraging is a strategy that utilizes power in one market to gain power or injure competition in another market. The classic example is tying (addressed in § 8.3c). Assume that widgets and gizmos are separate but complimentary products, that Z Co. owns a patent that confers lawful power in the widget market, and that the gizmo market is competitive. If Z Co. refuses to sell widgets except in a package bundled with gizmos it can effectively extend its lawful power in the widget market into the market for gizmos. Under conventional leveraging doctrine, these allegations raise several issues. First, consider Sherman Section 2. Do widgets and gizmos constitute one or two markets? The case law indicates that the markets are separate when there is "sufficient consumer demand so that it is efficient for a firm to provide [the first product] separately from [the second]."[59] Under Section 2 the next issue is whether Z Co.'s power in widgets constitutes or threatens monopoly. Now, consider Section 1 of Sherman. Are widgets and gizmos separate and distinct products? If so, and Z Co has sufficient power to enforce buyers wanting widgets to accept Z Co.'s gizmos, the conduct may be unlawful tying. At this juncture, under either Section 2 or Section 1 another issue emerges. When does leveraging power from one market or product to another cause sufficient competitive harm to violate the law?[60] If the charge is monopolization and any serious harm is done to competition in the gizmo market, *Kodak-Berkey* teaches that the offense is proven. But the Court's cryptic footnote in Verizon Communications Inc. v. Trinko would impose a stiffer standard: the question becomes whether Z Co.'s current share of the gizmo market is enough to

58. See Lorain Journal Co. v. United States, 342 U.S. 143, 72 S.Ct. 181, 96 L.Ed. 162 (1951); Aspen Skiing Co. v. Aspen Highlands Skiing Corp., 472 U.S. 585, 105 S.Ct. 2847, 86 L.Ed.2d 467 (1985); compare the discussion in Gifford, *Microsoft Corporation, The Justice Department, and Antitrust Theory*, 25 Sw. U.L. Rev. 621 (1996) and in Areeda & Kaplow, Antitrust Analysis, § 312 (5th ed., 1997).

59. Eastman Kodak Co. v. Image Technical Servs., 504 U.S. 451, 462, 112 S.Ct. 2072, 119 L.Ed.2d 265 (1992); cf. Jefferson

Parish Hospital Dist. No. 2 v. Hyde, 466 U.S. 2, 104 S.Ct. 1551, 80 L.Ed.2d 2 (1984).

60. The Second and Ninth Circuits have split on whether to violate Section 2 such leveraging conduct must threaten monopoly in the second market. See the discussion in § 15.8c. Such conduct would violate Section 1 upon a showing that it did serious competitive harm in the second market. Jefferson Parish Hosp. Dist. No. 2 v. Hyde, 466 U.S. 2, 104 S.Ct. 1551, 80 L.Ed.2d 2 (1984).

threaten monopoly there.[61] If the charge is tying under Section 1, once it is decided that defendant has sufficient power in one product to force purchases of the other product and that it is doing so, the offense is established under the bob-tailed *per se* rule for tying. As in the case of exclusive dealing, discussed in § 15.9e, the fact that the power Z Co. is leveraging is bottomed on intellectual property—that its leveraging device is a refusal to sell IP protected property unless the licensee accepts the tying conditions—is not relevant to whether the leveraging violates Sections 2 and 1.[62] Under the *Trinko* rule[63], whether Z's current gizmo market share is sufficient is, perhaps, a debatable matter. This ought to be resolved not by rules of thumb, but by looking realistically at the likely effect of the strategies in the target market. Will the strategy result in significant switching from the competing gizmos to Z's gizmos? How rapidly? Do MS's browser competitors have any defensive tactics open to them? What are they? How effective might they be? Is Z using any other tactics (for example, predatory pricing, such as by giveaways) that increase the policy of the leveraging tactic?

The 2001 Microsoft decision resonates with the gizmo hypothetical and the earlier charge that Microsoft bundling violated the 1995 consent decree. A plethora of IP-antitrust issues will continue to arise in the future if Microsoft seeks to link Windows to applications, the Internet, consumer products, programming tools and hardware. So long as Windows remains dominant and to the extent Microsoft succeeds in firming up such links, whenever Windows changes, everything linked to it will have to change. Then, only Microsoft, or those that have paid the price for its favor and received early information on upcoming changes, will be able to market products that remain compatible.[64]

15.8c3.   *Exclusive Dealing or Leveraging Attained Through Refusal to Deal*

Exclusive dealing and leveraging can each be accompanied in various ways, including by refusing to deal. The owner of any species of property has a presumptive right to refuse to deal,[65] but when that owner is a monopolist and the asserted right is exercised to protect or to extend the monopoly the presumption must give way.[66] There is no reason in

---

61. 540 U.S. 398, 415 n. 4, 124 S.Ct. 872, 157 L.Ed.2d 823 (2004) indicating that leverage theory is valid only if the plaintiff establishes a threat to monopolize the new market.

62. See IP–Antitrust Guidelines § 2.2. See also id. §§ 3.1, 3.4.

63. Alaska Airlines v. United Airlines, Inc., 948 F.2d 536 (9th Cir.1991), *cert. denied*, 503 U.S. 977, 112 S.Ct. 1603, 118 L.Ed.2d 316 (1992).

64. United States v. Microsoft Corp., 65 F.Supp.2d 1 (D.D.C.1999); D. Caruso, Digital Commerce: *Nimbly Microsoft has taken*

advantage of ignorance to reshape the world, NY Times, December 1, 1997, at C4.

65. United States v. Colgate & Co., 250 U.S. 300, 39 S.Ct. 465, 63 L.Ed. 992 (1919).

66. Piraino, *The Antitrust Analysis of Network Joint Ventures*, 47 HASTINGS L.J. 5 (1995) citing, Aspen Skiing Co. v. Aspen Highlands Skiing Corp., 472 U.S. 585, 601, 105 S.Ct. 2847, 86 L.Ed.2d 467(1985) as an example where the general right to refuse dealing is qualified in the case of monopolists. See also Otter Tail Power Co. v. U.S., 410 U.S. 366, 93 S.Ct. 1022, 35 L.Ed.2d 359(1973) and Lorain Journal Co. v. U.S., 342 U.S. 143, 72 S.Ct. 181, 96 L.Ed. 162

principle why IP should be treated differently from any other species of property in this regard. Thus, in circumstances where a refusal to deal shields a current monopoly position or leverages to extend the power of such a monopoly to another market, the analysis under Section 2 should parallel that which would apply if the exclusive were achieved by contract or the leveraging by a tie or either by other means than refusal to deal. However, a line of argument has recently developed that refusals to deal with IP should be exempt from conventional antitrust analysis. Indeed, on the basis of a recent amendment to the patent statute it might be contended that where a monopolist enforces exclusivity or achieves leverage merely by refusing to license a patent, that conduct is *per se* lawful regardless of any anticompetitive outcome.[67] A weaker version of the argument calls for a strong presumption of legality. This subsection evaluates these contentions.

Any claims that a patent or copyright owner has an unqualified right to refuse to license its intellectual property, even when the tactic is used to implement exclusive dealing or leveraging, must begin with statutory language. The most relevant provisions in the Patent Act concern the patentee's right to exclude[68] and a recent misuse provision that protects patentees from "misuse or illegal extension of the patent rights by reason of * * * [refusal] to license or use * * *."[69] In the case of copyright, the exclusive right to distribute[70] can be viewed as an analog to the patentees right to exclude.[71]

Next, the proponent of a *per se* right to refuse to deal must urge that exercising a statutory right granted under the Patent Act or Copyright statute cannot violate the antitrust laws. This broad proposition, however, is surely wrong. Even when the IP statute and the antitrust statute directly and unavoidably collide (as they do not here), the solution ought not to be that either the IP statute or the antitrust statute must give way totally.[72] The response most consistent with Congressional intent is to elect the resolution which, on the particular facts presented, is most consistent with the purposes that undergird both the antitrust and the intellectual property statutes: rational resource allocation that maximizes consumer welfare. Yet, vulnerable though it may be, a "patents always win" contention can be supported by broad language found in

(1951), other examples in which monopolists do not have the right to refuse dealing. See the discussion in §§ 3.4b3–b4.

67. Compare Appellant's Opening Brief in Image Technical Services v. Kodak, No.96–15293 & 96–15296, filed April 12, 1996 in the U.S. Court of Appeals for the Ninth Circuit, 21–27.

68. 35 U.S.C.A. § 154.

69. 35 U.S.C.A. § 271(d)(4).

70. 17 U.S.C.A. § 106(3).

71. There is no copyright statute analog to the patent misuse statutory provision.

72. Soma, Black & Smith, *Antitrust Pitfalls in Licensing*, 414 PLI/Pat 489 (1995) (noting the erosion of United States v. General Electric Co., 272 U.S. 476, 47 S.Ct. 192, 71 L.Ed. 362 (1926), in which the court permitted IP suppliers to include resale price maintenance provisions as a condition to licensees. The authors note that § 5.2 of the Antitrust Guidelines outlines a policy to enforce antitrust violations in nonconforming resale price maintenance license agreements).

Simpson v. Union Oil Co. of California[73] and in some court of Appeals opinions.[74] Finally, a "refusals are *per se* lawful" proponent can cite specific cases in which courts have refused to base antitrust liability on refusal to license.[75]

The major deficiency in a *per se* lawful claim for refusals to deal is its universality. Whether refusals are used to protect the monopolist's extant position through exclusive dealing,[76] or to leverage power into an adjacent market,[77] the claim of invulnerability is vastly overbroad. There are countless numbers of cases, both old[78] and new,[79] that support the IP-antitrust Guidelines teaching that intellectual property is treated like other property[80] and that standard antitrust analysis applies.[81] In its en banc appellate opinion in *Microsoft*, addressing arguments that a copyright freed the firm of antitrust restraints, the D.C. Circuit found this proposition "no more correct than the proposition that use of one's personal property, such as a baseball bat, cannot give rise to tort liability."[82]

Statutory provisions about IP exclusive rights are not definitive. A patentee's right to exclude and the copyright holder's right to distribute are both broad and general. To hold them uniformly determinative, regardless of context, is to strain their language. Section 271(d)(4) of the Patent Statute, the misuse provision, is more to the point, but it, too, speaks in generalized not in universal terms. Moreover, the section applies only to patents, not copyrights or other IP, and, at least literally, it changes the law only about patent misuse (a patent law offense discussed in § 15.11, that can render the patent unenforceable in any context until the misuse is purged), not about whether there is an

73. 377 U.S. 13, 24, 84 S.Ct. 1051, 12 L.Ed.2d 98 (1964) (patent laws modify the antitrust laws *pro tanto*).

74. E.g, United States v. Westinghouse Elec. Corp., 648 F.2d 642, 647 (9th Cir. 1981) (doing what patent law authorizes not antitrust vulnerable); SCM Corp. v. Xerox, 645 F.2d 1195, 1206 (2d Cir.1981), cert. denied, 455 U.S. 1016, 102 S.Ct. 1708, 72 L.Ed.2d 132 (1982).

75. E.g., SCM Corp. v. Xerox, supra note 75 at 1209; Data General v. Grumman Systems, 36 F.3d 1147, at 1185–86 (1st Cir. 1994); Miller Insituform, Inc. v. Insituform of North Am., Inc., 830 F.2d 606, 608–09 (6th Cir.1987), cert. denied, 484 U.S. 1064, 108 S.Ct. 1023, 98 L.Ed.2d 988; Service & Training, Inc. v. Data General Corp., 963 F.2d 680, 686 (4th Cir.1992).

76. Data General Corp. v. Grumman Systems Support Corp., 36 F.3d 1147 (1st Cir.1994).

77. Eastman Kodak v. Image Technical Servs., 504 U.S. 451 at 480, n. 29, 112 S.Ct. 2072, 119 L.Ed.2d 265 (1992).

78. Kobe, Inc. v. Dempsey Pump Co., 198 F.2d 416 (10th Cir.1952); *cert. denied*, 344 U.S. 837, 73 S.Ct. 46, 97 L.Ed. 651; United States v. Line Material, 333 U.S. 287, 68 S.Ct. 550, 92 L.Ed. 701 (1948); Automatic Radio Mfg. Co. v. Hazeltine Research, Inc., 339 U.S. 827, 70 S.Ct. 894, 94 L.Ed. 1312 (1950); International Salt Co. v. United States, 332 U.S. 392, 396, 68 S.Ct. 12, 92 L.Ed. 20 (1947) (a patent does not enable the patentee to evade the general laws applicable to all property).

79. E.g., Digidyne Corp. v. Data General Corp., 734 F.2d 1336 (9th Cir.1984) (copyrighted software which was used to "lock-in" purchases of CPU's was held a tie-in which yielded market power). Senza–Gel Corp. v. Seiffhart, 803 F.2d 661 (Fed.Cir. 1986).

80. IP–Antitrust Guideline § 2.0.

81. IP–Antitrust Guideline § 2.1.

82. United States v. Microsoft Corp., 253 F.3d 34, 63 (D.C. Cir. 2001)(en banc).

antitrust violation (which, when it exists, is normally remedied in ways that leave lawful enforcement of the patent open and unconstrained).[83]

Moreover, the conviction that patentee refusals to deal violate Section 2 when conventional rule of reason analysis would compel this conclusion is reinforced, not put in doubt, by a strong line of cases. The most salient recent authority is footnote 29 in Kodak v. Image Tech:[84]

> "Even assuming * * * that all manufacturers possess some inherent market power in the parts market, it is not clear why that should immunize them from the antitrust laws in another market. The Court has held many times that power gained through some natural *or legal advantage such as patent, copyright,* or business acumen can give rise to [antitrust] liability if a 'seller exploits his dominant position in one market to expand this empire into the next.'" [Citing], Times–Picayune Publishing Co. v. United States, 345 U.S. 594, 611, 73 S.Ct. 872, 97 L.Ed. 1277 (1953) (emphasis added).

Moreover, the particular means the intellectual property proprietor uses to leverage power to another market has consistently been held to be irrelevant.[85] Absent a vivid statutory mandate it is hard to fathom a reason why leveraging by refusal to deal about a patent or other IP would be segregated out for special treatment. As the court said in Atari v. Nintendo,[86] "[W]hen a patent holder uses his patent rights * * * to eviscerate competition unfairly" the patent holder becomes vulnerable under the antitrust laws.[87]

Of course, cases can be collected where courts have rejected claims by infringers or others who have been denied licenses that the patent or copyright proprietor is a monopolist guilty of exclusive dealing or leveraging. But a string cite of such cases does not show that a refusal to deal in IP never violates Section 2. Plaintiffs' theories of antitrust violation by refusing to license IP are not all good antitrust claims on both the facts and the law. Indeed, antitrust defendants typically prevail against almost all Section 2 claims. Claims based on monopoly leveraging or monopolization by refusal to deal are not exceptions, whether or not a patent or other IP is involved. Intellectual property proprietors have prevailed against refusal to deal claims not under a universal *per se*

---

83. Patent Misuse Reform Amendment, Pub. L. 100–703, 102 Stat. 4676 (1988) (amending 35 U.S.C.A. § 271(d)). Legislative Histories of U.S. Public Laws, 1988 Congressional Information Service Annual, Referencing S. Rpt. 100–83 on S.1200, 61–75 (discussing the need to reform patent misuse law because the judicially created patent misuse doctrine could potentially discourage licensing in situations where there are competitive benefits). Misuse is discussed more fully in § 15.11.

84. 504 U.S. at 480, n.29.

85. Image Technical Servs. v. Kodak, 125 F.3d 1195 (9th Cir.1997); Atari v. Nintendo, 897 F.2d 1572 (Fed.Cir. 1990); Unit-

ed States v. Univis Lens, 316 U.S. 241, 251–52, 62 S.Ct. 1088, 86 L.Ed. 1408 (1942); Mercoid Corp. v. Mid–Continent Inv. Co., 320 U.S. 661, 667, 64 S.Ct. 268, 88 L.Ed. 376 (1944); Berlenbach v. Anderson & Thompson Ski Co., 329 F.2d 782, 783–84 (9th Cir.1964), *cert. denied,* 379 U.S. 830, 85 S.Ct. 60, 13 L.Ed.2d 39 (1964).

86. See *Atari,* 897 F.2d at 1576.

87. See also Senza–Gel Corp. v. Seiffhart, 803 F.2d 661, 668 n.10, 86; Digidyne Corp. v. Data General, 734 F.2d 1336, 1338–39 (9th Cir.1984), cert. denied, 473 U.S. 908, 105 S.Ct. 3534, 87 L.Ed.2d 657 (1985).

lawful rule, but only when plaintiffs fail to make out a case under conventional antitrust principles. For example, MAI Systems Corp. v. Peak Computer, Inc.[88] held no more than that mere loading of an operating system diagnostic software from storage into ROM is sufficiently permanent to produce a copy that violates one of the copyright holder's exclusive rights and that the offense warrants injunctive relief. Triad Systems v. Southeastern Express[89] reiterated this holding and added that the fair use doctrine did not justify infringement even though the infringer was seeking to compete with the copyright holder. In neither was there even need to consider any antitrust issue.[90]

Data General[91] a recent First Circuit case, is closer to the point, but certainly supports no broadly applicable rule of *per se* validity for refusals to license. The Court held, in substance, that a copyright holder has a strong presumptive right not to license competitors seeking to compete with it in the very market in which it is exploiting its copyright. The case has no application at all to leveraging. It applies to efforts by a copyright proprietor to protect its own monopolized market in which it is exploiting IP that it was motivated to develop because of its potential value in that market. A strong presumption is warranted here. Certainly every copyright or patent successful enough to give its proprietor an economic monopoly should not, upon its success, be converted into an essential facility.[92] But *Data General* need not and should not be read as establishing a universally applicable presumption that a refusal to license is a presumptively valid business justification. Such a presumption would declare war on a basic goal of the copyright system—to promote a wide dissemination of copyrighted works to the public. Moreover, the *Data General* court was also right in declining to universally negate any antitrust duty to license *even in its own market*. Consider, for example, the MS hypothetical set forth in § 15.8c1. An intellectual property proprietor with an economic monopoly attributable in whole or in part to that IP should not be able to manipulatively use licensing terms or practices to block off normal market forces that might, over time, erode its power.

Any claim that recent case law can be read as supporting a *per se* rule or even a strong presumption protecting IP proprietor's refusals to deal from conventional antitrust inquiry is inconsistent with the *Image*

---

88. 991 F.2d 511, 518 (9th Cir.1993), *cert. denied*, 510 U.S. 1033, 114 S.Ct. 671, 126 L.Ed.2d 640 (1994). If an antitrust claim had been raised in *MAI Systems*, it would not have been a leveraging claim, but something more analogous to an exclusive dealing claim, because the IP proprietor was attempting to deny others access to the IP in order to protect its proprietary use in the market that the IP was developed to exploit.

89. 64 F.3d 1330, 1334 (9th Cir.1995), *cert. denied*, 516 U.S. 1145, 116 S.Ct. 1015, 134 L.Ed.2d 96 (1996).

90. In *Triad Systems* the district court separated antitrust claims for separate treatment and the Court of Appeals approved, labelling copyright and antitrust as "separate, complex bodies of law." Id. at 1338.

91. Data General Corp. v. Grumman Systems Support Group, 36 F.3d 1147 (1st Cir.1994).

92. See § 15.8c5. See also the discussion in § 15.8c1.

Tech dictum, inconsistent with the IP–Antitrust Guidelines, and the assimilation of both antitrust and intellectual property to the service of efficient resource allocation and protecting consumer welfare. An integrated rule of reason analysis taking account of both the ex ante and the ex post allocative effects can aid a court in reaching an appropriate outcome in such cases. Leveraging monopoly power into a distinct and separate market can do substantial ex post harm that should not be lightly justified as needed to encourage the R & D leading to the IP. In exclusive dealing situations the outcomes may be less determinate. If the IP proprietor is controlling the IP through exclusive dealing arrangements in the very market which the IP was produced to service, the ex ante interests in getting the IP on line will likely be significant, probably adequate to counter balance any ex post allocative harm. In any event, it is time to emphasize the common policy bases of antitrust and intellectual property. The period earlier in this century when overbroad antitrust *per se* rules could trump allocatively rational intellectual property rules is long since behind us. It would be a mistake to build similarly irrational and overbroad *per se* rules into the intellectual property system, and to allow these rules to overwhelm antitrust even when doing so would sacrifice rational resource allocation and consumer welfare, the common goals of both systems.

One additional observation is warranted. As shown in § 15.8c3, there are limited situations in which a single firm monopoly may appropriately be characterized as an essential facility, giving rise to a Section 2 duty by the monopolist to provide access to competitors on reasonable terms. The theme of this subsection is simple and direct: a single firm monopoly attributable solely and directly to intellectual property that excludes others from an economic market is not such a situation. For example, if the statutory reward for a particular patent is dominance of a market, the inventor or her assignee is entitled to exploit that dominance either by production and the exclusion of competitors or by licensing either to one licensee, to a few or to many. There are circumstances where monopolizing conduct by an IP monopolist may invite compulsory licensing as a remedy.[93] But unless and until a patent monopolist engages in unreasonable and avoidable conduct to protect, expand or exploit its power, it is free to exploit its IP alone, whether by production or licensing.

15.8c4. Exclusives, Leveraging and Related Tactics Challenged in the Government's Case Against Microsoft

The most important recent case involving antitrust and IP is the Justice Department's monopolization case against Microsoft. It raised

---

93. United States v. Automobile Mfrs. Ass'n, 307 F.Supp. 617 (C.D.Cal.1969) (consent decree resolving alleged conspiracy required compulsory licensing); United States v. Glaxo Group, 410 U.S. 52, 93 S.Ct. 861, 35 L.Ed.2d 104 (1973) (mandate for compulsory sales with reasonable licensing fees; Hartford–Empire Co. v. United States, 323 U.S. 386, 65 S.Ct. 373, 89 L.Ed. 322 (1945), supplemented, 324 U.S. 570, 65 S.Ct. 815, 89 L.Ed. 1198 (1945).

complex issues about both law and fact, about both power and conduct.[94] The D.C. Circuit's en banc 2001 opinion reversed and remanded the district court's holding of a Section 1 tying violation,[95] ordered the removal of the sitting district judge, and overturned the divestiture remedy subject to further remedial proceedings in the lower court. The lower court's holding of a Section 2 monopoly maintenance violation, however, was upheld in the most lengthy substantive portion of the en banc opinion. That violation was premised in large part on Microsoft's exclusionary conduct.

Determining Power—The government alleged that Microsoft through Windows had monopoly power in the market for operating systems for IBM-compatible desktop computers. The Government's case was based on opinion evidence and analysis from a prominent MIT economist, the perception of OEM customers that without Windows they could not stay in the desktop market, Windows' 95 percent market share, performance evidence such as Microsoft profits, entry barriers (especially scale advantages and network externalities), and conduct aimed at forestalling platform level software threats that show awareness of power and intent to protect and expand it. The district court accepted the Government's proposed definition and the 95 percent market share. On appeal, Microsoft argued that this definition improperly excluded from the market (1) non-Intel operating systems such as those used by Apple computers; (2) the operating systems used for handheld computers or personal digital assistants; and (3) middleware software products, such as Netscape browser or Java programing language, that could themselves be used to operate other applications software.

The court of appeals rejected Microsoft's arguments for a broader definition.[96] The non-Intel operating systems cost more and did not allow users to use the full range of software available for Intel computers. Handheld computers and devices had a much narrower range of potential uses than Intel computers. The court dealt somewhat more comprehensively with arguments that middleware programs should be part of the market. Microsoft's argument for including middleware programs in the market had some enhanced credibility because the Government, in its challenge to Microsoft's conduct, had taken the position that these middleware programs were a potential threat to Microsoft's dominance in the operating system market. The court agreed with the district court that middleware failed to meet the test of being "reasonably interchangeable by consumers." Middleware was not now a reasonable substitute for Microsoft operating software, and was not likely to become "the primary platform for software development at any time in the near future."[97]

---

94. See United States v. Microsoft Corp., 253 F.3d 34 (D.C. Cir. 2001)(en banc). See also district court's conclusions of law, 87 F. Supp. 2d 30 (D.C. 2000) and findings of fact, 84 F. Supp. 2d 9 (D.D.C. 1999).

95. This aspect of the 2001 en banc decision is addressed in § 8.3d1.

96. 253 F.3d at 52–55.

97. Id. at 54.

Conduct—The Government's conduct case had several inter-linking elements. It started with Microsoft's recognition of a possible threat to its dominance arising from two sources: (1) the growing importance of the Internet and Netscape's lead in the browser market achieved by its first entry in 1994 with a good product, Navigator; and (2) the extent to which the industry generally was responding to Sunmicrosystem's Java language, which, if it becomes the standard for application software, could make an OEM's choice of operating systems less relevant given that Java applications are compatible with any such system. The court of appeals opinion contains detailed review of the exclusionary conduct and strategic behavior that sustained the district court's holding that Microsoft had engaged in unlawful maintenance of its monopoly, both with respect to the browser market and Java language.

The appellate court sustained district court findings that Microsoft utilized its power from Windows to pressure OEM's not to equip their desktop computers with Navigator or, if they did, to give Explorer priority as the default browser. There was evidence that Microsoft pricing for Windows discriminatorily favored OEMs that supported Microsoft's efforts to exclude or inhibit Netscape, and that since 1996, Windows licenses have stopped OEMs from altering the opening screen of Windows viewed by the user (the Windows "cyber real estate"). This precluded OEMs, (for example, Hewlett Packard) from featuring their own or other factory installed software. Moreover, the tactic created a prime area on Windows; Microsoft could barter access to that area for exclusive rights from its licensee—rights that expanded or protected Microsoft's monopoly. And Microsoft exploited this opportunity. It imposed anticompetitive restraints in contracts with OEMs, Internet service providers, Internet content providers and others. A key point in the court's analysis was its recognition that Microsoft's conduct denied rival browsers of the most cost effective means of distribution.[98] With respect to Java language, the court rested on evidence that Microsoft used its license to Java to reconfigure this language and that, unlike systems written in conventional Java, applications systems written in Microsoft's altered Java were not compatible with systems other than Windows.[99]

Leveraging From Windows to Explorer—Perhaps the most complex element in The Government's conduct case was the claim that Microsoft persisted through sequential versions of Windows to forestall challenge form Netscape by leveraging its Windows power behind its sales of Explorer. Initially a tying tactic was used. Windows and the Explorer browser were separate products separately sold facing separate demand curves. But Microsoft packaged them for sale to OEMs, thus discouraging OEMs, having acquired and installed Explorer with Windows, from adding Netscape's browser. For the Windows 98 version Microsoft integrated Explorer into the operating system. The Government asserted that, when challenged under Section 2, the latter tactic is no more defensible than the former. Both entail the "forced" sale of a browser, a

98. Id. at 64.   **99.** Id. at 74–75.

competitive product, with the monopolized ("tying") product, the operating system. In the context of this industry, this had the effect not only of stifling browser competition but, by doing so, protecting Microsoft's operating system monopoly from erosion from the browser as a partial or potential substitute for Windows as more traffic moves to the Internet. The Government's evidence stressed that some Windows customers do not want the browser integrated (because integrating it will use memory otherwise available for other functions), that there is no technological reason to integrate, and that decisions about what linked functions to integrate into the operating system (and what competitive version of any feature to be so integrated should be used) in order to serve consumers best can better be made by customers, the OEMs.

Microsoft asserted that its practice, integrating the browser into its operating system, was a product design decision not subject to antitrust review. Because such market judgments involve myriad discretionary decisions and predictions about consumer convenience and preferences, the direction of innovation, and trade offs between present and future convenience and costs, they could not be knowledgeably or intelligently reviewed through judicial process.

Although these claims might have been clothed in a leverage theory, the Government chose to dress their claims instead as unlawful monopoly maintenance behavior. In most critical respects, the court embraced the Government's position (it did not, for example, establish separate tests for the contractual tying of two products and the integration of two products into one).[100] The analysis of the court was framed in terms of maintaining Microsoft's operating system monopoly, not in terms of extending that monopoly into new ancillary markets. Still, the court's analysis focused on these ancillary markets (browser market and Java language market). The very same conduct that a court might have condemned under a leverage theory was instead condemned because it entrenched Microsoft's operating system monopoly. Critical to much of the court's analysis of conduct was acceptance of the Government's factual premise that middleware such as browsers might, over time, be capable of providing competitive alternative to Microsoft's operating system.

Finally, the court of appeals rejected Microsoft's IP defense. Microsoft argued that the copyrights held on its programs, if properly obtained, effectively immunized any conduct related to the copyrights from antitrust limitations. The court of appeals was dismissive of this position, reasoning that a copyright holder was no more immunized from antitrust scrutiny than a baseball bat owner would be immunized from tort law.[101]

---

100. See, Grimes, *The Antitrust Tying Law Schism: A Critique of* Microsoft III *and a Response to Hylton and Salinger,* 70 ANTITRUST L.J. 199, 222–225 (2002)(addressing the distinction between product integration and contractual ties).

101. 253 F.3d at 63.

Six months after the court of appeals handed down this important decision, the Justice Department and Microsoft announced a settlement of the case. The settlement imposed various conduct restrictions on Microsoft, many of them designed to prevent the firm from coercing computer manufacturers to include Microsoft software in computers sold to the public. For example, the decree provides that Microsoft must offer its Windows operating system on uniform terms to all computer manufacturers. The decree contains provisions designed to prevent Microsoft from retaliating software providers that develop or use software that competes with Microsoft software and to prevent Microsoft from interfering with computer manufacturers or end users who wish to remove access to Microsoft middleware. The decree also requires Microsoft to disclose "Application Programming Interfaces" (APIs) that allow a middleware program to call upon the Windows operating system to perform various tasks. Finally, the decree set up a three-person Technical Committee designed to assist in carrying out and enforcing the terms of the decree.

The decree did not require structural change, nor did it require licensing of Microsoft copyrights on its software. Some thought the decree an inadequate response to the extensive strategic conduct that were found to violate Section 2 of the Sherman Act. Subsequent litigation involving nine states and the District of Columbia, parties to the suit against Microsoft, failed to result in any significant modifications to the negotiated decree.[102]

The 2002 settlement by no means suggests that all antitrust issues involving Microsoft's conduct have been resolved. There have been and continue to be significant private antitrust suits directed at Microsoft's conduct.[103] Outside the United States, the European Union and other jurisdictions continue to press competition law claims against the Microsoft Corporation.[104] The proper remedial relief, such as whether mandatory licensing could be viable and effective for a monopolist in Microsoft's position, remains a point of active discussion.

15.8c5. *Other Refusals To Deal By Intellectual Property Proprietors*

The owner of any property of any kind is presumptively entitled to decide for itself whether, when and with whom to deal.[105] But this privilege is not unqualified. The antitrust laws intrude upon it in various and significant ways.[106] Choices whether or not to deal when made

---

102. New York v. Microsoft Corp., 224 F. Supp. 2d 76 (D.D.C. 2002)(states remedy); United States v. Microsoft Corp., 231 F. Supp. 2d 144 (D.D.C. 2002)(U.S. consent decree). The appeal of Massachusetts was unsucessful. Massachusetts v. Microsoft Corp., 373 F.3d 1199 (D.C.Cir. 2004).

103. Significant examples of a private suits include In re Microsoft Corp. Antitrust Litigation, 185 F. Supp. 2d 519 (D. Md. 2002); Caldera, Inc. v. Microsoft Corp. 72 F. Supp. 2d 1295 (D.Utah 1999).

104. See the discussion in § 18.7e.

105. E.g., FTC v. Raymond Bros.-Clark Co., 263 U.S. 565, 44 S.Ct. 162, 68 L.Ed. 448 (1924); United States v. Colgate & Co., 250 U.S. 300, 39 S.Ct. 465, 63 L.Ed. 992 (1919).

106. E.g., Lorain Journal Co. v. United States, 342 U.S. 143, 72 S.Ct. 181, 96 L.Ed. 162 (1951); Otter Tail Power Co. v. United States, 410 U.S. 366, 93 S.Ct. 1022, 35 L.Ed.2d 359 (1973); United States v. Parke,

concertedly with competitors are often vulnerable.[107] Individual choices by holders of essential facilities can also be vulnerable.[108] Other monopolists or firms that threaten monopoly[109] can also be restricted in their choices about with whom they will deal. The materials discussed in this section concern restraints on decisions by intellectual property owners about whether to deal.

Non-Use and Suppression—In 1908, the Supreme Court held that a patentee does not forfeit her right to enforce her patent against infringers by failing to practice the patent herself.[110] Citing that case, the Court later held that the Commissioner of Patents could not lawfully deny a patent claim for components of a machine as to which it had allowed claims covering the whole machine, where petitioners sought the narrower claim in order to keep others from competing by using this part of their broader, protected device. On the strength of those two cases it is often said that patent law imposes no obligation to practice a patented invention. The claims by proprietors of copyrights, trade secrets, and rights of publicity not to be compelled to practice seem as strong.[111] Despite this consensus view, an antitrust question remains: Can non-use or suppression of IP violate Section 2 of the Sherman Act? Mere non-use cannot alone be vulnerable even for a monopolist. Consider, first, non-use of a patent. Many (perhaps most) patents are not practiced because they are not worth practicing. The antitrust laws do not impose on anyone, regardless of market power, the obligation to waste resources exploiting a patent that could increase cost without improving product. More broadly, the antitrust laws are not an apt instrument for second guessing market judgments, even by monopolists, about whether any given innovation could be profitable to exploit.

The suppression of a patent, by contrast, may imply something more than non-use. Suppose, for example, that current exploitation would have market value, but that the proprietor refuses either to use the patent or to license it to others who would pay a reasonable royalty, and that the proprietor acts this way in order to extract maximum returns from the proprietor's earlier capitol investment in current technology. Yet, even if a monopolist engaged in such conduct there could be social benefits that might exceed social harms. When viewed dynamically, allowing "suppression" as here defined, could yield a net benefit to the public as well as the monopolist because a rule forbidding such suppression could discourage investment in R & D. Even a monopolist (perhaps a monopolist especially) would be cautious about R & D investment if told by its lawyers that it would be compelled to use or license any

Davis & Co., 362 U.S. 29, 80 S.Ct. 503, 4 L.Ed.2d 505 (1960).

107. E.g., Fashion Originators' Guild of America v. FTC, 312 U.S. 457, 61 S.Ct. 703, 85 L.Ed. 949 (1941).

108. Otter Tail Power Co. v. United States, 410 U.S. 366, 93 S.Ct. 1022, 35 L.Ed.2d 359 (1973).

109. Lorain Journal Co. v. United States, 342 U.S. 143, 72 S.Ct. 181, 96 L.Ed. 162 (1951).

110. Continental Paper Bag Co. v. Eastern Paper Bag Co., 210 U.S. 405, 28 S.Ct. 748, 52 L.Ed. 1122 (1908).

111. Trademarks, by contrast, became invalid after a period of non-use.

successful innovation, despite damage to its own bottom line. No doubt aggregate social costs and benefits might be sorted out under the rule of reason. The fact finder would hear evidence supporting competing scenarios: on behalf of the plaintiff, why the monopolist's decision hurt resource allocation, injured competition and reduced consumer welfare, without an adequately offsetting business justification; on behalf of defendant, why given all relevant considerations and in view of the dynamics, the decision to withhold or delay commercialization was reasonable. On conventional Section 2 standards, only rather extreme facts would warrant a finding of unreasonable suppression by a single firm monopolist.[112] Suppose, for example, that the monopolist's current technology is vastly better than any available alternatives, and that the monopolist invents and patents new alternative technology significantly better than prior alternatives, but still not as good as its current technology. The monopolist licenses this alternative technology to a fringe competitor for three years at a high royalty rate with confidence that the competitor will timidly follow the monopolist's pricing leads and will earn only reasonable profits. Experience, however, diverges from this expectation. The fringe competitor does follow the monopolist's prices, but quickly succeeds in attaining lower costs, higher profits, better product quality, and higher market share. At the end of the three year term, the monopolist refuses to renew the license without a much higher royalty or to license the technology at all to any competitor at any royalty rate. Facts like these would invite a purpose and effect instruction based on *Aspen Skiing*,[113] and stressing the monopolist's change of strategy. On such an instruction the hypothetical facts would warrant a jury finding of monopolization. But because there is no patent law obligation to use, suppression in many situations might be a normal, profit maximizing reaction by the monopolist, and because any rule of reason inquiry would be complex, there should be a presumption that suppression, even by a monopolist, is lawful. Only if the suppression claim can be differentiated from the routine, as for example the last hypothetical can be, should a suppression claim raise a jury issue.

§ 15.9 Intellectual Property Transfers and Horizontal Restraints

This section sets forth an analytical framework (§ 15.9a) and then discusses three types of situations in which intellectual property transfers can raise horizontal antitrust issues. First, when the proprietor of a protected technology both practices it and licenses others to do so, the proprietor and its licensees come into a horizontal relationship; whether or not they were competitors before the license, they are actual or potential competitors through the license. If the license is unrestricted,

---

112. Here, as elsewhere in § 15.8, consideration is limited to single firm conduct. Conspiratorial non-use can give rise to very different issues. See Hartford–Empire v. United States, 323 U.S. 386, 65 S.Ct. 373, 89 L.Ed. 322 (1945), supplemented, 324 U.S. 570, 65 S.Ct. 815, 89 L.Ed. 1198 (1945).

113. Aspen Skiing Co. v. Aspen Highlands Skiing Corp., 472 U.S. 585, 105 S.Ct. 2847, 86 L.Ed.2d 467 (1985).

competition is plainly helped by the license. But if the license imposes restrictions on the licensee, for example as to the resale price, territory or field of use, resulting horizontal restraints and their effect on competition should be analyzed. Licenses in this category are discussed in §§ 15.9b and 15.9c (first the economics, then the law). Of course, such licenses have a vertical aspect, too.[1]

Second, some arrangements that entail technology transfers can raise significant antitrust issues by integrating previously competitive IP—that is, by placing it under common control. For example, two or more firms competing in the same product, research or technology market may pool their proprietary information through licenses to each other or by assignment or licenses to a joint venture or jointly owned subsidiary. Though these participants, too, are relating vertically as suppliers to each other as well as horizontally, the competitively significant characterization is horizontal. Arrangements of this type are discussed in § 15.9d.

Exclusive licensing can also raise horizontal issues because these licenses can foreclose the licensor's horizontal competitors from alternative technologies.[2] The licensee may compete with the licensor in a relevant goods market and may also control or be developing proprietary technology of its own which could substitute for the technology granted by the license. In such instances the exclusivity provision would for the license term both foreclose the licensee from competing with the licensor in that technology market and constrain the licensee in the technology choices it makes as a competitor of the licensor in the goods market.[3] On facts like these the competition issue raised by the exclusive license is properly characterized as horizontal. Such arrangements are discussed in § 15.9e.[4] Finally, grant back clauses in technology licenses can also raise

§ 15.9

1. The proprietor relates to the licensees not only horizontally, but, qua licensor, as a technology supplier. Some technology transfers may establish a relationship that is primarily or even solely vertical, and in which a competitive effect analysis must focus on this aspect. For example, the proprietor may engage solely in the business of producing and transferring innovative technology, which it never itself practices. This would leave at least a remote potential competition relationship if the proprietor controls and could lawfully use the technology itself. Even this possibility can be negated if the transfer were by assignment or by a license or licenses that inhibit practice by the proprietor. Such transfers, along with other vertical issues, are discussed in § 15.10.

2. If no licensee is an actual or potential competitor of the licensor either in the relevant technology market or in the goods market affected by the licensed technology,

the restraint is properly characterized as vertical. It can affect competition by foreclosing the goods and/or technology competitors of the licensor, but the licensees relate only vertically both to the licensor and the licensor's competitors. Compare the facts in Department of Justice and Federal Trade Commission, Antitrust Guidelines For the Licensing of Intellectual Property, Example 8 (1995), available at <http://www.usdoj.gov/atr/public/guidelines/0558.htm> [hereinafter the IP–Antitrust Guidelines or, where clear from the context, the Guidelines]. Exclusive licensing agreements of this kind are analogous to other exclusives (e.g., Tampa Electric Co. v. Nashville Coal Co., 365 U.S. 320, 81 S.Ct. 623, 5 L.Ed.2d 580 (1961) discussed in § 8.4).

3. Compare the fact situation in IP–Antitrust Guidelines Example 9.

4. If the licensor and licensee compete in the goods market in which the technology is used, but the licensee neither owns nor is developing a substitute technology,

horizontal issues, especially when the grant back is exclusive. These clauses are discussed in § 15.9f.

15.9a. Analytical Framework for Horizontal License Restraints

Case law involving antitrust and intellectual property has consistently used rule of reason analysis,[5] save in conventional *per se* situations where any claim of an IP related efficiency justification is a sham or manifestly trivial.[6] The Guidelines adopt this approach. The enforcement agencies will inquire "whether the [IP] restraint is likely to have anticompetitive effects and, if so, whether the restraint is reasonably necessary to achieve procompetitive benefits that outweigh [the anticompetitive effects]."[7] Nonetheless, no elaborate economic analysis will be needed if the "nature and necessary effect are * * * plainly anticompetitive."[8] In sum, conventional, modern antitrust analysis will be used, including the *per se* rule, a quick look, or a truncated rule of reason where appropriate. It is expected that courts, by and large, will accept this Guidelines approach.

15.9b. Economic Analysis: License Restrictions that Hurt Competition by Limiting Licensee Marketing Choices

If IP gives access to technology significantly more advantageous than competing technologies, it will have value that its owner could exploit in any of several ways: (1) by using the IP in competition against less advantageous technologies; (2) by assigning the IP for its market value (the value of the technology); (3) by not using but licensing others to use the IP technology; or (4) by both practicing and licensing others to use the technology. If the IP owner is not itself in the market where the IP has value, it will likely assign or license. If the owner is in that market, it may exploit alone, thus raising the value of its own output above, or reducing its own costs below, those of competitors. Alternatively, it may both use and license others for one or more of these reasons: to encourage wider use; to make its proprietary IP an industry standard; to share the capital costs and the risks of exploitation; or to reduce purchasers' risks by assuring them that there will be alternative sources

the exclusive license could still offset competition between licensor and licensee in the goods market by affecting licensee technology choices for the term. However, since the significance of this effect will be entirely a function of the competitive significance of foreclosing the licensee as a possible customer of the licensor's technology competitors, the issue raised is best characterized as vertical. See § 15.10.

5. Berkey Photo, Inc. v. Eastman Kodak Co., 603 F.2d 263 (2d Cir. 1979) (the market power of firms participating in joint research is a factor in antitrust analysis); Hennessy Industries v. FMC Corp., 779 F.2d 402 (7th Cir.1985); See also G. Sorbel, Exploitation of Patents and the Antitrust

Laws, 477 PLI/Pat 683 (1997) (discussing Adams v. Burke, 84 U.S. (17 Wall.) 453, 21 L.Ed. 700 (1873) (anticompetitive effects that are not *per se* violations of the law are reviewed in accordance with the rule of reason)).

6. E.g., Palmer v. BRG of Ga. Inc., 498 U.S. 46, 111 S.Ct. 401, 112 L.Ed.2d 349 (1990).

7. IP–Antitrust Guidelines § 3.4.

8. Id. (citing FTC v. Superior Court Trial Lawyers Ass'n, 493 U.S. 411, 110 S.Ct. 768, 107 L.Ed.2d 851 (1990) and National Society of Professional Engineers v. United States, 435 U.S. 679, 98 S.Ct. 1355, 55 L.Ed.2d 637 (1978)).

available. Licensing can yield procompetitive benefits. As the Guidelines state, IP "is one component [of an array of components utilized to achieve an output] * * * and derives value from its combination with complementary factors [such as] manufacturing and distribution facilities, workforces, and other * * * [assets, including other] intellectual property."[9] In general, licensing is socially preferable to exclusive exploitation by the proprietor. It can result in more rapid and wider exploitation as two or more firms link their IP each to a different set of complementary input factors. It can also lead to more competition in the relevant output market and wider diffusion of the IP technology during the protected term, thus increasing the likelihood of improvements and maximizing the chance that at term end the availability and utility of the product or the technology newly entering the public domain will be more widely appreciated and more quickly and effectively exploited.

The licensor will choose the best course not for the public but for itself. For example, it may be deterred from licensing, fearing that licensees, or some of them, may compete effectively enough to negate the licensor's cost advantage from license fees. Such a disincentive would be reduced if the IP owner could impose ancillary terms mitigating any competitive threat. Some typical license restrictions that could reduce such licensor risk would be: restrictions on the price charged by licensees for the licensed product or for products made with the licensed technology; restrictions on the scope of the licensee's geographic or product market; requirements that the IP proprietor supply key components, or provide customer service. There is an abundant literature on the competitive consequences of such license restrictions. The discussion below draws on the Guidelines and on an article by Louis Kaplow[10] which both summarizes and criticizes much of the earlier commentary.

15.9b1. Purposes and Effects of License Restraints Fixing Resale Prices

If the proprietor of an IP product (or process) that is better or cheaper than alternatives decides not to license and itself to exploit, the proprietor can extract any market power (large or small) conferred by the IP by pricing its output above marginal cost. If the market is otherwise competitive and the proprietor possesses all relevant information, it might be able to earn the same supracompetitive return by licensing only, or by both producing itself and by licensing. It could do this if: (1) it could determine the profit maximizing output it would have fixed and price it would have charged had it alone produced, and if its per unit costs at this output were the same as its per unit costs at the lower output it would itself produce when licensees shared production; (2) it set this profit maximizing price on its own output, if any; (3) it could determine the efficient production costs for its licensees; (4) it set a per unit royalty for licensees equal to the profit maximizing price, less

---

9. IP–Antitrust Guidelines § 2.3.

10. Kaplow, *The Patent—Antitrust Intersection: A Reappraisal*, 97 Harv. L. Rev. 1813 (1984).

the licensees efficient per unit cost of production; and (5) it granted sufficient licenses to assure sufficient competition among licensees to force them to sell at their cost. If the IP proprietor's information and calculations were correct, competition would force the licensees' prices to the desired profit maximizing level at which the IP owner priced its own output; for licensees this would be the sum of all costs, including the license fee, plus a reasonable competitive return. The aggregated profit-maximizing output would then be shared by licensor and licensees and the IP proprietor would earn its profit maximizing return—the same return it would earn if it alone produced the entire output at efficient cost and sold it at the profit maximizing price. Licensees would earn only a reasonable return on their costs. The full amount of the difference between production cost and selling price would go to the licensor, in the form of aggregate profits on its own production, plus license fees on licensee production. But note that this course is feasible only if the needed facts are knowable (and known), when all producers are able to operate at efficient scale, and when the market functions competitively.[11] The likelihood of meeting all of these conditions is very small.

Of course, an IP proprietor may not have confidence in its information and calculations about what royalty will extract all supracompetitive returns. Or, given scale economies, it may not be feasible to grant enough licenses to assure a competitive market. For any one or more of these reasons (or simply because it did not want to lose share even if maintaining profits) an IP proprietor may want to use price restricting licenses, an alternative and (if legal) less risky way to assure that its own profit maximizing price will not be undercut. The possible benefit from allowing price fixing licenses centers precisely here. Such an IP owner might hesitate to license at all unless all licenses contain a price restriction. If so, allowing the restriction would yield a social advantage; it would encourage licensing that would not otherwise have occurred. This widens knowledge of and experience with the technology and increases the chance of improvements and rapid deployment. Of course, in some instances, the licensor's incentives to license (lack of capital to exploit the full market alone; the need, in order to maximize orders, to assure buyers of a second source, etc.) may be so compelling that licensing would have occurred even if price restrictions, however strongly preferred by the IP proprietor, could not lawfully be negotiated. In those instances, allowing the proprietor to set a resale price for licensees would be gratuitous because it would yield no added social benefit. Nonetheless, denying the right to grant price fixing licenses may do little social good

---

11. Kaplow, supra note 10 at 1861–1862 shows that if all these assumptions are met, then even if one licensee is more efficient than the licensor, the licensor can still make this strategy work. The less efficient licensor need only designate the appropriate per unit price for the license. This per unit royalty extracts all supracompetitive profits of licensees with per unit costs comparable to those of the licensor. While this royalty will allow the more efficient licensee to price below the IP owner and other licensees, and thus to increase its share and its return, the resulting increase in the aggregate industry output will not reduce the amount that the IP owner earns per unit on both its own output and that of all licenses, including the more efficient one. Indeed, it will increase it. Compare IP–Antitrust Guidelines § 2.3.

even if the proprietor decides to license in any event. If the licensor holds strong and valuable IP and is, itself, a leading producer of the output product in an oligopolistic market, the proprietor is probably unlikely to face aggressive competition either from non-licensees (who are at a disadvantage due to lack of access to the IP) or from its licensees (who must rely on licensor goodwill for renewal). Such an IP owner, able with its IP to organize the industry by interdependent (and thus lawful) decisions to follow its own price leadership, may feel no need to fix resale prices.

Given the array of influences and possibilities, is it likely that, on balance, allowing price restricted licenses will be socially harmful? In those instances where licensing would not occur without price fixing, the practice yields a benefit, but not one it is possible to quantify. What of situations where allowing price fixing would be gratuitous, in that the licensor would license in any event? First, assume the IP is capable of yielding market dominance. In this case the licensor will want its full monopoly return, not to share it. If the licensor is a non-producer, its incentive will be to impose a maximum resale price that is as low as possible, while still attracting the licensees needed to fully exploit the market, and charging a per unit royalty high enough to extract as much of the supracompetitive return as possible. If the licensor produces itself, the licensor will have no incentive to raise the fixed resale price above licensee costs, including the license fee, for doing so would result in reducing output below the level that could yield the proprietor's maximum feasible monopoly return and force the licensor to share the monopoly return with licensees. But suppose the IP, though an improvement, is only one competitive alternative among a number. Here, the proprietor's incentives will be mixed. It cannot organize the industry around its technology without offering licensees an incentive of higher profits upon shifting to its proprietary technology. To attract licensees the proprietor may have to function, at least in part, as the equivalent of a cartel agent, setting a resale price and a cognate royalty rate that will yield some supracompetitive return to licensees (even though the proprietor which collects rather than pays license fees may take a larger portion of these returns).[12] The analytical problems may be further complicated by lack of enough structural information to decide where in the panorama of theoretical possibilities a particular instance fits.

One helpful indicator is whether the fixed resale price is a maximum price or a minimum price. If the licensor imposes a maximum resale price, this indicates that the licensor possesses market power in the licensed product or process. Without that market power, the licensor would likely be unable to impose a margin-squeezing price on its licensee. The possession of this market power may be exculpatory if it is solely a result of a lawfully exercised IP right. On the other hand, if the resale price imposed by the licensor is a minimum price, this circumstance suggests that the licensor lacks market power in the licensed

---

12. Compare IP–Antitrust Guidelines, Example 7; see also id. § 5.2.

product and may be imposing the minimum resale price as an entice-
ment for the licensee to choose its technology. The possibility that the
fixed resale price is a sham—that it is imposed not to exploit the
inherent monopoly in the IP right but to orchestrate a cartel among
rivals—is increased. Under these circumstances, vertical minimum price
fixing is likely to carry the same competitive risks and benefits that
attach outside the intellectual property context. See the discussion of
vertical minimum price fixing in § 6.6.

*15.9b2. Purposes and Effects of License Restraints Dividing Mar-
kets*

An IP owner planning to produce and license might wish to impose
either customer, territorial, product (or field of use) restraints on licensees, thus effectively reserving a segment of the market for itself. It may
also be willing (or even want) to protect each licensee's market niche
from entry by any other licensee (or even from the licensor itself). A
purpose and effect analysis of practices like these is comparable to that
concerning price restricted licenses. Neither territorial nor field of use
restraints will raise the licensor's return above the return it could
achieve by setting the royalty at the difference between efficient cost at
the profit maximizing output price, so long as the market is structured
competitively and the licensor has the information needed to calculate
the critical per unit royalty. But allowing such arrangements may reduce
the level of competition below where it would have been in instances
where licenses would have been granted even if such restrictions were
not allowed. And in some instances the proprietor may use such devices
to encourage the use of the proprietary technology and, in the process,
share monopoly returns with licensees.

15.9b3. Purposes and Effects of Restrictions Limiting Output

A license that restricts each licensee to a maximum output would
enable the licensor to adjust its own output to achieve a profit maximizing industry output. Doing this would affect price much the same way as
would a price fixing license or a license that divides the market into
territory or product categories or into other segments. Purposes and
effects would be similar.[13]

15.9b4. Cartelizing Through Restrictions

Prior discussions in § 15.8b assume that the IP has value at least as
an improvement, and that the license restraints are outcomes of negotiation between licensor and licensees in a market for the technology. But
IP licenses with restrictions such as those discussed above could also
serve as blatant cartelization devices. Suppose that a patented technology offers no cost or quality advantage over alternative technologies
already in the public domain. As a practical matter such IP is valueless.
Suppose, next, that despite this lack of value all or most firms in a

---

13. Id.

structurally competitive or oligopolistic industry agree to pay the patent holder a small license fee for licenses which fix resale prices at a level greater than aggregate costs. The only economically rational explanation would be that licensees are paying the patent holder for organizing and policing a price cartel.[14]

Real situations are not likely to be as stark as this hypothetical. But whenever an industry is structured so that it might be effectively competitive and is organized around a single patent (or other IP) through licenses containing price restrictions or dividing markets, the possibility of cartel-like motivations and effects is present.[15] If the licensed technology does not hold significant advantages over alternatives, cartelization is a likely explanation. Indeed, even if the technology is advantageous, though not profoundly so, an element of cartelization may lodge in a price fixing license (see § 15.9b1), especially when the proprietor attains industry standard status for its protected technology. In any situation where price, output or market segregating restrictions are imposed by the licensor, there is a possibility of consumer welfare injury. When price and output decisions for the industry are organized through licenses for technology of trivial value, there is reason for deep concern. Detailed analysis may also be warranted when the value of the technology is modest. If the purpose and effect is to reduce industry output below, and to increase overall industry return above, the level that could be achieved by the licensor fully and successfully exploiting the patent alone, the licenses distort allocation and raise prices.

15.9c. Applying the Antitrust Laws to Licenses that Restrict Licensee Marketing Choices

There have been swings in judicial attitude about the legality under the Sherman Act of various licensing practices.[16] Indeed, swings have

14. Id.

15. See United States v. New Wrinkle, Inc., 342 U.S. 371, 72 S.Ct. 350, 96 L.Ed. 417(1952). Compare Standard Sanitary Mfg. Co. v. United States, 226 U.S. 20, 33 S.Ct. 9, 57 L.Ed. 107 (1912). Standard, the leading firm in the market for enameled sanitary ware (sinks, bath tubs, toilets, etc.) held a patent which significantly improved its products. For a period it exploited the patent alone. Then it arranged to grant licenses to competitors the market shares of which, with its own, would aggregate about 85 percent of the market. The license would allow sales only at fixed prices, only to licensed jobbers who would resale at fixed prices and would preclude licensees from selling "seconds" to licensed jobbers or anyone else at reduced prices. The royalty provision included a penal amount that would be returned if the licensee complied. As the Court stated, the industry "was controlled from producer to consumer" with "fidelity

... secured ... by ... 'cash bail.' " Id. at 48. Compare Palmer v. BRG of Georgia, Inc., 498 U.S. 46, 111 S.Ct. 401, 112 L.Ed.2d 349 (1990), where the Court regarded as a sham a territorial division between horizontal competitors defended as ancillary to a copyright license.

16. See Rosen, *Intellectual Property and the Antitrust Pendulum: Recent Developments At the Interface Between the Antitrust and Intellectual Property Laws*, 62 ANTITRUST L.J. 669 (1994), which traces Antitrust Division developments from the period of the "nine-no-nos" in the 1970's through Chicago dominance in the 1980s to the focused and critical evaluations that characterized the more recent approach. See also Wilson, *Patent and Know How License Agreements: Field of Use, Territorial, Price and Quality Restrictions, Remarks Before Fourth New England Antitrust Conference*, speech reprinted in 213 PATENT, TRADEMARK & COPYRIGHT J. A–9 (1975); and

been wide enough to raise questions about whether there is any abiding and solid law to inform counselling and enforcement discretion. This section begins with an exploration of the case law and its implication, then makes suggestions about appropriate enforcement and counselling policy.

15.9c1.   Antitrust and Price Fixing Licenses

The first significant case about the validity of patent license restrictions was United States v. General Electric Co.[17] G.E., with patents completely covering the manufacture of the then most advanced electric light bulbs, manufactured these bulbs itself. It also licensed Westinghouse to manufacture them, but obliged Westinghouse to sell them only at prices fixed by G.E. In an opinion by Justice Taft the Court found no violation of Section 1:

> "We think [the patentee may limit the sales method and price charged by the licensee] * * * provided the conditions of sale are normally and reasonably adopted to secure the pecuniary reward for the patentee's monopoly. One of the valuable elements of the [patent] is to acquire profit by the price at which the article is sold * * *. When the patentee licenses another* * * [and] retains the right to continue to make and vend * * * the price at which his licensee will sell will necessarily affect the price at which he can sell his own patented goods * * *."[18]

This holding has had a checkered history. In 1948 a minority of four would have overruled it.[19] When challenged in *United States v. Huck Manufacturing Co.*, the decision against the Government below was affirmed by an equally divided court.[20] In that case the Government conceded that such a restriction might encourage licensing that would not otherwise occur and, in those instances, lead to better results than if the licensor exploited alone. But it contended that the restraints were often gratuitous—in that licensing would have occurred in any event—and that the restraint on competition resulting in such cases outweighed any long run competitive benefit from such additional licensing occasioned by the use of resale price restraints.

Bingaman, *Antitrust and Innovation in a High Technology Society*, 7 Trade Reg. Rep.(CCH) 48, 998 (1994). The current view of the enforcement agencies is expressed in the IP–Antitrust Guidelines. See generally § 15.7.

17.   272 U.S. 476, 47 S.Ct. 192, 71 L.Ed. 362 (1926).

18.   Id. at 490. Cf. Bobbs–Merrill Co. v. Straus, 210 U.S. 339, 28 S.Ct. 722, 52 L.Ed. 1086 (1908) (holding that when the publisher, a holder of a copyright on a book, sold the book with a notice stating the minimum price at which the buyer was licensed to resell, the copyright gave the publisher no cause of action against buyers who resold for less). Accord, Bauer & Cie v. O'Donnell,

229 U.S. 1, 33 S.Ct. 616, 57 L.Ed. 1041(1913) (patents). In effect G.E. gave a patent holder greater license to fix prices horizontally than it possessed to fix them vertically.

19.   United States v. Line Material Co., 333 U.S. 287, 68 S.Ct. 550, 92 L.Ed. 701 (1948).

20.   227 F.Supp. 791 (E.D.Mich.1964), *aff'd by an equally divided Court*, 382 U.S. 197, 86 S.Ct. 385, 15 L.Ed.2d 268 (1965). See also United States v. Univis Lens Co., 316 U.S. 241, 62 S.Ct. 1088, 86 L.Ed. 1408 (1942) where the Court held that an attempt by a patentee who sold patented lense blocks to control the price of finished lenses was not protected by *G.E.*

Ambivalence about the *G.E.* outcome on its own facts is certainly appropriate,[21] whether the IP is being exploited in the technology or the product market. If it be assumed that had price fixing been unlawful, licensing would have occurred without the price restriction, there is little question but that some dynamic and perhaps some immediate competitive harm results; allowing price fixing stifles whatever licensor-licensee price competition might otherwise develop, thus entrenching any licensor power. The *G.E.* court's reason for allowing such price fixing between competitors was less a matter of calculating harms and benefits than assuming that patent policy trumps the antitrust concern. The inference of harm, of course, depends both on structure and on the assumption that licensing would occur in any event. As to structure, if there are equally efficient alternative technologies readily available, a single price fixing license could not foreclose competition in the product market. Whether acting alone or in collusion with a single licensee the patentee would not be in a position to sustain supracompetitive prices. As to the assumption about licensing in any event, if the patentee would exploit alone, were it not lawful to restrict, allowing the restriction yields a better current deployment of the technology. Though having limited immediate social benefit (because of the price restriction), this may yield more competition once IP protection ends and may facilitate wider deployment and improvement during the term. Less obviously, the inference of harm is also dependent on the assumption that the licensee might, if unconstrained by the license, be tempted to price compete. If, as in *G.E.* the patent monopoly is available only to a two firm oligopoly, that assumption may be strained. Whether restricted by its license or not, it does not seem likely that Westinghouse would have challenged *G.E.* on prices. Whatever the structure after licensing, the situation is nevertheless at least somewhat better if the licensee has no contract obligation to follow the patent-holder's prices. An enforceable cartel is more of a threat than interdependence, even in a tight oligopoly. How much better this outcome would be than single firm exploitation by the patentee is also indeterminate. If Westinghouse had been denied patent access, how would it have reacted? Might it have invented around the patent and competed unconstrained? Might it have challenged the validity of the patent and won?

Note that patents do not always yield such market power as that in *G.E.*—indeed, some may yield none at all. Note, also, that the implicit assumption that allowing price fixing licenses may increase the patentee's reward and thus encourage investment in innovation is not overwhelmingly obvious. If the patent yields market power in either the technology or product market there will be alternative possible ways for the patentee to exploit that power. *G.E.* apparently determined the profit maximizing price on light bulbs, set that price itself, and required

---

21. The latest example of ambivalence is in the IP–Antitrust Guidelines. Section 5.2 asserts the *per se* illegality of vertical RPM. The supporting footnote simply states that "[s]ubsequent lower court decisions have distinguished the *G.E.* decision," though none of the cases cited in the note directly conflicted with *G.E.*

Westinghouse to set the same price. If the price restraint were illegal, G.E. might have used other strategies to attain maximum returns.[22]

G.E. is subject to a sham exception, as, indeed, is any license restriction fashioned in an effort to shield or disguise a blatant cartel.[23] If a patent has little or no economic value because alternative technology of comparable worth is in the public domain or available at competitive prices, the patentee may not lawfully organize a cartel by inducing competitors to accept its price fixing license.[24] Also, G.E. gains little or no credence when extended beyond a commitment by the licensee to sell the patented product manufactured by the licensee at the price specified by the licensor. The "first sale" doctrine stemming from Adams v. Burke[25] applies: the G.E. case does not protect the licensor if it is fixing prices at which buyers from the licensee may resell patented products. Also, a patent on any component (say, a part) of the licensee's finished product does not protect a licensor's attempt to fix the licensee's pricing of the integrated output.[26] Neither may a patent on a process warrant price fixing by the patentee on the products made with the process by the licensee,[27] although this, perhaps, is doubtful. Under the patent law the question ought to be, how should the protected market be defined? It is a question similar to market definition under antitrust, though the inquiry is not where ex post market power might exist, but what were the ex ante commercial expectations and goals that motivated the R & D leading to the IP.

Does G.E, within its narrow realm, remain reliable law? The question can be subdivided. In all likelihood, on the facts of G.E., there was, ex post (that is, after the patented technology was on line), both significant competitive harm and small possibility of offsetting benefit. In effect, the Court relied only on an ex ante analysis of G.E.'s patenting strategy; it apparently recognized that the ability to fix licensee pricing could influence G.E.'s original decision and thought this incentive to invest overwhelmed any ex post competitive harm. Thus, at a minimum, G.E. implies that price fixing licenses do not warrant an adverse *per se* response. So long as G.E. is not overruled pricing fixing licenses may be safe (though probably of little, if any, use to the patentee) if, given a competitive market structure, no plausible contention of competitive injury is available. On the other hand, though G.E. itself may imply that the reward granted by the patent statute includes a right to fix licensee prices and that all competitive concerns must always give way, a *per se* legal rule can no longer be assumed. The Supreme Court's later response

---

22. § 15.102a.

23. IP–Antitrust Guideline § 5.2 and n.33. Cf. United States v. Masonite Corp., 316 U.S. 265, 62 S.Ct. 1070, 86 L.Ed. 1461 (1942).

24. Cf. United States v. New Wrinkle, supra note 15.

25. 84 U.S. (17 Wall.) 453, 21 L.Ed. 700 (1873).

26. United States v. G.E. Co., 358 F.Supp. 731 (S.D.N.Y.1973).

27. Barber–Colman Co. v. National Tool Co., 136 F.2d 339 (6th Cir.1943); but see United States v. Studiengesellschaft Kohle, m.b.H., 670 F.2d 1122 (D.C.Cir.1981) (holding patentee is permitted to geographically restrict sales of goods made from licensed process).

in *Huck*, numerous post *G.E.* cases limiting or refusing to expand the patentee's privilege to fix prices, and the Guidelines assumption of *per se* illegality all counsel against any such assumption. Today, any price fixing license, though shielded by *G.E.*, can still face jeopardy if its effect is to unduly restrain competition in an appropriately defined market.[28] One cannot really know, since the Court has not addressed the question in either the Chicago or the current, post-Chicago era. If the structure is one in which output by licensor and licensee together aggregate to a substantial market share, prudence suggests that the patentee seek alternative ways of achieving its profit maximizing or market share protecting goals.[29]

15.9c2. *Antitrust and Field of Use Restrictions in Licenses*

Economic analysis suggests that the policies for restricting licensee pricing and market size should be similar if the practices have similar purposes and effects.[30] The law and enforcement policy, nonetheless, tend to respond with less hostility to territorial, field of use and customer restraints in licenses than to price restraints. Regarding patent licenses there are many cases and a specific statutory provision that is relevant. Subject to the same qualifications that apply to a price fixing license, the provision in the Patent Act authorizing exclusive licenses covering "any specific part of the United States"[31] can be and has been read as congressional permission for territorial restraints in licenses.[32] The qualifications are first, that the license restraint not be a sham to hide a cartel;[33] second, that the restraint not limit downstream firms buying from the first purchaser from the licensee. Licenses which divide markets by assigning separate product categories within which licensees may exploit the license or restricting the customers to whom licensees may sell have been upheld against challenge,[34] though there may be some limits.[35] Are there spillover effects in different product markets or at different vertical levels? If so the restraint may be vulnerable.

28. Cf. Windsurfing International v. AMF, Inc., 782 F.2d 995 (Fed.Cir.), *cert. denied*, 477 U.S. 905, 106 S.Ct. 3275, 91 L.Ed.2d 565 (1986).

29. Cf. HOVENKAMP, FEDERAL ANTITRUST POLICY: THE LAW OF COMPETITION AND ITS PRACTICE § 5.5.c (3d ed. 2005).

30. § 15.9b2.

31. 35 USCA § 261.

32. Ethyl Gasoline Corp. v. United States, 309 U.S. 436, 456, 60 S.Ct. 618, 84 L.Ed. 852 (1940).

33. Cf. Palmer v. BRG of Ga. Inc., 498 U.S. 46, 111 S.Ct. 401, 112 L.Ed.2d 349 (1990). The Court (per curiam) found *per se* unlawful a territorial division between bar review suppliers implemented through a transfer of copyright and trademark interests with territorial restrictions.

34. General Talking Pictures Corp. v. Western Electric Co., 305 U.S. 124, 59 S.Ct.

116, 83 L.Ed. 81 (1938) (field of use restriction is reasonably within the reward which the patent granted and to which the patentee is entitled, the test established in *G.E*). But cf. Automatic Radio Mfg. Co. v. Hazeltine Research, 339 U.S. 827, 70 S.Ct. 894, 94 L.Ed. 1312 (1950) where the Court, perhaps pointedly, avoided reaffirming General Talking Picture. Favorable lower court decision are numerous. E.g., Turner Glass Corp. v. Hartford–Empire Co., 173 F.2d 49 (7th Cir.), cert. denied, 338 U.S. 830, 70 S.Ct. 57, 94 L.Ed. 505(1949); Benger Lab., Ltd. v. R.K. Laros Co., 209 F.Supp. 639 (E.D.Pa.1962), *aff'd per curiam* 317 F.2d 455 (3d Cir.), *cert. denied*, 375 U.S. 833, 84 S.Ct. 69, 11 L.Ed.2d 64 (1963).

35. United States v. Consolidated Car-Heating Co., 87 U.S.P.Q. 20 (1950); Baldwin–Lima–Hamilton Corp. v. Tatnall Measuring Sys. Co., 169 F.Supp. 1 (E.D.Pa.1958)

The implication of *G.E.* and the holdings of *Ethyl and General Talking Picture* also shield patent territorial and field of use restrictions from *per se* vulnerability,[36] unless the arrangement is a sham.[37] As with price fixing, rule of reason analysis is called for, though a truncated one may be appropriate. Could the arrangement substantially restrain competition? If not, the inquiry should end. If so, the question becomes whether the restraint is excessive use of the power conferred by the patent. Certainly spillover effects to markets further downstream or to related products or process markets render the restraint vulnerable. If by the license the patentee achieves no restraint that exceeds what the patentee could lawfully accomplish by its own exploitation of the patent, the accumulated case law suggests that the restraint is lawful. In *Huck Manufacturing*[38] (involving price fixing, not a merely territorial or field of use restraints) the Government pressed for a different approach. It urged the Court to do a rule of reason analysis balancing ex ante and ex post concerns. If the restraint seriously impeded competition in the market in which the patent is utilized, the Government wanted a court to evaluate the likelihood that, but for a right to impose the restraint, the patentee would not have developed the technology. As yet, no court has embraced this approach, although in *Huck* four justices may have been ready to do so. In concept this approach is ideal; it resolves an antitrust-patent conflict by an allocative evaluation consistent with the goals of both systems. The problem is the practical one: how to determine whether or not the patentee would have made the same investment decision if it had had a different perception of the governing law. Whether such an approach might again be asserted by enforcers in the post-Chicago period is a matter for speculation.

In regard to license restraints for IP other than patents, there is no reason to impose stricter rules. Restraints in other IP licenses are not likely to be more restrictive of competition and may often be less. Copyright, for example (except in the case of a software copyright) is unlikely to foreclose competition in an economic market; neither is a trademark, except conceivably in unique circumstances or in aftermarkets for a single firm's product. Indeed, while field of use restrictions are very common in trademark licenses, antitrust challenges are extremely rare.

15.9d. Pooling and Cross–Licensing Intellectual Property

15.9d1. Possible Harms and Benefits

Separately owned and controlled IP can be actually or potentially competitive in a research market, a goods market or both. To place such

aff'd per curiam, 268 F.2d 395 (3d Cir. 1959), *cert. denied*, 361 U.S. 894, 80 S.Ct. 198, 4 L.Ed.2d 151(1959); United States v. Am. Linen Supply Co., 141 F.Supp. 105, 112–114 (N.D.Ill.1956).

36. See e.g, United States v. Studiengesellschaft Kohle, m.b.H. 670 F.2d 1122 (D.C.Cir.1981) (field of use restrictions a process patent subject to rule of reason).

37. See Palmer v. BRG, note 33 supra.

38. 227 F.Supp. 791 (E.D.Mich.1964), *aff'd*, 382 U.S. 197, 86 S.Ct. 385, 15 L.Ed.2d 268 (1965).

IP in common control can yield economies that will improve allocation and increase competition. Such arrangements can facilitate the effective use of complementary technologies, "unblock" blocking patents, link basic and improvement patents, reduce transaction costs, yield scale or scope economies, or facilitate contractual settlement, in many instances the least costly means of resolving conflicting IP claims. One or more such advantages can arise from bilateral or multilateral pooling of IP rights achieved by cross licenses between or among participants or by placing the rights in common control by means of a joint venture or a jointly owned subsidiary. But integrating the control of competing or potentially competing resources of any kind can also cause competitive harms. If, when combined, the previously competing technologies constitute a substantial share of a relevant goods or technology market, there is a direct reduction in horizontal competition that must be set off against, and that might overwhelm, any efficiency gain resulting from the pool. This is as true for joint control of IP as it is for joint control of any other capital asset.[39] The rule of reason task is to identify potential harms and benefits, each with manageable specificity, to consider the extent of concentration, and to make a judgment.[40] This process might be perfunctory if benefits overwhelm possible harm, as when, despite the integration, the relevant markets obviously remained competitive, or, conversely, when harms plainly dominate, as when the integration is clearly a sham. In some instances, however, careful market definition and analysis of harms and benefits may be essential.[41]

If an improvement patent is blocked by a primary patent held by a different patentee, there is a clear social advantage in dismantling the wall so that the improved technology can be practiced. This could be done by assignment by one of the two patent holders to the other, but neither patent holder may be willing to exclude itself from the combined technology. Cross-licensing in such a situation will be socially beneficial because it will facilitate exploitation of otherwise inaccessible technology. Situations of this kind should be presumptively lawful. However, if the technology market is concentrated, the possibility of adverse consequences should be considered.[42]

39. The Guidelines recognize that "collective price or output restraints in pooling arrangements, such as joint marketing of pooled intellectual property rights with collective price setting or coordinated output restrictions * * *" can harm competition. IP–Antitrust Guideline § 5.5. This paragraph of the Guidelines contrasts NCAA v. Bd. of Regents of Univ. Of Oklahoma, 468 U.S. 85, 104 S.Ct. 2948, 82 L.Ed.2d 70 (1984) with Broadcast Music, Inc. v. Columbia Broadcast System, Inc., 441 U.S. 1, 99 S.Ct. 1551, 60 L.Ed.2d 1(1979) as examples, respectively, of a harmful and a beneficial integration of IP. Contrast also examples 9 and 10 of the IP–Antitrust Guidelines.

40. See, e.g., Palmer v. BRG of Georgia, Inc., 498 U.S. 46, 111 S.Ct. 401, 112 L.Ed.2d 349 (1990).

41. See Standard Oil of Indiana v. United States, 283 U.S. 163, 51 S.Ct. 421, 75 L.Ed. 926 (1931). There is considerable literature on pooling. See Andewelt, *Analysis of Patent Pools Under The Antitrust Laws,* 53 ANTITRUST L.J. 611 (1985); Merges, *Contracting Into Liability Rules: Intellectual Property Rights and Collective Rights Organizations,* 84 CAL. L. REV. 1293 (1996).

42. United States v. Line Material Co., 333 U.S. 287, 68 S.Ct. 550, 92 L.Ed. 701 (1948). See IP–Antitrust Guidelines § 5.5; id. example 10.

By contrast, consider these facts: The product market is a seven firm oligopoly. The largest firms, A and B, each own proprietary technology that makes production significantly less expensive. A's technology is slightly better than B's and B is seeking to improve its alternative. Of the other firms, two hold two year licenses to A's technology and three hold licenses to B's technology. A and B transfer their IP and their rights under these licenses to a jointly owned subsidiary. On the face of it, this transfer could significantly harm competition in a relevant technology market. If the oligopolistic product market is an adequate surrogate for the technology market, significant competitive harm is clearly threatened. Placing the two competing technologies under unified control ends competitive licensing between A and B. In any patent pool—that is, any arrangement in which two or more patents controlled by two or more firms are placed in common control—the pool will end licensing competition among any patents in the pool that are actual or potential substitutes for each other. It may also dampen continuing research competition for improvements. But a complete analysis of the hypothetical would consider whether the goods market is an adequate surrogate for the technology market; firms not in the same goods market might be sources of technologies competing with the two placed in the pool. The analytical process could be perfunctory if it were quickly evident that no outside firms used or were working on comparable technologies. In that case, given the total end to technology competition within the goods industry, a truncated rule of reason analysis would be sufficient.[43]

In sum, the market effect of cross-licensing or pooling of competing patents varies with structure. If all or most of the low cost technologies available in a given industry were to come into common control, they would yield market power.[44] If the apparent purpose and effect is price fixing and no offsetting efficiency is proven, a *per se* reaction is called for. On the other hand, if there are several comparably efficient alternative technologies all controlled by different, independent hands, the adverse effect of a cross license or pool might be small, even trivial. Also if there is known to be one or more equally efficient technologies in the public domain, the pool could not significantly threaten competition unless scale or scope efficiencies or network externalities insulated the pool from those alternatives.

Suppose cross licenses or a pool were to noticeably increase concentration in a technology market, yet not bring it to a high level. Assume, for example, that the pool raises the HHI in the technology market from

---

43. See IP–Antitrust Guidelines § 5.1 and example 9. Where leading manufacturers assign competing, close substitute patents to a subsidiary, the discussion states that "the joint determination of royalties likely would result in higher royalties and higher goods prices * * *. In the absence of evidence establishing efficiency enhancing integration * * * the agency may conclude that the joint marketing * * * constitutes horizontal price fixing [that] could be challenged as * * * per se unlawful * * *." Cf.

United States v. New Wrinkle, Inc., 342 U.S. 371, 72 S.Ct. 350, 96 L.Ed. 417(1952).

44. Note, also, that cross-licensing or pooling of competing patents ends any incentive of any participant to challenge the validity of any patent in the pool, thus reducing (perhaps substantially) the likelihood that one of the patented technologies, upon being challenged, would be held to be in the public domain.

800 to 1100—that is, from unconcentrated to the low end of the moderately concentrated range (as characterized in the 1992 merger Guidelines).[45] If the patents are not blocking, what kinds of offsetting benefits might mitigate or outweigh the possible harm? There are numerous possibilities: integration efficiencies;[46] reduced transaction costs;[47] effective exploitation in a wider variety of fields;[48] economies of scale or scope in research or in commercializing R & D outputs.[49] Settlement of patent disputes about validity or priority can also justify pooling, for patent litigation can be costly and wasteful.[50] However, where the settlement pool covers enough of the relevant market to significantly increase concentration, and where the litigation being settled entails significant issues about validity of one or more patents, not just about priority, the competitive harms from settlement might be very high; if the litigation were carried on, one or more of the technologies might enter the public domain.[51]

Note, also, that where competitive harm is evident, the IP Guidelines require that the proponent of an integration of competing protected technologies carry the burden of proving both that the efficiency will stem from the integration, that it will, in fact, be achieved and that it could not be achieved by significantly less restrictive means.[52] In this respect the IP Guidelines presaged the approach taken to efficiencies in the 1997 revision of the merger guidelines.[53] If the agencies are diligent in applying these provisions there will be an effective screen for identifying competitive harms in technology markets—harms that should be challenged under the antitrust laws.

15.9d2.   The Relevant Case Law

Cross-licensing or IP pooling between or among horizontal competitors in technology or goods markets is vulnerable under the Sherman Act, Section 2 (and also under Section 1) if it achieves, expands, protects or threatens monopoly in a properly defined market.[54]

---

45. Paragraph 4.3 of the IP–Antitrust Guidelines contains a "safety zone" applicable to any licensing arrangement where a merger analysis is [not] applied. "In such cases, absent extraordinary circumstances, a license restraint will not be challenged if: (1) the restraint is not facially anticompetitive and (2) the licensor and licensees collectively account for no more than twenty percent of each relevant market significantly applied * * *."

46. The ABA Antitrust Section Commentary on the Licensing Guidelines suggests this example: license puts technology for a new drug in the hands better able to obtain regulatory clearance, manufacture and market. Id. 35. The general language of the Guidelines, § 2.3, suggests numerous other possible integration efficiencies.

47. Cf. National Cable Television Assoc., Inc. v. BMI, 772 F.Supp. 614 (D.D.C.

1991) (BMI's blanket license was not an unreasonable restraint to trade because the license agreement eliminated the need to negotiate with thousands of composers, and this efficiency outweighed any anti-competitive effects).

48. IP–Antitrust Guideline § 2.3.

49. Id.

50. Standard Oil of Indiana v. United States, 283 U.S. 163, 51 S.Ct. 421, 75 L.Ed. 926 (1931).

51. See the discussion in § 15.10c.

52. IP–Antitrust Guidelines § 4.1.

53. 1992 Merger Guidelines § 4 (As revised in 1997).

54. Harford–Empire, supra note 34; United States v. National Lead Co., 332 U.S. 319, 67 S.Ct. 1634, 91 L.Ed. 2077

In Northrop Corp. v. McDonnell Douglas[55] two aircraft manufacturers entered into a teaming agreement to jointly develop IP protected military aircraft of a type for which each possessed relevant experience lacked by the other. The agreement limited each participant's freedom to market aircraft developed through the joint effort. McDonnell was to sell only aircraft suitable for carriers, Northrop only land-based aircraft. When McDonnell begin selling land-based planes to foreign countries, Northrop sued under the agreement and McDonnell challenged the contractual restraint as an unenforceable violation of Sherman Section 1. The trial court found the restraint *per se* unlawful and granted summary judgment to McDonnell. The court of appeals reversed, holding that because the agreement brought complementary skills and efficiencies together the rule of reason applied. Moreover, the court of appeals used a truncated analysis to find for Northrop. Despite a concentrated global market for military aircraft, the court saw no significant restraint of trade; it thought that but for the teaming arrangement (which was facilitated by the restraint), each of the two firms would have stayed within its own specialization. They would not, in any event, have competed in selling land-based military aircraft. Given market dynamics, this conclusion under the rule of reason may be questionable. Is it so clear that explicit market separation was essential to attain venture participation? Might profit sharing terms of some kind have been sufficient, given that each participant had a strong incentive at the outset to gain the other's help? Beyond that, how could a court so confidently play economic counter-historian? Even without the teaming agreement McDonnell may have generated (or brought in from elsewhere) the know-how needed to bid on land–based military aircraft.

Discussing *Northrop*, commentators have noted that once sufficient integration occurs within a venture—that is, once a single enterprise has been established—Section 1 cannot have application to subsequent activities by the now unified enterprise.[56] At that point, because of *Copperweld*, the venture must be challenged only under Clayton Section 7 and is vulnerable only if under that section it was illegal in its essence.[57] A point can be passed where a venture becomes a single enterprise; after that any future intra-enterprise activities, as such, are not vulnerable

---

(1947). See § 15.8 for a more in-depth discussion of the application of Sherman § 2 to intellectual property. See also United States v. National Lead, 63 F.Supp. 513 (1945), aff'd, 332 U.S. 319, 67 S.Ct. 1634, 91 L.Ed. 2077 (1947); United States v. Vehicular Parking, 54 F.Supp. 828 (D.Del. 1944), *modified*, 56 F.Supp. 297 (D.Del. 1944). Also, cross-licensing doing significant competitive harm without approaching monopoly proportions is vulnerable under Section 1. United States v. New Wrinkle, 342 U.S. 371, 72 S.Ct. 350, 96 L.Ed. 417 (1952); United States v. General Instrument Corp., 87 Fed. Supp. 157 (D.N.J. 1949). Also, cross-licensing and horizontal IP pooling (whether through a subsidiary or joint ven-

ture) may be challenged under Section 7 of the Clayton Act. Automated Bldg. Components, Inc. v. Trueline Truss Co., 318 F.Supp. 1252 (D. Ore. 1970); Western Geophysical Co. v. Bolt Assoc., Inc., 305 F.Supp. 1248 (D.Conn.1969), *modified*, 305 F.Supp. 1251 (D.Conn.1969); United States v. Lever Bros. Co., 216 F.Supp. 887 (S.D.N.Y.1963).

55. 705 F.2d 1030 (9th Cir.1983).

56. P. MERGERS, P.MENELL, M. LEMLEY AND T. JORDE, INTELLECTUAL PROPERTY IN THE NEW TECHNOLOGICAL AGE at 1119 (1997).

57. Copperweld Corp. v. Independence Tube Corp., 467 U.S. 752, 104 S.Ct. 2731, 81 L.Ed.2d 628 (1984).

under Section 1.[58] For example, if separate firms merged into one and thereafter operated two previously competing retail stores under a single management that fixes prices for both, that would not be a price fixing conspiracy. But if the very formation of such an enterprise were vulnerable under Section 7 because the formulation resulted in an increase in concentration that threatened competition in a relevant market—an increase not offset by efficiencies generated by the integration—then *that formation* would remain vulnerable under Section 1 of the Sherman as well as Section 7 of Clayton. Also, if venture management entails ongoing interaction by the participating venturers acting each in its capacity as a separate market actor, agreements among them reached in that manner could remain subject to Section 1. There are differences, to be sure, between the competitive effects test under Sherman and that under Clayton. The one forbids unreasonable competitive harm, the other, said to be prophylactic, the threat of such harm. But in practical application the differences between these standards is seldom immense.[59] In any event, the extent of the integration achieved is not a basis for deciding whether Section 1 or Section 7 applies to the establishment of a single entity at the outset. That event can be tested under either or both statutes.

15.9e. Exclusive Dealing Licenses

Exclusive dealing involves the use of license terms preventing a licensee from gaining access to, developing itself, or licensing from others any technology competing with the technology covered by the license. Provisions with such effects always have a vertical element; they foreclose licensees as possible customers to competitors of the licensor.[60] Such provisions can be characterized as horizontal, however, when the licensee possesses, or has been developing, a competing technology. In those instances the licensee abandons to the licensor, a competitor, its position as a technology producer, thus ending actual or potential technology competition between them.

The Guidelines discussion of exclusive dealing only evaluates horizontal impacts resulting from vertical foreclosure effects on competitors and cites only cases based on such effects.[61] When a licensee is itself a competitor in the technology market, however, this directly horizontal element also belongs in the analysis. It should be considered under the rule of reason, much as cross-licensing or pooling would be. For the term of the license, concentration is increased by subtracting one competitor, the competing licensee, from among the firms participating in the

---

58. For an extreme and doubtful example, see Chicago Professional Sports Ltd. Partnership v. NBA, 95 F.3d 593 (7th Cir. 1996) which seems to strain NCAA in holding that NBA teams are not separate, cooperating actors but a single entity.

59. Cf. Brooke Group Ltd. v. Brown & Williamson Tobacco Corp., 509 U.S. 209, 113 S.Ct. 2578, 125 L.Ed.2d 168 (1993).

60. It is this aspect of exclusive dealing licenses that is discussed in the Guidelines.

61. E.g., Tampa Electric Co. v. Nashville Coal Co., 365 U.S. 320, 81 S.Ct. 623, 5 L.Ed.2d 580 (1961).

relevant technology market. That market may be concentrated or unconcentrated. The excluded firm may be significant or insignificant as a competitor or potential competitor. The license may yield integration benefits not otherwise available or it may not. If the licensee held a trivial share of an unconcentrated market, consented to the restraint to ease licensor fear that its know how might be usurped, in part, to improve the licensee's technology, when, in fact, it saw the technology as a better fit with its other resources, the license would be manifestly reasonable. If the technology market was concentrated, the licensee's technology significant, and the asserted efficiency benefits either trivial or capable of being achieved in less restrictive ways, the license restraint would fail under rule of reason evaluation.

15.9f. Grant Back Clauses

As noted in § 15.8b3, *Transparent-Wrap* rejected the contention that grant backs are intrinsically unlawful under the patent law.[62] When used by a firm which neither holds nor threatens to obtain monopoly power, can such clauses nevertheless violate Sherman Section 1? Grant back clauses can be narrowed (e.g., tightly specifying particular types of improvements that must be licensed to the patentee if an improvement patent is obtained) or wide (e.g., requiring assignment to the patentee of any improvement, patentable or not, even know–how loosely relevant to the technology licensed). They can be nonexclusive (thereby widening accessibility by assuring that at least one additional firm will have access)[63] or exclusive (thus predetermining that only the licensor, not even the inventor, will have access to the improvement).[64] They can be used in concentrated or unconcentrated markets. They can be used alone or as part of a pattern or sequence of restraints. Section 15.8b3 points out that perhaps alone, and certainly with other restraints, a grant back clause can violate Section 2. Alone or with other restraints they can also, as a matter of theory, violate Section 1. The question will always be whether, given structure, context and clause particulars, the grant back obligation threatens unreasonable competitive restraint in a relevant goods or technology market.[65] Conventional rule of reason analysis applies. Despite theoretical vulnerability, these practices are seldom, if ever, challenged except when they are part of a wider set of restraints. This may well be, in part, because counsel discourage the use of overbroad clauses (and, indeed, of any clause in contexts where, because of market share, they might seem particularly vulnerable).

62. Transparent–Wrap Machine Corp. v. Stokes & Smith Co., 329 U.S. 637, 67 S.Ct. 610, 91 L.Ed. 563 (1947).

63. Binks Mfg. Co. v. Ransburg Electro–Coating Corp., 281 F.2d 252 (7th Cir.1960), cert. granted, 364 U.S. 926, 81 S.Ct. 353, 5 L.Ed.2d 265 (1960); SCM Corp. v. Xerox Corp., 463 F.Supp. 983 (D.Conn.1978), aff'd 645 F.2d 1195 (2d Cir. 1981).

64. Transparent–Wrap Machine Corp. v. Stokes & Smith Co., 329 U.S. 637, 67 S.Ct. 610, 91 L.Ed. 563 (1947) (upholding grant back provision, in part because licensee was not restricted from using improvements for themselves); Santa Fe–Pomeroy, Inc. v. P & Z Co., Inc., 569 F.2d 1084 (9th Cir.1978).

65. United States v. General Electric (Carboloy) 80 F.Supp. 989, 1005–06 (S.D.N.Y. 1948), United States v. General Electric Co. (Lamps), 82 F.Supp. 753, 815–16 (D.N.J. 1949).

15.9g.   *Patent Settlement Agreements*

Patent litigation between competitors or potential competitors often leads to settlements that resolve the outstanding issues between the parties. These agreements, however, provide an opportunity of rivals to agree on matters that can effectively restrain competition between them. A number of cases have arisen in the drug industry in which a firm holding a patent on a drug reaches a settlement with one or more firms that have sought to bring competing generic drugs onto the market. The FTC has found that in some of these cases, the firm holding the patented drug would offer money to the generic firms in return for a commitment to delay entry of the generic drugs.[66] Other forms of anticompetitive settlements among litigants are of course possible, including division of markets.

§ 15.10   Vertical Restraints

Vertical restraints on IP that give rise to antitrust issues fall into two categories: foreclosing restraints which can harm competition at the licensor's level by depriving its horizontal competitors of downstream outlets, and restrictions on the competitive options of licensees which can harm competition at their downstream horizontal level. Foreclosing restraints involving intellectual property have already been discussed in the context of Sherman Section 2,[1] and also in contexts where the licensor and the licensee were horizontal competitors.[2] Restrictions on licensee competitive freedom, such as price, territory and field of use restrictions, have also been discussed when licensor and licensee relate horizontally.[3] Because those earlier sections describe analogous situations and because much of the analysis in those earlier sections has relevance also when licensor and licensee relate only vertically, discussion in this section can be brief.

15.10a.   Leveraging Power Through Tying or Package Sales

Tying is a familiar leveraging device. *Kodak v. Image Tech* defines it as an agreement to sell a product only "on the condition that the buyer also purchase a different (or tied) product, or at least agrees that he will not purchase [the tied product elsewhere]."[4] In § 8.3d, the possible defenses to tying are discussed in detail.[5] In § 15.8c2, tying and other leveraging by monopolists is considered.[6] Those materials show that

---

66. Abbott Laboratories and Geneva Pharmaceuticals, Inc., No. C–3945, C–3946 (May 22, 2000) available at www.ftc.gov/os/ 2000/03/abbot.do.htm. and www.ftc.gov/ os/2000/03/genevad & o.htm.; Hoechst Marion Roussel, Inc., D.9293 (May 8, 2001), available at www.ftc. gov/opa/2001/04/hoechst.htm. The Commission's order against Schering–Plough was vacated in Schering–Plough v. FTC, 402 F.3d 1056 (11th Cir. 2005), petition for rehearing en banc pending.

§ 15.10

1. § 15.8c.

2. §§ 15.9d, f.

3. §§ 15.9b-c.

4. 504 U.S. 451, 461, 112 S.Ct. 2072, 119 L.Ed.2d 265(1992).

5. §§ 8.3d1–d4. See especially § 8.3d9, addressing tie-ins and intellectual property.

6. § 15.8c.

tying can hurt competition and damage consumers in the tied product market by foreclosing competitors who may offer lower prices and better products than the tied market offerings of the firm with power.

The major point to be made here is that intellectual property can serve as a tying product or service and that when it does, it gains no privilege or special treatment because of its IP status.[7] Indeed, there are a number of cases, including Supreme Court opinions, in which a statutory IP right to exclude is treated as conclusive or presumptive of sufficient power to make a tie vulnerable under the antitrust laws.[8] The IP–Antitrust Guidelines in General Principle 2, reject this presumption.[9] Whatever the courts may do today, and certainly some opinions also press for integration of antitrust and IP jointly in the service of efficiency,[10] the enforcement agencies will not challenge an IP tie without a conventional showing of market power in the tying product.[11] It does not follow that single brand power will not be sufficient in aftermarkets for parts or service. The *Image Tech* opinion generally,[12] and especially footnote 29,[13] suggest that it can be.

The Antitrust–IP guidelines are "soft" on tying, at least in a non-monopolization context, in yet another respect. The Supreme Court majority has thus far declined to abandon its modified *per se* response to tying.[14] However, the Guidelines stress that tying may result in significant efficiencies and pro-competitive benefits.[15] Accordingly, the agencies as a matter of "prosecutorial discretion" will (at least in IP tying cases) consider both harms and benefits; they will likely challenge an IP tie only if there is power and if apparent harms are not outweighed by apparent benefits.[16] This resolution is consistent with the approach

7. International Salt Co. v. United States, 332 U.S. 392, 68 S.Ct. 12, 92 L.Ed. 20 (1947); Mercoid Corp. v. Mid–Continent Inv. Co., 320 U.S. 661, 665–66, 64 S.Ct. 268, 88 L.Ed. 376 (1944); Ethyl Gasoline v. United States, 309 U.S. 436, 456, 60 S.Ct. 618, 84 L.Ed. 852 (1940); Motion Picture Patents Co. v. Universal Film Mfg. Co., 243 U.S. 502, 37 S.Ct. 416, 61 L.Ed. 871 (1917); United States v. Loew's, Inc., 371 U.S. 38, 83 S.Ct. 97, 9 L.Ed.2d 11 (1962); Times–Picayune, Publishing Co. v. United States, 345 U.S. 594, 73 S.Ct. 872, 97 L.Ed. 1277 (1953). See also Eastman Kodak Co. v. Image Technical Services, 504 U.S. 451, 479 n. 29, 112 S.Ct. 2072, 119 L.Ed.2d 265 (1992).

8. United States v. Loew's, Inc., 371 U.S. 38, 83 S.Ct. 97, 9 L.Ed.2d 11 (1962); International Salt Co. v. United States, 332 U.S. 392, 68 S.Ct. 12, 92 L.Ed. 20 (1947). See the discussion in § 15.7.

9. Department of Justice and Federal Trade Commission, Antitrust Guidelines For the Licensing of Intellectual Property § 2.2 (1995), available at <http://www. usdoj.gov/ atr/public/ guidelines/0558.htm> [hereinafter the IP–Antitrust Guidelines or,

where clear from the context, the Guidelines].

10. Cf. USM Corp. v. SPS Technologies, Inc., 694 F.2d 505 (7th Cir.1982), *cert. denied*, 462 U.S. 1107, 103 S.Ct. 2455, 77 L.Ed.2d 1334 (1983).

11. IP–Antitrust Guidelines, § 5.3.

12. Eastman Kodak Co. v. Image Tech. Serv., Inc., 504 U.S. 451, 112 S.Ct. 2072, 119 L.Ed.2d 265(1992).

13. Id. at 479.

14. Jefferson Parish Hospital District No.2 v. Hyde, 466 U.S. 2, 104 S.Ct. 1551, 80 L.Ed.2d 2 (1984). We refer to this *per se* rule as structurally enhanced because proving tying conduct alone does not prove a violation. Plaintiff must also show market power. However, the *per se* norm brings the inquiry to an end when tying conduct and sufficient power are shown and possible offsetting efficiencies would be no defense. See § 8.3d1.

15. IP–Antitrust Guidelines, § 5.3.

16. Id.

suggested in § 15.1 that when claims based on antitrust seem to collide with rights claimed under an IP statute, the surface conflict should be resolved by evaluating the potential harms and benefits to allocation and consumer welfare, an approach consistent with the common goals of antitrust and IP.

Devices other than tying have been used to leverage power from one product market into a different market. It is clear from Zenith Radio v. Hazeltine Research, Inc.,[17] that a firm with power in a non-IP product may not leverage that power into another market by refusing to sell except to those that buy the forced product. Yet, two recent court of appeals cases have purported to find that owners of IP have a privilege to refuse to deal—a privilege lawful even if used to force buyers to accept a second, forced product in order to obtain the IP.[18] The Federal Circuit gave increased credence to this view in In re Independent Service Organizations Antitrust Litigation.[19] The plaintiff, an independent service provider that had serviced Xerox original equipment, brought Sherman Act claims against Xerox for its refusal to sell patented parts and copyrighted manuals and to license copyrighted software. In affirming summary judgment for Xerox, the court declined to apply *Image Tech* because the case involved a tying claim that had not been made against Xerox.[20] The court also interpreted broadly a patentee's right to refuse to license or sell, even when that refusal could result in substantial anticompetitive effects in a secondary market.

Independent Service Organizations has been criticized for extending the premise that an IP holder has the right not to license to the unjustified conclusion that it can license on terms that have an anticompetitive effect.[21] The tying behavior at issue in that case was challenged under Section 2, not as a Section 1 tying violation. But regardless of the which section is employed, allowing anticompetitive tying when achieved by refusal to deal is wrong.[22] Whether the modified per se rule is

---

17. 395 U.S. 100, 89 S.Ct. 1562, 23 L.Ed.2d 129 (1969); See also United States v. Loew's, Inc., 371 U.S. 38, 83 S.Ct. 97, 9 L.Ed.2d 11 (1962).

18. Virtual Maintenance, Inc. v. Prime Computer, Inc., 957 F.2d 1318 (6th Cir. 1992), *vacated*, 506 U.S. 910, 113 S.Ct. 314, 121 L.Ed.2d 235 (1992), on remand, 995 F.2d 1324 (6th Cir.1993); Datagate, Inc. v. Hewlett–Packard, Co., 941 F.2d 864 (9th Cir.1991); cert. denied, 503 U.S. 984, 112 S.Ct. 1667, 118 L.Ed.2d 388 (1992).

19. 203 F.3d 1322 (Fed. Cir.2000).

20. Id. at 1327.

21. Robert Pitofsky, Chairman, FTC, Antitrust and Intellectual Property: Unresolved Issues at the Heart of the New Economy, available at http://www.ftc.gov/speeches/pitofsky/ipf301.htm (Mar. 2, 2001).

22. On remand, Image Technical Services v. Eastman Kodak, 125 F.3d 1195 (9th Cir.1997) raises the same issue in an attenuated form. There, Kodak refused to deal with ISOs in respect to all parts, the great bulk of which were not protected IP, but some of which were patented or copyrighted. Kodak offered several business justifications for its conduct. When these justifications were rejected by the jury, Kodak, on appeal, stressed the IP status of some of the parts. This justification was found to be pretextual by the Ninth Circuit. See also Aspen Skiing Co. v. Aspen Highlands Skiing Corp., 472 U.S. 585, 105 S.Ct. 2847, 86 L.Ed.2d 467 (1985), which suggests that business justifications which might have been valid if they in fact motivated conduct provide no cloak for the conduct when they did not motivate it.

employed under Section 1 or a rule of reason like measure is employed under Section 2, the same result should ensue.

15.10b.   Resale Price Maintenance, Territorial and Field of Use Restraints Having Only Vertical Effects

Section 15.9c deals with license restrictions limiting the competitive decisions by the licensee in situations (not uncommon in marketing IP) where the licensee is an actual or potential competitor of the licensor. In some instances the relationship will be entirely vertical—for example, when the licensor is solely in the R & D business and the licensees do not engage in relevant R & D, but only in goods markets in which the licensor's IP has value.

In purely vertical situations, territorial separation imposed in an IP license would be evaluated under the rule of reason.[23] It can be inferred that in most situations the restraint would be reasonable.[24] In such situations the licensor will recover the full value of any power conferred by the IP from licensing fees, and has no incentive to protect licensees from competition with each other except to the extent that doing so will enable them to compete more effectively with horizontal competitors using alternative technologies. Certainly the licensor will have no incentive to enable licensees to raise their prices to levels yielding supracompetitive returns to them; this would reduce the licensor's return by reducing aggregate sales. Only if there is a basis for inference that the restraints are imposed as an accommodation to licensees seeking to cartelize is there reason for antitrust concern.

For similar reasons, vertical situations with no horizontal element give rise to no concern about field of use restrictions. If not imposed under pressure from licensees that are collectively seeking cartel profits, these arrangements, too, are not suspect.

Finally, if there is any situation where the *G.E. per se* lawful rule about price fixing licenses could be applied with little fear of adverse effect (or even expanded to cover constraints on the resale price of products made with or incorporating the IP), it would be situations where the licensor and licensee have no actual or potential horizontal relationship. However, such vertical price fixing, like such territorial or field of use restrictions, should be vulnerable as a cartel if it is initiated by licensees acting cooperatively. Despite its lack of serious threat in purely horizontal situations, such price fixing, even if initiated by the licensor for its own reasons, remains vulnerable under Dr. Miles.[25] Courts have construed *G.E.* very narrowly,[26] and the IP Guidelines state that "the Agencies will enforce the *per se* rule against resale price

23.   Continental T.V., Inc. v. GTE Sylvania, Inc., 433 U.S. 36, 97 S.Ct. 2549, 53 L.Ed.2d 568 (1977).

24.   See § 7.5c.

25.   Dr. Miles Medical Co. v. John D. Park & Sons, 220 U.S. 373, 31 S.Ct. 376, 55 L.Ed. 502 (1911).

26.   E.g., United States v. Univis Lens Co., 316 U.S. 241, 62 S.Ct. 1088, 86 L.Ed. 1408(1942); Ethyl Gasoline Corp. v. United States, 309 U.S. 436, 60 S.Ct. 618, 84 L.Ed. 852 (1940).

maintenance in the intellectual property context."[27] Wholly vertical IP price fixing is apparently to be evaluated by the enforcement agencies much as are cases with a significant horizontal element.

§ 15.11   Patent Misuse and the Copyright Analog

15.11a.   The Development and Present Status of the Patent Misuse Doctrine

There is a misuse doctrine long embedded in patent adjudication.[1] Under the doctrine, as originally developed, any effort by the patentee to exploit the patent in a way that extends beyond the specific monopoly granted by the valid patent claims constitutes misuse. Although the doctrine arose as "an extension of the equitable doctrine of unclean hands,"[2] it has frequently been applied in situations like tying when there might be an antitrust analog.[3] The standard equitable remedy for misuse is to withhold any remedy for infringing the patent until the misuse is abated and its adverse effects purged,[4] a displacement of patent protection available even at the behest of alleged infringers not themselves affected by the misuse.[5]

Although the analogy between misuse and Sherman or Clayton violation is evident, the misuse doctrine, as it was developed and applied, was an aspect of patent law. It could apply to any extension of patent exclusivity beyond the lawful scope of the patent, regardless of whether that extension caused sufficient adverse competitive effect to be subject to antitrust challenge.[6] Early on the antitrust tying offense was also subject to a *per se* rule which required no showing of competitive injury,[7] but more recently the Court has held that tying violates antitrust only when the defendant exercises sufficient market power to force the tie.[8] With this development the lack of any competitive effects test for misuse began to seem anomalous. Why enjoin the enforceability of a valid patent because of the patentee's mode of exploitation if all participants in the relevant transactions are making uncoerced market choices? During the

27. IP–Antitrust Guidelines § 5.2.

§ 15.11

1. See D. CHISUM, PATENTS § 19.04; Webb & Locke, *Intellectual Property Misuse Developments in the Misuse Doctrine*, 4 HARV. J. L. & TECH. 257 (1991).

2. United States Gypsum Co. v. National Gypsum Co., 352 U.S. 457, 465, 77 S.Ct. 490, 1 L.Ed.2d 465 (1957).

3. Motion Picture Patents Co. v. Universal Film Manufacturing Co., 243 U.S. 502, 37 S.Ct. 416, 61 L.Ed. 871 (1917) (a misuse of a motion picture projector patent to condition licenses upon use only to project specified films). Cf. International Salt Co. v. United States, 332 U.S. 392, 68 S.Ct. 12, 92 L.Ed. 20 (1947). (Leasing patented machine for dissolving rock salt and injecting salt into canned products on condition that they be used only with salt supplied by

the patentee violates Section 1 of the Sherman Act).

4. Morton Salt Co. v. G.S. Suppiger Co., 314 U.S. 488, 62 S.Ct. 402, 86 L.Ed. 363 (1942).

5. Id.

6. E.g., Mercoid Corp. v. Mid–Continent Investment Co., 320 U.S. 661, 64 S.Ct. 268, 88 L.Ed. 376 (1944). Accord Mercoid Corp. v. Minneapolis–Honeywell Regulator Co., 320 U.S. 680, 64 S.Ct. 278, 88 L.Ed. 396 (1944).

7. International Salt Co. v. United States, supra note 3.

8. E.g, Jefferson Parish Hospital District No.2 v. Hyde, 466 U.S. 2, 104 S.Ct. 1551, 80 L.Ed.2d 2 (1984).

1980s one circuit held,[9] and another announced its readiness to hold,[10] that competitive standards like those used in antitrust would be evoked in misuse cases. As yet, the Supreme Court has not addressed this issue.

During the years when misuse was unfettered by concerns about competitive effect, some of the broadest extensions of misuse doctrine occurred in contributory infringement cases and led to critical reaction which resulted in the enactment of Section 21 of the Patent Act.[11] In *Mercoid v. Mid–Continent*, Honeywell, holding a license to a combination patent on a heating system, exploited the license by making and selling one of the unpatented components for use in the system. When Mercoid made and sold the same component Mid–Continent, the patent holder, sued for contributory infringement. The Court of Appeals rejected a patent misuse defense, but the Supreme Court reversed.[12] It insisted that "this Court has consistently held that the owner of a patent may not employ it to secure a limited monopoly of an unpatented material used in applying the invention * * *."[13] The Patent Act of 1952 included a response to *Mercoid*. Section 271 affirmed in paragraph (b) that active inducement of infringement is a violation, stated in paragraph (c) that selling a non-staple article or commodity specifically made for use in a combination patent would constitute contributory infringement, but stated in paragraph (d) that no patent owner otherwise entitled should be denied relief or deemed guilty of misuse by reason of any one or more of the following: (1) deriving revenues from acts which, if done by another, would be contributory infringement; (2) licensing others to perform acts which, if not so licensed, would be contributory infringement; and (3) enforcing the patent against infringers or (unlicensed) contributory infringers.[14] The Court applied this section in Dawson Chemical Co. v. Rohm and Haas Co.[15] The patent involved was on a process for applying a herbicide well suited for rice. Because of the high transaction costs, licensing of the process to rice farmers was not feasible. Instead, the patentee exploited the patent by selling the unpatented chemical and licensing all purchasers to utilize the process. The alleged contributory infringement was the defendant's practice of selling to rice farmers the same chemical, a product not suitable for any other commercial use, knowing it would be applied through the patented process. The Court held that, given that the chemical was not suitable for any non-infringing commercial use, the patent holder was protected by Section 271(d) against a charge of misuse.

While the 1952 Patent Act thus narrowed the *Mercoid* scope for contributory infringement, it did not articulate any competitive effect

9. Windsurfing International Inc. v. AMF, Inc., 782 F.2d 995 (Fed. Cir. 1986), *cert. denied,* 477 U.S. 905, 106 S.Ct. 3275, 91 L.Ed.2d 565 (1986).

10. USM Corp. v. SPS Technologies, Inc., 694 F.2d 505, 511 (7th Cir.1982).

11. Patent Act of 1952, 35 U.S.C.A. § 21.

12. Mercoid Corp. v. Mid–Content Investment Co., supra note 6.

13. Id. at 664.

14. Patent Act of 1952, 35 U.S.C.A. § 271.

15. 448 U.S. 176, 100 S.Ct. 2601, 65 L.Ed.2d 696 (1980).

standard for misuse. Hence, any tie of another product to a patented product remained vulnerable, as did exploitation of a patent by sale as an input to the patented product or process of any component that was, in fact, "a staple article of commerce," and thus not protected by Section 271(d). Criticism of this continuing gap between antitrust and misuse standards led to judicial decisions such as in *Windsurfing*,[16] which required competitive harm for misuse. Then in 1988 Congress amended Section 271(d) once again. It added a new subsection (5) protecting patent holders against misuse for conditioning a license to a patent or the sale of a patented product on "the acquisition of a license to rights in another patent or purchase of a separate product, unless, in view of the circumstances, the patent owner has market power in the relevant market for the patent or patented product on which the license or sale is conditioned."[17]

It is now clear that the misuse defense will be available against a tying patentee only upon a showing of market power. Nothing in the language of the act alters the antitrust tying rule, however. The *Jefferson Parish* majority view is that a tie is a *per se* violation when the seller has sufficient power in the market for the tying product to force the tied product on the buyers.[18] Unless that case is overruled it remains law when IP ties are challenged under Sherman. The question is thus raised whether, given Section 271(5), the misuse standard—which for so many years required no competitive effects test at all—now imposes a tougher competitive effects test for tying than does the Sherman Act. One possible answer, probably the wisest one, is to recognize that the statute intended, when passed, to integrate into misuse doctrine the market power standards applied by antitrust courts. For this reason the two systems should be kept in accord.

The new statutory provision also raises the question whether the *Loew's* inference of market power from the mere possession of a intellectual property[19] can still prevail in cases where a patented product or process is used to achieve a tie. The broad sweep of the *Loew's* inference has long been anomalous and is facially inconsistent with the Court's recognition in *Walker Process*[20] that whether intellectual property conveys power depends on whether there are alternative, noninfringing products or processes which effectively compete with the patented one. Although the inference may be sound in tying cases, it may be inconsistent with the provision in Section 271(5) that requires a showing of power for misuse.[21]

---

16. Windsurfing International Inc. v. AMF, Inc., supra, note 9.

17. The Patent Misuse Reform Act, P.L. 100–703, 102 Stat. 4676, *codified in* 35 U.S.C.A. § 271(d)(5).

18. Jefferson Parish Hospital Dist. No.2 v. Hyde, 466 U.S. 2, 104 S.Ct. 1551, 80 L.Ed.2d 2 (1984) (tying under the Sherman and Clayton Acts is discussed in § 8.3).

19. E.g., United States v. Loew's, Inc., 371 U.S. 38, 83 S.Ct. 97, 9 L.Ed.2d 11 (1962).

20. Walker Process Equipment, Inc. v. Food Machinery and Chemical Corp., 382 U.S. 172, 86 S.Ct. 347, 15 L.Ed.2d 247 (1965).

21. See ABA Antitrust Section, Antitrust Law Developments 832 (3d ed. 1992).

15.11b. The Misuse Doctrine as Applied to Copyright

Doubt exists about whether there is an equitable misuse doctrine that can be used to enjoin the enforcement of a copyright when the holder is exploiting it beyond the scope of the protection granted by the copyright statute. Although the Supreme Court has alluded to the defense,[22] there is no high court case applying it. Among the courts of appeal, there is one recent case finding the defense a basis for enjoining copyright enforcement,[23] and one recent holding adverse to preliminary relief for copyright violation because the defendant was likely to prevail on a misuse claim.[24] There are also a handful of cases[25] sometimes cited as rejecting the misuse doctrine.[26] But if it be assumed that misuse requires an adverse competitive impact vulnerable under the antitrust laws, these seemingly adverse cases are better viewed as holding that (whether or not a copyright misuse doctrine exists) the conditions for its application were not established.[27]

The rationale for a copyright misuse defense tracks that for patent misuse and is based on the economic rationale for copyright itself. The copyright grant, like the patent grant, is limited in scope. The statute draws lines because it is intended to encourage sufficient innovation without offering gratuitously excessive constraints not needed to stimulate that innovation. Any constraint beyond the bounds of the statutory grant is, in this sense, excessive and unnecessary. Because in a competitive environment there will always be incentive to press for excessive protection, the misuse doctrine is needed to deter such efforts. In *Lasercomb* the copyright was licensed with an overbroad non-competition clause forbidding the licensee to develop any non-infringing but competing software for a period of 99 years, a potentially harmful and clearly excessive extension beyond the scope of the copyright. The Court, using an analysis "similar to but separate from the analysis necessary to a finding of antitrust violation * * *,"[28] labeled this effort to gain

See also IP–Antitrust Guidelines § 2.2. See the discussion in § 15.7.

22. United States v. Loew's, Inc., 371 U.S. 38, 44–51, 83 S.Ct. 97, 9 L.Ed.2d 11(1962); United States v. Paramount Pictures, 334 U.S. 131, 157–59, 68 S.Ct. 915, 92 L.Ed. 1260(1948).

23. Lasercomb America, Inc. v. Reynolds, 911 F.2d 970 (4th Cir.1990). See also Tamburo v. Calvin, 1995 WL 121539 (N.D.Ill.).

24. DSC Communications Corp. v. DGI Technologies, Inc., 81 F.3d 597, 601 (5th Cir.1996).

25. Triad Systems Corp. v. Southeastern Express Co., 64 F.3d 1330 (9th Cir. 1995); Data General Corp. v. Grumman Systems Support Corp., 36 F.3d 1147 (1st Cir.1994), Atari Games Corp. v. Nintendo of America, 975 F.2d 832 (Fed. Cir. 1992).

26. E.g, D.GIFFORD & L.RASKIND, FEDERAL ANTITRUST LAW: CASES AND MATERIALS 732–33 (1998).

27. Data General Corp. v. Grumman Systems Support Corp., supra note 25, held that it was not exclusionary in the anticompetitive sense and hence not an antitrust violation for Data General which used its copyrighted diagnostic software to provide service to users of its equipment to refuse to license Gruman to use the software to compete with Data General. If this holding about the reach of the antitrust laws was correct, and if misuse absorbs competitive effect standards from antitrust, the antitrust holding disposes of any misuse issue. *Triad Systems*, and *Atari Games* can be explained in similar terms.

28. Lasercomb America, Inc. v. Reynolds, supra note 23 at 979.

protection beyond the statutory grant "egregious."[29] Accordingly, and in conformity with the approach followed in patent misuse cases, the court enjoined enforcement of the copyright, and did so at the behest of a competitor that had not been party to the excessive licensing agreement. This response is theoretically defensible and sound as a matter of policy. Until the Supreme Court addresses the matter more specifically than it has done thus far, *Lasercomb* should be regarded as the best available statement of copyright misuse law.

29. Id.

Chapter XVI

GOVERNMENT ENFORCEMENT

Table of Sections

§ 16.1 Introduction

A unique feature of antitrust enforcement in the United States is the multiplicity of potential enforcers: there are three types: (1) federal agencies, (2) state and local agencies, and (3) private parties. Two federal agencies, the Antitrust Division of the Justice Department and the Federal Trade Commission, have overlapping jurisdiction to enforce most provisions of federal antitrust law. State and local governments, as well as private parties, may also bring suit to enforce the federal antitrust laws. Each of these parties, except the federal agencies, may also enforce various provisions of state antitrust laws.

To varying degrees, the federal agencies have set the tone for antitrust enforcement. Federal enforcers have brought many ground-breaking cases with substantial impact upon the development of the law. The expertise of the federal agencies often becomes a guide for federal and state courts, for state enforcement officials, for private litigants, and for attorneys giving advice. Yet this preeminence has not remained constant, nor is it uniform for all types of antitrust violations. Before the

Sherman Act, anticompetitive practices were challenged, if at all, by state or private enforcers bringing suit under state statutes or common law.[1] Since 1890, federal enforcement has ebbed and flowed with changes in the law, political philosophy, economic theory, and the institutional resources of the federal agencies. For example, beginning around 1980, merger enforcement became a primary focus of the federal agencies. This was the result of implementation of the premerger notification program, the level and type of merger activity, and of budgetary constraints that forced cutbacks in agency personnel.[2] Thus, while federal preeminence may have increased in merger enforcement, it may have waned in such fundamental areas as horizontal and vertical restraints. Monopolization cases were virtually abandoned by the federal agencies during the 1980s and have remained at low levels since.

The degree of federal preeminence also varies with the widely varying level of activity by state and private enforcers (discussed in § 16.3 and Chapter XVII).

§ 16.2 Federal Enforcement

As the United States' primary law enforcement agency, the Department of Justice assumed responsibility for enforcing the Sherman Act upon its enactment in 1890. Today, that responsibility is vested in the Antitrust Division of the Department of Justice, headed by an Assistant Attorney General. With its creation in 1914, the Federal Trade Commission, a collegial body with five voting commissioners, assumed overlapping responsibility for antitrust enforcement. Each agency, however, has its own enforcement methods and preserves unique enforcement responsibilities.

16.2a. The Antitrust Division of the Department of Justice

The Antitrust Division of the Department of Justice is the sole enforcer empowered to bring both civil and criminal proceedings under the Sherman Act.[1] The modern history of the Antitrust Division began under the leadership of Thurman Arnold, whom President Franklin Roosevelt appointed Assistant Attorney General in 1938.[2] In the years since, the Division has built and maintained a reputation of professionalism and excellence. The staffing of the Division has varied with available funds, reaching 421 attorneys in 1977 but falling to 229 attorneys by

§ 16.1

1. May, *Antitrust Practice and Procedure in the Formative Era: The Constitutional and Conceptual Reach of State Antitrust Law, 1880–1918,* 135 U.PA.L.REV. 495, 498–500 (1987).

2. The high percentage of agency resources devoted to merger review and enforcement appears not to have abated in the 1990s. FTC Chairman Pitofsky reported in 1998 that more than 2/3 of the agency's antitrust resources were devoted to merger review. Statement of the Federal Trade Commission, Hearings on Mergers and Corporate Consolidation in the New Economy, Sen. Jud. Comm. (June 16, 1998). See the discussion of the merger enforcement mechanism in Chapter X.

§ 16.2

1. 15 U.S.C.A. §§ 1, 2, 4.

2. In a clear reversal from earlier policies of the Roosevelt Administration, Arnold aggressively pursued cartel activity. See T. ARNOLD, THE BOTTLENECKS OF BUSINESS (1940).

1989.[3] During the 1990s, some of these lost positions were restored after a Bar Association Task Force criticized staffing levels as inadequate "to achieve antitrust policy objectives."[4] But inadequate staffing continues to plague both federal agencies as the conduct of premerger review occupies the bulk of each agency's resources. The Division's enforcement needs will continue to change, affected by factors such as the growth and globalization of the economy, the level of merger activity, and the allocation of enforcement responsibilities among government and private enforcers.

Although the Division pursues its own enforcement agenda, it cooperates with the FTC on a variety of projects, including the issuance of antitrust guidelines and the coordination of investigations to ensure that each acquisition is reviewed by a single federal agency. Occasionally, law enforcement files are transferred between the agencies, as occurred when a deadlocked FTC relinquished its files of Microsoft to the Antitrust Division in 1994.[5] In recent years, the Division has begun working more closely with State Attorneys General in pursuing investigations and certain litigated matters.[6]

In addition to its responsibilities of investigating and initiating enforcement proceedings, the Division carries out its responsibilities in a number of other ways. One is by intervening before federal agencies on regulatory matters where competition is an issue. Competition issues are often within the jurisdiction of other regulatory agencies, such as the Department of Transportation, the Federal Reserve, or the Federal Communications Commission. The Antitrust Division may serve as a competition advocate before these agencies. An example is the role the Division has played in advising the FCC on the implementation of deregulatory provisions of the Telecommunications Act of 1996.[7]

When antitrust issues are before the federal courts in privately initiated litigation, the Antitrust Division occasionally files amicus briefs. The Division's participation in private litigation is more likely when cases reach the Supreme Court. During President Reagan's eight years (1980–1988), all of the Division's amicus briefs were filed on behalf of defendants, a record that was criticized.[8]

---

3. MILTON HANDLER ET AL., TRADE REGULATION, CASES AND MATERIALS 100 (4th ed. 1997).

4. REPORT OF THE AMERICAN BAR ASSOCIATION SECTION ON ANTITRUST LAW TASK FORCE ON THE ANTITRUST DIVISION OF THE U.S. DEPARTMENT OF JUSTICE 19 (1989).

5. The history of the Microsoft investigation is described in Garza, *The Court of Appeals Sets Strict Limits on Tunney Act Review: The Microsoft Consent Decree*, ANTITRUST 21 (Fall 1995).

6. Address of Anne K. Bingaman, Assistant Attorney General, U.S. Dept. of Justice, Before the National Association of Attorneys General (Oct. 11, 1995) (describing

an "unprecedented level of cooperation with state attorneys general"); Comments of Kevin J. O'Connor, Assistant Attorney General, State of Wisconsin, in *Roundtable Conference With Enforcement Officials*, 65 ANTITRUST L. J. 929, 942–43 (1997).

7. Telecommunications Act of 1996, Pub. L. No. 104–104, 110 Stat. 56 (1996).

8. ABA Report, supra note 4, at 17–18 (suggesting that the Division's amicus briefs and other activities in support of a "minimalist" antitrust position send a "confusing" message about the Division's commitment to enforcement).

The Antitrust Division can influence antitrust compliance and enforcement in a number of other ways. A speech on a law enforcement topic delivered by the head of the Antitrust Division may affect the advice antitrust lawyers give to their clients. The various guidelines issued by the Division (more recently, jointly issued with the FTC) also shape antitrust law and the level of compliance. In addition to merger guidelines, the Division and the FTC have jointly issued guidelines addressing international operations, intellectual property, health care and, most recently, joint ventures among competitors. The Division has issued guidelines on criminal sentencing. Except for the Criminal Sentencing Guidelines, each of these documents purport to describe only the approach and standard used by the Division and the FTC in determining whether to challenge potentially anticompetitive conduct. But the impact of the guidelines can be much broader. Because of the agencies expertise and reputation, courts, state and local antitrust enforcers, and antitrust counselors may use the guidelines as a reference point and, often, as an authority.

16.2b.   The Federal Trade Commission

The Federal Trade Commission was created in 1914, the year of enactment of both the Federal Trade Commission and Clayton Acts. Partly as a response to the "rule of reason" approach announced in Standard Oil Co. of New Jersey v. United States,[9] Congress sought through the Clayton and Federal Trade Commission Acts to create more detailed standards of conduct and a body that could advise business on the line between prohibited and permitted conduct. But other proponents of the new Commission wanted to create a more effective agency for enforcement of the antitrust laws.[10] The result was a compromise in which the Clayton Act attempted to detail offenses relating to price discrimination, tie-ins, and acquisitions while Section 5 of the FTC Act contained very broad and flexible language granting the agency substantial enforcement discretion.[11]

The Commission is an independent regulatory agency governed by five commissioners, one of whom the President designates to serve as the chairman. No more than three of the five commissioners, who are appointed by the President with the advice and consent of the Senate, may be members of the same political party. The FTC has exclusive authority to enforce the FTC Act and concurrent authority (with the Antitrust Division) to enforce the Clayton Act. The broad wording of Section 5 ("unfair methods of competition") allows the FTC to reach any conduct proscribed by the Sherman Act as well as conduct that is beyond

---

9. 221 U.S. 1, 31 S.Ct. 502, 55 L.Ed. 619 (1911).

10. These conflicting goals are described in HENDERSON, THE FEDERAL TRADE COMMISSION: A STUDY IN ADMINISTRATIVE LAW AND PROCEDURE 21–23 (1924).

11. Because key provisions of the Clayton Act also contain phrases open to judicial

interpretation (e.g., where "the effect . . . may be to substantially reduce competition or tend to create a monopoly"), the goals of those who sought to create more certainty through precise legislative drafting have been largely unrealized. Id. at 48.

that Act. The Commission lacks criminal enforcement powers, although it may refer matters to the Justice Department for prosecution. Jurisdiction to enforce the Robinson Patman Act (codified as a part of the Clayton Act) is concurrent, but the Antitrust Division has ceded this responsibility to the Federal Trade Commission.

16.2c. Agency Investigations

Information leading to an investigation by the Antitrust Division or the FTC may be provided in a number of ways. Complaints may be made by a competitor, customer, or supplier; the Division may also learn of potential anticompetitive conduct through business or trade press, from investigations of related matters, from a congressional inquiry, or from a private suit. The premerger reporting program (discussed in § 10.2b) provides the information leading to almost all merger investigations.

Agency investigations may be informal—initial inquiries relying on public or voluntary sources—or formal—allowing the agency to invoke various forms of compulsory process. At some point before the Division initiates a formal investigation, it must decide whether that investigation will be criminal or civil.

For the Antitrust Division, the civil investigative demand ("CID") was authorized by legislation[12] after the Supreme Court held that grand jury investigations could not be used where the Division intended to proceed only in a civil proceeding.[13] As amended, the law enables the Division to use a CID to compel individuals and corporations to testify on interrogatories or depositions and to provide records relevant to a civil antitrust investigation. Demands are used by the Division to determine whether there is sufficient evidence to warrant filing a civil antitrust complaint. Civil investigative demands may be served in hand or by registered mail on any partnership, corporation, association or other legal entity, but may not be served on an individual. Like grand jury subpoenas, these demands may be served anywhere in the United States.[14] Firms who receive CID's have sought, with limited success, to challenge demands said to be beyond the jurisdiction of the Antitrust Division.[15]

The Federal Trade Commission also has subpoena power and discovery provisions similar to those of the Antitrust Division.[16] The Commis-

---

12. The Antitrust Civil Process Act, as amended, is set forth in 15 U.S.C.A. §§ 1311–14.

13. United States v. Procter & Gamble Co., 356 U.S. 677, 78 S.Ct. 983, 2 L.Ed.2d 1077 (1958).

14. The constitutionality of the statute authorizing civil investigative demands has consistently been upheld. E.g., Gold Bond Stamp Co. v. United States, 325 F.2d 1018 (8th Cir.1964); Hyster Co. v. United States, 338 F.2d 183 (9th Cir.1964).

15. Associated Container Transportation (Australia) Ltd. v. United States, 502 F.Supp. 505 (S.D.N.Y.1980)(allowing the plaintiffs limited discovery to test whether the CID was within the Division's jurisdictional reach). The litigation, however, failed to significantly restrict the reach of the CID when the court of appeals, on review of a district court order that had limited government access, reversed the lower court's holding. Associated Container Transportation (Australia) Ltd. v. United States, 705 F.2d 53 (2d Cir.1983).

16. 15 U.S.C.A. §§ 46, 49.

sion's subpoena power extends to witnesses and documentary evidence "relating to any matter under investigation." As in the case of compulsory process exercised by the Justice Department, efforts to challenge the scope of the Commission's investigative authority have generally been unavailing.[17]

No matter how long and careful an agency investigation may be, unless it results in enforcement action, the public may learn little or nothing about that investigation. Any lessons learned from that investigation may become the exclusive province of the agency attorneys and attorneys who represented the target of the investigation. Responding to criticism of this lack of transparency, the agencies have begun to take modest steps toward greater disclosure.[18]

16.2d. Department of Justice Criminal Proceedings

For criminal investigations, the Division usually relies on a grand jury with subpoena power. Grand juries are routinely used to gather information when criminal action is anticipated. Criminal actions have largely been reserved for *per se* horizontal violations such as price fixing. During the 1980s, the largest percentage of criminal indictments were for bid rigging in contracts for roads, airports, or other construction projects for local governments.[19] In the 1990s, criminal enforcement focused on international price-fixing conspiracies involving large firms in major industries. The Division has, however, occasionally broadened the class of criminal defendants beyond clear cut horizontal violations.[20] The Supreme Court has held that the Division must prove "criminal intent" to sustain a criminal prosecution under the Sherman Act,[21] a requirement that may preclude prosecutions unless a reasonable person knows or should know that the conduct is unlawful. Areas in which the law is unclear are generally unsuited for criminal prosecution.[22]

---

17. Relevance of a subpoena is measured by comparing the specifications of the subpoena with the resolution of the Commission announcing the purpose and scope of the inquiry. FTC v. Texaco, Inc., 555 F.2d 862, 874–77 (D.C.Cir.)(en banc), *cert. denied*, 431 U.S. 974, 97 S.Ct. 2940, 53 L.Ed.2d 1072 (1977); FTC v. Gibson, 460 F.2d 605, 609 (5th Cir.1972).

18. See the discussion in § 10.6b.

19. ABA Report, supra note 4, at 33 (noting that the bulk of horizontal restraints cases were criminal actions directed at bid rigging and similar conduct).

20. For example, in 1980, the Division brought a criminal action against Cuisinarts for vertical price fixing. In re Grand Jury Investigation of Cuisinarts, Inc., 516 F.Supp. 1008 (D.Conn.1981) affirmed, 665 F.2d 24 (2d Cir. 1981), *cert. denied*, 460 U.S. 1068, 103 S.Ct. 1520, 75 L.Ed.2d 945 (1983).

21. United States v. United States Gypsum Co., 438 U.S. 422, 98 S.Ct. 2864, 57 L.Ed.2d 854 (1978).

22. Criminal indictments need not be restricted to conduct subject to the *per se* rule. In United States v. Cinemette Corp. of America, 687 F.Supp. 976 (W.D.Pa.1988), the district court held that indictment was authorized notwithstanding the prevailing law in that circuit (there was a split in the circuits) that the *per se* rule did not apply to the conduct in question—an agreement among competing movie exhibitors not to compete for rights to show the same film. However, it was held in United States v. United States Gypsum Co., 438 U.S. 422, 98 S.Ct. 2864, 57 L.Ed.2d 854 (1998), that when conduct subject to the rule of reason is challenged criminally the government must prove that the defendant intended the act and its adverse competitive effect. For example, a criminal connection for a horizontal price verification agreement like that

The grand jury can subpoena witnesses and may issue a subpoena duces tecum to corporations or individuals.[23] The Division may begin with broad subpoenas, narrowing its inquiry in later stages of the investigation. After substantial documentary evidence has been obtained, the Division may bring individuals before a grand jury to testify as to crucial facts. This elaborate discovery may lead to an indictment of one or more defendants.

Grand jury proceedings are closed. Only the jurors, the government attorneys, and the witnesses are entitled to be present. Although witnesses are free to disclose their testimony, no one has a right to that testimony except to the extent a defendant is allowed discovery under the Federal Rules of Criminal Procedure.[24] An individual subpoenaed to testify may invoke the privilege against self-incrimination, though a corporation may not.[25] If an individual invokes the privilege, the United States Attorney, with the approval of the Attorney General, may obtain an order from the court requiring that the testimony be given; thereafter, the testimony or information provided under the order, or any information directly or indirectly derived therefrom, cannot be used against the individual in any criminal proceeding.[26]

The Antitrust Division has effectively implemented a Corporate Leniency Policy to offer incentives for co-conspirators to disclose their misconduct and cooperate with prosecutors.[27] The program has been successful in uncovering a number of major international cartels. Under this program, the first cooperating firm and its officers can receive amnesty from criminal prosecution. Other firms that agree to cooperate with the Justice Department will not receive amnesty but can receive reduced criminal sanctions, depending in part on the sequence of their voluntary action (the second firm to agree to cooperate will receive more favorable treatment than the third firm, and so on). In legislation enacted in 2004, full and candid cooperation with the government and with injured private claimants can also result in immunity from treble (but not from single) damages in private suits.[28]

in *Gypsum* would require proof that defendants entered into the agreement with the purpose and with the effect of dampening price competition between them.

23. Rule 17(a) and (c), Fed. R. Crim. P.

24. Rules 6 and 16(a), Fed. R. Crim. P.

25. Maricopa Tallow Works Inc. v. United States, 1968 Trade Cas. (CCH) ¶ 72,346 (9th Cir. 1967), *cert. denied*, 392 U.S. 926, 88 S.Ct. 2274, 20 L.Ed.2d 1385 (1968). The Supreme Court has on a number of occasions confirmed that the self-incrimination privilege does not apply to corporations. E.g., First National Bank of Boston v. Bellotti, 435 U.S. 765, 778, 98 S.Ct. 1407, 55 L.Ed.2d 707 (1978).

26. 18 U.S.C.A. § 6004.

27. U.S. Department of Justice, Antitrust Division, Leniency Policy for Individuals (Aug. 10, 1994), available at <http://www.usdoj.gov/atr /public/guidelines /0092.-htm>. U.S. Department of Justice, Antitrust Division, Corporate Leniency Policy (Aug. 10, 1993), available at <http://www.usdoj.gov/atr/public/guidelines/0091.htm>.

28. Antitrust Criminal Penalty Enhancement and Reform Act of 2004, 111 Stat. 665–668 (2004).

16.2d1.   *Criminal Sanctions*

Although the Justice Department has exercised its criminal authority under the Sherman Act to impose fines against individuals and firms guilty of violations, it seldom sought imprisonment of individuals before the 1970s. One source reports that from 1969 to 1977, fewer than twelve individuals were sentenced to more than 30 days of imprisonment.[29] Sentiment to make more frequent and stringent use of imprisonment was based on two incentives. One was to respond to discrepancy between treatment of white collar and blue collar criminals. White collar criminals were generating huge social loses with little risk of imprisonment while an individual convicted of robbery for even a small amount might be given a long sentence. Society's intolerance of crimes of violence may explain much of this discrepancy, but the other concern was that imprisonment would be a far more effective deterrent of major economic crimes such as price fixing. Short of bankrupting a firm, a result that most antitrust enforcers might regard as politically unacceptable, it was difficult to impose a criminal fine large enough to deter a price fixing scheme that might offer huge financial rewards. Substantial imprisonment, however, was viewed as an effective deterrent that reached the individuals responsible for price-fixing.

Before 1974, Sherman Act violations were misdemeanors that could lead to a maximum prison term of one year. In that year, the Antitrust Procedures and Penalties Act made violations of the Sherman Act felonies and substantially increased maximum sanctions: the maximum prison sentence to three years; the maximum fine for a person to $100,000; and the maximum fine for a corporation to $1,000,000.[30] Maximum fines were extended again in 1990—to $350,000 for individuals and $10,000,000 for corporations.[31] In addition, 1987 legislation set criminal fines for federal antitrust felonies at the larger of: (1) the amount set in the Sherman Act, as amended; or (2) twice the gross amount gained from the violation or lost by the victim.[32] These provisions have permitted the Division to obtain record-setting fines ($500 million against one firm and $250 million against another in the 1999 consent resolution of the vitamin cartel case).[33] In 2004, Congress adjusted the penalty limits upward again, allowing up to $100 million fines for corporations ($1 million for individuals) and prison terms up to 10 years.[34]

29. Baker & Reeves, *The Paper Label Sentences: Critiques*, 86 YALE L.J. 619, 623 n. 16 (1977).

30. Antitrust Procedures and Penalties Act, Pub. L. No. 93–528, 88 Stat. 1706, 1708 (1974).

31. The Antitrust Amendments Act of 1990, Pub. L. No. 101–588, 104 Stat. 2879, 2880 (1990).

32. 18 U.S.C.A. § 3571(d) (1994).

33. Department of Justice Press Release, May 20, 1999. By contrast, the highest criminal fine under the Sherman Act as of fiscal year 1991 was $2 million. Gary R. Spratling, Deputy Assistant Attorney General, Antitrust Division, U.S. Department of Justice, Criminal Antitrust Enforcement Against International Cartels, Address Delivered at the Advanced Criminal Antitrust Workshop, Phoenix, Ariz., 3 (Feb. 21, 1997).

34. 118 Stat. 668 (2004).

The Antitrust Division issued Sentencing Guidelines in 1977.[35] The Guidelines made clear that the Division would routinely seek imprisonment for individuals responsible for hard core violations such as price fixing and market allocation. The Guidelines also spelled out the deterrence rationale for such a sanction: businessmen who might dismiss a fine as a tolerable "license fee" for fixing prices would likely "view the threat of a substantial prison term more seriously."[36]

Incarceration beyond three years is also possible because each count of a conviction can add three additional years of imprisonment. The Sentencing Reform Act of 1984, a part of more comprehensive crime legislation, established the United States Sentencing Commission in the Judicial Branch.[37] The Commission's sentencing guidelines apply to all crimes that occurred after November 1, 1987, and establish a range of appropriate sentences for various crimes. The Guidelines are complex, establishing a matrix for adjusting sentences based on the level assigned to a particular crime and various extenuating or exacerbating factors. Section 2R1.1 provides that antitrust offenses will be assigned a base level of 10 which, assuming no prior criminal history, would produce a sentence from six to twelve months.[38] But the matrix allows for adjustment for a number of other factors, such as the level of affected commerce and whether the defendant has accepted responsibility for the offense. According to the Antitrust Division, application of these guidelines, which give the trial judge less discretion in sentencing, has produced somewhat longer sentences for antitrust crimes (for antitrust offenses subject to the Guidelines, the average sentence is said to have increased from 5 to 10 months).[39] A Supreme Court decision has found the sentencing guidelines to be unconstitutional, but still allows the guidelines to employed as advisory benchmarks.[40]

16.2e. Suits for Injunctive Relief

Both the Antitrust Division and the Federal Trade Commission can seek injunctive relief against conduct violating the antitrust laws. The Justice Department's authority to seek this relief is set forth in Section 4 of the Sherman Act and Section 15 of the Clayton Act.[41] In 1973,

35. Antitrust Division of the Department of Justice, Guidelines for Sentencing Recommendations in Felony Cases Under the Sherman Act (1977). The Guidelines have been supplanted by the more comprehensive guidelines issued by the U.S. Sentencing Commission in 1995. See note 34, infra.

36. 1977 Sentencing Recommendations, *supra* note 31.

37. Comprehensive Crime Control Act of 1984, Pub. L. No. 98–473, 98 Stat. 2017 (1984).

38. U.S. Sentencing Comm'n, Federal Sentencing Guidelines Manual § 2R1.1 (1995).

39. *60 Minutes with Anne Bingaman, Assistant Attorney General Antitrust*, 63 Antitrust L.J. 323, 329 (1994). See Antitrust Division, U.S. Dep't of Justice, Opening Markets and Protecting Competition For America's Businesses and Consumers: Goals and Achievements of the Antitrust Division (Fiscal Year 1993 through March 1996) (1996)(reporting an average sentence of 9 months during the 1993–1996 period).

40. United States v. Booker, 220 U.S. 543, 125 S.Ct. 738, 160 L.Ed.2d 621 (2005).

41. 15 U.S.C.A. § 25.

Congress added Section 13(b) to the FTC Act, authorizing the Commission to bring suits for injunctive relief in federal court to enforce the Clayton or FTC Acts.[42] Acting under this authority, the Commission may sue for a preliminary injunction (pending resolution of an administrative complaint filed by the Commission) or for a permanent injunction (in cases in which the Commission would generally not issue an administrative complaint). A unique aspect of the FTC's injunctive authority under Section 13(b) is its ability to seek ancillary relief, including the disgorgement of gains for restitution to victims of a violation of the FTC Act. In FTC v. Mylan Laboratories[43] the district court upheld the Commission's authority to seek disgorgement or restitution against defendants accused of using exclusive supply arrangements to raise the price of widely prescribed anti-anxiety drugs by 2000 to 3000 percent.

Although either agency may invoke its authority with respect to any threatened antitrust violation, a major use of the injunction authority is to prevent acquisitions thought to violate Section 7 of the Clayton Act (discussed in § 10.2d1). When an agency succeeds in obtaining a preliminary injunction to block consummation of a merger, that decision often results in the parties abandoning the merger rather than facing the high costs and uncertainty of prolonged litigation. Thus, hearings held on an application for a preliminary injunction regularly determine whether the acquisition proceeds.[44]

16.2f. FTC Administrative Complaints

The Commission may issue an administrative complaint to challenge violations of the FTC or Clayton Acts. In this complaint proceeding, the only remedy is a cease and desist order in the nature of an injunction; the Commission may not seek damages, nor may it pursue any form of criminal sanction.[45] The complaint is issued by vote of the Commission. After it issues the complaint, the Commission withdraws, allowing the matter to be prosecuted by complaint counsel (the staff of the Bureau of Competition) before an administrative law judge (ALJ). After the ALJ has issued a final decision, either complaint counsel or the respondent (the party named in the complaint) may appeal the decision to the Commission, which then sits as an appellate tribunal. The FTC's decision is final as to the complaint counsel, but the respondent may file a petition to review the FTC's decision in any court of appeal.[46] In a proceeding to review the Commission's decision, the reviewing court is to accept the Commission's findings of fact when supported by substantial

---

42. 15 U.S.C.A. § 53(b).

43. FTC v. Mylan Laboratories, 1999–2 Trade Cas. ¶ 72,573 (D.D.C. 1999).

44. An example is the decision of two office discount supply stores to abandon their proposed combination after the district court, based on a five-day evidentiary hearing, issued a preliminary injunction. FTC v. Staples, Inc., 970 F.Supp. 1066 (D.D.C. 1997).

45. The Commission may seek restitution in an action brought under Section 13(b), 15 U.S.C.A. § 53(b), but has so far done so in only one antitrust case. See note 43, supra. For a discussion of this issue, see Calkins, *An Enforcement Official's Reflections on Antitrust Class Actions,* 39 ARIZ. L. REV. 413, 431 & n. 112 (1997).

46. 15 U.S.C.A. § 45(c).

evidence in the record, but has de novo authority to rule on questions of law.[47]

Administrative litigation has proved to be drawn-out and costly, frequently lasting much longer than comparable antitrust litigation before a federal court. In 1996, the FTC proposed rules to expedite such administrative litigation, with the goal of making it at least as expeditious as proceedings in a federal court.[48]

The broadly worded Section 5 allows the FTC to pursue antitrust issues that could not be reached under other antitrust statutes. The Supreme Court has said that the Commission may act against conduct that conflicts with the basic policy of the Sherman and Clayton Acts "even though such practices may not actually violate these laws."[49] The scope of this power has never been articulated either by the Commission or any court. Perhaps it could be used to fill certain loopholes in Clayton Act coverage,[50] but the Commission's power cannot be open-ended. It would have to be cabined by norms or standards that could be objectively applied in counseling and by courts in reviewing Commission uses of the power. True, there are factors that make broad discretion under Section 5 less risky than would be open-ended power derived directly from the Sherman or Clayton Acts. The remedy for a Section 5 violation is a cease and desist order, so that the respondent cannot be punished for past conduct unless that conduct was subject to a prior such order.[51] In addition, the Commission's decision is less likely to be the basis of private treble damage suits. Collateral estoppel effect may not be given to the findings of the Commission in any ensuing litigation.[52] Furthermore, private parties may not enforce section 5 of the FTC Act, so any follow up action must be based on claims formulated under the Sherman or Clayton Acts. For all of these reasons, but primarily because of the broad wording of Section 5, the FTC could use its authority to attack anticompetitive practices not easily reached by other antitrust statutes. For example, in E.I. Du Pont de Nemours & Co. v. FTC, the Commission

---

47. 15 U.S.C.A. § 45(c). FTC v. Indiana Fed'n of Dentists, 476 U.S. 447, 454–55, 106 S.Ct. 2009, 90 L.Ed.2d 445 (1986); FTC v. Procter & Gamble Co., 386 U.S. 568, 581, 87 S.Ct. 1224, 18 L.Ed.2d 303 (1967); Hospital Corp. of America v. FTC, 807 F.2d 1381, 1384 (7th Cir.1986), cert. denied, 481 U.S. 1038, 107 S.Ct. 1975, 95 L.Ed.2d 815 (1987). See California Dental Ass'n v. FTC, 526 U.S. 756, 119 S.Ct. 1604, 1618–19, 143 L.Ed.2d 935 (1999)(Breyer, J., dissenting).

48. *FTC Announces Procedural Rule Change Streamlining Administrative Trial Process*, 71 A.T.R.R. 258 (1996); 61 F.R. 50640.

49. FTC v. Brown Shoe Co., 384 U.S. 316, 321, 86 S.Ct. 1501, 16 L.Ed.2d 587 (1966). In FTC v. Sperry & Hutchinson Co., 405 U.S. 233, 239, 92 S.Ct. 898, 31 L.Ed.2d 170 (1972), the Court may have interpreted the FTC's authority even more broadly,

finding that the FTC could "define and proscribe an unfair competitive practice, even though the practice does not infringe either the letter or the spirit of the antitrust laws."

50. For example Section 2 of the Clayton Act forbids certain price discriminations "in commerce," but not discriminations merely "affecting" commerce. Conceivably discriminations directly affecting commerce could be addressed as a violation of the unfair competition language in Section 5 of the FTC Act.

51. The Commission may seek penal sanctions for violation of a cease and desist order. § 19 of the FTC Act, 15 U.S.C.A. § 57(b).

52. 15 U.S.C.A. § 16(a).

sought to use its Section 5 authority to attack parallel behavior of oligopolists more difficult to reach under the Sherman Act. Although the Commission ruled that the conduct was unlawful, it was reversed in a decision by the Second Circuit.[53]

16.2g. FTC Reports

The FTC Act includes in Section 6 a grant of authority to the Commission to gather and compile information about "the organization, business, conduct, practices, and management" of persons "engaged in or whose business affects commerce."[54] The Commission's authority under Section 6 does not allow it to forbid or punish any business conduct. Rather this authority is designed to allow the Commission to better set enforcement priorities and to release such information about business activities as it deems in the public interest.[55]

Although the FTC's reporting authority has been used throughout its history, the Commission generated controversy during the 1970s through its aggressive efforts to collect from large firms and compile financial information that was broken down by line of business. The program was designed to fill loopholes in publicly available financial data. Firms that were engaged in multiple lines of business could mask accounting data from individual lines by reporting it in aggregate form. Even if segmented data was reported, it was not done consistently among firms in a manner that would allow compilation of data for particular industries. Assessments of the impact of antitrust policy on a particular industry, or the need for antitrust intervention in that industry, were crippled by the lack of a reliable data base for assessing industry performance.

The Commission's Line of Business ("LOB") program received support from economists and antitrust theorists with widely varying views.[56] The program survived a major court challenge by many of the firms required to submit LOB data.[57] Data was collected for the years 1974 through 1976 and was reported by the Commission in aggregate form (to prevent the dissemination of individual firm information).[58]

---

53. E. I. Du Pont de Nemours & Co. v. FTC, 729 F.2d 128, 139–42 (2d Cir.1984). The Second Circuit's constrictive reading of Section 5, while not precluding any application beyond the limits of the Sherman Act, requires that when challenging parallel conduct the Commission, if it cannot show a conspiracy, must establish anticompetitive intent or purpose and the lack of any independent business reason for the respondent's conduct. It was not reviewed by the Supreme Court.

54. 15 U.S.C.A. § 46(a).

55. 15 U.S.C.A. § 46(f).

56. See the comments of then Assistant Attorney General William Baxter, who noted that although he supported less antitrust enforcement in many areas, he favored the

LOB Program because antitrust policy should not be made while wearing "blinders." Oversight Hearings on the Antitrust Division, House Comm. on the Judiciary, Subcomm. on Monopolies and Commercial Law, 98th Cong., 1st & 2d Sess. 136 (1986).

57. Appeal of FTC Line of Business Rep. Litigation, 595 F.2d 685 (D.C.Cir. 1978), cert. denied, 439 U.S. 958, 99 S.Ct. 362, 58 L.Ed.2d 351 (1978).

58. In 1980, Congress added a proviso to Section 6 that prohibits the disclosure of information that would allow the identification of individual firm data. Federal Trade Commission Improvements Act of 1980 Pub. L. 96–252, 94 Stat. 374–75, adding the proviso to Section 6(f) and the last three undesignated paragraphs of Section 6.

During the 1980s, the Commission decided that it would make available in aggregate form the data that had already been collected but would not collect any more. Although there is at this point no comparable data source for measuring the performance of large businesses, over time, evolving and more refined standards that require segmented reporting of accounting data may provide some of the needed information.[59] Meanwhile, the Commission's authority to collect and disseminate information about American business survived the 1970s litigation largely unscathed. The Commission continues to exercise this authority.[60]

16.2h.   Consensual Resolution of Litigation

Enforcement initiatives of Antitrust Division and the Federal Trade Commission often result in negotiated settlements. For a variety of reasons, consent resolutions appear to be on the increase. One reason is the substantial leverage that each enforcement agency has in cases reviewed under the premerger notification program. The parties involved in a proposed acquisition generally have committed substantial resources to effecting a consolidation that cannot proceed without the government's consent, or a potentially long and uncertain litigation. Faced with government opposition, the parties usually seek a settlement rather than risk litigation. Outside the merger area, the Government may have less leverage, but costs and risks of litigation may still pressure a private party to negotiate a consent decree. Litigation costs may be prohibitive for relatively small firms or non-profit organizations.[61] Even large firms may find the risk calculus unfavorable. A litigated judgment against a defendant may open the door more widely to private treble damage suits because, in a suit by the Justice Department, any finding of a violation is prima facie evidence of a violation in subsequent suits.[62] Consent resolution, although not precluding subsequent private suits, forces a potential private plaintiff to bear the full burden of proof.

The procedures for these negotiated settlements vary. In the case of a criminal prosecution, the Antitrust Division may agree with the defendant on a plea bargain and negotiated sanction (usually a criminal fine). As a part of such a settlement, the defendant may ask the court to accept a plea of nolo contendere, a plea that cannot be used against the defendant in any related private antitrust suit. In civil matters, the negotiated settlement is often reached before the Division files any complaint. At this point, the Division will file a complaint along with a negotiated order resolving the issues. Court entry of the order allows the

---

59. Scherer, *Sunlight and Sunset at the Federal Trade Commission,* 42 Admin. L. Rev. 461, 480 (1980).

60. For example, see the Commission's Report on Pharmacy Benefit Managers: Ownership of Mail–Order Pharmacies (August 2005), available at <http://www.ftc.gov/reports/pharmbenefit05/050906pharmbenefitrpt.pdf>.

61. See Grimes, *The ABA Consent Decree: Reflections on Oversight of the Consent Process,* 10 Antitrust No.1, 25 (1995)(discussing the reasons why the American Bar Association may have been unwilling to litigate a matter involving the Association's regulation of legal education).

62. 15 U.S.C.A. § 16(a).

Division to enforce the terms of the settlement through court-imposed sanctions.

Whether the consent judgment with the Antitrust Division is agreed upon before the complaint is filed or after litigation is commenced, it will be subject to the safeguards of the Antitrust Procedures and Penalties Act, known as the Tunney Act.[63] The Tunney Act grew out of congressional concern that the Division, in the face of political pressure from the White House, had settled litigation during the Nixon Administration (in the early 1970s) on terms favorable to the defendant. The Act requires that the proposed consent order along with a competitive impact statement be filed with the court and open for public comment. After a period of 60 days, the court is instructed to enter the order if it determines "that entry of such judgment is in the public interest."[64] Tunney Act procedures would have more significance if the Antitrust Division immediately after investigating decided what conduct to challenge, filed its complaint and then started to negotiate. In practice this rarely, if ever, occurs. Once a civil investigation begins, the Antitrust Division and private attorneys (and possibly economists and executives) of the target firm start to interact. The Division is likely to share its concerns long before a complaint is drafted. Often the process of interactive negotiation clarifies issues and narrows contentions. It can also result, even before any suit is initiated, in agreement about what remedy will be acceptable to both parties. When this occurs, the complaint that is drafted will likely be no wider than needed to justify the pre-negotiated relief, and the competitive impact statement will focus only on harm resulting from the conduct challenged and the improvement attributed to enjoining that conduct.

Tunney Act procedures have generated controversy.[65] Compliance with the Act's procedural requirements is costly for the Antitrust Division already confronted with inadequate resources. The Division, in the interest of effective enforcement, has modified its practices to minimize the extent to which the Act limits its discretion. As a practical matter, the Act in most cases probably does not affect the decree that is entered. The Division has on occasion sought to avoid altogether the requirements of the Tunney Act. In the 1982 settlement of monopolization charges against AT & T, the Division sought to amend a preexisting consent decree (rather than enter a new one), in this way avoiding the Act's approval requirements.[66] The public interest standard for court

---

63. The Tunney Act is codified as 15 U.S.C.A. § 16(b)-(h).

64. 15 U.S.C.A. § 16(b), (e). (§§ 5(b)–5h of the Clayton Act).

65. For a discussion of early decisions applying the Tunney Act, see Branfman, *Antitrust Consent Decrees—A review and Evaluation of the First Seven Years Under the Antitrust Procedures and Penalties Act,* 27 ANTITRUST BULL. 303 (1982). For a discus-

sion of more recent developments, see Garza, supra, note 5, at 21.

66. United States v. American Telephone & Telegraph Co., 552 F.Supp. 131 (D.D.C.1982), *aff'd sub nom.* Maryland v. United States, 460 U.S. 1001, 103 S.Ct. 1240, 75 L.Ed.2d 472 (1983). Although the Antitrust Division argued that it was not bound by the Tunney Act, it nonetheless agreed to comply with the procedural requirements of the Act.

approval of a decree has also generated litigation. The vagueness of this standard may lead to the court's perfunctory approval of most consent orders, but on occasion has led to bolder judicial intervention. In *United States v. Microsoft Corp.*, the Division had negotiated a settlement with the defendant that the district court, after hearing from dissatisfied rivals of Microsoft, found not to satisfy the public interest standard.[67] The district court's decision raised questions about the nature of the public interest standard and the extent to which the court could second guess the Division's prosecutorial discretion. On appeal, the D.C. Circuit avoided constitutional separation of powers issues by construing the public interest standard narrowly.[68] The court held that a judge is not obliged to accept a decree that, "on its face, appears to make a mockery of judicial power. Short of that eventuality, the Tunney Act cannot be interpreted as an authorization for a district judge to assume the role of Attorney General."[69] In a case in which the judge believes the decree does not provide all the relief a third party should have received, the *Microsoft* decision limits a court's discretion to challenge the Division's settlement.[70] Other circuits may disagree.[71] And even *Microsoft* leaves room for third party challenges based upon failure of the decree to remedy matters addressed in the Department's complaint, or based upon alleged injurious effects of the decree on a third party.

The Federal Trade Commission also settles large numbers of matters by consent. The Tunney Act does not apply to FTC consent orders. Because many FTC matters settled by consent are not before a federal court, the consent orders are entered by the Commission without court participation. If the Commission has not yet filed an administrative complaint, a proposed complaint is served on the respondent, along with a proposed order indicating the relief the Commission would impose. If the parties reach an agreement, the Commission must provide a 60–day period for public comment, after which the order can be entered as a Commission order, subject to the same enforcement sanctions applicable to other Commission orders.[72]

16.2i. Regulatory Decrees

Closely linked to the increasing number of consensual resolutions to government antitrust investigations is the expanded use of regulatory decrees. All consent decrees are regulatory in the sense that they impose

67. 159 F.R.D. 318 (D.D.C.1995). Except for Judge Greene's refusal to countenance the Justice Department's effort to avoid the Tunney Act in *United States v. AT & T*, supra note 60, and for his insistence in that case that the proposed decree be modified in significant respects, Judge Sporkin's response to the Microsoft covenant decree is the high point of judicial use of the Act to affect outcomes.

68. 56 F.3d 1448 (D.C.Cir.1995).

69. Id. at 1462.

70. Id. at 1461–62.

71. In United States v. BNS Inc., 848 F.2d 945 (9th Cir.1988), the ninth circuit upheld a district court order preliminarily enjoining a proposed merger in order to study proposed effects of the merger going beyond markets that were addressed in the Justice Department's complaint. By implication, the decision would appear to allow use of the Tunney Act to question matters not addressed in the Department's complaint.

72. 16 C.F.R. § 2.34.

obligations on the parties for resolving past conduct said to have violated the antitrust laws. But many of these decrees also limit the future conduct of a firm, generating future agency and judicial regulatory oversight of the firm's actions.

None of this is entirely new. There is a substantial history for regulatory decrees in both federal agencies. The FTC's cease and desist orders often seek to prohibit not only repetitions of past conduct, but also related future conduct that could lead to similar anticompetitive consequences. Injunctions obtained by the Justice Department have been similarly employed. If one examines consent decrees negotiated during early post-war years, before deregulatory sentiment began to develop, some arrangements can be found that are considerably more intrusive than any negotiated today.[73] Accumulations of these regulatory decrees, some with no time limits on their operation, have led to periodic reviews and "house-cleanings" by the agencies and to efforts to write in sunset provisions that automatically terminate such provisions.

Although regulatory decrees have been criticized as inferior to "structural" relief,[74] they often afford the antitrust agency the best available remedy. For example, if a firm's market power is based on information advantages or brand loyalty, a structural remedy such as divestiture is inappropriate. When under such circumstances a firm has used a tie-in to exploit buyers, the most appropriate remedy to prevent future violations may be an injunction that directly forbids such conduct. Still, a number of commentators have noted a tendency among federal officials to rely on consent decrees laden with conduct restraints expensive to implement and enforce and with (perhaps) dubious procompetitive benefits.[75] Within any government agency, there may be a tendency to resolve differences of view among the staff by adding additional forbidden conduct to the consent decree. A desire to increase the agency's enforcement record may also lead it to insist on regulatory provisions when it realizes that structural relief is unwarranted or that there is substantial expense and risk in undertaking litigation aimed at such relief. A defendant, for its part, may prefer to accept such regulatory provisions as less onerous than structural relief and the cost and risks to it of continued litigation. Indeed, attorneys representing private parties may affirmatively promote a regulatory decree in order to forestall structural relief, as, for example, when the agency is weighing whether to seek an injunction to prohibit a pending merger. Whatever the reasons, regulatory consent decrees are an increasingly common outcome of negotiated settlements.[76]

73. See United States v. Gamewell, 95 F.Supp. 9 (D.Mass.1951) (contempt proceedings arising out of 1948 consent decree).

74. Baxter, *Separation of Powers, Prosecutorial Discretion, and the "Common Law" Nature of Antitrust Law*, 60 Texas L. Rev. 661 (1982). In United States v. AT & T, supra, note 66, the company apparently

concluded that divestiture would be preferable to extensive, ongoing regulatory oversight.

75. See the collection of views on regulatory decrees in 10 Antitrust, No. 1 (1995).

76. One of the authors has suggested the need for some additional control mechanism, perhaps within the Antitrust Division

An as yet unresolved issue is how to enforce these decrees. Neither alone nor collectively do the agencies have sufficient resources to monitor these regulatory decrees.

§ 16.3 State and Local Antitrust Enforcement

16.3a. State Enforcement

State attorneys general were challenging anticompetitive practices before the Sherman Act became law. According to one source, thirteen States had enacted antitrust statutes and a half dozen state suits had been successfully prosecuted against major trusts before the Sherman Act was passed.[1] Congress preserved and subsequently reinforced the state enforcement role. State or private enforcement was authorized under a provision of the Sherman Act that ultimately became Section 4 of the Clayton Act (authorizing suits for treble damages). Suits for injunctive relief are also permitted under Section 16 of the Clayton Act. During the first decade of the Sherman Act, state enforcers brought more antitrust suits than the Justice Department.[2] In the years after 1981 state enforcement, including cooperative efforts by several states joining as plaintiffs, again became more frequent and economically significant.[3]

Suits brought by a state attorney general can be based on federal or state antitrust statutes or on common law. Jurisdiction of any state suit based on federal antitrust would be in a federal court. A claim based on state antitrust law or common law could also be in a federal court if appropriately pendent to a federal claim. A federal antitrust claim may be brought on behalf of the state as an injured victim (e.g., as a buyer of a commodity subject to inflated monopoly or cartel prices) or as a protector of the public interest (*parens patriae*).

16.3a1. *Parens Patriae Actions*

As the Latin term suggests, a state attorney general brings a *parens patriae* action in a parental role protective of the public interest—to obtain compensation and or injunctive relief for injured members of the public. A state's *parens patriae* authority has venerable common law roots and may exist as a matter of both federal and state common law.[4] But for use in federal antitrust claims, these traditional forms of action appeared on shaky ground after two decisions limited a state's authority

---

itself, to constrain the tendency toward unwieldy and unnecessary regulatory provisions. Grimes, *The ABA Consent Decree: Reflections on Oversight of the Consent Process*, 10 ANTITRUST, No. 1, 25 (1995).

§ 16.3

1. May, *Antitrust Practice and Procedure in the Formative Era: The Constitutional and Conceptual Reach of Antitrust Law, 1880–1918*, 135 U. PA. L. REV. 495 at 499, 500.

2. Id. at 500–01.

3. Lande, *When Should States Challenge Mergers: A Proposed Federal/State Balance*, 35 N.Y. L. Sch. L. Rev. 1047, 1053–55 (1991).

4. Georgia v. Pennsylvania R. Co., 324 U.S. 439, 443, 445, 65 S.Ct. 716, 89 L.Ed. 1051 (1945)(acknowledging a state's federal and common law authority to sue on behalf of its citizens).

to use *parens patriae* to sue for damages caused by antitrust violations. The Supreme Court in 1972 declined to allow the State of Hawaii to recover damages for injury to its "general economy."[5] One year later, the Ninth Circuit declined to allow the State of California to recover damages on behalf of injured consumers.[6] While perhaps desirable, a state remedy of this sort, the Ninth Circuit suggested, should come through "legislation and rule making."[7] Citing the need to deter antitrust violations involving "small individual damages to large numbers of citizen-consumers," the Justice Department urged a legislative solution.[8] Congress responded by including in the Hart–Scott–Rodino Antitrust Improvements Act of 1976 language expressly authorizing treble damage *parens patriae* actions brought by an attorney general of a state.[9] Under Section 4C of the Clayton Act, a state attorney general may bring suit on behalf of natural persons, but not business entities, that have been injured by antitrust violations. This legislation also eased the task of establishing damages in parens patriae suits. Under Section 4D, the state attorney general may establish damages

> in the aggregate by statistical or sampling methods, by the computation of illegal overcharges, or by such other reasonable system of estimating aggregate damages as the court in its discretion may permit without the necessity of separately proving the individual claim of, or amount of damage to, persons on whose behalf the suit was brought.[10]

The states have made active use of the *parens patriae* provisions, often combining in multi-state actions coordinated by a task force of the National Association of Attorneys General. These efforts have included challenges to vertical price fixing,[11] joint ventures,[12] and mergers.[13] The Supreme Court has also interpreted Section 16 of the Clayton Act to provide a State attorney general the authority to obtain injunctive relief on behalf of citizens within the State's borders.[14]

---

5. Hawaii v. Standard Oil Co. of California, 405 U.S. 251, 261–64, 92 S.Ct. 885, 31 L.Ed.2d 184 (1972)(acknowledging a state's parens patriae authority to seek injunctive relief but not treble damages).

6. California v. Frito–Lay, Inc. 474 F.2d 774 (9th Cir.1973), *cert. denied*, 412 U.S. 908, 93 S.Ct. 2291, 36 L.Ed.2d 974 (1973).

7. Id. at 777.

8. H.R. REP. No. 94–499, 94th Cong., 1st Sess. 4 (1975)(quoting the testimony of Assistant Attorney General Thomas Kauper).

9. Section 4C of the Clayton Act, 15 U.S.C.A. § 15c. Given the broad authorization in Section 4D, the fact that Section 4C (15 U.S.C.A. § 15c) limits relief to natural persons, that the legislative history suggests intent to gain damages for antitrust injury to "citizen consumers" (id) and that the act was passed before Illinois Brick Co.

v. Illinois,431 U.S. 720, 97 S.Ct. 2061, 52 L.Ed.2d 707 (1977) was decided it seems clear that the passing on defense (§ 17.2c) should not avail in *parens patriae* actions.

10. Section 4D of the Clayton Act, 15 U.S.C.A. § 15d.

11. New York v. Nintendo of Am., Inc., 775 F.Supp. 676, 679 (S.D.N.Y.1991); Maryland v. Mitsubishi Electronics America, Inc., 1992–1 Trade Cases ¶ 69,743 (D. Md. 1992).

12. New York v. VISA U.S.A., Inc., 1990–1 Trade Cases ¶ 69,016 (S.D.N.Y. 1990).

13. Massachusetts v. Campeau Corp., 1988–1 Trade Cas. (CCH) ¶ 68,093 (D. Mass. 1988).

14. California v. American Stores Co., 495 U.S. 271, 110 S.Ct. 1853, 109 L.Ed.2d 240 (1990).

Parens patriae actions were intended to serve the twin goals of compensation and deterrence.[15] Like private class actions, *parens patriae* actions offer hope of reaching antitrust violations that spread antitrust injury among a large group of consumers in a manner that makes individual antitrust claims unlikely.[16] The federal antitrust agencies, it should be noted, either lack, or have not exercised, authority to pursue restitution on behalf of injured victims.[17] But as in the case of class actions that reach large classes of consumers with small individual damage claims,[18] calculation and distribution of such damages can be problematic. Although states have received substantial damage awards in some *parens patriae* actions, the awards often have cy pres (substitutes for direct payments to the injured buyer) characteristics, for example discount coupons for future purchases[19] or payments channeled to relevant charitable causes.[20]

16.3b.   Local Enforcement

In addition to actions brought by state attorneys general, local prosecutors sometimes bring antitrust actions. The majority of states expressly authorize local officials to institute antitrust actions.[21] But active enforcement is probably limited to a small number of prosecutors who employ antitrust specialists, usually within their consumer affairs division. For example, the Los Angeles District Attorney's office has an Antitrust Section as a part of its Consumer Protection Division. That office typically assigns two or three attorneys full-time to antitrust investigations. Other cities whose prosecutors have employed antitrust specialists include New York, Philadelphia, and San Diego. Often, local prosecutors have concurrent jurisdiction with the state attorney general to enforce the state's antitrust statute and may work closely with the attorney general's office in investigating and prosecuting cases.[22] Local

15. H.R. Rep. No. 94–499, 94th Cong., 1st Sess. 5 (1975).

16. In at least one case, a court refused to certify a class action on the grounds that a *parens patriae* action already underway was a superior way of litigating the antitrust claim. Pennsylvania v. Budget Fuel Co., 122 F.R.D. 184, 186 (E.D.Pa.1988).

17. As described in § 16.2e, the FTC might pursue restitution in actions brought under § 13(b) of the FTC Act but has so far done so in only a single case. There is no statutory provision authorizing the Department of Justice to seek restitution for private parties.

18. See the discussion of class action damage remedies in § 17.6b3. See also the comments in note 9, supra.

19. New York v. Nintendo of America, Inc., 775 F.Supp. 676, 679 (S.D.N.Y.

1991)($25 million in coupons for consumers and $3 million for antitrust enforcement for states).

20. New York v. Reebok Int'l, Ltd., 903 F.Supp. 532, 534 (S.D.N.Y.1995), *aff'd*, 96 F.3d 44 (2d Cir.1996)($8 million distributed to participating states for use in providing athletic equipment, services, and facilities).

21. According to a 1978 survey, 34 states expressly authorize both state and local officials to enforce provisions of the state antitrust law. Fellmeth & Papageorge, *A Treatise on State Antitrust Law and Enforcement: With Models and Forms*, Anti-trust & Trade Reg. Rep. (BNA), Supp. No. 1, 18 (Dec. 7, 1978).

22. An example of cooperation between state and local prosecutors is People v. Steelcase, Inc., 792 F.Supp. 84, 85 (C.D.Cal. 1992).

prosecutors may also pursue actions under federal law, at least when claims are brought on behalf of a government purchaser.[23]

16.3c. Use of State Antitrust Law

A state or local agency bringing an antitrust claim often has a choice, much as does a private party, whether to bring that claim under federal or state law. If state attorneys general are bringing a coordinated, multi-state action, they are likely to choose federal law so that uniform rules of law will prevail in determining the lawfulness of the conduct. Of course, pendent state claims may be joined to a federal claim and tried together in a federal court. Although state antitrust laws often are patterned after, and usually are interpreted in the same manner as, federal laws there are still notable differences.[24] Where such substantive differences make it easier for the state or local agency to prevail, or where it is to their advantage to bring the action in a state court, the claim may be made under state law.

Use of state antitrust enforcement can raise constitutional issues.[25] Congress has the authority to preempt state antitrust laws. But, as the Supreme Court has indicated, absent an express indication of Congress' intent to preempt, the Court will be reluctant to find preemption in an area such as monopolization and unfair business practices long subject to "state common law and statutory remedies."[26] State antitrust law may also be voided if it unduly discriminates against, regulates, or burdens interstate commerce.[27] The broadest argument in support of a preemption or Commerce Clause challenge to a state law antitrust claim is that the federal antitrust laws have occupied the field. This general claim seems unlikely to succeed,[28] but does not preclude a more specific claim based on a conflict between federal and state antitrust law.[29]

16.3d. Policy Issues Involving State and Local Enforcement

Despite venerable roots, state or local prosecutions probably play only a marginal role when measured against overall antitrust enforce-

---

23. Section 4C of the Clayton Act authorizes treble damage *parens patriae* actions brought by state attorneys general, but does not mention local government authorities. A local prosecutor might still attempt a *parens patriae* action under federal common law.

24. For example, state antitrust law often permits indirect purchasers to sue for antitrust injury, a result generally precluded under federal law. See § 17.2c4. Although the prohibition on indirect purchaser suits would not apply to *parens patriae* actions, a state or local agency suing in its proprietary capacity might be subject to the indirect purchaser rule under federal law. See note 9, supra.

25. See generally, ABA Antitrust Section, Monograph No. 15, Antitrust Federalism: The Role of State Law (1988).

26. California v. ARC Am. Corp., 490 U.S. 93, 100–01, 109 S.Ct. 1661, 104 L.Ed.2d 86 (1989).

27. The Supreme Court described this test in Brown–Forman Distillers Corp. v. New York State Liquor Authority, 476 U.S. 573, 578–79, 106 S.Ct. 2080, 90 L.Ed.2d 552 (1986).

28. California v. ARC Am. Corp., 490 U.S. 93, 109 S.Ct. 1661, 104 L.Ed.2d 86 (1989). See also Hovenkamp, *State Antitrust in the Federal Scheme,* 58 Ind. L.J. 375, 403 (1983)(concluding that "the assertion that federal law occupies the field will not be sufficient to preempt state antitrust law."). See, generally, § 14.6g.

29. The substantive provisions of state antitrust law are beyond the scope of this work. In many cases, however, state antitrust law is patterned after federal law discussed in this treatise.

ment. An obvious reason for this limited role is lack of resources. State enforcement had achieved relatively high levels in the 1980s after a long period of dormancy.[30] Still, most local prosecutors, and even some state attorneys general, do not have antitrust specialists and do not pursue antitrust claims. Those who have specialists may still lack the resources to maintain more than token enforcement. For example, during the period 1980 through 1994, only ten states were involved in more than one reported merger case.[31] State or local prosecutors can occasionally overcome resource shortages by combining to bring major antitrust suits. Nineteen states marshaled their resources in bringing the complaint in Hartford Fire Ins. Co. v. California,[32] a suit challenging the alleged cartel practices of the reinsurance industry. In the 1990s, state attorneys general have cooperated with the Antitrust Division of the Justice Department on a number of key cases.[33]

Although state and local enforcement expanded somewhat during the 1980s, these enforcers still remains relatively small players compared with either federal or private enforcement. The future of state and local antitrust enforcement probably lies in supplementing federal enforcement (often through joint enforcement undertakings with the federal agencies), in use of the *parens patriae* authority, often in multi-state coordinated suits, and in selective suits involving predominantly state or local issues. State agencies usually take positions consistent with those of the federal agencies. There continue to be cases, however, when the state or local prosecutor does not see eye to eye with the federal enforcement agencies. In the Microsoft litigation, nine states and the District of Columbia chose to continue pressing for a more comprehensive remedy after the Justice Department settled its claims against the firm in 2001. However noxious to defendants seeking to fend off antitrust liability, this demonstration of federalism can serve as a useful check on politically tainted settlements.[34]

---

30. Lande, supra note 3, at 1053–55.

31. Brodley, *Antitrust Standing in Private Merger Cases: Reconciling Private Incentives and Public Enforcement Goals*, 94 Mich. L.Rev. 1, 40 n.161 (1995).

32. 509 U.S. 764, 113 S.Ct. 2891, 125 L.Ed.2d 612 (1993).

33. Assistant Attorney General Anne K. Bingaman, *Antitrust Division Cooperation With State Attorneys General*, Address Before the Nat'l Assoc. of Attorneys General,

Oct. 11, 1995 (reporting 27 joint investigations that had to that point produced 4 joint decrees with states). The currently pending monopolization case against Microsoft is another example of federal-state cooperation.

34. For a description of the role played by the states, see First, *Delivering Remedies: The Role of the States in Antitrust Enforcement*, 69 Geo. Wash. L. Rev. 1701, 1728–30 (2001).

Chapter XVII

PRIVATE ENFORCEMENT

Table of Sections

---

§ 17.1   The Private Antitrust Claim

Section 4 of the Clayton Act says that "any person * * * injured in his business or property" by an antitrust violation shall be entitled to bring suit to recover "threefold" damages.[1] Section 16 says that "any person, firm, corporation, or association shall be entitled to sue for and have injunctive relief * * * against threatened loss or damage" due to such violation.[2] These provisions provide the basis for contemporary private enforcement of the federal antitrust laws. Many states also have provisions authorizing private suits to enforce their antitrust laws.

17.1a.   The History of Private Enforcement

Private suits challenging anticompetitive conduct have a long tradition. In the English courts, private litigation produced common law principles that were to evolve into contemporary antitrust law.[3] When the Sherman Act was drafted, legislators were attracted to a provision authorizing multiple damages for private parties bringing antitrust claims. The motivation of the framers seems to have been to provide deterrence or punishment for violators as well as compensation for victims. Referring to the trusts, Senator Reagan, a member of the Senate Judiciary Committee that drafted the bill, urged the committee to adopt a law "that will punish every man engaged in this business and that will give an adequate remedy in a convenient jurisdiction to every person who is damaged by these associations."[4] Senator Sherman, who thought that his original proposal for double damages was insufficient, urged that the multiple damages "be commensurate with the difficulty of maintaining a private suit."[5] The provision establishing treble damages for Sherman Act violations was approved as Section 7 of the Sherman Act, and later was extended in Section 4 of the Clayton Act to apply to violations of other antitrust laws.[6] Concerns that the original provision authorizing private suits had been ineffective led Congress in 1914 to give private litigants additional rights, including: the ability to use a favorable judgment in a government suit as *prima facie* evidence of a violation in a related private suit; suspension of the statute of limitations during the pendency of a government suit; and the ability to sue for injunctive relief (Section 16 of the Clayton Act).[7]

§ 17.1

1. 15 U.S.C.A. § 15(a).

2. 15 U.S.C.A. § 26.

3. The Schoolmasters' Case, Ct. of Com. Pleas, Hilary Term, 1410, Y.B., 11 Hen. IV, f. 47, pl. 21; Case of Monopolies, Ct. of King's Bench, 1602, 11 Coke 84, 77 Eng. Rep. 1260. See Letwin, *The English Common Law Concerning Monopolies*, 21 U. CHI. L. REV. 355 (1954)(finding common law roots to anti-monopoly law, but concluding that much of the English common law had been supplanted or modified by the time the Sherman Act was passed).

4. THE LEGISLATIVE HISTORY OF THE FEDERAL ANTITRUST LAWS AND RELATED STATUTES, VOL. I, 167 (E. Kintner, ed. 1978).

5. Id. at 114, 178.

6. The legislative history of federal statutes permitting private treble damage suits is reviewed in STUDY OF THE ANTITRUST TREBLE DAMAGE REMEDY, REPORT OF THE HOUSE JUDICIARY COMM., 98th Cong., 2d Sess. 6–9 (1984)(report prepared by G. Garvey for the Committee)(hereinafter, TREBLE DAMAGE REPORT.).

7. These provisions are found in the Clayton Act, Sections 5(A)(I), and 16, 15 U.S.C.A. §§ 16(a),(i), 26.

The statistical evidence suggests that private suits, although a high percentage of enforcement initiatives in the earliest years, were relatively infrequent throughout most of the first half century of the Sherman Act.[8] Growth in private suits occurred after the Second World War, apparently peaked in the late 1970s, and has abated in recent years.[9] The post war surge in private enforcement probably has a simple explanation: private plaintiffs were able to win a high percentage of suits that they initiated, a circumstance that was not present (or at least not to the same extent) in privately initiated suits brought either before or after that time. Proving an antitrust claim probably became easier after more generous discovery rules adopted in the late 1930s. The success of private plaintiffs was also linked to the general attitude of the federal courts toward antitrust. Indeed, the number of private suits may be a rough index of the receptivity of the federal courts to these claims.

Another key development for private enforcement was the evolution of the class action.[10] Adoption of Rule 23 of the Federal Rules of Civil Procedure in the late thirties, and critical amendments to that section in 1966, allowed attorneys to aggregate the claims of many small victims of antitrust violations, making it financially feasible to pursue actions that otherwise would have been left untouched. Grafted onto the private treble damage suit, class actions made it possible for private enforcers to have a much broader impact on conduct that caused substantial competitive injury. But class actions, just as private suits generally, have sparked controversy, raising concerns that too many resources are committed to antitrust enforcement, perhaps deterring beneficial or procompetitive conduct.

After the late 1970s, a number of developments contributed to a substantial decline in private litigation, albeit not down to the pre–1950 levels.[11] Among these were reduced reliance on fairness and increased reliance on efficiency as a key antitrust value, increased judicial leniency in evaluating defendants' summary judgment motions, development of rigorous standing, antitrust injury, and causation and damage standards, and a widespread disposition to rely more on markets and less on government action to influence resource allocation. In consequence the ratio of private to government claims decreased from 20:1 in the late 1970s to around 10:1 in the mid 1980s.[12]

17.1b. The Policy Debate Concerning Private Enforcement

Although more than ninety other nations have competition laws, few permit private enforcement. Even those nations that do authorize pri-

---

8. This statistical evidence is summarized in Treble Damage Report, supra note 6, at 10–15.

9. See the data collected by the Administrative Office of the U.S. Courts, set forth in Treble Damage Report, supra note 6, at 14.

10. See § 17.6 for a discussion of class action suits.

11. S. Salop & L. White, *Private Antitrust Litigation: An Introduction and Framework* in Private Antitrust Litigation, New Evidence, New Learning, 3–4 (L. White, ed. 1988)(reporting that private claims peaked in 1978 at 1611 cases).

12. Id. at 3.

vate suits (for example, Japan and Canada) do not experience anything approaching the United States' 10:1 ratio of private to government suits. Heavy use of private enforcement has sparked substantial criticism of the United States law,[13] including calls for abolition of private suits.[14] These criticisms, summarized here, are that private enforcement produces overdeterrence, that firms fearful of treble damage liability may forego legitimate competitive initiatives that would increase competition and benefit consumers, and that excessive enforcement generates "false negatives" or court rulings that condemn conduct that is on balance benign or procompetitive.[15] In any area of law undue deterrence is more likely when substantive requirements or possible sanctions are vague or uncertain. Even if an enforcement scheme only deterred clear anticompetitive conduct, such deterrence might be very costly. Stopping all antitrust violations would not be optimal deterrence if the cost of enforcement outweighed the harm from violations, particularly if the underlying conduct had procompetitive as well as anticompetitive effects. In addition, a system of private enforcement in which the enforcers are rewarded through multiple damages can create perverse incentives with unintended side effects.[16] A competitor as an antitrust plaintiff has been singled out for special criticism because the competitor has natural incentives to use any law (including the antitrust laws) to disadvantage a rival, even if the rival's conduct benefits competition and consumers.

These claims that private enforcement leads to overdeterrence have been directed mainly at private treble damage suits. Some have also criticized private suits seeking injunctive relief, such as a suit to enjoin a merger.[17] But overdeterrence is less likely if a suit seeks only injunctive relief because the absence of a possible multiple damage recovery reduces potentially perverse incentives. The lack of a damage recovery upon which to base attorneys fees means that such suits are less attractive to both plaintiffs and the bar. Suits in which the relief is limited to injunctive relief are more likely to be sparked by a threat of injury to the plaintiff's business. Of course, an injured competitor might still find it advantageous to seek to enjoin a rival's procompetitive conduct.[18] But a party's ability to delay the merging parties will depend on the strength of its case on the merits and whether the legal objections go to the core market involved in the merger or merely to tangential markets (for which narrowly tailored relief can easily be crafted).[19] If a plaintiff's only

13. For two influential articles criticizing private damage suits; see Breit & Elzinga, *Private Antitrust Enforcement: The New Learning*, 28 J.L. & Econ. 405 (1985) (hereinafter *Private Enforcement*); Breit & Elzinga, *Antitrust Enforcement and Economic Efficiency: The Uneasy Case for Treble Damages*, 17 J.L. & Econ. 329 (1974).

14. Austin, *Negative Effects of Treble Damage Actions: Reflections on the New Antitrust Strategy*, 1978 Duke L.J. 1353, 1372.

15. *Private Enforcement*, supra note 13, at 405–406 (summarizing some of the criticism of private enforcement).

16. Id. at 407–13.

17. Easterbrook & Fischel, *Antitrust Suits by Targets of Tender Offers*, 80 Mich. L. Rev. 1155 (1982).

18. Id. at 1169.

19. Brodley, *Antitrust Standing in Private Merger Cases: Reconciling Private Incentives and Public Enforcement Goals*, 94 Mich. L. Rev. 1, 23–24 (1995).

legal objection to a merger of two food producers is that they would have a large market share in the production of garlic salt, and that product represents a small percentage of the sales of each of the merging firms, a spin off might be arranged to counter this legal objection. The major focus of criticism of private enforcement remains the trebling of damages, a remedy the Supreme Court identified as designed both to punish and deter and to "counterbalance" private enforcement difficulties.[20] Congress has been responsive to criticism of trebling when heard from groups deemed vulnerable, important, or influential. Thus, the treble damage remedy has been curtailed for cooperative research,[21] certain aspects of export trade[22] and for municipalities.[23] Although the debate about trebling is sometimes intense, a comprehensive study of the remedy suggests caution in voicing either unrestrained criticism or praise of the current system.[24]

Both the premises and the conclusions of critics of private enforcement have been strongly challenged.[25] Concern that selfish motives may lead to claims having an anticompetitive impact has waned as antitrust standing doctrines have limited the access of competitor plaintiffs to the courts.[26] Constraints on how damages may be proved also reduce risk of overdeterrence. Even the premise that a treble damage recovery necessarily represents multiple damages, or even full compensation for the injured plaintiff, has been challenged. A plaintiff may be unable to prove the full extent of damages. Moreover, because prejudgment interest cannot be awarded for periods prior to the filing of the complaint, the plaintiff can receive no interest even if the defendant intentionally and successfully hid its conduct from the plaintiff for a long period of time. Some or all of the threefold damage award may be required to offset this loss. Also, the damage multiple should be sufficient to offset the plaintiff's risk of losing a meritorious claim based on evidentiary or procedural hurdles. Actual damages might not be a sufficient incentive for plaintiffs to file meritorious claims, given the risk of losing the law suit and the attendant costs associated with that unsuccessful claim.[27] Whether a treble damage remedy operates as a sufficient deterrent to

20. American Society of Mechanical Engineers v. Hydrolevel Corp., 456 U.S. 556, 575, 102 S.Ct. 1935, 72 L.Ed.2d 330 (1982). For review of proposals for detrebling, see Cavanagh, *Detrebling Antitrust Damages: An Idea Whose Time Has Come?*, 61 Tul. L. Rev. 777 (1987). But compare Lande, *Are Antitrust "Treble" Damages Really Single Damages?*, 54 Ohio St. L. J. 115 (1993).

21. The National Cooperative Research Act of 1984 is addressed in § 13.5.

22. The Export Trading Company Act of 1982 is addressed in § 14.3c.

23. The Local Government Antitrust Act of 1984 is addressed in § 14.3c.

24. See R. Pitofsky and S. Salop, *Forward* in Private antitrust Litigation: New Evidence, New Learning, note 11 supra, at xi.

25. Among the responsive literature is Lande, supra note 20, and Brodley, *Comment: Critical Factual Assumptions Underlying Public Policy*, in Private Litigation, supra note 11, at 252.

26. The possibility that antitrust standing doctrine unduly limits a competitor plaintiff's access to the courts is discussed in § 17.2b.

27. This point is developed in Brodley, *Comment*, supra note 25, at 255. For a discussion of the risk of detection and other variables that might affect the setting of an optimal antitrust penalty, see Breit & Elzinga, *Private Enforcement*, supra note 13, at 407–09.

antitrust violations has also been called into question.[28] To operate as an effective deterrent, a penalty for a violation must factor in the likelihood of detection. If, for example, there were only a one-in-four chance that a type of antitrust violation would be detected, each defendant caught might have to pay four times the profit gained from its illegal conduct in order adequately to deter future violations.

The case for private enforcement thus rests on twin goals: deterrence and compensation. Congress, both in 1890 and on more recent occasions, has seen compensation as a key goal of the enforcement scheme.[29] In 1976, Congress enacted Section 4C of the Clayton Act to allow state attorney generals to sue in *parens patriae* to obtain compensation for injured consumers.[30] Although Congress has enacted legislation limiting private suits challenging certain limited types of conduct or classes of defendants, Congress has never shown readiness to limit or discourage the private suit generally, nor has it wholly eliminated private suits in any area.[31]

The Supreme Court, too, has recognized that compensation and deterrence are both goals of private antitrust enforcement.[32] In *Blue Shield of Virginia v. McCready*, the Court described congressional intent underlying the private enforcement scheme as a design "that would deter violators and deprive them of the fruits of their illegal actions, and would provide ample compensation to the victims of antitrust violations * * *."[33] The Court said that, consistent with this congressional purpose, it had "refused to engraft artificial limitations on the Section 4 remedy," but rather had applied it "in accordance with its plain language and broad remedial and deterrent objectives."[34] In *Pfizer Inc. v. Government of India*, the Court extended the right to seek treble damages to foreign governments because of the enhanced deterrent effect of this broader class of plaintiffs.[35] In 2004, the Court offered a more limited reading of

---

28. Id. at 413.

29. See the discussion of the History of Private Enforcement in § 17.1.

30. Codified as 15 U.S.C.A. § 15(c) (1997).

31. For example, the Export Trading Company Act of 1982 preserves the right of an injured private party to sue an export trading company for actual damages and interest. 15 U.S.C.A. § 4016(b)(1). The National Cooperative Research Act of 1984 also allows suits for actual damages and interest from the date of injury. 15 U.S.C.A. § 4303(a). The Local Government Antitrust Act of 1984 bars private suits for damages, but leaves in place a private party's right to sue for an injunction. 15 U.S.C.A. §§ 35–36.

32. The Court has repeatedly acknowledged that deterrence is furthered by a dual system of enforcement that includes claims pursued by private attorneys general. See, e.g., Zenith Radio Corp. v. Hazeltine Re-

search, Inc., 395 U.S. 100, 130–31, 89 S.Ct. 1562, 23 L.Ed.2d 129 (1969), cited with approval in California v. American Stores Co., 495 U.S. 271, 284, 110 S.Ct. 1853, 109 L.Ed.2d 240 (1990); Illinois Brick Co. v. Illinois, 431 U.S. 720, 746, 97 S.Ct. 2061, 52 L.Ed.2d 707 (1977). Other cases are cited in Brodley, *Antitrust Standing in Private Merger Cases: Reconciling Private Incentives and Public Enforcement Goals*, supra note 19, at 12–13 & accompanying notes.

33. 457 U.S. 465, 472, 102 S.Ct. 2540, 73 L.Ed.2d 149 (1982).

34. Id. at 473.

35. 434 U.S. 308, 314–15, 98 S.Ct. 584, 54 L.Ed.2d 563 (1978). The Court also emphasized the importance of private enforcement in providing deterrence and compensation in Hanover Shoe, Inc. v. United Shoe Machinery Corp., 392 U.S. 481, 494, 88 S.Ct. 2224, 20 L.Ed.2d 1231 (1968). Relying in part on these dual goals of private enforcement, the Court refused to allow the

the role of private enforcement for non-U.S. plaintiffs in F. Hoffman–La Roche Ltd. v. Empagran S.A., holding that the U.S. courts lack subject matter jurisdiction over treble damage actions by persons who purchased abroad where the harm in the foreign market is independent of any harm in the U.S. market.[36]

17.1c. Comparing the Efficiencies of Private and Public Enforcement

Public enforcement enjoys certain efficiency advantages. Public enforcers are less likely to be motivated by the pocket-book motives that activate private plaintiffs. A public enforcer can fairly be assumed to be acting on the basis of its conception of the public interest in determining whether to bring an enforcement action. Public enforcement greatly reduces the risk that antitrust claims will be used for anticompetitive purposes and increases the likelihood that claims most helpful to the public will be pursued. But, as public choice theory suggests, public enforcers too have selfish motives. One of these is to bring cases that the agency will win, bolstering its record as an effective enforcer. Individual government attorneys who investigate cases also have a strong incentive to bring cases that can be won, thereby enhancing their chances for promotion or for outside employment offers. According to one researcher, the Antitrust Division tends to bring cases it can easily win, whether or not they have a significant economic impact.[37] Agency antitrust enforcement has also been criticized for its heavy reliance on regulatory decrees,[38] a shortcoming that, while not unique to public enforcement, may be exacerbated by a tendency for agency officials to seek regulatory relief as a way of declaring victory in cases in which structural relief is difficult to attain or implement. A private enforcer is more likely to seek a remedy of damages or injunctive relief that has a direct financial impact on the plaintiff or its operations.

As prosecutors, government agencies may enjoy some efficiency advantages, but also some key disadvantages. The Antitrust Division, for example, may have policy expertise and enforcement tools that enables it efficiently to investigate and prosecute antitrust cases. Still, it is unlikely that the Division will possess expertise in each and every industry involved in an antitrust investigation. Division attorneys must spend considerable time gaining that familiarity in order to reach sound prosecutorial decisions. By comparison, a competitor possesses industry expertise that might enable it quickly to discover a violation and knowledgeably to pursue an antitrust complaint. Although lacking the discov-

defendant to raise as a defense that the plaintiff had passed on monopoly overcharges to the plaintiff's customers. Id. See the discussion of *Hanover Shoe* in § 17.2c1.

36. 542 U.S. 155, 124 S.Ct. 2359, 159 L.Ed.2d 226 (2004). See the discussion of this case in § 18.2a4iii.

37. S. Weaver, Decision to Prosecute: Organization and Public Policy in the Anti-

trust Division 171–72 (1977). The innate caution of agencies may influence not only their decisions whether to prosecute, but also whether to pursue appeals of unsuccessful enforcement initiatives. It is possible, for example, that the paucity of government cases reaching the Supreme Court is due in part to this agency bias.

38. See the discussion in § 16.2i.

ery tools available to the Division at the investigatory stage, the competitor may have less need of such tools because of its in-house expertise.

Perhaps the most important concern with relying on public enforcement is its limited availability. With limited resources, agency decisionmakers must pick and choose among many potentially meritorious cases to investigate or prosecute. The Department of Justice and FTC, although possessing far more resources than state or local enforcers, report spending two-thirds or more of their available resources on premerger review and enforcement during the 1990s.[39] During a merger wave, any shortage of resources available for enforcement will be most acutely felt in non-merger enforcement areas. A policy bias may also result in abandoning entire categories of antitrust violations to private initiative. During President Reagan's two terms, the Antitrust Division devoted almost all of its enforcement resources to two categories: merger enforcement and horizontal violations of Section 1 of the Sherman Act. Even in areas in which an agency is active, a policy bias may lead to eliminating certain cases. The Division's merger enforcement cases during the 1980s were said by critics not to have fully enforced the Division's own Merger Guidelines.[40] Private enforcement can operate in a complementary fashion, filling enforcement gaps that are left because government agencies lack the resources or motivation to pursue enforcement. Given the propensity of agencies to bring only cases they are confident of winning, or the possibility of an agency bias against enforcement, a private party should be allowed to mount a challenge against anticompetitive behavior, even if that behavior has already been cleared by an antitrust agency. In R.C. Bigelow, Inc. v. Unilever N.V., the Second Circuit reversed a district court judgment for the defendant and allowed the plaintiff to pursue an injunction action against a merger involving firms that would give them 84 percent of the herbal tea market in the United States.[41] The FTC had previously cleared this merger on the premise that entry into the herbal segment was easy, at least for other manufacturers selling other types of tea. The Second Circuit concluded that herbal tea was an appropriate relevant market for purposes of deciding the summary judgment motion.[42]

There are large categories of cases that public enforcers seldom bring, even if the chances of prevailing are great. For example, cases in which anticompetitive conduct primarily affects small businesses or franchisees are generally not pursued by federal or state enforcers,

---

39. Statement of Robert Pitofsky, Chairman, Federal Trade Commission, 64 ANTITRUST L.J. 756, 757 (1996).

40. Krattenmaker & Pitofsky, *Antitrust Merger Policy and the Reagan Administration*, 33 ANTITRUST BULL. 211 (1988) (evaluating the Reagan Administration's antitrust policies and finding a significant decrease in merger enforcement).

41. 867 F.2d 102 (2d Cir.), *cert. denied*, 493 U.S. 815, 110 S.Ct. 64, 107 L.Ed.2d 31 (1989).

42. Another case in which the Second Circuit allowed a private party to pursue injunctive relief against a merger previously cleared by the FTC is Consolidated Gold Fields PLC v. Minorco, S.A., 871 F.2d 252 (2d Cir.1989). See also California's successful challenge to a supermarket merger that the FTC had cleared with more modest relief in California v. American Stores Co., 495 U.S. 271, 110 S.Ct. 1853, 109 L.Ed.2d 240 (1990).

perhaps because the injured party is thought capable of protecting it's and the public's interest, or because the consumer injury is thought less substantial than in other cases available to government agencies. Thus, tie-ins, exclusive dealing, or maximum vertical price fixing may distort allocation and injure consumers, efficient suppliers and franchisees, who themselves may be viewed as a class of consumers. But such actions are generally not on the menu for public enforcers.

To summarize the policy debate, there are expressed concerns that private litigants have incentives that lead them to bring cases that stifle rather than enhance competition. This could discourage legitimate competitive conduct and generate anticompetitive results. At the same time, reliance on a dual private-public enforcement mechanism is as old as the Sherman Act and has been reaffirmed on numerous occasions by the Congress and the Supreme Court. This reliance is justified not only because the antitrust laws serve a goal of compensating injured parties, but also because effective deterrence requires incentives, resources and expertise that government enforcers may lack.

Concern with the possibility that private suits might overdeter has had substantial, probably too much, influence on the Supreme Court's antitrust jurisprudence of the past quarter century. In the next section, we examine a number of limitations, mostly judicially imposed, on a private party's antitrust claims. The most important of these limitations—requirements of antitrust standing and standards for summary disposition of antitrust cases—have greatly inhibited private enforcement.

§ 17.2 Causation, Antitrust Injury, Statutory Standing, Passing-on, and the Business and Property Concept: Limitations on Private Enforcement

Section 4 of the Clayton Act speaks in widely inclusive terms. Any "person," broadly defined, that is "injured in his business or property" from an antitrust violation is granted a cause of action.[1] A cause in fact requirement is implicit in this language, indeed, is a prerequisite under Article III of the Constitution.[2] But the courts, for a variety of reasons, have construed Section 4 much more narrowly than its language invites and the constitutional reach of federal judicial power allows. Judicial interpretations of Section 4 have been steered by a conscious or subconscious desire to mitigate damage problems, limit access to federal courts, facilitate early termination of complex litigation, assure that plaintiffs

---

§ 17.2

1. 15 U.S.C.A. § 15(a).

2. U.S. Const. art. III, § 2, cl. 1. See America West Airlines v. Burnley, 838 F.2d 1343, 1344 (D.C.Cir.1988), where the court held that to establish Article III standing a plaintiff must show: (1) personal injury; (2) fairly traceable to the defendant; and (3) likely to be redressed by the remedy sought.

While constitutional standing questions are not likely to arise in antitrust cases, they can be hypothesized. If a firm challenges a merger by two of its competitors asserting only that defendants would engage in supracompetitive oligopolistic pricing, the pleading would fail to show a constitutionally sufficient basis for standing to sue.

recover only when harmed by an aspect of defendants' conduct that is itself anticompetitive, and constrain efforts to trace the harmful consequences of unlawful conduct through chains of distribution.

Theoretically, the initial question beyond the constitutional scope of standing would be, what standing limits have the courts read into Section 4. Chronologically, also, the courts first talked in standing terms about the range of issues considered here. Nevertheless, other concepts, such as "antitrust injury" and "passing-on" have been developed and are now used as tests that are differentiated from standing requirements. In the subsections following the materials are organized not chronologically as they evolved, but so as to facilitate exposition, comprehension and criticism.

The antitrust injury requirement performs a function that was originally performed by standing requirements, but the Supreme Court may and many lower courts now regard these requirements as cumulative limitations on plaintiff's access to the federal courts. Antitrust injury is treated first in § 17.2a because, of the several limitations that courts have imposed, it is the one best related to antitrust policy and because, if the power of this relationship were fully understood, it could become the norm against which to evaluate other standing limitations. In § 17.2b limitations developed under the standing concept before an antitrust injury standard was articulated and that have persisted, perhaps unnecessarily, are discussed and criticized. In § 17.2c the "passing on" or "indirect purchaser doctrine" is described and evaluated. Lastly, § 17.2d discusses "injury to business or property" as a possible limitation.

17.2a. Antitrust Injury

17.2a1. Development of the Antitrust Injury Concept

Section 4 of the Clayton Act allows any person "who shall be injured in his business or property by reason of anything forbidden in the antitrust laws" to sue for treble damages. This language could be read as merely restating the Article III standing requirement: the claimant must show actual injury and causation between that injury and the defendant's alleged illegal conduct. But the Supreme Court has read more into the language of Section 4. In 1978, the high point for private antitrust claims,[3] the Court held that Section 4 requires that a plaintiff establish *antitrust* injury—"injury of the type the antitrust laws were intended to prevent and that flows from that which makes defendants' acts unlawful."[4] In Brunswick Corp. v. Pueblo Bowl–O–Mat, Inc., the owners of three bowling alleys alleged that they suffered damage because defendant unlawfully acquired several competing bowling centers that, but for

---

3. S. Salop and L. White, *Private Antitrust Litigation: An Introduction and Framework, in* PRIVATE ANTITRUST LITIGATION, NEW EVIDENCE, NEW LEARNING, 1 (L. White, ed. 1988).

4. Brunswick Corp. v. Pueblo Bowl–O–Mat, Inc., 429 U.S. 477, 489, 97 S.Ct. 690, 50 L.Ed.2d 701 (1977).

the acquisitions, would have failed. The alleged injury was from the maintenance of competition, not from the loss of competition.

The plaintiffs satisfied the constitutional standing requirement. There seems little doubt that plaintiffs were alleging an injury in fact, and that the injury flowed from the allegedly illegal acquisitions. But the Supreme Court erected an antitrust injury requirement that bars recovery for an antitrust claim in which the plaintiff's injury does not flow from something that the antitrust laws were designed to prevent. Some antitrust violations result in competitive benefits as well as competitive harms. They are unlawful not because of the benefits but because the competitive harms outweigh the benefits. Thus, even assuming that the Brunswick company's acquisition of the bowling alleys was unlawful, the antitrust laws were not designed to prevent such competition as might flow therefrom. Had the plaintiffs alleged that the acquisitions gave the combined entity market power that would be exercised in a manner to suppress competition—say, for example, through strategic behavior that would have blocked plaintiff's access to customers or suppliers—the antitrust standing requirement set forth in *Brunswick* would have been met.

The *Brunswick* holding was not dictated by express language of Section 4. If one were concerned only about deterrence, the plaintiffs arguably should have been accorded standing, thereby raising the cost of unlawful mergers. Of course, once granted standing, a plaintiff would still have to prove that the merger was unlawful. But *Brunswick* was decided against a backdrop of concern with the burgeoning number of private suits. Standing concepts had been used before in efforts to limit claims by those least suitable to make them.[5] But these earlier efforts were less directly related to antitrust policy. Although even the antitrust injury requirement may not reflect statutory intent, limiting the class of plaintiffs to those whose injury is directly linked to the anticompetitive effects of illegal conduct is defensible as public policy. The Court seemed troubled by the possibility that the plaintiffs, in pursuing their claim, revealed an incentive to suppress acquisitions that could have net procompetitive effects. The Court did not directly address the possibility that the challenged acquisitions were truly anticompetitive and would harm consumers. Note, however, that this was not a suit to enjoin a merger. The Court correctly focused its attention on plaintiff's claims for treble damage relief. Assuming that the acquisitions were likely to have ill effects on the consuming public, those effects would not be directly redressed by granting multiple damages to the plaintiffs while leaving the acquisition untouched.

Because of its prophylactic design, Section 7 may not be well-suited for private damage claims. Even a meritorious claim of injury based on the merged firm's ability to engage in anticompetitive behavior will present problems, particularly when the anticompetitive injury is incipi-

---

5. See § 17.2d.

ent.[6] A smaller rival that is deterred from taking a competitive initiative because of a fear that it would be punished by the merged firm possessing market power will have only a hypothetical gain from an untried competitive initiative as a basis for damage relief. Even after an anticompetitive injury has occurred, the injured firm may have difficulty establishing a Section 7 damage claim. If the smaller rival begins discounting and the merged firm responds by making targeted price reductions aimed at the smaller firm's customers, the small firm can claim damages under Section 7—arguing that the harmful price reductions would not have occurred but for the market power obtained in the merger. But the statute of limitations on challenges to the merger may have tolled, and even if it has not, the plaintiff will be confronted with causation difficulties. The merged firm could argue that its allegedly unlawful actions were at worst a result of its predatory pricing behavior—conduct that would be antitrust vulnerable only if defendant possessed or threatened by its conduct to obtain monopoly power, not the result of the merger that occurred in the past, perhaps long before the predatory foray. Proving predation in violation of the Sherman Act may, of course, be far more difficult than establishing a violation of the incipiency standard of Section 7.[7]

The awkwardness of Section 7 as a basis for damage recovery tends to support the outcome in *Brunswick*, but these considerations do not apply if the private plaintiff seeks injunctive relief to block a merger before it is consummated. In Cargill Inc. v. Monfort of Colorado, Inc.,[8] nine years after deciding *Brunswick,* a divided Court chose to extend the antitrust injury requirement to Section 16 suits for injunctive relief. Section 16 authorizes suits for injunctive relief by any person who faces "threatened loss or damage by a violation of the antitrust laws."[9] As in the case of Section 4, the injunction provision does not expressly require antitrust injury, only a threatened loss causally linked to a violation of the antitrust laws (the same standard imposed by article III of the Constitution). The Court opted for a parallel interpretation of the two provisions, finding that it would be anomalous to allow "a private plaintiff to secure an injunction against a threatened injury for which he would not be entitled to compensation if the injury actually occurred." The Court saw the injunction and damage provisions as "complementary remedies."[10]

In *Cargill,* both of the lower courts had concluded that *Brunswick's* antitrust injury requirement applied to suits for injunctive relief, but

6. In cases arising before the antitrust injury doctrine had evolved, some lower courts debated whether Section 7 afforded a private remedy at all. See Isidor Weinstein Inv. Co. v. Hearst Corp., 303 F.Supp. 646 (N.D.Cal.1969); Bailey's Bakery Ltd. v. Continental Baking Co., 235 F.Supp. 705 (D.Hawai'i 1964), *aff'd per curiam*, 401 F.2d 182 (9th Cir.1968), *cert. denied*, 393 U.S. 1086, 89 S.Ct. 874, 21 L.Ed.2d 779 (1969) (no private action to enforce Section

7). Other courts, however, rejected that view. See e.g., Gottesman v. General Motors Corp., 414 F.2d 956 (2d Cir.1969).

7. See the discussion of predation in Chapter IV.

8. 479 U.S. 104, 107 S.Ct. 484, 93 L.Ed.2d 427 (1986).

9. 15 U.S.C.A. § 26.

10. *Cargill*, 479 U.S. at 112–13.

both also agreed that threatened antitrust injury was shown, and that the merger was likely to violate Section 7 of the Clayton Act. Monfort, the plaintiff in *Cargill*, owned and operated three integrated beef packing plants (integrated plants both slaughtered cattle and fabricated the beef for resale). It challenged the acquisition of the third largest by the second largest integrated beef packaging company. The plaintiff alleged that the acquisition violated Section 7 of the Clayton Act by impairing plaintiff's ability to compete both in buying cattle and in selling fabricated beef in the downstream market because defendant, to gain more market share at the expense of smaller rivals, "would bid up the price it would pay for cattle, and reduce the price at which it sold boxed beef," a "price-cost-squeeze" that would reduce its own profits, but eventually force smaller competitors from the market, after which defendant would recoup.[11] The district court agreed that threatened injury was shown and enjoined the acquisition. The Tenth Circuit affirmed. The Supreme Court overturned this holding. It ruled that the "kind of conduct * * * [alleged], competition for increased market share, is not activity forbidden by the antitrust laws." Hence, the plaintiff had failed to establish threatened antitrust injury.[12]

Extension of the antitrust injury requirement to Section 16 may satisfy a desire for consistency and simplicity of analysis. But this goal of uniformity is achieved at the expense of Section 7's design to protect against future (incipient) injury to competition. Although some of the jurisprudence of the 1960s and 70s that barred even minor increases of concentration in relatively unconcentrated industries has been discredited, there is no indication in the *Cargill* record that the Court considered or disagreed with the lower courts' holding that the combination of the second and third largest firms in the beef packing industry violated Section 7. Instead, the Court held that the plaintiff's theory of injury—through a price squeeze executed with the combined firm's market power—did not satisfy the antitrust injury requirement.[13]

The majority opinion can be read, as the dissent read it, as a requirement that the plaintiff establish a violation of the Sherman Act as a prerequisite for enjoining a merger. Construed in this manner, the holding is difficult to defend. The best that can be said in its favor is that in reaching the result it did the majority rejected the manifestly worse one that, as an *amicus* in *Cargill*, the Reagan Administration Department of Justice urged it to adopt: a *per se* denial of any competitor's standing to challenge any merger. Firms in a concentrated industry often exercise market power through concerted or parallel oligopolistic behavior, usually limiting output while raising or sustaining prices above a competitive level. Such oligopolistic behavior is more likely when one or two firms enjoy a position of power that allows them to punish smaller rivals who do not follow the larger firms' price leadership. Follow-the-leader pricing is not, by itself, a violation of Section 1 of the

11. Id. at 114.

12. Id. at 116–17.

13. Id. at 122.

Sherman Act as that Section is currently interpreted. But Section 7 has long been viewed as a tool that can stop these oligopolistic concentrations before they occur. The legislative history of Section 7, the jurisprudence of the Supreme Court, and the Merger Guidelines of the Antitrust Division and FTC all support a construction of that Section as a tool for preventing the creation of oligopolistic conditions.[14] If the federal agencies can enjoin a merger that produces oligopolistic concentration, but a private party cannot, the Court has created, as Justice Stevens said in dissent, a double standard for interpretations of Section 7.[15]

A more plausible reading of *Cargill* would still allow a plaintiff to plead antitrust injury from a merger that creates market power in an oligopoly. One way in which an oligopolistic industry might injure the plaintiff is through predation. The *Cargill* holding expressly left room for a plaintiff to challenge a merger based on likely predatory behavior by the combined firm—for example, cutting prices below average variable cost. But the *Cargill* plaintiff did not allege that such predation would occur, and the Court expressed skepticism that the required evidentiary showing could be made. Given the current hostility to price predation claims,[16] this opening may be meaningless in most merger cases. However, a merger-injunction plaintiff may still be able satisfy the antitrust injury requirement without alleging predation. A plaintiff might allege, for example, that the merged firm would gain market power enabling it to take strategic action, short of predation, that would injure competition. It is with respect to such non-predatory strategic conduct that the Court's holding seems most problematic.

In *Cargill*, the Court characterized the plaintiff's position as hinging on a likely price-cost squeeze designed to undermine the plaintiff's business.[17] Such a price-cost squeeze could indeed be a strategic tool to enforce a scheme of oligopolistic pricing, deterring competitive initiatives by the plaintiff. The Court seemed willing to see this price-cost squeeze only through the prism provided by one theoretical model (a model that regards oligopolistic pricing as benefitting all competing firms by providing an umbrella that shields high prices from competition). The problem with this model (aside from ignoring the clear consumer injury apparent from dynamic analysis of such pricing) is that oligopolistic price coordination will injure the plaintiff as a competitor because it now must act subserviently to the market leaders, accepting the price and market share that they are willing to allow. The Chicago theory response—that the smaller competitor plaintiff is protected by large firm power—is the very response that the defendants seek (and that Section 7 is designed to forestall): supracompetitive pricing through coordinated, cartel-like prices. True, a smaller plaintiff could be challenging a merger not out of fear of oligopoly pricing enforced by implicit threats of predation or a price squeeze, but because the merger yielded cost cutting efficiencies

14. See the discussion of Section 7 merger standards in § 11.2.

15. *Cargill,* 479 U.S. at 128–29 (Stevens, J., dissenting).

16. See § 4.1c.

17. *Cargill,* 479 U.S. at 118–19.

that the plaintiff could not match. But this issue can and should be resolved on the merits, as it would be if one of the enforcement agencies challenged the merger. If the merger yields efficiencies not attainable in less restrictive ways and these more than offset the threatened harm, the merger will be lawful.

The Court's failure in *Cargill* to recognize the potential injury from strategic scenarios in oligopolistic markets is troublesome. Still, the Court seems not to have wholly rejected strategic conduct as a basis for showing threatened antitrust injury. Had the plaintiff focused not on lost profits from a price cost initiative, but on its loss of independence needed to carry out competitive initiatives, it might have fared better. A line of cases in the Second Circuit, and scattered decisions in other circuits, suggests that plaintiffs that focus on the loss of competitive independence can be successful.[18] But other courts appear to read *Cargill* broadly, as a more comprehensive bar to competitor injunction suits.[19]

The Supreme Court addressed the issue of antitrust injury again in Atlantic Richfield Co. v. USA Petroleum Co.[20] Here, the plaintiff, a competitor, claimed injury based on Atlantic Richfield's maximum vertical price fixing agreement, at the time a *per se* violation of Section 1 of the Sherman Act, because it limited dealers' ability to raise retail gasoline prices. The plaintiff reasoned that, absent the agreement, Atlantic Richfield dealers could have raised their prices, placing less competitive pressure on plaintiff's retailers. As the Court stated, a "competitor is not injured by the *anticompetitive* effects of vertical maximum price-fixing * * * and does not have any incentive to vindicate the legitimate interests of a rival's dealer * * *." The Court concluded that a competitor would not have the proper incentives to protect the rights of Atlantic Richfield's dealers or consumers, either of whom the Court saw as potential plaintiffs with better antitrust credentials.[21] Maximum vertical price fixing is conduct associated with market power in the upstream seller exercised over the downstream reseller. Any allocative injury associated with maximum vertical price fixing, as the Court suggested, is likely to be associated with the seller-reseller relationship.[22] Thus, a suit brought by the seller's rival on a *per se* theory may seem an ill-suited vehicle to vindicate the alleged wrong.

---

18. Consolidated Gold Fields PLC v. Minorco, S.A., 871 F.2d 252, 258 (2d Cir.1989) (holding that a target company has standing to challenge a takeover by a rival because the target would lose "the power of independent decision-making as to price and output.") See also, R.C. Bigelow, Inc. v. Unilever N.V., 867 F.2d 102 (2d Cir.), *cert. denied sub nom.*, Thomas J. Lipton, Inc. v. R.C. Bigelow, Inc., 493 U.S. 815, 110 S.Ct. 64, 107 L.Ed.2d 31 (1989).

19. See e.g., Alberta Gas Chemicals Ltd. v. E.I. Du Pont De Nemours & Co., 826 F.2d 1235 (3d Cir.1987), *cert. denied*, 486 U.S. 1059, 108 S.Ct. 2830, 100 L.Ed.2d 930 (1988); Phototron Corp. v. Eastman Kodak

Co., 842 F.2d 95 (5th Cir.), *cert. denied*, 486 U.S. 1023, 108 S.Ct. 1996, 100 L.Ed.2d 228 (1988).

20. 495 U.S. 328, 110 S.Ct. 1884, 109 L.Ed.2d 333 (1990).

21. Id. at 345. Plaintiff's theory was that as the low cost marketer it was deprived of the fruits of its efficiency by defendant's strategy of getting its product to consumers at prices comparable to plaintiff's by unlawfully squeezing its own dealers.

22. See the discussion of vertical maximum price fixing in §§ 8.7, 8.9f.

17.2a2. Antitrust Injury and Incentive Incompatibility

Brunswick and *Atlantic Richfield* both stress the plaintiff's incentive incompatibility in holding that antitrust injury is not established. Although not focusing on incentive incompatibility, *Cargill,* too, could be seen as a holding that the plaintiff had incentives incompatible with the antitrust laws.[23] But an antitrust standing analysis cannot focus exclusively on incentive incompatibility. In many instances, plaintiffs may have a variety of incentives, some of them consistent, some of them inconsistent with the purposes of the antitrust laws. For example, a competing firm suing to enjoin an allegedly unlawful merger may fear the greater efficiencies generated by the merged entity. A fear of increased competition from a more efficient rival is an incentive inconsistent with the purposes of antitrust law. But it is quite possible that the same merger that generates efficiencies also generates market power. A plaintiff may quite logically fear that the market power will be exercised strategically to punish or deter a rival firm from exercising competitive initiative. Accordingly, the rival firm bringing suit to enjoin the merger may have mixed motives: some that are consistent, but others that are inconsistent, with the purposes of the antitrust laws. In such an instance, use of the antitrust injury requirement to dismiss the plaintiff's suit at the pleading stage is an unsatisfactory result. Many claimants with mixed motives may be knowledgeable, capable plaintiffs, able to efficiently prosecute antitrust violations. Incentive incompatibility ought to be determinative of antitrust injury only when a particular remedy sought by the plaintiff is consistent *solely* with an anticompetitive result, as at least arguably was the case in *Brunswick* and *Atlantic Richfield*. A better rule would be that a claim would be dismissed only if the plaintiff could have no credible and substantial procompetitive incentive.

17.2b. Antitrust Causation and Target Area Limitations

Well before it announced the antitrust injury requirement in *Brunswick*, courts held antitrust plaintiffs to more restrictive standing requirements than those implicit in Article III of the Constitution. As early as 1910 one court of appeals applied a fairly stringent test.[24] By the late 1950s courts often denied standing to parties whose loss was derivative where, for example, plaintiff qualified as an antitrust victim as a supplier,[25] landlord,[26] creditor,[27] franchisor,[28] employee[29] or stockholder.[30] Zenith

---

23. Brodley suggests that *Cargill* should be viewed as an incentive incompatibility case. Brodley, *Antitrust Standing in Private Merger Cases Reconciling Private Incentives and Public Enforcement Goals,,* 94 MICH. L. REV. 1, at 20–21 (1995).

24. Loeb v. Eastman Kodak Co., 183 Fed. 704 (3d Cir.1910).

25. Volasco Products Co. v. Lloyd A. Fry Roofing Co., 308 F.2d 383, 393–95 (6th Cir. 1962), cert. denied, 372 U.S. 907, 83 S.Ct. 721, 9 L.Ed.2d 717 (1963). But see South Carolina Council of Milk Producers, Inc. v.

Newton, 360 F.2d 414 (4th Cir.), *cert. denied*, 385 U.S. 934, 87 S.Ct. 295, 17 L.Ed.2d 215 (1966); Karseal Corp. v. Richfield Oil Corp., 221 F.2d 358 (9th Cir.1955).

26. Harrison v. Paramount Pictures, Inc., 115 F.Supp. 312 (E.D.Pa.1953), *aff'd per curiam*, 211 F.2d 405 (3d Cir.), *cert. denied*, 348 U.S. 828, 75 S.Ct. 45, 99 L.Ed. 653 (1954). But see Congress Bldg. Corp. v. Loew's, Inc., 246 F.2d 587 (7th Cir.1957).

27. Martens v. Barrett, 245 F.2d 844, 846 (5th Cir.1957).

Radio Corp. v. Hazeltine Research, Inc. required the plaintiff to establish that an antitrust violation be a "material cause" of the plaintiff's injury.[31] In *Hawaii v. Standard Oil Co. of California,* the Supreme Court in dicta suggested that antitrust causation requirements may be stricter than those flowing from Article III. The Court said that "lower courts have been virtually unanimous in concluding that Congress did not intend the antitrust laws to provide a remedy in damages for all injuries that might conceivably be traced to an antitrust violation."[32] Although perhaps signaling the Court's general view of antitrust standing, this dicta did not clarify the causation test in *Zenith.*

In searching for a suitable articulation of standing or causation the lower courts tried a number of formulas, including requiring that the injury to plaintiff must be direct, not indirect;[33] that the antitrust violation must be the proximate cause of the injury;[34] or that the plaintiff must have been within the "target area" that defendant "aimed at" or intended to hit.[35] Once the Supreme Court rejected a requirement that the private plaintiff show "public injury" as a standing requirement,[36] lower federal courts began using standing requirements as a sort of coarse-grained sieve to limit the number of private suits, on grounds which have a less satisfactory rationale than did the public injury test. The *antitrust injury* requirement announced in *Brunswick* has lessened the pressure to rely on these awkward causation requirements. Still, they have not disappeared.

In Blue Shield of Virginia v. McCready, a health insurance subscriber who had hired a psychologist alleged that her insurer had conspired with psychiatrists to exclude psychologists from the policy's coverage.[37] The defendant challenged her standing to bring the suit. A divided (5–4) Court upheld the plaintiff's standing. According to Justice Brennan's majority opinion, there were two relevant limitations on private suits under Section 4: (1) a risk of multiple recovery along with a subordinate

28. Nationwide Auto Appraiser Service, Inc. v. Association of Cas. & Sur. Companies, 382 F.2d 925 (10th Cir.1967); Billy Baxter, Inc. v. Coca–Cola Co., 431 F.2d 183, 187 (2d Cir.1970), *cert. denied,* 401 U.S. 923, 91 S.Ct. 877, 27 L.Ed.2d 826 (1971).

29. Reibert v. Atlantic Richfield Co., 471 F.2d 727 (10th Cir.), *cert. denied,* 411 U.S. 938, 93 S.Ct. 1900, 36 L.Ed.2d 399 (1973). Cf. Cordova v. Bache & Co., 321 F.Supp. 600 (S.D.N.Y.1970).

30. J. O. Pollack Co. v. L. G. Balfour Co., 1973–1 Trade Cas. (CCH) ¶ 74,339 (N.D. Ill. 1972). But see Kolb v. Chrysler Corp., 357 F.Supp. 504 (E.D.Wis.1973).

31. 395 U.S. 100, 114 n. 9, 89 S.Ct. 1562, 23 L.Ed.2d 129 (1969).

32. 405 U.S. 251, 263, 92 S.Ct. 885, 31 L.Ed.2d 184 (1972).

33. The first in this line of cases was Loeb v. Eastman Kodak Co., supra note 24.

34. Highland Supply Corp. v. Reynolds Metals Co., 327 F.2d 725, 732 (8th Cir. 1964).

35. E.g., Southern Concrete Co. v. United States Steel Corp., 535 F.2d 313 (5th Cir.1976); Calderone Enterprises v. United Artists Theatre Circuit, Inc., 454 F.2d 1292 (2d Cir.1971); South Carolina Council of Milk Producers, Inc. v. Newton, 360 F.2d 414, 418 (4th Cir.), *cert. denied,* 385 U.S. 934, 87 S.Ct. 295, 17 L.Ed.2d 215 (1966); Karseal Corp. v. Richfield Oil Corp., 221 F.2d 358, 362–64 (9th Cir.1955).

36. Radiant Burners, Inc. v. Peoples Gas Light & Coke Co., 364 U.S. 656, 81 S.Ct. 365, 5 L.Ed.2d 358 (1961); Klor's, Inc. v. Broadway–Hale Stores, Inc., 359 U.S. 207, 79 S.Ct. 705, 3 L.Ed.2d 741 (1959).

37. 457 U.S. 465, 102 S.Ct. 2540, 73 L.Ed.2d 149 (1982).

concern with the burdensomeness and complexity of determining damages; and (2) "the conceptually more difficult question 'of which persons have sustained injuries *too remote* * * * to give them standing to sue.' "[38] The Court found that neither of these limitations should foreclose the plaintiff's suit against its health insurer.

The risk of multiple recovery has little to do with causation. Citing its earlier decisions in Hawaii v. Standard Oil Co. of California[39] and Illinois Brick Co. v. Illinois,[40] the *Blue Shield* Court concluded that the risk of multiple recovery present in those cases was not evident here. The Court similarly concluded that the concern with "speculative, abstract, or impractical damages" was not applicable to the insurance subscriber's suit.[41]

The Court devoted more discussion to the second limitation that it identified: concern about the remoteness of the injury. On this causation issue, the Court found itself balancing the "avowed breadth of the congressional purpose" behind Section 4 with the "potency of the remedy," implying a need "for some care in its application." The Court went on to compare the remoteness analysis it was using to one "employed traditionally by courts at common law with respect to the matter of 'proximate cause.' "[42] The Court said:

> In applying that elusive concept to this statutory action, we look (1) to the physical and economic nexus between the alleged violation and the harm to the plaintiff, and, (2) more particularly, to the relationship of the injury alleged with those forms of injury about which Congress was likely to have been concerned in making defendant's conduct unlawful and in providing a private remedy under § 4.[43]

The required "physical and economic nexus" between the alleged violation and plaintiff's harm was present here because "denying reimbursement to subscribers for the cost of treatment was the very means by which it is alleged that Blue Shield sought to achieve its illegal ends."[44] The requirement of a relationship between the injury and the concerns Congress had in mind seems to be a restatement of *Brunswick's* antitrust injury requirement, and the Court seems to have seen it as such, intending perhaps to integrate the antitrust standing and antitrust injury issues.[45] The plaintiff's denial of health insurance benefits, while not equivalent to a monopoly surcharge, often the target of an antitrust plaintiff's suit, was an equally legitimate antitrust injury that flowed from "that which makes defendants' acts unlawful."[46]

38. Id. at 474–76.

39. 405 U.S. 251, 92 S.Ct. 885, 31 L.Ed.2d 184 (1972).

40. 431 U.S. 720, 97 S.Ct. 2061, 52 L.Ed.2d 707 (1977).

41. *Blue Shield*, supra note 37, at 475 n. 11.

42. Id. at 478.

43. Id. at 478.

44. Id. at 478–79.

45. Id. at 482–84.

46. Id. at 484 (citing *Brunswick*, 429 U.S. 477, 488, 97 S.Ct. 690, 50 L.Ed.2d 701).

A year after deciding *Blue Shield*, the Court handed down another antitrust standing decision in Associated General Contractors of California, Inc. v. California State Council of Carpenters.[47] The Court held that a labor union lacked standing to allege an unlawful boycott by a defendant contractors association charged with coercing its members not to deal with union firms. Although the injury was indirect, it seems beyond dispute that the union and its members would be injured if the firms for which they worked lost business. But the Court was obviously addressing more than simply the bare-bones causation required for constitutional standing. The Court raised a variety of questions about the plaintiff's suit, noting that the nature of the injury suffered was unclear, that there would be problems in tracing and apportioning the damages, and that the labor union may have been a second-best plaintiff (the union firms subject to the alleged boycott being the more directly injured parties).[48]

The *Blue Shield* and *Associated General Contractors* cases provide something less than clear guidance on the nature of the causation that must be shown to establish antitrust standing. These decisions do suggest some of the factors that the Court will scrutinize in determining standing: (1) the risk of multiple damages; (2) the complexity of determining damages; (3) whether better situated private plaintiffs exist; and (4) whether the injury was of the sort that the antitrust laws were designed to deter or compensate. When all of these factors are lumped together, as occurred in *Associated General Contractors*, lower courts receive little guidance as to how much weight is to be accorded each factor or how to resolve a case in which the various factors point in different directions. Indeed, *Blue Shield* and *Associated General Contractors* leave some doubt about the continuing relevance of earlier lower court cases that denied standing to plaintiffs for derivative injuries. The amorphous nature of the Supreme Court's multi-factored standing requirements and seeming inconsistencies in many lower court holdings demonstrate the need for a more administrable standard. The antitrust injury requirement, standing alone, might well have resolved many of these cases. Over time, antitrust injury might best serve as the central and exclusive test for determining antitrust standing. This theory based test would lessen litigation over standing issues and, even were it to allow an occasional non-meritorious case to survive the standing screen applied in response to the pleading, the standing issue could be quickly resolved at the summary judgment stage.[49] Significant problems about damage complexity or risks of multiple recoveries now dealt with as standing issues might be handled under rules and instructions tailored to these issues rather than being lumped into an amorphous factor test under the rubric of standing.[50]

---

47. 459 U.S. 519, 103 S.Ct. 897, 74 L.Ed.2d 723 (1983).

48. Id. at 537–46.

49. See the discussion of summary judgment standards in § 17.3.

50. See the discussion of damage § 17.7a-b.

Movement toward clarifying the antitrust standing test has been thwarted by *Blue Shield* and *Associated General Contractors*. A few lower courts have attempted to articulate a single test by treating antitrust injury as one of a number of factors to be assessed in determining whether standing exists.[51] But under the guise of a single, unified test, this approach captures all of the capricious variability associated with the factors to be weighed under *Associated General Contractors*. Meanwhile, the bulk of the lower courts decisions appear to require that a plaintiff separately demonstrate both that it suffered antitrust injury and that its economic nexus to the defendant's violation fits into a category giving it standing.[52]

17.2c. Indirect Purchaser or Passing-on Doctrine

17.2c1. *The Rejection of Passing-on and Its Rationales*

Questions of proof of damage have long occupied courts trying private antitrust suits. These issues, discussed in § 17.7, have produced yet another standing requirement for plaintiffs who bring private antitrust suits. The issue is passing-on. When a direct purchaser must pay an anticompetitive surcharge to a monopolist or cartelist it may not absorb the loss; it may pass it on in the form of a higher resale price. For example, the buyer may be a fabricator, middleman, or retailer, who following a general custom in the industry to mark up inventory by a given percent, may simply raise its resale price to capture the full amount of the overcharge paid to the seller. If more than one reseller is involved in the distribution chain, such passing-on may continue down the chain until it is paid, at last, by the consumer. The Supreme Court has now dealt with two questions regarding passing-on: (1) whether a defendant may defend against a claim of an overcharge by showing that the plaintiff passed-on part or all of the overcharge to its customers; and (2) whether an indirect purchaser to whom the overcharge was passed may sue the defendant who initiated the overcharge and received its benefit. The Court, subject to qualification, has now answered both these questions in the negative.

---

51. See R.C. Dick Geothermal Corp. v. Thermogenics, Inc., 890 F.2d 139, 146 (9th Cir.1989); Ashmore v. Northeast Petroleum Div. Of Cargill, Inc., 843 F.Supp. 759 (D.Me.1994).

52. Balaklaw v. Lovell, 14 F.3d 793, 798 n. 9 (2d Cir.1994); In re Lower Lake Erie Iron Ore Antitrust Litig., 998 F.2d 1144 (3d Cir.), *cert. dismissed sub nom.*, Bessemer and Lake Erie R. Co. v. Republic Steel Corp., 510 U.S. 1021, 114 S.Ct. 625, 126 L.Ed.2d 589 (1993), and *cert. denied*, 510 U.S. 1091, 114 S.Ct. 921, 127 L.Ed.2d 215 (1994); Greater Rockford Energy & Technology Corp. v. Shell Oil Co., 998 F.2d 391, 395 (7th Cir.1993), *cert. denied*, 510 U.S. 1111, 114 S.Ct. 1054, 127 L.Ed.2d 375

(1994). Some courts treat antitrust injury as an essential element of antitrust standing: Hodges v. WSM, Inc., 26 F.3d 36, 37–38 (6th Cir.1994); Lovett v. General Motors Corp., 975 F.2d 518, 520 (8th Cir.1992); Thompson v. Metropolitan Multi–List, 934 F.2d 1566, 1571 (11th Cir.1991); Bell v. Dow Chem. Co. 847 F.2d 1179, 1182–83 (5th Cir.1988); Thompson Everett, Inc. v. National Cable Advertising, L.P., 850 F.Supp. 470, 476 (E.D.Va.1994). For a listing of additional lower court cases, see SECTION OF ANTITRUST LAW, AMERICAN BAR ASSOCIATION, PROVING ANTITRUST DAMAGES, LEGAL AND ECONOMIC ISSUES 6–8 & nn. 4–5 (1996).

The Court held early in this century that a plaintiff's passing-on was not a defense to an antitrust suit. In *Chattanooga Foundry & Pipe Works v. City of Atlanta*, the city-owned water utility had paid overcharges on pipe used for water distribution.[53] Justice Holmes wrote for the Court rejecting a contention that the city was not injured because it passed on the overcharge through the rate-base used to compute consumer water charges. Justice Holmes elaborated on this theme in Southern Pacific Co. v. Darnell–Taenzer Lumber Co., stressing the law's need to simplify the inevitably complex myriad interrelationships of a dynamic economy. As he put it, the "general tendency of the law, in regard to damages at least, is not to go beyond the first step."[54] It does not hold the defendant liable for all the remote radiations of its wrong because that is too complex a business for a court to undertake with skill and social profit.[55] The Holmes opinion notwithstanding, lower federal courts in the "oil jobber" or "middleman" cases were not hesitant to deny recovery to a first purchaser when the evidence that the overcharge was passed on was convincing.[56]

All of this is a prelude to Hanover Shoe, Inc. v. United Shoe Machinery Corp.[57] In *Hanover,* a shoe manufacturer brought a treble damage action against United, a manufacturer of shoe-making machinery, alleging that the United's policy of leasing fabricating machines and refusing to sell them, a policy already held to constitute unlawful monopolization under Section 2 of the Sherman Act, had increased the cost of Hanover's manufacturing operations. In defense, United urged that Hanover was not injured because Hanover passed these costs on to buyers in the form of higher prices for shoes. The defense was rejected by the lower courts, and the Supreme Court agreed.

In rejecting the pass-on defense, the Court gave an altered emphasis to the view earlier announced by Justice Holmes.[58] The Court was concerned, as Justice Holmes was, with the complexity of determining whether an overcharge was passed on. Determining a reseller's ability to pass on an overcharge, the Court noted, would require knowledge of the elasticity of demand: if a higher resale price would result in lower sales, the reseller's ability to pass on the overcharge would be limited.[59] But the Court also gave weight to an overriding social policy (in addition to the policy of making judicially manageable rules) to make the treble damage remedy an effective deterrent to antitrust violations. In the context of the case, the Court found that shoe manufacturers were the

---

53. 203 U.S. 390, 27 S.Ct. 65, 51 L.Ed. 241 (1906).

54. 245 U.S. 531, 533, 38 S.Ct. 186, 62 L.Ed. 451 (1918).

55. Id. at 533–34.

56. E.g., Clark Oil Co. v. Phillips Petroleum Co., 148 F.2d 580 (8th Cir.), *cert. denied*, 326 U.S. 734, 66 S.Ct. 42, 90 L.Ed. 437 (1945); Northwestern Oil Co. v. Socony–Vacuum Oil Co., 138 F.2d 967 (7th Cir.

1943), *cert. denied*, 321 U.S. 792, 64 S.Ct. 790, 88 L.Ed. 1081 (1944); Twin Ports Oil Co. v. Pure Oil Co., 119 F.2d 747 (8th Cir.), cert. denied, 314 U.S. 644, 62 S.Ct. 84, 86 L.Ed. 516 (1941).

57. 392 U.S. 481, 88 S.Ct. 2224, 20 L.Ed.2d 1231 (1968).

58. Id. at 491–93.

59. Id.

most likely plaintiffs; the possibility of a suit by purchasers of shoes, to whom the overcharge was allegedly passed, seemed remote.[60]

Hanover Shoe, then, expresses two pragmatic goals. One is simplifying the proof of damages and protecting the courts from an unmanageable morass of complexity. The other is easing the course of a likely plaintiff with a significant interest in challenging the violation. The Court did not discuss an additional concern soon to be expressed: that allowing a pass-on defense might increase the risk of multiple liability because the defendant would have to account to plaintiffs at two or more levels. The Court did acknowledge a possible exception to its holding that no pass-on defense would be heard. Where the first purchaser makes its resales on cost-plus contracts, the defendant's pass-on argument would still be entertained.[61]

17.2c2. *Illinois Brick and the Indirect Purchaser Doctrine*

Hanover Shoe did not decide the issue of an indirect purchaser's standing to sue.

The reasoning of *Hanover Shoe* led in conflicting directions. If the Court's primary concern was avoidance of complexity and simplified judicial administration, that suggested indirect purchasers should not be allowed to sue. On the other hand, if the Court gave greater emphasis to the goal of providing maximum deterrence and compensation through private suits, that goal would favor allowing indirect plaintiffs, or at least some of them, to sue.

The Court addressed the indirect purchaser issue in 1977, the year Brunswick v. Pueblo Bowl–O–Mat was decided and, perhaps not coincidentally, at a point in time in which private treble damage actions reached peak numbers. In Illinois Brick Co. v. Illinois,[62] the State of Illinois and 700 local governmental entities sued producers of concrete block for illegal price fixing. The plaintiffs were indirect purchasers because the concrete block was sold by its producers to masonry contractors, who submitted bids to general contractors for the masonry portion of construction projects. The general contractors bid for construction projects with buyers such as the plaintiffs. A divided Court held that, subject to possible exceptions, an indirect purchaser could not maintain a suit for damages against the antitrust violator.[63] Both sides agreed on the need for mutuality: if pass-on was not to be available to the defendant as a defense, an indirect purchaser should not be able to use pass-on offensively. The plaintiffs in *Illinois Brick*, joined by the Justice Department in an amicus brief, argued for a more limited construction of *Hanover Shoe* that would allow indirect purchasers to attempt to show that the overcharge had been passed on to them. The Court rejected this approach for two reasons: (1) allowing offensive but not defensive use of pass-on would create a heightened risk of multiple liability for defen-

---

60. Id. at 494.

61. Id. at 491–93.

62. 431 U.S. 720, 97 S.Ct. 2061, 52 L.Ed.2d 707 (1977).

63. Id. at 746.

dants; and (2) offensive use of pass-on, just as defensive use, was likely to complicate litigation substantially, making judicial administration difficult.

The second of these grounds was indeed a basis of the Court's decision in *Hanover Shoe*. But *Hanover* was also grounded in the need to ensure a treble damage plaintiff is available to deprive violators of "the fruits of their illegality."[64] Placing a new spin on its prior holding, the *Illinois Brick* Court saw the attainment of effective private enforcement as better served "by concentrating full recovery for the overcharge in the direct purchasers rather than by allowing every plaintiff potentially affected by the overcharge to sue only for the amount it could show was absorbed by it."[65] As the dissent notes, this conclusion is open to question if a direct purchaser, already reluctant to sue its suppliers, is able to pass on a substantial portion of the increase to its customers.[66] A challenge by a direct purchaser may also be less likely if the direct purchaser buys under most-favored-nation clauses that ensure that each buyer will be given the same terms as its competitors.

17.2c3. Criticism of Illinois Brick

The Court's decision in *Illinois Brick* provoked an immediate and vigorous response. In Congress, hearings were held in the House and Senate Judiciary Committees on legislation to remove the bar on indirect purchaser suits. The legislation was supported by state and federal enforcement officials, but vigorously opposed by business groups. No federal legislation was enacted, but more than 25 states now permit indirect purchaser suits under state antitrust law, either through express legislation or through judicial interpretation of a pre-existing statute.[67]

Illinois Brick has been questioned by a number of commentators[68] and defended by others.[69] A central theme of much of the criticism is

64. Id. at 733 (citing *Hanover Shoe*, 392 U.S. at 494).

65. Id. at 735.

66. Id. at 764 (Brennan J. dissenting).

67. Bunker's Glass Co. v. Lorillard Tobacco Co., 75 P.3d 99, 104 (Ariz. 2003)(holding that indirect purchaser suits are allowed under Arizona law and listing 25 other states and the District of Columbia as allowing such suits).

68. Hovenkamp, *The Indirect–Purchaser Rule and Cost–Plus Sales,* 103 HARV. L. REV. 1717, 1723–1731 (1990) (defending some aspects of the indirect purchaser rule but urging a broader exception for "cost plus" contracts). Baker, *Federalism and Futility: Hitting the Potholes on the Illinois Brick Road,* 17 ANTITRUST 14 (2002) (questioning indirect purchaser rule, describing inconsistencies and risks in state responses, and suggesting federal legislation to respond to these problems); Harris & Sulli-

van, *Passing on the Monopoly Overcharge: A Comprehensive Policy Analysis,* 128 U. PA. L. REV. 269, 303–309 (1979) (offering a theoretical and empirical critique of the rule and supporting legislation to overturn it).

69. Landes & Posner, *Should Indirect Purchasers Have Standing to Sue Under the Antitrust Laws? An Economic Analysis of the Rule of* Illinois Brick, 46 U. CHI. L. REV. 602 (1979). See also, Landes & Posner, *The Economics of Passing On: A Reply to Harris and Sullivan,* 128 U. PA. L. REV. 1274 (1980); Viton & Winston, *Passing on the Monopoly Overcharge: The Welfare Implications,* 129 U. PA. L. REV. 1516 (1981); Cooter, *Passing On the Monopoly Overcharge: A Further Comment on Economic Theory,* 129 U. PA. L. REV. 1523 (1981). For responses from critics of the indirect purchaser rule, see Harris & Sullivan, *Passing On The Monopoly Overcharge: A Response to Landes*

that a broadly imposed bar on indirect purchaser suits will prevent consumers, a key-protected group under the antitrust laws, from redress through private antitrust suits. In addition, because many direct purchasers are insufficiently damaged by overcharges, or are unwilling to bring a law suit against their suppliers, the deterrent effect of private antitrust enforcement will be undermined. In *Illinois Brick,* the Court partially conceded this point by recognizing two exceptions to the bar on indirect purchaser suits: (1) when the direct purchaser has a cost-plus contract with its resale customers or (2) when the direct purchaser is controlled by the antitrust violator.[70] Unfortunately, these exceptions capture only a small percentage of the cases in which a direct purchaser's incentive to sue is diminished.

There are many situations in which direct purchasers will have weak incentives. One of the problems with the Court's reasoning is its failure to recognize that marginal cost pricing is not common in real markets. Under a model of perfect competition high elasticity of demand is assumed; a firm would use marginal cost pricing, or pricing that responds directly to buyer proclivity not to purchase a product if the price is raised. If demand were elastic, the direct purchaser would be unable to pass along a substantial portion of the price increase (and would presumably have a substantial incentive to sue the direct purchaser). But marginal cost pricing is especially unlikely in most down stream markets selling to consumers. For many firms, setting a price may be based more on supply side inputs—how much did it cost the firm to make this product. Demand side considerations may be accounted for more subjectively, in part because businesses do not have access to a precisely drawn demand curve of the type the model of competition assumes.[71] In consumer goods markets sellers often use a conventional mark up over cost. These conventions are routinely followed unless some significant distortion (e.g. excessive inventory build up) compels an alternative pricing response.

If the direct purchaser's resale price is based more on supply than demand side considerations, a direct purchaser facing increased cost for an input may not decrease its margin of profit—indeed that margin may actually increase if the direct purchaser uses a standard percentage mark up in setting its resale price. For example, if the direct purchaser routinely sets its resale price at 50 percent above the purchase price, an increase in the direct purchaser's price from $1.00 to $1.20 will result in the resale price rising from $1.50 to $1.80; instead of earning $.50 on each item sold, the direct purchaser will now earn $.60 per item. Under these conditions, if there is some elasticity of demand, the direct purchaser will still suffer loss. But the loss will be measured not by decreased profit per item, but by the loss of sales. To carry forward the example, the direct purchaser might sell 100,000 units at its $1.50 resale

and Posner, 128 U. Pa. L. Rev. 1280 (1980); Harris & Sullivan, *More on Passing On: A Reply to Cooter and to Vinton and Winston,* 129 U. Pa. L. Rev. 1533 (1981).

70. 431 U.S. at 725–27.

71. Harris & Sullivan, supra note 68, at 303–309 and n.81.

price, generating a total net revenue of $50,000 (100,000 units x $.50 per unit mark up). At the higher resale price of $1.80, the direct purchaser may sell only 80,000 units, generating a total revenue of $48,000 (80,000 units x $.60 per unit mark up). In this example, the direct purchaser has suffered a $2000 loss in revenue based on sales that it could no longer make.

If the direct purchaser's damages are measured in terms of lost sales, the complexity of damage allocation raised as a concern in *Illinois Brick* disappears. The damage to the direct purchaser would account only for sales that were lost because of the antitrust violator's surcharge. On the other hand, the damage to indirect purchasers would be based upon sales that were made. The indirect purchaser would base its damage recovery on the surcharge actually paid to acquire the item. Because both lost sales (allocation injury) and the surcharge paid by actual purchasers (wealth transfer injury) are legitimate and severable components of antitrust injury,[72] there is no duplicative recovery.[73]

One could defend the loss to deterrence and compensation goals to the extent the Court's concerns with complexity and multiple liability are valid. But as the above illustration suggests, there is likely to be a broad spectrum of cases in which a calculation and allotment of damages is relatively straightforward.[74] In *Illinois Brick,* the Court took an inauspicious turn. Fortunately that mistake has been mitigated to some extent by state statutes and judicial interpretations authorizing suits under state antitrust law for overcharge passed on to downstream buyers.

17.2c4.   *Exceptions to the Indirect Purchaser Rule*

Despite its questionable policy tradeoff, the indirect purchaser doctrine of *Illinois Brick* is prevailing law in cases brought under the Sherman Act. The Supreme Court, however, has acknowledged two exceptions to the rule that indirect purchasers may not sue: (1) where the direct purchaser is assured of selling a fixed quantity regardless of price because of a cost-plus contract; and (2) where the direct purchaser is owned or controlled by a seller accused of an antitrust violation.[75] Both exceptions arise because the direct purchaser has little or no incentive to challenge anticompetitive overcharges.

The second exception, for direct purchasers owned or controlled by an antitrust violator, is relatively straightforward. For example, if an antitrust violator sells to a direct purchaser owned or controlled by the violator, or if the person acting as a "direct purchaser" is nothing more than an agent for the violator, the next purchaser in line can sue

---

72.   See the discussion of allocation injury and wealth transfer injury in § 2.3b.

73.   Similar arguments are developed in H. Hovenkamp, Federal Antitrust Policy, The Law of Competition and Its Practice § 16.5c (3d ed. 2005).

74.   See generally, Harris & Sullivan, supra note 68.

75.   *Illinois Brick,* 431 U.S. at 730–35.

notwithstanding the indirect purchaser rule.[76] But it is an exception that by its terms is unlikely to apply in more than a small number of cases. The exception more susceptible to broad construction is that for a cost-plus contract. If, for example, a direct purchaser routinely prices by adding a percentage to its own purchase price, the incentive for such a direct purchaser to sue the seller is reduced and, arguably, the policy behind the cost-plus exception is met. But such arguments have not been well received.

In recognizing the cost-plus exception, the Supreme Court suggested that to fit within the exception both the cost and the quantity to be resold must be fixed.[77] In In re Beef Industry Antitrust Litigation the Fifth Circuit recognized a rigid formula for pricing as being within the cost-plus contract exception,[78] but plaintiffs were unable on remand to establish that such a rigid formula was used.[79] In an *en banc* decision of the Seventh Circuit, the court applied the cost-plus exception to allow the State of Illinois to sue as *parens patriae* for natural gas consumers.[80] The defendant was Panhandle Eastern Pipeline, which sold gas to distributors who sold it to users. The court applied the cost plus exception to consumers because it concluded that the distributors would be allowed to recoup their higher costs through the regulated rate-setting mechanism and because it believed consumer demand for natural gas was highly inelastic. But this argument for the "functional equivalent" of a cost-plus exception was rejected by the Supreme Court in Kansas & Missouri v. UtiliCorp United.[81] The high Court indicated that the rate-setting mechanism would not necessarily result in the distributor being able to pass along its full cost increases through a rate increase, and even if pass-on occurred after a time lag, the distributor would still be damaged by the price squeeze that occurred in the interim. These potential injuries suggested the need to preserve the distributor's own cause of action and, as in *Illinois Brick,* avoid the complexities of apportionment that would occur if indirect purchasers were also allowed to sue. The Court's reasoning seems to offer little hope of a more realistic assessment of the need for indirect purchaser suits to protect consumer interests and maintain deterrence. Nor does the Court suggest

---

76. Florida Power Corp. v. Granlund, 78 F.R.D. 441 (M.D.Fla.1978); In re Mid–Atlantic Toyota Antitrust Litigation, 516 F.Supp. 1287, 1292 (D.Md.1981).

77. The Court said that in the case of a cost-plus contract, "the purchaser is insulated from any decrease in its sales as a result of attempting to pass-on the overcharge, because its customers are committed to buying a fixed quantity regardless of price. The effect of the overcharge is essentially determined in advance without reference to the interaction of supply and demand that complicates the determination of the general case." *Illinois Brick,* 431 U.S. at 731.

78. 600 F.2d 1148, 1165 (5th Cir.1979), *cert. denied,* 449 U.S. 905, 101 S.Ct. 280, 66 L.Ed.2d 137 (1980).

79. On remand, the plaintiff's claim was dismissed. In re Beef Industry Antitrust Litigation, 542 F.Supp. 1122 (N.D. Tex. 1982), *aff'd,* 710 F.2d 216 (5th Cir.1983), *cert. denied,* 465 U.S. 1052, 104 S.Ct. 1326, 79 L.Ed.2d 721 (1984).

80. Illinois ex rel. Hartigan v. Panhandle E. Pipe Line Co., 852 F.2d 891, 897–99 (7th Cir.1988)(en banc), *cert. denied,* 488 U.S. 986, 109 S.Ct. 543, 102 L.Ed.2d 573 (1988).

81. 497 U.S. 199, 218, 110 S.Ct. 2807, 111 L.Ed.2d 169 (1990).

any willingness to consider whether simple apportionment formulas (such as allowing the direct purchaser to sue for interim damages while allowing indirect purchasers to sue for damages incurred after rates are hiked) would abate concerns with the complexity of apportionment. In cases involving regulated utility rates, the task of apportioning damages should be relatively straightforward through a well-documented rate regulation process.

Although not addressed by the Court in *Illinois Brick*, there are two other limitations to the rule that indirect purchaser may not sue. The first is that it does not apply to suits for injunctive relief. *Illinois Brick's* concerns with complex damage allocation formulas and multiple liability have no relevance when the plaintiff seeks only injunctive relief. Although the plaintiff in an injunctive suit must demonstrate threatened injury, there is no need for a court to get involved in damage allocation formulas merely to make a finding of threatened injury. It has been rightly held that injunctive relief is available to the indirect purchaser.[82]

Illinois Brick should also not apply when a suit for damages is brought against both the seller and the direct purchaser, alleging that each violated the antitrust laws. For example, in the case of a vertical restraint, both the seller and the direct purchaser are commonly alleged to be part of the conspiracy. The person purchasing from the direct purchaser should not be barred from suing the original seller for damages. But so too should the downstream seller be subject to suit. Because the conspiracy involved both the original seller and the direct purchaser, a plaintiff should be allowed to seek joint or several recovery against the conspirators. A number of courts have essentially taken this approach.[83]

In many cases involving vertical restraints, the conspiracy between the seller and the downstream purchaser subject to the restraint may be more fictional than real. For example, if a seller imposes vertical maximum price fixing, any leverage lies with the upstream seller, not the downstream direct purchaser that is subject to the maximum price.[84] If the direct purchaser can be seen as a part of an unreasonable, and thus unlawful, vertical conspiracy, its participation is not likely to be voluntary. In contrast, many cases of vertical minimum price fixing involve powerful retailers who impose their will on the upstream seller.[85] Here the upstream seller may be an involuntary participant in the conspiracy. These realities may complicate the application of the rule against suits by indirect purchasers. The better result may be to allow suits challenging vertical restraints against either the upstream seller or the downstream direct purchaser, but to refine the manner in which damages are calculated. The Third Circuit has held that in a case charging vertical

82. Mid–West Paper Products Co. v. Continental Group, Inc., 596 F.2d 573 (3d Cir.1979).

83. Reiter v. Sonotone Corp., 486 F.Supp. 115 (D.Minn.1980); Dart Drug Corp. v. Corning Glass Works, 480 F.Supp. 1091 (D.Md.1979).

84. See the discussion of maximum vertical price fixing in § 8.7.

85. See the discussion of minimum vertical price fixing in § 7.4.

price fixing against an automobile distributor, the dealer could sue the distributor for lost profits (because the higher resale price forced upon the dealer may have lessened its sales) while the consumer could sue for overcharge.[86]

The broadest avenue for avoiding *Illinois Brick's* proscription on suits by indirect purchasers is in those states that, either through legislation or judicial interpretation, allow indirect purchaser suits under state antitrust law. An indirect purchaser who has no remedy under federal antitrust law may simply frame a complaint under parallel provisions of state antitrust law. In California v. ARC America, Corp., the states of Alabama, Arizona, California and Minnesota sued in federal court for treble damages based on an alleged conspiracy to fix cement prices.[87] The states sued under the Sherman Act and under their parallel state antitrust provisions. The defendants argued that the Sherman Act claims were barred under the indirect purchaser rule and that state provisions that authorized suits by indirect purchasers were preempted by the Sherman Act. A unanimous Supreme Court, disagreeing with the lower court opinions, found no preemption. Justice White, who wrote the opinion in *Illinois Brick,* concluded that preemption should not lightly be inferred in cases in which Congress has legislated in an area traditionally occupied by the states. As to the concern with undue complexity in damage apportionment, the Court noted that this burden will usually fall on the state courts. Federal courts, it noted, are free to exercise their discretion not to exercise pendant jurisdiction over such complicated state claims.[88]

All of this suggests that the issue of indirect purchaser suits has not ended with *Illinois Brick*. Indirect purchaser suits brought under state antitrust law may prove a useful laboratory for exploring apportionment formulas and other risks that the Court found so formidable in *Illinois Brick*. Over time, a uniform and balanced approach to indirect purchaser suits under federal and state law seems wise. But absent federal legislation, that goals seems distant.

17.2d. Injury to Business and Property

Section 4 of the Clayton Act allows damage suits only for injuries to "business or property" giving rise to another standing question. The issue most debated, whether households that paid a higher price for consumer goods, food, monies, clothing, etc., suffered a requisite injury was resolved in favor of the plaintiffs in Reiter v. Sonotone Corp.,[89] a hearing aid case. In light of *Illinois Brick*, decided two years earlier,[90] any fear that consumer standing would open a litigation floodgate seems misplaced. Consumers will have standing against cartels (or monopolists) that either deal directly with consumers (say, NASDAQ market-making

86. Link v. Mercedes–Benz of North America, Inc., 788 F.2d 918 (3d Cir.1986).

87. 490 U.S. 93, 109 S.Ct. 1661, 104 L.Ed.2d 86 (1989).

88. Id. at 94.

89. 442 U.S. 330, 99 S.Ct. 2326, 60 L.Ed.2d 931 (1979).

90. See the discussion in § 17.2c2.

brokers) or that conspire with downstream firms to keep consumer prices up. But manufacturers, by and large, and many others will be protected against consumer suits under federal antitrust law by *Illinois Brick*.[91]

§ 17.3 Standards for Summary Disposition

If a defendant is unable to dispose of a private suit through a motion to dismiss based on standing or jurisdictional issues, its next line of defense is usually a motion for summary judgment. The standard for summary judgment is set forth in Rule 56(c) of the Federal Rules of Civil Procedure: Judgment is warranted if, based on the pleadings, admissions, results of discovery, or any affidavits, there "is no genuine issue as to any material fact" and that the moving party is "entitled to judgment as a matter of law." On its face, the rule suggests a uniform standard applicable to all types of litigation. Yet, antitrust claims have sometimes received special treatment. For a period beginning in the early 1960s antitrust claimants were given a degree of special protection against adverse summary judgment. More recently, the pendulum has swung the other way, perhaps too far.

In Poller v. Columbia Broadcasting System, Inc., the Court said that "summary procedures should be used sparingly in complex antitrust litigation where motive and intent play leading roles, the proof is largely in the hands of the alleged conspirators, and hostile witnesses thicken the plot."[1] The Court went on to note that in a trial with witnesses present and subject to cross-examination, "their credibility and the weight to be given their testimony can be appraised."[2] In his dissent, Justice Harlan, who had defended corporate clients in business litigation before taking his seat, anticipated the rising concern with the potential for abuse in treble damage suits. To Harlan, this case was a "not unfamiliar" example of casting "injury resulting from normal business hazards * * * in antitrust terms" in order that the plaintiff might take advantage of the treble damage remedy.[3] This concern with perceived abuse was to color later Court decisions on standing and summary judgment.

The concerns that moved the Court in *Poller* seem real, but by no means unique to private antitrust claims. They might, for example, apply as well to business torts or securities law claims involving questions of intent. This logic would suggest that general summary judgment principles should continue to apply to antitrust claims at least unless the

---

91. Conceivably business property issues could be raised by non-profit educational and other charitable institutions charged with violations, but thus far these issues have not been raised. Cf. United States v. Brown University, 5 F.3d 658 (3d Cir.1993). See also Improving America's Schools Act § 568, Pub. L. No. 103–382, 108 Stat. 3518, 4060 (1994); Charitable Gift Annuities Antitrust Relief Act of 1995, Pub. L. No. 104–63, 109 Stat. 687, 688 (1995) (precluding antitrust liability for agreements between tax exempt charities for concertedly fixing certain annuity rates).

§ 17.3

1. 368 U.S. 464, 473, 82 S.Ct. 486, 7 L.Ed.2d 458 (1962).

2. Id.

3. Id. at 474.

claims raise complex issues involving motive and intent, a reading that found some support in the Court's 1968 language in First National Bank v. Cities Service Co.[4]

By the 1980s courts were searching for ways of clearing crowded dockets and avoiding time-consuming jury trials. The statistics suggest that the number and percentage of summary judgments in antitrust claims increased, reaching a level near that for other civil claims.[5] This trend may have accelerated in 1986 when the Supreme Court decided Matsushita Electric Industrial Co. Ltd. v. Zenith Radio Corp., which could be read as making some antitrust claims especially vulnerable to adverse summary judgment.[6] In this lengthy proceeding with a massive record, Japanese producers of television sets were accused of an antitrust conspiracy to keep prices high in the Japanese market in order to suppress export prices and gain market share in the United States. While some commentators labeled this theory preposterous or audacious,[7] others have found it highly credible,[8] including one theorist whose familiarity with Japanese business and government practices allowed him to marshal additional materials in support of the plaintiffs' theory.[9] In any event, the Court, perhaps desirous of ending this elephantine proceeding, reversed the Third Circuit and reinstated the district court's grant of summary judgment for the defendants.[10]

Much of Justice Powell's opinion in *Matsushita* is a restatement of pre-existing principles governing summary judgment. But the opinion went beyond this. Justice Powell wrote: "[I]f the factual context renders respondents' claim implausible—if the claim is one that simply makes no economic sense—respondents must come forward with more persuasive evidence to support their claim than would otherwise be necessary."[11] The Court proceeded to analyze the plaintiff's theory by measuring it against an economic paradigm of predatory pricing that finds such behavior illogical and, therefore, unlikely.[12] It was this use of a controverted, deductive economic theory as a means of determining plaintiffs' claims lacked credibility that has generated most of the controversy surrounding *Matsushita*. Deductive theory is based on assumed premises about how rationale people are likely to act in situations having specified

---

4. 391 U.S. 253, 289–90, 88 S.Ct. 1575, 20 L.Ed.2d 569 (1968)(declining to read broadly applicable summary judgment principles out of antitrust cases).

5. Calkins, *Summary Judgment, Motions to Dismiss, and Other Examples of Equilibrating Tendencies in the Antitrust System,* 74 Geo. L. J. 1065, 1120–22 (1986) [hereinafter *Equilibrating Tendencies*].

6. 475 U.S. 574, 106 S.Ct. 1348, 89 L.Ed.2d 538 (1986).

7. *Equilibrating Tendencies,* supra note 5 at 1124 (citing Areeda); Easterbrook, *The Limits of Antitrust,* 63 Texas L. Rev. 1, 26–27 (1984)(the theory "does not make sense").

8. S. Ross, Principles of Antitrust Law 167–70 (1993).

9. First, *An Antitrust Remedy For International Price Predation: Lessons From Zenith v. Matsushita,* 4 Pac. Rim L. J. 211 (1995).

10. For discussion of the predatory pricing aspects of *Matsushita,* see § 4.5. The case's implications for conspiracy theory are discussed in § 5.2b.

11. *Matsushita,* 475 U.S. at 587.

12. The Chicago model of predatory pricing used by the Court is discussed in § 4.1c.

characteristics. Assuming that the underlying preconditions for application of such a theory are in fact met in a particular situation, such a theory can be a strong predictor of how people in that situation may act. But deductive theory describes tendencies or likelihood; it does not describe what in fact happened in any given past situation. Where there is conflicting inductive evidence about what happened, there is no apparent reason why the deductive theory should be thought so overwhelming as to keep the issue from the jury. This seems particularly true on the facts in *Matsushita*. The deductive theory was predicated on a conventional individualistic, western, short-term profit-maximizing assumption. The situation involved was set in an eastern commercial culture where concerns for national welfare may outweigh impulses for personal advantage, where cooperative activity is encouraged and valued, and where a long-range, industry and nation-oriented perspective is pervasive.

The *Matsushita* plaintiff's economic expert had outlined a detailed story that, at least in the view of the court of appeals, was credible. Justice Powell wrote for the Court, however, that there was a "consensus among commentators" that predatory pricing schemes "are rarely tried, and even more rarely successful."[13] To reach this conclusion, the Court had first to discount the views of the plaintiff's economic expert. Justice Powell suggested that the plaintiff's "expert opinion evidence * * * has little probative value" in comparison to the deductive economic model of predatory pricing that the Court was accepting.[14] Justice Powell simply ignored the views of theorists who had raised questions about the narrow view of predatory pricing.[15] If a court may pick and choose among economic models to find one most suited to granting summary judgment, a great deal of arbitrary power is vested in a district judge who likely has limited economic expertise and, perhaps, considerable interest in clearing the docket. Certainly a court-preferred economic theory, even one that has consensus support among current economists, should not trump a sensible alternative theory that also has professional support and the support of inductive evidence.

For a period *Matsushita* was sometimes read not only as establishing a more generous standard for granting summary judgment in antitrust cases, but also as an endorsement of the Chicago school economic approach to antitrust issues. In Eastman Kodak Co. v. Image Technical Services, Inc., the Court pulled back from any such reading.[16] The plaintiff claimed that Kodak was guilty of attempted monopolization and an unlawful tie-in. Kodak argued that antitrust violations were implausi-

13. *Matsushita*, 475 U.S. at 589.

14. Id. at 594 n. 19.

15. The Court found consensus in the views of theorists associated with the Chicago School (Bork, Easterbrook, Koller, and McGee), 475 U.S. at 589–90, and in Areeda and Turner's seminal article on predatory pricing. Areeda & Turner, *Predatory Pricing and Related Practices Under Section 2*

of the Sherman Act, 88 HARV. L. REV. 697 (1975). The Court ignored the rich body of criticism and commentary generated by the original Areeda & Turner article. See the discussion in §§ 4.1c–1d.

16. 504 U.S. 451, 112 S.Ct. 2072, 119 L.Ed.2d 265 (1992).

ble because under its economic model (analogous to that accepted by the Court in *Matsushita*), Kodak's small market share in the original equipment market would conclusively establish the lack of market power. The plaintiffs countered by offering a theory, and pre-trial evidence to support the theory, that information problems created market leverage that was exploited by Kodak. On an abbreviated record, the district court granted summary judgment for the defendant. The Ninth Circuit reversed the district court and the Supreme Court affirmed.

Writing for a divided (6–3) Court, Justice Blackmun found that the plaintiffs had offered evidence in support of a credible economic theory. According to the Court, *Matsushita* meant only that if "the plaintiff's theory is economically senseless, no reasonable jury could find in its favor, and summary judgment should be granted."[17] The Court rightly paid no attention to whether the theory fit a particular economic paradigm—only whether it was advanced by reputable theorists and had evidentiary support. In dissent, Justice Scalia was willing to give credence to only one economic model, the one tendered in argument by *Kodak*, and drawing Chicago School academic support. He also expressed fear of a rush of litigation if the plaintiff's theory were credited.[18]

The result in *Kodak* may suggest a return to generally applicable principles for deciding summary judgment motions, rejecting both expansive and constrictive summary judgment standards in an antitrust context. But the issue has not come fully to rest. In Brooke Group Ltd. v. Brown & Williamson Tobacco Corp.,[19] a divided Court once again gave credence to a disputed economic theory. In this predatory pricing suit brought by the fifth largest tobacco manufacturer against the fourth largest firm, the Court concluded, as it had in *Matsushita*, that predation schemes are rarely successful, and even more rarely so when the alleged perpetrator has a small market share.[20]

Summary judgment was held appropriate notwithstanding plaintiff's readiness to offer credible alternative economic models. The Court found that the plaintiff's expert testimony was not supported by evidence in the record: "Expert testimony is useful as a guide to interpreting market facts, but it is not a substitute for them."[21] But as the dissent pointed out, the plaintiff's theory of predation was not devoid of factual support in the record.[22] Far less did it lack support in the academic literature. In a tight oligopoly displaying patterns of follow-the-leader pricing, a targeted predatory foray is a well recognized means for disciplining any firm that breaks the pricing discipline.[23] Its language notwithstanding, the *Brooke Group* majority appears unwilling to permit a model of predatory pricing that might allow the plaintiff to survive summary judgment. *Brooke* thus leans back toward the Court's imbalanced view of the economics of predatory pricing, but it does not suggest a return to

---

17. Id. at 468–69.

18. Id. at 489.

19. 509 U.S. 209, 113 S.Ct. 2578, 125 L.Ed.2d 168 (1993).

20. Id. at 226.

21. Id. at 242.

22. Id. at 253 (Stevens J., dissenting).

23. Id. at 223–24.

Matsushita's use of different standards for summary judgment in antitrust than in other cases. The *Brooke Group* Court rested, however disingenuously, on the failings of the plaintiff's factual support, not on the unacceptability of its economic theory.

The law governing summary judgment for antitrust claims will most comfortably and wisely come to rest when efforts to grant special treatment for antitrust claims are discarded and when the Court uses economic theory circumspectly, and refuses to allow a deductive theory, even one supported by a well-established consensus, to foreclose a jury from evaluating a rational alternative which is supported by evidence in the record. Unfortunately, Supreme Court decisions from *Poller* to *Brooke* show the Court willing to reinterpret the standard for summary judgment based upon the substance of the antitrust claim and the Court's receptiveness to particular economic views supported at the time of decision by a salient academic elite. In *Kodak*, the Court showed an appropriate reluctance to choose among contested economic theories, at least as a basis for cutting off trial of the issues.

§ 17.4   Interstate Commerce

A federal antitrust law claim must be based on conduct that is in interstate or foreign commerce, or that affects such commerce. The Sherman Act, applies to restraints of "trade or commerce among the several States, or with foreign nations" language that the Court has held exercises congressional power over commerce "to the utmost extent."[1] The limitation, being constitutional as well as statutory, applies both to private suits and enforcement action initiated by the Government. We address the issue in the context of private enforcement because, although a number of earlier Supreme Court interpretations of the interstate commerce requirement entail government enforcement, most recent challenges have involved private claims, perhaps because such claims are more numerous and somewhat more likely to focus on localized conduct.

In the first half century of federal antitrust law, the interstate commerce requirement was a formidable constraint on enforcement. In United States v. E.C. Knight Co.,[2] the Justice Department's 1895 challenge to acquisitions that gave the acquirer control over most U.S. sugar refining failed; the Court held that the acquired refineries, all of which were located in Pennsylvania, did not restrain interstate or foreign commerce but only manufacture, and that control of monopoly in manufacturing was left to the states.[3] Even in instances in which distribution (as opposed to manufacturing) of goods was at issue, courts were quick to invoke the interstate commerce requirement as grounds for rejecting application of the Sherman Act. For example, after the Supreme Court in

§ 17.4

1. United States v. South–Eastern Underwriters Ass'n, 322 U.S. 533, 558, 64 S.Ct. 1162, 88 L.Ed. 1440 (1944).

2. 156 U.S. 1, 15 S.Ct. 249, 39 L.Ed. 325 (1895).

3. Id. at 11.

1911 held a vertical price fixing arrangement contravened the Sherman Act,[4] courts could avoid the issue by declaring that a particular vertical price fixing agreement did not involve interstate commerce.[5]

These early precedents, based on a restrictive reading of the Congress' power to legislate involving interstate commerce,[6] in shadow since South Eastern Underwriters,[7] were expressly overturned by the Court's 1948 decision in Mandeville Island Farms, Inc. v. American Crystal Sugar Co.[8] That decision confirmed that the Sherman Act extended to the full reach of the Commerce Clause of the Constitution (the Sherman Act has a "correspondingly broad reach").[9]

As originally phrased, neither the Clayton Act nor the Robinson–Patman Act were construed to exercise the full scope of the commerce power. These Acts applied only to activities "in commerce." In 1975, the Supreme Court held that Section 7 of the Clayton Act, did not reach the acquisition of two janitorial service firms by a rival in the Southern California market.[10] A year earlier the Court placed a limiting construction on similar language in the Robinson–Patman Act.[11] Construction of similar language in the FTC Act would be controlled by these authorities. Congress, however, responded. The FTC Act was amended in 1975 to cover matters "in or affecting commerce."[12] In 1980 Congress also amended Section 7 of the Clayton Act to reach acquisitions involving firms "engaged in commerce or in any activity affecting commerce."[13]

Today, the reach of both Section 7 of Clayton Act and the FTC Act is comparable to the reach of the Sherman Act. Since the FTC, in applying Section 5 of the FTC Act, can challenge conduct of the kind targeted by the Robinson–Patman Act and by Section 3 as well as Section 7 of the Clayton Act, all of these provisions, when invoked by the FTC, reach conduct affecting as well as in commerce. Thus, Sherman Act jurisdictional decisions now have implication for the full range of the FTC's antitrust enforcement under Section 5 of the FTC Act.

Sherman Act jurisdictional interpretation did not remain static following *Mandeville Farms*. The Court in 1967 gave a broad reading to

4. Dr. Miles Medical Co. v. John D. Park & Sons Co., 220 U.S. 373, 31 S.Ct. 376, 55 L.Ed. 502 (1911).

5. Fisher Flouring Mills Co. v. Swanson, 137 P. 144 (Wash.1913)(four manufacturers' price fixing contract with retailers beyond the reach of the Sherman Act for lack of interstate commerce).

6. Article I, § 8, cl. 3 of the Constitution gives Congress the power to "regulate Commerce with foreign Nations, and among the several States, and with Indian Tribes."

7. United States v. South–Eastern Underwriters Ass'n, supra note 1.

8. 334 U.S. 219, 68 S.Ct. 996, 92 L.Ed. 1328 (1948).

9. Id. at 231–35.

10. United States v. American Building Maintenance Industries, 422 U.S. 271, 95 S.Ct. 2150, 45 L.Ed.2d 177 (1975).

11. Gulf Oil Corp. v. Copp Paving Co., 419 U.S. 186, 95 S.Ct. 392, 42 L.Ed.2d 378 (1974).

12. Consumer Goods Pricing Act of 1975, 89 Stat. 801, Pub. L. 94–145. The "affecting commerce" language is set forth in 15 U.S.C.A. § 45(a)(1).

13. Antitrust Procedural Improvements Act of 1980, 94 Stat.1154, Pub. L. 96–349. The legislative history of this Act makes clear the intent to extend the coverage of Section 7 to the full extent permitted by the Constitution. H.R. Rep. No. 96–871, 2 (1980).

the Sherman Act's jurisdictional reach in Burke v. Ford.[14] Oklahoma liquor dealers sued wholesalers alleged to have divided up the wholesale market in the state. Summarily reversing a lower court holding that the jurisdictional threshold of the Sherman Act had not been crossed, the Court reasoned that the territorial restraints produced higher prices and lower sales to retailers, and this in turn would have led to fewer wholesaler purchases of liquor from out-of-state suppliers. Again, in 1975, the Court concluded that the Sherman Act casts a broad net in Goldfarb v. Virginia State Bar,[15] a case challenging the conduct of the Virginia Bar in setting rates for title searches performed by lawyers. Although the lower court had concluded that a title search on property located in Virginia could "never substantially affect interstate commerce,"[16] the Supreme Court reasoned that the money for the purchase of Virginia homes within the District of Columbia metropolitan area could come from the District of Columbia or Maryland and that loans were frequently guaranteed by the Veterans Administration or HUD, federal agencies operating out of the District of Columbia. According to Chief Justice Burger, the absence of evidence showing that home buyers were deterred by the high prices of title searches did not demonstrate that interstate commerce was not affected: "Otherwise, the magnitude of the effect would control, and our cases have shown that, once an effect is shown, no specific magnitude need be proved."[17]

The Supreme Court's most recent Sherman Act precedents dealing with the interstate commerce requirement, both involving private suits, also appear to follow *Mandeville Farms* in interpreting the Sherman Act to reach to the limits of the Commerce Clause.[18] But litigants continue to challenge this proposition and have won support from a minority of justices. In McLain v. Real Estate, a class action challenged alleged price fixing by real estate associations, firms, and brokers in the New Orleans area. The defendants moved to dismiss, arguing that the interstate commerce requirement was not met because, even if the defendants general conduct affected interstate commerce, the plaintiffs had not demonstrated that the alleged price-fixing conduct was an "integral and inseparable part" of the general conduct.[19] The Court appeared to reject this specific nexus test, pointing out that to require a showing that the challenged conduct itself had an anticompetitive effect on interstate commerce would convert the jurisdictional issue into a trial on the substantive issue.[20] But in apparent contradictory language, the Court added that to establish jurisdiction, the plaintiff must show that the challenged price-fixing activity "be shown 'as a matter of practical

---

14. 389 U.S. 320, 88 S.Ct. 443, 19 L.Ed.2d 554 (1967).

15. 421 U.S. 773, 95 S.Ct. 2004, 44 L.Ed.2d 572 (1975).

16. Id. at 783.

17. Id. at 785.

18. Summit Health, Ltd. v. Pinhas, 500 U.S. 322, 111 S.Ct. 1842, 114 L.Ed.2d 366

(1991); McLain v. Real Estate Bd., 444 U.S. 232, 100 S.Ct. 502, 62 L.Ed.2d 441 (1980).

19. *McLain*, 444 U.S. at 236.

20. Id. at 242–43 (the Court noted that a violation of antitrust laws may occur when the defendants act with anticompetitive intent, even if the anticompetitive effect is not achieved).

economics' to have a not insubstantial effect on the interstate commerce involved."[21]

The Court had an opportunity to clarify the ambiguity in Summit Health, Ltd. v. Pinhas, a case involving an ophthalmological surgeon's hospital privileges at a Los Angeles hospital.[22] After a dispute over the hospital's requirement that eye surgery be performed by two surgeons (a majority of local hospitals had, in response to a Medicare ruling, abolished the requirement that both a primary surgeon and surgical assistant be present), the hospital initiated peer review proceedings against Dr. Pinhas resulting in withdrawal of his attending privileges. Dr. Pinhas sued, alleging an unlawful boycott under the Sherman Act. The defendants argued that the Sherman Act did not reach individual peer review decisions with only a local impact. Picking up where the defendants in *McLain* left off, the hospital urged that a nexus be required, at the pleading stage, between the peer review decision and interstate commerce. There was no dispute that the hospital was generally engaged in a business that affected interstate commerce, but the hospital argued that the peer review decision affecting a single doctor did not affect commerce.

A divided Court held that the Sherman Act's jurisdictional threshold had been met. The Court restated the view offered in *Mandeville Island* that the Sherman Act reaches the full extent of congressional authority under the Commerce Clause.[23] But there may still be room for doubt—the Court's decision might be read as not deciding the "nexus" issue because the plaintiff's pleadings were read broadly as alleging an interstate commerce effect from the peer review action.[24] Justice Scalia's dissent (joined by three other justices) also argued for adoption of a nexus requirement as a means of maintaining a balance in federal-state responsibility for business torts.[25]

A nexus requirement is inconsistent with broader Commerce Clause holdings and with expressions of congressional intent.[26] For example, when Congress amended the Clayton Act to cover acquisitions that affect interstate commerce, it did so with the understanding that Section 7 of the Clayton Act would have the same jurisdictional reach as the Sherman Act—to the full extent of the reach of the Commerce Clause.[27] Although the Court seems to have rejected the nexus requirement in three consecutive holdings beginning with *Mandeville*, the issue has not disappeared. Recent Court decisions that appear to limit the reach of the

21. Id. at 246

22. 500 U.S. 322, 111 S.Ct. 1842, 114 L.Ed.2d 366 (1991).

23. Id. at 328–29 & n. 10.

24. Id. at 333 (The final sentence of the Court's opinion reads: "Thus, respondent's claims that members of the peer review committee conspired with others to abuse that process and thereby deny respondent access to the market for ophthalmological services provided by general hospitals in Los Angeles has a sufficient nexus with interstate commerce to support federal jurisdiction").

25. Id. at 340–343 (Scalia J., dissenting).

26. See Gavil, *Reconstructing the Jurisdictional Foundation of Antitrust Federalism,* 61 Geo. Wash. L. Rev. 657 (1993).

27. H. Rep. No. 96–871, 2 (1980).

Commerce Clause could generate further litigation involving antitrust statutes.[28]

§ 17.5   Statute of Limitations and Doctrines of Repose

Before 1955, lacking a federal statute of limitations for private antitrust actions, the federal courts borrowed state rules.[1] In 1955 Congress imposed a four year limitation period on private and government damage actions in Section 4B of the Clayton Act.[2] Under the statute, the limitations period begins running on the date "the cause of action accrued."[3] Although injunction suits brought under Section 16 of the Clayton Act are not governed by Section 4B, courts have held that the defense of laches may be available in injunction actions and that the four year statutory period should be used as a guideline in determining whether suit was brought within a reasonable time.[4] Not only laches, but other doctrines of repose can apply to private claims, usually, but not always, in conventional ways.[5]

17.5a.   Accrual of a Cause of Action

The application of the statute of limitations to discrete acts that violate the law and that do immediate and obvious injury would seem to present no particular difficulty. For example, if a seller is accused of a boycott, the cause of action accrues when a seller refuses to fill the order, not when the conspiracy was hatched or the plaintiff placed the order.[6] The plaintiff's repeated efforts to convince the seller to deal has been held not to delay the running of the statute as long as the initial refusal was final.[7] But many antitrust violations presuppose a continuing course

28. Among these decisions is United States v. Morrison, 529 U.S. 598, 120 S.Ct. 1740, 146 L.Ed.2d 658 (2000)(Violence Against Women Act unconstitutional because it exceeded Congress' constitutional authority to legislate under the Commerce Clause.)

§ 17.5

1. E.g., Chattanooga Foundry & Pipe Works v. Atlanta, 203 U.S. 390, 27 S.Ct. 65, 51 L.Ed. 241 (1906).

2. Section 4B of the Clayton Act, 15 U.S.C.A. § 15(b).

3. See generally, ABA SECTION OF ANTITRUST LAW, PROVING ANTITRUST DAMAGES, Chapter 3 (1996).

4. I.T. & T. Corp. v. G.T.E. Corp., 518 F.2d 913, 926–29 (9th Cir.1975).

5. E.g., Azalea Drive–In Theatre v. Hanft, 540 F.2d 713 (4th Cir.1976), cert. denied, 430 U.S. 941, 97 S.Ct. 1571, 51 L.Ed.2d 787 (1977) (collateral estoppel); United States v. United Shoe Machinery Corp., 110 F.Supp. 295, 343 (D.Mass.1953), *aff'd per curiam*, 347 U.S. 521, 74 S.Ct. 699, 98 L.Ed. 910 (1954) (res judicata).

6. Pioneer Co., Inc. v. Talon, Inc., 462 F.2d 1106 (8th Cir.1972) (action for refusal to deal allegedly violating antitrust laws accrued when manufacturer refused to fill orders, not when the orders were placed or when the conspiracy to refuse to deal was initially hatched). See Amey, Inc. v. Gulf Abstract & Title, 758 F.2d 1486, 1500–01 (11th Cir.1985), *cert. denied*, 475 U.S. 1107, 106 S.Ct. 1513, 89 L.Ed.2d 912 (1986)(antitrust action for inflated title search fees accrues at the point of plaintiff's obligation to pay, not when title search occurs or report is delivered to the plaintiff).

7. Kaw Valley Elec. Co-op. v. Kansas Elec. Power, 872 F.2d 931, 934 (10th Cir. 1989); David Orgell v. Geary's Stores, 640 F.2d 936, 938 (9th Cir.), *cert. denied*, 454 U.S. 816, 102 S.Ct. 92, 70 L.Ed.2d 84 (1981). Other courts have held that a continued refusal to deal would restart the statute of limitations: Bell v. Dow Chem. Co., 847 F.2d 1179 (5th Cir.1988); Charlotte Telecasters, Inc. v. Jefferson–Pilot Corp., 546 F.2d 570, 572 (4th Cir.1976). A continued refusal to deal linked to other acts

of conduct, such as a price conspiracy or interdependent pricing; indeed, the violation may even be predicated primarily on defendant's having a certain status—that of a monopolist. In cases such as these the point at which a plaintiff's cause of action accrues and the statute begins to run is not obvious.

In a continuing violation, the effects on the plaintiff may be insignificant at some periods, significant at others. Suppose plaintiff did nothing for four years after it had suffered some discernable harm and thus had a cause of action; does defendant have a defense to a later suit for other and perhaps more intensive damage which begins to occur after the four year period? In Zenith Radio Corp. v. Hazeltine Research, Inc.,[8] the Court insisted that the cause of action available to a plaintiff at any given time covers all past damage and such future damages as could then be proved and which would not be speculative. If a plaintiff which has begun to suffer damage allows four years to pass without bringing suit, it will be barred as to any damages—past or future—which it might have proved had it brought suit during the four year period. Only if there were elements of future damage which during the four years were too speculative to prove may the plaintiff hold off bringing suit; for these elements the cause of action accrues when the damage has actually been incurred.[9] Some lower courts have held, however, that the uncertainty of damages is not sufficient to prevent the running of the statute.[10] In Pace Industries v. Three Phoenix Co., the Ninth Circuit drew a distinction between "uncertain damages" and "uncertain extent of damage," reasoning that only the former precluded running of the statute.[11] The court held that a law suit filed to enforce an allegedly anticompetitive agreement began the running of the statute, barring the plaintiff's antitrust suit commenced more than four years later.

17.5b. Tolling the Statute

Under Section 5(I) of the Clayton Act, the running of the statute will cease during pendency of a government civil or criminal proceeding to enforce the antitrust laws, and for one year thereafter.[12] The Supreme Court has held that this tolling provision also operates during an administrative complaint proceeding brought by the FTC.[13] According to

would also restart the statute: Hennegan v. Pacifico Creative Serv. Inc., 787 F.2d 1299, 1300–01 (9th Cir.), *cert. denied*, 479 U.S. 886, 107 S.Ct. 279, 93 L.Ed.2d 254 (1986).

8. 401 U.S. 321, 91 S.Ct. 795, 28 L.Ed.2d 77 (1971).

9. Id. at 339–40.

10. Brunswick Corp. v. Riegel Textile Corp., 752 F.2d 261, 271 (7th Cir.1984), *cert. denied*, 472 U.S. 1018, 105 S.Ct. 3480, 87 L.Ed.2d 615 (1985)(the court wrote that once losses were "realized" and not merely "predicted," absent special circumstances, the statute of limitations begins to run).

11. 813 F.2d 234, 240 (9th Cir. 1987)("The question of whether there is a right to recovery is not to be confused with the difficulty in ascertaining the scope or extent of injury.")

12. Section 5(I) of the Clayton Act, 15 U.S.C.A. § 16(i).

13. Minnesota Mining and Manuf. Co. v. New Jersey Wood Finishing Co., 381 U.S. 311, 317–18, 85 S.Ct. 1473, 14 L.Ed.2d 405 (1965)(Section 5(I) operates with respect to FTC administrative complaint to enforce Section 7 of the Clayton Act); Donahue v. Pendleton Woolen Mills, Inc. 633 F.Supp. 1423, 1441 (S.D.N.Y.1986)(tolling operates

the statute, tolling occurs as long as the private claim is based "in whole or in part" on the matter addressed in the government proceeding. The Supreme Court has interpreted this language to require only that the matter raised in the private claim be substantially similar to that raised in the government proceeding.[14] The tolling periods for separate government suits (for example a civil and a criminal proceeding) may be combined to cover the period in which one or the other of the suits was pending.[15]

A statute of limitations is tolled not only by government proceedings, but also by fraudulent concealment of the cause of action.[16] A longer tolling may result from a combination of fraudulent concealment and government proceedings.[17] Many conspiracies are sub rosa. Such covert action may, under old and respected authority, be enough to toll the statute.[18] The cases generally hold that the plaintiff must have acted in a diligent and self-regarding way yet learned nothing of the violation during the statutory period.[19] But some courts have resisted the notion that a conspiracy is inherently self-concealing, requiring that the plaintiff show evidence related to the conspiracy, or unrelated to the conspiracy, that shows an intent to conceal.[20] Although some conspiracies may not be inherently secret (a conspiracy to tie the sale of one product to another may be established by the seller's very public coercion of the buyer), others almost always are (a conspiracy among rivals to rig bids or

with respect to FTC administrative complaint to enforce Section 5 of the FTC Act).

14. Zenith Radio Corp. v. Hazeltine Research, 401 U.S. 321, 337–38, 91 S.Ct. 795, 28 L.Ed.2d 77 (1971)(tolling operates as to all defendants in a conspiracy whether or not named in the government complaint); Leh v. General Petroleum Corp., 382 U.S. 54, 62–63, 86 S.Ct. 203, 15 L.Ed.2d 134 (1965), *reh'g denied*, 382 U.S. 1001, 86 S.Ct. 525, 15 L.Ed.2d 491 (1966)(despite differing parties and factual allegations as to time of conspiracy, claims were substantially similar). In Aurora Enters. v. National Broadcasting Co., 688 F.2d 689, 693 (9th Cir. 1982), the statute was not tolled because the private claim alleged a conspiracy and the earlier government claim did not.

15. Michigan v. Morton Salt Co., 259 F.Supp. 35, 50–51 (D.Minn.1966), *aff'd sub nom.* Hardy Salt Co. v. Illinois, 377 F.2d 768 (8th Cir.), *cert. denied*, 389 U.S. 912, 88 S.Ct. 238, 19 L.Ed.2d 260 (1967).

16. Early cases tolling the statute for fraudulent concealment include Westinghouse Elec. Corp. v. Pacific Gas & Elec. Co., 326 F.2d 575 (9th Cir.1964) and General Elec. Co. v. City of San Antonio, 334 F.2d 480 (5th Cir.1964).

17. Mt. Hood Stages v. Greyhound Corp., 616 F.2d 394, 407 (9th Cir.), *cert. denied*, 449 U.S. 831, 101 S.Ct. 99, 66 L.Ed.2d 36 (1980).

18. See, e.g. Bailey v. Glover, 88 U.S. (21 Wall.) 342, 22 L.Ed. 636 (1874). Compare the discussion in Holmberg v. Armbrecht, 327 U.S. 392, 66 S.Ct. 582, 90 L.Ed. 743 (1946).

19. Pinney Dock & Transp. Co. v. Penn Central Corp., 838 F.2d 1445, 1470–1480 (6th Cir.), *cert. denied*, 488 U.S. 880, 109 S.Ct. 196, 102 L.Ed.2d 166 (1988); New York v. Hendrickson Bros., Inc. 840 F.2d 1065, 1084 (2d Cir.), *cert. denied.*, 488 U.S. 848, 109 S.Ct. 128, 102 L.Ed.2d 101 (1988); Norton–Children's Hosps. Inc. v. James E. Smith & Sons, Inc. 658 F.2d 440, 443 (6th Cir.1981); In re Beef Indus. Antitrust Litig., 600 F.2d 1148, 1169 (5th Cir.1979), *cert. denied*, 449 U.S. 905, 101 S.Ct. 280, 66 L.Ed.2d 137 (1980); Laundry Equip. Sales Corp. v. Borg–Warner Corp., 334 F.2d 788 (7th Cir.1964).

20. Compare New York v. Hendrickson Bros., 840 F.2d 1065, 1084 (2d Cir.1988) (bid rigging schemes are self-concealing) with Texas v. Allan Constr. Co., 851 F.2d 1526, 1532–33 (5th Cir.1988) (acts at the time of conspiracy may demonstrate fraudulent concealment) and In re Catfish Antitrust Litig., 826 F.Supp. 1019, 1030–31 (N.D.Miss.1993) (concealment is not inherent in all price fixing and must be demonstrated by defendants affirmative acts).

otherwise fix prices in violation of the *per se* rule). To require that the plaintiff show evidence of the defendant's intent to conceal that is independent of the evidence proving such a conspiracy would severely undercut the fraudulent concealment doctrine.

Issues of enforcement policy are inherent in the application of the statute of limitations to covert conduct. To deprive a plaintiff of its action even against covert defendants, unless the plaintiff can show that diligence on its own part could not have brought the offense to light, would achieve two things. First, it would tend to impose costs on plaintiffs who were not as diligent as they might have been, thus encouraging their greater diligence to uncover wrongs against them. Second, it would tend to encourage defendants to go to greater lengths to disguise their wrongs during the four-year period. If, on the other hand, a plaintiff is allowed to preserve its action so long as the defendant's behavior is covert, the opposite effects would be expected. Absent any basis for deciding which policy would result in the greater deterrence of violations, the law, on the basis of its commitment not only to deterrence but also to compensating innocent victims, ought to favor the plaintiff who is generally diligent and self-regarding, even if unsuccessful in discovering the unlawful conduct during the four year period.

The courts can, in various ways, reach results consistent with this preference for the normally cautious plaintiff. For example, in an ongoing price-fixing conspiracy, each meeting in furtherance of that conspiracy might be held to be a new violation for purposes of the statute. Or, a court might conclude that the statute does not run on a price-fixing conspiracy until the last payment made to the conspirators.[21]

§ 17.6 Class Actions

When a group of similarly situated persons has been damaged by conduct violating the antitrust laws, a private claim can often be brought as a class action. Although the roots of the class action extend to old procedures for equitable relief, use of the class action in antitrust claims became feasible with the adoption of Rule 23 of the Federal Rules of Civil Procedure in 1937, and grew substantially after the 1966 amendments to that Rule. Class actions became a significant force because they allowed the aggregation of individual claims, too small to warrant individual plaintiffs bringing an action.[1] The aggregate damages, after trebling, produced damages well-beyond those awarded in most suits brought by individual claimants, providing a more substantial deterrent. Indeed, many class actions have followed criminal prosecutions by the

---

21. This was the holding in United States v. A–A–A Elec. Co., 788 F.2d 242, 245 (4th Cir.1986), a case in which the five-year criminal statute of limitations was applied (18 U.S.C.A. § 3282).

§ 17.6

1. The goal of the drafters of the original Rule 23 was to encourage more frequent use of the class action on behalf of persons who would not file individual claims. Advisory Committee Note to the original Rule 23, *reprinted in* 12 C. WRIGHT ET AL., FEDERAL PRACTICE AND PROCEDURE, appendix, at 406 (1st ed. 1973).

Justice Department and, after trebling, have yielded awards that usually substantially exceeded any criminal fines levied in the Justice Department prosecution.

The use of antitrust class actions may have reached a high point during the late 1970s and early 1980s. Constricting judicial interpretations of the antitrust laws and of Rule 23 probably contributed to the decline that began in the mid–1980s. But statistical data of the Administrative Office of the United States Courts suggests that antitrust class action claims, as a percentage of all class actions, started growing again in the mid–1990s.[2] Not all such actions enjoyed a high success rate. A survey of class actions found striking discrepancies in the rate at which such suits obtain class certification and a favorable settlement or judgment. Suits involving horizontal price fixing enjoyed the highest success rate, with monopolization cases and distribution restraints cases trailing significantly in their rates of success.[3]

17.6a.　Requirements for Class Action Suits

As amended in 1966, Rule 23 allows a class action if each of four prerequisites of Rule 23(a) are met and if the action falls within one of three designated categories in Rule 23(b). The four requirements of Rule 23(a) are: (1) the class be so numerous that joinder is impracticable; (2) there be common questions of law and fact; (3) claims of the class representatives typify those of the class; and (4) representative parties fairly and adequately protect the interests of the class. Of the three categories in Rule 23(b), the two most likely to be relevant in antitrust litigation are (b)(2), designed to protect a class that would benefit from injunctive relief, and (b)(3), which authorizes class actions when "questions of law or fact common to members of the class predominate" over other questions and when the class action would be "superior" to other possible ways of adjudicating the controversy. To make its findings under (b)(3), the court is to consider: (A) the interest of members of the class in individually controlling the prosecution or defense of separate actions; (B) the extent and nature of any litigation concerning the controversy already commenced by or against members of the class; (C) the desirability or undesirability of concentrating the litigation of the claims in the particular forum; (D) the difficulties likely to be encountered in management of a class action.

Courts occasionally certify antitrust class actions under (b)(2) where injunctive relief is feasible,[4] perhaps more frequently in cases involving a high risk of continuing abuse, such as in monopolization claims.[5] Certification under (b)(3) is usually the only available route when damages are sought in antitrust class actions. It is not unusual for an antitrust action

---

2. This data is presented in Calkins, *An Enforcement Official's Reflections on Antitrust Class Actions*, 39 ARIZ. L. REV. 413, 416–17 (1997) [hereinafter *Class Actions*].

3. Id. at 449–50.

4. In re NASDAQ Market–Makers Antitrust Litig., 169 F.R.D. 493, 517 (S.D.N.Y. 1996).

5. *Calkins*, supra note 2, at 450 n.189 (suggesting that injunctive relief is more likely in monopolization cases).

to be certified both under (b)(2) and (b)(3) when both injunctive and damage relief are appropriate.[6]

Rule 23(b)(3) has been controversial, critics asserting that inappropriate class suits have been maintained under this provision. Proposed amendments to Rule 23 are designed to curtail certain uses of the (b)(3) class action. In particular, a proposed new (b)(3)(A) would require the court, in determining whether a class action is superior to other available methods for the fair and efficient adjudication of a controversy, to weigh the practicability of individual class members pursing their own claims. According to an advisory committee note, the new factor would discourage, but not prevent, class certification when individual class members could practicably pursue individual actions.[7] A proposed new 23(b)(3)(F) would require the court to analyze whether probable relief to individual members "justifies the costs and burdens of class litigation." The advisory committee notes suggest that this language would "effect a retrenchment in the use of class actions to aggregate trivial individual claims."[8]

Rule 23(c)(1) requires that a court, "as soon as practicable after the commencement of an action," determine whether an action can be maintained as a class action. This "certification" is critical for most antitrust claims brought as class actions. Without certification, the attorneys bringing these suits are usually unwilling to prosecute the suit. For class actions certified under Rule 23(b)(3)—which includes most antitrust class actions—the court must direct notice to members of the class of their right to be excluded from the class (and to litigate their claims separately). The notice is to be "the best notice practicable under the circumstances."

Rule 23(e) mandates that the court approve a decision to dismiss or compromise a class action. Notice must also be provided to class members of a proposed dismissal or compromise. These provisions are a recognition that the attorneys bringing a class action may have selfish interests at odds with class members, as when a proposed settlement would pay attorneys' fees for the plaintiffs' attorneys but would provide little or no compensation to the class.

17.6b. Managing Antitrust Class Action Suits

Because of the size of the damage claims, the number of attorneys involved, and the court's special responsibilities for protecting class interests, class actions raise unique management problems for courts. Among these are problems in determining whether the class should be

6. E.g., *In re NASDAQ* supra note 4, at 515–16; Davis v. Southern Bell Tel. & Tel. Co., 1993–2 CCH Trade Cas. ¶ 70,480, 71,-604 (S.D. Fla. 1993).

7. Proposed Rule 23(b)(3)(A), advisory committee note. See Perry v. Amerada Hess Corp., 427 F.Supp. 667, 676 (N.D.Ga.1977) (denying class certification based on the view that individual plaintiffs could pursue antitrust claims).

8. Proposed Rule 23(b)(3)(F), advisory committee note. See In re Hotel Tel. Charges, 500 F.2d 86, 91 (9th Cir.1974) (rejecting certification after concluding that the class members would likely accrue "nonexistent, or minuscule, recoveries").

certified, giving notice to the affected class, honoring the rights of individual class members to opt out of the class in favor of individual litigation, and establishing and distributing the damage claims.

17.6b1. Certification

Certification of a class requires the court to determine whether the requirements of Rule 23(a) and (b) are satisfied. With some exceptions, courts have construed the rule generously, recognizing the purpose of the rule to save resources by aggregating large numbers of claims into a single efficiently managed law suit.[9] Impracticability of joinder, required by 23(a)(1) for all class actions, may be found whenever there is a substantial number of class members.[10] The courts look not for impossibility, but difficulty or inconvenience in effecting joinder.[11] Although numbers below 30 may be insufficient, there is no hard and fast minimum number for the class, particularly if the defendants alone have access to the data needed to estimate class size.[12] For example, a group of thirty or forty franchisees would, as a practical matter, be difficult to join; thus, if other prerequisites were met they would be an appropriate class.

Rule 23(a)(3) requires common questions of law and fact for all class actions. Because any antitrust class action will involve commonality on important issues of liability (e.g., market definition, power, conspiracy), this requirement is usually easy to meet in antitrust class actions. A single common issue, the resolution of which will affect all or most class members, may be sufficient.[13] Thus, allegations concerning the existence, scope, and effect of an antitrust conspiracy have been held to satisfy the commonality requirement.[14] As discussed below, a more difficult showing–the predominance of common legal and factual questions–is required if certification is sought under Rule 23(b)(3).

Typicality of the claims of the class representatives, required under 23(a)(3) for all types of class actions, means essentially that there be

9. A number of circuits follow the rule that in cases of doubt, a court should err in favor of allowing the class. Eisenberg v. Gagnon, 766 F.2d 770, 785 (3d Cir.1985), *cert. denied sub nom.* Weinstein v. Eisenberg, 474 U.S. 946, 106 S.Ct. 342, 88 L.Ed.2d 290 (1985); Horton v. Goose Creek Independent School Dist., 690 F.2d 470, 487 (5th Cir.1982), cert. denied, 463 U.S. 1207, 103 S.Ct. 3536, 77 L.Ed.2d 1387 (1983); Esplin v. Hirschi, 402 F.2d 94, 101 (10th Cir.1968); *cert. denied*, 394 U.S. 928, 89 S.Ct. 1194, 22 L.Ed.2d 459 (1969). See also Korn v. Franchard Corp., 456 F.2d 1206, 1208–09 (2d Cir.1972)(directing a broad construction of Rule 23).

10. E.g., Research Corp. v. Asgrow Seed Co., 425 F.2d 1059 (7th Cir.1970); Iowa v. Union Asphalt & Roadoils, Inc., 281 F.Supp. 391 (S.D.Iowa 1968); Illinois v. Harper & Row Publishers, Inc., 301 F.Supp.

484 (N.D.Ill.), *cert. denied*, 394 U.S. 944, 89 S.Ct. 1273, 22 L.Ed.2d 478 (1969); Siegel v. Chicken Delight, Inc., 271 F.Supp. 722 (N.D.Cal.1967), *order modified*, 412 F.2d 830 (9th Cir.1969).

11. Little Caesar Enters. Inc. v. Smith, 1997–1 CCH Trade Cas. ¶ 71,817 (E.D. Mich.), mag. recommended decision adopted, 172 F.R.D. 236 (E.D.Mich. 1997)(certifying a class of 458 franchisees).

12. *In re* NASDAQ, supra note 4, at 509 (S.D.N.Y. 1996) (one of the authors was a witness on the issue of manageability in the case).

13. In re Disposable Contact Lens Antitrust Litig., 170 F.R.D. 524, 529 (M.D.Fla. 1996).

14. Id. at 529; In re Potash Antitrust Litig., 159 F.R.D. 682, 689 (D.Minn.1995).

nothing significant which differentiates the claims of the representatives to a degree which might bring their interests into conflict with those of the class generally.[15] Thus, typicality refers to the nature of the claim of the class, not to the specific facts from which the claim arose; the requirement would be met provided that the class representative has the incentive to prove all the elements of the cause of action on behalf of individual members.[16] Related to typicality is the requirement in 23(a)(4) that class representatives be adequately representative of the class. According to the Supreme Court, representativeness requires the class representative to have interests that do not conflict with the class members interests and to have an attorney capable of prosecuting the action vigorously.[17] Generally, if the class representative satisfies the typicality requirement, the first prong of the representativeness test would also be satisfied.[18] The second prong of the representativeness test is met if counsel for the class representative is "qualified, experienced, and capable."[19]

When certification is sought under Rule 23(b)(3), additional requirements apply. Common issues of law and fact must predominate over issues affecting only individual claimants and a class action must be a "superior" method for adjudicating the controversy. Thus, although common questions of fact and law must be shown for any class action, predominance of these over other questions is a prerequisite only under 23(b)(3). "Predominance" under the rule means predominance in a practical sense; there is no need for a complete identity of legal or factual claims or anything approaching such extreme commonality.[20] Differences that bear only on the computation of damages for individual class members, for example, will not keep the class action from going forward.[21] To deal with individual member damage questions, courts may bifurcate liability from damage issues, appoint a special master, or rely

15. *Little Caesar*, supra note 11 (finding the typicality requirement met notwithstanding the named representative's active pursuit of his rights during pre-litigation period). Compare Siegel v. Chicken Delight, Inc., 271 F.Supp. 722 (N.D.Cal.1967), *order modified*, 412 F.2d 830 (9th Cir.1969) and West Virginia v. Chas. Pfizer & Co., 440 F.2d 1079 (2d Cir.), *cert. denied*, 404 U.S. 871, 92 S.Ct. 81, 30 L.Ed.2d 115 (1971) with Chicago v. General Motors Corp., 467 F.2d 1262 (7th Cir.1972).

16. *In re* NASDAQ Market Makers Antitrust Litig., supra note 4 at 510 (S.D.N.Y. 1996).

17. General Tel. Co. v. Falcon, 457 U.S. 147, 157 & n. 13, 102 S.Ct. 2364, 72 L.Ed.2d 740 (1982).

18. *In re* NASDAQ, supra note 4, at 512.

19. Id., citing Ross v. A.H. Robins Co., 100 F.R.D. 5, 7 (S.D.N.Y.1982).

20. Lumco Indus., Inc. v. Jeld–Wen, Inc., 171 F.R.D. 168 (E.D.Pa. 1997)(plaintiffs' allegations "will predominantly involve common issues of fact and law"); *In re* Disposable Contact Lens Antitrust Litig., supra note 13, at 529 (same); *In re* NASAQ, supra note 4, at 517 (S.D.N.Y. 1996)(predominance requirement satisfied "unless it is clear that individual issues will overwhelm the common questions and render the class action valueless").

21. E.g., Green v. Wolf Corp., 406 F.2d 291 (2d Cir.1968), cert. denied, 395 U.S. 977, 89 S.Ct. 2131, 23 L.Ed.2d 766 (1969); *In re* Disposable Contact Lens, supra note 13, at 531; Berland v. Mack, 48 F.R.D. 121 (S.D.N.Y.1969); Herbst v. Able, 47 F.R.D. 11 (1969), order amended, 49 F.R.D. 286 (S.D.N.Y.1970); Siegel v. Chicken Delight, supra note 10.

upon defendants' records that may be unavailable to the plaintiff before discovery.[22]

In determining whether a class action is a superior mode of litigation, a court is not limited to the factors listed in the rule. For example, courts have denied certification because the claims could feasibly be litigated in individual antitrust suits[23] or because the recoveries to class members were seen as too trivial to justify maintaining the class action.[24] These rulings anticipate the proposed amendments to Rule (b)(3), such as the proposed new (b)(3)(F) instructing the court to weigh whether relief to individual class members justifies the cost and expense of the action.

Under Rule 23(c)(1), certification of class actions is supposed to occur "as soon as practicable." The Supreme Court has said that a court may not "conduct a preliminary inquiry into the merits of a suit" in determining whether to certify a class action.[25] Yet for a variety of reasons, courts often examine one or more issues bearing on the merits before deciding whether to certify. That examination may come as a result of motions to dismiss filed by defendants, raising any of a variety of jurisdictional issues such as a challenge to the existence of antitrust injury or the application of the Sherman Act to conduct occurring outside the United States.[26] Plaintiffs in class actions face the same burdens as other plaintiffs in proving, in addition to a substantive antitrust violation, that the violation caused an antitrust injury to the plaintiffs translatable as actual damage to the plaintiff. This may be easier in cartel cases, more difficult in cases involving exclusionary conduct.[27]

In Hartford Fire Insurance Co. v. California, jurisdictional issues went all the way to the Supreme Court before the district court had addressed certification.[28] Even if defendants' motions do not require examination of the merits, the certification decision itself may do so. For example, in determining whether a class action is "superior" to other methods of litigation (as required under Rule 23(b)(3)), a court may find it necessary to visit the merits-related issues.[29] An example is *In re*

---

22. *In re* NASDAQ, supra note 4, at 522 (S.D.N.Y. 1996).

23. Perry v. Amerada Hess Corp., 427 F.Supp. 667, 676 (N.D.Ga.1977).

24. *In re* Hotel Tel. Charges, supra note 8, at 91.

25. Eisen v. Carlisle & Jacquelin, 417 U.S. 156, 177, 94 S.Ct. 2140, 40 L.Ed.2d 732 (1974).

26. E.g., McClain v. South Carolina Nat'l Bank, 105 F.3d 898, 903 (4th Cir. 1997)(affirming simultaneous rulings denying class certification and granting summary judgment); Davis v. Southern Bell Tel. & Tel. Co., 755 F.Supp. 1532 (S.D.Fla. 1991)(telephone consumers had antitrust standing to raise certain claims but were

barred from raising others under State Action doctrine).

27. See the discussion of these issues in §§ 17.7b–7c.

28. 509 U.S. 764, 113 S.Ct. 2891, 125 L.Ed.2d 612 (1993). The *Hartford* case began as a *parens patriae* lawsuit but grew to include a class of private plaintiffs as well.

29. As one court put it, "an analysis of the issues and the nature of required proof at trial [is required] to determine whether the matters in dispute and the nature of plaintiffs' proofs are principally individual in nature or are susceptible to common proof equally applicable to all class members." *Little Caesar*, supra note 11, 172 F.R.D. at 241.

Domestic Air Transportation Antitrust Litigation, in which the district court undertook such a preliminary inquiry notwithstanding its understanding that "it is not proper to reach the merits of a claim when determining a class."[30] Given the high judicial and litigant costs associated with class actions, it is inevitable and probably sound policy to permit such preliminary inquiries.

17.6b2. Notice

Usually as a part of the certification decision, a court must resolve issues of notice to the class members. In Eisen v. Carlisle & Jacquelin, a 1974 Supreme Court holding,[31] the plaintiff sought damages for himself and as a representative of all buyers and sellers of securities in odd lot transactions, alleging that defendants had conspired to monopolize trading in odd lots and had fixed commissions at excessive levels. The identified class consisted of about 6 million members, of whom about 2 million could be identified. The aggregate damage claim of $60 million would have produced an average return of $10 per class member. On the question of notice, the district court required that notice be given to every known class member with ten or more transactions during the damage period, to various financial institutions, and to 5000 others chosen randomly from the 2 million readily identifiable class members. All others were to be notified by publication. On the basis of a preliminary hearing on the merits, the district court assigned 90 percent of the costs of notice to the defendants. The Second Circuit held that the notice procedure (and a proposed method of distributing damages) violated Rule 23 and further held that the case was unmanageable as a class action.[32] The Supreme Court vacated that decision but dismissed the class action upon closely related grounds.[33] It held that Rule 23 required individual notice to all members of the class who could be identified through reasonable effort, not just to a sample of these, regardless of whether the cost of this notice would make the action impracticable; it also held that the cost of notice had to be borne by the plaintiff.

Although *Eisen* doubtless discouraged plaintiffs from bringing large class suits for which notification costs are high, class action plaintiffs continue to bring class actions involving 10 million or more members. For example, *In re* Domestic Air Transportation Antitrust Litigation involved a class that plaintiffs estimated at 12.5 million and defendants estimated at 50 million.[34] Although individual notice was required for members whose addresses were known, the court suggested that notice to other class members might be provided through publication in newspapers of general circulation or in the airlines own magazines.[35] In Disposable Contact Lens Antitrust Litigation, the plaintiffs obtained

30. 137 F.R.D. 677, 684 (N.D.Ga. 1991).

31. 417 U.S. 156, 94 S.Ct. 2140, 40 L.Ed.2d 732 (1974).

32. 479 F.2d 1005 (2d Cir.1973).

33. 417 U.S. 156, 94 S.Ct. 2140, 40 L.Ed.2d 732 (1974).

34. 137 F.R.D. at 694 & n.90.

35. Id. at 696

certification for a class between 15 and 18 million members notwithstanding an inability to identify (and notify) every class member.[36]

17.6b3. Damage Remedies

Once a court certifies a class and notice on class members is effected, the case may proceed through procedures more in accord with conventional litigation, albeit with a large cast of lawyers in attendance.[37] Of course, certification may greatly raise the stakes for defendants and bring additional pressure to settle. If the case is settled or litigated successfully, (although conventional damage rules apply), the court and the parties may face the difficult issue of the manner in which damage relief is to be distributed to class members. When the identity or address of large numbers of class members is unknown, it is impossible to distribute a judgement directly to the class. The administrative costs of distribution can be prohibitive even if class members can be located. Court approved remedies have been innovative, using allocation formulas for distributing a pool of damages, requiring the defendants to issue discount coupons, or simply requiring lower prices for a defined period.

Of course, distribution is not always complex. One case that involved unusually high distributions to the plaintiff class was Brand Name Prescription Drug Antitrust Litigation, where the court, after initially rejecting a proposed settlement involving damages of $408 million, approved a subsequent proposal that added injunctive relief against the drug companies.[38] Here, distribution of the award was relatively easy because the class, although involving tens of thousands of members, consisted of identifiable retail druggists whose individual claims were significant. Where the plaintiffs are consumers, distribution of damage awards becomes more problematic, not only because of the size of the class, but also because of the difficulty and expense in verifying relatively small consumer claims. Sometimes the courts are able to rely upon the defendants' data to identify and distribute damages.[39] In other cases, the courts have found more flexible approaches. In the *Domestic Air Transportation Antitrust Litigation,* a settlement required the defendant airlines to pay only $50 million in cash, but issue $408 million in discount coupons to air travelers (only 60 to 80 percent of which the court found were likely to be redeemed).[40] Other flexible remedies have been adopted

---

36. 170 F.R.D. 524 (M.D.Fla.1996).

37. According to Calkins, there were 169 attorneys listed in a class action brought by retail pharmacists against drug manufacturers. Calkins, *Class Actions,* supra note 2, at 421 (citing the record in In re Brand Name Prescription Drugs Antitrust Litig., 1996–1 Trade Cas. (CCH) ¶ 71,350 (N.D. Ill. 1996)).

38. Id. at 76,733–76,737.

39. In re Domestic Air Transportation Antitrust Litig., 137 F.R.D. 677, 692–93 (N.D.Ga.1991); In re Potash Antitrust Litig., 159 F.R.D. 682, 698 (D.Minn.

1995)(noting the possibility of using defendants' records to determine individual damages).

40. In re Domestic Air Transp. Antitrust Litig., 148 F.R.D. 297, 306, 315 (N.D.Ga.1993). The settlement was controversial because one airline that was not named as a defendant (Alaska Airlines) asked to be allowed to participate in the coupon program, suggesting to some observers that the coupon discount program was not a punishment but a sound marketing device beneficial to the participants.

or accepted by courts as a basis for settlement. For example, a hotel chain accused of price fixing[41]settled by agreeing to pay an aggregate recovery fund to be used to pay individual class members who were able to establish their claims and also to roll back room rates until a specified sum was paid over as a cy pres to future hotel patrons.[42]

17.6c. The Balance Sheet on Class Actions

Writing about the district court's decision in the *Eisen* case (before it was reversed), Professor Handler found that antitrust class actions were a net liability for antitrust, for federal courts, and for society generally.[43] The Supreme Court's disposition of *Eisen* may have been a response to some of those concerns. *Eisen* probably produced the results that the Court expected: it reduced the flow of class actions, particularly those for which, however powerful the deterrent effect, compensation achieved was small, so that the discernible financial advantage flowed primarily to the attorneys bringing the suit.[44] Because class actions generally tend to demand a high commitment from judges, the reduction in the flow of these suits will alleviate court congestion to some degree. The proposed amendment that would add Rule 23(b)(3)(F) may seem an endorsement of these benefits, giving courts a green light to dismiss class actions deemed to provide inadequate individual recoveries. But there is a cost of discouraging class actions such as *Eisen*. Dismissal gives up a potent deterrent against offenses doing massive aggregate allocative harm and, as Justice Douglas noted in a concurring opinion, will deny relief to numerous "consumers whose claims may seem *de minimis* but who alone have no practical recourse for either remuneration or injunctive relief."[45]

The value of antitrust class actions lies in their use: (1) to provide deterrence and compensation for antitrust injury that is not the subject of government enforcement; (2) to provide additional deterrence for actions subject of government enforcement and compensation for the victims of conduct that is challenged by government enforcers. Many

Caulkins, CLASS ACTIONS, supra note 2, at 442.

41. Colson v. Hilton Hotels Corp., 59 F.R.D. 324 (N.D.Ill.1972).

42. In re Antibiotic Antitrust Actions, 333 F.Supp. 278, 281 (S.D.N.Y. 1971)(requiring class members to verify their individual claims).

43. Handler, *The Shift from Substance to Procedural Innovations in Antitrust Suits–The Twenty–Third Annual Antitrust Review*, 71 COLUM. L. REV. 1, 5–13 (1971). The battle was joined by others who saw value in class actions. Kohn & Kaplan, *The Antitrust Class Suit: A Manageable Instrument for Social Justice*, 41 ANTITRUST L. J. 292 (1972); Note, *Managing the Large Class Action: Eisen v. Carlisle & Jacquelin*, 87 HARV. L. REV. 426 (1973).

44. The same year that *Eisen* was decided, the Ninth Circuit threw out a class action in which plaintiffs sought certification of a class of 40 million consumers said to have been overcharged an average of $2 per person for telephone services provided by hotels allegedly engaged in an antitrust conspiracy. Although a credible cy pres remedy had already been enforced against major defendants that had settled (text related to note 43, supra), the court found the recoveries likely to accrue to be "nonexistent, or minuscule" and the principal if not the only beneficiary of the action to be the attorneys for the plaintiffs. In re Hotel Tel. Charges, 500 F.2d 86, 91 (9th Cir.1974).

45. *Eisen*, 417 U.S. at 185.

class actions are follow-on actions, brought on the heels of government enforcement activity.[46] At one point, this may have represented the bulk of all class action antitrust suits.[47] For such follow-on suits, class actions would benefit society only to the extent that they provide additional deterrence to antitrust violations or compensation for the victims of the violations. Both questions deserve careful scrutiny.[48]

Recoveries in treble damage follow-on suits have tended to dwarf the fines assessed in Justice Department criminal proceedings. For example, in 1978 the Justice Department indicted North Atlantic shipping lines for unlawful cartel activity. The criminal proceedings were settled in nolo contendere pleas with the defendants paying substantial fines. But criminal fines were dwarfed by the $51.4 million in damages paid to settle follow-on private suits.[49] The Justice Department has gradually increased the level of fines and imprisonment imposed on hard core cartel violations.[50] If it could be inferred that criminal sanctions by themselves provides optimal deterrence of violations, treble damage judgments in private class action suits would be unnecessary for deterrent purposes. But because the gains from violations can be so high and the prospects of being discovered and found liable may be minimal, optimum deterrence cannot be assumed. Moreover, even if criminal sanctions alone were adequate deterrents, where violations occur they also do injury to others in the marketplace. The massive size of some damage awards shows substantial injury to victims.

Follow-on actions can have social value in efficiently providing compensation for those so injured. One class action that may have done this very well is the settlement of the *Brand Name Prescription Drug Antitrust Litigation,* which produced a damage settlement of $408 million to be distributed to retail pharmacists.[51] Others may not, as in suits that produce no direct payment to class members because the amount of the payment per member is too small to be efficiently distributed or when class members cannot be located.

In sum, it is hard to make a convincing case that class actions need to be scaled back by significant additional rule changes. Some class actions may be inappropriate and opportunistic strike suits that yield little benefit except to attorneys who bring and defend them. Also, in

---

46. A recent example of a follow-on action is Lumco Indus., Inc. v. Jeld–Wen, Inc., 171 F.R.D. 168 (E.D.Pa.1997) (granting class certification in a case challenging alleged price-fixing activity that had already been subject to a Department of Justice investigation).

47. Garth, et al., *The Institution of the Private Attorney General: Perspectives from an Empirical Study of Class Action Litigation,* 61 S. CAL. L. REV. 353, 376 (1988) (based on a study of class actions in the Northern District of California that were closed between 1979 and 1984, the author concludes that most antitrust and securities

suits depended upon federal investigative activity).

48. For a careful analysis of these issues, see Calkins, CLASS ACTIONS, supra note 2, at 437–451.

49. *Settlements of About $51.4 million Approved in Ocean Shipping Litigation,* 42 ANTITRUST & TRADE REG. REP. (BNA), No. 1052, at 370 (Feb. 18, 1982).

50. See § 16.2d1.

51. In re Brand Name Prescription Drugs Antitrust Litig., 1996–1 Trade Cases ¶ 71,350 (N.D. Ill. 1996). This class action suit was not a follow-on action.

some instances conflicts of interest may occur if classes and/or subclasses are too broadly defined. Yet the current rules provide ample basis for critical judicial evaluation and response to these problems.

Much of the criticism of antitrust class actions stresses that the typical suit follows after a successful federal enforcement action. But there are also class actions that precede or are contemporaneous with federal enforcement. For example, NASDAQ Market Makers Antitrust Litigation,[52] a private class action challenging as conspiratorial the wide spread between prices at which stock was purchased and sold, was an early response to scholarship that preceded both the Justice Department and SEC investigations into the conduct in question. *Brand Name Prescription Drug Antitrust Litigation*, which resulted in an unusually high settlement, was another independently generated case. Franchisee actions challenging unlawful tie-ins are a significant category of class actions that are unlikely to be follow-ons to government actions.[53]

The *NASDAQ, Prescription Drug,* and franchisee tie-in cases all involve conduct that one might characterize as non-hard core.[54] This suggests that class actions may have a social value in filling gaps that the enforcement agencies may lack the resources to fill.[55] Of course, if independently generated class actions are used to challenge non-hard core antitrust violations, there could be a risk that they will deter conduct having efficiency benefits. In the current antitrust climate, this risk is not substantial. Plaintiffs face an array of hurdles to establish antitrust injury, standing, and damages, all discussed elsewhere in this chapter. Courts are increasingly finding ways to take preliminary looks at the merits and dismiss or limit class actions before they are certified.

§ 17.7 Proving Damages

To be entitled to damages in a private antitrust action, plaintiff must prove that defendant's violation caused an injury to plaintiff's business or property and must establish the basis for a reasonable estimate of the amount of money necessary to compensate for the injury. The plaintiff's burden is preponderance of the evidence. Proof of an overcharge, an exclusion from a market, a termination or a loss of suppliers or customers or loss of business due to a monopolist's exclusionary conduct are illustrative of the kinds of things that may meet the burden.

---

52. *In re* NASDAQ, supra note 4.

53. An example is *Little Caesar,* supra note 11 (after an initial denial of certification, granting certification to a narrowed class of franchisees).

54. The NASDAQ case involving the buy-sell price spread could be seen as classic cartel activity, but the practice was traditional in American stock markets, leading the Justice Department to conclude, even

after it chose to pursue the matter, to use civil rather than criminal proceedings.

55. Another theorist who concludes that class actions help to fill gaps outside the area of hard-core violations is Calkins, CLASS ACTIONS, supra note 2, at 451 (concluding that class actions can play a useful role in deterring conduct that stops short of being criminal and would otherwise go unchallenged).

17.7a. Proving Damages Distinguished from Proving Injury

As early as 1931 the Supreme Court suggested a fundamental distinction between proof of an antitrust violation causing injury and ascertainment of the precise amount of that injury. In *Story Parchment Co. v. Paterson Parchment Paper Co.,* the Court sought to separate "the measure of proof necessary to establish the fact that petitioner has sustained some damage and the measure of proof necessary to enable the jury to fix the amount."[1] This distinction remains valid today, with heightened attention being paid to proof of antitrust injury[2] but more relaxed standards applicable to proof of the amount of that injury. Although eschewing "mere speculation or guess," the Court has held it sufficient to "show the extent of the damages as a matter of just and reasonable inference, although the result be only approximate."[3]

The Court followed these lines in Bigelow v. RKO Radio Pictures, Inc., again suggesting a flexible stance toward proof of the amount of damages.[4] The plaintiff had alleged an antitrust conspiracy that imposed discriminatory terms on the availability of motion pictures. To prove damages, the plaintiff introduced evidence of the profits of a nearby theater not subject to the discrimination, and also evidence of plaintiff's own profits during the pre-conspiracy period. Based on this evidence, the Supreme Court affirmed a jury verdict for the plaintiff.

The Court in *Bigelow* made a number of salient points. The first is that a difficult standard of proof for damages would enable the wrongdoer to profit by his anticompetitive acts, creating an inducement "to make wrongdoing so effective and complete in every case as to preclude any recovery, by rendering the measure of damages uncertain."[5] A second and related point is that the evidence needed for a precise computation of damages may rest in part with the defendants who have conspired to commit the anticompetitive act.[6] Indeed, the defendants may have taken action to destroy or obscure the evidence needed to ascertain the amount of damages. In *Eastman Kodak Co. v. Southern Photo Materials Co.,* the Supreme Court said that if the defendant's wrongful conduct has made ascertainment of the plaintiff's damages difficult, the defendant should not be heard to complain that damages "cannot be measured with the same exactness and precision as would otherwise be possible."[7]

§ 17.7

1. 282 U.S. 555, 562, 51 S.Ct. 248, 75 L.Ed. 544 (1931).

2. See the discussion in § 17.2a.

3. *Story Parchment*, 282 U.S. at 563.

4. 327 U.S. 251, 264, 66 S.Ct. 574, 90 L.Ed. 652 (1946)

5. Id. at 264.

6. Id.

7. 273 U.S. 359, 379, 47 S.Ct. 400, 71 L.Ed. 684 (1927). See also Zenith Radio Corp. v. Hazeltine Research, Inc., 395 U.S. 100, 124–25, 89 S.Ct. 1562, 23 L.Ed.2d 129 (1969), *reversed* 401 U.S. 321, 91 S.Ct. 795, 28 L.Ed.2d 77 (1971); United States v. General Dynamics Corp., 415 U.S. 486, 501, 94 S.Ct. 1186, 39 L.Ed.2d 530 (1974); J. Truett Payne Co., Inc. v. Chrysler Motors Corp., 451 U.S. 557, 565–67, 101 S.Ct. 1923, 68 L.Ed.2d 442 (1981).

17.7b. The Economic Debate Concerning the Measure of Damages

The economic debate about possible overdeterrence produced by private enforcement has spilled over into discussions about the proper measure of damages. A number of writers have addressed the concern that payment of damages to private plaintiffs may overdeter because any anticompetitive injury may be counterbalanced by efficiencies associated with the antitrust violation and because of the high costs associated with enforcement.[8] However, concerns that the costs of antitrust enforcement may exceed the benefits have already shaped both the law concerning antitrust injury,[9] and the law narrowing the scope of *per se* analysis to assure that efficiencies can be factored into decisions about liability.[10] Whether and to what extent these same concerns should influence the standards of proof for damages, or the way in which those damages are calculated, remains a matter of active theoretical discussion. Courts have so far largely ignored this debate.

As a matter of theory, one can isolate the factors that would be relevant for providing the ideal amount of deterrence for antitrust violations. According to Becker,[11] there are three costs to harmful conduct: (1) the costs imposed by the conduct (in the case of antitrust violations, inefficient allocation of resources and wealth transfers benefitting those exercising market power); (2) enforcement costs (including the cost of detection, investigation and adjudication); and (3) the costs of sanctions imposed on the violator. To achieve the ideal level of deterrence, the sum of these three costs must be minimized. That task is difficult because reducing one cost (costs related to enforcement) may increase another (costs resulting from antitrust violations). Increasing enforcement costs will decrease the cost of violations, but at some point the additional revenue spent on enforcement will no longer provide an offsetting return in reduced antitrust violations. Some writers conclude that monopoly pricing resulting in overcharges could best be deterred by a measure of damages that adds the amount of the overcharge (wealth transfer injury) to the deadweight loss (allocation injury).[12] Of course, any measure of damages designed to achieve the ideal level of deterrence will fail to compensate some victims of antitrust violations. At some point, additional dollars spent on enforcement will no longer provide

---

8. Prominent examples of this literature include: W. SCHWARTZ, PRIVATE ENFORCEMENT OF THE ANTITRUST LAWS: AN ECONOMIC CRITIQUE (1981); W. BREIT & K. ELZINGA, ANTITRUST PENALTY REFORM: AN ECONOMIC ANALYSIS (1986); Hovenkamp, *Treble Damages Reform*, 33 ANTITRUST BULL. 233 (1988); Page, *Antitrust Damages and Economic Efficiency: An Approach to Antitrust Injury*, 47 U. CHI. L.REV. 467 (1980).

9. See § 17.2a.

10. Broadcast Music, Inc. v. Columbia Broadcasting System, 441 U.S. 1, 99 S.Ct. 1551, 60 L.Ed.2d 1 (1979).

11. Becker, *Crime and Punishment: An Economic Approach*, 76 J. POL. ECON. 169, 181 (1968).

12. Page, *The Scope of Liability for Antitrust Violations*, 37 STAN. L. REV. 1445 (1985); H. HOVENKAMP, FEDERAL ANTITRUST POLICY, THE LAW OF COMPETITION AND ITS PRACTICE § 17.2b (3d ed. 2005). Hovenkamp points out that this rule is not adjusted to account for any efficiencies that are associated with an anticompetitive practice. Id.

sufficient additional deterrence to anticompetitive conduct, so some victims would bear their loss. But identifying these tendencies theoretically does not provide workable tools for policy. The Federal Reserve Board may be able to fine-tune interest rates by observing tendencies for inflation to increase or decrease because there are useful, if not ideal, measures of inflation. But antitrust enforcers cannot ratchet enforcement efforts up and down and observe the effect either on the frequency of violation or on the extent to which market actors back away from conduct in grey areas.

The preceding analysis does not account for the compensation goal, which has long been and should remain a major purpose of private enforcement.[13] As a society, we have chosen to provide compensation for most victims of conduct transgressing the law, be it criminal or civil law. Compensation of the victim, quite appropriately, has been the primary touchstone for court measures of antitrust damages. There is theoretical likelihood that using compensation of the victim as a damage measure will produce a level of deterrence other than ideal. But even if achieving the mythical ideal deterrence were the sole goal of private enforcement, any approach for achieving that goal would, in its implementation by the courts, surely fall well short of it.

As Hovenkamp points out, a damage measure that requires the court to determine the value of deadweight loss, overcharge, enforcement costs, and countervailing efficiencies associated with the defendant's conduct would force the court to address many imponderables and could greatly escalate the costs of litigation.[14] Simply stated, there is no readily available accounting data with which to determine the amount of deadweight loss or the extent of efficiencies associated with a transaction. When victim compensation is the primary measure of damages, the court will still have to address (in many cases) one of these issues–the amount of the overcharge–but will be spared any obligation to determine values for the remaining costs or efficiencies.

17.7c.   Damages for Cartel or Monopoly Overcharges

Although not without its difficulties perhaps the most manageable damage problem is that faced by the downstream buyers that pay supracompetitive prices to cartelists or monopolists (or their analogs, upstream sellers whose prices are depressed by a monopsonist or a buying cartel). When an antitrust violation injures a buyer of a product sold by a seller possessing market power, the proper measure of damages is the amount of the overcharge—that is, the amount by which the rigid price exceeded the free market price that would otherwise have prevailed. This would apply, for example, to a purchaser overcharged by a monopolist, overcharged by one or more participants in a cartel, or overcharged by a seller engaged in an unlawful tie-in or exclusive selling arrangement. Similar logic would apply to an antitrust plaintiff who is a

---

13. See the discussion of the goals of private enforcement in §§ 17.1b–1c.

14. HOVENKAMP, supra note 12, at § 17.2d.

seller of a product purchased by a buyer possessing market power (monopsony power)–the proper measurement of damages here would be the amount of the underpayment.

Although the logic of these overcharge cases is straightforward, conceptual problems emerge. The most basic is: what is the base price against which the overcharge is measured? As a matter of theory, the base price would be that which would result from competition: the marginal cost of producing the item.[15] Because establishing marginal cost based upon a theoretical model is problematic in real markets, courts are likely to look to other indicia. In the case of a cartel, courts may look to pre-cartel[16] or post-cartel prices,[17] adjusted, perhaps, to reflect identifiable ways in which pre-or post-conspiracy prices were affected by factors differing from those prevailing during the conspiracy. Use of this approach finds support in Supreme Court cases earlier this century,[18] but has been criticized as inconclusive, at least when other causal factors influence prices.[19] There is, of course, no assurance that the price charged before or after the conspiracy was not influenced by price leadership or other parallel conduct that pushed the price well above marginal cost (in which case its use would underestimate damages). But it is also possible that other factors (such as short-term oversupply) have unduly depressed prices during the pre-or post-conspiracy periods (in which case use of pre-and post-conspiracy prices might overstate the damages). The risk of such distortions is reduced (but not eliminated) if comparisons are drawn to both pre-and post-conspiracy prices.

Another approach to measuring cartel damages would be to compare prices charged by nearby sellers who are not involved in the conspiracy.[20] This measure will also under-compensate if these sellers are pricing above marginal cost under the umbrella of the cartel and, just as reliance on pre-and post-conspiracy prices, becomes less reliable as additional variables affect the prices in nearby markets. The willingness of courts to rely on such imperfect measures may be impelled by the realization that no reasonably attainable better measure is available, that many of the possible errors that can be identified would under-compensate, not

15. Marginal cost pricing is of course unlikely in real markets. See the discussion of the model of perfect competition in § 2.3a.

16. Cf. American Crystal Sugar Co. v. Mandeville Island Farms, Inc., 195 F.2d 622, 625–26 (9th Cir.1952) *cert. denied*, 343 U.S. 957, 72 S.Ct. 1052, 96 L.Ed. 1357 (1952).

17. E.g., Wall Products Co. v. National Gypsum Co., 357 F.Supp. 832 (N.D.Cal. 1973).

18. Eastman Kodak v. Southern Photo Materials Co., 273 U.S. 359, 378–79, 47 S.Ct. 400, 71 L.Ed. 684 (1927); Story Parchment Co. v. Paterson Parchment Paper Co.,

282 U.S. 555, 561, 51 S.Ct. 248, 75 L.Ed. 544 (1931).

19. Isaksen v. Vermont Castings, Inc., 825 F.2d 1158, 1165 (7th Cir.1987).

20. Cases employing a yardstick method include National Farmers' Org. v. Associated Milk Producers, 850 F.2d 1286, 1294–98 (8th Cir.1988), *cert. denied*, 489 U.S. 1081, 109 S.Ct. 1535, 103 L.Ed.2d 840 (1989); Metrix Warehouse, Inc. v. Daimler–Benz Aktiengesellschaft, 828 F.2d 1033, 1044 (4th Cir.1987), *cert. denied*, 486 U.S. 1017, 108 S.Ct. 1753, 100 L.Ed.2d 215 (1988); Home Placement Service, Inc. v. Providence Journal Co., 819 F.2d 1199 1205–1206 (1st Cir.1987).

over-compensate, and that the wrongdoer should not be allowed to avoid damages because of imperfections in the plaintiff's showing.

Many antitrust plaintiffs employ an economist to provide expert backing for a showing of damages based on a model (such as pre-or post-conspiracy prices). An economist may make use of regression analysis to assist in isolating the impact of cartel pricing.[21] Regression analysis allows an economist to take two or more variables and isolate the impact of one of those variables. For example, if the price of an item was likely to have been influenced by each of three factors (cartel behavior, shortage of supply of an input part needed to produce the item and introduction of a newly patented rival product), regression analysis provides a technique by which the impact of cartel pricing can be isolated. Although regression analysis is a highly respected statistical method, the analysis will produce sound results only to the extent it accounts for all of the relevant variables and uses reliable input data. Of course, defendants need not accept the views of the plaintiff's economic expert and typically offer their own economic evidence to question and critique the plaintiff's analysis.

Once the amount of the overcharge is determined, there is still the question of whether the full amount of the overcharge represents the plaintiff's damage. When the defendants are found to have engaged in unlawful cartel behavior, the accepted rule is that the plaintiff should be awarded damages based upon the full extent of the overcharge. But in the case of conduct that abuses a firm's monopoly position, the Second Circuit has held that compensation ought not to be based on the full extent of the monopoly overcharge.[22] Instead, the damages should be based on the increment in price created by defendant's abusive conduct. A monopolist, it is reasoned, has committed no violation of the antitrust laws merely by charging a monopoly price. The violation must be based on some additional conduct that constitutes an abuse of monopoly power.[23] But this approach may not be the wisest policy choice.

It is true that the possession of monopoly power by itself does not violate the Sherman Act. This feature of the law can be traced to a desire to reward innovative competitors who achieve monopoly power without abuse and to encourage entry. But a monopolist who seeks to retain its monopoly power through abuse is no longer engaged in procompetitive conduct. Such a firm has forfeited the right to retain an overcharge that is based upon classic antitrust injuries—the allocation and wealth transfer loss associated with monopoly power. A participant in a cartel cannot

---

21. See J. Greenfield & M. Polinsky, The Use of Economists in Antitrust Litigation (A.B.A. Mono. 1984). Hoyt, Dahl & Gibson, *Comprehensive Models for Assessing Lost Profits to Antitrust Plaintiffs*, 60 Minn. L. Rev. 1233 (1976).

22. Berkey Photo, Inc. v. Eastman Kodak Co., 603 F.2d 263 (2d Cir.1979), cert. denied, 444 U.S. 1093, 100 S.Ct. 1061, 62 L.Ed.2d 783 (1980). The *Berkey* holding was

followed in Allegheny Pepsi–Cola Bottling Co. v. Mid–Atlantic Coca–Cola Bottling Co., 690 F.2d 411, 415 (4th Cir.1982).

23. See § 3.4. The view that damages for unlawful monopolization should be limited to the price increment caused by abusive behavior is held by the writers of a well-known antitrust treatise. P. Areeda & H. Hovenkamp, Antitrust Law ¶ 710 (1994).

claim a right to retain a portion of its overcharge simply because it might have lawfully retained an overcharge based upon tacit, parallel conduct that did not meet the requirements for a conspiracy. Once a plaintiff shows that a defendant's conduct meets the requirements for an antitrust violation, the plaintiff ought to receive compensation for the full extent of the overcharge, although an exception may be in order for statutorily granted monopolies for copyrights or patents.

17.7d. Loss of Profits and Its Proof

Many other antitrust violations involve injuries not to buyers or sellers that deal with the violators but to their competitors. For example, a boycott or a monopoly predation may result in loss of business by one or more competitors, and there may be sufficient evidence to prove the violation and the fact of injury. If so, the indicated measure of damages may be loss of profits, but these may be difficult to estimate. Once again, "yard sticks" may be useful. The difference between a plaintiff's profits before the violation began and/or after it ceased and profits during the violation period are certainly relevant data. So, too, might the profits of the plaintiff itself during the violation period but in another market, one not impacted by the violation, where its operations were similar to those in the market where the violation occurred. If plaintiff itself is not active in any other comparable, unaffected market, perhaps it will be possible to identify another firm in such a market sufficiently similar in its operations to serve as an analog for plaintiff. All such approaches are problematical, and subject to challenge by rebuttal evidence challenging the similarities between the damage period and any analog period, the damage market and any analog market, and the defendant and its operations and those of any analog firm.[24] Plaintiff might also attempt to prove lost profits through expert evidence, always a problematical approach, especially when little or no profitable experience with the business can be established.[25]

§ 17.8 Private Enforcement Issues

17.8a. Prima Facie Evidence and Offensive Collateral Estoppel

Many private enforcement actions are follow-ons to government enforcement action, either announced investigations or actual cases filed by an enforcement agency. Congress has recognized and to a limited extent encouraged these follow-on actions through enactment of Section 5(a) of the Clayton Act.[1] That section allows a plaintiff to use final

24. See Parker, *Measuring Damages in Federal Treble Damage Actions*, 17 Antitrust Bull. 497 (1972). Note, *Private Treble Damage Antitrust Suits: Measure of Damages for Destruction of All or Part of a Business*, 80 Harv. L. Rev. 1566 (1967); Bigelow v. RKO Radio Pictures, Inc., 327 U.S. 251, 66 S.Ct. 574, 90 L.Ed. 652 (1946); Theatre Investment Co. v. RKO Radio Pic

tures, 72 F.Supp. 650, 656 (W.D.Wash. 1947).

25. Dominicus Americana Bohio v. Gulf & Western Industries, 473 F.Supp. 680 (S.D.N.Y.1979).

§ 17.8

1. 15 U.S.C. § 16(a).

judgments or decrees in a civil or criminal proceeding brought by the United States as prima facie evidence in a follow-on action against the same defendant "as to all matters respecting which said judgment or decree would be an estoppel as between the parties thereto." However, Congress severely limited the reach of this provision. No prima facie effect is to be given "to consent judgments or decrees entered before any testimony has been taken."[2] In addition, Section 5(a) provides that no collateral estoppel effect shall be given to findings of the Federal Trade Commission under the antitrust laws or under Section 5 of the FTC Act.

The offensive use of the doctrine of collateral estoppel is broader than Section 5(a) except that it, too, cannot be based on FTC findings. A plaintiff may make use of collateral estoppel not only with respect to prior Justice Department suits but also with respect to any private suit that has resulted in a judgment or decree against the same defendant. Offensive collateral estoppel is also a stronger doctrine than the prima facie evidence treatment in Section 5(a): estoppel may preclude the defendant from any further litigation on the relevant issues, whereas Section 5(a), when it applies, still allows the defendant to attempt to rebut the prima facie evidence. But the Supreme Court has imposed additional conditions on the application of collateral estoppel, requiring a showing that the plaintiff could not have easily joined the prior action, that the stake in the first action for the defendant was not very small, that there not be inconsistent rulings on the same issue in past actions against the same defendant, and that current action not afford the defendant procedural opportunities unavailable in the prior litigation.[3]

The logic behind Congress' decision to deny a Section 5(a) effect to any finding of the Federal Trade Commission should not go unchallenged. An FTC holding with respect to Section 5 of the FTC Act would not be directly useful to a private plaintiff because that section cannot be enforced in private suits. But the broader language of Section 5(a) of the Clayton Act precludes collateral estoppel effect even to holdings of the FTC Act governing other antitrust laws that the FTC can enforce, such as the Clayton Act. Here, the rationale for Congress' action is open to question. It is true that FTC findings are those of administrative tribunal (not of a federal court), but the procedural protections available in such an administrative proceeding are comparable to those available under Federal Rules of Civil Procedure. Moreover, a respondent subject to an adverse holding by the FTC may seek review of the Commission's decisions in a United States Court of Appeal and, finally, in the United States Supreme Court. There seems no convincing reason for treating the Commission's application of the Clayton Act differently from applications of federal courts.

17.8b. Joint and Several Liability and Contribution

Although Section 4 of the Clayton Act does not say so expressly, that Section (granting an injured "person" the authority to sue in a U.S.

---

2. Id.

3. Parklane Hosiery Co. v. Shore, 439 U.S. 322, 99 S.Ct. 645, 58 L.Ed.2d 552 (1979).

district court for "the district in which the defendant resides or is found * * * and * * * recover threefold the damages by him sustained")[4] has long been read as permitting a plaintiff to hold a defendant jointly and severally liable. This allows a plaintiff to identify a single participant in unlawful activity and sue that participant for threefold the damages suffered by the plaintiff, even if other unnamed participants were necessary for the success of the unlawful conduct (e.g., a conspiracy such as price fixing) and even if the true instigator of the conduct was one such unnamed participant. Such a result can be defended, for example, if the unnamed participants are judgment proof or beyond the jurisdiction of the court. Forcing a single defendant to pay threefold the damages caused by all participants in the conspiracy might be an awesome deterrent for any firm considering joining an unlawful conspiracy. But other participants in the conspiracy will pay no damages, so the deterrence claim is clouded. Whether or not joint and several liability enhances deterrence may turn on whether defendants tend to be risk averse: if defendants contemplating participation in a cartel are unwilling to take the gamble that they will escape all liability because of the risk of a much higher judgment against individual firms, then joint and several liability would increase deterrence.

Joint and several liability also gives the plaintiff discretion much like that held by a prosecutor to reward defendants who settle early or who, as a part of a settlement, provide evidence necessary to establish the violation. This may be the most important advantage of joint and several liability. It can allow plaintiffs to maintain successfully antitrust claims that could not be won without the inducement of attractive settlement terms for those that cooperate with the plaintiff.

But defendants rightly perceive a potentially more pernicious aspect of the settlement discretion resting in the plaintiff's hands. In what is described as a "whipsaw" tactic, plaintiffs usually escalate demands with each successive defendant who agrees to settle. Thus, the last firm to settle will generally pay a much higher amount than the first to settle. This can create disharmony among defendants, perhaps inciting one defendant to bid against another to be the first to settle. A defendant firm that perceives its conduct as lawful may wish to litigate, but as other defendants around it settle for low but increasing amounts, the risk for that defendant firm in declining to settle mounts steadily. Joint and several liability means that threefold the remaining unpaid damages will have to be paid by any defendant that abjures settlement, litigates, and loses. Unquestionably, this places additional risk on such defendants, at least some of whom may have sound defenses that, in the absence of joint and several liability, would inspire them to litigate. While responsible plaintiffs' attorneys may take the measure of a firm's culpability in negotiating damage settlements, there is no assurance that all plaintiffs' attorneys will be able to assess accurately, or choose to take account of, relative culpability. Injustices can occur if less culpable

4. Section 4 of the Clayton Act, 15 U.S.C.A. § 15.

defendants, who may have a greater incentive to litigate, are saddled with disproportionately high amounts of damage.

Concerns such as this led a defendant, who was the sole target of the plaintiff's antitrust claim, to seek to join other alleged co-conspirators to the law suit, asserting a right to obtain contribution from these firms in the event of the plaintiff established liability. In 1981, the Supreme Court addressed these facts in Texas Industries, Inc. v. Radcliff Materials, Inc.[5] The Court acknowledged that the original common law position that joint tortfeasors had no right of contribution had been eroded by state legislation and state court decisions. The Court also reviewed the policy arguments for recognizing a right of contribution, including the point that contribution can more justly allocate damages among culpable defendants. The Court also reviewed arguments against recognizing contribution rights, among them the complexity of determining the proper allocation formula among defendants, a complexity sure to lead to additional litigation and expense. Should damages be "allocated according to market shares, relative profits, sales to the particular plaintiff, the [defendant's] role in the organization and operation of the conspiracy, or simply pro rata, assessing an equal amount against each participant on the theory that each one is equally liable for the injury caused by collective action?"[6]

Without attempting to resolve the policy debate, the Court concluded that, absent an express or implied statement of congressional intent, there was no judicial power to graft a system of contribution onto an antitrust remedy that had existed for 90 years. It was, the Court concluded, a matter for Congress to resolve.[7]

Congress has so far not accepted the Court's invitation. There has been no lack of proposals put before the Congress. Perhaps the most seriously pursued bills would have instituted not a right of contribution but simply a formula for "claim reduction." As each successive defendant reaches a settlement with the plaintiff, the damage pool for the remaining defendants would be reduced by the full amount of the settling defendant's share regardless of the amount of the actual settlement. This approach would greatly reduce the plaintiff's leverage in pressuring defendants to settle early. It would also force the plaintiff to bear the loss of any initial settlement that did not meet the settling defendant's share of the damages. Although potentially less of a breeding ground for litigation than a contribution scheme, claims reduction proposals still face the nettlesome problem of determining the proper formula by which a settling defendant's share of the damages is set. Some proposals have sought to limit claims reduction to horizontal cartel cases, where damage share might be logically set based on market share. But if joint and several liability remains an important tool by which plaintiffs can successfully prosecute antitrust violations, it is counterintuitive to take away this pro-enforcement tool only in cases involving

---

5. 451 U.S. 630, 101 S.Ct. 2061, 68 L.Ed.2d 500 (1981).

6. Id. at 637.

7. Id. at 638–647.

hard-core cartel violations, but not for other antitrust claims involving potentially more complex or "gray" areas of the law.

Joint and several liability remains the law for private antitrust suits. Those who would change the law have so far been unable to craft a proposal for limiting or eliminating joint and several liability without significantly undermining enforcement incentives and complicating litigation.[8]

17.8c.   Evidentiary Limitations on Expert Witnesses

A significant issue for antitrust litigants (perhaps of particular concern to private plaintiffs because of possible cost and summary judgment implications) arises from Daubert v. Merrill Dow Pharmaceuticals.[9] This products liability case, replete with personal suffering, and equally painful realities about liability, resulted in a Supreme Court decision that will radiate through many other areas of law and policy. Antitrust is one of them. By lowering one bar to expert opinion testimony and raising another, the Court may have once again shifted the odds at least marginally against the shallow-pocket antitrust plaintiff.

Before *Daubert* scientific experts could qualify to testify if the methodology used was generally accepted in the scientific community, but not otherwise.[10] That so-called *Frye* standard entailed a delegation to recognized scientific communities: if peers would listen respectfully to the testimony so would the court (and could a jury). If not, the juridical system would not process the expert's claims at all. In *Daubert* plaintiff relied on attenuated science, a kind of a common sense deduction from a sequence of facts, made by a witness with scientific qualifications. The issue was whether this testimony should have reached the jury, despite its weakness in the category of peer acceptance.

In *Daubert* plaintiff challenged the *Frye* standard as too stringent and inconsistent with the openness to all relevant evidence that imbues the Federal Rules. Accepting this characterization, the Court labeled the old standard as rigid and capable of excluding opinion based on new scientific knowledge. But the Court, in fashioning a new standard to relax "traditional barriers to 'opinion' testimony",[11] structured an approach open to relevant but unconventional evidence, yet capable of excluding an opinion that a trial court finds to be unreliable.[12] If

---

8. Various reform proposals and their merits and deficiencies are considered in Cavanagh, *Contribution, Claim Reduction and Individual Treble Damage Responsibility: Which Path to Reform of Antitrust Remedies?* 40 VAND. L. REV. 1277 (1987).

9. 509 U.S. 579, 113 S.Ct. 2786, 125 L.Ed.2d 469 (1993).

10. Id. at 586 n. 4, which string cites cases using the "generally accepted" standard. The foundation case, Frye v. United States, 293 Fed. 1013 (D.C.Cir.1923) is discussed.

11. *Daubert*, 509 U.S. at 588.

12. Gavil, *After Daubert: Discerning the Increasingly Fine Line Between the Admissibility and Sufficiency of Expert Testimony in Antitrust Litigation*, 65 ANTITRUST L.J. 663 (1997). ("*After Daubert*") stresses the Court's purpose to lower the *Frye* barrier. But Gavil, by putting the qualification issue in the context of new practice rules accelerating trial time tables and the new readiness of Courts to decide economic issues in antitrust cases on their own, also shows that the *Daubert* rule will give rise to signif-

scientific evidence is offered, the trial court evaluates "whether the reasoning or methodology properly can be applied to the facts at issue * * *."[13] To decide, the court should consider several factors: testability of the expert's inference; the extent to which the expert's approach is subject to publication and peer review; any known or potential means of evaluating likelihood or error; the availability of controlling standards; and (directly reflecting the *Frye* test) the extent of peer acceptance of the approach.[14]

Initially, there may have been doubt whether *Daubert* applied to expert analysis of market structure and conduct. The Court's list of *Daubert* factors have the aura of hard science, the scent of the Bunsen burner. But the Court has now made evident that the scope of *Daubert* is broader.[15] The *Daubert* goal, to limit expert testimony to relevant opinions based on analysis and methodology that are reliable, applies beyond the laboratory. The new approach must now be taken to apply to all experts, presumably including economists. Given the rapidity with which the rules require discovery about intentions to use experts, the importance to outcomes of expert analysis of antitrust questions,[16] and the extent to which courts may rule as a matter of law on inductive or deductive issues more conventionally characterized as matters for the trier of fact,[17] the effects on antitrust litigation may be substantial.

icant case management issues both for parties and court.

13. Id. at 592.

14. Id. at 594.

15. Kumho Tire Co., Ltd. v. Carmichael, 526 U.S. 137, 119 S.Ct. 1167, 143 L.Ed.2d 238 (1999).

16. See Sullivan, *Post-Chicago Economics: Economists, Lawyers, Judges, and En-* *forcement Officials in a Less Determinate Theoretical World*, 63 ANTITRUST L.J. 669 (1995).

17. Matsushita Elec. Industry Co. v. Zenith Radio Corp., 475 U.S. 574, 106 S.Ct. 1348, 89 L.Ed.2d 538 (1986); but see Eastman Kodak Co. v. Image Tech. Services, Inc., 504 U.S. 451, 112 S.Ct. 2072, 119 L.Ed.2d 265 (1992). See the discussion in *After Daubert*, supra note 12.

Chapter XVIII

ANTITRUST IN GLOBAL MARKETS: THE EXTRA TERRITORIAL REACH OF UNILATERAL RULES; COMPARATIVE ANTITRUST; AND CONFLICTING NATIONAL REQUIREMENTS AND BILATERAL AND MULTILATERAL EFFORTS TO RESOLVE THEM

Table of Sections

---

§ 18.1 Introduction

No doubt other areas of antitrust, being dynamic, portend both risk and opportunity. Yet, none signifies greater hazard nor hope of constructive development than do conflicts in national competition policies in a global economy. Nor does any other area challenge theorists, officials and practitioners to draw on a wider range of the resources of law and policy to fashion workable solutions to existing tensions. Communication, information and productive technology have exploded, exports and imports have burgeoned among trading nations; capital ownership has been transformed and capital as well as product and service transactions have moved from more regulated national markets to less regulated international markets. All of this, along with the dismantling of trade barriers by international organizations including the GATT and the WTO, by the European Union and by regional free trade constructs has led to an increasingly integrated global capital market, to investments by major trading firms in plants abroad, to stimulated trading not only in final but also in intermediate goods and services, and to accelerated rates of international movement for all factors. There are several policy infrastructures important for this global market. One of these—one of several which is not yet adequately accommodating in its responses to globalization—is competition policy. If anything like a seamless global market is ultimately to emerge, the antitrust norms of major trading nations must either be better harmonized or at least made more transparent by greater substantive predictability or greater choice of law predictability, or both.

This chapter deals with some of the salient issues. It describes relevant areas of current U.S. antitrust law, criticizes it and points to possible paths for development. In § 18.2 the geographic reach of substantive U.S. antitrust, a series of developments and accommodations leading to the "purpose and effects test," the basic U.S. choice of law rule for antitrust, is examined. In this section the readiness of U.S. policy to protect U.S. markets from agitations that spread from foreign conduct is emphasized and contrasted with the relatively permissive U.S.

response to domestic conduct that causes competitive harm abroad. Comity is discussed, both conventional judicial conceptions and diplomatic or positive comity, efforts of U.S. and foreign officials to cooperate and accommodate. Because antitrust systems share a commitment to the goal of rational resource allocation and consumer welfare, room for cooperation is broad. But the scope, form and intensity of commitments to competition vary from nation to nation. The foreign system most like the U.S. system is that of the European Union. It, rather than Asian or other systems, will be used here for comparison. But competition policy even in the European Union—which is displacing U.S. antitrust as the model toward which countries throughout much of the world are turning when they seek to develop competition policy—evokes a more active governmental presence than does the U.S. system. Moreover, the European system, when compared to the U.S. system, has wider policy goals and looser theoretical guides to outcomes. Hence, conflict sometimes occurs and can be intense when officials in one system view internationally significant conduct as socially harmful while those in the other regard the same conduct as beneficial.

In § 18.2 the U.S. claim of competence to apply U.S. law to foreign conduct affecting U.S. markets is described. In § 18.3 the reciprocal claims of the EU to apply EU law to conduct in the U.S. that harms competition in the EU is noted. Section 18.4 considers whether EU law can be used to protect U.S. markets from anticompetitive conduct in Europe. Section 18.5 introduces possible defenses to U.S. antitrust available where a foreign government influences market outcomes. Section 18.6 compares substantive U.S. and EU antitrust policy in respect to single firm power, oligopoly, cartelization, consolidation and governmental participation in the economy. Section 18.7 examines some of the significant conflicts that have already occurred between the U.S. and the EU when officials in one system oppose particular market conduct while officials in the other either actively encourage or tolerate the same conduct because they regard it as falling into an area where unconstrained market choices must be allowed if efficiency is to be maximized. Section 18.8 brings the chapter to an end with a brief history of efforts, now active once again, to harmonize antitrust and to develop a multilateral antitrust code.

§ 18.2 The Extraterritorial Reach of U.S. Antitrust

18.2a. Foreign Conduct by Foreign Firms Affecting U.S. Imports

18.2a1. The Purpose and Effects Test: The Basic U.S. Rule for Imports

Issues about the international reach of antitrust can arise in either an import or an export context. In import situations, where the anticompetitive conduct is foreign but the adverse impact is felt here, the U.S. economic interest is strong. Yet, foreign government interests or sensitivities may also be palpable. Most cases involving issues about extraterritorial effects are cases where U.S. law is used to challenge foreign conduct affecting U.S. imports.[1] Because competition policy is made nationally and different nations have different views about the goals that markets should advance, conflict can occur where a transaction in one nation has significant effects in another. As a distinguished commentator has put it, when such conflict occurs, an affected country must make a choice. It can either try to resolve the question diplomatically (by seeking to persuade the other country to accept its rule, perhaps by offering some accommodation or, more aggressively, by threatening sanctions if it does not) or it can "simply apply its own law directly to the transaction."[2] The latter course leaves the conflicting foreign law unchanged, but uses available sanctions to compel foreign actors in the transaction to comply with the law of the affected country. Of course, "applying its own law directly to the transaction" need not be clamorously confrontational. The law, as well as diplomacy, has its means of accommodation: international law about national jurisdiction to prescribe, traditional judicial conflict of laws rules, and principles of comity. Accommodation might be achieved through the legal system as well as diplomatically.

To the extent that anything can be "settled" by a five to four Supreme Court decision generating critical commentary of both majority and minority opinions,[3] the basic U.S. rule was settled in Hartford Fire Insurance Co. v. California.[4] The Supreme Court adopted a seemingly unrelenting "purpose and effects" test to gauge the Sherman Act's extraterritorial scope of application. The plaintiffs were nineteen states and several private parties; the defendants included four leading U.S. insurance companies, some U.S. reinsurance companies, some U.S. brokers and trade associations (including ISO, an agency that gathers statistics and analyzes loss data for insurance companies), and a number of U.K. reinsurance companies operating in London. The issue addressed here, on which the Court split, is the applicability of Section 1 of the Sherman Act to policies of reinsurance issued by U.K. reinsurers on

---

§ 18.2

1. In export situations U.S. enforcement usually challenges conduct causing harm here, and has a territorial justification; hence, such enforcement seldom generates foreign resistance. There are some examples of foreign governments being resistant to antitrust constraints imposed by the U.S. on U.S. export trade. In Zenith Radio Corp. v. Hazeltine Research, 395 U.S. 100, 89 S.Ct. 1562, 23 L.Ed.2d 129 (1969), the damage to a U.S. exporter was based on evidence that a Canadian patent pool had the effect of reducing the plaintiff's export sales from the U.S. to Canada. Foreign states might also be critical where the U.S. does not enforce its antitrust rules against private restraints on exports because the harm done by such restraints occurs abroad.

2. Dam, *Extraterritoriality In An Age of Globalization: The Hartford Fire Case*, 1993 Sup. Ct. Rev. 289, 292–93, 323–25 (1993).

3. Dam, supra note 2; Kramer, *Note: Extraterritorial Application of American Law After The Insurance Antitrust Case: A Reply to Professors Lowenfeld and Trimble*, 89 Am. J. Int'l L. 750 (1995); Lowenfeld, *Comment: Conflict, Balancing of Interests, and the Exercise of Jurisdiction to Prescribe: Reflections on the Insurance Antitrust Case*, 89 Am. J. Int'l L. 42 (1995); Trimble, *Comment: The Supreme Court and International Law: The Demise of Restatement Section 403*, 89 Am. J. Int'l L. 53 (1995).

4. 509 U.S. 764, 113 S.Ct. 2891, 125 L.Ed.2d 612 (1993).

commercial general liability policies issued by the four insurance company defendants to U.S. policy holders.

Hartford and the other primary insurer defendants, as well as many other insurance companies, had for years issued "occurrence based" liability policies conforming to a standard form widely used by insurers and for which the ISO gathered and circulated loss data. Under these policies the issuer was liable for any loss resulting from a covered occurrence during the term of the policy, regardless of when the harm eventuated and a claim arose. The allegations (taken as true for the district court's dismissal of the claim) were that the defendant insurers wanted to stop issuing these policies and to substitute a "claims made" policy which would protect only against claims that were made during the policy term and arose during a period specified in the policy. Because insureds preferred the older "long tail risks" policies, the market would inhibit that change unless other insurers also stopped issuing occurrence based policies. To attain this outcome the defendant insurers induced ISO to agree to stop providing loss data on long tail policies, and also induced reinsurers, including those in London who wrote a large share of the reinsurance, to stop reinsuring long tail risks. The U.S. defendants relied on a statutory defense, the McCarran–Ferguson Act, a matter discussed elsewhere.[5] The London reinsurers raised the extraterritoriality issue. Although conceding that their conduct had a significant effect in the U.S., they contended that the Sherman Act did not govern their conduct because they were U.K. firms doing business in London in complete compliance with U.K. law, which did not subject them to constraints on agreements like that being challenged, but rather subjected them to a regime (based largely on industry self regulation) which approved cooperative decision making of the kind alleged in the complaint.

The district court[6] had accepted the reinsurers' extraterritorial defense on the basis of Timberlane Lumber v. Bank of America, N.T. & S.A.[7] *Timberlane* had held that U.S. antitrust covered some but not all foreign conduct affecting U.S. commerce, that at some point the interest of the U.S. was "too weak and the foreign harmony incentive for restraint too strong" to justify an extraterritorial assertion of jurisdiction by the U.S.[8] The *Hartford* court of appeals also saw the reinsurers' defense as raising a *Timberlane* comity question, but in a careful opinion for the court Judge Noonan concluded that the U.S. interests in protecting against adverse effects in the U.S. outweighed the British self regulatory interest.[9] However, the Supreme Court majority rejected *Timberlane* entirely. The opinion by Justice Souter flatly holds that conduct by foreign parties in a foreign nation that would violate the Sherman Act if engaged in here constitutes a violation by the foreign

5. See the discussion in § 14.3b.

6. The district court opinion is reported as In re Insurance Antitrust Litigation, 723 F.Supp. 464 (N.D.Cal.1989).

7. 549 F.2d 597 (9th Cir.1976).

8. Id. at 609.

9. California v. Hartford Fire Insurance Co., 938 F.2d 919 (9th Cir.1991).

parties if they intended the conduct to, and it did in fact, hurt competition in a U.S. market, subject only to a narrow and limited defense based on foreign legal compulsion. The majority saw it as no defense that foreign law conflicts with U.S. law merely in the sense that the foreign nation has "a strong policy to permit or encourage [the] conduct."[10] A comity defense for foreign conduct intended to have and actually having a significant effect here can be considered by a U.S. antitrust court only when the defendants' "compliance with the laws of both countries is * * * impossible."[11]

In reaching this result the *Hartford* majority took it as "well established * * * that the Sherman Act applies to foreign conduct" that satisfies an intent and effects test.[12] For the majority this disposed of any "jurisdictional" issue. Justice Scalia, in dissent, used a different analytical framework. He agreed that the lower court possessed subject matter jurisdiction—the issue under Section 1331 of the Judicial Code that was satisfied once plaintiffs "asserted nonfrivolous claims" under the substantive statute.[13] But for Justice Scalia the extraterritorial reach of the Sherman Act "has nothing to do with the jurisdiction of the courts * * *."[14] Whether the Sherman Act reached the conduct of the U.K. defendants in London was not jurisdictional, but a question on the merits. It should turn on the intent of Congress as expressed in the antitrust statute. But this intent issue did have a latent jurisdictional aspect—an issue not of judicial, but of "legislative jurisdiction," or "jurisdiction to prescribe,"[15] a matter conditioned by constitutional or international law constraints. The dissent answers this jurisdictional question in the affirmative also; the commerce clause gave Congress sweeping legislative jurisdiction to regulate commerce with other nations. For the dissent, this left the core concern: did Congress intend the Sherman Act to apply on facts like these?

On this issue of statutory construction, the Scalia dissent looked first to a canon to which the Court had recently given fresh vitality,[16] a presumption that unless a contrary intent appears, any act of Congress is intended to apply only within the territorial jurisdiction of the U.S.[17] But Scalia agreed with the majority that "it is now well established that the Sherman Act applies extraterritorially."[18] This, however, led him to another canon, one from *The Charming Betsy*,[19] an early nineteenth

---

10. 509 U.S. at 799.

11. Id.

12. Id. at 796. The Court cited United States v. Aluminum Company of America, 148 F.2d 416 (2d Cir.1945) (which does not bind it as a precedent, despite its special status), Matsushita Elec. Indus. Co., Ltd. v. Zenith Radio Co., 475 U.S. 574, 582, 106 S.Ct. 1348, 89 L.Ed.2d 538 (1986) (which is tangentially, not directly, relevant), and Continental Ore Co. v. Union Carbide, 370 U.S. 690, 704, 82 S.Ct. 1404, 8 L.Ed.2d 777 (1962) (which entailed both domestic and extraterritorial conduct by defendants).

13. 509 U.S. at 794.

14. Id. at 813.

15. Id. at 813.

16. See EEOC v. Aramco, 499 U.S. 244, 111 S.Ct. 1227, 113 L.Ed.2d 274 (1991).

17. 509 U.S. at 813.

18. Id. at 814.

19. Murray v. The Charming Betsy, 2 Cranch 64, 2 L.Ed. 208 (1804) (Marshall, C.J.).

century maritime case, that the dissent found dispositive: An " 'act of congress ought never to be construed to violate the law of nations if any other possible construction remains.' "[20]

Justice Scalia concluded from *The Charming Betsy* that international law did limit jurisdiction to prescribe. He accepted as governing the principle now announced in Section 403(1) of the Restatement of International Law[21] and exemplified by the holding in *Timberlane, supra.* The essence of his opinion is that prescriptive or legislative jurisdiction applied to extraterritorial conduct violates international law (as no statute should be construed to do unless its language compels) when such application would be unreasonable, taking account of all relevant factors, including: the extent of the activity in the regulating state; connections such as nationality, residence and economic activity between the regulating state and the regulated parties; the degree to which regulation of the kind involved is generally accepted as desirable; the extent to which another state has an interest; and the likelihood of conflict with regulation by another state. Justice Scalia found these Section 403(1) factors—essentially those which, with differing results, the court of appeals had evaluated under the aegis of *Timberlane*—to be dispositive against the application of U.S. law on the *Hartford* facts. He supported this conclusion only by a summary review of the factors, without indicating the direction in which he thought each factor disposed (hardly self evident points) and without disclosing in what respects he found the more detailed court of appeals analysis (which reached the opposite conclusion) to be faulty.[22]

After *Hartford*, some questions remain open. But given the unqualified tone of the majority opinion, there is little doubt about the basic rule, at least for now: if foreign conduct, even that of foreign firms, is taken with the intent to impact U.S. commerce, and if it does in fact significantly affect that commerce, that conduct is within the reach of the Sherman Act, subject only to the possible defense that foreign law compelled the foreign actors to engage in the conduct.[23]

18.2a2. Development of the Purpose and Effects Test

The Supreme Court's *Hartford* decision gives the antitrust bar a full blown black letter rule, although perhaps with some indistinct edges. This rule has a sinuous, if not a checkered, history—some of which may yet reassert itself. The applicability of the Sherman Act to conduct

---

20. *Hartford,* 509 U.S. at 814–15.

21. RESTATEMENT (THIRD) OF INTERNATIONAL LAW § 403(1).

22. *Hartford,* 509 U.S. 764 at 817–21, 113 S.Ct. 2891, 125 L.Ed.2d 612.

23. The text describes the defense as "possible" only because the Court did nothing to indicate its contours. Perhaps foreign compulsion would trump any conceivable U.S. interest in inhibiting adverse effects on U.S. markets. But perhaps not. An American court would be loath to put a firm in so vulnerable a position, but so, too, should the foreign sovereign. No doubt the Supreme Court would weigh unfairness to such a defendant heavily. It might therefore establish a conclusive presumption that foreign conduct compelled by a foreign sovereign does not violate the Sherman Act. But it might, instead, adopt only a strong presumption, one capable of being overcome by compelling U.S. interests. See § 18.5c.

abroad arose first in American Banana Co. v. United Fruit Co.[24] That case yielded an opinion for the Court by Justice Holmes that affirmed dismissal of a private antitrust claim on motion. American Banana alleged that defendant, United Fruit, had power in the banana market in South and Central America. When American Banana acquired property in Panama for banana trees and took other steps there and elsewhere to sell output in the U.S., United Fruit insisted that American Banana sell the Panama property to it. When American refused, United allegedly used tortious means to subvert foreign governmental activity in order to grasp the property. Notably, all of the challenged conduct occurred abroad and the only nexus to the U.S. was a possible future effect in a U.S. resale market. The Supreme Court, drawn to what it labeled as the "almost universal" conflict of laws or international law rule that the legality of an act "must be determined wholly by the law of the country where the act is done * * *," rejected American Banana's "surprising"[25] Sherman Act argument.

Despite *American Banana's* 1909 certainty about the U.S. judicial obligations to defer to the norms of other nations on a place of the tort principle, the Court modified this approach only five years later. In United States v. Pacific and Arabic Railway,[26] it held that a restraint on United States trade cannot escape the Sherman Act on the ground that part, although not all, of the relevant conduct occurred in a foreign country. This *Pacific-Arabic* view controlled again in United States v. Sisal Sales Corp.,[27] and was later tightly woven into Sherman Act tradition by Judge Hand's 1945 *Alcoa* opinion,[28] where the purpose and effects test (now regarded as settled both by the majority and the dissent in *Hartford*) was precisely articulated. In *Alcoa,* Limited, a Swiss corporation controlled by Alcoa's controlling stockholders, participated in a foreign cartel that affected U.S. prices. The court concluded that Alcoa, itself a U.S. corporation, did not control Limited and could not be held responsible for Limited's conduct. Hence, it faced the question whether Limited, a foreign corporation, violated the Sherman Act through its own conduct that took place only outside the United States, but that had a significant competitive effect within this country. Judge Hand phrased the issue much as did Justice Scalia in *Hartford*:

> "[W]e are concerned only with whether Congress chose to attach liability to the conduct outside the United States of persons not in allegiance to it * * * [and, if it did] whether our own Constitution permitted it to do so* * *. Nevertheless, * * * we are not to read general words, such a those in [the Sherman] Act, without regard to

---

24. 213 U.S. 347, 29 S.Ct. 511, 53 L.Ed. 826 (1909).

25. Id. at 355.

26. 228 U.S. 87, 33 S.Ct. 443, 57 L.Ed. 742 (1913).

27. U.S. v. Sisal Sales Corp., 274 U.S. 268, 47 S.Ct. 592, 71 L.Ed. 1042 (1927). See

also United States v. American Tobacco Co., 221 U.S. 106, 31 S.Ct. 632, 55 L.Ed. 663 (1911).

28. United States v. Aluminum Company of America, 148 F.2d 416 (2d Cir.1945).

limitations customarily observed by nations * * * [and] fixed by the 'Conflict of Laws.' "[29]

In exploring this issue, Judge Hand envisaged three distinct situations: where conduct elsewhere was not intended to but nevertheless did have a U.S. effect; where conduct elsewhere was intended to but did not have a U.S. effect; and where conduct elsewhere was intended to and did affect U.S. commerce. He rejected Sherman application in the first situation because of "the international complications" likely to arise from so broad a rule.[30] This was the opinion's only nod in the direction of comity. He declined to resolve his second hypothetical, but "for argument" assumed no violation. But "[w]here both [intent and effect] conditions are satisfied" he found ample support for liability in *Sisal* and other cases where a foreign defendant formed a purpose to restrain U.S. trade, performed relevant acts abroad and then, through an agent, performed relevant acts in this country.[31] He thought the "inanimate" means used by Limited to achieve its U.S. purpose left the company just as vulnerable to U.S. law as an animate U.S. agent would have done.[32]

After *Alcoa*, courts, including the Supreme Court, have consistently accepted the Hand view, subject, at least before *Hartford,* to the possibility of "jurisdictional" or "comity" defenses. Moreover, *Alcoa's* doctrinal reach is wide. Purpose is normally inferred from the foreign conduct and its U.S. effect; although more subjective purpose evidence would presumably be admissible, it isn't necessary and is seldom relied upon. Hence, the *Alcoa* test is sometimes referred to in short hand as the "effects test." Although the effects element may have been supposed, circa 1950, to be a significant limitation on the test's breadth, the effects requirement may not be much of a constraint today. In recent years there has been routine acceptance of deductive microanalytic reasoning as a surrogate for hard effect evidence. Also, increased economic sophistication displayed in suits both by the government and by private parties makes objective effects evidence less and less important. Quantitative analytical techniques can be used to measure effects statistically.[33] This may reduce to the vanishing point instances where inference of purpose is warranted and evidence of effect is deficient. The remaining constraint, the sensitivities Judge Hand eluded to by the phrase, "conflicts of laws," if it subsisted in the years between *Alcoa* and *Hartford*, did so under the aegis of comity. The extent to which the conflicts of law, international law and comity rubrics have actually limited the scope of the effects test, and whether there is any room for these concepts to have impact after the *Hartford* decision, is addressed in § 18.2a4.

29. Id. at 443.

30. Id.

31. Id. at 444.

32. Id. The Foreign Trade Antitrust Improvement Act, 96 Stat. 1233 (1982), 15 U.S.C.A. § 16a, discussed in § 18.2b, codi-fied the effects doctrine for foreign commerce action. The legislation, however, does not address the *Timberlane* issue.

33. See the discussion of regression analysis in § 17.7b.

18.2a3.   Purpose and Effect in Criminal Enforcement

Most claims alleging that foreign conduct by foreign nationals violates U.S. antitrust law have arisen in civil suits. Recently, after a federal district court concluded that a mens rea requirement precluded application of the *Alcoa* effects test in a criminal prosecution,[34] the First Circuit reversed. Its *Nippon Paper* opinion fully vindicated the Department of Justice's insistence that extraterritorial conduct is vulnerable to criminal challenge under the same test that applies in civil cases.[35]

On its own facts, *Nippon Paper* seems sound. It does not follow that a mens rea defense will never be available. Some years ago, United States v. Gypsum Co.[36] taught that where conduct challenged under the Sherman Act might either help or hurt competition depending on market structure—that is, in cases that had to be resolved after full-blown rule of reason analysis—the government's burden in a criminal proceeding requires proof beyond a reasonable doubt not only that defendants intended to do what they did, but that they intended its consequence. The charge in *Nippon Paper*, by contrast, involved blatant cartelization. If conduct such as that is proven, the inference that defendants intended the effect—that is, to fix prices—would be overwhelming. But more complex situations could arise in foreign commerce where the Government might be motivated to proceed criminally. In *Gypsum,* for example, the Justice Department so proceeded because it concluded that price fixing had occurred, and also alleged a rule of reason offence (the exchange of price data) as a back up. At the trial it prevailed only on the latter claim. On like facts in an international context today, the Department might decide to proceed much the same way. If so, to prevail on its back up rule of reason criminal charge, the Government would be required to prove that defendants were aware that given the relevant market structure the price exchange would facilitate oligopolistic pricing.

The effects doctrine can also play a role in determining criminal sanctions. The Department of Justice has indicated that in calculating criminal fines for international cartel violations, it will base those fines on the effects of the cartel on buyers within the United States. The fines can still be substantial. In the international vitamin cartel case resolved in 1999, the Department levied a $500 million fine against the Swiss firm of F. Hoffman La Roche and a $250 million fine against the German firm BASF.[37] In cases in which the Department has successfully prosecuted an international cartel, it has invited other nations to pursue sanctions against the cartel for the effects on those nations' buyers. Presumably, the Department would render enforcement assistance to enforcement agencies that took up this call.

Of course, one of the criminal sanctions that the Department frequently invokes against cartel activity is imprisonment of key officials

---

34. United States v. Nippon Paper Indus. Co., 944 F.Supp. 55 (D.Mass.1996).

35. United States v. Nippon Paper Indus. Co., 109 F.3d 1 (1st Cir. 1997).

36. 438 U.S. 422, 98 S.Ct. 2864, 57 L.Ed.2d 854 (1978).

37. Department of Justice Press Release, May 20, 1999.

involved in establishing and maintaining the cartel. See the discussion in § 16.2d. Officials in U.S. corporations involved in price-fixing or bid rigging are commonly sentenced to jail, but relatively few foreigners have been imprisoned. In the resolution of the 1999 vitamin cartel case, a key official of Hoffman La Roche agreed to submit to the U.S. court's jurisdiction and serve 4 months imprisonment and pay a $100,000 fine.[38] Without a consensual resolution, the Department would have difficulty prosecuting and imprisoning a foreign resident. The Department's ability to obtain consent resolutions is, however, enhanced by the leniency program that encourages cartel participants to come forward early and disclose the facts concerning cartel activity in return for more lenient treatment.

18.2a4. Conflicts of Law, International Law and Judicial Comity

18.2a4i. Before Hartford

The early *American Banana* opinion, like *Hartford*, spoke in terms of jurisdiction, but assigned to each nation the jurisdiction to prescribe only over its own territory. For Justice Holmes, this was an aspect of sovereignty.[39] Any other view would be "contrary to the comity of nations."[40] Judge Hand's *Alcoa* opinion, building on later Supreme Court decisions, found no such imperative either in international law or in the obligations of comity. He did, however, recognize "limitations customarily observed by nations ... [like] those fixed by the 'Conflict of Laws.'"[41] But not finding any such restraints applicable, the Hand opinion does not elaborate upon such limitations. Conceivably, the opinion could be read as saying that there is no conflict of law, international law or comity constraint unless the conduct being challenged "has no consequences within the United States"[42] or, if it does, was not intended to have such a consequence.[43] But a more natural reading suggests that Judge Hand was leaving this realm of inquiry, not directly presented on the facts and pleadings in *Alcoa*, open for another day. In any event, when, after *Alcoa*, the Department of Justice continued to press for extraterritorial application of the Sherman Act,[44] various U.S. trading partners, affected U.S. firms, and some American commentators criticized the *Alcoa* approach as overbroad and intrusive. Eventually the Ninth and other circuits addressed the comity questions apparently left open by *Alcoa*.[45]

38. Id.

39. *American Banana*, 213 U.S. at 355–57.

40. Id. at 356.

41. 148 F.2d 416 at 443.

42. Id.

43. Id. at 443–44.

44. The aggressive nature of U.S. extraterritorial enforcement and the large number of Justice Department cases has frequently been addressed. E.g., Wood, *The*

Impossible *Dream: Real International Antitrust*, 1992 U. Chi. Legal Forum, 277, 298; Atwood and Brewster, Antitrust and American Business Abroad § 2.23–24, § 6 (2d ed. 1981).

45. Timberlane Lumber Co. v. Bank of America, 549 F.2d 597 (9th Cir.1976); Mannington Mills, Inc. v. Congoleum Corp., 595 F.2d 1287 (3d Cir.1979). Montreal Trading Ltd. v. Amax, 661 F.2d 864, 869–70 (10th Cir.1981); O.N.E. Shipping v. Flota, 830 F.2d 449 (2nd Cir. 1987).

Timberlane[46] is the leading case and asserts that a comity defense may be available in some situations that meet the *Alcoa* purpose and effects test. The plaintiff, an American lumber company, alleged that its efforts to acquire a Honduran mill to be used in exporting to the U.S. were frustrated by tortious Honduran conduct (reminiscent of the conduct alleged in *American Banana*) that had been engineered by defendants, plaintiff's competitors, and an American bank. The district court had dismissed the case under the act of state doctrine, a ruling the Ninth Circuit found to be in error. However, the court of appeals considered whether, given the foreign locus, the Sherman Act applied. Doing so, it found the *Alcoa* effects test incomplete. Other countries involved "have sometimes resented and protested [U.S. enforcement] as excessive intrusions into their own spheres * * *." It is evident that at some point "the interests of the United States are too weak and [the reasons for resistance to U.S. enforcement] * * * too strong to justify an extraterritorial assertion of jurisdiction."[47] Accordingly, the court fashioned a " 'jurisdictional rule of reason.' "[48]It spelled out a set of factors to be considered, much like the factors (later reflected in the Restatement of International Law that Justice Scalia relied on in *Hartford*) to determine whether "considerations of international comity counsel against exercising jurisdiction in this particular case."[49]

In the years following *Timberlane* and before *Hartford* the appropriateness of a "jurisdictional rule of reason" was much debated. That global markets would profit from harmonization or transparency of rules about competition cannot be doubted. But is the *Timberlane* approach the way to attain this end? *Timberlane* does not aim at harmonization. Neither does it increase transparency—probably quite the opposite. Outcomes under substantive antitrust rules are sometimes hard to predict, but not always—as witness *per se* and truncated rule of reason analysis. Even when full blown rule of reason analysis is essential, microeconomic theory can provide a cohesive guide to outcomes. Many cases, international cartel cases among them, evoke the *per se* rule. Under *Alcoa*, likely outcomes in such cases are reasonably predictable. But if foreign activity having a purpose and likely effect on U.S. import commerce must be filtered through a jurisdictional rule of reason, predictability will be undermined. When there is foreign law more permissive to the conduct than the Sherman Act, a jurisdictional rule of reason will draw federal judges into diplomatic tasks of uncertain outcome. These are tasks, moreover, for which judges have little training or experience, and which are less judicial in character than most tasks federal courts are likely to be asked to do. Far from clarifying matters, using a jurisdictional rule of reason adds an additional layer of complexity. Judges are likely to react in differing and unpredictable ways when they apply an open-ended set of jurisdictional factors to complex facts. The differing substantive conclusions reached by the district court, the

---

46. *Timberlane*, supra note 45.

47. Id. at 609.

48. Id. at 613–15.

49. *Hartford*, 509 U.S. at 817–21.

court of appeals, and Justice Scalia in their respective *Hartford* opinions illustrate this problem.

18.2a4ii. After Hartford

The *Hartford* majority rejected not only the open-ended jurisdictional rule of reason, but also the analytical framework leaving room for conflict of laws first fashioned in *Alcoa* and restated in the Scalia *Hartford* dissent. This rejection of *Timberlane* may have little or no cost in respect of governmental antitrust enforcement. The DOJ and the FTC can and do factor comity judgments into their exercise of prosecutorial discretion. They continue to do so after *Hartford*. Moreover, these agencies may be better equipped than are courts with the kind of resources needed to perform this diplomatic function. They can more easily and freely gather relevant information and they could take (although probably would seldom seek) advice from diplomatic sources. This could be true, too, although less clearly so, for state attorneys general acting *parens patria* (as did the *Hartford* plaintiffs). But it is not true at all in the case of actions by private plaintiffs. Private plaintiffs must prove, and will have strong incentive to investigate, allocative and consumer welfare effects. Unless they hope to be able to prove competitive injury, antitrust injury and damages, they will have little incentive to sue. But under the *Hartford* purpose and effects test they would have scant incentive to hold off on bringing an otherwise compelling suit merely on comity grounds. However important these grounds might be to the public interest, they would not likely influence a treble damage plaintiff.

Does the *Hartford* majority opinion leave any room at all for *Timberlane* or Restatement-like factors that lower courts had earlier found significant and that Justice Scalia, in his *Hartford* dissent, thought compelling? The majority opinion in *Hartford* phrased the question as whether application of U.S. antitrust law on the facts alleged would amount to the "improper application of the Sherman Act to foreign conduct."[50] Apparently the Court saw the issue as one of subject matter jurisdiction; for it next asserted that the district court "undoubtedly had jurisdiction," citing cases based on the purpose and effects test.[51] It then went on to the comity question and rejected the existence of any such defense, absent inconsistent sovereign compulsions. It did, however, add (and it reads as an ambiguous afterthought), that "[w]e have no need in this litigation to address other considerations that might inform a decision to refrain from the exercise of jurisdiction on grounds of comity."[52] Unless that comment leaves room for questions of conflict of laws or international law constraints on Congress's jurisdiction to prescribe—questions of a kind that clearly would be accessible under both the Hand and Scalia frameworks—such questions are simply left out by the majority's decision structure. This may be what the majority

50. 509 U.S. at 784.

51. Id.

52. Id. at 799.

intended. Although arid seeming, such a rule would take federal judges out of international diplomacy except in severe, self defining situations where a private party is subject to diametrically inconsistent sovereign demands—situations so harsh that the application of the Sherman Act might even generate due process concerns.

If the Court in a future case addresses "other considerations," and looks again at conflicts, international law, or comity, it might find middle ground between the *Hartford* majority's bright line, and Justice Scalia's open-ended rule of reason. There are possible intermediate stopping points. In *Hartford*, the U.K. interest was solely that the insurance industry was a significant part of the economically dynamic London financial market. There was no active U.K. regulation of reinsurance at all. The only involvement of the U.K. government was passive, to allow a U.K. reinsurer to act concertedly when this would enhance profits. The other extreme—that in which UK law would result in a Sherman Act defense—can be easily modeled. Assume a U.K. regulator, acting under statutory powers, finds that reinsuring long-tailed policies puts U.K. reinsurers at undue risk, and therefore orders industry participants to form a crisis cartel to phase out such policies. Then because compliance with the U.K. regulatory order would not be possible without violating the Sherman Act, *Hartford* indicates that the foreign sovereign's compulsion would be a valid defense. But by changing the facts only slightly a middle ground dilemma can be presented. Assume that the U.K. law allows crisis cartels, but only if notified to a regulatory agency which has power to, but need not, forbid them. Reinsurers negotiate what they call a crisis cartel to phase out long-tail policies and submit it to the agency. The agency does not interfere and the cartel goes into effect. On these facts there are no conflicting sovereign compulsions, yet the conflict between U.K. and U.S. policy may be real and the interest of the U.K. may be pressing. Should there not be at least in private suits brought under American antitrust law some accommodation to foreign economic interests when they seem more formidable than U.S. interests? On the facts here hypothesized there is ambiguity about U.K. involvement, but it could be further investigated. Was the U.K. agency indifferent to whether or not a cartel was formed? Or did it investigate and make its own independent decision about anticompetitive risk before deciding to allow the cartel to function?

18.2a4iii. *Empagran*

The Court dealt most recently with comity issues in F. Hoffman–La Roche Ltd. v. Empagran S.A.,[53] a case involving purchasers of vitamins that were subject to a price fixing conspiracy by foreign and domestic suppliers of vitamins. The defendants moved to dismiss as to the foreign purchasers, five vitamin distributors from Ukraine, Australia, Ecuador, and Panama, each of whom purchased vitamins from the defendants for delivery outside of the United States. Applying language from the Foreign Trade Antitrust Improvements Act (FTAIA), the district court

53. 542 U.S. 155, 124 S.Ct. 2359, 159 L.Ed.2d 226 (2004).

had dismissed the claims of the foreign purchasers. The court of appeals reversed in a split decision.

The Supreme Court vacated and remanded the decision. In an opinion by Justice Breyer, the Court held that language in the FTAIA excluded foreign plaintiffs' claims to the extent that any injury to foreign plaintiffs from the price fixing conspiracy was independent of injury suffered by U.S. purchasers. The Court left the lower courts to address the issue, not addressed by the court of appeals, whether the anticompetitive conduct's undeniable domestic effects were linked to the foreign harm. The plaintiffs argued that vitamins were a fungible and readily transportable product and that, without adverse domestic effect (higher prices for U.S. consumers), there could be no international price fixing and foreign injury.

Would the spillover effects of foreign conduct on the U.S. market be sufficient to bring the foreign plaintiffs' claims within the language of the FTAIA? There is legislative history of the FTAIA that suggests such spillover effects are indeed a sufficient nexus for jurisdiction.[54] The Court's language in *Empagran*, however, suggests a renewed emphasis on comity concerns that might lead the Court to a different result. Justice Breyer cited amicus briefs filed by Germany, Canada and Japan, noting that other nations "disagree dramatically about appropriate remedies. The application, for example, of American private treble-damages remedies to anticompetitive conduct taking place abroad has generated considerable controversy." The Court took note of arguments that application of the U.S. treble damage remedy might lessen the incentive of firms to cooperate with foreign antitrust investigations in return for amnesty and concluded that "principles of prescriptive comity counsel against" an interpretation of the FTAIA that would allow jurisdiction.[55]

The status of foreign plaintiff antitrust claims remains in doubt after *Empagran*. Those claims will apparently survive if the plaintiff can establish an adequate nexus between the domestic and foreign injury. In support of U.S. jurisdiction, it can be argued that cartel damages to foreign purchasers from an international cartel often are not collected, limiting the deterrent effect of a U.S. based prosecution. But the Court's embrace of comity, in tension with the majority opinion in *Hartford*, suggests that doubt about the sufficiency of the nexus will be resolved in favor of defendants.

In dealing with extraterritorial issues there is, as yet, a lack of mid-level generalizations. *Aramco*,[56] which Justice Scalia cited in *Hartford*, posits a presumption that Congress is acting only to regulate conduct within U.S. territory—hardly a realistic presumption for any significant economic legislation in a world of integrated global markets. *Timberlane* teaches that when a U.S. law applies extraterritorially, anything done by

54. House Report 2–3, U.S. Code Cong. Admin. News 1982, 2487, 2487–88.

55. 542 U.S. at 169, 124 S.Ct. at 2369, 159 L.Ed.2d at 239.

56. EEOC v. Arabian Am. Oil Co., 499 U.S. 244, 111 S.Ct. 1227, 113 L.Ed.2d 274 (1991).

any nation to influence economic outcomes is open for analysis. *Hartford*, rejecting *Timberlane,* applies U.S. law extraterritorially, subject only to a very narrow and explicit constraint. The *Hartford* rule applied as written might work reasonably well in actions brought by the enforcement agencies (which make their own comity judgments), but in private actions it would seem wise to treat it as no more than a strong presumption, capable of being displaced by compelling evidence of interest on the part of another country. *Empagran* now opens the door for comity analysis in private suits, or at least those suits initiated by foreign plaintiffs and involving harm that is primarily outside the United States. But the Court has left lower courts with little in the way of guide posts in making open-ended comity analysis.[57]

Once a "compelling and conflicting" interest by another state is established, does it always trump U.S. antitrust? To affirm this would be to stay closer to simplicity; but to say no would be to edge closer to the possibility (if only that) of more sensible outcomes. Even compelling foreign interests conflicting with U.S. enforcement ought to be weighed against the significance to U.S. policy of attaining, in the specific case, the outcome that the U.S. antitrust laws mandate. In any given context the U.S. interest in effective competition may also be compelling. If it were weightier than the foreign government interest in constraining competition, there would be little basis for U.S. deference.[58] The deepest conundrum is whether any national court could ever objectively weigh such an issue.

18.2a4iv.   *Diplomatic Comity*

The concept of comity, a rubric under which to explore judicial deference in situations of international conflict, is a form of judicial diplomacy. At times, deference takes place through more conventional diplomatic media. As conflicts between nations about the application of competition policy have increased with globalization, such modes of deference—here called "diplomatic comity"—have become more frequent. We discuss three aspects: guidelines published by the U.S. enforcement agencies stating circumstances in which they will defer (and, incidentally, seeking to discourage courts from deferring when the agencies do not); bilateral agreements between the U.S. and some of its trading partners; and voluntary cooperation through the OECD, the WTO or other agencies.

---

57. On remand, the court of appeals held that the requisite effects on U.S. commerce had not been demonstrated and dismissed the case. Empagran S.A. v. F. Hoffman–La Roche Ltd., 417 F.3d 1267 (D.C. Cir. 2005).

58. The same kind of question can arise under the foreign sovereign compulsion doctrine accepted by the *Hartford* majority and often taken as of near universal validity. See § 18.5c. When there is a direct conflict between U.S. and foreign law that puts a foreign national in a position where it must violate one of them, should U.S. law always give way as the majority implies? Suppose the impact of giving way on U.S. interests would be very adverse, but that the foreign sovereign could give way with little harm to its interest. On those assumptions should a U.S. court apply the U.S. law, despite the dilemma facing the antitrust defendant, that it must violate one order or the other? See also § 18.2a1, note 23.

18.2a4v.   The International Guidelines

In 1995, the Antitrust Division and the FTC published a new, revised set of International Guidelines.[59] They stress that in enforcing the antitrust laws the Division, a part of the executive branch, and the FTC, an independent administrative agency, will take account of "international comity," defined as "respect among co-equal sovereign nations [that] plays a role in determining 'the recognition which one nation allows within its territory to the legislative, executive or judicial acts of another nation.' "[60] Section 2 of these guidelines sets forth a list of factors the agencies will consider. This list is based on previous guidelines and on a U.S.-European Union Antitrust Cooperation Agreement. It has an emphasis somewhat different from that reflected in the factor lists in *Timberlane* and the Restatement. Thus, the agencies will consider: competitive significance of the U.S. and foreign conduct; nationality of acting and affected parties; whether there was a purpose to affect U.S. markets; comparative significance of U.S. and foreign market effects; expectations furthered or defeated; extent of conflict with foreign law or economic policy; whether foreign enforcement action would be affected; and the comparative effectiveness of foreign and domestic enforcement. The illustrative examples set forth in the Guidelines suggest that the agencies will be quick to enforce against foreign cartels and recent enforcement initiatives confirm this inference.[61]

The Guidelines contain numerous illustrative examples. Yet, none that deal with import commerce identify a foreign law conflict or comity issue. Direct sales into the United States by foreign cartel members may be challenged,[62] as may sales by such a cartel to a non-U.S. intermediary that the cartelists know will resell into the U.S.[63] The agencies may also challenge a foreign cartel that seriously but indirectly damages U.S. manufacturers selling in the U.S. Thus, if a foreign cartel agrees to increase foreign prices and reduce U.S. prices in order to soak up excess capacity resulting from the cartel's increase in foreign prices, cartel participants will be vulnerable to an enforcement agency challenge even if the reduced U.S. prices are above cost and not vulnerable as "dumping." The Guidelines' illustrations respecting comity all deal only with a cartel of foreign buyers of U.S. exports.[64]

---

59.   U.S. Department of Justice and Federal Trade Commission Antitrust Enforcement Guidelines for International Operations § 3.11 (1995) [hereinafter the 1995 Guidelines], available at <http://www.usdoj.gov/atr/public /guidelines/internat.htm>.

60.   1995 Guidelines § 3.2, quoting from Hilton v. Guyot, 159 U.S. 113, 164, 16 S.Ct. 139, 40 L.Ed. 95 (1895).

61.   United States v. Nippon Paper Indus. Co., 109 F.3d 1 (1st Cir. 1997); United States v. Pilkington, 1994–2 Trade Cas. (CCH) ¶ 70,842 (D. Ariz. 1994); United

States v. F. Hoffman–LaRoche Ltd., Cr. No. 99–CR–184–R (N.D. Texas, May 20, 1999); United States v. Andreas, 39 F. Supp. 2d 1048 (N.D.Ill.1998).

62.   1995 Guidelines Illustrative Example A.

63.   1995 Guidelines Illustrative Example B. This conduct can be reached under (1) of the FTAIA test. See 1995 Guidelines § 3.12.1.

64.   1995 Guidelines Illustrative Example I.

It is interesting to speculate, using the § 3.2 factors as a guide, how the Justice Department or FTC might have evaluated the comity issue involved in *Hartford*. Neither enforcement agency challenged this conduct but there is no basis for assuming that a challenge was considered and rejected on comity grounds. An analysis under the Guidelines might have gone like this:

(1) significance of foreign and domestic conduct—of equal weight;

(2) nationalities—of equal weight;

(3) purpose to impact U.S. markets—weighs in favor of enforcement;

(4) comparative significance of U.S. and foreign effects—weighs in favor of enforcement because the adverse effect of the conduct on U.S. markets was palpable, whereas any adverse affect in the U.K. implicated only self-regulatory procedures;

(5) defeat of expectations—probably weighs in favor of enforcement, because U.S. insurance buyers expected to be able to obtain long-tail policies that some U.S. insurers were ready to write, and U.S. and U.K. firms were ready to reinsure while U.K. reinsurers may or may not have expected a U.S. antitrust challenge to their agreement to reject such policies;

(6) the extent of policy conflict—might weigh against enforcement (although it is difficult to evaluate this factor when, as here, it seems devoid of reference to market effects).

Going through this factor analysis in respect of a litigated case suggests that if comity decisions are left to enforcement agencies, they will be fused with a whole range of other factors that influence discretionary deployment of agency resources. It is also a reminder that agency comity decisions will seldom if ever be adequately disclosed so that scholars or the bar could learn from or criticize agency performance.

18.2a4vi.   *Bilateral Cooperation*

The United States has negotiated bilateral agreements on antitrust enforcement cooperation with the EU, Germany, Australia, Canada, Israel and Brazil.[65] In 1994, only after some of these agreements had been negotiated and signed, Congress authorized the enforcement agencies to enter into antitrust enforcement assistance agreements.[66] There are also general commitments to discourage restraints against competi-

---

65. The dates of the most recent agreements are: Australia (1982), Canada (1995), Germany (1976), Israel (1999), the European Communities (1991 and 1998), Japan (1999) and Brazil (1999). These agreements are available on the Antitrust Division's web site: http://www.usdoj.gov/atr.

66. International Antitrust Enforcement Assistance Act of 1994, Pub. L. No. 103–438, 108 Stat. 4037 (1994). The initial

agreement between the U.S. and the EU was executed, on the part of the EU, by the Commission. In French Republic v. Commission C–327/91, [1994], IECR 3641, [1994] 5 CMLR 362, the Court of Justice ruled that the Commission, acting alone, exceeded its authority to bind the community to another nation and that the agreement was void.

tion in some earlier bilateral agreements on economic cooperation.[67] The recent cooperation agreements require each signatory to assist the other in its antitrust investigations and to respect the confidentiality restriction imposed by the other. As Wood has emphasized, the goals are modest: conflict management (if not total avoidance), cooperation in enforcement within the limits of each country's enforcement powers and confidentiality laws, and the greater understanding that can come from consultations.[68]

The 1991 agreement with the EU, is more comprehensive than the ones that preceded it. EU commitments to antitrust have been more formidable and more akin to those of the U.S. than were the traditional commitments of European nations other than Germany.[69] There are significant differences between EU and U.S. antitrust,[70] arising mainly out of EU interest in accelerating national market integration, but in part out of the influence of European industrial policy. Nonetheless, the level of substantive agreement between the two systems should facilitate considerable accord in respect of enforcement. Despite this, there have been some substantial disagreements. These are discussed in § 18.7.

18.2a4vii. Multilateral Cooperation

OECD member countries, including the leading industrial nations,[71] have each mutually agreed to consider the interests of the others in accordance with OECD guidelines concerning practices affecting international trade.[72] Pursuant to these guidelines agencies of member nations responsible for antitrust enforcement should not take action that may affect important interests of another member country or its nationals until it notifies that other country. While neither the OECD recommendations nor the specific cooperation agreements with the EU or others contain either substantive or choice of law rules, they initiate the kind of consultation and interaction that could lead to greater understanding and accommodation when conflicting interests arise.[73]

67. Article XI, of the 1960 Convention of Establishment between U.S. and France and Article XVIII of the Treaty of Friendship, Commerce, and Navigation between the U.S. and Japan. These are cited and discussed in Wood, supra note 44, at 293–94. Even earlier, the agreements ending U.S. occupation of Germany and Japan after World War II required these countries to establish antitrust regimes.

68. Wood, supra note 44, at 294–97.

69. Fikentscher and Sullivan, *On the Growth of the Antitrust Idea* in W. Fik-entscher, Die Freiheit als Aufgabe 93–132 (Mohr Siebeck, 1997).

70. See § 18.6.

71. The fifteen EU nations plus Canada, Iceland, Japan, New Zealand, Norway, Switzerland, Turkey and the U.S.

72. OECD, Revised Recommendation of the Council concerning Co-operation between Member Countries on Anticompetitive Practices affecting International Trade, C(95)130 (July 27–28, 1995).

73. In Cases 89, 104, 114, 116–17 and 125–29/85 *Ahlstrom-Osakeyhtio v. Commission* (Wood Pulp), 1988 ECR 5193, 4 CMLR 901, the EU Court of Justice, in rejecting a defense that violators were subject to conflicting norms, those stemming from Webb Pomerene in the U.S., and the EU antitrust law, stated that U.S. authorities had been consulted by the Commission under OECD procedures and had expressed no objection to the EU enforcement proceeding.

18.2b.   Domestic Conduct By U.S. Firms Affecting U.S. Exports

Export restraints by some U.S. firms that impinge on the export opportunities of their other U.S. competitors are antitrust vulnerable.[74] Yet, U.S. extraterritorial antitrust enforcement, markedly aggressive when addressing foreign conduct hurting U.S. markets, is far less aggressive in dealing with U.S. domestic conduct affecting foreign markets. The extraterritorial reach of U.S. antitrust as applied to export commerce is limited in several ways. The Foreign Trade Antitrust Improvement Act of 1982 (FTAIA) explicitly states facts that must be proved to invoke the Sherman Act for foreign commerce. Section 7 of the Act states that the Sherman Act:

> "shall not apply to conduct involving trade or commerce (other than import trade or commerce) with foreign nations unless: (1) such conduct has a direct, substantial and reasonably foreseeable effect: (a) on trade or commerce which is not trade or commerce with foreign nations; or (b) on export trade or export commerce with foreign nations, of a person engaged in such trade or commerce in the United States;[75] [and] (2) such effect gives rise to a claim under the provisions of [the Sherman Act], other than this section."[76]

The language of the Act critical to coverage of U.S. exports is in subsection 1(b). Antitrust conduct (whether taken by U.S. or foreign firms and whether occurring in the U.S. or elsewhere) is at risk under the Sherman or FTC Acts if it has the required "direct, substantial and reasonably foreseeable effect" of restraining U.S. exports. Here is an example, one in which the possible violators are all foreign firms acting overseas. Assume that there are several widget manufacturers in Europe, that two of them are integrated to the distribution level and control an overwhelming share of distribution there, that U.S. widget manufacturers export to Europe and rely on these integrated European firms for distribution in Europe, that the U.S. producers are gaining wider market acceptance and that their aggregate share of the European market is increasing while that of European producers is falling, and that the two integrated European firms agree with each other to stop distributing in Europe for the U.S. exporters. There is obviously a direct and foreseeable adverse effect on U.S. export commerce. If that impact is substantial, the foreign conduct of the foreign competitors is vulnera-

---

74. This holding in Hazeltine Research v. Zenith Radio Co., 239 F.Supp. 51, 77 (N.D.Ill.1965), rev'd, 388 F.2d 25 (7th Cir. 1967), was not impinged upon by the Court of Appeals review.

75. Subsection 1(a) makes Sherman applicable in the event of harm to domestic commerce; Subsection 1(b), in the event of harm to a U.S. exporter, as in *Hazeltine*, supra note 70. If the commerce meets only the test of 1(b), not 1(a), than the Sherman Act applies only for "injury to export busi-

ness in the United States." See also United States v. Minnesota Mining & Mfg. Co., 92 F.Supp. 947 (D.Mass.1950).

76. Pub. L. No. 97–290, 96 Stat. 1233 (1982). The provisions of the Act are codified in various sections of U.S.C.A. titles 12, 15 and 30. Substantively comparable provisions apply to the application of Section 5 of the FTC Act to such commerce. 15 U.S.C.A. § 45(a)(3) (1988).

ble.[77] Of course, it would also be exposed if one of the firms cooperating to reduce distribution access to U.S. exporters was itself a U.S. firm. The statute does not make clear how substantiality is to be evaluated, nor do the Guidelines, except to suggest that the agencies would regard a nearly total exclusion of U.S. exporters from a foreign market as meeting that test. What of less manifest situations? One might evaluate substantiality purely in quantitative, monetary terms[78] but the more sensible response would be to evaluate the percentage of the relevant export market from which the U.S. firms are excluded.[79] If they could turn elsewhere for buyers the incentive for U.S. sanctions against foreign conduct would be reduced.

Note that a cartel among U.S. exporters that does not have a direct, substantial and reasonably foreseeable effect either on U.S. domestic trade, U.S. import trade or the export trade of U.S. exporters not participating in the cartel would not be covered by subsections 1(a) or (b) of the FTAIA. In sum, otherwise violative conduct by exporters in the U.S. escapes Sherman and FTC Act liability when it causes harm only in foreign markets. Of course, a cartel of U.S. exporters taking surplus production off the domestic market by selling in a foreign market at lower price could affect U.S. domestic trade by keeping prices up. Also, as national markets interpenetrate and global markets emerge, some of the distinctions the statute draws may fade or disappear. Harm to a global market that includes all or part of the U.S. should be characterized under the FTAIA as harm to a non-export or an import market in the U.S.

The earlier Webb Pomerene Act[80] is also potentially protective of export cartels in similar ways. It exempts otherwise violative conduct affecting the export of goods by an association of competitors, when the conduct does not have an anticompetitive effect in the U.S., injure domestic competitors of the association members, or "artificially or intentionally enhance or depress prices within" the U.S. To gain and maintain this exemption the association must file its articles of agreement and annual reports with the FTC. It is not clear from the cases how seriously the loss of exemption for enhancing or depressing domestic prices is to be taken. An *Alkali* association lost its exemption in part because its export of "surplus" domestic production at cartel prices "artificially" kept domestic prices high.[81] Microtheory suggests that any export cartel would have that effect if the cartel covered a substantial share of domestic production and the domestic and foreign market were not adequately integrated. On the analysis in *Alkali*, which is certainly sound theoretically, all such exemptions would be lost. However, the

77. See 1995 Guidelines, Illustrative Example D.

78. Compare Standard Oil of Calif. v. U.S., 337 U.S. 293, 69 S.Ct. 1051, 93 L.Ed. 1371 (1949).

79. Compare Tampa Electric Co. v. Nashville Coal Co., 365 U.S. 320, 81 S.Ct. 623, 5 L.Ed.2d 580 (1961).

80. 15 U.S.C.A. §§ 61–65.

81. United States Alkali Export Ass'n v. United States, 325 U.S. 196, 65 S.Ct. 1120, 89 L.Ed. 1554 (1945). The Court also held an exemption was lost because of the association's participation with a foreign cartel.

exemption has in fact been made available to associations with very large shares of domestic production.[82] There is need for litigation or a policy statement from the FTC to clarify this question, which should address the relevance of globalization and the integration of foreign and U.S. markets. No Sherman Act violation occurs in foreign commerce unless the conduct has effects on domestic or import commerce or on the export trade of U.S. exporters.

The Export Trading Co. Act of 1982 (ETA) also has pre-conduct review provisions. It authorizes exporters to obtain export trade certificates of review from the Secretary of Commerce with the concurrence of the Attorney General. Such a certificate only issues if the exporter shows that the proposed export conduct will not restrain U.S. trade nor substantially restrain trade of competing exporters, unreasonably affect prices in the U.S., constitute an unfair method of competition against competing exporters, or include conduct that may reasonably be expected to result in sale, consumption or resale within the U.S.[83] When a certificate issues any conduct covered by it enjoys a presumption of legality and, should it later be found to violate the Sherman Act, protects the exporter from treble damage liability. Moreover, private suits are discouraged. If conduct covered by the certification is challenged in a private antitrust action the prevailing party is entitled to recover attorney fees and damages.[84]

These statutes show that Congress has no interest in protecting foreign consumers from monopoly prices imposed by a U.S. export cartel. By contrast subsection 1(b) of FTAIA suggests that Congress did want the Sherman Act available to protect access by U.S. firms to foreign markets. While there was a thin but steady stream of cases aimed at opening closed foreign markets over the years, the Justice Department Enforcement Guidelines for International Operations, published in 1988, indicated that export conduct would not be challenged unless U.S. consumers were affected. In 1992, however, the Department deleted this statement, thus indicating a willingness to exercise the full jurisdiction

82. International Raw Materials, Ltd. v. Stauffer Chem. Co., 978 F.2d 1318 (3d Cir. 1992); United States v. Minnesota Mining & Mfg. Co., 92 F.Supp. 947, 964–66 (D.Mass.1950). See also, Pacific Forest Indust., 40 FTC 843 (1940); Export Screw Assn., 43 FTC 980 (1947); Phosphate Export Assn., 42 FTC 555 (1946). Note that Webb Pomerene sets up potential for a clash of policy between U.S. law, intended to encourage export cartels, and foreign antitrust law, seeking to protect foreign markets from cartel-like effects. In Cases 89, 104, 114, 116–17 and 125–29/85, Ahlstrom-Osakeyhtio v. Commission (Wood Pulp), 1988 ECR 5193, 4 CMLR 901, the EU Commission charged a Webb Pomerene association and other non-EC firms with cartelizing to raise prices on wood pulp exports to the EC. Finding that the participants, including the U.S. firms, intended their con-

duct to increase European prices and that this was the effect, the Commission applied an EC version of the effects test to find the foreign conduct vulnerable under EC antitrust. On review the Court of Justice affirmed on the jurisdictional issue and rejected the argument of the Webb Pomerene association that because of U.S. law association members found themselves "subject to contradictory orders" Judgment, ¶ 19. It saw no conflict because Webb Pomerene did not compel U.S. firm to cartelize, but merely exempted them from Sherman Act constraints. See also Hartford Fire Insurance Co. v. California, supra, note 4.

83. Pub. L. No. 97–290, 96 Stat. 1233, 15 U.S.C.A. §§ 4001–21.

84. The act is discussed more fully in 1995 Guidelines § 2.7.

Congress granted.[85] By what standard should a U.S. enforcement agency or court evaluate conduct that restricts the access of U.S. firms to foreign markets? For example, might widget exports, U.S. to U.K., constitute a market, or might the export market be U.S. to Europe, or even U.S. to any other nation? If U.S. exporters, cut out of the U.K., could seamlessly turn to customers elsewhere, whatever U.S. trade policy should seek to accomplish, it is highly doubtful that U.S. exporters should be granted an antitrust remedy. And what share of the market, as defined, must the stifled exports constitute before suit was warranted? Suppose exports constituted 5 percent of U.S. production, that 40 percent of these exports went to the U.K. and the rest elsewhere in Europe. Would U.K. conduct foreclosing 2 percent of U.S. widget production justify a suit? Would suit be warranted because 40 percent of U.S. widget export traffic was being foreclosed? Should the antitrust statutes be put in the service of U.S. trade policy if no harm to U.S. consumers is evident?[86]

§ 18.3 EU Antitrust and Domestic Conduct by U.S. Firms

As § 18.2b describes, firms in foreign markets adversely affected by U.S. export conduct distorting competition in those markets cannot expect to find protection through U.S. antitrust enforcement. Suppose the affected foreign market is the EU or a substantial part of the EU. Could the injured firms use EC antitrust to challenge conduct that took place in the U.S.?[1] Is the effects test a two way street?

The paradigm case is a cartel of U.S. exporters. Assume these facts: brimy-winkles are a crustation found only in U.S. waters. They are seldom consumed in the U.S. but are prized in France and Belgium. U.S. exporters form a Webb–Pomerene Association, file their articles, regularly report, obtain a certificate of review under Export Trading Company Act and steer a careful path around the shoals of the Foreign Trade

---

85. M. HANDLER, ET AL., TRADE REGULATION: CASES AND MATERIALS, "Note on Jurisdiction in Export Cases," 1208 (4th ed. 1997). The 1995 Guidelines contain no such provision.

86. See 1995 Guidelines § 3.11222 and Illustrative Examples D and E.

§ 18.3

1. Until 1992 what since that time has been called the European Union was the institutional outcome of three treaties establishing three communities, the European Coal and Steel Community (ECSC), established in 1951, the European Economic Community (EEC), established in 1957, and the European Atomic Energy Community (Euratom), established in 1957. The most important community, and the one whose treaty contained the antitrust provisions, was the EEC. In 1992 the Maastricht Treaty on European Union amended the EEC, ECSC and Euratom (redesignating the EEC as the European Community (EC)) and also established the European Union (EU). The EU now denotes the overall political entity within which the three existing communities repose. Those three treaties, as amended, now constitute the "first pillar" of the EU. Under the Maastricht Treaty, the EU has also taken on new responsibilities not comprehended in the earlier treaties, as amended, in the areas of common foreign and security policy (the "second pillar") and justice and internal ("home") affairs (the "third pillar"). This text resolves the nomenclature question presented by the interrelated EC and EU treaties by referring to the relevant antitrust provisions as part of the EC and its law, and referring to the EU only as a general reference to the territory of the fifteen member states or to those states in association as a separate political entity.

Antitrust Improvements Act.[2] They successfully reduced production (perhaps in the name of conservation), thus raising prices on export sales to France and Belgium. If these cartelizing exporters were gathering brimywinkles in another EU member state (say, Holland) and shipping them to France and Belgium, they would be liable for cartelization in violation of provisions of the EC Treaty.[3] If the U.S. association and its U.S. members have assets in the EU or can be found there, would they, like hypothetical Dutch cartelists, be vulnerable under Article 81 (old Article 85)[4] of the EC Treaty?

The EC Court of Justice recognizes that geographic markets merge into each other.[5] In *Dyestuffs*[6] the Court of Justice for the first time applied EC antitrust law to a non-EU defendant, the parent of an EU subsidiary. The court held that by using power to control its subsidiary within the EU, the parent did enough to subject itself to EC antitrust. In *Wood Pulp*[7] the Commission asserted jurisdiction over an agreement among Canadian, Finnish, and Swedish and U.S. firms (the latter exempt from U.S. antitrust law under Webb–Pomerene)[8] for fixing prices of wood pulp sold to EC buyers. The Commission found a violation based on evidence of cartel pricing and the Court of Justice affirmed the jurisdictional holding, stating that when firms outside the EC take "part in concentration which has the object and effect of restricting competition within" the EC they violate Article [81].[9] In so deciding, the Court rejected a comity defense.[10] The U.S. defendants contended unsuccessfully that because U.S. statutes (Webb–Pomerene and ETA) protected export cartels, there was a conflict between EC and U.S. antitrust that should stay the hand of the EC enforcer.[11]

Thus, EC antitrust has an international outreach much like the U.S. law announced in *Hartford*. So far as yet appears, the EC will not do any comity analysis comparable to that in *Timberlane* or the Restatement (to which Justice Scalia turned in *Hartford*). Of course, antitrust enforcement within the EU remains government-initiated, so the problems associated with U.S. private enforcement, the primary impetus for a

---

2. The Webb Pomerene Act, the ETA, and the FTAIA are described in § 18.2b.

3. E.g., Case 41/69 ACF Chemiefarma NV v. Commission (Quinine), [1970] ECR 661, [1967–1970] Common Mkt. Rep. (CCH) ¶ 8083, p. 654.

4. The articles of the EC Treaty were renumbered in 1999. The core antitrust provisions of the EC Treaty, Articles 85 and 86, became Articles 81 and 82, respectively. All EC decisions and documents prior to 1999 used the old numbers. All such pre–1999 references will be adjusted to the new numbers but surrounded by brackets to indicate the change. Thus, a reference to old Article 85 in a pre–1999 court decision will be presented as "Article [81]."

5. Case 26/76 United Brands v. Commission [1978] ECR 207.

6. Cases 48, 49, 51–57/69 Imperial Chem. Ind. Ltd v. Commission (Dyestuffs) [1972] ECR 619. [1972] CMLR 557.

7. Cases 89, 104, 114, 116–17 and 125–29/85 Ahlstrom–Osakeyhtio v. Commission (Wood Pulp), [1988] ECR 5193, 4 CMLR 901.

8. See § 18.2b.

9. *Ahlstrom-Osakeyhtio*, supra note 7 at ¶ 13; See Lange and Sandage, *The* Wood Pulp *Decision and its Implications for the Scope of EC Competition Law*, 26 CML Rev. 137 (1989).

10. Id. at ¶ 6.

11. On its face Webb–Pomerene does not purport to protect U.S. firms from foreign antitrust. Neither does ETA or FTAIA.

comity analysis, are unlikely to arise. If U.S. or other firms engage outside of the EU in conduct that, had it occurred within, would have violated Article 81 or 82 of the EC treaty, and that conduct has the purpose and effect of distorting competition within the EU, that conduct violates the antitrust provisions of the EC treaty and those provisions are directly enforceable against the violators, whether foreign or domestic. For the U.S. and the EU, the purpose and effects test is reciprocal.

§ 18.4 Conduct in Europe That Does Competitive Harm Abroad: Can EC Antitrust Be Used to Protect U.S. Markets?

As noted earlier, U.S. policy supports export cartels that may increase the profits of U.S. exporters, so long as no harm is done to competing U.S. exporters or to commerce within the U.S.[1] Does the EC antitrust have a comparable policy?

While there is no EC legislation equivalent to Webb–Pomerene, the language of Article 81 of the EC Treaty does not appear to put EU export cartels in jeopardy unless they have impacts within the EU. Article 81 prohibits concerted conduct having the "object or effect [of] the prevention, restriction or distortion of competition *within the common market * * *.*" (emphasis added). While this language could perhaps be read to cover distortion of export competition even if no other harm were done within the EU, it seems unlikely, in light of U.S. support of export cartels, that the Commission would be motivated to challenge exporters in the EU for increasing their returns on sales to U.S. buyers, or, if it did, that the Court of Justice would have any strong incentive to read Article 81 as forbidding such conduct.

§ 18.5 Can Foreign Governmental Undertakings Violate U.S. Antitrust Law?

Governments not only regulate, they sometimes act commercially. If they do, their undertakings or enterprises in or affecting U.S. markets could be subject to U.S. antitrust scrutiny. There are three possible antitrust defenses that can arise only when a significant element of the challenged transaction is influenced by the law or acts of a foreign sovereign. As an ABA monogram summarizes it:

"First, the Foreign Sovereign Immunities Act requires litigants affirmatively to prove one of a number of specific exceptions to the general principles of sovereign immunity in order to establish jurisdiction over a sovereign government, its agencies, or instrumentalities. Second, even where an exception to sovereign immunity can be shown, a United States court may be bound by foreign determina-

---

§ 18.4

1. § 18.2b. This policy may not be economically rational for the U.S. Like any trade war tactic it invites retaliation. Furthermore, increasing exporter returns through cartel profits means reducing exporter output, perhaps reducing export employment and increasing adverse trade balances.

tions of law or [may] abstain from exercising jurisdiction under the act of state doctrine where the litigation must question the validity of foreign acts. Third, the foreign sovereign compulsion doctrine creates an affirmative defense to liability where a private party was compelled to violate United States law as a result of a mandatory command of a foreign government, at least when the foreign government command applies to conduct within its own territory."[1]

In this section, these three defenses are briefly described.

18.5a. The Sovereign Immunities Act

The Foreign Sovereign Immunities Act of 1976 ("FSIA")[2] implicitly presupposes the existence of an international law doctrine binding on U.S. courts (the source and contours of which the statute does not articulate) that protects any sovereign from suit. The statute then specifies exceptions to that doctrine, situations in which a sovereign may be sued. Section 1605(a)(1–6) states that a U.S. court has jurisdiction over a foreign sovereign when the sovereign has (1) expressly or by implication waved immunity; (2) engaged in commercial activity; (3) expropriated property in violation of international law; (4) acquired rights to U.S. property; (5) committed certain torts in the U.S. (the act denies immunity for claims for money damages for personal injury, death or property damages); or (6) agreed to arbitration.

For an antitrust claimant the crucial exception is commercial activity, the only exception discussed here. Under FSIA commercial activity is characterized by the "nature of the course of conduct or particular transaction or act * * * ", not by reference to its purpose.[3] For example, a nation that socializes the extraction and sale of a natural resource would be engaged in commercial activity, regardless of whether it proceeded for reasons of conservation and environmental protection. The 1995 International Guidelines stress that "[a]s a practical matter" most marketplace activities of a foreign government-owned corporation are commercial and subject to the antitrust laws.[4] Although the Supreme Court has never considered the commercial exception in an antitrust case, the Court in Argentina v. Weltover[5] read "commercial", broadly:

> "[W]hen a foreign government acts, not as a regulator of the market, but in the manner of a private player within it, the foreign sovereign's actions are 'commercial' * * *. [T]he question is not

---

§ 18.5

1. ABA Section of Antitrust Law, Monograph 20, Special Defenses In International Antitrust Litigation (1995). The monograph also discusses the application of Noerr–Pennington and the First Amendment to efforts to influence foreign governments: "Only a few cases have considered whether Noerr–Pennington applies to the petitioning of foreign governments. These cases have produced more conflict than resolution." Id. at 123.

2. 28 U.S.C.A. §§ 1602 *et seq.* (1988).

3. Id. at § 1603(d).

4. U.S. Department of Justice and Federal Trade Commission Antitrust Enforcement Guidelines for International Operations § 3–31 (1995), reprinted in Appendix F (hereinafter the 1995 Guidelines) § 3–31.

5. 504 U.S. 607, 112 S.Ct. 2160, 119 L.Ed.2d 394 (1992).

whether the foreign government is acting with a profit motive * * * [but] whether the particular actions that the foreign state performs (whatever the motive behind them) are the *type* of action by which a private party engages in 'trade and traffic or commerce.' "[6]

But there is also a requirement that the commercial activity have a sufficient nexus with the U.S. to warrant application of FSIA standards. Thus, the statutory exception to the presupposed international law protection (whatever its scope may be) can apply to commercial conduct by the foreign state only in one of these circumstances: if the conduct occurs in the U.S.; or if an act by the sovereign in the U.S. is performed in connection with the state's commercial activity elsewhere; or if the commercial activity of the foreign state, although taken outside of the U.S., produces a "direct effect" within the U.S.[7] These requirements are analytically complex and can be factually ambiguous. The Supreme Court in Saudi Arabia v. Nelson[8] held, in effect, that the statutory requirement that the claim be "based on" the commercial activity imposed a tight nexus requirement between the commercial activity in the U.S. and the claim being sued upon. While this requirement may have little effect on antitrust suits, it may narrow the scope of the application in other areas.[9]

18.5b. The Act of State Doctrine

The conventional judicial responses to foreign law cited as influential or decisive in litigation in U.S. courts is to turn to conflict of laws rules, international law or comity. However, the Act of State Doctrine, as developed in a series of Supreme Court cases,[10] calls for a broader judicial abstention when the validity of the acts of a foreign state are questioned. The scope of protection sometimes granted cannot be fully explained by those conventional concepts.[11] The ABA Monograph spends seventy-three pages exploring the doctrine, the cases applying it, and the literature discussing it. That work yields ample material for either side's advocacy should the validity of a foreign act be at issue in antitrust litigation. But it does not provide the kind of guidance that leads to reasonably confident prediction. The most explicit statement in recent case law is

6. Id. at 614. See also, Siderman de Blake v. Argentina, 965 F.2d 699 (9th Cir. 1992), *cert. denied*, 507 U.S. 1017, 113 S.Ct. 1812, 123 L.Ed.2d 444(1993).

7. Section 18 of the Restatement (Second) of Foreign Relations Law, to which the legislative history refers, calls for a "direct, substantial and reasonably foreseeable" effect.

8. 507 U.S. 349, 113 S.Ct. 1471, 123 L.Ed.2d 47 (1993).

9. In *Nelson*, id., plaintiff had been employed by Saudi Arabia in the U.S. to work in a Saudi hospital. The suit claimed that when he blew the whistle on health and safety practices at the hospital he was detained and tortured by the government.

The Court majority thought the commercial activity of hiring *Nelson* in the U.S. was not closely enough linked with the tortious foreign conduct. See also Princz v. Germany, 26 F.3d 1166 (D.C.Cir.1994), *cert. denied*, 513 U.S. 1121, 115 S.Ct. 923, 130 L.Ed.2d 803 (1995).

10. Underhill v. Hernandez, 168 U.S. 250, 18 S.Ct. 83, 42 L.Ed. 456 (1897); American Banana v. United Fruit, 213 U.S. 347, 29 S.Ct. 511, 53 L.Ed. 826 (1909); Ricaud v. Am. Metal, 246 U.S. 304, 38 S.Ct. 312, 62 L.Ed. 733 (1918).

11. ABA MONOGRAPH 20, supra note 1, at 23–24.

found in W.S. Kirkpatrick & Co. v. Environmental Tectonics Corp., Int'l.[12] The Court said that the doctrine provides no exception to a court's obligation to decide controversies merely because doing so "may embarrass foreign governments," but does require that "the acts of foreign sovereigns taken within their own jurisdictions shall be deemed valid."[13]

The U.S. enforcement agencies' view of the doctrine, as expressed in the 1995 Department of Justice and Federal Trade Commission Enforcement Guidelines For International Operations, is instructive. The agencies will invoke the doctrine when the validity of the acts of a foreign sovereign presents an unavoidable issue. The doctrine applies only if the specific conduct complained of is a public act of the foreign sovereign within its territorial jurisdiction and on matters pertaining to governmental sovereignty. Even then, the doctrine does not compel dismissal, but abstention is "appropriate" where the court must " 'declare invalid, and thus ineffective as a rule of decision in the U.S. courts, * * * the official act of a foreign sovereign.' "[14]

Although the Guidelines are not explicit about this, it may be assumed, in light of the Foreign Sovereign Immunities Act distinction between commercial and governmental conduct, that FSIA standards will be utilized in deciding when a matter pertains to sovereignty and when it does not. Also (if it is correct that commercial conduct by a sovereign cannot be protected by the act of state doctrine any more than by FSIA), there is one statement in the Guidelines that may need modification. The Guidelines state that governmental "compulsion" is not necessary to invoke the doctrine.[15] But when a sovereign act comes into play in an antitrust suit it will likely be cited as a defense to private conduct that would otherwise constitute an antitrust violation. Given Hartford,[16] it would seem that such a foreign sovereign act would present "an unavoidable issue" only when that act compelled private conduct inconsistent with U.S. law.

In sum, though the refinement and application of the doctrine can be intricate, and in some situations questions about how it should apply will be confusing, it may be possible in antitrust applications to cut through this Gordian knot. If the governmental act in question is a market place commercial activity by the sovereign or its agencies, the doctrine ought not to apply. If the sovereign act is relied on by a private party to provide an antitrust defense for conduct by the private party, the outcome can turn on the validity of the act only if the act compels the private party to engage in the conduct that is alleged to have violated U.S. antitrust laws. Such a situation of compulsion could, of course, arise. If it did, there would at the theoretical level be an issue additional

---

12. 493 U.S. 400, 110 S.Ct. 701, 107 L.Ed.2d 816 (1990).

13. Id. at 409.

14. 1995 Guidelines § 3.33, citing *Kirkpatrick*, 493 U.S. at 405, which, in turn, quotes from Ricaud v. American Metal, 246

U.S. 304, 310, 38 S.Ct. 312, 62 L.Ed. 733 (1918).

15. 1995 Guidelines § 3.33.

16. *Hartford* is addressed in § 18.2a1.

to those canvassed in § 18.2a4, concerning whether the comity test in *Hartford* left room for balancing the U.S. interest against the foreign interest once compulsion was shown. It might be argued that whether or not balancing would remain appropriate under comity principles, it would be foreclosed by the act of state doctrine.

18.5c. Foreign Sovereign Compulsion

While the ABA monogram cites considerable case law and commentary about sovereign compulsion, little needs to be said here except that, until the Supreme Court itself adds to the literature, the *Hartford* case will be controlling. Foreign law protects foreign conduct from U.S. antitrust only when that law compels conduct within the foreign jurisdiction that, but for the compulsion, would violate U.S. antitrust.

§ 18.6 Comparative Antitrust: Similarities and Differences Between U.S. and EU Antitrust

18.6a. Basic Antitrust Ideologies

The dominant concern of U.S. antitrust is avoiding the abuse of market power that distorts allocative, productive and dynamic efficiency and shifts resources from consumers to firms with power. True, blatantly exclusionary conduct of a kind that yields no efficiency and often causes competitive harm may be challenged under a *per se* rule without a specific showing of either allocative or consumer injury; also vertical arrangements are vulnerable when, through foreclosure, they threaten upstream or downstream harm. But neither of these observations negates the generalization that the overwhelming concern of modern U.S. antitrust law is protecting market competition, not competitors.

The EC Treaty establishes the antitrust law applicable in the EU.[1] Articles 85 and 86 of the Treaty of Rome, renumbered as Articles 81 and 82 in 1999,[2] are the core competition law provisions. Article 81 forbids anticompetitive agreements while Article 82 addresses abuses of a single firm's dominant position. These provisions share with the U.S. antitrust law the goal of preventing abuse of market power that undercuts efficiency or innovation or transfers wealth to the power-wielding firm. But another important focus of EC law is integrating the markets of the member states. Competition policy is in service to the basic political goal of the common market: replacing commercial conflict between member states with an integrated, community-wide market. This results in some sensitivity to private arrangements that may inhibit cross-broader transactions or exploit different national demand curves by price discrimination. Such arrangements may be suspect even when they have little

---

§ 18.6

1. The EC treaty and the law (including antitrust law) established by that treaty will be referred to as the EC treaty and EC law or EC antitrust. However, general references to the fifteen member states as a political entity or references to the territory of all the member states is referred to by the term, EU. See § 18.3 n.1.

2. The revised numbering is used here. See § 18.3 n. 4.

apparent effect on market competition or efficiency. While this tendency is now easing, the EC antitrust tradition has included strict rules about single brand territorial separation, despite interbrand competition, and hostility to boundary-sensitive price discriminations that might well pass muster on an efficiency analysis and be lawful in the U.S. Also, although EC law values market competition as a process, consumer welfare is not the sole, nor necessarily the primary goal. The law is also responsive to fairness—sometimes to issues that might have been the stuff of a U.S. antitrust complaint half a century ago, but that might get short shrift in a U.S. court today—as well as to keeping markets open.

There are also significant differences in enforcement institutions, methods, procedure, sanctions and style. The European Commission is the administrative, enforcement, and rulemaking body that most closely corresponds to the Executive branch of the U.S. government. Each Commissioner oversees a Directorate General with substantive policy responsibilities. Directorate General IV for Competition (DG–IV) is the body directly responsible for the administration and enforcement of EU competition policy. DG–IV has no criminal enforcement authority but may, subject to court review, impose substantial administrative fines against those found in breach of Articles 81 or 82. A critical distinction from U.S. law is the relative absence of private enforcement A 2001 decision of the Court of Justice, however, suggests the potential for growth in private enforcement. In *Courage v. Crehan*,[3] a proprietor of a local establishment sued a brewer for damages arising out of a require-ments tie that prohibited the sale of competing beers. The brewer argued that a party to an unlawful agreement could not sue. The Court of Justice allowed the suit, holding that the "full effectiveness of Article [81] ... would be put at risk if it were not open to any individual to claim damages for loss caused to him by a contract or by conduct liable to restrict or distort competition." The Court said that such private suits could make a "significant contribution" to maintaining effective compe-tition.[4]

Although the national courts of member states are empowered to enforce Articles 81 and 82, enforcement initiatives had long been largely limited to DG–IV.[5] A new regulation adopted in 2003 provides for "shared competence" between the Commission and the member states.[6]

U.S. antitrust lawyers may view U.S. law as purer than that in the EU. Industrial policy, even international trade policy, is likely to influ-

---

3. Case C–453/99, [2001] ECR I–6297.

4. Id. at ¶ ¶ 26–27.

5. For a more comprehensive treatment of EC competition law, a useful source for American lawyers is E. Fox, Cases and Mate-rials on the Competition Law of the Europe-an Union (rev'd ed. 2002). See also V. Korah, An Introductory Guide to EC Competition Law and Practice (ESC Publishing Ltd., 4th Ed. 1990); B. Hawk, United States, Common Market and International Antitrust: A Com-

parative Guide (2d ed. rev. 1991); and K. Kole and A. D'Amato, European Law Anthol-ogy, Chapter 4 (1998). Regarding efforts to broaden enforcement responsibilities be-yond the Commission, see Klimisch and Krueger, *Decentralized Application of E.C. Competition Law: Current Practice and Fu-ture Prospects,* 24 European L.Rev. 463 (Oc-tober 1999).

6. Council Regulation 1/2003.

ence EC antitrust outcomes, a circumstance that suggests that EC antitrust law is wider ranging than U.S. law. But it would be difficult to support the proposition that that EC enforcers are protective of domestic industry, while U.S. enforcers are not.[7] As trading nations respond to globalization, one of the risks to antitrust is that it will be increasingly treated as an aspect of trade policy. That risk is probably no greater in the EU than it is in the United States. It should be resisted everywhere.

18.6b. Treatment of Firms with Power

18.6b1. *Single Firm Power*

The U.S. and EC both have power and conduct tests to determine if dominant firms are antitrust vulnerable. Monopolization in violation of Section 2 of the Sherman Act, the major U.S. offense, requires proof of market power and exclusionary conduct.[8] In the EU abuse of dominant position violative of Article 82 of the EC treaty requires proof of market dominance and of abusive conduct.[9] The two systems evaluate power in similar ways, by defining a market, evaluating shares and considering entry barriers.[10] But EC market definitions tend to be more consonant with views of practical business people, less theoretically rigorous than U.S. definitions.[11] This distinction may fade in response to DG–IV's 1997 statement on relevant market definition,[12] which in many respects emulates the approach to market definition set forth in U.S. horizontal merger guidelines.

Significant differences also are involved in the evaluation of conduct. Merely exploiting market power that was innocently obtained by charging monopoly prices does not violate U.S. antitrust law. Such "abuses" are left for the market to correct; courts need not function as regulating agencies or competitive "cops." Tolerance of a monopolist's conduct may have reached a new rhetorical peak with the Supreme Court's decision in Verizon v. Trinko.[13] Not so in the EC; although new Guidelines to be issued by the Competition Directorate may narrow the area of difference with US law, any excessive pricing by a single dominant firm can be an Article 82 violation,[14] as can charging higher prices in one geographic market than another, even if none are below cost.[15] Indeed, as compared

---

7. See the discussion in § 18.7.

8. In §§ 18.6b–6e, relevant EU materials will be cited, but reader familiarity with relevant U.S. materials (reviewed extensively in other parts of this book) will be assumed.

9. Case 27/76, United Brands Co. v. Commission, 1978 ECR 207.

10. Case 6/72, Europemballage Corp. v. Commission (Continental Can), 1973 ECR 215.

11. E.g., Case 22/78, Hugin Kassaregister AB v. Commission, 1979 ECR 1869; Case 226/84 British Leyland PLC v. Commission, 1986 ECR 3263.

12. Commission Notice on the Definition of the Relevant Market for the Purposes of Community Competition Law 1997 OJ (Sept. 12, 1997).

13. Verizon Communications, Inc. v. Trinko, 540 U.S. 398, 124 S.Ct. 872, 157 L.Ed.2d 823 (2004). See the discussion of this case in Chapter 3.

14. *British Leyland PLC v. Commission*, supra note 11.

15. Case 27/76, United Brands v. Commission, 1978 ECR 207.

with the U.S. concept "exclusionary conduct," the EC concept, "abuse," has a hair trigger. In situations when intrusion of U.S. law is unlikely, EC law has condemned not only unreasonably high or discriminatory pricing, but also refusals to deal, requirements contracts and exclusive arrangements, and loyalty rebates.[16]

Such differences take on large significance as markets are globalized. Powerful American firms operating in Europe must identify and carefully evaluate EC antitrust issues. To rely on judgments based on whether like conduct is acceptable in the U.S. could be folly.

18.6b2. Oligopoly

Oligopolistic, interdependent pricing is lawful, a major gap in the U.S. antitrust law.[17] There is an oligopoly gap, also, in EC antitrust,[18] but it is probably not as wide. An agreement must be inferred to invoke Article 81 in the EC system or Section 1 of the Sherman Act in the U.S.; the Commission and European Courts draw that inference more readily than their U.S. counterparts.[19]

18.6b3. Mergers and Other Consolidations

For some years merger was not a center of concern in EU competition law. Significant concentration, existing mainly at the national, not the community level, was viewed as a matter for deference to national policy. From the community perspective, negative effects from national concentration would be mitigated by the integration process that was building the common market, much as in the U.S. adverse competitive effects from, say, auto industry concentration, were abated by global market integration. Also, any mergers across member state lines would tend to reinforce the integration process. For these reasons representatives of member nations in the Council were slow to specifically cede power over mergers to the community. To an American eye, Article 81, forbidding anticompetitive agreements, and Article 82, forbidding abuse of a dominant position, would seem, together, to have conferred ample power to deal with anticompetitive mergers. Yet, when the possible need for a community control was recognized by DG–IV, it was, for the reasons above noted, widely believed otherwise.[20]

---

16. Case COMP/C–3/37.792,C Microsoft (2004); Case T–203/01 [2003], Michelin v. Commission, ECR II-4071; Case 395/87, Ministere Public v. Tournier, 1989 ECR 2521; Case 6—7/73 Istituto Chemioterapico Italiano SpA v. Commission, 1974 ECR 223; Case 27/76 United Brands Co. v. Commission, 1978 ECR 207; Case 85/76 Hoffman-La Roche & Co. AG v. Commission, 1979 ECR 461; Case T–69/89 Radio Telefis Eireann v. Commission, 1991 ECR II–485.

17. See § 5.1b.

18. See, e.g., Cases 89, 104, 114, 116–17 and 125–29/85, Ahlstrom–Osakeyhtio v. Commission (Wood Pulp), 1993 ECR I–1307, in which, when the Wood Pulp cartel

case was tried on the merits, evidence of coordination was held insufficient to support an inference of agreement on prices.

19. See, e.g., Cases 48, 49, 51–57/69, Imperial Chemical Industries, Ltd. v. Commission, (Dyestuffs), 1972 ECR 619, 1972 CMLR 557; Case 8/72, Vereeniging van Cementhandelaren v. Commission, 1972 ECR 977, 1973 CMLR 7; Cases 40–48, 50, 54–56, 111, 113–14/73, Suiker Unie v. Commission, 1975 ECR 1663, 1976 1 CMLR 295. But see Ahlstrom–Osakeyhtio, supra, note 18.

20. In the Commission Memorandum on Concentrations of 1966, the Commission distinguished between, mergers and acqui-

In the 1970's the Commission both challenged a merger under Article 82 and proposed to the Council a merger control regulation. The regulation was widely but critically discussed but not enacted. When the issue of whether Article 82 could apply to a merger reached the Court of Justice in *Continental Can*,[21] the Court held that Article 82 applies to a dominant firm that acquires a competitor and that such an acquisition, by expanding the dominant firm's power, constitutes abuse. The Court's more general language took an expansive view:

> The restraint of competition [e.g., two undertaking acting concertedly on prices] which is prohibited if it is the result of behavior falling under Article [81] cannot become permissible by the fact that such behavior succeeds under the influence of a dominant undertaking and results in the merger of the undertakings concerned.

> * * * [O]ne cannot assume that the Treaty * * * permits in Article [82] that undertakings, after merging into an organic unity, should reach such a dominant position that any serious choice of competition is practically rendered impossible * * *.[22]

This *Continental Can* language might have been construed to vitalize the use of both Articles 81 and 82 in a merger context. However, influenced, one may infer, by wide member state resistance to its proposed merger regulation, the Commission was cautious in challenging mergers under either Article. Not until 1987 did the Court of Justice consider the possible role of Article 81 in merger control, and then at the behest of a competitor, not the Commission.

British American Tobacco involved consolidation among firms marketing tobacco products in the EU. Rembrandt owned a holding company that owned Rothmans, a European tobacco supplier. Rembrandt agreed to sell half of this holding company to Phillip Morris and to share with Phillip Morris control of Rothmans. Since Rothmans and Phillip Morris both had large shares of a concentrated tobacco market, significant structural deterioration would result. When the Commission challenged this transaction the parties restructured it.

In the revised arrangement Rembrandt retained the holding company but that company conveyed to Phillip Morris 25 percent of the voting stock in Rothmans, plus sufficient non-voting shares to give it an aggregate equity of about 30 percent. Phillip Morris received no board representation and, on finding that Phillip Morris was motivated to maximize its own returns by maximizing its own market share, not by coordinating with Rothmans, the Commission characterized the Phillip

---

sitions, which it labeled "concentrations", and agreements, and expressed the view that Article [82] applied to concentrations, but that Article [85] did not. See Bernuni, *Jurisdictional Issues: EEC Merger Regulation, Member State Laws and Articles 85–86,* 1990 Fordham Corp. L. Ind. 611 (1991). See also V. Korah, An Introductory Guide to EEC Competition Law and Procedure § 4.3.2

(4th ed. 1990), noting that in the official texts in most languages Article [82] prohibits "abusive *exploitation* of power," which might require more than structural change tending to result in the possession of power.

21. Case 6/72, Europemballage Corp. v. Commission, 1973 ECR 215.

22. Id. at ¶ 25.

Morris investment as passive and found no violation of either Article 81 or 82. When competitors challenged this conclusion, the Court of Justice found no error. Nonetheless, the language of the court served to extend the scope of both Articles 81 and 82 as applied to mergers. Previously, application of Article 82 to concentration was taken to be limited to situations where the acquiring company gained control of the acquired company. In *British American Tobacco*, the Court stated that abuse of dominant position could result from the acquisition of legal or *de facto* control or the acquisition of a status providing influence over the target firm's commercial policy. In expansive language, the Court also indicated that Article 81 could apply to mergers and acquisitions, at least in a context such as that involved where the dominant firm did not acquire control. As to Article 81, the Court said:

> The Commission must display particular vigilance * * *. [It] must consider * * * whether an agreement which at first sight provides only for passive investment * * * is not in fact intended to result in a take-over * * * at a later stage, or to establish coopera-tion * * * with a view to sharing the market * * *. To hold that an infringement of Article [81] has been committed, it must [find on evidence] that the agreement has the object or effect of influencing the competitive behavior of the companies on the relevant market.[23]

While it is anything but clear how the merits of a comparable case would have come out under United States merger law, it is clear that both Sections 1 and 2 of the Sherman Act and Section 7 of the Clayton Act could apply. Also, it is probably a fair guess that either the Antitrust Division or the FTC would have been more cynical about the competitive risks arising on these facts than was the Commission. Marketing compe-tition in cigarettes is seldom price driven except in occasional price wars provoked by a firm's failure to follow price leadership. In such an industry Phillip Morris would not need to sacrifice any of its convention-al share building strategies based on brand differentiation advertising in order to coordinate more closely with Rothmans. Perhaps a stronger argument that the investment, absent legal or practical control, did not harm competition would be that the two competitors already had and probably acted on strong incentives to price cooperatively. But another difference should be noted. If this were a U.S. case and a competitor sought court review of a decision approving such a consolidation, the competitor might well have been denied standing for lack of antitrust injury.[24]

Although the Commission had not been unduly aggressive in using it, the fact that the Court had confirmed the existence of power to control mergers under Articles 81 and 82, as well, perhaps, as the increasing frequency of large, community-wide mergers led eventually to a shift in attitude about merger control in the Council. In late 1989, the

---

23. Cases 142, 156/84, British American Tobacco Co., Ltd. v. Commission, 1987 ECR 4487.

24. See Brunswick Corp. v. Pueblo Bowl–O–Mat, Inc., 429 U.S. 477, 97 S.Ct. 690, 50 L.Ed.2d 701 (1977). See the discus-sion in § 10.4b.

Council passed the EC Merger Control Regulation which became effective, September 21, 1990.[25] The regulation has several effects: the Commission has power under a vaguely worded standard to challenge consolidations (as defined) that exceed a specified turnover threshold. Planned transactions above the threshold must be promptly notified to the Commission and may not be consummated during a short post-notice waiting period, which the Commission may extend. If a transaction is a consolidation and exceeds the threshold, only the Commission has jurisdiction, unless the Commission releases the transaction to a competition authority of a member state. If a transaction is a consolidation, as defined, it is no longer subject to Regulation 17, which governs procedure for enforcing Article 81 and Article 82, even if it falls below the regulation's threshold.

In light of this provision the continuing significance of Articles 81 and 82 for mergers becomes clouded. Certainly Article 81 will continue to apply to agreements, such as some joint ventures, that do not constitute concentrations within the merger control regulation's definition. But the regulation may imply that any arrangement, including a venture, which is characterized as a concentration as defined will not be subject to either Article 81 or 82. This outcome would free all concentrations not meeting the regulation thresholds from antitrust review by the Commission, leaving them subject only to review under Member State (or possibly foreign—e.g., U.S.) law.

The definition of a concentration is broad. It covers all transactions, regardless of the form (merger, acquisition of shares or assets, contract committing to board representation, etc.), where two or more undertakings combine into a single undertaking or, although remaining separate undertakings, come under common control. It includes "concentrative" joint ventures, those having the purpose or effect of coordinating the competitive conduct of the ventures and those that perform the function of an autonomous undertaking on a lasting basis. However, it does not cover "cooperative ventures" that neither coordinate competition between the venturers nor establish a new autonomous undertaking. But the turnover threshold requires very high aggregate worldwide turnover by the merging firms and high community turnover. This focuses Commission merger jurisdiction on transactions with substantial community significance. Because a member state may not challenge any consolidations above the threshold unless the Commission defers to it, and because consolidations, as defined, even those too small to meet the threshold, are no longer subject to Regulation 17 (and thus one might infer to challenge under Articles 81 or 82), the regulation may shield all mergers from challenges by more than one sovereign within the community. This is markedly different from U.S. law in which a merger may be challenged both by federal and state authorities.[26] Of course the accumu-

---

25. Council Regulation 4064/89, 1989 O.J. (L 3951) (Dec. 30, 1989), corrected: O.J. (L 257/14) (Sept. 21, 1990).

26. See § 10.1. Despite "one stop challenges" for mergers in the EU, a merger large enough to be within the Commission's jurisdiction may also be subject to challenge

lated jurisprudence under Article 81 and 82 will be significant as an index of enforcement attitudes of DG–IV and the Commission, and of the Court's attitude about what kinds of concentration can cause serious competitive problems.

The 1990 regulation, of course, specifies a substantive standard for the Commission and the court to apply in evaluating concentration, but it is one that leaves these agencies a vast discretion. To decide whether to challenge a merger within its jurisdiction, the Commission must decide whether the merger is "compatible with the common market." The most specific substantive test is whether a concentration will "create or strengthen a dominant position as a result of which effective competition would be significantly impeded in the common market or a substantial part of it." In making this determination the Commission is to take account of a number of factors relevant to competition, including the need for competition, market structure, the economic and financial power of participants, alternatives open to their customers and suppliers, barriers to entry, and other such broad, generally stated factors. Thus far, Commission use of its discretion suggests a set of four rather mixed propositions, as described below.

First, the regulation warrants forbidding a merger that further concentrates an oligopolistic market, thus facilitating interdependent oligopolistic pricing. As the Commission put it in *Nestle-Perrier*, "the distinction between single firm dominance and oligopolistic dominance cannot be decisive for the application of * * * the merger regulation * * *."[27] Significantly, there was no evidence that the jointly dominant firms planned to price at supracompetitive levels. It was enough that deductive theory suggested this as a profit maximizing strategy and that there was no "explicit exclusion of oligopolistic dominance" in the language of the regulation. The merger regulation, in sum, has a prophylactic function, much as does U.S. merger law under the Clayton Act.

Second, the regulation warrants forbidding mergers that significantly increase leading firm scope that may seriously harm smaller competitors by providing commercial buyers with a broader range of "one stop shopping" options than smaller competitors can match.[28] Although a world market was involved, the merger was not challenged in the U.S. If it were challenged here, there would not likely have been focus on "one

in the United States or elsewhere. See §§ 18.2a, 18.7.

27. Commission Decision 92/553, 1992 O.J. (L 356/1) (Dec. 5, 1992) forbidding the acquisition of Perrier by Nestle which would result in joint dominance of Nestle and BSN in the bottled water market in France. Accord: *Gencor/Lowha* Commission Decision 97/26, [1997] CEL 2055.

28. *Aerospatiale-Alenia/De Havilland*, Commission Decision 91/619, 1991 O.J. (L

334/42) (Dec. 5, 1991), forbidding ATR, a leading supplier in the world and the community leader in the market and various sub-markets for turbo prop commuter aircraft from acquiring de Havilland, a Canadian supplier owned by Boeing (even though the continued operation of de Havilland was in doubt if the transaction was not approved).

stop shopping" which in the U.S. might have been defended as creating a scope efficiency.

Third, the regulation does not warrant forbidding a merger combining two suppliers each with about 40 percent of a telecom equipment sub-market in Spain, where the Spanish phone company is a monopsony buyer, where that buyer's preference for these suppliers is based on its minority equity positions in each of them, and where there are at least two other telecom suppliers currently making some sales in Spain, as well as a number of potential competitors that could expand into the relevant submarket. In essence: market shares should be evaluated in the context of other factors that can constrain power.[29]

Fourth, the regulation warrants challenging a merger combining the leading commercial jet aircraft firm, with 65 percent of the global market, with the smallest firm in that market, having 5 percent, when the merger would convert a three firm oligopoly into a two firm duopoly, given that the leading firm, by selling with long-term exclusive contracts, will be able to foreclose customers from its single remaining competitor, and where the leading firm may be able to cross-subsidize R & D for its commercial aircraft from its contracts for military aircraft. Although decided under Article 82, not under the new regulation, the Court of Justice decision in *Continental Can* was a strong precedent supporting the conclusion that an acquisition by a dominant firm that further concentrated the structure of the relevant market is hurtful to competition and thus "incompatible" under the regulation, as it would have been "abusive" under Article 82.[30]

A more recent development in EC merger law is the three 2002 cases in which merger prohibitions of the Commission were overturned by the Court of First Instance.[31] In Airtours v. Commission, the Commission had prohibited a merger that would have reduced from 4 to 3 the number of large competitors in the market for travel agencies that operated charter airlines and tours. The Commission acted because it concluded that the merger would increase transparency in the market, make mutual restrictions in capacity more likely, further marginalize already insignificant small operators that would no longer have access to the fourth firm's capacity, and produce higher prices as a result of the three remaining firms' collective dominance. Airtour's brought suit in the Court of First Instance to annul the Commission's prohibition.

The Court's decision reinforces the prohibition standard for European merger law. The Commission must establish (1) the creation or

29. *Alcatel/Telettra*, Commission Decision 91/251, 1991 O.J. (L 122/48) (May 17, 1991).

30. The proposition in the text is based, not on a Commission decision, but on the position DG–IV took during its investigation of the *Boeing/McDonnell Douglas* merger, which lead to a settlement. The conflict between the U.S. and the EU respecting this merger is discussed in § 18.7.

31. Case T–342/99, Airtours v. Commission, [2002] ECR II–2585; Cases T–310/01 and T–77/02, Schneider Electric SA v. Commission, [2002] ECR II–4201; Cases T–5/02 and T–80/02, Tetra Laval BV v. Commission, [2002]ECR II–4381, *appeal dismissed*, Cases C–12/03 P and C–13/03 P (Feb. 15, 2005).

strengthening of a dominant position; and (2) that the result of the merger is a likelihood that effective competition would be significantly impeded. The significance of *Airtours* and the other two 2002 decisions does not, however, lie in their interpretation of substantive merger law. Instead, those decisions placed the Commission on notice that it must comply with requirements for rigor of proof and due process. For example, the Court found that the Commission "did not provide adequate evidence in support of its finding that there was already a tendency in the industry to collective dominance and, hence, to restriction of competition, particularly as regards capacity setting. Second it did not take into account, as it should have done, of the fact that the main tour operators' market shares have been volatile in the past and that such volatility is evidence that the market was competitive."[32] The Court also found that the "Commission has failed to prove that the result of the transaction would be either to alter the structure of the relevant market in such a way that the leading operators would no longer act as they have in the past and that a collective dominant position would be created."[33]

Collectively, the three decisions of the Court of First Instance may move European merger law in the direction of U.S. law in terms of the burden of proof that is placed upon the agency that would challenge a merger. For example, the presumption of United States v. Philadelphia National Bank,[34] that large mergers in an already concentrated industry are anticompetitive, no longer carries the weight that it once did. U.S. Enforcers must offer a credible theory of why anticompetitive effects are likely and back it up with evidence showing that the necessary preconditions for application of the theory are present.[35] *Airtours* seems to impose a similar burden on the EC.

The EC has responded to these 2002 reversals with a number of reforms, including the appointment of a chief economist within the Competition Directorate, affording parties an earlier opportunity to review the Commission's investigation file, and the institution of more rigorous, in house review of proposed decisions. In 2004, a revised Merger regulation became effective.[36] Important changes instituted by this revision include language that reaches mergers in oligopolistic industries when the resulting industry would facilitate coordinated anticompetitive conduct *or* unilateral anticompetitive conduct by the merged firm (non-coordinated effects).

The 2004 revision also invites for the first time efficiency claims that might offset any anticompetitive effects of a merger. The requirements for honoring such efficiency claims are, however, quite strict. The efficiencies must benefit consumers (such as through lower prices) and must be merger specific, substantial, timely, and verifiable.

32. Id. At ¶ 120.

33. Id. at ¶ 293.

34. 374 U.S. 321, 83 S.Ct. 1715, 10 L.Ed.2d 915 (1963).

35. See the discussion in § 11.2d.

36. Council Regulation 139/2004.

Collectively, these changes may move European law closer to U.S. law. There remain, however, significant differences. Overall, it is clear enough that the Commission is disposed to challenge large horizontal mergers in concentrated markets. In both the *Aerospatiale-Alenia/De Havilland* and the *Boeing/McDonnell Douglas* mergers, there is indication that market advantage from a wider range of offerings may be viewed as a negative when it is attained by merger. Subject to the outcome of judicial review, the same can be said of the *GE/Honeywell* decision, discussed in § 18.7d.

18.6c. Horizontal Restraints

Article 81(1) prohibits all "agreements between undertakings, decisions by associations of undertakings and concerted practices which may affect trade between Member States and which have as their object or effect the prevention, restriction or distortion of competition within the Common Market, and in particular those which: * * * fix purchase or selling prices or any other trading conditions; limit or control production, markets, technical development, or investment; share markets or sources of supply; apply dissimilar conditions to equivalent transactions * * *; [or] make * * * contracts subject to acceptance * * * of [unrelated] supplementary obligations." All such agreements are void; however the provisions of 81(1) may "be declared inapplicable" by the Commission (although not by a court if the Commission has not acted) to transactions which contribute to "improving productions or distribution * * * or to promoting technical or economic progress, while allowing consumers a fair share of the resulting benefit," so long as the agreement does not impose greater restrictions than necessary to attain its benefits, nor enable undertakings to eliminate competition in a substantial part of the market for the products in question.[37]

Substantively, Article 81 aims at conduct similar to that caught by Section 1 of the Sherman Act. But there is much more effort to particularize in the EC treaty than in the Sherman Act, as the distinction discussed in § 18.6b3 between cooperative ventures (covered by Article 81) and consolidation (not covered) exemplifies. Also, the structure of EC law, as elaborated upon by Council Regulation 17, is more complicated than is application of Section 1 of the Sherman Act. Article 81(1) is read very broadly to cover vast ranges of cooperation among competitors, even including forms of cooperation that would confidently escape the Sherman Act under a truncated analysis. Subject to pending modernization plans, this coverage shifts comprehensive supervisory functions to the Commission. Under current regulations, any concerted action covered by 81(1) must be notified to the Commission. If the substantive criteria of 81(3) are met the Commission, the only agency empowered to grant relief under Article 81(3), may grant an individual exemption. If an agreement escapes even the broad sweep of 81(1), the Commission may grant a "negative clearance." Pursuant to Council

---

37. Article 81 of the EC Treaty.

regulations the Commission, acting under Article 81(3), has also issued block exemptions to general categories of agreements (such as specialization agreements some of which would arguably be *per se* unlawful divisions of markets under the Sherman Act), joint R & D and patent and know-how licensing, franchising, as well as in respect of various vertical restraints. This regulatory response became essential when an avalanche of notifications of agreements were stimulated by Regulation 17. There are also significant procedural, investigatory[38] and enforcement differences[39] between EC and U.S. antitrust law. While the competition provisions of the treaty can "produce direct effects in relations between individuals and create direct rights … which courts must protect,"[40] implicitly including money damages or injunctive relief where appropriate, there is in the EC procedural system no provision for private or parens patriae enforcement.[41]

Other than the distinction between consolidation and other agreements drawn in the EC and not in the U.S., substantive differences between the EC and the U.S. horizontal restraints law mainly affect readiness of EC authorities to infer agreement from structural circumstances and similar conduct, the breadth of one of the block exemptions, which can validate "specialization agreements" that might well be *per se* unlawful market division in the U.S.,[42] and perhaps the willingness of the EC to tolerate crisis cartels.[43]

18.6d. Vertical Restraints

Because integration of the members states into an internal European common market is the major objective of the EC treaty, vertical restraints, even though limited to a single brand facing interbrand competition, have been challenged under Article 81 because they may dampen cross-broader trade. *Consten and Grunding*[44] and *Pioneer*[45] both involved "airtight" exclusive distribution agreements in territories limited by national boundaries—agreements by which a manufacturer agrees to sell only to one distributor in a given Member State, agrees not to compete there itself, and also exacts commitments from each national

---

38. The Commission's broad investigatory powers are specified in Articles 11 and 14 of Regulation 17.

39. The Commissions power to impose penalties including fines up to 10 percent of overhead (see Cases 100–103/80, SA Musique Diffusion Francaise v. Commission,, 1983 ECR 1825) are found in Articles 15 and 16 of Regulation 17.

40. Certain "basic rights" have been protected by the Court of Justice, although not spelled out In the treaty or regulations. E.g., Case 136/79, National Panasonic (UK) Ltd. v. Commission, 1980 ECR 20335; Case 374/87 Orkem SA v. Commission, 1989 ECR 3283.

41. Private enforcement in the United States is addressed in Chapter XVII; parens

patriae enforcement is addressed in § 16.3a1.

42. Compare Commission Regulation No. 417/85, U.S. L53/1 (1985) with Palmer v. BRG of Georgia, Inc., 498 U.S. 46, 111 S.Ct. 401, 112 L.Ed.2d 349 (1990).

43. Stichting Baksteen, Commission Decision IV/34, 456 O.J. (L. 131/15)(May 26, 1994).

44. Case 56, 58/64, Consten and Grundig v. Commission, 1966 ECR 299. The Commission is in the process of revising its policy toward vertical restrains.

45. Case 100–03/80, SA Musique Diffusion Francaise v. Commission (Pioneer), 1983 ECR 1825.

distributor not to sell elsewhere. In both cases, these agreements were held to violate Article 81 because they stifle parallel imports.[46] Exclusive distribution with commitment by the manufacturer (e.g. not to sell to other distributors, dealers, or consumers in the distributor's exclusive territory) but containing no flat commitments by distributors not to transship and sell in other Member States, does not explicitly exclude parallel imports, but may discourage them. While these exclusive sales were not unlawful on their face, they could be vulnerable.[47] Manifestly, there is nothing in U.S. antitrust that would react so hastily to intra-brand distribution restraints, absent evidence of dominant market shares or parallel use by interbrand competitors which, together, aggregate a substantial market share. The EC adopted a new block exemption for vertical restraints in December 1999.[48] The regulation exempts certain vertical restraints from Article 81 if the supplier imposing them has a market share of 30 percent or less. When a seller makes a commitment to sell exclusively to a buyer, the market share threshold applies to the buyer's market share. The exemption does not apply to specified vertical restraints, including minimum vertical price fixing and certain territorial restrictions on a buyer's resale of goods.[49]

The Commission has also successfully challenged distribution arrangements which discriminate in price between buyers in different member countries even in circumstances where any challenge under Sherman Section 1 on analogous facts would be strained.[50] The very existence of block exemptions impact EC competition in ways that differ from effects of U.S. antitrust. Because Article 81(1) reads and is construed so broadly, because 81(2) renders contracts violating 85(1) void and unenforceable, and because the limited resources and burdensome case load of DG–IV render it highly unlikely that any agreement will gain an individual 85(3) exemption upon application to the Commission, firms engaging in transactions of a kind for which there is an existing block exemption must make their transaction comply, scrupulously, with that block exemption. In the area of vertical restraints, compliance with the December 1999 block exemption might seem relatively unproblematic for firms with a market share below 30 percent. Market definition, however, will be critical in counseling firms. A broadly defined market may suggest a low market share that appears to exculpate a firm's conduct, but be vulnerable to attack because the definition is deemed unduly broad. At least for firms comfortably falling within the 30 percent threshold, the new regulation should allow more flexibility for

---

46. The apparent severity of EU rules has been mitigated by recent Commission notices to the effect that it will not be enforced in instances where the single brand involved represents a very small share of the market.

47. See Case 19/77, Miller Int'l Schallplatton GmbH v. Commission, 1978 ECR 131 (contract stating that the distributor "shall as a rule refrain from exporting" held to violate Article 81(1)).

48. Regulation 2790/99, O.J.C. 336/21 (Dec. 29, 1999).

49. Id., Art. 4.

50. Cases 25, 26/84, Ford–Werke AG v. Commission, 1985 ECR 2725; Case 30/78, Distillers Company Ltd. v. Commission, 1980 ECR 2229. See also Brooke Group Ltd. v. Brown & Williamson Tobacco Corp., 509 U.S. 209, 113 S.Ct. 2578, 125 L.Ed.2d 168 (1993).

the efficient structuring of distribution, but may also invite competitive abuse. The threshold may exempt single-brand market power abuses, such as tie-ins or exclusive dealing, that are subject to challenge under U.S. law.

Selective distribution is another area in which Article 81 has differed from Section 1 of the Sherman Act. EC law is unhampered by the U.S. tradition that unilateral refusals to deal should be protected commercial rights.[51] Under U.S. law, a manufacturer can quite freely select the downstream outlets it wishes to handle its products and limit its sales to these outlets. The Commission has frequently granted negative clearances to selective distribution systems, but only when they are based on objective criteria used to select distributors.[52] The EC cases imply that if there is insufficient interbrand price competition in the market, selective distribution is vulnerable. It is also vulnerable if combined with pressure on distributors to maintain a high price level.[53]

18.6e. Regulatory Immunity or Preemption

In the United States, a state enterprise or regulatory regime can result in an exemption from federal antitrust law because the Supreme Court has fashioned a "state action doctrine" on the premise that Congress did not intend the antitrust laws to preempt conventional regulatory programs or business activities by states. The refinements and complexities of this doctrine are explored in § 14.6, but there is no question that the scope of the exemption is broad. For example, the state itself can never be in violation of the antitrust laws.

Similar issues arise in the EU when member state activity appears to impinge upon EC antitrust. As in the U.S., EC law is supreme and displaces inconsistent member state law.[54] Yet, as in the U.S., EC antitrust does not totally preclude member state intervention into markets. But the media through which a limitation on intervention is achieved are quite different from the U.S. state action doctrine. Discussion requires the construction of various EC articles other than the antitrust articles. These additional articles can put a member state itself into violation if it causes conduct by an undertaking that would violate EC antitrust norms, an outcome that could never occur in the U.S.

Under Article 88, if a member state "grant in aid" "distorts or threatens to distort EC competition by favoring certain undertakings or the production of certain goods", it is "incompatible with the common market," subject to exceptions for non-discriminatory aid to individual consumers, for natural disasters, or to redress disadvantage due to the division of Germany, and subject to power in the Commission to "consid-

51. United States v. Colgate & Co., 250 U.S. 300, 39 S.Ct. 465, 63 L.Ed. 992 (1919).

52. Case 26/76, Metro SB–Grobmarkte GmbH & Co. KG v. Commission, 1977 ECR 1875 ("Metro I") and Case 75/84, 1986 ECR 3021 ("Metro II") (Exclusion of discount chain as a distributor does not violate Art.

81 if the selection criteria are objective and the overall market is not structurally rigid).

53. Case 107/82, Allgemeine Elektricitats Gesellshaft AEG–Telefunken AG v. Commission, 1983 ECR 3151.

54. Case 6/64, Costa v. E.N.E.L., 1964 ECR 585, 1964 CMLR 425.

er to be compatible" aid for other specified purposes (such as to promote economic development areas, projects of common European interest, and for cultural and heritage conservation that does not affect trading conditions).[55] If aid violating these antitrust related standards is granted by a state, the state itself is in violation of the treaty.[56]

Also, under Article 86(1) no member state shall enact or maintain in force any measure violating the antitrust provisions in order to favor any public undertaking or private undertaking "to which the state has granted special or exclusive rights." However, Article 86(2) releases "[u]ndertakings entrusted with the operation of services of general economic interest or having the character of a revenue producing monopoly" from such rules insofar as application of the rules would "obstruct the performance * * * of the particular tasks assigned to them."[57]

It thus appears lawful for a member state to grant special or exclusive rights to either a state or a private undertaking. But if it does, two issues arise: First, it must be determined whether the member state has encouraged or caused anything (other than the exclusivity itself) that could constitute a violation of the EC antitrust provisions. Second, if the state has done this, then, under Article 90, the state itself is liable for the violation, unless applying the antitrust rules would obstruct a function "of general economic interest" assigned by the state to the undertaking.[58] Thus, a member state may grant an exclusive right to deliver mail and may lawfully forbid competitors from offering cream-skimming special services that would threaten the financial viability of the general postal service.[59] By contrast, while a state may establish an employment agency and forbid competitive private services, it may not enforce the prohibition against competitors offering a specialized employment service for executives when the services of the state agency are inadequate to the needs of employers seeking executives.[60]

Overall, EC law protects competition from state interference more broadly than does U.S. law, for the state action doctrine gives states in the federal union a license to interfere with markets that has no parallel for member states in the EC. On the other hand, it is not at all clear that there is, in fact, more state interference with competition in the U.S. than in the EU. Impressionistically, the opposite is likely true. First, the dirigisme tradition—an active state role in markets directing resource allocation through industrial policy—is entrenched in much of the EU. Second, deregulation has proceeded more comprehensively in the U.S. than in the EU.

55. Articles 92–94. See, e.g., Case 730/79, Phillip Morris Holland BV v. Commission, 1980 ECR 2671, [1981] 2 CMLR 321.

56. Id.

57. Article 86, EC Treaty.

58. Id.

59. Case C–320/91, Criminal Proceedings Against Corbeau, [1993] I ECR 2533.

60. Case C–41/90, Hofner and Elser v. Macrotron GmbH, [1991] I ECR 1979, [1993] 4 CMLR 306.

§ 18.7 International Conflicts and Efforts to Resolve Them

18.7a. IBM

During the 1970s, IBM used congeries of strategies to keep plug-compatible peripheral equipment manufacturers from seriously reducing IBM's share of the aftermarket for peripherals used with IBM mainframes. Among its tactics were frequent product changes that altered "interfaces," rendering rivals' products incompatible without sometimes expensive modification. Some such products with altered interfaces were brought to market without predisclosure, which inhibited competing peripheral suppliers' efforts to make timely adjustments in their offerings.[1] The U.S. had challenged this and related practices under Section 2 of the Sherman Act, but in the early 1980s, the newly appointed head of the Antitrust Division decided that IBM's conduct was not anticompetitive and/or that, due to industry changes after the suit was initiated, remediation was either not needed, or no longer feasible. Accordingly, the U.S., almost on the eve of the trial, dismissed its case against IBM.[2] The EC Commission, however, proceeded with its own concurrent investigation of whether IBM was guilty of abuse of dominant position in the EU. Because the issues were comparable to those raised in the dismissed U.S. suit, the U.S. Assistant Attorney General went to Brussels in an effort to dissuade DG–IV officials from proceeding against IBM, arguing that IBM's conduct was not anticompetitive, that forbidding it would discourage innovation, and that any relief granted against IBM under Article 82 would handicap this successful U.S. firm in world competition, with overspill into the U.S. market. This diplomatic effort failed.[3] The EC Commission went ahead, seeking to force IBM both to unbundle memory and mainframe and to pre-announce to EC competitors, on request, interface design changes on equipment offered in the Common Market.[4] Years of discovery, negotiation and a brief hearing followed. In the end, IBM agreed with the EC to unbundle and, for an approved fee, to provide peripheral equipment makers and users for all new products that IBM announced (but would not ship within four months) with any interface information that could be discovered after a product comes to market.[5]

The conflict between U.S. and EC enforcers in *IBM* was real, but not bitter. Such conflicts should not be surprising when unharmonized

§ 18.7

1. See e.g., Transamerica Computer v. IBM, 698 F.2d 1377 (9th Cir.), *cert. denied,* 464 U.S. 955, 104 S.Ct. 370, 78 L.Ed.2d 329 (1983), California Computer Products Inc. v. IBM, 613 F.2d 727 (9th Cir.1979).

2. See A.B. Lipsky, Jr., *Memorandum of Attorney General* (January 6, 1982), reprinted in Sullivan, *Monopolization: Corporate Strategy, the IBM cases, And the Transformation of the Law,* 60 TEXAS L. REV. 587 644–648 (1982).

3. See EEC Commission Will Continue with Antitrust Case Against IBM, 1982 Antitrust Trade Reg. Rep. (BNA) No. 1064 at 1030 (May 13, 1982).

4. E. FOX, L. SULLIVAN, CASES AND MATERIALS ON ANTITRUST 241–42 (1989).

5. See "IBM Settles Antitrust Suit With Common Market," THE WALL STREET JOURNAL, August 3, 1984.

national competition law is applied to transactions that span national boundaries.[6] So long as there is international trade there will be conflicting national interests, conflicting national antitrust policies, or conflicting views about how generally consistent policies can best be implemented. In the current world economy opportunities for such differences abound. There are also some examples where differences between national positions were evident, yet no international dispute occurred.

18.7b. Wood Pulp and Hartford

Wood Pulp,[7] the case in which the European Court of Justice adopted the effects test,[8] involved a potential conflict between EU and U.S. law. U.S. firms, acting pursuant to the Webb–Pomerene Act and exempt from Sherman Act challenge, participated, the Commission found, in an export cartel that injured European buyers. Although the U.S. defendants asserted the inconsistency of U.S. and EU law, U.S. authorities raised no objection to the European enforcement. On review, the EC Court gave the comity claim short shrift and applied Article 81. The findings, it might be noted, were analogous to those encountered later by the U.S. Supreme Court in *Hartford*.[9] Of course, *Hartford* was, itself, another conflicts case, in this instance between U.S. antitrust and U.K. law supportive of cartel-like conduct in the London reinsurance market. *Hartford* was similar to *Wood Pulp* in two respects: first, although defendants sought a comity-based inconsistency defense, the U.K. government (like the U.S. government in *Wood Pulp*) did not intercede on their behalf; second, although U.K. law was supportive of defendants' cartel, its approval (like the U.S. approval of American export cartels in *Wood Pulp*) was passive. In neither situation did any law or policy of the sovereign whose support for cartelization was claimed require the cartelization.

18.7c. Boeing–McDonnell Douglas

By contrast, the 1997 *Boeing-McDonnell Douglas* merger was the occasion for acrimonious disagreement between the U.S. and the EU authorities. Boeing held 65 percent of the global market for commercial jet aircraft. McDonnell Douglas held 5 percent, and Airbus, a European

---

6. The facts in *British Nylon Spinners v. Imperial Chemical Industries*, [1955] 1 ch. 37 (1954), [1953] 1 ch.19 (C.A. 1952), are suggestive. Imperial had been found to have violated the Sherman Act by an international market dividing cartel and enjoined from enforcing a relevant patent. While that suit was pending, Imperial had contracted with its subsidiary, Spinners, to convey the patent to Spinners. The British Court held that the antitrust decree could not deprive *Spinners* of its interest in the patent. While discussion here is limited to salient U.S.–EU conflicts, it must be remembered that over eighty countries have competition laws.

7. Cases 89, 104, 114, 116–17 and 125–29/85, Ahlstrom–Osakeyhtio v. Commission (Wood Pulp), 1988 ECR 5193, 4 CMLR 901. The opinion cited dealt with the jurisdictional issue. In a later opinion the Court found against the Commission on whether there was sufficient evidence of agreement. [1993] ECR I–1307.

8. See § 18.3.

9. Hartford Fire Insurance v. California, 509 U.S. 764, 113 S.Ct. 2891, 125 L.Ed.2d 612 (1993).

consortium, held 30 percent. The merger reduced the oligopoly from three firms to two and increased the share of the dominant firm to 70 percent. It also substantially increased concentration in the U.S. defense industry. The merger was notified to and investigated by the FTC in the U.S. and by the EC Commission in the EU. The FTC determined not to challenge the merger in July, 1997.[10] While all its reasons not to proceed may remain a matter of inference or speculation, the FTC concluded that the merger would cause no significant harm to any relevant market for civilian aircraft because McDonnell Douglas (with only 5 percent of the large civilian aircraft market) was too weak to remain a significant factor.[11] It may be that the FTC was also persuaded that greater consolidation in defense was needed to assure scale economies in the post-cold-war world and that the Defense Department, a monopsony buyer, had countervailing power to offset increases in concentration among those selling to it (a matter less and less obvious as arms sales abroad increase).

Looking at the same merger, DG–IV concluded that it violated the EC Merger Control Regulation.[12] There was precedent supporting the DG–IV contention that such an increase in concentration would be a violation.[13] DG–IV concluded that the merger would distort competition in two EC markets: that for new aircraft and that for repair parts and service for previously sold aircraft. It concluded that by greatly increasing concentration the merger would likely increase prices for new civilian aircraft and for repair, maintenance, parts and service for the large European stock of existing McDonnell Douglas planes. DG–IV thought these problems were exacerbated, moreover, by Boeing's recent practice of entering into twenty year exclusive supply contracts with major air carriers, a practice that the FTC may not have evaluated either as part of its merger investigation or separately.[14] DG–IV was also concerned that an integrated Boeing–McDonnell Douglas would be positioned to leverage power from its military aircraft monopoly in the U.S. to cross-subsidize its civilian operation, thus injuring competition in the market for new, large passenger planes—a market that the merger would reduce from a three firm to a two firm oligopoly.[15] Although the

10. 73 BNA TRADE REG. REP. 4 (July 3, 1997).

11. Matter of Boeing/McDonnell Douglas Corp., 5 Trade Reg. Rep. (CCH) ¶ 24,295 (July 1, 1997) (Commission Statement: no competitive harm because McDonnell Douglas no longer a competitive force). When the merger was announced there were reports that McDonnell Douglas had planned to withdraw from offering a full range of jet aircraft to find niches where it could prosper. The Aerospace Merger, N.Y. TIMES § A, p. 1 (Dec. 16,1996).

12. Council Regulation 4064/89, 1989 O.J. (L 395/1) (Dec. 30, 1989), *corrected:* 1990 O.J. (L 257/14) (Sept. 21, 1990). The new merger control regulation that DG–IV applied is discussed in § 18.6b.

13. Aerospatiale–Alenia/DeHavilland, Commission Decision 91/619, 1997 O.J. (L 334/42) (December 5, 1997).

14. These contracts might be independently challenged by the FTC under Section 5 or by the DOJ or any private party with standing (e.g., Airbus) as violation of Clayton Section 3 and Sherman Section 1. Analysis should weigh competitive harm resulting from foreclosing suppliers for twenty years against possible benefits due to planning and scale efficiencies, as well as mitigation from the possibility of competition for the long-term commitment.

15. Both cross-subsidy and the use by Boeing of long-term exclusive control, as DG–IV perceived it, could be devastating to competition over time because scale eco-

merger was between U.S. corporations and was occurring in the U.S., the EC had jurisdiction under its "effects test."[16] If the Commission were to find a violation and be affirmed, Boeing could be fined up to 10 percent of its EU sales, which could be enforced by impounding its EU assets, including new aircraft being delivered in Europe.

Despite the U.S.-EU cooperation agreement and efforts under that agreement to settle which sovereign's antitrust law should apply, dispute about this merger threatened a full scale U.S.-EU trade war. The likelihood of this eventually was high because in the aircraft industry, jousting between the U.S. and EU had been going on for years, with each side charging that the other subsidized civilian aircraft manufacturing in violation of GATT, either directly (the U.S. charge against the EU) or through defense expenditures (the EU charge against the U.S.).[17] Regardless of how disposed U.S. and EU antitrust officials may (or may not) have been to cooperate, trade representatives on each side seemed ready for a struggle. In this atmosphere, the merging firms in the United States and Airbus and others in Europe seem to have lobbied well beyond making presentations to antitrust enforcement officials, or even to trade representatives. In the United States, President Clinton threatened either a WTO complaint or unilateral trade sanctions if the EC disrupted the merger on antitrust grounds.[18] President Chirac of France was no less outspoken. He labeled the merger an attack on European commercial interests and insisted that DG–IV stand firm.[19] In the midst of this unpleasantness Boeing reached a settlement with DG–IV, consenting to significant relief with respect to each of DG–IV's concerns. It agreed: to abandon existing exclusivity clauses and not to negotiate any in the future; to hold separate the McDonnell Douglas commercial aircraft business (thus mitigating repair part problems); to license to competitors at reasonable royalties technology derived from military R & D; not to abuse relationships with customers and to report annually on projects benefitting from U.S. governmental financing.[20]

Why did this interaction between governments about antitrust standards deteriorate to an unseemly level? The short answer seems to be that whenever there are on both sides trade interests as significant as these, trade officials and trade thinking threaten to displace antitrust

---

nomics are of enormous importance in the R & D and design aspects of this industry. Whether development costs must be written off over an anticipated small number of units, or can be written off over a much larger number of units, makes a profound difference in the price that must be quoted for a new aircraft.

16. Cases 89, 104, 114, 116–17 and 125–29/85, Ahlstrom–Osakeyhtio v. Commission (Wood Pulp), 1988 ECR 5193, 4 CMLR 901. See § 18.3. Compare Hartford Fire Insurance Co. v. California, 509 U.S. 764, 113 S.Ct. 2891, 125 L.Ed.2d 612 (1993), discussed in § 18.2a1.

17. First, *The Intersection of Trade and Antitrust Remedies,* 12 Antitrust 17, 18 (Fall, 1997).

18. Mitchell, Clinton Warns Europeans of Trade Complaint on Boeing Deal, N.Y. Times § D, p.2 (July 18, 1997).

19. *European Experts Oppose Boeing Deal,* N.Y. Times § D, p.8 (July 17, 1997).

20. For conflicting views of the case compare Interview with A. Schaub, Director General For Competition, EC Commission, 12 Antitrust 13 (Fall, 1997); with, Interview with T.L. Boeder and B.S. Sharp, Attorneys for Boeing, 12 Antitrust 5 (Fall, 1997).

officials and antitrust thinking. U.S. trade officials have regularly championed Boeing in many trade contexts and were quick to enter into this dispute. The Department of Defense was also supportive of Boeing. Because Boeing was dominant in the global aircraft market, any wealth transfer from airlines to manufacturers would come from foreign as well as U.S. airlines and would go predominantly to Boeing's U.S. stockholders, management and employees. The EU, by contrast, focused on its airlines (facing higher equipment and service prices) and its travelers (facing higher fares due to higher airline equipment costs), and on Airbus, the European consortium in the civilian aircraft industry (which could suffer antitrust injury, even as the U.S. perceives it, if Boeing could support civilian development from defense industry research).

When U.S. trade relations with major trading partners are corrosive,[21] it is not surprising that tension also arises concerning antitrust conflicts, or that news commentators cease to notice a distinction between, on the one hand, trade negotiations (that might lead a frustrated country to choose between reciprocal sanctions, anti-dumping tariffs, or bringing a WTO case) and, on the other hand, conflicts of antitrust law (a failure of distinctive antitrust systems to align with each other, most appropriately resolved under rules about conflicts of laws).

There is no natural dividing line that assures that trade disputes on the one hand and disputes about which nation's antitrust law applies on the other will remain in comfortable separation. In the current international context both antitrust and trade policies reflect widely ascendant liberal conceptions about the economic and political function of markets. Despite that coalescence, antitrust is a system of law and is tuned at its theoretical level to insistent norms about rational resource allocation and unfettered markets, whereas trade policy, being more free of and less accustomed to responding to legal constraints, often celebrates its liberal goals only as vague, background principles, while it goes about the business of tough trade bargaining. Certainly, no manifest difference between an international disagreement about what antitrust rule applies and a trade policy conflict will be evident to the casual observer. Because of this, the press and the public viewed the Boeing dispute much as they viewed disputes about import rules that exclude genetically altered crops, beef treated with hormones, or the like. What needs to be more widely recognized, at least by trade officials and other political actors, is that antitrust has, to the apparent advantage of economies that have adopted it, captured important aspects of the liberal tradition and locked them into an understandable system of enforceable legal rules. It is a system that should be able to transcend the uncertainties and tensions of trade-off, threat, aggression, and dominance, which are the forces that so often mar trade negotiations, even among states that are committed to the liberal, free trade ideal and that are increasingly committed to developing systems of law for resolving these disputes.

21. See, e.g., Greenberger, *Trade Feuds Between US, Europe Rise*, WALL ST. J., p. A2, (July 25, 1997).

Charges that DG–IV was distorting antitrust to favor Airbus, its "national champion" in the global aircraft trade rivalry, seem unwarranted. The issues DG–IV raised were significant competition issues—indeed, issues that might well have been raised by the FTC—and the relief DG–IV attained was real antitrust relief. Moreover, if DG–IV reacted, in part, to the threat to the interests of Airbus as a competitor, its doing so was not a distortion of EC antitrust; its response in De Havilland,[22] discussed in § 18.6b3, was a precedent for this approach. EC antitrust draws no such sharp distinction between harm to competition and competitors as does US law, at least in the context where the competitor under attack is a significant, viable competitor in a highly concentrated market.[23] The basic assertion of DG–IV enforcers was that an acquisition of the smallest firm by the largest firm which reduced a dominated oligopoly into a dominated duopoly raised a serious antitrust problem. At least in this text, that proposition will not be doubted. Imploding market structure in a profoundly important industry *is* an antitrust concern. Structure, after all, is and must remain the basic tool of merger analysis. But neither did the FTC's decision run roughshod over competition analysis, although it may have been less tough-mindedly rigorous in some of its conclusions than that agency often is. But after the FTC decided and DG–IV disagreed, U.S. governmental activities in the interest of Boeing went well beyond antitrust enforcement, moving aggressively into a trade war posture.

There is a lesson to be drawn from this *Boeing-McDonnell Douglas* matter. Antitrust is a system of legal rules based on understandable theory. Antitrust can be objectively applied on the basis of inquiry into relevant facts. This has proven to be the case anywhere competition law systems have been allowed to develop with professional independence and expertise.[24] But in a global market, a system so conceived is inevitably fragile. So long as the antitrust systems of major trading partners lack either harmonization or agreed upon conflict rules that state with particularity which system defers and which prevails in given contexts, and so long as the intense trade interest of major sovereigns sometimes conflict, no trading nation can be sanguine about how and by whom antitrust norms are being applied. Currently, there is no system in place that can provide any degree of predictability or legal certainty to global market antitrust disputes.

Consider how the Boeing–McDonnell dispute—essentially, a conflict of laws problem—might have been resolved. Suppose it were addressed under the Restatement approach championed by Justice Scalia in *Hartford* or the related *Timberlane*[25] approach. The interests on each side are

22. Aerospatiale–Alenia/DeHavilland, Commission Decision 91/619 1997 O.J. (L 334/42) (December 5, 1997).

23. Id.

24. Although trade disputes not involving antitrust issues also arise in an environment increasingly legalized through GATT, WTO and national statutes dealing with dumping, trade disputes are far less likely than antitrust issues to be subject to recognized norms with considerable objective content.

25. Timberlane Lumber Co. v. Bank of America, 549 F.2d 597 (9th Cir.1976). See the discussion in § 18.2a4.

formidable. Would it be significant that the major U.S. interest is in defense and military aircraft and that the major EC interest is in the civilian aircraft market? This may well have had influence in the FTC's decision. Could benefits that the U.S. might anticipate—that is, defense related efficiencies—have been preserved without reenforcing Boeing's global civilian dominance by spinning off the civilian aircraft interests of both or in some less drastic way?

Next, consider how the FTC–EU dispute about the merger would have been resolved under the six factors specified in the U.S.-EU cooperation agreement (which, presumably, the FTC utilized).[26] The first factor compares the relative significance of conduct within each jurisdiction. This points to EU deference to U.S. enforcement because both Boeing and McDonnell Douglas are, after all, U.S. companies and most of their defense and civilian activities are with the U.S. or with U.S. firms. But does this mean that the EC, seeking to enforce, should also defer to U.S. non-enforcement? Or should this first factor integrate the *Hartford*[27] majority's notion that either of two involved nations may forbid a transaction, so long as the other nation is not compelling it? The second factor listed in the cooperation agreement evaluates purpose of the parties to affect consumers, suppliers or competitors within the enforcing sovereign's territory. This factor would clearly be permissive of U.S. enforcement if the U.S. had decided to enforce. But (unless it also confers significance on a U.S. decision not to enforce) it is also permissive of EC enforcement, for EU constituencies are certainly affected, perhaps even to the same degree as U.S. constituencies. The third factor evaluates relative significance of effects on the interests of the two sovereigns. As perceived by the FTC, benefits to the U.S. of non-enforcement are large; as seen by the EC harms of the merger are significant and enforcement yields large benefits without significantly impairing the merger's benefits in the U.S. Perhaps deference to U.S. non-enforcement is indicated; but not, if would seem, if U.S. interests could instead be protected in a way that left room for EC enforcement to protect EU interests. The fourth factor concerns expectations and seems, at most, weakly relevant here. The fifth factor evaluates consistency between a proposed enforcement and the laws of the other state. It must be noted that the EC's enforcement here is reasonably consistent with conventional U.S. merger law (the merger guidelines, for example, would presumptively call for enforcement). The only aspect of EC enforcement at all out of phase with US enforcement is EC focus on Airbus as an injured competitor. Overall, then, the fifth factor tends to validate EU enforcement. The final factor inquires into conflicting outcomes from enforcement initiated by the different sovereigns. Here a conflict arises from US non-enforcement set against EC enforcement. The factor does not indicate which of the signatory parties should give way, but case law

---

26. The text of the United States/EU Cooperation Agreement is available on the Antitrust Division's web site: http:// www.us-doj.gov/atr.

27. Hartford Fire Insurance Co. v. California, 509 U.S. 764, 113 S.Ct. 2891, 125 L.Ed.2d 612 (1993).

in both jurisdictions (*Hartford* in the U.S.; *Wood Pulp* in the EU) suggest that the non-enforcer (here, the U.S.) should give way to the enforcer (here, the EU). If the EC enforced, Boeing appealed, and if the Court of Justice responded as it did in *Wood Pulp*[28] and as the Supreme Court did in *Hartford,* both *Wood Pulp* and the majority opinion in *Hartford* would be air-tight precedents for validating EC enforcement against Boeing.

18.7d. General Electric–Honeywell

In what would have been the world's largest merger of industrial firms ($42 billion), General Electric proposed to merge with Honeywell International. Both firms were US based but had extensive international operations and business. Both firms were involved extensively in producing various parts for commercial and military aircraft, although the areas of direct overlap were relatively small. In May of 2001, the Department of Justice announced that it had cleared the proposed merger subject to a required divestiture of Honeywell's $200 million dollar helicopter engine business. The agreement also required the firms to authorize a new third-party service provider for overhaul and maintenance of Honeywell helicopter engines and auxiliary power units.[29]

The Justice Department and the EC's DG–IV had been cooperating in carrying out an investigation of this transaction, but the two authorities were unable to reach a common view on the anticompetitive risks of this large combination. Once the direct overlap in helicopter engines was addressed, the Justice Department apparently viewed this merger as procompetitive. In contrast, in July of 2001, the EC announced that it would block the transaction because it would create a dominant position in the markets for supplier and buyer furnished avionics and non-avionics equipment.[30] In reaching this conclusion, the EC relied on theories of leveraging (tying) and vertical foreclosure. For example, the EC reasoned that the merged entity, through its GE Capital Division, could promote the selection of Honeywell's avionics and non-avionics products on new aircraft platforms, "thereby denying competitors the possibility to place their products on such new platforms." The EC concluded that the "erosion of the market shares of GE and Honeywell's competitors resulting from the merger will impact the future strategic choices of the latter." This would undercut the competitors' profitability, seriously threaten their R & D investments, and "ultimately negatively impact competition."[31]

28. See Cases 89, 104, 114, 116–17 and 125–29/85, Ahlstrom–Osakeyhtio v. Commission (Wood Pulp), 1988 ECR 5193, 4 CMLR 901.

29. Department of Justice Press Release (May 2, 2001), available at <www.usdoj.gov/atr>.

30. General Electric/Honeywell, case COMP/M.2220 (July 3, 2001). The Court of First Instance upheld the Commission's de-

cision. Case T–209/01, Honeywell International, Inc. v. Commission (Dec. 14, 2005). The court questioned whether the Commission's decision could be sustained on bundling or conglomerate effects theories, but held that other independently sufficient grounds existed for the Commission's decision to prohibit the acquisition.

31. Id. at 97.

The Justice Department was strongly critical of the EC's reasoning and result. Assistant Attorney General Charles James saw the combined firm as one that would have offered "improved products at more attractive prices than either firm could have offered on its own" and one that would have provided an incentive to rivals "to improve their own product offerings."[32] Because the EC focused on competitors instead of competition, according to James, they concluded that inducing a customer to purchase more attractive and lower-priced GE/Honeywell products "was a bad thing of a sort that its antitrust law ought to prohibit."

The difference of view between the two enforcement agencies cannot be ascribed to the EC's failure to focus on competition. Instead, the difference turns on what each agency thought were the likely consequences of this merger. The Antitrust Division viewed this merger as one that would likely bring improved products and lower prices to buyers. The EC saw the merged firm exploiting strategic advantages to undermine Honeywell rivals' profitability, R & D capability, and long term survival. The Antitrust Division did not publicly address these concerns when it conditionally cleared the merger. In his subsequent address, Division Chief James conceded that inefficient Honeywell rivals might have been driven out of business, but even if they were, consumers would be "better off overall." James expressed confidence that rivals would not give up the battle but instead would compete harder by lowering their own costs and prices.

The James' comments were a statement of belief but do not squarely address the risk of strategic conduct by the merged firm that reduces competitors' options and raises their costs of competing. Nor do the comments address the risk that any efficiency gains of the merged firm might have been squandered in x-inefficiencies and not passed on to consumers. The EC believed that the all-important dynamic competition for new and improved products and services was best fostered by an industry structure in which no player had undue advantage in employing strategic conduct to raise rivals' costs.

The EC's remedy in General Electric–Honeywell was to block the merger of two U.S. based firms. This was a bold step that subjected to DG IV to controversy in the United States.[33] It stands in contrast to Boeing–McDonnell Douglas, where the EC allowed an objectionable merger of two U.S. based firms subject only to limited behavioral relief. A few years after the General Electric merger was blocked, the EC confronted another merger of U.S. based firms that the Justice Department found objectionable. When the Department lost its federal court

---

32. The quotations are from an Address by Assistant Attorney General Charles James, International Antitrust in the 21st Century: Cooperation and Convergence (October 17, 2001), available at <http://www.usdoj.gov/atr/public/ speeches/9330. htm>.

33. An example of this criticism is Patterson & Shapiro, *Transatlantic Diverence*

in GE/Honeywell: Causes and Lessons, ANTI-TRUST, Fall 2001, at 18, 21 ("Based on GE/Honeywell, we must conclude that mergers in the EU may be subject to an efficiency offense whereby they are blocked precisely because they provide incentives for the merged entity to set lower prices.").

action to obtain a preliminary injunction to block Oracle's acquisition of Peoplesoft,[34] the EC, despite earlier press releases suggesting serious concerns with the acquisition, quietly folded its tent and offered no opposition to this transaction.[35] While some might attempt a reconciliation of these inconsistent results, one commentator suggests that strong political forces are at work to discourage an antitrust agency from blocking a merger involving foreign-based firms.[36] The concern here is that the cost of intervention, even in cases of genuine conviction, may be deemed too high. Antitrust authorities may allow objectionable mergers to proceed rather than face the controversy of acting in situations in which there is no international consensus for action. Instead of the feared outcome that the country with the strictest antitrust regimen will control merger outcomes, the opposite may be true: the country with the most relaxed competition rules may frequently dictate the outcome, at least in instances in which that country has a direct and substantial connection with the merging firms. Of course, political pressure of various sorts, both domestic and international, has long been a factor in enforcement decisions. But any decision that departs from the relatively impartial professional judgment of enforcers can undermine the integrity of and respect for a competition enforcement system.

18.7e. Microsoft

Although the Justice Department has brought relatively few Section 2 Sherman Act cases in recent decades, when they do occur, they tend to involve very large firms with international reach. Thus, with respect to IBM and again with respect to Microsoft, there were investigations of target firm's conduct both here and abroad.

The Microsoft litigation in Europe and in the United States has sparked disagreements, although the difference of view here may be less one of substantive law and more over what constitutes an appropriate remedy. Both the Department of Justice and the EC have challenged Microsoft's conduct arising out of its monopoly/dominant position in operating software. The Justice Department 1998 claims, resolved by settlement in 2001, involved the Internet browser market and the Sun Microsystem's JAVA software.[37] The EC proceeding, initiated in 2001, focused on the markets for media player software and software for low end server markets. The complaints against Microsoft, as in the U.S. litigation, involve the use of Microsoft's power in the operating system market to raise the cost of rivals who compete in these two auxiliary software markets. Media player software, offered by RealNetworks and other firms, plays digital movies and other entertainment files. Low end server software is used by small businesses to link server terminals to a

34. United States v. Oracle Corp., 331 F. Supp. 2d 1098 (N.D. Cal. 2004).

35. Case COMP/M 3216 (October 26, 2004).

36. Fox, Remedies and the Courage of Convictions in a Globalized World: How Globalization Corrupts Relief, paper presented at Annual Conference of the American Antitrust Institute, June 21, 2005.

37. See the discussion of the U.S. Microsoft litigation in § 15.8c4.

central processing unit, allowing a network to exist among employees of the small business. Sun Microsystems had been the largest provider of such server software. Both RealNetworks (in the media player market) and Sun Microsystems (in the server market) lost substantial market share to Microsoft products before and during the EC proceedings.

In its 2004 decision, the Commission found that Microsoft's conduct constituted an abuse of its dominant position in violation of Article 82.[38] In particular, the Commission focused on Microsoft's bundling behavior in the sale of its media player software and on Microsoft's refusal to release interface information that would allow server software rivals to interconnect with Microsoft's operating system. These holdings reflect the EC's more sensitive standards for finding exclusionary conduct, but they seem generally consistent with the en banc decision of the appellate court in the Justice Department's suit against Microsoft.[39]

The Commission required Microsoft to sell to European customers a version of its Windows operating system that does not include its media player and to disclose to server software rivals complete interface information that would allow the interconnection of server terminals with a central computer using Microsoft's Windows operating system. As in the United States, the remedies for Microsoft's conduct have generated controversy, both by those who believe the remedy inadequate and those who feel it is overreaching. On the one side, critics complain that the requirement that Microsoft offer a Windows version without Microsoft's media player is insufficient. Since that version could be offered at the same price as the version that includes Microsoft's media player, purchasers would have little incentive to purchase it. A more effective remedy, for example, might have required Microsoft to sell its operating system with rival media players already included in the bundle. The requirement that Microsoft reveal code interfaces to rival server software firms may be difficult to enforce. Microsoft may make incomplete or delayed disclosure, substantially raising rivals' costs in supplying server software. There is risk of recurrent and ineffective regulatory interventions in what could be the intractable problem of obtaining meaningful compliance.

On the other side, the EC's remedies were criticized by the Justice Department for overreaching. Assistant Attorney General Pate complained that the code sharing provisions ran the risk of "chilling innovation" and competition, which should be protected even in dominant companies.[40] As in the General Electric/Honeywell disagreement, the U.S. and EC have different different perceptions of the risks of strategic conduct that powerful firms may use to implement exclusionary strategies. The Justice Department's critical comments in these cases does not, however, suggest a consensus among U.S. antitrust experts. Indeed, throughout the trial and appeal of the Justice Department's 1998 com-

---

38. Microsoft, Case Comp/C–3/37.792 (March 3, 2004).

39. United States v. Microsoft Corp., 253 F.3d 34 (D.C. Cir. 2001)(en banc).

40. Antitrust Division, U.S. Department of Justice, Press Release, March 24, 2004, available at <www.usdoj.gov/atr /public/press_releases/ 2004/202976.htm>.

plaint against Microsoft, the Department argued that Microsoft's exclusionary conduct would be harmful to innovation. Assistant Attorney General Pate's criticism of the EC remedy suggests a different view of a monopolist's incentives to develop and market innovative products.

In the next section, possible ways of bringing greater predictability and legal certainty to disputes like that in *General Electric–Honewell* or *Boeing-McDonnell Douglas* are explored.

§ 18.8 Unifying Efforts: an International Antitrust Code, Harmonization, or a Conflict of Laws Compact?

Law-oriented antitrust traditions have advantages not only over unstructured trade negotiation politics but also over less developed WTO litigation. The issue now faced by trading nations that share antitrust traditions is whether those advantages can be preserved in a global market. It may, indeed, be that as more and more transactions cross national borders and can no longer be managed as national antitrust issues, all issues upon which the views and interests of trading nations are discordant will have to be settled either like conventional trade disputes in give-and-take packages worked out amid threats of trade aggression or through lengthy WTO litigation. That would be a costly outcome, but may be one that can be avoided only if antitrust can be more effectively internationalized through substantive harmonization or a workable set of choice of law principles. Before addressing directly the question whether any such accommodation is feasible, some history is in order.

Although there are earlier analogs,[1] in the modern world antitrust was a uniquely U.S. phenomenon until after the Second World War.[2] In 1945, the Havana Charter was signed. The Charter would have established an International Trade Organization (ITO) and, in Chapter V, an international antitrust law.[3] This first international antitrust code never became law. The failure of the U.S. Congress to ratify, the most significant event leading to demise of the Charter, was due in part to congressional conviction that Chapter V was weak, compared with U.S. antitrust (then in a robust state) and that the U.S. was not ready to cede jurisdiction over U.S. firms to the ITO.[4]

Despite non-ratification of the Charter, the antitrust code in its Chapter V shaped national law in Germany and its basic principles,

§ 18.8

1. See § 1.2; Piotrecaski, Cartels and Trends: Their Origin and Historical Development from the Economic and Legal Aspect (1933).

2. See Sullivan and Fikentscher, *On The Growth of the Antitrust Idea*, in W. Fikentscher, Die Freiheit als Aufgabe 93–132 at 95 et seq. (Mohr–Siebeck (1997))[hereafter *Antitrust Idea*].

3. Set forth In Appendix A, UN Publication Sales No. 1948, II D.4. See generally C. Wilcox, A Charter For World Trade (1949), (where the text of the Charter is also reprinted at 227–327).

4. W. Diebold, Jr., *The End of The ITO* (Essays on Interaction Finance, No. 16, Princeton, 1952), Wood, *The Impossible Dream: Real International Antitrust*, 1992 U. Chi. Legal Forum 277, 281–84 (1992).

refined through German national experience, became the basis for the European Community antitrust embodied in the Treaty of Rome. Briefly, the history is this: the Western Allied powers used Chapter V to formulate decartelization requirements in their occupation zones in Germany. From 1947 to 1955 the occupation statute—the text formulated in one international treaty and imposed as law in Germany as a result of the peace treaty—was operative as national law in Western Germany.[5] After 1955 the same text became the law of the Federal Republic of Germany.[6] The provisions of EC antitrust law embodied in Articles 81 and 82 of the EC Treaty can also be traced, if less directly, to the Havana Charter. Of the original six member states, only Germany had a significant antitrust experience, and that was influenced by the Havana Charter. Also, the goal of the EC treaty, integration of the separate national markets of the member states, was a miniaturized model of the Havana Charter goal to integrate markets globally.[7] Other efforts to internationalize antitrust on a broader scale also began in the 1950s. The Economic and Social Council (ESC) of the UN addressed the topic and produced draft articles in 1953, modifications of those in the Havana Charter.[8] In 1980, lengthy negotiations in the UN Conference on Trade and Development (UNCTAD) resulted in General Assembly adoption of a voluntary restrictive business practice code that picked up parts of what had been in the Havana Charter.[9]

Recently, movement has been made toward the creation of a working group to begin development of a trade and competition agenda at the WTO. Here, too, the impetus came initially from private, academic initiatives. In 1991, the ABA Section on Antitrust Law published a report that discussed the idea of an international antitrust code. While regarding such a code as infeasible as a practical matter, the report encouraged the idea of greater harmonization of national law, identifying areas where consensus might be obtained.[10] In Europe, by contrast, private groups have been more hopeful about the possibility of an international code and some of their reports have been commented upon with favor by relevant public institutions. For example, in 1993 a group of academic experts mostly from Europe, but also from the U.S. and Japan, submitted a Draft International Antitrust Code and Report to GATT, with the view, mainly, of stimulating discussion.[11] Although consensus among all group participants was not achieved (American

---

5. *Antitrust Idea*, supra note 2 at 104–06.

6. Id. The first amendment to this German law took effect in 1958. The U.S. occupation in Japan also lead to an antitrust law there, but the Japanese experience with competition law was and remains unique.

7. *Antitrust Idea*, supra note 2, at 106–111, 126–132.

8. Wood, supra note 4, at 284–285.

9. Id. at 285–87.

10. ABA, Sec. on Antitrust Law, Report of Special Comm. On Int'l Antitrust ch.11 (1991).

11. Printed in 64 BNA Antitrust & Trade Reg. Rept. No. 1628, Spec. Supp. S1–S22 (August 19, 1993) (one of the authors was a member of this group). For a comprehensive critique from a Chicago perspective, see Gifford, *The Draft International Antitrust Code Proposed At Munich: Good Intentions Gone Astray*, 6 Minn. J. of Global Trade 1 (1996), which also reprints the code as an appendix.

members were resistant to propositions to which Europeans more readily committed), there were significant areas of accord. Moreover, the basic goal of the effort, to stimulate interest, was largely achieved. The WTO (successor to GATT) now has this topic on its agenda.[12] The WTO Trade Related Agreement on Intellectual Property (TRIP) contains antitrust rules applicable to intellectual property licensing[13] and the recent WTO accord on telecommunication contains what amounts to international antitrust rules for that sector.[14] Also, after the 1993 report, the EC Commission drew upon a group of European experts to prepare a 1995 report.[15] Responding to that report, the Commission addressed the topic affirmatively in its 1996 report on competition policy.[16] Then, in December, 1997, at a WTO Ministerial Conference in Singapore, the EU and other WTO members proposed creation of a working group to attempt to develop a WTO competition program.[17] That Group has met and prepared a report[18] to be reviewed at a WTO meeting in Seattle in November 1999, which will address what future steps the WTO may take. Meetings of academic experts have continued to exchange views on these topics (in Bruges, Belgium in 1997 and in Zurich, Switzerland in 1999).[19] Although the problems remain formidable, the negative view of the 1991 ABA Report may overstate them, especially in light of the incentives for finding accommodation.

It probably remains true that a broad antitrust code, negotiated through WTO and modeled on Havana, is not feasible. Although incentives to agree are stronger today, and the U.S. is not in the position of influence it occupied when the Havana Charter was negotiated, many of the reasons for U.S. rejection of that code continue to apply, and no doubt other trading nations with traditions even more different from Europe than is the current U.S. tradition would resist. Developing nations have their own concerns about a code, in part because many view the codification movement as simply an effort by trade officials from developed countries to pressure them to open internal markets that, for domestic political reasons, they do not wish to open. For many

12. Fox, *Competition Law and the Agenda for the WTO: Forging Links of Competition and Trade*, 4 Pacific Rim Law & Policy J. 1 (1995); *Antitrust Idea*, note 2 at 130–31.

13. Trade Related Agreement on Intellectual Property, Uruguay Round of Multilateral Trade Negotiations, April 15, 1994 at 6–19, 365–403 (GATT Secretariat, 1994).

14. Fourth Protocol to the General Agreement on Trade in Services, 36 Int. Leg. Mat. 354, 366 *et seq.* (1997).

15. Competition Policy In the New Order: Strengthen International Cooperation and Rules (1995).

16. XXV Report on Competition Policy of the Commission to the Ministers, On the Way to An International Competition Law, June 18, 1996, KOM (96) 284 Final.

17. See J. Klein, Internationalization of Antitrust, Bilateral and Multilateral Responses, (address presented at European University Institute Conference, Florence, Italy, June 13, 1997, U.S. Dept. of Justice, Antitrust Division).

18. Report (1998) of the Working Group on the Interaction Between Trade and Competition Policy to the General Council, World Trade Organization, WT/WGTCP/2.

19. Another of the authors of this text participated in and contributed a paper at the Bruges and at the Zurich meetings. The Bruges papers were published in COMPARATIVE COMPETITION LAW: APPROACHING AN INTERNATIONAL SYSTEM OF ANTITRUST LAW (H. Ullrich ed., 1998). The Zurich papers were published in TOWARDS WTO COMPETITION RULES (R. Zäch ed. 1999).

developing countries, competition law as practiced by the developed world is yet another tool that is applied in a discriminatory manner to their detriment, or is not applied at all (as when developed nations exempt from competition law export cartels that are selling to the developing nations).[20]

But lack of support for a multilateral instrument does not necessarily mean that there is no opportunity for positive steps toward harmonization. Greater progress might be made by creating a forum in which competition authorities (not trade officials) are the dominant players, by narrowing the issues to be addressed, and by a willingness to use, when appropriate, forums other than the WTO. Whatever approach is chosen, it is necessary to leave wide room for difference among, for example, large and small countries, long and newly committed capitalist states, states with a long established antitrust traditions and those without, etc. One forum that has already demonstrated promise is the OECD, an organization through which competition officials of leading trading countries have already worked collectively.[21]

Discussions thus far have led either to lack of hope or ambition[22] or to modest goals narrowed to areas like horizontal cartelization where consensus is largely in place already.[23] As Lang stresses in one of the 1997 Bruges papers, the current global information economy gives rise to complex issues about which national competition policies are significantly different.[24] Examples include leverage, foreclosure, access to infrastructure (whether "essential" or only important), and other vertical issues, especially where the challenged firm is dominant. Because of this, to "concentrate on horizontal agreements" and merely adopt " 'minimum standards' for national rules of reason" will not advance matters significantly.[25] If progress is to be made in addressing such formidable complexity, it will more likely begin with loosely structured discussions among informed, experienced people, without a set goal of achieving a detailed international code.

Where might such a discussion go substantively? Initially, it would be wise to identify alternative possible goals. The salient ones identified already are (1) a unifying code, (2) harmonization, and (3) cooperation (in such forms as shared information, discovery assistance, or even enforcement assistance). There is a fourth possibility, little discussed so far: agreement on choice of law principles for antitrust application to multinational transactions. Here, are brief comments about each.

International Code: There is much more interest in and support for a joint code among European nations than among others. Fifteen EU nations already have uniform, EC antitrust. Other Western European

---

20. Correa, *Competition Law and Development Policies* in Towards WTO Competition Rules, supra note 19 at 361.

21. Eg., *OECD, Draft Recommendation of the Council Concerning Effective Action Against "Hard Core" Cartels,* C(98)35 (April 27–28, 1998).

22. E.g. the ABA report, supra note 10.

23. E.g. the EU report, supra note 16.

24. Lang, *The Information Society and Economic Concentration,* in Comparative Competition Law, supra note 19, at 178.

25. Id. especially ¶ 2.3.

nations are committed to this law through European Free Trade Area agreements. Eastern European nations, now lined up hopefully seeking EU membership, have adopted or committed to essentially the same law. EC antitrust, moreover, suits European needs, interests and legal and procedural traditions. It is accessible. It is, moreover, law with an international code genesis in the Havana Charter. It is not surprising that European nations, projecting somewhat, should think in terms of a uniform multinational code as the appropriate response when seeking to bring accord among a wider group of nations. Americans, whether North, Central, or South, and Asians have very different traditions and experiences. But even the EC has apparently retreated from its view that a multinational code can be achieved in the short term.

Harmonization: Virtually all trading nations can agree on harmonization as a goal, so long as the discussion is kept sufficiently broad and general. Almost every nation, for example, can at a general enough level, take a stand against cartels, without implication about whether or when states may authorize crisis cartels or impose cartels by regulation (on the basis of natural monopoly theory or in the interest of goals alternative to allocative ones). But it is exceedingly hard to achieve consensus on any of the tough, cutting edge policy questions in antitrust.[26] Hard work by tough, informed, determined people will be essential to make even small progress here. Generalization will not advance matters very far.

Harmonization might come in small steps and, initially, on technical issues. A number of procedural issues arise because of the proliferation of premerger reporting requirements throughout the world.[27] For a merger involving one or more multi-national corporations, compliance with premerger notification can be difficult and costly because of the diverse reporting requirements of various antitrust authorities and because the waiting periods required under these schemes can vary substantially. At least in theory, a proposed merger that must be reported in, say, 15 different jurisdictions will be held up until the longest of the 15 waiting periods expires, even if the merger will have only minimal effects on consumers in the nation with the longest waiting period. International discussions, already underway in the OECD and other forums, may lead to some progress in harmonizing the content of premerger filings. Here, as in other areas, there is no point in seeking total uniformity. Each nation will have its own unique interests in a particular merger and should retain the discretion it deems necessary to properly analyze the transaction. But agreement on a standard core filing, with each nation free to request additional information, might greatly ease the burdens on filing firms. It might also be possible to come up with some agreement on a standard waiting period that might be imposed on the parties after a premerger filing is made. Here again,

26. Id. at 178–79.

27. For an overview of the major merger laws of the world, see ROWLEY & BAKER (EDS.), INTERNATIONAL MERGERS: THE ANTITRUST PROCESS (1991). It is difficult for any printed material to keep pace with newly adopted and amended antitrust laws throughout the world.

nations might reserve the right to extend the waiting period for good cause related to a particular merger investigation.

Cooperation Agreements: Cooperation agreements have been negotiated and implemented. This process should and probably will continue. As the *Boeing* experience shows, agreements to cooperate will not insulate the signing nations against severe tension or even a trade war when significant national interests collide. But bilateral agreements may serve a number of purposes. They may regularize and professionalize exchanges between competition authorities. The procedures for cooperation can serve as a laboratory for testing modes of cooperation. If certain tools prove effective, they are likely to be widely copied. The procedural or substantive rules in these agreements may also become a sort of international common law that will be followed even by those nations that are not parties to an agreement.

Conflict Principles: International law scholars often discuss conflict of law and comity issues of the kinds that flowed into the *Hartford Insurance* litigation and the *Boeing* dispute. Antitrust officials, practitioners and scholars seldom do.[28] It is time that they became more involved. Any sovereign with a strong, basic commitment to markets as resource allocators, and with generally successful, long term experience with antitrust enforcement as a means for attaining and protecting competition (in short, at *least* the EU and the U.S.) ought to be confident that the whole liberal, market oriented antitrust system will not fall apart if, in any given case, one such country has to defer to another (in short, if the U.S. has to defer to the EU, or the EU to the U.S.). That being so, any sovereign (again, at least the EU and U.S.) ought to be able to defer, one to the other, under a set of reasonable, adequately specific (and hence, capable of objective, consistent application) choice of law rules, if such rules were agreed upon in advance and set in place as guides for resolving antitrust conflicts. On those assumptions, the only thing that could inhibit deference in any given case would be a decision by one of the participants that the stakes, on the particular occasion, were high enough to warrant acting in bad faith and risking the continued stability of the established choice of law system. Once such a system were in place and if it had operated successfully for a time, such a high price for faithlessness would strongly deter any such temptation to breach.

Certain rudimentary conflict principles are already taking shape as a matter of common law development. For example, the effects doctrine extending but also limiting a nation's competition law jurisdiction to

---

28. Other than the spate of commentary from international law and conflict scholars (as distinguished from antitrust authorities) that followed the *Hartford* decision, we know of few significant articles addressing conflicts of law in the context of competition policy. One exception is Trautman, *The Role of Conflicts Thinking in Defining the International Reach of American Regulatory* *Legislation,* 22 Ohio. St. L. J. 586 (1961). A more recent one is First, *Towards an International Common Law of Competition* in TOWARDS WTO COMPETITION RULES, supra note 19, at 95 (discussing international common law development of substantive and conflict of law rules for competition issues).

conduct that has a substantial effect on its consumers or (in some cases) on its firms' export commerce. The effects doctrine (the impact on a nation's consumers) has also been used as a basis for calculating fines against firms involved in an international cartel. Meanwhile, a number of nations, including the United States, appear to draw back from applying their competition laws to benefit foreign consumers by providing exemptions from antitrust law for export cartels. These developments are all consistent with a common law conflicts rule that each nation can and should act to protect its own consumers. More express international recognition of this rule might provide developing nations, often victimized by international or export cartels, an incentive and an opportunity to develop an enforcement mechanism to protect their consumers.

Another example of an evolving conflict principle also deserves mention. In the area of merger control, precedent suggests that any nation objecting to a merger is free to impose its law on the merging firms as long as the sanctions are reasonably related to the perceived anticompetitive harm from the merger and within the power of the nation to impose. The Boeing/McDonnell Douglas combination is a case in point. See § 18.7c. Of course, there must be limits to such a common law rule. A nation that objects to the merger of two firms that have no major facilities on its territory might decide to impose an import duty on all of the merged firm's products imported into the nation. Such an import surcharge might well be seen as unrelated to (and perhaps disproportionate to) the likely anticompetitive effect of the merger. There is, in any event, some doubt whether this principle is followed consistently as a matter of international common law. In General Electric–Honeywell, the EC determined to prohibit a merger (conditionally approved by the Department of Justice) notwithstanding that both firms were heavily U.S. based.[29] A few years later, the EC chose not to challenge at all the Oracle acquisition of PeopleSoft, notwithstanding the U.S. Justice Department's view that the combination of these two U.S. based firms would violate Section 7 of the Clayton Act. So far at least, the consistency needed to provide a precedential base for such a conflicts rule appears lacking.

If these ruminations are accurate, or even might be, then it would be useful, at this stage, for the antitrust community to turn its attention to the development of plausible choice of law rules for deciding what national antitrust regime should govern particular global market transactions.

29. See the discussion in § 18.7d.

Appendix A

Researching Antitrust Law

Analysis

Section 1. Introduction

The Law of Antitrust: An Integrated Handbook provides a strong base for analyzing even the most complex problem involving issues related to antitrust law. Whether your research requires examination of case law, statutes, administrative decisions, expert commentary, or other materials, West books and Westlaw are excellent sources of information.

To keep you informed of current developments, Westlaw provides frequently updated databases. With Westlaw, you have unparalleled legal research resources at your fingertips.

Additional Resources

If you have not previously used Westlaw or if you have questions not covered in this appendix, call the West Reference Attorneys at 1–800–REF–ATTY (1–800–733–2889). The West Reference Attorneys are trained, licensed attorneys, available 24 hours a day to assist you with your Westlaw search questions. To subscribe to Westlaw, call 1–800–344–5008 or visit westlaw.com at **www.westlaw.com**.

Section 2. Westlaw Databases

Each database on Westlaw is assigned an abbreviation called an *identifier*, which you can use to access the database. You can find identifiers for Westlaw databases in the online Westlaw Directory and in the printed *Westlaw Database Directory*. When you need to know more detailed information about a database, use Scope. Scope contains coverage information, lists of related databases, and valuable search tips.

The following chart lists selected Westlaw databases that contain information pertaining to antitrust law. For a complete list of antitrust law databases, see the online Westlaw Directory or the printed *Westlaw Database Directory*. Because new information is continually being added to Westlaw, you should also check the tabbed Westlaw page and the online Westlaw Directory for new database information.

Selected Antitrust Law Databases on Westlaw

Database	Identifier	Coverage
Combined Materials		
Federal Antitrust and Trade Regulation–Combined Federal Antitrust and Trade Regulation Materials	FATR–ALL	Varies by source
Federal Antitrust and Trade Regulation–Code and Regulations	FATR–CODREG	Varies by source
Case Law		
Federal Antitrust and Trade Regulation–Federal Cases	FATR–CS	Begins with 1789
Federal Antitrust and Trade Regulation–Supreme Court Cases	FATR–SCT	Begins with 1790
Federal Antitrust and Trade Regulation–Courts of Appeals Cases	FATR–CTA	Begins with 1891

Federal Antitrust and Trade Regulation–District Courts Cases	FATR–DCT	Begins with 1789

Briefs, Pleadings, and Other Court Documents

Andrews Antitrust Litigation Reporter Court Documents	ANANTILR–DOC	Begins with 2000
Antitrust Trial Motions	ATR–MOTIONS	Begins with 1997
Antitrust Trial Pleadings	ATR–PLEADINGS	Begins with 1997
Microsoft Antitrust Appeals Documents	MICROAPP–DOC	Begins with June 2000
Microsoft Trial Transcripts	MICROSOFT–TRANS	Begins with October 1998

Statutes, Legislative History, and Rules

Federal Antitrust and Trade Regulation–U.S. Code Annotated	FATR–USCA	Current data
Legislative History–U.S. Code, 1948 to Present	LH	Begins with 1948
Arnold & Porter Standards Development Organization Advancement Act of 2004	STDOAA–LH	Full history
Federal Rules	US–RULES	Current data
Federal Orders	US–ORDERS	Current data

Administrative Materials

Federal Antitrust and Trade Regulation–Code of Federal Regulations	FATR–CFR	Current data
Federal Antitrust and Trade Regulation–Federal Register	FATR–FR	Begins with July 1980
Federal Antitrust and Trade Regulation–Final, Temporary, and Proposed Regulations	FATR–REG	Varies by source
Federal Antitrust and Trade Regulation–Antitrust Releases	FATR–ANTI	Begins with January 1994
Federal Antitrust and Trade Regulation–Consumer Product Safety Commission Materials	FATR–CPSC	Begins with 1981
Consumer Product Safety Commission Regulated Products	FATR–CPSCRP	Current data
Federal Antitrust and Trade Regulation–Department of Justice Business Review Letters	FATR–BRL	Begins with 1975
Federal Antitrust and Trade Regulation–Federal Trade Commission Decisions	FATR–FTC	Begins with 1949
Federal Antitrust and Trade Regulation–News Releases	FATR–NR	Begins with January 1994
Federal Trade Commission (FTC)–Annual Reports	FTC–ANRPTS	Begins with 1916
Federal Trade Commission–Closing and Other Public Letters	FTC–CPLETTERS	Begins with 1999
Federal Trade Commission–Franchise and Business Opportunities	FTC–FBO	Begins with 1995

Legal Texts, Periodicals, and Practice Materials

Antitrust and Trade Regulation–Law Reviews, Texts, and Bar Journals	ATR–TP	Varies by publication
Acquisitions Under the Hart–Scott–Rodino Antitrust Improvement Act	AHSRA	Current data
Antitrust	ANTITR	Selected coverage begins with 1986 (vol. 1)

Antitrust and American Business Abroad	ANTITRAABA	Third edition
Antitrust Basics	ANTITRBAS	Current data
Antitrust Law Handbook	ANTITRHDBK	Current data
Antitrust Law Journal	ANTITRLJ	Begins with 1982 (vol. 51)
Callmann on Unfair Competition, Trademarks, and Monopolies	CALLMANN	Fourth edition
Corporate Compliance Series: Antitrust	CORPC–ATR	Current data
Federal Trade Commission	FEDTRCOMM	Current data
Health Care and Antitrust Law	HTHATRL	Current data
Intellectual Property and Antitrust Law	IPANTITRST	Current data
Intellectual Property Litigation Guide: Patents and Trade Secrets	IPLITGUIDE	Current data
Journal of Competition Law and Economics	JCOMLE	Full coverage begins with 2005 (vol. 1)
Loyola Consumer Law Review	LYCLREV	Selected coverage begins with 1990 (vol. 3) Full coverage begins with 1994 (vol. 6, no. 2)
Modern Licensing Law	MODLICENLAW	Current data
PLI Antitrust Reference Books Multi-base	PLIREF–ATR	Current data
Restatement of the Law–Unfair Competition	REST–UNCOM	Current data
Sedona Conference Journal	SEDCJ	Full coverage begins with 2000 (vol. 1)

News and Information

Andrews Antitrust Litigation Reporter	ANANTILR	Begins with November 1996
Antitrust and Trade News	ATRNEWS	Varies by source
NAAG Consumer Protection Report	NAAGCPR	Begins with January 1995
Privacy and Information Law Report	GLPRINLR	Begins with September 2000
Westlaw Topical Highlights–Antitrust	WTH–ATR	Current data

Directories

West Legal Directory®–Antitrust and Trade Regulation	WLD–ATR	Current data

Section 3. Retrieving a Document with a Citation: Find and Hypertext Links

3.1 Find

Find is a Westlaw service that allows you to retrieve a document by entering its citation. Find allows you to retrieve documents from any page in westlaw.com without accessing or changing databases. Find is available for many documents, including case law (state and federal), the *United States Code Annotated*® (USCA®), state statutes, administrative materials, and texts and periodicals.

To use Find, simply type the citation in the *Find this document by citation* text box at the tabbed Westlaw page and click **GO**. The following list provides some examples:

To find this document:	**Access Find and type:**
United States Postal Service v. Flamingo Industries (USA) Ltd.	
124 S. Ct. 1321 (2004)	**124 sct 1321**
United States v. Microsoft Corp.	
253 F.3d 34 (D.C. Cir. 2001)	**253 f3d 34**
15 U.S.C.A. § 1	**15 usca 1**
28 C.F.R. § 50.6	**28 cfr 50.6**

For a complete list of publications that can be retrieved with Find and their abbreviations, click **Find** on the toolbar and then click **Publications List**.

3.2   Hypertext Links

Use hypertext links to move from one location to another on Westlaw. For example, use hypertext links to go directly from the statute, case, or law review article you are viewing to a cited statute, case, or article; from a headnote to the corresponding text in the opinion; or from an entry in a statutes index database to the full text of the statute.

Section 4. Searching with Natural Language

Overview: With Natural Language, you can retrieve documents by simply describing your issue in plain English. If you are a relatively new Westlaw user, Natural Language searching can make it easier for you to retrieve cases that are on point. If you are an experienced Westlaw user, Natural Language gives you a valuable alternative search method to the Terms and Connectors search method described in Section 5.

When you enter a Natural Language description, Westlaw automatically identifies legal phrases, removes common words, and generates variations of terms in your description. Westlaw then searches for the concepts in your description. Concepts may include significant terms, phrases, legal citations, or topic and key numbers. Westlaw retrieves the documents that most closely match the concepts in your description, beginning with the document most likely to match.

4.1   Natural Language Search

Access a database, such as the Federal Antitrust and Trade Regulation–Federal Cases database (FATR–CS). Click **Natural Language** and type the following description in the text box:

predatory pricing under the sherman act

4.2   Browsing Search Results

Best Mode: To display the best portion (the portion that most closely matches your description) of each document in a Natural Language search result, click the **Best** arrows at the bottom of the right frame.

Term Mode: Click the **Term** arrows at the bottom of the right frame to display portions of the document that contain your search terms.

Previous/Next Document: Click the left or right **Doc** arrow at the bottom of the right frame to view the previous or the next document in the search result.

Section 5. Searching with Terms and Connectors

Overview: With Terms and Connectors searching, you enter a query consisting of key terms from your issue and connectors specifying the relationship between these terms.

Terms and Connectors searching is useful when you want to retrieve a document for which you know specific details, such as the title or the fact situation. Terms and Connectors searching is also useful when you want to retrieve all documents containing specific terms.

5.1 Terms

Plurals and Possessives: Plurals are automatically retrieved when you enter the singular form of a term. This is true for both regular and irregular plurals (e.g., **child** retrieves *children*). If you enter the plural form of a term, you will not retrieve the singular form.

If you enter the nonpossessive form of a term, Westlaw automatically retrieves the possessive form as well. However, if you enter the possessive form, only the possessive form is retrieved.

Compound Words and Abbreviations: When a compound word is one of your search terms, use a hyphen to retrieve all forms of the word. For example, the term **along-side** retrieves *along-side*, *alongside*, and *along side*.

When using an abbreviation as a search term, place a period after each of the letters to retrieve any of its forms. For example, the term **f.t.c.** retrieves *FTC*, *F.T.C.*, *F T C*, and *F. T. C.* Note: The abbreviation does not retrieve the phrase *Federal Trade Commission*, so remember to add additional alternative terms such as **"federal trade commission"** to your query.

The Root Expander and the Universal Character: When you use the Terms and Connectors search method, placing the root expander (!) at the end of a root term generates all other terms with that root. For example, adding the ! to the root *monopol* in the query

monopol! /s market

instructs Westlaw to retrieve such terms as *monopoly*, *monopolize*, *monopolizing*, and *monopolization*.

The universal character (*) stands for one character and can be inserted in the middle or at the end of a term. For example, the term

withdr*w

will retrieve *withdraw* and *withdrew*. Adding three asterisks to the root *elect*

elect* * *

instructs Westlaw to retrieve all forms of the root with up to three additional characters. Terms such as *elected* or *election* are retrieved by this query. However, terms with more than three letters following the root, such as *electronic*, are not retrieved. Plurals are always retrieved, even if the plural form of the term has more than three letters following the root.

Phrase Searching: To search for an exact phrase, place it within quotation marks. For example, to search for references to *trade secret*, type **"trade secret"**. When you are using the Terms and Connectors search method, you should use phrase searching only if you are certain that the terms in the phrase will not appear in any other order.

5.2 Alternative Terms

After selecting the terms for your query, consider which alternative terms are necessary. For example, if you are searching for the term *cooperative*, you might also want to search for the term *noncooperative*. You should consider both synonyms and antonyms as alternative terms. You can also use the Westlaw thesaurus to add alternative terms to your query.

5.3 Connectors

After selecting terms and alternative terms for your query, use connectors to specify the relationship that must exist between search terms in your retrieved documents. The connectors are described below:

Type:	To retrieve documents with:	Example:
& (and)	both terms	**collusion & oligopol!**
a space (or)	either term or both terms	**compet! non-compet!**
/p	search terms in the same paragraph	**yard-stick /p damages**
/s	search terms in the same sentence	**restrain! /s trade**
+s	the first search term preceding the second within the same sentence	**burden +s prov! proof**
/n	search terms within *n* terms of each other (where *n* is a number from 1 to 255)	**vertical! /5 integrat!**
+n	the first search term preceding the second by *n* terms (where *n* is a number from 1 to 255)	**summary +3 judgment**
" "	search terms appearing in the same order as in the quotation marks	**"in pari delicto"**

Type:	To exclude documents with:	Example:
% (but not)	search terms following the % symbol	**r.i.c.o. 'puerto rico"**

5.4 Field Restrictions

Overview: Documents in each Westlaw database consist of several segments, or *fields*. One field may contain the citation, another the title, another the synopsis, and so forth. Not all databases contain the same fields. Also depending on the database, fields with the same name may contain different types of information.

To view a list of fields and their contents for a specific database, see Scope for that database. Note that in some databases not every field is available for every document.

To retrieve only those documents containing your search terms in a specific field, restrict your search to that field. To restrict your search to a specific field, type the field name or abbreviation followed by your search terms enclosed in parentheses. For example, to retrieve a U.S. Supreme Court case titled *Eastman Kodak Co. v. Image Technical Services, Inc.*, access the Federal Antitrust and Trade Regulation–Supreme Court Cases database (FATR–SCT) and search for your terms in the title field (ti):

ti(kodak & image)

The fields discussed below are available in Westlaw case law databases you might use for researching issues related to antitrust law.

Digest and Synopsis Fields: The digest (di) and synopsis (sy) fields summarize the main points of a case. The synopsis field contains a brief description of a case. The digest field contains the topic and headnote fields and includes the complete hierarchy of concepts used by West's editors to classify the headnotes to specific West digest topic and key numbers. Restricting your search to the synopsis and digest fields limits your result to cases in which your terms are related to a major issue in the case.

Consider restricting your search to one or both of these fields if

- you are searching for common terms or terms with more than one meaning, and you need to narrow your search; or

- you cannot narrow your search by using a smaller database.

For example, to retrieve federal cases that discuss damages for misappropriation of trade secrets, access the FATR–CS database and type the following query:

sy,di(misappropriat! /p "trade secret" /p damages)

Headnote Field: The headnote field (he) is part of the digest field but does not contain the topic names or numbers, hierarchical classification information, or key numbers. The headnote field contains a one-sentence summary for each point of law in a case and any supporting citations given by the author of the opinion. A headnote field restriction is useful when you are searching for specific statutory sections or rule numbers. For example, to retrieve headnotes from federal district court cases that cite 15 U.S.C.A. § 13(a), access the Federal Antitrust and Trade Regulation–District Courts Cases database (FATR–DCT) and type the following query:

he(15 +s 13(a))

Topic Field: The topic field (to) is also part of the digest field. It contains the hierarchical classification information, including the West digest topic names and numbers and the key numbers. You should restrict search terms to the topic field in a case law database if

- a digest field search retrieves too many documents; or

- you want to retrieve cases with digest paragraphs classified under more than one topic.

For example, the topic Monopolies has the topic number 265. To retrieve federal courts of appeals cases with headnotes classified under *Monopolies* that discuss misuse of patents, access the Federal Antitrust and Trade Regulation–Courts of Appeals Cases database (FATR–CTA) and type a query like the following:

to(265) /p patent /5 misus!

To retrieve cases with headnotes that may be classified under more than one topic and key number, search for your terms in the topic field. For example, to retrieve recent federal cases with headnotes discussing restraint of trade, which may be classified to such topics as Contracts (95) and Monopolies (265), access the FATR–CS database and type a query like the following, adding a date (da) restriction to your search:

to(restrain! /s trade) & da(aft 2004)

For a complete list of West digest topics and their corresponding topic numbers, access the Custom Digest by choosing **Key Numbers and Digest** from the *More* drop-down list on the toolbar.

> *Note*: Slip opinions and cases from topical services do not contain the West digest, headnote, and topic fields.

Prelim and Caption Fields: When searching in a database containing statutes, rules, or regulations, restrict your search to the prelim (pr) and caption (ca) fields to retrieve documents in which your terms are important enough to appear in a section name or heading. For example, to retrieve federal statutes relating to exemptions from antitrust laws, access the Federal Antitrust and Trade Regulation–U.S. Code Annotated database (FATR–USCA) and type the following query:

pr,ca(exempt! /p anti-trust)

5.5   Date Restrictions

You can use Westlaw to retrieve documents *decided* or *issued* before, after, or on a specified date, as well as within a range of dates. The following sample queries contain date restrictions:

da(2005) & restrain! /s trade

da(aft 1998) & restrain! /s trade

da(11/14/1990) & restrain! /s trade

You can also search for documents *added to a database* on or after a specified date, as well as within a range of dates, which is useful for updating your research. The following sample queries contain added-date restrictions:

ad(aft 2002) & restrain! /s trade

ad(aft 11/9/2001 & bef 6/23/2002) & restrain! /s trade

Section 6. Searching with Topic and Key Numbers

To retrieve cases that address a specific point of law, use topic and key numbers as your search terms. If you have an on-point case, run a search using the topic and key number from the relevant headnote in an appropriate database to find other cases containing headnotes classified to that topic and key number. For example, to search for federal cases containing headnotes classified under topic 265 (Monopolies) and key number 12(16.5) (Efforts to Influence Governmental Action; Litigation), access the FATR–CS database and type the following query:

265k12(16.5)

For a complete list of West digest topics and their corresponding topic numbers, access the Custom Digest by choosing **Key Numbers and Digest** from the *More* drop-down list on the toolbar.

> *Note*: Slip opinions and cases from topical services do not contain West topic and key numbers.

6.1 Custom Digest

The Custom Digest contains the complete topic and key number outline used by West attorney-editors to classify headnotes. You can use the Custom Digest to obtain a single document containing all case law headnotes from a specific jurisdiction that are classified under a particular topic and key number.

Access the Custom Digest by choosing **Key Numbers and Digest** from the *More* drop-down list on the toolbar. Select up to 10 topics and key numbers from the easy-to-browse outline and click **Search selected**. Then follow the displayed instructions.

For example, to research issues involving trade regulation, scroll down the Custom Digest page until topic *382 Trade Regulation* is displayed. Click the plus symbols (+) to display key number information. Select the check box next to each key number you want to include in your search, then click **Search selected**. Select the jurisdiction from which you want to retrieve headnotes and, if desired, type additional search terms and select a date restriction. Click **Search**.

6.2 KeySearch

KeySearch is a research tool that helps you find cases and secondary sources in a specific area of the law. KeySearch guides you through the selection of terms from a classification system based on the West Key Number System® and then uses the key numbers and their underlying concepts to provide a query for you.

To access KeySearch, click **KeySearch** on the toolbar. Then browse the list of topics and subtopics and select a topic or subtopic to search by clicking the hypertext links. For example, to search for cases that discuss the application of antitrust law to the Internet, click **Antitrust and Trade Regulation** at the first KeySearch page. Then click **Computers, Software, and Internet** at the next page. Select the source from which you want to retrieve documents and, if desired, type additional search terms. Click **Search**.

Section 7. Verifying Your Research with Citation Research Services

Overview: A citation research service, such as KeyCite, is a tool that helps you ensure that your cases, statutes, regulations, and administrative decisions are good law; retrieve cases, legislation, articles, or other documents that cite them; and verify the spelling and format of your citations.

7.1 KeyCite for Cases

KeyCite for cases covers case law on Westlaw, including unpublished opinions. KeyCite for cases provides the following:

- direct appellate history of a case, including related references, which are opinions involving the same parties and facts but resolving different issues

- negative citing references for a case, which consists of cases outside the direct appellate line that may have a negative impact on its precedential value

- the title, parallel citations, court of decision, docket number, and filing date of a case

- citations to cases, administrative decisions, secondary sources, and briefs and other court documents on Westlaw that have cited a case

- complete integration with the West Key Number System so you can track legal issues discussed in a case

7.2 KeyCite for Statutes and Regulations

KeyCite for statutes and regulations covers the USCA, the *Code of Federal Regulations* (CFR), statutes from all 50 states, and regulations from selected states. KeyCite for statutes and regulations provides

- links to session laws or rules amending or repealing a statute or regulation

- statutory credits and historical notes

- citations to pending legislation affecting a statute

- citations to cases, administrative decisions, secondary sources, and briefs and other court documents that have cited a statute or regulation

7.3 KeyCite for Administrative Materials

KeyCite for administrative materials includes materials such as the following:

- National Labor Relations Board decisions
- Board of Contract Appeals decisions (varies by agency)
- Board of Immigration Appeals decisions
- Comptroller General decisions
- Environmental Protection Agency decisions
- Federal Communications Commission decisions
- Federal Energy Regulatory Commission (Federal Power Commission) decisions
- Internal Revenue Service revenue rulings, revenue procedures, private letter rulings, and technical advice memoranda
- *Public Utilities Reports*
- U.S. Merit Systems Protection Board decisions
- U.S. Patent and Trademark Office decisions
- U.S. Tax Court (Board of Tax Appeals) decisions
- U.S. patents

7.4 KeyCite Alert

KeyCite Alert monitors the status of your cases, statutes, regulations, and administrative decisions and automatically sends you updates at the frequency you specify when their KeyCite information changes.

Section 8. Researching with Westlaw: Examples

8.1 Retrieving Law Review Articles

Recent law review articles are often a good place to begin researching a legal issue because law review articles serve as an excellent introduction to a new topic or review for an old one, providing terminology to help you formulate a query; as a finding tool for pertinent primary authority, such as cases, statutes, and rules; and in some instances, as persuasive secondary authority.

Suppose you need to gain background information on vertical mergers.

Solution

- To retrieve law review articles relevant to your issue, access the Antitrust and Trade Regulation–Law Reviews, Texts, and Bar Journals database (ATR–TP). Using the Terms and Connectors search method, type a query like the following, restricting your search to the title field (ti):

ti(vertical & merger)

- If you have a citation to an article in a specific publication, use Find to retrieve it. (For more information on Find, see Section 3.1 of this appendix.) For example, to retrieve the article found at 25 Hofstra L. Rev. 261, access Find and type

25 hofstra l rev 261

- If you know the title of an article but not the journal in which it was published, access the ATR–TP database and search for key terms in the title field. For example, to retrieve the article "What Goes Up Must Come Down: The Dizzying Height of Vertical Mergers in the Entertainment Industry," type the following Terms and Connectors query:

ti(dizzying & height & "vertical merger")

8.2 Retrieving Case Law

Suppose you need to retrieve recent federal courts of appeals cases discussing tying arrangements.

Solution

- Access the FATR–CTA database. Type a Terms and Connectors query such as the following, adding a date (da) restriction to your search:

tying /s arrangement agreement & da(aft 2000)

- When you know the citation for a specific case, use Find to retrieve it. For example, to retrieve *In re Visa Check/MasterMoney Antitrust Litigation*, 280 F.3d 124 (2d Cir. 2001), access Find and type

280 f3d 124

- If you find a topic and key number that is on point, run a search using that topic and key number to retrieve additional cases discussing that point of law. For example, to retrieve federal courts of appeals cases containing headnotes classified under topic 265 (Monopolies) and key number 17.5(2) (Tying Agreements in General), access the FATR–CTA database and type the following query:

265k17.5(2)

- To retrieve opinions written by a particular judge, add a judge field (ju) restriction to your query. For example, to retrieve federal courts of appeals opinions written by Judge Sotomayor that contain headnotes classified under topic 265 (Monopolies), access the FATR–CTA database and type the following query:

ju(sotomayor) & to(265)

- You can also use KeySearch and the Custom Digest to retrieve cases and headnotes that discuss the issue you are researching.

8.3 Retrieving Statutes and Regulations

Suppose you need to retrieve federal statutes dealing with penalties for restraint of trade.

Solution

- Access the FATR–USCA database. Search for your terms in the prelim and caption fields using the Terms and Connectors search method:

pr,ca(penalty & restrain! /p trade)

- When you know the citation for a specific statute or regulation, use Find to retrieve it. For example, to retrieve 15 U.S.C.A. § 1, access Find and type

15 usca 1

- To look at surrounding sections, use the Table of Contents service. Click **Table of Contents** on the Links tab in the left frame. To display a section listed in the Table of Contents, click its hypertext link. You can also use Documents in Sequence to retrieve the sections following section 1 even if the subsequent sections were not retrieved with your search or Find request. Click **Tools** at the bottom of the right frame and choose **Documents in Sequence** from the menu that is displayed.

8.4 Using KeyCite

Suppose one of the cases you retrieve in your case law research is *MetroNet Services Corp. v. U.S. West Communications,* 329 F.3d 986 (9th Cir. 2003). You want to make sure it is good law and retrieve a list of citing references.

Solution

- Use KeyCite to retrieve direct history and negative citing references for *MetroNet Services Corp.* Access KeyCite and type **329 f3d 986**.

- Use KeyCite to display citing references for *MetroNet Services Corp.* Click **Citing References** on the Links tab in the left frame.

8.5 Following Recent Developments

If you are researching issues related to antirust law, it is important to keep up with recent developments. How can you do this efficiently?

Solution

One of the easiest ways to follow recent developments in antitrust law is to access the Westlaw Topical Highlights–Antitrust database (WTH–ATR). The WTH–ATR database contains summaries of recent legal developments, including court decisions, legislation, and materials released by administrative agencies. When you access the WTH–ATR database, you automatically retrieve a list of documents added to the database in the last two weeks.

You can also use the WestClip® clipping service to stay informed of recent developments of interest to you. WestClip will run your Terms and Connectors queries on a regular basis and deliver the results to you automatically. You can run WestClip queries in legal and news and information databases.

*

Appendix B

FEDERAL AGENCY ENFORCEMENT GUIDELINES

U.S. Department of Justice and Federal Trade Commission, Antitrust Enforcement Guidelines for International Operations, http://www.usdoj.gov/ atr/public/ guidelines/internat.htm

U.S. Department of Justice and Federal Trade Commission, Antitrust Guidelines for Collaborations Among Competitors, http://www.ftc.gov/ os/2000/04/ ftcdojguidelines.pdf

U.S. Department of Justice and Federal Trade Commission, Antitrust Guidelines for the Licensing of Intellectual Property, http://www.usdoj.gov/ atr/public/ guidelines/0558.htm

U.S. Department of Justice and Federal Trade Commission, Horizontal Merger Guidelines, http://www.usdoj.gov/ atr/public/guidelines /hmg.htm

U.S. Department of Justice and Federal Trade Commission, Statements of U.S. Enforcement Policy in Health Care, http://www.usdoj.gov /atr/public /guidelines/1791.htm

*

Table of Cases

E

Portac, Inc., United States v., 869 F.2d 1288 (9th Cir.1989)—§ **5.1, n. 21.**

Potash Antitrust Litigation, In re, 159 F.R.D. 682 (D.Minn.1995)—§ **17.6, n. 14, 39.**

Premier Electric Const. Co. v. National Elec. Contractors Ass'n, Inc., 814 F.2d 358 (7th Cir.1987)—§ **14.4, n. 15.**

Principe v. McDonald's Corp., 631 F.2d 303 (4th Cir.1980)—§ **8.9, n. 50.**

Princz v. Federal Republic of Germany, 26 F.3d 1166, 307 U.S.App.D.C. 102 (D.C.Cir.1994)—§ **18.5, n. 9.**

ProCD, Inc. v. Zeidenberg, 86 F.3d 1447 (7th Cir.1996)—§ **15.4, n. 33.**

Procter & Gamble Co., United States v., 356 U.S. 677, 78 S.Ct. 983, 2 L.Ed.2d 1077 (1958)—§ **16.2, n. 13.**

Professional Real Estate Investors, Inc. v. Columbia Pictures Industries, Inc., 508 U.S. 49, 113 S.Ct. 1920, 123 L.Ed.2d 611 (1993)—§ **14.4; § 14.4, n. 10; § 15.8, n. 14.**

PSI Repair Services, Inc. v. Honeywell, Inc., 104 F.3d 811 (6th Cir.1997)—§ **3.3, n. 39; § 8.3, n. 137; § 8.9, n. 22.**

Q

Queen City Pizza, Inc. v. Domino's Pizza, Inc., 129 F.3d 724 (3rd Cir.1997)—§ **8.9, n. 24, 63.**

Queen City Pizza, Inc. v. Domino's Pizza, Inc., 124 F.3d 430 (3rd Cir.1997)—§ **3.3, n. 39; § 8.3, n. 137; § 8.9; § 8.9, n. 14, 21, 59, 86.**

R

Radiant Burners, Inc. v. Peoples Gas Light & Coke Co., 364 U.S. 656, 81 S.Ct. 365, 5 L.Ed.2d 358 (1961)—§ **5.8, n. 5, 33, 65; § 14.4, n. 17; § 17.2, n. 36.**

Radio Corp. of America, United States v., 358 U.S. 334, 79 S.Ct. 457, 3 L.Ed.2d 354 (1959)—§ **14.5; § 14.5, n. 1, 80.**

Radio Telefis Eireann v. Commission of the European Communities (C241/91 P), 1991 WL 837519 (CFI 1991)—§ **18.6, n. 16.**

Ramsey v. United Mine Workers of America, 401 U.S. 302, 91 S.Ct. 658, 28 L.Ed.2d 64 (1971)—§ **14.3, n. 24.**

R.C. Bigelow, Inc. v. Unilever N.V., 867 F.2d 102 (2nd Cir.1989)—§ **10.4, n. 18; § 10.5, n. 29; § 17.1; § 17.1, n. 41; § 17.2, n. 18.**

R.C. Dick Geothermal Corp. v. Thermogenics, Inc., 890 F.2d 139 (9th Cir.1989)— § **17.2, n. 51.**

Realty Multi–List, Inc., United States v., 629 F.2d 1351 (5th Cir.1980)—§ **3.4, n. 54.**

Red Lion Medical Safety, Inc. v. Ohmeda, Inc., 63 F.Supp.2d 1218 (E.D.Cal. 1999)—§ **8.3, n. 141; § 8.9, n. 25.**

Reibert v. Atlantic Richfield Co., 471 F.2d 727 (10th Cir.1973)—§ **17.2, n. 29.**

Reid Bros. Logging Co. v. Ketchikan Pulp Co., 699 F.2d 1292 (9th Cir.1983)— § **5.1, n. 21.**

Reiter v. Sonotone Corp., 486 F.Supp. 115 (D.Minn.1980)—§ **17.2, n. 83.**

Reiter v. Sonotone Corp., 442 U.S. 330, 99 S.Ct. 2326, 60 L.Ed.2d 931 (1979)— § **17.2; § 17.2, n. 89.**

Remington Products, Inc. v. North American Philips, Corp., 755 F.Supp. 52 (D.Conn.1991)—§ **10.4, n. 16.**

Remington Products, Inc. v. North American Philips Corp., 717 F.Supp. 36 (D.Conn.1989)—§ **10.5, n. 28.**

Research Corp. v. Asgrow Seed Co., 425 F.2d 1059 (7th Cir.1970)—§ **17.6, n. 10.**

Reynolds Metals Co. v. FTC, 309 F.2d 223, 114 U.S.App.D.C. 2 (D.C.Cir.1962)— § **11.3, n. 32.**

Ricaud v. American Metal Co., 246 U.S. 304, 38 S.Ct. 312, 62 L.Ed. 733 (1918)— § **18.5, n. 10, 14.**

Ricci v. Chicago Mercantile Exchange, 409 U.S. 289, 93 S.Ct. 573, 34 L.Ed.2d 525 (1973)—§ **14.5; § 14.5, n. 1, 61.**

Rice v. Norman Williams Co., 458 U.S. 654, 102 S.Ct. 3294, 73 L.Ed.2d 1042 (1982)—§ **14.6; § 14.6, n. 66.**

Rice Growers Ass'n of California, United States v., 1986 WL 12562 (E.D.Cal. 1986)—§ **10.5, n. 11.**

Richardson v. Buhl, 77 Mich. 632, 43 N.W. 1102 (Mich.1889)—§ **10.3, n. 1.**

Rockford Memorial Corp., United States v., 898 F.2d 1278 (7th Cir.1990)—§ **10.5, n. 11; § 13.4; § 13.4, n. 41.**

Roland Machinery Co. v. Dresser Industries, Inc., 749 F.2d 380 (7th Cir.1984)— § **8.4; § 8.4, n. 24, 28, 31.**

Ross v. A.H. Robins Co., Inc., 100 F.R.D. 5 (S.D.N.Y.1982)—§ **17.6, n. 19.**

Rothery Storage & Van Co. v. Atlas Van Lines, Inc., 792 F.2d 210, 253 U.S.App. D.C. 142 (D.C.Cir.1986)—§ **5.2, n. 69; § 5.5; § 5.5, n. 20; § 13.1, n. 5; § 13.3, n. 4, 8; § 13.4, n. 3; § 14.5, n. 44.**

Russell Stover Candies, Inc. v. FTC, 718 F.2d 256 (8th Cir.1983)—§ **7.2, n. 14.**

Russ' Kwik Car Wash, Inc. v. Marathon Petroleum Co., 772 F.2d 214 (6th Cir. 1985)—§ **5.2, n. 63.**

Ryko Mfg. Co. v. Eden Services, 823 F.2d 1215 (8th Cir.1987)—§ **7.3, n. 17; § 7.4, n. 50; § 8.4, n. 31.**

S

SA Musique Diffusion Francaise v. Commission, 1983 ECR 1825—§ **18.6, n. 39, 45.**

*

Index

References are to Pages

†